www.wadsworth.com

www.wadsworth.com is the World Wide Web site for Wadsworth and is your direct source to dozens of online resources.

At *www.wadsworth.com* you can find out about supplements, demonstration software, and student resources.
You can also send email to many of our authors and preview new publications and exciting new technologies.

www.wadsworth.com
Changing the way the world learns®

Social Work Processes

Seventh Edition

Beulah Compton

Burt Galaway
Professor Emeritus, University of Manitoba

Barry Cournoyer
Indiana University

THOMSON
BROOKS/COLE

Australia • Canada • Mexico • Singapore • Spain
United Kingdom • United States

THOMSON

BROOKS/COLE

Executive Editor: Lisa Gebo
Assistant Editor: Alma Dea Michelena
Editorial Assistant: Sheila Walsh
Technology Project Manager: Barry Connolly
Marketing Manager: Caroline Concilla
Marketing Assistant: Mary Ho
Advertising Project Manager: Tami Strang
Project Manager, Editorial Production: Katy German
Art Director: Vernon Boes
Print Buyer: Barbara Britton

Permissions Editor: Kiely Sexton
Production Service: Forbes Mill Press
Text Designer: John Edeen
Copy Editor: Robin Gold
Cover Designer: Roger Knox
Cover Image: Celia Johnson
Cover Printer: West Group
Compositor: Linda Weidemann, Wolf Creek Press
Printer: West Group

Printed in the United States of America
1 2 3 4 5 6 7 08 07 06 05 04

For more information about our products, contact us at:
Thomson Learning Academic Resource Center
1-800-423-0563

For permission to use material from this text,
contact us by:
Phone: 1-800-730-2214   **Fax:** 1-800-730-2215
Web: http://www.thomsonrights.com

Library of Congress Control Number: 2004104220

SE ISBN 0-534-36559-0

IE ISBN 0-534-63218-1

Brooks/Cole—Thomson Learning
10 Davis Drive
Belmont, CA 94002
USA

Asia
Thomson Learning
5 Shenton Way #01-01
UIC Building
Singapore 068808

Australia/New Zealand
Thomson Learning
102 Dodds Street
Southbank, Victoria 3006
Australia

Canada
Nelson
1120 Birchmount Road
Toronto, Ontario M1K 5G4
Canada

Europe/Middle East/Africa
Thomson Learning
High Holborn House
50/51 Bedford Row
London WC1R 4LR
United Kingdom

Latin America
Thomson Learning
Seneca, 53
Colonia Polanco
11560 Mexico D.F.
Mexico

Spain/Portugal
Paraninfo
Calle Magallanes, 25
28015 Madrid, Spain

Dedicated to Beulah Roberts Compton

March 29, 1919–August 13, 2002

Contents

Exhibits

Preface

This is the seventh edition of a text first published in 1974. Thirty years is a long time! Since publication of the sixth edition, we have undergone several personal changes. Most significantly, our extraordinary colleague and dear friend Beulah Compton passed away. Her contributions to the profession and the thousands of students whose lives she touched are literally incalculable. We will miss her knowledge and especially her wisdom. Her presence, however, remains palpable. In considering changes, we routinely asked, "What would Beulah think?" Somehow, she would provide an answer in a way that we understood. Readers will continue to find much from Beulah in this as in earlier editions.

Burt Galaway also completed a transition. He has retired from the University of Manitoba, spends much of his time in the mountains surrounding Denver, Colorado, does volunteer work, spends time with grandchildren, enjoys opera and theater, and travels. Finally, the "we" has also changed. Barry R. Cournoyer, who teaches at Indiana University School of Social Work—where Beulah received her MSW degrees many years earlier—joins us as co-author.

As in earlier editions, we organize the material around three key concepts: ecosystems, social work as a problem-solving process, and client-and-worker partnership. Enmeshed within this framework is material on social support, the development of helping communities, spirituality, the development of client competence, and the strengths perspective. In this edition, we elaborate on the philosophical and scientific bases for our model, incorporate biological information as well as additional content on cultural competence, explore the relevance of evidence-based practice, and establish solution seeking as a fundamental aspect of the problem-solving processes. We maintain a generalist perspective and continue to encourage social workers to attend to the personal and the environmental in both small and large social systems. We continue to use several hyphenated terms in this edition. Among others, we regularly refer to person-in-situation, people-in-situation, or person-in-environment, problem-solving, and client-worker or client-and-worker. Of course, the concept of process pervades all aspects of the text.

Part I includes chapters intended to provide a general overview and contextual introduction to social work practice. In Chapter 1, we introduce you to our view of generalist social work practice and some of the core ideas and themes associated with problem-solving processes. In Chapter 2, we explore the ecosystems perspective—and elaborate on the fundamental person-in-situation concept. We also consider how to apply knowledge borrowed and adapted from the biopsychosocial sciences in social work practice. In Chapter 3, we provide a general overview of the problem-solving process as fundamental to our model of practice. In Chapter 4, we explore the partnership between worker and client in considerable depth. We use the hyphenated term "client-and-worker" to capture the essence of this mutual, collaborative relationship of such importance to social work practice. In Chapter 5, we examine the sources of authority in social work, along with the various conflicts that emerge when different stakeholders hold opposing views and expectations about means and ends. In an effort to promote ethical as well as effective practice, we use Chapter 6 to consider the values and ethics of the profession, some of the laws that affect practice, and the conflicts that may occur among them. In Chapter 7, we build on the client-and-worker partnership theme to explore the aspects of the helping relationship that plays such a significant role in the success or failure of our service to people-in-situations.

In Part II, we explore how clients-and-workers decide what to do and how to do it. In Chapter 8, we discuss the dynamics, tasks, and functions of the engagement process in social work practice. In Chapter 9, we consider the challenges associated with communication in general and cross-cultural communication in particular. We also introduce the idea of cultural competence as a fundamental aspect of ethical and effective social work practice. In Chapter 10, we build on our exploration of communication and cultural competence to examine the data collection and assessment processes in practice. In Chapter 11, we consider the processes by which social workers-and-clients may construct a service agreement that forms the basis for work toward solutions.

In Part III, we review some of the ways and means that social workers-and-clients may pursue goals reflected in the service agreement. We explore the processes of intervention, evaluation, and ending. In Chapter 12, we consider methods to mobilize client power. In Chapter 13, we explore case management and the identification and access of formal social supports. In Chapter 14, we consider means to mobilize informal social supports, and in Chapter 15, we consider how to foster the development of helping communities. In Chapter 16, we examine teamwork in social work practice—including interdisciplinary teamwork. In Chapter 17, we explore the processes associated with evaluating the effectiveness of our programs and services. In Chapter 18, we consider the tasks and dynamics associated with ending processes in social work practice. Finally, we use Chapter 19 to explore the issue of social worker self-care, including how to maintain balance and equilibrium in our personal and professional lives and how to avoid burnout.

Part IV contains assorted readings to complement and supplement materials presented in the text. Most are original works created exclusively for this text by prominent authors in various field of practice. For this edition, we included two new case studies. Reading 1 contains a portion of George Bernard Shaw's play "Mrs. Warren's Profession." Reading 2 is Dennis Saleebey's "The Strengths Perspectives: Principles and Practice." Reading 3 is "The House on Sixth Street" by Francis P. Purcell and Harry Specht. This is a classic case study that has been used for about four decades in social work education. Reading 4 is Jane F. Gilgun's "An Ecosystem Approach to Assessment." Reading 5 is "Social Work and the Medicine Wheel Framework" by Lyle Longclaws. Readings 6 and 7 are case studies— "The Birky Family" and "The Stover Family," respectively. Reading 8 is "Variations on the Problem-Solving Theme" by Ralph Woehle. Reading 9 is another case study, "Betty Smith." Reading 10 is Susan Steiger Tebb's "The Record of Change: Client-Focused Recording." Reading 11 is the poignant "Four Pennies to My Name" by Addie Morris. Reading 12 is Craig Rennebohm's "Approach and Companionship in the Engagement Process." Reading 13 is "Basic Communications Skills for Work with Groups" by Barry R. Cournoyer and Katharine V. Byers. Reading 14 is "A Framework for Establishing Social Work Relationships Across Racial/Ethnic Lines" by Joan Velasquez, Marilyn E. Vigil, and Eustolio Benavides. Reading 15 is "Family Group Decision Making" by Gale Burford,

Joan Pennell, and Susan MacLeod. Reading 16 is Cynthia Franklin and Catheleen Jordan's "The Clinical Utility of Models and Methods of Assessment in Managed Care." Reading 17 is Michelle MacKenzie's "A Brief Solution-Focused Practice Model." Reading 18 is "Goal Setting with Biological Families" by Edith Fein and Ilene Staff. Reading 19 is Anthony N. Maluccio's "Action as a Vehicle for Promoting Competence." Reading 20 is "The Social Work Process of Social Care Planning" by Miriam M. Johnson and W. David Harrison. Reading 21 is Reima Ana Maglajlic's "Social Work, Social Care, Care Management, and User Involvement." Reading 22 is Elija Mickel's "Self-Help in African American Communities: A Historical Review." Reading 23 is Robert W. Weinbach's "Does My Intervention Make a Difference?" Reading 24 is "Termination in Context" by Howard Hess and Peg McCartt Hess. Reading 25 is "Burnout: An Occupational Hazard for Social Workers" by Jan L. Hagen. Reading 26 is a case study entitled "Leonard Timms" by Robert B. Bennett. Reading 27 is a case study entitled "The Omar Family" by Khadija Khaja.

As have most aspects of human life, social work practice has undergone many changes during the last 30 years. Indeed, the speed and magnitude of change appear to increase with each passing year. Contemporary social workers must be extraordinarily adept at learning, unlearning, and relearning (Toffler, 1983) to provide the best possible services to and with the people we serve. In effect, social workers must be consummate problem-solvers as we prepare for and participate in the problem-solving activities of the individuals, families, groups, organizations, communities, and societies we serve.

In recognition of the increasing importance of information technology, we use many materials accessible through the World Wide Web. In particular, we incorporate content from InfoTrac® College Edition— a sophisticated set of bibliographic databases and full-text materials. Accompanying this book is a password that entitles you to a subscription to InfoTrac College Edition. Once registered, you will be able to search for and retrieve articles from professional journals that pertain to the content presented in *Social Work Processes*.

As in earlier editions, we conclude each chapter with a set of learning exercises to strengthen and enhance your learning. Many require the use of InfoTrac College Edition and other valuable Internet resources. The exercises reflect the professional obligation to remain current with the ever-expanding information explosion and the importance of thinking critically about the value, credibility, and relevance of knowledge for practice. They require scholarly investigation, critical thought, and considerable creativity. They involve quite a bit of writing, which we believe supports clear thinking and problem solving. We urge you to word-process your responses so that when you have completed this course and finished the text, you have a portfolio of writings—in computerized format—that you may refer to again and again over the years. Learning portfolios serve a number of useful functions (Cournoyer & Stanley, 2002) both during your formal education and subsequently in your professional career. You might call the collection your "Social Work Processes Portfolio." Your writings should contribute significantly to your growth and development as a skilled social worker and problem-solver.

We adopt an informal writing style in this text and try to be conversational in tone. We often use "you" to address the reader individually or sometimes collectively as a group of aspiring social workers. Occasionally, "you" means the "client-and-worker" as collaborative partnership. The "we" often refers to the co-authors of the book and sometimes to the group of aspiring and practicing social workers to which we—you and each of us—belong. Occasionally, "we" means the entire population of human beings of which we all are a part.

Once again, we express our sincere gratitude to the many social work faculty and students who have of-fered helpful suggestions regarding this text. We invite you to use the form at the back of the book to forward your comments and suggestions about this edition. Outstanding social work scholars, to whom we extend our deep appreciation, have prepared several original readings for the text. We also thank Alma Dea Michelena, Caroline Concilla, and Lisa Gebo of Thomson Brooks/Cole for their wise advice, support, and friendship. Finally, we have been enriched and guided by colleagues who have provided reviews for this edition. Thanks for suggestions and comments go to the following reviewers:

Roni Berger, Adelphi University
Susan Clark, Abeline Christian University
David Cousert, University of Southern Indiana
Kevin DeWeaver, University of Georgia
Goldie Kadushin, University of Wisconsin, Milwaukee
Sonja Matison, Eastern Washington University
Gary Paquin, University of Cincinnati
Nora Smith, Monmouth University
Wade Taylor, Northwestern State University of Louisiana

We hope this latest edition serves as a solid foundation for your generalist social work practice in the 21st century.

Beulah R. Compton
Burt Galaway
Barry R. Cournoyer

In Memory of
Dr. Beulah Roberts Compton
March 29, 1919 to August 13, 2002

We dedicate the seventh edition of *Social Work Processes* to Beulah Compton, our long-time friend and professional colleague. Beulah was an inspiring teacher, prolific writer, respected lecturer, and workshop leader and was untiring in her commitment to social work students—especially students who had experienced discrimination or poverty. Beulah's life is testimony to the power of dedication and commitment. She was able to overcome challenges in her own life. Her father died of tuberculosis when Beulah was five. Her mother struggled with medical bills and support for Beulah and her younger brother. At a young age, Beulah assumed major responsibility for care of the family home and for her younger brother. Beulah's mother died when Beulah was 19 and a freshman in college. She worked her way though Illinois Wesleyan University and then completed an MSW degree at the Indiana University School of Social Work. Beulah subsequently earned a doctoral degree at the University of Chicago School of Social Service Administration—after she had already established a national reputation as a respected social work educator.

As an undergraduate, Beulah often worked two jobs to pay tuition and living costs. Limited library hours did not give her enough time for library study. She therefore began her lifelong practice of purchasing all the social work books and journals she required. Two entire rooms in her last home were devoted to her library. She installed actual library-style bookshelves in one. Beulah freely shared her books and journals with students who frequently called at her home to study with her and to borrow various resource materials. She donated her entire social work library to Rusk College—a traditionally black college—where it remains available to students.

Beulah had a long and distinguished academic career at the University of Minnesota School of Social Work. She initially retired from that university. However, she did not stop working. Beulah went on to postretirement careers at the Indiana University School of Social Work, the University of Alabama School of Social Work, and the University of Southern Mississippi School of Social Work where she served as director. During her tenure at the University of Minnesota, she spent a sabbatical year helping to establish the MSW program at Southern Mississippi. Beulah enjoyed the South and spoke warmly about her life in Alabama and Mississippi. She is buried in Mississippi.

Beulah's views and values about social work have been preserved in this book as well as in the previous six editions. The values have been shaped by her early life experiences, her work with the St. Paul Family Center Project in the late 1940s and early 1950s, and her study with Helen Harris Perlman at the University of Chicago. Beulah's professional papers have been donated to the University of Minnesota Archives.

Beulah died after a lengthy illness. We have said good-bye to Beulah's body, but her spirit and influence live on to inspire the many students and colleagues who have been touched by her.

Burt Galaway

Chapter 1

Introduction

◆ Social Work Practice and Context

Social Work

Welcome to the exciting world of social work. Helping others is among the most satisfying of human endeavors. It can also be one of the most challenging. It is certainly among the most complex.

This book is about generalist social work practice. The principles, themes, and ideas introduced here should serve as a solid foundation for your professional service to others. We refer to this practice approach as the problem-solving model. It is a view of practice that places strong emphasis on process in relationships and the processes involved in problem solving. In other words, the "means" or processes by which clients-and-workers pursue "ends" are of paramount importance. Regardless of the desirability of the goals, unless the processes reflect fairness, honesty, dignity, and respect for the people involved, the results will be tarnished and fundamentally unsatisfactory.

Before we delve further into the topic of practice, let us explore the idea of social work itself. *Social* and *work* are two simple words. Each is easy to understand. The term *social* is derived from the Latin *socius,* which means companion, ally, or associate (Merriam-Webster, 2003). In contemporary usage, social usually refers to more than one person or human system and to the interpersonal or intersystemic relations between or among them. Dyads, families, groups, organizations, communities, and societies are included within the concept, as are the exchanges among them.

Work derives from the old English *werc* or *weorc* meaning activity (Merriam-Webster, 2003). Today, work tends to refer to purposeful undertakings—those intended to achieve a goal, obtain a result or effect, or perhaps create or distribute a product. Combining these two words into "social work" should not yield an especially complex idea. Nonetheless, when joined, considerable ambiguity remains.

What is social work? Is it a profession? If so, how is it different from other helping professions? These are challenging questions indeed! The wide range of social work settings, roles, and functions, and the various forms of practice make them especially difficult to answer. Most of us can easily characterize medical doctors. Their job is to heal the human body—typically through the prescription of medications or perhaps surgical procedures. We also know that lawyers represent people and organizations in legal matters—often through the preparation of carefully written documents, negotiation with others, or in legal proceedings such as courtroom trials. Few of us have any difficulty understanding what teachers do. Their job is to educate students.

However, what about social workers—what do they do? Answers to such questions tend to be more difficult for social workers than for doctors, lawyers, and teachers. Indeed, it has been a topic of debate and discussion for most of its history.

At the turn of the 20th century, voluntary philanthropy gave rise to scientific philanthropy as social reform shifted from a religious-based auspice to an educational one. With it came the 14-year debate (1909–1923) between Jane Addams, a leader of the settlement house movement targeted at eradicating poverty, and Mary Richmond, who advocated social reform by providing services to individuals based on need, giving rise to casework as we know it today. (Holosko, 2003b, pp. 273–274)

About 50 years ago, Harriet Bartlett undertook perhaps the most ambitious and certainly the most famous attempt to define the profession (Bartlett, 1958, 2003). In her essay entitled "Working Definition of Social Work," she suggests that the purposes of social work are

- To assist individuals and groups to identify and resolve or minimize problems arising out of disequilibrium between themselves and their environment.
- To identify potential areas of disequilibrium between individuals or groups and the environment in order to prevent the occurrence of disequilibrium.
- In addition to these curative and preventive aims, to seek out, identify, and strengthen the maximum potential in individuals, groups, and communities. (Bartlett, 2003, p. 268)

In the working definition, Bartlett suggests that social work, "like the practice of all professions, is recognized by a constellation of value, purpose, sanction, knowledge, and method. No part alone is characteristic of social work practice nor is any part described here unique to social work. It is the particular content and configuration of this constellation which makes it social work practice and distinguishes it from the practice of other professions" (Bartlett, 2003, p. 267).

Bartlett's observation that the particular parts of social work practice are not unique to the profession helps explain the difficulty in defining social work as distinctly different from other helping professionals. As might be expected from a profession that seeks to address both the personal and the social, criticisms of Bartlett's working definition emerged (Bartlett, 1970; Boehm, 1958, 1959; Gordon, 1962, 1965, 1969). Discussions about a common conception of social work continued throughout the 1970s, leading to the dedication of an entire issue of the journal *Social Work* to the topic of conceptual frameworks for the profession (National Association of Social Workers [NASW], 1977) and another in 1981 (NASW, 1981a). Like the issue about whether or not social work is a profession (Austin, 2001; Bitensky, 1978; Brill, 2001; Flexner, 1915, 2001; Franklin, 2001; Gambrill, 2001; Glaser, 2001; Holosko & Leslie, 2001; Mizrahi, 2001; Rullo, 2001; Sowers & Ellis, 2001; Wong, 2001), debates about a common definition of social work or social work practice continue at the beginning of the 21st century just as they did at the dawn of the 20th. In February 2001, the University of Kentucky School of Social Work sponsored a conference (University of Kentucky

School of Social Work, 2001) entitled "Reworking the Working Definition," and in May 2003, a special issue of the journal *Research on Social Work Practice* was dedicated to an exploration of the working definition (Holosko, 2003c). In that issue of the journal, numerous prestigious authors examine the strengths and weaknesses of the working definition and explore potential themes for further development of a conception of the social work profession (Bidgood, Holosko, & Taylor, 2003; Feit, 2003; Gambrill, 2003; Holosko, 2003a, 2003b; Leslie & Cassano, 2003; Ramsay, 2003; Risler, Lowe, & Nackerud, 2003; Sallee, 2003; Turner, 2003; Wakefield, 2003). The most recent definitions of the profession reflect several themes developed in these important articles. For example, the International Federation of Social Workers (IFSW) suggests,

The social work profession promotes social change, problem-solving in human relationships and the empowerment and liberation of people to enhance well-being. Utilising theories of human behaviour and social systems, social work intervenes at the points where people interact with their environments. Principles of human rights and social justice are fundamental to social work. (IFSW, 2000, Definition of Social Work)

The federation recognizes the difficulties associated with efforts to define the profession by noting, "social work in the 21st century is dynamic and evolving, and therefore no definition should be regarded as exhaustive" (IFSW, 2000, Definition of Social Work, footnote).

The National Association of Social Workers (NASW) states that social workers attempt to

enhance human well-being and help meet the basic human needs of all people, with particular attention to the needs and empowerment of people who are vulnerable, oppressed, and living in poverty. . . . (They) focus on individual well-being in a social context and the well-being of society . . . (and) . . . promote social justice and social change with and on behalf of . . . individuals, families, groups, organizations, and communities. Social workers are sensitive to cultural and ethnic diversity and strive to end discrimination, oppression, poverty, and other forms of social injustice . . . (through) direct practice, community organizing, supervision, consultation, administration, advocacy, social and political action, policy development and implementation, education, and research and evaluation. Social workers seek to enhance the capacity of people to address their own needs . . . (and) promote the responsiveness of organizations, communities, and other social institutions to individuals' needs and social problems. (NASW, 1999, Preamble)

In the Educational Policy and Accreditation Standards (EPAS), the Council of Social Work Education (CSWE) states,

> Social work practice promotes human well-being by strengthening opportunities, resources, and capacities of people in their environments and by creating policies and services to correct conditions that limit human rights and the quality of life. The social work profession works to eliminate poverty, discrimination, and oppression. Guided by a person-in-environment perspective and respect for human diversity, the profession works to effect social and economic justice worldwide. (CSWE, 2001, p. 3)

There are many other formal definitions of social work and social work practice. Although they differ in certain specifics, all emphasize the *social* dimensions of service by using terms and phrases such as "social systems," "social institutions," "social justice," "social change," "social action," "society," and "social problems." Several refer specifically to certain social problems in particular: "poverty," "discrimination," "oppression," "social and economic injustice," and "abuses of human rights." The definitions also reflect the importance given to the dignity and well-being of people both individually and collectively. "Respect for human diversity," "quality of life," "dignity," and "human rights" all convey a special value for each person and all peoples.

You may notice that these definitions of social work do not specifically refer to the effects and effectiveness of social work practice. In discussing this lapse, Gambrill suggests,

> We use a definition of social work that reflects guidelines in our code of ethics, in which services to clients are emphasized, and that we can be most attentive and faithful to our code if we adopt a client-focused, outcome definition of social work practice. . . . A client-oriented outcome definition would go something like this: Social work practice consists of helping clients achieve outcomes they value via provision of effective, efficient, and ethical services. (Gambrill, 2003, pp. 318–319)

Cournoyer adopts a similar view in suggesting that evidence-based social work involves

> the mindful and systematic identification, analysis, and synthesis of nomothetic and ideographic evidence of practice effectiveness as a primary part of an integrative and collaborative process concerning the selection, application, and evaluation of service to members of target client groups. The evidence based decision-making process includes consideration of professional ethics and experience as well as the cultural values and personal judgments of consumers. (Cournoyer, 2004, p. 4)

We concur with these conceptions in their recognition of the importance of clients' input into the definition of problems and goals as well as their emphasis on evidence of safe and effective outcomes. Indeed, these points are consistent with our problem-solving approach to social work practice. We anticipate that future definitions of the profession will incorporate both of these aspects.

Given current formal definitions, it appears that social workers help people address and resolve social problems. In their efforts to help, social workers routinely attend to people individually or collectively and to social systems with which they interact.

Okay then, social workers help people resolve social problems. That is a clear idea. However, if we adopted this view, everyone would be a social worker. People everywhere routinely engage in problem-solving activities of one kind or another and most of us regularly help each other—our children, siblings, friends, colleagues—in those efforts. True enough. Human beings do regularly engage in various problem-solving activities and, as social creatures, often help others along the way. Parents everywhere share child-care or child transportation responsibilities. Teenagers help one another with homework assignments. Friends consult each other about personal relationships and occupational problems and offer support to those who suffer losses. Colleagues collaborate to solve work-related problems. Many people voluntarily help others by providing food to the hungry, money to the poor, or shelter to the homeless. Others offer solace to the grieved, guidance to the bewildered, and information to the ignorant.

The fact that people have problems and help one another with them represents a primary reason that the terms *social work* and *social worker* are difficult to define. Actually, most professions confront the same issue. Humans everywhere have health concerns and routinely offer "medical advice" to others. As a parent, I might say to my child, "You've got a cold. Drink some orange juice." Does that make me a medical doctor? An older sister might help her younger brother learn to "calculate the circumference of a circle." Is she therefore a teacher? You might advise a friend to "get the agreement in writing." Do you become a lawyer? Of course not! Doctors, teachers, and lawyers are specially prepared to help others deal with health, educational, and legal issues, respectively, and they all pledge allegiance to their professional code of ethics. Similarly, social workers are carefully educated to help others resolve social problems. Sophisticated knowledge about social problems and the effects and effectiveness of initiatives undertaken to prevent or resolve them as well as expertise in the skills of social problem-solving processes, and adherence to our professional code of ethics make us professional social workers. The fact that we help people solve social problems is only a part of what distinguishes us from the public and from other professionals.

The nature of the social problems faced by people and communities varies widely according to type, severity, duration, circumstance, and urgency. Sociologists tend to view social problems as "conditions within a society that endanger life or its quality, threaten core societal values, and generate a sense that something ought to change" (Cournoyer, 2004, p. 25). Social workers adopt a similar view but also recognize that people play a central role in determining what is and what is not problematic for them. Different people and groups may experience similar events in quite different ways. Indeed, they may apply unique meaning to and be affected differentially by exactly the same phenomenon. A major problem to one person may be a minor irritant to another, "just part of life" to someone else, and "a stimulating experience" to yet another. Members of one cultural group may be highly insulted by a particular nonverbal gesture whereas those of another group may be oblivious to its significance.

As social workers, then, we need to know a great deal about social problems and the effectiveness of programs, practices, and policies intended to solve them. In addition, we must possess truly advanced knowledge and expertise in processes needed to help others define, address, and resolve social problems. We need competence and judgment to select or construct relevant change strategies and the necessary skills to apply them in practice (Bisno, 1969). As Kidneigh suggests, social workers must be skilled in both deciding-what-to-do and doing-the-decided (Kidneigh, 1969). In other words, clients-and-workers make decisions about what needs to be done and how it should be done, and then proceed to implement their decisions. That is why we speak of social work as a problem-solving process or, more completely, a *social problem-solving process*.

Process

As the title of this text suggests, we view process and processes as fundamental aspects of ethical and effective social work practice. The term *process* derives from the Latin word *processus* to mean a "continuing activity or function . . . (or) a series of actions or operations conducing to an end . . . (or) a continuous operation . . . (or) the whole course of proceedings" (Merriam-Webster, 2003). In social work practice, we use the concept of process to refer to the entire series of encounters and activities that occur during the course of professional service to others. We view the social work process as a continuous and integrated whole that includes developing a collaborative client-and-worker partnership for problem solving. Although it is somewhat artificial to divide the process into component parts, we identify several subordinate processes to promote understanding. You may also refer to these as stages or phases of practice. However, please note that we view these processes as spiral-like. Sometimes, the client-and-worker revisits earlier processes to pursue them in a different or perhaps more complex manner. In our view, social work practice reflects the processes of (1) engagement, (2) assessment, (3) intervention, and (4) evaluation. Each of these processes involves numerous tasks, issues, and activities and requires sophisticated professional knowledge and skill. Some tasks and activities tend to occur within specific processes but others, such as the client-and-worker partnership, apply throughout the entire process—from the beginning to the end (or more precisely, from before the beginning to after the end).

Social Welfare

We know that the concept *social* relates to people or groups of people and the relations between and among them. The term *welfare* derives from the Middle English *wel faren,* which means to "fare well" (Merriam-Webster, 2003). Today it usually means "well-being." In a general sense, then, social welfare refers to the well-being of society and the individuals and groups of people that make up society. In our efforts to promote or maintain social welfare and to care for one another, human cultures establish organized sets of norms and institutions. Some target the prevention, management, or resolution of social problems. Others promote protective factors thought to enhance well-being. Informal social systems such as families, friends, and neighbors conduct many social welfare activities, and formal institutions and organizations carry out others. The formal social welfare system includes a vast array of publicly and privately funded organizations, agencies, and programs. Child and family service organizations, criminal justice services, homeless programs, refugee and immigrant services, teenage-pregnancy prevention programs, substance abuse treatment facilities, and mental health centers make up only a small part of the formal social welfare system.

Formal and informal social welfare activities sometimes conflict with each other and, in resource-rich societies, formal organizations may supplant roles and functions previously undertaken by families or communities. For example, in cultures where strong extended family and clan relationships exist, members routinely provide care for dependent children or aging persons. Formal systems, legislated policies, and financial incentives may be unnecessary or unwanted, and if introduced, they may profoundly affect the nature of established cultural patterns and social relationships. Dependent children may be placed with employed foster caretakers rather than with extended family members, and elderly persons may enter nursing homes instead of residing with a niece or grandson.

Formal social service systems hope to enhance the general social welfare. However, they sometimes yield unintended adverse consequences. This potential, explored in greater depth in a later chapter, weighs heavily on professional social workers. We recognize the complex implications of formalizing previously informal services. As professionals, we are morally obligated to support rather than supplant functional informal systems, to consider and counter potential negative effects on both the society as well as the people served, and to provide services that are substantially superior to those available through informal systems.

The total cost of health and social welfare services in the United States each year exceeds one trillion dollars in public and private monies (Morales & Sheafor, 1998, p. 15). More than two million people work in social service occupations (Franklin, 1997, Table 4, p. 48) and that figure does not include persons employed in health and education. There are approximately one-half million educated social workers in the United States (U.S. Bureau of Labor Statistics, 2003). Although some work elsewhere, most occupy professional positions within the formal social welfare system—especially if

heath and education are included. The relationship of social workers to the social welfare system is similar to that of teachers to the educational system, or doctors and nurses to the health care system.

Interestingly, the words *political, policy,* and *police* all share similar etymological origins. The term *policy* comes from the Latin *politia* (Merriam-Webster, 2003) and refers to rules or regulations instituted by political, governmental, or institutional bodies. Legislatively enacted policies typically involve funding for programs and services. Sometimes they include specific objectives along with deadlines for their accomplishment and criteria for evaluation. Typically, social welfare policies appear as written documents such as laws and administrative rules that describe the desired ends and authorize organizations to pursue them. Such policies may establish programs to provide income and health insurance coverage to dependent children or provide protective services to vulnerable populations.

As social workers, we have special responsibility for the social welfare system—just as doctors do for health care and teachers for education. We should have a sophisticated understanding of its policies, institutions, programs, and services. You should acquire that knowledge during your social work education. However, we encourage you to go beyond basic understanding to develop and articulate a philosophical perspective about important social welfare issues.

◆ The Ecosystem (Person-in-Situation) Perspective

Our model of social work practice builds on three core themes: (1) the ecosystem (person-in-situation) perspective, (2) the problem-solving process, and (3) client-and-worker partnership. These themes reflect well-established traditions within social work and provide an integrated framework for practice with diverse populations in various settings.

The ecosystem perspective with its emphasis on person-in-situation emerged as a framework for social work practice during the 1950s and has gathered philosophical and intellectual momentum within the profession ever since. Gordon's (1969) view (see Exhibit 1-1) is representative of conceptions of social work from the 1950s, 1960s, and 1970s in directing social work intervention toward the interaction between and among individuals and their environments (Baer

---

EXHIBIT 1-1
A Person and Situation Focus for Social Work Practice

The central focus of social work traditionally seems to have been on the person-in-life-situation complex—a *simultaneous* dual focus on persons and environments. This focus has been concentrated at some times on the side of the organism as interpreted by psychological theory and at other times on the side of environment as interpreted by sociological and economic theory. The mainstream of social work, however, has become neither applied psychology nor applied sociology.

The simultaneous dual focus on organism and environment, however unbalanced at times in terms of trying to adjust one to the other, has remained essentially non-normative. So far, social work has avoided identifying with or setting specific norms of human behavior or specifications of an ideal environment beyond the most general notion of human freedom and availability of resources for meeting basic needs. In oversimplified terms, emphasis has been on individualizing the person-situation complex in order to achieve the best match between each person and environment, in which either person-behavior or environmental situation may deviate widely from the typical or normative.

We conclude, therefore, that the central target of technical social work practice is *matching some-*

thing in person and situation—that is, intervening by whatever methods and means necessary to help people be in situations where their capabilities are sufficiently matched with the demands of the situation to "make a go of it." While social work has never very explicitly defined what is regarded as "making a go of it," there has been, again with some imbalance, a simultaneous dual concern for outcome or consequences for both the individual and environment. Some of the consequences desired for individuals are verbalized as satisfaction, maintenance of a sense of dignity and feeling of worth, relief of stress, et cetera. Regarding the consequences of the environment, more is implied than stated in the term, "living a socially productive life." We conclude, therefore, that the social work perspective in its practice is consequence—or outcome-oriented with the simultaneous dual focus on person and situation maintained in the outcome of the matching.

Source: Gordon, W. E. (1969). Basic concepts for an integrative and generative conception of social work. In G. Hearn (Ed.), *The general systems approach: Contributions toward an holistic conception of social work* (pp. 5–11). New York: Council on Social Work Education, pp. 6–7.

& Federico, 1978; Boehm, 1958; Germain, 1973; Meyer, 1970; Peterson, 1979; Pincus & Minahan, 1973).

The NASW implicitly endorses the ecosystems perspective in suggesting, "The purpose of social work is to promote or restore a mutually beneficial interaction between individuals and society in order to improve the quality of life for everyone" (NASW, 1981b, p. 6).

Social workers focus on person-and-environment in interaction. To carry out their purpose they work with people to achieve the following objectives:

- Facilitate interaction between individuals and others in their environment.
- Help people enlarge their competence and increase their problem-solving and coping abilities.
- Influence social and environmental policy. (NASW, 1981b, p. 6)

These conceptions are consonant with Schwartz's mediational approach (1961), Germain and Gitterman's life model (1980, 1996; Gitterman, 1996), and Bartlett's position that social work should focus on social functioning, defined as the "relation between the coping activity of people and the demand from the environment" (1970, p. 116). For Bartlett, social functioning does not refer exclusively to the functioning of individuals or to the functioning of social groups and system. Rather, social functioning involves the interactions and exchanges between and among people and the environment. Thus, people and environment represent a single integrated concept. We social workers must constantly consider them together. Social workers use the hyphenated term *person-in-situation* or *person-in-environment* (PIE) to capture the indivisible linkages.

The consensus, then, is that social work focuses on the interactions between and among humans and their environments. Social workers adopt a person-in-situation perspective as they help people address problems, needs, and aspirations associated with three social dimensions: (1) life transitions, (2) the environment, and (3) obstacles that impede successful accomplishment of transitional and environmental tasks (Germain & Gitterman, 1980, 1996). The life or ecosystems model in social work "integrates the treatment and reform traditions, by conceptualizing and emphasizing the dysfunctional transactions between people and their social and physical environments" (Germain & Gitterman, 1980, pp. 10–13). In adopting an ecological perspective, social workers-and-clients pay special attention to the transactions between and among individuals and their environments. We view them together in a constant state of reciprocity, each affecting the other. From this view, people experience problems when there is a poor fit between their needs and wants and the resources available in their environments (e.g., family, neighborhood, community, or society).

Should social workers work toward change in the person or change in the situation (Wood & Middleman, 1991)? An issue of long and heated debate in social work circles (Fook, 1993; Franklin, 1990; Lee, 1929), the practical answer is obvious. Social workers do, and should do, both.

A dual focus on people and environments is fundamental to the empowerment tradition in American social work (Simon, 1994). Indeed, most practicing social workers appear able to integrate clinical and social orientations in their work (Reeser, 1991, 1992; Taber & Vattano, 1970). Moreover, focus on the person-situation interaction is consistent with concepts of politically progressive casework (Barber, 1995). A "radical casework approach would mean not merely obtaining for clients social services to which they are entitled or helping them adjust to the environment, but also trying to deal with the relevant people and institutions in the clients' environment that are contributing to their difficulties" (Rein, 1970, p. 19).

In a study of 226 children seen at a child guidance clinic where childhood problems were the expected focus of attention, researchers found a high frequency of family and social problems. The authors conclude, "These findings provide support for a traditional social work concept—the person-in-environment perspective . . . a focus on only the individual yields an incomplete picture. Social workers need to provide a sufficiently comprehensive assessment to detect problems in the broader social context" (Proctor, Vosler, & Sirles, 1993, p. 261). Another study of 864 adolescents and their families obtained findings that suggest the social environment affects both parenting and delinquency (Stern & Smith, 1995). Results of these and other studies seem to confirm the obvious conclusion. In most instances, social workers direct interventions toward the social or situational context in which the person or family lives as well as to internal psychological or family processes (Coady, 1993).

In the 1990s, Karls and Wandrei (1992b, 1994a, 1994b) published a taxonomy of social problems from a person-in-situation perspective. Congruent with social work's dual focus on people and environment, the *PIE Manual* allows social workers-and-clients a means to classifying problems in two primary areas: (1) social role functioning and (2) environmental problems or conditions.

The Biopsychosocial Sciences

If social workers wish to understand people and social problems from a person-in-situation perspective, three main types of knowledge are relevant: (1) knowledge about the person—individual characteristics, biological conditions, development, behavior, patterns of adaptation, beliefs, and so on; (2) knowledge about the situation—groups, organizations, communities, cultures, formal and informal social systems, assets, and resources; and (3) knowledge about interpersonal, interactional, cross-cultural, and intersystemic dynamics, patterns, and processes to help us understand "transactions between people and environments that, on one hand, promote or inhibit growth, development, and the release of human potential and, on the other hand, promote or inhibit the capacity of environment to support the diversity of human potential" (Germain, 1981, p. 325).

The social work profession uses a great deal of knowledge about the person and the situation from the social, behavioral, and, increasingly, the biological sciences. Scientific disciples such as sociology, psychology, political science, economics, anthropology, and biology produce knowledge about the nature of human beings, the human condition, and society. Drawing on knowledge from the biopsychosocial sciences, social workers attempt to understand the nature of human beings as individuals and as members of families, groups, organizations, communities, and societies; appreciate the dynamics and processes of growth, development, and change; and, importantly, grasp the significance and complexity of the interactions between and among social institutions and human beings. In addition, social workers also generate knowledge of considerable use to people interested in helping others address social problems. Increasingly, social workers conduct small research studies as a routine part of their services and often share findings with colleagues. In addition, each year the profession produces a few hundred more Ph.D. and Doctor of Social Work (DSW) graduates trained to conduct sophisticated research studies. The profession benefits from all kinds of research about the nature and effectiveness of programs, practices, and policies intended to help people resolve social problems. Each bit of new information—whether from an aggregation of single-system studies conducted by a small group of social workers, a program evaluation, or a large research project comparing the outcomes of different forms of service—contributes to knowledge base of the profession.

A growing number of social workers view research as an integral part of their professional work. However, social work is not a science. Like other helping professions, social work's primary mission is service; knowledge generation is secondary—although it may well contribute importantly to the effectiveness of our efforts. The primary mission of the scientific disciplines is the production of knowledge; the service implications are secondary.

Nevertheless, as we discuss in subsequent chapters, social workers have a responsibility to generate knowledge and to use it in combination with that from the biopsychosocial sciences. The professional practice of social work requires a high degree of intellectual sophistication. We must be able to understand and analyze complex scientific studies, conduct some research ourselves, and adapt the findings for use in service to others. Indeed, contemporary social workers must be both expert practitioners and competent researchers.

Professional Focus

For more than one hundred years, social workers have debated the proper mission of the profession. Some seek an emphasis on societal problems while others prefer to focus on the needs of individual human beings. Based on our conclusion that the personal affects the social and the social affects the personal, we believe social workers must develop practice competence in both areas. The social worker depicted in "The House on Sixth Street" (Reading 3) helped to organize apartment building tenants to work toward social change in the form of improved housing conditions. In different circumstances, however, the same social worker might focus on individual change by assisting a particular family to relocate to a better residence.

Social work advocates for rehabilitation and proponents of prevention have also engaged in intense arguments. Critics argue that social workers spend too much time with the casualties of our society—those people affected by social problems—instead of investing in prevention efforts. The issue may be somewhat analogous to private versus public health activities in medicine. Most medical doctors and facilities focus on curing or reversing the effects of illnesses and injuries. We go to doctors when we have a heart attack, break a leg, or contract HIV. We hope that medications and various other medical treatments will cure or heal our ailments. Public health initiatives seek to prevent or reduce the harm caused by various diseases. By improving sanitation conditions, we reduce the likelihood of a number of illnesses. Vaccines inoculate populations from the deadly effects of several viral and bacteriological diseases. The debate is similar among social workers. Should we focus on policies, programs, and services that might reduce the extent and severity, or perhaps even eradicate targeted social problems? Alternatively, should we attend to the individuals and groups of people affected by those problems and help them recover?

The debate is reminiscent of the tension between social workers who focus on social change and those who attend to the well-being of individual people. Prevention often involves social and environmental change, whereas rehabilitation helps individuals to cope or recover from the personal effects of social problems. We believe that social work is and should be both preventive and rehabilitative in approach. Helping an abused child may prevent development of subsequent problems—such as post-traumatic stress— or perhaps reduce the likelihood that the child will become abusive as an adult. Serving a person who abuses children may lead him to a more satisfying life or reduce the length of a prison sentence but may also prevent him from inflicting abuse on children in the future. Similarly, efforts to provide vulnerable persons with adequate nutrition, clothing, housing, and social stimulation serve both rehabilitative and preventive purposes.

◆ Problem Solving

Methods and Interventions

Historically, we organized social work according to a preferred method of practice: casework, group work, community organization, and, more recently, family work. Even today, methods based on the size of the client system remain well entrenched in university and college curricula. Unfortunately, practice organized by system size may encourage a focus toward one end of the individual-to-society continuum to the exclusion of the other. If we concentrate our studies on practice with individuals, we may neglect the broader social context; if we concentrate on the social, we may forget the person. Furthermore, our understanding of the nature, extent, and effects of social problems throughout a society may be limited. For instance, we might fail to consider the effects of social problems such as racism on systems other than those on which we concentrate. If we consider only how families are affected by racism, we may neglect institutional racism or racist processes that extend into health care, education, employment, or housing. Finally, by focusing excessively on system size in efforts to help clients, we may obscure the range of problem definitions and solutions that clients-and-workers may consider.

Schwartz (1961) thinks it inappropriate to define the method based on the number of persons or the size of the social system served. He suggests that we regard casework, group work, and community organization as aspects of the relational system within which service occurs rather than as methods of practice. According to Schwartz, method is "a systematic process of ordering one's activity in the performance of a function. Method is function in action" (p. 148). In other words, method is the systematic way in which social workers mediate between the individual and the social environment in efforts to help people address social problems. Separating social work practice into an "individual method," "family method," "group method," "community method," or, conceiv-

ably "organizational method" and "societal method" may divert us from a true person-in-situation focus.

The so-called law of the instrument suggests that the available tool often determines the action. "Give a small boy a hammer, and he will find that everything that he encounters needs to be pounded. It comes as no particular surprise to discover that scientists formulate problems in ways which require for their solution just those techniques in which they themselves are especially skilled" (Kaplan, 1964, p. 23). We find the same tendency in social work, especially when we equate practice with specific models, conceptions, or methods of intervention.

In our approach, clients-and-workers define and assess problems before selecting solutions or interventions. Then, based on the collaborative assessment, they construct the best plans for intervention. Intervention is a conscious, planned effort to produce change. As such, it is only one aspect of social work practice. Before intervening, clients-and-workers must reach a common understanding of the nature of the problem, formulate goals and targets for change, and consider the pros and cons of potential solutions. Intervention before mutual understanding and consensus about the problem of concern and the planned solution violates our view of the professional social work process.

Certainly, associating social change with community organization and individual change with casework represents an oversimplification. We can direct social work with individuals toward change in the social environment and direct work with communities toward helping an individual person (Rein, 1970). However, this distinction is easily lost in academic courses and in actual service delivery. Social workers who work with individuals tend to focus on change within the person. Those working in communities usually direct attention toward change in the environment. Those who serve some groups (e.g., clinical) generally focus on change within individual group members, and those serving other groups (e.g., social action) often focus on change in the environment. Strict adherence to a particular practice method can divert focus from the person-in-situation to either the person alone or the situation alone.

The ecosystem perspective encourages a different view of practice and contributes to the idea of a generalist social worker who, through a collaborative process with prospective clients, assesses problems in the person-situation interaction and considers a range of possible solutions (Kemp, Whittaker, & Tracy, 1997). The array of potential solutions can include traditional practice methods but may involve combinations (e.g., family work, group work, and community organization) or different approaches and strategies altogether.

In social work, the term *intervention* refers to deliberate planned actions undertaken by clients-and-workers to prevent or resolve social problems. We also use it to identify one of the major processes in the problem-solving approach to practice. Thus, intervention occurs after the problem and the desired solution are determined through a collaborative process between clients-and-workers.

An intervention model is an organized set of procedures that clients-and-social workers anticipate, often on the basis of nomothetic evidence, will solve a defined social problem. As we have already noted, intervention is a part, but not the whole, of social work practice. Some social workers mistakenly assume that practice is primarily intervention. As a result, they may focus too intently on the change strategy and neglect other fundamental aspects of the process. Some also adopt a favored intervention method and apply it indiscriminately, without regard for the definition of the problem or for client aspirations. Exclusive loyalty and allegiance to the intervention approach may impede their ability to consider other options—perhaps to the detriment of clients' well-being. Life would indeed be much simpler—at least for us social workers—if we could adopt a single change strategy and use it repeatedly with all clients. Thus far, however, we have yet to discover a magic solution that applies to all people, all problems, all circumstances, and all time. In the 19th and 20th centuries, liquid elixirs and potions sold as medicine were often called "snake oil" to emphasize the fact that they were medically ineffective. We have the equivalent of thousands of such "snake oils" on the market today. Watch and listen to virtually any so-called infomercial or advertisement on television and you will find dozens of half-truths, false promises, and sales tricks intended to separate your money from yourself. Many of us routinely fall prey to such seductive practices. We want to be healthier, more attractive, smarter, more vigorous, and richer than we think we are.

Shocked at the ease with which people are deceived—whether by the latest special psychic reader, the newest incredible nutritional supplement, or the most recent psychotherapeutic fad—we are also sobered by the realization that we social workers can, perhaps unwittingly, participate in the same kind of charlatanism.

Absent a universal magic potion or solution for all the world's social problems, we prefer to view intervention models and methods as tools or instruments to accomplish certain specific tasks. Like hammers, they do not work for all people, all problems, or all situations. Sometimes a screwdriver works better than a wrench. We believe that universal or haphazard application of any intervention model—regardless how attractive—violates the integrity of the professional social work process and reduces the likelihood of an effective outcome.

Social Work Processes

As suggested earlier, we view social work process as a broad concept that encompasses the whole of practice. The term *process* (singular) incorporates several subordinate processes (plural)—each constituting an integral part of the whole of social work practice.

We think that the processes of engagement, assessment, intervention, and evaluation associated with the problem-solving model represent a useful framework for generalist social work practice. The model applies equally well to work with individuals, families, and other groups—including community groups, organizations, and societies—to resolve social problems.

Social workers engage collaboratively with clients in problem-solving activities to help resolve social problems in the interactions between and among persons and their situations. We view problem solving as a rational, goal-directed process that includes actions to define the problem, collect information to inform assessments and decisions, establish goals and construct plans to pursue them, produce change, and evaluate progress.

Problem Solving, Strengths Discovery, and Solution Seeking

The problem-solving model is directed toward solutions—solutions to social problems. The word *solve* is derived from the Latin *solvere* meaning to solve, dissolve, loosen, or release (Merriam-Webster, 2003). The words *soluble, solution,* and *resolution* come from *solvere*. Our conception of problem solving reflects attention to *solutions-to-problems*. We do not focus on problems alone or, for that matter, on solutions alone. Ours is not a problem-focused model nor is it an exclusive solution-focused model. Rather, it is a solutions-to-problems focused model. We do not prescribe solutions based on our own view of problems nor presume that we possess magical solutions that apply to all problems and all people under all circumstances at all time. Rather, we focus on solutions-to-problems as defined and understood through a collaborative client-and-worker partnership.

We view our clients as genuine partners in the problem-solving process. We think that people generally have access to an extraordinary wealth of strengths, assets, information, and resources. Furthermore, and perhaps more importantly, we believe that people are free agents who possess the potential to influence as well as be influenced by the world around them. Free agency, in our view, represents both a capacity to construct, experience, and affect events in the world and a basic human right. In other words, people have a right to treatment based on an assumption they are free and capable of making their own decisions and taking their own actions. We also believe that the nature and extent of human agency can grow and expand. That is, people can enhance their freedom by developing their capacity and expertise in decision making and action taking, and by constructing environmental conditions that promote human freedom (Bandura, 1989; Musolf, 2001). Certain personal characteristics and various factors in the social and physical environment affect the nature and degree of human agency. An infant cannot exercise free agency in the same way or to the same extent as can a 30-year-old adult. People denied access to educational or employment opportunities cannot assert their free agency to the same degree as do those who can enroll in assorted academic programs or accept employment in their families' businesses. People who are hungry or incarcerated in prisons and those who live in oppressive societies are unable to manifest their human agency in the same ways that well-fed, free, non-oppressed persons can.

We base our view of the collaborative partnership in work with people on the assumption of the right to human agency. The strengths-perspective reflects a similar view (Cowger, 1994; Rapp, 1997a; Saleebey, 1992, 1996, 1997, 2002; Weick, 1992; Weick, Rapp, Sullivan, & Kisthardt, 1989; Weick & Saleebey, 1995). Whitley, White, Kelley, and Yorke (1999, pp. 110–111) summarize Saleebey's (1997) five primary principles (see Exhibit 1-2) of strengths-based case-management practice.

Some proponents of the strengths perspective in social work practice have criticized the problem-solving model by asserting that a focus on problems obscures client strengths (Weick, 1992). We welcome the contributions of the various strengths- and solutions-oriented perspectives. Indeed, we believe they complement our problem-solving approach. We emphasize the search for and discovery of solutions-to-problems in our work. During the engagement phase, we move very quickly to identify a preliminary goal. The term "solving" in problem solving reflects the emphasis on solutions. The problem-solving approach is fundamentally goal-oriented in nature. We direct our efforts toward finding solutions to agreed-upon problems.

Although problems in the person-situation interaction are the basis for the initial engagement between client and worker, the ensuing formulation and implementation of solutions calls on client strengths, strengths in the environment, and worker strengths. Assessment involves a systematic identification of strengths as they relate to the desired goals, and the intervention plans draw on these strengths. The identification and use of strengths has always been a part of the problem-solving process. As problem-solving practitioners, we embrace the emerging literature on the strengths perspective (Chapin, 1995; Rapp, 1997a, 1997b; Saleebey, 1992, 1997, 2002).

The search for and recognition of strengths, however, should never be used to minimize or deny the reality of people's experience or the nature and extent of oppression and social injustice. The profession of social work exists because there are real social problems. In recognizing strengths, we must not overlook the nature and extent of human suffering and social injustice throughout the world, nor should we distort for our own purposes the pain and discomfort experienced by others. When a child falls from a bike, scrapes her legs and arms, and runs bleeding and crying to us as caring parents, we do not say, "It does not hurt" or "The pain will make you stronger." Rather, we accept the tears, the blood, and the reality of her hurt and try to provide love and comfort. When a schoolchild comes to us as school social workers and reports that a teacher used a racial epithet to insult him, we do not immediately try to redefine it in a positive light. Rather, we attempt to explore and understand the event as experienced by the child—whatever the nature of that experience. People usually meet social workers because they experience a problem. Clients-and-workers start with a

EXHIBIT 1-2
Five Principles of Strengths-Based Case Management

First, case managers must recognize that all individuals, groups, families, and communities have strengths. The challenge often is to discern those strengths when there appears to be only adversity. For clients' strengths to be recognized and appreciated, case managers must have a good understanding about the clients' experiences, the environment, and cultural makeup of the family and its community.

The second principle stated by Saleebey (1997) is that adversity can be a source of challenge and opportunity. Case managers should recognize that many families . . . have faced trauma and abuse previously and have survived it. The challenge is to help clients draw on those same resources not yet realized to address their current issues. This principle speaks to the level of resiliency . . . many families possess and use to manage and overcome numerous hardships in their lives. . . .

A third principle espoused by Saleebey (1997) is that case managers do not possess all the power to move their clients to a state in which they are capable of bringing about change in their lives. Rather, it is the job of case managers to understand clients' motivations and aspirations for change and to use that motivation as a basis for providing support. . . . (T)his principle emphasizes the power of the client's emotional state to bring about change. Understanding the source of the client's motivation is an essential factor that case managers need to identify, accept, and incorporate in the support process. A highly motivated client is more likely to be successful than one who has little motivation or is presented with goals they are compelled to accept.

The fourth principle of strengths-based case management is the recognition that the support process must be a collaborative one between case managers and clients (Saleebey, 1997). This principle acknowledges that a partnership needs to develop between the client and case manager; a partnership that recognizes the experiences and knowledge of clients, as well as the skills of case managers. Together, a process for support is inferred that is likely to be more effective because it lessens the potential for dependency on case managers.

The final principle that Saleebey (1997) identifies is that strengths can be found in any environment. Although many communities are the result of great social and economic injustices that require change extending from sources external to that environment, this principle takes into account that such communities also have many persons with talents, aspirations, and ideals. These communities also have established institutions that are stable and capable of providing different types of resources. These . . . should be identified and utilized for the benefit of the client. Too often clients are portrayed as "products" of dysfunctional communities (e.g., areas with high crime rates, low school attendance, high teen pregnancy, and a disproportionate number of female-headed households). This principle implores case managers to leave the security of their offices and seek out the positive resources of communities in which their clients reside.

Source: Whitley, D. M., White, K. R., Kelley, S. J., & Yorke, B. (1999). Strengths-based case management: The application to grandparents raising grandchildren. *Families in Society: The Journal of Contemporary Human Services, 80*(2), 110–119, pp. 110–111.

problem—some sense of distress or discomfort in the relationship between people and their social environment. Exploration of the problematic experience and circumstances conveys respect for the people and their fundamental human agency. However, we do not obsess about the problem. Once we have a consensual understanding of its nature, duration, severity, and the urgency with which to proceed, we move collaboratively to identify and implement solutions.

Solutions-to-problems call on strengths brought by the client, the environment, and the social worker. As are many other contemporary social workers (Benard, 1997a; Berg-Weger, Rubio, & Tebb, 2001; Blundo, 2001; Chapin, 1995; Clark, 1997; Cohen, 1999; Cowger, 1994,

1996; de Jong & Miller, 1995; Fast & Chapin, 1997; Graybeal, 2001; Kisthardt, 1993; Larsen & Mitchell, 1980; Rapp, 1997a, 1997b; Rowlands, 2001; Rupe, 1997; Russo, 1999; Saleebey, 1996, 1997, 1999, 2002; Weick, 1992; Weick et al., 1989; Westbrooks & Starks, 2001; Whitley et al., 1999; Wolin, 2003), we too are extremely interested in strengths, assets, resiliencies, and resources that appear within the person-in-situation and could apply to solutions. Strengths discovery is a very important part of the data collection and assessment process, and incorporating strengths represents a fundamental part of service planning. We consistently seek to identify and use the strengths of the person-in-situation as part of the problem-solving process. However, just as we are not obsessed with problems, we are not fixated on all strengths or those that cannot contribute to solutions. Instead, ours is a strengths-for-problem-solving or strengths-for-solutions-to-problems focused perspective.

Social Work and Case Management

Like many concepts in social work, the term *case management* carries multiple meanings—perhaps because *management* is often associated with administration, supervision, or control. To some, it involves assisting clients to access and use resources—that is, to manage the resources of their communities (Rose, 1992; Rose & Moore, 1995). To others, it means managing the client; it often carries the connotation of rationing or controlling access to community resources, usually formally organized resources. We endorse the first conception of case management as an array of processes associated with assisting clients to access and use the various resources of their communities. Formal service agencies and professional providers as well as friends and neighbors, extended family members, clubs and organizations, churches and other religious groups, and recreational and mutual aid groups are representative of the kinds of resources that may be helpful (Dinerman, 1992). Such a view of case management is entirely consistent with the person-in-situation perspective and our view of social work practice.

Social Work and Psychotherapy

The growth of psychotherapy within North America during the last 100 years has been nothing short of extraordinary (Crampton, 2002). The psychological revolution (Gross, 1978) and the popularization of psychotherapy (Caplan, 2001) have dramatically transformed perceptions among large segments of the general population. Just a few decades ago, people seeking or needing mental health services were subject to considerable stigma. Today, it is nearly normative behavior and a sign, among middle- and upper-class persons, of a certain status and a source of some pride. It is now common to hear people refer quite casually and perhaps with a bit of pride to their therapy: "My psychotherapist says . . ." begins many sentences in conversations.

The popularity of psychotherapy has, of course, both positive and negative consequences for society. In part, its growth may be associated with the industrial and the technological revolutions, and more recently the medicalization of various social problems (Bartholomew, 2000; Conrad & Schneider, 1992; Lee, 2003; Santiago-Irizarry, 2001; Timimi, 2002). People are more mobile, families smaller, communities less cohesive, and relationships more transitory. Mainstream society and mass media emphasize individual and personal happiness in what Lasch calls a culture of narcissism (1979, 1981). In some instances, people seek out a counselor or therapist to meet their needs for a close friendship in which they may talk about themselves without any obligation to reciprocate. Such relationships may have a "buy a friend" quality to them that, at some point, becomes profoundly unsatisfying to both provider and consumer.

Furthermore, psychotherapy is marketed widely in business-like fashion (Caplan, 1995; Kutchins & Kirk, 1997)—at times, in a "snake oil" kind of manner. We are not surprised that many well-to-do, self-centered and self-absorbed people living in a narcissistic culture frequently seek services that involve individual self-exploration, self-attention, self-aggrandizement, and self-love—especially if those services are widely available and highly promoted.

We hope to balance this somewhat cynical view, however, with our sincere acknowledgement that many psychotherapeutic services indeed aid hundreds of thousands of people affected by a range of psychological and behavioral problems. People who experience specific phobias such as fear of public speaking, heights, or closed spaces can benefit from certain psychotherapeutic treatments that reflect extremely high success rates (Bourne, 1998; Bruce & Sanderson, 1998). Several other problems can effectively be treated through some forms of psychotherapy (Chambless et al., 1998; Chambless et al., 1996; Seligman, 1995; Seligman, 1994; Thyer, 1996) and, of course, medications have dramatically reduced the suffering of millions of people affected by severe forms of mental illness.

Interestingly, the growth and popularity of psychotherapy is undoubtedly associated with the growth and popularity of social work. Master's-level social workers are among the large and expanding group of helping professionals who provide psychotherapeutic services. Indeed, some social workers prefer to identify themselves as psychotherapists or therapists rather than as social workers—perhaps because of their perception that the former titles convey greater status and prestige than the latter do.

In the book *Unfaithful Angels,* Specht and Courtney (1994) chastise social workers and the social work profession for abandoning its traditional mission to build community, improve social conditions, and promote the general social welfare. Specht asserts that an overemphasis on psychotherapy has led social workers to focus disproportionately on the individual at the expense of the social. He argues that, as social workers,

> Our mission must be to build a meaning, a purpose, and a sense of obligation for the community, not one by one. It is only by creating a community that we establish a basis for commitment, obligation, and social support. We must build communities that are excited about their child care systems, that find it exhilarating to care for the mentally ill and the frail aged. Psychotherapy will not enable us to do that. (Specht, 1990, pp. 354–355)

We agree with Specht that the mission of social work must include community building and the promotion of social justice. However, we disagree with the conclusion that service to individuals, families, and groups does not or cannot contribute to these efforts. We think they do—just as community workers improve the welfare of individuals and families. Indeed, we hope that many of you become community workers. Work with individual clients, however, can also contribute to various forms of social and community development. We anticipate that your person-in-situation focused service will lead many clients to become more active and involved members of their community and contribute to the general welfare. Our vision of practice—even when it involves work with individual clients—includes consistent attention to the social and environmental aspects of the person-in-situation. We fully recognize the dangers associated

with self-oriented psychotherapies and believe that our approach to practice helps to counteract the promotion of self-centeredness, self-absorption, and selfishness. Indeed, before you adopt any change strategy that fails to consider both the personal and the social dimensions of human experience, we urge you to assess carefully its implications for both consumers and for others potentially affected by its use. Unfortunately, several of the psychotherapies, perhaps inadvertently, seem to further "me first" and "I want what I want when I want it" attitudes and behaviors. Imagine the consequences if we encouraged parents of babies and young children, teachers, doctors, bus drivers, electricians, pilots, or sanitation workers to adopt a self-first style of life. As social workers, we bear a special obligation to contribute to a sense of community and connectedness between and among people and groups. It would be truly ironic, and profoundly sad, if we social workers participated in promoting even more self-centered attitudes and behavior in a mainstream culture that celebrates and reveres narcissism.

Settings for Practice

Social work is one of the fastest growing professions (Silvestri, 1997). Social workers serve in virtually all areas of society and the range of settings increases each year. In the United States alone, social workers

> held about 468,000 jobs in 2000. About 1 out of 3 jobs were in state, county, or municipal government agencies, primarily in departments of health and human services, mental health, social services, child welfare, housing, education, and corrections. Most private sector jobs were in social service agencies, hospitals, nursing homes, home health agencies, and other health centers or clinics. Although most social workers are employed in cities or suburbs, some work in rural areas. (U.S. Bureau of Labor Statistics, 2003)

Of the nearly one-half million U.S. social workers employed in 2000, some 281,000 or 60% worked in child or family welfare and school settings; about 104,000 or 22% in medical and public health, and approximately 83,000 or 18% served in mental health and substance abuse settings (U.S. Bureau of Labor Statistics, 2003). However, these three general categories fail to capture the incredibly wide and diverse range of social work settings. The breadth of potential roles, functions, and positions is truly enormous

---

EXHIBIT 1-3
Generalist Social Work Practice Compared with Method-Focused Agency Practice

GENERALIST SOCIAL WORK FOCUS		*AGENCY METHOD FOCUS*
Not predefined	←PROBLEM→	Predefined by setting
No client system until contract	←CLIENT→	Presumed to be agency client
Not predetermined	←CLIENT→	Predetermined (whether family, group, couple, individual, etc.)
Target = client system and/or others	←CLIENT→	Client = sole target
Includes environment as potential target of social worker action	←ASSESSMENT→	Environment viewed primarily in terms of client responses and behavior
Not predefined; multimethod	←METHODS→	Predefined
Includes client and social environments as targets; multilevel interventions	←INTERVENTION→	Primary focus on client as target
Social worker: generally multiple primary roles (such as counseling and/or linking to resources and/or case management)	←STAFF ROLES→	Technical: generally one primary role (such as counseling or information services)

Source: Rosemarie Carbino, Clinical Professor, School of Social Work, University of Wisconsin, Madison.

---

and helps to explain the increasing attractiveness of the social work profession.

Generalists and Specialists

Earlier, we observed that social workers need skills for deciding what to do and skills for doing the decided. We also suggested that the problem-solving model provides solid guidance for generalist social work practice in diverse contexts. This text will not prepare you for specialized social work practice. However, it should serve as a solid foundation on which to develop advanced expertise in service to selected population groups affected by particular social problems.

All professions, including social work, need generalists and specialists. In our profession, a generalist is "a social work practitioner whose knowledge and skills encompass a broad spectrum and who assesses problems and their solutions comprehensively. The generalist often coordinates the efforts of specialists by facilitating communication between them, thereby fostering *continuity of care*" (Barker, 2003, p. 176). Generic or generalist social workers tend to adopt an

orientation that emphasizes a common core of knowledge and skills associated with social service delivery. A generic social worker possesses basic knowledge that may span several methods in social work. Such a social worker would not necessarily be a specialist in a single

field of practice or professional technique but would be capable of providing and managing a wider range of needed client services and intervening in a greater variety of systems. (Barker, 2003, pp. 176–177)

As distinguished from generalists, a social work specialist is a "practitioner whose orientation and knowledge are focused on a specific problem or goal or whose technical expertise and skill in specific activities are highly developed and refined" (Barker, 2003, p. 414). Such specialists usually engage in advanced study at the graduate level and complete additional training in a carefully defined area.

In our view, generalist social workers are especially well prepared to help people decide what to do. Unencumbered by a preconceived commitment (see Exhibit 1-3) to a particular aspect of the person-in-situation (e.g., individual, family, small group, community) or to a preferred change strategy (e.g., social action, behavior modification), generalists are free to consider personal, situational, and interactional factors as part of the data collection and assessment processes. As a result, generalists may be more open to a greater array of potentially innovative solutions to social problems.

Clients deserve access to effective change strategies for doing the decided. In many situations, the generalist practitioner possesses competence in the appropriate intervention and may personally provide the service. In other circumstances, the generalist calls in specialists for consultation, collaboration, or service delivery. Sometimes the consulting specialist is another social worker and sometimes an expert from another profession. In many instances, the generalist—in case management fashion—retains primary responsibility for coordinating the overall plan as the specialist provides the specialized intervention. On other occasions, the specialist assumes primary responsibility as the generalist participates in a secondary fashion—perhaps as a member of the intervention team.

There are hundreds of specializations among the helping professions. A medical doctor, for example, might specialize in cardiology, brain surgery, or perhaps pediatrics. A lawyer might specialize in labor law, civil rights, or perhaps criminal trial work. Social workers may also specialize in various ways. Master of Social Work (MSW) programs often offer concentrations to help prepare social workers for specialized forms of practice.

Some MSW programs continue the tradition of organizing their educational concentrations according to method (e.g., individual work, family work, group work, community organization, administration). Some adopt a population focus (e.g., children, adolescents, adults, aged, gays or lesbians, immigrants, African Americans), whereas others organize by social problem (e.g., mental illness, substance abuse, domestic violence, crime, poverty, child abuse). Several organize their concentrations or specializations by setting or field of practice (e.g., child welfare, mental health, corrections, family services, schools, hospitals). Interestingly, however, researchers who studied more than 2,500 MSW-level social workers found that the frequency with which the workers performed 131 specific tasks was essentially the same—regardless of their field of practice (Raymond, Teare, & Atherton, 1996). Although these findings raise questions about the value of concentrations based on fields-of-practice, they support the value of preparation for generalist practice—if we address the knowledge, skills, and tasks common across practice settings. We believe that the problem-solving approach to social work practice explored in this text will equip you for service in a wide variety of settings.

Knowledge Development, Research, and Practice

Advanced education, sophisticated knowledge and skill, and adherence to a code of ethics distinguish professionals from nonprofessionals. To claim professional status, social workers must be thoroughly familiar with knowledge needed for practice and maintain currency with developments that pertain to your clients and services. Indeed, the NASW Code of Ethics states that social workers "should strive to become and remain proficient in professional practice and the performance of professional functions . . . critically examine and keep current with emerging knowledge relevant to social work . . . routinely review the professional literature and participate in continuing education relevant to social work practice and social work ethics" (NASW, 1999, Section 4.01.b) and "base practice on recognized knowledge, including empirically based knowledge, relevant to social work and social work ethics" (NASW, 1999, Section 4.01.c).

To practice legally throughout most of the United States and Canada, social workers must acquire licenses through their state, province, or territory. In most locales, eligibility for a social work license requires an earned degree from an accredited college or university program and a passing score on a standardized examination.

In addition, most licensing laws require that social workers engage routinely in lifelong professional learning or continuing professional education. Ongoing supervision and participation in workshops, seminars, and institutes help meet the legal requirements. As professional social workers, however, we also carry a moral and ethical obligation to seek, review, and analyze current and emerging information so we can base our professional activities on evidence of practice effectiveness (Cournoyer, 2004; Cournoyer & Powers, 2002; Cournoyer & Stanley, 2002). Knowledge is not static. Things we assumed to be true just a few years ago, we now know to be false. At one time, for example, professionals believed that schizophrenia resulted from "devil possession." Later, we thought that overinvolved mothers were the primary cause. Currently, we recognize schizophrenia as a medical condition of the brain. Knowledge about the particular parts and processes of the brain affected by the disease is growing rapidly. Informed by these discoveries, new medicines and treatments are under development.

The number of falsehoods once considered truths is virtually limitless. We can readily identify dozens in our own lives and, undoubtedly, you can do the same in yours. Recognition that knowledge changes in an evolutionary manner helps us maintain considerable humility. As social workers, we cannot afford to hold inflexible or absolutist views about the nature of knowledge and truth. Unless we continue to learn, unlearn, and relearn, the quality and effectiveness of our services will undoubtedly decline. For clients, the consequences of our ignorance can be disastrous.

In addition to learning from others by, for example, reviewing research studies published in professional journals, you may also learn by evaluating the effectiveness of the services you provide. Indeed, the NASW Code of Ethics requires us to do much more than simply consume knowledge. Social workers must also "contribute to the knowledge base of social work and share with colleagues their knowledge related to practice, research, and ethics . . . (and) seek to contribute to the profession's literature and to share their knowledge at professional meetings and conferences" (NASW, 1999, Section 5.01.d).

We believe that "knowledge is power." We also think that the magnitude and potential impact of knowledge-based power grows as the information and technology revolution increases in speed and size. As a form of power, we can apply knowledge in any of the ways that people have traditionally used other forms of power. Knowledge can promote liberation or maintain repression; be generously shared or selfishly hoarded. As persons in possession of sophisticated knowledge, we social workers can use our knowledge to maintain a prestigious status relative to clients or share it in collaboration and partnership. We could use knowledge to control or manipulate others for our own ends. Use of knowledge in such ways would, however, violate social work values and ethics as well as the integrity of the processes we hold dear. In our view, social workers are ethically obligated to share knowledge generously and openly as an integral part of professional practice. We often do so as a natural part of the problem-solving process and, of course, knowledge dissemination may contribute to empowerment, liberation, social justice, and community development.

In the client-worker partnership that is so central to social work practice, we avoid using our expertise to consolidate our personal power, enhance our status, or control others. Instead, we share knowledge with clients to assist them in the decision-making and planning processes.

We generally produce professional knowledge through research studies. Some social workers make a distinction between research and practice or between researchers and practitioners. We do not. In our view, social work practice involves research and social work practitioners are researchers. Practice involves careful definition of a problem, collection of data to understand the problem and work toward a solution, formulation of clearly stated goals, development of an intervention plan, implementation of that intervention plan, and evaluation of the effects. Research consists of precisely the same processes, although we may use different language to describe them.

What we call dependent variables in research studies are, in social work practice, identified as service goals or objectives. The practice intervention is analogous to the independent variables in research. In practice, as in research, we formulate hypotheses and make predictions—we predict that the interventions will solve the problem of concern.

The research plan is a description of how the investigators intend to implement the research project. It is essentially the same as the service plan, which is a description of how to carry out the intervention. There are many research methods, just as there are many intervention strategies. We believe that competent social workers are both practitioners and researchers because good quality practice represents a form of research as well as a form of service.

◆ The Client-Worker Partnership

Collaborative Processes

The client and social worker function as collaborative partners throughout all aspects and processes of problem solving. We use the hyphenated terms *client-and-worker* or *client-worker* to capture the nature of a collaborative partnership based on mutual respect and reciprocity. Social workers do not assume a superior position to clients. Rather, we encourage clients to participate actively as full collaborative partners from beginning to end.

The concept of partnership is well established in the field of community economic development (CED). This area of social work practice evolves from our community organization roots through a merger of community, social, and economic development. In this work, social workers assist whole communities—often underdeveloped and marginalized—to develop and manage their own resources and gain greater control over their destinies. These efforts often require partnerships with people and organizations outside the communities. External partners may include banks, foundations, consultants, or governmental agencies (see Exhibit 1-4). Of course, such collaborations can

---

EXHIBIT 1-4
Governments as Community Economic Development (CED) Partners

Populations are generally aware of factors affecting their fragile economy but the citizens usually do not engage actively in altering the conditions which cause the economies of their communities to be forever insecure and reliant upon extraordinary measures. They view such work as belonging to government. Thus, announcements of plans from above are the perennial expectation of a population which has learned to be helpless. Governments as partners in CED must take into account the current state of learned helplessness and follow processes to enable the population to see and take hold of ways to transform their community through its economy.

   Development of communities, and especially less advantaged communities, must follow a strategy which places responsibility for formulating and realizing change firmly in the hands of the people of the community who, in turn, learn to grasp and deal with that responsibility. Ideally, this approach involves all levels of the nation's governmental and corporate forces. First and foremost, it requires citizens to understand the facts of

their economic circumstances and the causes of their underdevelopment. It then requires them to identify, choose, and act on their development options. To place responsibility more squarely in the hands of citizens does not mean that governments must abandon their responsibility for economic development. Rather, government is situated as a stage-setter, as an enabler, and as the sponsor of a process which will transform a community according to the choice and determination of its population. Government is the force to handle those functions and activities which are otherwise impossible for citizens to handle themselves. The role of specialists is shifted from being decision makers who specify development policy to being the major source of support for citizens who would determine the direction of development in their local economy. This is a formidable role shift.

Source: MacNeil, T. (1994). Governments as partners in community economic development. In J. Hudson & B. Galaway (Eds.), *Community economic development: Perspectives on policy and research* (pp. 178-181). Toronto: Thompson Educational Publishing, p. 179.

---

involve considerable challenge and conflict as well as cooperation.

   All partners offer resources needed for the project. Although the nature or form may vary, each partner contributes something of value. Lockhart discusses the dialectical nature of the partnership between an insider and outsider working toward a community economic development plan for a Canadian Aboriginal community:

> If a current fashionable term "social impact assessment" is to mean anything beyond a cheap strategy to usurp the ability of a community to determine what kinds of development are most consistent with its own sense of being, then such assessment must ensure that community insiders learn as much about themselves from the process as do any outsiders who may be involved. (Lockhart, 1982, p. 167)

We will return to the notion of assessment as joint learning and joint decision making in later chapters.

At this point, however, we want simply to reiterate our view that all social work processes involve the collaborative efforts of the client-and-worker partnership; none is the exclusive jurisdiction of the worker.

Values for Practice

In addition to scientific knowledge, ecosystems and problem-solving process perspectives, evidence of practice effectiveness, and the input of our client-partners, certain values also guide social work practice. During the more than 100 years since the origin of social work, several common values have emerged.

> The mission of the social work profession is rooted in a set of core values. These core values, embraced by social workers throughout the profession's history, are the foundation of social work's unique purpose and perspective:
>
> ■ Service
> ■ Social justice

- Dignity and worth of the person
- Importance of human relationships
- Integrity
- Competence (NASW, 1999, Preamble)

We plan to explore these values in greater depth and consider the professional ethics and legal obligations that pertain to practice in subsequent chapters. At this point, however, we ask you to keep these core values in mind as you proceed through the text. Consider them in relation to our approach to social work practice. We believe you will find them reflected consistently throughout the discussion of our model.

Readiness for Partnership

Consistent with an ecological (person-in-situation) perspective and especially important for client-worker partnerships, the person of the social worker represents a major factor in the success or failure of collaborative problem-solving activities. Numerous personal factors may affect both process and outcome. Characteristics such as age, sex, race, ethnicity, language, physical ability, and appearance may have an influence, as may personal beliefs, attitudes, stereotypes, personality, and interpersonal style. An extraordinarily large number of factors may affect your relationship with clients and the effectiveness of your collaborative work together. At this point, let us consider two dimensions that relate to your readiness for social work practice: self-awareness and self-discipline.

Self-Awareness and Self-Discipline Social work practice requires a deep and sophisticated level of self-understanding. As social workers, we must know a great deal about our personal values, our preferences and biases, stereotypes, our tender spots, and the circumstances that trigger defensiveness or competitiveness. We need to be aware of our relationship tendencies, issues, and patterns. For example, it helps to know how we tend to react when we are aggressively confronted. Do we cower, withdraw, or perhaps respond in annoyance or anger? It helps to know if we have control issues that could affect our views and experience of others. In the absence of self-awareness, we might unwittingly exploit clients or interact in ways that interfere with the collaborative partnership and the problem-solving process.

Like other professionals, social workers often begin relationships with first time applicants with an aura of good will. Partly because many potential clients encounter us during crises or periods of vulnerability, they tend to trust our motives and expect that we will be competent—unless, that is, they have first- or second-hand negative experience with unethical, impaired, or incompetent professionals. Where nonprofessionals often have to earn trust, we usually have to make serious mistakes before we lose it. Many such errors result from a lack of personal deliberation or discipline. Spontaneous comments that would be insignificant in a conversation with a friend can profoundly damage client-and-worker partnerships, obstruct problem solving, or result in genuine harm to others. Reactive expressions or gestures can do the same.

As social workers, we use ourselves as the major tool or instrument for service. We cannot prescribe medicine or engage in surgical procedures, and we usually cannot offer money as incentives for change. We rely on our selves, our words, and our actions, to assist others in problem-solving activities. Therefore, we must be exceptionally skilled at using ourselves in careful, precise, and controlled ways. Despite common references to "natural healers" or "born helpers," we doubt that the ability to help others "comes naturally." Indeed, social workers—like doctors and nurses—can hurt as well as help others. You may have heard of hospital patients who receive the wrong medicines or surgical patients who have a good limb amputated instead of the bad. Well, social workers also make mistakes and sometimes, like doctors, our errors result in severe injury or death. You may have read newspaper reports about a social worker who failed to check on a child in foster care and did not know someone had kidnapped the girl weeks earlier. Perhaps you have heard stories about social workers who became sexually involved with clients. You might even know a social worker who failed to notice signs that a client planned to commit suicide or homicide. Regretfully, stories about incompetent, unprofessional, or negligent professional behavior are far too common. Although we all make mistakes, social workers who are self-aware and self-disciplined probably make fewer errors with less adverse consequences.

Many of the skills needed for social work practice may seem quite new, unfamiliar, and perhaps even unnatural to you. Careful listening, for example, is highly unusual in many North American cultures. How often do you feel genuinely heard and understood in your conversations with others? How often do you think others feel you have genuinely heard and understood them? If anything, it is more natural and common in everyday conversations to listen half-heartedly, picking up bits and pieces of others' words and gestures, and guessing at the meaning. Many of us typically pay much more attention to what we are thinking than to what others are saying.

Learning to listen carefully requires discipline, systematic practice, and evaluative feedback. You should become a proficient listener through your social work courses—if you complete the assignments and exercises. After graduation, however, you will not receive a course grade based on the quality of your listening skills. You will probably not often tape record and others will not often observe your interviews with clients. Unless you are self-aware and disciplined, you could easily slip back into old patterns of half-hearted listening. The people that feel unheard and misunderstood may recognize you are listening poorly but—unless you build in processes to maintain self-awareness and discipline—you may not even realize it yourself.

◆ Chapter Summary

In this initial chapter, we introduced you to our view of generalist social work practice and the social work processes that accompany problem solving. We discussed several ideas and concepts, and presented the following three core themes that support and guide our approach to social work practice:

- An ecosystems perspective provides a useful framework for social work practice where the person-in-situation is the fundamental focus of attention. A focus solely on the person or solely on the situation diverts us from our primary mission.
- The function of generalist social work practice is to facilitate a problem-solving process that includes engagement, assessment, intervention, and evaluation processes. We pursue these processes in efforts to assist clients in resolving social problems. Neither exclusively problem-focused nor exclusively solution-focused, we focus on solutions-to-problems that affect people-in-situations.
- A collaborative client-worker partnership reflects the values of the profession and contributes to effective problem solving.

In addition to these core themes, we also identified the following ideas:

- Professionals are distinguished from nonprofessionals less by the nature of the problems of concern than by their advanced educational preparation, sophisticated knowledge and expertise, and their allegiance to a code of ethics.
- Social workers are associated with the social welfare system—just as teachers are with the educational system. Therefore, we have a special obligation to be knowledgeable about social welfare policies, institutions, and issues.
- Practice methods and intervention strategies based on the size of the social system served or theoretical perspective do not constitute the whole of social work practice. Social work practice encompasses all components of the problem-solving process, including deciding what to do and doing the decided. Models of intervention relate only to doing the decided—that is, to carrying out a plan designed to produce change.
- Excessive allegiance to a particular intervention model or method can lead to disproportionate attention to either the person or the situation end of the person-in-situation continuum. The selection of intervention should follow and derive from a collaborative client-worker assessment of the person-in-situation.
- Social workers serve within an incredibly wide and diverse range of practice settings—usually within the context of an agency or program. Agency mission and program goals affect the nature, scope, and kinds of available services.
- Social work generalists and specialists fulfill important functions within the social service delivery system. Generalist social workers may be especially well prepared to help people address a wide range of problems within various aspects of the person-in-situation (e.g., individual, family, small group, community) because of inclusion consideration of personal, situational, and interactional factors as part of the data collection and assessment processes.
- The growth in the rate of knowledge generation derived from practice relevant research studies is astonishing. Social workers must continue to learn throughout their professional lifetimes and bear personal, moral, ethical, and legal responsibility to maintain currency with emerging knowledge pertinent to their fields of practice.
- All social workers are case managers in the sense that a primary mission involves linking

people with the formal and informal resources of their environments.

- The person of the social worker affects the client-worker relationship and the nature and outcome of the problem-solving process. Readiness for social work requires extraordinary levels of self-awareness and self-discipline.

Learning Exercises: Readings, InfoTrac, and the Web

The learning exercises that conclude this and subsequent chapters support and supplement the material presented in the text. Several require access to the World Wide Web and many involve the use of the InfoTrac® College Edition bibliographic resources. You will need access to a computer that has an Internet connection. The exercises involve reading, thinking, and writing. We encourage the use of a word-processing program so that you may easily save your responses to a storage device (e.g., hard drive, floppy, zip disk) for later retrieval and review. When you have completed all the exercises in the text, you will have a large collection of computerized word-processed files that, in effect, document your learning in the form of a *Social Work Processes Portfolio.*

Before you begin the exercises, please use the instructions that accompany this text to activate your InfoTrac College Edition account at http://www .infotrac-college.com. Take a few minutes to review the extraordinary resources available through the InfoTrac College Edition Web site and review the guidelines for conducting bibliographic searches. You will need some knowledge and skill in conducting database searches to retrieve some of the supplemental readings.

1. Use your word-processing computer program to enter the important terms and concepts presented in this chapter. At this point, simply list them in alphabetical order. Place a question mark by any terms that you do not clearly understand. Save your document as EX 1-1 so that you can easily recognize that it is your response to the first exercise of the first chapter.

2. Log on to the World Wide Web and go to the site of the International Federation of Social Workers at www.ifsw.org. Briefly explore the structure of the Web site and then locate the IFSW *Policy Statement on Human Rights.* Read and reflect on the policy. Write a one-page essay in which you explore the implications of the policy for social workers in North America. Save your document as EX 1-2.

3. Log on to the World Wide Web and go to the site of the National Association of Social Workers at www.socialworkers.org. Notice how NASW organizes the Web site and then locate two documents: The *NASW Code of Ethics* and the *NASW Procedures for Professional Review.* If you do not already have a copy of these documents, you may wish to make one for your own professional use. Read each document and reflect on their meaning for you as a social worker. In a one-page essay, explore those aspects of the documents that you had not previously considered. Save your document as EX 1-3.

4. Log on to the InfoTrac College Edition Web site. Conduct a keyword search (using either Keyword Search or Advanced Search) to locate the full-text article entitled "Empowering African American Custodial Grandparents" (Cox, 2002). Read the article and, in a one-page essay, reflect on the similarities and differences between the reported practice approach and the model presented in Chapter 1. Save your document as EX 1-4.

5. Log on to the InfoTrac College Edition Web site. Conduct a keyword search (using either Keyword Search or Advanced Search) to locate the full-text article entitled "Strengths-Based Recovery Practice in Chemical Dependency: A Transpersonal Perspective" (Moxley & Washington, 2001). Read the article and reflect on its implications for social work and social work practice in a one-page essay. Save your document as EX 1-5.

6. Turn to **Reading 1, Mrs. Warren's Profession** to find a brief excerpt from George Bernard Shaw's controversial play. Read and reflect on the contents. Write a one-page essay in which you identify the people-and-situations in the contemporary world that approximate those of Mrs. Warren in her day. Save your document as EX 1-6.

7. Turn to **Reading 2, The Strengths Perspective: Principles and Practices.** Review the article by Dennis Saleebey, and reflect on the contents, then

write a one-to-two page essay in which you explore the potential strengths and possible limitations of a strengths perspective for social work practice. How does the strengths perspective presented by Saleebey fit with the problem-solving model? Does problem solving necessarily imply an emphasis on deficits and an inadequate acknowledgement of strengths? Save your document as EX 1-7.

8. Go to your university library to locate the article "Social Work and the Popular Psychotherapies" by Harry Specht.[1] The article was published in the journal *Social Service Review* (1990). Reflect on the contents and then write a one-to-two page essay in which you explore the implications of Specht's challenges to the profession. Explain how Specht's concept of developmental socialization relates to the ecosystem perspective or the person-in-situation focus discussed in this chapter. Discuss the utility and relevance of Specht's views of social work assessment and intervention.[2] Save your document as EX 1-8.

9. Turn to **Reading 3, The House on Sixth Street.** Reflect on the contents and then write a one-to-two page essay in which you address the case in relation to the following issues: (a) The ecosystem or person-in-situation perspective, (b) the problem-solving process, (c) the client-worker relationship, and (d) the shift in professional focus from the individual to the community. How does this illustrate a shift in perspective from working with individuals to working with communities? How does it illustrate the idea of a social work generalist who brings in specialists when necessary to accomplish objectives? In what ways did the social worker in the case of the House on Sixth Street involve clients in decision making? Save your document as EX 1-9.

10. What implications does the idea of a collaborative partnership with clients have for your responsibilities as a professional? Try to summarize these implications in a one-page essay. Save your document as EX 1-10.

---

[1] Professor (deceased), School of Social Welfare, University of California, Berkeley.

[2] You may also be interested in Harry Specht and M. E. Courtney's provocative book *Unfaithful angels: How social work has abandoned its mission* (1994, New York: Free Press).

Chapter 2

The Ecosystem Perspective and the Use of Knowledge

◆ Systems Theory

Conceptual frameworks used for social work practice should help the client-and-worker understand the problem of concern within the context of the person-in-situation and contribute to the problem-solving process. Systems theory meets some of these requirements by shifting attention from linear cause-and-effect relationships to the person-and-situation as an interrelated whole. Less interested in whether the environment causes the person to behave in a particular manner or the person affects the environment in a certain way, we view the person as an integral part of his or her total life situation. The person-in-situation is a whole in which the person and the situation are both cause and effect in a complex set of relationships. These dynamic interactions, transactions, and organizational patterns are critical to the functioning of both the individual and the situation. However, they are observable only when we study the whole system.

The whole is more than the sum of its parts. We cannot adequately understand a problem in social functioning by simply adding together a separate assessment of the individual and a separate assessment of the environment. Rather, we strive to understand the complex interactions between the client and other social systems. Therefore, we need conceptual frameworks that enable us to identify problems in the dynamics, processes, and transactions of the system as a whole. This is different from thinking of problems as forms of individual or family pathology. The terms *dysfunctional individual* or *dysfunctional family* are incongruent with a systemic view because they do not reflect the interactional nature of individuals, families, and their environments.

The term *system* comes from the Greek work *systema* meaning to combine. In contemporary usage, system refers to "a regularly interacting or interdependent group of items forming a unified whole . . . a group of interacting bodies under the influence of related forces . . . that is in or tends to equilibrium" (Merriam-Webster, 2003). Although primarily interested in human systems, social workers-and-clients consider relevant physical systems (e.g., air, water, food supplies, buildings, communications, and transportation) as well. Mature human systems tend to reflect relatively stable and predictable processes. However, they also constantly respond and adapt to internal and external processes in pursuit of goals, equilibrium, survival, and identity (Allen-Meares & Lane, 1987; Bowler, 1981; Brooks & Shaw, 1973; Buckley, 1967; Capra, 1996; Compher, 1982; Davidson, 1983; De Hoyos & Jensen, 1985; Ford & Ford, 1987; Fordor, 1976; Greene, 1991; Hanson, 1995; Laszlo, 1996; Meyer, 1983b; Miller, 1978; Skyttner, 2001; Sutherland, 1973; Tracy, 1989; Warren, Franklin, & Streeter, 1998).

You may compare a system to a tuning fork: "When you strike one end, the other end reverberates" (Kaplan, 1986, p. 16). Similarly, individuals within a social system are also integrally connected. Affect one and you affect others as well. As a conceptual framework, systems theory serves the purpose of the social work profession well by shifting attention from either the person alone or the environment alone to problems in the systemic interaction within the person-in-situation. The phrase "the process is the problem" captures this notion. Rather than assigning causal responsibility or blame to an individual, systems theorists view problems as the result of systemic processes. The implications of this view are clear: if we change or "fix" the process, we might solve the problem.

Explanatory rather than prescriptive in nature, systems theory does not identify specific change strategies that clients-and-workers might adopt in problem-solving activities. However, it serves as a conceptual base from which to develop a rich and expansive repertoire of relevant intervention models and approaches. Strike a tuning fork in one place and the whole thing vibrates—perhaps including the hand holding it and the eardrums hearing the resulting tone.

This systems principle—that everything affects everything else—is extremely useful in social work. We often serve people who have made many unsuccessful attempts to address social problems that affect them. A systems perspective helps us to consider new change strategies for old problems, and to identify different points for intervention. By thinking systemically, social workers find it easier to collaborate creatively with clients in identifying a range of change targets and strategies as part of the problem-solving process.

System Dimensions

In attempting to understanding human social systems, clients-and-workers often consider several aspects or dimensions and use certain concepts. These include system of concern, boundaries, purpose, development, organizational structure, roles, rules, communications, incentives, and power (Bowler, 1981; Capelle, 1979; Davidson, 1983; Hanson, 1995; Skyttner, 2001; Von Bertalanffy, 1969; Von Bertalanffy & LaViolette, 1981; Weinberg, 1975).

System of Concern The system of concern refers to the systemic layer or layers that draw the attention of the client-and-worker. Typically, the definition of the problem and goal, and the locus of likely solutions, help identify the system or subsystems of concern. Systems reflect layers or levels that begin within the person and extend to the most general aspects of the situation. In generalist social work, we commonly think about the following layers: intrapersonal, interpersonal, group, intergroup, organization, interorganization, community, inter-community, society,

and inter-society. Of course, these layers are not static, either in nature or in terminology. At times, a particular layer may be better conceptualized as, for example, a couple, family, tribe, culture, neighborhood, or nation. Furthermore, the system of concern may involve more than one layer as a problem or solution manifests in adjacent systemic levels. Finally, the system of concern may change during the problem-solving process as the problem-definition is refined or the potential solutions modified.

We may regard an individual person as a system or a subsystem of other social systems within the person-in-situation system. People are part of political systems, cultural systems, community systems, family systems, friendship systems, neighborhood systems, occupational systems, economic systems, religious systems, and many more. Of course, people as individuals are also composed of biological systems, belief systems, emotional systems, motivational systems, and decision-making and problem-solving systems, along with numerous others. In theory, every system is simultaneously a subsystem and a suprasystem in a hierarchical arrangement of layered systems.

In observing the layered quality of systems, Simon (1952) points out that individuals, primary groups, organizations, communities, and societies may be viewed as nests of Chinese blocks, in which any activity taking place in one system at one of these layers operates simultaneously in at least one other system at another level. Each system nests within one or more larger systems and serves as a nest for smaller ones.

Exchange of information, energy, and resources occurs in both directions throughout the nested systems so that larger as well as smaller both give and receive. The smaller systems are not necessarily swallowed-up by the larger. Sometimes the smaller systems incorporate and assimilate the larger system. Indeed, not only do we find people in the environment, we also see the environment in people. For example, when asked to introduce themselves, people from cultures where the personal freedom and autonomy are prized are likely to use the word "I" and talk about themselves as individuals—their beliefs, ambitions, or experiences. People from cultures where family and community are highly valued may use "we" instead of "I" and refer to their social world.

Culture is part of a larger system surrounding the individual but also very much part of the individual. Each level in a system faces both ways—toward the smaller systems within and toward the larger system of which it is a part. Any action may affect the whole system and may then spread like ripples toward both the inner and outer layers. From a systems perspective, then, your interaction with an individual person affects the person and spreads to the family, community, and other related social systems. Similarly, subsystems within the individual—physical, psychological, cognitive, spiritual, and so on—influence each other as well. In exploring these interactions, however, system thinkers typically avoid traditional linear questions such as "Do feelings need to change before behavior can change?" Systems thinkers assume that behavioral change affects feelings—just as emotional change influences behavior.

Of course, the degree of influence varies according to factors such as the nature of system and subsystem boundaries, functionality, developmental level, and maturity. The performance of one part of a system can affect the whole—perhaps bringing everything to a halt (Magnusson & Allen, 1983a). Consider, for example, the immediate consequences of the September 11, 2001, attacks on the United States. Governmental officials discontinued all airline travel for a period and, of course, substantial changes in procedures have continued to this time. The economic and social consequences have been profound—but not surprising. Strategists—whether terrorist, military, political, social, financial, or athletic—are systems thinkers and planners. In planning, strategists attend to vital subsystems and major systemic processes. In military operations, soldiers target bridges and airports to block travel, radio and television facilities to block communications, and perhaps basic supply networks to block access to food and water. Terrorists do much the same in targeting those people, groups, and places likely to produce the greatest social and emotional fear and pain among the population. Of course, disrupting systems is much easier than building or repairing them. However, the principles are the same: pay special attention to the vital subsystems and major systemic processes.

Family systems reflect these dynamics as well. When a vital subsystem fails to fulfill its functions, the entire family system is affected. Sometimes, adjustments in other subsystems can compensate—at least temporarily—but occasionally the whole family's ability to function can be severely impaired. Suppose a single parent loses her job so that the family's income stream is blocked. The systemic effects can be profound. To return to its previous level of functioning, the family must regain regular access to external resources from the larger social system—perhaps by securing other employment. Of course, numerous social and economic factors affect its likelihood—many of which are typically beyond the control of a particular individual. Nonetheless, most communities take action against parents who fail to feed, cloth, or educate their children or if parents acquire resources to fulfill those functions in undesirable ways (e.g., prostitution, drug sales, robbery).

Boundaries   We use the term *boundary* to identify the places where one system or subsystem ends and another begins. Nations, states and provinces, and cities and towns stake out boundaries or borders. Landowners have boundaries to their property—often demarcated by fences. Houses, buildings, and rooms have walls. The human body has skin—often highlighted with clothes, ornaments, or markings of various kinds. Although many people regularly use the term in reference to physical entities, boundaries appear in social and symbolic systems as well. Members of athletic teams and armies wear identical uniforms to distinguish themselves from others. Gang members and business executives do essentially the same with their colors or their suits, respectively. Language, social customs, and nonverbal behaviors can all serve boundary functions as well.

We may graphically depict systemic boundaries with lines and drawings on paper or with a software program. For example, we may draw a circle around the names of three people to show they are members of a household or family. Recognizing that boundaries—like the doors and windows of a home—may be opened or closed partially or fully to control the flow of information, energy, or resources between systems, we like to draw different kinds of lines to reflect the degree of openness and closedness. A solid line _____ indicates a closed boundary where the identity of the system is extremely clear and intersystemic exchanges are blocked. A dashed line _ _ _ _ _ suggests an open boundary where the system's identity is clear and intersystemic interaction occurs through regularized processes. A dotted line . . . . . . reflects extreme openness—so open that the system's identity is unclear or ambiguous and intersystemic exchanges occur freely in unpredictable ways and forms.

All systems develop repetitive interactional patterns. These patterns result in routine interactive behaviors between various subsystems. Patterns can be either rigid or flexible. Next time you are a member of a class, observe the seats that members take at the first and subsequent sessions. Free to sit wherever they wish, people nonetheless tend to take the same seats each time—presumably meeting some personal and perhaps social purpose. Such patterns are recognizable in all systems—even in those that appear chaotic (Abraham, 1995; Davies, 1999; Kiel, 1996; Robertson, 1995; Williams, 2002; Williams, 1997).

Systems generally function better when their patterned behaviors reflect a balance between flexibility and continuity. Access to several patterns and readiness to adopt new patterns enhance the system's capacity to adapt to new or dynamic situations. During times of change and crisis, inflexibility can endanger a system's survival. On the other hand, absence of continuity tends to engender anxiety and perhaps confusion. For example, suppose you are a student in a college or university course. Imagine that it is now two to three months into the semester. The seating pattern is well established. Everybody takes the same seat at the beginning of each class. What do you think would happen if you came early and took a seat usually occupied by someone else? How do you think that person would react when she or he entered the room and saw that you had that seat? What nonverbal expressions would you expect? How would others in the class react—the people adjacent to your previous seat and those near the one you took today? How might the professor respond?

Many social patterns—such as the classroom seating patterns—operate just below our conscious awareness. Such patterns reflect boundaries of their own—albeit they may be more symbolic than territorial in nature. Pattern boundaries may also be fixed, open, or fluid. Patterns with fixed boundaries are easier to identify than those with fluid boundaries but their disruption often generates greater disequilibrium than equivalent disruption to open or fluid pattern boundaries. Furthermore, unanticipated pattern-change tends to generate greater discomfort and uncertainty than does anticipated change. Imagine the reactions of your classmates if you informed them in advance that you planned to sit in a different seat today to conduct a social experiment. How would those reactions compare with the unanticipated change?

Rigid boundaries insulate closed systems from other systems. Limited by impermeable boundaries,

they neither accept input from nor provide output to other systems. As such, closed systems are vulnerable to decay. Characterized by entropy, their component parts and processes tend toward sameness. Lacking diversity and differentiation, closed systems gradually lose their ability to adapt and function. They become static and usually die.

To grow, develop, and survive, systems must be open to input from other systems. They require permeable boundaries that permit exchange of information, energy, and resources necessary for survival. Of course, systems reflect different degrees of openness or closedness. Human systems in particular are rarely completely closed or completely open. Rather, they are more or less open at certain points, at different times, or perhaps in particular areas.

Indeed, the capacity to open or close partially or completely contributes to a system's adaptability. For instance, when a deadly virus arises in one part of the world, public health officials often quarantine the area. Other nations may temporarily restrict travel to or from the infected areas. These measures help to protect one system from the dangers of another and may encourage provision of medical care to those within the quarantine. Under other circumstances, nations may loosen policies to encourage immigration of people who have specialized expertise to contribute to their system's productivity.

Social workers sometimes notice these phenomena in efforts to serve families affected by domestic violence. Rigid, closed boundaries often separate family members from external systems—with the exception of the primary violence initiator who may interact with selected outsiders. Absent input from other systems in the community, insulated family members may conclude that domestic violence is acceptable.

Prisons and institutional facilities, such as nursing homes and residential treatment centers, also reflect closed system characteristics. Their guarded boundaries—in the forms of gates, fences, curfews, security measures, and censorship—tend to inhibit intersystemic exchange. Closed processes are evident in numerous aspects of human life and may have differential effects. For example, social workers reflect closed processes when they maintain clients' privacy and confidentiality. Generally considered desirable, the secrecy of the process may produce certain undesirable characteristics common among closed systems.

You are probably familiar with communities and cultures that are very conscious of their identity and are unwilling to tolerate strangers or new attitudes and behavior. In time, such communities, with relatively closed boundaries, may suffer some of the effects of entropy. On the other hand, you may also recognize social systems that are so open that their borders are effectively invisible. Lacking in identity and structure, and rules and routines, the system becomes increasingly chaotic and may eventually disappear into the background. Human systems that thrive tend to reflect clear and open or (i.e., dashed line) boundaries with capacities to adjust the degree of openness—closedness according to intersystemic circumstances.

Let us consider how these boundary concepts might apply in social work. Suppose you visit a family because a child is in trouble with the school or community. A parent greets you at the door and says, "I don't like outsiders interfering in my personal business. I can take care of my own children just fine." At this point, you already have two pieces of important data: First, you know that this parent is probably the person in the family charged with boundary maintenance. Second, you know that at the time of first contact the boundaries around this family appear closed.

Given this information, you may wonder if the family system might lack sufficient access to and input of new information and energy. You may question if the family system boundaries are generally closed to outsiders—perhaps because of previous experiences or cultural traditions—or specifically closed to you—perhaps because of the organization you represent or the purpose of your visit. Whatever the cause of the rigidly closed boundaries, you might wonder if the welfare and social functioning of the family might improve if its boundaries become more flexible and open.

In your work as a social worker, you may also encounter families whose boundaries are ill defined and unguarded. You and others may be allowed to enter and exit at will—perhaps even without greetings or goodbyes. Inside, you could find yourself sitting in the midst of chaotic patterns among a loose collection of individuals. You may be unable to determine who is, and who is not, part of the family or household system. Inadequate boundary maintenance can lead to just as many problems as too much—although they may manifest in quite different forms.

Obviously, social workers and clients also constitute a social system. As such, various boundaries are required. During the early part of the process, for example, clients-and-social workers establish conceptual boundaries around the phenomena that require their attention. These help to identify the system of concern. Typically, the definition of the problem and the identification of the system of concern are inextricably related. In effect, the client-and-worker must define the problem, determine its general location among the various parts and processes of the person-in-situation system, and identify those parts and processes that might become part of the solution. For example, suppose a person seeks your help with a particular problem. Let us say a parent is concerned about alcohol use by her 13-year-old son. The client-and-worker could view the problem from several perspectives and locate it and any potential solutions within many different places or processes. A common hypothesis would be that the drinking problem is located within the person of the child. In other words, the child *has* a problem or *is* the problem. The child is the system of concern. Because of such a determination, you might well begin to consider services directed toward change in the child—particularly about the drinking behavior. The child, then, is both the system of concern and the focus of change.

However, other perspectives are also plausible. For example, you might hypothesize that the family system boundaries are insufficiently clear about certain matters. The child, a subsystem of the family, may be uncertain what is and what is not acceptable. He may have received mixed or inconsistent messages about drinking or perhaps about the degree of autonomy he may exercise.

Of course, several alternate hypotheses could apply. Some might involve the child's peer group system, the neighborhood, school system, community, or perhaps even the mainstream culture. Others might relate to developmental processes or perhaps systemic pattern changes that have occurred. For instance, a favorite grandmother may have died, an elder sibling may have left the household to join the army or go to college, or parents may have separated.

In determining the boundaries of the system of concern, the client-and-worker identify the systemic location of both the problem and any potential solutions (Klenk & Ryan, 1974). Obviously, they could define the problem and identify the system of concern in many different ways. How they do so significantly affects what happens next in the problem-solving process.

Purpose All systems reflect purpose—a raison d'être or reason to exist. Sometimes the purpose is explicit, such as an organization's mission statement or a nation's constitution, but it is often implicit, such as might be the case for a person, a family, or a neighborhood. Whether written or unwritten, the system's purpose and function contribute a sense of direction and priorities that help in the identification and definition of problems and solutions.

Most social workers understand that systems tend to reflect certain purposes and goals. Appreciation of the system's mission and function provides context for the specific goals associated with the identified problems of concern. We judge your attempts to help in relation to both the general systemic purpose and the specific problem-solving goals. If you fail to identify or if you ignore either, you may find yourself involved in ambiguous exploration processes or perhaps tempted to impose goals without the full participation and consent of the client. Ideally, solutions not only resolve the problem but also support the system's general purpose and goals.

Equifinality is the capacity to achieve the same results from different initial conditions. In other words, there are many ways to fulfill identical purposes, accomplish similar goals, or attain the same end state. The concept of *multifinality* suggests an opposite principle: Similar initial conditions may lead to dissimilar results. Alternatively, the same actions may lead to quite different outcomes.

A few purposes seem to be common to most if not all systems. For example, most social systems seek to sustain its members, survive as a social entity, and grow in size, prestige, security, or resources. As social workers, we believe that each system's purposes are ultimately determined by its members as informed by people and systems affected by its activities. Of course, social workers sometimes encourage clients to consider various options and help elucidate some of the implicit purposes that we might otherwise overlook.

Development Human systems reflect constant change, movement, and development. Indeed, living systems' goal-directed actions involve change, as do adjustments to various internal and external demands. In addition, systems at all layers change as they proceed through various developmental stages and processes. Some involve natural aspects of growth and aging whereas others reflect the maturity of particular systemic patterns and processes. Obviously, the tasks, dynamics, and purposes of a 2-year-old person differ considerably from those of a

57-year-old. Those of a recently committed couple vary a great deal from those of a family with teenage children or a family with adult children and grandchildren. A new organization—for example, a social service agency—confronts different demands from those of a 100-year-old family service agency or children's bureau.

Similarly, patterns and processes reflect strains and satisfactions associated with growth and aging. For example, most of us would expect some problems following the installation of a new communications network—whether it involves a single gadget-laden telephone, a complex series of connected computers, a different way for family members to talk with one another, or a revised set of guidelines for international peace negotiations.

As a systemic process, problem solving also reflects developmental aspects. Because all systems experience problems, all systems require problem-solving processes. Indeed, most problem-solving activities occur without the involvement of professional helpers. Social workers tend to become involved only when usual systemic problem-solving processes fail. We sometimes forget the obvious significance of this reality when we neglect to explore previous problem-solving efforts or suggest simplistic solutions that clients have already tried.

In considering the developmental aspects of problem-solving processes, clients-and-workers examine factors such as whether and to what degree clients have (1) acknowledged, accepted, and assumed ownership of the problem; (2) assessed, analyzed, and defined the problem and goals; (3) developed motivation to pursue goals; (4) considered various solutions; (5) undertaken solution-focused activities; and (6) evaluated the outcomes. Later, we will explore the transtheoretical stages of change developed by Prochaska and colleagues (Budd & Rollnick, 1996; Prochaska, 2000; Prochaska, 1999; Prochaska & DiClemente, 1982; Prochaska, Norcross, & DiClemente, 1994) and the motivational-enhancement strategies often associated with those stages (Miller, Benefield, & Tonigan, 2001; Miller & Rollnick, 1991, 2002; Rollnick, 2002; Rollnick & Miller, 1995).

As systems proceed through various developmental processes and change in response to internal and external demands, they seek a dynamic equilibrium—a *steady state*—somewhat like a thermostat does in our homes to maintain a relatively stable temperature. The furnace comes on when the temperature drops and stops when the temperature reaches a certain level. Forces that promote change and those that maintain order and stability are both essential to systems. The system tends to use change forces to pursue goals, if environmental factors do not block them. Thus, instead of attempting to oppose a force within the client, you may be concerned with finding ways to ally your strength with client strengths to overcome the obstacles to growth. If the direction of the client's movement appears to be destructive, you must first examine—and perhaps renegotiate—system goals. You may be able to use your strengths in conjunction with the system's natural inclination toward growth.

Organizational Structure All systems reflect organizational structures. We may depict them graphically in the form of charts and other drawings. Formal systems, such as social service agencies, actually prepare organizational charts to depict the identity and status of various members or positions, and the nature of the communications or relationships among them. Often organized in hierarchical fashion, executives may be at the top, program directors at the next level, supervisors at the third, and direct service providers at the fourth. Informal groups also reflect organizational structure. We use lines to reveal who reports to or communicates with whom.

Although members of informal systems seldom create written organizational charts, they also reflect structures. In family systems, for example, parents often—although not always—occupy superior positions relative to children. Social workers often use genograms, eco-maps, social network maps, and other graphical schemes to capture the organizational structure of family systems.

People as individuals also reflect structural aspects. Individual personality, for instance, may be organized so that executive functions occupy one status, emotional expressiveness another, and rule keeping yet another. We may graphically depict these as well. Use of a Transactional Analysis perspective, for example, may yield a three-circle, "snowman" type figure to illustrate the relative size and strength of the Parent, Adult, and Child ego-states.

Some theorists apply a family-metaphor (Schwartz, 1995; Subby, 1990; Whitfield, 1987) or object-relations perspective (Blanck & Blanck, 1986; Goldstein, 2001; Gomez, 1997) to intrapersonal structures on the basis that the internal personal systems tend to approximate the person's external interpersonal relationships.

Roles "A role is a set of ideas associated with a social *status* that defines its relationship with another position in a *social system*. The role of teacher, for example, is built around a set of ideas about teachers in relation to students" (Johnson, 2000, pp. 263–264). In assuming the role, teachers tend to incorporate "*beliefs* about who they are, *values* related to goals they are supposed to pursue, *norms* about how they are supposed to appear and behave, *attitudes* about their emotional predispositions toward their work and students" (Johnson, 2000, p. 264). The term *status* is integral to the concept of role in that it refers to "a position occupied by an individual in a *social system* . . . status is a purely relational term, which means that each status exists only through its relation to one or more other statuses" (Johnson, 2000, p. 309). To have meaning, the status of "son" or "daughter" requires the existence of "mother," "father," or "parent." Similarly, a "pitcher" requires a "batter" or "catcher" within the social system known as a baseball team. In the absence of other players, to whom would the pitcher pitch?

Statuses fall into two general categories: *acquired* and *ascribed*. An achieved or acquired status refers to the occupation of a position within a social system at some point following birth. One cannot be "born into" or "inherit" an acquired status. Rather, we gain, earn, or attain it in some way. For instance, we earn the status of social worker through education and perhaps licensure. On the other hand, we cannot earn or achieve an ascribed status. We receive it at or before birth. Usually permanent characteristics such as race, sex, nationality, ethnicity, and sometimes religion form the basis for ascribed statuses. As such, they are often involved in various forms of oppression and other forms of social injustice.

Social workers may find it useful to distinguish between the concept of *role*—a set of ideas about a status—and *role performance*—which involves behavior and outcomes. For instance, based on an unconventional philosophy, a parent may adopt an atypical approach to child rearing. Perhaps the mother homeschools the children and prohibits access to television, video games, computers, and telephones. To enrich the description, let us say she also works nights as a nude dancer in a strip club. At variance with contemporary mainstream conceptions of the parent role, others may judge her as strange, weird, sinful, or irresponsible. However, based on behavior and outcomes, the parent's role performance could be outstanding. The children may feel loved, respected, and attached. They may be well nourished, well developed, socially adept, and above grade-level on various academic indicators.

Roles represent the basic building blocks of social systems. Indeed, systems are essentially a network of statuses and their associated roles. Social role expectations powerfully influence human experience and behavior. They affect what we think, feel, and do as we interact with other people—whose thoughts, feelings, and behavior, and feelings are also largely determined by role expectations (Perlman, 1961, 1962, 1968). In open systems, general rather than specific role prescriptions allow for adaptation in performance that, in turn, may lead to significant systemic change. Roles are also important to interactional processes because individuals relate to one another within and between social systems through their roles. In addition to performance, social workers tend to be interested in role strain, conflict, and congruity.

We may sometimes classify roles, like social systems, on a formal-to-informal continuum. Formal roles (e.g., father, daughter, company president, social worker) generally reflect greater clarity of duties and responsibilities than do informal roles (e.g., class clown, family scapegoat, social secretary). Informal roles may modestly affect external systems and larger systemic layers, but formal roles—even those within small systems—may powerfully affect the individual, the immediate system, and larger external systems. The quality of role performance of a father or mother, for instance, may directly or indirectly affect the family, the neighborhood, the community, and even the society. Partly because of the importance of such roles, larger social systems (e.g., religions, governments, cultures) establish fairly elaborate rules, patterns, and expectations for their implementation.

Larger systems usually depend on smaller systems for input and often have the power to give or withhold opportunities for growth. For example, our unconventional, homeschooling, nude-dancing mother may be punished by a larger system for violating society's expectations for the parent role, even though the immediate system—the family—is well and happy. Thus, larger systems often offer opportunities to smaller systems, but they also impose limitations through their power to define role expectations and punish deviation. Both larger and smaller systems construct notions about how to fulfill various roles. Those conceptions may vary a great deal. However, the larger systems—communities, cultures, and societies—often have the power to impose their role definitions on individuals, families, and groups. Of course, many larger systems also recognize the importance of small system role performance to their own well-being (Biddle & Thomas, 1966).

Role positions reflect meaning through their relationships with other statuses within a system. One cannot be a grandparent without a grandchild or a spouse without a partner. Systemic stability and integration requires some mutual understanding about role expectations between or among these reciprocal relationships. In large manufacturing companies, for example, people in management and those in labor often prepare formal, collective bargaining agreements about role expectations to maintain stability and productivity. Similarly, spouses in two-parent family systems typically negotiate how to fulfill their spousal and parental roles. Usually such understandings involve some division of labor as well as authority to make decisions in certain areas.

Consensus about role expectations and reliable role performance contribute to systemic equilibrium by engendering a sense of security and trust. When we can depend on others to do what we expect them to—based on their roles—we feel more comfortable and optimistic. The world seems coherent and integrated.

Role expectations tend to address needs related to internal system maintenance and to relations with external systems. In families, for example, children need protection, nurturance, and sustenance if they are to survive, grow, and thrive. The system must determine how these tasks and responsibilities will be fulfilled and by whom. The system also must negotiate transactions with other systems to give or receive information, for example, or perhaps to exchange labor for resources. These intersystemic encounters are often complex. The system must determine who will conduct the transactions and how, where, and when they will occur. The nature and number of roles varies, partly because of system size. Smaller systems generally require fewer roles. As social systems grow in size, the number of distinct roles tends to increase and they, in turn, become more specialized.

Depending on the degree of permitted individual interpretation and the nature of the role, expectations can inhibit or encourage growth. Some systems routinely limit opportunity access to certain statuses. For instance, officials in certain schools, neighborhoods, or clubs may deny admission to people of certain racial or ethnic minority groups while actively recruiting those of some other ascribed status. The nature and degree of access determine the quantity, quality, and range of experiences that affect the course of individual and system development. For instance, children who grow up in environments that lack written materials are unlikely to learn to read. Later, when those children enter situations where books and magazines are plentiful, they may then develop reading proficiency. However, the total amount of time and effort required to learn is usually much greater because of the earlier deprivation.

Roles, status, and expectations play a part in our professional relationships as well. What do we expect of ourselves when we assume the role of social worker? What do others and especially clients expect of us? What do we expect of clients? Do we expect them to be dependent, deferential, grateful, and compliant, or do we expect clients to engage us as active, competent partners? How do we communicate our expectations and how do we elicit theirs? May our respective expectations be negotiated and, if so, how and to what degree?

The answers to these questions about role expectations play a major part in both the process and outcome of our professional efforts to help clients. However, these issues apply in all relationships and all systems. When role expectations are rigid and inflexible, people in those positions tend to feel constrained and inhibited. When they are unclear and fluid, the uncertainty may contribute to stress and anxiety associated with unpredictability. Examples of these tensions abound. Discrimination tends to generate not only fear among the oppressed but frustration and anger as well. When oppressed people begin to assert themselves, those who previously occupied favored positions may experience some of those same feelings. Simultaneously, both groups tend to experience great uncertainty about the future.

The term *role set* refers to the array of statuses that people fulfill at a given point in time (Johnson, 2000; Merton, 1968). For instance, a person might be a mother, a daughter, a wife, a sister, a social worker, a supervisor, a church member, and a singer in a local choral group—all at the same time. *Role conflict* "occurs when people are confronted with contrary or incompatible role expectations in the various social statuses they occupy in their lives" (Johnson, 2000, p. 264). For example, your role as employee may conflict with your role as family member—resulting in *status strain*. You might also experience competing demands within a single status—generating *role strain*. For instance, in your role as student you might be expected to produce several papers on different topics by the same due date.

Another form of role conflict—sometimes called *role incongruity*—occurs when two or more people disagree about the expectations associated with a particular role. Some clients, for example, expect their social workers to agree with and support all the decisions they make—regardless of the implications. Some social workers view their responsibilities differently, however, and encourage clients to consider likely consequences of various decisions and actions. Similarly, some students expect their professors to transmit expert knowledge for them to record and remember. Some professors, however, expect students to seek out, discover, and construct their own knowledge. Both of these scenarios produce role incongruity, which, by the way, may sometimes enhance and sometimes impede individual growth and development.

In practice, role incongruity may arise when a social worker's expectations for a client differ from those of the client or when a client's expectations for a social worker differ from those of the social worker. A client may expect direction whereas the social worker may anticipate a collaborative partnership. Social workers serving in correctional or criminal justice organizations may genuinely view themselves as professional helpers but clients often expect surveillance and control.

Role incongruity frequently occurs when people from different cultures interpret the expectations of a given role. They may hold competing—or conflicting—views about the attitudes and behavior appropriate to the role. This can lead to serious and often unrecognized problems in social work. For example, a Native American social work student offered services to a Native American woman who desperately needed medical care but was too frightened to go to the clinic. In an attempt to act as a broker, the student visited the European American doctor on her client's behalf. The interview with the doctor left her feeling angry and frustrated. She felt that the doctor had been rude, suspicious, and rejecting. She told her field instructor that the doctor immediately began to inquire about the client's medical condition by asking one specific question after another. The Native American student social worker found this behavior upsetting because it was incongruent with her expectations about the way strangers should treat each other. Her view of the doctor's role differed considerably from that of the doctor—who, presumably, was trying to obtain information needed to assess the client's health status.

Role ambiguity exists when a person is uncertain about the behaviors associated with a particular role. For example, a young father may be unclear about his expected child-care responsibilities. An applicant for social services may be uncertain about the nature, depth, or breadth of information to share. Role ambiguity may occur because we have not clearly communicated expectations or we did so but others misunderstood. Role ambiguity is especially common during times of transition—for example, starting a new job, retiring, forming a new partnership, joining an organization, graduating from college, or starting or concluding an intimate relationship.

Keep this in mind when you meet with prospective clients for the first time. Too much role ambiguity can make an already anxiety-provoking situation for clients even more so. Take some time to explore expectations about the respective roles of client and social worker. Try to discover what they expect of you and what they think you expect of them. Clarify what you do expect and, if there are differences in perspectives, acknowledge and try to resolve them. Early clarification about role expectations helps moderate unnecessary anxiety and reduce the chances for subsequent misunderstanding.

Although specific to client–social worker beginnings, role clarification processes also apply to later phases of practice. Indeed, most relationships—including those between social workers and clients—periodically require discussions about respective role expectations. Exploration about anticipated roles and preparation for them are usually helpful whenever clients plan to try something new—whether it involves job applications, social relationships, court appearances, admissions to a residential facility or a nursing home, or placement with a foster family. People are often unclear about new roles. Exploration, clarification, and preparation reduce anxiety and facilitate transitions. For example, young people about to enter correctional facilities for the first time tend to be fearful about what might happen to them and are often unclear about how they should behave. Similarly, young children taken into protective custody because their parents or guardians neglected or abused them are often petrified with uncertainty.

Social workers often facilitate difficult transitional processes by providing information and support.

Related to role clarification and preparation for new experiences, *social support* and *social network* are also central concepts in social work practice. Social support involves the provision of various kinds of help, aid, nurturance, or sustenance from others within the recipient's social network. For instance, following the death of Joan's mother, friends and family members gather to provide sympathy and understanding, prepare meals, deal with routine chores, and help with funeral arrangements. Social support requires a social network, although the existence of a social network does not guarantee social support. We may characterize social networks by factors such as size, density, distance, and diversity. We use terms such as *nodes* and *links* or *linkages* to describe the structural aspects of social networks. Social support provided by other persons in their social network enables people to cope with environmental demands and life transitions. There are at least four types (Cameron, 1990; Cameron & Rothery, 1985; Rothery, 1993):

- *Instrumental* supports include the goods and services used to cope with life's demands, such as money, child care, or homemaker services.
- *Informational* supports involve knowledge about relevant phenomena, processes, and community resources.
- *Emotional* supports include companionship, intimacy, compassion, understanding, and opportunities to explore experiences, consider options, and discuss feelings in the context of secure relationships.
- *Affiliation* supports involve associations and relationships that provide a sense of identity, importance, and belonging.

People receive social support through formal or informal sources (Cameron, 1990; Erickson, 1984; Whittaker & Garbarino, 1983). Formal sources include people and organizations such as helping professionals, private and public social service agencies, and religious groups. Informal sources include people such as family members, friends, work colleagues, and neighbors. Clients' social networks and social supports are fundamental to a person-in-situation perspective and represent a core aspect of social work practice. Genograms, social network maps, and eco-maps are widely used by clients-and-workers in efforts to understand the nature and extent of social supports for potential application in problem-solving activities.

In certain circumstances, clients-and-workers may decide to

- Add additional people and linkages to increase the size, scope, or diversity of the informal social network.
- Enhance clients' experience of social support by increasing or intensifying the type of social support provided.
- Reconfigure the social network by removing some links, reducing or discontinuing contact with unsupportive persons, and increasing or adding contact with those capable of providing support.
- Change the nature or style of relating with people to increase the number, enhance the quality of supportive encounters, and decrease the number of unsupportive exchanges.
- Recognize the reciprocal nature of social relationships by providing as well as receiving social support.

Social networks and social support are among the most essential elements of the person-in-situation perspective. They constitute means and contexts for both understanding and for problem-solving.

In summary, role theory provides clients-and-social workers with several useful ideas. For example,

- The social system may prescribe certain behaviors based on our position within that system.
- Every role involves our own expectations and abilities as well as those of one or more other people.
- The notion of role expectation implies norms that set the outside limits of congruent, non-conflicted interactions and transactions between positions within the system and across systems.
- Both the person occupying the role and others have emotionally charged value judgments about how people carry out their roles.
- We may view social functioning as the sum of the roles performed by a human system.
- We may use the concepts of role, role functioning, role expectations, and role transactions to increase the knowledge base for assessment of the problem situation.

- Role failure and role conflict tend to occur when
  - Resources necessary for a person's ability to perform a role are lost or absent.
  - People assume new roles without knowing the role expectations.
  - Interacting systems reflect a conflict in role expectations.
  - People experience a conflict of role expectations within their cluster of roles.
  - Other systems reflect ambiguity about role expectations.
  - The individual as a system, or as a member of a social system, does not have physical, intellectual, or social capacities adequate to the role.
  - Strong feelings or crises disrupt previously effective role patterns.
- Individuals receive instrumental, informational, emotional, and affiliational social support through interaction with other persons in their role set. These interactions and the flow of social support provide a focus for social work assessment and intervention.

Rules Social *norms* are cultural rules that guide and determine the attitudes, beliefs, feelings, appearance, and behaviors permitted, expected, or prohibited by people occupying particular roles. Certain rewards and punishments are associated with rule conformity or nonconformity. Often informal in nature, these sanctions tend to control or regulate social life through various social consequences.

> Norms have a variety of social purposes. They regulate behavior and appearance and thereby help to create the recognizable patterns that distinguish one *social system* or situation from another. In doing so, they help define and maintain *boundaries* that separate insiders from outsiders, since visible conformity to norms is a sign of membership in a social system and the violation of norms can result in being excluded or expelled. Norms also support cultural *values* by attaching sanctions to the alternatives from which people choose how to behave. (Johnson, 2000, pp. 209–210)

Most social systems are guided by "implicit and unwritten; indirectly expressed and inferred; recurring over time; self-perpetuating" rules (Kaplan, 1986, p. 18). These rules vary from culture to culture. For example, all cultures provide rules about how women should fill the role of mother within a family system.

However, these rules vary according to the family's cultural heritage. They also evolve as the culture changes over time.

Cultural rules represent a parsimonious way of dealing with the complexity of interaction. There are two types of rules: (1) rules about appearance and behavior; and (2) rules about how to make rules. The first category involves content, and the second involves process.

Consider a family in which parents and an adolescent girl routinely engage in quarrels about how often she may date during the week. Although the argument may appear to be about content—the weeknight dating rule—it probably includes tension about process—how the family establishes rules. The teenager may wish to have greater participation in the rule-making process.

Suppose this family seeks the help of a social worker. During the first interview, the worker "goes round" and asks each family member to discuss the issue of concern. When the teenager girl's time came, the mother answered for her. This pattern recurred each time the worker asked the daughter a question and may reflect a family rule as well as reveal something about family roles and boundaries. Of course, an interview with a social worker is, for most families, an atypical experience. We cannot determine from one meeting if the rules reflected during the first interview also apply to other contexts. They may, however, lead to hypotheses about family operations that may be useful for assessment and problem-solving.

People tend to internalize the external rules of their cultures and, therefore, take these rules as they move from one system to another. Often accepted as truth or fact, as the way things work, or perhaps, as the way things should work, social norms tend to become essential aspects of people's core belief systems. Our psychological experiences reflect the sociological aspects of our culture. Of course, the reverse is also true as our individual beliefs and behaviors appear within and influence our cultures.

When entering a new community or a different family, people routinely experience a form of culture shock. When two young adults form a union, they often bring conflicting rules into their new family system. If both assume that theirs are the right and true rules, conflict is inevitable. If they do not develop processes to discuss and decide on their own family rules, they may become stuck in a chronic state of tension.

Communications   Members in social systems require ways and means to exchange information. In the context of systems, communications refers to all the various verbal, nonverbal, and technological processes used to express and understand thoughts, feelings, and information. Social workers are also interested in the nature, quality, amount, and effectiveness of communications relative to systemic purpose and function as well as to individual and social well-being.

The importance of communications for systems and for social work practice is difficult to overstate. In pursuit of jointly agreed-upon goals, social workers communicate with clients and with others on their behalf. The quality of and effectiveness of those communications are fundamental and indeed essential for successful outcomes.

We will explore communications in greater depth in subsequent chapters. At this point, however, let us consider a few relevant concepts from the communications literature that we think apply to all social systems.

Communications involve the quality of *intentionality*. They may be intentional or unintentional. Indeed, some communications may be unknown to the sender but known to receivers, known to the sender but unknown to receivers, known to both, or unknown to both the sender and targeted receivers. Human beings and other social systems often do not realize they are transmitting information when they are. You may think of this as the "open microphone" phenomenon. Thinking that the microphone is off, a speaker might make a remark to a colleague that an entire audience overhears. The speaker might be quite shocked to realize that everyone heard the supposedly private comment. Similarly, during a telephone exchange, a speaker may assume that the listener both clearly hears and understands everything said. However, the listener may actually hear and understand only partial fragments because of a phone malfunction.

Intentional communications may be *direct* or *indirect*. The contents and meaning of direct messages are clear, straightforward, and easily understood. The entire message is explicit. Hidden, subtle, double, or mixed messages do not occur. Indirect messages, however, contain messages within messages. The covert message may sometimes be more important to the sender or the receiver than is the overt message. For instance, a small group of three people might discuss dinner plans. The first says directly, "I'd like Mexican food." The second person asks the third, "What would you like?" This question may be a direct expression of interest in the third person's preference or it could be an indirect request for another kind of food. The third person might say, "I certainly like Mexican food and if everybody wants that I'll go along. I also really like Thai food and eat that every chance I get." This message seems to contain both direct and indirect elements. It would be more clear and direct to say, "I like Mexican food too, but I'd rather have Thai food this evening."

Social workers often use concepts from *assertiveness* skills training in an effort to understand communications or to enhance their quality (Alberti & Emmons, 1995; Davidson, 1997; Smith, 1975). Assertive messages involve clear, direct, accurate expression of one's thoughts, feelings, preferences, or requests in a manner that respects both the sender and the receiver. "I messages" represent the prototypical form: "I feel annoyed at myself when I think I am not performing up to my potential." "I love you." "I prefer oatmeal to bran flakes." "I want you to call me Professor."

Passive messages tend to be unclear, incomplete, indirect, or false expressions in a manner that increases the value of the receiver at the expense of the sender. Examples of typical passive messages include, "Whatever you'd like." "Please go first." "If you want to." "What do you think?" "You decide." Even when the sender has a strong feeling, belief, or preference, it remains unexpressed so that others inevitably assume greater power, authority, or responsibility.

Aggressive messages certainly involve direct expression of one's thoughts, feelings, preferences, or requests. However, they occur in a manner that diminishes the worth of others while inflating the value of the message sender. Examples include, "You jerk!" "I said, DO IT NOW!" "Because I said so!" Aggressive communication may induce fear, intimidation, or subordination. As such, we may sometimes consider aggressive expression as a form of assault or violence. On occasion, of course, aggressive messages serve functional purposes. For instance, a parent might yell aggressively at a child who is in the path of an oncoming car: "Get out of the way of the car!"

Although direct assertive communications have numerous advantages, in some circumstances indirect expressions serve important functions as well (Tingley, 2001). Indeed, as we will explore in later chapters, social workers sometimes transmit messages indirectly as part of the problem-solving process.

We may use active or passive *voice* to send written or verbal messages (Merriam-Webster, 1989, pp. 720–721). You may remember these concepts from language courses. In active voice, the subject of the clause performs the action of the verb as in, "José cradled the baby." In passive voice, the speaker or writer proceeds indirectly into the sentence. The subject does not perform the action of the verb and often remains unidentified, as in "The baby was comforted." In this sentence, we cannot determine who provided the comfort. Phrases such as "it is believed" or "the message was delivered" leave the actors undetermined. We do not know who believes or who delivered the message. Sometimes, the intent of passive voice is to reduce personal responsibility. If we cannot identify the actors, we certainly cannot hold them accountable.

On occasion, however, speakers or writers may wish to emphasize the object of the action more than the subject does. Through the phrase "the baby was comforted," a speaker may indeed intend to accentuate the fact that the baby—perhaps after a long delay—was finally comforted. The identity of the comforter may not have been important to the message sender.

Sanctions As social systems attempt to fulfill their purposes and accomplish their goals, they knowingly or unknowingly establish means and methods to motivate people and to reward and punish certain conditions, appearances, or behaviors. Organizations may use money or titles as incentives, or perhaps the fear of loss of status or position (e.g., demotion or exclusion). Communities may use censure, fines, or imprisonment in efforts to control unwanted behavior. Families may use praise, recognition, affection, or freedom as incentives and disapproval, rejection, withdrawal of affection, or restriction as punishers. Individuals also motivate, reward, and punish themselves by, for example, imagining potential benefits of certain desirable behavior or the negative consequences of the undesirable. Guilt or fear or apprehensive may inhibit certain thoughts, feelings, or behavior, and pleasure, joy, or excitement may encourage others.

Consistent with a person-in-situation perspective, incentives may be internal or external to the system and may precede or follow the targeted condition or behavior. For instance, a heterosexual teenage boy may encourage feelings of sexual excitement by carefully examining the photograph of a nude woman. In this instance, the picture precedes and presumably accompanies the pleasure. It stimulates the desired condition. On other occasions, rewards or punishments—that follow behavior—encourage the condition or action.

Power   Power is an aspect of all life, and its exercise is a major process within social systems. There are many types of power. For example, the power of authority refers to the legal or social status or right to control or influence events or other people. The power of competence involves the knowledge, skill, and ability to undertake some action or cause an effect.

Police and judges possess obvious authoritative power but so do helping professionals such as doctors, lawyers, and social workers. Our status as authorities immediately engenders implicit power, and in some settings, such as child welfare, the community authorizes social workers to exercise truly remarkable influence and control. Think about the extraordinary power that social workers exercise when, for example, they remove at-risk children from their own homes to a safer place. In the absence of legal authority to do so, the same behavior would constitute kidnapping.

Indeed, larger systems often have the power to oppress or liberate smaller systems and to block or provide access to growth-enhancing opportunities. This is a key concept in analyzing the relationships among various levels of systems (Ullman, 1969). As social workers, we must often consider the relationship between power, powerlessness, and the processes of human growth and development. Larger social systems may deprive smaller systems of vital resources. Individuals within those smaller systems may lack access to information, energy, or assets needed to solve problems of social functioning. Simply put, few individuals have power and control over all aspects of their lives. People may have the personal qualities and strengths to cope effectively with life but the larger social system may deprive them of needed opportunities and resources.

Processes

Living systems process information, energy, and resources in pursuit of purpose and survival. In considering systemic processes, social workers consider inputs, throughputs, outputs, and feedback.

Inputs   Inputs refer to any external event, information, energy, or thing that affects the system. Food, water, and air are inputs for people as are, presumably, social contact and stimulation. Automobile factories require the input of steel, plastic, and various other materials. Schools and universities need the input of money and students.

Outputs   Outputs refer to effects that the system has upon other systems in the surrounding environment. Humans, for example, emit carbon dioxide, nitrogen, heat, and various waste products into the environment. Some families produce children, socialize them, and prepare them for roles in the external world. Schools and colleges produce graduates. Automobile factories produce cars. Farms produce food. Many outputs serve as inputs for other systems.

Throughputs   Throughputs are the systemic processes that transform or convert inputs into outputs. Digestion and respiration represent throughputs within the human body. Socialization of children in families, the teaching of children in schools, and the manufacture of automobiles from component parts are all throughput processes.

A system may undertake numerous such processes leading to multiple outputs.

Feedback   Feedback refers to information gained about the effects of a throughput process that leads to change in that process. Feedback "produces action in response to an input of information and *includes the results of its own action in the new information by which it modifies its subsequent behavior*" (Deutsch, 1968, pp. 390–391).

Human systems are goal-directed and feedback controlled "since it is the deviations from the goal state itself that direct the behavior of the system" (Buckley, 1967, p. 53). The goal-directed feedback loop underlying self-directing human and social systems involves receiving external information about the effects and effectiveness of our outputs, analyzing that information in relation to desired outcomes, and adjusting our processes to move closer to accomplishing our goals. Thus, feedback is central to the interaction between a system and its environment. In a complex adaptive system, there are multistage mediating processes between the reception of feedback and its use (Buckley, 1967).

Feedback may be negative or positive. Both forms are useful because they guide the nature, direction, and extent of change. Beware of the temptation to view negative feedback as "bad" and positive feedback as "good." Indeed, both forms are essential aspects of systemic process. Negative feedback conveys information that the throughput processes are not producing the desired outputs at the preferred quality or in the expected quantity. Systems may incorporate that information and make changes to the processes so that outputs more closely approximate its goals. Positive feedback confirms that the throughputs are indeed producing outputs of the desired kind, quality, and quantity and encourages continuation of the same processes. In effect, negative feedback encourages change, whereas positive feedback encourages stability or perhaps an increase in the frequency or intensity of those processes currently in place.

Tension represents a form of feedback and is characteristic of all living systems. As feedback, tension serves several vital functions. We should not view its absence as desirable or its presence as undesirable. Rather, "some level of tension must be seen as characteristic of and vital to such systems although it may manifest itself as now destructive, now constructive" (Buckley, 1967, p. 53). Chronic, extremely high levels and continuous long-term minimal levels of tension can be destructive, but modest levels of tension tend to be constructive.

Systems and Social Work Practice

Social workers tend to apply principles and concepts from systems theory to client systems. However, social workers do some of their most important, time-consuming, and demanding work with people other than clients. If you serve as a social worker in child welfare, you interact with court systems, medical services, neighbors, police, attorneys, the school officials, foster parents, and other child-care services. Of course, the social service agency where you work is a system as well. Its characteristics and processes certainly affect you as well as the clients you serve in very significant ways.

Social workers often think of clients as the primary beneficiaries of their helping efforts. However, as you begin to work with people, ask yourself a few questions. Who authorizes you to become involved? Who might benefit most from your service? Who or what must change? Who is the real client? These can be challenging questions indeed. Consider, for example, who might be the client in a child abuse investigation?

Who is the client when parents identify their teenage son's drug use as a problem? Who is the client when a teacher sends a student to the school social worker? Who is the client when a judge requires a 38-year-old man convicted of voyeuristic "peeping" to receive counseling services from a social worker?

These are extraordinarily difficult questions partly because they reflect the complexity of social work practice. Most of our services involve multiple systems—each of which may have different purposes, rules, expectations, and objectives. Some hold conflicting views about what you the social worker should do, how you should do it, and what should be the outcomes. You must develop ways and means to deal with different agendas among several related social systems. As social workers, we rarely interact exclusively with people formally identified as clients. Most of the time, our service to clients involves contact with several other people and sometimes numerous other systems.

Pincus and Minahan (1973) suggest that social workers interact with four types of social systems: (1) the change agent system, (2) the client system, (3) the target system, and (4) the action system. We add a fifth category—the professional system.

Change Agent System   Social workers are change agents employed for the purpose of planning and working with other systems. You may think of your agency or organization as the change agent system. Obviously, the change agent system strongly influences your professional behavior through policies, procedures, constraints, and resources.

Client System   People become part of a client system when they ask for or agree to accept social work services. Although many people voluntarily seek professional help, some become consumers in other ways. For instance, a powerful social system may expect you to serve someone. If you work in corrections, child welfare, or adult protective services, people may be required to receive your services. In such circumstances, who the client is may not be clear. Is the client the recipient of services or the powerful other? Might the actual client be the community at large, a judge, a prosecutor, or family members who have some degree of authority over the service recipient?

When a supervisor or program director within your agency assigns you to address a community need, it may not be clear whether the community or the change agent system—your agency—is the client. People identified as the targets of your efforts are not clients—unless or until they provide informed consent for you to intervene in their lives. In the absence of such an agreement, we may view them as a target system or perhaps as potential clients. However, they do not yet meet our definition of a client system.

Target System A target system includes the people or social systems that change agents "need to change or influence in order to accomplish their goals" (Pincus & Minahan, 1973, p. 58). If the agreed-upon goals for service involve change in the client system then the client system is simultaneously the target system as well. However, much of social work practice involves work with a client system toward change in another system—the target system. We believe that people do not become clients without their consent. If you approach a person at the request of someone else, or a person comes to you because he or she is required to do so, the person to whom you direct your change efforts is a target system rather than a client system.

Action System The action system consists of those with whom the social worker participates in problem-solving efforts. Sometimes a single person or group is simultaneously the action system, target system, and client system. However, frequently problem-solving activities involve people and systems other than the client or the target. Others may join in the change efforts—often in a cooperative manner because of shared views and goals. Social workers routinely collaborate with numerous action systems, such as neighborhood or community groups, advocacy organizations, family groups, mutual aid groups, self-help and support groups, or interdisciplinary professional teams.

Professional System The professional system includes social work associations; schools and departments of social work; social work accreditation and licensing bodies; and the values, ethics, laws, and sanctions that pertain to social workers and their practice. The knowledge, values, and culture of the professional system strongly influence the nature of the actions you may undertake and the manner in which you do so. The professional system largely determines what social workers must do and what they may do—what is required and what is permissible. As such, the

professional system often serves as a valuable member of the action system as you advocate for social change. Of course, the professional system may sometimes constitute your client system—when, for instance, you provide service to the National Association of Social Workers (NASW). On occasion, it might become a target system—when you seek change in association policies.

◆ Ecosystems

Person-in-Situation

Social workers tend to adopt a multilevel systems perspective in attempts to appreciate and understand people in their environmental context. We refer to this view as the ecosystems or person-in-situation perspective. *Ecology* refers to the study of the patterns of interactions and relationships between and among organisms and their environments (Merriam-Webster, 2003). *Human ecology* involves the study of "the spatial and temporal interrelationships between humans and their economic, social, and political organization" as well as "human communities and populations especially as concerned with preservation of environmental quality (as of air or water) through proper application of conservation and civil engineering practices" (Merriam-Webster, 2003).

Bronfenbrenner (1977, 1979, 1989, 1992, 1997, 2000) refers to ecological systems in his analysis of human development. Germain and Gitterman (Germain, 1973, 1976, 1978, 1979a, 1979b, 1981; Germain & Gitterman, 1980, 1995, 1996; Gitterman, 1996) draw on Bronfenbrenner's work to formulate an ecological or ecosystems model for social work practice. This approach, known as the *life model,* has been widely adopted and expanded by several other scholars (Bernier & Siegel, 1994; Brower, 1988; Brower & Nurius, 1993; Clancy, 1995; Fraser, 1996, 1997; Hartman, 1979; Henry, Stephenson, Hanson, & Hargett, 1993; Kelley, McKay, & Nelson, 1985; Kemp et al., 1997; Lenqua, Wolchik, & Brauer, 1995; Maluccio, Washitz, & Libassi, 1992; Mattaini, 1990; Meyer, 1988; Minahan, 1993; Osterman & Benbenishty, 1992; Peterson, 1979; Rothery, 1993; Stern & Smith, 1995).

Biological scientists use the term *ecosystem* to refer to "the complex of a community of organisms and its environment functioning as an ecological unit"

EXHIBIT 2-1
Key Ecosystem Concepts

The ecosystem perspective in social work embodies a balanced emphasis on person and environment and is characterized by the following concepts:

1. The environment is a complex environment-behavior-person whole, consisting of a continuous, interlocking process of relationships, not arbitrary dualisms.
2. The mutual interdependence among person, behavior, and environment is emphasized.
3. Systems concepts are used to analyze the complex interrelationships within the ecological whole.
4. Behavior is recognized to be site-specific.
5. Assessment and evaluation should be through the naturalistic, direct observation of the intact, undisturbed, natural organism-environment system.
6. The relationship of the parts within the ecosystem is orderly, structured, lawful, and deterministic.
7. Behavior results from mediated transactions between the person and the multivariate environment.
8. The central task of behavioral science is to develop taxonomies of environments, behaviors, and behavior-environment linkages and to determine their distribution in the natural world.

Source: Allen-Meares, P., & Lane, B. A. (1987). Grounding social work practice in theory: Ecosystems. *Social Casework: The Journal of Contemporary Social Work, 68*(9), 515–521, p. 518.

(Merriam-Webster, 2003). Social workers maintain the same general meaning while incorporating psychological and social factors (see Exhibit 2-1 for a brief summary of key ecosystems concepts). An ecosystems perspective is a "conceptual lens through which the social worker can note the systemic relatedness of case variables. The ecosystems perspective offers no prescription for intervention but as a meta-theory attempts to depict phenomena in their connectedness and complexity. This perspective permits multiple practice theories, approaches, and practitioner roles" (Barker, 2003, p. 137).

Although criticized as unnecessary and less useful than domain-specific theories (Wakefield, 1996a, 1996b, 1996c), the ecosystem perspective serves widely as a contextual guide for practice in many settings and with many different clients, including communities (Figueira-McDonough, 1995), schools (Clancy, 1995), families (Maddock, 1993; Rothery, 1993), groups of clients with sickle cell disease (Kramer & Nash, 1995), persons with dementia (Minahan, 1993), foster care (Osterman & Benbenishty, 1992), suicidal adolescents (Henry et al., 1993), children with behavior problems (Bernier & Siegel, 1994; Fraser, 1996, 1997), and children adjusting to divorce (Lenqua et al., 1995). We believe that the ecosystems perspective supports social work's assumption of interdependency between people and environments and complements our problem-solving approach to practice.

In exploring the person-in-situation, social workers consider internal and external demands, personal coping or adaptive abilities, and environmental supports. Problems typically develop when there are gaps between a person's coping abilities and the demands of the environment, or between personal wants and environmental resources. Goodness-of-fit results when a person's wants and abilities match the demands and resources of the surrounding environment.

Germain and Gitterman (1980, 1996) suggest that problems often occur during life transitions when role demands increase but coping abilities or environmental supports remain static. The classification system developed by Karls and Wandrei reflects an ecosystem perspective (1992b, 1994a, 1994b, 1995). Their person-in-environment (PIE) scheme provides social workers-and-clients a means to classify problems in two primary areas: (1) social role functioning and (2) environmental problems or conditions. Social functioning is defined as "a person's overall performance in his or her social roles" (Karls & Wandrei, 1994a, p. 7). Karls and Wandrei also identify four categories of social problems: (1) family, (2) other interpersonal,

(3) occupational, and (4) specialized situation. Social problems or conditions may occur within six environmental systems: (1) economic and basic needs; (2) education and training; (3) judicial and legal system; (4) health, safety, and social services; (5) voluntary association system: and (6) affectional support (1994a).

Change efforts may be directed toward reducing personal or environmental demands, increasing environmental supports, strengthening individual coping abilities, or—as is usually the case—some combination thereof. In general, then, social work services address social problems that result from a lack of fit between individuals and their environments. From an ecosystems perspective, clients-and-workers work toward change in the environment, the person, or the interaction between the two.

We should not dichotomize the individual and the environment. They are not separate entities. The person is part of the environment and the environment is part of the person. Indeed, the structures and cultures of society emerge in the self and life of each person just as each person affects the environment. In our appreciation for this profound interdependency, however, social workers recognize that each person's life is unique—a reflection of self as well as society. Human beings experience the world from their own personal perspectives with idiosyncratic opportunities, meanings, feelings, identities, and myths—which they internalize and selectively apply as internal and external circumstances warrant (Levinson, 1978).

What Is the Person?

The person is a complex biopsychosocial system within the person-in-situation constellation. Although social workers often focus upon understanding the psychology of the person, knowledge about biological and spiritual aspects are equally relevant. Indeed, scientific discoveries associated with the genome project have dramatically increased our appreciation of genetic factors and biochemical processes in the context of the ongoing debates about "nature versus nurture."

Biological Factors   Social workers have long recognized the relevance of biological factors in efforts to understand and assist people with various social problems. In serving parents concerned about the psychosocial development of their children, knowledge of common developmental milestones helps social workers distinguish normative processes from those

of genuine concern. Understanding the influence of biochemical factors on adolescent development and behavior helps in this regard as well. Basic understanding of the biological needs of pregnant women and developing fetuses, infants, and children are often extremely relevant in service to families with a limited knowledge base. Many social workers serve in public health, family planning, and teenage pregnancy programs. Others work in prevention programs to reduce the prevalence of SIDS, HIV/AIDS, lead-based poisoning, and damage to mothers and infants caused by tobacco, alcohol, and drug consumption. Recognition of common genetically based as well as environmentally influenced illnesses and conditions enable social workers to refer underserved populations to needed medical services. Understanding of diseases and disease processes are central to many aspects of social work service in health and mental health settings. Many social workers serve people and families affected by cancer, diabetes, lung and liver diseases, dementia and Alzheimer's syndrome, and illness or injury-based disabilities of all kinds. Social workers who serve in correctional agencies increasingly recognize that many people incarcerated for criminal behavior are affected by brain damage, learning disabilities, and other conditions influenced by genetic factors, physical injuries, or illness. The incredible advances in neuroscience and brain research have led many social workers to reconsider long-held beliefs about the relative importance of nature in the nature-nurture continuum. Similarly, genetics research has contributed to the development of genetics counseling as an important subspeciality within social work. The truly outstanding advances in knowledge growing out of the human genome project reinforce our recognition of the systemic relationship among biological, psychological, social, and environmental factors (Harris, 1998; Pinker, 2002; Ridley, 2003).

Begun formally in 1990, the U.S. Human Genome Project is a 13-year effort coordinated by the U.S. Department of Energy and the National Institutes of Health. The project originally was planned to last 15 years, but rapid technological advances have accelerated the expected completion date to 2003. Project *goals* are to

- *identify* all the approximate 30,000 genes in human DNA,
- *determine* the sequences of the 3 billion chemical base pairs that make up human DNA,
- *store* this information in databases,
- *improve* tools for data analysis,

- *transfer* related technologies to the private sector, and
- *address* the ethical, legal, and social issues (ELSI) that may arise from the project. (U.S. Department of Energy Human Genome Program)

In the contemporary context of professional social work practice, genuine expertise in one's field of practice is expected. Social workers must be familiar with biological factors associated with the people-and-environments they serve. Indeed, the Council on Social Work Education (CSWE) requires accredited programs to educate students about "theories and knowledge of biological, sociological, cultural, psychological, and spiritual development across the life span" (CSWE, 2001, p. 11).

Psychoanalytic Constructs Sigmund Freud first outlined the principles of psychoanalytic theory. From this perspective, human beings are dynamic energy systems consisting of basic drives and instincts. From birth, largely unconscious drives push humans toward the satisfaction of basic desires. Humans are typically unaware of these dynamic forces because various defense mechanisms keep them from conscious awareness. Nevertheless, they influence human thoughts, feelings, and behavior and affect the way humans relate to others. Thus, human personality is primarily an elaboration of inborn unconscious drives along with various adaptations to the vicissitudes of early childhood.

According to psychoanalytic theory, the human personality is a semi-closed energy system that conserves energy by resisting change. Unconscious forces drive and motivate individuals who struggle to maintain a homeostatic balance. Consequently, durable personal change after childhood can only come through experiences that reach the deepest levels of personality.

Freud organized the personality into three divisions. "The id comprises the psychic representatives of the drives, the ego consists of those functions which have to do with the individual's relation to his environment, and the superego comprises the moral precepts of our minds as well as our ideal aspirations" (Brenner, 1955, p. 45). The ego gradually evolves during childhood to serve an executive function within the personality, dealing with impulses from the id and moral signals from the superego, as well as with the realities of the environment. However, the primary forces determining thoughts, feelings, and actions remain largely unconscious—beyond the ego's conscious awareness and control.

Ego Psychology Constructs Several theorists questioned the central assumptions of psychoanalytic theory. Ego psychologists hold that an autonomous ego, present at birth, plays a powerful role in determining thoughts, feelings, and behaviors. Emphasizing the rational processes of the ego rather than the instinctual forces of the id, the personality develops and becomes differentiated in relation to environmental interactions, unconscious needs and, importantly, conscious goals and aspirations. Less deterministic than psychoanalytic theory, human development and behavior is much more than a manifestation of powerful unconscious drives. Rather than being fixed early in life, personality constantly develops throughout life.

Eric Erikson (1968), a foremost ego psychologist, believed that although early childhood experiences were certainly significant, the personality system adapts throughout the course of life to meaningful internal and external experience. According to Erikson, biopsychosocial developmental tasks and demands continually present human beings with opportunities for change and growth. This view represented a fundamental departure from central psychoanalytic beliefs. The manner in which humans respond to various developmental opportunities influences personal and social behavior and affects how well they negotiate subsequent life tasks (Hartman, 1970).

Ego psychologists challenge the psychoanalytic notion of a semi-closed system and the conservation of energy principle by asserting that the personality reflects characteristics of an open system in which the ego purposely seeks to experience the environment. Thus, personality development occurs as the result of active interaction with the environment. Ego psychologists argue that although people need some stability, they also seek new experience in pursuit of growth and development. In addition, ego psychologists emphasize the role of the ego as a conscious, powerful executive officer of personality—the part that makes decisions and takes action. "The main categories of ego functions are its clusters of cognitive, affective, motoric, executive, and integrative operations" (Perlman, 1975, p. 214).

The *cognitive* functions of the ego include content and process aspects. Cognitive contents include facts, beliefs, notions, concepts, memories, and assumptions. Cognitive processes involve the means by which contents are acquired, processed, stored, retrieved, organized, and reorganized. The *affective* functions involve feelings and feeling processes.

Various theorists and researchers have attempted to organize the hundreds of distinct human emotions into various categories or classifications such as anger, fear, guilt, hate, love, caring, and excitement. Although this work is far from complete, it appears that humans from all races, ethnic groups, and cultures reflect a common core of basic emotions. The *executive* functions of the ego involve judgment, decision making, and action taking. Judgment and decision making rest on the abilities to perceive the natural and external environment accurately, think logically and analytically, and integrate thoughts and feelings into a conclusion. Action taking requires motivation and skill needed to implement the decision through goal-directed activity.

The ego functions are interrelated. Each affects the others. Feeling affects thinking, thoughts affect emotions, and actions affect and are affected by both. Indeed, action can bring significant change in both thinking and feeling. Thus, in efforts at deliberate change, we may target thoughts, feelings, or behavior or combinations of the three. Indeed, clients-and-workers engage their own executive ego functions when they analyze the problem of concern and the person-in-situation to decide where and how to begin.

In sum, several ideas from ego psychology may be useful as clients-and-workers attempt to understand the developing person within the person-in-situation context. For example:

- If the ego has its own needs, drives, and is autonomous, and if the human personality develops over the life cycle, efforts directed to present life experiences are particularly important.
- If the personality is an open system, day-by-day input from transactions with the environment is highly significant; the client needs to be actively involved with the environment.
- The idea that the individual strives for competence and mastery offers an optimistic view of the possibilities of human growth and change, while stressing the importance of input from other social systems and the environment.
- In ego psychology, individuals actively and consciously participate in their own destiny, rather than simply reacting to stimuli or to needs beyond their control. This leads to the concept of partnership between the social worker and the client.
- The idea that human beings intentionally seek to control their own destinies provides guidance

for assessment, demands that clients be active participants in planning and change, supports the social work values of self-determination and respect for the individual, and suggests that hope serves as a stimulus for problem-solving.
- When combined with the notion that motivation is what the client wants and how much he or she wants it, the systemic concept of purpose highlights the importance of client goals and client self-determination.
- The human search for meaning in life suggests the importance of considering clients' transpersonal and spiritual experiences.
- Research in ego psychology indicates that a continuous relationship from a caring adult plays a key role in the development of resiliency in children and youth.

Competence, Mastery, and Efficacy   Several theorists and researchers expand on the idea that individuals are motivated from childhood to interact with and explore the environment in search of new experience and a sense of competence, achievement, and efficacy (Bandura, 1977, 1989, 1992, 1995a, 1995b, 1997; Bandura & Walters, 1963; White, 1959, 1963). The notion of competence seeking is viewed as much more than a motive to satisfy needs and drives such as hunger, thirst, dominance, and sex. Marking a distinct departure from the deterministic assumptions of psychoanalytic theory, humans are free agents capable of autonomous decision-making and, indeed, free will.

People develop a sense of competency and efficacy as they gain experience and master new skills in line with their personal and cultural standards. Social approval often accompanies mastery experiences and enhances the innate motivation to attempt new and more complex tasks.

This motivational force represents a push toward mastery (White, 1959). Experiences of competency result in a sense of self-efficacy—a generalized belief or expectation that one can influence other people and affect events and conditions in the world (Bandura, 1977). These concepts support the notion that, given a relatively benign environment, people actively seek control of their lives and welcome new experiences. From this perspective, humans possess the capacity for free agency (Bandura, 1989, 1992).

Motivation   Motivation refers to forces operating inside or outside a person that initiate or stimulate action toward some end or goal. Biological, psychological, and social factors affect motivational intensity. Basic or primary motives include hunger, thirst, sex, avoidance or minimization of pain and perhaps fear, and possibly others. Secondary motives develop through experience or socialization. Such learned motives, among numerous others, include motives for achievement, power or dominance, and competency, efficacy, or mastery. Some theorists use the terms "push" and "pull" to refer to the perceived source of energy. From this perspective, push motives emanate from internal states such as hunger or thirst, whereas pull motives reflect attractions and opportunities within the environment. Most motivated behavior results from a combination of the two forces (Petri, 1996).

Researchers from several disciplines and theorists from biological, behavioral, and cognitive perspectives offer concepts and hypotheses about motivation. Expectancy and attribution constructs fall within the cognitive tradition. "According to expectancy-value theory, behaviour is a function of the expectancies one has and the value of the goal toward which one is working [expressed as B = f(E × V)]. Such an approach predicts that, when more than one behaviour is possible, the behaviour chosen will be the one with the largest combination of expected success and value" (*Motivation. Encyclopædia Britannica,* Cognitive motivation section, para. 1). From this perspective, motivated behavior (B) is a function (f) of Expectancy (E) times the Value (V) of the goal. The motive to avoid failure moderates the motive to succeed. An accumulation of successful initiatives contributes to a generalized expectancy that one's actions positively affect events or conditions in the world, and a history of failed efforts may lead to an expectation that one's actions do not affect events or conditions.

A sense of mastery—or control over one's internal reactions and relevant external events—is a significant force in motivating human behavior (Liberman, 1978). "When individuals are involved in situations where personal competence can affect . . . outcomes, they tend to perform more actively and adequately than when . . . situations appear less controllable" (Lefcourt, 1966, p. 188). "Insofar as individuals believe that their actions and inactions affect their well-being, the achievement of a sense of mastery becomes a major goal throughout their lives" (Liberman, 1978, p. 36).

Self-efficacy, mastery, internal locus of control, and competency represent a few of several concepts that relate to the topic of cognitive motivation—which is

increasingly recognized as central to problem-solving (Baer, Kivlahan, & Donovan, 2000; Miller et al., 2001; Miller & Rollnick, 1991, 2002; Rollnick, 2002; Rollnick & Miller, 1995). The relevance of motivation, capacity, and opportunity to human behavior and development have long been recognized in social work (Deci & Ryan, 1980; French, 1952; Moore-Kirkland, 1981; Oxley, 1966; Ripple, 1955; Ripple & Alexander, 1956; Ripple, Alexander, & Polemis, 1964; Sachs, 1991). Social workers routinely enhance client motivation and encourage hopefulness early in the problem-solving process (Ripple et al., 1964). People are much more likely to take action if they believe it will help them achieve their own important goals. Goals that others have for them and insignificant goals tend to generate less motivational energy.

The relative balance between hope and discomfort affects the degree of motivational commitment. Optimistic predictions about goal achievement and some level of discomfort enhance motivation. Too much discomfort, however, decreases hope. Clients who repeatedly experience failure in various aspects of life and feel incompetent in problem-solving efforts may develop an all-pervasive sense of discomfort, helplessness, and apathy. Excessive discomfort and diminished optimism reduces the likelihood of goal-directed activity (Compton, 1979).

Hope buffers stress and discomfort. People who optimistically believe they can effectively achieve their goals often willingly forego other wants and needs. Therefore, establishing a tentative goal represents an extremely important part of the first interview. By exploring and identifying clients' initial goals early in the process, social workers encourage motivation (French, 1952; Perlman, 1957; Ripple & Alexander, 1956; Ripple et al., 1964; White, 1959, 1963).

Beginning in the 1950s, social workers at the University of Chicago began to explore the relationship of motivation, capacity, and opportunity to clients' effective use of social work services. They concluded that the combination of clients' hopefulness and the kind and extent of opportunities are critical to successful outcomes. Interestingly, neither the personality functioning of the client nor the type of problem seems especially significant. As a result, they encouraged social workers to engage clients in a careful assessment of the balance between hope and discomfort while exploring the nature of available opportunities. They also recognized that our words and actions as social workers during the early stages of client-worker interaction could influence—for better or worse—the crucial hope-discomfort balance (French, 1952; Ripple, 1955, 1957; Ripple & Alexander, 1956; Ripple et al., 1964).

Frustration involves disappointment, discomfort, and perhaps discouragement associated with a realization that we have not or cannot achieve a desired goal. The experience of frustration tends to affect motivational energy. Occasionally, frustration can enhance motivation—especially when an action has been partially successful. However, severe and repeated frustration may diminish motivation to take goal-directed action or even to make commitments to do so. Over time, cumulative frustration may lead to pervasive feelings of incompetence, hopelessness, and helplessness.

Learned Helplessness and Learned Optimism The concept of learned helplessness (Seligman, 1975) relates to the topic of frustration and helps us to understand apathetic clients. In general, apathy and limited motivation result from insufficient environmental opportunities for competency experiences. If people are to develop competence and autonomy in social functioning, they must be able to make valid predictions about the response of the environment to their actions. They must have some confidence that they can do something about problems or opportunities, and that their efforts can make a difference. If people decide that events and conditions in the world are beyond their ability to influence, hopelessness and helplessness may result. People may conclude that nothing they do now or in the future will make any difference in their lives. "Learned helplessness produces a cognitive set in which people believe that success and failure is independent of their own skilled actions" (Seligman, 1975, p. 38). To develop competence, initiative, and autonomy, the responses of the environment to our actions must reflect a certain degree of comprehensibility and consistency. Even when circumstances are unpleasant, people who believe they have some control over the aversive conditions experience much less stress than do those who conclude they have no control. Belief in their ability to exert some influence over aversive circumstances serves as a stress buffer (Greer, Davidson, & Gatchel, 1970).

As social workers, we should not be surprised when some people whose coping strategies have produced inconsistent responses or failure appear hopeless or helpless. Before we label any clients "unmotivated," however, we must examine their life circumstances and experiences. What kind of control do they have over life events? How does the environment respond, if at all, to their efforts? How much predictability and consistency is reflected in the environment? Simply put, people who believe their actions do not make a difference are less motivated to try. "Learned helplessness may develop when individuals believe they have no control over events—even when those events could actually be affected by their behavior" (Hooker, 1976, p. 194).

Hope, self-efficacy, or learned optimism (Seligman, 1991) represents the antithesis of hopelessness, apathy, and learned helplessness. We may consider this along an optimism-to-pessimism continuum.

> The defining characteristic of pessimists is that they tend to believe bad events will last a long time, will undermine everything they do, and are their own fault. The optimists, who are confronted with the same hard knocks of this world, think about misfortune in the opposite way. They tend to believe defeat is just a temporary setback, that its causes are confined to this one case. The optimists believe defeat is not their fault: Circumstances, bad luck, or other people brought it about. Such people are unfazed by defeat. Confronted by a bad situation, they perceive it as a challenge and try harder. (Seligman, 1991, pp. 4–5)

Resiliency The topic of resiliency naturally follows the discussion of learned helplessness and learned optimism. Resiliency is the ability to adjust, adapt, or recover from change or adversity. It is the capacity to "bounce back" from troubles. In systems terms, it involves an efficient return to a state of balance or equilibrium following exposure to disequilibrium.

Adverse life experiences in early life have long been associated with later social and psychological difficulties. In particular, deprivation of love and other forms of social and emotional contact during infancy may profoundly affect human development and well-being (Bowen, Martin, & Nelson, 2002; Bowlby, 1947, 1951, 1979, 1982, 1988; Harlow, 1974, 1979, 1986; Spitz, 1959, 1965, 1983). Intriguingly, experiences that place one person at high risk for damaging repercussions may have little or no adverse impact on another—perhaps because of their different perceptions and conclusions about the events, their genetic predisposition, or the psychosocial environment in which they grow and live (Anthony, 1987; Dugan, 1989; Fraser,

1997; Hetherington, 1996; LePage-Lees, 1997; Masten, 1994; Rutter, 1987; Shirilla, 2002).

Epidemiological studies have revealed a series of risk factors for children's mental health outcomes. These include parental and marital discord, father's low-skilled and unskilled employment, familial overcrowding, paternal criminal behavior, maternal mental illness, and children's admission to out-of-home care (Rutter, 1979, 1987; Rutter, Maughan, Mortimore, Ouston, & Smith, 1979). Moreover, the likelihood that youngsters will be exposed to stressful life events, their intellectual functioning, general competency, ability to engage with others and with activities, and tendencies toward disruptiveness are all related to the socioeconomic status of their family and its familial stability, cohesiveness, and organization (Garmezy, 1987). Interestingly, a substantial number of children seem to adapt successfully despite childhood adversity. Less than half of all children exposed to significant risk factors develop serious disability or chronic problems (Werner & Smith, 1992). Some children seem to be invulnerable to the effects of various familial and environmental risk factors. Despite the adversity and stressors, they somehow develop characteristics and attitudes indicative of "competence: good peer relations, academic achievement, commitment to education and to purposive life goals, early and successful work histories" (Garmezy, 1971, p. 114). These children reflect the qualities of hardiness (Kamya, 2000; Lifton, Seay, & Bushko, 2000; Maddi, Wadhwa, & Haier, 1996) or resiliency (Anthony, 1987; Dugan, 1989; Fraser, 1997; Hetherington, 1996; LePage-Lees, 1997; Masten, 1994; Rutter, 1987; Shirilla, 2002). Somehow, they are strengthened rather than weakened by adversity.

Indeed, "at least 50 percent and usually closer to 70 percent of these children and youth from high-risk environments grow up to be not only successful by societal indicators but have personal strengths usually falling in the following categories: social competence and connectedness, problem-solving and meta-cognition skills, a sense of autonomy, and a sense of purpose and future" (Benard, 2002, p. 215). A large sample of young adults who had received foster care services in New York City fared no better or worse than did a control group of young adults from a similar class background, except with respect to education and employment where the foster care graduates were at a disadvantage. Interestingly, fostered youngsters who spent more time in foster family settings fared better than did those

served in group-home care (Festinger, 1983). A British researcher found that 75% of adults who had received foster-home care during childhood manifested largely satisfactory outcomes from their experiences in care (Triseliotis, 1980). Similarly, a study of 585 graduates of long-term foster care for children and youth with troubled behavioral patterns and multiple placement histories revealed that they often achieved levels of comfort and well-being in young adulthood that could not have been predicted from the adversity of their early experiences (Fanshel, Finch, & Grundy, 1990).

The development of resilience appears to depend on how youngsters integrate potentially damaging events into their worldviews. They seem to benefit from repeated opportunities to develop a meaningful view of their histories. In one study of female incest survivors, those women who could make sense of the incestuous victimization were more likely than those who could not to exhibit effective adult coping, including less psychological distress, better social adjustment, and higher levels of self-esteem (Silver, Boon, & Stones, 1983). People from family backgrounds characterized by child maltreatment (Herrenkohl, Herrenkohl, & Egolf, 1994) and parental mental illness (Beardslee, 1989) fare better during adulthood if they can construct some meaningful understanding of their childhood history and realize they do not bear responsibility for the shortcomings of their parents and family.

What are the characteristics and factors that enable some people to survive and thrive in adverse environmental conditions? What are the protective factors and what are the risk factors (Fraser, 1997)? There seem to be several biological, psychological, and social factors associated with hardiness or resiliency. Warshaw and Barlow (1995, pp. 3–4) offered the following 10 components of resiliency: (1) unambivalent commitment to life, (2) self-confidence, (3) adaptability, (4) resourcefulness, (5) willingness to risk, (6) acceptance of personal responsibility, (7) perspective, (8) openness to new ideas, (9) willingness to be proactive, and (10) attentiveness. Adopting an optimistic view, Warshaw and Barlow assert that people can learn resiliency through adaptive practice. Indeed, resilience among children seems associated with flexibility or adaptability. Flexible children can break free from and let go of failure experiences, avoid self-defeating repetitions of previous unsuccessful behavior, and experiment with alternate problem-solving strategies in their efforts to cope (Murphy & Moriarity,

1976). One researcher found that resilient children shared three categories of protective factors:

- Relate easily with others, feel good about themselves, believe they are in control of their lives, and exhibit self-reliance.
- Have a warm relationship with at least one adult in their family, feel the members of their family are close, and experience their families as organized and orderly.
- Have a support system in the neighborhood or elsewhere in the community that includes role models with whom the youngster can identify and that help them move toward self-defined goals. (Garmezy, 1987)

Rutter (1987) and Garmezy (1987, 1993) consider various ways and means to help children and youth become more resilient—what Warshaw and Barlow refer to as "learned resiliency" (1995). Rutter proposes resiliency-building experiences that

- Alter exposure to or involvement in risk experience
- Reduce the likelihood of chain reactions from risk encounters
- Promote self-esteem through service and supportive personal relationships or successful task accomplishment
- Expand the type and range of opportunities (Rutter, 1987, p. 329)

Benard (2002, pp. 215–216) suggests that social workers who provide services to youth promote the core ideas that

- Most high risk youth make it.
- All individuals have innate resilience.
- People and places make a difference!

She suggests that social workers adopt a strengths perspective in which they undertake the following processes with their youthful clients:

- Listen to their story
- Acknowledge the pain
- Look for strengths
- Ask questions about survival, support, positive times, interests, dreams, goals, and pride
- Point out strengths
- Link strengths to client's goals and dreams
- Link client to resources to achieve goals and dreams
- Find opportunities for client to be teacher/paraprofessional. (Benard, 2002, p. 217)

Stress and Coping Clients often first engage social workers during highly stressful situations when they have exhausted their coping strategies and resources. Clients may feel extraordinarily anxious or perhaps depressed and apathetic because the troubles appear impossible to resolve. Social workers may view stress as the tension that arises in a system—individual, family, or group—from the perception that an event involves uncertainty and risk. However, authors have proposed dozens of definitions—often based on the discipline of the theorist or researcher—and use the concept in multiple ways for multiple purposes (Doublet, 2000). From a systems perspective, the idea of stress makes sense as a form of input or feedback that generates disequilibrium.

Interestingly, stress is not always problematic. At times, stress may be biologically beneficial as well as psychologically and socially functional. Selye referred to this as *eustress* (good stress) (1976a, 1976b). Stress becomes distress (bad stress) when the intensity or severity is extremely high or continues for a long time. At moderate levels, stress may actually improve the quality of problem-solving activities. Sometimes stress involves some element of pleasure or excitement as people prepare to meet a challenge. Of course, some stressors can be debilitating. The sudden, unexpected loss of a loved one or the experience of a personal violation such as rape or torture may be more stressful than most people can manage. Even in circumstances such as these, however, the perception and perspective may mitigate the degree of experienced stress. As the stories of prisoners of war, concentration camp survivors, and victims of atrocities reveal, some people naturally or perhaps willfully perceive events in such a way that overwhelming distress is moderated (Frankl, 1963). Some people, however, routinely interpret even modest stressors as beyond their coping capacity and, therefore, experience considerable distress. Indeed, in a state analogous to that of learned helplessness, they may become immobilized—unable or unwilling to take steps to resolve the stressful problem or to manage the distress.

Coping processes and coping resources may moderate distress and enhance the effectiveness of problem-solving activities. As social workers, we may encourage clients to explore their coping styles and patterns as well as enhance their ability to mobilize them in distressful circumstances. The beliefs and attitudes about life that people possess or adopt serve as powerful personal coping resources. Ability to moderate the biophysical experience of excessive tension may contribute as well. People who believe that life is orderly and purposive, that processes can be understood, and that outcomes are generally for the best suffer less debilitating illness than do others, no matter how severe the level of distress. Perhaps the most powerful coping mechanism is a belief in life (Antonovsky, 1980).

Other personal coping resources include (1) knowledge, history of successful experience with life tasks, and cognitive capacities such as the ability to reason; (2) the ability to modulate and use emotional responses to stress; and (3) skills to carry out planned action (Antonovsky, 1980). Wealth and power represent important environmental resources for coping with distressful life events. Money provides the means to purchase services or products we may need. Power enables us to exercise considerable control over our own destinies. A substantial social network that provides access to social support represents another powerful coping resource. In time of crisis or distress, family, friends, neighbors, and colleagues can provide emotional support, information, and other resources. In efforts to help clients cope with distress and engage in problem-solving activities, social workers routinely assist in identifying, accessing, strengthening, and developing informal systems of social support.

Transpersonal Psychology and Spirituality "Transpersonal psychology is concerned with the study of humanity's highest potential, and with the recognition, understanding, and realization of unitive, spiritual, and transcendent states of consciousness" (Lajoie & Shapiro, 1992, p. 91). Transpersonal refers to phenomena beyond the individual, person, or self and therefore includes the domain of spirituality. Carl Jung, one of Freud's contemporaries, believed that spirituality is a primary human drive. Rejecting several Freudian notions—including the pleasure principle—Jung postulated the existence of an "inner deity" and argued that "the wheel of history must not be turned back, and man's advance towards a spiritual life, which began with the primitive rites of initiation, must not be denied" (Jung, 1933, p. 123).

Many clients find meaning in their lives through their religious and spiritual beliefs and traditions. Often that involves reference to God, Jesus, Mohammed, a "higher power," "the God within," or perhaps contact with the universe, universal, or infinite. In some traditions, ancestors, spirits, or mystical energy sources relate to spirituality and, of course, some refuse to use a name to identify God. Spiritual beliefs and practices represent a central part of cultural life for many people. It is hardly surprising then that clients frequently reflect problems that relate in some way to their religious and spiritual traditions. Helping people as they seek meaning and purpose in life often involves exploration of spirituality (Frankl, 1963; Guttman, 1996). Spirituality may represent a source of comfort and serve to aid problem solving. For instance, Alcoholics Anonymous and 12-step programs for people addicted to or abusive of alcohol commonly refer to and incorporate the concept of a "higher power" (Berenson, 1987; Krystal & Zweben, 1989). Social work service that incorporates spirituality may help clients deal with a sense of alienation, hopelessness, grief, and a range of other issues and problems (Berg & Miller, 1992b; Breen, 1985; Canda, 1988a, 1988b, 1991, 1995; Cascio, 1998; Cowley, 1993; Cowley & Derezotes, 1994; Derezotes, 1995; Hodge, 2001; Klein, 1986; Levinson, 1978; Moxley & Washington, 2001; Sermabeikian, 1994; Sheridan, 2002; Wolin, Muller, Taylor, & Wolin, 1999). Siporin offers the following definition of spirituality that transcends any particular religious ideology:

> The spiritual element of the person is the aspect of an individual's psyche, consciousness and unconsciousness, that is also called the human soul. It is in terms of the spiritual dimension that a person strives for transcendental values, meaning, experience and development; for knowledge of an ultimate reality; for belonging and relatedness with the moral universe and community; and for union with the immanent, supernatural powers that guide people and the universe for good and evil. The spiritual aspect of the person is not subsumed or dealt with in psychoanalytic ego theory or in cognitive theory, though it has a place in Jungian and existentialist therapies. (Siporin, 1985, pp. 210–211)

In serving clients, social workers frequently participate in explorations of life's meaning and related issues of a spiritual nature. Clients-and-workers may also find it useful to incorporate transpersonal beliefs and practices during intervention processes. For many people,

> Spirituality is a human need; it is too important to be misunderstood; avoided; or viewed as regressive, neurotic, or pathological in nature. Social workers must . . . acknowledge that spirituality in a person's life can be a constructive way of facing life's difficulties. (Sermabeikian, 1994, p. 181)

Spiritual beliefs and rituals may help individuals cope with life challenges. However, they may also contribute to a sense of wholeness and connectedness throughout a culture (Yellow Bird, 1995). Indeed, a lack of fit between a person's desire for meaningful transpersonal experience and the opportunities available in society may lead to spiritual crises or malaise (Cowley & Derezotes, 1994; Sermabeikian, 1994). If social workers lack sensitivity to the transpersonal environment, they may misinterpret some spiritual experiences as symptoms of mental illness or perhaps deviance. Until relatively recently, the transpersonal and spiritual environments received limited attention in social work (Derezotes, 1995; Sheridan, Bullis, Adcock, Berlin, & Miller, 1992). However, social workers are increasingly recognizing its significance for practice (Canda, 1995; Garland, 1995; Gelman & Schnall, 1995; Sheridan, 2002; Van Hook, 1995). Indeed, 82% of 284 educators from 25 U.S. schools of social work favored the inclusion of spirituality content within the social work curriculum (Sheridan, Wilmer, & Atcheson, 1994).

Incorporating spiritual or religious beliefs and practices within professional social work practice, however, requires great sensitivity and rather extraordinary judgment. Some clients become involved in cults and religious-like organizations that exert nearly total control over their decisions, actions, and resources. Rather than supporting connectedness with the universe and the infinite, the net effect is similar to imprisonment where guards monitor and control thoughts and actions. In addition, some religious traditions promote views and behavior that deprive others of basic human rights. Some religious teachings convey messages that women are not the equal of men, nonbelievers may be tortured and murdered without fear of divine punishment, men may marry girls as young as 9 years of age, or people of certain groups may buy and sell people from other groups as slaves. As social workers, we are interested in social justice as well as individual and cultural rights. At times, the religious beliefs and practices of certain individuals and groups profoundly violate the human rights of others. Our professional values and principles require that we explore the implications and effects of such practices on social justice and social welfare. As we support the potentially life-enhancing qualities of spirituality, we cannot naively ignore the adverse consequences of those religious traditions that promote discrimination, oppression, and violence toward other peoples (Ellis, 1986, 1989a, 1990; Ellis & Yeager, 1989).

What Is the Environment?

In social work practice, we may define the environment as a combination of people and their social and environmental interactions in a particular personally, culturally, and socially constructed geographic space. The exchanges occur over a particular period in the individual and family's life and in the life of the social and cultural system (Germain, 1979a, 1979b; Pincus & Minahan, 1973; Siporin, 1975). Exhibits 2-2 and 2-3 illustrate the complexity of the interaction between person and environment. As complex as Exhibit 2-2 appears, it deals only with the social environment, which consists of several levels—the individual, the group, the family, the community, class, and the culture. Social workers attend to all of these as well as to the physical environment, consisting of the natural world, such as geography or climate, and the constructed world, such as the shelters or roads we build.

Social workers incorporate systems and ecosystems thinking in our efforts to understand and influence environmental events and conditions. We also consider temporal dimensions of the person-in-situation. Because human life is both finite and lived within certain geographical parameters, time and space are critical environmental qualities. We may consider the time-space continuum from general and personal perspectives. By general, we mean the time and space experience commonly agreed to by most people. For example, the current 365-day calendar, the 24-hour day, and distances measured by kilometers or miles illustrate the general time-space realities. The personal experience of time and space, however, may vary quite distinctly from the general. You have probably had experiences where an hour seemed to last forever or a year just flew by. Perhaps you have also felt disoriented and not known exactly where you were. Cultures vary in these dimensions as well. In some contexts, clock time is highly valued and measures all sorts of human activity. Other cultures experience time more rhythmically—perhaps associated with the rising and setting of the sun—and less associated with watches and clocks.

Most human beings construct shelters to protect themselves from the physical environment. In so doing, they also construct a personal or family space that gives them some privacy from the group. The

EXHIBIT 2-2
The Multifaceted Individual

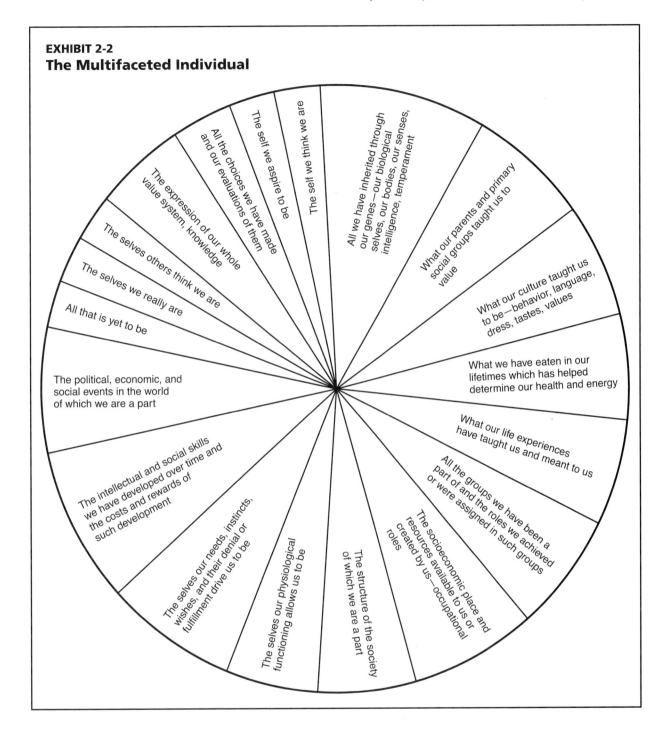

construction of shelter and the marking of private space may differ from culture to culture. In North America, we prefer attractive shelters that provide adequate warmth or coolness, afford access to our places of employment or education, and contain certain electrical appliances. The private spaces we create affect our internal experience, including comfort level but also thoughts and feelings about ourselves.

Environments and ecosystems that contain greater diversity generally reflect greater strength than do those

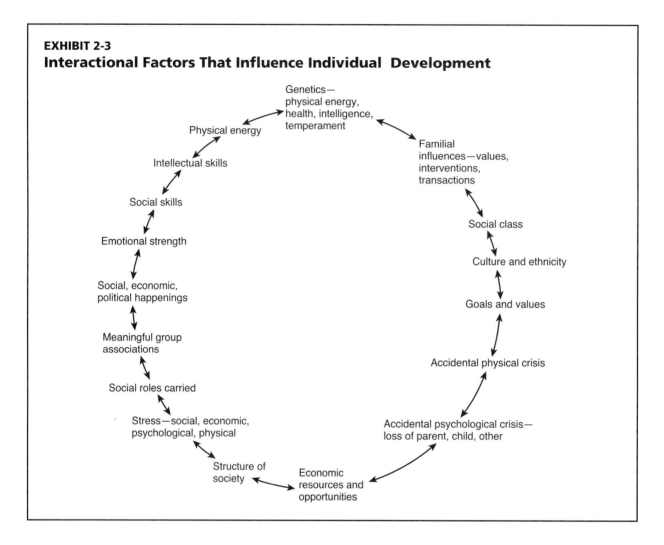

EXHIBIT 2-3
Interactional Factors That Influence Individual Development

reflecting greater homogeneity. Physical ecologists and environmentalists recognize this when they feverishly work to save certain botanical and biological species from extinction. Humans can and often do endanger the life of our own species as well as the well-being of the earth as an ecosystem when our actions lead to dramatic changes in the composition and diversity of the living organisms that also inhabit this planet. Social systems tend to reflect a similar principle—diversity usually adds to rather than detracts from systemic well-being.

Human beings of all races and ethnicities reflect the same basic genetic make-up. *Homo sapiens* represent a single species that originated in Africa and gradually spread throughout the world. We lost our cousins, *Homo erectus* and *Homo neanderthalensis,* some 50,000 years ago. Although humans may vary slightly

in skin color and certain facial characteristics—leading to notions of race and sometimes ethnicity—and we can usually distinguish males from females and one individual from another—we are clearly one people. Biologically and genetically, the differences among us are miniscule. However, nurture as well as nature affects humans. Indeed, we can only understand much—although far from all—human behavior and development from the perspective of family and community experience. Culture refers to the customary and shared beliefs, practices, and goals of a social group. Socialization reflects the way in which people learn to operate within the cultural context of the group and its surrounding environment.

Culture includes but is not limited to religious or spiritual beliefs and practices. Nonreligious interpersonal and social customs, characteristics, and behavior such as language, body decoration, clothing, art, music, literature, recreation, and pastimes also reflect a group's culture. Representing a clear integration of the person and the situation, culture resides within the minds of individuals as well as within the collective memory and records of the group. Therefore, social workers need to comprehend how cultures develop, and how, over time, opportunities and deprivation shape cultures, and how people from various cultures interact with one another. We also need to appreciate the importance of difference in the development of human societies, to understand that human organizations develop through the expression of individual differences and to respect diversity. To appreciate and understand individual people, we must understand the cultural contexts of their growth, development, and behavior. Social workers require standards and measures of health and normality that include a broad range of coping behaviors and values to accommodate individual diversity and cultural or ethnic differences (Greene & Frankel, 1994).

All cultural groups appear to engage in oppressive practices. Human beings in possession of power and resources relative to others often seem to use it to subjugate, abuse, exploit, or exterminate others—typically those who differ from themselves in some way. Although the kinds of power vary widely and may include cattle, land, physical strength, knowledge, education, or a certain status, those with power often apply it against those without it. *Ethnocentrism* refers to the belief that qualities and characteristics of one's own group are superior to those of other groups. *Egocentrism* reflects a similar assumption—that one is fundamentally superior to or more important than others are and should be the primary or exclusive focus of attention. *Xenophobia* involves the fear of foreign people and things. *Rankism* involves the abuse of power, status, or rank (Fuller, 2002). More powerful individuals and groups tend to reflect egocentric, ethnocentric, xenophobic, and rankist attitudes and behaviors toward less powerful people.

Patterned role expectations, inertia, and homeostatic forces operate to resist change, diversity, and difference. Most human systems prefer stability and predictability. Knowledge that others will behave as we expect them to reduces the discomfort of uncertainty and permits people and systems to make plans. As a result, people tend to internalize role expectations as value systems and may judge relatively neutral behavior as right or wrong—regardless of benefits they may have for the development and welfare of the system.

Family systems illustrate this process. Society cannot exist without some system for the creation, protection, and socialization of children. Families serve as the primary means for fulfilling these functions. However, people from different cultures often hold quite different views about what constitutes a family and what behaviors are necessary to safeguard and socialize children. In North America, middle-class European American families usually assign this role to mothers. However, families could also assign it to an aunt, grandmother, uncle, father, or neighbor. The "mothering" role might be fulfilled equally well by other people, but some European Americans make judgments about the rightness or wrongness of the assignment on the basis of their own internalized role expectations and cultural traditions. Indeed, sometimes people use other evaluation schema and determine that a person, family, or community is not only wrong but also deviant, criminal, abnormal, dysfunctional, or perhaps sick.

People, especially those in power relative to others, often make judgments based on ethnocentric bias rather than reflective thought and analysis. In some communities, grandmothers, uncles, cousins, and close friends are part of the family just as in some well-to-do communities nannies become family members. As social workers, we often hold implicit or explicit power in relation to other people. Therefore, we must be especially careful to distinguish between our own internalized expectations of role performance and those based on critical analysis and evidence. Otherwise, we could—perhaps unknowingly—serve as de facto representatives of powerful others in processes and activities that contribute to oppression rather than to social justice.

People, such as social workers, who adopt the view that all people are equal and entitled to certain fundamental human rights—such as those outlined in the Universal Declaration of Human Rights (General Assembly of the United Nations, 1948)—may find it difficult to apply it in practice. Egocentric, ethnocentric, xenophobic, and rankist socialization may interfere with our willingness and ability to experience each person as both unique and equal. The position that "everyone is equal but different" is both uncommon and challenging to adopt and live. It is much easier to adopt the more popular ethnocentric position that "people like me are equal."

Some people negotiate this dilemma by concluding, "everyone is the same and, therefore, everyone is equal." Many of us find it difficult to acknowledge individual and cultural differences. This may partly result from the way the human brain functions and the socialization processes we experience. Humans tend to learn by classifying people, objects, events, conditions, and experiences within certain categories. Assuming that things and phenomena within particular categories reflect essential similarity, we often refer to categorical labels in communication with others. For example, when we speak of a tree, others usually know that we mean a certain kind of growing plant. However, a forestry expert would not only have access to numerous other subordinate categories—various types of trees—but would also be able to recognize idiosyncratic characteristics and essential uniqueness of the individual tree. Indeed, some features of the particular tree might not even fall within any known category or subcategory. As the forestry expert notices additional unique characteristics, the tree becomes more and more an individual—distinctly different from other living organisms from the same kingdom, phylum, class, order, family, genus, and species.

As specialists in human interaction, social workers cannot be satisfied with broad classifications based on innate characteristics such as sexual organs, skin color, or even presenting problem. We cannot assume that members of a particular ethnic group, religion, social status, or nationality are alike. Rather, we must appreciate the uniqueness of each individual person and celebrate the enormous diversity that such a realization implies. Cultural competence includes valuing individual differences while recognizing cultural commonalities. "*Cultural competence* refers to the process by which individuals and systems respond respectfully and effectively to people of all cultures, languages, classes, races, ethnic backgrounds, religions, and other diversity factors in a manner that recognizes, affirms, and values the worth of individuals, families, and communities and protects and preserves the dignity of each" (NASW National Committee on Racial and Ethnic Diversity, 2001, p. 11).

The NASW emphasizes cultural competence in its Code of Ethics by requiring social workers to

> understand culture and its function in human behavior and society, recognizing the strengths that exist in all cultures . . . (and) . . . have a knowledge base of their clients' cultures and be able to demonstrate competence in the provision of services that are sensitive to clients'

cultures and to differences among people and cultural groups . . . (and) . . . obtain education about and seek to understand the nature of social diversity and oppression with respect to race, ethnicity, national origin, color, sex, sexual orientation, age, marital status, political belief, religion, and mental or physical disability. (NASW, 1999)

Integration of Person and Environment

We cannot view the environment as something separate from and distinctly outside ourselves. People do not occasionally bump into the environment. Rather, environment is part of us and we are part of it. Air and water are inside as well as outside our bodies, and we depend upon the environment for our very survival. From the time of birth, the environment affords us the material from which we construct our lives. The world provides the context in which we make decisions and undertake our journeys.

Consider, for example, two 18-year-olds who have just graduated near the top of their respective high school classes. John and Richard look very much alike. Both are attractive and in good health. John comes from an established professional family with more than adequate financial resources. Throughout his childhood, John's family expected him to complete high school, attend a prestigious university, and pursue a professional career. When John attended his father's alma mater and became a professional man, his family and primary social systems conveyed support. He had adopted the expected life path. Deviations would have been extremely difficult.

Richard, by contrast, was the oldest of five siblings. His family had owned a farm but had to sell it to pay for his father's care during a long terminal illness. His mother and the children then lived in a small rural community, where his mother worked in a small grocery store. Money was extremely tight. The father did not own health, life, or social security insurance. Richard was very bright and much interested in farming. He wanted to attend a university and major in agribusiness. However, the university was 100 miles away, and Richard could not see any way to pay for his education. In addition, his mother needed both his financial and emotional support. Therefore, Richard took a job in the local creamery. After 10 years, he became manager of the creamery. It was a good, steady, and adequately paying job and allowed Richard to have daily contact with the farm life he loved. However, it was far short of the life about which he had dreamed.

These two men constructed their lives from the opportunities available to them within their respective environments. At the time of graduation from high school, they reflected similar personal abilities. However, their life paths diverged primarily because of the different resources, expectations, and opportunities they could access and, of course, the choices they made. Richard might have decided to leave his mother and siblings to support themselves while he went to college. He probably could have paid for college through loans and part-time jobs. However, such a decision would have been as inconsistent with his personal beliefs and culture as it would have been for John to take a job at the creamery instead of going to college.

Thus, the choices we make in response to available environmental opportunities shape the course of our individual lives. In turn, we shape the environment through our choices and activities. Richard was concerned about how certain farm practices damaged the topsoil and deprived birds and small animals of their habitat. He organized a group of concerned farmers and arranged for an agricultural expert to educate them about environmentally sound land use practices. The farmers accepted the new information and adapted their farming procedures to protect the land. Interestingly, they also increased their profit margins and grew more prosperous.

Through their decisions and actions, Richard and the farmers influenced the physical environment. Simultaneously, they also affected the social environment. The farmers' relationships with each other and with Richard became more satisfying. They worked on other projects together and the community as a whole became more socially active and harmonious. The processes reflected by Richard and the farmers apply to us all. Our personal decisions and activities shape both our own personal futures as well as that of the environment. Many social workers recognize this reality and regularly help clients to change environmental conditions that affect problems of concern.

Adaptedness and *adaptation* are useful concepts for considering the transactions between any level of human system and the larger surrounding systems. *Adaptedness* describes a "relationship between an organism and its environment in which the *goodness of fit* supports the needs of both" (Barker, 2003, p. 6). Adaptedness refers to a state or condition whereas *adaptation* refers to

The active efforts of individuals and species over their life spans to survive, develop, and reproduce by achieving goodness of fit with their environments. Adaptation is also a reciprocal process between the individual and the environment, often involving changing the environment or being changed by it. Social workers oriented to systems theories consider that helping people move through stressful life transitions by strengthening or supporting their adaptive capacities is a central part of their intervention strategies. (Barker, 2003, p. 6)

Sometimes adaptation is viewed as a process in which a smaller system capitulates to the power of a larger system—that is, as a form of submission. However, submission is only one of many forms of adaptation. In theory at least, the adaptive options are limitless. They include the entire array of transactional processes through which people shape and are shaped by their physical and social environment.

The Environment as a Series of Mediating Layers

We may define the environment as "the circumstances, objects, or conditions by which one is surrounded . . . the complex of physical, chemical, and biotic factors (as climate, soil, and living things) that act upon an organism or an ecological community and ultimately determine its form and survival . . . the aggregate of social and cultural conditions that influence the life of an individual or community" (Merriam-Webster, 2003). In effect, environment includes "all the influences, conditions, and natural surroundings that affect the growth and development of living things" (Barker, 2003, p. 144). The concept encompasses a great deal indeed! To facilitate understanding, you may think of environment as a set of nested boxes, each enclosed within a larger box. The environment of a single box includes not only the next larger box but also the even larger boxes that enclose them all. However, each box reflects its own unique characteristics that are different from—but shaped by—both the smaller boxes within and the larger boxes that constitute its environment. All the intervening boxes mediate the impact of the largest box on the smallest box. The environmental influence of a community on an individual person is then mediated through the next larger box—usually the family.

We find it helpful to distinguish four layers or levels of environment surrounding each person. These include the (1) *situational,* (2) *micro,* (3) *meso* or *mezzo,* and (4) *macro* levels. Each layer contains others, and the functioning of each layer is determined largely by its interaction with adjacent layers (Bronfenbrenner, 1979; Magnusson & Allen, 1983a, 1983b). The *situational* layer is the part of the immediate environment perceived by a person at any given moment. "It is in actual situations that we encounter and form our conceptions about the world and develop specific kinds of behavior for dealing with it." Situations present "the information that we process, and they offer the feedback necessary for building valid conceptions of the outer world. Knowledge about the actual situations that an individual has encountered, along with the accompanying physical, social, and cultural microenvironments, will help us understand behavior at different stages of development" (Magnusson & Allen, 1983b, p. 11).

The *micro* layer involves "that part of the total physical and social environment that an individual is in contact with and can interact with directly in daily life during a certain period of time" (Magnusson & Allen, 1983b, p. 11). This includes the person's experiences in his or her family, at school or work, during leisure time, and so forth. The microenvironment is largely specific to the individual, in that no one else experiences the same environment in the same way. As you might anticipate, the microenvironment is vital to the survival of babies and children and critical to human biopsychosocial development. Although humans at birth are far from a *tabula rasa,* blank slate, or "white paper" (Locke, 1689) upon which experience writes, nurture interrelates with nature. For instance, most human beings are biologically prepared at birth to learn language. Although such readiness is the result of "nature," language proficiency is not. Nurture provides the experiences that enable humans to sign, speak, or write the particular language of their culture. Raised apart from other humans, a person would not acquire language proficiency and, after some time, the natural readiness for language acquisition would disappear (Harris, 1998; Pinker, 2002; Ridley, 2003). People in the microenvironment play numerous roles vital to the biopsychosocial development of human beings. Absent their nurturing input, people individually and collectively could not survive or thrive.

The *meso* layer is "that part of the total environment that in some way or another influences and determines the character and functioning of the microenvironment" (Magnusson & Allen, 1983b, p. 11). It includes groups, organizations, and institutions that people encounter in their daily lives, such as school, work, religion, recreation, and community resources. The *macro* layer includes the physical, social, cultural, economic, and political structure of the larger society, including technology, language, housing, laws, customs, and regulations.

Four ecological layers from the situation to the macrosystem surround each person. The whole reflects each of its parts and all parts complement aspects of the whole. Language, for example, is a critical part of each individual, the situation, and the micro, meso, and macro layers of the environment. As intellectually obvious as this interconnectedness may be, social workers often overlook the meaning and relevance of the macroenvironment in their zeal to serve individual human beings.

The actual environment affects human potential by providing or limiting access to resources and opportunities. Human beings simply cannot survive without food, water, and social stimulation. However, perception of and selective attention to certain aspects to the exclusion of others also affect people's experience of the environment. Thus, clients-and-workers must be concerned about three environments:

- Actual environment
- Client-perceived environment
- Worker-perceived environment

Each of these is "real." Unperceived strengths, assets, and resources in the actual environment are just as unavailable to clients-and-workers as if they did not exist. Similarly, social workers may conclude that their perceptions of the environment are accurate and those of clients are biased or distorted. Such conclusions often lead to distorted perceptions and selective attention. Furthermore, they may diminish our ability to understand and appreciate the meaning that clients assign to their perception.

Systems theory and the ecosystem perspective provide a useful organizing framework for social work for these reasons:

- The concepts that relate to the development, function, and structure of systems are equally applicable to all clients served by social workers, including individuals, families, groups, organizations, communities, and societies.
- Systems theory clarifies the range of elements that bear on social problems, including the social units involved, their interrelationships, and

the implications of change in one element for all the others.

- Systems theory shifts attention from the characteristics possessed by individuals or their environments to interfaces, interactions, and communication processes.
- Social work considers individuals and their environments as part of a complete whole.
- Systems theory views people as active systems capable of self-initiated behavior and able to contribute to changes in their environment or even to the creation of new environments. Adaptation of the environment is as much a property of human systems as is the tendency to respond to the environment. These concepts negate the tendency to see disturbances as pathology and encourage social workers to attend to the present life of the client.
- Social workers who recognize that systems are purposive and subject to the processes of equifinality and multifinality tend to become open to the possibilities for change. These concepts encourage self-determination, client participation in the change process, and consideration of client purpose and goals in assessment and planning processes.
- Living, open systems require constant exchange with other systems and the environment for progressive development. Social workers must provide and maintain interactional and transactional opportunities for all clients.
- Social workers must be aware of those populations and systems proceeding toward isolation and closure, and recognize societal strains and forces that contribute to entropic processes.
- Change, tension, and conflict are inherent in open systems. Social workers must explore why the system resists desirable changes and how such changes become unbearable for a system. This entails accepting clients as they are and fostering self-determination. From this perspective, tension or conflict is not pathology.
- The concept of system boundaries provides a means to assess the systems with which we work. Healthy systems tend to respond to external influences with caution and a degree of testing. Systems that reflect either too much openness or too much closedness are a cause for concern. Showing respect for clients' rights, we carefully consider how to cross clients' boundaries.

- Recognition that change in one part of a system can affect the whole means that we must be aware of the impact of intervention on the clients' broader transactions.
- From a systems perspective, the agency is a social system, and the agency, the worker, and the client are all in the same transactional field. Social workers constitute a social system and are components of the social agency system.
- The person-situation system exists within a hierarchical arrangement of systems that extends from the individual to the macro level of society and culture.

◆ Knowledge for Use

Sophisticated knowledge is a distinguishing characteristic of professionalism. However, the selection and application of knowledge for use in helping human beings address social problems are complex endeavors. Helping people is much more than a technical activity or ad hoc experiment. We cannot simply take action and hope for the best. Rather, we must encourage clients to join us in thinking analytically and reflectively about the most relevant credible knowledge for application to their particular circumstances. Although trained for professional practice, social workers and other helpers sometimes act before they think. As a result, they may fail to use knowledge as a basis for action. Alternately, certain social workers may possess expertise in a specific intervention model or technique and apply it indiscriminately to all situations, regardless of the problem, the goal, or the capacity of the system. As distinguished from the technician, bureaucrat, or amateur, professional social workers consult with clients to select interventions that fit the unique characteristics of the problem and the person-in-situation as informed by knowledge and guided by rational analysis. As social workers, we routinely face complex, dynamic, and unexpected problems and circumstances. Simplistic and routine application of intervention techniques conveys disrespect to clients and suggests that practice is a technical rather than a professional endeavor.

In contrast to the basic sciences that seek knowledge for its own sake, the professions seek knowledge for use (Bartlett, 1964). The mission and purpose of social work help define "the boundaries of relevant knowledge as well as stimulating the search for new knowledge. Part of what makes a given profession distinctive is the nature of action or practice evolving from placing knowledge within a particular frame of reference" (Kamerman, Dolgoff, Getzel, & Nelson, 1973, p. 97). The purposes and values of the profession help to determine that frame of reference.

Indeed, knowledge and purpose have an interactive relationship. As professional purposes evolve, we seek new knowledge to deal with those changes. Similarly, as knowledge expands, our professional purpose may change. For example, during the middle part of the 20th century, the introduction and widespread use of the polio vaccine dramatically reduced the number of children crippled by polio. Hospitals and facilities that provided treatment and rehabilitation to polio patients became irrelevant, as did the helping professionals who specialized in those services. They had to reconsider their missions. One major center adapted its mission and retrained its professionals to provide rehabilitative services to persons with spinal cord injuries or brain damage. Many professionals did the same. In effect, new knowledge led to new purpose.

Social workers often find it difficult to establish the parameters of our professional knowledge base. Our mission is broad and our purposes wide and varied. The formal definitions of social work provide a basis on which to identify pertinent areas. We could apply deductive reasoning to the concepts and principles common to the definitions to identify relevant essential knowledge. We could also study what social workers actually do and, through inductive analysis, identify knowledge in that manner. In developing nationally standardized licensing examinations, the Association of Social Work Boards (ASWB) adopts the latter approach in determining relevant content.

Interestingly, the two processes tend to yield similar results. The ASWB-sponsored licensing examinations test applicants in the following content domains:

- Human Development and Behavior in the Environment
- Issues of Diversity
- Assessment in Social Work Practice
- Direct and Indirect Practice
- Communication
- Professional Relationships
- Professional Values and Ethics
- Supervision in Social Work
- Practice Evaluation and Use of Research
- Service Delivery
- Social Work Administration. (ASWB, 2004)

We also need credible information about the nature, extent, and effects of particular social problems and knowledge about the effectiveness of various approaches and strategies intended to prevent or resolve them. A focus on particular social problems is, of course, entirely consistent with our generalist problem-solving perspective. Indeed, expertise about any social problem requires sophisticated knowledge from all ecosystem layers. Similarly, knowledge about practice effectiveness involves appreciation for the systemic principle of feedback about what works for people affected by a particular problem. We believe that knowledge about the effects and outcomes of problem-solving activities—whether they involve social policies, community action, neighborhood development, family or group work, or service to an individual person—represents both a moral and an ethical requirement for professional helpers (Allen-Meares, Deroos, & Siegel, 1994; Bilsker & Goldner, 2000; Corcoran, 2000, 2002; Cournoyer, 2004; Cournoyer & Powers, 2002; Franklin & Jordan, 2002; Gambrill, 1999; Gibbs, 2002a, 2002b; Klein, Bloom, & Chandler, 1994; Rosen & Proctor, 2002; Smokowski & Wodarski, 1996; Thyer, 2002; Vandiver, 2002; Wodarski & Dziegielewski, 2002).

Knowledge for use in efforts to help people affected by social problems may come from many different sources. The information and technology revolution has dramatically increased the total amount of knowledge and profoundly diminished time and distance between people and societies. Human beings with access to university and research libraries and to the World Wide Web can retrieve a quantity and quality of information never before known in the history of humankind. Such accessibility may contribute to the liberation of the oppressed, to the empowerment of disenfranchised populations, and to the enlightenment of consumers. We have observed such processes among patients conducting sophisticated searches for information about medical illnesses that afflict them. As consumers of medical services, they become extraordinarily knowledgeable about the latest scientific research—often becoming as expert as some physicians. Sometimes they learn about the pre-eminent researchers and practitioners in the field and initiate direct correspondence. Occasionally, when standard treatments reflect unfavorable prognoses, they volunteer to participate in research studies of experimental medical drugs or procedures. Their consumer-based knowledge about the illness and especially the effectiveness of medical treatments enable them to challenge doctors and advocate on their own behalf.

Sometimes patients with specific illnesses and their families join to form consumers or advocacy groups. As a collective, they search for, collect, and analyze evidence about the efficacy and effectiveness of services and share their findings with each other and with interested professionals. In the information age, knowledge need not be limited to a select few. Indeed, we believe that inequitable distribution of access to knowledge represents a form of social injustice and oppression that social workers must address. Otherwise, the information age might increase rather than alleviate the disparity between those who have and those who have not. Knowledge poverty may become as much of a social problem as financial poverty is today. If social workers in the 21st century do not become expert information workers, our profession may become essentially irrelevant in societies guided by knowledge.

> Over the course of the past decade, we have become convinced that *learning how to learn* and *lifelong learning* are, on balance, even more important for social work students than the acquisition of professional knowledge itself. Unless social work students become active, self-directed, and collaborative learners during their B.S.W., M.S.W., or doctoral programs, they will be unlikely to engage energetically in lifelong learning opportunities following graduation. As a result, the quality and effectiveness of their service to clients will certainly diminish over time. . . . New information emerges so rapidly that all helping professionals must be prepared to discover, analyze, and, if relevant, apply innovative knowledge in their service to others. To serve clients and society competently, social workers must be enthusiastic lifelong learners—reading, observing, listening, studying, reflecting, conversing, collaborating, analyzing, synthesizing, and evaluating—during academic programs of study and continuing throughout their professional lives. (Cournoyer & Stanley, 2002, pp. ix–x)

Based on person-in-situation and evidence-based perspectives, social workers seek knowledge for use in understanding people, environments, and the transactions between and among people and their environments as they relate to the assessment and resolution of social problems. We are especially interested in knowledge about social problems, the

people, and population groups affected by or at-risk of them, and the nature, effects, and effectiveness of policies, programs, and services intended to prevent or resolve those social problems. We are social workers rather than social scientists. As such, our primary mission is to help people engage in social problem-solving activities.

Research and Practice

Early social workers, in effect, learned by doing; they gained practice wisdom through their experiences. As their numbers grew, more experienced social workers began to supervise and train novices through an apprenticeship system. Senior social workers possessed more experience and more practice wisdom. They were in positions to share their authority-based knowledge to less-experienced workers. This had been a traditional means of transmitting knowledge in the trades, crafts, and professions. Medicine and law had also adopted apprenticeship models of training. However, fostered by industrialism, technology, the growth and expansion of institutions of higher learning, and the scientific revolution, some social workers began to question the value of authority-based knowledge and practice wisdom alone. Scientists of the early-to-middle 20th century tended to believe that accurate knowledge about the world must derive from empirical observations and that "all disagreements about the world could be resolved, in principle, by reference to observable facts. Propositions which were neither analytically nor empirically testable were held to have no meaning at all. They were dismissed as emotive utterance, poetry, or mere nonsense" (Schon, 1983, pp. 32–33). Some promoted empirical science as the only source of positive knowledge in the world. "According to the positive epistemology of practice, craft and artistry had no lasting place in rigorous practical knowledge" (Schon, 1983, p. 34). A few social workers embraced this perspective, sometimes known as logical positivism, and became competent research methodologists. They learned how to conduct scientific research and developed expertise needed to examine and test phenomena. Unfortunately, only a small number of the few social workers who acquired competency in scientific research methods conducted practice-relevant research. In other words, the research-based knowledge generated held little value for social work practitioners—who sought information about how best to help people in need.

Furthermore, science-based publications typically included reference to research designs, sample selections, and statistics, which seemed foreign to many social workers. Because of these and other factors, a schism developed within the profession. Perhaps reflecting ethnocentric thinking, researchers and practitioners tended to view each other with skepticism and sometimes derision. Practitioners accused researchers of not producing knowledge that would be useful for practice (Bergmark & Oscarsson, 1992); researchers, in turn, accused practitioners of not being interested in hard knowledge and of lacking discipline and intellectual rigor.

During the middle to latter portion of the 20th century, other factors contributed to this split. The few social workers actively conducting research were usually associated with universities—contributing to a "town" and "gown" differentiation. The postmodern movement in philosophy and literature spread into the academic disciplines raising questions about the objectivity of traditional scientific methods (Belenky, Clinchy, Goldberger, & Tarule, 1986; Fraser, Taylor, Jackson, & O'Jack, 1991; Goldberger, Tarule, Clinchy, & Belenky, 1996; Hartman, 1990; Sands & Nuccio, 1992; Weick & Pope, 1988; Wolf, 1992). Often associated with views that men and women see and experience the world differently (Gilligan, 1984), postmodernists asserted that ethnographic and other forms of qualitative research were every bit as valuable as traditional forms of quantitative research. As social work approached the 21st century, the tensions among different kinds of researchers and between researchers and practitioners were palpable. Some of the strain continues today. Practitioners continue to be involved in the often messy and uncontrolled problems of human life. They often speak of experience, trial and error, practice wisdom, intuition, and even of muddling through. Researchers—whether qualitative or quantitative, or male or female—remain interested in critical analysis, scholarship, and evidence to support conclusions. Unquestionably, some researchers—perhaps especially academics—adopt a patronizing attitude toward practitioners, and some practitioners reject any and all forms of research, refuse to consider its potential utility practice, and avoid critical analysis of the nature, quality, and effects of their service. However, several factors and forces currently operate that may encourage greater respect and common purpose among these factions within the profession.

Ethical and educational standards have changed considerably over the years. In addition to our ethical obligation to keep abreast of emerging knowledge, most licensing laws require social workers to complete a certain amount of continuing professional education each year. Similarly, through its Educational Policy and Accreditation Standards (EPAS), the Council on Social Work Education expects graduates of school work programs to "use theoretical frameworks supported by empirical evidence to understand individual development and behavior across the life span and the interactions among individuals and between individuals and families, groups, organizations, and communities . . . (and) . . . evaluate research studies, apply research findings to practice, and evaluate their own practice interventions" (CSWE, 2001, p. 9). Graduates of accredited programs should use "empirically based interventions designed to achieve client goals" . . . (apply) . . . "empirical knowledge and technological advances" . . . (and evaluate) . . . "program outcomes and practice effectiveness" (CSWE, 2001, p. 12).

Furthermore, third-party payers (e.g., managed care and insurance companies), governmental agencies, and other funding sources (e.g., United Ways and other philanthropic organizations) increasingly require service providers and programs to demonstrate that they are adopting evidence-based practices and evaluating the outcomes of their service efforts. Members of consumer action groups are intensifying their advocacy for effective services for themselves and their family members. Agency supervisors and administrators have begun to consider service outcomes in their evaluations of both programs and practitioners. It has become a common requirement that social workers and program coordinators produce evidence not only that they served a great number of people or worked a certain number of hours but also that they actually helped rather than harmed people in their care. The outcomes of several lawsuits have also led social workers to place greater emphasis on accountability and effectiveness. These and other factors have contributed to a somewhat greater consensus among social workers that research related to practice effectiveness has value and that ethical practice must incorporate evaluation (i.e., research) processes. Indeed, seeking feedback about the relevance, utility, and outcome of activities represents both a natural part of systemic thinking and a fundamental aspect of social work practice. When clients-and-social workers evaluate the effects and effectiveness of their problem-solving activities, they are conducting research. Contemporary social workers must increasingly both deliver services and evaluate practices. In effect, they serve as scientist-practitioners or practitioner-researchers (Hess & Mullen, 1995).

Problem-solving processes represent a natural means by which to integrate scientific inquiry and practice. Practitioners, researchers, and the increasing number of practitioner-researchers are, in effect, problem-solvers (Allen-Meares & Lane, 1990; Hess & Mullen, 1995). Scientific inquiry involves an attempt to understand and solve a problem, and social work practice seeks to do the same in collaboration with a client. In this respect, the process of research and practice are similar. In both endeavors, problems are defined, hypotheses or assessments formulated, data collected, plans developed, action taken, and outcomes evaluated.

The rapidly growing movement toward empirical or evidence-based social work practice reflects this trend toward integration of research and practice (Blythe, 1992; Blythe & Briar, 1985; Corcoran, 2000, 2002; Cournoyer, 2004; Cournoyer & Powers, 2002; Davenport, 1992; Davis, 1989; Fischer, 1993; Franklin & Brekke, 1994; Franklin & Jordan, 2002; Gambrill, 1999; Gibbs, 2002a, 2002b; Ivanoff, Blythe, & Briar, 1987; Ivanoff, Robinson, & Blythe, 1987; Jayaratne & Levy, 1979; Mullen & Goldstein, 1992; Reid, 1992, 1994; Rosen & Proctor, 2002; Rothman, 1991; Siegel, 1984; Thyer, 1996; Thyer & Wodarski, 1998a, 1998b; Wodarski & Bagarozzi, 1979; Wodarski & Thyer, 1998).

> Evidence-based social work is the mindful and systematic identification, analysis, and synthesis of evidence of practice effectiveness as a primary part of an integrative and collaborative process concerning the selection, application, and evaluation of service to members of target client groups. The evidence-based decision-making process includes consideration of professional ethics and experience as well as the cultural values and personal judgments of consumers. (Cournoyer, 2004, p. 4)

From this perspective, evidence of what helps clients achieve goals comes from both nomothetic and ideographic sources. The term *nomothetic* refers to general conclusions such as might result from studies of groups, and *ideographic* involves specific information from the study of a particular client. In seeking evidence of "what works" then, a social worker conducts scholarly reviews of the professional research literature in search of nomothetic information relevant to a particular person-in-situation. Then, the worker

and client consider the relevance and applicability of the service approaches that reflect evidence of effectiveness for similar people in similar circumstances. They select or adapt an approach that is usually effective for others and apply it to the problems of concern. While implementing the approach, the client-and-worker team evaluates its effectiveness. In evaluating the outcomes of their work together, they produce ideographic evidence that they may use to improve their outcomes or to share with others who are addressing similar problems.

In the contemporary world of professional practice, social workers do not always need to conduct the scholarly reviews of the literature by themselves. A large number of such reviews and several meta-analytic studies have already been completed and published. In addition, social workers and other helping professionals that serve similar client groups are beginning to form journal clubs or study groups to maintain currency in the most recent evidence of practice effectiveness. Some even pool the results of their ideographic practice evaluations to produce, through aggregation and additional analysis, nomothetic evidence. It is hardly surprising that the phases of evidence-based social work fit so readily within the problem-solving process. Together, they represent a means by which social workers may fulfill their ethical responsibilities to contribute to the profession's knowledge base and simultaneously increase the quantity, quality, and relevance of research for practice (Lindsey & Kirk, 1992).

Theory and Practice

Is theory essential for practice? Social work professors occasionally debate this question (Simon & Thyer, 1994). There are pros and cons on each side of the issue. In general, we agree with Briar and Miller, "the choice for the practitioner is not whether to have a theory but what theoretical assumptions to hold" (Briar & Miller, 1971, p. 53). Humans seem to be meaning-making by nature. Invited or not, we regularly attribute meaning to and formulate hypotheses about events in the world. We adopt or construct opinions, views, and perspectives that serve as conceptual screens or lens through which to observe and interpret events in the world. We may not identify them as such and we may be unaware that we use them. However, they serve the same kind of functions that sophisticated formal theories do.

As do the rest of us, clients also routinely hypothesize about the causes of problems and, based on them, generate ideas about solutions. Indeed, one of the functions of the data collection, exploration, and assessment processes in social work practice is to come to an understanding of the causes and effects of the problem. In effect, the client-and-social worker collaboratively work out an informal theory that fits the perceived facts and circumstances and helps them predict what might happen, "if and when" they take problem-solving action. Sometimes, they refer to formal theories from disciplines such as sociology, psychology, economics, or perhaps biology. Theories related to systems, communications, learning, or human and social development often help in their meaning-making endeavors. Occasionally, however, the client-and-worker decide on an informal theory—unrelated to any academic or scientific perspective—that fits with the client's personal, familial, cultural, or spiritual tradition and experience. Such ideographic theories often hold special value for clients and frequently have great meaning to social workers who participate in their creation or application.

Several social workers have proposed heuristic rubrics for considering or comparing theories for use in social work practice (Fischer, 1971; Kettner, 1975; Meyer, 1983a). For example, Trader (see Exhibit 2-4) suggests that social workers consider several themes and ask ourselves particular questions when considering the relevance and applicability of a theory for use in service to oppressed peoples.

Knowledge and Values

What is knowledge and what are values? Answers to these apparently simple questions may not come easily. Because our values influence our perception, interpretation, evaluation, and utilization of knowledge, we may sometimes confuse them with knowledge itself. Values are beliefs about what we consider desirable; what we think should or ought to be. We typically have considerable emotional investment in the values we adopt or choose. Knowledge refers to what is, to what is real, true, genuine, or factual. Values imply a preference for certain "means, ends and conditions of life, often accompanied by strong feeling" (Pumphrey, 1959, p. 23). Knowledge, on the other hand, is information about the world and its qualities, about people and their interrelationships.

Values relate to the question of whether a proposition is right or wrong, whereas knowledge relates to the question of whether it is true or false. This distinction is very important to social work. For instance, suppose an adult client highly values personal liberty and individual freedom. Based on that value, the client adopts a parental style in which children are free to find and select their own food, choose where and when they sleep, what they wear, where they wander, and what they do. Imagine the potential consequences if a 2-year-old child received such freedom. Many of us might well call that parental style child neglect. Indeed, if the child died from malnutrition or was killed by a passing car after wandering onto a busy street, we might wonder about personal negligence. Social workers who understand the biological, emotional, and social needs of developing children would use that knowledge in exploring the question of how much and what of kind of personal freedom is best for raising children of different ages and capacities. Most of us would quickly recognize the potential risks to children if their parent's value-based emphasis on individual freedom remained untempered by the knowledge that children, as they develop, also need protection, continuity, and consistent limits. When our values coincide with knowledge, we feel comfortable because of the congruence. However, when knowledge conflicts with our preferred values, we usually experience internal discomfort or dissonance. The same process may occur within the client-and-worker partnership. Sometimes the worker's personal or professional values conflict with the client's knowledge. Professionals, of course, are obligated to transcend their personal preferences in deference to professional values and ethics but after negotiating that internal dilemma, a conflict between the worker's professional values and the client's knowledge may remain. Similarly, a client's values sometimes conflict with the worker's knowledge. For instance, many parents believe they have the right and duty to discipline their children through various forms of corporal punishment. Social workers may be aware of findings from research studies about the permanent brain damage that often occurs when people shake babies. They may also be familiar with research-based knowledge about the differential effects of punishment when compared with systems based on incentives. Value-knowledge conflicts appear within and between

EXHIBIT 2-4
Considering a Theory for Use in Social Work Practice

Pathology-health balance. Do the concepts focus on illness or deficit rather than on well-being and strengths? Are the definitions of pathology and health based solely on the expectations of the dominant group in society? Do standards for health include a range of potentials that allows for group differences? Are class differences implied or stated in the models for either normality or abnormality?

Practitioner-client control balance. Does the theory suggest that the worker carries more responsibility than the client in the process of changing the client's situation? Are clients perceived, even subtly, as being inferior to practitioners? Are practitioners seen as being obliged to use their knowledge and skills to increase clients' coping abilities? Does the theory view human beings as primarily dependent, interdependent, or independent? Can the theory allow for shared control? From what source does the practice derive its legitimacy?

Personal-societal impact balance. Does the theory embody a personal-deficit model rather than a societal model in assigning causation for problems? Does the theory take into account historical as well as current societal conditions? Can the theory account for political-economic influences on behavior? Does the theory assign importance to variations in socialization experiences among oppressed groups? Does the theory allow for linking of the personal to the social and environmental aspects of behavior?

Internal-external change balance. Does the theory emphasize internal, psychic change in preference to changes that occur in society? Does the theory assume that the nature of society is primarily punitive rather than supportive? Are the definitions for change based primarily on the dominant societal patterns, or do they allow for a variety of patterns? To what extent is the view of change synonymous with adjustment?

Rigidity-flexibility balance. Does the theory allow for the adjustment of concepts to the needs of particular groups? Do abstract principles lend themselves to creative and differential application in practice? Can the theory accommodate new information about oppressed groups? Does the theory relate to a view of the class structure of society? Does the theory demand an uncritical adherence to its postulates? Are there built-in criteria for continual assessment of the utility of the theory?

Source: Trader, H. P. (1977). Survival strategies for oppressed minorities. *Social Work, 22*(1), 10–13, p. 11.

---

larger size systems as well. Social workers may know that abject poverty, inadequate nourishment and nutrition, and insufficient social stimulation can cause severe and often permanent damage to the physical, psychological, and social well-being of children reared in such circumstances. However, the larger social system—perhaps in the form of the opinions of a majority of voters or those of elected or appointed officials—may place great importance on the value that people should be personally and individually responsible for themselves and their children. Based on the value of personal responsibility, rather than knowledge about children's biopsychosocial needs, social policies that might reduce poverty, enable access to nutritious food, and provide adequate social stimulation are excluded from consideration.

Most democratic societies reflect the general value-based principle that people have the right to think for themselves and adopt, choose, or create their own values. However, behavior based on those values is often limited. Although we can think anything, we can actually only do certain things. For example, laws prohibit child abuse, even for those who believe children should be corporally punished; child neglect, even for those who believe in absolute individual freedom; and sex between adults and children, even for those who believe that girls may marry at age nine. Knowledge about the values of other systems or the larger societal system as well as research-based knowledge may be relevant to the issues addressed by the client-worker team.

Gordon (1962, 1965) explored two general kinds or categories of knowledge: (1) knowledge that has been confirmed by empirical testing or observation; and (2) assumptive knowledge—knowledge that is accepted and acted on as though it were true but has not yet been confirmed, although the intent is to confirm it eventually. Similarly, Gambrill (1999, 2001) discussed the distinction between authority-based and evidence-based knowledge. She suggested that much information taught and learned in social work education programs is authority-based rather than evidence-based in nature. She also argued that the teaching and learning processes that transmit authority-based information might be more accurately characterized as indoctrination rather than education.

Assumptive or authority-based information may be true or false. In effect, it reflects the ideas, wisdom, and opinions of the people who assume them true. These assumptive notions often contribute to the generation of useful questions or hypotheses for qualitative or quantitative research studies. If confirmed through research studies, assumptive knowledge may become empirical knowledge. However, until subject to careful scrutiny and investigation, we might well view assumptive positions more as a reflection of value or opinion rather than knowledge and fact. A great deal of the information used by social workers is assumptive or authority-based in nature. The establishment of empirical knowledge is conditioned on our willingness to conduct research and analyze the findings. Until that occurs, social workers should recognize and distinguish authority-based from evidence-based knowledge, which holds greater professional credibility than do the opinions of even our most prestigious authorities.

Acting on Incomplete Knowledge

Although the quantity and quality of practice-relevant research continues to grow at an ever-accelerating rate (Thyer, 1996, 2000), there are many circumstances where social workers must, like other helping professionals, intervene in people's lives on the basis of incomplete knowledge. This raises extraordinarily challenging issues and dilemmas of an ethical, legal, practical, and often personal nature. In the absence of certain knowledge, we may question our

right as well as our ability to provide helpful service to others. How can people feel optimistic about their work with us if we are uncertain? How can we doubt our effectiveness and still be effective? Some social workers handle this kind of discomfort by forgetting what they do not know. In other words, they decide that their value-based opinions and assumptive ideas are actually truths. They become dogmatic, certain of their own knowledge, and confident. As a result, they may indeed feel less discomfort and more optimistic about their effectiveness. However, dogmatic strategies often lead to closed boundaries that inhibit growth and learning. Why would we consider new information if we already possess certain knowledge and absolute truth?

Social workers may adopt other strategies in attempts to manage the discomfort associated with uncertain knowledge. Some focus on their ignorance and uncertainty, and adopt a passive, hesitant, or ambiguous approach in their efforts to help others. In other words, they become an excessively open, borderless-system. When social workers are reluctant to assume responsibility, their clients suffer from the lack of an active, secure helper. Some social workers blame the profession or their educational programs for their discomfort. Critical that they did not receive more or better knowledge, they find themselves in a profession about which they have limited confidence or identification. Such a position is truly uncomfortable. Feeling replete with cognitive dissonance, they may adopt a cynical perspective about their profession, education, work, and perhaps even their clients. By cynically placing blame on external factors, such social workers may fail to recognize that all professions lack certain knowledge and all professionals must negotiate the dilemmas that accompany that reality. Furthermore, such cynicism may result in professional negligence if the social worker fails to learn about relevant evidence-based knowledge, which, after all, continues to expand at a dizzying pace.

As helping persons in arguably the most ambitious profession, we routinely find ourselves in complex dynamic situations trying to assist unique people address incredibly challenging social problems without the advantage of certain knowledge. Indeed, successful management of this kind of dilemma is characteristic of effective professionals of all kinds. Although social workers may adopt several strategies in attempts to control their discomfort in this regard, we encourage you to adopt an open-system, problem-solving per-

---

EXHIBIT 2-5
A Social Work Pledge in the Face of Incomplete Knowledge

In my professional work with clients, I hereby pledge to

- Carefully and critically analyze and evaluate the nature and quality of information for use in practice
- Distinguish my personal from my professional values and assumptive or authority-based information from empirical or evidence-based knowledge
- Incorporate relevant evidence-based knowledge as part of the problem-solving process in my efforts to serve clients
- Evaluate the effects and effectiveness of problem-solving activities and use the results as feedback for improvement

- Manage discomfort associated with incomplete knowledge in ways that enable me to remain open to emerging knowledge and treat others with dignity and respect
- Assume responsibility for my actions
- Enthusiastically engage in lifelong learning in efforts to seek, discover, analyze, and apply evidence-based knowledge for practice
- Base professional decisions on scholarly understanding and open-minded critical analysis of available knowledge in consultation with clients
- Resist temptations to make decisions on the basis of personal values, opinions, ideology, self-interest, or personal feelings

---

spective and enthusiastically commit to a professional lifetime of active learning in which you continually seek, discover, analyze, and apply evidence-based knowledge in your efforts to help others. You could also consider the pledge reflected in Exhibit 2-5.

◆ Chapter Summary

In this chapter, we considered several aspects of the person-in-situation focus that are central to our model of practice. We referred to dimensions of general systems theory, reviewed various systemic processes, and explored the relevance of systems thinking for social work. We also reviewed elements of the ecosystems perspective, including aspects of the person as well as the environment, and considered how they constitute an integrated whole.

We explored several challenging issues associated with the use of knowledge for practice. We considered the relationships between research and practice, and attempted to distinguish knowledge from values, personal from professional values, and assumptive or authority-based from empirical or evidence-based information. Finally, we considered the challenges associated with the use of incomplete or uncertain knowledge and explored various means for managing the stress-inducing questions that accompany that reality.

Learning Exercises: Readings, InfoTrac, and the Web

1. Use your word-processing computer program to enter the important terms and concepts presented in this chapter. At this point, simply list them in alphabetical order. Place a question mark by any terms that you do not clearly understand. Save your document as EX 2-1.

2. Turn to **Reading 4: An Ecosystemic Approach to Assessment.** Review the article by Jane Gilgun and reflect on its implications for social work and social work practice. Address the following questions in a one-page essay: What are the differences, if any, between the approach she describes and the major key concepts we identified in Chapter 2? How might you modify the way you carry out an ecosystemic assessment to reduce any possible discrepancy between her approach and the model of practice we are discussing? Save your document as EX 2-2, and then log on to the InfoTrac College Edition Web site. Conduct a keyword search (using either Keyword Search or Advanced Search) to locate the full-text article entitled "Treating Powerless Minorities Through an Ecosystem Approach" (Chung & Pardeck,

1997). Read the article, including the case description, and consider it in light of Gilgun's article. Discuss your thoughts in a paragraph or so, and add it to EX 2-2.

3. Turn to **Reading 5: Social Work and the Medicine Wheel Framework.** Read the article by Lyle Longclaws. Reflect on its implications for social work and social work practice in a one-page essay. Save your document as EX 2-3. If the idea of medicine wheels intrigues you, use the InfoTrac College Edition resources to locate and review the article entitled "Medicine Wheel" by F. Whiseyjack (2000). If you do so, you might add a few more comments to your essay.

4. Turn to **Reading 6: The Birky Family.** Read the section entitled "Initial Contact" to learn about this Appalachian family who resettled in a southern city. In a one-page essay, explore how environmental factors affect the family. Be sure to address the following questions: What messages have the parents internalized from their rural environment that may be interfering with their ability to improve the fit between their current needs and environmental resources? If you were this worker, which problem would you prefer to address first? Why? What would be your second area of focus after the family makes some progress with the first? Why? Save your document as EX 2-4. After that, complete an abbreviated genogram and eco-map based on the guidelines suggested by Jane Gilgun in Reading 4. You may draw the genogram and eco-map by hand or use the features of your word processing program.

5. Turn to **Reading 7: The Stover Family.** Read the case record and reflect on its implications for social work and social work practice in a one-page essay in which you address these questions: When did Mrs. Stover become the client? What did the worker do that helped Mrs. Stover decide to accept service? What (or who) is the target system? Save your document as EX 2-5.

6. Log on to the InfoTrac College Edition Web site. Conduct a keyword search (using either Keyword Search or Advanced Search) to locate the full-text articles entitled "On Science, Antiscience, and the Client's Right to Effective Treatment" (Thyer & Myers, 1999); "Social Work Research and the Quest for Effective Practice" (Rosen, Proctor, &

Staudt, 1999); and "Differential Effectiveness of Prevalent Social Work Practice Models: A Meta-Analysis" (Gorey, Thyer, & Pawluck, 1998). Read and reflect on their implications for social work and social work practice in a two-page essay. Save your document as EX 2-6.

7. Log on to the InfoTrac College Edition Web site. Conduct a keyword search (using either Keyword Search or Advanced Search) to locate the full-text article entitled "The Inclusive Workplace: An Ecosystems Approach to Diversity Management" (Mor Barak, 2000). Read and reflect on its implications for social work and social work practice in a one-page essay. Save your document as EX 2-7.

8. Log on to the InfoTrac College Edition Web site. Conduct a keyword search (using either Keyword Search or Advanced Search) to locate the full-text article entitled "Demographic and Clinical Correlates of Client Motivation Among Substance Abusers" (Rapp, Li, Siegal, & DeLiberty, 2003). Read the article and reflect on its implications for social work and social work practice in a one-page essay. Save your document as EX 2-8.

9. Log on to the InfoTrac College Edition Web site. Conduct a keyword search (using either Keyword Search or Advanced Search) to locate the full-text article entitled "Perceptions of Goal-Directed Activities of Optimists and Pessimists: A Personal Projects Analysis" (Jackson, Weiss, Lundquist, & Soderlind, 2002). Read the article and reflect on its implications for social work and social work practice in a one-page essay. Save your document as EX 2-9.

10. Log on to the InfoTrac College Edition Web site. Conduct a keyword search (using either Keyword Search or Advanced Search) to locate the full-text article entitled "Resilience in Adult Children of Alcoholics: A Nonpathological Approach to Social Work Practice" (Palmer, 1997) or "Stress, Coping, and Resilience in Children and Youth" (Smith & Carlson, 1997). Read one or both of the articles and reflect on its (or their) implications for social work and social work practice in a one-page essay. Save your document as EX 2-10.

11. Log on to the World Wide Web and go to the Web site of the Association of Social Work Boards at www.aswb.org. Locate the page that contains the ASWB Examination Content Outlines. Review the

content areas addressed in the bachelor's and the master's level examinations. Reflect on the range of knowledge expected of licensed social workers and then write a brief outline of those content areas that you will need to study. Save your document as EX 2-11.

12. Prepare a one-page essay in which you consider the social worker and client as a system and think about your present understanding of social work practice. Address these questions: What factors might contribute to the client-worker system becoming closed? What circumstances might lead to an excessively open client-worker system? What potential dangers emerge if the systemic boundaries become too closed or too open? How can these conditions be prevented? Save your document as EX 2-12.

13. Turn again to **Reading 3: The House on Sixth Street.** You previously read it for an earlier exercise. Review it again. This time, prepare a one-page essay in which you address these questions: How does this illustrate the layering of systems? Who or what is the client? What (or who) is the target system? What other means might the change agent and client have used to accomplish their objectives? Save your document as EX 2-13.

Chapter 3

Problem Solving: A Process for Social Work Practice

◆ Problem Solving as a Life Process

The word *problem* has a long history. The term *problema* in Latin and Greek means "an obstacle." It is derived from a combination of the words *pro,* meaning forward, and *ballein,* meaning "to throw." Problem, therefore, means "to throw forward" (Merriam-Webster, 2003). This definition approaches our interpretation of the term. We define problem as *an event, condition, or experience that stimulates a sense of disequilibrium and a corresponding motivation to regain a sense of equilibrium through thought or action or both thought and action.* Our definition does not suggest or convey a value judgment. Problems are neither good nor bad. They do not necessarily convey anything negative about the person, family, group, organization, community, or society that experiences them.

The American philosopher John Dewey (1910) observed that human beings use "intelligence in operation" to respond to problems they confront. Although we may react initially with feelings of discomfort, disturbance, or uncertainty, we fairly quickly seek to eliminate the difficulty and reduce the discomfort associated with our experience of the problem. As part of this problem-solving process, we *think.* Indeed, "The origin of thinking is some perplexity, confusion, or doubt. Thinking is not a case of spontaneous combustion; it does not occur just on 'general principles.' There is something specific which occasions and evokes it" (Dewey, 1910, p. 12).

> Thinking begins in what may fairly enough be called *a forked-road* situation, a situation which is ambiguous, which presents a dilemma, which proposes alternatives. As long as our activity glides smoothly along from one

thing to another, or as long as we permit our imagination to entertain fancies at pleasure, there is no call for reflection. Difficulty or obstruction in the way of reaching a belief brings us, however, to a pause. In the suspense of uncertainty, we metaphorically climb a tree; we try to find some standpoint from which we may survey additional facts and, getting a more commanding view of the situation, may decide how the facts stand related to one another.

> *Demand for the solution of a perplexity is the steadying and guiding factor in the entire process of reflection.* Where there is no question of a problem to be solved or a difficulty to be surmounted, the course of suggestions flows on at random. . . . But a question to be answered, an ambiguity to be resolved, sets up an end and holds the current of ideas to a definite channel. Every suggested conclusion is tested by its reference to this regulating end, by its pertinence to the problem in band. This need of straightening out a perplexity also controls the kind of inquiry undertaken. A traveler whose end is the most beautiful path will look for other considerations and will test suggestions occurring to him on another principle than if he wishes to discover the way to a given city. *The problem fixes the end of thought* and *the end controls the process of thinking.* (Dewey, 1910, pp. 11–12)

In Dewey's view then, thinking begins in response to a problematic condition and involves consideration of how to resolve this problem. Ideas or suggestions about solutions to the problem may pop quickly to mind.

If the suggestion that occurs is at once accepted, we have uncritical thinking, the minimum of reflection. To turn the thing over in mind, to reflect, means to hunt for additional evidence, for new data, that will develop the suggestion, and will either, as we say, bear it out or else make obvious its absurdity and irrelevance. . . . The easiest way is to accept any suggestion that seems plausible and thereby bring to an end the condition of mental uneasiness. Reflective thinking is always more or less troublesome because it involves overcoming the inertia that inclines one to accept suggestions at their face value; it involves willingness to endure a condition of mental unrest and disturbance. Reflective thinking, in short, means judgment suspended during further inquiry; and suspense is likely to be somewhat painful. . . . (The) most important factor in the training of good mental habits consists in acquiring the attitude of suspended conclusion, and in mastering the various methods of searching for new materials to corroborate or to refute the first suggestions that occur. To maintain the state of doubt and to carry on systematic and protracted inquiry—these are the essentials of thinking. (Dewey, 1910, p. 13)

Effective thinking for problem solving requires rationality and reflection. Otherwise, we may act uncritically or impulsively, leap to inappropriate conclusions, mistake the nature of the problem, or search for the answer to the wrong problem. Any of these behaviors can compromise our capacity to cope with the situation and reduce the likelihood of a successful resolution (Campbell, 1995; Hart, 1993; Herman, 1943; Hickman, 1997; Leffers, 1993; Mead, 1934; Pappas, 1993).

Dewey organized the processes of effective problem solving into a sequence of well-defined and orderly steps that naturally yield a preferred solution. He referred to these as the five phases of reflective thinking:

1. Recognize the difficulty
2. Define or specify the difficulty
3. Raise suggestions for possible solutions and rationally explore the suggestions, including data collection
4. Select an optimal solution from among many proposals
5. Carry out the solution

Dewey's approach to reflective thinking and problem solving can be applied to many different fields and contexts. For example, Bennis suggested a problem-solving perspective for planning systemic change (Bennis, Benne, & Chin, 1969) in business and industry, and Basadur proposed an eight-step model (see Exhibit 3-1) for organizational problem solving.

In the early 1940s, Polya (1957) introduced a four-phase model for addressing mathematical problems:

1. Understand the problem, including the problem situation, the goal of the problem solver, and the conditions for solving the problem
2. Devise a plan by which the goal might be attained
3. Carry out the plan
4. Evaluate the implementation of the plan and the results

As Helen Harris Perlman (1957, 1970, 1986) and many other social workers concluded, the problem-solving approach seems especially well-suited to the needs and tasks of clients-and-social workers in efforts to resolve issues of concern (Compton & Galaway, 1984, 1989, 1994, 1999; Fortune, 1979; Hoshino, 1994). Dewey did not explicitly include evaluation of the effectiveness of the attempted solution as a separate stage, although Polya certainly did so. Recognizing its importance to living systems, we also include evaluation of intervention effects as a separate process so that adaptations to solution strategies may be guided by feedback information. We organize the problem-solving process for social work practice into four primary phases:

- Engagement
- Assessment
- Intervention or action
- Evaluation

Each of these phases can be further subdivided. For example, Cournoyer outlines a seven-step process: (1) preparing, (2) beginning, (3) exploring, (4) assessing, (5) contracting, (6) working and evaluating, and (7) ending (Cournoyer, 2005). Clients-and-workers tend to address specific tasks and activities during each phase.

The meaning of problems and the idea of problem solving in social work practice are frequently misunderstood. For example, some people think of problems as necessarily "bad." They may believe that all problems can be avoided or prevented if we are simply good or careful enough. In other words, morally decent competent people should not have problems. Such a position is naïve and unrealistic. Challenging things happen to good and bad people alike. Deprived of food and water, all people feel hunger and thirst. Floods, tornadoes, earthquakes, fires, and droughts can affect everyone. Even the most innocent of people can be victimized by crime, infected by viruses, and affected by economic and political change. Difficult

---

EXHIBIT 3-1
The Simplex System to Improve Organizational Problem Solving

Step 1: Problem finding. A skilled problem finder learns to uncover problems rather than waiting to be overwhelmed. For example, a single customer complaining may be enough to reveal a potential problem in the distribution process.

Step 2: Fact finding. Once a problem has been identified, all the relevant information needs to be gathered to understand the size and importance of the problem. Useful questions to answer are: "How often . . . ?"; "How much . . . ?"; and "How long . . . ?" Beware of taking facts for granted; some may turn out to be assumptions.

Step 3: Problem definition. This requires stating the problem in a way that can be resolved. "How might we . . . ?" is often a good way of defining a problem.

Step 4: Idea finding. This requires the generation of a number of alternative approaches to achieve a desired goal. Brainstorming is a useful way of avoiding the premature exclusion of certain options.

Step 5: Evaluation and selection of solutions. Sifting the possible solutions down to the best approach usually requires listing the criteria against which various options will be evaluated. Eventually the best overall approach is adopted.

Step 6: Action planning. Finding a solution is not enough; it has to be implemented. Develop a specific action plan, including who will do what and when. The plan must be realistic and take account of organizational constraints.

Step 7: Gaining acceptance. Action planning usually identifies people who have to provide approval—or even active support—for the plan to succeed. Many proposals for change fall apart because of inadequate attention to how to win over the necessary people.

Step 8: Taking action. Finally, the time comes to take action. Set a deadline, share your plans with others, and break big tasks into smaller pieces.

Source: Basadur, M. (1995). *The power of innovation.* Langham, MD: Pitman.

---

things happen to everybody—even to "rich and beautiful people" with svelte bodies driving expensive cars, residing in enormous mansions, and living privileged lives. Problems in living are, quite simply, inevitable. Their occurrence does not suggest that someone necessarily made a mistake or committed a sin or a crime. Frequently, no one is to blame. Furthermore, problems often lead to positive change. Indeed, we believe that humans must experience certain problems before we can grow, develop, and thrive.

Some social workers define the purpose of social work as meeting client needs rather than helping to resolve problems. When used as a noun, the term *needs* generally refers to the various conditions required for biopsychosocial survival. Food, water, shelter, human contact, and social stimulation represent some human needs. The kind and number vary according to the conception, definition, and measurement of needs. For instance, social achievement, personal or economic security, good health, or per-

haps a passing grade on a college examination may be included within some conceptions of human need.

In perhaps the most well-known exploration of the topic, Abraham Maslow (1943, 1979, 1982) proposed a hierarchy of needs. He believed that people must meet or satisfy the needs at lower levels before they could address those at higher stages. Maslow conceptualized them in the form of a pyramid. At its base are physiological needs, followed in turn by needs for safety, belongingness, esteem, and at the very top of the hierarchical pyramid is self-actualization. Maslow adopted an optimistic view about human beings and humanity. Believing that people are basically good, he was more interested in exploring human strengths and success rather than pathology and failure.

The hierarchy of needs makes intuitive sense. We expect people who are hungry and thirsty to first satisfy those physiological needs before considering others. Hungry enough, humans might well risk their safety, status, or reputations to secure food and

---

EXHIBIT 3-2
Who Determines Client Needs?

Mr. K's wife had to be hospitalized, leaving him without care for three preschool children. Following a court hearing, a judge required Mr. K to receive help from a social services agency to meet the children's need for child care. The judge's primary concern was the welfare of the children. The agency worker who received the assignment accepted the referral information that Mr. K needed to secure care for his children while his wife was in the hospital.

Mr. K recognized the need for child care, but he was distraught with worry about his wife's illness. Terrified that she might die, he wanted desperately to understand the cause and the course of the illness, and to learn when she could come home. By focusing on child care, the worker attempted to meet the needs of the children for supervision. However, the worker's attempts to meet those needs were not related to Mr. K's most pressing problem and the kind of help he wanted. The worker ignored Mr. K's questions about his wife's illness and his intense worry about her well-being, and continued to focus on the children's need for care. Perhaps because of deepening fear and con-

cern about his wife, Mr. K began to exhibit behavior that the worker considered strange. He would pace around the room during their meetings. He seemed preoccupied with other things and sometimes tears rolled down his face for no apparent reason. The worker wondered if Mr. K might suffer from a psychiatric illness and questioned his fitness as a parent.

Needless to say, neither Mr. K nor the social worker was satisfied with the experience. The worker wanted Mr. K to acknowledge that the need for child care was paramount. The client wanted to learn about his wife's condition and perhaps how to cope with the intense fear and worry he experienced about her well-being. Had the worker paid some attention to his wants, instead of the externally defined needs, they may have been able to obtain information and allay his fears through a few phone calls. At that point, Mr. K may have been in a much better position to address issues related to the children's care. As it was, neither the worker nor the client achieved their goals because they had not reached a common understanding of the problems, wants, or goals.

---

water. Well-nourished people with access to basic resources could shift their attention to security and safety. They might create doors with locks; build walls, fences, moats, or gated communities; or invent various weapons or alarm systems and organize armies, police forces, or security guards. Well-fed and feeling more physically secure, people might begin to consider the emotional, social, psychological, spiritual, cultural, and artistic aspects of life. Indeed, we imagine that growth of communities and civilizations reflected similar processes during their development.

The term *need* can also be used as a verb as in the phrase "I need . . ." or "They need to . . ." When used in this fashion, the object to which the verb refers may become artificially associated with fundamental survival needs. "I need a face-lift" or "They need to paint their house" does not seem equivalent to the need

that a starving person has for food, or that children caught in a war zone have for safety.

As social workers, we are especially interested in encouraging community development to ensure that people everywhere have access to nutritious food, water, and housing as well as education, employment, health care, and personal safety and political freedom. However, there are risks associated with the use of terms such as *needs* when applied by one person or group to another (see Exhibit 3-2). As you well know from earlier chapters, we prefer the term *problems* to the term *needs* and, within that context, seek to understand problems and to determine clients' wants and goals from a person-in-situation perspective.

Like Dewey, we believe that life itself is a problem-solving process. Reid (1978, p. 26) says it well: "A want . . . experienced without satisfaction becomes a problem." Human *wants* then is a more expansive term than *needs*. Our wants are endless. When one is satisfied, another immediately takes its place. If not satisfied, the new want becomes a problem. Thus, problems abound in our daily lives and we are constantly involved in problem solving. We solve so many problems in such an automatic and natural way, that many people are consciously unaware of the steps to the process. As long as we solve problems and achieve our desired results, we may be quite uninterested in exactly how we do so. We may adopt preferred patterns of problem solving that we use over and over again—until, that is, we confront a problem that exceeds our capacity or competence and for which our usual problem-solving strategies prove ineffective. At that point, we may seek the assistance of a helping professional—who, we hope, can help us address the problem we are unable to solve through our usual means.

Effective problem solving tends to proceed in a fairly predictable process. First, we perceive a want. If unsatisfied, the want becomes a problem that requires a solution. Defined problems lead naturally to goals that could resolve the problem. Satisfactory solutions must relate to these goals. We gather data related to the problems and the situation, and then envision goals. As we consider solutions, we review the acquired data and begin to envision possible plans to reach our goals. We make decisions about the best solution and then take action accordingly. We simultaneously evaluate the results of our actions, so that we can learn from the process. Through evaluation, we attempt to determine whether our actions have moved us toward the goals we selected.

If our evaluation is negative, we often retrace our steps to determine which aspects of the problem-solving process were ineffective. We might realize that we perceived or defined the problem incorrectly or that we did not have the knowledge and information necessary to reach an appropriate decision. Sometimes our method of action was ill-chosen or improperly applied. Some of us suffer a great deal at this point in the problem-solving process because we hold ourselves responsible for the negative outcome and feel guilty. Of course, we are rarely fully responsible because we must necessarily approach all problems in living with incomplete knowledge. We can never be absolutely certain of the solution or the outcomes. However, we can be certain about the process. Indeed, we believe that social workers must be exceptionally knowledgeable and skilled in all aspects of the problem-solving process, including activities associated with its steps, stages, or phases. We suggest that ethical, effective social workers must consciously and deliberately follow a coherent problem-solving process in their efforts to help clients address the problems that concern them.

◆ Problem Solving in Social Work

Perlman (1957, 1970, 1986) first proposed a problem-solving framework for social work practice. Social workers everywhere are forever in her debt for helping the profession emerge from a conception of practice that involved an almost-obsessive focus on past experience. Perlman encouraged social workers to attend to present problems and issues and invest energy in taking action to resolve them. From an optimistic and, indeed, solution-oriented perspective, she helped us reconsider the value of intensive and extensive exploration about past events and circumstances as a means for solving contemporary problems in living.

Much of Perlman's work—completed nearly 50 years ago—represents a logical precursor to current trends in cognitive-behavioral, strengths-based, and solution-focused forms of practice. A principal difference between our approach and Perlman's is that we extend the problem-solving process to families, groups, organizations, and communities through the integration of systems and ecosystems principles. We broaden the model to include more emphasis on transactions with, and changes in, systemic layers beyond the person. Perlman tended to limit the application of the problem-solving approach primarily to individual clients and emphasized the worker's responsibility for carefully thinking about the facts, diagnosis, and planning.

We view the problem-solving process as a solid foundation for generalist practice with systems at multiple layers of society and stress the collaborative nature of all phases of the problem-solving process, including assessment and intervention. We agree with Perlman that social work professionals must possess sophisticated knowledge, including the know-how to secure additional pertinent information, and should use their intelligence to contribute to the process. This represents a basic professional responsibility. However, the client also brings to the process extremely relevant knowledge, an ability to access other information, and intelligence. Ideally, the client and the worker combine and synthesize their knowledge and ideas through a collaborative, thinking-together, partnership. Indeed, the worker is obligated to share his or her expertise and analysis with clients. Failure to do so abrogates the principle of partnership and represents a form of "doing to" or "doing for" rather than "joining with" clients.

Perlman viewed problem solving both as a process and a helping method. We see it as a process that includes selecting appropriate intervention strategies. Perlman emphasized the enabling or facilitating role of the worker, whereas we expect social workers to engage in a much broader array of helper roles. We also attempt to provide greater distinction between the various stages of the process. Unlike Perlman (1957) and several other helping theorists, we disagree with the notion that treatment begins with the first glance between worker and client. We strongly believe that work toward change cannot and should not proceed until the applicant agrees to participate in the process, concurs with the assessment, and provides explicit consent to implement the intervention plan.

Phases of the Problem-Solving Process

Each phase of effective problem solving requires accomplishing certain tasks before clients-and-workers can usefully proceed to the next phase. As social workers, we use specialized social work skills in undertaking tasks associated with each phase of practice:

- Engage clients, explore the presenting problem, and identify preliminary goals
- Collect data, assess the situation, establish goals, and develop an action plan
- Implement the action plan
- Evaluate the effects and effectiveness of the action plan and disengage with clients

Please note that we identify goals at two phases. We do so initially during the engagement phase and again during assessment. Inherent in the experience of a problem is a want. The preliminary goal represents a statement of what the client initially wants. Although their preliminary goals often change later, many clients know what they want to happen at the time of first contact. They may have already constructed one or more possible solutions. Exploration of preliminary goals represents a natural complement to exploration of the presenting problem. By exploring goals as well as problems early in the process, clients-and-workers

are likely to feel more motivated and future oriented, and clients are more likely to feel understood. Early identification of preliminary goals contributes to the sense of the client-and-worker as a collaborative partnership and often enhances active client engagement and participation. Of course, the preliminary goals are reconsidered as part of the assessment process—when final goals are conjointly established.

Guided by the values and ethics of the profession, the problem-solving process involves a series of interactions between client-and-social worker and usually people from other systems as well. The process reflects an integration of feeling, thinking, and doing as guided by and directed toward an agreed-upon goal that, if achieved, results in a solution to the problem. Effective problem solving includes access to and application of knowledge as well as skill. Establishing a collaborative relationship and sense of genuine partnership between client-and-worker represents an essential aspect of the process. Relationship and understanding do not automatically develop just because people find themselves together in a meeting. Relationship is embodied in emotions and attitudes that sustain the problem-solving process as client-and-worker work together in partnership toward a mutually agreed on goal or objective. Thus, the problem-solving process rests on the ability of each partner to relate and communicate with the other to exchange information, energy, and other resources needed to pursue the agreed-upon goal. For instance, clients typically have information about

- What brings them into contact with the social worker
- The emotions, fears, and conflicts generated by the problem
- What they expect and hope will result from this contact and the social worker

Social workers typically have

- Knowledge about various social problems and programs, practices, the services used to address them
- Access to resources that may pertain to problem resolution
- Competence in the social work helping skills and expertise in some models and methods of change
- An orderly way of proceeding toward solutions to problems

We believe that troubles in living stem from difficulties in effectively coping with specific situations in daily life. Difficulties in coping may stem from a combination of motivation, capacity, and opportunity:

- *Motivation:* An imbalance of hope and discomfort in relation to an imagined solution to the problem—a goal
- *Capacity:* The needed knowledge, social skills, rational skills, relationship with external reality, and interplay of current and past biopsychosocial factors in development
- *Opportunity:* Access to support systems, needed resources, and helping relationships

From this perspective, progress toward a desired goal depends on the motivation and ability of people individually or collectively to engage in a problem-solving process and to use or develop opportunities in the environment. The dimensions of motivation, capacity, and opportunity were first formally organized in social work by professors at the University of Chicago School of Social Service (Ripple, 1955; Ripple & Alexander, 1956; Ripple, Alexander, & Polemis, 1964). As did Perlman, they also anticipated elements of contemporary practice—particularly motivational enhancement (Baer, Kivlahan, & Donovan, 2000; Miller, Benefield, & Tonigan, 2001; Miller & Rollnick, 1991, 2002; Rollnick, 2002; Rollnick & Miller, 1995).

The experience of problems in living and their solution always involves emotions, the knowledge that we have available to us, our perceptions of the world, and an orderly way of thinking. These elements interact in a complex way. We feel discomfort, frustration, fear, and perhaps anger along with other emotions when confronting a problem that we cannot solve alone, a problem that represents a serious threat to our goals, or a problem that seriously threatens the needs and wants of those around us. The emotions may obscure parts of the problem, interfere with data collection and consideration of alternative solutions, or block effective action toward a solution. Emotions may seriously diminish or perhaps even paralyze problem-solving ability. When immobilized by intense emotions, people cannot truly participate as full collaborative partners. Therefore, social workers often help moderate emotions before proceeding with problem solving. Occasionally, extreme emotions are themselves the problem so that the goals for work might be something such as "learning to manage emotions." Amelioration of intense feelings, however, is usually insufficient by itself to resolve problems. Clients typically require additional knowledge or perspective about the problem, resources, and, of course, completion of actions needed to achieve goals.

Powerful emotions, of course, should not necessarily be viewed as negative phenomena. Indeed, all effective helping processes draw on the feelings of both clients and workers. When accompanied by feelings, learning is often more durable. We remember things that have an affective dimension much better than those that occur in a dry, sterile, emotionless context. Emotions represent an important part of problem solving. They become problematic only when they are so intense or so minimal that they obstruct thought and action. Feelings create the climate in which helping and solution seeking take place. Problem solving, however, remains a rational process that involves feelings and occurs within the context of emotions.

The problem-solving model requires rational thought and analysis. Accordingly, you may suppose that it is appropriate only for clients who have the sophisticated cognitive ability to weigh and measure alternative courses of action. Nothing could be further from the truth. Even on those occasions where social workers assume primary responsibility for the intellectual or analytic work, we must also ensure that clients participate as active partners in decision making and action taking. Fraser (1995), for example, discusses the relevance and importance of cognitive problem solving in both family preservation service and in work with aggressive youth. We have also successfully incorporated this approach with families judged by other professional helpers from schools, mental health clinics, and social agencies to be unreachable and beyond help.

Engagement The engagement phase[1] of practice involves those dynamics, dimensions, and activities associated with initial contacts with potential clients. Engagement includes personal and professional preparation for the meeting; introductions and orientation to the process; review and consideration of policy and ethical factors; and activities directed toward understanding the nature of the presenting problem and identifying a preliminary goal—usually in terms

---

[1] We explore the engagement phase in greater depth in Chapters 8 and 9.

of what the applicant[2] wants. Successful engagement results in an agreement with the applicant to proceed to assessment for the purposes of specifying the problems for work, establishing final goals, and developing a service plan. This agreement constitutes a preliminary contract between client-and-worker.

Early during the engagement phase, social workers encourage applicants to describe and discuss the problem of concern in their own words and in their own ways. We hope to gain some understanding of the views and experiences of those people most affected by the problem. Social workers sometimes find this difficult when we become so concerned with understanding the problem from our own perspective that we neglect to understand it from the perspective of consumers. We might, for example, be so intent on applying a particular theory to understand the problem or perhaps in attempting to classify or diagnose that we effectively block our capacity to understand others' experience. Indeed, workers sometimes remain unaware that their understanding of the problem differs from that of the applicant's. Consider the implications of a circumstance where a helping professional holds one view of the problem and the consumer holds another. A social worker could conceivably conclude that their work together was a great success. "We solved the problem as I defined it!" However, the consumer considers it a total failure and a waste of time, energy, and money. "We didn't solve the problem as I defined it!"

Effective outcomes usually require active engagement and participation of both consumers and social workers. We believe that activity, participation, and motivation tend to increase when workers seek to understand and appreciate applicants' expectations and problem definitions. During initial encounters with social workers, some people may be reluctant to share their thoughts, feelings, and experiences about the problem or potential solutions. Indeed, many people have little reason to believe that helping professionals will be either respectful toward or helpful to them. Understandably, many associate relatively high-status helping professionals with powerful larger systems intent on judgment, control, punishment, and perhaps

oppression of others. When social workers define problems for people and then proceed to act on the basis of those problem definitions, we, of course, confirm such opinions.

People often describe problems in terms of basic needs for food, clothing, shelter, or medical care. Repairing a broken refrigerator and obtaining a new stove are worthy objectives—easily as worthy as building self-esteem or enhancing communication skills. Their accomplishment may well contribute to an easier and more satisfying life and often require considerable professional skill. Interestingly, requests for help with basic needs or similar concrete problems are common during initial encounters—even when the "true" or "deeper" nature of the problems concern different aspects of human living. A spouse may initially identify a problem as "my partner doesn't help around the house" and identify a preliminary goal as "getting him to contribute to the household chores." A teenager required by a judge to visit a social worker may view the problem as "unfair treatment by the judge" and identify a preliminary goal as "getting out from under that judge's control." By exploring and discussing the concern and preliminary goal from clients' perspectives, we convey respect, encourage development of a genuine partnership, increase motivation, and enhance understanding. Our successful efforts toward resolution of initial goals can increase trust and generate a sense of success and optimism, which can contribute significantly when other, more complex problems and goals emerge. "Starting where the client is" represents a long-held social work principle that is especially applicable during the engagement phases. Interestingly, many helping professionals find it difficult to respect that principle (see Exhibit 3-3), preferring instead to "start where the social worker is." Indeed, social workers who are unable or unwilling to start where people are may find it impossible to adopt the problem-solving model and develop collaborative partnerships with clients.

Exploration of applicants' view and experience of the problem and identification of preliminary goals represent critical aspects of engagement. They form a frame and context for the work you undertake together. Although the definitions of problems and goals may change during the process of exploration and data collection, agreement about the preliminary goal enables you and the applicant to begin working together. At that point, applicants-and-workers have an

---

[2] We use the term *applicant* to identify people who come into contact with a social worker but have yet to agree to work toward problem-resolution or goal attainment.

EXHIBIT 3-3
Starting Where the Client Is

Suppose that we were out in the woods and we came upon a man who had accidentally got his foot caught in a bear trap. There he is, howling and carrying on frightfully, weeping and straining in a most profane fashion. Then two psychologists come by and one of them wants to give the man the Rorschach test and an intelligence test and take a case history. The other psychologist, however, has undergone a different kind of training; and he says, "No let's start intensive psychoanalysis right now." So, they talk it over. They have their differences, of course, but they agree eventually that what this man in the bear trap needs is obviously psychotherapy. If he would just be trained to be a more mature individual; if he could have the release therapy he needs; if he would undergo the needed catharsis, achieve the necessary insight,

and work through the essential abreaction, he would develop more maturity, he would understand the difficulty he is having, and he would then be able to solve his problem himself. Obviously, the psychologists agree, that is the only sound way to deal with the poor fellow. Suddenly, however, a farmer comes by and lets the man out of the bear trap.

To the utter amazement of the psychologists, the man's behavior changes greatly and quickly. Besides, he seems to take a great liking to the farmer, and goes off with him, evidently to have a cup of coffee.

Source: Johnson, W. (1951). Being understanding and understood: Or how to find a wandered horse. *ETC.: A Review of General Semantics, 8*(1), 161–179, pp. 176-177.

---

agenda. The problem and preliminary goal provide direction and purpose for data collection. Without them, the exploration and data collection processes can become unfocused and incoherent. Their absence also increases the likelihood that the professional will assume control of the process such that applicants become more like subjects and less like collaborative partners.

Assessment   The assessment phase[3] of practice involves those dynamics, dimensions, and activities associated with data collection, analysis, goal setting, and planning. It includes activities directed toward more complete and thorough mutual understanding of the nature, extent, severity, and development of the problem and prior attempts at problem solving within the context of clients' lives and circumstances. Successful assessment results in a clear and specific service plan along with an agreement or contract with clients to proceed to the intervention phase when work toward goal achievement effectively begins.

Assessment involves use of information to make decisions about the problem and what can be done about it. It involves refinement and clear specification of the problem and corresponding goal, consideration of alternative problem-solving approaches, selection of a change strategy, and development of a detailed action plan to accomplish the goal. A successful assessment results in a service plan collaboratively developed and agreed on by client-and-worker.

Although some practitioners regard data collection and assessment as two distinct phases in the problem-solving process, we consider them as intertwined. The information client-and-worker collect often leads them to alter their evolving assessment during the process, and the developing assessment frequently guides them to seek information they otherwise might not have sought. Therefore, we include both data collection or exploration and analysis within the assessment phase.

Although the precise form of data collection varies according to the client-defined problem and preliminary goal and the agency setting, kind of social problem, unique characteristics of the client and situation, and the dynamic, evolving nature of the data collection-analysis process, we generally collect information about

---

[3] We explore the assessment phase in greater depth in Chapters 10 and 11.

- The origin and development of the problem
- Thoughts and feelings about the problem
- Previous attempts at solving the problem and their outcomes
- Desired outcomes and potential solutions, especially those of the client but also those of other significant people and systems affecting the client—including those of the social worker
- Characteristics and developmental aspects of the client system and the relevant systems within which the client functions
- The situational context, including relevant information about primary and secondary social systems and other relevant ecological or environmental factors
- Abilities, capacities, assets, strengths, skills, and other resources available within the client and related systems that may help in problem resolution and goal attainment

Assessment—like engagement—involves a collaborative process through which the client-and-worker reach some mutual understanding about and explanation of the problem, decide on the goals for their work together, consider various means and methods by which to pursue those goals, and agree on a plan to achieve the agreed-upon goals. The desirable number of alternative intervention plans or solutions to consider varies according to several factors—such as the complexity and urgency of the problem, evidence of practice effectiveness, legal and ethical principles, and client culture, motivation, capacity, and opportunity. There are advantages and disadvantages to both large and small arrays of alternate intervention approaches. Too many options with similar risk-benefit ratios may lead to confusion; too few alternatives reduce the opportunity for genuine choice.

Intervention The service plan collaboratively developed during the assessment process includes an action plan for implementation by the client-and-worker during the intervention phase.[4] Knowledge about the nature and effectiveness of various prevention and intervention programs, policies, practices, services, methods and models, and protocols continues to increase exponentially as the information and technology revolution races ahead. Consistent with an ecosystem perspective and the principle that goals emerge through client-worker collaboration, change efforts may be directed toward people, people-in-situation interactions, or the environment. Therefore, social workers require a truly sophisticated base of knowledge about a wide range of intervention approaches, evidence of their relevance and effectiveness relative to various problems, and expertise in seeking, discovering, and analyzing emerging practice relevant information (Cournoyer, 2004).

Evaluation The evaluation phase[5] of practice involves those dynamics, dimensions, and activities associated with review, evaluation, and ending. It includes activities directed toward considering the nature, process, and outcomes of the collaborative work toward problem resolution and goal attainment. Importantly, the evaluation phase also includes a planned process of disengagement through which clients and workers may conclude their work together and say their goodbyes.

Ideally, the evaluation phase results in a clear, mutual understanding of the nature and extent of progress toward goal achievement, what and how the client-and-worker attempted to attain those goals, and a satisfactory conclusion to the process.

Although we use the term *evaluation* to identify the final phase of the problem-solving process, evaluation of progress toward goal attainment occurs during the intervention phase as well. Indeed evaluation is a fundamental part of both the service plan and the work undertaken by the client-and-worker. Consistent with our emphasis on systems principles, we consider evaluation as an essential part of the collaborative work. The client-and-worker regularly review action steps and evaluate progress toward goal attainment. Sometimes evaluation data reveals unexpected results that lead to major revisions in the service agreement. Following evaluation, the partners may modify the action plan, reformulate the problem definition, or perhaps revise goals, if necessary. In addition to ongoing evaluation, we also incorporate a final review as part of the conclusion of service. The client-and-worker may terminate service because they decide the goals have been accomplished, determine they are unlikely

---

[4] Chapters 12 through 16 contain exploration of a selected range of intervention approaches.

[5] We explore the evaluation phase in greater depth in Chapters 17 and 18.

to be accomplished, or decide that another worker or agency may better serve the client.

We present problem solving as an orderly, sequential, interactional process. Each phase depends on the successful completion of the preceding phase. In actual practice, however, you may operate in more than one phase at once. The phases follow each other in an approximate sequence, but the tasks of one phase are not always complete before work in another phase begins. Problem solving in social work often proceeds in spiral fashion. Action does not always wait for the completion of assessment, and assessment often begins before data collection is complete. In fact, you may become aware that you have not collected enough facts, or the proper facts, only after you attempt to synthesize what you know. When you and your client begin to take action toward a particular goal, you may realize you chose the wrong problem or selected an unworkable course and must start all over again. However, you begin again with the distinct advantage of additional knowledge and experience, and often an improved working relationship.

Social workers generally find that problem solving is a squirming, wriggling, living process that embraces the social reality between our clients and ourselves and the systems within which we operate. Occasionally it may be difficult to identify and track each phase in the sequence or to discern the logic of the process. Nonetheless, we carry a central professional responsibility to comprehend where we are in the process and to ensure that we deal with all phases. Impulsive leaps from the tasks and functions of one phase to those of another compromise the integrity of the process and reduce the probability of success. Actions taken without reflection or consultation usually lead to unintended consequences.

Problem solving may be characterized as the process by which worker-and-client determine the following:

- The problem or issue to address
- The goals or objectives for their work together
- The factors that seem to account for the problem's persistence despite the client's desire for change
- The plans, strategies, or procedures to attempt to resolve the problem
- The specific actions, tasks, or steps needed to implement the plans, strategies, or procedures

- The means to evaluate the effects and effectiveness of the actions, tasks, or steps and overall progress toward goal achievement

For the social worker, successful problem solving calls for skill and the ability to keep both a clear head and an understanding heart. However, the problem-solving framework does not prescribe specific strategies or procedures. Rather, it promises that this type of thinking and exploring, conducted consciously and knowingly, in about this order, increases the probability of finding an effective resolution that is consistent with the client's goals. The nature of the solutions depends on the problem or issue, clients' wants and circumstances, and the knowledge, understanding, motivation, resources, opportunity, and capacity for collaborative action that you and clients can apply to the process.

◆ Clients, Applicants, Prospects, and Respondents

The term *client* has historically been used in the profession to describe a very broad category of people with whom the social worker interacts. Imprecise use of terms, however, can prove problematic in professional practice. The words we choose and the way we use them have very real consequences.

We concur with Perlman that people who come to an agency for help are not yet clients. Rather, they are *applicants*. They become *clients* only after they reach an agreement with a social worker to work on one or more identified problems. We agree with this distinction and hope to extend it somewhat further.

Social workers first meet people interested in possible service under markedly different circumstances. We can identify at least three major categories:

- People initiate a request for service. For instance, a couple may contact a family service agency for assistance in resolving relationship difficulties. Parents might approach an agency for help in managing a rebellious adolescent, or a young adult could seek assistance in coping with symptoms of depression.
- Social workers reach out to offer services to people who have not requested the services. In a sense, this involves marketing agency services. For example, outreach workers may establish contact with youth gangs or young people who may be attracted to gangs, homeless persons to

---

EXHIBIT 3-4
Joe, A Potential Suicide

Joe, an 18-year-old young man, was temporarily admitted on an involuntary basis to the hospital for psychiatric evaluation. The evidence suggested that he represented a danger to himself. Two nights before, Joe attempted suicide by slashing his wrists. Tonight, Joe made another attempt by self-inflicting wounds on his right arm (2–3 inches long), the left side of his abdomen (3–4 inches long), and his sternal chest area.

During admission, he explained that he recently broke up with his girlfriend (Karen). He said that he went to a party earlier this evening and discovered his former girlfriend with a new boyfriend. According to Joe, Karen is pregnant with his child. He said

he couldn't stand seeing her with someone else so he left, feeling very upset. He reported that he broke into Karen's home and took a kitchen knife to injure himself.

Joe indicated that he neither wants nor needs psychiatric help. Therefore, the attending physician asked me, in my role as social worker, to contact Joe's parents and ask if they would petition the court to have him committed for inpatient psychiatric treatment. The physician believed that Joe would almost definitely attempt suicide again if released and concluded that involuntary hospital commitment represents the only way to save his life.

---

connect them with services, or prostitutes to encourage safe sex practices or offer other services. The outreach approaches vary and may include newspaper advertisements, flyers, public announcements, or perhaps neighborhood or community meetings.

- People are required, under pressure of outside authority, to see a social worker. Mandatory referrals of this kind may be associated with crime, drug abuse, child neglect, sexual offenses, or occasionally some psychiatric conditions (see Exhibit 3-4 for an example of the latter).

The interactions and role relationships between social workers and clients differ during different phases of the work—for example, when you are exploring whether a problem exists and when you are implementing an intervention. Perlman (1957) recognized this difference when she distinguished between applicants and clients. Other social workers have also noted the need to make distinctions among those with whom practitioners work (Gambrill, 1983; Germain & Gitterman, 1980; Reid, 1978).

Nevertheless, any person, family, group, or organization with whom the social worker interacts for purposes of defining a problem or producing change still tends to be referred to as a client. Such use of the term shows little regard for the differing sources of authority for the interaction, the differing circumstances

under which the interactions occur, the differing levels of client desire for the interactions, and the difference between interactions for purposes of problem definition and interactions for purposes of intervention. We believe the profession must develop a more precise nomenclature as a step toward clarifying our thoughts and actions.

In this book, we define *client* as any individual, group, family, organization, or community with whom the social worker has collaboratively negotiated an explicit agreement regarding the nature of the problem to address and a corresponding intervention plan. Thus, there is no client until we have a clear agreement regarding the problem and the steps to resolve it.

We therefore use the following terms to clarify the various paths toward clienthood:

- An *applicant* is a person, group, or organization that voluntarily seeks our services.
- A *prospect* is a person, group, or organization to which we reach out.
- A *respondent* is a person, group, or organization that is required to interact with us.

Having made these distinctions, we need a concise way of referring collectively to applicants, prospects, and respondents. We are going to adopt the convention of using the term *applicant* to mean any potential client, unless the context clearly suggests that prospect or respondent would be a more appropriate term. Similarly, for the sake of brevity, we will use the term *person* to mean an individual, family, group, organization, or community.

The problem-solving approach has been challenged over the years. Some assert that the process is too linear, that it is too "rational" or diminishes the value of emotions, or that it fails to emphasize strengths. We argue that the problem-solving model is spiral rather than linear in nature, and a professional rather than a bureaucratic or technical endeavor. The social work processes are not a set of techniques by which experts who understand what is wrong seek to improve, enlighten, plan for, manipulate, or "do to" clients. Rather, they represent an attempt "by one human being with specialized knowledge, training, and a way of working to establish a genuinely meaningful, democratic, and collaborative relationship with another person or persons in order to put one's special knowledge and skills at the second person's (or group's) disposal for such use as can be made of it" (Lerner, 1972, p. 11).

Decisions about what individuals and groups of individuals should be, have, want, and do are cognitive decisions in which "every person is a legitimate expert for oneself and no person is a legitimate expert for others" (Lerner, 1972, p. 161). The model rests on the assumption that every human being has a desire to be active in his or her own life—to exercise meaningful self-control for his or her own purposes.

The model recognizes—but does not emphasize—people's irrational and instinctive characteristics. Indeed, studies in mental hospitals have found that even the most regressed psychotic patients are at least as responsive to changes in external reality as to their internal fantasies. Altering their external reality alters their ways of coping and "given a chance to participate in making decisions that affected their lives, inmates generally did so in a responsible manner and with constructive results for all concerned—professionals as well as themselves" (Lerner, 1972, p. 161).

We assert that living systems are purposive. Practitioners are more effective when we start with applicants' goals and aspirations, the obstacles to their achievement, and their envisioned solutions. The push toward change comes from the discomfort of unfulfilled wants, but the pull toward change comes from hope that these wants can be achieved. This does not imply ignorance about unconscious and irrational factors or a failure to appreciate intense emotions. Rather, the practitioner begins with the consciously recognized and rationally described problems, goals, and solutions as experienced and expressed by the people we serve. Indeed, solution seeking represents an obvious and fundamental part of the problem-solving process. It is not coincidental that the term "solving" is part of its name.

We value the problem-solving framework for a number of reasons:

- A priori assumptions about the cause, nature, location, or meaning of problems are eschewed. Thus, problems may be associated with the client, other systems with which the client interacts, lack of social resources that should be supplied by the environment, or transactions among these factors. The existence of a problem does not imply impaired personal or psychological functioning.
- The framework is based on a belief in the growth potential of all human systems. Attention is directed toward social transactions and human struggles toward growth.
- The model is not based on any particular theoretical orientation and allows you and your client to agree on methods of intervention appropriate to the problem and its locus, the goals and objectives, the client, and your competence and resources.
- The framework emphasizes client goals and objectives. This is congruent with social work values such as the importance and uniqueness of each person, respect for individual and cultural differences, and self-determination.
- The way that problems and goals are identified and defined determines the emphasis and direction of inquiry. This facilitates data collection that is relevant, salient, and individualized, and minimizes unnecessary intrusion into clients' private lives.
- The framework supports the client's right to participate in the identification and definition of the problem. If you have a different view, you must negotiate a joint statement of the problem for work. You and the client must agree on what you are going to undertake together.
- The problem-solving process applies to a wide variety of situations, settings, and client systems of different sizes and types. Client-and-worker tasks and activities are specifically stated and directly relate to client goals and objectives. Such specificity often contributes to problem resolution and goal attainment.

EXHIBIT 3-5
Phases of the Problem-Solving Process

Engagement Phase

- Preparing for engagement
- Making contact
- Clarifying purpose and expectations
- Inviting applicants' participation and encouraging development of collaborative partnerships
- Exploring and seeking to understand applicants' views of presenting problem and situation
- Exploring and seeking to understand applicants' wants and frames of reference
- Reaching agreement about preliminary goals
- Agreeing to work together through a collaborative problem-solving process

Assessment Phase

- Collecting and exploring data related to the problem, situation, and possible solutions
- Discovering strengths
- Organizing, analyzing and synthesizing data
- Partializing and prioritizing problems and goals
- Considering various action strategies
- Collaborative decision-making
- Collaboratively developing a service agreement that outlines the
  - problem for work
  - goals and objectives to pursue
  - respective roles and responsibilities
  - action plan

Intervention Phase

- Introducing optimistic energy; enhancing hope and motivation
- Anticipating obstacles and envisioning successful resolutions
- Implementing agreed-upon action plans that typically involve both worker tasks and client tasks
- Reviewing action steps and considering their effects
- Monitoring progress toward goal achievement
- Modifying action plans and action steps as needed

Evaluation Phase

- Reviewing the process and the implementation of action plans
- Evaluating progress toward mutually agreed-upon goals and objectives
- Celebrating progress and recognizing areas for further work
- Deciding whether to
  - conclude services through termination, transfer, or referral (disengagement)
  - renegotiate the service agreement and continue to work together (reengagement)
- Saying goodbye or reengaging

◆ Chapter Summary

In this chapter, we reviewed the problem-solving process that underlies our approach to social work practice. We explored four key ideas:

- Problem solving is an orderly life process directed toward the solution of problems and the achievement of goals.
- In social work, practitioners interact with a wide range of people, under a wide range of circumstances. We find it more precise and often more useful to distinguish between applicants, prospects, and respondents—who often travel some-

what different paths en route to assuming the status of client.
- The application of the problem solving process routinely incorporates strengths within the person-in-situation context.
- The problem-solving process involves several phases that often emerge in spiral-like fashion.

Specific social work skills and activities are required for each phase of the problem-solving process. The skills and activities for the four phases—engagement, assessment, action or intervention, and evaluation—are summarized in Exhibit 3-5.

Learning Exercises: Readings, InfoTrac, and the Web

1. Use your word-processing computer program to enter the important terms and concepts presented in this chapter. At this point, simply list them in alphabetical order. Place a question mark by any terms that you do not clearly understand. Save your document as EX 3-1.

2. Log on to the InfoTrac College Edition Web site. Conduct a keyword search (using either Keyword Search or Advanced Search) to locate the articles entitled "Recalling John Dewey: Has He Left the Building?" (Novak, 2002) and "John Dewey's Social Psychology and Neopragmatism: Theoretical Foundations of Human Agency and Social Reconstruction" (Musolf, 2001). Read these two articles and reflect on their implications for social work and social work practice in a one-page essay. Save your document as EX 3-2.

3. Log on to the InfoTrac College Edition Web site. Conduct a keyword search (using either Keyword Search or Advanced Search) to locate the articles entitled "Seven Habits of Reclaiming Relationships" (Laursen, 2002) and "Recasting Problems as Potentials in Group Work" (Laursen & Oliver, 2003). Read these two articles and reflect on their implications for social work and social work practice in a one-page essay. Save your document as EX 3-3.

4. Turn to **Reading 8: Variations on the Problem-Solving Theme.** Review the article by Ralph Woehle and reflect on its implications for social work and social work practice in a one-page essay. In your response, be sure to explore those differences or distinctions between Woehle's view of establishing action steps or tasks and our emphasis on a collaborative partnership process. Save your document as EX 3-4.

5. Turn to **Reading 9: Betty Smith.** Review the circumstances of the case and then, in a one-page essay, address the question "Who is the client?" in this case. Provide a thoughtful rationale for your position. Save your document as EX 3-5.

6. Refer to **Exhibit 3-2: Who Determines Client Needs?** In a one-page essay, explore how you might have approached the situation in a different manner? Save your document as EX 3-6.

7. Refer to **Exhibit 3-4: Joe, A Potential Suicide.** The attending physician asked the social worker in this case to contact Joe's parents to see if they might sign a petition to commit their son to inpatient psychiatric treatment. In a one-page essay, address the following questions: Who is the client in this case? Is it Joe, the physician, the hospital, Joe's parents, society, or some other person, group, or organization? Provide a thoughtful rationale for your position and explore the professional dilemmas associated with this situation. Save your document as EX 3-7.

8. Refer to **Exhibit 3-5: Phases of the Problem-Solving Process.** Carefully examine the extended outline of the problem-solving process in social work practice. In a one-page essay, consider what other activities or skills might be applicable to the process reflected by the outline. Save your document as EX 3-8.

Chapter 4

Client-Worker Partnership

◆ Nature of the Client-Worker Partnership

A collaborative client-worker partnership is crucial to our model of practice. Collaboration occurs throughout all phases of ethical, effective practice. Without a strong sense of partnership, both the process and outcome of problem-solving processes are jeopardized. Three aspects of the collaborative client-worker partnership are especially relevant:

- Partnership and client self-determination
- Collaborative decision making
- Partnership and human dignity

In her history of the empowerment tradition in American social work, Simon (1994) observes that a collaborative relationship with clients has been one of the key elements of empowerment. Collaboration means working together, and working together creates a partnership in which worker and client both participate to achieve the goal of the problem-solving effort. Through participation, people claim power, develop their strengths, assume responsibility, and contribute to a democratic process.

Other authors also describe the relationship between worker and client as a partnership (Coady, 1993; Maluccio, Washitz, & Libassi, 1992; Reid, 1978, 1992; Reid & Epstein, 1977). Bricker-Jenkins (1991) refers to the client-worker partnership as open, egalitarian, and mutual. Clients are viewed as capable of making their own decisions and integral to all decision making. Worker and client enter into a collaborative relationship based on trust, respect (Coady, 1993), and mutual involvement (Tebb, 1991). Applicants and clients are involved and participate in all decisions, including assessment and the development of intervention plans (Valentine, 1993).

The elements of mutuality and equality, necessary for genuine partnership, are also central to feminist approaches to social work practice (Bricker-Jenkins, 1991; Collins, 1986; Nes & Iadicola, 1989; Rosewater & Walker, 1985; Russell, 1989). Mutuality is also critical in work with Native people (Kelley, McKay, & Nelson, 1985) and necessary for balancing the power differential between social workers and clients. Although the partners may make different but equally important contributions to the problem-solving process, collaborative decision making occurs throughout.

Negotiating Decisions

Partnership, in effect, means that clients and social workers jointly negotiate key decisions during the problem-solving process. In particular, they agree on a definition of the problem to be solved, the goals to be pursued, and the plans to accomplish those goals. Partnership means negotiation, not unilateral decision making. Social workers do not stipulate the nature of the problem or goals, nor do we passively accept the applicants' perception of them. Generally, we do work within applicants' conception of the problem and wants—when they appear consistent with our professional responsibilities. On occasion, however, we must ask applicants to consider different problem statements or alternate goals. For instance, a client might seek to solve a problem by committing a crime or violating others' human rights. We could not ethically endorse such a solution.

EXHIBIT 4-1
Client Self-Determination and End-of-Life Decisions

NASW's position concerning end-of-life decisions is based on the principle of client self-determination. Choice should be intrinsic to all aspects of life and death.

The social work profession strives to enhance the quality of life; to encourage the exploration of life options; and to advocate for access to options, including providing all information to make appropriate choices.

Social workers have an important role in helping individuals identify the end-of-life options available to them. This role must be performed with full knowledge of and compliance with the law and in accordance with the NASW Code of Ethics (National Association of Social Workers, 1996). Social workers should be well informed about living wills, durable power of attorney for health care, and legislation related to advance health care directives.

A key value for social workers is client self-determination. Competent individuals should have the opportunity to make their own choices but only after being informed of all options and consequences. Choices should be made without coercion. Therefore, the appropriate role for social workers is to help patients express their thoughts and feelings, to facilitate exploration of alternatives, to provide information to make an informed choice, and to deal with grief and loss issues.

Social workers should not promote any particular means to end one's life but should be open to full discussion of the issues and care options. As a client is considering his or her choices, the social worker should explore and help ameliorate any factors such as pain, depression, need for medical treatment, and so forth. Further, the social worker should thoroughly review all available options including, but not limited to, pain management, counseling, hospice care, nursing home placement, and advance health care directives.

Social workers should act as liaisons with other health care professionals and help the patient and family communicate concerns and attitudes to the health care team to bring about the most responsible assistance possible.

Because end-of-life decisions have familial and social consequences, social workers should encourage the involvement of significant others, family, and friends in these decisions. Social workers should provide ongoing support and be liaisons to families and support persons (for example, caregivers, significant others) with care to maintain the patient's confidentiality. When death occurs, social workers have an obligation to provide emotional and tangible assistance to the significant others, family, and friends in the bereavement process.

Source: National Association of Social Workers. (2003). Client self-determination in end-of-life decisions. In National Association of Social Workers (Ed.), *Social work speaks: NASW policy statements, 2003–2006* (6th ed., pp. 46–49). Washington, DC: NASW Press, p. 48.

Exhibit 4-1 contains an excerpt from the National Association of Social Workers' (NASW) most recent policy regarding end-of-life decisions by persons with terminal illnesses. Note that the policy acknowledges the right of competent individuals to make their own choices—but only after being informed of all the available options. Such discussions provide a context for social workers to encourage collaborative exploration and consideration of alternatives with people intent on ending their own lives.

In negotiating decisions, the partners share their respective points of view and try to find common areas of agreement in defining the problem statement, goals and solutions, and the action plan. Despite our efforts to equalize the relationship, many applicants view us as people of power because of our professional status, the position we occupy in the agency, and the expertise we bring to the partnership. Accordingly, we must take care to express our views in ways that enhance applicants' participation and self-determination. Generally, we encourage applicants to share their views before we express ours. When our ideas match theirs, we can offer support and concurrence. If they do not, we may introduce our views as alternatives for exploration. Of course, we frame them as options for consideration rather than as directives to be followed.

In negotiating with applicants, be careful to avoid (1) controlling the process by failing to create a climate in which applicants can express their viewpoints; (2) expressing your views too early or too authoritatively; and (3) uncritically accepting applicants' views without sharing your own knowledge and professional opinions—which deprives them of needed information and indirectly impedes self-determination.

Different but Equal Contributions

Although applicants and social workers do not usually bring the same things to the problem-solving work, our respective contributions are equally important to the process. In general, applicants bring

- Knowledge regarding themselves and the situation
- Knowledge about the origin and development of the problem
- Expectations regarding how you can help
- A network of social relationships
- Views about what they would like to accomplish
- Strengths for use in pursuing goals

Social workers usually bring

- Expert knowledge to help assess the situation and select service plans most likely to resolve problems and accomplish goals
- Skills in the problem-solving process
- Professional opinions and ideas for consideration by the applicant
- Skills to help applicants formulate solvable problems
- Skills to assist applicants in mobilizing internal and external strengths for use in pursuing goals
- Skills to create a relationship context in which applicants can actively participate
- The resources of your agency and connections to other community resources

It is not your job to "fix" clients. Rather, you help them set and work toward goals. You assist them to recognize and use person-in-situation strengths and resources for problem solving and goal attainment. By encouraging collaborative decision making, clients become active participants in the problem-solving process. The partners contribute to the problem-

solving work. Neither the worker's nor the client's contributions are sufficient—both are essential.

Partnership and Professionalism

The concept of collaborative partnership with applicants or clients may require you to reconsider popular views about professionals' role and function. Given our specialized education and professional status, we may sometimes be tempted to conclude that we know what is best for people, to impose our knowledge, or to use our expertise to control clients. Gordon (1969) argues that social work is nonnormative in the sense that we hold only very general concepts of the ideal or "well" person, healthy situation, or optimum environment (see Exhibit 1-1 in Chapter 1). The notion of nonnormative practice supports the diversity that enriches us all and runs counter to the idea of social workers as experts about what is best for people.

Several qualities and characteristics exhibited by social workers seem to contribute to the development of effective and beneficial client-worker partnerships:

- Genuine concern for clients, purposeful expression of feelings (Biestek, 1994), and an optimistic attitude that encourages clients to create change for themselves.
- Acceptance—a nonjudgmental attitude; recognition of others' dignity, equality (Biestek, 1994), and uniqueness; sensitivity to clients' feelings; and respect for clients' wants and preferences.
- A sense of commitment or loyalty to the plan (Biestek, 1994). Such fidelity is needed if the goals are to be achieved.
- Empathy. By seeing and expressing understanding of the problem from clients' points of view, empathic workers demonstrate respect and acceptance, and discover strengths, assets, resources, and options.
- Authority—recognition of and comfort with your role and position as a professional social worker, including your right and obligation to contribute to decisions regarding issues pertinent to the client-worker partnership (McIvor, 1991). Authority does not mean authoritarian—decisions affecting clients require their informed consent (Palmer, 1997).

The concept of a client-worker partnership in problem solving helps distinguish social work from other professions. We consciously use our authority, sophisticated knowledge, and expertise to contribute to a collaborative process that enhances client empowerment and competence. We eschew the notion of "doing to" or even "doing for" in favor of the idea of "doing with."

Social Work Values

A value may be viewed as "something (as a principle or quality) intrinsically valuable or desirable" (Merriam-Webster, 2003). Gordon (1965) notes that values denote things that are preferred; Levy (1973) suggests that values reflect preferred conceptions of people, preferred outcomes for people, and preferred instrumentalities for dealing with people. In other words, values can be thought of as beliefs about people and appropriate ways of dealing with them.

Professionals tend to reflect a cluster of values that guide their philosophies and behavior. Based on an extensive literature review, an English sociologist concluded that the helping professions operate using tenets of faith concerning the nature of people (Halmos, 1966). Halmos argues that these values represent a form of faith because they are accepted without proof. Nonetheless, like other faith-based values, they provide guidance and direction for the profession. Thus, professional values are unproved—and probably unprovable—beliefs about human nature that provide direction to practitioners' day-to-day work.

What are the core social work values? Are there certain values that all social work practitioners must accept? Are there certain common values that distinguish the social work profession from others? Are there intervention approaches, strategies, or techniques that social workers should not use because they violate our professional values? These are challenging questions indeed. Miller, Baum, and McNeil (1968), for example, identify some of the value dilemmas encountered by social work practitioners and suggest that we withdraw from settings in which treatment is imposed or coerced. Salomon (1967) explores the possibility of inherent conflict between the humanistic stance of social work and the principles and procedures of scientific methodology. Briar and Miller (1971) advance the intriguing suggestion that client self-determination might be conceptualized as a treatment technique rather than a value, on the basis that clients in one-to-one relational systems make faster progress when they are extended maximum opportunities for self-determination. In other words, self-

determination might be viewed as a means of facilitating client progress rather than exclusively as a fundamental social work value.

Are a profession's values the source of its uniqueness? We think not. The social work profession, for example, exists within a larger cultural context and reflects the values extant in society. Indeed, societal norms may actually limit professional social work practice (Schwartz, 1961). We live and work in an extremely complex culture characterized by a wide range of values, some of which conflict. Social workers do not adopt all the myriad values. Rather, we select those values that reflect and support our perspectives and practices. Although, we may select and operationalize values in a distinctive way, the values themselves are far from distinct. Rather, we share them with other parts of the culture.

One way of thinking about values is to picture an inverted triangle (see Exhibit 4-2). The broad top of the triangle represents values in a remote, general, or abstract sense, and the narrow bottom corresponds to proximate, specific, and concrete values. If values are to guide practice, the challenge is to take abstract concepts—such as self-determination, human rights, or social justice—and apply them in specific situations. We can move from the general to the specific by asking "How?" questions. "Why?" questions tend to produce explanations of actions that move us from the specific to the remote. In general, the higher the level of abstraction, the easier it is to reach consensus. Disagreements are much more likely as people begin to consider specific details. For example, many social workers would readily support the abstract principle of client self-determination. However, there may be considerable controversy about how to implement this principle in attempting to help a 15-year-old who wants to steal cars.

If values are unproven and probably unprovable beliefs that guide the work of professionals, what are the value premises with which the social work profession identifies and how are these premises operationalized? Most social workers do indeed share several values. These are reflected in social work codes of ethics, educational standards, and other formal documents. We will examine them later in considerable depth. At this point, however, let's consider two values that are especially applicable to client-worker partnerships. Social workers tend to believe strongly in (1) human dignity and uniqueness and (2) self-determination.

EXHIBIT 4-2
Abstract and Concrete Values

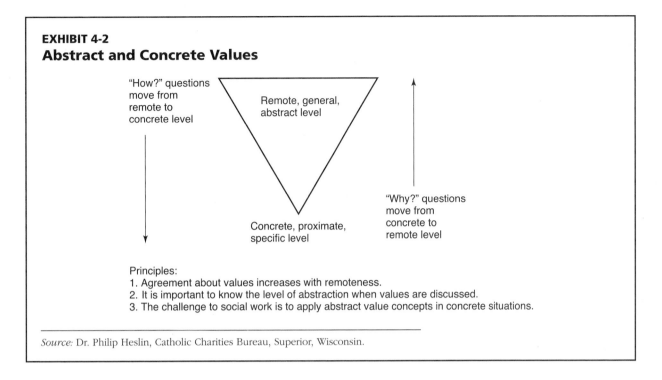

"How?" questions move from remote to concrete level

Remote, general, abstract level

"Why?" questions move from concrete to remote level

Concrete, proximate, specific level

Principles:
1. Agreement about values increases with remoteness.
2. It is important to know the level of abstraction when values are discussed.
3. The challenge to social work is to apply abstract value concepts in concrete situations.

Source: Dr. Philip Heslin, Catholic Charities Bureau, Superior, Wisconsin.

◆ Human Dignity and Uniqueness

Social workers believe that each person deserves respect as a unique individual with an inherent human dignity. People must not be treated as objects or as means to other ends. Diversity is welcomed. Tillich (1962), a theologian and philosopher, referred to human uniqueness as our existential nature. Gordon's concept of social work function (see Exhibit 1-1 in Chapter 1) derives from the same notion. He suggests that the social work profession should not strive for some ideal conception of either the person or the environment but instead seek to establish linkages between people and their environments without attempting to limit the uniqueness or diversity of either (Gordon, 1969).

How can the premise that every person is unique and all people have a right to respect and dignity be applied in specific social work situations? Social workers can operationalize this value in practice by

- Treating people as individuals and recognizing the risks associated with labels and classifications
- Encouraging active participation throughout all phases of the problem-solving process

- Discovering and making use of client strengths
- Holding people—including ourselves—accountable
- Carefully considering what our communications convey about dignity and respect

Dignity Through Individualization

Social workers often find it challenging to balance our responsibility to respond to people as unique individuals and the processes of assessment and classification. Classification involves the organization of apparently similar phenomena into groups or categories. For example, children soon learn to group objects by their color, size, and shape: blue, red, yellow; large, medium, small; triangles, squares, circles, rectangles, and so forth. Of course, humans learn to categorize by many other dimensions as well. We might classify situations as safe or dangerous, warm or cold, familiar or unfamiliar, or perhaps predictable or unpredictable. We often group people as well—perhaps by sex, height, weight, hair texture, skin color, or dimensions such as friendly or unfriendly, introverted or extraverted, generous or selfish, or "us" and "them." Once we classify, categorize, or group people, things, or events, we often hold expectations because of the class rather than the individual. Indeed, the process of generalizing beyond individuals and organizing phenomena by common characteristics helps us make sense out of a mass of raw data. Otherwise, we might well be overwhelmed with the enormity of so many idiosyncratic details. When we classify people, however, we may begin to respond to them as representatives of a particular category rather than as individuals. The consequences of this have been documented in a body of sociological literature about labeling, stereotyping, and deviance (Becker, 1963; Lemert, 1967; Platt, 1977; Rubington & Weinberg, 1968; Schur, 1973; Simmons, 1969; Tannenbaum, 1951). Labeling or classification tends to diminish individual uniqueness and may endanger human dignity. Once labeled deviant, individuals may find that they encounter responses determined by the label rather than by any of their particular characteristics. A self-fulfilling prophecy may result so that people become or are perceived to be what the label says they are (Merton, 1968). Indeed, Shireman and Reamer (1986) raise the possibility that the juvenile justice system may unwittingly promote crime by its labeling practices. Toch states the problem succinctly:

> Playing the classification game in the abstract, as is done in universities, is a joyful, exhilarating experience, harmless and inconsequential. Classifying people in life is a grim business which channels destinies and determines fate. A person becomes a category, is processed as a category, plays the assigned role, lives up to the implications. Labelled irrational, the person acts crazy; catalogued dangerous, the person becomes dangerous or stays behind bars. (1970, p. 15)

In your practice, you are likely to encounter the American Psychiatric Association's *Diagnostic and Statistical Manual of Mental Disorders (DSM)* (American Psychiatric Association, 2000). Many social workers (Jahn, 1986; Kline, Sydnor-Greenberg, Davis, Pincus, & Frances, 1993; Williams, 1981, 1995) find the *DSM* useful for social work, but others question its use on both ethical and professional grounds (Kirk & Kutchins, 1994; Kutchins & Kirk, 1986, 1987, 1989a, 1989b, 1993, 1995, 1997). Kirk and Kutchins (1992) assert that the *DSM* is essentially a political document intended, in part, to lend credibility to psychiatrists' claim that they are scientific. The famous psychiatrist Karl Menninger wondered about the *DSM* as well:

A committee of our worldly national body has just published a manual containing a full description of all the bewitchments to which all human flesh is err, with the proper names for each one, the minute suborder and subspecies listed and a code number for the computer. The colleagues who prepared this witch's hammer manual are worthy fellows—earnest, honest, hard-working, simplistic; they were taught to believe that these horrible things exist, these things with Greek names and Arabic numerals. And if patients show the stigmata, should they not be given the label and the number? To me this is not only the revival of medieval nonsense and superstition; it is a piece of social immorality. (Menninger, 1968, pp. 117–118)

Social workers confront complex issues regarding the *DSM*. For example, is it appropriate to relate to people through the lens of a diagnostic label? May social workers use a typology or classification scheme developed by and for another profession? Should we agree with Salomon (1967) that the scientific imperative to order and classify is inconsistent with the humanism of social work? Toch suggests, "the point of concern rests in any labels that lead to sorting or disposition" (1970, p. 15). Toch takes the position that although labels help us to theorize and analyze, they are less useful for deciding what to do to help individual persons. When professionals decide what should happen to people based on the category into which they have been placed, we run the risk of violating their uniqueness and dignity. However, this is precisely where classification appears most useful. Professionals' assessments or diagnoses often serve as guides for selecting appropriate interventions. What a complex dilemma! Some focus on diagnostic classifications may help us identify effective change strategies and approaches. Too much, however, may lead us to neglect the human dignity and uniqueness of the individual person in our attention to the label. We may reduce the danger somewhat by adopting person-first language and consistently collaborating with applicants and clients in developing mutual understanding of the problem and a service plan based on that understanding. In effect, classifications may be useful but only within the context of an individualized understanding of the people, problem, and situation.

The person-in-environment (PIE) system for classifying adults' problems in social functioning (Karls & Lowery, 1997; Karls & Wandrei, 1992a, 1992b, 1994a, 1994b, 1995) represents an innovative social work approach to classification. PIE helps us classify problems within an ecosystem framework and provides a means of classifying problems according to (1) social role functioning and (2) environmental problems or conditions. When problems are conceptualized according to these two dimensions, workers and applicants or clients may draw from various theoretical perspectives and change strategies to design an individualized intervention plan.

Dignity Through Strength

Collaborative partnerships tend to reduce our occupational temptation to focus on weaknesses, deficiencies, and problems. In Chapters 1 and 3, we encouraged social workers to incorporate strengths, assets, and resources as integral aspects of the problem-solving process. Attending to and using strengths may help to resolve problems, achieve goals and contribute to improved quality of life (Coursey, Farrell, & Zahniser, 1991). In studies of social workers' and clients' perceptions of service outcomes and client functioning, Maluccio found,

> Clients presented themselves as pro-active, autonomous human beings who are able to enhance their functioning and competence through the use of counseling service along with the resources operant in themselves and their social networks. Workers, on the other hand, tended to view clients as reactive organisms with continuing problems, weakness, and limited potentialities. (1979, p. 399)

What disturbing findings! Perhaps reflecting an obsessive focus on problems and negative labels, they hardly suggest respect for human dignity and uniqueness or a collaborative approach to assessment. One way to counter these limiting tendencies is to incorporate strengths-discovery as part of assessment and use strengths and resources during the intervention phase (de Jong & Berg, 1998, 2001, 2002; de Jong & Miller, 1995; C. A. Rapp, 1997; R. Rapp, 1997; Saleebey, 1992, 1996, 1997, 1999, 2001a, 2001b, 2002; Weick, 1992; Weick, Rapp, Sullivan, & Kisthardt, 1989; Weick & Saleebey, 1995). Although we recognize deficiencies, weaknesses, and pathologies, we also seek, identify, celebrate, and mobilize strengths, assets, resiliencies, and resources in our collaborative efforts to understand and resolve social problems. Think about how you respond when people you care about discuss your talents and special qualities. How do you react when they focus on your mistakes, failures, and deficiencies? Most of us find it easier to address weaknesses when explored in the context of our strengths. Indeed, "there is a need to shift the focus in social work education and practice from problems or pathology to strengths, resources, and potentialities in human beings and their environments. If this shift occurs, practitioners would be more likely to view clients as capable of organizing their own lives" (Maluccio, 1979, p. 401).

Dignity Through Participation

Participation in decision making, planning, and action is essential to human dignity. Acknowledging this, the United Nations has included the right of children to participate in decisions in Article 12 of the *Convention on the Rights of the Child* (Exhibit 4-3). Weick and Pope (1988) suggest that social work practice needs to regard the client's own knowledge as primary to counteract the traditional emphasis on professional expertise. Incorporating clients' knowledge and wisdom as part of the problem-solving process contributes to self-determination, establishment of a caring partnership, and effective service (Biehal, 1993; Itzhaky, 1991; Itzhaky & York, 1994). These are keys to good social work practice.

In our culture, most exchanges with professionals occur in a context where the decision-making authority of clients or patients is overshadowed by the status and expertise of the professional. In effect, consumers only retain the authority to accept or reject the professional's advice. In social work, however, we try to share power and authority for decision-making. Generalist social workers' primary expertise lies less in the content area of knowing what is best for the client and more in the process area of assisting clients to develop alternatives for themselves, make decisions among the alternatives, and implement the decisions. Social workers and other helping professionals may be especially susceptible to the dangers of rescue fantasies, which involve:

> A feeling that the therapist is the divinely sent agent to pull tormented souls from the pit of suffering and adversity and put them back on the road to happiness and glory. A major reason this fantasy is so destructive is that it carries the conviction that the patient will be saved only through and by the therapist. When such a conviction is

---

EXHIBIT 4-3
Children's Right to Be Heard

Article 12:

1. States Parties shall assure to the child who is capable of forming his or her own views the right to express those views freely in all matters affecting the child, the view of the child being given due weight in accordance with the age and maturity of the child.

2. For this purpose, the child shall in particular be provided the opportunity to be heard in any judicial and administrative proceedings affecting the child, either directly, or through a representative or an appropriate body, in a manner consistent with the procedural rules of national law.

Source: General Assembly of the United Nations. (1989). *Convention on the rights of the child.* New York: United Nations.

---

communicated to patients, verbally or otherwise, they have no choice other than to rebel and leave or become even more helpless, dependent, and sick. (Dumont, 1968, p. 6)

Exhibit 4-4 presents a stunning example of nonparticipatory decision making. As you review the situation, consider when, where, and how J. J. might have participated in the process.

The temptation to assume a superior, expert, "I know what's best" attitude is strong indeed. Some of us social workers find it difficult to resist and may occasionally assume the role of "savior," "guru," "good parent," or perhaps "wise professor." It requires considerable humility to recognize that clients are the chief problem solvers. We play a major part in helping clients through the process and may, at times, introduce extra energy, enthusiasm, and optimism. Indeed, a passive approach to practice is essentially inconsistent with the value self-determination and respect for individual dignity. In effect,

> The worker should learn to expect a little bit more than the client expects of himself. Social workers are very well versed in beginning where the client is but perhaps too often tend to stay where the client is. If they instead assume the responsibility for leadership and imparting realistic hope, they may more effectively strengthen a client's ego and help him to reach to achieve his full potential and assume social responsibility. (Oxley, 1966, pp. 432–437)

Schwartz (1961) refers to this as lending a vision. Expecting and encouraging participation tends to enhance strengths and dignity.

Dignity Through Accountability

Accountability is an aspect of dignity that may easily be overlooked. When we regard people as both capable of and responsible for their thoughts, decisions, and behaviors, we convey respect for their dignity and autonomy. We use the term *accountability* to convey this sense of respect rather than as a euphemism for negative consequences or penalties. In some fields, such as juvenile and criminal justice, the concept of accountability is used to justify harsh punishments. In other contexts—for example, in some hospital or residential settings—professional staff may systematically control consequences in an effort to mold behavior. A view of accountability as the manipulation or imposition of penalties or punishments is inconsistent with our view of social work practice.

On the other hand, social workers should usually not attempt to protect or insulate people from the natural consequences of their actions. We know from systems theory that behaviors produce reactions in the environment. As part of the exploration process, social workers appropriately encourage consideration of the likely consequences of particular courses of action. Clients-and-workers commonly consider the probable effects of various options—from doing nothing or making dramatic changes—as part of the assessment and planning processes. Once decided, however, social workers should neither protect clients from nor deliberately manipulate the natural consequences of their actions in an effort to control their behavior or obtain a certain outcome—even a desirable one. As we suggested earlier, the ends do not justify the means.

EXHIBIT 4-4
Nonparticipatory Decision Making

J. J. is a white, 14-year-old ninth grader at a suburban junior high school. His teachers and principal have identified him as an aggressive youth who is failing in the classroom, lacks motivation, and displays poor attendance and social skills. Until this year, J. J. did not have a history of problems and had been able to achieve satisfactory grades. All attempts to promote acquiescence within the school setting, by detention, suspension, tutoring, and other means, have failed. The staff has been in frequent contact with the mother, who is verbally supportive but has been unable to change J. J.'s current behavior. She has refused referral to outside assistance because a previous experience resulted in the loss of her job. At a case conference involving the principal, teacher, attendance clerk, and social worker, the consensus was that, if his behavior continued to decline, J. J. was in danger of failing ninth grade and being summoned before the juvenile court on a truancy petition. The staff was hesitant to adopt drastic action because they believed J. J. could be retracked toward appropriate behavior. He reflects above-average intelligence and considerable athletic prowess, and an engaging and personable social style. Negative sanctions or stigmatization through the court might increase his level of frustration and prove harmful in the long run. Thus, he was temporarily assigned to a small group of delinquent, acting-out students in an attempt to discover whether he would be willing to discuss and work-through various problems in a group of students in similar situations.

Source: MSW student, School of Social Work, University of Minnesota.

How then, can accountability enhance dignity? The partnership between the applicant or client and the social worker implies that each party has legitimate—often explicit—expectations of and responsibilities to the other. When the behavior of either workers or clients is inconsistent with those expectations, they can be properly held accountable by the other. For example, if workers do not keep their promises, they should explain and, where appropriate, apologize, and commit to more reliable behavior in the future. Similarly, when clients do not follow through with commitments, the social worker may and indeed should explore what happened and clarify expectations regarding future commitments.

For example, let's imagine that the J. J. case outlined in Exhibit 4-4 had occurred in a different way. Let's say that the principal and teacher called the attendance, performance, and behavioral problems to the attention of the school social worker, who then made contact with J. J. In these circumstances, J. J. would be a prospect (see Chapter 3). He would only become a client if he decided to work with the social worker. Let's assume that's what happened: J. J. and the worker explored the problem areas and reached consensus about a preliminary goal. Furthermore, J. J. agreed to participate in the group as a means of addressing the problems and pursuing the goal. However, J. J. did not show up for the group meeting. Under these circumstances, the worker might convey respect for J. J.'s dignity through accountability by contacting him to explore the factors associated with the missed meeting and his plans for future meetings, and to reinforce and maintain the expectation that J. J. can keep his commitments because he has the strength to do so. This view of accountability does not require that the social worker judge J. J. or impose punishments for nonattendance. The worker asks what happened in a matter-of-fact way. Judgmental, "why didn't you show up" questions usually do not contribute to the process. They tend to generate defensiveness, place clients in a one-down position, and encourage justifications or rationalizations rather than genuine exploration. "What" or perhaps "how" questions are usually more effective. Questions such as, "What got in the way of your plans to attend the meeting?" would tend to encourage J. J. to explore nondefensively what prevented him from doing what he said he was going to do.

EXHIBIT 4-5
Language That Invites Participation

Language may encourage or discourage participation by the individuals and families we serve.

Out with the Old	In with the New
Resistant families	Families with unmet needs
Dysfunctional families	Families that are overwhelmed and underserved
Case management	Service coordination
"We offer this"	"What do you need?"
Staffing a case	Families and professionals creating intervention plans together

Out with the Old	In with the New
Disturbed child	Child with emotional reactions (person-first language)
Professionals as providers	Families as preferred providers
"We need a placement for this child; where to next?"	"Let's develop a community plan with this child and family"
"That's your job"	"Let's work together."
SED, CCRS, etc.	Say the words!

Source: Adapted from Learn to Talk. (Winter, 1995). *Network News: The Newsletter of the Family Support Network.* Charleston, South Carolina.

Communicating dignity through accountability often involves the social work skills of asking open questions, empathic listening, and confrontation. Widely misunderstood, the skill of confrontation does not include anger, judgment, or attack. Rather, the social worker matter-of-factly observes a discrepancy or inconsistency between aspects of clients' words and behaviors. For instance, if a client makes a promise but does not keep it, then we have a discrepancy between that person's words and actions. The social worker might use the skill of confrontation by observing the inconsistency with the client. However, confrontation should never be expressed in anger, which is usually associated with a personal judgment of the person (e.g., he was irresponsible) and a desire to punish, reject, or shame. Client accountability is more likely to result from reasonable exploration of the behavior and reinforcement of expectations rather than from angry comments or punishments.

Accountability in partnerships goes both ways. Clients have a right to expect you to be accountable. However, most clients find it difficult to confront us when we behave irresponsibly—when we fail to make telephone calls we said we would, secure information we promised to obtain, remain available when we agreed to be, or follow through on other commitments we made. Accordingly, we social work-ers must acknowledge our own lapses and mistakes, apologize for our failures, and explicitly identify our plans to rectify or remedy the problem. As human beings, people—clients and workers alike—are fallible. Sometimes, we fail to do what we promised. When this happens, we can nondefensively acknowledge our own accountability, accept responsibility, apologize, and move ahead to correct the situation or improve our performance.

Communicating Dignity

Individualization, strength, participation, and accountability are aspects of dignity that social workers attempt to convey in our communications with applicants and clients. The importance of communications cannot be over-emphasized. The messages clients-and-workers send and receive represent the primary means and context for problem solving. Indeed, communications people receive about themselves powerfully influence their self-images (Rose, 1962). If people view themselves as persons of worth and have a sense of their own strengths and capabilities, they may be better able to deal constructively and appropriately with issues in their environment. Communications are so vital to the client-worker relationship and the problem-solving process that we social workers have a special obligation to constantly review what and how we talk, listen, and relate. Do our words, gestures, and demeanor invite participation and enhance dignity? Exhibit 4-5 provides a few examples of such language. Does our behavior communicate that our applicants and clients are highly prized, unique individuals worthy of our time and respect?

The worker's attitudes about privacy—reflected both in the way the interview is conducted and the manner in which material gained from interviews is handled—communicates a powerful message about the esteem in which the interviewees are held. McFadden (1992) concludes that respecting the dignity of the child requires us to refrain from therapeutic interventions that invade privacy unless we have the child's permission. When attempting to operationalize the value of individual dignity, you may find it useful to repeatedly inquire, "What do my actions communicate to clients about my perception of them?"

◆ Self-Determination

The principle of self-determination has a long history in social work. In fact, the NASW *Code of Ethics* includes a specific passage within the section entitled Social Workers' Ethical Responsibilities to Clients: "Social workers respect and promote the right of clients to self-determination and assist clients in their efforts to identify and clarify their goals" (NASW, 1999, Section 1.02).

> Broadly defined, self-determination refers to the right of individuals to have full power over their own lives. It encompasses concepts that are central to existence in a democratic society, including freedom of choice, civil rights, independence, and self-direction. A more contemporary definition of self-determination reflects its operation at both individual and collective levels, embracing the notion that although all citizens have the right to control their own lives, they exist within communities (defined as families, neighborhoods, cities, states/regions, and countries), in which their decisions affect others and others' decisions affect them (Falck, 1988; Pierce, 2001). (Cook & Jonikas, 2002, p. 87)

Although applicants and clients usually make responsible decisions that are consistent with their own welfare and that of the community, sometimes social workers must encourage them to explore more fully the potential effects of their actions (Ewalt & Mokuau, 1996), and occasionally we have to assume consid-

erable responsibility for others. The NASW Code indicates, "Social workers may limit clients' right to self-determination when, in the social workers' professional judgment, clients' actions or potential actions pose a serious, foreseeable, and imminent risk to themselves or others" (NASW, 1999, Section 1.02). This obligation to safeguard human life may, in some circumstances, complicate our view of a collaborative client-worker partnership. Freedberg (1989) wonders if social workers' assumption of the roles of both client advocate and agent of a sometimes-oppressive society reveals a fundamental contradiction. Nevertheless, barring some clear-cut indication of danger to others, social workers in day-to-day contact with clients generally attempt to maximize opportunities for client self-determination. Thinking of the people you serve as consumers of social services rather than as patients or even clients may help to enhance self-determination (Moore & Kelly, 1996; Tower, 1994).

Self-Determination and Options

Self-determination involves making choices and, therefore, cannot occur without options. The nature and number of options and the resulting degree of self-determination, however, may be limited by several factors. For example, time limitations may preclude an adequate search for alternatives; insufficient external or internal resources and capacities may diminish the range of options (Abramson, 1988), as may divergent interests between clients and agencies or other social institutions. Closed-minded thinking and entrenched institutional practices are also major limiting factors.

Social workers routinely participate with applicants and clients to develop new alternatives and resources within the environment or to develop new ways of responding to environmental demands. Increasing opportunities in the environment may also enhance the nature and scope of self-determination. We may, for instance, work to remove social and physical barriers, develop resources and capacities, and help people develop skills to maximize use of environmental opportunities. The search for options and expansion of opportunities for choice and self-determination may be constrained if people believe there is nothing they can do to influence events. In such circumstances, social workers often first seek to help the applicants or clients reconsider their pessimistic beliefs and conclusions and begin to exercise choice. Internal impediments may include stereotyped and fixed cognitive structures or processes that inhibit consideration of other perspectives and options—including alternative ways to think, feel, and behave.

Self-Determination and Client Values

The concepts of human dignity and self-determination imply respect for a great diversity of applicant and client value systems. However, such principles can be difficult to implement in practice. For example, if we believe in the self-determination of all people, how do we respond when clients violate the dignity or interfere with the rights of others? What do we do about clients whose values—sometimes culturally or religiously based—encourage or require subordination of women to men, severe corporal punishment of children, denial of services to men, or death to people who are racially, ethnically, or religiously different? In respecting self-determination, must we quietly accept and tolerate abuse, oppression, violence, slavery, and genocide because they are based on and derive from cultural or religious values?

Levy (1972) identifies a number of areas in which social workers favoring planned change have value conflicts with applicants. There may be times when your conceptions of human dignity and client self-determination are inconsistent with applicants' cultural or religious values. When such differences arise, they become a matter for discussion and negotiation. Ideally, they can be clarified and resolved before intervention efforts begin.

Hardman (1975) suggests that values themselves become an appropriate target for change when they conflict with the welfare of others or with clients' ability to achieve agreed-upon goals. He recognizes that unless professional helpers examine and come to terms with this issue, they are likely to experience existential discomfort and remain essentially uninvolved with the people they purport to serve. In work with a parolee, Hardman noticed that his client's values regarding sexual activity were likely to damage the dignity and feelings of other people and probably result in criminal behavior. Hardman was personally unaffected by that reality until he realized that the other person could be his daughter. At that point, he became profoundly aware that the rights and well-being of others are indeed relevant to his service to clients. Hardman had to confront not only the difference between his own values and those of the parolee but also the relationship between his professional responsibility regarding the rights of his clients and those of other people.

Self-determination issues arise in many aspects of social work practice. Consider, for example, the role of women and children. People of certain religions and cultures believe that women are and should be subservient to men, and that wives must subordinate their rights and preferences to those of their husbands. In some cases, violations of such cultural values may lead to banishment, public humiliation, stoning, or perhaps death. Some communities believe that children are, in effect, owned by their parents. As a form of property, then, children may be treated as objects rather than people, or perhaps as slaves who must do manual labor for long hours without pay. Failure to obey parents may lead to severe corporal punishment and deprivation. How can social workers address these forms of social injustice and human indignity while adhering to the principle of self-determination?

When issues emerge regarding the self-determination rights of clients versus those of others, we suggest that the client-and-worker consider the following:

- How personal or cultural values may restrict progress toward achievement of the agreed-upon goals
- Possible options or solutions and the potential implications and consequences of their implementation
- The rights and well-being of others

The principle of self-determination does not mean that social workers adopt a passive, noncommittal role in relation to the rights of others. We cannot avoid personal or professional responsibility by keeping silent while clients espouse beliefs and engage in behavior that violates the rights, dignity, and well-being of others. Rather, we introduce alternate perspectives, identify options, and share ideas. Just as we resist the temptation to make decisions for others, we also counter the temptation to focus solely on the rights and preferences of applicants and clients to the detriment of other people and groups. Our passivity and silence may suggest acceptance or approval. Failure to share your knowledge and judgment may leave applicants and clients unaware of options that may relate to their own decision making. About 60 years ago, Charlotte Towle noted, "The social worker's

---

EXHIBIT 4-6
Worker Values and Frustration

Alice is a social worker who works as a community organizer. I remarked that it certainly must be satisfying to be part of a process where people come together to work toward a common goal. I was surprised when Alice shook her head slowly and said in a somber tone of voice, "No, 99% of the time there is very little glamour to organizing." When I asked her to elaborate, she said that it is hard, hard work and she often feels discouraged by the realization that often the people she tries to

organize aren't necessarily looking to change the system but rather to become part of the system. Usually that means playing the same games that those in power play. She talked further about the frustration she deals with constantly. I, too, began to feel that organizing was not the glamorous, romantic job I had pictured it to be.

_____

Source: BSW student.

---

devotion to the idea that every individual has a right to be self-determining does not rule out valid concern with directing people's attention to the most desirable alternative" (1945/1965, p. 26). You have an obligation to share your own thinking—and perhaps your own experiences—with clients and applicants. However, you must take care to present your input as information to be considered, rather than as edicts to be followed or commands to be obeyed. Schwartz (1961) offers some helpful suggestions. In contributing data—facts, ideas, and value concepts—acknowledge the natural limitations concerning the validity, reliability, and potential applicability of the information. Also, relate the data to the purpose of your work with the applicant. Opinions should be clearly labeled as such and not represented as facts. Successful practitioners share their knowledge and ideas in a nonjudgmental manner that enables others to accept or reject them without fear of censure.

Social workers cannot support client behavior that injures or violates the human rights, dignity, or well-being of other people or groups even if it is based on clients' personal, religious, or cultural values. We cannot sit passively by while children are abused, enslaved, or murdered; while women are oppressed or mutilated; or people of one religious faith are terrorized by those of another. Social workers cannot use the principle of self-determination to condone or encourage—however indirectly—atrocities by one person or group toward another. We take the position that self-determination can exist only when the rights and dignity of all human beings are fully respected. Self-

determination, therefore, must always be considered within the context of human rights and social justice.

Worker Self-Determination

Some social workers confuse client self-determination with worker self-determination. Social workers and other helping professionals voluntarily agree to limit their own rights when they assume professional responsibilities. Social work codes of ethics, including those of the NASW (U.S.) and the Canadian Association of Social Workers (CASW), limit social workers' freedom of choice and action—including their right to self-determination. As a social worker, you must practice within the knowledge and skill base of the profession. You give priority to service over self-interest and willingly limit your range of options to provide professional quality service to others. In a sense, you sacrifice some of your own rights and preferences. For example, suppose you are bilingual but prefer English to Spanish. In an interview with a family that only speaks and understands Spanish, you would obviously speak their language—even though you might prefer English. As social workers, we frequently make adjustments and manage our personal preferences to improve the quality of our service. We may, for instance, refrain from expressing our anger toward the action of a property owner or a banker when such restraint might help clients secure housing or loans. Alice (see Exhibit 4-6) struggles with the difference between her own goals and preferences and those of the people she serves.

◆ Legal Authority and Self-Determination

Social workers' commitment to client self-determination may prove especially complex in certain fields of practice. In some contexts and under certain circumstances, social workers may possess legal authority to coerce respondents to modify their behavior or to exact penalties if they fail to conform. Such legal authority is typically mandated to (1) protect dependent or vulnerable people, including minor children, persons with developmental disabilities, and infirm older people; and (2) force people who have violated societal norms to receive rehabilitation services. For example, juvenile and adult offenders, persons with chemical dependency problems, and people affected by certain mental illnesses may be required to undergo some form of treatment, rehabilitation, correctional, or educational experience.

Use of Authority to Protect

Social workers fulfill protective as well as helping functions. The protective role is often quite distinct from the helping role. Indeed, the two functions sometimes conflict (Kelly, 1994; Murdach, 1996; Reid & Epstein, 1977). Respondents have a right to information about both of these functions—even when they primarily seek help rather than protection. Our authority extends to the protection of others as well as applicants, respondents, or clients and may include the protection of people from themselves. For example, suppose you learn that a teenage student plans to commit suicide following an academic disappointment. As a school social worker, you possess the legal authority to protect the teenager from self-harm. In so doing, you infringe on her right to self-determination. However, in fulfilling your protection function you also try to consider your helping responsibility as well. You may be able to enlist her in considering how to secure her safety from self-harm in ways that are least restrictive or least likely to cause unnecessary stigma. Similarly, children removed from their homes because of abuse may be encouraged to participate in decision making regarding alternative living arrangements. They might well be able to help decide which of various options would best meet their needs and preferences. We noted earlier that the United Nations Convention on the Rights of Children explicates children's right to express views on matters affecting them. Involving children in

decision making may reveal resources—such as relatives and neighbors—previously unknown to the social worker. For instance, Arthur (see Exhibit 4-7) suggested the Jelneck family.

Occasionally, physically ill older people may become unable to care for themselves in their own homes, despite their wishes to do so. As a social worker, you may have to exercise your responsibility to ensure the safety of persons whose condition or circumstances leave them unable to care for themselves. Although the need for protection limits their self-determination, you may well be able to encourage such respondents to participate in the selection of an alternative living arrangement. Nicholson and Matross (1989) suggest ways in which social workers can enhance self-determination in persons—such as those with senile dementia and persons with advanced AIDS—who live beyond their ability to make autonomous decisions. For example, durable powers of attorney, living wills, and prerecorded oral communications, may enable individuals to provide advance instructions regarding their care after their decision-making ability has been impaired by disease.

When applying coercive power to protect a respondent, you must be clear about the knowledge that justifies use of authority and about the source and extent of that authority. You must also communicate these matters clearly to the respondent. Such authority can lead to abuse of power (Szasz, 1994) by social workers, especially if they are not sensitive to the possible consequences of their actions (Diorio, 1992). Because of the potential for abuse of power, respondents should have an opportunity to request an appeal and review of your decisions. The involvement of independent courts, guardians (Downes, 1992), or ombudspersons helps counter potential misuse of authority. As individuals and as a profession, we social workers must continually assess whether the use of coercive authority is truly necessary to protect respondents. Possession of such enormous power may easily be misused to impose a personally preferred standard of behavior rather than ensure the protection of at-risk people.

Use of Authority to Force Participation in Service Programs

The use of authority to force respondents to receive rehabilitation services creates a serious dilemma for social workers. We may attempt to resolve this

---

EXHIBIT 4-7
Finding a Foster Home for Arthur

Just after graduation, I secured a job as a new probation officer. Arthur, a 16-year-old inmate of the State Training School was one of my first clients. His record revealed a history of truancy from school and episodes when he ran away from home. He was ready for release into foster care. However, previous officers had not yet located an appropriate placement. When I met Arthur, I asked him if he knew any families—relatives or friends—that might serve as a temporary placement. He seemed a bit hesitant at first but then mentioned the Jelneck family. During previous summers, he had lived with and worked for the Jelnecks. I explored this as much as I could with Arthur. He believed he got along well with the family but did not know whether they would be interested in letting him live with them. After some further discussion, we jointly concluded that we should at least contact the Jelnecks to explore the possibility of a placement with them. Arthur agreed to write a letter to the Jelnecks to describe his situation and indicate that I would be in contact with them.

I waited about a week and then called the Jelnecks. Mrs. Jelneck indicated that they had received a letter from Arthur and agreed to let me come out and talk with her and her husband about parole planning.

During my visit with the Jelnecks, we talked at length about their past contact with Arthur. They, like Arthur, viewed their previous involvement in a positive light. I indicated that we did not believe it would be appropriate for Arthur to return home. They agreed with this. When I asked if they might be in a position to consider letting Arthur live with them, they agreed to mull over the possibility.

---

dilemma in at least two distinct ways: (1) integrating the authority and service roles and, within the limitations imposed by the setting, expanding opportunities for self-determination; and (2) withdrawing from coercive efforts to require rehabilitation services.

Social workers usually adopt the first strategy by attempting to integrate the authority and service functions (Behroozi, 1992; Hardman, 1960; Hatcher, 1978; Ivanoff, Blythe, & Tripodi, 1994; Klockars, 1972; Overton, 1965; Rooney, 1988, 1992, 1993). In exercising legal authority, we typically have some flexibility so that we may encourage client self-determination in at least some areas. For example, a social worker serving as a probation officer may enforce the legal requirement that probationers must report in on a scheduled basis. This is not a matter for self-determination. However, the worker may enlist the probationer in deciding about the nature of the schedule, the frequency of or interval between visits, time and length of interviews, and the topics for discussion. Similarly, social workers may encourage residents of correctional settings to help decide how to best use any available services. Prisoners may exercise some self-determination by helping to decide on the problems and goals they want to pursue—rather than having them determined by the prison system or the social worker.

Based on their analysis of juvenile justice policy, Shireman and Reamer (1986) conclude that opportunities exist for social workers to work with respondents within required rehabilitative programs. Rooney (1988, 1992, 1993) outlines a process to help respondents become clients through the negotiation of a mutually acceptable service plan. Creative social workers may help people who begin as respondents to find an area in which they can voluntarily agree to work and thus become clients. Of course, all respondents decide whether to respect or ignore the requirements of the authority. Some may choose to accept the consequences for failure to conform—which may sometimes mean imprisonment. Respondents also decide how much they will invest in the process. Many choose to do the bare legal minimum, but others do a great deal more.

Obviously, some respondents refuse to negotiate service plans and continue to meet with social workers solely because of the external coercion to do so. In such circumstances, we may regard the state and its formal institutions (e.g., courts, hospitals, prisons)

EXHIBIT 4-8
Self-Determination in Prison

The principle of self-determination, the freedom to choose one's own destiny is based on an assumption of individual dignity . . . The recognition of people's right to free choice guarantees that he may choose to run his life as he sees fit. His choice may run counter to society's welfare and even his own, yet essentially, it is his choice and his prerogative. Society may censure, but it cannot take his right; nor should society strip him of his dignity by its censure. The criminal then has a right to say "Crime is my choice and I am willing to pay the price. If you send me to prison, I am paying my debt to society and refuse to submit to your attempts to reform me." The principle of self-determination makes it incumbent upon society to honor such a plea.

There are large numbers of inmates in correctional institutions who recognize a need for reha-

bilitation and are willing to become involved in programs for that end. An inmate's voluntary recognition of a need for assistance does not, in turn, give officials a free reign in outlining the inmate's rehabilitation program. It is reasonable that the offender have input into the definition of his own "problem" and have this included in the official assessment. He should have the opportunity to say what type of program would assist him and who should provide the services. Further, it seems appropriate that the inmates have a right, in part, to determine the conditions under which the services are delivered.

_____

Source: O'Connor, G. (1972). Toward a new policy in adult corrections. *Social Service Review, 46*(4), 582–596, pp. 585–586.

---

as the client. Googins and Davidson (1993) suggest that the organization may be the actual client for social workers practicing in employee assistance programs (EAPs). Coercive power often exists in more subtle forms within EAPs than in correctional settings. Social workers' authority to intervene in these settings derives from a contract with the employing organizations. The goals of service tend to involve the reduction of behaviors that negatively affect organizational productivity or profitability. Typically, then, employees who meet with the EAP social worker are the targets of change.

Some social workers feel uncomfortable with the notion that the state or the organization is the true client because it explicitly acknowledges the social control function of the profession. We certainly understand the discomfort. However, we believe that straightforward acknowledgement of the nature of the relationship between the worker and the organization or the state actually helps respondents to understand and perhaps adapt to the coercive aspects of the encounter. Forthright clarification and discussion about the conditions under which you, as a social worker, may forcibly intervene in the life of the respondent often furthers the working relationship. By describing the nature and limits of your power and authority, and outlining the rights

and obligations of the respondent, you set the stage for genuinely informed decision-making. Under such circumstances, respondents become more likely to participate actively and perhaps become clients truly interested in using the proffered services.

Earlier, we mentioned that social workers might demonstrate respect for the value of client self-determination by withdrawing from coercive services (Miller, 1968). Indeed, some social workers might refuse to participate in programs of social control on grounds that they violate basic rights of self-determination. We might also advocate for the development of genuinely voluntary social services to substitute for programs of forced rehabilitation (see Exhibit 4-8).

Raynor (1986) contrasts two scenarios for probation work. In one scenario, derived from the model of coerced treatment, probation services are essentially repressive and controlling in nature. In such circumstances, social workers have relatively little involvement, except to provide an ideological justification for social control. In the second scenario, relationships between probation officers and probationers become partnerships. The partners mutually negotiate terms and conditions. They direct their change efforts toward the development of social support networks and mobilization of community resources to pursue goals jointly identified by the partners.

Respondents' willingness to work in partnership with social workers—and thus become clients—depends on the type of services and the manner in which they are offered. Many who would resist predetermined rehabilitation programs are quite willing to work with social workers to resolve personal problems they identify on their own. This is also true for children (Silverman, 1977) and people with severe forms of mental illness (Coursey et al., 1991).

Social workers will, of course, debate issues related to client self-determination for decades to come. We are inclined, however, to raise questions about the appropriateness of social workers' involvement in coerced rehabilitation services and advocate for the development of social structures, policies, and programs that permit voluntary associations between respondents and social workers. Such efforts are consistent with the principle of client self-determination. We do not mean to suggest that people who are guilty of crimes should be exempt from appropriate societally sanctioned punishment. Consequences for violations of law represent an entirely legitimate function of society. As social workers interested in human rights and social justice, we consider the nature and extent of penalties. We seek assurance that punishments are fair and humane. We investigate the effectiveness of policies and ask, for example, whether widespread imprisonment of large segments of the population represents the best investment of societal capital that might otherwise fund health, social welfare, and educational services. Social workers may ask if penalties are restorative and healing or alienating and divisive in nature (Galaway, 1981; Galaway & Hudson, 1996; Van Ness & Strong, 1997; Zehr, 1990). Many of us wonder if our society might rely excessively and perhaps unnecessarily on the criminal justice system and punishment when less formal social sanctions and incentives might be at least as effective in deterring criminal behavior.

◆ Chapter Summary

In this chapter, we developed the notion of a client-worker partnership as a fundamental aspect of our model of social work practice. This concept of collaborative partnership embodies two major social work values—respect for the uniqueness of each individual person and encouragement of client self-determination. The key ideas about partnership include the following:

- The client and social worker jointly participate in decision-making about the problems and goals for work and negotiate the plans by which identified goals may be pursued.
- The client and social worker bring different but equally important resources to the problem-solving work.
- Social workers are experts in facilitating a problem-solving process and securing client participation. Although social workers may be expert in certain social problems or intervention methods, we do not presume to know what is best for our clients.
- Professional values are preferences. As such, they cannot be proven true or false. Social work values are not unique. Rather, they are adapted from the larger culture.

We identified two fundamental values of social work practice: (1) the innate dignity of each individual person, and (2) the importance of client self-determination. To respect human dignity and uniqueness, we

- Respond to people as individuals rather than as diagnoses, disorders, problems, diseases, or cases.
- Incorporate strengths, assets, and resources in the problem-solving process.
- Encourage maximum client participation throughout the process.
- Maintain joint accountability with the client.
- Conscientiously communicate respect for others in our words, gestures, and actions.

To maximize client self-determination, we

- Actively collaborate with our partners in a quest for options. Without options, we cannot truly make decisions or genuinely exercise the right to self-determination.
- Attempt to increase the nature and range of decision-making opportunities for applicants and clients. We do not presume to know what is best for people and consequently we avoid making decisions for them. Rather, we use our knowledge and expertise within the context of collaborative decision making.
- Share our knowledge, perspectives, and suggestions with applicants and clients as ideas for consideration rather than as commands or directives.

- Encourage applicants and clients to reconsider their values if they endanger their own or others' welfare or represent an obstacle to their goals.
- Distinguish client self-determination from worker self-determination. When we assume professional responsibility, we sharply limit our own range of options to serve the best interests of applicants, clients, and other people.

The principle of client self-determination becomes difficult to apply in work with respondents who are legally required to meet with social workers. Involuntary respondents may receive protective services because of their perceived vulnerability and dependency or rehabilitation services to learn to control socially proscribed behavior. To honor the principle of client self-determination in work with respondents, social workers

- Recognize the potential for abuse of their power and authority.
- Clearly explain the limits to respondent choice and outline the rights and opportunities that remain.
- Identify and maximize respondent options and decision-making opportunities.
- Whenever possible, work within the framework of respondent wants and preferences.
- Recognize the importance of respondents' access to appeal or review processes.

Learning Exercises: Readings, InfoTrac, and the Web

1. Use your word-processing computer program to enter the important terms and concepts presented in this chapter. List them in alphabetical order. Place a question mark by any terms that you do not clearly understand. Save your document as EX 4-1.

2. Log on to the InfoTrac College Edition Web site. Conduct a keyword search (using either Keyword Search or Advanced Search) to locate the articles entitled "The Capabilities Perspective: A Framework for Social Justice" (Morris, 2002) and "Preserving End-of-Life Autonomy: The Patient Self-Determination Act and the Uniform Health Care Decisions Act" (Galambos, 1998). Read the articles and prepare a two-page essay in which you reflect

on their implications for client self-determination within the context of social work and social work practice. Save your document as EX 4-2.

3. Log on to the InfoTrac College Edition Web site. Conduct a keyword search (using either Keyword Search or Advanced Search) to locate the articles entitled "Unjustified Seclusion of Psychiatric Patients Is Breach of Human Rights" (Dyer, 2003), "Informed Consent, Parental Permission, and Assent on Pediatric Practice" (American Academy of Pediatrics Committee on Bioethics, 1995), and "Making Decisions with Children: A Child's Rights to Share in Health Decisions Can No Longer Be Ignored" (Rylance, 1996). Read the articles and prepare a two-page essay in which you reflect on their implications for client self-determination within the context of social work and social work practice. Save your document as EX 4-3.

4. Turn to **Reading 10: The Record of Change: Client-Focused Recording.** Review the article by Susan Steiger Tebb and reflect on its implications for social work and social work practice in a one-page essay. In your response, be sure to explore those aspects of the CREW format with which you agree and disagree. Save your document as EX 4-4.

5. Turn to **Reading 11: Four Pennies to My Name: What It's Like on Welfare.** Review the essay by Addie Morris and reflect on its implications for social work and social work practice in a one-page essay. In your response, be sure to explore your personal reactions to Ms. Morgan's experience. Also discuss how you could have interacted with Ms. Morgan and her children in a manner that might convey more respect for their human individuality and dignity. Save your document as EX 4-5.

6. Go the Web site of the United Nations at www.un.org. Search for and locate (1) the United Nations Universal Declaration of Human Rights, (2) the United Nations Convention on the Rights of the Child, and (3) the United Nations Convention Against Torture and Other Cruel, Inhuman or Degrading Treatment or Punishment. Reflect on the principles contained within these three documents in light of topics addressed in this chapter. Prepare a one- to two-page essay in which you discuss their implications for the social work profession and for your service as a social worker. Save your document as EX 4-6.

Chapter 5

Authority for Social Work Practice

In earlier chapters, we introduced the conceptual framework for our model of social work practice: an ecosystems perspective, social work practice as a problem-solving process, and a collaborative client-worker partnership. In this chapter, we discuss three sources of authority for our efforts as social workers to help people address social problems. We also consider how to resolve dilemmas that arise when the expectations of these sources of authority conflict. Sometimes our attempts to resolve such conflicts may require change in agency policies and procedures, or perhaps professional practices.

Social workers receive authority to provide professional service from

- Clients
- The social work profession
- Social agencies

◆ Authority from Clients

You will not be surprised to read that clients are one of three sources of authority for your social work practice. Earlier, we suggested that applicants do not become clients until they reach an explicit agreement with a social worker concerning the problem to address, the goals to pursue, and the service plan to accomplish the agreed-upon goals. Through this agreement, the new client authorizes you to carry out actions.

The likelihood of change increases when all parties agree to the nature of the change effort. Therefore, during the engagement process we try to find a common area for work—even when the applicants

are respondents or prospects—to obtain direct authority from the people we hope to serve. Earlier, we mentioned the importance of focusing on applicant wants rather than needs. Such a perspective often makes it easier for prospective clients to authorize you to provide services.

Focusing on Wants

The social work literature is replete with references to clients' needs. However, the process by which those needs are or should be determined remains quite unclear. Implicit in the ambiguity is an assumption that professionals know or should know what clients need. Reid suggests that social workers should consider clients' wants rather than their needs (see Exhibit 5-1). He describes a want as a "cognitive affective event consisting of an idea that something is desirable and a feeling of tension associated with not having it" (Reid, 1978, p. 25).

"When a want is experienced without means of satisfaction at hand or in sight, one has the sensation of having a problem" (Reid, 1978, p. 25). We agree with Reid that clients' *wants* provide a more useful focus for social work than do clients' *needs*. By focusing on clients' wants rather than needs, social workers are less likely to do to people what they do not want done. Even well-motivated efforts to meet people's needs may violate individual liberties (Gaylin, Glasser, Marcus, & Rothman, 1978; Szasz, 1994). Partly in response to such violations, students, patients, inmates, gay and lesbian persons, and several other peoples have organized groups and initiated advocacy movements to ensure their rights. Such movements serve a

---

EXHIBIT 5-1
Wants as a Focus for Social Work

A focus on wants rather than needs may give us a different perspective on the unmotivated client. Usually, he is unmotivated to be what social workers or others believe he ought to be. He lacks "motivation" to be a better spouse or parent, or to be more law abiding. To our dismay we see vast numbers of people who do not have motives for self-betterment, as we define it. While many clients lack motivation in these terms, few lack wants. If the client's wants are our concern, then the essen-

tial questions become: What does the person want? Can we help him get it? Should we do so? Should we try to create wants he does not have? If so, by what means? These questions are not easily answered, but they may help clarify our position and thinking about the many people who are less than enthusiastic about our efforts to help them.

_____

Source: Reid, W. J. (1978). *The task centered system.* New York: Columbia University Press, pp. 25–26.

---

feedback function for human service agencies and organizations that—despite their usually noble and idealistic missions—sometimes fail to consider the best interest of individual persons. By focusing on wants that people experience rather than the needs attributed to them by some external agency, social workers demonstrate respect for client self-determination and human dignity and are more likely to secure clients' authority for intervention.

Agency or Society as Client

Social workers frequently attempt to serve people who do not initially grant authority to intervene on their behalf. Earlier, we used the terms *respondent* and *prospect* to capture their nonvoluntary status. During the engagement phase, you may reach an agreement with some applicants who consequently become clients. Others, however, may never authorize you to provide service.

Initially, you may find work with respondents and prospects challenging because the relationships begin on an involuntary basis. You may establish contact to carry out a legal mandate or to proffer a service. Two approaches may help you address these challenges: First, you may attempt to seek some common ground through which the partners can agree on the problem, goals, and a service plan (Ivanoff, Blythe, & Tripodi, 1994; Rooney, 1988, 1992, 1993). If successful, these efforts transform respondents or prospects into clients. Second, you may rely on your agency's authority to carry out a mandated service. Under such circumstances, it would be inappropriate to refer to

the people you serve as clients. Rather, they are targets of change or, as we suggested earlier, target systems. The actual client is society or, more specifically, your agency, which possesses a social mandate to carry out change efforts on behalf of society. Even when the agency is your client, you must still function within the knowledge and ethical limits of the profession. For example, you cannot carry out actions intended to harm people. You must respect the rights of people targeted for change, attempt to enhance self-determination by creating opportunities for choice, adopt the least restrictive methods possible, and use the minimal intervention necessary to carry out the organization's mandate. Agencies authorized to provide mandated services often have broad legal power to intervene in people's lives. This raises the potential for abuse of power (Coursey, Farrell, & Zahniser, 1991). Although laws, policies, and our professional social work ethics limit the ways we may exercise our mandated authority, we should also integrate additional processes to protect at-risk people from the misuse of power.

◆ Authority from the Profession

Professions tend to serve specific societal functions for which their members are accountable (Schwartz, 1961). In social work, these functions relate to certain complex social problems whose solutions require sophisticated knowledge and skill. Such expertise may be so specialized, advanced, or esoteric that people served may be unable to judge the adequacy of ser-

EXHIBIT 5-2
Selected Social Work Professional Associations

National Association of Social Workers (U.S.)
750 First Street NE, Suite 700
Washington, DC 20002-4241
Tel: 800-638-8799
Fax: 202-628-6800
Email: info@naswdc.org
URL: www.socialworkers.org

International Federation of Social Workers
Postfach 6875, Schwarztorstrasse 20
CH-3001 Berne, Switzerland
Tel: (41) 31 382 6015
Fax: (41) 31 381 1222
Email: secr.gen@ifsw.org
URL: www.ifsw.org

Canadian Association of Social Workers
383 Parkdale Avenue, #402
Ottawa, Ontario K1Y 4R4
Tel: 613-729-6668
Fax: 613-729-8608
Email: casw@casw-acts.ca
URL: www.casw-acts.ca

vices received. Indeed, professionals commonly demand the autonomy to make judgments and take actions independent of lay control. They often consider themselves accountable only to their professional peers. Society tends to grant professions considerable autonomy based on the assumption and expectation that its members will act with concern for the welfare of their clients and the community in general. Recognizing that condition, the helping professions establish ethical principles and processes for monitoring the behavior of its members. Ethical codes invariably contain requirements for service to others and to the community to mitigate professional self-interest and self-aggrandizement, and to ensure that the profession fulfills its social function. For its part, the community sanctions professionals' right to practice after fulfilling certain requirements such as

- Completing a prescribed course of formal education
- Successfully passing a sponsored examination
- Receiving a license, registration, or certificate

Professional Associations

All professions have associations that serve various functions. Composed of dues-paying members, a professional association may work to

- Improve the performance of individual practitioners
- Police the behavior of its members to safeguard clients and the community, and to maintain or enhance the reputation of the profession
- Protect members' exclusive right to practice their profession and maintain or increase its service domain
- Promote public policies consistent with the profession's mandate

The primary professional association in the United States is the National Association of Social Workers (NASW), a national association with chapters in each state and territory, and some international regions as well. Qualified social workers may join NASW and affiliate with an appropriate state or territorial chapter. In Canada, social workers may join one of the provincial or territorial associations and thereby become members of the Canadian Association of Social Workers (CASW). The Québec association (Ordre professionnel des travailleurs sociaux du Québec), however, recently discontinued its affiliation with CASW.

Social workers in several other countries have established professional associations. The International Federation of Social Workers (IFSW) links the various national groups (see Exhibit 5-2). Professionals of all kinds and perhaps social workers in particular tend to

---

EXHIBIT 5-3
Selected Social Work Education Associations

Council on Social Work Education
600 Duke Street
Alexandria, VA 22314
Tel: 703-683-8080
Fax: 703-683-8099
Email: info@cswe.org
URL: www.cswe.org

Canadian Association of Schools of Social Work
1398 chemin Star Top Road
Ottawa, Ontario K1B 4V7
Tel: 613–792–1953
Fax: 613–792–1956
Email: cassw@cassw-acess.ca
URL: www.cassw-acess.ca

---

recognize the value of organizing themselves for collective action. We encourage you to consider a student membership in a professional social work association. In addition to numerous individual benefits, your membership entitles you to participate in conferences and various public policy initiatives.

Social work educators have also established organizations to promote improvements in professional education and to accredit academic programs that meet certain standards of quality. These organizations maintain relationships with college and university accreditation bodies as well as professional social work associations. The Council on Social Work Education (CSWE) serves as the accrediting body for schools and departments of social work throughout the United States. The Canadian Association of Schools of Social Work (CASSW) serves a similar function in Canada (see Exhibit 5-3). Members in CSWE and CASSW include departments, schools, or faculties of social work, along with faculty members who teach or administer social work education programs and other interested social work professionals. Each organization publishes lists of accredited social work education programs.

There are more than 635 accredited social work educational programs in the United States and approximately 35 in Canada. The applications of several others are under review. Some unaccredited programs offer courses in social work. However, their graduates do not qualify for state or provincial social work licensure or for membership in professional social work associations. Therefore, social work education programs—and the colleges and universities that sponsor them—highly value their status as accredited programs. They invest a great deal of time, energy, and resources to maintain accreditation.

Licensure of Social Work

Licensing is a legal procedure that restricts who may practice social work and who may refer to themselves as social workers (Hickman, 1994). All states in the United States and some territories have enacted social work licensing legislation. Some Canadian provinces have done so as well. Although eligibility requirements for licensure in the United States vary somewhat from state to state, applicants must possess at least an earned degree from a social work educational program accredited by the Council on Social Work Education. Most also require candidates to pass a social work licensing examination. States may also require applicants to submit letters of reference and other relevant background information and documentation. Once licensed, social workers are legally required to participate annually in a certain number of continuing professional educational experiences to maintain some currency with emerging knowledge.

Some states license a single level of social work practice, whereas others may offer several. In Colorado, for example, social workers and mental health practitioners must possess a license to practice psychotherapy. Indiana regulates two levels of social work practice and offers a Licensed Social Worker (LSW) and a Licensed Clinical Social Worker (LCSW) credential depending on the qualifications and experience of the candidate. Minnesota provides for four levels of licensure.

The scope of social work licensure is far from comprehensive. Some states exempt certain workers from licensing requirements if, for example, they are employed by a state-sponsored public welfare agency, religious organization, or some medical settings. Social work professors are usually not required to possess a license to teach social work—although several groups advocate such a requirement.

The Association of Social Work Boards (ASWB) links representatives of the various states and some provincial social work licensing organizations. ASWB also sponsors the development and maintenance of a series of standardized social work licensing examinations in wide use. The ASWB Web site at www.aswb.org maintains information about social work licensure and specific requirements throughout the United States and some Canadian provinces. The site also contains information about licensing examinations.

As a social work student, you should know about the licensing requirements in your state, province, or territory. Well before you graduate, contact your social work licensing board for information and, if applicable, application materials. The NASW and the CASW, along with the state, provincial, and territorial chapters, also possess relevant information about licensing including proposed changes or amendments to the regulations and laws. We urge you to learn as much as you can about social work licensure in your locale before completing your program. Such knowledge should prove especially useful as you begin your professional social work career.

Professional Autonomy

Social work, like several other professions, maintains that its practitioners possess a knowledge and skill base of such sophistication and distinction that nonsocial workers cannot truly understand, appreciate, or evaluate the performance of social workers. Most professions seek professional autonomy. Nurses now supervise and evaluate the performance of nurses, although at one time many were subordinate to medical doctors. Similarly, contemporary social workers tend to view themselves as independent professionals and social work as an autonomous profession. They do not believe that other professionals—including those with doctoral degrees—can adequately supervise them or evaluate the quality of their practice. Rather, only more highly qualified and experienced social workers can effectively supervise junior social workers.

Another aspect of professional autonomy involves the right of individual practitioners to direct and control the content and terms of their work free from mandatory supervision. Although legal statutes, professional association policies, or agency regulations require most social workers to receive regular supervision, some highly qualified and experienced social workers may be eligible for completely autonomous and independent practice. However, most independent social workers voluntarily secure supervision or participate in consultation groups.

Although professional autonomy conveys considerable status and prestige, there are potential dangers. Greater autonomy may be associated with the emergence of a hierarchy of institutionalized expertise (Friedson, 1970, pp. 71–92) and bureaucraticization. Furthermore, independence, autonomy, and separation are characteristic of closed systems that often reinforce rigidity, conformity, conservatism, and stagnation or decay. Such processes may adversely affect the profession and perhaps the people it serves. Traditional practices may continue long after research studies conducted by scholars from other disciplines clearly demonstrate their ineffectiveness or harmfulness. Excessive professional autonomy accompanied by closed attitudes and secrecy may insulate the profession and its members from useful knowledge, feedback, and resources.

Stimulated in part by various consumer rights movements, individuals and groups increasingly demand a more open or transparent form of professional accountability. Consumers argue forcefully they have the right to judge professionals by the nature and outcome of the service. Concerned that self-regulation may enable professionals to protect each other at the expense of clients and the community and to suppress information about incompetent practitioners, consumers increasingly advocate for open access to disciplinary records and membership on license review boards. In addition, a growing number of consumers submit complaints to professional associations and licensing boards about the nature or quality of the social work services they received. Simultaneously, the number of lawsuits alleging social work malpractice or professional negligence increases each year.

Professional Culture

Through our educational experiences, membership in professional associations, and formal and information relationships with other social workers, we tend to use a common language and adopt particular ways of thinking and acting. In other words, we become part of a professional culture and internalize the norms and values of the profession. We feel obligated to operate in accordance with established professional practice. The internalization of professional values and culture—a process known as socialization—represents an important aspect of professional education and helps provide some protection to clients. During the helping process, you rely primarily on your own knowledge, judgment, and expertise. No one intervenes to safeguard clients. The community entrusts you with the authority and responsibility to serve others based on the premise that your actions and judgments stem from social work values and knowledge acquired through immersion in the professional culture.

◆ Authority from the Agency

The profession and practice of social work emerged, grew, and developed within the context of agency structure. Although the independent, private practice of social work is growing, most social workers continue to work in agencies and organizations. Those who do practice privately tend to operate on a part-time basis while working full-time within agencies. In reality, social work practice is agency-based practice. Indeed, society authorizes agencies to fulfill certain functions. Our authority to provide service derives partly from our professional status as social workers and partly from our status as agency employees. Therefore, we must understand the agency context as an important element of social work practice. Community agencies offer resources for the resolution of clients' problems and specify policies under which those resources become available.

Agency policies and practices may encourage or impede client access to resources and affect certain aspects of social workers' professional practice. Therefore, our service to and relationships with clients are integrally linked to the agency, its mission and purposes, and its policies and procedures. Effective service requires that social workers understand agency structure and process and skillfully use agency resources in their efforts to serve clients.

An Interstitial Profession

Social workers are concerned with the interactions between the individual and society and the social problems that emerge within a people-environment context. In this sense, social work is an interstitial

profession—serving both clients in need and the society at-large. An ambitious and idealistic mission, the dual focus on both people and their world complicates the life and work of social workers. The agencies (public or private, traditional or nontraditional, nonprofit or for-profit) that employ social workers receive their sanction from and are accountable to the society, community, organization, or group that sponsors them. The parameters of each agency's mandate, mission, and goals determine the nature and scope of the services that social workers may provide.

Social workers commonly use two general types of tools in their work. The first involves professional knowledge, values, judgment, and skills that may be enhanced and refined by study and practice. In effect, professionals sell these valuable information resources to support themselves. Some professionals, such as certain lawyers and doctors, sell their services directly to clients or patients. However, the society or community funds the services of most social work services that are—at least in theory—available to all members of the community including those who cannot afford to pay. In some circumstances, social workers may also dispense community or societal funds directly or indirectly to aid clients in need. The funds that support social work services are not the property of social workers. They belong to the people, community, or organization that provides them. Understandably, funding sources expect service providers to use their resources efficiently and responsibly and to produce effective outcomes.

People who visit a lawyer or a doctor may look elsewhere for help if they receive inadequate service. As the direct purchaser of professional services, they may express their displeasure by hiring another attorney or physician. Professionals in such circumstances must satisfy their customers or lose income. The effects are direct and often immediate. Social workers, however, seldom experience the same kind of consequences. Most social work clients do not pay the full cost for services and do not directly pay the social worker. If clients discontinue service because of worker incompetence, the social worker is unlikely to suffer an immediate financial loss. The effects, if any, may come only after a large number of clients discontinue services or submit complaints. Under those circumstances, a poorly performing social worker might receive a reprimand or perhaps be discharged—usually following a complex and lengthy process. In effect, most social workers and the human service agencies that employ them are relatively unaffected by client feedback and evaluation because much of the funding for programs and staff salaries comes from other sources. Earlier, we discussed the risks associated with closed-systems and inadequate feedback processes. This is precisely the context in which much social work takes place. Knowledgeable about the importance of frequent, direct feedback for system functioning, social work administrators and supervisors as well as an increasing number of funding sources have begun to institute more sophisticated evaluation processes often based on multiple indicators of performance such as consumer satisfaction, client goal attainment, and various outcome measures. Indeed, social workers who possess competence and expertise in practice and program evaluation are becoming increasingly valuable to agencies that must provide evidence that their services are effective.

The agency, then, is the context in which social workers practice their profession. In your efforts to provide clients the best possible service, you must understand the mission, structure, processes, policies, and procedures of the organization for which you work. Human service agencies are, of course, among the social systems that can or do affect clients' lives and circumstances. The agency is part of the situation in the person-in-situation perspective. On occasion, therefore, clients and social workers direct their change efforts toward one or more aspects of the agency itself. To do so effectively, you must understand the possible points of intervention. Three major factors affect the organization of agencies: source of support, source of sanction, and areas of concern. Agencies obviously cannot operate without a source of funds. Funds may come from public tax funds, private voluntary contributions, and fees for services. The nature, source, and adequacy of funding influence agencies' mission, programs, organizational structure, policies, and procedures. Most human services agencies lack sufficient funds to meet the goals and aspirations reflected by their missions. As a result, managers and directors must routinely make extraordinarily difficult decisions. Some, for example, must decide which of several desperately needed programs and services should be downsized or even discontinued.

Public agencies generally depend on legislative appropriations for operating funds and must conform to governmental policies and regulations. In some cases, elected officials such as a mayor or governor appoint the members of public service boards or commissions, and the administrators of public agencies. Chief executive officers of public agencies, perhaps in consultation with governmental officials and legislators, establish the processes and procedures needed to implement the legislatively mandated policies that establish and maintain the agency. If you work in a public agency—such as a state or provincial child and family welfare department—you should be familiar with both the legislative and the organizational policies that guide the operations of your agency and ultimately the services you provide.

Many social workers, of course, work in other kinds of agencies and organizations. Schools, hospitals, some police departments, certain businesses, and several religious organizations routinely employ social workers. Although their primary mission may be educating students or healing patients, many such agencies employ a large number of social workers and sometimes organize specific social work departments or programs. For example, a school may have a social work department or a hospital may offer a social services program. In such contexts, the dominant profession in the host agency, rather than social workers, may determine the mission as well as the nature and extent of financial support (Dane & Simon, 1991). As "guest" professionals, social workers in such settings often have somewhat less autonomy and status than in organizations whose primary mission is social service.

Private agencies usually operate under the general policy directives of a board of directors. Boards of directors have three primary functions: (1) establish and authorize agency implementation of programs and services, (2) determine overall agency policy, and (3) fund raising. Boards tend to be composed of an elite group of members who have special status or recognition within the community. Nominated and elected by current members, however, some board members may possess little knowledge about the people who need or receive agency services and the social problems that affect them. Some boards lack diversity, and many include neither client or staff representation. Few members receive formal training in the duties, functions, or operations of boards of directors. Indeed, relatively few realize the legal obligations and potential liability associated with board membership.

Boards of directors hire the chief executive of the agency and may have some role in other personnel decisions as well. Dependent on and accountable to the board, some agency executives seek to satisfy board members—sometimes at the expense of program quality—to maintain implicit authority to run the agency their own way without board interference. Such executives may limit staff access to the board and control the nature and flow of information. They may even frustrate social workers and clients' attempts to provide board members with meaningful data and perspective concerning the realities of conditions and service delivery.

Agencies have both functions and programs. The community defines the agency functions, which are usually described in a formal mission statement. Programs consist of the ways in which the agency carries out the designated functions.

Even if an agency's functions remain constant, its programs often change in response to changing needs and conditions. An agency whose primary function is the care and treatment of children may initially offer programs for orphaned children. Over time, however, the agency may find that child abuse has become a more pressing social problem and redesign its programs accordingly.

Agency Function

Agency mission and function have traditionally influenced social work practice. Indeed, the functional school of social casework, popular within the profession from the early 1930s to the late 1950s, held that the primary role of the social caseworker was to provide the specific services offered by the agency according to its socially mandated function (Smalley, 1967, 1970; Taft, 1935). By contrast, advocates of the diagnostic school (Hamilton, 1940, 1951) placed less emphasis on the importance of agency function. They also practiced in agencies but believed that the primary role of the agency was to provide the resources—such as office space and secretarial support—that practitioners require to diagnose and treat various psychosocial ills. The debates between social workers affiliated with the diagnostic and the functional schools of social work reflect an interesting part of social work history. Although some issues remain, adopting a generalist problem-solving practice model resolves most of the major areas of disagreement.

Nonetheless, agency function remains a major part of contemporary social work practice. As agency-based professionals, most social workers provide services that support their organization's mission. You may work in an agency that reflects a particular function or work in a program that provides a specific service such as child protection, child welfare, offender supervision, residential treatment of disturbed youth, care for aging persons, independent living for disabled individuals, violence prevention, organization of migrant workers, community development, or advocacy for people in poverty.

A public child welfare agency, for example, may include such specialized units as foster home recruitment and supervision, foster care placement, child protection for preschool children, child protection for adolescents, and independent living services. When we discussed the nesting and layering of systems, we noted that higher-order systems provide both opportunities and limitations to lower-order systems. As a social system, your agency also offers resources that clients and workers may use in their efforts to resolve problems and achieve goals. However, the nature and scope of your agency's functions may simultaneously limit what you and your client can do.

Exhibit 5-4 illustrates a conflict between agency function and applicant wants. Constrained by the agency's narrow definition of function, the social worker was unable to start with the applicant's wants and develop a suitable preliminary goal. As a result, the applicant became angry and the family failed to receive needed agency services.

In such situations, you may encourage your agency to expand or revise the current interpretation of its mission or function. Remember the Birky family (Reading 6)? The social worker initiated contact because of concerns about 4-year-old John's behavior in the agency's preschool as well as possible child neglect. During the first telephone call, the worker learned that the youngest child in the Birky family died the day before. He had drowned in an uncovered ditch near the housing development where they lived.

Following the earlier death of another child, city officials had promised to cover the ditch. However, they failed to do so. Suppose that Mr. and Mrs. Birky and the worker decided to focus on the ditch, which continues to present a hazard to children. The preliminary goal is clear—to cover the ditch and thus produce a safe environment for children. The worker and the family could consider a number of possible solutions to accomplish this goal. For example, they might contact the city council member who represents the area, visit the mayor to describe the danger, organize a group of neighbors from the housing development to

EXHIBIT 5-4
Conflict Between Agency Function and Applicant Wants

Mrs. Iverson called to request services for Jody, her 15-year-old daughter, whom she described as being out of control. According to the mother, the daughter was attending school on a sporadic basis, lying, and stealing. The mother is a single parent currently separated from her second husband, who is not the child's father. The stepfather was reported by the mother to be chemically dependent and the children did not get along with him. There is one other child in the family, a son, who is currently not living in the family home. The mother works full time as an aide at a nursing home. She wanted some type of temporary placement for her daughter. The intake worker explained that the purpose of our program is to keep children in the home. The mother expressed a willingness to give the program a try.

After receiving the referral from intake, I contacted the mother and set up a meeting in the family home. I learned that the mother had recently kicked her daughter out of the home and the girl was staying with an adult friend.

The daughter was not present, apparently because of the mother's refusal to allow Jody back in the home. Mrs. Iverson told me that she does not trust her daughter because she lies and steals, and fails to follow house rules, which include doing chores and being home by curfew. Limited financial resources are also a factor contributing to the stress between mother and daughter. Jody is responsible for some bills that the mother cannot afford to pay. This led to Mrs. Iverson's decision to kick Jody out of the home.

Mrs. Iverson's recent marital separation resulted in the loss of a second income; financial ends are not being met even though she took on a second job. I asked about her marital situation. She stated that they had been separated for about two months and she intended to file for divorce.

I inquired about mother's support network at this point in her life. She stated that she had a sister with whom she is very close. This sister was recently diagnosed with cancer, and Mrs. Iverson feels very concerned. She also talked about a close woman friend who has children. Both she and her daughter have talked with this woman in the past and it was helpful, although she feels that the situation has gotten so bad now that even this friend cannot help.

I asked her about possible community resources. She stated that she and her estranged husband briefly saw a Christian marital counselor, but stopped because it did not help with their problems. She and her daughter also saw a counselor once about a month ago. Mrs. Iverson said she does not believe in counseling.

Mrs. Iverson reported that she does not spend very much time with her daughter because she works in the evenings. When they do talk, they argue a lot. I asked what in the past, if anything, had helped to alleviate some of the problems between them. Mother told me about a written contract that was drawn up at the suggestion of her woman friend. The contract dealt with house rules such as curfew, chores, and not yelling at her mother. The mother stated that her daughter was good about following the contract for a few days but then she started breaking it on a regular basis. As a consequence, the mother grounded the child, but she could not consistently follow through because of her work schedule.

I told the mother that I hoped I could be of some assistance to both her and her daughter and I asked her how she thought I could help. The mother stated that she didn't know how I could help and that she basically saw the situation as pretty hopeless.

At this point I felt as if I needed to begin applying some pressure on Mrs. Iverson to start formulating some concrete steps toward getting her daughter back in the home. As I did this I was very conscious of two things: The mother did not want the child back in the home and the goal of the program is to keep children in the family home and avoid placement.

I told the mother that since she was the child's legal guardian she was responsible for caring for the child, and that part of that care was to allow

(continues)

EXHIBIT 5-4
Conflict Between Agency Function and Applicant Wants *(continued)*

the child to come back home. I again asked the mother what she saw as my role in this situation and how I might possibly be able to help. The mother did not provide any concrete response. I told her once again that I did not view the situation as hopeless, but that some hard work needed to be done before any real changes would be made.

I asked the mother what would have to happen in order for Jody to be able to return home. She stated three things: (1) get a part-time job, (2) follow house rules regarding chores and curfew, and (3) go to school on a regular basis. I felt very positive about the fact that she had identified these concrete stipulations.

The mother appeared to be fairly resistant to exploring possibilities for goal setting and also seemed apathetic to the idea of having a social

worker involved, stating that she did not know what good it would do. I felt frustrated by the negative attitude of mother, but also tried to be empathetic.

After spending about an hour talking, the mother was providing both nonverbal and verbal feedback indicating that she did not see any real solutions nor did she particularly see where I could be of assistance. Before the meeting had completely ended, I suggested a meeting with the mother, daughter, and myself. The mother agreed to this if I was willing to set it up. We ended with the understanding that I would contact the daughter and get back to the mother about a specific meeting date and time.

———————

Source: Anonymous MSW student.

take collective action, or secure an attorney to file a lawsuit against the city. However, the social worker works for a center whose function is to provide day-care services. Covering ditches near public housing developments is not part of the agency's mission. What should the social worker do about the discrepancy between agency function and the Birky family's wants?

Social workers seem to view problems in such a way that they fit within their agency's purpose. Workers in child-placement agencies tend to assume that placement represents a desirable solution for childhood problems; those who work for hospitals view hospitalization in a similar fashion; and social workers employed by psychiatric clinics often view psychotherapy and medication as an optimal solution. Narrow agency-based foci can do great harm to applicants and clients by limiting the range of problem definitions and the array of potential solutions. While respecting agency function and program purpose, social workers must beware of closed-mindedness. Although it is clearly impossible to offer all services within a single—often underfunded—agency, we may sometimes interpret agency function in an innovative manner, encourage revision of agency mission or program purpose, or refer applicants to an agency better

suited to address their concerns. Willingness to consider alternate problem definitions and solutions outside the scope of our own agency's mission represents one of the hallmarks of a generalist approach to social work practice.

The Agency as a Bureaucracy

Most formal organizations function as bureaucracies. Characterized by a distinct hierarchy of authority; inflexible norms, rules, and procedures; and clear distribution of specialized responsibilities and functions, bureaucratic structures and processes represent the most common means to organize work. Nearly 60 years ago, sociologist Max Weber (1947) used the Roman Catholic Church, the modern army, large-scale capitalistic enterprises, and various charitable organizations to illustrate bureaucratic systems where an employee's promotion depends on the judgment of superiors.

Even today, most people view bureaucracy as the most efficient way to organize large groups of people. Indeed, there are many functional aspects. However, bureaucracies also tend to encourage "timidity, delay, officiousness, red tape, exaggeration of routine, and limited adaptability" (Wilensky & Lebeaux, 1958).

Bureaucracies try to achieve efficiency by breaking tasks into smaller and smaller parts and standardizing activities so that processes are duplicated in precisely the same way time after time. Standardization, specialization, and routinization enable manufacturers to produce high-quality, durable, and reliable automobiles, computers, and refrigerators. It is less clear that such bureaucratic practices apply as well in efforts to help human beings address highly idiosyncratic, complex, and often dynamic, social problems. Bureaucratic agencies tend to be organized around "abstract, standard parts: specific programs organized around specific problems that are dealt with by specific procedures" (Lerner, 1972, p. 171). Clients may then be "defined in terms of the particular problems around which programs are organized" and "processed to and through those programs and subjected to the various procedures and techniques which constitute them" (p. 173). Under such conditions, clients' own goals and expectations may be lost in the bureaucratic process.

Conflicts between helping professionals who provide direct services to clients and program administrators are almost inevitable in any bureaucratically organized agency.

> Professionals share a desire for and expect a large degree of autonomy from organizational control; they . . . tend to look to other professionals to gain some measure of self-esteem, are not likely to be devoted to any one organization, and accept a value system that puts great emphasis on the client's interest.
> Bureaucrats are different from professionals. They perform specialized and routine activities under the supervision of a hierarchy of officials. Their loyalty and career are tied up with their organization. Therefore, conflict results when professionals are required to perform like bureaucrats. (Weissman, 1973, p. viii)

In social work, professionals and bureaucrats are not two different sets of people. Professional persons commonly occupy bureaucratic positions and serve administrative functions. Indeed, bureaucratic forms of organization are useful in social services because no other feasible organizational model has properties as well suited to carrying out the very complex functions required of social services (Pruger, 1973, 1978). Each agency has some form of bureaucratic structure to organize tasks and stabilize operations.

An executive director serves as the primary administrative officer and holds direct responsibility for the day-to-day functioning of the agency. Executive directors are usually responsible for securing funding to run the agency. At times, this obligation may occupy most of their time and energy. Executive directors report to a board of directors or a public official, commission, or perhaps legislative committee. Executive directors often cooperate with other agencies and organizations in pursuit of various community goals and often actively attempt to enhance the visibility and public reputation of the agency.

Subordinate to the executive director may be assorted administrators. Large agencies sometimes have a large array of division, department, and program directors; unit managers; direct line supervisors; and perhaps some consultants. Small organizations may have three levels of hierarchy: the executive, supervisors, and workers. The workers provide services to clients. Administratively, workers tend to focus primarily on the relationship with their direct supervisor. Supervisors fulfill several functions, two of which may seem contradictory: First, supervisors serve an educative function and help workers develop, improve, and maintain the knowledge, judgment, and skill needed to provide high-quality service and achieve effective outcomes. Second, supervisors evaluate the performance of the workers under their supervision. In this latter role, they apply assorted criteria in an effort to determine the quality and effectiveness of workers' performance. This is a difficult combination of functions: supervisors educate, coach, train, support, and guide—often under extraordinarily challenging circumstances—but then must evaluate or grade the quality of work based on certain standards of performance. Like workers, supervisors differ in personality and approach. Some may be essentially conservative—interested more in job security and promotion than in the actual circumstances of clients, the quality of service, or workers' needs for support and learning opportunities. Others are genuine advocates for clients and workers alike. They may join workers in efforts to help resolve difficult problems or advocate with higher-level administrators for additional resources. The experiences beginning workers have with their first supervisor often profoundly affect their views of clients, agencies, and social work practice. Beware of the tired, cynical, or arrogant supervisor. Seek out those who reflect a genuine interest in clients, workers, and lifelong learning. You may benefit enormously from competent supervisors who can help to increase your professional knowledge and skill, enhance your self-awareness and personal maturity, and develop a professional helping style and identity. If you are lucky, your supervisors may also encourage you to develop and implement an ongoing plan for lifelong professional growth and learning.

The challenges of social work practice are such that you may need considerable support from supervisors in dealing with day-to-day job frustrations. Wasserman (1970) found that workers' practice in a large public agency was determined more by structural constraints than by their professional knowledge and skill. Eight of the 12 new workers studied left the agency within two years of initial employment. He observed that the "two principal feelings expressed by the 12 new professional workers during the two-year period were frustration and fatigue . . . they were exhausted by having day after day to face critical human situations with insufficient material, intellectual and emotional resources and support" (Wasserman, 1970, p. 99). Supervisors certainly cannot wave magic wands and undo the structural constraints on your capacity to help; however, they can offer support, emotional encouragement, and intellectual and material resources to help you learn how best to help people affected by challenging social problems.

Social workers serve within bureaucratically organized agencies. Bureaucracies reflect both strengths and weaknesses—but they are not enemies. Demolition of bureaucratic structures would probably lead to chaos rather than nirvana. It helps neither clients nor workers to view bureaucrats and bureaucracies as adversaries. Try to understand them from a person-in-situation perspective. Bureaucracies are complex social systems in which clients, social workers, and bureaucrats function as subsystems. As a social worker, you must learn to work within the bureaucratic context, use its resources on behalf of clients, and, where necessary, advocate for change and improvement in agency mission, function, policies, or procedures. In the long run, viewing yourself as "good" and bureaucrats or bureaucracy as "bad" may be detrimental—not only to you personally but also to the people you hope to serve (Pruger, 1978).

◆ Managing Conflicts Among the Sources of Authority

Earlier, we introduced the topic of role theory and the notion of role set. As a social worker, you function within a role set that includes the applicant or client,

profession, and agency. Each of these communicates information about how you should fulfill your professional role. These expectations sometimes conflict with or contradict one another (Drolen & Harrison, 1990; Globerman & Bego, 1995; Harrison, Drolen, & Atherton, 1989). Sometimes the expectations of the agency—derived from its function or bureaucratic structure—conflict with the expectations of the profession or perhaps the wants of a client. At other times, applicants may hope you will do something that the profession's code of ethics prohibits. These conflicts, inconsistencies, and contradictions occur frequently enough that you should develop some means and processes to resolve or manage them. Otherwise, the tensions among them may become burdensome and perhaps reduce your practice effectiveness.

Conflict Between Agency and Professional Expectations

On some occasions, the solutions clients and workers identify conflict with the functions and parameters of the agency. Indeed, certain compromises are unavoidable. Over time, however, the discrepancies between your plans and the agency's policies and resources can become extremely frustrating. The better you understand the bureaucratic context within which you practice, the greater will be your ability to manage the frustrations and perhaps even improve agency effectiveness.

Accountability and Evaluation   Weissman encourages professionals to recognize the difference between nonprofit and profit-making organizations: "Money serves as an alarm system in private enterprise" (1973, p. vii). When revenues decline, people immediately pay serious attention to any matters that might be involved. However, nonprofit organizations reflect only an indirect connection between production and revenue. Therefore, they lack an early warning alarm system that focuses attention to matters of concern. Lacking a bottom-line based on profits, nonprofit agency executives and professionals may decide from among a range of performance indicators. Some may keep track of factors such as the number of clients served or the amount of time invested. Many agencies report such figures in their annual reports to boards of directors. An increasing number of agencies, however, have begun to track service outcomes in the form of the number and percentage of clients that achieve identified goals. Many contemporary agency executives recognize that they accomplish their mission and function without an effective accountability system—analogous in some ways to the fiscal alarm system within for-profit organizations. The continuing information and technology revolution, managed care, and mounting pressures from communities and consumers have greatly increased pressure for accountability and practice effectiveness. As forms of systemic feedback, we applaud efforts to improve both the efficiency and effectiveness of our programs and services. However, we should incorporate clients' conceptions of problems and goals among our measures of outcome effectiveness. If the effectiveness indicators do not adequately reflect clients' issues and wants, we may inaccurately claim success or failure based on irrelevant evidence. Consistent with our professional values and ethics as well as our view of the importance of inclusion and collaboration, we believe that clients and workers must participate in determining the means by which to evaluate success or failure and effectiveness or ineffectiveness.

Certainly, agency executives and professional staff, boards of directors, and community representatives may develop goals appropriate to agency mission and function. However, these goals must be sufficiently abstract that they may reasonably incorporate the individualized goals jointly determined by clients and social workers. Indeed, agency goals often help to provide a context in which workers and clients develop specific goals for their work together. In this sense, agency policy becomes an important part of goal setting with clients.

Means and Ends   Specialization of tasks, standardization of processes, and rational distribution of labor in accordance with a coherent overall plan are central to bureaucratic organizations (Weber, 1947). Collective tasks may be broken down into smaller actions that lead to collective ends. Two assumptions underlie this concept. First, the organization possesses a clear, consistent, complete, and generally agreed-upon definition of the ultimate ends toward which it aspires. Second, the ends are achievable through standardized means (Lerner, 1972).

We mentioned earlier that social agencies often frame their ultimate ends in the form of general goals that support their mission and function. Described in abstract terms, their accomplishment is difficult to evaluate. Imagine how challenging it would be to de-

termine the effectiveness of an agency that purports to "strengthen families" or "prevent child abuse." Programs or services sponsored by agencies may identify goals as well. Somewhat less general and abstract than agency goals, their achievement nonetheless generally remains difficult to measure. In some ways, progress toward the goals that clients and workers jointly establish may represent the easiest to evaluate.

Some contemporary agencies attempt to integrate the different levels of goals through a kind of inductive-deductive, back and forth process in which stakeholders consider aggregated client-and-worker goals in light of more abstract program goals and still more abstract agency goals. As the reality of clients' circumstances and goals emerge in greater clarity through the process of aggregation, some adjustments in programmatic and agency goals may become warranted. Furthermore, if specific client-and-worker goals link to and support those at the program and agency levels, evaluation of progress toward their achievement simultaneously yields evidence of progress toward the more abstract goals as well.

The information and technology revolutions have led to a remarkable increase in the knowledge about what works, when, for whom, and under what circumstances. In other words, we may access considerable information about effective programs and practices for certain people affected by several social problems. The empirically based and evidence-based practice movements within the helping professions have contributed to our awareness of what works for what and for whom (Brown, Dreis, & Nace, 1999; Cournoyer, 2004; Cournoyer & Powers, 2002; Gorey, Thyer, & Pawluck, 1998; Hubble, Duncan, & Miller, 1999; Roth & Fonagy, 1996; Thyer, 1996, 2000, 2002; Thyer, Isaac, & Larkin, 1997; Thyer & Wodarski, 1998a, 1998b; Wodarski & Thyer, 1998). Our predictive abilities are not absolute, however. We may be able to predict that more that 75% of people who experience a particular problem and wish to address that problem can successfully do so through a particular practice intervention. However, we usually cannot determine whether an individual person or family will be among the more than 75% who resolve the problem or the fewer than 25% that do not.

In serving human beings, we cannot guarantee, "if we do X, then Y will happen." We work with probabilities, not certainties. There are far too many variables in each ecosystem to make guarantees. A profession works by applying principles and methods to resolve problems determined by unique client input and professional judgment, rather than by employing standardized procedures toward some predetermined end established by a hierarchical authority. The goals that clients-and-workers jointly develop should fit within the agency's mission and general goals. However, we should not violate clients' wants or the integrity of the collaborative partnership by forcing a general agency goal on clients. Rather, the client-and-worker determined goals represent specific statements about desired outcomes for a particular client in a particular situation at a particular time. Fortunately, most client-worker goals readily fit within one or more general agency or program goals. Of course, a thorough understanding of agency mission and program goals greatly facilitates this process.

Orientation Toward Authority The term *authority* refers to the "power to influence or command thought, opinion, or behavior" (Merriam-Webster, 2003). Often associated with a particular status or position within an organization or other social system, the term *authority* may convey alternate meanings. For instance, a social worker might view authority as the power that derives from one's professional knowledge, expertise, and competence. A bureaucrat might view authority as the power and influence that result from one's rank, status, or office. Of course, some professionals, perhaps because of seniority, consider themselves superior to other professionals who are junior and accordingly assume greater authority—even though they may not possess advanced knowledge or skill. Professionals from one discipline may view themselves in higher esteem than they view others—perhaps because they earn more money or have more years of advanced education. Similarly, many professionals view themselves in positions of authority relative to the clients they serve. These latter examples illustrate forms of status authority, and the first represents a form of authority derived from competence and expertise.

Understandably, social work professionals tend to focus primarily on the best interests of clients, but bureaucrats often look after the best interests of the organization. Professionals usually identify with their professional colleagues, both on an individual basis and in their professional association. Bureaucrats often identify with the bureaucracy. Of course, many bureaucrats are also professionals, and many professionals serve bureaucratic functions. Extreme dichoto-

mization of professionals on one end of a continuum and bureaucrats on the other has limited utility. Nonetheless, it is probably fair to suggest that in exercising power and authority, "the professional norm is to influence clients and peers by modes which are oriented toward the pole of free exchange while the bureaucratic norm is oriented toward the pole of coercion supported by invoking of sanctions" (Morgan, 1962, p. 115).

Working Within the Bureaucracy

When you accept a position on an agency staff, receive a salary from the agency, and use agency resources to help clients, you cannot disregard agency policies and procedures. Those policies guide your behavior. Indeed, the NASW *Code of Ethics* contains numerous principles related to the responsibilities social workers hold in relation to colleagues and employers. Section 3.09 is entitled "Commitments to Employers." Among other obligations, social workers should

- Adhere to commitments made to employers and employing organizations (NASW, 1999, Section 3.09a)
- Be diligent stewards of the resources of their employing organizations, wisely conserving funds where appropriate and never misappropriating funds or using them for unintended purposes (NASW, 1999, Section 3.09g)

If you conclude that agency policies are unacceptable, you must either work to change them while remaining bound by them or else leave the agency and work for change from the outside. Indeed, the NASW Code requires social workers to "work to improve employing agencies' policies and procedures and the efficiency and effectiveness of their services" (NASW, 1999, Section 3.09b).

If you stay, Pruger (1973) urges that you become a "good bureaucrat" by developing the qualities and tactics summarized in Exhibit 5-5.

Social workers communicate the policies and practices of our agencies to clients through our words and actions. How you handle yourself, as a concerned professional, becomes important to clients when they have to deal with less than adequate resources. As an agency representative and a professional social worker, you possess some flexibility in the interpretation and implementation of policy. Well-conceived policies, procedures, and rules reflect some room to

EXHIBIT 5-5
The Good Bureaucrat

Qualities of the good bureaucrat:

1. Staying power. Things happen slowly in complex organizations, but whatever changes workers have in mind cannot be implemented if they do not stay in and with the organization.
2. Vitality of action and independence of thought. Organizational life tends to suppress these qualities. Workers must resist such pressure.
3. The ability to provide room for insights and tactics that help individuals preserve and enlarge the discretionary aspect of their activity and, by extension, their sense of personal responsibility.

Tactics used by the good bureaucrat:

1. Understand legitimate authority and organizational enforcement. Most organizations' regulatory policies and codes allow individuals considerable autonomy if they recognize it. Within the limits of legitimate authority, individuals may expand their discretionary limits.
2. Conserve energy. Change agents should not thrash around and feel discouraged because they do not receive, in a large organization, the kind of support they receive from their friends. Also, master the paper flow of the organization. You should describe what can be changed and work on it, rather than bemoaning what cannot be dealt with.
3. Acquire a competence needed by the organization.
4. Don't yield unnecessarily to the requirements of administrative convenience. Keep in mind the difference between that which serves the organizational mission and that which serves the organization. Rules, standards, and directives as to the way things should be done are means that serve ends. In organizations, means tend to become ends, so that a worker may be more concerned about turning in the mileage report than about the results of the visit to a client. Ends and means should be clearly distinguished.
5. Remember that the good bureaucrat is not necessarily the most beloved one.

Source: Adapted from: Pruger, R. (1973). The good bureaucrat. *Social Work, 18*(4), 27–32.

---

maneuver and often implicit or explicit processes to seek waivers, exemptions, or exceptions. Maintain your integrity and honor your commitments to the agency but also remain open to creative and innovative means to access resources on behalf of clients. Agencies are not monolithic organizations. Bureaucracies are also systems and, as such, are amenable to change. Establish relationships with significant agency people, develop ways and means to influence agency policies and procedures, and take advantage of change opportunities when they emerge.

Questioning Agency Culture Social workers must possess an accurate understanding of the policies and procedures of our agencies to maximize clients' access to services. You should thoroughly understand the parameters of agency policies, the sources of authority, and the processes for reconsideration, interpretation, and appeal.

Polices are broad statements that must be interpreted by someone before they can be applied in service to people. Social workers often rely on more senior colleagues or supervisors for policy interpretation. However, your colleagues and supervisors may have acquired the interpretation in the same way—asking others. They may simply repeat what they heard— perhaps years before. We suggest a different process:

- Clarify problems and goals through a collaborative partnership with an applicant or client.
- Locate and personally review the relevant written policy.
- Analyze the policy, reflect on its actual meaning, generate alternate ways to interpret and apply the policy.
- Consider the alternate policy interpretations in relation to the problems and goals established with the client.

- Choose the interpretation that best enables you to help the client resolve identified problems and achieve agreed-upon goals.
- Prepare a written interpretation of the policy and its application to the client situation.
- Submit a copy of the statement to your supervisor for information or approval and include it as part of the record of service to the client.

Accepting colleagues' or supervisors' policy interpretations without completing these steps may diminish your role as an autonomous professional. Because bureaucracies tend toward conservative and routine processes, you may expect that others' informal perspectives about policy may well limit what you can do and what clients can access. When policies are ambiguous, administrators may make arbitrary decisions. Often, "no" is easier to say than "yes." It is difficult to change established processes and procedures when workers rely on traditional messages about policies that circulate through the agency grapevine. Reliance on and acceptance of such informal interpretations may lead workers to gripe about "bad" policies and procedures when the formal written policies actually make good sense. Unless you personally examine, analyze, and reflect on the actual policy, you may frustrate yourself and your clients through false, incomplete, or outdated interpretations. You can help energize bureaucratic agencies by becoming genuinely knowledgeable about agency policies and conducting your own reviews and analyses.

Some years ago, one of us conducted a study of an agency to determine whether clients received the aid they needed. We asked agency workers about conditions. They routinely complained about the limitations of agency policies. They reported that the policies prevented them from really helping their clients. When we investigated further, however, we found that the average client of that agency received less than half of the services and resources that agency policies allowed. In other words, clients typically received only a modest proportion of what they could legitimately obtain. The policies themselves did not limit clients' access to services and resources. Rather, the narrow and traditional interpretations of policies by workers and supervisors effectively deprived clients of their due.

Professional service does not begin and end with your visits with clients. Some of the most important work, requiring considerable self-discipline and com-mitment, involves advocating and brokering with the agency's bureaucracy. Although many social workers prefer to deal with people than with paper, preparation of written documents represents an essential part of our professional responsibilities. Indeed, social workers sometimes fail their clients because we lack skills to prepare written proposals. Most of us recognize the importance of the interpersonal skills of talking and listening for social work, but reading and writing are also essential. Frequently, one of the most effective aspects of practice involves reading statements of policy and preparing written analyses and interpretations that enable clients to access needed services and resources.

Changing Agency Policy   Sometimes, of course, the problem is not misinterpretation of agency policies but the policies themselves. When actual agency policies do not permit adequate service to clients, social workers must attempt to make changes. The NASW Code indicates that social workers "should not allow an employing organization's policies, procedures, regulations, or administrative orders to interfere with their ethical practice of social work . . . (and) . . . should take reasonable steps to ensure that their employing organizations' practices are consistent with the NASW Code of Ethics" (NASW, 1999, Section 3.09d). In attempting to influence agency policy change, you approach the situation in very much the same way that you help clients. Use the problem-solving processes to choose an approach that reflects the greatest likelihood of success. Prepare a written position paper but also consider the systemic implications. Target influential people; organize a committee, task force, or working group; and adopt empowerment strategies (Shera & Page, 1995). Recognize that griping and whining tend to accomplish little. Neither do passionate expressions of feeling and emotion. Policy change involves a serious and persistent set of problem-solving activities. Concisely define the problem and provide tangible evidence of its nature, extent, and consequences for clients and workers as well as for the agency and community. Document this definition in some detail, by organizing and verifying data. Be clear about what to change, likely obstacles to change, and costs and benefits of both the problem and your proposed solution. Carefully consider the potential consequences if your proposal is adopted. There are far too many examples of new or revised policies that worsen rather than improve conditions.

Imagine a situation where a social worker concludes that clients are poorly served by an agency policy. Angry and frustrated, the worker resigns in protest. A newspaper reporter learns of this and interviews the worker. Hoping to use the power of public opinion to influence change for the better, the worker describes the agency's problems to the reporter. When published, the newspaper story creates a great stir throughout the community. People are upset about the situation. However, they do not respond as the social worker expects. Instead, influential community members read the story as evidence of professional incompetence. Officials fire the executive director, cut funding to the agency, and establish stringent rules and regulations to govern social workers' behavior. Then, they hire a business manager to reduce costs, decrease the number of programs and the range of services, and replace professional staff with paraprofessionals and volunteers. The social worker's resignation certainly affected agency policies and procedures. Unfortunately, the impact was negative rather than positive and resulted in palpable harm to clients and staff alike.

The worker in this scenario did not thoroughly investigate the situation before resigning and talking to the press. The executive director and the board members were seriously concerned about the same problematic policies that frustrated the worker. However, their analysis of the situation led them to conclude that attempts to make changes at this particular time would prove counter-productive and result in costly backlash from influential community members. Therefore, they had established contact with national private and public sources of potential support. In other words, the agency director and the board were working quietly to address the issue in a way that might prove successful. The community response to the worker's actions effectively blocked those efforts.

Of course, sometimes we anticipate a backlash but proceed anyway. Before doing so, however, estimate the nature and approximate strength of the likely negative reaction and develop plans to meet and counter it. The freedom fighters of the 1960s civil rights movement in the United States predicted the violent reactions to their activities. They knew what would happen and prepared themselves to respond to violence in nonviolent ways. We should also prepare for potential reactions and consequences of our efforts to change policy. Identify those likely to feel threatened by the change. Determine the forces inside and outside the

organization that maintain the problematic policy. Identify those who possess the power and authority to make change and discover if they are simply unaware of the problem, strongly invested in the present policy, or opposed to change because of conflicts of interests and values. Timing can be crucial. Like individuals, agencies are most often open to change during times of crisis. The probability of change grows when budgets expand or contract, client numbers increase or decrease, leadership changes, or several transitions occur at about the same time.

Social workers might use advocacy, collaborative, or combined strategies in our efforts to influence policy change. Advocacy strategies can involve various intervention tools—some of which may include public confrontation. For example, you might call on citizen groups, unions, and professional organizations to join in litigation, picketing, bargaining, and pressure-building activities. You might contrive a crisis, influence external authorities to bring sanctions, or encourage policy noncompliance, work slow-downs, or strikes by workers and clients.

Collaborative strategies tend to be less confrontational in nature. Social workers may work collaboratively to

- Obtain administrative support to establish a committee, task force, or work group to conduct a thorough, rational, and scholarly study of the situation and make recommendations for changes.
- Secure administrative assurance that people who participate in the group's work are protected from negative repercussions.
- Collect and disseminate factual information about the nature, extent, and consequences of the problematic policy.
- Consider the current policy and practices in relation to professional values and ethics, legal obligations, and scientific knowledge.
- Offer innovative interpretations of current policy or propose new or revised statements of policy.
- Develop alternate strategies for policy implementation and analyze their likely effects.
- Design, secure approval, and implement an experimental pilot project to demonstrate the effects of your favored proposal.

In attempting to influence agency policy development, understand the processes through which change takes place. Recognize that initiating change often requires a different strategy than implementing or maintaining change. Workers sometimes work long and hard to initiate the process but fail to invest the necessary time and energy to ensure that the agreed-upon change actually occurs and lasts. Given the systemic tendency to return to traditional ways of thinking, feeling, and doing, maintaining change requires considerable effort as well.

Clients and Policy Change

Clients themselves can sometimes be a powerful force for policy change. Agency policies and practices directly affect clients' lives and welfare. Experiencing the immediate effects of the policies, clients can serve as powerful advocates for change. Their involvement, however, does not relieve us of our responsibility to work for change. Clients may choose to take individual action or organize themselves into social action groups. They may write letters or develop position statements about troublesome policies. A relatively small number of telephone calls or letters from clients to a legislator, mayor, or governor can produce significant action. Social workers should not view clients as helpless victims of circumstance nor see ourselves as rescuers or saviors. Clients invariably reflect enormous strength and resilience. We must recognize that they can act for themselves independently or collaboratively with us to address various problems—including those associated with unfair or inadequate agency policies.

Some contemporary agencies employ client advocates, ombudspersons, or consumer representatives to ensure that dissatisfied clients have someone to contact. Client advocates tend to assume a partisan role by actively working on clients' behalf. Ombudspersons typically take a neutral perspective in investigating complaints and making recommendations. They usually lack authority to require action. Consumer representatives also investigate complaints and grievances and often possess authority to take corrective action when clients receive poor quality treatment. If consumer protection personnel and services are available in your agency, be sure to inform applicants and clients of their availability.

Many agencies establish processes by which applicants and clients may appeal decisions they believe are incorrect, unfair, unjust, or inconsistent with agency policy. Paradoxically, some agencies and a few social workers hesitate to share appellate policies and procedures with applicants and clients. Although few workers like to have their decisions challenged, the right to appeal is a necessary protection against the abuse of power. Indeed, an opportunity to appeal decisions represents a fundamental aspect of due process. All clients should receive full and complete information about their rights of appeal and the processes by which they may exercise those rights.

In some situations, clients and applicants may have recourse to litigation. As child protection work shifts from a helping to an adversarial process, an increasing number of parents challenge agency decisions in court. The high cost and long delays of court proceedings lead some parents and agencies to seek help from external mediators to resolve their disputes (Barsky, 1995, 1997a, 1997b). Although mediation is a well-established means to resolve disputes between businesses and customers, property owners and tenants, and divorcing spouses, it has only recently emerged as a way to address disagreements between clients and social agencies.

Alternative Structures for Practice

Prompted by the difficulties of practice within bureaucratic agency structures, some social workers seek alternate contexts for service. Private or independent private represents one such venue. Approximately 3% of NASW members functioned as private practitioners in the early 1970s. By the early 1990s, more than 30% of NASW members engaged in full- or part-time private practice (Karger & Stoesz, 1994). Interestingly, a survey of MSW students and faculty in graduate social work programs indicated that a majority of students expected to practice privately at some point in their careers. However, the professors generally did not purport to prepare students for private practice (Brown & Barker, 1995).

The popularity of private practice among graduate social work students raises concerns that the profession may eventually focus more on psychological than social problems and on private rather than public concerns. The attractions of office-based, psychotherapeutic practice with medically insured people from middle- and upper-class economic groups may represent a threat to social work's historic mission to serve poor, disenfranchised, and underserved populations. However, some emerging developments may allay these concerns.

The potential contexts and roles for private social work practitioners are rapidly expanding. Individual and family counseling and psychotherapy represent one of many emerging contexts. Independent social workers increasingly serve as consultants, trainers, researchers, lobbyists, and activists. Many agencies and some businesses and industries now hire social workers on a contract basis to perform discrete services. These contract workers essentially operate as private practitioners but may conduct risk assessments, complete child-custody evaluations, interview and assess potential foster-care or adoption families, or undertake program evaluation and research studies. The growing need and demand for conflict resolution in a wide variety of settings lead many social workers to offer private mediational services. Some independent social workers conduct assessments and prepare reports for defense attorneys' use at disposition or sentencing hearings for juvenile or adult offenders. Private practitioners may also find work as case managers in service areas such as child welfare, juvenile and adult justice, and services for injured or ill persons or those with developmental disabilities. We can safely predict an enormous increase in the demand for generalist social work and case management services for elderly people and their families during the next few decades. Agency-based practitioners cannot possibly meet the enormous service needs of a rapidly growing elderly population. We will need independent practitioners as well.

Changes in funding patterns may increase access of low- and moderate-income persons to private practitioners. As government agencies, insurance companies, and other third-party payers increasingly purchase services from various organizations and practitioners, access to alternate providers may increase. The use of vouchers may also enable clients and applicants to purchase services directly from either agency-based or private practitioners (Bertsch, 1992). Free from the large administrative costs of bureaucratic structures, private practitioners—in theory—can sometimes provide services at lower cost.

Small collectives represent another alternative to large bureaucratic organizations. In these arrangements, all staff members participate in nonhierarchical decision making. Such "flat" organizational structures, however, can be quite inefficient because of the time required to discuss matters fully and to reach a consensus. Obviously, collectives cannot grow beyond a relative small number of staff members. Larger numbers make decision making practically impossible.

Another approach involves transforming bureaucratic structures to encourage greater responsiveness. Formation of teams and quality circles may enable small groups of workers to assume joint responsibility for a set of activities (Ketzenbach & Smith, 1993; Manz & Sims, 1995). This approach attempts to introduce collective decision-making processes into bureaucratic structures. Unless carefully organized, however, team meetings can absorb large quantities of time that could go to client services. Many corporations eliminate entire levels of middle management to streamline and reduce costs. This type of downsizing flattens the organizational structure and reduces hierarchical rigidity, but requires highly competent, self-directed workers at the line level. We anticipate that governmental and nonprofit agencies will follow the corporate lead by experimenting with flatter organizational structures (Peters, 1992; Treacy & Wiersema, 1995).

◆ Chapter Summary

In this chapter, we introduced the sources of authority for social work practice, explored the possibility of conflict among these sources, and reviewed some approaches to conflict resolution. We discussed the following:

- Social workers' most important source of authority is our clients, who reach an agreement with us to work jointly toward the achievement of mutually agreed-upon goals. You are most likely to secure authority from clients if you respect client wants.
- A second source of authority is the social work profession, which provides guidance for competent practice.
- Another source of authority is the agencies that employ social workers to carry out their socially mandated functions.
- The various demands and expectations of these sources of authority sometimes conflict. For example, your clients may expect you to provide services that your agency prohibits. You may also experience conflicts between client expectations and your professional values. Some clients may expect you to do things that you think are professionally unsound; others may expect you to refrain from doing things you

believe represent legal or professional obligations. The agency may expect you to adopt an outdated, ineffective approach to service while the social work profession expects you to base your practice on current evidence of practice effectiveness. If conflicts between agency policy and professional values emerge, you may seek to change agency policies and practices. In doing so, we recommend that you

- Recognize how the agency's approach to service delivery affects clients.
- Obtain and carefully review the written policies of your agency. Do not accept informal interpretations of agency practices that circulate throughout the organization. Personally conduct an analyis of the policy itself.
- Document problems associated with current policies. Prepare a written proposal for change. Try to do this collaboratively with a group of colleagues, preferably with the knowledge and approval of administration.
- Provide a legitimate and rational reason along with data to support how your proposal for change will benefit the agency by rectifying problems, strengthening the agency's function, improving service quality, or increasing public support.
- Try to avoid publicly embarrassing the agency. Use public censure only as a last resort. Such techniques often result in strong reactions against you personally and perhaps against the agency and its clients.
- Inform clients of their rights to appeal decisions and of the availability of client advocates, ombudsmen, or client representatives within the agency.

Learning Exercises: Readings, InfoTrac, and the Web

1. Use your word-processing computer program to enter the important terms and concepts presented in this chapter in alphabetical order. Place a question mark by any terms that you do not clearly understand. Save your document as EX 5-1.

2. Log on to the InfoTrac College Edition Web site. Conduct a keyword search (using either Keyword Search or Advanced Search) to locate the article entitled "Should Licensure Be Required for Faculty Who Teach Direct Practice Courses?" (Thyer & Seidl, 2000). Read the article and prepare a one-to-two-page essay in which you reflect on the implications for social work, social work practice, and social work education. Be sure to describe your own position on the issue. Save your document as EX 5-2.

3. Log on to the InfoTrac College Edition Web site. Conduct a keyword search (using either Keyword Search or Advanced Search) to locate the articles entitled "Understanding Adjudication: Origins, Targets, and Outcomes of Ethics Complaints" (Strom-Gottfried, 2003) and "Ensuring Ethical Practice: An Examination of NASW Code Violations, 1986–97" (Strom-Gottfried, 2000). Read the articles and prepare a one-to-two-page essay in which you reflect on their implications for social work and social work practice. Discuss how you might manage your own risk of potential violations. Save your document as EX 5-3.

4. Go to your university library to locate the article "Organizational Tinkering" by Edward J. Pawlak. The article was published in the journal *Social Work* (Pawlak, 1976). It may take you some time to locate—it was published more than 25 years ago! Read the article and prepare a one-page summary of the various ways social workers might influence the organizations in which they function. Save your document as EX 5-4.

5. Turn to **Reading 6: The Birky Family.** Review the section entitled "Service Plan for the Birky Family." Recall that the social worker for this family was employed by a preschool. As the worker, you have some concern as to whether this intervention plan is within the function of your agency. Prepare a memo to your supervisor to defend this service plan and explain why you think it should be followed. Save your document as EX 5-5.

6. Log on to the World Wide Web and go to the home page of the Association of Social Work Boards (ASWB) at www.aswb.org. Search the Web site to locate licensing information about United States or Canadian jurisdictions. Many states and provinces sponsor Web sites that contain a great deal of pertinent information. For

example, the State of Indiana maintains a Web site at www.in.gov/hpb/boards/mhcb. A visit reveals that the state regulates two levels of social work practice: Licensed Social Worker (LSW) and Licensed Clinical Social Worker (LCSW). The Social Worker, Marriage and Family Therapist and Mental Health Counselor Board is responsible for governing social work licensure and practice in the state. Search for a jurisdiction that interests you—perhaps where you go to school, where you live, or where you hope to work. Locate information about the licensing requirements in that locale. Also, determine how and where you can find the actual statute that establishes legal regulation of social work and any administrative rules or regulations that pertains to professional practice of social work. Summarize that information in a brief one-page report. Save your document as EX 5-6.

7. Prepare a one-page essay in which you identify at least three ways in which professional autonomy may conflict with the bureaucratic organization of most agencies. Save your document as EX 5-7.

8. Review the case description contained in Exhibit 5-4. Assume that you are the social worker with Mrs. Iverson. Prepare a one-page essay in which you address the following questions: How might you have handled the agency's limited definition of services differently in this case? What steps might you take within the agency to try to change agency policy? Are any of the techniques for influencing the agency suggested by Edward Pawlak in "Organizational Tinkering" potentially useful? Why or why not? Save your document as EX 5-8.

9. Turn again to **Reading 11: Four Pennies to My Name: What It's Like on Welfare.** Prepare a one-to-two page essay in which you address the following questions: How could the various agency representatives who came in contact with Mrs. Morgan have been more helpful? How could they have communicated a different climate in the agency, without any change in agency policy or procedures? Suppose Mrs. Morgan decided to organize and lead a group of former welfare clients in an effort to humanize the welfare agency; how might you, as a social worker, assist her in doing so? What are the risks of helping Mrs. Morgan develop an organization of welfare clients if you are employed by one of the public agencies she encountered? What could you do to reduce these risks? Save your document as EX 5-9.

Chapter 6

Ethical Practice

In this chapter, we explore the professional duties of social workers—our ethical obligations. Developed, maintained, and published by professional associations, codes of ethics are formal documents of considerable significance to practitioners, consumers, and the public. Social workers have ethical responsibilities to clients, colleagues, employers, the profession, community, and society. Conflict among these various obligations is inevitable. Therefore, we must develop rational and deliberate means to process ethical issues and resolve ethical dilemmas. These are complex matters requiring both sophisticated knowledge and considerable intellect to analyze multiple facets and dimensions. Some social workers regularly participate in ethics discussions and an increasing number of agencies establish special committees to help practitioners address challenging ethical issues and dilemmas. Indeed, some agencies employ professional ethicists as well as lawyers as consultants to aid staff with especially difficult ethical circumstances.

◆ Values and Ethics

We define values as unprovable assumptions or tenets of faith that guide social work practice. Levy (1973) categorizes values as preferred conceptions of people, preferred outcomes for people, and preferred ways to deal with people. In our discussion of innate human dignity and self-determination, we focused on means to incorporate these values in day-to-day social work practice. Accordingly, it might seem that these values fall into the category of preferred ways to deal with people. These values, however, also incorporate preferred conceptions of people. They suggest that people are capable of making decisions and participating actively in the process, deserve respect for individual differences and diversity, and can choose among alternatives. We have said little about the preferred outcomes for people, except to suggest that they should be consistent with these fundamental value premises. In effect, the goals of service provisions involve values and emerge through negotiation with applicants and clients.

The concept of professional ethics relates to the notion of values. Professional ethics, usually codified, describe the duties of professionals in their relationships with other persons—including clients, other professionals, and the general public. They involve obligations that we accept when we assume the role and status of a professional. There are several different codes of ethics in social work. The various licensing boards, the major social work professional associations, and several specialized social work organizations publish codes that are binding on members. Barker (1988) concludes that these various social work codes are essentially equivalent in nature.

When you join a professional social work association or earn a license, you become subject to the relevant code of ethics. You accept the obligations and duties contained in the code. Although the codes of ethics of the National Association of Social Workers (NASW) (U.S.) and the Canadian Association of Social Workers (CASW) differ in structure and organization, their contents are remarkably similar. Exhibit 6-1 contains an outline of the organizational structures of the two codes. The NASW code "does not specify which values, principles, and standards are most important

EXHIBIT 6-1
Organization of the NASW and CASW Codes of Ethics

NASW Code

Preamble

Purpose of code

- Identifies core values
- Summarizes ethical principles
- Designed to help identify relevant considerations when professional obligations conflict or ethical uncertainties arise
- Provides ethical standards
- Socializes practitioners to mission, values, ethical principles, and ethical standards of the profession
- Articulates standards to assess whether social workers have engaged in unethical conduct

Ethical principles derived from values of the profession

- Social workers help people in need and address social problems
- Social workers challenge social injustice
- Social workers respect the inherent dignity and worth of the person
- Social workers recognize central importance of human relationships
- Social workers behave in a trustworthy manner
- Social workers practice within area of competence; to develop and enhance professional expertise

Ethical standards

- Ethical responsibilities to clients
- Ethical responsibilities to colleagues
- Ethical responsibilities in practice settings
- Ethical responsibilities as professionals
- Ethical responsibilities to the social work profession
- Ethical responsibilities to the broader society

CASW Code

Definitions

- Best interest of client
- Client
- Conduct unbecoming
- Malpractice and negligence
- Practice of social work
- Social worker
- Standard of practice

Preamble

- Philosophy
- Professional practice conflicts
- Nature of this code

Ethical duties and obligations

- Primary professional obligation to client
- Integrity and objectivity
- Competence in the provision of social work
- Limit on professional relationship
- Confidential information
- Outside interests
- Limit on private practice

Ethical responsibilities

- Responsibility to the workplace
- Responsibility to the profession
- Responsibility for social change

and ought to outweigh others in instances when they conflict" (NASW, 1999, Purposes section). The Canadian code, however, establishes seven ethical duties and obligations, and three ethical responsibilities. The ethical duties and obligations are of higher priority than the ethical responsibilities. Violation of the former can subject the worker to disciplinary action.

◆ Duty to Clients

Social work codes consistently emphasize our primary ethical duty to clients. You must place their best interests above most others—including your personal preferences and often your personal values. Your obligation to clients may also sometimes conflict with your responsibilities to your agency. Recall the situation of Mrs. Iverson (Exhibit 5–4 in Chapter 5). Her request for service clearly conflicted with agency policy.

Carrying out your duty to serve the best interest of clients requires that you identify who is the client. This is often a difficult task. Suppose, for example, you serve in a child-protection capacity with a public agency. You routinely work with children at risk of abuse or neglect. However, you also work with family members, schoolteachers, doctors, neighbors, and other people involved with the kids. An agency employs you, the citizens pay you through their tax dollars, a legislature authorizes funding and establishes legal parameters, and judges make decisions and issue rulings that affect you and the children and families you serve. The identity of the client is not at all clear. Is the client the children, the parents, the family, the agency, the judge, the legislature, or the taxpaying citizens?

When you serve couples in a spousal dispute, is the client the couple or one spouse or the other? These are challenging questions that sometimes remain unanswered. However, in each situation, you should clarify where your primary responsibility rests and discuss it with the people involved. Early exploration of these matters makes it easier to address conflicts that may subsequently emerge between your duty to the client and the wishes of other people. Consider the complicated circumstances involved in work with respondents—people required to receive your services. Suppose a judge decides that an offender may attend group work services in lieu of a prison term. You serve as the group leader. Is the offender your client? Might it be the judge or perhaps the agency that employs you? Where does your primary ethical duty lie? In some settings—such as child protection or corrections—social workers have legal power to impose requirements on the service recipients. This creates a context ripe with potential for the abuse of power. Although we do not like to think that social workers ever misuse our authority, we sometimes do. Consequently, we must learn how social workers use and abuse power, and remain alert to the possibility that any of us might knowingly or unknowingly succumb to the temptations associated with our status and authority.

Consider, for example, the experiences of Native peoples in North America for nearly 100 years. In an obvious abuse of power, social workers needlessly consigned thousands of Native children to boarding schools—essentially against the wishes of the children, their families, and their communities. To guard against such abuse, we urge you to consider two principles:

First, use the least intrusive intervention possible, especially when you are relying on legal power to impose a requirement. Exhibit 6-2 contains a brief description of the wrongful removal of children from their home late at night. Presumably because of ignorance and insensitivity, the worker misused power by taking the children into custodial care. The worker could easily have remained in the home with the youngsters or arranged for someone else to supervise them until the parents returned. At that point, a social worker could explore the allegations of abuse. Such a course of action would have been more respectful to the people involved, more ethical, and would have spared both the children and the parents the trauma of their removal from familiar surroundings.

Second, avoid taking precipitous action without first consulting the people involved—whether applicants, respondents, or clients—and carefully considering their views. Exhibit 6-3 contains a few illustrative examples of social workers' and social agencies' misuse of power, extracted from the files of a private child-placement agency. If the social workers involved had taken the time to secure the wishes and views of the respondents before making a decision, these abuses may never have occurred.

Social workers often hold considerable legal power relative to other people. Possession of such authority may tempt us to misuse it for our own conscious or unconscious purposes. In an effort to help you manage the potential for abusing your own power, we suggest that you routinely incorporate the following guidelines:

- Be aware and regularly remind yourself that social workers can and unfortunately sometimes do abuse the power and authority we possess; recognize that you as well as other social workers are susceptible to the temptations associated with power.
- Choose the least intrusive services possible when you must use your power and authority to protect or manage other people, or require them to receive service.
- Obtain and carefully consider respondents' views before you use power to force people into service.

EXHIBIT 6-2
Abuse of Power—Terrified Toddlers Taken from Home

Nackawic, N. B.—A family is angry and shaken after three terrified toddlers were spirited away in the night by a social worker who mistook birthmarks for bruises.

Joshua Martin, 3, Jason, 2, and 10-month-old Lolita were returned home with an apology after social workers confirmed the blue marks on the children's backsides were birthmarks, said their father, Denis Martin.

But that was after 12 hours of anguish that has left the children upset and unable to sleep.

Last Thursday, Martin and his Philippines-born wife, Gloria, hired a 17-year-old baby-sitter to care for the children while the couple went grocery shopping in Fredericton, about 40 kilometers to the south.

"When we got back, the baby-sitter was gone and so were the children," said the 36-year-old father.

"And there was a note from a social worker."

Martin said he tried to persuade authorities of their mistake and even spoke to the social worker who took the children. But he was told nothing could be done until morning.

"We told them most children in the Philippines get that birthmark," said Martin.

"But they didn't buy that. They wouldn't even discuss it."

The Canadian Medical Association's Home Medical Encyclopedia says the birthmarks—called Mongolian blue spots—are commonly found on Asian and black children.

The encyclopedia describes them as blue-black pigmented spots found singly or in groups on the lower back and buttocks at birth and notes they "may be mistaken for a bruise."

Russ King, health and community services minister, defended the actions of his staff.

"We did review the situation and the (Family Services) act was complied with fully," King said Wednesday. "The department also has protocol procedures and these were complied with."

Asked if it's normal procedure to remove children when the parents aren't home and leave a note, he said: "The act was followed."

Replied Denis Martin: "Their procedure may have been followed, but the procedure they had was lousy as far as coming into my house and taking my children when we weren't home. They should wait until the parents come home."

Source: Terrified toddlers taken from home. (1 October 1992). *Winnipeg Free Press*, p. A16. Reprinted with permission by *The Canadian Press*.

◆ Duty of Competent Practice

Both the NASW and CASW codes require that you practice within the parameters of the profession and the limits of your knowledge and skill. Sometimes called the "duty of care," the development and maintenance of competence is an ethical obligation. To meet this duty, you must be an active lifelong learner who keeps up with findings from relevant research studies, regularly reads pertinent professional journals, participates in postgraduate learning opportunities, and routinely secures supervision, training, and consultation from experts in the field. You must also inform prospective clients of both your areas of expertise and those about which you have limited knowledge or skill.

The NASW code clearly describes social workers' responsibility to maintain familiarity with the current professional research literature. The CASW code implicitly does so as well. Many social workers fail to meet this responsibility to keep current with advances in knowledge and to apply it in practice. Surprisingly few social workers regularly read research articles in professional journals (Gerdes, Edmonds, Hoslam, & McCartney, 1996; Holosko & Leslie, 1998; Kirk, Osmalov, & Fischer, 1976; Penka & Kirk, 1991; Richey, Blythe, & Berlin, 1987; Sheldon & Chilvers, 2000). This is especially unfortunate during an era when knowledge related to the effectiveness of programs, policies, services, and practices continues to increase at such a rapid rate and is so readily

---

EXHIBIT 6-3
Abuses of Power in Child Placement

1. Jane, 16 years old, was doing very well in her foster home and her school. She was also active in her community; among other things, she volunteered at a homeless shelter. At a shopping center one day, she had an unexpected encounter with her mother, who pressured her to come home. Jane felt ambivalent about this, and discussed her confusion with the public child welfare caseworker. The worker became angry, in the belief that Jane did not appreciate the good home she was in, and took steps to move her to a more restricted setting: The worker telephoned the foster parent on the day after the meeting and told her to pack Jane's clothes. The worker planned to pick up Jane and her clothes when Jane returned home from school and to move her to a shelter, where she would remain until there was an opening in a group home. Jane had no warning of this pending change.

2. Jose, 7 years old, and Carlos, 9 years old, were placed in a Spanish-speaking home in the city where their mother lived. The mother maintained contact with Carlos and Jose, as well as with the foster mother; her behavior was sometimes inconsistent and disturbing to the youngsters, but the foster mother was able, with the assistance of the private agency social worker, to help the mother become more dependable and clear in her communications to Carlos and Jose. One of the public agency workers who had previously served the boys disliked the mother intensely and saw her as undermining placements; the worker had also had conflicts with the private agency social worker who supervised the foster home around the mother's involvement with the two boys. Further, this worker had two older siblings of Carlos and Jose placed with a non–Spanish-speaking home about 200 miles away. This public agency worker successfully pressured her colleague, who had Carlos and Jose on her caseload, to move the boys from the culturally appropriate placement close to their mother and place them with their older siblings in the English-speaking family 200 miles away.

3. Eric, a 16-year-old who identified himself as gay, had completed a residential treatment program for sexual offenders. Extensive planning had been completed—including a number of preplacement visits—to place Eric with a foster family that was comfortable with his sexual orientation. Arrangements had been completed for him to receive counseling from a therapist in the community; school coordination had been completed, so he was ready to start school. When he had been in the placement about a month and was preparing for the opening of school, the administrator of a public agency that had legal and financial responsibility for Eric became angry that the private agency would not negotiate a lower rate for Eric, overrode the placement decision of his own social worker, and ordered that Eric be immediately removed from the foster home.

Source: Disguised case records of an anonymous social agency.

---

accessible (Cournoyer, 2004; Cournoyer & Powers, 2002; Thyer, 1996, 2000).

Rosen (1994) studied 73 social workers as they met with 151 clients of family service agencies. He investigated the kinds of knowledge social workers used to make decisions about problems and goals and the selection of interventions. Rosen found that the social workers most frequently relied on value-based, normative assertions or assumptions to make decisions. They made some use of theories and policies, but routinely failed to incorporate research-based knowledge in decision making. Furthermore, they used research knowledge even less frequently to decide about interventions than for other decisions.

Generating and Sharing Knowledge

The NASW code includes an ethical obligation to share the knowledge arising from your practice by making presentations at professional conferences and

---

EXHIBIT 6-4
Selected Professional Writing Resources

American Psychological Association. (2001). *Publication manual of the American Psychological Association* (5th ed.). Washington, DC: Author.

Beebe, L. (1993). *Professional writing for the human services.* Washington, DC: National Association of Social Workers.

Coley, S. M., & Scheinberg, C. A. (1990). *Proposal writing.* Newbury Park, CA: Sage.

Dowling, L., & Evanson, J. L. (1990). *Writing articles: A guide to publishing in your profession.* Dubuque, Iowa: Kendall/Hunt.

Hopkins, G. (1998). *The write stuff: A guide to effective writing in social care and related services.* Lyme Regis: Russell House.

Knatterud, M. E. (2002). *First do no harm: Empathy and the writing of medical journal articles.* New York: Routledge.

NASW Press Staff. (2004). *An author's guide to social work journals* (5th ed.). Washington, DC: NASW Press.

Prince, K. (1996). *Boring records? Communication, speech, and writing in social work.* London: Jessica Kingsley.

Szuchman, L. T., & Thomlison, B. (2004). *Writing with style: APA style for social work* (2nd ed.). Belmont, CA: Brooks/Cole.

---

writing for professional journals. This duty may also be inferred from the CASW provision that "a social worker shall promote excellence in the social work profession" (1994, p. 23). Writing is an essential social skill for communication and advocacy and a means to sharpen thinking skills (Walker, Carroll, & Roemer, 1996). Williams and Hopps (1988) encourage practicing social workers to participate more in research and publication as a means to expand relevant professional knowledge. Exhibit 6-4 contains a brief list of resources that might help social workers prepare our work for dissemination and publication.

Take seriously your ethical obligation to present materials at professional conferences and submit materials for publication. "Professing" to and sharing with others represents an integral aspect of professionalism. Of course, preparation of manuscripts for publication differs somewhat from other types of professional writing: Generally written in a more formal style, they usually include a summary review of the literature, presentation of case material or other data, and an analysis or interpretation of the contents or findings.

Abstracts are especially important professional products. They capture the essential elements of manuscripts submitted to professional journals or conferences. Conference program committees typically accept or reject presentation proposals on the basis of the nature and quality of submitted abstracts. Prepa-

ration of conference presentation abstracts and their associated papers often represents a major step toward publication. Exhibit 6-5 contains some information about abstract preparation. We encourage you to develop abstracts for scholarly papers you prepare for your college courses. In addition to providing you some practice opportunity, the exercise should improve the quality of your written work and perhaps even secure you a better grade.

Reacting to Incompetent Practice

In addition to the numerous other ethical obligations, social workers also bear some responsibility for the performance of their colleagues. For example, you must take action when you become aware of colleagues' impaired, incompetent, or unethical professional behavior. Under most circumstances, you should first approach the colleague to discuss his or her incapacitation, incompetence, or unethical behavior and, if applicable, develop a plan for remediation. If this action proves unsuccessful, you should then file a complaint with the relevant professional association—NASW or CASW. If your colleague practices in a jurisdiction that licenses social workers, you may also have a duty to file a complaint with the licensing board. Make sure of the facts before you make an allegation and provide as much documentary evidence as possible. Use descriptive language in

EXHIBIT 6-5
Preparing Abstracts

Abstracts are intended to provide readers with sufficient information to make decisions about whether the publication will be of use in their work or help a conference committee decide whether to invite the writer to prepare a complete paper or deliver a formal presentation. Abstracts should be both short and specific. Try to avoid general terms that do not convey clear meaning. Use as few words as possible, and avoid repetition.

Sample Abstract: Draft Version

There are a number of dimensions that are common to professions. The author examines the concept of a profession through exploration of literature sources and interviews with persons who consider themselves to be professionals. A group of five particular dimensions is noted. The article discusses these five dimensions and arrives at an operational definition of a profession. The author then explores the operability of this definition by applying it to the practice of social work.

Sample Abstract: Revised Version

A definition of the concept "profession" is developed by examining five dimensions—body of knowledge, particular skills and techniques, delivery of service to clients, common culture, and public sanction. Elements of all five dimensions are found in social work, although body of knowledge and skills and techniques may be less apparent than the other dimensions.

---

your report; avoid speculations and inferences. It helps to adopt a highly professional, somewhat formal attitude, and a matter-of-fact style of presentation. Although it is an awkward and personally as well as professionally difficult process, we have a duty to our profession, the clients we collectively serve, and to the society to take reasonable corrective action when we become aware of our colleagues' impaired, unethical, or incompetent practice.

Historically rare, allegations of social work malpractice—in the form of lawsuits, complaints filed with licensing boards or complaints filed with professional associations—are increasing modestly in number each year. At some time during your professional career, you may be the subject, rightly or wrongly, of a formal complaint or lawsuit. As a prudent practitioner, you should conduct yourself to reduce the risk of a successful malpractice action against you (Bullis, 1990; Houston-Vega & Nuehring, 1996; Reamer, 1994, 1995a, 1995b, 1995c). Exhibit 6-6 provides some tips about how you might do this. In general, your case records represent the best evidence of competent, ethical practice and the best defense against frivolous complaints. Therefore, be sure to maintain professional quality notes and records. Keep them up to date and ensure that they are complete, clear, concise, well organized, and written in descriptive and objective language (Gelman & Reamer, 1992).

The case records should support decisions made and actions taken. Record keeping is an essential part of your professional service to clients. It is not "extra," and it is certainly not optional. The American Professional Agency, which handles most social workers' malpractice insurance, recommends that you take the following steps should you be subject to a malpractice suit (Bogie & Coleman, 2002):

1. Report any likely threat of a suit or actual suit to your malpractice insurance agency.
2. Limit your conversations on the potential or actual claim to those persons who have a privileged status such as your attorney.
3. Do not contact or try to work things out with the plaintiff or his or her attorney.
4. Do not alter or destroy your files or records.
5. Recognize that litigation of any type takes time to resolve.
6. Make efforts to alleviate stress you may be experiencing.
7. Remember that litigation is a contemporary symptom of our society and not necessarily a reflection on you.

EXHIBIT 6-6
Tips for Avoiding Successful Malpractice Actions

Carole Mae Olson, social worker and member of the Board of Directors, National Association of Social Workers, offers the following rules for risk management:

1. Don't even think about writing an incorrect diagnosis.
2. Take threats of suicide seriously.
3. Know your areas of skill and competence and refer clients to other practitioners if you are not qualified to provide the service they need.
4. Follow up on referrals; do not abandon the client.
5. Reveal complete information about your practice to the client, including qualifications, business practices, and confidentiality limits.
6. Monitor the fees due; don't let bills mount up.
7. Avoid dual relationships.
8. Obtain the necessary signed releases.
9. Establish a simple written contract with a client.
10. Use consultation often.

Source: Malpractice: How to sidestep the pitfalls. (1997, February) _NASW News_, p. 5.

◆ Duty to Advocate for Social Justice

Social workers bear an ethical obligation to promote social justice and human rights (Benn, 1991; Brown, 1990; Council on Social Work Education [CSWE], 2001; Ezell, 1991, 1993, 1994, 1995; Hardina, 1995; International Federation of Social Workers [IFSW], 2003; Poppendieck, 1992; Specht, 1990; Specht & Courtney, 1994; Stoesz, 1986; Wakefield, 1988a, 1988b). Many social workers engage in social justice efforts through various forms of case and class advocacy. In social work, advocacy involves goal-oriented activity carried out on behalf of clients and aimed at influencing systems that threaten or impede clients' survival, freedom, equal opportunity, or dignity. Case advocacy is partisan intervention on behalf of a particular client in efforts to improve services and resources. Class advocacy differs from case advocacy in that the workers' partisan efforts focus on enhancing services and resources for a particular class or group of people. Both forms of advocacy have a long tradition in social work (Ad Hoc Committee on Advocacy, 1969; Gilbert & Sprecht, 1976; Rothman, 1985; Wood & Middleman, 1991).

The mission of social work has traditionally incorporated both the promotion of social justice and the delivery of direct services. Some authors worry that contemporary trends may threaten this dual mission (McCullagh, 1987; Schriver, 1990; Strom & Gingerich, 1993), and others urge the development of less bureaucratic and more humanistic organizational structures to better address the needs and interests of both clients and workers (Fabricant & Burghardt, 1992; Hoff, 1995). A few scholars wonder if increased opportunities for private practice and employment in for-profit organizations may threaten the profession's social justice mission. Private, profit-making firms have begun to provide health and social welfare and correctional services (Karger & Stoesz, 1994; Schriver, 1990; Specht & Courtney, 1994; Stoesz, 1994; Wakefield, 1988a, 1988b). Social workers now work in such diverse practice arenas as employee assistance firms, health maintenance organizations, home health corporations, and health management companies (Karger & Stoesz, 1994). Although several authors are concerned about the growth of independent private practice, it represents only one aspect of the trend toward privatization of services. Schriver (1990) believes a clinical gentry of social workers who feel little or no commitment to the NASW code of ethics may soon dominate the profession.

These concerns and the discussions about them resemble those of the early 20th century when settlement house reformers accused the charity organization societies of taking the "social" out of social work (Axinn & Levin, 1982; Leiby, 1978; Lubove, 1977; Trattner, 1989). Lee (1929), however, asserted that both cause (social reform) and function (direct practice) are legitimate aspects of the social work mission. We agree wholeheartedly with Lee's perspective and, indeed, routinely observe social workers engaged in both kinds of activities.

Social workers express their commitment to social justice and human rights in various ways—although political action does not seem to represent a major means. Borenzweig (1981) found that the majority of social workers in both private and public practice reported no involvement in political activities. Interestingly, those in private practice were just as likely to be involved in political advocacy as were those in public practice. On the other hand, Wolk (1981) found that social workers were more politically active than the general population. The most politically active social workers were likely to be white, older, of higher educational and economic achievement levels, and involved in macro practice. Ezell (1991) found that administrators were more involved in advocacy than were caseworkers. In an investigation of the significance of role orientation, Reeser (1991, 1992) discovered that neither those social workers holding agency (bureaucratic) nor those reflecting professional-role orientations favored social activism. However, those adopting a client-role orientation did tend to support socially active reforms, especially if they also held a professional orientation. Wagner (1989) observed that idealistic social workers who felt a strong commitment to social justice often believe their views represent a minority position in the social work community.

In a study of social workers' voluntary contributions to community service, Hoff, Huff, and Ord concluded, "social workers in the public and non-profit sectors may be in as much danger of losing their commitment to social justice and reform as those in private practice" (1996, p. 59). However, they also found that 68% of the social workers in private practice or working in for-profit agencies reported doing pro bono work. Interestingly, only 12% of those working in nonprofit and public agencies reported offering voluntary service.

Conflicts Between Class and Case Advocacy

Many social workers attempt to promote social justice through both class and case advocacy. However, class advocacy raises complex issues (Torczyner, 1991). At the extreme macro level of advocacy, you might work and speak for thousands of people. You could not possibly secure the full and informed consent of each individual member of the class. As a result, you risk infringing on the self-determination rights and wants of those for whom you claim to speak. In class advocacy, we again face those familiar questions: Who is the client? Who decides the purpose and objectives of your actions? Who determines what actions to take?

Suppose, for example, that you serve a large number of low-income clients of Southeast Asian heritage. Would you be ethically justified in advocating for the installation of a free food shelf or pantry to provide foods that meet your clients' nutritional needs and preferences? If successful, your advocacy efforts might significantly enhance the lives and welfare of your Asian clients. They would undoubtedly consume and probably enjoy the food, and use their limited resources for other purposes. However, the foodstuffs would probably not appeal to low-income persons from several other cultures. If funds are limited such that the pantry cannot offer a diverse range of cultural foods, other groups might suffer. In advocating for your Southeast Asian clients, you might violate—at least to some degree—your obligation to pursue equal opportunity and access for all human beings. When resources or opportunities are finite, advocacy for individual people or specific groups may sometimes adversely affect the dignity, freedom, and well-being of others. Hoshino provides another illustration of this dilemma in Exhibit 6-7. Because of limited public funds for income maintenance, when certain clients receive more than their entitlement, the amount available for other equally needy persons decreases.

Requests for advocacy may generate value conflicts within the client-social worker partnership. Suppose, for example, a group of refugees asked their social worker to advocate for the repeal of legislation that prohibited the marriage of children under the age of 16. The refugees claim that the law infringes on their right to maintain traditional practices and customs. In their culture, most young women marry early, usually at the age of 12 or 13. The social worker faces a conflict of values. She certainly believes her clients have the right to preserve their cultural heritage and exercise their right to self-determination. However, she does not support the marriage of children at such an early age. The practice conflicts with her personal and cultural views about the proper age of sex and marriage. As a social worker, however, she also believes that early marriage represents a considerable health risk to the young girls especially because of the refugees' strong cultural preference for large families. Many girls become pregnant shortly after marriage but

---

EXHIBIT 6-7
The Means Test: A Dilemma in Social Work Practice

In a session on the means test, I gave the example of a professional social worker in a family service agency counseling a public assistance recipient and learning in the confidential relationship that the client was earning a weekly income from baby-sitting. How should the worker handle the situation? One student said he had been an eligibility worker, and used to tell his clients, in effect, "Don't tell me anything I shouldn't know." Another student fell back on the confidentiality rule: What went on between the worker and the client in the interview room was strictly confidential; otherwise, how could the client relate to the worker? It was pointed out that there is a difference between confidentiality in the professional sense and privileged communication in the legal meaning, which applies to the attorney-client, doctor-patient, priest-confessor, husband-wife, and certain other relationships. But even those are not absolutes; for example, doctors must report suspected child abuse.

Assuming that they know what the general public assistance policies are, including the responsibility of the recipient to report any changes in income that affect eligibility, how should social workers behave? In a strictly applied means test program, any increase in income and assets reduces the amount of the grant or disqualifies the recipient. One student even mentioned that he had lived with a woman who was a recipient. Did his presence and any support he provided the woman and her children constitute income or resources? Would they affect the grant?

As the discussion proceeded, it was clear that the students tended to resort to various subterfuges to get around the effects of the means test: It is the recipient's responsibility to report; it is not a concern of the worker. If the worker becomes aware of income or assets in the course of his or her professional relationship with the client, he or she has a responsibility to inform the client of the requirement to report additional income. What if the client refuses to notify the public assistance agency and so advises the worker? Our county, for example, has a general policy that all staff who learn of unreported income must report that information to the public assistance unit, whether or not the client does. Some students stated that, if they informed the client that they were reporting the income to the public assistance agency, the client would terminate service immediately. Thus, the dilemma: How can the worker maintain the relationship with the client and, at the same time, ensure that the laws are obeyed? What happens when the worker, while encouraging the client to find work and get off assistance, is told by the client that this would mean loss of Medicaid protection for herself and her children, since most jobs that public assistance recipients can obtain do not include health insurance coverage? Some recipients would regard the advice that they should get a job as simply insane, since they also would have the added cost of day care, which few could afford.

Source: Dr. George Hoshino, Professor Emeritus, School of Social Work, University of Minnesota, Minneapolis.

---

before their youthful bodies are developmentally ready for the stresses of pregnancy and childbirth.

Advocacy work can also lead to conflicts between social workers and their agencies. Consider, for example, the situation of several social workers who work in a shelter for undocumented Central American refugees. Although they provide numerous other social services, the agency prohibits the workers from advocacy to reduce violence toward and harassment of

the refugees by neighbors. The agency hopes to maintain a low profile in the community—because of the undocumented refugees' and their own legal vulnerability. Indeed, the social workers themselves are in some legal jeopardy and conflict between the law and their commitment to their clients. If they decide to advocate publicly on behalf of their Central American refugee clients, authorities might prosecute the social workers for felony conspiracy to shield undocumented aliens. They might lose their jobs as well. Under the law, the workers must refrain from affiliation with undocumented residents in ways that aid or abet their continued presence in the country. Should the social workers respect the agency policy and abide by the law or risk their jobs and the possibility of a jail term to advocate for their clients?

Other issues surround decisions related to the transition of case to class advocacy. Suppose, for instance, that a social worker works in a school where majority students routinely assault and harass Native American students en route to and from school. Conversations with other school social workers reveal that similar attacks take place almost daily in other communities as well. Despite her already heavy workload, she begins to consider ways to advocate for the safety and welfare of the Native students. She wonders whether to devote attention to individual cases of victimization or direct her advocacy energies toward larger-scale change. If she focuses only on protecting students enrolled in her school, those from other communities remain at risk. If she engages in class advocacy—which typically requires enormous time and energy—some of her own students may suffer during the interim. Of course, both forms of advocacy extend her stretched personal and professional resources and may interfere with her regular day-to-day school social work with students, their families, and teachers.

These are complex and challenging issues. They illustrate how social work is professional rather than technical or bureaucratic work. The intellectual requirements associated with decision making in circumstances such as these—especially because our decisions affect the lives and welfare of real human beings—are substantial indeed. A key to working through complex ethical issues is to maintain an open-mind and consider the situation from multiple perspectives. Conscientious reflection and analysis may prevent you from thoughtlessly charging ahead in some undirected attempt to correct a wrong or rescue a victim.

We suggest that you begin your efforts to address ethical issues and dilemmas with a firm awareness of fundamental social work values. Although few values are absolutely or universally applicable in all situations, it is useful to remember the principle of client self-determination when reflecting on ethical complexities. Whenever possible, seek as much client input as you can by

- Attempting to understand the full meaning of clients' wants
- Using all the clients' available skills and resources
- Respecting clients' ideas in planning advocacy efforts
- Teaching skills necessary for clients to represent and advocate for themselves
- Increasing clients' access to resource-rich systems

You should take additional measures to promote client self-determination when engaging in class advocacy. When feasible, seek as much class input as you can by

- Working with client representatives
- Keeping the larger population informed of actions taken on their behalf
- Monitoring group sentiment regarding these actions and their consequences

Recall the school social worker whose Native American students were regularly harassed while traveling to and from school. In respecting the principle of client self-determination, the worker should speak to the Native students before proceeding to class advocacy. She should involve as many students, parents, and colleagues as possible to identify the nature and extent of the problem and generate a range of potential solutions. As a school social worker, she should regard her role as advocate in this situation as temporary and transitional. At some point during the process, she will step aside as the clients assume primary responsibility for self-advocacy. At first, however, the school social worker might form a task force of Native American youth to address the problem of victimization and help them develop the knowledge and skills to advocate for themselves. This approach both enhances client self-determination and facilitates the development of their self-advocacy skills.

Deliberate Misdiagnosis

Some social workers resort to deliberate misdiagnosis to meet a client's perceived need for services within the context of funding limitations. Although it occurs in social welfare and educational contexts as well, the phenomenon occurs more commonly in health and especially mental health services. Kirk and Kutchins (1988) conducted a survey of a random sample of professionals whose names appeared in the NASW Register of Clinical Social Workers and obtained the following findings:

- 70% of the respondents thought that the *Diagnostic and Statistical Manual (DSM)* of the American Psychiatric Association did not help them to diagnose marital and family problems
- 64% indicated that they primarily used the *DSM* to secure third-party reimbursement
- 80% acknowledged that third-party requirements often influenced their diagnoses
- 72% revealed that deliberate overdiagnosis occurred frequently or occasionally to help clients qualify for reimbursement from insurance companies
- 86% reported they had deliberately used an individual psychiatric diagnosis from the *DSM* when the primary issue was a family system problem

In effect, deliberate misdiagnosis or overdiagnosis represents a means to defraud a third-party payer—either an insurance company or the taxpayers through governmental sponsored health funding programs—to secure payment for services social workers believe their clients need. The ethical issues concerning diagnosis are analogous to those reflected in the means test dilemma presented in Exhibit 6-7. Most social work clients have small incomes and limited resources. Many social workers are understandably tempted to assign diagnoses or classifications that enable clients to receive services for which they would otherwise be ineligible. Those workers whose individual income is directly related to third-party funding also derive personal financial benefit when assignment of a "covered" rather than a "true," a general rather than a specific, or perhaps a more severe diagnosis results in payments. Social workers in private practice derive income from client fees that are often provided partly or wholly by third parties. Under such circumstances, some professionals may be motivated to misdiagnose by a personal desire to generate income for themselves.

The practice of misdiagnosis raises a number of ethical—as well as legal—questions. Is the system really so inflexible that social workers must cheat to secure services for their clients? Who should be able to determine the types of mental health care that clients need—social workers, clients, or insurance companies or governmental departments? What are the criminal penalties for defrauding managed care or insurance companies, or the government? Could misdiagnoses lead to the provision of unneeded or even harmful services? How many clients suffer lifetime stigma because they receive more severe diagnoses to secure payment? Does the long-term damage of misdiagnosis exceed the short-term gains? Social workers who intentionally misdiagnose take enormous legal and ethical risks—even when they do so to benefit their clients rather than themselves.

Duty to Provide Voluntary Public Service

As a social worker, you have a duty to provide voluntary public service that benefits society as a whole. Regard this as paying your civic rent or public dues. We all benefit from community life and, therefore, bear some responsibility to give something back (Bergel, 1994). You may make voluntary contributions to the community and society in many different ways: pro bono service, class advocacy, political action, or voluntary membership on public boards and commissions. As you continue in your professional education and career, consider how you might make a positive difference in your community.

◆ Dual Relations

Both the CASW and NASW codes provide clear boundaries for and limits to the professional relationship. For example, you must not violate the personal privacy of clients by seeking information beyond that necessary to meet the goals of your work together. The risks associated with dual relationships are also recognized. You may not engage in sexual relationships with clients or former clients. Interestingly, the CASW code specifies that the status of client expires two years following the conclusion of service. This passage leaves room—at least theoretically—for the possibility of ethically acceptable intimate relationships some years after clients and workers complete their work together. The NASW code also indicates that social workers should not provide professional service to any person with whom they have previously had a sexual or social relationship.

Dual relationships, including social relationships, are discouraged. A dual relationship exists when you also know a client as a neighbor, employee or employer, colleague, and so forth. Kagle and Giebelhausen (1994) view dual relationships as boundary violations that endanger clients, assert that both current and posttermination friendships between workers and their clients are harmful, and recommend disciplinary action against workers who engage in dual relationships.

In small rural communities, however, most social workers simply cannot avoid dual relationships (Brownlee & Taylor, 1995; Delaney, Brownlee, Sellick, & Tranter, 1997). They commonly see people as clients at one point and as fellow participants in community activities at another time. They regularly meet informally on the street, in stores and restaurants, at school meetings, and so forth. Under these circumstances, the proper and ethical management of dual relationships becomes the primary concern. We suggest a frank discussion with clients about the likelihood of encountering each other in different contexts. Try to reach an understanding about the best way to handle these inevitable meetings.

Ethical difficulties with dual relationships are more common in some service settings than in others. Social workers involved in community organization, community and neighborhood development, political action, class advocacy, and mobilization of informal systems of social support typically experience few ethical problems with dual or multiple relationships. Indeed, such relations may be essential for their work. Social workers in health, mental health, addictions, and child and family welfare work, however, often struggle with the complex implications of dual relationships.

Bodde and Giddings (1997) suggest that the prohibition against all forms of nonsexual dual relationships may be impossible and impractical in today's practice environment. They encourage social workers to engage in free, open, rational, and scholarly discussion of the ethical implications of dual relationships within the profession. As a way to initiate the conversation, they suggest that social workers should do the following:

- View nonsexual dual relationships from a neutral perspective to facilitate professional discussion of the topic.
- Acknowledge the complexities of the issue and differentiate between appropriate and inappropriate nonsexual dual relations.
- Focus on ways and means to prevent the exploitation, coercion, and manipulation of clients within the context of dual relationships.

◆ Confidentiality

Both the NASW and CASW codes establish social workers' duty to hold material shared by clients in confidence. Many social workers treat confidentiality as a fundamental value of the profession, on the same level as client self-determination and respecting human dignity. We also value clients' right to confidentiality. Indeed, some social work licensing laws provide clients the right to privileged communications—which represents a higher standard than confidentiality alone. United States federal laws and regulations also establish clear guidelines for the protection of clients' confidential information regarding their education, health, mental health, and substance use. The Health Insurance Privacy Protection Act (HIPPA) regulations significantly strengthen both the requirements and the penalties for failure to safeguard clients' confidential information.

However, professionals' ethical obligation to maintain client confidentiality is far from absolute or universal. Rigid adherence to confidentiality obligations may result in unintended negative consequences, and numerous exceptions, qualifications, and caveats accompany the principle (Dickson, 1997). For example, both the CASW and the NASW codes establish duties to report matters such as child maltreatment or abuse of vulnerable people, to warn persons at risk of harm from clients, and to protect clients from self-inflicted harm.

Duties to Report, Warn, and Protect

The duties to report, warn, and protect sometimes lead social workers to breach clients' right to confidentiality. All states and provinces require people to report evidence of child abuse and neglect to governmental agencies, and many mandate reporting of abuse and exploitation of vulnerable adults as well. Social workers and other professionals often bear special legal responsibility in these areas and may receive substantial penalties for failure to report. However, the duty to report often creates ethical dilemmas for social workers: Do we maintain the principle of client confidentiality or violate it to meet our obligation to report or protect someone from harm? What happens when a family is our client but one member of the family shares confidential information that involves a spouse, parent, or child? Indeed, the tensions between confidentiality and other duties become especially acute in service to families (Butz, 1992; Watkins, 1989).

The legal duty to warn emerged largely from court decisions associated with the Tarasoff case (Fulero, 1988; Gelman & Reamer, 1992; Kagle & Kopels, 1994; Kopels & Kagle, 1993; Lamb, Clark, Drumheller, Frizzell, & Surrey, 1989; Recent cases, 2001; Vande-Creek & Knapp, 1993, 2001; Weil & Sanchez, 1983). In that case, Prosenjim Toddar confided to his therapist that he intended to kill a woman when she returned from vacation. The therapist took the matter seriously and contacted both his supervisor and the police, who briefly detained the man but had insufficient grounds to hold him. Toddar subsequently killed the woman, Tatiana Tarasoff. Tatiana's family successfully sued the therapist, arguing that he failed in his duty to warn her of the danger from Toddar. Court decisions in Tarasoff and several similar cases (Schwartz, 1989) provide the legal basis for social workers' duty to warn third parties when clients represent a clear and present danger to them—even if the evidence of risk emerges within the context of a confidential relationship. However, the application of duty to warn is profoundly more complex than the duty to report. You must exercise considerable professional judgment and perhaps consult with supervisors and colleagues to help determine the relative seriousness, probability, and immediacy of the danger. Even when the evidence indicates a real and imminent danger, you must also consider when and how to warn potential victims and whether to inform clients that you are planning to or already have violated their right to confidentiality to warn others of the danger. Many social workers face difficult ethical decisions when serving clients infected by the HIV virus or suffering from AIDS (Reamer, 1988, 1991). Do social workers have a duty to warn past, current, or future partners of HIV-infected clients (Abramson, 1990; Gelman & Reamer, 1992; Gray & Harding, 1988; Lamb et al., 1989; Reamer, 1988, 1991, 1993a, 1993b; Ryan, 1988; Schlossberger & Hecker, 1996; Taylor, Brownlee, & Mauro-Hopkins, 1996)? Exhibit 6-8 contains descriptions of three challenging scenarios.

In such circumstances, we suggest that you recognize the importance of confidentiality regarding clients' medical status, acknowledge the potential for discrimination against infected persons, and appreciate the intricacies of the duty to warn. The legal issues in these matters are not yet fully resolved. Social workers would be wise to study carefully the relevant state, provincial, and national laws in this area. For example, in some locales, health care professionals are bound to report incidences of dangerous infectious diseases to public health officials responsible for prevention or containment of epidemic conditions. Confidentiality is so highly valued, however, that disclosure of clients' information without their consent should occur only after considerable reflection. The risks of nondisclosure must be serious and severe indeed to warrant disclosure of protected information without client permission. Unless the law specifically requires a report—as is the case for indications of child abuse—or the danger to life is imminent, social workers should usually seek legal consultation before taking action that might violate clients' rights to privacy and confidentiality.

Challenging for all social workers, confidentiality is especially difficult for social workers practicing in police settings (Curtis & Lutkus, 1985) and in schools (Berman-Rossi & Rossi, 1990; Garrett, 1994). Findings from a New Jersey survey suggest that social workers are more likely than psychiatrists or psychologists to breach confidentiality in circumstances involving the duty to warn and protect others (Lindenthal, Jordan, Lentz, & Thomas, 1988). Despite the exceptions to the principle, many clients assume that all information that emerges in the context of the client-worker relationship must remain confidential. Therefore, social workers should provide applicants and clients with accurate information about the nature, extent, and limitations of their right to confidentiality. Do so as early as possible in the process. Printed documentation may contribute to improved understanding but cannot serve as a substitute for actual discussion. Later, should you need to breach confidentiality to warn, report, or protect, your clients should not be unduly surprised. Whenever it is possible and safe to do so, discuss with clients why you plan to reveal confidential information, precisely what you intend to disclose, and with whom you plan to share it.

Negative Consequences of Confidentiality

Confidentiality may have negative as well as positive consequences. It is, after all, a form of secrecy—an aspect of some closed systems. As such, adherence to the confidentiality ethic may deprive applicants and clients of responsibility for and the natural consequences of their own words and actions. Warren (see Exhibit 6-9), the client, is both personally capable of and responsible for acknowledging the earlier lies and correcting the record with the court. He is

---

EXHIBIT 6-8
Confidentiality and HIV-Positive Clients

1. Joe is a social worker in an HIV anonymous testing clinic. Susan, a 24-year-old married woman, tested HIV+. Joe encouraged Susan to inform her husband Frank of her positive status, and to abstain from unsafe sex practices until she had discussed her health with him. Two weeks later, Susan returned to see Joe. She was very distraught and confused. Susan told Joe that she had been having unprotected intercourse with her husband so that he would not suspect anything was wrong. She still had not found the courage to tell Frank about her status for fear of losing him. Joe is unclear how to proceed in his role. He could take more time with Susan toward disclosing her HIV+ status to her husband, but he is also concerned about warning Frank so that he can protect himself.

2. Mary is a student social worker placed at a community college. She has been working with an HIV+ student for seven months. Mary has been helping Steve to cope with the pressures of school, health and relationships. Steve is afraid to inform new partners of his HIV+ status for fear of being rejected. Recently, Mary has discovered that Steve's new partner of three weeks is a male friend of hers. To her knowledge, the friend is not aware of Steve's HIV+ status. Mary wonders if Steve would inform his partner of his positive status if the couple were to engage in sex. Mary feels obligated to work with Steve toward disclosure, but is inclined to inform her friend about Steve's status. She is also considering removing herself from a position of conflict of interest.

3. Barb is an addiction counselor in a drug/alcohol treatment center. She has been working with Michelle for three months. Michelle is an HIV+ recovering injection-drug user. Barb has recently learned that Michelle is using again. Barb has also received reports of Michelle prostituting herself to raise drug money. Further, she has been sharing her needles with other users. Barb realizes that relapses happen and wants to work with Michelle toward recovery. Barb also feels a responsibility to report Michelle's behavior to the proper authorities. However, Barb wonders if it should be up to Michelle's sexual and needle-sharing partners to protect themselves responsibly.

Source: Taylor, S., Brownlee, K., & Mauro-Hopkins, K. (1996). Confidentiality versus the duty to protect: An ethical dilemma with HIV/AIDS clients. *The Social Worker/Le travailleur social, 64*(4), 9–17. Copyright © 1996 Canadian Association of Social Workers, pp. 9-10.

---

also personally responsible for the consequences should his misrepresentations lead to perjury charges or more severe penalties. Might we diminish his dignity and his potential for growth by keeping his secret? Could Warren actually accrue more long-term benefits from disclosure than from secrecy? Might nondisclosure indirectly reinforce the practice of deceit, deception, and misrepresentation as a reasonable way to cope with life's challenges?

The client-and-worker partnership constitutes a system. Under conditions of strict confidentiality and secrecy, the system becomes closed. Earlier, we explored some dangers of closed systems. The rigid boundaries associated with secrecy may deprive the system of information, feedback, resources, and opportunities for growth and change through open-

exchange with other systems. Application of the confidentiality principle may sometimes even prevent use of larger support systems and social networks.

Imagine a situation where an incoming applicant says, "I would like to tell you something, but I want you to keep it secret." You could say, "Certainly, anything you say to me is confidential." If you do so, however, you run the risk of learning something that involves a danger to someone's life and almost immediately breaking your promise to meet your duty to report, warn, or protect. You might say, "No, I can't accept those terms. You better not tell me anything more." Alternately, you might reply, "I cannot promise absolute confidentiality at this point. I am obligated to try my best to protect human life. If you share information that leads me to believe someone's

---

EXHIBIT 6-9
Does Warren Have Confidentiality?

Warren Duffy, a 15-year-old six footer, was charged with armed robbery. In a juvenile court hearing Warren denied this charge. He claimed complete innocence and suggested that this might be a case of mistaken identity. He was remanded to Youth House while the charge was investigated. Orlando Corrado was assigned to be his social worker. While Mr. Corrado was evaluating his background, Warren admitted that he committed the crime with which he was charged. Corrado suggested that it might be best if Warren himself informed the judge of this. Warren refused to do so and added that what he had told the social worker was said in strictest confidence.

_____

Source: Loewenberg, F., & Dolgoff, R. (1988). *Ethical issues for social work practice* (3rd ed.). Itasca, IL: F. E. Peacock, p. 57.

---

life is in danger, I would be obligated to take action to save that person—even in it means breaking your confidentiality. You should understand that before you decide what to share with me."

We urge you to value the principle of confidentiality and familiarize yourself with relevant legal and ethical obligations. However, please become equally familiar with the exceptions that sometimes apply and the limitations and potential negative consequences implicit in excessive or inappropriate secrecy. Finally, be sure to provide clients accurate information about the status of their right to confidentiality. They should know early in the process that you might have to break confidentiality under certain circumstances. Indeed, there many situations where the client-and-worker together may jointly decide to share confidential information as an important part of their work toward problem resolution and goal attainment.

◆ Ethical Decision Making

Social workers routinely consider and incorporate ethical principles in most aspects of their daily practice. As a professional, you must adhere to a wide range of ethical and legal obligations under sometimes extraordinarily complex circumstances. To maintain your ethical integrity, you must be thoroughly familiar with the fundamental social work values and the specific ethics of your professional code (Reamer, 1998, 1999, 2002). You should also understand the legal duties that apply generally to helping professionals as well as the laws governing the practice of social work in your locale. When dealing with the lives and welfare of human beings, ignorance of legal and ethical obligations is no excuse.

Knowledge of the values, principles, and duties should enable you to identify ethical issues and recognize which obligations apply in particular practice situations. Sometimes all the applicable responsibilities align in a complementary fashion so that you may simply fulfill your duties in a relatively straightforward way. Quite frequently, however, the obligations are incompatible and contradictory. In other words, to meet one duty you must necessarily violate another. How are we to decide which to respect and which to ignore? When two or more ethical obligations compete or conflict, which takes precedence? Which is more important (Proctor, Morrow-Howell, & Lott, 1993)? Although the NASW and CASW codes of ethics do an excellent job describing our ethical responsibilities, they provide little direction for resolving ethical conflicts. Therefore, we must look elsewhere for guidance.

Resolving Ethical Dilemmas

A number of scholars encourage social workers to follow a sequence of logical steps in making ethical decisions (Congress, 2000; Levy, 1993; Loewenberg, Dolgoff, & Harrington, 2000; Mattison, 2000; Reamer, 1999; Reamer & Conrad, 1995; Rhodes, 1986). Congress, for example, introduces the ETHIC model of ethical decision making that contains five steps:

   E Examine relevant personal, societal, agency, client, and professional values.

T Think about what ethical standard of the NASW code of ethics applies, as well as relevant laws and case decisions.

H Hypothesize about possible consequences of different decisions.

I Identify who will benefit and who will be harmed in view of social work's commitment to the most vulnerable.

C Consult with supervisor and colleagues about the most ethical choice. (Congress, 2000, p. 10)

Levy (1993) believes that social work practice inevitably involves conflict and identifies six tasks to complete as you struggle with your conflicting duties:

1. Identifying ethical principles in a situation.
2. Establishing priorities among the principles.
3. Assessing the potential risks and consequences of a course of action.
4. Identifying compelling conditions that could supersede normal application of ethical principles.
5. Enumerating provisions and precautions necessary to cope with a course of action.
6. Evaluating decisions in the context of ethical and professional responsibility.

Reamer suggests a seven-step process for ethical problem solving:

1. Identify the ethical issues, including the social work values and duties that conflict.
2. Identify the individuals, groups, and organizations . . . likely to be affected by the ethical decision.
3. Tentatively identify all possible courses of action and the participants involved in each, along with possible benefits and risks for each.
4. Thoroughly examine the reasons in favor of and opposed to each possible course of action, considering relevant: ethical theories, principles, and guidelines; codes of ethics and legal principles; social work practice theory and principles; personal values (including religious, cultural, and ethnic values and political ideology), particularly those that conflict with one's own.
5. Consult with colleagues and appropriate experts (such as agency staff, supervisors, agency administrators, attorneys, ethics scholars).
6. Make the decision and document the decision-making process.
7. Monitor, evaluate, and document the decision. (Reamer, 2000, p. 361)

Several social work authorities suggest that we organize our ethical obligations into a hierarchy of values or principles. Then, when conflicts occur, we may assign greater weight to the more highly ranked obligations (Loewenberg & Dolgoff, 1988, 1992, 1996; Loewenberg et al., 2000; Reamer, 1993, 1994, 1999, 2002; Reamer & Conrad, 1995). Exhibit 6-10 contains an illustrative example of one such hierarchy of ethical principles.

Sorting out your ethical duties to individual clients, families, colleagues, your agency, and society is a complex task. You will need to give careful thought to ethical decision making; we hope that you will have regular conversations about this matter with your professional colleagues and your supervisor. You might encourage your agency administrators to conduct an ethics audit, as proposed by Reamer (2000).

Distinguishing Ethical from Practice Issues

In some circumstances, social workers confuse practice issues and ethical dilemmas. Challenging circumstances do not always involve ethical conflicts. Frequently, the difficulties we confront are actually practice issues—or the result of failures to follow basic principles and processes of traditional, good social work practice. Re-read the situation described in Exhibit 6-9. Although we have limited information, we wonder about the social worker's approach to practice. For instance, we cannot find any indication that the worker discussed the purpose for the meeting, her role as the social worker, or the guidelines that governed the meeting. She apparently failed to describe Warren's rights in the process or to discuss the nature and limits of confidentiality. The question, "who is the client?" remained unstated and unexplored. It appears obvious that the juvenile court judge is the de facto client, but Warren may have easily concluded that he was a client. However, Warren was clearly a respondent rather than a client. He did not agree to work with the social worker and indeed did not consent to receive services. The judge ordered him to Youth House—which, in turn, assigned him a social worker. The description seems to illustrate numerous practice errors rather than an ethical dilemma. The worker found herself in a personal and perhaps a moral dilemma when Warren demanded that she keep confidential the information he shared.

Exhibit 6-11 contains a description of another practice situation that could be confused with an ethical

---

EXHIBIT 6-10
A Hierarchy of Principles to Guide the Resolution of Ethical Dilemmas

1. Rules against basic harms to the necessary preconditions of action (such as life, health, food, shelter, mental equilibrium) take precedence over rules against harms such as lying or revealing confidential information or threats to additive goods such as recreation, education, and wealth.
2. An individual's right to basic well-being (the necessary preconditions of action) takes precedence over another individual's right to freedom.
3. An individual's right to freedom takes precedence over his or her own right to basic well-being.
4. The obligation to obey laws, rules, and regulations to which one has voluntarily and freely consented ordinarily overrides one's right to engage voluntarily and freely in a manner which conflicts with these laws, rules, and regulation.
5. Individuals' rights to well-being may override laws, rules, regulations, and arrangements of voluntary associations in cases of conflict.
6. The obligation to prevent basic harms such as starvation and to promote public goods such as housing, education, and public assistance overrides the right to retain one's property.

Source: Reamer, F. G. (1993). *Ethical dilemmas in social services* (2nd ed.). New York: Columbia University Press, pp. 60-65.

EXHIBIT 6-11
Debbie's Pregnant

Debbie Roberts, a 12-year-old sixth grader, is 10 weeks pregnant. She has been a good student. Her teacher reported that she never has had any trouble with her. Until now she has not been known to the school social worker. She was sent to the worker only because she refused to talk to the school nurse about her condition. In her conversation with Debbie, the social worker learned that Debbie did not want to have an abortion, but wanted the social worker to help her make arrangements so that she could carry to full term. She stressed that she did not want her parents to know that she was pregnant.

Source: Loewenberg, F., & Dolgoff, R. (1988). *Ethical issues for social work practice* (3rd ed.). Itasca, IL: F. E. Peacock, p. 30.

---

dilemma. Based on the limited information, we cannot see how this represents an ethical conflict. In our view, good practice dictates that the worker joins with Debbie as prospect or respondent to plan how to discuss the matter with her parents. We cannot find any evidence to suggest that Debbie's parents represent a danger to her safety or that her father or another family member impregnated her, which might lead us to take action to ensure her protection from her family. We do not see anything in the description that suggests Debbie was a victim of rape or child sexual abuse. We would certainly explore those possibilities to ensure that Debbie is safe. Based on the description, however, the major safety issues appear to involve the 12-year-old girl herself and the pregnancy. We do not find evidence that she has received medical care or advice. Everything suggests that she is currently at greatest risk because of the crisis she faces, the stress that generates, and the effects of pregnancy on a 12-year-old female body. These appear to be the major areas of risk. Competent social workers know, understand, and appreciate how people respond to crises. We should be sensitive to others' stress reactions, understand the nature of pre-teens' thought processes, appreciate the risks of pregnancy to 12-year-olds, and recognize the expected and normal tensions between early adolescents and their families. A social worker should apply these basic elements of professional knowledge to this practice situation in a timely fashion because the girl and her parents need to proceed quickly to assess the situation and develop plans. The social worker should facilitate that process rather than obsessing how to maintain inappropriate secrecy from the girl's parents.

Several factors contribute to the tendency to portray poor quality practice as an ethical dilemma. First, social workers may be confused about who is the client. For instance, Warren (Exhibit 6-9) is clearly a respondent, and Debbie (Exhibit 6-11) is probably a prospect and possibly a respondent. Neither is a client. In both situations, another party asked the social worker to intervene. The judge or court is the de facto client in the former situation, and Debbie's parents are in the latter. Good practice requires us to share this fact with prospective clients and then proceed according to basic principles and knowledge. We cannot find evidence that this occurred in either example.

Second, some social workers may misunderstand the nature of confidentiality and—based on the misunderstanding—may distort its practice implications. We cannot possibly guarantee that all information shared can or should remain secret. Therefore, voluntary applicants, respondents, prospects, and clients should receive accurate information about their respective rights to and limits of confidentiality. Clients have greater confidentiality rights than do respondents and prospects, but there are numerous exceptions even for clients.

Third, some social workers believe they cannot and should not share their professional knowledge and expertise or offer suggestions and guidance. Nothing could be further from the truth! A genuinely collaborative partnership requires input from the worker as well from as the applicant or client. It cannot be a one-way street. As professionals, we are or should be equipped with a sophisticated knowledge base and expertise in facilitating the problem-solving process. We must draw on and share our professional knowledge with people in our care. Unreflective acceptance of and compliance with applicants' initial requests without drawing on practice knowledge not only constitutes poor practice, it reflects unprofessional practice. Suppose you were to explore the situation further with Debbie, the pregnant 12-year-old. She tells you that about three months earlier, she began to have consensual sex with her 13-year-old boyfriend. She

became pregnant almost immediately. She says her parents are loving and supportive; however, she knows her pregnancy will hurt them terribly. She expects that they will feel extraordinarily guilty and responsible. Debbie says, she loves her boyfriend and wants to have his child. She remains adamant that her pregnancy remain a secret. Under these circumstances, we cannot see how a social worker could or should comply with her request for secrecy. Competent practice requires that you first inform Debbie that you cannot and will not keep the secret, that Debbie's health and safety are at risk, and that you hope she will join you in talking with her parents, but that if she does not wish to participate, you will tell them anyway. If Debbie believes that her parents, other family members, her boyfriend, or anyone else might become violent or abusive toward her because of the information, you should offer to ensure her safety by making protective service arrangements, if necessary. You might also identify a medical doctor with expertise in and sensitivity about pre-teen and early teen pregnancies. Such information might prove useful as you continue to explore the situation with Debbie, her parents, or both parties together.

◆ Chapter Summary

In this chapter, we introduced the idea of professional ethics as a set of obligations that we voluntarily accept when we assume the role of social worker. These duties are published in formal codes of ethics and reflected in licensing laws. Social workers should obtain a copy of the relevant codes and keep them handy for ready reference as you confront practice and ethical issues in your day-to-day service.

Your primary ethical duty is to your clients. You have an obligation to be competent in your professional practice. You must possess a basic level of knowledge and expertise and continue to learn actively throughout your professional career. You should find means to discover and apply emerging knowledge from research studies relevant to your practice areas. You should also contribute to the knowledge base of the profession—perhaps by participating in small research studies or program and practice evaluation projects and presenting them to colleagues, possibly at conferences or as articles in journals. In addition, you must take reasonable steps to ensure the competence of other social workers and take action to protect the public from impaired, incompetent, and unethical practitioners.

As social workers, we are concerned with people and society. Therefore, we have a special obligation to promote social justice and human rights. Your work toward these ends may take many forms, including case and class advocacy. In advocating for others, however, recognize the potential conflicts that may emerge between your duty to individual clients and your duties to society as a whole.

Dual relationships may increase clients' vulnerability to coercion, manipulation, and exploitation. Therefore, social workers should avoid them whenever possible. If you work in small communities or in close-knit cultures and neighborhoods, however, complete avoidance is impossible. Under such circumstances, you have a special obligation to explore the issue with applicants and clients and incorporate the reality of the dual-relationship in your collaborative work together. In practice settings where our roles and functions involve advocacy, social or political action, and community and neighborhood development, dual relationships usually complement rather than complicate our professional practice. Clients are usually most vulnerable when dual relationships occur within the context of health and mental health, certain child and family welfare, correctional, and some educational services.

Social workers are also obligated to maintain client confidentiality. This ethical and legal principle receives considerable attention in professional codes of ethics. However, we must recognize the conditions, exceptions, qualifications, and ramifications associated with application of the ethic of confidentiality. We serve many people who are not—or at least are not yet—clients. As such, their confidentiality rights are seriously limited. The duty of confidentiality often conflicts with other obligations, such as the duties to report, warn, and protect when human lives are at risk. Furthermore, you should appreciate that confidentiality is not a universal or absolute good. Confidentiality can represent a form of secrecy commonly associated with closed systems. In some situations, secrecy may actually undermine the work of traditional cultures and informal social support networks that could otherwise provide resources and support for problem solving.

Social workers sometimes confuse practice issues and ethical dilemmas. Adopting basic social work principles of good practice prevents or mitigates the emergence of ethical conflicts and dilemmas. As a social worker, however, you have multiple ethical duties to a wide range of constituents: clients, colleagues, your agency, the profession, and society. These numerous responsibilities sometimes conflict with each other so that you cannot simultaneously meet some without violating others. Under such circumstances, you must decide which obligations should take precedence over others through what is, in effect, a problem-solving process. As such, you may often collaborate with applicants and clients in exploring ethical issues and involve your colleagues and supervisors as well. Place the topic of ethics and ethical decision making on your professional agenda. Encourage discussion in school and the agency, form a book or journal club, and establish an ethics committee to promote knowledge and expertise in ethics. As professionals, we must adopt rational, reflective, and deliberate processes of ethical decision making and recognize their real and potential impact upon the people we serve.

 Learning Exercises: Readings, InfoTrac, and the Web

1. Use your word-processing computer program to enter the important terms and concepts presented in this chapter in alphabetical order. Place a question mark by any terms that you do not clearly understand. Save your document as EX 6-1.

2. Obtain copies of the following codes of ethics: (1) The *Code of Ethics* of the National Association of Social Workers, (2) The *Code of Ethics* of the Canadian Association of Social Workers, and (3) the most recent draft or approved version of the *Ethics of Social Work: Statement of Principles* of the International Federation of Social Workers. You may access copies of the NASW code through the World Wide Web at www.socialworkers.org/pubs/code/code.asp and the IFSW Code at www.ifsw.org. Information about how to obtain a copy of the CASW Code is available at www.casw-acts.ca. Carefully read these documents and reflect on the areas of similarity and difference. Prepare a one-page essay to capture your thoughtful observations and reflective reactions. Save your document as EX 6-2.

EXHIBIT 6-12
Dual Relationships and Confidentiality

You are a child protection social worker. Recently you apprehended two young children against their father's wishes. On more than one occasion he threatened harm to you and your family, to the police and the Family Court judge. After the court session, the police officer involved said that "the man was under stress, probably didn't mean what he said, and nothing could be done unless a criminal act occurred."

Later that week you obtain quotes to have your kitchen floor repaired, sign a contract with a local firm, and pay a deposit. The work crew arrives and quite unexpectedly the young man whose children you recently apprehended is in the crew to work in your house. You have to go to a very important meeting that morning and are just leaving as the workers arrive. Your baby-sitter will be at home with your two young children. Given the constraints of professional ethics and confidentiality, how would you handle this situation?

———————
Source: Brownlee, K., & Taylor, S. (1995). CASW Code of Ethics and non-sexual relationships: The need for clarification. *The Social Worker/Le Travailleur Social, 63*(3), 136.

---

3. Log on to the InfoTrac College Edition Web site. Conduct a keyword search (using either Keyword Search or Advanced Search) to locate and read the articles entitled "Confidentiality after Tarasoff" (Kagle & Kopels, 1994), "Health Care Providers' Duty to Warn" (Regan, Alderson, & Regan, 2002), and "Protecting the Confidentiality of the Therapeutic Relationship: *Jaffee v. Redmond*" (Lens, 2000). Prepare a two-page essay in which you discuss your reflections about the implications of the article for confidentiality and the duty to warn in social work practice. Save your document as EX 6-3.

4. Log on to the InfoTrac College Edition Web site. Conduct a keyword search (using either Keyword Search or Advanced Search) to locate and read the article entitled "Boundary Issues in Social Work: Managing Dual Relationships" (Reamer, 2003). Prepare a one-page essay in which you discuss the implications of the article for your approach to social work practice. Save your document as EX 6-4.

5. Turn to **Reading 26: Leonard Timms.** Review the case study by Bob Bennett and reflect on the value and ethical issues facing a social worker providing services to Leonard Timms and his family. Prepare a one-page essay to explore your observations and reactions. Save your document as EX 6-5.

6. Turn to **Reading 27: The Omar Family.** Review the case study by Khadija Khaja and reflect on the value and ethical issues facing a social worker providing services to the Omar family. Prepare a one-page essay to explore your observations and reactions. Save your document as EX 6-6.

7. Read the vignette described in Exhibit 6-12. Carefully consider the practice and ethical implications, and then reflect on the question contained in the last sentence. Refer to the NASW or CASW codes of ethics to identify any passages that offer guidance. Prepare a one-page response to the question about what you would do. Be sure to incorporate references to relevant sections of the ethical code. Save your document as EX 6-7.

8. In the section on advocacy as an ethical duty, we identified a conflict of values between a social worker and a group of refugees who wanted assistance in changing legislation so as to permit girls younger than 18 to marry. Prepare a one-page essay in which you address the following questions: Do these clients have a right to advocacy? How does the social worker reconcile her own beliefs about early marriage and pregnancy with her loyalty and responsibility to her clients? If the social worker refuses to advocate for her clients, should she also refuse any assistance that might aid their legal action, which she believes is potentially harmful to many young women? It's

likely that, even if the legislation is not changed, the practice of early marriage will continue. Does that information influence your views? Save your document as EX 6-8.

9. In Exhibit 6-7, George Hoshino describes an ethical dilemma posed by the means test. Prepare a one-page essay in which you describe how you would resolve this dilemma. Explain your reasoning. What provisions of either the CASW or NASW codes guide your decision making? Save your document as EX 6-9.

10. Review the instances of abuse of power in Exhibit 6-3. Put yourself in the position of a social worker at the private agency serving the young people who have been subjected to these abuses by workers at the public agency. Prepare a one-page essay in which you address the following questions: What action would be appropriate for you to take? Is your decision influenced by the fact that your salary and other expenses of the private agency depend on the fees paid by the public agency for your services? Save your document as EX 6-10.

11. Prepare a one-page essay in which you discuss how you might manage any conflicting legal and ethical duties when working with the HIV-positive clients described in Exhibit 6-8. Save your document as EX 6-11.

Chapter 7

Relationship in
Social Work Practice

In this chapter, we explore the helping relationship that develops between worker and client. Earlier, you learned how living systems of all kinds must interact with other systems in the world around them to survive and grow. You also considered the importance of partnership and collaboration between client-and-worker for their problem-solving work together. Our approach incorporates both of these dimensions and emphasizes the central role of relationship to all forms and aspects of social work practice.

◆ Development of Relationship

Toward a Definition

Early theorists recognized the importance of the relationship between worker and client in their conceptions of social work practice (Pumphrey, 1959, 1991; Pumphrey & Pumphrey, 1961; Reynolds, 1963; Richmond, 1899, 1917). Biestek considers the relationship between worker and client as "the channel of the entire casework process; through it flow the skills in intervention, study, diagnosis and treatment" (1957, p. 4). He defines the casework relationship as "the dynamic interactions of attitudes and emotions between the caseworker and the client, with the purpose of helping clients achieve better adjustments between themselves and their environments" (1957, p. 12).

Perlman distinguishes the relationship from other aspects of the helping process and asserts that the hallmark of a professional relationship is "its conscious purposiveness growing out of the knowledge of what must go into achieving its goal" (1957, p. 64). She con-

siders authority an important aspect of the client-worker relationship and states, "all growth-producing relationships . . . contain elements of acceptance and expectation, support and stimulation" (p. 68). Perlman suggests that social workers help people address problems through (1) the provision of resources, (2) the problem-solving work, and (3) the therapeutic or working relationship. She defines the latter as the "climate and the bond" between workers and clients that "acts to sustain and free clients to work on their problems" (1971, p. 58). In distinguishing the professional working relationship from others, she suggests that the client-social worker relationship involves authority and is purposeful, time-limited, controlled, and fundamentally *for* the client (1979, pp. 48–77).

Coyle defines relationship within the context of social group work as "a discernible process by which people are connected to each other, and around which the group takes its shape and form" (1948, p. 91). Konopka (1963) describes the elements of the client-worker relationship in work with small groups as purpose, warmth, and understanding. Keith-Lucas defines the client-worker relationship as "the medium which is offered to people in trouble and through which they are given the opportunity to make choices, both about taking help and the use they will make of it" (1972, p. 47). He suggests that effective helping relationships reflect (1) mutuality, (2) reality, (3) feeling, (4) knowledge, (5) concern for the other, (6) purpose, (7) a "here and now" quality, (8) opportunity to consider or experience something new, and (9) a lack of personal or moral judgment. Pincus and Minahan view relationship as an affective bond between workers and other systems with which they are engaged and may involve an "atmosphere of collaboration, bargaining or conflict" (1973, p. 73). They identify the common elements of all social work relationships as (1) purpose, (2) commitment to the needs of the client system, and (3) objectivity and self-awareness by the worker.

Some authors refer to the helping relationship as a working or therapeutic alliance (Bachelor, 1995; Bachelor & Horvath, 1999; Barnard & Kuehl, 1995; Horowitz, 1991; Kokotovic & Tracey, 1990; Marziali, 1984; Marziali & Alexander, 1991) and most recognize its critical importance to service effectiveness. Coady (1993), however, wonders whether social workers' historical emphasis on the helping relationship has moderated in recent years. He encourages us to reestablish our focus on and attention to relationship factors. Horowitz (1991) believes that the helping relationship, although difficult to measure, represents the heart of long-term psychiatric rehabilitation. From a review of the psychotherapy research, Marziali and Alexander (1991) conclude that a productive relationship includes (1) a clear agreement between the professional and client regarding the goals of therapy, (2) understanding and consensus about the tasks to accomplish those goals, and (3) an interpersonal bond between the professional helper and client.

Descriptions of the professional relationship have largely focused on one-to-one or one-to-group relationships. As Pincus and Minahan (1973) point out, however, social workers engage in many other types of relationships. In working on behalf of their clients, workers may interact with property managers, teachers, employers, legislators, bankers, assorted bureaucrats, religious leaders, boards of directors, and agency executives, among many others. In some circumstances, social workers who engage in administration, policy, planning, and organization activities may regard the system they engage as their client. However, social workers' responsibilities within these relationships differ somewhat from those in the direct services. Direct service workers often help people resolve personal problems or provide growth experiences within the context of a close, professionally intimate relationship. Workers seeking to change the professional policies and programs of another (target) system may develop formal or informal relationships of considerable importance, but they rarely reflect the closeness or intimacy that results from work on highly personal issues. Nonetheless, all social work relationships involve elements of power and authority and all

reflect professional purposes and values such as self-determination, dignity, and human rights. Social workers who demonstrate an ability to develop and maintain effective professional relationships tend to exhibit self-awareness, self-discipline, personal integrity, and a capacity for free, genuine, and congruent use of self. Sensitivity to and empathy for others' problems, experience, situation, and aspirations contribute immeasurably to the development of productive working relationships. Indeed, the qualities of authenticity or genuineness, empathy, and respect or positive regard represent the core relationship conditions in counseling and psychotherapy (Asay & Lambert, 1999; Carkhuff, 1984; Lambert, 1982, 1983; Rogers, 1957, 1975; Truax & Mitchell, 1971; Truax & Carkhuff, 1967; Weinberger, 1993, 1995, 2003). Of course, social workers regularly fulfill other roles in addition to counseling and therapy. Nonetheless, with modest adaptations to accommodate different purposes, roles, and contexts, these qualities should serve you well in virtually all professional circumstances (see Exhibit 7-1).

Through focus group research with public child welfare clients and workers in Missouri, Drake found considerable agreement between clients and workers regarding the worker competencies required for child welfare: "The most frequently mentioned competencies, both by social workers and clients, involved the worker's ability to foster an appropriate relationship with the client" (1994, p. 595). The competencies identified by workers and clients are summarized in Exhibit 7-2.

Purpose

All relationships are purposeful. Even friendships and family relations reflect a purpose—although they often remain unstated. In social work relationships, however, the purpose and goals are conscious, usually explicit, and support the mission and value system of the profession. Earlier we suggested that social workers help people address and resolve social problems. In our efforts to serve, social workers routinely attend to people individually or collectively and to social systems with which they interact through relationships that consistently reflect the purpose and values of the profession. Our working relationships, then, are clearly and consistently purposeful, reflecting both the general mission and values of the profession (normative purpose) and the specific goals as determined

EXHIBIT 7-1
Variables Affecting How the Social Work Relationship Is Used

1. The purpose of the relationship.
2. The position of the practitioner in the change agent system.
3. The role of the worker and the role of the other in interaction.
4. The role and position of the other in the larger social systems of which both worker and other are a part (the community, church, social groups).
5. The goal toward which the social worker is directing change activities.
6. The goal toward which the other systems are directing their activities. Note that, in the relationship between client system and change agent system, it is assumed that the goal is to develop a relationship that allows for working together. However, relationships between the change agent and individuals in the target system or the action system may involve relationships of cooperation, negotiation, or conflict.
7. The form of communication. In the direct helping relationship between an individual client and the practitioner as the change agent, communication is usually verbal. However, in the relationship between practitioners and their own change agent system, or between the change agent and action or target systems, many other forms of communication—such as letters and reports—may be used. It is important that the practitioner be skilled in the use of all methods of communication.
8. The skill of the worker in decision making and the use of appropriate intervention methods.
9. The type of system with which the worker interacts. Practitioners may work toward change in a client system that consists of an individual, group, organization, or community; or may work with individuals or groups representing nonclient systems.

Source: Adapted from Fraley, Y. L. (1969). A role model for practice. *Social Service Review, 43*(2), 145–154.

collaboratively by the partners involved in the problem-solving process (operational purpose).

Numerous factors (refer again to Exhibit 7-1) influence the development of each working relationship and result in an operational purpose that is, theoretically, unique. A social worker who lobbies state government for an increase in special education funding, one who helps to organize migrant farm workers, and another who counsels a middle-aged woman affected by alcohol addiction reflect distinctly different operational purposes in their working relationships. Although all three have common normative purposes, their distinct operational purposes determine the kind, nature, context, intensity, duration, and characteristics of their respective working relationships. In addition, each social work relationship has an *immediate purpose* that varies from time to time—sometimes within a single meeting or interview. For example, Mrs. Jones and a social worker may agree to work together toward the goal of enhancing and strengthening her

marriage. The operational purpose of the client-worker relationship is to pursue and attain that goal. However, when Mrs. Jones and the worker meet today, she wants to explore a specific incident that occurred with her spouse earlier in the morning. She especially wants help in understanding her reaction and developing an alternate way to respond when her husband makes a critical comment. This represents an immediate purpose for the relationship during today's meeting. Although the immediate purpose usually relates to and supports progress toward the operational purpose, occasionally the client-and-worker decide to use the relationship for one that does not directly contribute. Nonetheless, both operational and individual purposes always fall within and reflect the normative purposes of the profession. For instance, an outreach worker for a community center may engage members of a street gang in discussions about using the center for its meetings. An immediate purpose may be to provide the group with a safe meeting

EXHIBIT 7-2
Relationship Competencies for Child Welfare Practice

Competencies Identified by Child Welfare Clients

Workers must show clients basic human respect.

Workers must not be pushy or rude.

Workers must ask permission of clients to look in rooms or examine contents of cupboards.

Workers must be willing to spend time with clients.

Workers must be consistently honest with clients.

Workers must be aware of the dehumanizing context of child welfare work.

Workers must be able to effectively communicate with clients.

Workers must speak at the client's level.

Workers must use direct language.

Workers must be able to really listen to what the client says.

Workers should be able to use small talk as an aid to establishing effective communication.

Workers must be able to develop a comfortable relationship with clients.

Workers should have the ability to develop relationships that are warm, not simply nonhostile.

Workers must use an empathic presentation.

Workers must not prejudge families on the basis of reports from other workers or the nature of the initial report.

Workers must have the ability to remain calm and to defuse client anger, especially in initial meetings.

Competencies Identified by Child Welfare Workers

Workers must be able to express an appropriate attitude.

Workers must avoid presenting a judgmental or blaming demeanor.

Workers must not impose their own values on clients.

Workers must be able to see the situation from the client's point of view.

Workers must project an attitude that is assertive but not aggressive.

Workers must be able to effectively communicate with clients.

Workers must use clear, unambiguous language.

Workers must relate to clients at the client's level.

Workers must use body language and eye contact appropriately.

Workers must avoid the use of threatening terms.

Workers must use good listening skills.

Workers must not prejudge situations.

Workers must understand situations as they see them and should be open to input from clients.

Workers must not base their assessments on prior occurrences as documented in the case files.

Workers must clearly acknowledge the client's right to participate in the process.

The client's role must be explicitly delineated.

The worker must allow the client to define the situation as he or she sees it.

Workers must have an awareness of the impact of child protective services (CPS) intervention.

Workers must understand the intrusive nature of CPS intervention.

Workers must have skill in dealing with and diffusing anxiety.

Source: Drake, B. (1994). Relationship competencies in child welfare services. *Social Work, 39*(5), 595–602. Copyright © 1994, National Association of Social Workers, Inc., pp. 597, 599.

place. Helping the gang develop less destructive activities might be an operational purpose. Both purposes are consistent with the mission of the social work profession.

Although the normative purposes of any social work relationship usually remain implicit, the operational and immediate purposes should be explicitly articulated so that clients and workers may provide informed consent and use them to guide their problem-solving activities. Indeed, the outcomes of your work may depend on your ability to formulate clearly the immediate purposes of professional contacts with others and to describe those purposes in an easily understandable fashion. Mayer and Timms (1970) conclude that clients' lack of understanding of the purposes and values of the professional may obstruct the development of a helping relationship. The unique purpose of the helping relationship should certainly emerge through mutual exploration with the client, but social workers must ensure that purpose is established, articulated, clearly understood, and mutually agreed upon.

Be especially sure to clarify the operational purpose of the relationship when your primary role is not that of helping. For instance, when a court, community, or other institution expects you to control or modify the behavior of a family that endangers others and causes community distress, you must state clearly and honestly the purpose that brought you to the family's door. The statement of purpose often leads to a discussion of the authority that permits you to make the visit. You must explain carefully and clearly to the family why you are there, your responsibilities to agency or institution or community, and the nature, extent, and limits of your authority.

Purpose affects two other related issues: (1) your role as helper and (2) confidentiality. When you enter a situation on an uninvited basis, do not pretend that your only motivation is to help the family. Families readily recognize this as untrue or, at least, not the complete truth. They realize you have other responsibilities. If they perceive you as dishonest right from the beginning, they may well conclude that dishonesty is quite acceptable—particularly in this relationship. In effect, you encourage the family to be dishonest in turn. Be honest and straightforward. You must communicate that you are entering the situation primarily for other than helping purposes. You may add that you want to and intend to help within the context of your major purpose. Also realize that the idea of "help" can mean very different things to different people—especially for respondents. Many families have had bad experiences with various helping professionals and may regard the word with considerable apprehension and skepticism.

Suppose, for instance, that you want to serve an offender in the criminal justice system. You introduce yourself to him and offer to help. The offender has every reason to be suspicious of your motives. Do you actually want to help him pursue his wants and goals? Could you really be interested in modifying the offender's behavior so that—from our perspective—he can lead a better life? Clarification of purpose becomes essential in such circumstances and affects the nature, scope, and extent of confidentiality. You must address the parameters of confidentiality very early in the relationship. Respondents in particular should understand what information may be shared outside your relationship, how it will be shared, with whom it will be shared, and whether they will be informed when it is shared. This is another aspect of honesty and integrity. Most people respond favorably to this approach.

Directness in communications conveys respect for others' right to express themselves based on an accurate understanding of the confidentiality limits, removes any misconceptions and uncertainty about what happens to information, and often leads to more open and natural interaction. Do not proclaim trustworthiness in a "You can trust me" fashion or push respondents to trust you. Instead, invite them to decide about your trustworthiness for themselves as you work together.

When you initially explain your purpose to respondents, you may receive reactions of anger, distrust, and rejection. Prepare yourself for such possibilities and develop skills to manage your own personal feelings and responses. If you can maintain a sense of calm and reasonableness, you may demonstrate to angry respondents that possibly, just possibly, they may be able to trust you.

Working Together

Relationship does not emerge spontaneously out of some mysterious interpersonal chemistry. Rather, it develops out of purposive interaction—out of the business with which worker and applicant concern themselves. Applicants meet with social workers to resolve problems. They are not looking for a special kind of relationship. The relationship develops from communication about and work toward solution to the problems of concern. A pleasant, friendly, or personally satisfying relationship with applicants and clients is not an essential requirement for problem resolution. Sometimes the solutions emerge within a context of reactivity, anger, ambivalence, or fear. Keith-Lucas writes, "the attempt to keep the relationship on a pleasant level is the greatest source of ineffectual helping" (1972, p. 18). Your goal is not to establish a positive satisfying relationship, it is to help people resolve problems and achieve agreed-upon goals. However, a productive helping relationship often results from your demonstration of respect, understanding, concern, and willingness to take active steps to help. Because the working relationship develops from purposeful activity, it grows and changes over time. The relationship changes as the operational or immediate purposes change, and when its purposes are fulfilled, it ends. In addition to purpose, the nature of the relationships that develops between applicants or clients and workers is influenced by the following:

- Setting in which you and the applicant come together
- Time limits of the process
- Individuals or groups involved and the interests that they represent
- Capacities, motivations, opportunities, expectations, and purposes of those involved
- Problem that brings you and the applicant together and the goals each has for its resolution
- Qualities you bring, including your knowledge and skills
- Actual behaviors of the parties to the relationship in transactions over time

Helping relationships may be used in various ways. The relationship itself may help sustain clients as they work toward problem resolution. The honesty, dignity, respect, understanding, and predictability of the relationship with the worker often serves as a form of coping mechanism to support people during times of stress, change, confusion, transition, or crises. The way the social worker behaves in the relationship and the nature of the relationship itself constitute a kind of model or example that people may consider for application in their own lives. On occasions, the working relationship itself may become the subject of analysis—when it relates to the agreed-upon purpose, problems, and goals. The way applicants or clients use

the relationship may approximate the way they relate to others. Awareness of such patterns within the context of the working relationship may enhance understanding and motivate change in other meaningful interactions. Applicants often identify relational styles and relationship problems as issues for work. They are especially common in work with families and groups. Of course, the relationship between worker and client and those that emerge in work with families, groups, organizations, and communities represent an ideal context for practicing new ways of relating to other people.

As human beings, social workers and clients bring irrational elements (bits and pieces from past relationships and experiences that do not fit the present), nonrational elements (emotion, feeling, affect), and rational elements (intellectual and cognitive qualities) to the relationship. Goldstein (1973) suggests that these come from:

- Past experiences that have influenced the ability of the individuals to relate to others
- The here-and-now physical and emotional states of those involved
- The here-and-now thoughts or mental images of each individual about self, the process, and the problem
- Each person's anxiety about the present situation
- Each person's expectations of how to behave and what should come out of the interaction
- Each person's perception of the others involved
- The values and ideals shared by the participants in the process
- The influence of other social and environmental factors

As a helping professional who participates in the exploration of troubling concerns, meaningful aspirations, and often the private thoughts and feelings of vulnerable people, you carry special responsibility for self-awareness and self-discipline. These qualities help us to manage the unhelpful or harmful tendencies that could otherwise emerge within the context of the helping process.

◆ Elements of Relationship

Findings from research studies completed during the last half century suggest that professional helpers who reflect certain qualities tend to be more helpful to clients than are those helpers who fail to demonstrate these qualities (Asay & Lambert, 1999; Carkhuff, 1984; Lambert, 1982, 1983; Rogers, 1957, 1975; Truax & Mitchell, 1971; Truax & Carkhuff, 1967; Weinberger, 1993, 1995, 2003). The qualities workers manifest in the client-worker relationship represent an important element for change. Certainly, there are other important factors as well (Asay & Lambert, 1999; Lambert, 1982, 1992, 2003; Lambert & Bergin, 1994; Lambert & Cattani-Thompson, 1996; Lambert, Christensen, & De-Julio, 1983; Ogles, Lambert, & Masters, 1996). Perhaps the single most important category of change factors involves the strengths, "assets, resources, challenges, and limitations within the client and client's external situation. These extra-therapeutic factors—what clients bring with them to the relationship with the helping professional" (Cournoyer, 2005, p. 7) appear more significant than any other. The expectancy, optimism, enthusiasm, and hopefulness that the work will be successful also play an important role, as does the selection and implementation of the intervention model, strategy, or approach (Lambert, 1992). However, the characteristics "of the helping professional and the resulting relationship between the client and helper . . . may have the second most significant effect upon client outcomes (Lambert, 1992)" (Cournoyer, 2005, p. 7). The first involves the attributes, assets, strengths, and resources that people and their social systems bring to the working relationship. The relationship factors account for approximately the same proportion of effectiveness as do expectancy factors and the intervention approach combined (Lambert, 1992).

The relative effect of relationship factors on outcomes is clearly associated with the qualities exhibited by helping professionals. Authorities and researchers tend to include qualities such as acceptance, affirmation, caring, empathy, encouragement, nonpossessive warmth, and sincerity among the characteristics of effective helpers (Hubble, Duncan, & Miller, 1999). These attributes may be classified into seven groups: (1) concern for the other, (2) commitment and obligation, (3) acceptance, (4) expectation, (5) empathy, (6) authority and power, and (7) genuineness and congruence.

Concern

Concern involves a sincere caring for and about others, and a genuine interest in their experiences. Of course, as a professional helper, you must demonstrate that you care in a way that others recognize, understand, and appreciate as sincere. Concern that

appears false or superficial, or that goes unnoticed, does not contribute to the relationship. Expression of your concern usually emerges through an unconditional affirmation of others' lives and needs. You truly want them to be all they can be and do all they want to do, for their sakes. Unconditional affirmation may be especially difficult when you enter a situation at the request of a court, a community, or an agency. The people you encounter may be angry and hostile, and may behave or dress in ways that you find offensive. In such circumstances, you must be aware of your negative feelings and judgments so that you can manage your reactions and express concern rather than defensiveness, annoyance, or disgust.

Caring for others is not the same as affection or approval. You do not have to like everyone and you certainly do not need to approve of everyone's life choices or behavior. If you believed that you must like all your clients, you might be inclined to deny or repress your feelings, rather than to manage or perhaps change them. Concern is a sense of so caring for the other that personal feelings of liking or disliking become irrelevant (Keith-Lucas, 1972).

We almost always become truly personally and somewhat emotionally involved with people in our efforts to help. In so doing, however, we risk becoming over-involved, perhaps out of a desire to see people we care about do or feel better. When you take on others' problems as your own and focus on what you want rather than what they want, you have probably entered into the realm of over-involvement.

Concern for another in the helping relationship means that we offer our skills, our knowledge, ourselves, and our caring for clients to use (or not use, if they choose) in their movement toward agreed-upon goals. It means that we respond as they need us to (within the limits of purpose, time, and place) rather than as our need to help demands, and we leave them free to fail. Most of us find it easier to take action or do something rather than stand by and wait. On occasion, however, active waiting with others may be the most appropriate expression of concern. Genuine concern means that we are willing to be the "agent of a process rather than the creator of it" (Keith-Lucas, 1972, p. 104). Beware of the temptations to play the role of hero, savior, or winner. Let clients be the victors and the heroes in their own lives.

Concern for others means respecting applicants' and clients' privacy rights. We only seek as much information about others as needed to help resolve the issues of concern. More is not always better and greater depth is not always beneficial. The degree or extent to which clients reveal intimate or personal material does not accurately reflect the quality of helping relationships. Successful resolution of problems and accomplishment of goals represents the best measure. Sharing private information with a helping person is never easy, and it may give rise to feelings of shame or violation. Seeking knowledge of others for the sake of personal curiosity makes them an object rather than the subject of our efforts.

We communicate concern and respect by being on time for interviews and conferences. Home visits represent an especially powerful message of concern because they show you are willing to leave your territory to go to theirs. We communicate concern by ensuring that interview or conference rooms are as private, comfortable, and attractive as possible, by dressing in a culturally appropriate manner, and by concerned listening. Concerned listening is not passive. It involves careful listening and observing in an effort to receive messages accurately and to understand the meaning in others' communication. Careful listening involves attending physically, expressing concern nonverbally, and demonstrating that you have heard and understood what another has expressed. Reflections or restatements of their messages and relevant questions based on their expressions rather than on your thoughts tend to reflect concern for others.

Concern means that you view the people you serve as uniquely valuable human beings and relate to them with reverence. It involves transcending your own needs and views in a genuine intention to invest yourself in service to the interests and purposes of others.

Commitment and Obligation

You cannot enter into working relationships with others without assuming several professional responsibilities. Applicants and workers enter into an agreement of understanding—a kind of contract—that involves commitments and obligations so that the purposes of the relationship may be achieved. The terms of this agreement should be explicit so that the partners truly understand their mutual and respective responsibilities. When applicants commit to the conditions and purposes of the relationship, they typically begin to feel a sense of coherence and direction. They and we know where we are heading. As we noted earlier, applicants become clients at the point

of commitment. Less uncertain and more secure, they can turn their attention and energy to the tasks at hand rather than to self-protection.

People seeking help tend to be well aware of the need to accept commitments and obligations as part of the problem-solving process. Indeed, fear and anxiety about those commitments and obligations often keep them from asking for help. Applicants may be concerned that they will be unable to do what is needed, they will not succeed, or they will embarrass themselves in the process. When we clarify clients' general obligations, they frequently feel an enormous sense of relief and a noticeable increase in motivation and optimism. In general, we expect clients to explore the problems of concern in an open and honest fashion, to describe their situations and their ways of coping, to participate in the process of defining goals, and to work with us toward their achievement. We expect them to meet with us at the times and in the places we agree on, and to try their best to do what they say they will in working toward goal attainment. However, we do not expect them to do more than they can do, be who they are not, or succeed in each and every step they take.

Social workers, of course, also assume commitments and obligations in the working relationship. We have explored several of these already. For the relationship, however, social workers make a commitment to

- Be present at prearranged times and places and be available in certain emergency situations
- Keep the focus of the work on the agreed-upon problems and goals
- Offer a relationship that is conducive to sharing, growth, and change

Most applicants and clients question our commitment as social workers if we violate these fundamental relationship obligations without adequate reason and explanation. They may well conclude that we do not value or respect them, that we do not care, or perhaps that we are impaired or incompetent. Our commitment cannot be qualified by our idiosyncratic personal needs, feelings, beliefs, or preferences. When we voluntarily take on the role of professional social worker and freely enter into a working relationship with another, we assume these fundamental obligations. We cannot neglect or abandon them because a working relationship is unpleasant or unsatisfying. Professional commitment cannot be intermittent, inconsistent, or unreliable. Rather, it is expressed through determination, consistency, constancy, dependability, integrity, and mature acceptance of responsibility and accountability for our own behavior.

You can hardly expect respondents and prospects to feel an immediate sense of obligation during the early portion of the relationship. After all, you are entering their lives at the request of a third party. They have not sought and may not want your help. Nonetheless, you remain responsible for fulfilling your commitments even if or when they do not agree to any of their own. Many people are quite suspicious of professionals in general and especially those whose services they have not requested. Under such conditions, they may well monitor your integrity to determine the degree to which you can be trusted. Moreover, they may decide to test you in some way. Although you may feel personally uncomfortable under such scrutiny and suspicion, realize that many respondents and prospects are simply reacting to their previous experience with other professionals. We must earn trust, not expect it. Keep every promise you make—no matter how small. Any lapse of consistency and reliability is likely to reinforce previous suspicions.

Acceptance

Within the context of the social work relationship, acceptance involves the communication of a nonjudgmental attitude and an ability to differentiate between people and their actions. In addition, however, acceptance means to regard as true, to believe in, to receive what the other offers. If we accept others, we receive what they offer of themselves, with respect for their capacity and worth, with belief in their capacity to grow and mature, and with an understanding that their behaviors are attempts at survival and coping. Such acceptance involves the qualities of knowing, trusting, and individualizing. *Knowing* relates to your efforts to take in and understand other people's reality, experience, values, needs, and purposes and to acquire some idea of where other people come from—some idea of their life and frame of reference. In other words, to come to *know* them. *Trusting* involves the faith, hope, and optimistic attitudes you hold in people's capacity for self-determination and self-direction, growth, change, and development (Drake, 1994). *Individualizing* refers to the capacity to see the person as a unique human being, with distinctive feelings, thoughts, and experiences that differ from all others, including us. We must resist tendencies to make assumptions about others based on generalized notions about a group, class, culture, or race. Although it is certainly important to understand the manner in which various biological, social, economic, and cultural factors influence client-worker transactions, we use such sociological information as possibilities or perhaps hypotheses. Individuals always vary from the general, average, or modal characteristics of the group.

Acceptance does not mean that we must always agree with others' views, values, decisions, and actions. Nor does it suggest that others' behavior should be excused because of the challenging circumstances in which they live. Rather, acceptance involves genuine suspension of control over and evaluative judgment of others. Knowing, trusting, and individualizing are dimensions of acceptance. Although it is extraordinarily difficult to do, we try our best to sincerely let people be who they are, have the views they hold, and do what they do.

Expectation

Expectations of the future affect present well-being and behavior, which, in turn, influence future well-being and behavior. Expectations represent a potent force. We must account for them in all our transactions with other humans.

As a social worker in relationship with others, consider the following:

- Your own expectations about the applicants' and clients' ability or willingness to change
- Your expectations of your own ability to contribute to the change process
- Applicants' and clients' expectations of you and your behavior
- Applicants' and clients' expectations about the outcomes of the helping process

Your expectations that others can grow, change, learn, and solve problems enhance your effectiveness. Ripple, Alexander, and Polemis (1964) found that clients tend to continue with social workers who are encouraged and optimistic about outcomes. Bland or neutral attitudes are associated with discontinuation. The most effective social workers truly believe and anticipate that their clients will resolve problems and achieve goals. Our optimism can make a difference.

Applicants' and clients' expectations about the roles and functions of social workers and their expectations about the future also influence outcomes. Consider this example:

> My husband's gambling was driving me around the bend and I thought maybe the Welfare could help me do something about it. But all the lady wanted to do was talk—what was he like when he gambled, did we quarrel and silly things like that. She was trying to help and it made me feel good knowing someone cared. But you can't solve a problem by *talking* about it. Something's got to be done! (Mayer & Timms, 1970, p. 1)

Although the woman in this vignette believed the social worker genuinely cared about her, she discontinued contact after a few sessions. Evidently, she could not see that anything could change through conversation alone. Rightly or wrongly, progress rarely occurs until or unless clients' expectations about what should happen in their transactions with social workers matches what actually does happen. Fortunately, clients and workers can adjust and negotiate those expectations. As their respective notions about the way they should work together become more congruent, the effectiveness of the work itself tends to improve (Marziali & Alexander, 1991).

Applicants' expectations about outcomes affect actual outcomes. You have probably heard about the placebo effect or the self-fulfilling prophecy. A substantial percentage of ill people who believe they have received an effective medicine improve even though they actually took an inert substance. Faith and optimism are powerful factors indeed. Findings from a study of mental health clients revealed a positive correlation between their scores on a hopefulness scale and the degree of progress following six weeks of service (Gottschalk, 1973). In another study, patients' scores on an acceptance scale before open heart surgery were found to be considerably better predictors of postoperative recovery than were the actual severity of their diseases (Frank, 1978).

The nature of expectations become especially critical when you intervene at the request of third parties. Individuals, families, groups, organizations, or communities may well view your arrival as yet another problem, rather than as part of the solution. If you enter with a pessimistic attitude, you may prove them right. When both parties have negative expectations, they tend to infect and reinforce each other so that an impasse results. Take responsibility for changing your

own views. That should help. You can also encourage respondents to reconsider their expectations as well. You may, for instance, carefully explore respondents' expectations and attempt to discuss and perhaps correct inaccurate perceptions. Manage any defensiveness you might feel and avoid proclamations that you are different from or better than other social workers they may have encountered. Trying to enhance your status by diminishing others tends to backfire. Demonstrate your competence rather than talking about it. Try to understand how the respondents' reached their views about helping professionals. If they seem angry, recognize that it is directed toward others and results from expectations they have based on their previous experience.

You may also encourage clients to give you a chance to earn their trust by asking them to compare their expectations with your actual behavior. If you keep your promises and treat respondents with dignity and respect, over time they may entertain the possibility that you are indeed different from what they expected (see Exhibit 7-3).

Empathy

Empathy involves the capacity to enter into the feelings and experiences of another—to know what the other feels and experiences—without losing oneself in the process (Rogers, 1966, 1975). Social workers use the understanding that results from empathy to appreciate others' world and reality as part of the helping process (Keith-Lucas, 1972). Rather than pity or sympathy, empathy involves feeling the experiences of another as if they were our own but without claiming them as such (see Exhibit 7-4).

> Derived from the Greek word *empatheia*, empathy may be described as a process of joining in the feelings of another, of feeling how and what another person experiences. Empathy is a process of *feeling with* another person. It is an understanding and appreciation of the thoughts, feelings, experiences, and circumstances of another human being. (Cournoyer, 2005)

Empathy requires an ability to feel an emotion deeply and yet to remain separate enough from it to be able to use the resulting knowledge. These may seem paradoxical: feel deeply with another but keep some part of yourself separate. However, that is fundamental to empathy. Clients value workers who can genuinely understand them and with whom they feel a strong personal bond (Drake, 1994; Marziali &

EXHIBIT 7-3
Challenging a Respondent's Inaccurate Perception of the Worker

In an interview, a social worker encouraged a young Native American prisoner to enroll in some of the prison's vocational training groups. The man refused. The following conversation ensued.

Client: There's no need to try and do anything with you people. You are all alike.

Worker: What do you mean, we are all alike?

Client: You all lie to us. You never do anything that you promise to do. We can't trust you.

Worker: When have I lied to you? When have I failed to follow through on a promise?

Client: You haven't, but everybody else around here does.

Worker: But I am not everybody. I am me. If I haven't lied to you or failed you, then I think you should try trusting me until I do. When I do fail, I want you to tell me about it so I can change. But until that time . . .

EXHIBIT 7-4
Pity, Sympathy, and Empathy

Consider three reactions to someone who has told us that he strongly dislikes his wife. The sympathetic man would say, "Oh, I know exactly how you feel. I can't bear mine, either." The two of them would comfort each other but nothing would come of it. The pitying man would commiserate but add that he himself was most happily married. Why didn't the other come to dinner sometime and see what married life could be like? This, in most cases, would only increase the frustration of the unhappy husband and help him to put his problem further outside himself, onto his wife or his lack of good fortune. The empathetic person might say something like, "That must be terribly difficult for you. What do you think might possibly help?" And only the empathetic person, of the three, would have said anything that would lead to some change in the situation.

Source: Keith-Lucas, A. (1972). *Giving and taking help*. Chapel Hill: University of North Carolina Press, pp. 80–81.

Alexander, 1991) but who are not overwhelmed by the same feelings and experiences they have. If we could incorporate fully the experience of our clients, we would—in effect—become a mirror image of them, as stuck as they are.

Authority and Power

We explored the topic of authority earlier at some length. You may recall that we identified three sources of social work authority: the client, agency, and profession. Derived from the power granted you by clients and society, you acquire authority to offer and provide certain services and to influence people and situations through the application of your pro-

fessional position, knowledge, and expertise. Within the context of the helping relationship, your authority has an institutional aspect—derived from your position and function within the agency and your status as a professional—and a psychological aspect—derived from applicants and clients who accept you as a source of knowledge, expertise, and guidance. A person in need seeks someone who possesses and reflects the authority to help. Power and authority within the working relationship contribute to rather than detract from the process. Indeed, they are always present in some form or another. Applicants tend to become suspicious about workers who say they lack authority or adopt a pretense of powerlessness. They may wonder why you are unwilling to acknowledge the obvious. Confident assumption of authority engenders a sense of congruence between what the applicants know and what you say and contributes to the feeling of safety and security within the relationship.

When you refer clients elsewhere, when you say, "We will meet once a week on a Monday if that is convenient for you," or when you decide to include another family member in service, you are setting the conditions of the relationship. You are exercising your authority.

Goldstein points out that when one requires from another what "cannot be obtained elsewhere—whether one is seeking the adoption of a child, financial assistance, help with a personal problem, or professional services to assist in a social action enterprise—the relationship cannot be equalized" (1973, p. 83). Because the worker's needs have no relevance to the task, "the seeker cannot reciprocate or supply the provider with any reward that can restore the balance" (p. 84). Clients tend to view workers as considerably more competent and knowledgeable than themselves.

Questions of power and authority are particularly relevant when we are required to enter a family situation by court order or agency decision. Prior experiences of the misuse of professional authority may underlie the family's negative expectations, lack of trust, and fear of commitment. When we intervene in people's lives at the request of others, we must be prepared to explain very clearly—many times, if necessary—the nature, extent, and means by which we will use our power and authority. Our own feelings about authority may complicate matters. However, social workers must be able to deal comfortably with both our own and others' exercise of authority. We cannot afford psychological "issues with authority." They can too easily interfere with our ability to serve others and effectively fulfill our professional responsibilities. You must be able to accept the legitimate authority of others just as you expect others to accept yours.

Genuineness and Congruence

Genuineness, congruence, or authenticity involves saying what we mean and doing what we say. Honesty, integrity, consistency, openness, and sincerity are elements of genuineness; arrogance, "putting on airs," pretense, and superiority represent its polar opposite. Surprisingly often, clients routinely spot social workers who are slick, deceitful, or phony and just as often recognize those who are real, honest, honorable, and trustworthy. In our efforts to become and remain congruent, genuine, or authentic, we must seek three things:

- Honest knowledge about and acceptance of ourselves
- Clear understanding of our professional roles and functions, and our agency's policies and procedures
- Internalization of our concern for and acceptance of clients, commitment to their welfare, and acknowledgement of and comfort with our authority and the authority of others

Those social workers who are real, genuine, and congruent in helping relationships understand themselves, accept that self-knowledge, and are comfortable with who they are. They can initiate contact with others without having something to prove or protect; understand and accept others' ideas, experience, and emotions; and interact without defensiveness or hubris. However, social workers' expression of authenticity should not be impulsive, reactive, instinctive, or uninhibited. We cannot say whatever comes to mind or share any feelings we might experience. The idea of genuineness in helping is not a *carte blanche* to "let it all hang out." Professionalism requires perspective, personal awareness, discipline, and judgment within the context of a relationship that is purposeful. Reflecting about our thoughts, reactions, and feelings before expressing them does not make us less real or authentic—it enables us to be genuine within our roles and functions as professional social workers. Professionalism and objectivity, however, do not mean coldness, cautiousness, or aloofness. Those attitudes are as insincere and false as unbridled reactivity. An unfeeling, detached, impersonal style of relating and an undisciplined expression of transient notions, reactions, and impulses are equally incompatible with congruence and genuineness in the helping relationship.

Consider the example of a world-class figure skater. Spectators feel the spontaneity and creative force of her performance—it appears instinctive and effortless. However, the apparent naturalness of the performance required years of slow and painful learning—self-discipline, persistence, gradual growth, and change in the use of self. This skater's free and creative movements are the result of training and disciplined practice.

Yet, the skater does not think about or reflect on each movement or gesture. She has so internalized the demands of the task that she can give herself to it entirely and unself-consciously. She can respond freely and spontaneously to what is within herself in the here and now. The skater knows herself and her capacity, and there is a joy in what she does. Similarly, social workers enter their professional relationships with a clear knowledge of what can and cannot be done, a sense of competence, and a belief in what they are doing. Effectively helping others demands no less preparation, work, discipline, and self-knowledge than does virtuoso figure skating.

◆ The Helping Person

Social work practitioners bring about change through their use of self—of who they are and what they have made a part of themselves, including their thoughts, their feelings, their belief systems, and their knowledge. Many people do not have the capacity to help others, in the same way that many people lack the capacity to design computers or to perform surgery. None of these jobs is simply a matter of knowledge. They call for certain kinds of people with certain kinds of talents.

According to Keith-Lucas (1972), people will not be effective helpers if they are

- More interested in knowing about rather than serving people
- Motivated by strong personal needs to control, feel superior to, or be liked by others
- Involved in service to people in need of help for problems they have addressed or solved but have forgotten what it cost them to do so
- Primarily interested in retributive justice, preaching, and moralizing

Effective helpers reflect quite different kinds of qualities and attributes. The truly helpful professional exhibits maturity and courage, creativity, self-awareness, and sensitivity and acceptance of difference.

Maturity and Courage

The most effective helping people are deeply involved in the process of becoming and learning. They find change and growth exciting rather than threatening. They do not exclude themselves from the human condition but view all people, including themselves, as engaged in problem solving. They enjoy being alive despite all the complexities and struggles involved in life and living. Able to manage their levels of anxiety and tension and balance the multiple aspects and dimensions of their lives, they are free to take on new experiences. They are mature human beings who can accept others' control over their own lives.

Maturity requires self-awareness and personal discipline. We explored these aspects of professionalism earlier. They become extraordinarily important aspects of the maturity required to develop productive working relationships within the context of racial, cultural, age, gender, or social class differences. Despite the gradual evolution and development of social tolerance and acceptance of diversity within North American society, it is difficult to imagine that anyone can be truly immune from the influence of racism, sexism, ethnocentrism, ageism, classism, homophobia, lookism, ableism, xenophobia, and other "us versus them" forms of closed-system thinking. Most people—including social workers—maintain thoughts, feelings, reactions, and behaviors associated with various forms of "rankism." Fuller (2002) adopts the term "rankism" to characterize the abuse of power or authority by people of higher rank, "somebodies," toward people of lower rank, "nobodies."

> The feelings of shame, humiliation, indignity, or inferiority felt by a "nobody" when abused, oppressed, enslaved, imprisoned, or exploited or even when addressed with superiority, arrogance, or condescendence by a "somebody" are pretty much the same whether it appears as racism, sexism, ageism, ableism, lookism, heterosexism, or other insidious "isms." When a professor demeans a student, a colonel ridicules a private, an employer humiliates an employee, a Senator ignores a citizen, a social worker belittles a client, or the people of one culture deny the humanity of another, the resulting dehumanization frequently has long-lasting effects. (Cournoyer, 2005, p. 129)

Maturity involves self-awareness of rankest tendencies, the willingness to acknowledge them, the discipline to manage them, and the courage to make amends when they occur despite our best intentions. Rankist patterns of thought, feeling, reaction, and behavior persist partly because they are irrational conditioned responses acquired through socialization and involvement in our society. All of us live and grow in a society with numerous, insidious, pervasive forms of irrational rankism. We all absorb, to a greater or a lesser extent, the irrational attitudes of our society. These attitudes become a part of us. The fact that they are irrational makes them all the more difficult to recognize, understand, manage, and possibly, just possibly, eradicate.

Social work with families, groups, organizations, and communities requires special self-awareness and maturity. Each person in the group may trigger a different response from you. You need to be aware of favoritism, rejection, avoidance, and demands for special attention. In addition, you must monitor power and status problems, sibling rivalries, competitions, and aggressions. You need self-awareness, self-discipline, and other aspects of maturity to maintain your focus and purpose, while weaving the many strands of individual needs and rivalries into a meaningful process. It takes particular skill to remain focused on the needs of others when certain members of a group question or challenge your judgment and authority. Family, group, organization, and community work requires enormous self-discipline based on an understanding of your own needs for status and control, your needs to save "face" and avoid embarrassment, and your patterned reactions to open conflict.

Be conscious of feelings and responses aroused through transactions in your work with clients. In particular, recognize your own dependency needs and feelings about authority and their relation to those of clients. You must be conscious of grandiose, superior, or arrogant attitudes; feelings of omnipotence, "specialness," or entitlement; needs for client affection and approval; and tendencies to assume too much or too little responsibility with your clients.

Problems in the helping relationship may be caused by lack of self-awareness about attitudes toward racial, ethnic, age, status, or gender differences and other aspects of rankism. Davenport and Reims (1978) found that stereotyped reactions to women clients were not correlated with social workers' theoretical perspective but were associated with their personal biased belief systems. We must be aware of our own personal ideologies and assumptions about people who differ from us. It is far too easy to confuse our personal beliefs with professional knowledge.

Gender roles are particularly relevant to social work. For example, how do we feel when a middle-aged woman comes to us repeatedly with tales of spouse abuse and brutality but refuses to leave the situation? Do we recognize the social, economic, and moral constraints that may hold her in place, despite a strong desire to change her situation? Cooper (1978) points out that white people "influenced by a culture rampant with racism and unfamiliar with the intricacies and nuances of the lives of ethnic people may, even with the best of intentions, fail to recognize when social and cultural factors predominate" in their professional attitudes. By contrast, "ethnic therapists are vulnerable to the opposite form of clinical error. Because they are so centrally involved, they may exaggerate the importance or impact of ethnic factors" (p. 78). Cooper (1978) also discusses the unavoidable guilt experienced by white practitioners who are aware of their privileged position in a segregated society and cautions that this guilt may lead them to "unrealistic rescue fantasies and activities—a form of paternalism" (p. 78). When white guilt remains unconscious, it can lead to overcompensation, denial, reaction formation, an intense drive to identify with the oppressed, and a need to offer them special privileges and relaxed standards of behavior that are no more acceptable to their communities than to the general population.

Gitterman and Schaeffer (1972) suggest that institutional racism results in social distance between worker and client. This distance must be bridged if we hope to encourage the development of a genuine partnership characterized by mutual understanding and collaboration. Goodman says,

> The profession of social work cannot afford to sustain practices that would diminish the humanity of any group. It must deny that only blacks can treat blacks, or only whites can treat blacks, or only people of the same culture can understand each other well enough to provide help. Social work must . . . propagate a multiracial set of identities that will continue and extend the search for a common basis in humanity. (1973, p. xiii)

Maturity involves courage as well as self-awareness and personal discipline. The mature social worker accepts the risks that inevitably accompany working relationships: the risks of failing to help; becoming involved in difficult, emotionally charged situations that people do not know how to handle; having your comfortable world and ways of operating upset; being blamed and criticized; being constantly involved in the unpredictable; and sometimes being physically threatened. Mature courage is not based on ignorance or insensitivity, nor is it a search for thrills and excitement. We are fully aware, yet do what must be done.

We need courage to think honestly about ourselves and others and to confront clients with the reality of the problems and circumstances they face. Honest expression, even in efforts to help and support, can often seem threatening and hurtful. Courage involves accepting responsibility for our failures and mistakes as well as for our accomplishments, and sometimes requires a willingness to risk job, status, and perhaps reputation to do the right thing in the right way at the right time in the right place.

Creativity

Creativity involves originality, expressiveness, and imagination. Social workers require creativity because effective practice involves a search for alternative ways to define and resolve problems. Applicants come to us because they are stuck. Their usual ways of defining and solving problems have in this instance become ineffective. We cannot help if we imagine only pedestrian definitions and solutions. Most clients have already considered and attempted them. Indeed, social workers tend to lose much of their credibility by proposing solutions clients have already attempted. Clients must think, "What kind of professional is this—suggesting something that didn't work when we tried it ourselves?" We must contribute something new. Creativity involves openness to all life experiences, diverse perspectives, and emerging knowledge; a gentle skepticism about tradition; and a curiosity about life that remains forever unsatisfied.

Creativity involves a certain degree of nonconformity in thought and action. Social workers cannot simply accept prevailing opinions, fads, or ideologies as truth. Ideological chauvinism hinders our search for new solutions and openness to learning. However, we must distinguish nonconformity from counter conformity—an unthinking, reactive rejection of authority and tradition—which may be motivated by personal insecurity and hostility.

Effective social workers regard most solutions to life problems as tentative and provisional. Intellectual openness and receptivity involve a freedom to reconsider accepted theoretical positions or systems of thought. Creative professionals commit themselves to finding solutions to problems rather than to particular solutions or methods. Despite the heavy investment made to educate themselves, they recognize the dynamic and tentative nature of knowledge.

Maintaining a creative, open-minded perspective represents a real challenge to our maturity because we tend to hold tenaciously to our preferred beliefs and assumptions. It can be quite anxiety provoking to accept complexity and ambiguity. Most people find simplicity and certainty more comforting. Mature creative people tend to enjoy complexity and almost joyfully maintain a sense of openness in the face of contradictory or obscure information.

Sensitivity and Reverence

People tend to enter into relationships with a helping professional with much ambivalence and considerable anxiety. Applicants often find beginnings particularly awkward, uncomfortable, and stressful. Help seeking is complicated by complex feelings about the problems, their views and judgments about themselves as people with problems, and the threat of the unknown in the helping process. Accordingly, social workers must be especially sensitive to people and the situation—particularly during engagement—but throughout the entire problem-solving process as well. Observe even small movements and changes in others, try to avoid stereotyped judgments or generalizations, and accept the reality that people differ in the way they think, feel, react, and behave during times of uncertainty. Be sensitive to others' experience and reactions to differences in gender, sexual orientation, race, age, class, and culture on the professional relationship. Unlike social workers, applicants and clients are not obligated to pursue self-awareness, personal discipline, and maturity in an effort to better serve others. They may react to our differences and diversity. If we are sensitive enough, we may notice such reactions and—when the timing and circumstances are right—address them to ensure that clients receive the best possible service. Cultural norms related to differences are powerful, often irrational, forces embedded deep within people. They seem absolutely right and true—at least to us. Sensitivity to clients' culturally developed beliefs and traditions help social workers recognize, appreciate, and, where consistent with the problems and goals for work, encourage clients to reconsider them.

Such acute sensitivity to the experience of others requires a truly extraordinary degree of respect for and acceptance of each person's fundamental uniqueness. Woodruff (2001) uses the term "reverence" to describe "the capacity for awe in the face of the transcendent" (Moyers & Woodruff, 2003). When applied to social work relationships, reverence "involves an attitude of deep respect or awe and humility in the presence of another. Although reflecting a religious or spiritual connotation, as in reverence toward a higher being, it aptly captures the special attitude social workers manifest as they evolve toward cultural competence and acceptance of others" (Cournoyer, 2005, p. 59). As social workers, we may access this experience of reverence when we become awestruck by another's story—when we lose any sense of self-consciousness or evaluation to accept the person and the narrative fully, with neither reservation nor judgment.

◆ Chapter Summary

In this chapter, we explored the nature and significance of the working relationship as part of the problem-solving process in social work. We reviewed various aspects and dimensions of this important theme, and established that the professional relationship involves a purposeful exchange of thoughts, feelings, and perceptions between worker and client within the context of their problem-solving work. We considered relationship as the medium through which most social work practice occurs. We made the following key points:

- The professional relationship can be thought of as a climate between worker and client that is characterized by open communication of thoughts, perceptions, and feelings.
- The worker bears the primary responsibility for developing conditions under which a constructive relationship can develop.
- Relationship is purposeful. Its purpose is to accomplish goals jointly determined by the applicant and worker, within the scope and function of the agency and the mission of the profession. The nature of the relationship depends on the problems and goals.
- The relationship evolves through clarity of purpose and collaboration as the problem-solving work with applicants and clients progresses.
- There are seven essential elements of a professional relationship: (1) concern, (2) commitment and obligation, (3) acceptance, (4) expectation, (5) empathy, (6) authority and power, and (7) genuineness and congruence.
- Qualities conducive to a professional relationship include maturity and courage, creativity, and sensitivity and reverence.

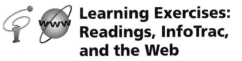

Learning Exercises: Readings, InfoTrac, and the Web

1. Use your word-processing computer program to enter the important terms and concepts presented in this chapter in alphabetical order. Place a question mark by any terms that you do not clearly understand. Save your document as EX 7-1.

2. Log on to the InfoTrac College Edition Web site. Conduct a keyword search (using either Keyword Search or Advanced Search) to locate the article entitled "Client's View of a Successful Helping Relationship" (Ribner & Knei-Paz, 2002). Read the article and prepare a one-page essay in which you reflect on its implications for social work practice. Save your document as EX 7-2.

3. Log on to the InfoTrac College Edition Web site. Conduct a keyword search (using either Keyword Search or Advanced Search) to locate the article entitled "Reconceptualizing Multicultural Counseling: Universal Healing Conditions in a Culturally Specific Context" (Fischer, Jome, & Atkinson, 1998). Read the article and prepare a one-page essay in which you reflect on its implications for social work practice. Save your document as EX 7-3.

4. Turn to **Reading 11: Four Pennies to My Name: What It's Like on Welfare.** Review the essay by Addie Morris and reflect on its implications for topics addressed in this chapter. Consider what responsibilities you might have as a social worker to try to improve the climate that clients experience at your agency. Prepare a one-page essay to explore your observations and reactions. Save your document as EX 7-4.

5. Turn to **Reading 9: Betty Smith.** You reviewed this reading earlier when you addressed the question, "Who is the client?" for a learning exercise at the end of Chapter 3. Examine the reading again. This time, look for ways that the worker established conditions under which a productive working relationship might develop with Ms. Smith—who is, after all, a respondent. Prepare a one-page essay in which you summarize the worker's relationship-building activities. Also, identify any other means that a worker

might use to cultivate a relationship with respondents and prospects. Save your document as EX 7-5.

6. Turn to **Reading 26: Leonard Timms.** Review the case study by Bob Bennett and reflect on the relationship issues facing a social worker providing services to Leonard Timms and his family. Prepare a one-page essay to explore your observations and reactions. Save your document as EX 7-6.

7. Turn to **Reading 27: The Omar Family.** Review the case study by Khadija Khaja and reflect on the relationship issues facing a social worker providing services to the Omar family. Prepare a one-page essay to explore your observations and reactions. Save your document as EX 7-7.

8. Prepare a one-page essay in which you explore the idea that the way professionals dress communicates concern and respect for others. Discuss the implications of this idea for you as a social worker. Save your document as EX 7-8.

9. Prepare a one-page essay in which you describe and discuss the differences between a relationship with a friend and one with a client. Also, discuss the differences in ways each kind of relationship develops. Save your document as EX 7-9.

Chapter 8

Engaging Potential Clients

In this chapter, we discuss engagement, the first phase of the problem-solving process. Engagement begins as we establish communication with an applicant, respondent, or prospect and ends when we have a preliminary agreement to work together. The preliminary agreement also includes tentative goals or objectives. Engagement is a process, not a set amount of time. It may take only a few minutes for some applicants, a full interview for others, or perhaps several weeks or months for respondents and prospects. Engagement may require one meeting or several and often occurs in quite different ways with different people. The processes tend to vary with applicants, respondents, and prospects. Engagement requires sophisticated communication skills. Accordingly, we start this chapter with a discussion of communication and its barriers.

◆ Communication

Basic Principles

Engagement requires communication, an interactional process that involves sending, receiving, and feedback (Exhibit 8-1). *Encoding* involves transforming a message into symbolic form in preparation for transmission. *Transmitting* is the process of sending the encoded message. *Receiving* and *decoding* are the processes of receiving and interpreting the stimuli that were sent. *Noise* consists of extraneous influences that may have distorted reception of the message transmitted. *Checking-out* or *feedback* provides a way of overcoming problems created by noise, by inadequate

encoding or decoding, or by faulty transmission or reception. The essential checking-out phase is fundamentally equivalent to the feedback processes we described earlier in our discussion of systems theory.

The feedback process operates something like this: Suppose that A sends a message to B, which B receives. How does B know that the message received is the message A intended to send? Perhaps B's receptors were faulty; perhaps A's transmitter was faulty; or perhaps there was noise or interference between A and B that distorted the message. B checks out the message by telling A what has been received (Brown, 1973).

Feedback occurs in various ways within the communication process. Social workers often paraphrase, reflect, or summarize applicants' words to let them know that we are listening carefully, trying to understand. We frequently ask others to correct us if we misunderstand their intended meaning. This process is often referred to as "active listening." Through your restatements, you serve as a mirror to reflect others' messages. You might restate what you have heard in similar but fewer words, submit a tentative summary of the applicant's discussion, or connect things that the applicant has left unconnected. At times, you may go somewhat beyond what has been said or offer a tentative interpretation: "Is it possible that what you are telling me means . . . ?" Be careful about proclamations of understanding, such as "I see . . ." or "I understand . . ." Also, attempts to reassure or offer support in ways that subtly convey evaluation may generate discomfort in some people and perhaps suggest a powerful differential between you and them. For example, "That is hard . . ." or "Most people would be upset . . ." or "That's good . . ." implies a

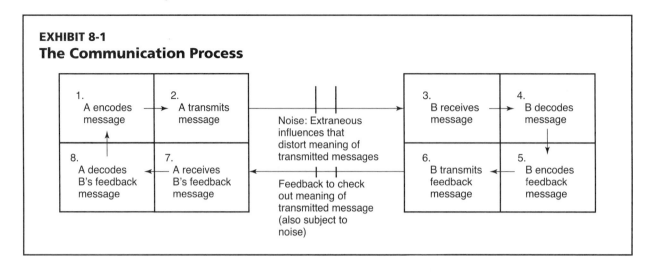

EXHIBIT 8-1
The Communication Process

form of judgment that may distinguish you as an evaluator, perhaps even a superior, rather than as a genuine partner in the process. We hope to establish a collaborative relationship rather than a doctor-patient or professor-student kind of relationship. Especially before you and an applicant have reached an agreement concerning problems and goals, limit your use of comments that suggest judgment. Even positive or favorable judgments may unnecessarily limit your role and the relationship. Therefore, when using reflections, try to remain as close as possible to the actual message and meaning intended by the sender. As you move away from others' frames of reference, the feedback value of your reflections decreases. Also, be careful about timing when you attempt to paraphrase a message. Look for a genuine pause in the applicant's communication, perhaps at the end of a paragraph. If you cut off applicants in mid-sentence or attempt to reflect too often, they may begin to wonder if you are truly interested in what they have to say.

Social workers also often seek feedback (Cournoyer, 2005) from clients, especially during the engagement phase when expectations are explored and parameters established. For instance, after a brief description of the agency's policy regarding confidentiality, you might ask, "Is that clear?" or "Does that make sense?" or "What questions do you have about the policy?" You might also seek feedback following one of your own attempts to summarize an applicant's message. After you do so, you might add, "Do I have that right?" "Is that what you mean?"

As you might imagine, the types and forms of potential communication problems that may occur in social work are, virtually limitless. Indeed, many communication difficulties emerge during the engagement phase. For instance, Cormican (1978) describes difficulties associated with the use of different dialects. One party may use a dialect such that the other party might be unable to decode the encoded and transmitted symbols or does so incorrectly. The message is misinterpreted and misunderstood. Lewis and Ho illustrate another problem through reference to nonverbal communication with Native American clients:

> In an effort to communicate more fully, the social worker is likely to seat himself facing the client, look him straight in the eye, and insist that the client do likewise. A Native American considers such behavior to be rude and intimidating; contrary to the white man, he shows respect by not staring directly at others. (1975, p. 380)

Cormican (1978) asserts that labels such as *borderline state, depression,* and *personality disorder* can obstruct communication processes. If, for example, we interpret applicants' messages through the lens of a diagnostic label rather than from their actual point of view, we may easily misunderstand their meaning. In effect, we may distort the decoding process through the cognitive screen of our labels. Regularly check to determine whether you received and understood the message the sender intended.

Empathic communications derive from your understanding of another's frame of reference and may involve reflections of content, feeling, thinking, and

---

EXHIBIT 8-2
Feedback as a Communication Problem

The client in treatment struggles to express a feeling or thought that troubles her. She finally manages to say something that perhaps approximates what is on her mind. The social worker's response is, "I really appreciate where you are coming from." What does the social worker's response mean? What does it reveal and what does it conceal? What contribution, positive and negative, does this remark make toward furthering the treatment of the client and fostering a therapeutic relationship? This phrase is a duplicitous expression of confusion, concealment, and lack of understanding and empathy. If one were to ask the therapist

what he intended to convey to the client by using the phrase, he would presumably say something like, "I mean that I understand what the client is feeling." But his every word proves otherwise. First, nobody can truly understand what another person is feeling. One can come close, and such approximations of empathy are surely what social workers strive toward in their work, but understanding inevitably remains an approximation.

Source: Bloom, A. (1980). Social work and the English language. *Social Casework, 60*(6), 332–338.

---

meaning. Reflection skills may be used with client systems of any size to check the accuracy of messages received. As illustrated in Exhibit 8-2, however, feedback processes are subject to the same potential problems as any other form of communication.

We can never truly and completely understand what another means, believes, or feels, and we should not delude ourselves into thinking otherwise. However, we have a basic professional responsibility to facilitate understanding in whatever way we can. We must strive to improve clarity in our communications and make it as easy for others to understand our messages. As Bloom suggests, "Communications to clients ought to be simple, clear, accurate, and direct. Social workers should choose words that are precise and cannot be misunderstood, words that are not evasive and vague" (1980, p. 337).

Communications occur simultaneously on many levels—verbal and nonverbal, overt and covert. We sometimes speak of the denotative and meta-communication levels of messages. The denotative level refers to the literal content of the symbols used—usually words. Meta-communications are messages about the message; voice inflection, gestures, manner of speaking, and other factors all provide clues to the intended meaning. The ability to communicate several messages simultaneously provides opportunities for the famous double bind—the simultaneous transmission of contradictory messages—so that the receiver thinks, "I'm damned if I do, and damned if I don't" (Bateson,

Jackson, Haley, & Weekland, 1963; Esten & Wilmott, 1993). For example, people may say the words "Yes," while shaking their heads "No." Someone might say "Hello" while walking away, or "Yes, I'm very interested in a conversation with you" while absorbed in active television channel surfing.

Barriers to Communication

Barriers to communication may occur at any phase in the communication process—encoding, transmitting, receiving, decoding, and checking out. Many of these barriers are obvious: inability to conceptualize and use symbols (encoding problems), speech impediments (transmitting problems), hearing or receptor impediments (receiving problems), failure to understand the concepts received (decoding problems), and environmental influences (noise that interferes with the messages between transmitter and receiver). There are also a series of more subtle but equally serious barriers to communication. In addition to applicants' ambivalence—which, of course, affects communication—we also consider five worker barriers to engagement: anticipation of the other, assumption of meaning, failure to clarify purpose, premature change activities, and inattentiveness.

Anticipating Others   We do not listen carefully if we believe we know what the other person is going to say—that is, if we anticipate the message. Anticipating

---

EXHIBIT 8-3
Stereotypes in a Case Summary

The family has been known to the agency for the past 15 years, primarily because of the husband's failure to provide financial support and episodic incarcerations. The family consists of Mr. Shasta (age 32), Mrs. Shasta (age 27), and six children. Mr. Shasta has been in and out of court since a young boy because of delinquent and antisocial behavior. He received a dishonorable discharge from the army. In the last few years, his drinking has increased to near alcoholism. Mrs. Shasta came from a family also long known to the agency. She married Mr. Shasta at age 17 to escape an alcoholic father.

Recurring pregnancies, health trouble, and abuse by her husband have left her in poor shape to cope with him, let alone rear a child and manage the home. The case is looked on by staff as one of the most unpleasant in the agency because of several incidents of fraud, misuse of funds, and Mr. Shasta's refusal to seek and keep work. Mr. Shasta is avoided by workers as much as possible because of his violent temper and drinking. Returning him to employment is seen as hopeless. He has quit or been fired from at least 20 jobs. Mr. Shasta's drinking seems to affect his attitudes about looking for work and his wife and children. Adequacy of child care is a concern, with reports that the mother neglects her children. Neighbors have reported that the father beats the children when drunk while Mrs. Shasta tries to protect them. Health problems of the mother and children remain ongoing issues but the family is indifferent to the need for medical care.

---

others diminishes understanding because of selective reception and decoding. We may think we know what others are about to say and, in effect, operate as if they have already said it. Anticipation of meaning may occur for various reasons. We may, for instance, have heard a person tell a story that we think we have heard them tell before. We may have heard similar stories from other people. People may remind us of other people or describe problems and circumstances with which we are familiar. As a result, we can expect them to say the same things others did before. We might have a label or stereotype in mind to characterize a person or problem and, therefore, anticipate they will express messages that support the label or conform to the stereotype (Cormican, 1978).

Stereotyping can be very subtle. You may notice similarities among several applicants and begin to develop a stereotype of a particular kind of person or group of people. The stereotype may then interfere with your perception of new applicants so that you cannot receive or understand communications that are inconsistent with the stereotype. Anticipation of others occurs when we permit our expectations, predictions, or existing stereotypes to distort the current communication. Although we develop many stereotypes from our personal and cultural experiences, we can also do so through our own practice experiences, or from summaries or background information provided in case records or by agency colleagues. For example, suppose that you have been asked to provide service to the family whose agency record contains the summary displayed in Exhibit 8-3. Such a summary leaves powerful impressions that can affect your interpretation of communications from the Shasta family.

Remember, though, that this summary contains merely a description of certain discrete behaviors of Mr. and Mrs. Shasta. Without additional data, you cannot know enough about the situation to make inferences about the meaning of the behavior for the Shastas. You would be well advised to listen carefully to what they have to say.

Assuming Meaning Assuming meaning occurs when you receive an ambiguous message, fail to check its meaning with the applicant, and proceed on the basis of a meaning that you have assumed. The words themselves may be ambiguous, the way in which they are uttered may convey unclear feelings or thoughts, or the applicant's behavior may be inconsistent with the words. Checking out the meaning with the applicant may prevent you from making erroneous assumptions that interfere with communica-

> **EXHIBIT 8-4**
> ## Failure to Respond to Client's Concerns
>
> When Mr. Allen came into the office, I was completely surprised at the growth on his head. Actually, Mr. Allen gave the appearance of having two heads, one on top of the other. I asked about it and Mr. Allen said that it had just started, but that wasn't what he had come to see me about. He came because he wanted to pay his taxes. He said he had saved some money out of his grant, and with the extra $5 this month, he had "settled" with the tax offices. He declared Mrs. Allen still wouldn't pay taxes, but he was going to. I told him we would budget the entire tax bill in his grant, and that he would receive a $4 raise or a total of $37. I again asked about his head. Mr. Allen said that when he was a baby he had fallen off the bed and has had a small knot since. He said he wanted to keep his taxes current, and would never again be talked out of paying them. I assured him henceforth his taxes would automatically be included in his grant. I then asked when this knot on his head had started growing again. Mr. Allen said it suddenly started getting bigger about two months ago. Before taking a breath, he started talking about the taxes again. He must have had a hard time saving
>
> enough money to pay the accumulated tax bill. He said they "settled" for $18, and he had a "clean slate." He described how he had gone without his newspaper, hadn't been running his electric fans much nor watering his flowers as he should. I said I wished he had come to us sooner, but now that the taxes were paid, and the future ones budgeted, I suggested we talk about the growth on his head. I asked what he had he done about it. He replied he had not done anything, and again changed the subject to taxes. I told him I noticed each time I mentioned his head, he changed the subject to taxes. I said, it made me wonder if he didn't want to talk about his head, or if there was some connection between his head and taxes. He looked surprised, and then slowly, as if explaining to a child, said, "Long ago the doctors told me if this ever started growing in a hurry I would have to have it cut off. I am 77 years old and may or may not get out of that operating room. If I die, my wife can live on her old age pension if she has a home, if not, she can't. So, I have to get those taxes paid before I go to a hospital or even see a doctor."

tion and engagement. As an example, consider this brief excerpt from an interview with a respondent—a 16-year-old boy just released from an institution on parole:

> I asked how things had gone this past week. He looked at me with a grin and said, "Fine." He added that he had "not done anything!" During this exchange, he leafed through a magazine and pointed out someone's picture to me. At this point, I told him that we were here to talk and that he should put the magazine away. It is very obvious that this boy knows very little or at least practices few of the common social courtesies of everyday life.

Because the boy grinned and leafed through a magazine, the worker assumed that he was trying to avoid conversation. However, the worker acted on this assumption without first checking it. In a similar situation, you might take a minute to ask the boy

about the magazine or perhaps even to wonder aloud, "I get the impression that you might not be very interested in talking with me just now." Seeking clarification helps avoid assumptions of meaning and helps you determine if your impressions are accurate. Simple steps like these clarify the situation, contribute to understanding, and encourage a successful engagement process.

Failing to Clarify Purpose If you fail to make the purpose of an interview explicit, you and the applicant may have different—perhaps even contradictory—ideas about the reason for the meeting. As a result, you may interpret each other's communications in the light of your different expectations and reach extraordinarily distorted conclusions. Consider the example presented in Exhibit 8-4. Mr. Allen says clearly that he has come to pay his taxes. However, the social worker is concerned about his health. It takes several questions before the worker understands the importance of responding to the applicant's concerns.

Premature Change Activities Social workers are committed to change. Difficulties occur, however, when we initiate change efforts without clearly understanding what the applicant wants and whether that change is feasible. Change efforts should be considered only after the applicant and worker define the problem, establish goals, and agree to work together. Suggestions for change and interventions before the partners reach such an understanding constitutes a form of "treatment without consent." You would not want your medical doctor to offer a prescription for medication or give you an injection before you understood what it was, what it was for, how it related to your health concerns, and provided your explicit consent. The principle is similar in social work. The purpose of engagement is to gain a mutual understanding of the presenting problem, jointly establish goals, and collaboratively consider various solutions. Urging change prematurely tends to impede the engagement process and limit access to and exploration of important information relevant to decision making. Furthermore, early attempts at persuasion and advising are seldom effective until some sense of trust develops.

Inattentiveness If your mind wanders during an interview—if you start thinking about other cases, say, or planning future activities—you create a barrier to continued communication with the applicant. Applicants should be able to expect professionals to give undivided attention to their present communications. As a social worker, you must honor that entirely reasonable expectation. Of course, even the most experienced workers have moments when thoughts wander and attention wanes. Walsh recommends owning up to the occasional inattention: "Despite most therapists' fears of revealing such incidents, clients are probably aware of these lapses anyhow, and the admission wins respect for its honesty" (1981, p. 461). For example, a worker might say,

> Excuse me, Frank. What you were saying made me think of something else that's going on, and I haven't been paying close attention for a minute, here. Can you go over that again? I was with you up to the point where you said Jan had no business interfering with the kids. (Walsh, 1981, p. 461)

Applicant Ambivalence The barriers to communication that applicants reflect may sometimes signal fear, resentment, lack of motivation, or perhaps reluctance to enter into a problem-solving process with a social worker. Most people experience some level of ambivalence when first meeting a helping professional—even when they initiate the contact. There are numerous forms and degrees of ambivalence, sometimes referred to as "resistance." The term *resistance* has a complicated history and equally complex connotations. Although it has many dictionary definitions, helping professionals tend to use it in a psychological sense to mean:

1. *Avoidance* behavior used by a client to defend against the influences of the social worker.
2. In *psychoanalytic theory,* the mental process of preventing one's *unconscious* thoughts from being brought into the consciousness. Resistance may be *conscious* or unconscious, and the client uses it for protection against self-realization. It is an inevitable facet of therapy. (Barker, 2003, p. 369)

Resistance may stem from the usual discomfort and anxiety involved in dealing with a strange person and a new situation or perhaps from cultural and subcultural norms regarding involvement with service agencies and asking for help. Studies have found that whereas some cultural groups feel relatively comfortable about seeking help from professionals, others prefer to rely on their informal support systems (Cleary & Demone, 1988; Daniel, 1985; Griffith & Villavicencio, 1985; Logan, Freeman, & McDay, 1990; Marlow, 1990; McGoldrick, 1988). Because of cultural norms, some persons may find it particularly difficult to admit the existence of a problem and to seek services from a helping professional or agency.

Agencies may exacerbate cultural differences by establishing procedures that intensify applicant discomfort. An emphasis on precisely scheduled appointments and office visits, for example, may heighten resistance of clients from lower socioeconomic groups and hamper their ability to use traditional social service agencies. Frankenstein (1982) notes that what is recorded as applicant resistance may instead be an indication of agency resistance—that certain agency practices and worker expectations inhibit communication with troubled families. Of course, some applicants may secure a degree of gratification or perhaps "secondary gain" from certain as-

---

EXHIBIT 8-5
Communication Turn-Offs

- Unsolicited advice: "Let me tell you what I'd do . . ."
- Prophesies: "You're going to hate yourself tomorrow."
- Hijackings: "You think you had a bad day? Let me tell you what happened to me!"
- Reassuring squelches: "A year from now you'll look back on this and laugh."
- Contradictions: "You're not tired; you couldn't be."
- Cutesipation: "Of course I think your little stories are worth reading; they're charming."

- Interrogations: "Why did you do that? Why didn't you talk to me first? What was going on in your head?"
- Evaluations: "You lost your job because you weren't willing to turn in your work on time."
- Diagnoses: "You're only saying that because you're tired; you don't really mean it."
- Sermons: "The money you spend on suits would clothe an orphanage."

Source: Elgin, S. H. (1993). *Genderspeak*. New York: Wiley.

---

pects of the problem or situation. This may interfere with their ability to communicate, diminish their self-determination, and make problem solving considerably more difficult.

Overcoming Barriers to Communication If obstacles to communication arise, you must deal with them promptly so that problem-solving work can begin. Exhibit 8-5 contains a list of common communication turn-offs to avoid during engagement and other phases of social work practice.

A few additional thoughts about communication:

- The questions you ask determine the range of potential answers and, as a social worker, it is your responsibility to explore problems, situations, and potential solutions.
- Behavior represents a form of communication. Your behavior in the presence of applicants communicates something about your view of the relationship with them. Applicants' behavior in your presence suggests something about their views as well.
- Silence is as much a part of human communication as what and how something is expressed. Therefore, listen and observe carefully to recognize significant topics and issues that go unsaid or unexplored. Applicants, of course, interpret your silences in their own ways as well.
- Applicants may experience a decrease in initiative, autonomy, and sense of personal responsibility when you assume responsibility for their thinking, feeling, and planning. On the other hand, your reluctance or refusal to complete reasonable tasks for or on behalf of applicants may interfere with establishment of a collaborative partnership, strengthen their sense of resistance, decrease their motivation, or deepen their apathy.
- Nonverbal communication may be as effective and sometimes more effective than verbal communication during the engagement process (Middleman & Wood, 1991). Indeed, most applicants probably understand more about our intended messages through our behavior and our nonverbal meta-communications than through the words we say. If you wish to communicate the elements presented in Exhibit 8-6 in a way that applicants can understand, you complement your words with nonverbal and behavioral messages as well.

◆ Getting Started

Potential clients and social workers usually come together in one of these ways:

- Individuals, families, groups, organizations, and communities may reach out to a social worker or agency for help with a problem they have identified as being beyond their means of solution.

EXHIBIT 8-6
Elements of the Worker's Presentation of Self

1. Compassion: I deeply care about you.
2. Mutuality: We are here on a common human level; let's agree on a plan, and then let's walk the path together.
3. Humility: Please help me to understand.
4. Respect: I consider you as having worth. I treat your ideas and feelings with consideration. I do not intrude upon your person.
5. Openness: I offer myself to you as you see me: a real, genuine, and authentic human being.
6. Empathy: I am trying to feel what you are feeling.
7. Involvement: I am trying to share and help in the problem-solving work.
8. Support: I share my optimism, encourage your efforts, and recognize your progress.
9. Expectation: I have confidence that you can achieve your goals.
10. Limitation: I must remind you of your agreed-upon obligations.
11. Confrontation: I must ask you to look at yourself.
12. Planning: I will always bring suggestions and proposals, but I would rather have yours.
13. Enabling: I am here to help you become more able, more powerful.
14. Spontaneity and control: I will be as open as possible, yet I must recognize that, in your behalf, I need to exercise some self-control.
15. Role and person: I am both a human being like you and represent an agency, with a special function to perform.
16. Science and art: I hope to bring you professional skill, which must be based on organized knowledge, but I am dealing with people, and my humanity must lend art to grace the science.

- A social worker may reach out to offer services to persons who are not initially seeking help.
- Someone else may conclude that an individual, family, group, organization, or community is affected by a serious problem that threatens their own or others' welfare and request that a social worker or agency intervene to provide services.

Preparing for Engagement

Your initial contact may involve an interaction with an individual, a family, group, organization, or community. To prepare, you should collect and review any pertinent data you can access about the applicant, the presenting problem, the situation, and the purposes of the forthcoming encounter. In addition, you may want to discuss with others in your agency the kinds of help the agency can offer. Beginnings often establish patterns for ongoing relationships. First impressions can be incredibly long lasting. Thus, you should do everything possible to reduce unnecessary obstacles to communication—especially during the engagement phase. Establish a clear understanding about the time, place, and circumstances for the meeting. If you have some control over the physical conditions—such as you

might in an agency office, school, or some public place—ensure that the meeting will be comfortable, private, and as free from interruptions as possible. If you visit applicants in their homes or communities, prepare yourself to be as confidently professional as possible to contribute to their comfort level as well as your own.

Also think about how to prepare for contact with collaterals—people other than applicants, whose knowledge, interest, or participation may relate to the problem or solutions. For example, referral sources may have additional information than they originally expressed. Similarly, family members, colleagues, and friends of applicants may contribute in various ways to the helping process. Before you contact them, prepare a tentative agenda about the purpose of the contact, questions you plan to ask, and information you hope to obtain. Respect for the integrity of the process and the people involved require that you discuss the purposes for any collateral contacts with applicants and clients before doing so. Approach the issue about who, whether, and if so, how, to contact significant others as an opportunity for collaborative exploration and decision making. In most contexts, you must secure applicants' and clients' formal consent before communicating with other persons. Sometimes, though, there may be compelling reasons for a collateral contact before your first encounter with an applicant.

In these circumstances, we suggest the following guidelines:

- Consider applicants as a primary source of information, although not necessarily the only source.
- Do not seek collateral information that you would be unwilling to share with applicants. Be prepared to disclose to and discuss with applicants the process by which you obtained the data and the reasons you chose that approach.
- Share collateral information that pertains to some particular aspect of the problem with applicants before you ask them about the topic. In this way, you provide an opportunity for applicants to reconcile what you know with what they think and feel before taking a position. This approach follows due process and avoids "setting-up" applicants through a technique often used by police officers or attorneys to catch or trap people in lies.
- If, for compelling reasons, you must seek information in advance of an initial contact with an applicant, limit the inquiry to the situation that brings you and the applicant together. Accumulation of large amounts of data from collateral sources—especially if unrelated to the problem—tends to diminish the role of the applicant as the primary source.
- Usually, you can wait until after the first encounter with applicants before seeking information from other sources. At that meeting, you can jointly establish the need for such information and the purposes it serves. Indeed, most collateral data collection takes place after you and the applicant agree to work together and have a preliminary definition of the problem and goal—that is, after applicants become clients.

Initial contacts may occur without notice in face-to-face fashion or be scheduled in advance by telephone, letter, or perhaps even electronic mail. Remember that the process of scheduling the initial contact may be the very first communication the potential client has with your agency. Try to ensure that it is clear, specific, easily understood, and conveys a positive, professional, and welcoming impression. If you must write letters to make such arrangements, be specific as to date, time, and place, use agency letterhead, and prepare them in a professional manner in grammatically correct and well-written fashion. However, adopt an informal style that sets the stage for developing a collaborative relationship. You might use first and second person language: "I" and "you." If you have not spoken directly with an applicant before the first meeting—perhaps because it was scheduled by letter or by another staff person—try to telephone sometime ahead of time to confirm the appointment, briefly respond to any questions that have come up about the appointment, and indicate that you are looking forward to the meeting. This short person-to-person communication helps to establish a foundation for engagement. Of course, there are certain circumstances where preliminary telephone calls are inappropriate and perhaps unsafe. In some domestic violence circumstances, for instance, a victimized person may wish to keep information about the meeting private. Be sensitive to such possibilities so that your phone call does not somehow increase applicants' risk to themselves or others.

Some agencies and programs may expect you to make unannounced home visits, perhaps because of child abuse allegations. In general, we discourage this practice because it tends to violate the integrity of the process and often unnecessarily escalates respondents' anger. If circumstances are dangerous enough to warrant a sudden, surprise visit, it usually means that the police should be involved. We encourage you to work within your agency to develop policies that permit you to telephone in advance—if only a few hours—to inform respondents of your forthcoming visit.

If required, unannounced visits can become a part of the plan negotiated with and agreed to by the respondent during the engagement process. That way, the ground rules are clear and understood by the people involved. In child protective service work especially, you may have to make the first contact through an unannounced home visit—perhaps because respondents lack telephone service. Under such circumstances, start the visit by briefly introducing yourself and your agency, displaying your agency identification card and providing a business card, establishing whether the person who answered the door is the parent or caretaker of the child in question, and clearly stating your purpose and role. Indicate that you are responsible for ensuring the safety of children in the community and need their assistance to determine if a child in the household is safe from abuse or neglect. Ask permission to enter the residence and interview the child. Most respondents, perhaps reluctantly, permit you to do your job—especially if you present yourself in a confident, professional manner, and convey through your respectful words and actions that you intend to conduct a genuinely impartial investigation. As you cross the threshold to the residence, you simultaneously cross social and psychological boundaries as well. Indeed, through the engagement process, social workers inevitably cross certain boundaries. Relationships involve exchange of energy and information between and among various systemic boundaries—including those of applicants and workers. What you say and do, and how and when you say and do it during the engagement process affects the development of the relationship and your ability to be helpful. Successful engagement requires that you always be sensitive to and respectful of the meaning of applicants' physical, psychological, or social boundaries.

Engaging Applicants

Unlike respondents, applicants voluntarily seek help from you and your agency. Thus, we suggest that you start with a relatively brief exploration of the presenting problem. Most applicants expect and want to talk about the issue that led them to initiate contact. It makes sense to begin there (Pilsecker, 1994) rather than exploring other aspects of the people or situation first—which may frustrate applicants who anticipate an early opportunity to discuss their concerns. Following the introductions and brief description of purpose and key agency policies, you may ask a relatively open-ended question about the presenting problem. For example, you might say, "What led you to contact us at this particular time?" Explore the nature of the problem, its severity, frequency, and duration along with previous efforts at resolution. After these initial explorations, shift attention to what the applicant wants to accomplish—to goals. Many applicants prefer to focus more on desired solutions rather than on the problem of concern.

During the engagement phases, encourage preliminary discussion of what the applicant expects from you and what you expect from the applicant. In the engagement process, all these discussions—about presenting problems, desired solutions, and expectations—are preliminary, but they provide a necessary starting point for data collection, assessment, and service planning. In beginning, appreciate what it means to give and receive help. Keith-Lucas (1972) describes help as something offered by one person or group to another in such a way that it contributes to a resolution of the issue at hand. Help, therefore, has several important elements: (1) what is given, (2) how it is given, and (3) how it is used. To be helpful, what is given must be of value to the recipients, and it must be given in such a way that the recipients are free to use it in their own ways, without loss of self-esteem or loss of control. Applicants become clients when they choose to accept the offered help. In our culture, accepting help from professionals can imply a considerable loss of self-esteem or "face," which may increase if the problem is attributed to some personal defect of the applicant such as a moral failure, character flaw, psychological disorder, or personality dysfunction.

Asking for help may be especially difficult for people who have been exploited or oppressed, or who have made previous unsuccessful attempts to resolve problems. On the other hand, some parents readily enroll their children in developmental and educational programs sponsored by schools, religious organizations, and social service agencies. Many people find it easier to acknowledge a need for help in indirect ways, perhaps by attributing the cause of the problem to external or temporary factors. Similarly, people may comfortably participate in neighborhood group activities and seek social workers' help to advocate for change in another system—perhaps in a school or housing development while indirectly hoping their involvement helps them manage their own issues. Recognize that the social problems of poverty and unemployment are often regarded as the consequences of moral failure or psychological pathology; individuals, families, and groups wrestling with these problems may feel ashamed to ask for help. Have you ever driven through miles of confusing streets before finally stopping to ask for directions? If so, you may wonder why you wasted so much time, gas, and energy before you admitted you were lost and needed help. Have you ever worried for hours or days about an assignment before asking for help from a colleague or a professor? Did your procrastination represent an attempt to preserve a sense of adequacy, self-esteem, or "the reputation you have with yourself"? Was your ambivalence and reluctance to ask for help greater when you thought the problem might be the result of a permanent defect of character? Was it less when you viewed the issue as a temporary condition caused by other people or circumstances? Most of us experience help seeking in just such a manner. If you understand what it is like for people to ask for assistance from a helping professional, you should find it easier to approach them with sensitivity, generosity, and reverence.

Social workers can only be helpful if we understand what applicants seek to change or accomplish. During the engagement phase, applicants and workers must clarify the problem for work, establish preliminary goals, and explore respective expectations. Applicants should understand the nature, realities, and limits of your abilities and the agency's resources as well as some realistic appreciation of the work required to pursue the agreed-upon goals.

Engaging Prospects

Engaging prospects is different from engaging applicants. Whereas applicants seek service from you or your agency, you reach out to prospects with an offer for service. Prospects may not want service, and often are unaware of your potential helpfulness. The reasons for ambivalence vary widely. Some may be concerned about cost. Others may be concerned about scams, con artists, and certain sales people. Some may have received services previously but were unsatisfied. As you attempt to engage prospects, be sensitive for signs of ambivalence and adopt an especially respectful manner. Social workers and their agencies may identify various vulnerable or at-risk population groups as potential prospects. Runaway youth, homeless populations, individuals with severe mental illness, and people with alcohol and drug problems represent common social work prospects. Many such prospects consider themselves helpless and their circumstances hopeless. If you hope to engage them, you must exercise considerable communication skill, patience, and persistence to overcome apathetic and pessimistic attitudes. In particular, you must be accessible and available (Snell, 1991) to prospects at times and in places they find convenient, and in a manner they can accept. Outreach workers attempting to engage youth gangs must be on the streets, accessible, and in places where young people congregate. Making contact with roadside prostitutes means getting out on the road to meet and talk with these young women. These approaches require persistence, consistency, and patience. Meaningful contact rarely results from a single walk through a neighborhood, an evening out where young people congregate, or one visit to the roadside rest stops where prostitutes solicit business. To engage prospects under such circumstances, you must patiently establish a regularly, continuing, predictable presence that invites a certain degree of trust.

Successfully engaging prospects often requires the offer and provision of concrete services and resources. For example, you might initially offer prostitutes free condoms or arrange for free medical care to reduce the risk of sexually transmitted disease. This may serve as a stepping-stone to conversations about problems and concerns for which you may be able to offer services. Cohen (1989) found that engagement with individuals who are homeless and mentally ill requires a clear offer of service provided on a voluntary basis that addresses client wants. Actively engaging such prospects requires a commitment to empowerment forms of practice where prospects maintain control over the helping process.

In some respects, social workers' efforts to engage prospects are similar to those of salespeople—although the overall purposes of the two professions are quite different. For social workers, profit is usually a secondary motive; for salespeople, it is usually the primary and sometimes the only motivation. Despite the different functions and motives, effective social workers, like good salespeople, tend to be persistent, consistent, and patient in making contacts. Social workers must also be skilled interviewers to determine what prospects want and then to offer services to secure those wants. Often overlooked, the process of reaching out to and engaging prospects represents an aspect of social work practice that has profound social justice implications. Social work prospects include the most alienated, marginalized, disenfranchised, and vulnerable people of our society. They are quite likely to remain so unless we effectively reach out, engage them, and offer relevant services.

Engaging Respondents

Social workers encounter respondents because someone else recognized a problem and either asked you to intervene or required the respondent to seek service from you. If you serve as a social worker in many agencies, most or all of the people you serve begin as respondents. We hope that many of them also become your clients.

When someone refers a respondent, use the opportunity to explore the referral source's view of the situation and reason for the referral. Take some time to ask questions such as these: What does the referral source see as the problem? How did the referral source decide it is a problem? What facts relate to or help to explain the problem? What goals and solutions would the referral source prefer? Be cautious, however, about providing the referral source any assurance that you intend to pursue those goals. You must also consider the respondent's view of the problems and goals. Furthermore, you may decide that the preferred goals of the referral source are inappropriate, unethical, or impossible. Under such circumstances, you might—following discussion with the respondent—propose alternate goals to the referral source and secure authorization to intervene on that basis. For example, a child protective services (CPS) worker could not immediately agree to a referral source's demand that six children be placed in a foster home because of a neighbor's allegations that their parents have neglected them. The CPS worker would, of course, need to visit the family, interview the children, talk with the parents, and collect much more information before reaching the conclusion that an out-of-home protective placement is required. Social workers court disaster when we accept the referral source's problem definition, goal, or solution before gaining a full understanding of the meaning of the referral to the respondent and reaching our own professional assessment. Of course, some respondents may be unwilling to provide an opinion regarding the problem. Some may be unaware that the referral source already provided some information about the problem or may be uncertain about its exact nature. Consequently, you should share the advance information with respondents and, if it is legal, ethical, and safe for the people involved, identify its source as well. Sometimes you cannot legally or ethically reveal the identity of the informant—for example, in cases involving child neglect and abuse and certain sexual offenses where public identification might endanger someone's life. Suppose, however, that you serve as a social worker in a juvenile or family court. You work with youth who come to the attention of the judge because of allegations of delinquent or criminal offenses. Imagine that you have a young man in your office. He has been accused of stealing a car and going for a joy ride. You have the police report of the car theft in your hands. Begin the interview by showing him the police report and asking him about it. Does he agree with it? Are there statements that should be corrected? If his story differs

markedly from that of the police officer, you may suggest the discrepancy be clarified during the court hearing, when both parties are under oath.

It is not your function as a social worker to catch people in lies or distortions. Rather, you try to establish honest and open communication. When respondents, such as people on probation or under court order, are required to report to you, encourage them to discuss the process that led them to this point. What do they recall about the court hearing? What did the judge or other referral source say about the reason for the referral? Did they receive formal documents? Many respondents are remarkably unclear about the reasons for the referral or the expected outcomes of the service. Exploration of these topics helps respondents clarify their understanding. You may introduce alternative perspectives if you believe respondents' recollections or perceptions are incomplete or distorted.

By beginning the discussion with respondents in this relatively neutral way, you may then proceed to discuss their views about problems and wants. Through a study of family preservation services with families of abused children, Rooney found "that the interaction with the social worker who explains services and helps to create a contract may be the critical factor as a family moves from varied levels of skepticism to a generally favorable view about the services" (1993, p. 14). The nature of the initial experience with a social worker had a greater impact on the family's decision to accept or reject services than did their initial status as applicant or respondent (see Exhibit 8-7 for suggestions about engaging families in cases of alleged child abuse).

Through our communications with respondents, we encourage them to participate as partners in the problem-solving process. We seek to share power with respondents rather than maintain authority over them. Asking permission represents a good strategy. Drake (1994) notes that when workers ask permission, child welfare clients feel respected and empowered. In child welfare work, you can ask for permission to enter the house or to see a child. More generally, you can ask for permission to explore areas of concern. For example, instead of saying to a youth, "I'd like to talk about the offense," you could ask, "Is it all right if we talk about the offense?" Instead of saying, "How are things going at home?," you might ask, "Would it be all right with you if we talk about how things are going at home?" Through these simple measures, you may

EXHIBIT 8-7
Engaging Respondents in Situations of Alleged Child Abuse

Begin the interview by introducing yourself. Be direct and clear in explaining who you are and why you are there (Baily & Baily, 1983). An example is: "My name is Debbie Scora. I am a social worker from Child and Family Services. I have come because it has been reported that Nicolas is in potential danger. Are you Nicolas's mom?"

At this point, attempt to gain entry into the house. You could say, "It must be awkward for you with me standing in the doorway like this. Would you like to discuss this inside?" The parent may let you in; or refuse to talk anymore and shut the door; or continue to talk, but not let you in the door. In the latter case, try to gain trust by explaining that you are there to learn what happened and you need the parents' help. You should make it clear that this is something you can work on together. As you develop more of a relationship with the parent, you should again request access to the house. If the parent refuses to talk at all or consistently refuses to grant entry, you must go back to the agency and get the necessary court order or other authority to take protective action.

Once inside the house, you should refrain from accusing the parents of abuse. Instead, state your concern for the child and explain that it is your job to protect children (Bross, Krugman, Lenherr, Rosenburg, & Schmitt, 1988). Ask the parent for help in understanding this mutual problem. Remember that you have walked uninvited into this situation. Most people would be annoyed. You could say, "I understand some bruises were noticed at school today. I need your help in understanding how he may have gotten these bruises. Have you noticed them?" Encourage the parent to talk with you. You may ask for an explanation of the situation from the parent's point of view. For example, "How do you think Nicolas got those bruises?" Kadushin and Martin (1988) believe that the primary focus should be on what the agency and the parents can do together to help the child. They recommend that you make the following assumptions during the initial contact:

1. The parents are not deliberately willful in their behavior. Neglect, abuse, and exploitation are responses to the social and/or personal difficulties that the parents face.
2. Change is possible.

3. The parents recognize something is wrong and want to make changes but are defensive and suspicious about your involvement.
4. Initial efforts should be directed at helping the parents make the changes that would permit the children to remain in their own home without danger.

You should now ask directly and assertively to see the child (Kadushin & Martin, 1988). Although you may have the legal authority to interview the child without the parents' permission, encourage a voluntary process. If at this time, or at any other time during the interview, parents express resentment, you should acknowledge their feelings and reinforce their role as parents (Oppenhein, 1992). An example of this is: "I understand how difficult it must be to see your son hurt. Maybe it would be easier for Nicolas if you hold his arm while I examine him." Examine the child carefully, in the presence of the parent, who preferably is involved in the process (Oppenhein, 1992). Reassure the child during the examination and attempt to gain a sense of the child's general well-being. Also, gather information about the nature of the parent-child relationship (Oppenhein, 1992).

If you see the child alone, reassure the child that you have the permission of the parent to talk to the child and that what the child says to you will not be shared with the parents unless the child agrees (Kadushin & Martin, 1988).

Examine the child for any physical injuries, including missing teeth, bruises or other skin discoloration, scabs covering healing cuts, rope burns, pin marks, scratches, and any difficulties the child might display in walking or manual dexterity (Kadushin & Martin, 1988). If there is any evidence of injury, tell the parent that you must make an appointment with a pediatrician. Encourage parental participation in this process. Oppenhein (1992) gives an example of this: "We have a problem here. To me it looks like someone has deliberately hurt him. He will have to see a doctor. I can help arrange that. We need to be clear about how and when these injuries happened. Could someone in the household have hurt him?" This statement is straightforward, but does not blame the parent.

Source: Debbie Scora, BSW student, Faculty of Social Work, University of Manitoba, Winnipeg, Manitoba.

encourage respondents to share in decision making and participate as genuine partners. Of course, asking for permission creates the possibility that respondents may say "No." When you stand on the front step and ask, "May I come in?" the family may refuse. If you ask, "May we talk about the offense?" the answer may be: "No, I'd rather not." Although such refusals are relatively rare, when they do occur, you have several options. One option is to honor the respondent's request but leave the option of returning to the subject later. For example, you might say, "All right, we don't need to talk about that now, but I'd like to ask you again later." A second option is to explore what lies behind the respondent's refusal. You might ask, "Would you be willing to talk about your reluctance to invite me in just now?" or "Could we talk about the reasons you'd rather not talk about the offense right now?" By asking about the reluctance, you may shift the focus from the refusal to what might lie behind it. Try to avoid asking "why" or "why not" questions. Unless you adopt an extremely gentle tone of voice in asking them, "why" questions tend to produce angry or defensive responses, strengthen barriers, and increase emotional distance. We are usually less interested in respondents' justification for decisions than in understanding the reasons for them. A third option involves persuasion. You could explain your reasons for the request in an attempt to encourage the respondent to reconsider the refusal. If you outline your reasons in a rational manner, you may be able to avoid resorting to your authority. We prefer the second option, exploring what lies behind the respondent's decision. If the respondent appears uncomfortable with that, try the first or third options if possible. Use the fourth option—that of exercising your legal authority—only after other options have failed.

Referral sources often expect social workers to provide reports about our services to respondents. In particular, you must usually let the referral source know whether you made contact with the respondent and reached an agreement to work together. However, exercise caution in reports to referral sources. Do not share information about respondents until they clearly understand what will be communicated and provide their consent, or realize that your reports are required by law or court order. If you conclude that the respondent does not need your services, that you cannot help, or that the respondent is unwilling to participate, discuss the situation with the referral source to decide how to proceed. In some circum-

stances, the referral source may become the client. For example, parents who seek help for a child's problem quite often become clients so that the child is never directly served. Or, suppose a neighborhood group expresses concern about the behavior of a family that recently moved into the neighborhood. A social worker's visit reveals that the new family is functioning well but differently from the neighbors. In such a situation, the neighborhood group might become the client and the problem redefined as difficulty accepting difference. Or, an initial contact may reveal that the respondent really does want help with some difficulties, but the needed services do not fall within the scope of your agency's mission. In that case, you may suggest that the referral source seek help elsewhere. Be sure to do so in a courteous and orderly fashion. At times, you may help the referral source identify other programs that might be better suited to provide the needed services.

When you intervene in people's lives at the request of third parties, you may provoke anxiety and perhaps anger. People may find it difficult to engage with you until they understand why you came, what you know about them, and what you hope to do. If you expect them to answer your questions, you must first share your purpose with them. There must be no hidden agenda. Many respondents have had previous experiences with social agencies or other institutions that left them feeling rejected, inadequate, ashamed, judged, or betrayed. Their initial response to you may be shaped by negative images of social workers and what they do to people.

There are three important principles here. First, appreciate the fact that you are an uninvited and usually unwanted guest. Respondents have the right to feel angry and every reason to challenge your authority. In fact, such reactions often represent quite appropriate attempts to secure their own system boundaries. On the other hand, respondents who threaten you with physical violence and those who overenthusiastically welcome you may have poor boundary structures. Do not placate respondents, nor try to allay their anger by talking about your desire to help. Instead, deal openly, realistically, and compassionately with the problem as you understand it. Try to send a message such as, "This is my understanding of what brought me here. I know my coming into your life may bring trouble. But if we can agree on the reality of the problem and what can be done about it, we might be able to figure out some way to resolve it."

The second principle concerns your feelings about the role. Many of us have been socialized to hint at difficult issues, minimize conflict, and avoid confrontation. We may feel quite hesitant to speak directly about the realities of challenging situations and problems. Indeed, we may have limited personal experience in direct, assertive communication. As professionals, we need to learn to share negative facts with compassion and caring. Our words may transmit difficult information, but our voices, bodies, and behavior should convey interest and concern. You may need to practice before you can comfortably share unwanted news in a matter-of-fact manner.

The third principle involves sharing negative facts and evaluations as if they are problems to address. Describe the information to respondents and refer to it as "the report," "the allegation," or "the information I have." Resist any temptation to view information from referral sources as the "truth" and do not uncritically accept respondents' word that it is false. Both perspectives are likely to have some accuracies and some inaccuracies. You do know, however, that you have information that creates a problem for both the respondent and for you. Perhaps the two of you might address the problem together.

Transfers

Thus far, we have explored the processes associated with engaging applicants, respondents, and prospects as if these were individuals or groups new to your agency. Sometimes, however, supervisors transfer cases—perhaps because of retirement, illness, or to improve the quality of service. Occasionally, you may engage people who have previously received service from current or former workers with your agency. These individuals and groups are often well known to the agency and may have established case records. Many are clients because they previously agreed to a problem definition, goals, and service plan. Others, however, may remain applicants, respondents, or perhaps prospects.

Ideally, the transfer process involves at least one joint meeting with you as the new worker, the previous worker, and the individual or group being served. The previous worker can introduce you and facilitate your engagement. Such meetings provide an ideal opportunity to discuss problems, goals, and plans and to review progress to date. Unfortunately, this ideal process may not be followed. Sometimes you may simply be handed a case file, perhaps with a transfer summary, and instructions to provide service to the individual, family, or group. Under such circumstances, you must consider how to best use the existing case records, how to make the first contact, and how to facilitate the engagement process. We suggest that you read the case file and begin the interview by offering the applicant a brief summary of what you learned from the file. Then ask for comments and suggested corrections or revisions. By beginning in this manner, you clearly demonstrate that you have indeed read the case file and have some information. We prefer this to a general question about the problem. On one memorable occasion, such an inquiry prompted a long sigh accompanied by this response: "You are the fifth worker I have had, and you all ask me to start over. Don't you people ever write anything down?" At termination, another client commented, "The most important thing is that you cared, and I knew that you did because the first time we met, you told me you had read our case file and you still came out to help. We had been in such a mess for so long that I was surprised to know that anyone who knew about us would think we were worth coming to see." The discussion of the case file need not be long or tedious. Most of the time, you can quickly move to explorations about current status, next steps, and how you might best participate in the problem-solving process.

◆ The Tasks of Engagement

Inviting Participation

Partnership is one of the underlying principles of our approach to social work practice. Applicants and workers participate together in decision making and other aspects of the problem-solving process. The principles of collaboration and participation imply respect for the dignity of each applicant. One of your tasks in engagement is to create a climate that invites and encourages the development of a collaborative partnership. If you talk too much, you deprive applicants of the opportunity to participate and may subtly suggest a power differential where you assume the superior position. To begin, you must exchange introductions; identify yourself, your professional affiliation, and your agency; and describe a preliminary purpose for the meeting. You should also outline relevant policies, such as the nature and limits of confidentiality.

Respondents need additional information about the referral source and information, prospects deserve some information about how they were selected for contact, and transfer clients value a brief summary based on information gained from the previous worker or contained in the case record. Following any information you present, seek feedback to determine if something is unclear, incomplete, or incorrect. Practice these beginning tasks so you can complete them easily, comfortably, and concisely—preferably in a few sentences—but avoid delivering this content as a "canned speech." Try to make it new and real with each new beginning. Otherwise, people may recognize it for what it is—a memorized routine spoken in bureaucratic fashion. After seeking and receiving feedback, follow up with an open-ended question that encourages free expression about the problems or issues of concern. Open-ended questions are framed so that they cannot be answered with a "yes," "no," or an extremely short response.

The following suggestions may encourage applicants' participation:

- Provide a brief introduction, identify a preliminary purpose for the meeting, outline pertinent policy matters, and then ask an open-ended question designed to secure applicants' views and perceptions about the problem of concern.
- Explore the problem and situation, and gradually shift the focus to wants, goals, and solutions.
- Do not offer an assessment and avoid giving advice or direction at this early stage of the process.
- Try to be comfortable with silences and occasional discussions of information that seems somewhat off-topic—let applicants tell their own stories, in their own way, at their own pace.
- Be aware that many of us talk too much and often unnecessarily attempt to control others, especially when we are uncomfortable.
- Remember that one of your tasks is to create a welcoming climate in which applicants feel encouraged to participate.

Applicant participation may be impeded through evaluative comments or overuse of reassurance, especially in early phases of work. Reassurance is seldom appropriate during engagement, even though you may experience a strong urge to comfort applicants who feel distressed. Try to remember that your purpose is the resolution of a jointly defined problem.

It is not necessarily the amelioration of personal discomfort.

Understanding the Presenting Problem

Starting with Applicants' Perspective Social workers use interviewing and communication skills to understand an applicant's experience, view, and perception of the problem of concern. Active listening and other forms of empathic reflection represent a fundamental means by which social workers gain some understanding of others' experience. Applicable throughout all phases of the problem-solving process, empathic reflections are especially useful during the engagement phase to encourage exploration and participation. Sincere empathy requires us to put all other considerations aside and fully attend to what an applicant says—the words used, the feeling carried by the words, and the unspoken messages conveyed by body language. Although you must provide some structure to the interview to collect relevant data, too much structure is counterproductive. If the applicant is able to share, it is better to listen than to question. Make brief empathic comments and ask simple questions related to what the applicant has just said to encourage further expression. Let applicants tell their stories in their own ways, while you seek to understand.

Avoid preoccupation with the collection of information to complete bureaucratic tasks or formulate theoretical hypotheses. During the engagement phase, the critical issue is to understand the applicant's view of what brings you together (Pilsecker, 1994). If you do not understand immediately, seek further clarification or ask for elaboration. On some occasions, you may simply admit your difficulty in understanding, and ask the applicant to help you do so. Indeed, when working with applicants different from you in culture, language, and experience, it would be unrealistic to expect immediate mutual understanding. Reach into yourself and try to recall an occasion when you felt something similar to what the applicant expresses. You may not have lost a spouse or a child—as an applicant may have—but you have probably suffered some loss that left you in despair. The depth of feeling may be different, but the similarities can help you to understand. The commonalities of human emotions and experience allow us to relate to one another. Remember, however, that the purpose for tapping into your own experience is to

---

EXHIBIT 8-8
Mr. Keene: Disparate Worker and Client Goals

Mr. Keene sought the worker's help in regard to financial matters. He looked to the worker as to a parent to decide on specific expenditures. His major problems in financial management were an uncontrollable impulse to overspend on useless gifts to his wife and an inability to deny the children toys, sweets, and recreation jaunts. He would agree with the worker when she carefully figured out with him what would be reasonable and appropriate spending on these items, but he consistently overspent. He talked persistently about his wife, about the fact that he had not known she was ill, about not knowing the cause of her illness, about his concern as to when she would come home. The worker did not respond directly to these concerns but concentrated on the children's needs. After 12 months, however, Mr. Keene was able to afford a housekeeper.

His relationship to the children was characterized by anxious fretting over them, indulging them, and demanding the utmost in care for them from the housekeeper. At times he would be strict, but those occasions would be quickly followed by indulgence. He became extremely worried about rou-

tine childhood illnesses or normative developmental behavior changes. Certain comments indicated that he connected the children's symptoms with their mother's behavior. He persisted in taking the children to visit their mother even though the worker advised against it and he agreed that the visits meant little to his wife. They also exhausted and disturbed the children. The worker's efforts to help him largely involved acknowledging his desire to be a good parent and using his concern for the children's welfare to argue for consideration of their health and emotional comfort. Mr. Keene typically presented problems to the worker with an earnest request for advice, and the worker readily provided sound child guidance information and advice. However, Mr. Keene was generally unwilling or unable to apply the worker's advice.

The worker observed repeatedly that Mr. Keene was very devoted to his wife. He visited regularly, perhaps excessively, taking gifts and writing letters. He talked repeatedly of her eventual return. He would react to any slight improvement in her

(continues)

---

further understanding of the applicant's experience. It may contribute to your own self-understanding, but that is a secondary purpose. Your first priority is the applicant. Also, be extremely careful about the temptation to assume that you understand an applicant because you had a similar experience or, worse, that what helped you solve your issue should necessarily work for the applicant. No two people experience the same event in the same way. If you are to be of help, you must understand the applicant's experience and frame of reference.

The process may easily go astray if you become so focused on your definition of the problem that you do not genuinely listen and try to understand applicants' perspectives. Without applicant input, the goals that you adopt cannot reflect what the applicant wants. Absent a common purpose for your work together, you cannot expect to make much progress. Indeed, you will invariably head in different directions and, in

attempting to explain the failure, each party may well blame the other. The applicant may refer to the worker's incompetence while the worker refers to negative characteristics of the applicant—neither recognizing that the primary cause of the difficulties lies in disparate goals.

Mr. Keene (Exhibit 8-8) was referred to a family social service agency following the psychiatric hospitalization of his wife. The court believed that Mr. Keene would need help in caring for the three children, ages 4, 2, and 1. Following 14 months of work with Mr. Keene, the worker continues to focus on a solution to the child-care problem. However, Mr. Keene seems to experience the absence of his wife as the primary problem. He appears to feel considerable guilt about what happened and does not seem to fully comprehend the nature of his wife's illness. We may expect continued difficulties with the child care issue as long as the worker fails to recognize Mr. Keene's

---

EXHIBIT 8-8
Mr. Keene: Disparate Worker and Client Goals *(continued)*

condition with great optimism and with urgent demands for her discharge. Recently he brought her home against medical advice. She became disturbed, and after she disrupted a smoothly running home, he was forced to return her to the hospital. It was recorded that he often referred to his wife's competence before her illness, adding, "And I didn't know she was ill." This statement was not explored.

Mr. Keene's relationships with various housekeepers have been problematic. The first housekeeper probably was incompetent, but this was not clear because of Mr. Keene's nagging and his constant comparisons of her activities with those of his wife. He fired this woman because she was unkind to the children.

The second housekeeper, a competent person who got along fairly well with the children, quit because she could not endure his excessive demands. She also thought he undermined her efforts with the children. Mr. Keene was remorseful about this, recognizing too late that she was a good housekeeper and mother substitute.

The third housekeeper was a competent, motherly woman who got along smoothly with Mr. Keene through joking with him, mothering him, and bossing him. She mended his clothes and packed his lunches. She allowed the children to play without restraint, and they became more quiet and contented. Mr. Keene assumed more responsibility with chores and reported enthusiastically to the worker that now his problems were solved and he would not need help much longer. Impulsively, without consulting the worker or the housekeeper,

he brought his wife home from the hospital with grudging medical consent because he reported favorable conditions for her care at home. Later he justified his actions through saying that he had been unhappy that his wife was not at home to enjoy everything with them. The housekeeper could not put up with the wife's very disturbed behavior and threatened to leave. Mr. Keene turned to the worker, who helped him face the fact that his wife was not ready to live outside of a hospital. In returning her to the hospital, Mr. Keene had to call plainclothes police and win her cooperation through deception.

Now, following this episode, Mr. Keene is anxious and undecided about future plans. He thinks he probably can mend matters with the housekeeper, but she still feels angry and fearful, and appears to be on the verge of leaving. He wonders how he will ever be able to bring his wife home if no one will give her a chance. Will his wife ever get well? He realizes that this is a good housekeeper, and he should probably urge her to stay. However, he remains annoyed that she did not show more patience with his wife, even though Mrs. Keene was irrational and clearly unable to assume responsibility for herself or the children. The worker introduced the possibility of foster home care for the children but Mr. Keene thought he could not survive without seeing his children every day. Following preliminary consideration of the pros and cons of the two plans—foster care and a continuation of the present plan—Mr. Keene left the interview somewhat undecided but leaning toward another trial of the housekeeper service.

---

feelings and understand his perspective about the problem. If we sincerely want to be of help, we must start with applicants' experience and views. Even in emergency situations and those where we are uninvited guests, we can almost always seek to understand while working to ensure the safety of those at risk.

Partializing and Reaching Common Ground Applicants frequently identify several problems of con-

cern. Try your best to explore them all. At some point, however, the shear number of problems exceeds our processing capacity. We cannot address everything all at once. Under such circumstances, you must engage the applicant in deciding which problem to address first. Partialization leads to selecting a specific problem to receive initial attention. You may refer to it as the problem for work. This process improves the likelihood of finding common ground. You and the applicant need not reach immediate agreement to work on all the problems, just on the first—perhaps the most urgent or the most important to the applicant. The applicant's preference represents the ideal starting point. However, you may sometimes recognize a problem that involves risk to life or identify a core issue that deserves higher priority. Selecting where to start involves collaborative problem solving, and you may share your views as well as encourage applicants to share theirs.

Engagement cannot occur without a common understanding of and agreement about a problem to address. We refer to this as "finding common ground." It represents an essential step in the problem-solving process. Consider Mr. Keene's situation (Exhibit 8-8). In that case, the worker apparently believed that child care represented the primary problem and the place to start whereas Mr. Keene experienced the problem and priority in a different way. Although we can easily recognize and distinguish their different views—based on the brief case description—applicants and workers often fail to notice they hold disparate views. Consequently, they may continue to struggle with the process—uncertain about what is actually happening.

Sometimes common ground emerges quickly, at other times it occurs only through a series of interviews and negotiations, and occasionally common ground cannot be found. Without a common place to begin, however, you and the applicant cannot proceed. Under such circumstances, both parties may need to acknowledge the fact and decide what to do. For example, you might consider a transfer to another worker, referral to another agency, or perhaps temporary or even permanent termination of the process. In situations where you have a court mandate to provide supervision or service, and the respondent has a legal mandate to report his or her activities, you may consider at least two possibilities. You may return to the court, acknowledge the impasse, and request that the court decide the next steps. This may be wise if, for example, you have been mandated to work with a mother who continues to abuse her child and you are concerned about the child's physical well-being. Alternatively, you may agree to meet only the responsibilities mandated by the court. In either of these situations, however, the possibility of future negotiations should be left open.

When exploring problems and situations, be alert for causal hypotheses. They often resemble problems. Consider the case of a 13-year-old boy, James: (1) He was just arrested for stealing a car, (2) his father recently died in an automobile accident, and (3) his mother reports that she may overprotect her son. Many social workers—knowledgeable about family dynamics and social systems, adolescent development, and the effects of loss and grief may identify the mother's overprotectiveness and the father's death as the problem for work. However, the central and most pressing problem at the moment is that the boy has just been apprehended by the police while driving a stolen car. If you focus on the mother's overprotectiveness, you shift the problem definition from the son's behavior to the mother's. Moreover, you may be terribly wrong in your hypothesis that events in the family caused the boy to steal the car. Indeed, the car theft may have been an initiation requirement for membership in a neighborhood gang. In an attempt to partialize problems and seek common ground, both the mother's and the son's explanations may be considered. Over time—perhaps after you and the family deal with the auto theft issue—you and the family may redefine the problem for work as the mother's overprotectiveness.

Of course, the death of his father may represent another underlying cause of James's behavior, possibly mediated by his mother's feelings and actions. Should you therefore identify James's or perhaps the mother's feelings of grief as the problems for work? Probably not—at least not yet. Engagement leads to the identification of common ground and an initial problem for work. We therefore begin there—with the jointly agreed-upon preliminary problem and associated goals. At this point, we try to maintain focus on the problem rather than on possible causes. As we proceed, the worker and the applicant—who, because of the agreement, has become a client—continue to collect and explore additional information on which to formulate a more comprehensive assessment and service plan.

Understanding Applicant Wants

Applicants hope something beneficial will result from your work together on the problem of concern. Indeed, most have some conception of a desired end or outcome; they know what they want to happen. If you understand their wants as well as their views about problems, you may often proceed quite quickly to problem-solving action steps. Indeed, applicants want help to implement a particular solution, rather than to examine various solution options. This makes

---

EXHIBIT 8-9
Engaging a Respondent

John, age 16, was sentenced to a term of open custody for five months for charges of breaking and entering and theft.

The initial session began with discussion about what problem areas John would like to focus on during our meetings. I explained that we would try to define one to three target problems that he felt were of the most importance to him.

John immediately indicated that his primary goal was to obtain a review of his sentence in order to get out of custody early. John felt that the problem was: "Being in custody for five months prevents me from showing others that I can manage my life well without getting into further trouble."

We held a brief discussion on some of the requirements that would be expected by a judge in granting a review and felt that in most cases, they were both desirable and within John's means to achieve.

I continued to initiate discussion around John's interest in showing others of what he was capable.

John described that people viewed him as having a negative attitude—that he often wants things his way and doesn't care to compromise, that he is impatient and won't follow rules or requests that don't suit him, that he is too sarcastic in his tone with others, and that he is jeopardizing his schooling. John stated that he wanted to show them that he could follow rules and get along and could complete his schooling. His goal was to show others (parents, teacher, authority) an improved attitude. I pointed out how closely linked this issue was with his interest in a review in order to strengthen motivation and rationale for this goal.

John indicated that not obtaining his schooling was a serious problem for him. His goal was to attend school full time and continue to work toward his diploma.

Source: Kallies, L. (1997). Task-centered social work with young offenders. MSW practicum report, Winnipeg: Faculty of Social Work, University of Manitoba.

---

sense. When confronted with a problem, most of us tend to seek solutions. Goal seeking gives the problem-solving process energy, thrust, and purpose. Consideration of applicant wants, goals, and solutions represents an important aspect of the process. During the early part of the engagement process, however, explore the problem separately from the goal or solution. For example, suppose a mother comes to your child welfare agency and says she wants to give up her child for adoption because that will solve several problems. Another person may view suicide as a resolution for depression. Someone else may identify dropping out of school as a solution to poor grades. Sometimes initial ideas about solutions reflect an attempt to cope with the stresses associated with problems. Before accepting them as goals, identify and explore the problems for which they represent solutions. Exploration may generate other, better, easier, or more effective options. Do not reject or dismiss applicants' wants and proposed solutions. Rather, seek to separate them from the problem for the purposes of exploration and engagement (see Exhibit 8-9).

Understanding Applicants' Frames of Reference Social workers' most severe obstacle to problem solving may be our tendency to define applicants' problems from our own personal or professional frame of reference. Indeed, when applicants hesitate to accept our view, we may label them resistant or perhaps conclude they are in a state of denial. Most of us tend to adopt fairly durable perspectives about people, life, and problems. Sometimes our conceptual lens become fixed in such a way that we become trapped in them, blocked from even considering alternate points of view. Try to complete the puzzle contained in Exhibit 8-10.

After attempting to solve the puzzle, turn to Exhibit 8-11 on the next page for the solution. Are you surprised? Most of us fail to find a solution because we assume that the dots compose a square and that the solution must fall within the boundaries of the square. Thus, our failure stems from self-imposed assumptions that interfere with effective problem solving. Try to transcend your preconceived assumptions and perspectives so you can appreciate and accurately understand applicants' frame of reference.

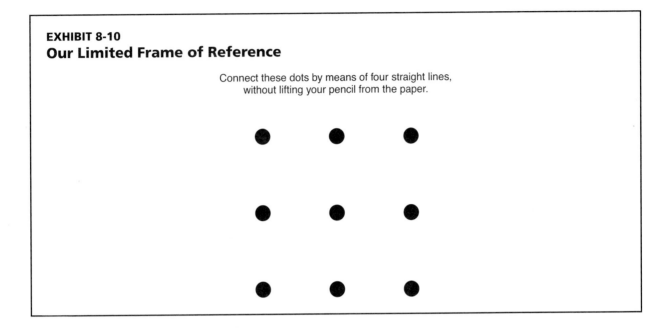

EXHIBIT 8-10
Our Limited Frame of Reference

Connect these dots by means of four straight lines,
without lifting your pencil from the paper.

Levels of Goals and Objectives There are different levels of goals. Social workers and applicants or clients may be concerned with an optimal or ultimate goal—the final desired outcome to which their efforts are directed. Or, you may be concerned with interim objectives that serve as significant steps on the journey toward the optimal goal. Frequently, these intermediate objectives provide a way of testing the soundness of the ultimate goal.

In Exhibit 8-12, we see how consideration of different levels of goals leads to discovery of common ground. Each of the significant participants in Ms. Bates' case has a personal view of the problem and a corresponding goal or solution. The professionals want her to come to terms with the inevitability of her physical deterioration and accept a realistic plan for care—although they differ on the plan. Ms. Bates, desperately needing to deny the prognosis, is determined to get well and return to teaching. She wants acknowledgement of this goal and help to achieve it. How can these disparate goals possibly be reconciled? Sometimes we can reach consensus about interim objectives—even if we cannot agree about ultimate outcomes—that enables us to further the process of problem solving.

The professional people want Ms. Bates to participate in rehabilitative efforts to maintain her functioning as well as possible for as long as possible. These same efforts are necessary if she is to achieve her ul-

timate goal of returning to teaching. The worker may inform Ms. Bates (1) that the medical staff and she see the problem differently; (2) that they are in strong disagreement about the ultimate goals; (3) that the worker questions whether Ms. Bates can return to full-time teaching; but (4) that the place to start is with her ability to work on objectives that are necessary to either ultimate goal. If she wants to return to the classroom, she must struggle to walk again, to read Braille, and to care for herself physically. Eventually, there will come a time when the worker and Ms. Bates put the results of their efforts together and develop a long-term plan to either return to the community as an independently functioning person, or make a transition into at least partially sheltered care.

Through her attempts at self-care, Ms. Bates soon discovered that she would be unable to return to the classroom. She then decided that part-time work in a nursing home was a realistic objective. The worker did not have to force this change in goals. Ms. Bates made her own decision based on the experience she gained in pursuing the intermediate objectives.

If you insist that applicants' long-term goals are unrealistic, you may diminish their hope and motivation, and fail to reach consensus. If you can begin with intermediate objectives, applicants may voluntarily abandon unrealistic goals as they gain experience. During the engagement phase, objectives—rather than ultimate goals—often form the basis for common

EXHIBIT 8-11
Solution to Exhibit 8-10

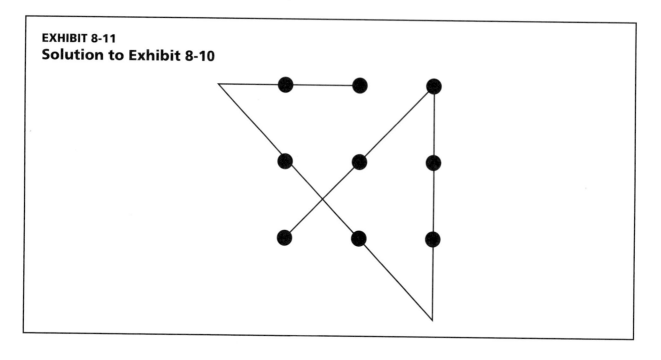

EXHIBIT 8-12
Conflicting Goals

Ms. Bates, a 29-year-old schoolteacher, was admitted to a rehabilitation service following a massive stroke. She has been diabetic since she was 5 years old, and despite constant medical attention and rigid personal self-discipline in diet and medication, the disease was becoming progressively worse. During the past five years, she has been losing her sight, and now she is considered legally blind. The stroke, which was also related to the diabetic condition, resulted in paralysis of her right side. Ms. Bates has always been a very goal-directed person. Despite an ever more disabling illness, she earned an advanced degree in the education of children with disabilities. She sees her problem as one of getting well quickly so she can return to her classroom. She has a somewhat unrealistic notion of what is involved in such an accomplishment, denying the hard and difficult work associated with learning to (1) walk with a cane and (2) read Braille. She often becomes angry with the nurses and frequently refuses to cooperate with them because she feels that they are trying to keep her dependent. Her prognosis (which has been shared over and over again with her) indicates that she is in the last stages of an irreversible terminal condition. It is obvious that she will never return to teaching. The doctors and nurses view the problem as Ms. Bates's unwillingness to accept the prognosis and behave accordingly. They are frustrated that the patient refuses to acknowledge the reality of her condition and and will not participate with them in the small, painful, and difficult tasks necessary to achieve minimal self-care. The social worker sees the problem as (1) securing welfare funds for Ms. Bates because her personal savings are almost exhausted and (2) engaging Ms. Bates in planning for a move to a nursing home, as the rehabilitation facility cannot keep her much longer.

ground. Agreement about objectives may lead to an initial service plan. The problem-solving model requires that applicants' purposes and expectations be explored and understood. Lack of attention to their views about problems, wants, goals, and objectives tends to contribute to unsuccessful engagement and ultimate failure in the helping process (Mayer & Timms, 1969).

Clarifying Expectations and the Preliminary Agreement

The engagement process culminates in a preliminary agreement between applicants and social workers about the presenting problem and the initial goals or objectives. In addition, you must clarify the realities and boundaries of what can be offered and help the applicant understand the nature of your work together. As you convey to the applicant any limits on the service offered, you should also express confidence about your ability to help—within the scope of your agency's mission and your own expertise. Do not promise more than you can deliver but maintain a general attitude of optimism. Applicants tend to join us in problem-solving action only if we can offer hope that something can be done about the problem of concern.

Applicants are often confused about how the helping process actually works. They may wonder, "What do social workers do?" There is no visible technology to offer clues. Explanations and descriptions may help, however, our behavior during engagement provides an example of social work in action. The respectful collaborative processes reflected during engagement illustrate how we intend to operate throughout all phases of the problem-solving process.

◆ Chapter Summary

Engagement involves communications between social workers and applicants, prospects, or respondents that lead to an understanding of presenting problems and their desired solutions. The process involves encoding, transmitting, receiving, decoding, and checking-out the accuracy of communications. Understanding may be impaired by communication barriers such as the following:

- Anticipating others
- Assuming meaning

- Failing to clarify purpose
- Premature change activities
- Inattentiveness
- Applicant ambivalence

The tasks of engagement include the following:

- Creating a climate in which the other person can participate
- Understanding the presenting problem and situation as perceived by the applicant
- Understanding what the applicant wants and the solutions he or she perceives
- Developing an initial agreement to continue working together.

The process of engagement varies somewhat according to whether the prospective clients are applicants, prospects, or respondents. Applicants actively seek service, and you can usually begin with a straightforward discussion of their perceptions of the problem and situation, and gradually on to their desired solutions. Respondents typically require greater clarity about the social worker's purpose, role, and responsibilities. You may spend considerable time exploring respondents' views of the presenting problem and their desired solutions but you must also discuss their perceptions of the situation and your presence in it. In efforts to engage prospects, you seek to establish communication and to learn what they want that might be accessible through your agency programs and services.

Engagement lays the groundwork for all future work and establishes the partnership essential for effective social work practice. You seek to understand applicants' perceptions of their situation, their presenting problems, and their desired solutions. Engagement ends when you have a preliminary agreement to collect data for use in formulating plans to achieve the desired goals and objectives.

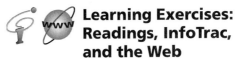

Learning Exercises: Readings, InfoTrac, and the Web

1. Use your word-processing computer program to enter the important terms and concepts presented in this chapter in alphabetical order. Place a question mark by any terms that you do not clearly understand. Save your document as EX 8-1.

EXHIBIT 8-13
Beginning a First Interview

I introduced myself to David and he shyly acknowledged the introduction. He looked apprehensive but seemed to maintain an air of cockiness about him. I also had the impression that David viewed me with suspicion. I asked him to sit down. I sat across from him where I proceeded to interpret my role and my interest in working with him and his family. I told him that I knew about the events that led to his placement here at the Hillside School and that I was here to begin planning with him for his return home. I also told David that I would be talking to him and his parents to help them with any problems that they may have. I also related to David that I had seen his mother, and that I had planned to see both his mother and father as soon as possible.

---

2. Log on to the InfoTrac College Edition Web site. Conduct a keyword search (using either Keyword Search or Advanced Search) to locate the article entitled "Engaging and Retaining Women in Outpatient Alcohol and Other Drug Treatment: The Effect of Referral Intensity" (Loneck, Garrett, & Banks, 1997). Read the article and prepare a one-page essay in which you reflect on the implications of coercive referral and engagement procedures for principles such as dignity, client self-determination, and due process within the context of the social work profession and social work practice. Also address the relative effectiveness of low- and high-intensity referral processes for women affected by alcohol or other drug (AOD) problems. Save your document as EX 8-2.

3. Turn to **Reading 12: Approach and Companionship in the Engagement Process.** Review this article by Craig Rennebohm and reflect on its implications for topics addressed in this chapter. In particular, discuss the processes by which to reach out to and engage people affected by mental illness and homelessness. Prepare a one-page essay to explore your observations and reactions. Save your document as EX 8-3.

4. Turn to **Reading 13: Basic Communications Skills for Work with Groups.** Review this article by Barry R. Cournoyer and Katharine V. Byers and reflect on its implications for topics addressed in this chapter. Several communication skills are explicated. Identify those that seem especially pertinent to the engagement phase. Be sure to distinguish between two general forms of communication—empathic and expressive. Prepare a one-page essay to explore your observations and reactions. Save your document as EX 8-4.

5. Turn again to **Reading 3: The House on Sixth Street.** In that case, Mrs. Smith came to a neighborhood service center to complain that there had been no gas, electricity, heat, or hot water in her apartment house for more than four weeks. At the time she asked the agency for help, Mrs. Smith was 23 years old and the mother of four children, three of whom had been born out of wedlock. At the time, she was unmarried and received public assistance. She came to the center in desperation because she was unable to run her household without utilities. Prepare a one-page essay in which you address the following questions: What were the differences between Mrs. Smith's and the worker's views of the presenting problem? How did the differences get resolved? How did the presenting problem and the problem for work differ? Save your document as EX 8-5.

6. Reread the brief case description of Mrs. Iverson and her daughter contained in Exhibit 5-4. Prepare a one-page essay in which you address these questions: What happened as the worker moved from topic to topic in an attempt to find a focus for the work? How did Mrs. Iverson respond? How might you have done things differently in an attempt to engage Mrs. Iverson? Save your document as EX 8-6.

7. Read the paragraph contained in Exhibit 8-13. This excerpt is from the summary of an interview by a social worker responsible for discharge planning and community supervision of youth released from a juvenile correction institution. This

---

EXHIBIT 8-14
A Failure of Engagement

The campers arrived in the afternoon and were registered and assigned sleeping quarters. At 7:00 P.M., the orientation program began. Camp staff and volunteers were introduced, and the purposes and goals of the camp were outlined. Various activities were described. One involved the creation of a half-acre vegetable garden on the campsite.

At this announcement, the campers from district C became restive. Staff believed tiredness was the cause of the behavior, but soon district B campers started to react in the same fashion. The campers said that they were not informed at district level of the activities at the camp and were not prepared for such hard physical labor. They asked for immediate transportation back to their homes. However, their request could not be granted. The buses that brought the groups had long since departed.

The campers began to vandalize the property. The camp director summoned the police, who arrested 25 participants. The police spent the rest of the night at the camp to maintain law and order.

---

is the first interview between David and the worker. Prepare a one-page essay in which you address these questions: What, if anything, troubles you about this interview? How might this social worker have started the interview differently? Save your document as EX 8-7.

8. Read the contents of Exhibit 8-14. It contains a description of an incident that occurred when 200 Caribbean youth from four different districts arrived at a summer camp. Prepare a one-page essay in which you address these questions: Why did the engagement process proceed so poorly? If you were a management-level staff member at this summer camp, how would you have handled the engagement differently to engage these young people as you find them, not as you would like to find them? Save your document as EX 8-8.

9. Suppose you serve as a social worker at the youth drop-in center located in a local shopping mall. Sixteen-year-old Leslie spends a great deal of time hanging out in the mall and at the center. Leslie has been experiencing serious conflict with her parents and is suspected of engaging in prostitution. You have had several brief, informal contacts with Leslie but now at the center you hope to engage Leslie in discussion about what's really going on and whether Leslie wants to make changes. Prepare a brief half-page summary of what you would do and say in attempting to engage Leslie in this context. Identify the tasks you hope to complete and the issues you anticipate. Save your document as EX 8-9.

10. Eric, age 16, just pled guilty in juvenile court to a charge of home burglary and has been placed on probation. Suppose that you serve as his probation officer. He is about to report to you for the first time. Prepare a brief half-page summary of what you would do and say in attempting to engage Eric in this context. Identify the tasks you hope to complete and the issues you anticipate. Save your document as EX 8-10.

11. Cynthia, a 19-year-old single woman, has scheduled an appointment with a neighborhood counseling service to discuss persistent feelings of sadness, which she has experienced over the past several weeks. Assume you are the social worker about to see her for the intake session. Prepare a brief half-page summary of what you would do and say in attempting to engage Cynthia in this context. Identify the tasks you hope to complete and the issues you anticipate. Save your document as EX 8-11.

12. Assume that you serve as a child protection services worker who is visiting a home for the first time on a cold winter day. Earlier in the day, you received a report that a 5-year-old child may be at risk because of neglect. The report indicates that the home lacks adequate heat and the child goes without sufficiently warm clothing. Prepare a brief half-page summary of what you would do

and say in attempting to engage the family in this context. Identify the tasks you hope to complete and the issues you anticipate. Save your document as EX 8-12.

13. Suppose you serve as a school social worker visiting with the mother of 10-year-old Carlos, who has been in five fights with peers in the last two weeks. The teachers believe that Carlos is the aggressor in these situations. You have telephoned to schedule a home visit and have arrived at the home to discuss this matter. Prepare a brief half-page summary of what you would do and say in attempting to engage Carlos' mother in this context. Identify the tasks you hope to complete and the issues you anticipate. Save your document as EX 8-13.

Chapter 9

Communicating Across Cultures

Engaging people from different cultures requires considerable sensitivity, openness to difference, willingness to acquire knowledge of other cultures, and understanding of self (Dungee-Anderson & Beckett, 1995). These matters surface in the engagement process but are part of all cross-cultural communications in social work. Your educational program probably includes a great deal of content and many learning experiences on the subject of human diversity. Numerous books and related materials about the relationship of cultural diversity to social work and the organization of social services are now available (Asamoah, 1997; Devore & Schlesinger, 1996; Ewalt, Freeman, Kirk, & Poole, 1996; Fong & Furuto, 2001; Harper & Lantz, 1996; Herberg, 1995; Leigh, 1998; Lum, 2003; Lynch & Hanson, 1992). Furthermore, the social work professional and educational associations have increased their emphasis on cultural competence (Council on Social Work Education, 2001; NASW National Committee on Racial and Ethnic Diversity, 2001).

In this chapter, we explore issues that arise as we engage and work with persons from other cultures and consider means to

- Recognize different styles of communication
- Develop cross-cultural competence through study, cultural guides, and applicants themselves
- Avoid pitfalls such as failure to recognize that variations exist within as well as between cultural groups, that certain cultural practices may be a source of stress for some clients, that culture is only a part of identity, and that not all clients want a worker of the same culture or gender

◆ Different Communication Styles

Differences in Help-Seeking Behavior

People from various cultural traditions tend to reflect differences in help seeking behavior and in the type of help sought. For instance, African Americans (Boyd-Franklin, 1989; Daniel, 1985; Lewis & Kissman, 1989; McGoldrick, 1988; Moon & Williams, 1993), Caribbean Canadians of African ancestry (Allen, 1995; Brice-Baker, 1996; Gibson & Lewis, 1985; Ho, 1993), and Latinos (Griffith & Villavicencio, 1985; Vazquez-Nuttall, Romero-Garcia, & DeLeon, 1987) often prefer to seek help from family, friends, and churches. These attitudes may be reflected in communication patterns during engagement. African Americans and Caribbean Canadians, for example, may become inarticulate or belligerent (Brice-Baker, 1996; Christiansen, Thornley-Brown, & Robinson, 1982; Daniel, 1985), may see questions as prying (Chapman, 1995), and may take more time than do whites to become comfortable with the worker and to develop trust (Boyd-Franklin, 1989; Gibbs, 1980). Latinos' cultural norms concerning privacy may discourage discussion of family matters with children and strangers (Dana, 1993, 2000). Persons from some Asian cultures are likely to deal with problems by internalizing them to avoid loss of face (LeResche, 1992; Tamura & Lau, 1992). In addition, many Asian immigrants distrust officials (Duryea & Gundison, 1993) and therefore tend to avoid contact with agencies. Jewish Americans, by contrast, may be quick to seek help, including psychotherapy, because they are less likely to regard it as a sign of weakness (McGoldrick, Garcia-Preto, Hines, & Lee,

---

EXHIBIT 9-1
Misdirected Advocacy

A worker was asked to advocate on behalf of Southeast Asian immigrants for increased support services during their resettlement. The worker immediately directed her attention toward increasing psychological support services, through the enlistment of numerous psychologists and psychiatrists, on the assumption that psychological support was a desired component of support services. The result of this action was that the clients immediately severed their relationship with the worker and declined all further offers of assistance from her agency. The clients felt that they had been misrepresented by the worker in her efforts to seek support services and felt deeply insulted. In their culture, a referral to a psychologist or psychiatrist meant that a person was crazy or deranged. To these Southeast Asians, support services were associated with financial, material, or educational assistance.

Source: Kathleen Behrens, MSW student, School of Social Work, University of Minnesota, Minneapolis.

1989; Sanua, 1995; Srole, Langer, Michael, Opler, & Rennie, 1962).

Understanding differences in help-seeking styles and preferences helps us to interpret initial reactions from applicants. In particular, people from cultures that discourage help seeking from outside agencies may be reluctant to meet with or open up to social workers. Furthermore, certain services may seem unacceptable—perhaps because they are associated with a sense of embarrassment or shame. Persons comfortable discussing problems with family members, friends, and other informal helpers may find it acceptable to use you to sort through advice they received from others. Be careful about recommending services such as psychiatric or psychological counseling that may have negative connotations. Exhibit 9-1 provides a cautionary example and illustrates the problems that occur when we assume we know the meaning of others' words and experiences. This worker might have proceeded differently if she had checked out what the immigrants meant by support.

Taylor, Neighbors, and Broman (1989) analyzed 1979–1980 U.S. survey data regarding the use of social service agencies by African Americans. In a sample of 2079, 64% (1322) indicated having serious personal problems at some time in their lives. Of these, 90% sought help from at least one member of their informal network, and 49% (631) sought professional assistance. Only 91 received help from social services. Extended kin networks are important sources of service for African Americans (Billingsley, 1992; Dilworth-Anderson, 1992; Luckey, 1994), as well as

Puerto Ricans (Delgado, 1995). Providing services to African Americans and other cultural groups often requires developing and maintaining positive relationships with gatekeepers (members of stature and trust in these communities), who help to link persons who need services with agencies (Gibbs, 1993).

Distinctive Communication Styles

Cultural styles of communication are often distinctive. Failure to understand the common styles and customs may result in miscommunication and misunderstanding. In many Native American cultures, direct eye contact is considered insulting and should be avoided. Many European Americans, however, experience avoidance of eye contact as a signal of evasion or dishonesty. Likewise, many American and Canadian native cultures value noninterference. Direct questioning may be perceived as a violation of this value.

Indirect approaches—including use of analogy, stories, and hypotheticals—are often more acceptable (Tafoya, 1989). Use of metaphors and folk sayings *(dichos)* may facilitate communication with Latino clients (Zuniga, 1992, 2001, 2003). Many Asian cultures expect a period of polite conversation at the beginning of a visit; rushing to the reason for the visit, without exchanging pleasantries, is considered rude. In some cultures, failure to accept coffee or tea would be discourteous. Some cultures place importance on silence as a form of respect; others tend to be very expressive. Indeed, white social workers sometimes misunderstand the expressiveness of some

African Americans. A white social worker who worked in a nursing home noted with concern that many African American seniors spent so much time in religious activities—singing hymns, prayer, and Bible study—that they did not have time to meet with her. The white worker may have misunderstood the importance of this expressive behavior for the African American seniors. If she were less preoccupied with a particular style of helping, she might be more able to assist these seniors in a manner consistent with their own traditions and culture.

Recognize that cultures differ in their patterns of communication, in the meaning of words, in the way things are said, and in the meaning of gestures. Be sensitive to these differences as you work to engage people from other cultural backgrounds. As you learn more about the cultures of the particular clients you serve, you will become more effective at engagement and helping. No one can be expected to be conversant with all cultures. You should, however, become knowledgeable about the cultures of the people you serve.

◆ Cultural Competence

"Cultural competence refers to the process by which individuals and systems respond respectfully and effectively to people of all cultures, languages, classes, races, ethnic backgrounds, religions, and other diversity factors in a manner that recognizes, affirms, and values the worth of individuals, families, and communities and protects and preserves the dignity of each" (NASW National Committee on Racial and Ethnic Diversity, 2001, p. 11). The elements of cultural competence include (Cross, 1988):

- Acceptance and respect for difference
- High esteem for culture
- Continuous self-assessment
- Attention paid to the dynamics of difference
- Seeking to expand knowledge of cultures and their strengths

Recognizing culture as a resource and a source of strength for people is a necessary condition for cultural competence. Culture is an important—though not the only—contributor to our sense of identity. People can draw from the resources of their culture—for example, the expressive singing, prayer, and Bible study of the African American seniors in our earlier example—to help cope with stress and life transitions.

Social workers' understanding and appreciation of clients' cultures tend to increase with experience of and exposure to diverse populations. You can become aware of the strengths, assets, and resources of other cultures and use them in efforts to serve. Take advantage of opportunities to increase your understanding of cultural diversity through immersion experiences, published materials, Internet resources, field study, cultural guides from your community, and your clients themselves.

Research and Study

Earlier, we noted your ethical duty to keep current through regular reading of the practice relevant research literature. This obligation includes knowledge about the cultures of your clients. Bibliographic databases, such as those provided through the InfoTrac College Edition subscription that accompanies this textbook, provide extraordinary access to valuable resources. A large body of material is also available on the World Wide Web (see Exhibit 9-2).

You may also learn about diversity through participation in cultural events and celebrations—African American church services, powwows, Cinco de Mayo parades, Catholic feast day events, Chinese New Year, Kwanzaa (Karenga, 1995), and so forth. Large cultural groups often have their own newspapers where you may gain regular information about upcoming social events for you to experience. Your local library can also put you in touch with cultural organizations in your community.

Cultural Guides

A cultural guide (Lynch & Hanson, 1992) is a person familiar with a culture to whom you can turn for advice and assistance, especially when messages from your applicants or clients seem confusing or your work with clients from another culture has stalled. The guide may be a worker within your agency, another professional colleague, or a friend or acquaintance. Normally, people enjoy talking about their cultures. You can generally expect helpful responses to authentic inquiries. You may also serve as a guide for others regarding your own culture.

Clients as Resource

Applicants and clients are usually the most expert source of information about their situations, including

---

EXHIBIT 9-2
Human Diversity and Cultural Competence: Selected Online Resources

AAC&U DiversityWeb, www.diversityweb.org

Agency for Healthcare Research and Quality (AHRQ), www.ahcpr.gov/research/minorix.htm

American Political Science Association Race and Ethnicity Online, www.apsanet.org/~rep

American Civil Liberties Union (ACLU), www.aclu.org

American Public Health Association (APHA), www.apha.org

Association of Asian Pacific Community Health Organizations (AAPCHO), www.aapcho.org

Anti-Defamation League, www.adl.org

Black Health Care, www.blackhealthcare.com

Caring for Hispanic Patients (CHISPA), http://itdc.lbcc.edu/chispa

Center for Cross Cultural Health, http://www.crosshealth.com

Center for Healthy Families and Cultural Diversity, www2.umdnj.edu/fmedweb/chfcd

Center for the Health Professions, www.futurehealth.ucsf.edu/home.html

Center for World Indigenous Studies, www.cwis.org/index.html

CLNet Diversity Page, http://clnet.sscnet.ucla.edu/diversity1.html

Cross Cultural Health Care Program, www.xculture.org

Cultural Survival, www.cs.org

English Server Race and Ethnicity, www.eserver.org/race

Ethnic Medicine, www.ethnomed.org

GLBT Health WebPages, www.metrokc.gov/health/glbt

Lesbian and Gay Community Services Center, www.gaycenter.org

Library of Congress Federal Research Division Country Studies, http://lcweb2.loc.gov/frd/cs/cshome.html

Multicultural Pavilion, www.edchange.org/multicultural

National Alliance for Hispanic Health, www.hispanichealth.org

National Center for Cultural Competence, www.georgetown.edu/research/gucdc/nccc/

National Center for Cultural Healing, www.culturalhealing.com

National Center for Multicultural Education, www.nameorg.org/

National Multicultural Institute, www.nmci.org

National Organization for Women, www.now.org

PrevLine, www.health.org

Provider's Guide to Quality and Culture, http://erc.msh.org

Resources for Cross Cultural Health Care (DiversityRx), www.diversityrx.org

Simon Wiesenthal Center, www.wiesenthal.org

Transcultural Nursing, www.culturediversity.org

U.S. DHHS Office of Civil Rights, www.hhs.gov/ocr/index.html

U.S. DHHS Office of Minority Health, www.omhrc.gov

World Health Organization, www.who.int/en

WWW Virtual Library on Indigenous Studies, www.cwis.org/wwwvl/indig-vl.html#general

WWW Virtual Library on Migration and Ethnic Relations, http://www.ercomer.org/wwwvl/index.html

---

the cultural aspects of relationship. Like cultural guides, clients often enjoy sharing their culture with you. Gently ask a question when you do not understand or when you sense that communications are strained. Remember that directness is considered rude in some cultures. Many clients may be reluctant to say anything that might be critical of you. Indirect questions may be more appropriate: "How is this usually handled in your culture?" "How is disagreement usu-ally dealt with in your culture?" "How do people express unhappiness in your culture?"

◆ Some Pitfalls

Pitfalls to avoid in cross-cultural work include the assumption that cultures are homogeneous, extreme views of cultural relativism, the idea that human personality can be reduced to cultural identity, and the assumption that applicants always want a worker of the same culture.

Misconceptions About Cultural Homogeneity

You need to be aware of two types of cultural variation: (1) variation within a culture and (2) variation in individual cultural identification. Differences within cultures may be as great as those between cultures. For example, there are significant cultural differences between Latinos of Mexican, Cuban, Puerto Rican, and other South and Central American ancestry (Santiago, 1993). There are more than 300 Native American tribes in the United States and more than 50 in Canada, with "tremendous variation among tribes regarding gender roles, language, religion, acculturation, and relationship with non-Indians" (Tafoya, 1989, p. 73). The culture of African Americans differs from that of Caribbean American populations, and differs again from the cultures of recent African immigrants. There are also many very diverse Asian cultures, all with long histories (Berg & Miller, 1992a). Social workers must become aware of both intracultural as well as cross-cultural similarities and differences within our service communities.

People also differ in the degree to which they identify with a particular cultural tradition. Many Latinos, for example, remain active in cultural organizations, speak Spanish at home, and actively identify with their cultural tradition. Others identify more with the mainstream culture. Some Native Americans practice their traditional religions, participate in cultural ceremonies, and keep their language alive, but others practice Christianity and speak English exclusively. Longclaws (1996) identifies the following categories of cultural identification among Native Americans: traditionalists, transforming or new traditionalist, assimilated, universalist, and anomic.

Recognize and respect applicants' and clients' wishes regarding their cultural identification. Remain sensitive about the extent to which a particular client identifies with his or her cultural background, whether the client wishes to have a closer identification, and whether the client wishes to take on a different identification.

Misconceptions About Cultural Relativism

In the extreme, cultural relativism suggests that all values are culture specific and must only be considered within the context of a particular culture. Indeed, if we define values as unprovable assumptions or tenets of faith and each culture develops its own norms and mores based on and sufficient for its own needs (Benedict, 1959), then values of one culture could not reasonably be applied to others. Therefore, cross-cultural absolutes could not exist. The idea of cultural relativism regularly emerges within the context of ongoing international debates about human rights. If all values are culturally relative, how could there be a common set of values or a universal standard of human rights? Obviously, most social workers disagree with this extreme version of cultural relativism. For example, the International Federation of Social Workers (IFSW) states,

Every human being has a unique value, which justifies moral consideration for that person. (IFSW, 2000, Section 2.2.1.)

Each individual has the right to self-fulfillment to the extent that it does not encroach upon the same right of others, and has an obligation to contribute to the well-being of society. (IFSW, 2000, Section 2.2.2.)

Each society, regardless of its form, should function to provide the maximum benefits for all of its members. (IFSW, 2000, Section 2.2.3.)

The IFSW (2003, Section 3) also endorses

The Universal Declaration of Human Rights, www.unhchr.ch/udhr/index.htm

The International Covenant on Civil and Political Rights, www.hrweb.org/legal/undocs.html#CPR

The International Covenant on Economic Social and Cultural Rights, www.unhchr.ch/html/menu3/b/a_cescr.htm

The Convention on the Elimination of all Forms of Racial Discrimination, www.hrcr.org/docs/CERD/cerd2.html

The Convention on the Elimination of All Forms of Discrimination Against Women, www.hrcr.org/docs/CEDAW/cedaw.html

The Convention on the Rights of the Child, www.unicef.org/crc/crc.htm

Indigenous and Tribal Peoples Convention (International Labour Organizations convention 169), www1.umn.edu/humanrts/instree/r1citp.htm

Social workers cannot condone genocide, slavery, torture, or oppression of peoples in the name of cultural relativism. We advocate for social justice and actively challenge "negative discrimination on the basis of irrelevant characteristics such as ability, age, culture,

---

EXHIBIT 9-3
Cultural Relativism and Assessment

PIE attempts to avoid defining social roles in a culture-specific context. It is imperative that the social worker using the system takes into account the specific cultural and societal role definitions influencing the client. For example, in the African American community, physical punishment of children may be viewed as a more socially acceptable method of disciplining a child than in some other communities. To determine whether or not an African American parent has a parent role problem, the social worker must take into account whether the parent's discipline of the child would be considered excessive within the norms of the client's reference group and, of course, whether the discipline meets the legal conditions of physical child abuse.

_____

Source: Wandrei, K. E., & Karls, J. M. (1994). Structure of the PIE system. In J. M. Karls & K. E. Wandrei (Eds.), *Person-in-environment system: The PIE classification system for social functioning problems* (pp. 23–40). New York: NASW Press, pp. 24–25.

---

gender or sex, marital status, political opinions, skin colour or other physical characteristics, sexual orientation, or spiritual beliefs" (IFSW, 2003, Section 4.2.1). However, our advocacy for human rights and social justice must be tempered with respect for cultural diversity. For example, cultures reflect quite different views about child rearing and child abuse (Beavers, 1986; Moon & Williams, 1993). Especially, when social workers serve in positions of legal authority and power, we may confuse our own cultural values with professional values. In child protection services, we must consider cultural context when we investigate situations involving possible child abuse or neglect. The person-in-environment (PIE) classification system (Exhibit 9-3) attempts to recognize situational factors while ensuring the fundamental human rights of individuals and communities.

In preparing yourself to communicate across cultures, become informed about and sensitive to cultural differences but avoid romanticizing our own or others' cultures. All cultures reflect strengths and weaknesses; all have the potential to oppress or liberate their members. Consider your clients as valuable resources who can help you discover the features of their culture they find empowering and want to strengthen and those they consider oppressive and would like to change.

Misconceptions About Identity

Even though culture is an important factor in the development of human identity, it is far from the only determinant. Earlier, we explored the concept of role set and our simultaneous assumption of many roles, all of which contribute to our sense of identity and to our behavior. We may be a member of the dominant culture or one of the many other cultures. However, we may also be straight or gay, urban or rural, employed or unemployed, or a spouse or parent. We are more than our culture. Who we are depends on the relative value we assign to our various roles. Some people may consider cultural identity the most important aspect so that it dominants and permeates all other roles. Others, however, may adopt their occupational role or perhaps their family role as their primary identification. Many lesbians and gay men are active in groups based around sexual orientation, which may be more important to them than is their identification as European American, Latino, Asian American, or African American. Some people identify primarily with their religious affiliations and wear clothing and symbols to reflect that identification. Communication with clients improves when social workers recognize that cultural identification based on race, ethnicity, or religion is not always primary. Remain open to learning from clients what they perceive as the most important contributors to their sense of personal and cultural identity.

Two additional factors complicate cultural considerations. First, we are born into some cultures and we may adopt others. Perhaps you were born into a particular Latino or Native American culture, but then you may choose to adopt other cultures—gay culture, rural culture, a professional culture, and so forth. Social workers must sort out this complex interplay with each client, and make decisions about which cultural identities are most important. Many clients routinely draw from several cultures and multiple roles. Second, an increasing number of persons reflect mixed racial and ethnic heritage. This cultural complexity may seem problematic, but it creates an opportunity for individuals to select strengths from various cultures and to make deliberate decisions about who they are and what they want to be (Gibbs & Moskowitz-Sweet, 1991; Weaver, 1996, 2001, 2003).

Misconceptions About Client-Worker Similarity

Research studies about whether clients benefit more when served by workers of their own rather than a different culture reflect mixed findings (Davidson, 1992; Morrow-Howell, Chadiha, Proctor, Hourd-Bryant, & Dore, 1996; Morrow-Howell, Lott, & Ozawa, 1990; Terrell & Terrell, 1984). A study of 53 Veterans Administration counselors found that both white and nonwhite counselors perceived themselves as about equally effective in their work with white clients, but that white counselors perceived themselves to be less effective than did nonwhite counselors in work with nonwhite clients (Davis & Gelsomino, 1994). Taylor et al. (1989) found that of the 62% of the African Americans who received social services received them from a white worker, 26% would have preferred an African American social worker, 15% did not want an African American social worker, and 59% indicated that it made no difference. Arguments that it may be easier to communicate with a worker of the same culture or gender must be weighed against the risk of creating segregated services in which African Americans serve African Americans, Latinos serve Latinos, women serve women, and so forth. Indeed, disproportionate emphasis on worker-client similarity or difference may inadvertently suggest that workers are unable to transcend culture differences and could diminish social workers' motivation to develop the knowledge and skills needed to work effectively with diverse populations.

If you sense that an applicant is uncomfortable with you because of differences in ascribed role (e.g., race, ethnicity, age, sex), initiate a discussion of the topic. Your willingness to discuss the matter openly may satisfy many applicants. The nature of the problem of concern may sometimes suggest that a worker of similar—or perhaps different characteristics may be better suited for the work. Applicant preference is also a factor for potential consideration. However, social workers should not uncritically accept applicant preference to the exclusion of other factors. For instance, suppose an adult male convicted of violent assault and rape of several young women indicates a preference for a young female social worker rather than a middle-aged adult male social worker. Or, suppose a teenager who believes in white supremacy requests a white worker. Should we accept their preferences simply because they have expressed them? Probably not. These issues require exploration and discussion rather than automatic endorsement.

Thus far, we have considered the topic of cross-cultural communication primarily from the perspective of a worker from the dominant culture working with persons from other cultures. However, increasing numbers of African Americans, Native Americans, Latinos, Asian Americans, and others enter the profession and provide service to white clients. Their familiarity with the dominant culture should help in communicating across cultures. Nevertheless, considerable sensitivity is needed and, of course, a great deal of self-awareness. For example, Davis and Gelsomino (1994) found that social workers, no matter what their cultural backgrounds, generally tend to perceive the source of white clients' problems as internal and the source of other clients' problems as external. Obviously, some people of European-heritage experience extra-personal problems, and some of African, Native, Latin, or Asian heritage experience problems of an intra-personal nature. Assuming otherwise reflects a bias that may interfere with competent service.

◆ Chapter Summary

In a sense, all communication is cross-cultural because each individual person is different from all others. As a social worker, you seek to engage others, establish communication, and work toward the solution of problems they experience in their ecosystems. But communication is made more difficult to the extent that we do not share a common pool of symbols, styles, and gestures. Thus, the greater the dissimilarity in life experiences and culture between social workers and applicants, the greater is our responsibility to work at understanding the applicant's experiences and perspectives. This requires an ability to accept difference and hold in abeyance our own preconceptions, and an active

EXHIBIT 9-4
Interacting with a Person Affected by a Disability

- Relax, act naturally; be yourself. If you aren't sure how to behave, ask the person what you should do.
- Don't assume the person needs or wants your assistance, but don't be afraid to ask politely—not patronizingly—if she does.
- In meeting or parting, shake whatever the person offers: hand, prosthesis, hook, or elbow.
- If the person is visually impaired, immediately identify yourself and anyone with you.
- Remember that most people with visual impairments are not hard of hearing; use a normal tone of voice when addressing them.
- If the person is deaf or hard of hearing, look directly at her when you talk rather than at any interpreter or other assistant who may be present.

Don't shout; that distorts your voice and makes it even harder to understand.
- Remember that people who are deaf depend heavily on facial expressions, hand gestures, and body language for communication.
- If the person is visually impaired or hard of hearing, don't avoid words like see or hear; she doesn't. Stumbling for other words to use will make an otherwise natural conversation awkward.
- Above all, remember that people with disabilities are people first; their disabilities are only one part of who they are.

Source: Burgess, L. (1994). Myths are the greatest barriers. _Modern Maturity, 37_(1), 6–7.

and sensitive willingness to seek to understand others. The American Association of Retired Persons' Disability Initiative (Exhibit 9-4) offers some suggestions for communicating with persons affected by a disability.

In this chapter, we made these points:

- Cultural differences may affect both help-seeking behavior and communication styles.
- You reflect cultural competence when you respect differences, have high esteem for culture, conduct a continuous assessment, pay attention to the dynamics of difference, and seek to expand your knowledge of cultures and their resources.
- You can enhance your cultural competence by reading, participating in cultural events, consulting with cultural guides, and talking with clients about their cultural experiences and expectations.
- Cultures are not homogenous, individuals vary in their sense of identification with a particular culture, and there are definite limits to assumptions of extreme cultural relativism.
- Race, ethnicity, religion, and geography are not the only determinants of identity.
- Applicants do not always prefer nor always benefit more from workers of the same culture.

Learning Exercises: Readings, InfoTrac, and the Web

1. Use your word-processing computer program to enter the important terms and concepts presented in this chapter in alphabetical order. Place a question mark by any terms that you do not clearly understand. Save your document as EX 9-1.

2. Log on to the InfoTrac College Edition Web site. Conduct a keyword search (using either Keyword Search or Advanced Search) to locate the articles entitled "Defining Cultural Competence: A Practical Framework for Addressing Racial/Ethnic Disparities in Health and Health Care" (Betancourt, Green, Carrillo, & Ananeh-Firempong II, 2003), "Native Hawaiian Traditional Healing: Culturally Based Interventions for Social Work Practice" (Hurdle, 2002), "The Myth of Cross-Cultural Competence" (Dean, 2001), and "Cultural Competence versus Cultural Chauvinism: Implications for Social Work" (Taylor-Brown, Garcia, & Kingson, 2001). Read the articles and prepare a two-to-three page essay in which you reflect on its implications for social work and social work practice. Be sure to comment on areas of agree-

ment and disagreement, and offer your own considered opinions. Save your document as EX 9-2.

3. Turn to **Reading 14: A Framework for Establishing Social Work Relationships Across Racial/Ethnic Lines** by Joan Velasquez, Marilyn E. Vigil, and Eustolio Benavides. The authors provide a framework for cross-cultural communication and offer some suggestions for communicating with Latino families. Review the article and reflect on its implications for topics addressed in this chapter. Prepare a one-page essay to explore your observations and reactions. Save your document as EX 9-3.

4. Turn to **Reading 27: The Omar Family.** Review this case study by Khadija Khaja and reflect on the cultural issues facing a social worker providing services to the Omar family. Suppose that you were the social worker in the situation. Given your own racial, ethnic, and cultural characteristics, how would you have attempted to address the cultural similarities and differences. Prepare a one-page essay to explore your observations and reactions. Save your document as EX 9-4.

5. Some Eastern governmental leaders have resisted international efforts to promote human rights, arguing that concepts of individual freedom and human rights are derived from Western thought and do not match Eastern values that emphasize the needs of society, the group, and the family. Leaders of some religion-controlled nations in the Middle East also argue that individual human rights violate certain fundamental religious precepts. Sometimes the discussion of divergent cultural values includes reference to northern (developed) versus southern (developing) societies. At other times, the debates reflect a religious versus secular flavor. Some leaders have called on the United Nations to reconsider the Universal Declaration of Human Rights arguing that it represents an imposition of Western values and limits developing nations' autonomous right to adopt governmental structures consistent with their cul-

tural values—especially their religious beliefs. Earlier (Learning Exercise 4-6), you reviewed the Universal Declaration of Human Rights along with other human rights documents. You prepared an essay about their implications for social work practice. Reconsider them again. This time prepare a one-to-two page essay in which you address the following questions: Under what circumstances might the universal principles of individual human rights conflict with the rights of cultural groups to determine their own governing structures and processes? Does the worldwide dissemination of Western, and especially North American, culture through mass media and technology represent a form of cultural colonialism? Are nations founded on the basis of a single religious perspective justified in limiting individual human rights if those restrictions are consistent with their religious principles? Are members of a national group that view Westerners as infidels and Western culture as a threatening manifestation of Satanic forces be justified in blocking access to certain books, magazines, movies, and television shows? Are Western societies justified in prohibiting prominent display of religious symbols such as Muslim hijabs, Jewish yarmulkes, or large Christian crosses in public schools? If so, under what circumstances would they be justified? Do fundamental social work values—such as confidentiality, individual dignity, and self-determination—assume greater importance than other important values such as family and group solidarity, religious integrity, and cultural survival? If so, does social work's greater emphasis on certain values constitute a form of oppression? Save your document as EX 9-5.

6. Select a cultural group and do a search of the InfoTrac College Edition bibliographic resources to identify materials that might help you understand that culture. Then do a search for additional material on the World Wide Web. Keep track of the citations and Web sites you identify and record them in a document labeled EX 9-6.

Chapter 10

Assessment

In this chapter, we consider the process of assessment. Social workers and applicants or clients collect, explore, and consider information needed for decision making and problem solving. Assessment is a collaborative process that involves the exploration, organization, and analysis of information for decision making about the problem and its solution. Although applicants and clients are often the primary source, the worker contributes information, and data may be collected from other people and through other means as well. We collect information about strengths, assets, resources, and potentials of the applicant and the situation as well as data about the nature, duration, intensity, and urgency of the problem. The partners also consider potential solutions in relation to nomothetic and ideographic evidence of probable effectiveness, ethical considerations, and the applicant's personal and cultural preferences (Cournoyer, 2004).

◆ Exploration and Assessment

Definition

Assessment involves the collection, exploration, organization, and analysis of relevant information for use in making decisions about the nature of the problem and what is to be done about it (Cournoyer, 2005; Ivry, 1992). Applicants or clients and social workers collaborate in all aspects of the process, including analysis of the collected information. The assessment process leads to the development of a service plan that includes a statement of the problem for work,

goals or objectives and plans to achieve them, and a means by which to evaluate progress.

Data and Information We make a distinction between data and information. Data are the bits and pieces of perceptions, thoughts, and feelings collected about applicants, problems and situations, and potential solutions. However, data are of no use until they have been organized for use—at which point they become information. Think back to the case of Mr. Keene described in Exhibit 8-8. Several bits and pieces of data were collected during the 14 months: Mr. Keene depended on his wife to handle the household finances and the children. When Mrs. Keene was hospitalized, he could not accept the seriousness of her condition and found it difficult to make needed changes to care for the children and the household. Although these data were available, they had not been organized to guide intervention.

Information is processed data. Assessment is the process of exploring, organizing, and processing data and then making decisions based on the information derived from the data. The relationship between data and information is illustrated in Exhibit 10-1.

The Purpose of Assessment

The purpose of assessment is to reach an understanding of the presenting problem, applicant wants and solutions, and the person-in-situation so that worker and applicant can construct a plan to alleviate the problem. Understanding is not pursued for its own sake. Rather, we seek understanding to develop

EXHIBIT 10-1
Information as Processed Data

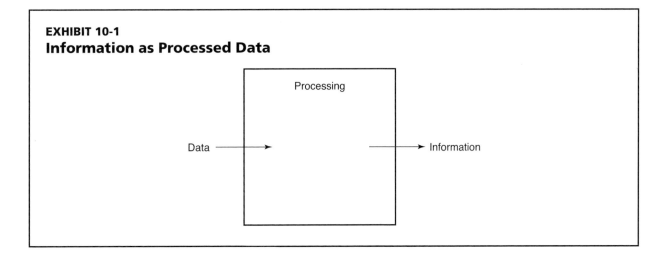

action plans to pursue and accomplish agreed-upon goals and objectives.

The process of assessment involves a collaborative attempt to

- Comprehend the nature, scope, duration, severity, and urgency of the problem situation
- Understand the meaning of the problem to the applicant
- Understand the applicant's desired outcome
- Identify strengths, resources, and potentials within the applicant and the environment
- Collect data and thoughtfully consider information—including professional knowledge—to clarify targets of changes, refine goals and objectives and determine their relevance and feasibility, and develop plans to reach goals and evaluate progress toward their achievement

Assessment and Diagnosis

Some professionals view assessment as a process of classifying, categorizing, or labeling applicants or clients. We adopt a different perspective. We consider assessment to be systemic in nature. Rather than focusing on the client alone, we consider the problem, desired solutions, and the person-and-situation as an integrated whole. Systems theory suggests that problems are often the result of interactions among systemic variables. To focus on only one aspect or to seek a single ultimate cause or reason invites frustration and failure. Our aim is to organize information about the

client-situation-problem for the purposes of decision making concerning goals, solutions, and actions.

Some social workers still speak of *diagnosis* (Turner, 1994, 1995). We prefer the term *assessment*. Perhaps because of its long association with medicine, *diagnosis* often suggests some form of pathology—usually within the person. Even if we were to use the term *social diagnosis* (Richmond, 1917), the presence of something pathological remains an underlying assumption. We believe that some problems occur as a natural part of human existence. The absence of personal or social pathology would not lead to the disappearance of all problems. Some problems would still occur.

The concept of diagnosis also suggests that decisions about the nature of the problem and what should be done are determined through an examination by a professional person. Professionals make independent decisions, assign diagnostic labels (Mattaini & Kirk, 1991; Weick, 1983, 1986, 1987), and offer prescriptions. Diagnoses do not emerge through a dynamic collaborative process. Indeed, they may be more related to agency and agency function than to client circumstances (Desgranges, Desgranges, & Karsky, 1995; Kirk & Kutchins, 1988; Kutchins & Kirk, 1986, 1989a, 1993, 1997; Safer, 1995).

The debate about diagnosis within social work often involves reference to the *Diagnostic and Statistical Manual (DSM)* of the American Psychiatric Association (American Psychiatric Association, 2000). Some social workers, especially those working in mental health settings, routinely use the *DSM* (Jarman-Rohde, McFall, Kolar, & Strom, 1997; Williams, 1981,

---

EXHIBIT 10-2
Arguments for and Against the Use of the *DSM-IV*

Arguments for

1. Most widely used classification of mental disorders
2. Provides a common language for mental health professionals and researchers
3. Meets administrative requirements of clinical, governmental, and reimbursement agencies
4. Descriptive criteria contribute to improved diagnostic reliability

————————

Source: Williams-Finch, B. W., & Spitzer, R. L. (1995). Should DSM be the basis for teaching social work practice in mental health? Yes! *Journal of Social Work Education, 31*(2), 148–153.

Arguments Against

1. Many phenomena included as mental disorders are more usefully explained in terms of social, economic, or environmental terms.
2. Psychiatric labels often lead to lifetime stigmatization.
3. Diagnostic reliability remains suspect.
4. May not contribute to practice effectiveness.

————————

Source: Kutchins, H., & Kirk, S. A. (1995). Should DSM be the basis for teaching social work practice in mental health? No! *Journal of Social Work Education, 31*(2), 159–165.

1995; Williams-Finch & Spitzer, 1995). Others argue just as strongly that *DSM* is inappropriate for social work (Kirk & Kutchins, 1988, 1992, 1994; Kirk, Osmalov, & Fischer, 1976; Kirk & Reid, 2001; Kirk, Wakefield, Hsieh, & Pottick, 1999; Kutchins & Kirk, 1986, 1987; 1989a; 1993, 1995, 1997). The arguments for and against the use of the *Diagnostic and Statistical Manuals* of the American Psychiatric Association are summarized in Exhibit 10-2.

The idea of the social worker as an independent psychiatric diagnostician runs counter to our notions of partnership, collaboration, and the person-in-situation perspective. However, we hold the same views about other classification systems and terminology. It is not just the *DSM*. We believe it would be just as incomplete and improper for a social worker to categorize or label applicants "noncompliant," "child abusers," or "victims" as it would be to classify them "schizophrenics" or "personality disordered." The terms themselves are less the problem than is the process by which they emerge and how they are used. For example, suppose an applicant says, "I am an alcoholic and I need help." Another might say, "I suffer from bipolar disorder." Both may find the terms meaningful, useful, and extraordinarily helpful. However, when we professionals apply diagnostic terms to applicants or clients, we lose our sense of partnership and collaboration as well as our person-in-situation perspective. To counter such tendencies, some social workers adopt "person-first"

language to reduce the potential for bias and prejudice. The terms "racist," "pedophile," "batterer," and "gifted" are not person-first. They increase the probability of stereotyping. The phrases, "people who sometimes espouse views that members of one race are inherently superior to those of another" or "people who sometimes engage children for their sexual gratification" appear in person-first form. Clients and workers could use the *DSM-IV-TR* or other classification systems in a collaborative manner—especially if person-first language was used. However, these systems tend to be used in diagnostic fashion where the professional makes the decision and assigns the classification. Although all classifications systems may be misused, we appreciate the person-in-environment (PIE) system (Karls & Lowery, 1997; Karls & Wandrei, 1992a, 1992b, 1994a, 1994b, 1995; Williams, Karls, & Wandrei, 1989). Developed specifically for social work, the system incorporates person-and-situation factors. Interestingly, the PIE system also provides room for the inclusion of *DSM* classifications if appropriate. Of course, social workers could use the PIE—as some use the *DSM*—to apply classifications to people rather than as a possible conceptual tool for potential use by the partners in a collaborative process of decision making. We encourage person-first thinking and speaking and urge you to maintain the integrity of the partnership process—regardless of the relevant terms or classification system.

Assessment as a Continuous Process

Earlier, we described problem solving as a spiral, rather than a linear step-by-step process. Social workers engage potential clients in assessment and intervention on several different levels at the same time, and often in regard to several different problems. The process is dynamic. Clients and workers continue collecting and processing new data throughout their work together. This may result in a reassessment or a reconsideration of the problem for work, the desired goals and objectives, or the action plan. New problems and wants may emerge or those that reflected lower priority may become more urgent and require immediate attention. Assessment of problems and situations is a dynamic process that continues until termination.

Types of Assessment

Depending on how your agency defines its function and the limits it places on your work, three types of assessment are possible:

- Service specific
- Applicant specific-global
- Applicant specific-focused

A *service specific assessment* is conducted to determine if an applicant is eligible for the service provided by your agency. This is sometimes referred to as eligibility determination (Kropf, Lindsey, & Carse-McLocklin, 1993; Leutz, Abrahams, & Capitman, 1993). Obviously, some applicants do not meet the agency-based eligibility criteria for service. However, social workers maintain responsibility for providing information about and referral to other relevant agencies or programs.

Applicant specific-global assessment begins with a problem as presented by the applicant. The assessment then expands to encompass a review of the applicant's person-situation interaction. The focus is on the presenting problem and the situation rather than on the service provided by the agency. The applicant and worker proceed through an extensive data collection phase to review the person-in-situation interaction before arriving at a service plan.

Applicant specific-focused assessment begins with the presenting problem, moves quickly to what the applicant wants done about the problem, and then addresses the feasibility of accomplishing applicant goals. For this type of assessment, you focus on collecting data needed to understand the presenting

problem, consider the feasibility of applicant objectives, and determine the most effective ways of accomplishing the agreed-upon goals. You work within this limited framework, rather than attempting a more comprehensive review of the person-in-situation.

In reality, you must always consider agency function and applicant eligibility. In some agencies, however, the function is sufficiently broad that clients and workers have considerable flexibility in service planning. Other agencies or programs offer a narrow range of services under a specific, limited set of eligibility criteria. Regardless of setting, however, assessment processes vary somewhat according to the unique characteristics of the applicant, problem, and situation.

◆ Types of Data

In adopting an ecosystemic and problem-solving perspective, social workers usually collect data regarding the following:

- The presenting problem as perceived by the applicant and other significant participants in the process
- The applicant's wants and goals or objectives and previous attempts at problem-solving
- The situation—including strengths, assets, and potential opportunities and resources
- The applicant—including strengths, capacities, competencies, potentials, and level of hope and discomfort

Data collection for assessment continues from the process of engagement. Engagement leads naturally into data collection, exploration, and then to analysis. Thus, you and the applicant continue your efforts to understand the presenting problem and determine how best to pursue its resolution. You collaboratively consider applicant wants and objectives, collect data to determine their feasibility, and identify alternative methods of achieving them. Thus, you look for strengths brought by the applicant, strengths brought by you, and the opportunities and strengths available in the environment.

Client Wants and Desired Solutions

In the engagement phase, we encouraged you to identify and discuss the applicant's initial wants. What does the applicant want to accomplish? What are the goals or desired outcomes? The engagement process ends with a preliminary agreement in which these wants and goals are formalized. Typically, the preliminary agreement provides a basis for collecting data needed to make decisions about how best to pursue the identified goals and objectives.

Desired outcomes may be conceptualized as goals or objectives. Indeed, many social workers attempt to distinguish between the two. Some view goals as the long-term outcomes or end states that applicants or clients and social workers hope to accomplish. These goals are often stated in general terms: "The overarching goal is generally broad and inclusive, such as 'return to community' or, later 'maintain in the community setting' . . . and should be broad enough to encompass many possible objectives" (Rothman, 2002, p. 306). Other examples might be to have a happy marriage, obtain a good job, become more assertive, or make an important contribution to the community. Some view objectives, by contrast, as short-term, immediate, specific, and concrete outcomes. For instance, to complete an application for a job with the Acme Manufacturing Company by the end of the week would be an objective rather than a goal. However, these distinctions are often lost in general practice. Indeed, many professionals may use terms such as *long-term* and *short-term goals* rather than *goals* and *objectives*.

Regardless of the terms used to describe them, considerable evidence suggests that establishing goals generally contributes to an improved process and better outcomes (Locke, 1996; Locke & Latham, 1990, 2002; Maher, 1987; Monkman, 1991; Taussig, 1987). Goals help people maintain their focus (Locke, Shaw, Saari, & Latham, 1981) and contribute to the development of action plans (Collins, Mowbray, & Bybee, 1999; Earley & Kanfer, 1985; Earley & Perry, 1987; Smith, Locke, & Barry, 1990). Specific goals, compared with those phrased in general terms, are associated with improved outcomes (Locke et al., 1981), and those of moderate difficulty contribute to greater motivation and goal-directed activity than do easy goals (Locke & Latham, 1990).

General goals often add a sense of direction and coherence to the work, and specific goals help generate energy, motivation, and action. We may refer to the acronym SMART to help clients and workers establish goals that are *Specific, Measurable, Action-Oriented, Realistic,* and *Timely*. Indeed, clients and social workers often focus on accomplishing particular, short-term

goals. Considerable evidence indicates that many people approach agencies for concrete services (Drake, 1994; Goldberg & Stanley, 1985). Even when more general goals are sought in the long term, establishing short-term SMART goals tends to increase motivation and improve the likelihood of problem-solving action. Long-term goals may provide a framework in which to develop short-term objectives. In practice, your agency mission and function may provide a basis for long-term goals. For example, the long-term goals of the foster family care agency in Exhibit 10-3 provide a direction for the agency's services and supply a framework within which the social workers and clients can develop individualized objectives.

In considering and formulating SMART goals, applicants or clients and workers require data about strengths and resources that might contribute to their attainment as well as about potential obstacles or barriers. Strengths may reside within people—individually or collectively—or in other forms, such as money, property, or access to knowledge. The range and scope of potential strengths is virtually limitless. As Saleebey observes (see Reading 2) in outlining the principles of a strengths-perspective,

- Every individual, every family, every community has strengths, assets, and resources.
- Trauma and abuse, illness, and struggle may be devastating, but they also may be opportunities for growth and sources of challenge and opportunity.
- Assume that you do not know—nor can you know—the upper limits of any individual's capacity to grow and change.
- Take individual, family, and community visions and hopes seriously.
- Every environment is full of resources.

Saleebey (2001b, 2002) and de Jong (de Jong & Berg, 2002; de Jong & Miller, 1995) suggest numerous ways and means to search for strengths and resources within the person and environment. We social workers are interested in those strengths that may contribute to problem resolution and goal achievement.

We also seek data about obstacles or impediments to solutions. Barriers to goal attainment may be within you or your knowledge, attitudes, or skills; the applicant or the applicant's situation; the limitations imposed by your agency or profession; or the general state of knowledge and expertise. For example, an applicant's strong feelings of worthlessness may impede

---

EXHIBIT 10-3
Whimspire Mission and Goals

The mission of Whimspire is to assist young people to achieve social integration and prepare them to live in a democratic society by serving as an alternative to institutional care and providing opportunities to live in family settings. The mission will be accomplished to the extent that we can assist young people in our care to move toward outcome goals necessary for interdependent adult living in a democratic society. As an adult, the person will

1. Work and be self-supporting.
2. Actively participate in the community, including voluntary associations, recreational interest groups, religious organizations, or other community organizations, and contributing to the benefit of the overall community.
3. Respect the rights of others, appreciate difference, and avoid victimizing others through illegal behavior.
4. Live in a family or other intimate relationship where one gives and takes emotional support.

5. Manage personal and household matters including budget, cleaning, shopping, cooking, and laundry.
6. Accept responsibility for one's own behavior including taking steps to make amends for mistakes and omissions.

These are long-term outcome goals. Whimspire services will contribute to assisting young people to accomplish these goals. Youths who emancipate from Whimspire programs into interdependent adult living will be relatively skillful in all of these areas. Youth who are discharged to some permanency plan other than emancipation should be further along towards accomplishing these outcomes than when they came into the Whimspire program but they cannot be expected to have sufficient skills to fully accomplish the goals.

Source: Whimspire, Inc. (1997). *Whimspire Practice Guide: A Social Integration Model.* Grand Junction, CO: pp. 1–2.

---

progress toward a goal of strengthening communication with a neighbor or friend. High crime rates may serve as a barrier to older persons' goals of engaging in neighborhood activities outside the home. In that case, you would need to collect data to establish whether the barrier is in fact the high crime rates (a barrier in the situation) or an exaggerated fear of crime (a barrier within the applicant). To illustrate the barriers that social workers bring, recall the Birky case (Reading 6). The worker was employed by a day-care center that might have a limited conception of its purpose and function. As a result, the agency might attempt to restrict or prohibit the worker's involvement in advocacy or political action.

Legal or ethical principles may also prevent you from consenting to certain action plans. Suppose you are working with an agency that serves African refugees and immigrants. Some of these families, new to your community, may ask you to help them arrange for the clitoral circumcision of their prepubescent daughters, a traditional practice in their cul-

ture. Could you ethically help them do so? You are also likely to encounter requests in which the action plan—the means used to achieve the objectives—poses ethical difficulties. Recall the description contained in Exhibit 6–7, in which a woman on public assistance declined to report external sources of income. Could you ethically support the deception?

Collecting data about goals and potential solutions may lead to some disagreement between you and the applicant. For instance, you might disagree about the relative importance of various goals or perhaps the means to pursue them. Such differences are not uncommon (Abramson, Donnelly, King, & Mailick, 1993) and, like other issues, should be discussed and negotiated with applicants or clients. Share your opinion as something for collaborative decision making. If agreement proves impossible, you may be able to reach consensus about a different goal or plan. You could start there and then return to others at a later point in time.

You and the applicant also need data about solutions. You hope to identify an action plan most likely

EXHIBIT 10-4
Selecting a Tree

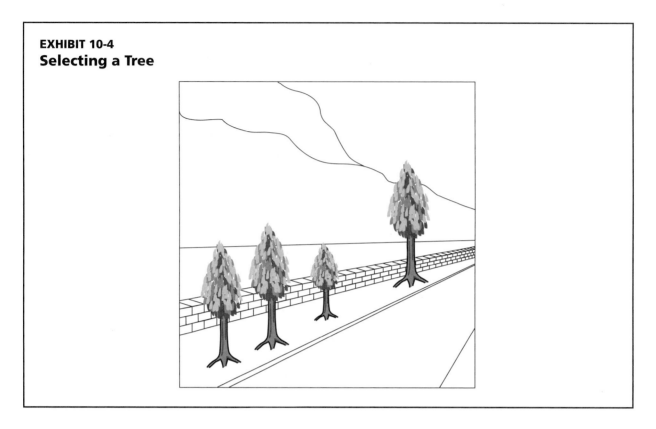

to achieve the goal. As we discussed earlier in the context of systems theory, the principle of equifinality suggests that there are many ways of reaching the same goal. Consider Exhibit 10-4. If your goal is to take home the tallest tree, which tree do you select? To make sure that you have selected the proper tree, please take a measuring stick and determine the height of all of the trees. Are you surprised? Failure to consider alternatives often results in an unsuccessful action plan. Our vision is limited by past experience, preferred courses of action, and our own biases. Carefully considering alternative action plans is one step toward overcoming these limitations and, as we suggested earlier, choice among alternatives constitutes self-determination. Further, the experience of choice enhances motivation (Deci & Ryan, 1980; Deci, Spiegel, Ryan, Kowstner, & Kauffman, 1982).

When discussing the Birky case (Reading 6), most social work students recognize an initial goal of resolving the grief associated with the tragic death of their young son. Many students, however, find it difficult to identify alternative action plans by which this objective might be achieved. There are at least five:

(1) counseling by the worker; (2) referral to a grief counselor in the community; (3) support and help in resolving the grief from members of their extended family; (4) support and assistance from neighbors, clergy, or members of religious organizations in their community; and (5) connecting the family to a mutual aid group of parents who have lost young children to tragic accidents. There are numerous variations within each of these categories and, of course, applicants and clients may contribute potential solutions as well. Part of the assessment process involves analyzing data regarding which of these or other options reflects the greatest likelihood of success and best matches Mr. and Mrs. Birky's personal and cultural preferences.

Do you need to systematically consider all alternatives? Are there any situations in which you may simply accept the preferred alternative and pursue that, without considering others? Including all logical alternative courses of action could become very tedious and might discourage applicants who, after all, come to us for a resolution of their problems. They may have limited patience for exploring options or may experience decision making as yet another problem to address. You can reasonably rule out any alternatives that make no sense to you and the applicant and those for which there exists strong evidence of harm or ineffectiveness. For example, you are not likely to agree to help an unemployed youth hold up a convenience store, even though that might accomplish the objective of obtaining enough money to buy food. We generate and explore options to avoid being entrapped by blinders that limit choice or reduce client self-determination and empowerment. However, do not overdo the process. Whenever possible, consider a manageable range of options that reflect promise of effectiveness and consistency with clients' personal and cultural preferences.

Indeed, considering alternative solutions is unnecessary in some circumstances. If an applicant proposes a course of action that seems reasonable and coincides with practice effectiveness evidence, you may simply concur and proceed to take action. If the proposed course of action proves ineffective, you may introduce other options later. As we have noted, problem solving is a spiral process. Clients and workers commonly reconsider action plans, goals and objectives, and even problem statements when their efforts prove ineffective.

Exploring the Presenting Problem

Focusing on Solutions Notice that we focus somewhat more on the examination and assessment of goals and desired solutions than we do on the presenting problem. We do so because we place greater emphasis on goals, objectives, wants, and solutions than on problems. Ours is a problem-solving rather than a problem-focused model for practice. Attention to goals and solutions tends to enhance motivation and hope and encourages action.

Of course, goals, solutions, and problems are inseparable. Discussion of desired outcomes naturally leads to exploration of the presenting problem. Such exploration enhances both applicants' and social workers' understanding of the problem, its origin, duration, severity, and urgency. In so doing, the partners adopt different perspectives and theorize about possible causes for and factors associated with the problem. These tend to emerge as informal hypotheses about the nature of the problem, desired outcomes, and alternative ways of reaching the solution. Whether generated by the applicant, the worker, or both, the partners consider these hypotheses in light

of the available data and information, reject some, and refine others (Meyer, 1992, 1993, 1995).

Applicants come to agencies because they experience problems. Respondents are sent to agencies because someone else believes there is a problem. Social workers reach out to prospects because we and our agency believe there is a problem. Thus, we collect data regarding their experience of and views about the presenting problem:

- What does the applicant want to change? What would represent an ideal resolution?
- When and under what circumstances did the problem first occur? How long has it existed? How often does it occur? What factors are associated with its occurrence and those occasions when it does not occur?
- How severe or intense is the problem? What factors are associated with an increase or decrease in severity? How urgently should the problem be addressed?
- What attempts have been made to resolve the problem? What were the results of those efforts?

Proponents of a solution-focused approach suggest that the worker should move very quickly to specifying the solution desired by the applicant and trying to accomplish that solution (Berg & de Jong, 1996; Birdsall & Miller, 2002; Cowger, 1994; de Jong & Berg, 2002; de Jong & Miller, 1995; de Shazer, 1988a, 1988b; de Shazer & Berg, 1988; Miller, Hubble, & Duncan, 1996; Selekman, 1993, 1997). We agree that early attention to goals and solutions has numerous advantages. However, most applicants want an opportunity to tell their stories and discuss the problem as they experience it. If we move too quickly, applicants may feel misunderstood and perhaps disrespected. Some may feel that you do not fully appreciate the nature of the problem or its meaning to them. They may think that you are minimizing the seriousness of the problem or even denying its existence. Also, in the absence of genuine understanding of the problem, we could easily formalize goals and solutions for the wrong problem. Problems and solutions are, or at least should be, integrally linked. Otherwise, we might easily create and implement a terrific solution that fails to address the problem of concern. Exploration, assessment, and definition of the problem allow you and the applicant to determine whether the proposed solution could conceivably resolve the problem. We find the following guidelines helpful:

- Explore and communicate understanding of the applicant's experience of and views about the presenting problem.
- Ensure that you and the applicant agree on the problem of concern.
- Explore possible past and present factors associated with the presenting problem in light of their implications for potential solutions and the applicant's envisioned future.
- Collect and explore data about desired solutions.
- Ensure that the plans reflect a reasonable probability of successfully resolving the problem.

The Person-in-Environment (PIE) Classification System

We have discussed some of the dangers associated with the potentially stigmatizing and limiting effects of labeling and the misuse of classification systems. Of course, such conceptual schemes have numerous benefits as well. You need only visit your university library and imagine what it would be like to find books without the Dewey Decimal or the Library of Congress Classification systems. As we mentioned earlier, our obligation as professionals is to maintain a people-first perspective. We therefore consider the usefulness of particular classification systems for particular problem-solving purposes.

Several social workers have proposed problem classification schemes that reflect some consistency with an ecosystem perspective. They may sometimes be useful to you and your applicants in the exploration and assessment processes. For example, Perlman (1968) described three categories of human problems: (1) deficiencies or deficits in tangible material means, deficiencies in personal capacity that restrict or thwart role performance, and deficiencies of knowledge and preparation; (2) personality disturbances or mental disorders; and (3) discrepancies in roles, including discrepancies between several valued roles, between expectations of self and others, or between personality needs and role requirements and inconsistencies that result from ambiguous and contradictory role definitions. Reid and Epstein (Reid, 1978; Reid & Epstein, 1977) developed a classification scheme of eight problem categories amenable to the task-centered model of practice: (1) problems of interpersonal conflict, (2) dissatisfaction in social relationships, (3) dissatisfaction with formal organizations, (4) difficulties in role performance, (5) decision problems, (6) reactive emotional distress, (7) inadequate resources, and (8) psychological and behavioral problems. Building on Reid and Ep-

stein's classifications, Northen (1982) added loss of relationships and cultural conflicts. Germain and Gitterman (1996) introduced a classification system to match their life or ecological model for social work practice. They identified three categories of problems: (1) life transitions involving developmental changes, status role changes, and crisis events; (2) unresponsiveness of social and physical environments; and (3) communication and relationship difficulties in families and other primary groups.

As we mentioned earlier, Karls and Wandrei propose a PIE classification system (Karls & Lowery, 1997; Karls & Wandrei, 1992a, 1992b, 1994a, 1994b, 1995) that draws heavily from role theory.

> *Person-in-environment (PIE)* is a system for describing, classifying, and coding the problems of social functioning of the adult clients of social workers. Developed under a grant from NASW, PIE uses the organizing construct of person-in-environment to provide a system of brief, uniform descriptions of a client's interpersonal, environmental, mental, and physical health problems. The system also includes an assessment of the client's ability to deal with these problems.
>
> PIE balances client problems and strengths. For each of the client's interpersonal problems, the social worker can note the extent of the disruption caused by the problem and the strength of the client to deal with the problem. PIE is not a behavior theory-based diagnostic system producing a formal diagnosis, but rather a system for identifying, describing, and classifying the common problems brought to the social worker. Problems are viewed not as existing in the person only but in the total person-in-environment complex. PIE is intended for use in all fields of social work practice and by practitioners of varying theoretical orientations. (Karls & Wandrei, 1995, p. 1818)

The PIE system is a four-factor system that incorporates the concept of social functioning and recognizes the importance of interpersonal and environmental problems as well as those in the mental health and physical health domains (Karls & Wandrei, 1994a, 1994b, 1995).

- Factor I: Social Functioning Problems
- Factor II: Environmental Problems
- Factor III: Mental Health Problems
- Factor IV: Physical Health Problems

Factor I includes "problems in social role functioning, defined as the performance of activities of daily living required by the culture or the community for the individual's age or stage of life" (Karls & Wandrei,

---

EXHIBIT 10-5
Social Roles Used for the PIE System

Social Role	Codes	Social Role	Codes
Family Roles	1000.XXX	Worker Role—Volunteer	3300.XXX
Parent Role	1100.XXX	Student Role	3400.XXX
Spouse Role	1200.XXX	Other Occupational Role	3500.XXX
Child Role	1300.XXX	Special Life Situation Roles	4000.XXX
Sibling Role	1400.XXX	Consumer Role	4100.XXX
Other Family Role	1500.XXX	Inpatient/Client Role	4200.XXX
Significant Other Role	1600.XXX	Outpatient/Client Role	4300.XXX
Other Interpersonal Roles	2000.XXX	Probationer/Parolee Role	4400.XXX
Lover Role	2100.XXX	Prisoner Role	4500.XXX
Friend Role	2200.XXX	Immigrant Role—Legal	4600.XXX
Neighbor Role	2300.XXX	Immigrant Role—Undocumented	4700.XXX
Member Role	2400.XXX	Immigrant Role—Refugee	4800.XXX
Other Interpersonal Role	2500.XXX	Other Special Life Situation Roles	4900.XXX
Occupational Roles	3000.XXX		
Worker Role—Paid Economy	3100.XXX		
Worker Role—Home	3200.XXX		

Source: Karls, J. M., & Wandrei, K. E. (1994). *PIE manual: Person-in-environment system: The PIE classification system for social functioning problems.* Washington, DC: NASW Press, pp. 7–8.

1995). Factor I problem descriptions address five dimensions: (1) social locus, (2) type, (3) severity, (4) duration, and (5) client strengths. All five dimensions may be captured within a classification code. Multiple problems may be identified. Exhibit 10-5 includes a list of the four categories and subcategories of roles in which problems of social functioning may occur. The PIE manual (Karls & Wandrei, 1994a) also provides descriptions of nine different types of role performance problems: (1) power, (2) ambivalence, (3) responsibility, (4) dependence, (5) loss, (6) isolation, (7) victimization, (8) mixed, and (9) other.

Factor II includes "problems in the client's environment as they affect the client's social functioning" (Karls & Wandrei, 1995). Both social as well as physical aspects of the environment are incorporated within the PIE system. Factor II problems address three dimensions: (1) social system, (2) severity, and (3) duration. Multiple environmental problems may be identified within six environmental systems (Exhibit 10-6).

Factor III may be used to identify "any current mental disorder or condition that is potentially relevant to understanding the client's problem. Such conditions are listed on Axes I and II of DSM-IV" (Karls & Wandrei, 1994a, p. 5). Factor IV may be used to record "any cur-

rent physical disorder or condition that is potentially relevant to understanding or managing the client's problems. Ideally, the social worker should use the terminology and coding contained in the ICD-9-CM" (Karls & Wandrei, 1994a, p. 5).

We find the PIE system attractive for social work because it

- Presents a problem classification scheme consistent with the person-in-situation or ecosystem focus of social work.
- Incorporates applicant strengths, coping abilities, and the environmental sources of problems and reduces potential for labeling or stigmatizing people.
- Provides social work with a classification scheme of its own.
- Encourages collection, aggregation, organization, analysis, and research regarding the types of social functioning and environmental problems that social workers help applicants and clients address.

The authors of the PIE system suggest that problem classification is the responsibility of the worker. According to Karls and Wandrei (1994b), the social worker

---

EXHIBIT 10-6
Environmental Systems Used for the PIE System

Environmental	Systems Codes	Environmental	Systems Codes
Economic/Basic Needs System	5000.XX	Health/Mental Health	8100.XX
Food/Nutrition	5100.XX	Safety	8200.XX
Shelter	5200.XX	Social Services	8300.XX
Employment	5300.XX	Discrimination in Health, Safety, and Social Services System	8400.XX
Economic Resources	5400.XX		
Transportation	5500.XX	Voluntary Association System	9000.XX
Discrimination in Economic/ Basic Needs System	5600.XX	Religion	9100.XX
		Community Groups	9200.XX
Education and Training System	6000.XX	Discrimination in Voluntary Association System	9300.XX
Education and Training	6100.XX		
Discrimination in Education/ Training System	6200.XX	Affectional Support System	10000.XX
		Affectional Support	10100.XX
Judicial and Legal System	7000.XX	Discrimination in Affectional Support System	10200.XX
Justice and Legal	7100.XX		
Discrimination in Judicial/ Legal System	7200.XX		
Health, Safety, and Social Services System	8000.XX		

Source: Karls. J. M., & Wandrei, K. E. (1994). PIE manual: Person-in-environment system: *The PIE classification system for social functioning problems.*. Washington, DC: NASW Press, pp. 24–25.

---

should record what he or she perceives as a problem, even if the client would not necessarily agree. As you know, we prefer a collaborative process of assessment and believe that problem classification can and should be undertaken as a joint activity of applicant and worker. In addition, a comprehensive four-factor PIE assessment process may sometimes be incompatible with the demands of particular applicant circumstances. Many applicants and respondents expect prompt action to address the problems they are experiencing. Accordingly, we prefer to view assessment as a step-by-step, ongoing process, through which we can begin to take action on the basis of initial agreements concerning problems and goals. However, this does not preclude the use of the PIE system. Once you and the applicant identify one or two problems, you can begin to identify solutions and action plans. Later, you may jointly decide to return to other areas.

Linking Problem Classification to Objectives and Action Plans
Classification represents a useful step in organizing data for use in generating potential solu-

tions. Much research regarding the effectiveness of policies, programs, services, practices, and interventions are targeted toward problems classified according to various conceptual schemes or taxonomies. Indeed, this is often how we locate nomothetic evidence about the safety and effectiveness of various services—we search for studies related to a problem classification such as child abuse or posttraumatic stress. As we suggested earlier, however, labels and classifications cannot possibly capture the essence of a person, family, group, organization, community, or society. Even when a preponderance of scientific evidence indicates that a certain practice approach is effective for a large majority of people affected by a particular problem, it may not fit with the personal or cultural preferences of a particular applicant or client. Or, the practice may need to be modified somewhat to address the unique characteristics of a problem or the idiosyncratic circumstances of the person-and-situation.

When classifications accurately match the problems jointly defined by the applicant and worker, they serve as a genuine aid to action planning. Our central obligation, however, is to help people resolve the agreed-upon problems rather than address the general characteristics of a particular classification. Frequently, people experience problems that do not neatly fit within one or more categories. Medical doctors sometimes confuse "helping the patient" with "treating the disease." Social workers may similarly lose track by focusing so intently on the classification that we forget that our primary obligation is to help human beings. Formulating a problem for work with the client is not the same as deciding on a problem classification or diagnosis. We offer the following guidelines to help you distinguish defined problems from classification categories:

- Maintain a consistent focus on the jointly defined problems for work.
- Recognize that classifications seldom precisely match the particular characteristics of the jointly defined problems.
- Beware of any temptations to force a jointly defined problem into a preexisting problem classification.
- When an agreed-upon problem for work does fit a problem classification scheme and nomothetic evidence from research studies indicate that certain practices are safer or more effective than others in resolving problems, you should share this information with the applicant. Such knowledge is a resource for collaborative use by applicants and social workers rather than a source of power or authority that permits us to control applicants or the process.
- Recognize that nomothetic evidence of effectiveness reveals a certain probability that the practice or intervention will lead to successful resolution of the problem with a particular applicant or client. Policies, programs, services, and interventions do not reflect a 100% effectiveness rate. Unfortunately, some clients do not benefit from services that work for most other people (Rubin & Babbie, 1997).
- The systems theory principle of equifinality suggests that there are several ways to reach a particular goal. You and the applicant must jointly reflect on the agreed-upon problems and goals within the context of particular person-and-situation characteristics. Your collaborative planning should incorporate consideration of these unique factors in adopting or adapting an evidence-based approach or in creating your own individualized action plan.

Exploring Causes   At one time, most social workers believed that in-depth exploration of the historical causes of problems was essential. We spent a great deal of time and energy taking detailed histories of childhood development and family life experiences. Derived in part from medical and psychoanalytic traditions, many social workers believed that understanding the original or historical causes of a problem was necessary to determine a solution. However, this belief rests on questionable assumptions. It now seems quite likely that in-depth understanding of and sophisticated hypotheses about the causes of problems are not essential for problem solving (de Shazer, 1982, 1988a; Kaplan & Girard, 1994; O'Hanlon & Weiner-Davis, 1989; Reid, 1978). Social workers seek to help people solve problems and accomplish goals to enhance social functioning and quality of life in the present and future. Although exhaustive data collection about past causes that cannot be changed may be a stimulating intellectual exercise, it rarely contributes much to present day problem solving. That remains our primary function. We should move as efficiently as possible to data collection that aids in the resolution of problems and attainment of goals.

Tracking the sequence of events leading to, accompanying, and following problems, however, often does contribute useful information. Sometimes referred to as antecedent or stimulus conditions, knowledge about events or circumstances that occur before the onset of the problem may help when formulating goals and solutions. Events and conditions that accompany or follow an episode of the problem may also be considered consequences or reinforcers that maintain the problem once it has occurred. Tracking the antecedents and consequences associated with experiences of the problem often yields pertinent data. Although it is typically helpful to track the initial or early occurrences, it is especially valuable to track more recent episodes of the problem. Indeed, many problems have current origins or have occurred only once.

It also helps to track occasions when the antecedent conditions failed to trigger the problem and times when the problem occurred but was successfully avoided, minimized, managed, or resolved in some way. These data pertain directly to problem-solving related information.

Discovering Strengths

De Jong and Berg (1998, 2001, 2002; de Jong & Miller, 1995) suggest that developing well-formed goals involves uncovering strengths, because goal accomplishment ultimately depends on them. Exploration and clarification of competencies and resources, rather than complex causes, also leads to problem-solving related information (Miley, O'Melia, & Dubois, 1995). We recommend a systematic discussion of the strengths and resources available to the applicant that pertain to the identified problems and goals. This may take considerable patience and skill because many people are unaccustomed to thinking about their strengths (de Jong & Berg, 2002). Also explore strengths and resources in the applicant's environment. Consider resources associated with both formal and informal social network. Of course, primary social systems and relationships with family, friends, neighbors, or others often represent major sources of support and strength. Social workers also bring a wealth of strengths including those agency and community resources you can access.

Searching for exceptions, an approach developed in solution-focused brief therapy (de Shazer & Berg, 1988; Miller, 1992; Molnar & de Shazer, 1987), is useful for identifying strengths. Similar to the process of tracking the problem sequence discussed earlier, we ask applicants to describe exceptions to the problem. When does the problem not exist? What is different about those times? As exceptions emerge, you may be able to identify how the applicant or the situation contributes to the exceptions. In Reading 17, Michelle MacKenzie illustrates the use of this approach with a family disturbed by the aggressive behavior of the 7-year-old son. Once the family was able to discover times when the behavior was not a problem, they were able to use their strengths to recreate those circumstances. The search for exceptions underlines the importance of carefully considering times when things are going well, describing these times, and working at expanding and replicating these positive experiences.

Strengths discovery requires different questions than typically asked during traditional problem exploration:

> Instead of asking, "what's wrong with this family?" the question becomes, "what are the strengths in this family that will help them grow and change?" Instead of asking, "why is this person mentally ill or delinquent or abu-

> sive?" the question can be, "what do they need to develop into more creative and loving adults?" (Weick, Rapp, Sullivan, & Kisthardt, 1989, p. 354)

An example of the strengths discovery process is provided in Exhibit 10-7.

◆ Data Collection

Locating Data

Applicants are usually a primary source of data for assessment and decision making. They are, after all, the experts about their own situation. They have struggled with the problem and often attempted various solutions. They also are in the best position to know what they want. We place great value on applicants' understanding of and perspectives about the facts and circumstances. In general, we assume that people express what they believe to be a truthful and accurate representation. In other words, we believe their stories (Cowger, 1994, 1996).

You and the applicant may also find it helpful to collect data from various collateral sources such as family members, friends, employers, and schools; and from other community professionals, agencies, and organizations. Remember that a primary goal of data collection is to identify strengths and resources within the applicant and community. In the case of the Birky family (Reading 6), it might be helpful to collect data about the availability of churches that the family could comfortably attend. The move to the city has disrupted their prior support systems. Involvement in a religious organization and its activities might help provide some support needed to cope with the loss of their child.

The files and records of your own agency may also contain pertinent data. Applicants and clients may have previously received services. In examining case records, however, retain an open mind. They tend to contain historic data that may now be inaccurate or obsolete. We are primarily interested in present functioning and future goals. Moreover, file material may not bear on the present problem, may confuse the matter if it was gathered for an unrelated purpose, and may reflect the biases, selective perceptions, and evaluations of the people who collected it. People change and grow; the agency record may no longer accurately reflect the applicant or the circumstances.

EXHIBIT 10-7
Strengths Assessment

Harry, a 45-year-old man, grew up in rural Kansas. He had been referred to the community support program upon discharge from the state hospital. Harry had been hospitalized 20 years ago, and carried a diagnosis of chronic schizophrenia. He had been placed in a board-and-care home that was located in a large urban area.

The community support staff became worried about Harry. It was reported that he was non-communicative, had poor hygiene skills, and was hallucinating regularly. These problems were compounded by a report from the boarding home that Harry was packing his bags each night as if to leave. The staff predicted imminent rehospitalization.

Harry was referred to a social worker trained in the strengths perspective. Through the process of a strengths assessment, Harry's knowledge of and interest in farm work came to the fore. The social worker took seriously this expression of interest and began working with Harry to find a place where he could use his skills.

They located a ranch on the edge of town where the owner was happy to accept Harry as a volunteer. Harry and the owner became friends and Harry soon established himself as a dependable and reliable worker. After a few months Harry recovered his truck, which was being held by his conservator, and began to drive to the farm daily. To the delight of the community support staff, Harry began to communicate and there was a marked improvement in his personal hygiene. At the time of termination with the case the owner of the ranch and Harry were discussing the possibility of paid employment.

Source: Weick, A., C. Rapp, W. P. Sullivan, & W. Kisthardt. (1989). A strengths perspective for social work practice. *Social Work, 34*(4), 350–354, pp. 353–354.

Case records tend to reflect the orientations of the professionals who create them. Older records or those prepared by senior social workers may not reflect an emphasis on strengths or a focus on data directly applicable to problem solving. Indeed, many older case records may be little more than a catalog of problems and deficits and may have limited use in your current practice. If you do secure data from agency records, however, please inform the applicant—as your partner in the process—and discuss the information in an open fashion. The applicant may disagree with some of the material and should have the opportunity to include an addendum with corrections.

The principle of informed consent and the nature of a genuinely collaborative partnership require applicants' involvement in discussions about potential data sources and the reasons they are relevant. If at all possible, applicants' permission should be secured before any sources of data are accessed. The applicant should be fully informed about the sources, the data sought, and how the data relates to the task at hand. This is, of course, entirely consistent with our notion of partnership.

Interviewing in Social Work

There are five general sources of data: (1) applicants' accounts; (2) accounts of others; (3) questions and tests, either verbal or written; (4) observations; and (5) records of other professional or institutional systems. The most widely used tool for data collection is the individual or group interview with an applicant, in which questions and observations generate data. You must decide the purpose of face-to-face meetings, what data are sought, and how to structure the meeting. At one extreme is the nondirective interview or meeting, in which you follow the feeling and thinking of the interviewee or allow the group to reveal itself as it will. At the other extreme is the highly structured interview or meeting, in which you ask a series of predetermined questions. You provide some structure to the interview when you decide where and when it takes place, establish ground rules and norms for content and participation, and even when you arrange chairs for the persons involved. Give careful thought to the location of the first meeting. If at all possible, determine whether it would better serve the function to meet on the applicant's turf, yours, or perhaps some neutral territory.

The nondirective interview enables applicants to tell their own stories in their own ways and at their own paces. It is an important context for securing data that usually cannot be gained by direct questions. Careful listening and observation of body language, gestures, and movements enhances our understanding of the applicant's experience of the problem. If you listen and observe closely, you may begin to recognize certain cognitive patterns—the kind of reasoning the applicant or client uses—and associated problem-solving strategies. Also seek to identify applicants' coping devices and relationship patterns—which often emerge naturally during exploration about and accounts of situations and problems, their origin and development, and attempts to address and resolve them.

Social workers also use the interview format to collect data from sources other than the applicant. Carefully consider potential sources for the data they can provide and their potential utility. Recognize that some sources may expect you to share data in return. You should discuss any data sharing with the applicant in advance. If you are unwilling to share data, you must make this known to the source when the interview is requested.

Excellent books have been written on the topic of helping interviews (Benjamin, 1987; Cormier & Cormier, 1985; de Jong & Berg, 2002; Epstein, 1985; Evans, Hearn, Uhlemann, & Ivey, 1998; Garrett, 1995; Gordon, 1992; Hersen & Hassett, 1998; Ivey & Ivey, 2003; Kadushin & Kadushin, 1997; Pedersen & Ivey, 1993; Schubert, 1991), and social work educational programs usually devote considerable time to learning about and practicing interviewing skills. Distinguished by several features, the social work interview reflects the following:

- *A context or setting.* Interviews often occur within an agency context and sometimes within applicants' homes, the offices of other agencies or organizations, or in informal community settings. The context provides certain parameters to the interview and influences the nature, scope, extent, and sometimes the quality of communications.
- *Purpose and limits.* Social work interviews are conducted to accomplish specific purposes. They are not casual exchanges of information or

informal conversations. Communications are limited to those purposes. The purpose contributes additional parameters to the interview and serves to screen out irrelevant or extraneous material.
- *Specialized role relationships.* The worker and applicant interact with each other on the basis of their specialized roles. These roles further clarify parameters. Their interactions tend to conform to the expected behaviors of their specialized roles.

Interviewing as Data Collection   Earlier, we described communication as an interactional process that involves giving, receiving, and checking out meaning. Interviewing is a specialized form of communication that is contextual, purposeful, and limited and involves specialized role relationships. You interview to secure data for use in decision making about the nature of the problem, desired solutions, and the service plan.

You must be concerned about the reliability and validity of your data collection procedures (Marlow, 1998; Rubin & Babbie, 1997). *Reliability* is the extent to which the interview produces consistent information. If different messages are received from applicants at different times, consider whether the differences reflect actual changes in perspective or circumstances, or whether they might result from your interviewing style. Different sources may also provide contradictory information. Some inconsistency is a natural outcome of the different perspectives of multiple sources. Too much inconsistency, however, may raise questions of reliability. *Validity* is the extent to which the information obtained reflects the actual perceptions, thoughts, feelings, and behaviors of the source. If applicants and collaterals do not accurately share actual perceptions, thoughts, feelings, and behaviors, questions of validity arise. You may have to adjust the interviewing techniques or use alternate data collection formats. Concerns about validity and reliability surface, for example, when interviewing children about sexual abuse. Separated from familiar settings and support systems and subjected to repeated interviewing and leading questions, the child may provide reports intended to please the interviewer, rather than accurately describe what took place. Recovery of repressed memories specifically and the retrieval of recollections generally may be influenced by the verbal and nonverbal communications

---

EXHIBIT 10-8
Common Communication Errors

- Interacting in a patronizing or condescending manner
- Interrogating rather than interviewing by asking questions in rapid, staccato fashion
- Focusing on ourselves (e.g., formulating questions before understanding the other's message, self-consciously monitoring our internal experiences, evaluating our own performance)
- Attending predominantly to a single dimension of a person's experience (e.g., just thoughts or just feelings; only the personal or only the situational; just the negative or just the positive)
- Interrupting frequently with a comment or question
- Failing to listen or remember, or selectively listening with an "agenda" so that messages are interpreted to match our own beliefs and opinions
- Neglecting to use a person's name, mispronouncing or changing it (e.g., referring to "Catherine" as "Cathy" or "Josef" as "Joe"), or assuming a degree of formality or informality that does not match that of the client's (e.g., "Mr. Jones" when he would prefer "Bill" or "Jane" when she prefers "Mrs. Smith")
- Neglecting to consider the cultural meaning of the interview for a particular person or family
- Failing to demonstrate understanding through active listening

- Using terms that stereotype people or groups
- Offering suggestions or proposing solutions too early in the process (on the basis of incomplete or inaccurate understanding of the person-issue-situation)
- Making statements in absolutist terms (e.g., *always, never, all,* or *none*)
- Disclosing our own personal feelings and opinions or sharing life experiences prematurely
- Confronting or challenging a person before establishing a base of accurate understanding and a solid relationship
- Speculating about causes of issues before adequately exploring the person-issue-situation
- Prematurely pushing for action or progress from a person
- Using clichés and jargon
- Making critical or judgmental comments, including pejorative remarks about other persons or groups (e.g., other professionals, agencies, and organizations)
- Displaying inappropriate or disproportionate emotions (e.g., acting extraordinarily happy to meet a new client or sobbing uncontrollably when a person expresses painful feelings)

Source: Cournoyer, B. R. (2005). *The social work skills workbook* (4th ed). Belmont, CA: Thomson Brooks/Cole, pp. 131–132.

---

of professionals (Baker, 1988; Wasel-Grimm, 1995). As interviewers, we are responsible for creating a climate in which applicants may share valid and reliable information.

Creating a Productive Climate By creating a climate in which the applicant can comfortably share thoughts, feelings, and perceptions, you increase the likelihood of securing valid and reliable data. This requires considerable communication skill, careful observation, and judgment to ensure that your verbal and nonverbal behavior encourages full and open sharing. It is remarkably easy to consciously manipulate or unconsciously affect others' expressions. We may also make communication mistakes that affect

the interview. Exhibit 10-8 contains a list of communication errors commonly made by social workers.

A productive climate that encourages participation is integral to the development of a collaborative helping partnership characterized by full and open communications. The context of the interview, the questions you ask, the nature of your responses, your body language and gestures all influence applicant participation.

Providing a Focus With the applicant's participation, you need to establish a purpose early and focus the interview in relation to the purpose. When pursuing what the applicant has said, you should detect areas related to the interview's central focus. Try to avoid irrelevant and tangential material, but make note of events, subjects, and themes that arise. They may suggest a focus for subsequent interviews.

Rosen and Lieberman report an experimental study of the content relevance of workers' responses—that is, "the extent to which the content of an interactive response is perceived by a participant to be relevant and in agreement with the participant's own definition and expectations of the content to be dealt with in the treatment relationship" (1972, p. 398). Workers with more training did significantly better at maintaining content relevance with compliant clients. Interestingly, workers with less training reflected more content-relevant responses with aggressive clients. However, many of their responses were harsh and retaliatory and failed to promote communications. These findings point to the need for clear worker and client understanding of the purpose of the interview (Rosen & Lieberman, 1972).

Communications Modes   During interviews, try to recognize applicants' preferred modes of expression. People tend express themselves in the following modal domains:

- *Perceptual*—interactions and communications about applicants' observations or perceptions, usually through sight or hearing but sometimes through other senses as well.
- *Cognitive*—interactions and communications about applicants' thoughts or images. This mode includes both the words people say to themselves—conclusions, interpretations, and hypotheses—as well as things we imagine in the form of mental pictures.
- *Affective*—interactions and communications about applicants' feelings and emotions as well as associated internal sensations. Anxiety, for instance, involves both an emotional as well as a physiological experience.
- *Behavioral*—interactions and communications about applicants' past, current, or anticipated behavior—often considered as excesses or deficits. For example, one person might engage in too much aggressive behavior, and another might engage in too little assertive behavior.

People express themselves in and communicate about all four modes but may reflect a preference for one or another. Some applicants in crisis might well express themselves in a highly emotional manner, but others may remain very cognitive or intellectual in both mode and content. Indeed, many applicants prefer to express themselves cognitively before expressing feelings and emotions.

Imagine, for example, that you are interviewing Chan, a 16-year-old boy who frequently argues with his father. Following a recent argument, Chan stormed out of the house and drove off in a neighbor's car. In discussing the situation, Chan might begin by saying that he and his dad do not get along, that his dad does not understand him, or that his dad is unfair. These are all cognitive statements. They reflect his interpretation of perceived events. Some interviewers might simply accept Chan's interpretation and move quickly to another topic or perhaps encourage expression of feeling. However, Chan's perceptions deserve further exploration: What took place? What did Chan see and hear? What did his father say? What did Chan think? What did Chan say? What happened then? After exploring the incident in detail, you and Chan are both prepared to consider alternative interpretations of the events. After moving back to the perceptual level ("What did you see and hear?") and reconsidering the cognitive level ("What meanings do you attach to what you saw and heard?"), you may move the interview to the affective level ("What did you feel when this was occurring? Do I detect a note of anger in your voice? As you look back on it now, what kinds of reactions are you having?"). And from the feeling level, the next logical step is to behavior ("What did you do when this happened? As you look back, what might have been other ways of handling yourself? In view of such experiences, if you and your father have future arguments, what are ways in which you think you might behave?"). Take some time to explore the incidents in some detail before considering Chan's feelings and behavior. Failure to collect perceptual and cognitive data often leads to flawed decisions based on insufficient information.

Interviewing Techniques   We regard interviewing as a disciplined art. You may wonder if discipline interferes with spontaneity or perhaps if development of interviewing skills could leave you feeling technical or mechanical rather than warm and human. We do not think so. Indeed, we believe that learning appropriate communication skills tends to increase spontaneity for two reasons: (1) In the process of learning about interviewing, you become aware of—and able to correct—common communication errors in your interactions with others, and (2) you expand the repertoire of potential responses available to you. The larger menu of potential skills permits increased spontaneity. As Kadushin suggests, "Technical skill is not antithetical to spontaneity. In fact, it permits a higher form of spontaneity; the skilled interviewer can deliberately violate the techniques as the occasion demands. Technical skill frees the interviewer in responding as a human being to the interviewee" (1972, p. 2). As we have already noted, the graceful figure skater could not become spontaneous and free without many hours of disciplined practice. So it is with interviewing skills. Spontaneity and creativity in communications emerge through learning and disciplined practice.

Consider three interviewing skills for data collection, which are designed to encourage applicant participation, expression, and exploration: (1) open-ended questioning, (2) seeking clarification, and (3) active listening.

Open-Ended Questions   Open-ended questions provide applicants opportunities to express and explore a topic with considerable freedom. These questions cannot easily be answered with a "yes," "no," or a brief response. A few examples: "What is your relationship with your son like?" "How did you reach that conclusion?" "What would you like to accomplish through our work together?" Closed-ended questions yield brief responses: "What is your telephone number?" "Do you prefer to meet at our agency office or in your home?" "Are you in a relationship right now?" Unless it is an emergency situation where you must quickly obtain specific data, open-ended questions are generally preferred because they allow applicants to participate more fully and freely. If an applicant hesitates, you can come back with a more focused question. An interview can be thought of as a funnel; it begins with broad, open-ended questions and becomes more focused as you and the applicant narrow in on specific areas of concern. In the following example, a student describes her attempt to interview a social worker about her work. Starting this interview with an open-ended question might have both invited participation and brought focus to the purpose.

> Following a brief statement concerning the purpose of and time frame for the interview, I asked my first real question. "Do you view your work as social work?" In response, Joan asked, "What is your definition of social work?" I replied that rather than define social work at this point I would prefer to learn more about the work that she is doing, and perhaps at some time in another interview we could approach the topic of social work as it relates to her work. At this point in the interview I felt briefly that our roles in the interview situation had been reversed.

Recognize that questions may reveal your biases or assumptions. Effective data collection requires considerable objectivity or neutrality. As Cournoyer and Byers suggest (Reading 13), you must

> be aware that some questions may contain an implied suggestion or judgment. For example, you might say to a group member, "John, have you told your mother yet?" You may intend this as a simple request for information. However, John . . . might interpret this as a suggestion that, if he has not yet done so, he *should* tell his mother as soon as possible.

Tone of voice and nonverbal communications can betray bias as easily as your choice of words can. The purpose of the data collection interview is to secure reliable and valid information about the applicant's perceptions, interpretations, feelings, and behaviors as they relate to the problem and goals. Objectivity or neutrality is especially important at this stage. If you share opinions, offer advice, reveal stereotypes, or reflect bias, applicants would likely alter their communications. The data could well become less valid or reliable. Later, when you have explored the applicant's views and experiences, you may consider offering your own knowledge and judgment to the applicant, when various intervention strategies are under consideration.

Social workers generally avoid asking "why" questions. Unless your tone of voice and nonverbal behavior convey sincere concern and genuine neutrality, asking "why" tends to produce defensive reactions, justifications, or rationalizations. People are often interested in learning the answer to "why" questions but usually cannot answer them directly—perhaps especially during the early stages of work. Rather than asking "why," we usually ask "how" or "what" questions: Particularly for problem solving, descriptions are typically more useful than explanations. Questions such as the following tend to be more productive: "What happened then?" "How did you respond?" "What did you do?" "What was that like?" "How did you feel?"

Seeking Clarification   In seeking clarification, you invite applicants to say more about a particular topic, to elaborate or perhaps to specify. An open-ended

---

EXHIBIT 10-9
Seeking Clarification

Suppose that a client says, "I don't get along with my father." Here are some possible responses that meet two important requirements of interviewing: (1) encouraging the client to participate and (2) helping to provide structure to the interview.

- How do you feel about this?
- You don't get along with your father.
- What do you mean when you say . . . ?
- Give me an example of how you . . .
- Tell me more about this.
- Oh?
- For instance?
- When did you first notice that . . .
- What are some of the things you and your father disagree about?
- What is your father like?
- You seem to be very upset about this.

- Perhaps you could share some of your ideas about what has caused these problems.
- If your father was here, what would he say about this problem?

And here are three guidelines:

1. Avoid asking a question that calls for a yes or no answer.
2. It probably never helps to ask the question why. If clients knew why they were having trouble, they wouldn't be seeing you.
3. Silence is a possible probing response. Because it tends to provoke anxiety, especially in adolescents, it generally loses its effect if too prolonged.

Source: Richard J. Bealka, M.D., psychiatrist, Mental Health Institute, Independence, Iowa.

---

question, such as "What do you mean when you say 'it hurts your feelings'?," involves a request for clarification. It relates to something the applicant has said and provides an opportunity for exploration at a somewhat greater depth or specificity (see Exhibit 10-9).

Active Listening Active listening represents a concrete indication that you are genuinely trying to understand the applicant's perceptions, thoughts, feelings, or behaviors. Unlike questions, it is a tangible reflection of empathic understanding. Active listening is a key dimension of the essential feedback loop between you and the applicant. It helps applicants determine if you understand their comments and helps you assess if your understanding is indeed consistent with what applicants mean to convey. If you fail to communicate understanding through active listening or if you do so inaccurately, applicants tend to become inhibited, uncomfortable, or perhaps annoyed. People hope and expect to be understood when they consult a helping professional. If you do not periodically listen actively, they may feel acutely discouraged. However, if you accurately communicate understanding, people tend to feel hopeful and become more expressive. The best active listening responses are equivalent reflections of others' messages.

You listen carefully and communicate your understanding of a speaker's messages by reflecting or mirroring them back. In essence, you paraphrase the client's message. Ideally, your words should be essentially equivalent to or synonymous with those of the client. If factual information is expressed, your active listening response should convey that factual information. If feelings are communicated, your active listening response should reflect those feelings and should be of equivalent intensity. If ideas are expressed, you should paraphrase those ideas so that the other's meaning is accurately captured. (Cournoyer, 2005)

You may use certain lead-in phrases to signal your attempts at active listening: "I hear you saying . . ." "You feel . . ." "You think . . ." At first, active listening may seem somewhat awkward or artificial because it is seldom used in everyday conversation. However, its use dramatically decreases misunderstandings and encourages applicants to continue the process of expression and exploration. Rosen and Lieberman examined the use of such skills among social workers by comparing "the extent to which a response by one participant in the relationship provides feedback to the other participant that the message sent was actually received" (1972, p. 398). They found that trained workers maintained a higher rate of congruent responses than untrained workers. This suggests that the skill may be acquired and improved through training.

Other Data Collection Tools

Observation As social creatures, people tend to observe people in their daily interaction with others and may formulate hypotheses or perhaps conclusions about them on that basis. Indeed, "people watching" is a common pastime. As a social worker, however, you must become a sophisticated observer who thinks critically about the meaning of data obtained in that fashion. Observations may occur in a structured or unstructured fashion and the observer may be an unnoticed observer, a noticed but uninvolved observer, a participant observer, or an active observer who leads and initiates. For example, you may give a group of children a game to play and then observe and record their actions without participating in the game. You might serve as a committee member who participates and observes or as a committee chairperson who provides leadership as well.

You might well wonder how effectively you could both participate in or lead an interactive experience and simultaneously engage in careful observation. However, this is often what social workers must do. Of course, like data collected through other methods, the quality of observational data is subject to the bias and selectivity of the observer. No one can possibly observe all the behaviors of a person or group. Imagine how difficult it would be to track solely the facial expressions and changes in posture of a single interviewee. You cannot possibly observe all behaviors of other people, so you must focus on certain kinds of data. For example, in a family meeting, social workers might observe the proximity and positions of the family members relative to each other and to the worker, or perhaps the facial expressions of members as they communicate with each other member. Another social worker might observe the exchanges between a parent and an allegedly abused child—perhaps tracking the frequency and proportion of expressions classified as empathic, demanding, critical, hostile, supportive, and so forth—in an attempt to assess the quality of the relationship. Identify the theoretical or, preferably, the research based framework that guides your selection of observational targets. Recognize and acknowledge your own biases, stereotypes, preconceptions, and expectations; manage them; and resist the temptation to

reach fixed conclusions based on small samples of data observed under atypical circumstances. Generally speaking, information derived from interviews and observations are primarily useful for generating hypotheses rather than for determining truth or validity. Like most other people, helping professionals cannot consistently distinguish truthful from deceptive responses (Ekman & O'Sullivan, 1991; McDermott, Tseng, Char, & Fukunaga, 1978).

Questionnaires Scales, surveys, questionnaires, and other assessment instruments may contribute relevant data as well (Marlow, 1998; Oppenheim, 1992; Rubin & Babbie, 1997). Agencies often require new applicants to complete intake forms. Anonymous written questionnaires or surveys may help a group or committee determine priorities or agenda items. Written exercises may be used in family work to allow members to express themselves without the risk of directly confronting other members. Surveys may help generate data for use in community organizing. Increasingly, social workers incorporate rapid assessment instruments (RAIs) for the purposes of data collection and evaluation of progress toward goals (Corcoran & Fischer, 2000a, 2000b; Fredman & Sherman, 1987; Hudson, 1982). When combined and integrated, data collected through multiple methods—interviews, observations, and instruments—from multiple sources, at different times, and in different contexts reflects a greater likelihood of validity and reliability. Common sense dictates that data obtained from a single interview, based on verbal exchanges that occur under the atypical conditions in which applicants and social workers meet, would rarely reveal a full and accurate understanding of a problem or situation and certainly not of a person, relationship, family, group, organization, or community. The data collected through interviews, observations, and instruments serve as indicators and stimuli for generating questions and hypotheses that may then be examined through various means over time.

Data Collection by Applicants

We usually think of the social worker as the collector of data. However, applicants may also be involved. Indeed, we urge you to encourage applicant participation in data collection processes whenever possible. Applicants may be able to secure reports from other agencies, collect data from friends and neighbors, and research neighborhood resources to locate mutual aid groups, religious organizations, and so forth (Delgado, 1996). Applicants may keep logs, write diaries, or track the frequency and intensity of certain phenomena. In community organization work, you might involve residents in data collection from other community members regarding matters that need to be changed and the desired goals. Reconsider the Birky family case (Reading 6). Suppose that the social worker and the family decide to organize tenants in the housing development to repair the open ditch and reduce other neighborhood hazards to children. Mr. and Mrs. Birky could assist in data collection by talking with neighbors to identify hazards to children and by helping to organize a neighborhood forum on the subject. We suggest that, in the assessment process, you and the applicant discuss your data needs, formulate the questions you want to answer, and develop a plan that addresses how the data will be collected, by whom, and when.

You may also ask other persons to collect data. In some situations, a person close to the applicant and knowledgeable about the situation may interview the applicant, collect observational data, or provide a paper-and-pencil assessment instrument. Other professionals may also be asked to administer oral or written tests to collect data about applicants and clients. Psychologists, for instance, may conduct sophisticated psychological examinations, neurologists may test for the presence of brain anomalies, ophthalmologists may test for visual problems, audiologists for hearing problems, and other experts for various additional conditions.

◆ Processing Data and Decision Making

Data are collected to guide decision making about the nature, scope, severity, or urgency of the problem; the goals; and the action plan. Given our emphasis on collaborative partnerships, we believe that applicants should play an essential role in the decision-making process. However, views about the role of applicants in decision making span a continuum from no involvement on one extreme to primary decision maker at the other. At one of these poles, Franklin and Jordan (Reading 16) imply that social workers collect data and take responsibility for decision making. They do not refer to applicant involvement. This may be partly because of their focus on workers in managed care behavioral health. Of course, applicants could be involved in any of the assessment models that they describe.

At the other pole, Burford, Pennell, and MacLeod (Reading 15) describe a Canadian experience with family group conferences. Family group conferences originated in New Zealand as a way of responding to youthful offenders and to children in need of care and protection (Hudson, Maxwell, Morris, & Galaway, 1995). In this approach, social workers and other professionals perform two functions. They facilitate a process of family decision making, and they provide the family members with data for consideration in their decision making. The family also has data available from its own members and, in the case of youthful offenders, from the victims. The family then meets privately to develop a plan to deal with the youthful misbehavior or to provide for the safety, protection, and nurturance of their children. The plan that results from the family's assessment is presented to the professionals for their feedback and consent.

Family group conferences and other participatory approaches to assessment empower families and often enhance motivation to carry out the plan. Applicant participation in decision making also ensures that the applicant's frame of reference is genuinely considered and facilitates recognition of applicant strengths (Cowger, 1994; de Jong & Miller, 1995; Saleebey, 2001a, 2001b, 2002). We courage you to seek active client participation in all phases of problem solving, including assessment (Dean, 1993). Exhibit 10-10 contains 12 guidelines for strengths assessment that incorporate client participation. They provide an alternative to existing normative and deficit models of diagnosis and treatment.

Use of Knowledge

Assessment is an active thinking, hypothesis-generating, and testing process that integrates understanding and knowledge for problem solving and goal attainment. A sound assessment contributes to the development of an action plan. Assessments result from the organization and analysis of data collected through interviews, observations, instrumentation, or other means. Certain questions and hypotheses guide the process. They emerge from the material applicants share; your professional knowledge of individual and social biopsychosocial development, human behavior,

---

EXHIBIT 10-10
Guidelines for Strengths Assessment

1. Give preeminence to the client's understanding of the facts.
2. Believe the client.
3. Discover what the client wants.
4. Move the assessment toward personal and environmental strengths.
5. Make assessment of strengths multidimensional.
6. Use the assessment to discover uniqueness.
7. Use language the client can understand.
8. Make assessment a joint activity between worker and client.
9. Reach a mutual agreement on the assessment.
10. Avoid blame and blaming.
11. Avoid cause-and-effect thinking.
12. Assess; do not diagnose.

Source: Cowger, C. D. (1994). Assessing client strengths: Clinical assessment for client empowerment. *Social Work, 39*(3), 262–267, pp. 265–267.

---

change processes; the genesis and course of the problem; and the effects of prior responses to the problem situation. Of course, you also draw on knowledge from relevant research studies regarding the nature of the identified problem, the characteristics of the population from which the applicant comes, and the effectiveness of programs, policies, services, or practices designed to address the problem.

In assessment, you consider the relevance and applicability of generalized knowledge to particular situations. You ask questions to determine how each applicant's situation matches or differs from those of others in similar circumstances and those reflected through nomothetic evidence. For example, if an applicant is dealing with the recent death of her husband, you might refer to generalized knowledge regarding thoughts, feelings, and life tasks that commonly accompany such a loss. You seek to assess how she is coping and to determine if the tasks and feelings represent problems for the applicant. Thus, you might say, "I imagine you have experienced many changes since your husband passed away," or ask questions such as, "What has it been like since your husband's death?" or "How do you handle the chores your husband used to do?" In such a situation, it may be easier to first ask for descriptive information before talking about feelings. Feelings may emerge spontaneously in response to these descriptive questions. If not, you may explore feelings more directly later.

The problem-solving model asks you to consider the duration, previous occurrences, and precipitating factors of the problem. Applicants who have struggled with a problem over a long period usually develop patterns of adjustment or accommodation. They may find it difficult to consider alternate perspectives or approaches. Problems with a recent onset are often easier to understand and address because applicants have yet to establish fixed patterns of adaptation. If an applicant sighs and says the problem seems to have gone on forever, you may wonder how much energy or motivation is available to invest in solution seeking. The applicant may have a sense that the problem is unmanageable. In formulating assessments, applicants or clients and workers must determine whether assumptions abstracted from general knowledge apply to their particular circumstances.

Applicants have different motives and intentions for meeting with social workers. If you can answer the question, "Why are they here?," you may learn a great deal. Something may have recently changed to increase distress, enhance motivation or hope, or provide new urgency. Perhaps the situation reached a point where the applicant feels unable to go on without some relief. Sometimes established patterns of adjustment or accommodation to long-standing problems gradually or suddenly become ineffective so that people experience new levels of discomfort.

Data about previous occurrences of the problem and prior attempts to address it permit some estimate of applicants' capacity to plan, anticipate consequences and outcomes, and invest energy in problem-solving activities. Such information also provides an indication of applicants' understanding of change processes and social situations, and their ability to apply social and problem-solving skills. Of course, numerous environmental factors may affect the effectiveness of problem-solving actions. Data about aspects of the situation that have contributed to or interfered with problem resolution represent key material for assessment. While collecting and organizing data, social workers attempt to develop empathic understanding of applicants' experience—whether expressed verbally or nonverbally, or through other means. These data often naturally lead to questions or hypotheses guided by various research findings and theories within the professional knowledge base.

To illustrate the use of professional knowledge, reconsider Mr. Keene's situation as presented in Exhibit 8-8. Assume that, at the point of the last recording, the worker left the agency and you were assigned to serve Mr. Keene. A visit is scheduled for tomorrow. In preparing for the meeting, you review the information generated by the previous worker and develop a preliminary plan or agenda for the interview. You fully recognize that the preliminary plan is subject to change based on your actual meeting with the client.

In preparing, make note of the previous worker's recorded definition of the problem and assessment of the situation. Based on the record, it appears that the worker focused on Mr. Keene's level of functioning relative to an idealized notion of how fathers should relate to their children. The record did not reveal attempts to assess systemic factors and processes, or to recognize the nature and extent of Mr. Keene's internal distress. The previous worker appeared to view Mr. Keene as a rather impetuous, dependent man, who was inconsistent in his relationship with the children and impulsive in his relationship with his wife. The record does not reflect an understanding of Mr. Keene's experience of the situation, the knowledge he had of the problem, or his social skills in dealing with the multiple systems with which he suddenly had to interact. In attempting to develop a tentative assessment of the situation, you might return to the factors that precipitated onset of the problem.

If you did, you might notice that the problem began as a crisis for Mr. Keene. His wife suddenly lost contact with reality and had to be hospitalized. Suppose you asked questions such as the following: How are people affected by crises? How do crises affect people's abilities to cope? How are their thought processes and judgment affected? Might some people become more emotionally and socially dependent during periods of crisis? What might happen if you explore with Mr. Keene what his wife means to him,

how her illness affects him, and what the hospitalization might suggest about the future? What could occur if you explore the origin and development of the relationship between Mr. Keene and his wife? What if you ask Mr. Keene about his understanding of the nature and prognosis of his wife's illness and find, as it seems from the record, that he is largely ignorant about her condition? Can we expect applicants to deal effectively with a problem when they do not have or do not comprehend the facts of the situation? What might happen if you ask Mr. Keene if he would like you to talk with the hospital staff or perhaps join him in a visit to his wife?

What if you applied professional knowledge about the effects on people of the sudden loss of their spouses and used that knowledge to communicate understanding and provide support? Might he become more able to fulfill his parental responsibilities if he receives help to cope with the crisis associated with the hospitalization of his wife?

Our professional knowledge might inform you that, in many instances of death and illness, family members feel remorseful, angry, deserted, or fearful. Is it possible that Mr. Keene's inconsistent relationship with the children and his wife comes from remorse, anger, or fear? We might also recognize that intense feelings may restrict the ability to hear, understand, and process information. What might happen if you help Mr. Keene to lower the intensity of his feelings before discussing difficult topics that require decisions and actions?

According to the case description, the worker seemed to concentrate on Mr. Keene's responsibility to care for the children and did not address his experience of crisis about his wife and their relationship. Such an understanding seems critical to the assessment of the situation. Additional questions may be important: What is Mr. Keene's notion of the roles of husband and father? Does the macro system from which he comes set forth these roles in ways that conflict with the worker's and housekeepers' notions? Does Mr. Keene have an extended family support system? Can he turn to his neighbors? As you think about the plan for the first interview with Mr. Keene, what do you identify as the most helpful way to approach him? Your plan for the first interview might look something like the one presented in Exhibit 10-11. In reviewing the plan, observe how assessment questions have been used as a guide? Also notice how assessment of Mr. Keene's

---

EXHIBIT 10-11
An Interview Plan Reflecting a Systems Perspective

A. Problems for exploration
1. Reactions to change in workers
2. Problems of grief and loss
3. Problem of transition to single parent
4. Care of children

B. Climate of the interview
1. Convey concern and respect for Mr. Keene and his feelings
2. Communicate acceptance and support
3. Remain empathic and responsive
4. Convey recognition of the value of his statements

C. Pace of interview
1. Adopt a relatively relaxed pace, try to match Mr. Keene's tempo

D. Data collection
1. Be alert to vocal and nonverbal clues
2. Attempt to expand, amplify, and clarify Mr. Keene's experience with his wife's illness and the meaning it holds for him

3. Encourage identification of support networks and hospital contacts
4. Explore Mr. Keene's knowledge of mental illness
5. Explore Mr. Keene's understanding of his children's psychosocial development needs and their need for adequate care

E. Plan of interview
1. Establish a beginning contact with Mr. Keene
2. Learn more about Mr. Keene's struggles, worries, and stresses
3. Offer help to Mr. Keene to understand his wife's illness
4. Offer appropriate support to Mr. Keene
5. Recognize Mr. Keene's struggles

F. Goal of interview
1. A beginning understanding of the problems for work
2. A preliminary agreement with Mr. Keene that allows for work on the problem to proceed

---

loss, remorse, and pain about his wife's illness affects the plan for the interview and its pace.

Assessment Instruments

The various assessment instruments available (Boughner, Hayes, Bubenzer, & West, 1994; Corcoran & Fischer, 2000a, 2000b; Hudson, 1982; Reichertz & Frankel, 1993; Van Hook, Berkman, & Dunkle, 1996) can be grouped in three categories: (1) instruments that facilitate data collection, (2) instruments that aid in organizing and processing data, (3) instruments that contribute to decision making.

Instruments designed to facilitate data collection, including questionnaires and application forms, are used to accelerate data collection. They may be computerized to enable rapid processing and tabulation for agency communication and statistical reports. Often useful, forms and instruments should be carefully reviewed for validity, reliability, relevance, readability, and linguistic and cultural sensitivity. Are they balanced? Do they provide data that are actually needed? For example, an application form that asks

for a description of the presenting problem should also ask what the applicant wants done about the problem. A form that has a checklist for problem behaviors should also include a checklist for applicant strengths.

Instruments for presenting and processing data include outlines for organizing information. The format for the service plan presented in Chapter 11 (Exhibit 11-5), the sample case plan presented in 'Reading 18 by Fein and Staff (Exhibit R18-3), and genograms and eco-maps (Reading 4) are examples. These are tools for organizing data to generate information needed for decision making.

Instruments that contribute to decision making are usually designed to measure some underlying concept—self-esteem, social support, anger, family functioning, and so forth—that may be subject to change efforts. These instruments are usually scales or indices. The scale provides a score indicating the extent to which that concept is present or absent. Such assessment instruments should be used with considerable caution and interpreted with understanding of psychometric principles and properties.

Even tools with solid evidence of validity and reliability are never completely accurate. There is some probability of false positives and false negatives. Suppose, for instance, there is a scale to measure a potential for abusive behavior toward children. Findings from aggregated data suggest that a certain probability—usually considerably less than 100%—exists that a person scoring 85 or higher reflects a strong potential for child abuse. Some of the people who score in that high range are not actually likely to abuse children. Their scores are false positives. Imagine the consequences if a social worker concluded and reported those results without accurately and completely explaining the nature of probability and the potential for error. A person might easily be inaccurately labeled a potential or actual child abuser. The consequences could be extreme: loss of family, job, or reputation might ensue.

Findings from aggregated data also suggest that a certain probability—again typically much less than 100%—exists that a person scoring 35 or lower reflects a low potential for child abuse. However, some people who score in this low range are, in fact, quite likely to abuse children. Their scores are false negatives. Suppose a social worker concluded that a person reflecting a low score is free from any abuse potential and may safely interact with children. Imagine the consequences if that person subsequently abused a child so severely that the child died. How would you feel if you were the social worker?

Like interviews and observations, scales cannot make 100% determinations in individual cases. They can only be used to estimate probabilities (Rubin & Babbie, 1997). When using a scale, examine the studies that determined its validity and reliability. Consider the nature of the participants in those original studies. Scales are standardized for one or more populations. They may not be valid and reliable for other populations—although they are often used for other groups. You may feel more comfortable using scales that have been standardized with several different populations, at several different points in time, and that have produced relatively consistent evidence of reliability and validity.

You have a professional responsibility to be thoroughly familiar with any assessment instruments employed. You must have detailed knowledge about how the scale was developed, populations for which it has been standardized, and its known reliability and validity. We strongly recommend that you discuss any

results of the tests and instruments with the applicant and treat this as information for consideration. Remember to incorporate the issue of probability and false negatives and false positives. You and the applicant should jointly decide whether the results from the assessment instrument are useful for your problem-solving purposes.

Assessment as Negotiation

The purpose of assessment is to develop a service plan acceptable to you and the applicant. This is most likely to occur if you collaboratively negotiate the definition of the problem, the desired goals, and the appropriate action plan with applicants. Negotiation has been recognized as a way of working with respondents (Murdach, 1980), resolving differences of opinion regarding the problem, reaching consensus about goals (de Jong & Miller, 1995), and making decisions about the action plan. Negotiation requires a communication process and respect for the views of those involved.

◆ Assessment as a Continuous Process

Assessment involves collecting data, processing and organizing data, and negotiating decision making between social workers and applicants or clients. Indeed, these processes continue throughout your work as applicants make the transition into the role of client. Assessment, therefore, is a continuous process. Given new data, new information, or new perspectives, you and the client may decide to pursue different goals. As a result, service plans may require revision.

Partialization

Partialization is the process of selecting which of the problems brought by the applicant should be addressed first. You cannot do everything at once. Applicants and workers must make decisions about where to begin. For example, the Birky family (Reading 6) faces a very large number of problems. Working with more than one or two at a time could easily overwhelm both the family and the worker.

But how do you partialize? As with most decisions, this is a matter to be negotiated between you and the applicant. One possibility is to start by asking what issues are troubling the applicant and what solutions are sought. You may start with either problems or solutions. The two are integrally linked. The applicant can make a list, and you may suggest changes or additions from your own observations and experience. If the applicant disagrees with your perception of a problem area, you have two options: (1) You may withdraw your proposal but indicate that you would like to return to it at a later time, or (2) you may explore the differences of view between you and the applicant. Be open to the possibility that your perception could be incorrect. In the early contacts with applicants, the first option is preferable, unless the matter is very urgent and may involve the safety of others. You can always raise the topic again when the client is more comfortable with you.

Once you have generated a list, ask where the applicant would like to start. Try to begin with the applicant's choice, if at all possible. Such a process tends to enhance client motivation and increase the likelihood of success.

Sequencing of Service Plans

How many problems can you and the client attempt to resolve at one time? We suggest that you focus initially on a single problem area, along with the associated goals and action plans. As you make progress in that area, you and the client may then take on additional problems, solutions, and actions. These may be items from your original list, matters that you held for reconsideration, or new problems that emerge during your work together. You can discuss, negotiate, and phase in new service plans as you proceed. As clients begin to experience some success and progress, their motivation often increases. Avoid overwhelming people with more and more issues and goals. If you are unsure whether a client is ready to move to another area, ask. Clients are often the best source of information about themselves.

◆ Chapter Summary

Assessment is the use of information to make decisions about the nature of the problem, what should be done about the problem, and how this should be accomplished. It includes the collection and organization of data to provide information needed for decision making. Applicants actively participate as full

partners in the process. Potentially stigmatizing labels are used with great caution and within the context of person-first thinking and language. Classification schemes such as the *DSM-IV* may help social workers and applicants and clients access authoritative and research-based information about conditions and effective practices but must always be recognized as conceptual tools that rarely match the actual experience of individual people. The person-in-environment (PIE) system has considerable potential, especially if used in partnership with applicants and clients.

Data collection responsibilities may be shared with applicants. Indeed, applicants are often the primary source of data. Data collection usually involves interviewing, observing, and sometimes instrumentation. You are responsible for creating a climate in which the applicant can share, providing a focus for data collection, distinguishing among various communication modes (perceptions, cognitions, behaviors, and feelings), and using interviewing skills that encourage applicant participation. We recommend that your data collection efforts be guided by the following principles:

- Applicants are the primary, although often not the only, source of data.
- Applicants should be informed about your data collection activities.
- Data are collected for use in problem solving.
- Applicants have a right to know what you know and to review data that you collect.

Assessment is a collaborative attempt to collect data and analyze information about the nature, scope, duration, severity, and urgency of the problem situation; the meaning of the problem to the applicant; the applicant's desired outcome; and the strengths, resources, and potentials within the applicant and the environment for use in clarifying targets of changes, refining goals and objectives and determining their relevance and feasibility, and developing plans to reach goals and evaluate progress toward their achievement. Decision making is participatory and collaborative. Assessment involves negotiations directed toward the development of a jointly agreed-upon service plan that reflects a reasonable probability of effectively resolving the identified problem and achieving the desired goals. Assessment sometimes involves partialization. Many applicants and clients face numerous problems and issues that cannot reasonably be addressed simultaneously. A process of selection and prioritization is required. Finally, assessment is a continuous process. As you and clients work together, new data may emerge—perhaps in the form of recent research studies or evaluations of the effects of your work together—so that new decisions must be made.

Learning Exercises: Readings, InfoTrac, and the Web

1. Use your word-processing computer program to enter the important terms and concepts presented in this chapter in alphabetical order. Place a question mark by any terms that you do not clearly understand. Save your document as EX 10-1.

2. Log on to the InfoTrac College Edition Web site. Conduct a keyword search (using either Keyword Search or Advanced Search) to locate the article entitled "Family Processes as Predictors of Adolescents' Preferences for Ascribed Sources of Moral Authority: A Proposed Model" (White, 1996). Also access the articles entitled "Collaboration with Families in the Functional Behavior Assessment of and Intervention for Severe Behavior Problems" (Peterson, Derby, Berg, & Horner, 2002) and "Clinical Practice Guideline: Diagnosis and Evaluation of the Child with Attention-Deficit/Hyperactivity Disorder" (American Academy of Pediatrics, 2000). Read the articles and prepare a two-page essay in which you reflect on their implications for assessment processes within the context of social work and social work practice. Save your document as EX 10-2.

3. Turn to **Reading 15: Family Group Decision Making.** Authors Gale Burford, Joan Pennell, and Susan MacLeod describe the application of family group conferences, an assessment process that shifts power and authority for decision making to families. The social worker and other professionals provide data to the family; the family processes the data and develops a plan. The family undertakes the assessment, although the plan that results from their assessment is subject to approval by the professionals. Review the article and reflect on its implications for topics addressed in this chapter. Prepare a one-page essay to explore your observations and reactions. Save your document as EX 10-3.

4. Turn to **Reading 16: The Clinical Utility of Models and Methods of Assessment in Managed Care.** Cynthia Franklin and Catheleen Jordan discuss four assessment models—psychosocial, cognitive behavioral, life models, and family systems—and develop a fifth, which they call technical eclecticism, to integrate methods from the other four models. Prepare a one-page essay to explore your observations and reactions to the authors' approach to assessment. Consider the strengths as well as the weaknesses of the assessment models, and contrast the role of the professional with that reflected in Reading 15, "Family Group Decision Making," by Gale Burford, Joan Pennell, and Susan MacLeod. Save your document as EX 10-4.

5. Review Exhibit 10-11, which contains a plan for the interview with Mr. Keene. Prepare a one-page essay in which you address the following questions: How have questions related to assessment been used to guide the interview? How might exploration and assessment of Mr. Keene's loss, remorse, and pain concerning his wife's illness affect the climate and the pace of the interview? Save your document as EX 10-5.

6. Look again at Readings 3, 7, and 9. "The House on Sixth Street" reflects service to applicants who are seeking help, and the Stover family and Betty Smith cases involve respondents referred by an agency or institution. Prepare a one-page essay in which you compare the process of problem identification and description in these cases. How did the processes differ? What evidence do you see of negotiation? What do you find useful and what do you question in the problem identification process for each case? Save your document as EX 10-6.

7. Look again at Readings 7 and 9. Prepare a brief report comparing the coping resources of Ms. Smith and Mrs. Stover. Explore the similarities and differences in how they use those resources to address their respective situations? Also prepare an eco-map of each client situation. Save your document as EX 10-7.

8. Turn to **Reading 26: Leonard Timms** and **Reading 27: The Omar Family.** Review the case studies again to consider and reflect on the ways the social workers collected data and undertook the

assessment processes. Prepare a two-page essay to explore your observations and reactions. Be sure to discuss any hypotheses that you might have formulated to guide your search for additional data. Save your document as EX 10-8.

9. Interview two social workers, one from a mental health setting and one from another setting, about the *DSM-IV-TR*. Prepare a two-page report in which you summarize their views about the use of the *DSM-IV-TR* in their practice. Explore if, and if so, how they use the *DSM-IV-TR*. Discuss what they see as the strengths of *DSM-IV-TR* and what they consider its limitations for social work. Save your document as EX 10-9.

Chapter 11

The Service Agreement

Engagement, data collection, and assessment culminate in the formulation of an explicit service agreement. At that point, the applicant becomes a client. An explicit service agreement guides subsequent intervention activities. However, as new assessments or reassessments arise, you and the client may modify the service agreement accordingly. In this chapter, we integrate the major themes from the chapters on engagement and assessment by considering three components of the service plan:

- The statement or definition of the problem for work
- Agreed-upon goals or objectives
- The action plan to accomplish the identified goals or objectives.

The action plan includes the specific activities needed to accomplish the objectives. Typically, action plans include an outline of tasks or action steps for both the client and the worker, identification of roles that the worker will assume, and description of the change strategy or intervention approach.

◆ Aspects of the Service Agreement

Definition

Terminology We have previously used the term *service contract* (Compton & Galaway, 1989). Despite its wide currency (Bassin, 1993; Goulding, 1990; Maluccio & Marlow, 1974; Preston-Shoot, 1989; Reid, 1996; Rowe, 1996; Saxon, 1979; Shulman, 1992; Thomlison & Thomlison, 1996; Turner & Jaco, 1996;

Wickman, 1993), the concept of contracting has provoked some controversy (Croxton, 1988; Davis, 1985; Hoshino, 1994; Miller, 1990; Rojek & Collins, 1987, 1988). Critics argue that because of the more powerful position of the worker, applicants are not genuinely free to negotiate what they truly want and cannot always hold the worker accountable. Some suggest that the concept of contract does not accurately reflect the complexity of work with certain clients. On the other hand, some writers suggest that contracting encourages more ethical practice by making goals explicit and by recognizing that applicants have options (Bloom & Fischer, 1982; Ivanoff, Robinson, & Blythe, 1987; Tutty, 1990). Wood (1978) has linked the lack of an explicit contract with negative results from service.

Concerns about contracts are legitimate. However, we believe they are addressed by the principle of partnership that we emphasize. Power sharing and collaboration between worker and applicant is very different from the notion of coercive contracting, sometimes practiced in corrections agencies and schools, in which people are told what they must do and warned of the consequences for failure to comply. In an attempt to convey the mutuality of the process and avoid the legalistic implications of the term *contract,* we now use the term *service agreement* to capture the elements of the understanding reached between applicant and worker. The *action plan* is the part of the service agreement that describes the actions to be undertaken to reach the goals. In some portions of the professional literature, action plans may be called treatment plans, treatment contracts, intervention plans, or perhaps service plans.

Mutuality We have emphasized the collaborative nature of the partnership between worker and applicant or client in all phases of the problem-solving process—engagement, assessment, intervention, and evaluation. In the service agreement, however, the partnership concept is fully developed and made explicit.

The service agreement is

the explicit agreement between the worker and the client concerning the target problems, the goals, and the strategies of social work intervention, and the roles and tasks of the participants. Its major features are mutual agreement, differential participation in the intervention process, reciprocal accountability, and explicitness. In practice these features are closely interrelated. (Maluccio & Marlow, 1974, p. 30)

The concept of partnership does not mean that you and the client contribute the same knowledge, understanding, feeling, and activity. Your respective contributions usually differ in kind or degree.

As we have noted, an initial or exploratory agreement is developed in the engagement phase to facilitate data collection. The differences between an exploratory agreement and a working agreement are explained in Exhibit 11-1.

Negotiation The service agreement calls for input, decision making, planning, and commitment from both applicants and workers. It is your responsibility to respect applicants' individuality and to maximize opportunities for their self-determination in the process of arriving at a service agreement. You provide applicants with opportunities for meaningful decisions about self and situation through discussions, negotiations, generation of alternatives, and decision making. Consider the following questions as you negotiate service agreements:

1. Should the problem for work differ from the one that was initially identified?
2. What is the desired solution? Specifically, what goals or objectives should guide the action plan?
3. How will this solution be achieved?
4. What role or roles will the social worker assume?

Remember that the applicant may be an individual, family, group, organization, or community and that you may interact with applicants in a variety of settings.

In negotiating service agreements, social workers and applicants often confront differences—of perception and perspective—that must be resolved (Murdach, 1980, 1982; Seabury, 1976, 1979, 1985). Do not try to avoid conflicts. Instead, view them as a natural part of the process. Skirting or minimizing differences tends to corrupt the contracting process (Seabury, 1979). Try to tease out differences and then negotiate them. Even if the conflict cannot be resolved and an agreement cannot be reached, at least you and the applicant will not waste time or energy on a flawed agreement. In fact, a decision between you and an applicant not to pursue service because of recognized differences represents a legitimate agreement.

To be helpful, social workers must find some common ground with the applicant regarding problem definition, goals, and an action plan. This frequently involves bargaining and negotiating and often calls for patience and perseverance. Workers who close cases after a single contact with applicants because an agreement could not be reached may not fully understand the nature of the negotiation process. Agreements often take some time to work out.

The Problem for Work

Developing a service agreement involves joint assessment and decision making. During the engagement phase, you and the applicant arrived at an initial identification of the problem, set preliminary goals, collected relevant data, and explored the problem and potential solutions. On that basis, you and the applicant must now define the problem for work, what can be done, and how you are going to do it. This involves organizing the available data, information, and knowledge into a coherent form that explains the problem and suggests a number of possible solutions. This process includes two components: "analysis of a situation to identify the major factors operating within it" and "identification of those factors which appear most critical, definition of their interrelationships, and selection of those to be dealt with" (Bartlett, 1970, p. 144). Social workers and applicants must work hard and think critically to assemble and analyze the information and to make judgments about its meaning. Indeed, this represents a professional obligation for social workers.

The problem for work—as defined by you and the applicant on the basis of the completed assessment—may be the same as the initial presenting problem, may reflect a further specification or restatement of that problem, or may be entirely different. The target of change

---

EXHIBIT 11-1
Ingredients of a Social Work Service Agreement

A working agreement is essentially an understanding between at least two people and should cover:

1. The objectives or goals (the what) toward which each party shall work. These objectives should be specific, discrete, and, whenever feasible, observable.
2. The specific responsibilities of each party to the agreement in terms of rights and obligations.
3. The technique or means (the how) to be used in achieving the objectives.
4. The administrative procedures to be involved—when to meet, where to meet, and so on.

These four ingredients cover the essential terms of an agreement and should be explicit and detailed, so that each party knows clearly what is expected. It is possible to specify at least two types of agreements: *exploratory* and *working*.

1. The exploratory agreement represents a commitment, by both parties, to explore and ne-

gotiate the terms of a working agreement. No other commitment is made at this stage.
2. A working agreement may or may not grow out of an exploratory agreement; this will depend on the negotiation that takes place.

Therefore, it is possible to specify the following sequence:

1. Acceptance of an *exploratory* agreement.
2. The development of a *working* agreement.
3. Review and evaluation of the accomplishments of the working agreement.
4. Renegotiation resulting in a new working agreement or termination. This is essentially a repetition of stage 1.

Source: Joe Hudson, Professor, Faculty of Social Welfare, University of Calgary, Calgary, Canada.

---

may or may not be the applicant. Depending on the circumstances, the problem for work may be defined as residing within the applicant, outside the applicant, or as the result of the applicant-situation interaction.

Ideally, the definition of the problem suggests an effective solution that is incorporated with a formal, written problem statement (Reid, 1992). Here are several questions to ask about problem statements:

- Does the statement describe something in the applicant's current situation as a source of discomfort that the applicant wants changed?
- Is the statement specific and explicit? A broad general statement—for example, "Tom does poorly at school"—is not useful. A much more specific statement is: "Tom is failing mathematics" or "Tom has been absent 25 of the last 60 days of school."
- Is the applicant in the problem statement? If not, it may be someone else's problem. For example, a service plan for the applicant cannot be supported by a problem statement such as, "The mathematics teacher has too high a grading standard" or "The staff at the school do not like Tom."

A useful statement would be "Tom feels disliked by his teachers" or "Tom's mathematics skills do not meet passing standards for his class." Either of these latter statements would allow for action plans directed toward changing Tom's behavior, changing the mathematics standards, or changing the way teachers relate to Tom.

- Do you and the applicant have the capacity, power, and resources to solve or reduce the problem? It is not useful to formulate problems that lack possible solutions.
- Does the statement describe a problem for work, rather than a solution? The problem statement should suggest possible solutions but should not itself be a statement of the desired solution. Avoid statements such as "Tom needs to pass his mathematics course" or "Tom needs to improve school attendance."

Goals and Solutions

What are the desired goals of the joint work? What is the appropriate solution for the problem? To answer these questions, adopt the same process as you do when defining problems for work. Your first responsibility is to use interviewing skills to discover applicants' views of desired solutions. You may then share your view of a desired goal with the applicant. If the two views are incompatible, negotiate the differences, just as you resolve incongruent perceptions of the problem. Do not proceed to take action until or unless you and the applicant arrive at mutually agreeable goals and solutions. Lack of agreement invariably leads to frustration and often to failure.

Unfortunately, some professionals believe that only highly competent persons are able to participate in the problem-solving process. We strongly disagree. All human beings want something—if only to be rid of the worker! Regardless of their level of sophistication, wants of all kinds can be transformed into goals or objectives. For many applicants, securing essential resources needed for survival represents their only goal. Helping clients obtain food, shelter, clothing, medical care, or basic education represents an entirely worthy objective.[1] All people can participate in problem solving—regardless of the complexity of the problem—and benefit from the experience of collaborative partnership in the process. In our view, applicants must be actively involved in thinking about and agreeing to problems, goals, and plans. Social workers who think that small concrete objectives are unimportant or that obtaining basic needs for apathetic, withdrawn, depressed, or angry people need not involve mutual problem definition and goal-setting should reexamine their assumptions about the nature of professional social work.

Research into the outcomes of social work practice indicates that failure is often linked to a divergence of purpose between worker and applicant (Goldberg & Stanley, 1985; Lerner, 1972; Mayer & Timms, 1969; Polansky, Bergman, & de Saix, 1973). Indeed, difference of opinion about goals and solutions represents a core ingredient of what is often called "resistance." Many people hold specific expectations about the kinds of services social workers and agencies provide. They may be quite confused if you offer something they did not expect or do not understand. Indeed, a surprisingly large number of applicants often leave agencies in frustration following a disappointing initial visit.

Earlier, we indicated that engagement includes identifying the solutions that applicants want for the problems they are encountering. Through assessment, you consider these solutions—and, if appropriate, other possible solutions—and estimate their likely effectiveness. Record your joint decisions regarding the desired goals or objectives and solutions in the service plan. The agreed-upon solutions may emerge in the form of applicants' initial wants, a reframed or revised version of those wants, or an entirely different set. Regardless, they are jointly negotiated by you and the applicant and have the expressed consent of both parties (Berg & de Jong, 1996; Berg & Miller, 1992a, 1992b; Cowger, 1994).

In a qualitative study of workers' initial contact with applicants, Kenemore (1987) found that many social workers were uncomfortable with the prospect of negotiating the nature of goals and services. We hope that you come to view the negotiation process as a natural part of the process. It is essential to the development of a collaborative partnership and, we believe, substantially increases the probability of an effective outcome.

In negotiating goals, as in defining problems for work, look for common ground with the applicant. As the worker, your task is to find a common goal toward which you and the applicant can direct your change efforts. Begin with a goal that is important to the applicant and consistent with your professional obligations—even if there are others that you deem more significant. Anticipate that opportunities to introduce other goals will occur naturally during the course of your work together.

Consider the case of Mrs. Troy as described in Exhibit 11-2. The Troy family is experiencing what Germain and Gitterman call "problems and needs associated with tasks involved in life transitions" (1980, p. 32). From the worker's viewpoint, important goals would include Mrs. Troy's development of skills needed to cope with stress and to manage her children. After exploration and negotiation, however, the worker agreed with Mrs. Troy's goal to get John out of the house. Working toward this objective provided an opportunity for the worker to provide immediate assistance for Mrs. Troy. The objective also meets two important tests: (1) specificity and (2) attainability. Let's consider these two qualities.

First, goals should be sufficiently specific and concrete to be measurable. Indeed, explicitness represents an important criterion for all parts of the service

---

[1] This may well entail pursuing changes in the environment, which runs counter to a tendency in social work to define problems and objectives by personal qualities of the applicant (Rosen, 1993).

EXHIBIT 11-2
Getting John Out of the House

Mrs. Troy was referred to this agency for help in coping with her children. She was referred by a welfare department social worker who is providing brief individual counseling for Margaret, the 16-year-old daughter, regarding plans for her 2-month-old baby. The family consists of Mrs. Troy, age 42; John, age 19; Joe, age 17; Margaret, age 16; Robert, age 2 months (Margaret's baby); Marcel, age 14; and Raymond, age 12.

The social worker who made the referral thought Mrs. Troy needed help in handling the kids, especially the oldest boy, John. Before I saw Mrs. Troy, a second referral was made by the nurse who helps Mrs. Troy to manage her diabetes. The nurse stated that Mrs. Troy would become so upset with the kids, John in particular, that she would forget to take her medication. She said that Mrs. Troy was at her wit's end and was threatening to leave the kids and disappear.

Mrs. Troy was not as desperate when I interviewed her two days later. She did, however, make it clear that she wanted some help to get John out of the house. She also wanted the other kids to do

what they were told. Mrs. Troy saw John as the main problem. He deliberately aggravated the other kids and ordered them around as if he was in charge. He would sit around the house all day, have his friends over, refused to obey her, and called her profane names. Mrs. Troy's boyfriend moved out a few months ago because of the frequent arguments he had with John. She also felt that John's bad example contributed to the other kids' misbehavior.

Mrs. Troy's primary request was for help in getting John to move out of the house, but she didn't seem to feel there was much hope of doing it. She had tried putting his clothes out, locking him out, and changing the locks. Each time, John persisted in his efforts to get back in by shouting and pounding on the doors and windows. Mrs. Troy, feeling powerless and seeing no alternative, would let him in. On one occasion when John became belligerent after coming home drunk, she called the police. They simply drove him a few blocks away and released him.

---

plan—problem statement, goals, and action plan (Lundy, 1993). Establishing measurable objectives is necessary to integrate social work practice with research and evaluation (Greene, 1989). It permits applicant and worker to determine whether the objectives have been accomplished and provides the basis for accountability within the profession. Broadly stated goals or aspirations—such as "feeling better," "increasing opportunities for recreational activities," or "improving parent-child relationships"—do not usually provide the relief wanted by applicants. They are simply too ambiguous (Berg & Miller, 1992b; Epstein, 1980; Reid, 1992).

Second, there should be a reasonable chance of accomplishing the objective. The probability of success depends on several elements, including the applicant's degree of interest and abilities as well as the nature and extent of available resources. These factors are sometimes referred to, respectively, as motivation, capacity, and opportunity (Ripple, 1955; Ripple &

Alexander, 1956; Ripple, Alexander, & Polemis, 1964). In some circumstances, increased motivation, capacity, or opportunity in a particular area might be identified as an objective.

Feminist scholars and other researchers note the benefits of selecting small objectives, which have a relatively high probability of accomplishment, rather than large goals, which may be difficult to achieve and discouraging for the applicant (Berg & Miller, 1992b; Russell, 1989). However, excessively easy objectives can also discourage applicants, who may conclude "I cannot do any better" and feel unsatisfied at the achievement of an insignificant objective "that anybody could accomplish." Objectives should involve some challenge, require some investment of time and energy, and clearly relate to the problem of concern. Short-term objectives that can be accomplished within a few days or weeks are usually more attainable than are longer-term goals, which are usually stated in general terms. Thus, we suggest that you

---

EXHIBIT 11-3
Well-Formed Goals

1. The goals are important to the client.
2. The goals are expressed in interactional terms so that others could also notice changes.
3. The goals reflect a focus on change in specific situations or contexts rather than "everywhere" or "always."
4. The goals seek the presence of some desirable behavior or condition rather than the absence of problems.
5. The goals reflect beginning steps rather than final results.
6. The goals include a role for clients to change some aspect of their thinking, feeling, or doing.
7. The goals are concrete, behavioral, and measurable.
8. The goals are realistic and achievable.
9. The goals represent a challenge to clients and involve their hard work.

Source: de Jong, P., & Berg, I. K. (2002). *Interviewing for solutions* (2nd ed.). Pacific Grove, CA: Brooks/Cole, pp. 78–84.

EXHIBIT 11-4
Recipe File for Mrs. Stover?

Mrs. Stover brought up a further problem in connection with running the household. As she gets more interested in cooking, she is realizing how little she knows. She attempted to cook a goose for the family but spoiled it through lack of proper cleaning. She claims the food that she knows how to prepare is plain and unattractive. The children do some complaining about the food; George recently pointed out that other children he knows get more variety. I arranged to bring Mrs. Stover a recipe file containing a large variety of recipes and some instructions on food preparation and menus.

---

focus on short-term, immediate objectives. Once you have successful experiences, you and your clients can always develop new service agreements. Exhibit 11-3 contains a list of criteria for well-formed goals.

The Action Plan

The action plan lays out the steps that you and the applicant intend to take to solve the problem and achieve the goals. Social workers and applicants determine the action plan through a process similar to that used to define the problem and establish objectives. You first discover what the applicant would like to do to reach the solution. Then you convey your ideas about how to accomplish the objectives—including references to your role as well as the applicant's. Any differences in your respective views are then negotiated and, if possible, resolved.

The principle of equifinality suggests that there are many routes to any desired end state. A common error in social work is to offer an action plan without considering options with your applicant. Consider Exhibit 11-4, which is an excerpt from the Stover case (Reading 7).

Worker and client agree that the problem is Mrs. Stover's lack of knowledge about cooking and concur that the goal is for her to prepare more attractive meals. However, the worker precipitously arranges to provide Mrs. Stover with a recipe file. A better process would have been to involve Mrs. Stover in the discussion. What steps might enable her to improve her cooking skills? She might know of friends, relatives, or neighbors from whom she could request recipes. Perhaps she could make use of the public library or visit a county extension agency. Some other organization might provide the services of a home economist. A

EXHIBIT 11-5
A Sample Service Agreement with Mrs. Stover

Date: February 3

Problem: Mrs. Stover is unable to prepare an attractive variety of meals for her family.

Objective: By February 10, Mrs. Stover will be able to prepare and serve her family a dish she has not previously prepared.

Action plan:

1. On February 4, Mrs. Stover will invite her neighbor to coffee and make inquiries about recipes for preparation of low-cost main dishes.
2. By February 5, Mrs. Stover will call at the public library and check cookbooks for two or three new recipes.
3. Worker will contact the county extension agency to determine if: (a) the service of a home economist consultant is available; and (b) the agency has recipes available for low-cost main dishes.
4. February 7. Worker will telephone Mrs. Stover to review progress on securing recipes. We expect that Mrs. Stover will be able to select a recipe to try over the weekend.
5. February 8 or 9. Mrs. Stover will prepare a new dish for her family.
6. February 10. Mrs. Stover and worker will meet at 10 A.M. to evaluate the plan and to decide about next steps.

---

possible action plan that might emerge from such a collaborative process is summarized in Exhibit 11-5.

Proposing a plan or taking action too quickly prevents applicants from active participation in the process of planning and working toward solutions. Precipitous suggestions deny them an opportunity to display their strengths and exercise their competence. The development of a service plan should include a systematic review of applicant strengths. Develop a list of strengths and discuss with the applicant how these might be used to accomplish each objective. Strengths, of course, include the applicant's personal resources, as well as the resources of family, friends, and neighbors and cultural resources. Examples of strengths for Mrs. Stover might include these: "talks at least once a week with her mother," "occasionally has coffee with the neighbor," and "has visited the local public library."

Time Limits Note that the agreement in Exhibit 11-5 contains time limits for completing the tasks. We encourage applicants and workers to establish dates for the accomplishment of all activities in the service plan. This allows you and the applicant to evaluate whether the plan was implemented as scheduled. Deadlines tend to motivate people. Reid and Epstein (1972) call this the "goal gradient effect." When deadlines approach, people's efforts increase. Think of your own

experience in completing course assignments. How much of the work would get done without deadlines?

Working with Families and Groups Though several of our illustrations have involved individual clients, social workers routinely develop service plans in work with families (Anderson & Stewart, 1983; Fox, 1987; McClendon & Kadis, 1990; Shulman, 1999), other groups (Preston-Shoot, 1989; Wickman, 1993), and organizations. Group dynamics introduce additional complexity to the process. Family and group members may have different views about problems, goals, solutions, and action plans. Working as a mediator, you assist the group or family to resolve these differences, so that a service agreement can be negotiated. Some group or family members may have hidden agendas that interfere with the process. Exhibit 11-6 offers some ideas for helping families and groups reach decisions.

Focusing on Results Campbell (1969) distinguishes between two types of agency administrators. Trapped administrators are so concerned with a particular program or set of activities that they cannot adapt or change. Experimental administrators, on the other hand, are committed to accomplishing the mission and goals of the agency. They are prepared to change, to adapt, and to replace programs and activities as necessary to achieve the objectives.

EXHIBIT 11-6
Helping a Group Reach a Decision

1. State the problem clearly.
   Examples: "The purpose of this meeting is . . ."
   "Our job for today is . . ."
2. If a statement is not clear, ask for clarification.
   Examples: "I'm not sure I completely followed you just then. Would you elaborate?"
   "I'm sorry, I missed that point. Will you say it again?"
3. Stay on focus and help others to do so.
   Examples: "That's an important point. I wonder, though, if we might save that for later so we can get back to the major issue for today's meeting."
   "It seems to me we're digressing."
4. Summarize.
   Examples: "Here are the points we have made so far . . ."
   "Thus far we have agreed . . ."
5. Test the workability of proposals.
   Examples: "Do you think the members would support that proposal?"
   "Where would we get the money to do that?"
6. Test willingness to carry out the proposal.
   Examples: "Would you be willing to . . ."
   "Who can take this responsibility?"
7. Test readiness for decision.
   Examples: "Do you think we could decide this issue now?"
   "Well, are we ready to make that decision?"
8. Call for the decision.
   Examples: "Are we agreed, then, that . . ."
   "Will someone put this into a motion?"

There are also trapped practitioners—social workers who focus on particular activities or services rather than on accomplishing goals and objectives. They tend to see every problem in terms of a particular role, intervention approach, or technique. Social workers must be able to consider alternative courses of action if we want our clients to do so. Further, by generating a number of possible solutions to a problem, we are likely to reach higher-quality decisions (D'Zurilla, 1986; Heidrich & Denny, 1994; Nezu & D'Zurilla, 1981).

To avoid becoming a trapped practitioner, follow these guidelines:

- Be open to action plans that applicants propose.
- Whenever possible, respect applicants' personal preferences and cultural traditions.
- Carefully consider alternative action plans to accomplish any objective.
- Incorporate nomothetic evidence of practice effectiveness in considering alternate intervention approaches, policies, programs, services, and strategies or techniques.
- Seriously consider action plans that call for knowledge and skill beyond your current expertise. In such circumstances, you may need to make referrals or perhaps seek additional training and supervision.

Limitations on Worker Activity When negotiating action plans with applicants and clients, consider the dimensions of time, skill, ethics, and agency function.

Time You cannot responsibly commit yourself to activities that extend beyond the time you have available. Clients have a right to expect that you will do what you say you will do. Consider this incident. A social worker placed a 14-year-old boy in a foster home. Knowing that the youth might have some initial adjustment problems, the worker indicated that they would meet weekly to talk about them. Burdened by a heavy caseload, however, the worker did not visit the boy for a full month. The boy, disillusioned and angry, rejected the worker's efforts to become involved. The youth ran away and eventually became institutionalized. Had this worker made a realistic agreement—to see the boy once a month instead of once a week—client and worker might have been able to maintain communication and to engage in more effective problem solving. Do not confuse intensity of service with quality of service. Poor-quality service is virtually guaranteed when social workers make commitments we cannot meet. Similarly, frequent contact between workers and clients does not necessarily imply high-quality service. Plan your time carefully so that you do not make promises you cannot keep.

Skill Do not enter into service agreements calling for activity that exceeds your skills. When a client requires a specialized skill that you do not possess—such as marriage counseling or bargaining with a large bureaucracy—the negotiated action plan should include the participation of an appropriate expert or specialist. In the proposed service agreement for Mrs. Stover (Exhibit 11-5), for example, the worker secured information about a home economist with relevant expertise. We do not usually expect social workers to be experts in cooking or nutrition.

Ethics Committed to our social work code of ethics, we avoid involvement in intervention plans that would commit us to unethical behavior. For example, an applicant's economic crisis might be alleviated by embezzlement of funds from his workplace. Obviously, you could not endorse or participate in such an action. Neither could you to agree to plans that involve exploitation of or discrimination against other people or groups.

Agency As we noted earlier, social services tend to be organized around specific agency functions (Wilensky & Lebeaux, 1958) that establish natural parameters for worker-client agreements (Murdach, 1982). Of course, as a professional, you have some leeway to interpret agency function and may request exceptions to agency policies and procedures. You may also work within your agency to secure a broader definition of its functions. However, as long as agencies have community-sanctioned functions, you must consider these limitations when making commitments to clients.

Written Agreements

The service agreement, including the action plan, may be in oral or written form. Written agreements have some clear advantages. As Barker (1987b) notes, written agreements, although underused in social work, are effective tools for explicating objectives and mutual expectations. They help clarify ambiguities and

improve the specificity of the plan, reduce the likelihood of misunderstanding, and contribute to evaluation (Wilcoxon, 1991). Written agreements contribute more to goal achievement than do oral agreements (Klier, Fein, & Genero, 1984; Tolson, 1988). Putting agreements in written form also represents a useful learning experience, especially early in your career.

Another important consideration is that workers, like clients, are more likely to follow through on written agreements. We believe that clients have a fundamental right to hold social workers accountable for the nature and quality of our service. We encourage you personally and collectively to ensure that clients understand how to file complaints against workers who fail to keep commitments. All agencies should have such procedures and, of course, clients should be informed about means to submit grievances with professional associations and licensing boards.

◆ Intervention Roles

Definition

Social workers may take on a variety of intervention roles in our efforts to serve others. The intervention includes those activities undertaken subsequent to the development of a service agreement in pursuit of the goals or objectives specified in the service agreement. Some social workers use the term more globally to refer to all social work activities, including data collection and assessment. However, we strongly believe that intervention cannot and should not begin until we have reached an agreement with the applicant. We distinguish intervention from earlier processes in an effort to maintain focus on this important principle. Intervention roles are characterized by the expected responsibilities, activities, and behaviors of the worker by both client (individual, family, group, organization, or community) and worker to accomplish agreed-upon goals or objectives.

We consider five fundamental intervention roles—social broker, facilitator,[2] teacher, mediator, and advocate. Others may conceptualize the common roles

---

[2] In earlier editions, we used "enabler" to capture this role. Perhaps unfortunately, the terms "enabler" and "enabling" have become so strongly associated with substance use that we now adopt the term "facilitator."

differently or perhaps include additional roles. For example, Grosser (1965) has discussed the roles of broker, enabler, advocate, and activist in community development work. The literature also includes references to additional roles such as therapist (Briar, 1967), encourager (Biddle & Biddle, 1965), ombudsman (Payne, 1972), bargainer (Brager & Jorcin, 1969), lobbyist (Mahaffey, 1972), and validator (Tobias, 1990).

The intervention roles of broker, facilitator, teacher, mediator, and advocate provide a framework for thinking about intervention activity with systems of any size, from individual to community. This framework is independent of specific change models, strategies, or techniques that change over time—often through practice effectiveness research studies (Cournoyer, 2004; Thyer, 1996).

Social Broker

Brokers serve as intermediaries between one person or party and another—often conducting negotiations to resolve problems and achieve goals. Stockbrokers assist clients to define their resources, assess risk tolerance, and develop investment objectives. They then use their contacts and knowledge of the market to select stocks consistent with clients' objectives. Real estate brokers explore prospective home buyers' needs, wants, and resources to identify a desired type or category of house and then draw on their knowledge of the market to locate appropriate homes. Similarly, in serving as a social broker, social workers link clients with other community resources to accomplish the objectives specified in the service agreement. Social brokerage requires a broad knowledge of community resources, as well as knowledge of agency operating procedures, so that effective connections can be made. You serve as a social broker when you arrange for clients to receive marital counseling, job placement services, or improved housing; when you bring outside experts to provide valuable information to groups; or when you assist community organizations by identifying sources of program funding.

Information and referral are basic activities of the social broker. In many cases, the most important service you can provide is to help a client find and use a needed resource—not only formal social agencies and community programs but also clubs, organizations, and associations in which they might wish to participate.

Facilitator

In the facilitator role, you assist clients to find and use the coping strengths and resources within themselves to produce changes outlined in the service agreement. Change occurs because of client efforts. Your responsibility is to facilitate—or enable—the client to make the desired change. You may facilitate change within clients or within their patterns of relating with others. However, the facilitator can also help the client find ways of altering the environment.

You serve as a facilitator when you assist a group of neighborhood residents to determine the need for a day-care center, explore factors to consider in establishing the center, and plan its creation; when you help a group identify sources of internal conflict that obstruct progress toward its goals and then discover ways to resolve these difficulties; or when you assist a mother to enhance her relationship with her child.

Facilitators may encourage verbalization and expression of feelings, examine the pattern of relationships, offer encouragement and reassurance, or engage in logical discussion and rational decision making. What Tobias calls the validator role may also be an aspect of facilitation: "The function of the validator is to confirm, legitimize, substantiate, or verify the feelings, ideas, values, or beliefs of the client as well-grounded, correct, or genuine within the client's system" (1990, p. 357). Tobias sees this role as particularly important for work with mentally ill clients, "who from the onset of their illness have experienced confusing and painful feelings and ideas, distorted perceptions, and impaired judgment . . . compounded by years of institutional delegitimization, disqualification, and negation" (p. 357). The facilitator role primarily involves contacts with the client, rather than with external systems.

Teacher

In the teacher or educator role, you may provide clients with new information necessary for coping with problem situations, assist clients in practicing new behaviors or skills, or model alternative behavior patterns. You perform a teacher role when you supply low-income parents with shopping and nutritional information or provide parents with information regarding child development milestones; when you role-play different ways that adolescents might respond to teacher; when you teach a neighborhood

---

EXHIBIT 11-7
A Drop-In Neighbor

Mary Maki resides in a high-rise apartment building. Other residents constantly drop in on her, and she feels her privacy is being violated. On several occasions, Mary has become angry with these visitors. She wants to find a balance between protecting her privacy and maintaining friendships.

The worker and Mary agree that alternative responses to anger are needed. Thus, Mary and the worker role-play situations through which Mary can learn to communicate with unwanted drop-in neighbors in a respectful, assertive manner.

---

group how to request more frequent garbage collection services from the city council; or when you describe effective interpersonal skills and model clear communication. Exhibit 11-7 illustrates the use of role-playing.

Like the facilitator, the teacher strengthens clients' abilities to cope with and address problems in their situations. Whereas the facilitator helps clients to mobilize existing resources, however, the teacher also contributes new knowledge, expertise, and resources. Teaching is an important aspect of social work practice. In some cases, sharing knowledge alone may be sufficient to accomplish the objectives. However, we share information in the form of input for clients to consider and use or not, as they see fit. Schwartz (1961) offers three important suggestions:

- Recognize that the information you offer is only a small part of the available social experience.
- The information should be related to the problem being addressed.
- Opinions should be clearly labeled as such and not represented as facts.

Mediator

Mediation involves efforts to resolve disputes between the client system and other persons or organizations. Suppose a young person has been expelled and the service agreement reflects a goal of returning to school. You may need to serve as a mediator between the young client and school authorities. Suppose members of a community wish to construct a playground for their children. Two subgroups develop plans that cannot be integrated. A stalemate results. You might mediate between the two subgroups. Exhibit 11-8 illustrates mediation.

In serving as a mediator, you assist clients and others to find common ground on which to reach a resolution of the conflict. There is growing literature on mediation and conflict resolution (Dillon & Emery, 1996; Folger, Poole, & Stautman, 1993; Kruk, 1997; Leviton & Greenstone, 1997; Moore, 1986; Nugent, Umbreit, Winamaki, & Paddock, 2001; Parsons, 1991b; Savoury, Beals, & Parks, 1995; Severson & Bankston, 1995; Tolson, McDonald, & Moriarty, 1992; Umbreit, 1994, 1995). You facilitate communication between the parties, share information, offer alternate perspectives, and attempt to negotiate resolutions—often through win-win solutions (Brams & Taylor, 1999; Jandt, 1985).

In serving as a mediator, social workers attempt to

- Bring about a convergence of the conflicting parties' perceived self-interests
- Help each party recognize the legitimacy of the other's interests
- Assist the parties to identify their common interest in a successful outcome
- Avoid situations in which issues of winning and losing are paramount
- Localize conflicts to specific issues, times, and places
- Break conflicts into separate elements or issues

Social workers often assume a mediational role in helping to resolve disputes *within* client systems such as families, groups, organizations, and communities. Such mediation can also be regarded as a dimension of facilitation because resolving intrasystem disputes permits the client to mobilize resources and move toward the objectives of the service agreement.

Like counseling or psychotherapeutic service, mediation requires specialized expertise. Some social workers serve primarily as mediators, perhaps mediating parent-adolescent conflicts, child-custody arrange-

---

EXHIBIT 11-8
Mediating a Conflict in a Board and Lodging Home

Ida Wick lives in a rooming house. She collects mementos and keeps old newspapers. The owner asks Ida to dispose of the newspapers because of fire regulations. They become irritated with one another and cannot reach a resolution. The social worker assumes the role of mediator. The worker first discusses the problem with Ida and then makes a request for a joint meeting with the owner. In the meeting, the worker negotiates a settlement by which the fire safety standards can be met: Ida is provided with a storage cabinet, in which to keep her more important mementos and a scrapbook for newspaper clippings.

EXHIBIT 11-9
Advocacy with Social Security

Hullie Mutton's benefits from the Social Security office have been summarily decreased on the grounds that she received an overpayment. The Social Security office admits the error was theirs. The social worker discusses the decrease with the client and offers to contact the office on Mrs. Mutton's behalf. The worker stresses to the representative, Miss Jones, that the error was not the client's and that the reduction places Mrs. Mutton in considerable financial jeopardy. Further, the worker requests information on the appeal process and indicates that the client wishes to begin the proceedings. Miss Jones agrees to take a further look at Mrs. Mutton's situation and says that she will ask her supervisor for an exception.

---

ments, divorce settlements, termination agreements, or even labor-management issues. All social workers periodically call on mediation and conflict resolution skills in our service to others and occasionally refer certain clients to mediational specialists.

Advocate

As an advocate, you present and argue the client's cause when necessary to accomplish the agreed-upon goals or objectives. In social work, as in the legal profession, the advocate is not neutral but, rather, a partisan representative for the client (Grosser, 1965). Advocacy may be defined as

> an attempt, having a greater than zero probability of success, by an individual or group to influence another individual or group to make a decision that would not have been made otherwise and that concerns the welfare or interests of a third party who is in a less powerful status than the decision makers. (Sosin & Caulum, 1983, p. 12).

As advocate you argue, debate, bargain, negotiate, and manipulate the environment on behalf of the client. Advocacy differs markedly from mediation. The mediator attempts to secure a resolution through give and take on both sides. The advocate, however, seeks to gain a victory for the client. Advocacy efforts are frequently directed toward securing benefits to which the client is entitled (Exhibit 11-9). Most social workers use advocacy (Ezell, 1994), although perhaps less frequently than other roles (Herbert & Levin, 1996).

Unlike the broker, facilitator, teacher, and mediator roles, advocacy can be used without the direct involvement of the client. This creates the risk of proceeding without having a clear agreement with the client to do so (Torczyner, 1991). Lawyers do not become the representatives for clients until clients have retained them and authorized them to extend this service. Similarly, as a social worker, you should have an explicit agreement with clients before engaging in advocacy on their behalf.

EXHIBIT 11-10
How to Discipline Jimmy?

Mrs. B complained of Jimmy's misbehavior and her uncertainty about how to discipline him. She told me she took Jimmy to the child guidance center. She said a doctor tested Jimmy and then told her that the problem might be hers rather than Jimmy's. He said that she was lonely and insecure and maybe needed some guidance in handling her children. She discussed this freely and admitted that this might be true. I asked her if she would like me to discuss ways to handle Jimmy. She said definitely yes, that she couldn't do a thing with him.

Generalist Practice

The generalist social worker reflects competence in the roles of broker, facilitator, teacher, mediator, and advocate. If you understand and can effectively assume these roles, your clients may access an enhanced range of potential means to address problems and pursue goals. Exhibit 11-10 contains a portion of a conversation between a social worker in a Head Start program and Mrs. B, who wants to enroll her child in the program. Note the development of a preliminary service contract. The partners agree that Mrs. B finds it difficult to manage Jimmy. They decide on a goal: Mrs. B will learn new ways to discipline him. They also agree that the worker will provide information about possible ways to manage Jimmy.

In helping Mrs. B purse the goal, the worker would adopt the facilitator and teacher roles. However, the roles of broker, mediator, and advocate might also apply. For example, further exploration about the visit to the child guidance center, her perceptions of what the doctor said, her thoughts and feelings concerning the experience, and her willingness to return to the center could lead to an action plan in which the worker serves as a broker between Mrs. B and the center. If a problem or conflict emerges with the center, the worker might assume a mediator role to resolve the dispute or an advocate role to serve on Mrs. B's behalf. The overall goal remains the same: Mrs. B will learn new ways to manage her son. However, the action plan may involve facilitating or educating Mrs. B, serving as a broker to link Mrs. B and the center, mediating differences between Mrs. B and the center, or acting as Mrs. B's advocate and representing her interests to the center. The ability to use all the intervention roles and your willingness to consider various approaches and perspetives provide a wide range of options for action.

Intervention plans may combine elements of various roles. For example, the referral process represents a major part of the social broker role. Referral involves four distinct steps: (1) preparation of the client, (2) preparation of the referral organization, (3) contact, and (4) follow-up. In preparing the client, discuss what the referral process entails and what the referral agency expects. Adopting facilitator and teacher roles, you help prepare the client to make effective use of the referral agency.

In preparing the referral agency, you share information about the client, problem, situation, and any preliminary goals. Of course, you do so with the client's full knowledge and consent. In some situations, agencies may express reluctance to accept a referral. You may then assume mediational or advocacy roles. After the client makes initial contact with the referral organization, follow up with both the client and the organization. Ideally, follow-up should be a part of the initial planning. As a result of follow-up, you may learn about obstacles to successful engagement, which may call for facilitation, teaching, mediation, or advocacy skills.

This model of social brokering, supplemented by the other intervention roles, is central to the use of formal social support and social care. To provide a useful service, you must be skilled at involving clients in developing service agreements and helping them find and use the resources necessary to meet the agreed-upon goals. Such an approach requires the ability to humanize the ways in which services are delivered and to assist agencies in meeting their responsibilities to clients.

◆ Chapter Summary

The service agreement is negotiated between worker and applicant. The agreement includes a definition of the problem for work, goals or objectives, and an action plan designed to resolve the problem and achieve the desired outcome. The service agreement reflects a commitment by both the worker and applicant to implement the plan. Changes, of course, may be jointly negotiated. Here are three important principles:

- Negotiation of the service agreement involves input from both worker and applicant. Social workers' professional judgment, experience, and background represent legitimate sources of knowledge and information that should be made available to the applicant as part of the decision-making process. Seek to reach a service agreement that represents the best collective judgment of both you and the applicant.

- Social worker and applicant should remain alert to a wide range of potential goals, objectives, and intervention approaches. The target of change may be the applicant, the environment, or their interaction. No single social worker can be expected to master all change strategies. However, we must be aware of the repertoire of change strategies available to the profession and be able to help clients select the most appropriate approach. If you cannot provide the service, you should be able to locate it elsewhere in the community.

- The development of a service agreement is a cognitive process involving thinking, reasoning, and decision making. Feelings and intuitions are important human experiences. They should be valued and respected. However, planning is primarily a rational activity. Intervention efforts should be based on a deliberate rational service agreement negotiated with the client.

Intervention involves social workers' actions directed toward achievement of the agreed-upon goals or objectives. We discussed five intervention roles: social broker, facilitator, teacher, mediator, and advocate. Different roles may sometimes be used to reach similar goals. Expertise in these roles reflects a generalist perspective that permits social workers and clients to consider alternative approaches to intervention. These roles may be combined or integrated. Social workers and clients typically partialize problems and then pro-

ceed sequentially from problem to problem. Therefore, we routinely negotiate and phase in appropriate service agreements and action plans relevant to each problem and goal. Of course, service agreements must be flexible enough to be renegotiated as the client needs and wants change (Shulman, 1992; Tolson, Reid, & Garvin, 1994). New or revised agreements build on what you have learned through your work together (Rothery, 1980).

 ## Learning Exercises: Readings, InfoTrac, and the Web

1. Use your word-processing computer program to enter the important terms and concepts presented in this chapter in alphabetical order. Place a question mark by any terms that you do not clearly understand. Save your document as EX 11-1.

2. Log on to the InfoTrac College Edition Web site. Conduct a keyword search (using either Keyword Search or Advanced Search) to locate the articles entitled "The Use of Individualized Goal Setting to Facilitate Behavior Change in Women with Multiple Sclerosis" (Stuifbergen, Becker, Timmerman, & Kullberg, 2003), "African American Mothers' and Daughters' Beliefs About Possible Selves and Their Strategies for Reaching the Adolescents' Future Academic and Career Goals" (Kerpelman, Shoffner, & Ross-Griffin, 2002), and "Values and Goal-Setting with Underserved Youth" (Martinek & Hellison, 1998). Read the articles and prepare a two-to-three page essay in which you reflect on their implications for service agreements within the context of social work and social work practice. Save your document as EX 11-2.

3. Log on to the InfoTrac College Edition Web site. Conduct a keyword search (using either Keyword Search or Advanced Search) to locate the articles entitled "Opportunities and Barriers to Empowering People with Severe Mental Illness Through Participation in Treatment Planning" (Linhorst, Hamilton, Young, & Eckert, 2002) and "Documentation of Client Dangerousness in a Managed Care Environment" (Callahan, 1996). Read the articles and prepare a two-page essay in which you reflect on their implications for service agreements within the context of social

work and social work practice. Save your document as EX 11-3.

4. Turn to **Reading 17: A Brief Solution-Focused Practice Model.** Review this reading by Michelle MacKenzie and prepare a one-page essay in which you address the following questions: What are the risks and benefits associated with assisting applicants to define the solutions they desire and moving quickly to accomplish these solutions? What aspects of this approach might complement problem-solving models of practice? Save your document as EX 11-4.

5. Turn to **Reading 18: Goal Setting with Biological Families.** Review this reading by Edith Fein and Ilene Staff and prepare a one-page essay in which you address the following questions: What are the similarities and differences between the authors' approach to the goal-setting process and the process outlined in this text? Which of their suggestions do you find most meaningful to you and most applicable to your service as a social worker? Save your document as EX 11-5.

6. Turn to **Reading 3: The House on Sixth Street.** Become familiar with the case description again. This time, prepare a one-page essay in which you briefly comment on the use of outside experts. Following that, use the format presented in Exhibit 11-5 to prepare a service plan that includes the problem for work, the goals or objectives, and the action plan. Save your document as EX 11-6.

7. Turn to **Reading 7: The Stover Family.** Become familiar with the case description again. This time, prepare a one-page essay in which you address the following questions: What can you learn from the process used to develop a mutually acceptable goal or objective with Mrs. Stover? How does this case illustrate high-quality but low-intensity service? Save your document as EX 11-7.

8. Turn to **Reading 26: Leonard Timms.** Become familiar with the case description again. This time, prepare a one-page essay in which you address the following questions: Who is the client? How does the service agreement with Leonard Timms emerge? What can you learn about goal setting from the process? Save your document as EX 11-8.

9. Turn to **Reading 27: The Omar Family.** Become familiar with the case description again. This time, prepare a one-page essay in which you address the following questions: How does the service agreement with the family emerge? What can you learn about goal setting from the process? Save your document as EX 11-9.

10. Turn to the brief case description presented in Exhibit 11-2. Mrs. Troy and the worker reached agreement on the objective of getting John out of the house, but no action plan was developed. Put yourself in the place of a worker and think about possible action plans. Prepare a one-page essay in which you address the following questions: What possible strengths might you explore with Mrs. Troy? What are alternative ways to accomplish the objective? Following that, use the format outlined in Exhibit 11-5 to draft a possible service agreement. In an attempt to keep this task from becoming a one-sided effort, imagine that Mrs. Troy is by your side and actively contributing ideas and suggestions. Pay particular attention to your ability to identify and focus Mrs. Troy's strengths in relation to the objective and your ability to explore with her alternative courses of action that might be used to reach the objective. Save your document as EX 11-10.

11. Read the case example contained within Exhibit 11-11. Prepare a one-page essay in which you convert the oral service agreements reflected in the description into written form. Be sure to specify the goals or objectives and the action plans. Save your document as EX 11-11.

EXHIBIT 11-11
Objectives and Intervention Plan with a Spouse Abuse Client

Jackie called the Geneva Women's Center early one morning and left a message on the answering machine saying she needed help and would like to meet with someone after work. Later that afternoon she came to the Center. I met with Jackie, who said that she had to come in because she couldn't take it anymore. Jackie detailed numerous incidents of physical, verbal, and emotional abuse by her husband Joe in the last two years. The last incident occurred over the weekend. Joe had come home drunk, found her sleeping, and flipped their double bed over with her in it. He then began screaming and shouting at her, calling her names, and saying that she was no good, lazy, and that he "ought to take care of her." The episode ended when Joe literally threw her out of the bedroom and slammed the door. Jackie eventually slept on the couch but decided she had to leave. She believed that Joe would come after her if he knew she was trying to leave, which is why she waited until he would be working to take any action. Jackie had heard about the Center from a woman at work and wanted help finding a place to stay until she could decide what to do.

I explained to Jackie about the shelter in Bluegrass (60 miles away) and the safe home network here in Geneva. Jackie felt she wanted to stay in Geneva so she could keep working. She was pretty sure Joe would not bother her at work. I told her that a safe home could be arranged. After determining Jackie's particular needs (smoker, not allergic to animals, no children, no personal items), I excused myself and alerted other staff, who began to make the arrangements. It was necessary to begin work on this immediately because of the lateness of the hour.

When I returned to the room, Jackie was crying. She said she didn't really want to leave, that she loved Joe, but she couldn't handle getting beat up all the time. She just didn't know what to do. I asked Jackie if she had thought about different things to do. Her list of possibilities included help for Joe, reconciliation and salvaging their marriage, and divorce. She hadn't made a decision as to which she should pursue. Jackie said she thought Joe would be mad if she didn't come home, but that she didn't feel she could return there until things changed.

We discussed the resources she had available to her through the Center: emotional support, assistance with filing an Order for Protection (OFP), legal advocacy, and assistance with financial and housing needs. I also mentioned the counseling program for abusive men offered by the Mental Health Center. We talked at length about an OFP and the functions it provides: removing an abuser from the home, ordering counseling or treatment, ordering financial support, preventing the abuser from further assaults or threats of assault, and so on. I explained that one of the primary functions of the order was to provide safety for the victim and to give up to one year for decision making.

After further review of the process of obtaining an OFP, Jackie thought she would like to file, but wanted to think about it for a while. I said that would be fine. Our discussion was interrupted by a staff-person who related that safe home arrangements had been made. I asked Jackie if she was ready to go; she was, and I drove her to the safe home. After getting Jackie settled, I gave her written information about the things we talked about and assured her that the woman she was staying with could answer any questions she might have. We then made arrangements to meet at the Center the next day, when she got off work, to see if she'd made any decisions.

Jackie and I met the next day. She reported that she hadn't slept very well the night before, but that the woman she was staying with was very nice. Jackie also said she called Joe, who was wondering where she was and asked her repeatedly to come home. He said that he loved her, that he was sorry, and that they could work things out. Jackie said she wanted to believe him but couldn't, and that she told him she needed some time to think about things. Jackie went on to tell me that she thought the OFP was a good idea and that she wanted to file. She thinks that Joe might get help if the court orders him to, and maybe things would work out. She wanted to include exclusive occupancy in the order until Joe shows that he's really willing to change.

Jackie and I filled out an OFP form before she returned to the safe home. We agreed that the following day she would get off work early and file with my assistance. I would call the court administrator's office and let them know we were coming and pick Jackie up after work. In the event the order could not be served to Joe that same day, Jackie would arrange to stay at the safe home one more night.

Source: Ellen Holmgren, MSW student, University of Minnesota School of Social Work.

Chapter 12

Intervention Methods
to Mobilize Client Power

In the last chapter, we introduced the idea of intervention roles. In this chapter, we focus on several specific methods to assist clients in mobilizing their power. Empowerment is a prominent theme in the social work practice literature (Breton, 1994a, 1994b; Browne & Mills, 2001; DuBois & Miley, 1996; Gutierrez, 1996; Gutierrez, GlenMaye, & DeLois, 1996; Hartman, 1993; Kondrat, 1995; Lee, 1994; Mondros & Wilson, 1994; Moreau, 1990; Parsons, 1991a; Parsons & Cox, 1994; Pinderhughes, 1983; Rose, 1990, 2000; Simon, 1994; Staples, 1990). Key elements of our practice model—partnership, working toward client wants, emphasizing client strengths—are consistent with this tradition. We do not view power as something social workers *give* to clients. Social workers do not empower people. Rather, we engage in a collaborative process of mobilizing client power. This process of enhancing client power through active participation and collaboration occurs throughout the engagement, assessment, and service planning phases, and continues during intervention as well. During the intervention phase, we help clients mobilize the power they need to resolve problems and achieve goals.

Pinderhughes (1983) defines *power* as the ability to exert a beneficial influence on forces that affect one's life; *powerlessness* is the inability to exert such influence. Parsons (1991a) speaks of empowerment as an active process through which clients become strong enough to participate in, take control of, and influence institutions and events that affect their lives. DuBois and Miley note, "empowerment implies exercising psychological control over personal affairs as well as exerting influence over the course of events in the socio-political arena" (1996, p. 26). Parents with emotionally troubled children reflect at least three aspects of empowerment though development of greater ability to (1) solve problems and manage their children at home; (2) deal with service providers, especially about access to information about conditions and services and their right to make decisions about services for their children; and (3) influence the service system and community to secure better services (Koren, DeChillo, & Friesen, 1992). Mobilizing client power means helping clients assume responsibility for and assert control over their own lives and circumstances, and secure the resources needed to resolve problems and achieve goals.

In this chapter, we identify several intervention methods to help clients mobilize power:

- Securing resources
- Enhancing self-awareness
- Strengthening social skills
- Accessing information
- Facilitating decision making
- Finding meaning

◆ Securing Resources

The social context in which people function shapes our lives. Our capacity for problem solving depends on our ability to secure needed resources, our power to counter negative effects of environmental conditions, and our capacity to maximize opportunities. Productive interventions may be directed toward changes in (1) the environment, (2) the client, or (3) the interaction between aspects of the client system and the environment.

EXHIBIT 12-1
Who Will Care for Mr. Sandstone?

Mr. Sandstone, a 37-year-old Native American, is quadriplegic. He was injured two years ago, when he was struck by a truck while crossing the street. After an 18-month hospital rehabilitation program, Mr. Sandstone was discharged into the community. The rehabilitation counselor and social worker found him a wheelchair-accessible apartment and some furniture. They also took him shopping for clothes. Mr. Sandstone needs assistance with most aspects of daily living, including bathing, transfers, positioning, and bowel and bladder voiding. A home care assistant visits three times a day, seven days a week. His back-up caregiver is his 75-year-old mother who has heart problems. The mother feels obliged to stay and care for her son, who is the youngest of her children. On several occasions, the mother indicated that she is too old to provide adequate care for her son. She also says that her son drinks a lot. This disturbs her because she never drank alcohol in her life. She feels she should no longer live with her son. However, she remains the only back-up caregiver and has not attempted to leave. Mr. Sandstone is dependent on his mother for everything.

Actively Supplying Resources

Earlier, we discussed the role of social broker, in which you bring clients together with resources. At times, you may go further and actually secure concrete resources for clients. As social workers, we sometimes engage in tasks for clients as well as helping them undertake tasks for themselves. When we do so, we may increase the amount of time and energy available for clients to engage in other problem-solving activities. Their lives may become less hectic. They may feel more comfortable or perhaps more able to cope and may experience a corresponding increase in self-worth. If clients are able to actively seek out and use resources on their own or perhaps with our joint involvement, so much the better. However, do not adopt the position that clients must always do things on their own. Sometimes clients are simply too distressed, distraught, or overwhelmed. Under such circumstances, requiring clients to complete all tasks by themselves may increase client helplessness, pessimism, and lead to yet more failure experiences.

Some social workers hypothesize that we make clients dependent when we secure resources for them rather than expecting them to do for themselves. We disagree. If clients are fully engaged in deciding who will do which problem-solving tasks, they are unlikely to become either passive or dependent. We also challenge the presumption that human independence represents an ideal state. We view human beings as essentially social creatures. We depend on each other for virtually all aspects of life. A more useful and probably accurate ideal conception would involve human interdependence: people capable of effectively interacting with others. Excessive independence is easily as problematic as extreme dependency. People who function well in life are capable of both autonomous and cooperative behavior. Neither exclusively independent nor exclusively dependent, they choose when and how to complete tasks alone or with others as the goals and circumstances demand. We urge you to adopt such a perspective as you and clients decide about problem-solving tasks and activities. Sometimes, clients do for themselves, sometimes we do for them, and sometimes we do things together.

The social worker reflected in the case vignette contained in Exhibit 12-1 may actively work to secure a back-up care provider for the client. The client's 75-year-old mother may also need assistance to make a decision about her living arrangements. She probably would find it easier to make the decision after she feels comfortable that adequate care is available for her son.

Direct Intervention

At times, you may intervene directly with other systems. For example, you might discuss a child's problems with school officials. As a result, you could help the parents and the child better understand the school's perspective or perhaps interpret complex information. When intervening directly with other systems, be sure to share relevant information with

---

EXHIBIT 12-2
Opportunities

What does this say?

OPPORTUNITYISNOWHERE.

---

clients about the contacts and their outcomes. Of course, their informed consent is usually required and clients often accompany us when we meet with other systems—assuming as active a role as possible.

Sometimes clients benefit from an alternate view of their situation (Gutierrez, 1995; Moreau, 1990). Look at Exhibit 12-2. What did you see at first? Opportunity is nowhere? Or opportunity is now here? Many clients fail to see the resources available in their environments. As well as identifying and making resources accessible to clients, you can help them to identify opportunities where initially they see none.

Organizing

You may also help clients secure needed resources by organizing (Breton, 1994b). In Reading 3, The House on Sixth Street, for example, the worker helps clients organize to improve the quality of their housing. In Reading 6, The Birky Family, the worker and client might include an action plan to organize the neighborhood to secure a safe environment for their children. In organizing, social workers use intervention methods such as obtaining information, facilitating decision making, strengthening social skills, and various aspects of the broker, facilitator, teacher, mediator, and advocate roles. In the description contained in Exhibit 12-3, a social worker and a lawyer help a group of clients take political action to secure resources. Social workers often assist clients to function within the political system. This sometimes includes helping clients to organize people with similar interests to pursue social, political, or legal action.

Here is another example. A social worker became aware of a proposed change in state rules governing long-term boarding care facilities for adults affected by severe mental illness. Under the new rules, the worker's facility would be redefined as transitional rather than long term. Residents would be required to move after a limited period. News of the pending rule change made the residents upset and anxious. However, they were uncomfortable with the idea of testifying at an upcoming hearing on the subject. The social worker suggested that they have their statements videotaped for presentation at the hearing. They agreed, the social worker made the arrangements, and the videotapes made a very powerful impact at the hearing.

◆ Enhancing Self-Awareness

Enhancement of client self-awareness may be an explicit goal within the service agreement or perhaps an aspect of an action plan. Sometimes clients do not fully understand that their behavior—including their thoughts and feelings—may contribute to the problem or that their own strengths could be mobilized for problem solving. In such circumstances, social workers may work to enhance clients' self-awareness (Furstenberg & Rounds, 1995; Hepworth, 1993). Several techniques are available, and most involve the process of feedback.

Earlier we discussed feedback as a fundamental element of living systems and communication processes. Through feedback, social workers may help clients become more aware of themselves and how they interact with others. Of course, all interactions include some feedback and have potential to enhance self-awareness. When clients express themselves, they *hear* themselves. As social workers respond verbally and nonverbally to clients' messages, clients learn a bit more about themselves and perhaps something about us as well. When we actively listen in an authentic,

EXHIBIT 12-3
Social Action with Hmong Veterans

A social action effort has been initiated with Hmong veterans who fought as allies of the United States in Southeast Asia.

The Hmong lived peacefully as farmers in the highland region of Northern Laos before the Vietnam War. In 1960, with a growing fear of the spread of communism in Southeast Asia, the CIA began to recruit the Hmong to help contain the spread of communism in Laos and to provide surveillance of North Vietnamese troop movements. By 1975, an estimated 30,000 Hmong soldiers had been trained, equipped, paid, fed, and directed by the U.S. (Robbins, 1987).

The war disrupted the Hmong economy, leadership patterns, and family structure. Approximately 10% of the population died as a direct result of the war or through related disease and starvation. When the United States withdrew its troops in 1975, those Hmong remaining in Laos were faced with the threat of extermination by the communists; thousands fled to Thailand for safety (Tou-Fou, 1983).

Between 1975 and 1985, over 50,000 Hmong resettled in the United States (Reder, 1985). Life was very difficult for them; their devastating losses could never be forgotten and the barriers to acculturation were immense. Moreover, the United States never officially recognized the role that the Hmong played as its ally in Southeast Asia. Allegedly, the CIA made promises of care and support, should the Hmong ever lose their homeland, but nothing was done (Castle, 1979).

According to Rothman and Tropman (1987), social action represents the efforts of disadvantaged groups to gain the redistribution of resources, power, and/or decision-making capabilities. For the Hmong, the goal of social action was not to gain benefits associated with services rendered to the United States. Rather, there was hope that, through recognition, they would be able to derive some meaning from their contributions and sacrifices.

The advocacy effort began with a mobilization to present a resolution on the subject at Minnesota precinct caucuses. The resolution was based on information provided by Hmong veterans and a lawyer who was surveying Hmong veterans in the Minneapolis–St. Paul metropolitan area.

Although the resolution was only passed in a few precincts, it did serve some important functions: It provided a sampling of community sentiment on the subject, highlighted the specific features of the proposal that were most likely to evoke resistance, and helped to identify individuals who were interested in the issue and willing to participate in further efforts. Most importantly, the precinct venture revealed the need for increased planning and coordination; because of the eleventh-hour preparations, numerous opportunities to strengthen the caucus turnout were missed.

The first order of business following the caucuses was to organize a task group to facilitate planning for future actions. The task group was relatively small (5–8 people), so that coordinating meetings and activities would not be overly complex. A high priority was placed on gaining Hmong veteran representation, since Hmong interests would be most affected by the social action. Furthermore, the group wanted representation from Vietnam veterans, since they tend to be the most sympathetic to the Hmong's situation. All members of the group identified the problem for work as the lack of support offered by the U.S. government to Hmong veterans for their services in Southeast Asia.

The agreed-upon long-term goal of the social action was to obtain U.S. veterans' benefits for Hmong veterans who fought in alliance with the U.S. between 1960 and 1975. Attention was then directed toward assessing the feasibility of the goal. Critical areas for data collection and investigation were identified, and responsibility for gathering the needed information was delegated. The group decided to identify other similar efforts, potential obstacles and areas of resistance, resources and allies, and to identify unintentional consequences that might arise from the action.

Source: Kathleen Behrens, MSW student, School of Social Work, University of Minnesota.

accepting, empathic, and accurate fashion, clients may learn even more about themselves and their messages. Indeed, most aspects of communication contribute to self-understanding. However, several forms are especially useful for providing feedback: reflecting, going beyond, asking about process, responding with immediacy, interpreting, limit-setting, looking for strengths, and confrontation.

Reflecting

When you paraphrase another's message, you restate the communication you received. You reflect back or mirror what the other expressed. This demonstrates that you genuinely want to understand and enables clients to reexperience their own expressions. Accurate reflection requires you to listen and observe carefully for the basic message, then paraphrase it in an essentially equivalent form. Although you use your own words—rather than simply mimicking theirs—your reflected message should match theirs. You should not add your own ideas or speculate about feelings or meanings. You operate as a mirror—reflecting rather than interpreting the communication.

Large messages are difficult to paraphrase. Indeed, it would seem artificial to try to reflect the entirety of a several-paragraph expression. In such circumstances, you may reflect a portion of the large message—perhaps the part that seems most important to the client or possibly the last part. Alternately, you may summarize the major elements of a large message. You may reflect a simplified, outline version of the expression. Always be tentative in your synthesis. You are submitting it for clients' approval, amendment, or rejection. When reflecting clients' messages, watch carefully for clues that either confirm or deny the accuracy and helpfulness of your restatements. Summarizing can be used to check your understanding and to encourage clients to explore the material more completely.

Going Beyond

Going beyond what is said builds on the understanding of clients' experience in the form of a modest extension to what they have actually expressed. Rather than reflecting an equivalent message, you add slightly to their expression to put an unexpressed feeling or idea into words. In going beyond, however, remain focused on clients' experience and perspective.

It is still an empathic response. Do not introduce new feelings or ideas that come from your frame of reference. Instead, put into words the unstated experience of the client.

Suppose, for example, a client talks with you about the recent funeral of her daughter. She discusses the expenses and wonders how she can pay for everything. She expresses anger, frustration, and stress. In addition, however, her eyes begin to water and a tear falls upon her check. After reflecting the meanings and feelings associated with the financial concerns, you might go beyond by saying, "And you also feel terribly sad that your daughter is gone."

In going beyond, you do not speculate, interpret, or offer opinions about what clients express. Rather, you put into words what they probably think, feel, or experience but have yet to communicate.

Asking About Process

Like reflections, questions of all kinds may contribute to client self-awareness. When we ask about process, however, enhanced self-understanding becomes even more likely. Earlier, we referred to process as a series of ongoing interactions. If we inquire about the way people search for, discover, and select information; formulate opinions; reach conclusions; or make decisions, clients may explore aspects of their internal processes often overlooked. You might ask questions such as these: "How did you reach that conclusion?" "What was the first thing you experienced when your daughter said that to you?" "How did you choose to focus on that aspect of the problem?" "How do you usually go about making decisions in this area of your life?"

Feelings also reflect processes that may be explored. Feelings contain both sensory and cognitive elements. Human beings experience some bodily sensation such as muscular tension or increased heart rate and almost simultaneously associate a thought or image so that we have a feeling or emotion. In some circumstances, the feelings we experience are strongly influenced by our interpretations of events in the world or our bodily sensations. For instance, one student might receive a grade of B and experience great pleasure and joy. Another student might get the same grade and experience profound disappointment. When jogging, a client may interpret a rapid heart rate and flushed skin as a normal, healthy response to exercise. However, when the same bodily sensations occur when engaged in a conversation at a dinner party, the client may view them as signs of anxiety or perhaps embarrassment. By exploring the specific processes by which clients come to experience feelings, we may help them become more self-aware and, in some circumstances, more able to manage their emotions.

Responding with Immediacy

When social workers respond with immediacy to clients, we share an observation or an idea about what is happening in the moment. For instance, you might observe that a client's rate of speech decreases and head lowers as you begin to discuss a particular topic. Or, when you notice a nonverbal reaction when you mention that your work together will end after two more meetings, you might ask, "I wonder what you're thinking and feeling right now as we talk about concluding our work together?"

In responding with immediacy, you encourage

exploration of the client's experiences and feelings about you, your relationship, or the work you are engaged in, *as they occur.* In responding with immediacy, you focus on the client's experience of what is occurring here and now between the two of you. These thoughts and feelings become the subject for immediate exploration. Responding with immediacy makes things real. It intensifies the relationship and encourages the client to explore relational concerns as they emerge. (Cournoyer, 2005, p. 393)

The term *immediacy* refers to the "here and now with me" aspect of the communication. To the degree that you make observations or share ideas about clients' past or future behavior or experience, you become less immediate. Those expressions may also contribute to enhanced self-awareness. When you respond with immediacy, however, clients have a current, specific example of their own behavior or experience that coincides with your expression. Clients are often more able to consider such input seriously—because it is happening right now.

Despite the atypical circumstances that surround the client-and-social worker relationship, sometimes clients relate to us in a fashion that reflects the way they relate to others. Their general relationship patterns may emerge in the relationship with you. For example, suppose that a client who identifies failed relationships as the problem of concern, talks in a virtually nonstop manner, and on those few occasions when you can make a comment, the client routinely interrupts you before you can complete a sentence. You might wonder if this pattern also occurs with other people. In such a situation, responding with immediacy might contribute to the client's self-awareness and perhaps lead to consideration of alternate ways of communicating.

Responding with immediacy is not applicable each and every time you notice something that could contribute to greater client self-awareness. Interventions should relate to the agreed-upon problems of concern and the goals for work. Enhancement of general self-awareness is rarely a primary goal for social work clients. Generally speaking, therefore, you should only respond with immediacy when clients' behavior with you relates to the problems and goals. In addition, assess the client's capacity to handle the stress associated with this, sometimes new, information and the increased intimacy that often results from immediate responses. When we talk with clients about what is happening right here and right now in our relationship, we immediately become more intimate. Some clients may lack the resources to manage such intimacy—particularly if you are in the early stages of the working relationship. Therefore, the skill of responding with immediacy usually occurs within the context of a well-established relationship after clients come to recognize that you have their best interests in mind and sincerely want to help rather than judge them.

Interpreting

Interpreting involves proposing an alternative explanation about events and phenomena so that clients may consider its relevance for themselves. Expressed as a hypothesis—never as if it were established fact—the interpretation may enhance self-awareness and growth. You may begin the interpretation with an "I wonder . . ." lead in phrase. Consider, for example, a client who is a high school student with great academic potential. She regularly procrastinates, fails to turn in homework assignments, and studies only enough to pass the exams. You might offer an interpretation in the following way: "I wonder if you might be afraid to succeed? After all, if you started to get grades of A and B, you'd have to start thinking about college—where you would go, what would be your major, and how you would pay for your education."

Through interpretation, you introduce your idea of what the client's message or behavior might mean.

This requires considerable skill. We suggest the following guidelines:

- Offer the interpretation in a tentative fashion—as a hypothesis for consideration.
- Ensure that the interpretation relates in some way to the agreed-upon problems and goals, or the action steps.
- Use simple language and try to keep it succinct. Clients may experience lengthy explanations as lectures.
- Seek feedback from the client after you offer the interpretation.
- Avoid debates with the client about the accuracy, validity, or pertinence of the interpretation. If the client seems uncomfortable or skeptical, accept that reality and go on.

Limit Setting

Setting limits within a nurturing relationship may also facilitate client self-awareness. Specifically, the appropriate use of limits may help clients better understand and gain greater control of their impulses. Limits may also build a sense of worth, by demonstrating that we care enough to risk conflict and that we believe clients are strong enough to accept the limits. You do not have to carry the entire burden of limit setting in work with groups and families. Group members often set limits, either on the behavior of particular members, or for the entire group. Some groups' preoccupation with rules indicates the importance of limits for the growth of the system. In work with individuals, too, rules or limits can be discussed and used to assist clients.

Looking for Strengths

Searching for strengths involves the discovery and recognition of clients' capacities, abilities, potentials, and achievements (de Jong & Miller, 1995). Clients often fail to attend to or appreciate their strengths. They may be unaware of their own competence or even their own successes. In looking for strengths, first encourage clients to engage in self-exploration that leads them to discover their own strengths. If clients have difficulty, you may have to point out some of their strengths to them. During the intervention phase, we seek to discover strengths that could contribute to resolution of the problems, attainment

of goals, or completion of planned action steps. We generally do not encourage clients to explore or recognize any and all of their strengths. Rather, we look for strengths that might aid in problem solving.

Clients routinely reflect extraordinary strength and resilience as they live their lives and cope with problems that would overwhelm many other people—including most social workers! Nonetheless, be cautious about pointing out strengths. If your observations about positive aspects sound at all disingenuous, clients may well feel diminished rather than supported. Insincere compliments may come across as a form of pity or perhaps condescension. Excessive praise for small steps can have a similar effect. Indeed, some clients experience compliments from social workers as neither positive nor complimentary. Whenever possible, help clients discover their own strengths. You may often do so by asking about competencies, social support, successes, and life lessons (Cournoyer, 2005). For example, you might ask questions such as these: "If you were to identify a special talent or ability that you have that few people know about, what would it be?" "You've dealt with these problems for quite some time. What talents or abilities have you drawn on to cope with these challenging issues?" "Who are the people you can turn to when you need support?" "What do you consider to be your greatest accomplishment or your biggest success?" "You've dealt with one problem after another for a long time. Somehow you've survived and you've probably learned some important lessons about life during the process. What have you learned that enables you to keep going in the midst of all these difficulties?"

Confrontation

Confrontation involves pointing out distortions, discrepancies, contradictions, or inconsistencies in clients' feelings, experiences, or behavior. Confrontations must be undertaken in a careful and caring manner because they involve considerable risk to clients' coping capacities. No other technique offers social workers such a tempting opportunity to act out our own feelings. Confrontation does not involve expressing anger, frustration, disapproval, superiority, or spite. Rather, the technique is expressed as an observation that clients may or may not find accurate, relevant, or useful. For example, to a client who hopes to lose weight as a way to help control his diabetes, you might observe something like this: "Joe, if I understand correctly, you

---

EXHIBIT 12-4
Using Feedback to Promote Personal Growth

1. Focus feedback on the behavior, not the person. Focusing on behavior is less threatening because it implies that change is possible.
   Example: Say: "Jordan talked considerably during the meeting."
   Not: "Jordan is a loudmouth."

2. Focus feedback on observations rather than interferences or interpretations.
   Example: Say: "I noticed you left the meeting early."
   Not: "You didn't seem to think the meeting was very important."

3. Focus feedback on a description of the process rather than a judgment.
   Example: Say: "I noticed you frequently changed the subject and often looked at your watch."
   Not: "You didn't want to be here today."

4. Focus feedback on behavior related to a specific situation, the here and now. Feedback is usually most helpful when it is given soon after the observation is made, thus keeping it concrete and relatively free of distortions.
   Example: Say: "You didn't answer me just now when I asked . . ."
   Not: "You never answer me when . . ."

5. Focus feedback on the sharing of ideas and information rather than on advice giving. Let the other person decide the most appropriate course of action given the ideas and information you have provided.
   Example: Say: "Mrs. S. from the school just called and said she's tried to reach you several times and you haven't returned her calls."
   Not: "You should return your calls every day."

6. Focus feedback on the amount of information you think the listener can use, not the amount that you would like to give. If overloaded, the person is less likely to use the feedback effectively.

7. Consider the appropriate time and place when offering feedback. Excellent feedback presented at an inappropriate time can do more harm than good.

---

hope to manage the diabetes by losing some weight. You planned to weigh yourself twice daily—once in the morning and once in the evening. However, today you say you've haven't checked your weight at all during the past two weeks. What do you make of this?"

When you consider using confrontation, ask how it could contribute to problem resolution and goal attainment or toward the completion of agreed-upon action steps. Like other intervention techniques, confrontation should not be used unless it supports the service agreement. Done poorly, with a vulnerable system, confrontation can lead clients to feel embarrassed or ashamed, guilty, self-conscious, afraid, rejected, or defensive and angry. Some clients may quickly accommodate to your views but adopt a passive, submissive attitude thereafter. Others might angrily withdraw from contact. Neither contributes to the problem-solving process. Confrontation involves some risk to clients' equilibrium. Therefore, its use should be based on a careful assessment of clients' capacity

to use the information gained through the confrontation and a similar assessment of the strength of your relationship with them. Confrontation is seldom useful until a solid working relationship between client and worker has been established. Also, try to precede and follow confrontations with empathic reflections. This helps clients recognize that you truly are interested in understanding their thoughts and feelings and are not solely attempting to point out inconsistencies.

These feedback techniques—reflecting, going beyond, asking about process, responding with immediacy, interpreting, limit-setting, looking for strengths, and confrontation—may help clients develop greater self-awareness and contribute to personal growth. Exhibit 12-4 contains several guidelines for the use of feedback to encourage personal growth.

Feedback that involves descriptive information is usually easier for clients to consider than are evaluative comments (Fatout, 1995; Millstein, 1993). Behavioral descriptions are nonjudgmental observations.

EXHIBIT 12-5
Behavioral Descriptions

The skill of behavior description depends on accurate observation, which, in turn, depends on being aware when you are describing and when you are inferring. A statement must pass two tests to qualify as a behavioral description.

1. A behavioral description reports specific, observable actions rather than generalizations about the person's motives, feelings, attitudes, or personality traits. It states what was observed. It does not infer about why. Here are examples:

Behavioral Descriptions	Inferences
Bob's eyes filled with tears.	Bob had a cold, Bob was depressed, or Bob felt sorry for himself.
Becky did not respond when Bill asked her a question.	Becky did not hear Bill, Becky resented Bill's question, or Becky was embarrassed.

2. A behavior description is nonevaluative. It should not indicate or imply that what happened was good or bad, right or wrong. Evaluative statements (such as name calling, accusations, judgments) usually express what the speaker is feeling and convey little about what behavior was observed. Here are examples:

Behavioral Descriptions	Evaluative Statements
Jim talked more than others on this topic. Several times, he interrupted others before they finished.	Jim is rude or Jim wants to be the center of attention.
Bob, you disagreed with Sally about almost everything she's said today.	Bob, you're just trying to show Sally up or Bob, you're being stubborn.
Fran walked out of the meeting 30 minutes before it was finished.	Fran doesn't care about others or Fran is irresponsible.
Sam interrupted me before I finished.	Sam deliberately cut me off or Sam was rude.

They are quite rare in everyday life. Many people process observations and reach conclusions based on judgments of others' motives, attitudes, or perhaps character. We may even be unaware that we are making inferences and reaching conclusions based on interpretations of small amounts of data. Exhibit 12-5 contains a few examples of behavioral descriptions, as well as some corresponding inferences or evaluative statements.

◆ Strengthening Social Skills

Many problems, goals, and action steps involve social and communication skills. Numerous relationship, family, work, school, and community issues require well-developed skills in talking and listening, expressing understanding, making requests, addressing differences of opinion, resolving conflicts, and providing support to others. Consider, for example, the complex social and communication skills required to fulfill the roles of parent, employee, student, or friend. Most social roles require sophisticated interpersonal competence. Many of the intervention techniques used to enhance clients' self-awareness may be used as part of a plan to strengthen social and communication skills. Once aware of their social and communication patterns, clients may deliberately work to accentuate desired behaviors and diminish undesired behaviors. Knowledge about communication processes and understanding of common misconceptions (see Exhibit 12-6) may contribute as well.

Teaching

Although self-awareness and knowledge about social and communication processes help strengthen social skills, more is usually needed. Social workers often assume an active teaching role to encourage skill development. Teaching goes well beyond the simple provision of information. Coaching, training, and encouraging practice are additional aspects of the teach-

---

EXHIBIT 12-6
Ten Misconceptions About Communication

1. Words have meanings.
   Wrong: Meanings are created in the human mind; different people associate different meanings with the same word.
2. Communication is verbal.
   Wrong: Communication is both verbal and nonverbal.
3. Telling is communication.
   Wrong: Telling is only half of communication; the other half is receiving.
4. Communications can solve all our problems.
   Wrong: Communication may create more problems than it solves. Careful attention needs to be given to what and how much is communicated.
5. Communication is a good thing.
   Wrong: Communication is neither good nor bad; it is a tool to facilitate what we want to relay, and this may be good or bad.
6. The more communication, the better.
   Wrong: Quality is more important; quantity should not override quality.

7. Breakdown can occur in communication.
   Wrong: Cars break down; communication does not. The more likely problem is that the listener did not hear what he or she wanted to hear or did not understand.
8. Communication is a natural ability.
   Wrong: Communication skills—both sending and receiving messages—are learned.
9. Interpersonal communication is intimate.
   Wrong: Intimate communication involves sharing very personal beliefs or feelings with other people.
10. Communication competence equals communication effectiveness.
    Wrong: Knowing how to communicate does not guarantee that the result will be the one desired.

Source: Adapted from Barnes, D. (1994). Survival tips when the diagnosis is poor communication. *Family-Centered Care Networks, 11*(1), 4–5. (Published by National Center for Family-Centered Care, Bethesda, MD.)

---

ing needed to help clients develop skills for influencing their environments in purposeful ways (Evans, 1992; Murphy & Schneider, 1994). Some clients may benefit from training in responsible assertive communication strategies, others from daily living skills, and many from problem-solving processes and techniques. Helping clients strengthen social skills is a complex undertaking. Clients vary in their readiness, motivation, and learning styles. Teaching may require individualized learning plans to accommodate the unique needs of particular clients. Even within family and group contexts, some individualization of instruction may be need.

When teaching, social workers must defend against the tendency to adopt a superior or condescending attitude. Try to avoid lecturing or preaching. Instead, enlist clients as co-learners in a collaborative process of teaching and learning. Attempt to maintain the partnership relationship while teaching. Although such a cooperative approach usually requires more time and patience than does the traditional superior teacher-subordinate student relationship, it often leads to greater learning. Clients who feel hopeless, powerless, and incompetent often find the collaborative learning experience enormously valuable. In addition to developing needed social and communication skills, clients may also gain a sense of optimism and self-control.

Modeling   Social workers frequently serve as models of human behavior for clients. Consciously or unconsciously, clients frequently view us as examples to adopt, adapt, or reject. Through their observations of our behavior and interactions, clients may learn something of value in their work toward problem resolution and goal attainment. For example, when you demonstrate nondefensiveness when confronted or challenged, display patience while explaining complex ideas, or gentle strength when maintaining agreed-upon limits, clients may consider your behavior for their own possible use.

Social workers may also planfully incorporate modeling as part of the teaching role. For instance, during a role-play or simulation, you might adopt the role of client in communicating with a spouse, employer, teacher, or other significant person to demonstrate alternate social and communication skills. Certainly, clients are free to adopt, adapt, or reject your example. However, you serve as a model nonetheless. You should remain extremely aware of the potential effect of your demeanor, words, gestures, interpersonal patterns, and other forms of behavior on clients' learning. For better or worse, your example often constitutes a most powerful lesson for clients.

Rehearsing Rehearsal incorporates coaching, modeling, and practicing aspects of teaching. You may assume the role of significant persons in clients' lives to provide an opportunity for them to practice a new communication skill before they engage others for real. In groupwork, you may ask clients to practice carrying out a task in the protected social environment of the group. Rehearsal in role-play simulations enables clients to enact the social and communication skill, identify any obstacles that may appear, and develop means to overcome them. Rehearsal represents a key aspect of teaching because intellectual understanding and self-awareness usually must be accompanied by experiential learning. Otherwise, the ideas about how to engage socially may not transfer into clients' real-world experience.

◆ Accessing Information

Sharing Information, Opinions, and Advice

Social workers may legitimately provide information and guidance to clients—when it relates to the service agreement. Advice giving is an entirely proper and appropriate professional function. The principle of client self-determination is often misconstrued to mean that social workers may not share knowledge and offer advice. On the contrary, failure to provide relevant information and sound professional guidance may, in some circumstances, represent a form of malpractice. The knowledge and opinions shared should support the goals and plans identified in the service agreement. Furthermore, you should encourage clients to participate in the discovery or analysis of information, and the consideration of suggestions. In family and group contexts, members may share information and opinions with each other and may collaborate in making decisions about how best to use the input.

There are several common purposes for sharing information, suggestions, and opinions. For example, they may be used to

- Establish a common understanding about a situation
- Present clients with an alternate view of the situation—based on your analysis
- Propose actions that clients may consider and perhaps choose to try
- Provide new knowledge about a situation

You might, for instance, suggest alternatives to clients' usual ways of functioning and explore how these alternatives might be used in specific circumstances. You could provide perspectives about important aspects of the problem or its solution. You might dispense information about community resources, including the names of contact persons, eligibility requirements, and some idea about what to expect when attempting to access relevant resources.

Advice giving is not exactly the same as providing information. You may provide information in a neutral manner so that clients are clearly free to accept, modify, or reject its relevance for themselves. However, clients often feel less freedom to decline social workers' advice or recommendations. Clients may feel vulnerable or perhaps obligated to accept your suggestions. Despite your efforts to establish a collaborative partnership, you maintain your position as someone in authority. Clients may demonstrate their rejection of your advice in an indirect manner—perhaps in an effort to deflect your disappointment or disapproval. For example, they may forget your suggestion or fail to follow through.

Avoid giving advice before you truly comprehend clients' wants. When clients ask for advice, try to understand the reason or motive for the request before responding. Premature advice is often off-target and multiple suggestions—one right after another—tend to lose value and credibility. When you do offer advice, identify it as your opinion and suggest that together you consider its potential for use in this situation. Clearly indicate that clients are free to accept, modify, or reject your advice.

Self-Disclosing

Self-disclosure represents a special form of information sharing because it involves revealing part of your own personal history and life experiences with a client. It goes well beyond sharing information and opinions about a specific situation that the client faces. Many feminist counselors (Bricker-Jenkins, 1991; Collins, 1986; Rosewater & Walker, 1985; Russell, 1989) believe that self-disclosure of personal life experiences by helping professionals strengthens the client-worker relationship, improves communication, and facilitates client progress. However, some workers wonder if self-disclosure is ever appropriate or, if so, under what conditions. In considering these questions, it is helpful to differentiate between worker-initiated self-disclosure and client-initiated self-disclosure.

Worker-Initiated Self-Disclosure Some social workers see self-disclosure as an essential part of practice (Freud, 1992; Lundy, 1993; MacDonald, 1988; Russell, 1989; Valentich, 1986). They argue that self-disclosure allows the practitioner to share relevant personal experiences and to respond emotionally to clients' experiences. Some assert that such personal revelations are necessary for building openness and trust (Lundy, 1993). Further, self-disclosure can assist in identifying common social conditions shared by both client and worker (Worell & Remer, 1992). Worker self-disclosure and expression of emotions may be essential to the search for mutual understanding between worker and client (Bricker-Jenkins, 1991) and may reduce the role distance and power difference between worker and client (Worell & Remer, 1992).

Worker-initiated self-disclosure may also confuse clients and lead them to adopt goals that they judge to be important to you, though not to them (Wells, 1994). Some clients may, for example, adopt an approach to growth or recovery that is more *your* path than *their* path. Other clients may experience social workers' self-disclosure as indication that we need as much help as they do. Indeed, some clients may begin to offer care and support to social workers perceived as needy or vulnerable. We urge caution in using worker-initiated self-disclosure. Carefully analyze your motives and purposes in considering self-disclosure. Be certain that it is *for* the client rather than for you and is clearly congruent with the goals and plans outlined in the service agreement. Much of the time, other forms of information sharing can accomplish the same purposes with fewer risks. The following guidelines may be helpful when you consider worker-initiated self-disclosure:

- Determine that the self-disclosure is not motivated by your personal need to share.

- Do not use self-disclosure to establish your own credibility.
- Be sure that the self-disclosure clearly relates to the client's issues and the agreed-upon goals or plans and is meaningful to the client in the current situation.
- If the client appears uncomfortable or uninterested, discontinue self-disclosure.

Client-Initiated Self-Disclosure Some clients may ask personal questions of you. In other words, they initiate a request for self-disclosure. In some circumstances, such questions may be based on a sincere interest in you and represent honest efforts to secure information. On other occasions, however, clients may be engaged in a testing process of some sort—perhaps in an effort to validate their own points of view. For example, an adolescent client might ask, "Have you ever used cocaine?," or a couple seeking relationship counseling might inquire, "Are you married and have you ever been divorced?"

In certain circumstances, you may decide that the question represents a reasonable request and readily respond. Some questions may refer to your educational background, professional qualifications, and areas of expertise. These, of course, are entirely legitimate. Indeed, clients should not have to ask to access such information. Some personal questions are similar in this regard: "Do you speak Spanish?" "Have you worked with people with these kinds of problems before?" These questions are quite reasonable and pertain to the work at hand. Other questions, however, are clear requests for personal information unrelated to the issues of concern. You are not obligated to answer these personal questions. You could respond with a statement such as, "I am uncomfortable discussing my personal life." You could then follow with a question of your own. You might, for example, say, "What leads you to ask?"

If you conclude that it would contribute to the process by responding to a client's request for personal information, and you feel comfortable doing so, answer with a short statement followed by a question about the reason for asking. In response to an adolescent client's question about your past use of cocaine, you may say simply, "Yes, I did," or "No, I didn't. What leads you to ask?" Do not volunteer information that might provide impetus for clients to continue problematic behavior or place yourself in legal jeopardy. Although you must protect clients' right to confidentiality, they are not obligated to maintain the confidentiality of things you say. Indeed, clients commonly discuss with friends and family members what social workers say to them during meetings. Client-initiated requests for self-disclosure are perhaps more challenging because you have less time to consider whether and how to respond. You might anticipate the kinds of personal questions clients might commonly ask so you can prepare some general responses. Consider the following guidelines when responding to personal questions from clients:

- Do not respond if your answer would be unhelpful or harmful to the client, or place you in legal jeopardy.
- Do not respond if you are uncomfortable with the question. Simply indicate your discomfort about discussing personal matters.
- If you do respond, keep your answer short, factual, and truthful. Do not elaborate on, explain, or defend your behavior.
- Whether you respond or not, ask about the reason for the request. Explore what lies behind the client's question and interest in this personal information about you.

Truth Telling

Honesty, of course, is a hallmark of professionalism. Social workers frequently share important information with clients. We tell the truth in doing so. Our codes of ethics require us to do so. Nonetheless, truthfulness is not the only factor in service to clients. We consider other aspects as well—including the service agreement and the duty to provide competent care. It would be brutal to say to a distraught client, "You look terrible today." As Exhibit 12-7 illustrates, the cruelty of an honest statement need not be deliberate.

The principle of honesty does not mean that you may attack or otherwise damage clients with your words. "I'm just being honest" does not excuse social workers from our professional duty to provide high quality, competent care that supports the goals reflected in the service agreement. We suggest the following guidelines:

- Whatever you do say should be truthful. Do not tell lies.
- Do not share "the whole truth" if it does not relate to the service contract or might cause damage—perhaps because a client is unprepared or fragile.
- Consider the manner in which you communicate the truthful information. Be sensitive to timing and client readiness.
- Do not use honesty as an excuse to attack or disparage another person. Do not adopt an angry, judgmental, disapproving, or demeaning attitude in expressing yourself. Frame your comments in as neutral a manner as possible.

◆ Facilitating Decision Making

Clients may find it difficult to make decisions for a number of reasons: lack of experience, inability to weigh options or analyze evidence, or discomfort about taking risks. Decision making involves risk and responsibility. We always run the risk of making an unwise choice. Indeed, even wise decisions often yield unintended consequences—some positive, some negative. Many people prefer to avoid the risk and responsibility through procrastination or perhaps by deciding not to decide. Some clients may ask you, directly or indirectly, to make decisions for them. For example, sometimes clients ask for advice or information in such a way that it actually constitutes a request that you make a decision for them. Be extremely careful to avoid making decisions for clients. Doing so would profoundly change the nature of the partnership. In effect, you would assume the role of parent or guardian, rather than social worker, and take on primary responsibility for the decision and its consequences. When clients find it difficult to make a particular decision, encourage them to consider including it as a problem for work. Then, the partners may negotiate an appropriate service plan; Exhibit 12-8 provides an example. Having made a decision, the client negotiates with the worker another plan to implement the decision.

Decision Making as Problem Solving

Decision making is a logical problem-solving process. You can involve clients in discussions of the advantages and disadvantages of one option compared with the advantages and disadvantages of another. Lists may be helpful. Try to determine which of the advantages are most important to the client and which of the dis-

EXHIBIT 12-7
Too Much Honesty

Source: Baby Blues cartoon by Jerry Scott and Rick Kirkman © 1997 King Features Syndicate, Inc.
Reprinted with special permission of King Features Syndicate.

advantages might be neutralized or reduced. In some cases, the plan may be to gather additional information to improve the quality of decision making.

Force field analysis (Exhibit 12-9) may help clients to organize their thinking and arrive at a decision. You may need to encourage clients—or even give them permission—to take risks. Let clients know that risk taking is an essential part of life. So are mistakes and bad choices. Most are not life threatening. We can usually recover from poor decisions and often learn a great deal from them. Avoiding decisions tends to limit our learning, growth, and development. Furthermore, if we do not make decisions for ourselves, we become susceptible to unreasonable influence and control by others who are often more than willing to make decisions for us.

Assisting clients to make decisions may seem a cumbersome process. However, the skills are transferable. As clients learn how to make decisions in one area, their abilities and willingness to engage in decision making in other areas of their lives tend to increase as well.

Logical Discussion

Logical discussion helps build clients' capacity for rational decision making, planning, and deliberate action by encouraging thoughtful reflection about events and actions—past, present, or future. Many clients find the process contributes to their growth and maturity as well as serving as an aid to coping with challenging circumstances. You may adopt the questioning processes associated with Socratic dialogues to stimulate reflection and analysis. According to Plato, Socrates taught by asking questions rather than by lecturing (Santas, 1979). Often referred to as the Socratic method, we may similarly encourage clients to analyze and reflect on the assumptions, premises, and principles that guide their actions. This approach is especially useful in work with families and groups where members can offer alternative views and support each other to examine the conceptual sources of their assumptions.

Challenging Irrational Beliefs Some clients hold beliefs and ideas about themselves, other people, or the environment that unnecessarily limit their range of opportunity or action. These beliefs are irrational in the sense that they interfere with the pursuit of their goals and aspirations. Clients may base self-limiting beliefs on erroneous information or perhaps derive them from distorted thinking. You can challenge irrational beliefs by means of logical discussion, confrontation, Socratic dialogue, or by tracking the sequence of events associated with various automatic thoughts (Burns, 1980). Such processes may enable clients to consider alternate perspectives and behaviors that may contribute to rather than inhibit goal

---

EXHIBIT 12-8
A Service Plan to Assist in Decision Making

Background:

Richard is the 10-year-old son of Jon and Bonita Jasper. Jon is a merchant seaman and is at sea for extended periods, leaving Bonita as the primary provider of child care. Richard has been staying out late at night, is refusing to do household chores, and recently was gone from home overnight. Bonita, in her efforts to control Richard, has used harsh discipline, including beating him with a belt that left welts. The school made a referral to child protection; the child protection agency is holding the case open because Bonita has asked for services from the family service unit of the Maritime Union. This initial plan was developed by Bonita and Sally Harlow, the worker, during a home visit.

Date: March 5

Problem:

Bonita is having difficulty managing Richard without anger, is resorting to harsh punishment, and is considering requesting an out-of-home placement.

Objective:

Bonita will be able to decide whether to request placement for Richard or to develop a service plan to retain Richard at home.

Service Plan:

Task	Who Will Do?	To Be Completed by:
1. Meet twice in Bonita's home to discuss the choices available and the pros and cons of each choice.	Bonita and Sally; Sally will visit Bonita at her home for these meetings.	1st meeting on March 12; 2nd meeting on March 19
2. Bonita will make a decision between these: a. requesting placement b. developing a service plan for retaining Richard in the home c. discontinuing service	Bonita	March 23
3. Telephone conference to discuss the decision and schedule another meeting if Bonita decides for (a) or (b).	Worker will call Bonita	March 24

---

achievement. Exhibit 12-10 contains examples of several irrational beliefs along with possible challenges.

◆ Finding Meaning

Social workers often encounter clients who feel hopeless, pessimistic, and unable to find meaning or purpose in life. In serving young people, you may notice that some experience a powerful sense of psychological or social anomie (Durkheim, 1951; Merton, 1968). Social anomie involves feelings of alienation from the general society that may reflect societal breakdown, fragmentation, or rapid change. Psychological anomie relates to individuals' inability to find personal meaning in the world around them or to

---

EXHIBIT 12-9
Force Field Analysis

Force field analysis is a structural method for making a decision about a course of action:

1. Identify the situation as it is now.
2. Specify a clear objective (the situation as you would like it to be).
3. Identify the forces operating in the situation that tend to push toward the objective (positive forces), those that tend to push against attaining the objective (negative forces), and those that are neutral or uncommitted (neutral forces). Use a brainstorming technique: Name the forces as fast as possible, with no evaluation. Don't worry about repeating what has already been said. Discussion, clarification, and evaluation come later.

4. Rank the forces by the following:
   a. Their relevance to the desired objective
   b. Their potential to effect change
   c. Their feasibility
   d. The clarity or tangibility of the force
5. Devise action alternatives for altering some of the negative forces, especially those you ranked highest. Consider whether some of the neutral forces could be made positive and how to strengthen the positive forces.

Force Field Analysis
Forces for (+)
Uncommitted or neutral forces (0)
Forces against (−)

---

adopt values and principles to guide life choices. Some experience life as existentially meaningless without value, reason, or purpose. Frankl (1963) suggested that the search for meaning in life represents a fundamental human endeavor. Based partly on his experience as a Nazi concentration camp prisoner, he developed logotherapy to assist people in finding meaning in life (Guttman, 1996).

The function of spirituality in assisting people to find meaning in life is recognized in transpersonal approaches to social work practice (Canda, 1991; Cowley & Derezotes, 1994; Derezotes, 1995; Derezotes & Evans, 1995; Lantz & Greenlee, 1990; Moxley & Washington, 2001; Randour, 1993; Sermabeikian, 1994). From this perspective, spirituality is viewed as wholeness or integrity, irrespective of religious belief or affiliation (Cowley, 1993). Transpersonal approaches appear well suited to help clients whose problems or goals are spiritual in nature, relate to changing moral values in a violent society, or involve the sense of helplessness engendered by the threat of terrorism, HIV/AIDS, homelessness, and dispiritation (Cowley, 1993; Cowley & Derezotes, 1994; Smith, 1995; Stretch, 1967).

Transpersonal practice attempts to integrate spiritual experience into the larger understanding of human development (Smith, 1995). From this perspective, the concept of the person-in-environment expands to include transcendental reality (Canda, 1988b). Mystical experiences are acknowledged for their potential to contribute to human growth and awareness. Some advocates of transpersonal practice challenge the assumptions that linear thinking represents a useful standard for optimal cognitive development, that individual autonomy reflects an ideal form of psychosocial maturity, or that ordinary waking consciousness is associated with optimal mental processing (Canda, 1991).

Existential discontent associated with a lack of meaning or purpose in life may motivate people to pursue their goals (Brown, 1980). Indeed, some social workers and clients focus so intently on concrete goals that they sometimes miss the often more important development of a sense of meaning, direction, or purpose that may accompany personal growth (Horowitz, 1991). The transpersonal approaches encourage social workers to recognize clients' spiritual or philosophical development during the problem-solving process. Social workers often help clients find meaning in life by imparting hope, dispelling apprehension, and nurturing the belief that the future beckons with the promise of change (Horowitz, 1991). Your attitudes and actions may contribute to clients' optimism, liberation, empowerment, and spiritual identity.

EXHIBIT 12-10
Some Irrational Beliefs

Irrational Beliefs That Lead to Unassertive Responses

I must be loved and approved by every significant person in my life; if I'm not, it's awful.

It would be awful if I hurt the other person.

It is easier to avoid life difficulties than to face them.

I need someone stronger than myself on whom to rely.

Emotional misery comes from external pressure, and I have little ability to control or change my feelings.

Examples of Ways to Challenge Irrational Beliefs

Why would it be terrible if the other person rejected me? How does that make me a worthless, hopeless human being? What do I really have to lose by telling my partner that I don't like the way he behaves toward me? If the worst happens and he leaves me, how would that make me a failure, a reject? And what's the evidence that, if this relationship ends, I'll never find another person who will treat me better?

How can I really hurt another person, or become a bad person, simply by making my own well-being and comfort as important as that person's? Who says life should be easy? It isn't. Change is risky, and the status quo is only easier in the short run—not in the long run.

It might be nice to have someone to rely on, but what law is there that says I can't—even at this late stage—learn new coping skills and take care of myself, if necessary?

No one makes me feel anything; I control my own thinking and feelings.

Irrational Beliefs That Lead to Hostile or Aggressive Responses

When other people behave badly or unfairly, they should be severely condemned, they are rotten individuals.

It is catastrophic when things are not the way that I like them to be—when I am treated unfairly or rejected.
The world should be fair and just.

Why should the other person roast in hell for behaving badly? This behavior doesn't mean she is a totally despicable human being. How can I express my displeasure without calling this person names?

People are going to act the way they want—not the way I want. I don't like their behavior, but I can stand it.

Why should the world be fair? It would be nice if it were, but it isn't. How can I try to change what I can change, and lump (or leave) the rest?

(continues)

EXHIBIT 12-10
Some Irrational Beliefs *(continued)*

Irrational Ideas That Lead to Depression or Self-Downing for Assertive Failures

Things and situations should turn out better than they do, and it's terrible if I don't find good solutions to life's grim realities.

I must be thoroughly competent, adequate, and proficient at all times.

Examples of Ways to Challenge Irrational Beliefs

What law of the universe says that because I dislike something it shouldn't exist? How does getting myself upset over things really help me to effectively go about trying to change them? Like it or not, the world isn't fair; and I'd just better accept that, trying to change what I can and learning not to upset myself over what I can't change.

Why is it awful if I behave nonassertively (or aggressively)? How does that make me, as a human being, hopeless, worthless, or demeaned? Won't I stand a lot better chance of changing my poor habits and behavior by focusing on where I went wrong—and trying to figure out what to do differently next time—than by beating myself over the head and making myself depressed?

Source: Adapted from: Ellis, Albert. (1975). *A new guide to rational living*. Englewood Cliffs, NJ: Prentice-Hall.

In efforts to help clients find meaning in life, consider exploring existential themes through questions such as the following:

- What do you perceive to be the primary purpose of life? In particular, what gives your life meaning? In reference to these notions of purpose and meaning, what do you most hope to accomplish during your life?
- What is your view of the concept of spirituality? How does spirituality relate to your life's purpose?
- What is your view of religion? How do your religious traditions contribute to meaning and purpose in life?

Many clients find meaning through creative work, family life, or service to others. People often hope to "leave a mark" or make a contribution to their community, children or grandchildren, or perhaps help younger persons or possibly those whose lives have been less fortunate. Where appropriate, you may help clients find ways to express themselves artistically—perhaps through painting, sculpting, making music, or writing; develop more intimate relationships with their families and friends; or provide community service—possibly through volunteer efforts with civic or religious organizations.

◆ Chapter Summary

You can help clients to mobilize power—to take control of their own lives and decision making and to secure the resources they need—by drawing on a range of intervention skills and techniques. For example, you may help clients

- *Secure resources.* You may directly provide resources to clients by doing things for them, assisting them to find resources in their environments, and helping them to organize themselves collectively to pursue their common interests.

Assisting people to participate through social and political action represents an integral aspect of much social work practice.

- *Enhance self-awareness*. You may help clients become more knowledgeable about their own patterns of thought and behavior and their effect on others. You may provide feedback to clients by using the skills of reflecting, going beyond, asking about process, responding with immediacy, interpreting, limit setting, looking for strengths, and confrontation.

- *Strengthen clients' social and communication skills*. Well-developed social and communication abilities may enable clients to increase control over their own lives and influence their situations. You may adopt a teaching role and use modeling and rehearsing skills to facilitate clients' development in these areas.

- *Access information*. Information is empowering, although it must be shared in a way that leaves clients free to accept, adapt, or reject it. This is particularly important for advice or suggestions that may engender a sense of obligation in clients. Be cautious about initiating self-disclosure as a means to share information and opinions. Worker initiated personal revelations may be motivated less by client wants than by our own wants and needs. Offering brief, truthful responses to clients' questions about your own life and experience may sometimes be appropriate, as long as your responses contribute to the agreed-upon service goals, are not harmful to the client, and do not cause you personal discomfort.

- *Facilitate decision making*. Your efforts to help clients make decisions often involve both logical discussion, with evaluation of the pros and cons of alternative courses of action, and examination of clients' beliefs that may interfere with choice making and action. Resist the temptation to make clients' decisions for them. Your role is to assist clients in making their own choices and assuming the risks and responsibilities associated with them.

- *Find meaning in life*. Life without meaning or purpose often contributes to a profound sense of pessimism, cynicism, and perhaps despair. Alienated or anomic clients may benefit from explorations about life's meaning and purpose, spirituality, and perhaps their religious views

and practices. For some people, creative work, family relationships, or service to others provides meaning, direction, and purpose in life. Explore these possibilities with clients and, if they so choose, help them find a way to express them in some tangible manner.

Learning Exercises: Readings, InfoTrac, and the Web

1. Use your word-processing computer program to enter the important terms and concepts presented in this chapter in alphabetical order. Place a question mark by any terms that you do not clearly understand. Save your document as EX 12-1.

2. Log on to the InfoTrac College Edition Web site. Conduct a keyword search (using either Keyword Search or Advanced Search) to locate the articles entitled "Enhancing Relationships in Nursing Homes Through Empowerment" (Ingersoll-Dayton, Schroepfer, Pryce, & Waarala, 2003) and "Effects of a Cognitive-Behavioral, School-Based, Group Intervention with Mexican American Pregnant and Parenting Adolescents" (Harris & Franklin, 2003). Read the articles and prepare a two-page essay in which you reflect on their implications for social work and social work practice. Save your document as EX 12-2.

3. Log on to the InfoTrac College Edition Web site. Conduct a keyword search (using either Keyword Search or Advanced Search) to locate the articles entitled "Harm Reduction: A Social Work Practice Model and Social Justice Agenda" (Brocato & Wagner, 2003) and "Child Sexual Abuse: Prevention or Promotion?" (Bolen, 2003). Read the articles and prepare a two-page essay in which you reflect on their implications for social work and social work practice. Save your document as EX 12-3.

4. Turn to **Reading 19: Action as a Vehicle for Promoting Competence.** Review this article by Anthony Maluccio and reflect on its implications for topics addressed in this chapter. Prepare a one-page essay in which you describe your observations about and reactions to the six suggested means for enhancing clients' problem-solving

skills and promoting competence through action. Save your document as EX 12-4.

5. Turn to **Reading 9: Betty Smith.** Become familiar with the case description again. This time, prepare a one-page essay in which you address the following questions: How does the worker confront Betty Smith about the inadequacy of her care for the children? How does this affect their work together? Share your observations and reactions. Save your document as EX 12-5.

6. Turn to **Reading 26: Leonard Timms.** Review this case study by Bob Bennett and reflect on the intervention strategies and methods used by the social worker in providing services to Leonard Timms and his family. Prepare a one-page essay to explore your observations and reactions. Save your document as EX 12-6.

7. Turn to **Reading 27: The Omar Family.** Review this case study by Khadija Khaja and reflect on the intervention strategies and methods used by the social worker in providing services to the Omar family. Prepare a one-page essay to explore

your observations and reactions. Save your document as EX 12-7.

8. Re-read the description presented in Exhibit 12-1: Who Will Care for Mr. Sandstone? Prepare a one-page essay in which you address the following questions: How would you go about sharing with Mr. Sandstone your views about his need for a back-up care provider and any arrangements you are making for this? How will the fact that Mr. Sandstone is a Native American client influence the way in which you share information with him? Share your observations and reactions. Save your document as EX 12-8.

9. Read the description presented in Exhibit 12-11: What's Next for Jim? Prepare a one-page essay in which you identify which of the methods discussed in this chapter you would use to assist Jim to explore and change how he copes with stress. Describe in some detail how you would use the methods you select and discuss how these will help Jim mobilize power. Share your observations and reactions. Save your document as EX 12-9.

EXHIBIT 12-11
What's Next for Jim?

Jim, a 45-year-old inmate at Meadow River prison, is married and has three adolescent children. When Jim first approached the worker, he identified the problem as fear and anxiety. Jim was afraid to speak to others and to leave his room. In addition, he suffered from panic attacks. Because of this, it was difficult for him to talk about himself. After a few weeks, however, he became more comfortable and he began to open up. He stated that he was wild when he was younger and often got into trouble with the law. At one point he was incarcerated at a correctional institution for the criminally insane. He remembers physical, psychological, and sexual abuse during that incarceration and believes that much of what happened at the institution caused his current fears.

Six years ago, Jim was arrested again. He stated that on the way to the police station he became fearful that he would be sent back to the institu-

tion for criminally insane. He managed to escape by assaulting the police officers. He was later re-arrested and is currently serving time for this offense. While in prison, Jim has joined AA and has become involved with a church.

During the first few meetings, Jim said that his children were doing well in school and excelling in sports. Soon after, he began discussing their problems bit by bit. Before the holidays in December, Jim broke down and said that two of his children were in foster care and that all of them were continually running away and getting into trouble with the law. He also mentioned that his wife was an alcoholic. By this point, Jim had managed to overcome a lot of his fears and was insistent about the help that he wanted for his family.

(continues)

EXHIBIT 12-11
What's Next for Jim? *(continued)*

He began to be quite demanding that someone contact his wife to help her find additional support. Phone calls were made to his wife; however, they were never returned.

In December, Jim was granted four-hour temporary absences from the institution to attend family counseling in the community. He was also given permission to spend Christmas day with his family. During this visit, his family began fighting and he went to his room, pulled out a gun, and said that he was going to shoot himself if everyone didn't sit down and shut up. He felt that this was the only way to calm everyone down. He stayed there the remainder of the day but his wife later called the institution. Jim was quickly transferred from the minimum-security camp to maximum security, where he faces more charges and is expected to stay until his release. This transfer was difficult for Jim because the maximum-security unit controls most daily activities. Jim's feelings of extreme anxiety have returned.

Chapter 13

Case Management and Formal Social Support

Earlier we reviewed several intervention methods you can use to help people mobilize power and effect changes in themselves and their environments. In this and the next chapter, we explore how you can assist people to access various forms of social support (Streeter & Franklin, 1992). In this chapter, we will

- Define the concepts of social support and social support networks
- Distinguish between formal systems of social support and informal social support networks
- Explore how social workers provide case management services to coordinate formal systems of social support
- Discuss the process of making effective referrals

◆ Social Support

Social support has been defined "as the existence or availability of people on whom we can rely, people who let us know that they care about, value, and love us" (Sarason, Levine, Basham, & Sarason, 1983, p. 127). Support involves the provision of the care and assistance necessary for a person to carry out their social roles. Four specific types of social support may be distinguished (Cameron & Rothery, 1985; Cohen & Wills, 1985; Gorlick & Pomfret, 1993; Rothery, 1993; Sarason, Sarason, & Pierce, 1990):

- *Affiliational support*—a sense of being tightly bound with another person or persons, of being

esteemed and valued, and of belonging in and with a group.
- *Informational support*—provision of knowledge and skill (including information about resources) to help people understand and cope with challenges or exploit opportunities.
- *Emotional support*—a sense that it is safe to express feelings and discuss emotionally charged events within the context of one or more social relationships.
- *Instrumental support*—provision of financial aid or other essential goods and services.

Social support systems and networks include those individuals, groups, and organizations with whom people exchange social support. In reality, of course, people do not interact with organizations but, rather, with people within those organizations. We can draw social support from both formal and informal sources (Cameron, 1990; Erickson, 1984; Whittaker & Garbarino, 1983). Formal support comes from organizations and agencies. Service providers are usually paid to do so through their employment in formally organized structures. Informal social support occurs through those individuals—family members, friends, neighbors, colleagues, members of community groups, and so forth—with whom people interact in everyday life. Informal social support involves processes of social exchange as individuals within systems and networks both give to and receive from each other.

◆ Case Management and Formal Social Support

Case Management

One function of social work is to locate, coordinate, and obtain formal social support (Lauber, 1992; Moore, 1990) through the provision of case management services. This involves assisting clients to identify their social support wants and needs, determine where and how these needs may be secured within the community, and secure appropriate formal services (Davies, 1992; Douville, 1993; Frankel & Gelman, 1998; C. A. Rapp, 1997; Rose, 1992). Exhibit 13-1 contains a summary of the functions and principles of case management services for families with children.

Case management is the "process of planning, organizing, coordinating, and monitoring the services and resources needed to respond to an individual's health care and social service needs" (American Hospital Association, 1987, p. 2). Case management may be defined as a service delivery system that

> organizes, coordinates, and sustains a network of formal and informal supports and activities designed to optimize the functioning and well-being of people with multiple needs. Through these activities the case manager seeks to accomplish the following goals:
>
> - To promote when possible the skills of the client in accessing and utilizing these supports and services;
>
> - To develop the capacity of social networks and relevant human service providers in promoting the functioning and the well-being of the client, and
>
> - To promote service effectiveness while attempting to have services and supports delivered in the most effective manner possible. (Moxley, 1989, p. 17)

Social work case managers serve diverse client groups, including children and families (Halfton, Berkowitz, & Klee, 1993; Long, 1995; Thompson & Peebles-Wilkins, 1992; Werrbach, 1996), older individuals (Hennessy, 1993; Soares & Rose, 1994; Sullivan & Fisher, 1994), persons with mental illness (Belcher, 1993; Bertsch, 1992; Degen, Cole, Tamayo, & Dzerovych, 1990; Hornstra, Bruce-Wolfe, Sagduyu, & Riffle, 1993; Rubin, 1992), people who are homeless (Mercier & Racine, 1995), persons with AIDS (Indyk, Belville, Lachapolle, Gordon, & Dewart, 1993; Roberts, Severinsen, Kuehn, Straker, & Fritz, 1992), and persons who abuse drugs or alcohol (Freng, Carr,

& Cox, 1995; Sullivan, Hartman, Dillon, & Wolk, 1994; Sullivan, Wolk, & Hartman, 1992). Case managers are social workers who help clients navigate the complex network of specialized services that evolved as a result of the following:

- A historical tendency of policymakers to categorize social needs and problems
- Administrative pressure toward differentiation of structures and services to enhance efficiency in the distribution of labor and resources
- Specialization associated with professionalization of services

Case management involves the coordination of multiple services on behalf of individuals, families, and groups so that they may be efficiently and effectively directed at defined problem areas. Through case management, coordination and integration of services occurs at the client level. Policy change and program planning efforts at administrative or macro-system levels may facilitate service delivery—although they are not typically conceptualized as a fundamental part of case management practice. For example, developing multiservice centers and multi-agency teams that provide one-stop client access to multiple social, health, legal, or educational services facilitates coordinated helping activities (Healy, 1991). Certain critics argue that case management's focus on identified clients may lead some workers to neglect important social issues such as the scarcity of affordable housing, high rates of unemployment and underemployment, inadequate or poor quality services, and counter-productive social welfare policies (Belcher, 1993; Moore, 1992; Netting, 1992). Other authors express concern about the application of case management processes to regulate and control clients' access to services (Austin, 1993; Dinerman, 1992; Korr & Cloninger, 1991; Moore, 1992), especially in managed care (Brennan & Kaplan, 1993). As the term implies, managed care involves managing the provision of services—often through gate-keeping procedures. Devised as a means for employers and insurance companies to contain the escalating costs of medical services, managed care processes have expanded throughout health, mental health, and addictions service delivery systems and are making inroads within both child welfare and juvenile justice as well.

As managed care grows more prevalent, this approach to case management provokes increasing concern among many social workers (Shapiro,

---

EXHIBIT 13-1
Functions and Principles of Case Management for Families and Children

Case management has five basic functions:

1. *Assessment*—the process of determining needs or problems.
2. *Planning*—the identification of specific goals and the selection of activities and services needed to achieve them.
3. *Linking*—the referral, transfer, or other connection of clients to appropriate services.
4. *Monitoring*—ongoing assurance that services are being delivered and remain appropriate, and the evaluation of client progress.
5. *Advocacy*—intervention on behalf of the client to secure services and entitlements.

Five important case management principles selected by parents are

1. Parents should have a major role in determining the extent and degree of their participation.
2. Case managers should have frequent contact with child, family, and other key actors.
3. A single case manager should be responsible for helping families gain access to needed resources.
4. Parents and children should be involved in decision making.
5. Case manager roles and functions should support and strengthen family functioning.

Source: Adapted from Early, T. J., & Poertner, J. (1993). Case management for families and children. *Focal Point,* 7(1), 1–4. Published by the Research and Training Center on Family Support and Children's Mental Health, Portland State University, Portland, Oregon.

1996). However, the impact of managed care is not entirely negative. For example, such processes may reduce inappropriate provision of intrusive and expensive services such as institutional care and may indirectly encourage focus on client's strengths and informal social support networks. Furthermore, social, political, and legal action contributes to the development of policies and regulations to reduce certain abuses in medical managed care, including arbitrary limits on access to certain kinds of health care, gag agreements that prohibit service providers from sharing information regarding all available services or treatments, and rigid limits on the duration of services.

As a social worker, your first ethical duty is to your clients—even if you happen to work in a managed care environment. Thus, you work in partnership with clients to determine their social support wants and to secure resources in the community. Through such collaborative processes, you may reduce the potential for conflict with managed care companies. Disagreements tend to arise when social workers seek intrusive and expensive services for clients because of the social worker's views about what is needed. Of course,

when managed care organizations deny services that you and your clients collaboratively decide are needed, you may assist clients to use appeal or other remediation processes. You should also document these limitations as part of the means to advocate for change in managed care policies and procedures. Action to improve policies has always been part of our social work obligation (Richmond, 1917).

◆ Effective Referrals

Coordination of formal social support often requires that social workers invest considerable time making and supporting referrals to other services. As we discussed earlier, the social broker role involves

- Securing information about available resources
- Preparing clients for contact with other systems and providers
- Preparing referral agencies and providers to receive clients
- Facilitating contact
- Follow-up contact and evaluation

Information About Resources

As a social worker, you frequently operate at the interface between the individual and the formal resource system. Effective referrals require that you know what resources and services are available, where they are located, who provides or sponsors them, what kinds of help they offer, and who is eligible to receive services. Develop and continually update an inventory of important resources—perhaps through a computerized database. Become familiar with various access routes to the resources and introduce yourself to key contact people. Discover eligibility requirements and appeal procedures in case clients are denied service. Determine formal and informal policies and become familiar with service delivery processes and procedures. Cultivate relationships with social workers and other professionals from potential resource organizations so you can serve the long-term interests of your clients (Middleman, 1973). If you maintain contacts with responsive agencies and work to improve the sensitivity and receptivity of nonresponsive agencies before a crisis occurs, your ability to tap resources when a particular client faces a critical need becomes much more feasible.

Preparing Clients

Preparing clients includes discussion of the process and the expectations of the referral agency. Orientation and preparation help build clients' competence and enhance their readiness and ability to make maximum use of services (Moore, 1990; Painter, 1966; Soares & Rose, 1994). You explore the range of available resources and services that are appropriate to clients' unique needs and collaborate in weighing the pros and cons of each option. Consider how the resources may benefit the client and determine those services to which the client might be entitled. Prepare the client for the likely reception at the agency. For example, suppose you know that Mr. Washington at a particular agency is an especially effective youth employment counselor. He is particularly adept at establishing rapport with young people and routinely helps many obtain their first jobs in the community. However, youth referred to Mr. Washington must initially encounter a receptionist who tends to be curt, perfunctory, and hostile. Many feel diminished and fail to show up for subsequent appointments. Through your follow-up contact with the youth, you

learn about their experiences with the receptionist. Based on that information, you begin to prepare young people for the reception they might expect at Mr. Washington's office. You might use role-play simulations to help them learn how to ignore rude behavior and request an appointment with Mr. Washington in a firm but respectful manner. You might also consider the possibility of advocacy with the management of Mr. Washington's agency to discuss the reception of clients. However, you might decide against this approach to avoid jeopardizing the emerging working relationship between the two agencies. Also, preparing the youth to deal with the receptionist results in potentially valuable learning that might apply to other circumstances as well. All of us encounter rudeness and insensitivity. Many young people find that developing assertive communication skills enhances their abilities to function effectively in various social situations.

Preparing Agencies

Preparing the agencies involves sharing information about referred clients—with their full knowledge and consent. Sometimes, of course, agencies are reluctant to accept a referral and provide services to which your client may be entitled. Under such circumstances, you may engage in mediation or advocacy. Clients frequently require your support and encouragement throughout the referral process.

Typically, you prepare agencies through telephone conversations. Try to make these calls in the presence of your clients so they may overhear what you say and learn what you do. If this proves impossible, be sure to inform the client fully about information you share with the agency. Occasionally, a face-to-face meeting with an agency staff person may be needed. However, these meetings are time consuming and usually no more useful than a phone call—unless the client accompanies you to the meeting. Under those circumstances, the referral process may be considerably enhanced.

You may sometimes need to communicate with agencies by letter—perhaps by preparing a summary report or a referral request. Exhibit 13-2 contains two versions of a letter sent by a social worker to an attorney. Both the social worker and attorney serve the same client and have the client's consent to correspond with each other about the matter. Written in an officious style, the first version contributes little to the

---

EXHIBIT 13-2
A Letter on Behalf of a Client

Here are two versions of a letter written by a social worker.

Version 1

Dear Ms. Trojan:
RE: Nesti, James

As per discussion on April 30, 1993, please be advised that the writer has interviewed said youth on Tuesday, May 4, between 10:00 A.M. and 12:30 P.M. at the Youth Center. Another interview was undertaken on the same date from 2:00 P.M. to 3:00 P.M. at 100 Horseshoe Avenue with the parents. All parties have agreed to hold a family group conference and the first available date is Sunday, May 16, 1993 from 2:30 P.M. to 5:30 P.M.

A concern is that the aforementioned conference cannot be held at the parties' first choice, which is their residence, because once bail is denied there is no provision for writer to escort the youth from the Youth Center to the location proposed for the family group conference.

Therefore, arrangements for the family group conference will have to be made for same date and time at the Youth Center. There are no foreseen difficulties with such arrangements.

The people who have agreed to participate in the family group conference are parents, siblings, sister-in-law, other extended family members, previous teacher and a counselor, Native Community Elders, and possibly victims (in either case, victim impact reports will be available).

The agenda for the family group conference is as follows:
a) session begins with open circle pipe ceremony
b) youth discloses circumstances of the offense; and c) participants determine recommendations for disposition.

Trusting this is in order, please confirm whether as Counsel you are able to attend.
Sincerely,

Social Worker

Version 2

Dear Ms. Trojan:
RE: Nesti, James

I interviewed James on Tuesday, May 4 at the Youth Center, and later that day also visited his parents at their home. James and his parents have agreed to a family group conference scheduled for Sunday, May 16, from 2:30 P.M. to 5:30 P.M. here at the Youth Center. I had hoped to hold the meeting at the Nesti residence but I could not secure permission to escort James to and from the Center. We would value your attendance.

We expect participants in the family group conference to include James, both parents, siblings, a sister-in-law, other extended family members, a previous teacher, a counselor, Native community elders, and possibly victims. Victim impact reports will be available.

The agenda for the family group conference is:
a) begin session with an open circle pipe ceremony;
b) James discloses the circumstances of the offense; and
c) conference members determine recommendations for disposition.

Please confirm whether you are able to attend.
Sincerely,

Social Worker

---

development of a cooperative working relationship. The second version reflects a more straightforward style that readers tend to appreciate.

Writing represents an advocacy tool that frequently helps clients secure needed services (Waller, Carroll, & Roemer, 1996). In writing referral reports and summaries, avoid jargon, present descriptive and factual information without overgeneralization, label opinions as such, and include client strengths. Describe the specific reasons for and purpose of the report. Identify goals and objectives you would like to see addressed and outline the nature of your continuing involvement with the client. Organize content according to topical themes (Cohen, 1986). Use active voice and present tense, share observations in a straightforward manner, and apprise recipients of the likely validity and reliability of information. Provide a copy of the letter or report to your client.

Facilitating Contact

A substantial proportion of people referred to other agencies fail to establish contact or receive services. Despite preparation of both clients and agencies, various obstacles may obstruct contact. Clients may lack transportation, child care, or financial resources. Some may have trouble with directions or find it difficult to negotiate competing demands and obligations. Many clients cannot afford to attend meetings scheduled for times that conflict with their employment. Others may become anxious or agitated about first visits to strange places, buildings, or unknown people.

Such impediments may require you to facilitate contact by such activities as providing transportation, securing child care, finding financial support, arranging for meeting times that do not conflict with clients' work schedules, or accompanying clients to the initial visit with the new agency. Indeed, by joining clients in first meetings, you can use the trip to the agency to help them prepare and, upon arrival, ensure that contact occurs. After the meeting, you can use the return trip to discuss the experience.

Follow-Up

Follow-up contact with clients and agencies represents an essential aspect of effective referrals. Whenever possible, establish a plan and schedule a date to follow up with both parties when you first arrange the referral. Follow-up provides an opportunity to review clients' experience with the new agency and to conduct an informal evaluation. You may discover, for example, that a client discontinued services after a short period, or that an agency became reluctant to provide service. In the event of difficulties, you may engage in various problem-solving activities and assume facilitator, teacher, mediator, or advocate roles as needed. Of course, you may also receive favorable feedback from clients, service providers, or both. Such

positive information tends to encourage subsequent referrals to the agency.

If you still see the client as part of the service plan, follow-up can occur within the context of a regular meeting. If not, you may do so by telephone if the client has access to one. If not, a visit may be needed. In any event, postreferral follow-up represents an essential part of the service you provide.

◆ Chapter Summary

Social support involves the provision of care and assistance necessary so people can fulfill social roles. There are four major forms of social support: (1) affiliational, (2) informational, (3) emotional, and (4) instrumental. In this chapter, we explored aspects of formal social support, which is usually provided by employed staff of service organizations and agencies. Case management involves the coordination of formal social support services to assist clients in reaching their goals.

Case management involves adopting the social broker role in helping clients obtain needed community services—often through well-planned processes of referral to other agencies or providers. Effective referrals require familiarity with community resources, provision of appropriate information, preparation of both clients and agencies for the referral, and follow-up to ensure that the client is receiving the necessary services. Of course, clients serve as collaborative partners throughout the process of identifying and securing formal social support.

 **Learning Exercises: Readings, InfoTrac, and the Web**

1. Use your word-processing computer program to enter the important terms and concepts presented in this chapter in alphabetical order. Place a question mark by any terms that you do not clearly understand. Save your document as EX 13-1.

2. Log on to the InfoTrac College Edition Web site. Conduct a keyword search (using either Keyword Search or Advanced Search) to locate the articles entitled "Iowa Case Management: Innovative Social Casework" (Hall, Carswell, Walsh, Huber, &

Jampoler, 2002) and "Strengths-Based Case Management: Individuals' Perspectives on Strengths and the Case Manager Relationship" (Brun & Rapp, 2001). Read the articles and prepare a two-page essay in which you reflect on their implications for social work and social work practice. Save your document as EX 13-2.

3. Log on to the InfoTrac College Edition Web site. Conduct a keyword search (using either Keyword Search or Advanced Search) to locate the articles entitled "Examining the HIV/AIDS Case Management Process" (Chernesky & Grube, 2000) and "Knowledge for Direct Social Work Practice: An Analysis of Trends" (Reid, 2002). Read the articles and prepare a two-page essay in which you reflect on their implications for social work and social work practice. Save your document as EX 13-3.

4. Turn to **Reading 20: The Social Work Process of Social Care Planning.** Review this article by Miriam Johnson and David Harrison. Social care is a British term (Huxley, 1993); social care planning is a form of case management. Prepare a two-page essay in which you address the following questions: What are the major elements and dimensions of social care? What kinds of actions were undertaken by the social worker in providing social care service to the Milton-Clay extended family? What intervention roles did the social worker adopt? How were decisions made about what to do about problems that emerged during the course of the client-worker relationship? How similar is the authors' view of social care to the problem-solving approach to social work described in this text? How might Ms. Arthur have done better in making use of the model? Do you think Ms. Arthur was justified in taking such an active role in seeking emergency help when Ms. Clay sounded suicidal? How do you think each of the Miltons and Clays would have described the family situation before and after they worked with Ms. Arthur? Do you think that the Miltons should have been involved in the written family care plan outlined in Exhibit R20-1? What do you think of the plan? Do you think that Ms. Arthur should have pursued neighborhood, church, or other local resources more vigorously? As you conclude your essay, summarize your thoughts and observations about social care planning and identify those aspects of the process that you think would be the most rewarding as well as those that would be the most challenging. Save your document as EX 13-4.

5. Turn to **Reading 21: Social Work, Social Care, Care Management, and User Involvement.** In this article, Reima Maglajlic discusses the development and status of care management for persons with disabilities in the United Kingdom. Prepare a one-page essay in which you address the following questions: How may care management be distinguished from traditional social work? What do you think about this distinction? How do political and ideological factors affect the nature, scope, and process of service delivery? How are social workers who engage in social care management affected by changing policies and procedures? What does the author suggest that social workers do to improve the quality of social care management services under these circumstances? Save your document as EX 13-5.

Chapter 14

Mobilizing Informal Social Support

Earlier, we made a distinction between formal and informal social support. In this chapter, we explore informal social support and consider:

- A definition of informal social support
- The benefits of informal social support
- Ways to strengthen informal social support systems and networks
- Means to create and change informal social support networks
- The use of mutual aid or self-help groups
- Ways to integrate formal and informal support

◆ Informal Social Support

Definition

Informal social support refers to the care and assistance provided by families, relatives, friends (Adams & Blieszner, 1993), and neighbors that collectively form an informal social support network. Specht (1986) defines a social support network as the specific set of interrelated persons with whom an individual engages in social interaction. Informal social support is also offered through leisure, recreational, and religious activities that provide opportunities for socialization (Joyce, Stanley, & Hughes, 1990; Morrison, 1991; Nakhaima, 1994) and through self-help or mutual aid groups (Gitterman & Shulman, 1994; Kurtz, 1990; Schubert & Borkman, 1991; Strauss et al., 1984). Informal social support embraces a broad range of activities, including assistance with self-care, resource management, home maintenance, assistance with

daily activities such as transportation and meal preparation, and emotional support. Human beings appear to need informal social support throughout life, although the particular forms vary according to circumstances and phase of life cycle development.

The composition of social support networks also fluctuates as a result of factors such as members' death or relocation (Gold, 1987). Informal networks consist of "self-help groups, friends, neighbors and communities who provide, without payment, a wide range of aid including support, advice, advocacy, transport, friendship, compassion, to those who seek it" (Olsen, 1986, p. 15). Informal social support involves "help that is provided within the context of one's personal social network of family, friends and neighbors" (Wilson, 1986, p. 176). The informal social support network includes "a set of interconnected relationships among a group of people that provides enduring patterns of nurturance (in any or all forms) and provides contingent reinforcement for efforts to cope with life on a day to day basis" (Whittaker, 1986, p. 41). Informal social support involves "a range of interpersonal exchanges that provide an individual with information, emotional reassurance, physical or maternal assistance and a sense of the self as an object of concern" (Garbarino, 1986, p. 35).

Informal social support is often provided by natural helpers in the environment (Memmott, 1993; Nakhaima, 1994; Patterson, Germain, Brennan, & Memmott, 1988; Patterson, Memmott, Brennan, & Germain, 1992; Wilcox & Taber, 1991). Natural helpers are unpaid people who because of their concern, interest, and understanding assist others during difficult times (Patterson & Brennan, 1983). Informal social

---

EXHIBIT 14-1
Informal Social Support

Jerry: I've been HIV-positive for 10 years now. About one year ago, I was diagnosed with AIDS. I've been able to manage up to now with the help of my incredible friends.

Social Worker: How have your friends been helpful during these last several months?

Jerry: They have been amazing! These five people have been so incredibly generous. I've felt more affection, love, and understanding in the last year than I did in the previous 32 years of my life. It's been a blessing that I'll never forget. As my health deteriorated—especially during the last month, one of the five of them has stayed overnight with me every single night. They created a schedule among themselves. They take turns. During the daytime, one of them comes to make lunch and then usually 2 or 3 of them come to prepare dinner. They help me go to the toilet, wash my body, clean my sheets, and take care of the house. They've made sure my bills were paid, coordinated arrangements with my doctor, and brought me to the hospital this morning.

They're my real family, and before I die I'd like to somehow let them know what their love and support has meant to me.

---

support is usually provided through face-to-face contact but can also be provided through telephone (Goodman, 1990; King, 1991; Meier, Galinsky, & Rounds, 1995; Rounds, Galinsky, & Despard, 1995; Wiener, Spencer, Davidson, & Fair, 1993) and computer networks (Finn & Lavitt, 1994; Weinberg, Schmale, Uken, & Wessel, 1995).

Benefits of Informal Social Support

There seems to be a generally positive correlation between supportive social networks and physical and psychological well-being. Informal social support increases immunity to physical and psychological health problems (Specht, 1986). Extensive social support systems may even help ward off common colds (Cohen, Doyle, Skoner, Robin, & Gwaltney, 1997). Interactions with significant others in a social network can satisfy social and emotional needs, provide socialization and recreation, and protect against loneliness and isolation. People with ready access to supportive human relationships respond better to stressful life events such as divorce (Hughes, Good, & Candell, 1993; Kunz & Kunz, 1995) or job loss (Jones, 1991) and to chronic hardships (Cassel, 1974; Koeske & Koeske, 1990; Ladewig, McGee, & Newell, 1990).

Informal social support serves as a buffer against stress for some individuals during major life events or life transitions (Specht, 1986). For example, spouses of military personnel on deployment tend to seek social support from friends and neighbors rather than from formal programs (Saulnier, 1996). A supportive network may facilitate recovery from an acute illness or may promote adaptation to chronic illness. Informal social support enhances personal well-being, life satisfaction, and quality of life. It contributes to individual feelings of self-esteem, connectedness or belonging (Specht, 1986), and a sense of purpose (Schilling, 1987). Informal social support may enable older people to live independently in the community (Novak, 1997), slow health deterioration (Choi & Wodarski, 1996), and reduce the number of admissions to long-term care facilities (Connidis & McMullin, 1994). Older individuals' informal support networks generally consist of spouses, children, and friends but may also include church groups, self-help groups, or activity groups. Exhibit 14-1 contains a description of an exchange between a medical social worker and Jerry, a young man just admitted to the hospital because of the severe illnesses associated with advanced AIDS. Notice how his friends' social support enables him to maintain a sense of dignity while he struggles with the illness.

Isolation of neglectful parents from formal and informal support networks may contribute to child abuse. Conversely, expanding and strengthening these networks of social support may help to prevent child maltreatment (Beeman, 1997; Festinger, 1996; Fuchs, 1993; Gaudin, Polansky, Kilpatrick, & Shilton, 1993; Gaudin, Wodarski, Arkinson, & Avery, 1990; Moncher,

EXHIBIT 14-2
Social Support for Neglectful Parents

A 1981 study of neglectful parents (Polansky, Chalmers, Buttenwieser, & Williams, 1981) pointed to their isolation from informal and formal support networks as a core problem that should be addressed by child welfare providers. Subsequent reports have provided support for this conclusion (Gaudin, Polansky, Kilpatrick, & Shilton, 1993; Polansky, Ammons, & Gaudin, 1985; Zuravin & Greif, 1989). The findings on re-entry in this study strongly underscore the same theme. Yet when the workers in this study were asked to identify caregivers' service needs, counseling or therapy was given the highest priority, consistent with findings from an earlier report (Jones, Neuman, & Shyne, 1976), while parent support groups occupied a much lower priority. With people as disconnected as the caregivers of

re-entrants appear to be, ways must be explored to help them begin to make connections.

Various useful approaches to reducing isolation and to enhance parenting skills have been described elsewhere (Boutilier & Rehm, 1993; Carlo, 1993; Fein & Staff, 1993; Gaudin, Wodarski, Arkinson, & Avery, 1990; Lewis, 1991; Polansky et al., 1981; Walton, Fraser, Lewis, Pecora, & Walton, 1993). Yet there is an ongoing challenge to develop ways of reaching out that are sensitive to diverse ethnic and cultural values affecting parental practices as well as family life as a whole (Maluccio, Fein, & Davis, 1982; National Research Council, 1993).

Source: Festinger, T. (1996). Going home and returning to foster care. *Children and Youth Services Review, 18*(4/5), 383–402, p. 398.

1995; Thompson, 1995). Exhibit 14-2 contains information regarding the relationship between parents' informal social support and neglected children.

Social support may help reduce homelessness (Marin & Vacha, 1994) and delinquency (Shields & Clark, 1995). A Maryland study of 150 adult drug offenders released from custody found that 73% returned to their former neighborhoods. Interestingly, this factor alone was not associated with a return to drug use. However, unemployment and dissatisfaction with family life were (Slaght, 1999). These findings suggest that released drug offenders may benefit from employment and family enhancement services along with other efforts to strengthen social support as a means to refrain from drug abuse relapse.

A study of 864 delinquents and their families found that delinquency was affected by the family's natural environment. Factors such as disadvantaged neighborhoods, life distress, social isolation, and lack of partner support were associated with delinquent behavior. These findings indicate that strengthening social support in the surrounding environmental context as well as within the family system itself may help to diminish the likelihood of delinquent behavior (Stern & Smith, 1995).

◆ Strengthening Informal Support Networks

Strengthening informal social support networks involves several interrelated aspects: (1) increasing the number of persons with whom clients interact, (2) expanding the number of interactions with network members, and (3) enhancing the quality of social interactions so they become more helpful to clients. Exhibit 14-3 explores the informal social support network of a 37-year-old single parent diagnosed with schizophrenia. Systematic consideration of Michelle's social network revealed strengths in relationships with her brother and a niece. The student social worker helped her to develop a plan to strengthen these connections. Responding to her neighbor's greeting may lead to other opportunities for increased social contact. The student social worker might use some of the change methods we explored earlier to help Michelle become more comfortable in conversations. For example, education, role playing, and rehearsal may help Michelle become more socially skillful, which might, in turn, lead to a stronger, larger, and more satisfying social support network. The worker might also help Michelle

---

EXHIBIT 14-3
Social Support for a Woman with Schizophrenia

Michelle is a 37-year-old woman with schizophrenia. She and her 4-year-old son, Jacob, reside with her 75-year-old father, who supports them financially. Because of the severity of her illness, Michelle's father has been Jacob's primary caregiver. Michelle is unable to adequately care for her son on her own. Michelle does assist in parenting Jacob and usually takes Jacob to the local day care center several days a week. Since being diagnosed with schizophrenia 15 years ago, Michelle has lost contact with all of her friends and has not been able to form new friendships. She is now almost totally socially isolated, especially since the death of her mother last year. Michelle's relationship with her father is currently strained.

Because there were many areas in Michelle's life that she wanted to work on, our first step was deciding where to start. Michelle thought the main problem was boredom; she had too much free time and no one to visit. I explored these two problem areas with Michelle. She said that she would like to find a job or enroll in a job training program, although she was concerned about how others would perceive her and if she could make friends within these environments. I also asked Michelle how important it was for her to have friends and she stated that this was very important. I asked Michelle whether finding work or forming friendships was more important at this time. Michelle felt that having friends was more important. The problem for work was then defined. Michelle lacks social companions.

The next step was to set objectives. The objectives developed by Michelle include:

- finding a friend to have coffee with
- engaging in some social activities
- building self-esteem, through interacting with people other than professional service providers
- utilizing appropriate communication skills, in order to feel more comfortable in social situations

Several other possible objectives were mentioned, but Michelle didn't want to take on too much at once. She felt that the objectives were attainable and would improve her life.

We then began to develop an intervention plan. We discussed the concept of informal social supports and ways in which they could be utilized. Michelle initially didn't perceive any informal social supports available to her. In exploring, however, we discovered that she had a close relationship with her brother and with a niece who came over to help baby-sit her son when her father was out of town. Michelle stated that her brother came over once a week for dinner and she looked forward to his visits. When I asked what she enjoyed about her brother's company, she said that he made her laugh, often gave her advice, would always give her a ride if she needed to go somewhere, and acted on her behalf if she was having difficulties with her father. Michelle spoke highly of her niece. She and Jacob enjoyed her niece's visits; they often played games or went out to the movies or to dinner.

(continues)

---

become more involved with her son's day-care center, which could further expand opportunities for her to both receive and give informal social support. The student social worker, however, might remember the notion of partialization and collaboration. Michelle might be overwhelmed in attempts to undertake too many tasks simultaneously. In her efforts to strengthen her social support system, Michelle might find it more manageable to complete one task before proceeding to the next.

People both give and receive social support. The process is reciprocal in nature (Tracy, 1990). Part of your work may involve educating clients about social support and interaction, and helping them strengthen their abilities to be supportive and helpful to others. For example, if Michelle (see Exhibit 14-3) volunteers at her son's day-care center, she may help others and receive social support as she does so. If Jerry (see Exhibit 14-4) becomes active in organizing an AA group, he might both help himself and provide an important

EXHIBIT 14-3
Social Support for a Woman with Schizophrenia *(continued)*

We also discussed other people who might be part of her informal social network. She said that one of her neighbors frequently said hello to her and seemed friendly, although they never engaged in conversation. She also mentioned a mother at Jacob's day care, who recently invited Jacob and Michelle to her son's birthday party, although Michelle wasn't sure if she felt comfortable going.

We then considered ways she might use these supports. Michelle thought that she could call her brother more if she was having a bad day or if she just wanted to talk. Since Michelle only saw her niece when her father went out of town, we discussed Michelle calling her more often and perhaps getting together on a more regular basis to enjoy social activities. We discussed methods by which she could practice her communication skills and become more comfortable in social situations.

She felt that she could do this by initiating phone calls to her brother and niece and by saying hello to her neighbor and the mother at the daycare. I also presented the possibility of Michelle attending a local support group of mothers with young children. Michelle agreed. We also discussed Michelle volunteering at her son's day care one half day a week. This would give her a chance to meet other mothers and allow her to practice her communication skills. Michelle thought that it would be rewarding to work with children. We also discussed how Michelle's strengths—such as her friendly disposition, her caring attitude toward others, and her desire to make positive changes in her life—would be beneficial in attaining her goals.

Source: BSW student, Faculty of Social Work, University of Manitoba, Winnipeg, Manitoba.

EXHIBIT 14-4
Assisting Jerry to Organize an AA Group

Jerry, age 35, is physically disabled as a result of a skiing accident three years ago. He is paralyzed from the waist down, with the full use of the left arm but only 40% use of his right arm. He suffered no cognitive impairment. Currently, Jerry lives in an apartment building in which 80% of the residents have a physical disability. The remaining 20% are able-bodied. Because Jerry had no private disability insurance, he has had to rely on home care service provided by public social assistance. This has resulted in a tight schedule, with very limited flexibility.

Jerry has had trouble coping and has become psychologically and emotionally depressed. Over the past three years, he has developed an alcohol problem and has retreated from both friends and family. He currently refuses to discuss his problems with anyone. Jerry is a heavy smoker and occasionally smokes marijuana. He is unemployed and does no volunteer work.

Jerry was referred by the manager of his apartment building for drunken and unruly behavior in the halls. Jerry claims that he is tired of being told what to do. His life mostly centers around the home care he receives, which includes bathing, cooking, getting him up from bed, turning him in the middle of the night, shopping for food, and cleaning. Jerry has admitted that he might have a problem with alcohol and has shown a desire to change, but is uncertain how. He says that he feels depressed and tends to do drugs and alcohol with others in the building. This appears to be Jerry's way of avoiding total isolation.

Jerry and I negotiated the short-term objective that he would quit drinking, stop his abusive behavior, and re-integrate with family and friends. The longer-term goal would be for Jerry to re-enter the mainstream of society. This would involve

(continues)

EXHIBIT 14-4
Assisting Jerry to Organize an AA Group *(continued)*

training for a job, in order to eventually achieve financial independence and control over his life.

The focus of the plan is to link Jerry with his environment and to enable him to cope. We agreed to begin by linking Jerry with his family, friends, and groups within his immediate environment. Essentially, Jerry's role will be to accept face-to-face contact with family and friends and to assume responsibility for his past and present behavior.

Jerry agreed to attend Alcoholics Anonymous, to access information on the problems associated with alcohol and drug abuse, to learn what resources are available for him, and to participate with others in the community. At the initial meetings, Jerry felt encouraged by the progress of other chemically dependent persons. He visited the library and spoke with some residents of a treatment program.

Jerry then expressed an interest in meeting other disabled persons in his building who are chemically dependent. Such networking could help him develop his self-esteem and coping mechanisms to a point where he no longer perceives his disability as a hindrance to life within the community.

I provided Jerry with information regarding the possibility of setting up meetings with other tenants who feel they may have a problem with alcohol or drugs. Thus encouraged, Jerry decided to organize a twelve-step group there in the building. To do so, Jerry would need access to a meeting room once a week. We agreed that, given management's low opinion of Jerry, I would advocate on his behalf regarding the meeting room.

Jerry decided to post notices on every floor to inform other tenants about the meetings. He planned to include his phone number, so that he would be directly responsible for organizing the meeting and arranging for other tenants to attend. Jerry initially intended to limit the group to disabled tenants. At my suggestion, he agreed to open the meetings to all tenants, disabled or not. We also agreed to seek out nondisabled tenants to help post the notices. This would not only help Jerry logistically but encourage him to interact socially with nondisabled individuals.

Source: BSW student, Faculty of Social Work, University of Manitoba, Winnipeg, Manitoba.

---

service to others. As you identify client strengths, you may discover many ways that clients can simultaneously help themselves, serve others, and contribute to the well-being of their communities.

Listening and empathy seem to be two of the most important qualities in the provision of social support, followed by helping, assisting, and guiding (Byrne & Sebastian, 1994). The support provider must convey respect, objectivity, and a nonjudgmental attitude. Social support is characterized by problem solving, assistance with decision making, and an ability to be present with an individual (Byrne & Sebastian, 1994). Exhibit 14-5 contains a list of informal helping behaviors developed from research interviews with 40 single mothers receiving public assistance (Gottlieb, 1978). At times, you may assist clients in developing necessary skills to help and support others.

◆ Creating and Changing Informal Support Networks

Increasing the size of clients' informal support networks may be necessary. However, greater size alone is insufficient. Social workers often need to help clients improve the quality of their social relationships or perhaps help them create new networks. Indeed, some social support networks may have negative consequences (Galinsky & Schopler, 1994; Gurowka & Lightman, 1995). For example, an adolescent might participate in a youth gang that engages in criminal behavior. A child might live in an abusive family system. Whether a youth gang or a troubled family, social support systems may have both beneficial and harmful aspects. You and your clients must carefully assess each social network before concluding that

EXHIBIT 14-5
Informal Helping Behavior

Category	Definition	Example
A. Emotionally Sustaining Behaviors		
A1 Talking (unfocused)	Airing or ventilation of general concerns about reference to problem specifics.	"She'll talk things over with me."
A2 Provides reassurance	Expresses confidence in other as a person, in some aspect of other's past or present behavior, or with regard to the future course of events.	"He seems to have faith in me."
A3 Provides encouragement	Stimulates or motivates other to engage in some future behavior.	"She pushed me a lot of times when I was saying, 'Oh, to heck with it.'"
A4 Listens	Listening only, without reference to dialogue.	"He listens to me when I talk to him about things."
A5 Reflects understanding	Signals understanding of the facts of other's problem or feelings.	"She would know what I was saying."
A6 Reflects respect	Expresses respect or esteem for other.	"Some people look down on you; well, she doesn't."
A7 Reflects concern	Expresses concern about the importance or severity of the problem's impact on other or for the problem itself.	"Just by telling me how worried or afraid she is" (for me).
A8 Reflects trust	Reflects assurance of the confidentiality of shared information.	"She's someone I trust and I knew that it was confidential."
A9 Reflects intimacy	Provides or reflects interpersonal intimacy.	"He's just close to me."
A10 Provides companionship	Offers simple companionship or access to new companionships.	"I've always got her and I really don't feel alone."
A11 Provides accompaniment in stressful situation	Accompanies other in a stressful situation.	"She took the time to be there with me so I didn't have to face it alone."
A12 Provides extended period of care	Maintains a supportive relationship to other over an extended period of time.	"She was with me the whole way."
B. Problem-Solving Behaviors		
B1 Talking (focused)	Airing or ventilation of specific problem details.	"I'm able to tell him what's bugging me and we discuss it."
B2 Provides clarification	Discussion of problem details, which aims to promote new understanding or new perspective.	"She makes me more aware of what I was actually saying other than just having the words come out."

(continues)

EXHIBIT 14-5
Informal Helping Behavior *(continued)*

	Category	Definition	Example
B3	Provides suggestions	Provides suggestions or advice about the means of problem-solving.	"He offered suggestions of what I could do."
B4	Provides directive	Commands, orders, or directs other about the means of problem-solving.	"All Rose told me was to be more assertive."
B5	Provides information about sources of stress	Definition same as category name.	"She keeps me in touch with what my child's doing."
B6	Provides referral	Refers other to alternative helping resources.	"Financially, he put me on to a car mechanic who gave me a tune-up for less than I would pay in a garage."
B7	Monitors directive	Attempts to ensure that other complies with problem-solving directive.	"Making sure that I follow through with their orders."
B8	Buffers from source of stress	Engages in behavior that prevents contact between other and stressor.	"He doesn't offer it (alcohol) to me anymore."
B9	Models or provides testimony of own experience	Models behaviors or provides oral testimony related to the helper's own experience in a similar situation.	"Just even watching her and how confident she seems has taught me something."
B10	Provides material aid or direct service	Lends or gives tangibles (food, clothing, money) or provides service (babysitting, transportation) to other.	"He brought his truck and moved me so I wouldn't have to rent a truck."
B11	Distracts from problem focus	Temporarily diverts other's attention through initiating activity (verbal or action-oriented) unrelated to the problem.	"Or he'll say, 'Let's go for a drive,' some little thing to get my mind off it."

C. Indirect Personal Influence

	Category	Definition	Example
C1	Reflects unconditional access	Conveys an unconditional availability to other (without reference to problem-solving actions).	"She's there when I need her."
C2	Reflects readiness to act	Conveys to other readiness to engage in future problem-solving behavior.	"He'll do all he can do."

D. Environmental Action

	Category	Definition	Example
D1	Intervenes in the environment to reduce source of stress	Intervenes in the environment to remove or diminish the source of stress.	"She helped by talking to the owners and convincing them to wait for the money a while."

Source: Gottlieb, B. H., & Todd, D. M. (1979). Characterizing and promoting social support in natural settings. In R. F. Muñoz, L. R. Snowden & J. G. Kelly (Eds.), *Social and psychological research in community settings* (pp. 183–242). San Francisco: Jossey-Bass, pp. 189–191. Copyright © 1982 Jossey-Bass, Inc. Reprinted with permission.

EXHIBIT 14-6
Diminished Social Network After a Life Transition

Mrs. P, aged 78, was brought into hospital after falling and breaking her hip. Before her hospitalization, she lived alone in elderly housing. Her husband died almost two years ago. Mr. and Mrs. P raised two children, Karen and Chris, on a farm in rural Manitoba. Karen, 50 years old, is married and lives in Winnipeg; Chris, 47, has been living in Calgary, Alberta, for the past 22 years. Mrs. P came to Canada from Ukraine with her family when she was just a baby. She has two brothers, John and Mike, and a sister Mary, who recently passed away. John (84) has Alzheimer's and lives in a nursing home; Mike (73) lives alone in Winnipeg. Mrs. P was raised and married in rural Manitoba where she and her husband lived together for 58 years. Mrs. P never worked outside of the home; however, she greatly enjoyed helping on the farm and cooking for her family. Their farmhouse was located in a close-knit Ukrainian community, which strongly supported the Catholic Church. Mrs. P gave up the farm and moved to Winnipeg shortly after husband died. She was diagnosed with cancer three months ago, but up until now has remained independent. Mrs. P will be discharged from hospital next week with a wheeled walker.

In conversations during her hospital stay, Mrs. P reports having a hard time adjusting to the changes in her life. She misses her friends, neighbors, and church from her old community. Also, she doesn't see Karen and her family any more than she did while living on the farm. Mrs. P feels she cannot talk to her daughter about her illness because she thinks Karen cannot accept it so soon after losing her father. Mrs. P also believes Karen is too busy with her own family to deal with any other problems. This is upsetting to Mrs. P who, since losing her husband, realizes more than ever how important family is to her.

---

increased interaction alone will yield positive outcomes. For example, Mrs. P (see Exhibit 14-6) might benefit from an expanded social support system after a life transition. Establishment of connections with people from the local Ukrainian community and a Catholic church might represent an initial step toward development of a social support system (Nakhaima, 1994).

Persons with chronic mental illness sometimes gain informal social support through participation in clubhouse communities (Beard, Propst, & Malamud, 1982; Dougherty, 1994; Jackson, Purnell, Anderson, & Sheafor, 1996; Mastboom, 1992; Propst, 1992). These organizations emerged during the 1950s. More than 180 clubhouses currently operate in the United States (Lamb, 1994) and provide supportive relationships and opportunities to members. They are characterized by

- Respect and equality among members and staff
- Attention to all aspects of each member's life
- Emphasis on the importance of work and acceptance of personal responsibility
- Focus on members' strengths and competencies (Jackson et al., 1996)

Each community is designed to promote recovery from social isolation (Beard et al., 1982) and is located in a clubhouse building that provides for a full range of members' needs, including food, clothing, shelter, social interaction, meaningful work, and medical care. Supportive relationships develop among members and staff as they participate in the work necessary to operate the clubhouse (Propst, 1992).

◆ Mutual Aid Groups

People come together in mutual aid groups to share a common concern and to help one another cope with or resolve problems related to that concern (Toseland & Hacker, 1985). For example, the common concern may be recovery from alcoholism, mental health problems, parenting issues, or coping with the stress of a specific illness. Most mutual aid groups provide support to members. Some also engage in social and political action (Cox, 1991). Certain groups may include a social worker in an advisory or consultative role. Mutual aid groups can provide a network of supportive human relationships for clients and may be included in service planning (Gitterman & Shulman, 1994; Kurtz, 1990; Powell, 1990; Schubert & Borkman, 1991). They provide a potential resource to help clients mobilize power.

Social workers often work with mutual aid groups by making referrals, serving on advisory boards, providing consultation on request, and initiating efforts to establish new groups (Silverman, 1986). Many social workers are involved with mutual aid groups (Gartner & Reissman, 1984) and fulfill functional roles such as educator, resource provider, referral source, link to the greater community, consultant, and group facilitator (Coplon & Strull, 1983). To help clients effectively use this valuable resource, social workers must understand the internal workings and ethos of mutual aid and its social and political context. We may need to speak a language of empowerment to participate and collaborate with the self-help and mutual aid movement. Otherwise, professional terminology and jargon may create barriers between "us" and "them" and interfere with the development of productive relationships (Rappaport, 1985).

Findings from one survey of social workers suggested that most held a positive view of mutual aid groups and valued the attributes of peer support, reciprocal sharing of practical ideas for coping, long-term support, and lack of stigma. However, 60% of the respondents believed that self-help groups are biased against professional help and that the groups discourage members from seeking additional help. Interestingly, 80% thought that mutual aid groups were underused by professional social workers. The researchers concluded that social workers need education about the availability and potential use of mutual aid groups (Toseland & Hacker, 1985). Unfortunately, the attitudes of some professionals may impede involvement (Salzer, McFadden, & Rappaport, 1994), despite indications that they may work collaboratively with self-help groups (Thompson & Thompson, 1993). Developing and strengthening lines of communication between social workers and mutual aid groups might prove beneficial to many people.

Explore the range of self-help and mutual aid groups available in your community. Listings may be published in local newspapers, and information and referral programs may maintain databases of such resources. Mutual aid groups may meet by telephone (Goodman, 1990; King, 1991; Meier et al., 1995; Rounds et al., 1995; Wiener et al., 1993) and through the Internet (Finn, 1995; Finn & Lavitt, 1994; Weinberg, Schmale, Uken, & Wessel, 1996; Weinberg et al., 1995). Modern computer technology makes informal social support available even in sparsely populated areas. In serving clients, you may sometimes find it appropriate to explore their previous experience with or interest in participation with mutual aid or self-help groups. Some of your clients, like Jim (see Exhibit 14-4), may be interested in providing leadership to organize a mutual aid group.

◆ Integrating Formal and Informal Support

Although social workers commonly work with informal social support networks, this aspect of practice does not always receive the attention it deserves. During a BSW practice seminar, for example, students were asked to prepare a definition of social support based on a scholarly review of the literature, and then to develop a service plan that included strengthening a client's social support system. Although several students noted the distinction between formal and informal social support in their definitions, none of the 18 students addressed the informal social support system in their service plans. Instead, they focused exclusively on aspects of the formal social support system.

We intentionally explored formal and informal support in separate chapters to emphasize the importance of the latter. In serving clients, however, you often work to strengthen both formal and informal social support (Choi & Wodarski, 1996; Koslyk, Fuchs, Tabisz, & Jacyk, 1993; Olsen, 1986; Spence, 1991; Thompson & Peebles-Wilkins, 1992; Whittaker, 1986). Indeed, the focus for work with many clients often gradually shifts from formal to informal social support.

◆ Chapter Summary

Informal social support—care and assistance by unpaid people in the client's network of family, relatives, friends, and neighbors—represents an important resource. Social support serves as a buffer against hardships and stressful life events. Of course, interactions in the client's informal social support network are not always positive. At times, clients may benefit from reduced contact with certain people or by introducing new relationships into their social support networks. Goals for intervention may include

- Increasing the size of the informal social support network
- Increasing the frequency or intensity of interactions within the network
- Changing the quality of interactions within the network
- Developing new relationships for incorporation within the network

Social support is reciprocal. Many clients seek to enhance their abilities to provide help and support to others. Mutual aid groups provide accessible forms of social support and can be found in even the smallest of communities.

Although we explored formal and informal social support in separate chapters, social workers commonly work to strengthen both formal and informal social support with most clients. As work with any client proceeds, the balance is likely to shift from securing appropriate formal support to enhancing informal support.

Learning Exercises: Readings, InfoTrac, and the Web

1. Use your word-processing computer program to enter the important terms and concepts presented in this chapter in alphabetical order. Place a question mark by any terms that you do not clearly understand. Save your document as EX 14-1.

2. Log on to the InfoTrac College Edition Web site. Conduct a keyword search (using either Keyword Search or Advanced Search) to locate the articles entitled "Factors Contributing to the Survival of Self-Help Groups" (Wituk, Shepherd, Warren, & Meissen, 2002) and "The Benefits of Mutual Support Groups for Parents of Children with Disabilities" (Solomon, Pistrang, & Barker, 2001). Read the articles and prepare a two-page essay in which you reflect on their implications for clients you might serve. Save your document as EX 14-2.

3. Turn to **Reading 22: Self-Help in African American Communities: A Historical Review.** Review this article by Elijah Mickel and reflect on the implications for topics addressed in this chapter. Prepare a one-page essay to explore your observations and reactions. As we noted in Chapter 9, many people of color, especially African Americans and Latinos, prefer to seek help from informal networks. Consider carefully how you might encourage these practices and strengthen their informal networks. Save your document as EX 14-3.

4. Log on to the World Wide Web and visit the Web site of the International Center for Clubhouse Development at www.iccd.org. Prepare a one-page summary of the philosophy, mission, nature, and scope of the clubhouse movement. Be sure to answer these questions: What is a clubhouse? What is the name and location of the nearest ICCD certified clubhouse? Save your document as EX 14-4.

5. Log on to the World Wide Web and search for the Web site of Elizabeth M Tracy, a social work professor who, along with James K. Whittaker, incorporates the use of social network maps in her work and teaching. You will probably find information about Dr. Tracy at http://msass.cwru.edu/ faculty/etracy. You should also be able to find and download relevant forms and directions for preparing a social network map at http://msass .cwru.edu/faculty/etracy/networkmap.pdf. You may also find these resources in an article entitled "The Social Network Map: Assessing Social Support in Clinical Practice," which was published in the journal *Families in Society: The Journal of Contemporary Human Services* (Tracy & Whittaker, 1990). Prepare a one-page summary outline of the directions for preparation of a social network map. Save your document as EX 14-5.

6. Read the applicant's description of a problem situation contained in Exhibit 14-7. Prepare a one-page list of possible ways to strengthen the informal social support network for the applicant. Offer other suggestions as well. Save your document as EX 14-6.

EXHIBIT 14-7
My Mother Doesn't Want to Know

Applicant: My mom and dad divorced about 15 years ago. My father remarried almost immediately, but my mother has lived alone. She hadn't dated much at all until she met Jack about eight months ago. It's been a whirlwind affair. She just fell head over heels in love with him. I was really happy for her for quite a while. Heaven knows she deserves some happiness after all those years with my father and then being alone for so long. Jack's moved into my mother's house, doesn't contribute to the living costs, and travels a lot in his work. He's away three or four nights each week. Yesterday, during lunch at a restaurant, I saw Jack at another table with a woman about his age, a woman about my age, and an old high school friend of mine. They didn't see me. Last night, I called my old friend to say I had seen her in the restaurant. I also asked about the people at lunch with her. She told me that it was John and Mary and their grown daughter Jenny. She said they live in her neighborhood. I asked if John and Mary were married. She said, "Oh yes. They've been happily married for nearly 30 years. I just went to their anniversary party the other night."

I was so shocked, I nearly dropped the phone. My first impulse was to call my mom and tell her what I learned about Jack—or John—but I thought I'd better talk with a professional before I do so. This news will break her heart.

Chapter 15

Building
Helping Communities

The social work profession in the United States celebrated its centennial in 1998. The first formal training program for social workers was established by the New York Charity Organization Society in the summer of 1898. Our 100-year history has been marked by conflict between those who advocate for community development and social action and those who emphasize services to persons experiencing stress and crisis (Franklin, 1990). The literature on community organization and community development reflects a clear distinction between societal change efforts and direct work with individuals and families (Banks & Mangan, 1997; Buffum & MacNair, 1994; Fisher, 1994; Galaway & Hudson, 1994; Homan, 1994; Mandros & Wilson, 1994; Meenaghan & Gibbons, 1998; Midgley, 1995, 1996; Rothman & Tropman, 1987; Tropman, 1997; Weil, 1997; Weil & Gamble, 1995; Wharf & Clague, 1997; Woliver, 1993). Finding means to integrate these two traditions represents a major professional challenge (Adams & Nelson, 1995; Barber, 1995; Elliott, 1993). In this chapter, we consider ways that you and your clients may work together to develop helping communities that may benefit all.

Although community organization is sometimes regarded as a distinct form of practice that differs markedly from direct service to individuals and families, we prefer to consider them as different facets of an integrated, generalist approach to professional social work. Whenever feasible, we encourage you to integrate community development activities into your work with individuals and families.

Within the context of providing direct services, you and your clients may also strengthen your communities by

- Contributing to social capital
- Seeking advice and consultation from natural helpers
- Initiating and facilitating communications
- Contributing to peaceful conflict resolution
- Organizing to meet community wants and needs

◆ Contributing to Social Capital

Social scientists developed the concept of social capital to help explain why community action succeeds in some contexts and fails in others (Fabricant & Fisher, 2002; Freedman, 1997; Livermore & Neustrom, 2003; Schneider, 2002). Physical capital refers to tangible resources, equipment, and infrastructure. Human capital may include people, their energy, knowledge, and expertise. Despite the presence of opportunities and resources, efforts at community organization and development sometimes fail—even when the benefits of collective action are obvious (Putnam, 1993, 1995b, 2000, 2002; Putnam, Feldstein, & Cohen, 2003; Putnam, Leonardi, & Nanetti, 1993).

One of the most important and most original developments in the field of social science during the past 30 years has been the idea that the concept of physical capital as embodied in tools, machines, and other productive equipment can be extended to include human capital as well (Becker, 1964; Schultz, 1961). Just as physical capital is created by changes in materials to form tools that facilitate production, human capital is created by changes in people's knowledge and abilities that enable them able to act in new ways.

Social capital, however, comes about through changes in the relations among persons that facilitate action. If physical capital is wholly tangible, being embodied in observable material form, and human capital is less tangible, being embodied in the skills and knowledge acquired by individuals, social capital is less tangible yet, for it exists in the *relations* between persons. Just as physical capital and human capital facilitate productive activity, social capital does as well. For example, a group that reflects a strong sense of trust among members is able to accomplish much more than a comparable group that lacks trust (Coleman, 1988, pp. S100–S101).

Putnam and colleagues conducted a study of several Italian regional governments that were newly created in 1970. Some were enormously successful but others failed miserably (Putnam, 1993; Putnam et al., 1993). Putnam attributed the difference to the presence of social capital in the successful communities (Exhibit 15-1). Social capital consists of networks of social relationships—what we earlier called systems of informal social support. Communities with dense social networks tend to reflect considerable social capital whereas those with sparse social networks possess limited social capital. The density of the social networks increases as people in a community participate in more social networks, as a greater proportion of the members of the community engage in the social networks, and as the social networks reflect greater overlap so that there is interconnectedness within the community.

Access to social capital tends to enhance family well-being (Boisjoly, Duncan, & Hofferth, 1995), whereas diminished social capital and the withering of community life may contribute to emotional disorders (Maher, 1992) and crime (Bellair, 1997). Variations in social control, individual involvement in crime, and crime rates correlate with social support—that is, the availability of social networks offering coping resources for citizens. As social support increases, crime rates within communities tend to fall (Cullen, 1994). Communities that involve their citizens in mutual ties of trust, empathy, and obligation insulate them from the social precipitators of crime (Braithwaite, 1989; Cullen, 1994; Messner & Rosenfeld, 1994). Crime rates may even be lower in communities that encourage citizens to participate in altruistic activities (Chamlin & Cochran, 1997).

If social capital increases as people participate in informal associations and social networks, then clients

can contribute to the social capital of their communities by participating in sporting clubs, recreational organizations, neighborhood groups, religious organizations, parent associations, and so forth. The kind of group or organization seems less important than the degree of involvement. Social capital depends on active participation rather than passive observation. Playing on a team, joining a community chorus, or serving as a volunteer strengthen social capital whereas attending a concert, watching a baseball game, or going to a movie do not. You can enhance your service to many clients by exploring the ways they do or might contribute to the social capital of their communities. If their connections are tenuous or sparse, consider means to increase their participation in informal associations and social networks.

◆ Consulting Informal Helpers

At times, clients may benefit from consultation with and advice from family, friends, and community members (Memmott, 1993). Human beings are social creatures. Few live isolated lives or rely totally on professionals for guidance and assistance. Most feel comfortable discussing challenging topics with family members and friends. For example, a 1997 survey of mid-life Americans found that 64% of the respondents did not anticipate difficulty talking with their aging parents about the parents' ability to live independently, although 68% had not yet done so (Barrett, 1997). Of the 29% who had spoken with their aging parents, 70% reported that it was easy to do.

All of us must make important decisions in our lives, some of which are truly difficult. We can often benefit from the advice of natural helpers in our informal support networks (Patterson, Memmott, Brennan, & Germain, 1992). Some of our friends and relatives have extensive life experiences or special expertise, and others have alternative viewpoints or philosophical perspectives. Most people appreciate being asked for advice and consultation, and often feel more connected as a result. Indeed, the processes associated with informal help seeking and help giving tends to strengthen support networks.

Professionals sometimes actively or passively discourage clients from seeking advice from friends, neighbors, and family. For example, in Exhibit 12-8, where a mother needed to decide whether to request the placement of her 10-year-old son or to seek

---

EXHIBIT 15-1
Social Capital and Civic Engagement

The norms and networks of civic engagement also powerfully affect the performance of representative government. That, at least, was the central conclusion of my own 20-year, quasi-experimental study of subnational governments in different regions of Italy (Putnam et al., 1993). Although all these regional governments seemed identical on paper, their levels of effectiveness varied dramatically. Systematic inquiry showed that the quality of governance was determined by long-standing traditions of civic engagement (or its absence). Voter turnout, newspaper readership, membership in choral societies and football clubs—these were the hallmarks of a successful region. In fact, historical analysis suggested that these networks of organized reciprocity and civic solidarity, far from being an epiphenomenon of socioeconomic modernization, were a precondition for it.

No doubt the mechanisms through which civic engagement and social connectedness produce such results—better schools, faster economic development, lower crime, and more effective government—are multiple and complex. While these briefly recounted findings require further confirmation and perhaps qualification, the parallels across hundreds of empirical studies in a dozen disparate disciplines and subfields are striking. Social scientists in several fields have recently suggested a common framework for understanding these phenomena, a framework that rests on the concept of *social capital* (Coleman, 1988, 1990; Granovetter, 1985; Jacobs, 1961; Loury, 1987; Putnam, 1993). By analogy with notions of physical capital and human capital—tools and training that enhance individual productivity—"social capital" refers to features of social organization such as networks, norms, and social trust that facilitate coordination and cooperation for mutual benefit.

For a variety of reasons, life is easier in a community blessed with a substantial stock of social capital. In the first place, networks of civic engagement foster sturdy norms of generalized reciprocity and encourage the emergence of social trust. Such networks facilitate coordination and communication, amplify reputations, and thus allow dilemmas of collective action to be resolved. When economic and political negotiation is embedded in dense networks of social interaction, incentives for opportunism are reduced. At the same time, networks of civic engagement embody past success at collaboration, which can serve as a cultural template for future collaboration. Finally, dense networks of interaction probably broaden the participants' sense of self, developing the "I" into the "we," or (in the language of rational-choice theorists) enhancing the participants' "taste" for collective benefits.

Source: Putnam, R. D. (1995). Bowling alone: America's declining social capital. *Journal of Democracy, 6*(1), 65–78, pp. 66–67.

---

assistance in managing his behavior within the home, the service plan only included consultation with the social worker. Exhibit 15-2 provides an alternative service plan for the same client, which includes consultation with her minister, a sister, and two friends.

As professionals, we must remember that people in our clients' informal support systems represent important resources for consultation about decisions. Informal helpers remain a stable part of clients' communities long after social workers have come and gone. Helping clients benefit from these natural resources involves three sets of activities:

- Identifying individuals or groups within clients' informal networks that may be helpful sources of advice
- Incorporating potentially helpful natural helpers as part of the service plan
- Reviewing advice received from natural helpers and assisting clients in determining its potential relevance and utility

Help clients understand that they are not bound by the advice received from helpers—whether natural helpers from their community or from formal helpers

EXHIBIT 15-2
Revised Service Plan to Assist Bonita to Make a Decision

Background:

Richard is the 10-year-old son of Jon and Bonita Jasper. Jon is a merchant seaman and is at sea for extended periods of time, leaving Bonita as the primary provider of child care. Richard has been staying out late at night, is refusing to do household chores, and recently was gone from home overnight. Bonita, in her efforts to control Richard, has used harsh discipline, including beating him with a belt that left welts. The school made a referral to child protection; the child protection agency is holding the case open because Bonita has asked for services from the family service unit of the Maritime Union. This initial plan was developed by Bonita and Sally Harlow, the worker, during a home visit.

Date: March 5

Problem:

Bonita is having difficulty managing Richard without anger, is resorting to harsh punishment, and is considering requesting an out-of-home placement.

Objective:

Bonita will be able to decide whether to request placement for Richard or to develop a service plan to retain Richard at home.

Service Plan:

Task	Who Will Do?	To Be Completed by:
1. Meet twice in Bonita's home to discuss the choices available and the pros and cons of each choice.	Bonita and Sally; Sally will visit Bonita at her home for these meetings.	1st meeting on March 12; 2nd meeting on March 19
2. Consult with the following people to seek their advice regarding decision: ■ Rev. Clarke, minister of Bonita's church ■ Bonita's sister, Anna ■ Bonita's two friends, Corie and Denise	Bonita	March 19
3. Bonita will make a decision between these: a. requesting placement b. developing a service plan for retaining Richard in the home c. discontinuing service	Bonita	March 23
4. Telephone conference to discuss the decision and schedule another meeting if Bonita decides for (a) or (b).	Worker will call Bonita	March 24

EXHIBIT 15-3
Fear of Helping Children

Ralph Smith, a nationally known child advocate from Philadelphia, was just a daddy one afternoon, picking up his son at child care.

He walked toward the back, near the bathrooms when a girl walked out, tights around her ankles, an unhappy look on her face. No one else was there. He bent down to help her pull the tights up. Then he froze. What if someone saw this tableau and misinterpreted it?

"I pulled the tights up so fast," he says now, embarrassed at his fear.

How do we help other people's children? Adults' inability to nurture or correct someone else's kids is "one of the most tragic social changes to impact on children," said David Popence, co-chairman of the Council on Families in America and a sociology professor at Rutgers University.

Source: Dubin, M. (1996, July 23). Adults fear helping kids of others. _Omaha World-Herald,_ p. 42.

EXHIBIT 15-4
Semi Silences SOS Pleas

An elderly Gretna couple frantically trying to wave down help by the roadside were ignored by several motorists—some of whom even swerved to avoid them—before they were finally run over and killed.

But RCMP [Royal Canadian Mounted Police] say no one stopped for Jacob Neufeld, 78, and his wife Mary, 77, until it was too late.

RCMP Cpl. Richard Graham said the Neufelds were struck down after they moved onto the road in an effort to get a semi-trailer to stop at about 8 P.M. on an isolated strip of the highway about 13 kilometres south of Morris.

Graham said the couple was on their way home to Gretna after having dinner at their daughter's home in Grunthal. He said it appears they turned off Highway 75 and onto a side road by mistake, then got stuck in a ditch when they tried to turn around.

Graham said the couple walked about half a kilometre back to the main highway and—likely cold and exhausted—began trying to flag down passing vehicles, waving their arms and walking onto the highway.

"People are afraid to stop for anyone these days," he said.

Source: Wiecek, P. (1995, February 4). Semi silences SOS pleas. _Winnipeg Free Press,_ p. 1. Reprinted with permission.

---

such as yourself. Rather, clients make their own decisions after taking into consideration the information obtained and suggestions received from others.

◆ Building Trust Through Communication

North American societies reflect a pervasive fear and profound sense of distrust. A 1995 national survey in the United States found that only 35% of respondents believed that most people could be trusted. In 1964, that figure had been 76% (Morin & Balz, 1996). The apprehension and suspicion may inhibit us from engaging with others (see Exhibits 15-3 and 15-4).

Community development and other forms of social capital require a considerable degree of trust and a certain amount of personal and social risk. Building trust tends to grow through grassroots action as people take responsibility for their own lives, neighborhoods, and communities and begin to communicate with others. Social workers and clients may work to reduce fear and distrust in several ways. Carefully consider whether you and your clients might overemphasize fear or exaggerate danger in your work together. People must inevitably balance possible risks with potential rewards in many aspects of human life, perhaps especially within the context of social and community relations. The fact that some teenagers commit violent crimes need not lead us to conclude that all youth are dangerous. Some women are abused by their male partners. However, that does not mean that all men are violent. Fear and distrust tend to be contagious and often grow exponentially through gossip, urban myths, and, of course, the popular media, which often seems to present information without perspective or context in the name of "news." A single crime, highly publicized on the front page of newspapers or in nightly TV news shows may prompt fears about a "crime wave" even when statistics about annual rates reveal a steady decline. Absent contextual information, the "news" nonetheless contributes to increased suspicion and social isolation. Fear thrives on inaccurate, distorted, biased, and incomplete information. Knowledge helps to moderate disproportionate apprehension. Indeed, fear may be overcome through collective action, social contact, and communication.

We may facilitate clients' participation with others by taking strolls in their neighborhoods, getting to know neighbors, spending time on the streets, and visiting public places. There are many ways to engage rather than avoid other people, even strangers. Although it may be common to walk around a group of teenagers loitering in a shopping center, we could say "good morning." We could stop for a few minutes to chat with a panhandler instead of speeding up to avoid contact. A friendly greeting can help us develop comfort and skill in reaching out to others.

Encourage clients to resist temptations to jump quickly to conclusions based on appearances or mannerisms. Making assumptions about other people is an especially dangerous practice—for clients and social workers alike. As Exhibit 15-5 illustrates, we can easily be mistaken in our assumptions.

◆ Peacemaking

Bishop Tutu and the South African Truth and Reconciliation Commission provide a powerful example of peacemaking under extraordinarily difficult circum-

stances (Truth and Reconciliation Commission, 2001). Families have been able to forgive those who admit to torturing and killing family members during Apartheid. Perpetrators have avoided prosecution by facing the families, sharing the truth, and helping to locate remains. The reconciliation process provided many victims' families the opportunity for closure and healing. Some critics complain that justice was incomplete because perpetrators went unpunished. However, Bishop Tutu argues that reconciliation promoted healing and spared the nation from further bloody conflict and many additional deaths.

Nelson Mandela and Bishop Tutu follow in the peacemaking tradition reflected in the work of Mohandas Gandhi, Martin Luther King, Jr., and the social worker Jane Addams. What might happen if more people transcended our apparently human tendency for vengeance and punishment against transgressors? What if we emphasized peace and understanding more than victory and domination? Imagine a community where people acknowledged responsibility for damage we caused and offered forgiveness when harmed. Few human beings are perfect. Most of us routinely make mistakes. You may help clients contribute to peace by assisting them to accept responsibility for their errors, extend apologies to persons they have harmed, and develop and implement plans to make amends. Indeed, accepting responsibility for harm we cause others is one of the twelve steps on which Alcoholics Anonymous and similar self-help programs are based (Alcoholics Anonymous, 2003). Taking personal responsibility for our actions is integrally related to the issue of forgiveness (A Campaign for Forgiveness Research, 2001; International Forgiveness Institute, 2003). Indeed, our ability to accept apologies, consider redress, and offer forgiveness when harmed by others may contribute to our personal growth (Di Blasio, 1993; Di Blasio & Proctor, 1993) and to the development of helping communities (Norell & Walz, 1994). Of course, both apologies and forgiveness should not be coerced. Unless they are freely and sincerely offered, they are unlikely to promote anyone's peace and reconciliation.

◆ Organizing Helping Communities

Social workers and clients may contribute to the development of helping communities by fostering and participating in

---

EXHIBIT 15-5
Dangerous Assumptions

Client: I learned something about myself that I truly dislike. I'm really embarrassed and would like your help to change. I've always thought I was open-minded, but the other day I realized I am really quite judgmental.

There's a group of teenagers that hang out on a street corner near the supermarket where I shop. I walk by them several times a week. They wear dark clothes and display pierced ears, noses, tongues, and who knows what else. Both the boys and girls wear black and white make-up and dye their hair in purple and orange colors. Most also wear leather collars around their necks.

I'm ashamed to say that I've been disgusted and revolted by these teenagers. They seemed so self-centered, lazy, and arrogant. Anyway, the other day I was walking back home with my grocery cart. Just as I was passing the teenagers, a young boy on a bicycle was hit by a car. It happened right in front of us. I wasn't sure what to do, but those teenagers were amazing. Three of them went right over to the boy to provide comfort while another used a cell phone to call 911 and provide precise directions to the accident. One young man instructed the others to refrain from moving his neck, back, or limbs in case they were broken. Another talked quietly with the still-conscious boy asking his name and encouraging him to remain still until medical help arrived. One girl held his hand and offered soothing words. Her compassion was absolutely transparent. Another boy comforted the driver—who was physically uninjured but emotionally distraught. Meanwhile the other teenagers directed traffic so that additional accidents wouldn't occur.

The kids were simply incredible—full of concern for other people, capable and confident, and mature beyond their years. I was so impressed and felt a powerful affection for them. I wanted to hug each of them and take them home to dinner. But I also felt profoundly ashamed about my previous assumptions. Apparently, I am a very superficial person—even though I'm 71 years old. I guess I've always had this tendency to judge people quickly based on their looks and appearance. I hope I'm not too old to change.

- Mentoring and support organizations
- Community economic development organizations
- Consumer and social action organizations

Mentoring and Support Organizations

Altruism reflects a human motivation (Schwartz, 1993; Wakefield, 1993) that often underlies mutual assistance programs. For example, mentoring programs that help multicultural urban youth enhance school performance and develop positive self-identification tend to reflect altruistic and social connection themes (Freedman, 1993; Keenan, Dyer, Morita, & Shaskey-Setright, 1990; Mech, Pryde, & Rycraft, 1995; Zippay, 1995). Parents of one family may assist with stress management and the development of parenting skills, and serve as mentors to other parents whose children are at risk of abuse or neglect (Kiam, Green, & Pomeroy, 1997). In some communities, seniors provide volunteer services to older seniors and assist with transportation, food preparation, and other needs (Fort & Associates, 1990). Many clients experience personal growth, meaning, and satisfaction through volunteer service in their communities (Rosemond, 1996; Vorrath & Bendtro, 1985).

Churches and other religious organizations often engage in support services for low-income families and others in vulnerable or oppressive circumstances. Exhibit 15-6 contains a brief description of a helping community intended to provide supervision and support for offenders.

The promise and potential of helping communities may be enhanced when helpers gather together in coordinated efforts (Delgado & Rose, 1994). In this context, social workers and clients may

- Join and participate in a network of associations within the community

---

EXHIBIT 15-6
One Church–One Offender

One Church–One Offender provides an alternative to incarceration for nonviolent offenders through placement with volunteer committees sponsored by local churches. Our mission is:

- To offer nonviolent offenders a better alternative to overcrowded, expensive jails through a partnership with judicial, social and religious agencies cooperating to provide a program of community based advocacy, health care, education and spiritual nurture.
- To encourage positive behavior and to provide an environment conducive to the growth of self-esteem, confidence, independence and hopefulness in the offender.
- To intervene in the client's life to influence productive ways of living useful to the client and the community.

Trained committees of caring people work with a nonviolent offender to help that person become a productive citizen. The program rests on the willingness of community volunteers to become involved in addressing the current rate of crime and on the determination of the courts to resolve problems of overcrowding in jails and prisons that do nothing to reform behavior. It also relies on the desire of the individual offender to change and work for a better life for him and his family. One Church–One Offender is making a difference in the lives of offenders and making our neighborhoods a better place to live.

Source: One Church–One Offender, Inc., 111 West Columbia Street, Fort Wayne, IN 46802. Phone: 260-422-8688.

- Help community groups organize mentoring and support programs
- Use existing mentoring and support services
- Explore clients' strengths and determine how they may contribute to helping communities so that some may become providers of mentoring and support services

Community Economic Development

Community economic development (CED) reflects efforts to integrate social development, community development, and economic development (Galaway & Hudson, 1994; Midgley, 1996). Typically involving small-scale, local activities designed to improve economic conditions, increase participation within communities, and enhance opportunities, CED initiatives may strengthen social capital. We can learn much from CED efforts in Africa that focus on creating economic and social infrastructure and enhancing productive activities and social well-being (Kabadaki, 1995). Although eradication of poverty requires a massive national effort, "community programs that seek to enhance incomes and improve social conditions at the local level have an obvious . . . role to play" (Midgley, 1993, p. 277). In your work with individual

clients, two aspects of community economic development may be particularly helpful: microbusinesses and cooperatives.

Microbusinesses Some clients, including young people entering adulthood, may be interested in establishing small businesses and developing markets for their services (Else & Raheim, 1992; Raheim, 1996). Individuals can often offer services—such as day care, word processing, home maintenance and repair, home cleaning, and yard maintenance—at more competitive rates than can large organizations because of lower overhead and administrative costs. Self-employment may enhance economic empowerment and self-sufficiency for women (Raheim & Bolden, 1995). However, many clients need help to develop skills in business planning, marketing, and financial management. They may also require funds to establish a small business. Even modest home-operated businesses need a certain amount of capital. Microlending programs address both of these limitations.

Microlending initiatives are well established in Asia and Africa as a mechanism for making modest loans to enable low-income persons—often women—to establish small businesses and move their families out of poverty (From sandals to suits, 1997). As a condition

---

EXHIBIT 15-7
Microlending and Microenterprise Resources

ACCIÓN International, www.accion.org
ACCIÓN USA, www.accionusa.org
Appalachian Center for Economic Networks (ACENET), www.acenetworks.org
Aspen Institute Microenterprise Fund for Innovation, Effectiveness, Learning and Dissemination (FIELD), www.fieldus.org
Association for Enterprise Opportunity, www.microenterpriseworks.org
Building Healthier Communities, www.mcauley .org/bhconline/index.htm
Canadian Community Economic Development Network, www.canadiancednetwork.org

Centre for Community Enterprise, www .cedworks.com
Community and Economic Development Toolbox, www.cardi.cornell.edu/cd_toolbox_2/ cdindex.cfm
Corporation for Enterprise Development, www .cfed.org
The Microenterprise Journal, www .microenterprisejournal.com
USAID Microenterprise, www.usaidmicro.org
Women's Initiative for Self Employment, www.womensinitiative.org/index.htm

---

of the loan, microlending programs often require participants to complete a course in basic business practices. The course participants form a group that provides support and encouragement to each other. In some programs, the group itself guarantees the loans to individuals. Therefore, all group members have a stake in helping each business succeed. Pilot microlending programs have recently emerged in North America to provide similar forms of assistance to low-income persons. If microlending programs are available in your community, you may choose to help clients access them as a step toward self-support. Absent such programs, you and other social workers may seek to develop them as a means to help people become active participants in the market economy (see Exhibit 15-7).

Cooperatives Participation in cooperatives may also be appropriate for some clients (Fairbairn, Bold, Fulton, Ketilson, & Ish, 1991; Fulton, 1989; Quarter, 1992). There are both producer and consumer cooperatives. In producer cooperatives, people who produce goods or market services band together to jointly market and sell the goods or services. Farmers in North America for example, have formed producer cooperatives to market their products. In consumer cooperatives, consumers organize themselves into a collective to buy and distribute goods or services. Examples include babysitting clubs, food purchasing clubs, cooperative grocery stores, service

stations, credit unions, and even cooperative funeral services.

Cooperatives can generally offer services at lower costs than other businesses can. In addition, cooperatives provide opportunities for members' active participation in the business. Some cooperatives require members to donate a certain amount of time and energy, which helps to lower costs. Most clients tend to be more interested in consumer cooperatives than in producer cooperatives, unless several have successfully established related businesses and can market their services together. Some clients may want to initiate a cooperative in their neighborhood or community to meet a specific need. Information about organizing cooperatives is readily available on the Internet (see Exhibit 15-8).

Social Action Groups

Participation in collective action to promote change is fundamental to a democratic society. Part of your service to clients may involve helping them identify and join social action groups whose goals they share. Groups of social service consumers have successfully secured policy change and created helping communities for their members (Breton, 1995; Checkoway, 1995; Cohen & Wagner, 1992; Cox, 1991; Tower, 1994; Weiss, 1993). When appropriate, ask clients about their involvement in consumer or social action organizations. Some may be interested to learn about

---

EXHIBIT 15-8
Cooperatives Resources

Canadian Cooperative Association, www.coopcca.com

Coady International Institute, www.stfx.ca/institutes/coady

Cooperatives 101, www.rurdev.usda.gov/rbs/pub/cir55/cir55rpt.htm

Cooperative Development Foundation, www.coopdevelopment.org

Co-operatives Secretariat, www.agr.gc.ca/policy/coop/home_e.phtml

Committee for the Promotion and Advancement of Cooperatives (COPAC), www.copacgva.org

International Cooperative Alliance, www.coop.org

University of California Center for Cooperatives, www.cooperatives.ucdavis.edu

University of Wisconsin Center for Cooperatives, www.wisc.edu/uwcc

U.S. Department of Agriculture, Rural Development, Cooperative Services, http://www.rurdev.usda.gov/rbs/coops/csdir.htm

---

and participate in relevant associations. You may also consider ways that clients may actively involve themselves in consumer organizations to promote the kinds of helping communities they desire.

Social action organizations that address clients' concerns may not yet exist at the local level. For example, the Birky family (Reading 6) might not find a local organization prepared to take on the problem of the uncovered ditch. Mrs. Iverson (Exhibit 5-4) may not find an organization prepared to lobby for a foster home placement for her daughter. Social action organizations often focus on changes in larger systems—at the national, regional, or state or provincial level. These are important initiatives. However, many problems that clients encounter occur at the local level. For example, the need for traffic lights, more frequent garbage pickup, adequate street lighting, and increased availability of teachers for parent consultation are local community issues. Under such circumstances, you may help clients assume leadership in change efforts and serve as an advisor, consultant, and participant in those efforts.

◆ Chapter Summary

Participation in helping partnerships is a key theme of this book. In this chapter, we expanded the notion to include clients' participation in their communities. In large part, we build helping communities through active participation with others in areas of common interest.

Social workers and clients may participate in our communities by

- Becoming active in voluntary associations and organizations, and thereby contributing to the social capital of the community
- Seeking advice from friends, neighbors, and respected community members
- Striving to reduce fear through communication with others—especially strangers—in the community
- Becoming a peacemaker—both by accepting responsibility for our errors and apologizing and by offering forgiveness when others do the same
- Organizing helping communities—by using and offering services as a mentor or volunteer, participating in community economic development, and participating in social change groups

Many clients benefit themselves and their communities through various forms of social action and participation. In providing social service, you may often encourage and facilitate clients' community organization and development activities. Even when the problems and goals of concern do not directly involve community matters, you may learn about clients' social action efforts. Remain alert to the possibility that you might do or say something that could somehow impede or obstruct clients' community participation (Swenson, 1994). Give careful thought to the following questions. What am I doing that might:

- Encourage clients to consider the possibility of making peace within their communities by acknowledging and apologizing for their own errors and forgiving those who erred against them?

- Encourage clients to consider the advisability of providing volunteer community service, joining cooperatives, and participating in social action organizations?

- Inhibit or interfere with clients' participation in voluntary associations and community organizations?

- Discourage clients from discussing personal matters and key decisions with trusted family members, friends, or others?

- Exaggerate or increase clients' fear, apprehension, suspicion, xenophobia, or social isolation?

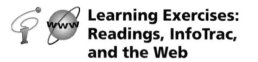

Learning Exercises: Readings, InfoTrac, and the Web

1. Use your word-processing computer program to enter the important terms and concepts presented in this chapter in alphabetical order. Place a question mark by any terms that you do not clearly understand. Save your document as EX 15-1.

2. Log on to the InfoTrac College Edition Web site. Conduct a keyword search (using either Keyword Search or Advanced Search) to locate the articles entitled "Innovation in Social Policy: Collaborative Policy Advocacy" (Sherraden, Slosar, & Sherraden, 2002) and "Social Work Advocacy in the Post-TANF Environment: Lessons from Early TANF Research Studies" (Anderson & Gryzlak, 2002). Read the articles and prepare a two-page essay in which you reflect on their implications for social work and social work practice. Save your document as EX 15-2.

3. Log on to the InfoTrac College Edition Web site. Conduct a keyword search (using either Keyword Search or Advanced Search) to locate the articles entitled "Social Support and Parenting in Poor, Dangerous Neighborhoods" (Ceballo & McLoyd, 2002) and "Reducing Depression in Pregnancy: Designing Multimodal Interventions" (Cunningham & Zayas, 2002). Read the articles and prepare a two-page essay in which you reflect on

their implications for social work and social work practice. Save your document as EX 15-3.

4. Log on to the World Wide Web. Conduct a search for the International Forgiveness Institute. You should find a reference to Institute's Web site at www.forgiveness-institute.org. Prepare a one-page summary in response to the following questions: What is forgiveness? What is the Institute's forgiveness process model (see www.forgiveness-institute.org/IFI/Whatis/process_model.htm)? Save your document as EX 15-4.

5. Log on to the World Wide Web. Conduct a search for the Asset-Based Community Development (ABCD) Institute. You should be able to find the Institute's Web site at www.northwestern.edu/ipr/abcd.html. Download the following publications: "A Twenty-First Century Map for Healthy Communities and Families" by John L. McKnight (1996) at www.northwestern.edu/ipr/publications/papers/century.pdf, and "Mapping Community Capacity" by John L. McKnight and John P. Kretzmann (1990) at www.northwestern.edu/ipr/publications/papers/mcc.pdf. Read the two papers and then prepare one-page abstracts of each. Save your document as EX 15-5.

6. Log on to the World Wide Web. Conduct a search for the Coady Institute at St. Francis Xavier University. You should be able to find the Institute's Web site at www.stfx.ca/institutes/coady/ie_index.html. Locate the publication, *From Clients to Citizens: Asset-Based Community Development as a Strategy for Community-Driven Development* (Mathie & Cunningham, 2002). Read the paper and then prepare a one-page abstract. Save your document as EX 15-6.

7. Log on to the World Wide Web. Conduct a search for the "Agents of Social Change Online Exhibit" at the Sophia Smith Collection, Smith College. You should be able to find the Collection's Web site at www.smith.edu/libraries/libs/ssc/exhibit/ Review the exhibit and in a one-page essay, summarize information that was new to you. Save your document as EX 15-7.

8. Prepare a one-page essay in which you explore how the social work profession and social work practice might contribute to fear in communities. Also, briefly discuss how social workers might

---

EXHIBIT 15-9
Absentee Human Service Systems

The current remote and bureaucratized systems must be changed in order to end the economic mistargeting of our existing human-service spending. In any poor urban neighborhood, tens of millions of dollars are spent each year on human needs—health services, foster care, recreation, environmental clean-up, drug education and treatment, nutrition and housing improvements.

Almost every dollar of this investment currently goes to teachers, police officers, day care providers, nurses, outreach workers, probation officers, foster families, social workers, health care professionals, planners, managers, landlords, administrators, and service contractors who live some place else. The second time these dollars are spent, they are spent somewhere else. We are used to decrying the problems of absentee landlords and absentee merchants, but we have largely ignored the absentee human-service system we have so consistently sustained. Community-planned and community managed human-service systems would not only work better for clients, they would also contribute jobs, enterprise, and development to the neighborhoods that need them most.

———————

Source: Annie E. Casey Foundation. (1994). Community empowerment: Making human services a community enterprise. *AEC Focus, 4*(1), 3. Published by the Annie E. Casey Foundation, One Lafayette Place, Greenwich, CT 06830.

---

counteract such reactions and help communities become less suspicious of us and our profession? Save your document as EX 15-8.

9. Review the brief commentary presented in Exhibit 15-9. In a brief one-page essay, explore your thoughts and reactions to the piece. In your essay, discuss whether you agree or disagree with the position. Also, comment about the idea social workers should be expected—or required—to live in their clients' neighborhoods. Save your document as EX 15-9.

Chapter 16

Teamwork for Social Work Practice

The capacity to operate as a productive team member represents an important social work practice ability. Social workers often serve as team members when we act as brokers to link clients with various services beyond the scope of our agencies. Indeed, teams of providers may deliver some of the programs and services that your agency sponsors. Increasingly, social workers function as members of intraprofessional and interdisciplinary teams to ensure effective service delivery.

In this chapter, we consider

- Teamwork as a problem-solving process
- Intraprofessional and interdisciplinary teams
- Natural helper teams
- The downside of teamwork

◆ The Problem-Solving Approach to Teamwork

Teamwork as a Resource

Teamwork involves the cooperative effort of an organized group to achieve a common goal. Teams use the various capacities of its members to expand the range of knowledge and skills available to clients for problem solving. A focus on the agreed-upon problems and goals enables team members to maintain a sense of identity and direction and fosters purposeful communication. Team members must develop functional relationships and communication processes to provide clients the most effective help possible.

Professionals tend to talk outside the presence of clients in a different manner than they do when clients are present (Sands, 1994). Teams of practitioners sometimes meet by themselves to pool their knowledge of the problem and decide how to proceed. Sometimes clients are informed about these meetings. Often, they are not. We think clients should be actively involved in considering how different professionals can help and should be told about all relevant professional consultations (Saltz & Schaefer, 1996). We prefer to offer clients the opportunity to participate in deliberations with other professionals so that they may speak for themselves if they so choose (Williams, 1988).

Engage clients in discussions about the nature and degree of their potential involvement with a team. Explore what the team might be able to offer, how it may be used, and what information might be shared. Typically, social workers and clients provide team members with information needed to understand and work toward problem resolution. However, sharing data with others is not a simple issue. We must always consider how others might use what we share. For instance, supposed you serve on an interdisciplinary, interagency team that helps to determine where children in need of foster care should be placed. Consider the importance of the decisions and the process by which they are reached. The stakes are incredibly high. Placing children in foster homes involves extremely complex and difficult issues. The needs of the child and the resources and capacities of the foster care family or facility are identified, assessed, and evaluated to determine the goodness-of-fit between the child and the placement. There are numerous stakeholders to the process. Biological parents, siblings, or grandparents; a court, judge, or state agency;

prospective foster parents or providers in a foster care facility; and the child him or herself are potential participants. In most cases, clients must provide informed consent before you may share information outside your agency. Keep clients fully aware of what is being shared, and why and whenever possible, involve them in the process itself.

Case conferences are often extremely useful for joint planning, coordination, and evaluation of services when more than one worker and agency are involved with the same client system. Clients should be informed about these conferences and invited to participate. They should also receive reports about conference outcomes—preferably in written form. In considering whether or not clients should attend and participate in case conferences, social workers and clients should consider whether the conference is likely to

- Help clients better understand or analyze the problems of concern, goals, intervention strategies, or evaluation tools and instruments.
- Help clients develop a sense of control over their own destiny.
- Overwhelm clients with the professionals, the process, the context, or the topics.
- Address issues of meaning and relevance to clients.
- Address unrelated agency policies and practices.
- Provide opportunities for clients to offer meaningful input to the conference.

The Team Leader

When more than one agency or professional is involved with the same client, the participants should develop policies and procedures to guide their meetings. These guidelines should be established before meetings that may affect clients. In many circumstances, case conferences are high-stakes endeavors that may dramatically influence peoples' lives and situations. Haphazard organization or ad hoc processes place clients at considerable risk. Indeed, failure to adopt reasonable procedures and due process could constitute professional malpractice.

At a minimum, a team leader must be chosen or appointed to coordinate and facilitate the case conference. The leader should possess authority to undertake several basic responsibilities in a competent manner. The leader should ensure that

- All agencies and persons involved are invited to and included in the conference
- The purpose and focus of the conference are clearly defined and outlined—perhaps in the form of an agenda
- All participants have an opportunity to share their knowledge and expertise
- Decision-making and conflict resolution processes are coherent, fair, and understood by all participants
- Action plans that emerge from the conference include specific information about exactly what is to be done, who is to do it, and when it should be completed
- Records about the process and outcomes of the conference are accurate, complete, accessible to eligible participants, and maintained in a secure environment

The case conference should result in group agreement about the plan, including the part each agency is to play and the goals each is to pursue. The plan should be recorded in written form. All participants should receive a copy and have a chance to make corrections. Once the corrected plan has been adopted, each agency becomes formally obligated to fulfill its responsibilities. The team leader coordinates and monitors implementation of the plan by each agency. The leader should be selected before the team begins the action phase of the work with or on behalf of the client. Granted power and authority, the team leader must be willing to use them in a responsible manner. Conflicts among the members of the team and relationship difficulties must be approached as problems to be solved and addressed as such. If the team functions in a dysfunctional manner, it may negatively affect the client (Fargason, Barnes, Schneider, & Galloway, 1994; Sands, Stafford, & McClelland, 1990; Sessa, 1996).

Types of Teams

Social workers commonly serve on many different kinds of teams (Exhibit 16-1). You may serve on interdisciplinary teams. For example, in a hospital setting, social workers often join medical doctors and nurses to coordinate services for a patient (Poulin, Walter, & Walker, 1994). You may also participate on intraprofessional teams. For instance, several social workers representing different agencies may meet to coordinate services to a family. You could also join a

---

EXHIBIT 16-1
Typology of Teams

	Within your organization (intra-agency)	**With another organization (interagency)**
Social work team	**Type A** Example: Foster care worker and adoption worker from the same agency work together to develop and implement a permanent plan for a child in foster care	**Type B** Example: Child protection worker, school social worker, and probation officer meet regularly to coordinate services for a family in which youth behavior problems relate to a pattern of intrafamily abuse
Interdisciplinary team	**Type C** Example: Hospital social worker, nurse, doctor, and physical therapist meet to coordinate discharge plans for a client/patient	**Type D** Example: Public health nurse, adult protection worker, and senior citizen center worker meet to develop a protection and activity plan for a vulnerable older person living alone
Natural helper team	**Type E** Example: Social worker and foster parent develop service plans for youth in care	**Type F** Example: Social worker and Parent Anonymous mutual aid group work to provide mutual aid and support to parents who, under stress, may abuse their children

---

team of social workers, paraprofessionals, and natural helpers associated with your own agency. For example, you may work with foster parents, agency volunteers, or mental health consumers as peer service providers (Solomon & Draine, 1996). You might even serve on a team that includes social workers and natural helpers outside your agency. For instance, you might participate with consultants, leaders, and perhaps members of self-help or mutual aid groups. The enormous growth in the number and kinds of mutual aid groups creates numerous opportunities for collaboration.

◆ Intraprofessional and Interdisciplinary Teams

Social workers have long been concerned about the fragmentation of helping services. There have been periodic efforts to establish methods of collaboration among various community agencies. In the early 1900s, Dr. Richard Cabot encouraged hospitals to employ social workers to work with doctors and nurses and aid patients with the social aspects of their medical conditions. Social workers have collaborated with other professionals ever since. However, interdisciplinary engagement is not necessarily beneficial. Like other activities, collaboration across professional lines reflects the potential to enhance or detract from the quality of service. Contemporary social workers routinely deal with multiple agencies, programs, and service providers in their attempts to help clients. Absent effective coordination and teamwork, consumers of health, educational, and social services may be caught in a nightmarish fragmentation of care (Compher, 1987). Clients often must struggle with a great deal more than the issues they identify as concerns. They frequently also face the burden of resolving professional conflicts, reconciling incongruities, and acting on contradictory advice from diverse agencies and providers.

Obstacles to Effective Teamwork

A man crossing the street was hit by a truck. When passers-by rushed over to help, they saw the man crawling away as fast as he could, on hands and one knee, dragging one leg helplessly. They said, "Where are you going? Don't you realize you've just been hit by a truck. You need help." The man replied, "Please leave me alone. I don't want to get involved."

Like the man, social workers may be reluctant to participate on teams. However, collaboration with others often improves service effectiveness. Team membership can also serve as a form of social support, buffer stress, and enhance personal and professional satisfaction (Poulin et al., 1994). Why is it, then, that many social workers find it difficult to work on teams—perhaps especially on interdisciplinary teams? Let's look at some of the obstacles to effective teamwork.

The Myth of Good Intentions Social workers sometimes assume that good intentions and a cooperative attitude are sufficient to ensure effective teamwork. If we are friendly, respectful, and considerate of others, surely good interdisciplinary collaboration must follow? This rests on the assumptions that getting along with others is a relatively simple and natural ability, that teamwork depends primarily on personal characteristics, and that specific knowledge and skills are nonessential. We view collaboration with others as a complex process that involves a great deal more than good intentions and desirable personal qualities. We think that knowledge and skills for effective teamwork must be learned and refined.

Helplessness in the Face of Authority Many social workers serve in host settings dominated by another profession. Teachers are more dominant in schools, and doctors are more dominant in hospitals. In such settings, some social workers report a sense of helplessness because of the dominant profession's authority (Dane & Simon, 1991). Exhibit 16-2 contains an example. In such settings, social workers may come to believe that we can do little to influence decisions when we possess such limited power.

There are at least two types of authority: authority of position and authority of competence. Certain positions and statuses convey authority that may or may not be deserved. Doctors, professors, judges, mayors, governors, presidents, and social workers possess authority by virtue of their positions. The authority of competence, however, derives from actual performance, the manner in which we carry out our responsibilities, and our reputation for professionalism and effectiveness. Such authority is granted by colleagues and others with whom we interact during the course of our work. We convey authority to others—just as they do to us. All professionals need power and authority if we are to provide effective service. While granting other professionals authority needed to fulfill their duties, we must retain the authority that we need to carry out our responsibilities. Authority is neither good nor bad; however, it is essential if we are to help. Social workers sometimes see ourselves as powerless when we could readily assume considerable authority through a simple change in perspective or attitude.

Professional Boundaries Professionals who serve on helping teams tend to have both distinct and common areas of expertise. Indeed, some tasks can be completed by team members from several professions or disciplines. Because of the overlapping responsibilities associated with these common tasks, specific negotiation is required to avoid misunderstanding, conflict, and duplication of effort. Some professionals, including certain social workers, view their turf as large and expansive. They may consign other team members from other professions and disciplines to peripheral roles. Some other professionals may eschew specialization and insist that all members of the team—regardless of discipline—can deal effectively with any problem. Neither extreme seems especially productive. Teams reflect diverse talents and abilities. Effective service often requires a combination of specialized and general expertise. Teams benefit from recognition and use of members with special competence and clarification about who should do what within those common areas that overlap. Role negotiation is an important collaborative skill that contributes greatly to team functioning and service quality.

Professional Differences Professions differ in their perspectives about human growth and development, the genesis of human problems, and the approaches and strategies for problem resolution. Each profession selects theories and knowledge that most relate to its societal function and best support its methods of practice. As a result, professions may hold different beliefs, assumptions, and expectations about human nature and human conduct. Correspondingly, each profession

---

EXHIBIT 16-2
Reluctant Team Members

The social worker is part of a multidisciplinary team at a long-term care facility. The client is a 75-year-old woman. Her diagnosis includes schizophrenia (delusions and paranoia), dementia, and Parkinson's disease. The physical assessment reveals that she ambulates and transfers independently and that her hearing and vision are good. The mental functioning and psychological assessment reveals that she is alert and oriented to person and place, reflects poor cognition and perception, is paranoid with new people, periodically yells and screams at others, occasionally exhibits aggressive hitting-out behavior when she feels threatened, and frequently sings when anxious. Her social skills are limited to one-on-one interactions (loves to talk about clothing). She becomes agitated and anxious in groups. Her verbal skills are limited. Only one of her six siblings visits occasionally.

The client began to experience problems as a teenager. Her mother died when she was 21, and she lived in group homes until admission. She has worked in a sewing room and in a cafe. Because of behavior problems, she was admitted on September 22 for a probationary six-month trial. The first case conference was held in December. The social worker made the following recommendations: adopt a calm and gentle approach; let the client make the first move; keep voice level low; respect the client's right to privacy and allow her to decide whether to have her door open or closed; and praise client regarding appearance and behavior. Shortly after the meeting, the social worker observed that her recommendations had not been included within the care plan and that the staff continues to leave the client's door open at all times and enter without knocking. The social worker spoke to the head nurse, who said it was not necessary to include these recommendations because all staff members are aware of the approach to use with residents.

---

develops different styles of communication and methods of problem solving. Professions may also have different notions of what constitutes an effective outcome. Thus, conflicts between team members may arise out of different beliefs and expectations about how people act and how they should be treated (Sands et al., 1990). For example, an interdisciplinary team serving children in a psychiatric setting can become confused when some staff adopt a linear, cause-and-effect approach to problems and others operate from an interactive, systemic, and relational perspective (Parker, 1987).

All team members do not need to view things from the same perspective. Diverse perspectives and focal points can represent an enormous strength. If I suffer a broken leg in an automobile accident, I want the medical doctor at the scene to address the physical damage, immobilize the leg, and try to repair the fracture. I do not want the physician to focus on the existential meaning of the injury or its psychological and social implications. However, if I experience extensive and disabling injuries, I might very well want a social worker to help me address the psychosocial consequences. The medical doctors and nurses would focus on my physical well-being while the social workers might help me cope with the psychological, social, economic, and perhaps spiritual issues associated with the injuries. Although these foci differ, they are not incongruent or incompatible. However, professionals may disagree about which viewpoints are more relevant or important. In our service as members of teams, we should recognize the inevitability and use of diverse perspectives and opinions, and learn to negotiate them, in the best interests of clients and their families (Fargason et al., 1994; Sands et al., 1990).

Competition

Both cooperative and competitive dynamics tend to emerge when helping persons, groups, or organizations work together to help a common client address a common problem. A study of interdisciplinary teams that experienced conflict found that members saw themselves primarily as representatives of their own discipline, rather than as members of a team (Sands et al., 1990). For example, one team member might say, "I understand the needs of those children better than the foster mother or the teacher." Another might assert that, "My work is more important to the client's welfare than yours," "My supervisor knows more than your supervisor," or "I have a doctorate and you don't." Competition may occur at times and places where it is inappropriate, unprofessional, detrimental to clients, and sometimes even contrary to the self-interest of the competing individuals.

Findings from game theory experiments reveal much about these patterns and processes in human interaction and decision making. Consider, for example, situations involving nonzero-sum games. In contrast to zero-sum games, where there are individual winners and losers, these games are structured so that uncooperative play is patently absurd. Players who decline to cooperate cannot win and stand a good chance of losing. Despite the rational absurdity, uncooperative play is surprisingly common in nonzero-sum games. Astonishingly, players often become increasingly competitive as the games continue and the negative effects of competition become more apparent (David, 1970).

What explains this behavior? Players can be classified into three categories: (1) *maximizers,* who are interested only in their own payoffs; (2) *rivalists,* who are interested only in defeating their partners and are not concerned with the result of the game itself; and (3) *cooperators,* who are interested in helping both themselves and their partners. Comparison of nonzero-sum games under different communication conditions reveals that greater communication increases cooperation only among cooperators. Increased communication fails to change the behavior of maximizers or rivalists (David, 1970).

Unlike participants in games, clients may suffer substantial damage as a result of competitive relationships among practitioners. Social workers can work toward cooperation by establishing a climate where each team member is recognized as a valuable part of the group. Unfortunately, teams often reflect a hierarchical structure based on authority of position or status. Lower status team members—who often possess a wealth of information based on direct observation—are often ignored. For example, in children's residential settings, paraprofessional staff who carry the daily stress of living with and caring for troubled children often find that their knowledge and ex-

pertise remains unrecognized by the professionals, who assume only they can truly understand the needs of the children. Social workers who serve as team members or team leaders are well suited to cultivate cooperative relationships. After all, we routinely establish collaborative partnerships with the clients we serve. Consistent with the principles and processes of problem solving, we may recognize the potential value of new ideas from diverse sources and encourage all participants to contribute alternate perspectives and options. Such cooperative attitudes and collaborative processes, however, require considerable maturity. Self-interest and competitive rivalry can be devastating to teamwork. Members' ego involvement with their own professional orientations may block their ability to consider the opinions or perspectives of others (Mouzakitis & Goldstein, 1985). Team members and leaders must transcend personal and professional self-interest and competitiveness to develop relationships that foster trust and mutual respect (Mouzakitis & Goldstein, 1985). Teams must also be clearly focused on their primary purpose and goals to harness the expertise of individual members in the interests of problem solving. As a social worker, you may occasionally restate the overarching purpose to enhance the group's awareness of common intent.

Each practitioner brings to the team different value systems, principles, frames of reference, jargon, and conceptions of what constitutes good practice (Abramson, 1984). Strong disagreements may surface about topics such as the degree of client involvement in treatment planning or which party in a client system should receive advocacy services (e.g., child or parent, victim or offender). In such circumstances, decisions may be reached through compromise rather than consensus—even though all members of the team bear responsibility. Effective teamwork requires members who can share a common value base, language, and conceptual framework that incorporates or transcends their professional orientation. A sense of collective responsibility in interdisciplinary collaboration may emerge when team members establish shared meanings of ethical concepts such as confidentiality and autonomy, a hierarchy of values and ethical principles, and a regular procedure for analyzing complex ethical dilemmas and practice issues (Abramson, 1984). Team members who still cannot agree with the rest of the group may formally record their dissent and be excused from the particular case in question (Sands et al., 1990). However, silent disagreement does not excuse team members from their responsibility for group decisions.

A commitment to team functioning sometimes leads members to avoid disagreement at all costs. This may lead to the phenomenon of groupthink in which individuals feel less accountable for what happens and consequently become less thorough (Janis, 1982; Kowert, 2002). Teams may counter this tendency by assigning certain team members on a rotating basis to the role of devil's advocate. If decisions are routinely challenged, the chances of overlooking potential problems can be reduced.

Differences in Professional and Agency Culture

Effective collaboration requires that professionals demonstrate respect, trust, and acceptance of others in their interactions. As social workers, we learn the importance of accepting and respecting clients, but we rarely consider how these principles might apply to our colleagues. Professional ethics and concern for the quality of service to clients require that we also pay attention to collegial relationships as well.

Professional education and staff development initiatives often includes efforts to socialize workers to their profession and their agency. As you internalize the values and culture of the profession, you naturally begin to conform to certain expectations and adhere to particular processes and procedures. These socialization processes help to protect clients as practitioners internalize their professional culture. However, internalization can cause problems in interagency collaboration, unless we identify our own socialized values and culture and learn to recognize and respect the values and culture of other professions and agencies.

The agency, its value system, and its operational practices help shape the way social workers define problems for work. As a professional, you must become an integral part of your agency while remaining analytical about its policies and procedures. As a leader or member of a team, you cannot afford a narrowly focused perspective or ideology. To work effectively with other community services, you must understand the structure, values, and operating practices of those agencies. Otherwise, different conceptions about people, problems, and practices can lead to bitter conflict.

Teamwork often provides an intimate glimpse into the hearts and minds of our colleagues. We may gain heightened appreciation for people we previously underestimated and, conversely, come to question the competence of colleagues we admired. This can be an especially touchy issue, especially if the person has more power and authority, or serves as a supervisor (Abramson, 1984). Many social workers stress the need for skill building in this area. All participants need to understand the basics of effective teamwork. It does little good for one professional to strive for an atmosphere of mutual respect if others assume roles of self-appointed authorities. Agencies and organizations can contribute enormously to enhanced team functioning. If agency leaders endorse team process and clearly communicate that cooperation is expected and required, teamwork tends to become more collaborative and productive (Nason, 1983). This support can be demonstrated by various incentives and forms of recognition as well as staff development training in group problem solving and team building.

Teamwork and Advocacy

Exhibit 16-3 contains an illustration of some challenges in teamwork. The social worker on an interdisciplinary team feels caught between the views of the team and those of the client about an appropriate discharge plan. Interdisciplinary teams commonly confront dilemmas of this kind (Abramson, Donnelly, King, & Mailick, 1993).

Consider the following suggestions for integrating the advocacy and teamwork aspects of social work practice. You may find them useful.

- Become comfortable with the areas of competence and expertise that you bring to the team. Recognize that all team members bring valuable competencies and that no team member is omnipotent. Advocate on behalf of clients within your area of competence.
- Consider time and context as you decide when and how to advocate on behalf of clients. Establish priorities to guide decisions about which issues are of such importance that you will fight hard and long, which may be deferred, and which require some but not complete action. Deciding about the timing of advocacy initiatives requires considerable political acumen.
- Learn how to advocate. As in other settings, an important skill is the ability to present a well-reasoned position in an assertive manner with-

---

EXHIBIT 16-3
Disagreements Regarding Discharge Planning

Tom, a 22-year-old African American, entered the Regional Treatment Center about six months ago, through a district court commitment for mental illness. At the time of hospitalization, Tom was in a decompensated state, with significant disorganization of thought. Early treatment was complicated by difficulties in adjusting medications, with severe side effects. Tom consistently denied the mental illness and did not acknowledge any dysfunctional thoughts or behavior. Tom's family support is strong. The family includes the patient's mother, an infant grandchild in her care, and an adult daughter who lives outside the home. The treatment team perceives the family as mistrustful; their interactions with team members have been abrupt and conflict-filled. Discharge planning was underway at the time the case was assigned to me.

Tom's condition is considered stabilized. He is participating in selected group programs, his mood is generally consonant with the situation, his thinking is organized and lucid, and he is responsible in providing for his basic needs. Tom has been unable to specify goals beyond his desire to leave the treatment center. He is compliant with the medication, but disagrees about its necessity or bene-

fits. He often talks about undesirable side effects, although he acknowledges they have been worse in the past. Tom has had no significant experience with independent living. The team is recommending discharge to a group home, because of Tom's history of poor medication compliance and need to monitor side effects. Tom reports he is ready for discharge but disagrees with the team's plan. He would prefer to return to the family home.

I am responsible for implementation of the discharge plan and have had four interviews with Tom on the subject of discharge. Tom expressed many negative ideas about group homes. He agreed to visit a group home to expand his information and clarify perceptions about group homes. Although the visit seemed to reduce Tom's apprehension, he remains determined to return to his mother's home. The significant disagreement regarding discharge planning is producing conflict and alienation between the treatment team and Tom and his family.

Source: Paulette Anderson, MSW student, School of Social Work, University of Minnesota, Minneapolis.

---

out becoming aggressive, defensive, submissive, or passive-aggressive (Mailick & Ashely, 1981).

◆ Natural Helper Teams

Social workers also work with teams of natural helpers. For instance, you may serve as a team member, leader, or perhaps professional consultant with volunteers, child care workers, and foster parents associated with your own agency or with various natural helper groups within the community such as members of clients' informal social support networks and mutual aid or self-help groups. Although natural helpers may not possess professional credentials, they nonetheless often bring considerable knowledge, expertise, experience, and wisdom to the teamwork process.

The ideas we discussed about interdisciplinary and intraprofessional teams also apply to participation with natural helper teams as well. Some social workers find it difficult to work with such groups—perhaps because it involves sharing power and authority with nonprofessional team members (Blüml et al., 1989; Hazel, 1989; Hazel & Fenyo, 1993). However, most professionals soon come to appreciate the wisdom that natural helpers bring to the endeavor. After all, teams essentially function as task-centered groups or committees. If the goals are clear, well understood, and agreed to by all team members, we have a solid basis on which to operate. As a social worker serving as a member, leader, facilitator, or consultant, you assist the team in reaching decisions and developing plans to best accomplish the goals (see Exhibit 11-6).

Suggestions for working cooperatively with natural helper teams are provided in Exhibit 16-4. Consider

---

EXHIBIT 16-4
Facilitating a Natural Helper Team

1. Recognize differing expertise.
2. Share all information.
3. Involve all team members in all phases of planning.
4. Allow team members to express differing opinions.

5. Discuss differences of opinion, and negotiate action plans.
6. Expect responsible behavior from all team members.
7. Discuss performance problems openly.

---

these principles in relation to a situation involving a social worker and a foster parent team. Approximately six months ago, 16-year-old Rose was placed with a foster family because of sexual assaults by her stepfather. She had made a good adjustment to her new living circumstances. Recently, however, she began to exhibit some signs of depression and social withdrawal. Based on an interview with Rose, an agency psychologist recommended family therapy for Rose and the foster parents. The foster parents want Rose to receive individual counseling services but believe family therapy with them is unnecessary. Suppose you are the social worker in the situation and bear responsibility for Rose's care and well-being. How would you handle this situation with the foster parents—who, after all, are members of the natural helper team? Would you expect them to undergo therapy with Rose and attempt to enforce this as a condition of their service? If not, how would you address the changes in Rose's mental and social status? And, how would you deal with the psychologist?

In this instance, we believe the psychologist's recommendation that the foster parents undergo family therapy with Rose was premature. We would prefer that the social worker engage the natural helper team—of which Rose would probably be a part—to explore the symptoms of depression and social isolation and consider various options. The team might well consider the potential use of the psychologist's suggestion as part of their decision making process but would be ill-advised to view the recommendation as a prescription or directive.

Consider another example. Jack, age 16, has been in foster family care for about two months. You serve as Jack's social worker and have responsibility for coordinating his care. He is making a reasonably good

adjustment. Jack's biological mother, whom he sees irregularly, promised to visit him over the weekend. On Thursday, she telephoned to say she would not be able to visit. On Friday, Jack skipped school. You wonder if Jack skipped school because of his disappointment about his mother's cancelled visit. You do not think that any disciplinary action is necessary. The foster parents, however, told Jack that he must spend all day Saturday in the house studying. As the social worker, how would you address the differences between your point of view and those of the foster parents—who are members of the natural helper team?

In this instance, we believe that the social worker should respect the foster parents' decision for several reasons. First, being grounded for a day and required to study does not seem an unreasonable response to skipping school. Second, the social worker and the team can generate alternative ways to address Jack's disappointment with his biological mother—without creating a power struggle between the worker and the foster parents. A team meeting might be used to develop an appropriate plan. It might also be a context for establishing a process by which the social worker and the foster parents might consult with each other about matters such as this in the future.

In your work with natural helper teams, remember to respect all members' knowledge, perspective, and expertise. Natural helpers often spend a great deal more time with clients than do professionals. Although it is difficult to quantify the various therapeutic factors, foster and adoptive parents often play an extremely powerful role in helping children in their care overcome various psychosocial difficulties. Indeed, their day-to-day involvement may be more meaningful to many children than the comparatively infrequent contact with professionals (Exhibit 16-5). The same may

EXHIBIT 16-5
Helping Foster and Adoptive Children

The Team Approach

There is often an unnecessary, irrelevant and counterproductive boundary between therapist, caseworkers and the family. Many traditional interventions focus in one of two directions: one, individual psychotherapy of the child with token consultation to the parents; and two, family therapy that has a "submerged" goal of smoking out problems in the parents or in their marriage. In the former case, the oft-times well-intended therapist unwittingly undermines the placement through efforts at forming an exclusive "special relationship" with the child. Involvement with the parents is reduced to informing them about the highlights of therapeutic progress. In the latter case (in family therapy), treatment is directed away from the problem child and onto the parents (foster/adoptive) as the core of the problem. With disturbed children such approaches are myopic and amount to a "prescription of failure." We have often heard, much to our chagrin, that psychotherapy was successful right up to the time that the placement failed—a failure in fact which is laid on the already hunched shoulders of the beleaguered parents.

Overanalyzing of the parents and solo treatment of the child are hazardous in the special situation of disturbed foster and adoptive children. Faced with the task of parenting and treating the formerly maltreated child, it is critical that all forces come together. The inherent differences and distrust that often underlie the relationships between and among the family, agencies and professionals must be put aside.

We have found that a therapeutic team comprised of mental health professional, family, caseworker and school personnel—all striving with unified goals—has great synergistic power. That is, their helping impact is greater than the sum of individual parts. In a collaborative approach, they are less apt to be "split" apart from each other by the child's attempts to ally with some and to reject others. The acknowledgement and support of members of the team can inflate deflated parents, offer support and advice, and, in a sense, inoculate them against "imported pathology."

The Family as Primary Agent of Change

There is not a school teacher, nor a therapist, nor a friendly neighbor, nor any other well-intended individual that can make the difference in the disturbed child's life the way his family can. (In many instances this is the foster and adoptive family. However, sometimes this may also involve the biological family, in situations where they are still an active part of the child's life.) While many individuals can have a positive place in the child's world, the changes each can make are at times secondary. It is the moment-by-moment, interaction-by-interaction, day-to-day struggles that primarily lead to the building of bonds, the mitigation of past injuries and abuses and the re-socialization of the child. Given the importance of the family—foster or adoptive— it is mandatory that they be supported, nurtured, respected and recognized for their primary role in treatment of the child.

Source: Delaney, R. T., & F. R. Kunstal. (1997). _Troubled transplants: Unconventional strategies for helping disturbed foster and adopted children_ (2nd ed.). Oklahoma City, OK: Wood 'N Barnes, pp. 66–67.

be said for child-care staff, volunteers, and clients' neighbors and family members. As a professional social worker, you may sometimes best help clients by offering support and assistance to the natural helpers. Frequently, these efforts naturally complement any direct intervention services you might provide.

◆ The Downside of Teamwork

Social workers must carefully weigh the risks and disadvantages as well as the potential benefits associated with teams and teamwork. Poorly functioning teams in which differences among professionals remain

---

EXHIBIT 16-6
The Sadistic Team Leader

- Schedules excessively long meetings regardless of the topic.
- Has no clear purpose.
- Has no bathroom breaks (best when combined with coffee).

- Schedules meetings for Friday afternoons or lunchtimes.

Source: Adams, S. (1996). *The Dilbert Principle.* New York: HarperCollins, pp. 222–223.

---

unresolved may be more destructive than constructive and may negatively affect clients (Huslage & Stein, 1985; Parker, 1987). Separate meetings among the conflicting parties or consultation with an experienced group worker or team leader may help to resolve legitimate differences. Occasionally, dissolution of a team and reconstitution of another may be needed. Exclusion of clients from team meetings represents a serious risk and raises questions about due process. We believe that social workers should ensure that clients are routinely invited to participate in team meetings. At a minimum, clients should be fully informed about the team meeting and have some means to provide input and offer feedback regarding decisions that might affect them.

Teamwork is also expensive. Imagine the hourly cost when several professionals meet to discuss a single case situation. Unless the proceedings occur in an efficient manner and yield productive outcomes, the cost-benefit ratio may make team meetings fiscally impractical (Poulin et al., 1994). For example, a case conference that involves five professionals meeting for two hours (not to mention travel time) consumes the equivalent of more than a full workday. This time might have otherwise been available to provide direct services to clients. During a field placement in a child protection agency in a rural county, a student observed that child protection teams—consisting of a social worker from social services, a police officer, a public health nurse, and a school official—spent more time talking among themselves than interacting with the family about the allegations of child abuse or neglect. Social workers should evaluate carefully whether the benefits of a team meeting justify the costs. Coordination of services, for example, may be more efficiently and effectively conducted by a case manager than by a team (Kane, 1982). Indeed, teamwork does not necessarily ensure more effective out-

comes (Schmitt, Farrell, & Heinemann, 1988). Some professional teams use meetings to meet their own needs, rather than those of clients (Sands et al., 1990). Some leaders and some members are unprepared or unwilling to work hard on team business. Some may use meetings to protect their professional turf, maintain the status quo, or avoid work. Conversing with colleagues is often easier than actually providing service to people struggling with social problems. Talking about problems—rather than doing something about them—is characteristic of many teams, committees, and other task-oriented groups. Indeed, some leaders use meetings to punish team members (see Exhibit 16-6).

◆ Chapter Summary

In this chapter, we explored teamwork as a means to help clients in problem solving. You may work with intragency teams, interagency teams, interdisciplinary teams, and teams with natural helpers and mutual aid groups. Seek to involve clients as direct participants in team decision making. At a minimum, inform clients about team meetings so that they have an opportunity to raise matters for discussion, provide input, and offer feedback regarding the outcomes of meetings.

Obstacles to effective teamwork include the misguided belief that a spirit of cooperation and good intentions are all that is required, a feeling of helplessness when the team includes a person of considerable power or authority, disputes about professional boundaries, and clashes between the values and assumptions of different professions. Competition among team members must be minimized if teams are to serve clients effectively. Divergent professional and agency cultures may negatively influence team process and reduce its effectiveness. Conversely, disproportionate loyalty to team decisions may limit your ability to serve as an effective client advocate.

Social workers often help coordinate natural helper teams. Natural helpers include foster parents, volunteers, clients' neighbors and friends, and mutual aid groups. View these helpers as potentially valuable resources rather than as competitors. As you do with applicants and clients, engage them as collaborative partners in problem-solving processes. In many cases, the natural helpers may function as primary service providers, while you provide them with support and assistance. Finally, recognize the potential risks and disadvantages of teamwork, including the harmful effects of dysfunctional teams, the relatively high costs, and the possibility that teams may exist to serve the needs of professionals rather than clients. Good quality case management service can sometimes accomplish the purposes for which a team might be created in a more efficient and effective manner.

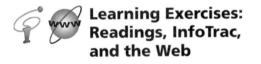

Learning Exercises: Readings, InfoTrac, and the Web

1. Use your word-processing computer program to enter the important terms and concepts presented in this chapter in alphabetical order. Place a question mark by any terms that you do not clearly understand. Save your document as EX 16-1.

2. Log on to the InfoTrac College Edition Web site. Conduct a keyword search (using either Keyword Search or Advanced Search) to locate the articles entitled "Interdisciplinary Teams in Health Care and Human Services Settings: Are They Effective?" (Schofield & Amodeo, 1999) and "Disagreements in Discharge Planning: A Normative Phenomenon" (Abramson et al., 1993). Carefully read the articles and prepare a two-page essay in which you share your reactions and discuss the implications of these articles for your approach to teamwork. Save your document as EX 16-2.

3. Go to your university library to locate the article "The Dance Beyond the Family System" by John V. Compher, which was published in the journal *Social Work* (1987). Read the article and prepare a one-page summary of the four dysfunctional patterns of interaction among agencies and social

workers that can interfere with effective service to families: (1) the blind system, in which agencies do not know what the other agencies are doing; (2) the conflicted system, characterized by battles between agencies that set up divergent goals for the client; (3) the rejecting system, in which agencies are focused on their own operational needs, rather than on clients' needs; and (4) the underdeveloped system, which can be strengthened by providing clients with careful, coordinated referrals. Save your document as EX 16-3.

4. Return to Exhibit 16-2: Reluctant Team Members. The vignette illustrates a problem in team performance. Prepare a one-page written plan in which you discuss how you would go about addressing and resolving the problem. Organize your plan according to the format for service agreements introduced earlier (see Exhibit 11-5 or Exhibit 15-2). Include a statement of the problem for work, at least one goal or objective, and an action plan. Save your document as EX 16-4.

5. Review the code of ethics of the National Association of Social Workers (available online at www.socialworkers.org) or the Canadian Association of Social Workers regarding participation on intra- and interdisciplinary teams. Prepare a one-page summary of your ethical obligations as a member of such teams. Save your document as EX 16-5.

6. Suppose that you serve as a member of a small interdisciplinary team in a child welfare agency. During a team meeting with a 13-year-old youth about to be placed in foster family care, another social worker said this to the teenager: "Part of my job is to make sure the foster parents do what they are supposed to." Write a brief reaction to the other worker's statement. Address these questions: What might lead a social worker to make such a remark? How do you think the teenager would experience the comment? How might such a statement affect team functioning? Save your document as EX 16-6.

7. Suppose that you serve as a professional member of a natural helper team sponsored by a child welfare agency. During a team meeting, one of the paraprofessional members said, "This foster parent reprocesses things two or three times, her phone calls are lengthy, and she rambles on. She

---

EXHIBIT 16-7
Occupational Trainees

In a Caribbean nation, young people, ages 16–25, can apply to a one-year occupational training program. Entrance is voluntary but, once accepted, the young people are expected to adhere to program rules. No trainee is allowed to leave the campus during school days between 8 A.M. and 5 P.M. unless there is a medical or domestic emergency at home. Any trainee wishing to go home for a weekend must apply by 4 P.M. Wednesday for a weekend pass. The application is to be made through the director of the residence hall to the social service department. While off campus, every trainee is expected to be in possession of a leave card, signed by the social worker. Only the social worker is authorized to grant leave.

However, many of the trainees attempt to manipulate the system. They go to the health services and pretend to be ill. The nurse then sends a permission slip to the social worker, who automatically issues passes. Some trainees pursue relationships with the nurse, so that she will regularly grant permission slips. Some trainees have sent telegrams to themselves reporting a death or sickness in the family, which they then use as a basis for requesting emergency leave. Others have sought to trick the gate guard into letting them come and go without passes.

Instead of applying for weekend passes on Wednesday, large numbers of trainees have begun to come into the office on Friday and pressured the social worker to grant weekend leaves. Some bring fraudulent letters from parents requesting permission to leave campus. If the social worker denies leave, trainees go to the nurse or the gate guard, or simply climb over the fence. Some trainees have forged the social worker's signature on leave passes.

---

tends to call during the evening even though there is not a specific crisis. During these discussions, I often feel emotionally exhausted." Prepare a brief response to these questions: What words would you use in responding to the paraprofessional helper? What is your rationale for responding in that way? How do you think the paraprofessional would react to your words? Save your document as EX 16-7.

8. Read the description contained in Exhibit 16-7. Prepare a one-page essay in which you formulate an assessment of the relationship of the trainees' behavior to patterns of staff interaction, and to agency policies and procedures. You may refer to ideas presented in John Compher's article. Suppose you worked as a social worker in this training center and called a general staff meeting to address this issue. Summarize what you might suggest to the staff as a way to respond to the trainees' behavior. Save your document as EX 16-8.

Chapter 17

Evaluating Practice

Evaluation is the final phase of the problem-solving process. Through this process, social workers and clients monitor service implementation and evaluate progress toward goal attainment. On the basis of the evaluation, clients and workers may redefine the problems for work, change the goals or objectives, adjust the service plan, or perhaps carry out the service plan in a different way.

Social workers and other helping professionals bear an ethical obligation to evaluate the effectiveness of the services they provide. We must determine if clients benefit from the service and whether goals and objectives are achieved. Importantly, we must remain alert to the possibility that our efforts may not have any favorable effect or could cause real harm. Unless social workers and clients engage in evaluation of goal attainment, we may not know the impact of our interventions. Evaluation processes also help us determine the relative cost of services in money, time, and other resources (Moore, 1995). In this chapter, we explore the following topics:

- Program and practice evaluations
- Practice research
- Unintended consequences
- Record keeping

◆ Program and Practice Evaluations

Program evaluation refers to efforts to determine the effectiveness or efficiency of various program services, such as counseling, case management, or foster family care. Practice evaluation is carried out by individ-

ual social workers and clients to determine the degree of progress, if any, toward resolution of identified problems and achievement of agreed-upon goals. The processes of program and practice evaluation approximate one another, although different terms may be used for analogous operations. There are three general stages or phases of program evaluation (Yegidis, Weinbach, & Morrison-Rodriguez, 1999).

- *Needs Assessment*—determining "by objective methods if a program being considered is really needed or if an existing program is still needed. Typically, a needs assessment defines the problem of concern, describes actual conditions and how they differ from what is desired, identifies unmet needs, and diagnoses the obstacles that might prevent a program from being effective in meeting them" (Yegidis, Weinbach, & Morrison-Rodriguez, 1999, p. 252).
- *Evaluating Program Implementation*—"securing data about whether a program is operational as planned and, if it is, how well it is operating. This form of program evaluation is referred to as *process evaluation* or, sometimes, *formative evaluation*" (Yegidis, Weinbach, & Morrison-Rodriguez, 1999, p. 253).
- *Evaluating Program Outcomes*—"determining whether a program actually achieved its objectives and accomplished what it was supposed to accomplish at a reasonable cost. Thus, this kind of evaluation often involves a dual-focused emphasis on program effectiveness (achievement of objectives) and program efficiency (the relationship of outcome to expenditure of efforts

and resources)" (Yegidis, Weinbach, & Morrison-Rodriguez, 1999, p. 255). This form of program evaluation may be termed *summative evaluation.*

Evaluation involves the application of research procedures to assess change processes and their outcomes. Program evaluation and practice evaluation reflect similar processes that are directed toward slightly different but overlapping targets. Both forms of evaluation involve attempts to determine the outcomes—or dependent variables—of programs or interventions. At the program level, social workers may assess the nature and impact of services such as child protection, family counseling, violence prevention, unwanted teen pregnancy reduction, HIV prevention, or community development. At the practice level, social workers attempt to determine the nature and outcomes of service to a particular client system.

An Evaluation Model

Some social workers find the specialized language used in the program evaluation literature somewhat difficult to understand. Although the terminology varies somewhat, we may adopt the same conceptual framework for either program or practice evaluation. Hudson and Grinnell (1989) offer a useful model (Exhibit 17-1). The structure of both program and practice evaluation involves four sets of variables: inputs, activities, outputs, and outcomes.

Inputs include the resources necessary to implement programs or interventions. At the program level, inputs may include money, equipment, space, personnel such as licensed social workers, and, of course, clients or customers for the service. At the client-worker level, inputs include time, expertise, and access to the information and resources required by the service plan.

At the program level, *activities* include the actions agencies take to produce change. Programs and services, such as intake interviewing, counseling, and referral represent programmatic activities. At the client-worker level, activities include those steps that social workers and clients take to implement service plans. Intervention processes are practice activities. From this perspective, activities correspond to the independent variables identified in research projects.

Outputs include those products that emerge from the programmatic or practice activities. In a sense, outputs are processed inputs. Outputs are often mea-sured by number of clients served, people contacted, materials distributed, or perhaps the number of hours worked. As such, output indicators do not reflect the value or benefit of the activities to service recipients.

Outcomes reflect the "benefits or changes for individuals or populations during or after participating in program activities. They are influenced by a program's outputs. Outcomes may relate to behavior, skills, knowledge, attitudes, values, condition, or other attributes. They are what participants know, think, or can do; or how they behave; or what their condition is, that is different following the program" (United Way of America, 1996, Introduction to outcome measurement, para. 7). Unlike outputs, outcomes refer to the effects of the services on consumers or perhaps the community at large. The difference between outputs and outcomes is not always clear. Outputs are generally stepping-stones to some further benefit, whereas outcomes provide the socially justifying reason for the intervention or program. Outcomes stand on their own and do not require further justification. For example, at the program level, an intervention designed to enhance employment among unemployed single parents with young children might successfully increase the number of low-cost, high-quality child-care facilities throughout the community. However, unless service activities actually lead to greater levels of employment among the single parents, enhanced child care alone may not constitute sufficient justification for the program.

The desired output or objective of the intervention plan outlined in Exhibit 15-2 is a decision by the client to proceed in one direction or another. A desired outcome might well be improvement in parent-child relations or stable living arrangements for the adolescent. Outputs and outcomes represent dependent variables or the desired effects of the program or practice. Occasionally, a variable might be both independent and dependent, depending on where it lies in the causal chain of events. For example, finding employment may be a dependent variable for an intervention. We hoped the service would help a client secure a job. However, getting the job also constitutes an independent variable in that it may also lead to increased self-support, financial security, optimism, and perhaps self-esteem. Bonita's decision (Exhibit 15-2) represents an outcome or dependent variable of the work undertaken with the social worker. However, the decision is also an independent variable that may influence Bonita and Richard's future.

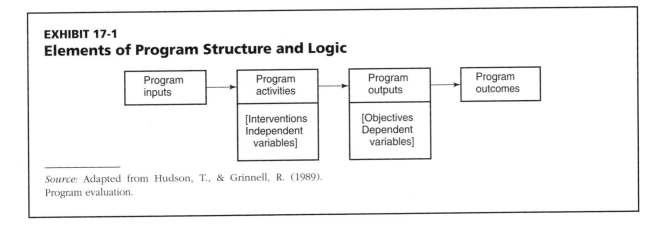

EXHIBIT 17-1
Elements of Program Structure and Logic

Source: Adapted from Hudson, T., & Grinnell, R. (1989). Program evaluation.

A Logic Model

A logic model usually binds the four key concepts of inputs, activities, outputs, and outcomes in the form of a graphic illustration. In effect, logic models are arguments (Hernandez, 2000; Renger & Titcomb, 2002). We may claim, for example, that (1) if inputs are provided, activities will occur; (2) if the activities occur, outputs will accrue; and (3) if the outputs accrue, desirable outcomes will result. For example, suppose a policy advocate asserts that providing subsidized day-care services for young children of working parents could dramatically reduce the number of persons on public assistance. Federal funding may be identified as a necessary resource (input) to finance the establishment of programs (activities) to provide day care for a certain number of children (output), which frees their parents to secure employment and graduate from public assistance programs (outcome). A complete logic model should explain how increased federal appropriations can expand the number of day-care facilities available for children of unemployed or underemployed, low-income parents that will, in turn, result in a reduction in the public assistance caseload. Such a logic model or argument might make sense to people interested in decreasing the number of people receiving public assistance or reducing the amount of money expended in such programs. Other people might anticipate other outcomes as well. For instance, some might expect that employment could contribute to greater optimism, enhanced parent-child relationships, improved living conditions, and a better quality of life. Still others might predict that reducing expenditures for public

assistance will effectively decrease the quality of life of low-income persons by eliminating access to subsidized medical care and social services.

As another example, intensive family intervention programs (activities or independent variables) may be promoted as a means of curtailing out-of-home placement of children and youth (output or dependent variable). Advocates may suggest that professionally trained social workers (inputs) are needed to carry out such programs. The logic model should explain why professionally trained social workers are necessary for intensive family intervention and how intensive family intervention will reduce out-of-home care. To be complete, the logic model should also establish a connection between the output (reduction of out-of-home care) and some socially justified outcome, such as enhancing the safety and life quality of children and youth, improving their prospects for a more secure future, or perhaps reducing the crime rate throughout the community.

A logic model involves a thesis or an argument that explains the connections. Many social policy and program proposals, and their corresponding evaluation designs, are essentially illogical or incomplete. Some fail to establish a rational linkage between the component parts of input, activity, output, and outcome. Others fail to include outcomes in the model, evidently assuming that outputs are sufficient justification for programs and services.

Summative evaluation processes attempt to determine the extent to which activities, programs, services, or interventions accomplish their goals and objectives. Formative evaluation efforts seek to improve the quality of activities—usually during the course of service delivery (Chen, 1996; Wholey, 1996). These two forms overlap and relate to two other approaches: (1) outcome evaluation and (2) process evaluation. Outcome evaluations attempt to identify the impact or results of some activity. They may go beyond assessment of goal achievement to include other effects as well. Process evaluations involve efforts to determine the specific nature of the activities, programs, services, and interventions. These may involve monitoring activities, quality control processes, fidelity checks, or perhaps attempts to determine the relative significance of various components or dimensions of the program or services.

Sophisticated efforts tend to incorporate both formative and summative kinds of evaluation. Determining goal achievement is an essential aspect but knowledge about how they are accomplished is also important. Similarly, beneficial or perhaps harmful effects of services might remain unknown unless evaluation efforts extend beyond assessment of goal attainment alone. Learning that certain goals are not achieved becomes more meaningful if we can identify which interventions fail to produce the desired outcomes. Suppose, for example, that you find a reduction in child abuse after a parent skills training program. You might celebrate and assert that a laudable goal has been accomplished. The finding is of little practical value, however, unless you clearly understand the nature of the training program that apparently led to the reduction in abuse. You cannot replicate the program and duplicate the positive outcomes unless you know what was done and how it was implemented. Furthermore, if you can establish a clear, specific, and replicable description of the program—perhaps in the form of a practice manual—you can then determine that replications reflect fidelity to the described program (Barkley, 1997; Halle, 1998).

Assisting with Program Evaluation

Practitioners commonly contribute in several ways to program evaluation within their agencies. You might participate in quality improvement initiatives by submitting aggregated data, participating in focus groups, or perhaps by formulating questions to be addressed through evaluation processes. Social workers sometimes serve as members of quality improvement teams or program evaluation committees, and some function as researchers to collate and analyze direct and indirect evidence of outcomes. Administrators, super-

visors, direct service providers, and clients can benefit enormously from the findings of well-designed program evaluations.

As various agency personnel participate in planning a particular program evaluation effort, different views of agency mission, goals, objectives, and outcomes may emerge. Indeed, people may hold divergent views about the general purpose of evaluation itself (Exhibit 17-2). Agencies that have yet to create or publish a clearly described mission statement that contains specific goals and objectives tend to reflect considerable confusion when attempting to undertake a program evaluation. In the absence of a shared mission and common goals, agencies may be uncertain about what actually constitutes a successful outcome.

Earlier, we discussed the ethical obligation to maintain familiarity with emerging theoretical and empirical knowledge related to the services we provide and the clients we serve. Such continuous professional learning contributes to social workers' knowledge about effective, ineffective, and potentially dangerous practices. Current familiarity with the professional research literature complements findings from your practice evaluations and from the agency's program evaluations. Ideally, these various forms of information contribute to the improved client satisfaction and service outcomes.

◆ Practice-Research

Evaluation as Client Service

In providing services to clients, social workers also function as researchers. As a helping professional, you must apply sound scientific methods to understand interventions and evaluate outcomes (Rosen, 1996). Social workers and clients should routinely attempt to answer questions such as these: What are our service goals (dependent variables)? What intervention activities (independent variables) should we undertake to pursue those goals? How can we determine if we are faithfully adhering to our planned intervention actions and accomplishing our agreed-upon goals (evaluation). Earlier, we referred to our professional and ethical obligations to contribute to the profession's knowledge base and adopt sound research processes in our efforts to evaluate the effectiveness of programs and practices. In effect, we must be competent researchers as well as proficient helpers. Indeed,

---

EXHIBIT 17-2
Differing Views About Objectives and Evaluation

Helping Families, Inc., is a small (eight professional staff plus a director) family service agency that provides family counseling, relationship counseling, individual counseling, and family life education services. The agency receives funds from the United Way, fees, and several service contracts. Recently, the United Way and the local welfare department, which purchases services from Helping Families, mandated that all agencies develop a plan for evaluation of their services. The evaluation plan must include procedures to determine if the agency is accomplishing its goals.

Helping Families has never formulated very clear outcome goals, other than its broad mission statement having to do with helping individuals and families cope with the strains of living. The agency has created a committee to address the evaluation mandate. A program evaluation researcher has been retained as a consultant and is helping the committee formulate objectives that are reasonably measurable. The committee members have strong views about evaluation:

Sally Dogooder, a social worker, is committed to helping clients. She doesn't think there is a need for evaluation and is concerned that the effort may

consume some of the already limited time available to serve clients.

Gene Helpinghand, also a social worker, is moderately favorable to evaluation. He agrees that the agency needs to develop a better understanding of what it is doing, both to provide information to the community and to improve the delivery of services. Gene is concerned about the basis for evaluation, however, and believes strongly that assisting clients to feel better is the primary mission of the agency.

I. M. Hardpressed, the harried executive of Helping Families, is frequently called on to defend the agency to the community and to justify expenditures. She wants to know if services are being delivered in the most efficient manner possible and is particularly interested in being able to document services and costs.

Francis Powerstructure, president of the board of Helping Families and a leading member of the business community, is interested in documenting that the agency is delivering a useful product and wants to know if the agency is providing the community with a worthwhile service.

---

research-based evaluation processes represent a fundamental aspect of professional social work practice. Meeting these obligations is complex and challenging (Elks & Kirkhart, 1993; Gerdes, Edmonds, Hoslam, & McCartney, 1996; Owens & Nease, 1993).

Efforts to assess outputs and outcomes may be premature unless we simultaneously engage in process evaluations directed toward determining the specific nature of interventions. The programs, practices, services, or interventions—the independent variables—require clear conceptualization. Studies of change activities are essential to the development of the profession's knowledge base and often serve as a prerequisite to formative and summative evaluations. To determine effectiveness, we need to answer a series of questions about the program activity or practice intervention:

- What do we hope to accomplish? What are the goals or objectives for the program or intervention? Clarity about goals and objectives is essential for any evaluation.
- What population is expected to benefit from the service? The client or targeted beneficiaries may be individuals, families, groups, organizations, neighborhoods, communities, or even larger aggregations.
- What components of the program or intervention are necessary to accomplish the goals or objectives for the client or targeted beneficiaries? The description should include specification of all relevant program or intervention components.
- How do the components of the program or intervention fit together? Do some need to precede others? Are some concurrent? Step-by-step

descriptions and sequential flow charts help illustrate the relationships among the various parts and often reveal linkages between discrete activities and goals or objectives.

■ What theoretical, logical, and empirical evidence supports the thesis that the intervention activities are likely to result in goal accomplishment? Programs and practices reflect hypotheses that a particular action will yield a certain outcome. Evaluation processes test these hypotheses to determine if they actually produce the anticipated results.

For example, consider the senior citizens who hope to increase public safety in their neighborhood. They would like to take afternoon and evening strolls and visit friends. However, they feel insecure because of concern about muggings and purse snatchings. As a step toward realizing the goal of increased public safety, they identify as an objective the assignment of at least one pair of police officers to conduct foot patrols of the neighborhood from 3 to 11 P.M. each day. The seniors then develop an intervention plan to accomplish the objective. The first action step of their plan is to request the police chief's support for the notion of a foot patrol. Their second step is to petition the city council for additional neighborhood resources. They must bring two kinds of pressure to bear—factual and political—to influence the chief and the city council. The seniors need to assemble facts concerning the number of crimes against seniors in the neighborhood and determine the extent to which seniors' activities are limited by fear of street crime. Even with that knowledge, they may need to mobilize a show of political support if they are to get the city council's attention. After considerable brainstorming and planning, the seniors may develop an intervention plan similar to the one outlined in Exhibit 17-3. This simplified flow chart indicates the various components (activities or independent variables) of the intervention plan and their relationship with each other and the objectives. They may also incorporate a plan to monitor completion of each component task or activity. Collection of such process information should enable the group to determine what went wrong if the plan to influence the police chief and the city council proves unsuccessful.

The plan, of course, could be fully implemented as planned but still fail to produce the desired outcomes. If so, the seniors may decide that the plan itself was

not appropriate. They could then consider alternative plans and strategies. For instance, they might work to unseat some city council members or form coalitions with other organizations to bring additional political pressure to bear.

This example also illustrates the distinction between outputs and outcomes, and goals and objectives. The output or objective of the intervention is the assignment of a team of foot-patrol officers to the neighborhood. The desired outcome or goal is a reduction in crime against senior citizens. We hypothesize that accomplishing the objective will contribute to goal attainment. However, we cannot be certain unless we evaluate both outputs and outcomes.

Fidelity Checking

Fidelity checking represents a form of process evaluation that addresses a key question: Is the program activity or service plan being implemented as designed? An increasing number of research studies yield information about the effectiveness of policies, programs, services, and practice models. Earlier, we noted that social workers bear an ethical obligation to remain current with such findings and apply that knowledge in service to clients. However, if social workers implement a policy, program, or practice in an inconsistent manner that does not conform to the evidence-based guidelines, it is likely to be less successful than it was in the research studies. In other words, the implementation lacks fidelity.

The same principles apply to service plans individually negotiated between social workers and clients. In such cases, we establish fidelity by attempting to determine the degree to which what actually occurs conforms to what was planned. We evaluate whether the participants did what they agreed to do in the way they indicated they would. In other words, we attempt to determine the degree of adherence to the service plan.

Social work practice often involves exploring whether—and if so, how—the agreed-upon service plan was carried out. Clients and social workers may or may not follow through with their commitments. For example, a fidelity check of the intervention plan outlined in Exhibit 17-3 might reveal that Committee A did not collect the necessary evidence or did not do so in a timely fashion. The intervention described in Exhibit 15-2 may not have occurred because the worker was unable to schedule a second visit with

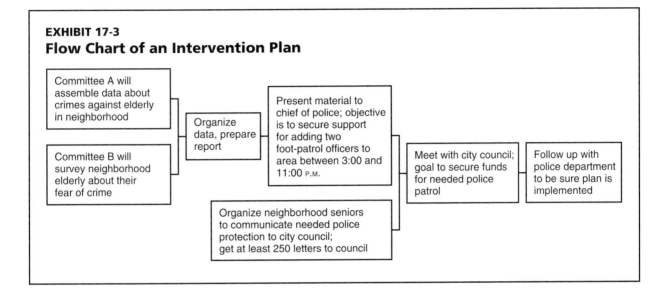

EXHIBIT 17-3
Flow Chart of an Intervention Plan

Bonita. If the evaluation reveals that the plan has not been implemented as scheduled, decisions about how to proceed must be made.

Consider the example of 16-year-old Ron. He broke into a small owner-operated business and caused nearly $500 in damages. As part of the service plan, Ron and the social worker, Mr. Garcia, agreed to meet with the victim to negotiate a way of making amends (Exhibit 17-4). Mr. Garcia followed through on his part of the plan by contacting the victim. He learned that the victim is willing to meet with Ron and scheduled a meeting. Mr. Garcia informed Ron by telephone who agreed to the meeting time and place. Ron, however, failed to meet with Mr. Garcia to prepare for negotiation and did not attend the meeting with the victim. The plan was not implemented as agreed.

What do we do? Fidelity checks provide data that may lead you to accept responsibility for your failure to meet your commitments or to engage clients in an exploration of what prevented them from fulfilling theirs. Confrontation is a specialized skill that social workers may use to address discrepancies between statements and actions. Exhibit 17-5 contains guidelines for confrontation. Essentially, you gently but firmly draw attention to the discrepancy between words and actions. You do not express anger or make any type of judgment about the client. Confrontation involves an observation conveyed in a matter of fact manner that leads to discussion. Once the discrepancy has been noted and explored, you involve the client

in a problem-solving process to resolve the issues that led to the failure to fulfill the commitment.

When Ron failed to attend the scheduled meeting with the store owner, Mr. Garcia contacted Ron and made arrangements to visit him the next evening. On that occasion, the following conversation ensued:

Garcia: Ron, I'd like to discuss what happened that prevented you from meeting with Mr. Higby.
Ron: OK.
Garcia: Ron, you said you would make the meeting but you didn't. What happened?
Ron: I don't know, I just didn't make it. [Silence.]
Garcia: You didn't make the meeting and you don't know why?
Ron: Yeah. I kind of forgot about it.
Garcia: Ron, I wonder if you might be uncomfortable or embarrassed about talking with Mr. Higby?
Ron: Not really, I can handle it.
Garcia: What do you mean by "I can handle it?"
Ron: I can meet with the guy.
Garcia: Ron, we can ask Mr. Higby if he is willing to set another meeting. I'm not sure he will agree, but we can try. However, before we do, let's estimate the likelihood that you would attend the meeting if we can arrange it. What do you think the chances are that you'd get there this time?
Ron: I'll make it this time.

EXHIBIT 17-4
A Service Plan for Ron

Date: January 20.

Problem:

Ron has committed a burglary and has been told by the judge that he will be expected to make restitution to the victim.

Objective:

To develop and present to the court a restitution plan that is acceptable to both the victim and Ron.

Service Plan:

What is to be done?	By whom?	When?
1. Meet with Mr. Higby (victim) to determine if he is willing to meet with Ron to work out a restitution plan. Try to secure his agreement to meet.	1. Mr. Garcia (social worker)	1. February 1
2. Telephone Ron to let him know results of meeting with Mr. Higby and to schedule meetings 3 and 4.	2. Mr. Garcia	2. February 2
3. Meet at office to prepare for meeting with Mr. Higby.	3. Ron and Mr. Garcia	3. February 7
4. Meet with Mr. Higby to develop restitution plan; Mr. Garcia to serve as mediator.	4. Ron and Mr. Garcia	4. February 15
5. Present restitution plan to judge at disposition hearing.	5. Ron, with assistance from Mr. Garcia as needed	5. February 20

EXHIBIT 17-5
Guidelines for Confrontation

1. The purpose of confrontation is to point out a discrepancy between a verbal commitment and behavior and to engage clients in addressing the implications of the discrepancy.
2. Confrontation is not an expression of worker anger or frustration.
3. Confrontation relates to specific behavior and involves descriptive rather than inferential language.
4. Limit confrontation to the behavioral discrepancy; do not make any judgments about the person.
5. Do not offer answers or explanations for the discrepancy.
6. Explore—and, whenever possible, use—clients' solutions to the discrepancy as the basis for reinstituting or revising the plan.

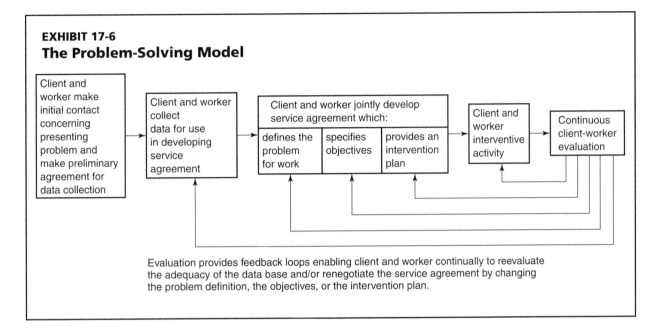

EXHIBIT 17-6
The Problem-Solving Model

Client and worker make initial contact concerning presenting problem and make preliminary agreement for data collection → Client and worker collect data for use in developing service agreement → Client and worker jointly develop service agreement which: defines the problem for work | specifies objectives | provides an intervention plan → Client and worker interventive activity → Continuous client-worker evaluation

Evaluation provides feedback loops enabling client and worker continually to reevaluate the adequacy of the data base and/or renegotiate the service agreement by changing the problem definition, the objectives, or the intervention plan.

This led to some further exploration about what might happen during the meeting, how Ron handles himself in unpleasant situations, and how he might ask to make restitution in this situation. Mr. Garcia helped Ron prepare for the meeting, which was rescheduled for the following week. Ron attended that meeting, made a formal apology, and offered to make amends. He and Mr. Higby developed a plan for Ron to provide 45 hours of labor to the business as payment for the damages.

This case illustrates some important elements of confrontation. The worker did not ignore or minimize the situation. Mr. Garcia addressed it in a direct and matter-of-fact manner by focusing on the specific behavior rather than on Ron's character. The discrepancy became the focus of exploration, which, in turn, led to the development of a plan, a new commitment, and renewed motivation to meet with Mr. Higby.

Evaluation as a Continuous Process

Evaluation of services produces a flow of data for ongoing reassessment of goals and objectives, intervention plans, and even problem definitions. Before you can institute evaluation processes, you need a clear conceptual picture of the intervention activities, an understanding of how they would lead to the chosen goals or objectives, and how progress could be mea-

sured. Evaluation generates feedback data that are so essential to the problem-solving process. The information enables social workers and clients to assess the nature and effects of the process (Exhibit 17-6). The data may reveal a need to redefine a problem for work, reconsider goals or objectives, modify the intervention plan, or perhaps, even adjust the evaluation processes and procedures. The evaluation feedback loops encourage a systemic, dynamic, and interactive view of the problem-solving process. However, changes to the service agreement that arise from evaluation data must be negotiated with clients and require their full understanding and consent. Changes cannot be made unilaterally.

Clear specification of goals or objectives and identification of measurement procedures are prerequisites for evaluation. Without them, progress evaluation is impossible.

Goal Attainment Scaling

Operational specification of concrete goals or objectives and identification of means to assess progress toward their achievement can be challenging. Goal attainment scaling (GAS) was developed to facilitate evaluation of patient progress in mental health programs (Kiresuk & Sherman, 1968; Kiresuk & Garwick, 1974; Kiresuk & Lund, 1977; Kiresuk, Smith, & Cardillo,

---

EXHIBIT 17-7
Goal Attainment Follow-Up Grid

Program using goal attainment scaling _____	Date of scale construction _____ Follow-up date _____			
Levels of predicted attainments	**Scale headings and scale weights**			
	scale 1 ($w_1 =$)	scale 2 ($w_2 =$)	scale 3 ($w_3 =$)	scale 4 ($w_4 =$)
Most unfavorable results thought likely				
Less than expected success				
Expected level of success				
More than expected success				
Most favorable results thought likely				

1994). However, the GAS procedures may be used in any situation that involves goal setting. They are well suited for practice in child welfare, hospitals, the criminal justice system, and other service settings (Fleuridas, Leigh, Rosenthal, & Leigh, 1990; Karr, 1990). Indeed, they may be used to assess student progress toward learning goals or evaluate agency progress toward organizational objectives. Goal attainment scaling is particularly useful for social work because it permits individualized goals or objectives. Social workers and clients identify and work toward goals individually tailored to particular situations. Predetermined or standardized objectives are not imposed

The GAS procedures, however, measure the extent of goal or objective attainment. They do not reflect the importance or priority of the objectives, nor do they determine the intervention methods. The grid used in goal attainment scaling (Exhibit 17-7) provides for the development of scales and time frames for accomplishing each goal or objective. The scales reflect five possible levels or categories of attainment. The categorical levels range from the most unfavorable on one end of the continuum to the most favorable result on the other. The expected result appears at the midpoint of each scale.

At least one scale should be identified and developed for each objective. Each scale is labeled and follow-up dates are established to indicate the expected amount of progress by that time. The most unfavorable, most favorable, less than expected, and

more than expected results at follow-up are also recorded. Specification of the five levels must be objective enough to permit reliable scoring. Quantification is desirable but not absolutely essential. Ensure that each scale is both exhaustive and mutually exclusive. In other words, the scale levels should account for all outcome possibilities, and none of the five levels should overlap.

Once developed, the scales may be set aside until the designated follow-up date. At that point, the worker and client use them to rate the amount of progress toward goal attainment. Kiresuk and Garwick (1974) present a formula for calculating an overall goal attainment scale score and discuss procedures for weighting scales when some reflect greater importance than others. Exhibit 17-8 illustrates a set of goal attainment scales that might be used in conjunction with service to Mrs. B and Jimmy (see Exhibit 11-10).

Single-System Designs

Evaluation of service to a single client system involves a sample of one. We refer to this form of research as a single-system design to distinguish it from research designs that involve one or more groups of participants (Barlow & Hersen, 1984; Berlin, 1983; Blythe, 1995; Blythe & Tripodi, 1989; Garcia & Floyd, 1999; Grinnell, 1997; Ruckdeschel & Farris, 1981; Thyer, 1993; Tripodi, 1994, 2002; Tripodi & Epstein, 1980). Single-system designs may be identified by other terms, such as time-

EXHIBIT 17-8
Goal Attainment Follow-up Grid: Case Example

Program using GAS ___Intercity Head Start___

Client ___Mrs. B___

Date of scale construction ___August 1___

Follow-up date ___September 1___

Levels of predicted attainments	Scale headings and scale weights			
	Scale 1: Relation to Jimmy ($w_1 = 3$)	Scale 2: Relation to Loneliness ($w_2 = 2$)	Scale 3: Return to Clinic ($w_3 = 1$)	Scale 4 ($w_4 = $)
Most unfavorable results thought likely	Mrs. B reports angrily yelling at Jimmy daily or more often during last week in August.	No action or discussion of Mrs. B's loneliness.	No action or discussion about returning to clinic.	
Less than expected success	Mrs. B reports angrily yelling at Jimmy more than three times but less than daily during last week in August.	Mrs. B discusses her loneliness but cannot make plans to deal with it.	Mrs. B is discussing her reaction to the clinic but has not formulated plans to return.	
Expected level of success	Mrs. B reports angrily yelling at Jimmy no more than three times during last week in August.	Mrs. B is discussing her loneliness and making plans to join a group.	Mrs. B has discussed her reaction to the clinic and plans to secure a return appointment.	
More than expected sucess	Mrs. B has discontinued angrily yelling at Jimmy but has not discovered another way to discipline him.	Mrs. B has initiated contacts with a group.	Mrs. B has telephoned the clinic for a return appointment.	
Most favorable results thought likely	Above, and Mrs. B is using another form of discipline before becoming angry with Jimmy.	Mrs. B has attended one group meeting.	Mrs. B has been to the clinic for a return appointment.	

series, $N = 1$, single case, ideographic, or single-subject research. They differ from case studies because of the systematic nature of the evaluation process. Case studies tend to capture the conceptual content and interactive flow or process between the worker and client in the form of a narrative that typically excludes formal measurement or evaluation of progress toward goal attainment (Blythe, 1995).

Contemporary application of single-system designs varies according to their purposes. For example, a client and worker might be primarily interested in evaluating progress toward goal achievement. They might adopt a design that involves formal assessment at three points in the process: (1) pre-intervention, (2) post-intervention, and (3) follow-up. Assessment tools might include goal attainment scaling, self-reports, or perhaps one or more standard measures. Improved scores from pre- to post-intervention reflect progress toward goal achievement. If the follow-up scores—conducted some time after the conclusion of service—remain at or close to the post-intervention levels, then we have evidence that progress was maintained. This process serves the worker and client well—for the purpose of evaluating overall progress toward goal achievement. Professionals who understand basic principles of research, however, might quickly point out that such a design fails to control for several threats to validity. We could not conclude that the intervention itself resulted in the favorable outcomes. The three-point, time-series design cannot determine causality. We can only establish an association or correlation between the intervention and progress as indicated by improved scores on the various measures. Nonetheless, both the worker and the client may be quite satisfied with the results. Furthermore, the findings are much more likely to represent an accurate indication of actual progress than would be the case if the worker and client adopted an informal, nonsystematic, and impressionistic review of progress at the conclusion of their work together.

Other forms of single-system research control for several threats to validity and reliability and help determine a causal linkage between interventions and outcomes. For example, "multiple-baseline design, natural withdrawal reversal design, or intensity designs" (Tripodi, 2002, p. 751) may be used for that purpose. However, these single-system designs are usually more appropriate in applied research settings rather than in agency-based practice. In day-to-day service to individuals, families, groups, organizations, and communities, most social workers find the three-point time-series design serves them and their clients quite well.

◆ Unintended Consequences

Practice and program evaluations usually focus on the degree to which we achieve our goals and objectives. We tend to focus on goal accomplishment. In emphasizing outcomes, however, we sometimes neglect to look for the unintended and perhaps harmful consequences of our programs and practices. Sieber (1981) argues that social intervention may have unintended consequences. *Side effects* result from the intervention but have no direct bearing on the problem itself. For example, in medicine, some chemotherapies for cancer may cause hair loss, dizziness, nausea, or other reactions that do not relate directly to the cancer itself. Side effects may be classified as positive, neutral, or negative.

Some side effects may benefit the client, although they do not directly address the problem for work. Earlier, for example, we discussed a possible service plan for the Birky family (see Reading 6) that might include helping them to organize their neighbors politically, with the goal of covering the ditch in which their son died. Possible positive side effects from such a plan might be an expansion of the Birkys' informal support system.

Regressive effects have a direct bearing on the identified problem but contribute to a worsening rather than an improvement in the condition. They represent an unintended, negative consequence. For example, young people at risk of delinquent or criminal behavior may participate in programs such as "Scared Straight" that include scheduled visits to prisons and conversation with adult prisoners. Proponents believe that first-hand exposure to the inmates and prison life deters future antisocial behavior. Unfortunately, the research does not appear to support this view. In a systematic review and meta-analysis of nine randomized or quasi-randomized research trials, reviewers concluded, "Programmes like 'Scared Straight' are likely to have a harmful effect and increase delinquency relative to doing nothing at all to the same youths. Given these results, agencies that permit such programmes must rigorously evaluate them not only to ensure that they are doing what they purport to do (prevent crime)—but at the very least they do not cause more harm than good" (Petrosino, Turpin-Petrosino, & Buehler, 2003, Abstract section, para. 7).

Single-session psychological debriefing services are commonly offered to persons possibly affected by potentially traumatic events such as school shootings, natural disasters, youth suicides, and terrorist acts. Based on an assumption that immediate intervention reduces the likelihood of posttraumatic stress disorder, service providers are unquestionably motivated by good intentions. Unfortunately, the research evidence does not currently support the effectiveness of single-session psychological debriefing services. In a systematic review of 11 randomized research studies, reviewers found, "Single session individual debriefing did not reduce psychological distress nor prevent the onset of post traumatic stress disorder (PTSD). . . . There was also no evidence that debriefing reduced general psychological morbidity, depression or anxiety" (Rose, Bisson, & Wessely, 2003, Abstract section, paras. 6–7). Rose and colleagues concluded, "There is no current evidence that psychological debriefing is a useful treatment for the prevention of post traumatic stress disorder after traumatic incidents. Compulsory debriefing of victims of trauma should cease" (Rose et al., 2003, Abstract section, paras. 8).

Future studies may, of course, provide additional information and clarification about services such as "Scared Straight" and single-session psychological debriefings. However, studies such as Petrosino et al. (2003) and Rose et al. (2003) highlight the importance of considering unintended, negative consequences in our service to others. Social workers routinely deal with vulnerable people under severe distress. We discuss intimate details of clients' lives and circumstances and intrude within their social systems. Such activities involve a potential for harm as well as benefit (Burr & Christensen, 1992; Durst, 1992; Howitt, 1993; McNulty & Wardle, 1994). We must acknowledge this possibility and take reasonable steps to prevent regressive effects. Genuine collaborative partnerships with clients and critical thought help us anticipate potential consequences. Clients' active participation in decision making reduces the risk of taking actions that may have harmful effects.

◆ Record Keeping

Keeping records is, of course, a professional responsibility. It also represents an important client service. Records contain data that support decisions made and actions taken. Records are necessary to evaluate practice, to document that services have been provided (Corcoran & Gingerich, 1994; Gelman, 1992), to provide data for program evaluation, and to provide information needed to ensure accountability.

Tebb (see Reading 10) describes an intriguing form of record keeping in which clients participate in writing the case record. This creative approach furthers the important notion of partnership. Even when clients participate in the process, however, social workers are responsible for ensuring that records are accurate, complete, and prepared in a timely fashion. Exhibit 17-9 contains an overview of the topic of social work recording. Although some social workers experience record keeping as an onerous chore, we urge you to consider it as a fundamental part of practice that contributes to the quality of service provided to clients. Record keeping often helps professionals reflect on and critically think about their processes and practices. And, of course, by reviewing records before meetings with clients, you can refresh your recollections and focus on the work at hand. Clients tend to value social workers who remember their names and circumstances and recall what's gone on before.

We encourage you to take recording as seriously as other parts of your practice. Here are some guidelines:

- Keep your records up to date. It is much easier to keep records current than to try to catch up after you have fallen behind.
- Record all contacts whether they occur via telephone, letter, email, or face-to-face. At a minimum, track the date, time, and place or form of the contact and the names of the participants.
- Keep your records factual and descriptive. Base the records on your observations and the statements of clients or others involved in the service. Distinguish reported from observed information. Routinely use phrases such as "the client said," "the client reported," or "I observed."
- If you form opinions or hypotheses, reach conclusions, or offer recommendations, identify them as such through phrases such as "In my opinion," "I wonder if," "I conclude," or "I recommend." Personal opinions and conclusions that lack supporting evidence should not be included as part of the record. Avoid nonessential adjectives and vague terms such as *uncooperative, euphoric, bizarre, resistant,* or *stubborn.*
- Keep your records as short as possible but do not leave out any crucial information.
- Record any agreements made by you or your client that require follow-up.
- Be sure your recording relates to the purpose at hand.

The format used to organize data should be logical and coherent. Most agencies adopt a particular recording structure for their professional employees. Many have adopted computerized forms of record keeping so that social workers may type information directly into a database (Modai & Rabinowitz, 1993).

Recording can also be a useful tool for professional development. Process recording (Graybeal & Rulf, 1995) represents an effort to capture the exchanges between a social worker and client. The social worker prepares a written recollection of who said or did what in a transcript-like fashion. On the basis of process recordings, a supervisor, instructor, or consultant can help identify practice strengths and weaknesses and recommend ways to improve service quality. At one time, process recordings were based exclusively on workers' recollections. In contemporary practice, however, direct observation and electronic (video or audio) recording are now also widespread. Process recording

EXHIBIT 17-9
Social Work Recording

Why Keep Records?

In all contacts with clients, their families, and community resources, it is necessary to record what took place so that (1) the worker remembers what happened; (2) other people may know; (3) service program and objectives may be reviewed; and (4) teaching and learning may occur. Thus, records are for use.

What Goes into a Record?

A case record—the account of what the social worker did in a particular situation—should fit the needs of the case. The purpose of the recording should determine its length and scope, and what is written should meet the interests of its intended readers. Good recording is based on factual reporting, good thinking, and sound evaluative judgment. The social worker is not a journalist but might apply the fundamental journalistic questions: What? Who? Where? When? How? Why? The last of these is the most difficult; heed the researcher's dictum not to go beyond data—that is, to support any speculations with at least some relevant facts.

The Forms of Recording

There are three major forms of recording: (1) narrative; (2) summary; and (3) assessment and evaluative.

Narrative

Narrative recording—sometimes known as process recording—is used when it is necessary to report as many facts as you can remember—for example, in a critical situation or transaction that others, including a supervisor or a psychiatrist, need all the information possible to evaluate it. A narrative recording of an interview may also be used in order to make sense of the interaction and to better understand the associated dynamics. Narrative recordings can be useful tools for learning, especially early in the worker's career.

However, they will waste the worker's time, the secretary's time, and the supervisor's time if done routinely, mechanically, and without a specific purpose. Thus, narrative recording in social work practice should be used sparingly. Workers may sometimes find it helpful to record an interview in narrative form, so as to become more aware of the interaction. For most ongoing treatment, though, summary recording is preferred.

Summary

There are several types of summary recordings:

1. Intake summaries succinctly state what brought the client to the agency, including the nature of the presenting problem and what is asked of the agency. Agencies usually provide an outline to guide the worker in this phase. A complete biography or family chronology is not necessary in the first interview. However, a foundation for future work with the client should be laid, with a focus on the problem and what can be done about it.

2. Discharge summaries put the discharge plan in writing, so that there can be no misunderstanding about the situation and about what interventions are planned for the future. The discharge summary should be geared to the future prospects of the case and should spell out at least some of the factors that led to the discharge plan.

3. Transfer or closing summaries state why a case was closed or transferred, review briefly what was accomplished, and say what remains to be done by the client, with or without further help. The nature of the closing contract—how it was fulfilled and what the client's understanding is—should be specified. In all discharge, transfer, or closing summaries, it is necessary to summarize what went on during the social work contact, why the case was closed, and what the closing or transfer arrangements were.

4. A block summary encapsulates all the contacts over a period of time. How often such block summaries should be done—especially in periods when there is little contact or little change in a situation—depends on the nature

(continues)

EXHIBIT 17-9
Social Work Recording *(continued)*

of the case. Allowing months to go by without recording client contacts may create the erroneous impression that a case situation has been completely dormant. To minimize time-consuming narrative recordings, block recordings can be interspersed with narratives of particularly important transactions.

Assessment and Evaluative Statements

In a sense, all recordings contain elements of judgment, perception, and applications of knowledge; accordingly, all recordings, except transcriptions from tapes, are impressionistic in one way or another. To introduce adjectives and adverbs is to make evaluative comments. This is all to the good,

but you must provide evidence for your thinking. It is often helpful to include a brief paragraph of impressionistic assessment at the end of a particular recording. Clinical diagnosis is not necessary, but there is no reason why the worker cannot state an informed opinion.

Basically, recordings, whatever their form, should at some point convey the worker's impression of how the client looks, feels, thinks, and acts. Inclusion of the worker's own reaction to the client is also appropriate.

Source: John Goldmeier, Professor, School of Social Work and Community Planning, University of Maryland.

---

may be required in your field practicum experiences. Following graduation, you may find them useful as part of an ongoing supervision or consultation process. Of course, if you decide to make an electronic record of meetings with clients, you need to secure their permission.

◆ Chapter Summary

As a social worker, your evaluation efforts proceed on two levels. In your work with clients, you continuously evaluate progress toward achievement of the agreed-upon goals as outlined in the service agreement and remain alert to the possibility of unintended, negative effects. As an agency professional, you also routinely contribute to program evaluation initiatives that provide information about the effectiveness of various services. Both practice and program evaluation efforts require an explicit statement of goals and a clear, precise description of the interventions and services.

Client progress may be evaluated through several means, including rapid assessment instruments (Corcoran & Fischer, 2000a, 2000b; Hudson, 1982) and goal attainment scaling (Kiresuk & Sherman, 1968; Kiresuk & Garwick, 1974; Kiresuk & Lund, 1977; Kiresuk et al., 1994). Careful record keeping represents a

fundamental professional responsibility. Case records hold data necessary for evaluation, for practitioner and agency accountability, and as tools for professional development.

Learning Exercises: Readings, InfoTrac, and the Web

1. Use your word-processing computer program to enter the important terms and concepts presented in this chapter in alphabetical order. Place a question mark by any terms that you do not clearly understand. Save your document as EX 17-1.

2. Review the code of ethics of the National Association of Social Workers (available online at http://www.socialworkers.org) or the Canadian Association of Social Workers regarding our obligations to evaluate our policies, programs, and practice, and to base our services on professional empirical knowledge. Prepare a one-page summary of your ethical obligations for evaluation. Save your document as EX 17-2.

3. Go to your university library to locate the articles "Do No Harm: Policy Options that Meet Human Needs" (McKnight, 1989) and "A Practical

Approach to Program Evaluation (Lee & Sampson, 1990). Read the McKnight article and prepare a one-page essay about how public policies that intend to produce positive benefits may actually have serious unintended negative consequences. Explore the implications of basing policy and practice decisions on the basis of good intentions. Read the Lee and Sampson article and prepare another one-page essay about how you might incorporate program evaluation to reduce the likelihood of harm. Save your document as EX 17-3.

4. Log on to the InfoTrac College Edition Web site. Conduct a keyword search (using either Keyword Search or Advanced Search) to locate the articles entitled "Evaluating Practice: Assessment of the Therapeutic Process" (Baer, 2001) and "Using Single System Design for Student Self-Assessment: A Method for Enhancing Practice and Integrating Curriculum" (Garcia & Floyd, 1999). Read the articles and prepare a two-page essay in which you reflect on their implications for social work practice evaluation. Save your document as EX 17-4.

5. Log on to the InfoTrac College Edition Web site. Conduct a keyword search (using either Keyword Search or Advanced Search) to locate the article entitled "Instituting an Outcomes Assessment Effort: Lessons from the Field" (Mecca, Rivera, & Esposito, 2000). Read the article and prepare a one-page essay in which you reflect on its implications for social work practice evaluation. Save your document as EX 17-5.

6. Turn to **Reading 23: Does My Intervention Make a Difference? Single System Research.** In this article, Robert Weinbach introduces single case designs as a tool for practice evaluation and argues it is compatible with good social work practice. As an illustration, he applies this design to the evaluation of a group program for pediatric diabetes clients who need to reduce their sugar intake. After reviewing the reading, reflect on its implications for topics specifically addressed in this chapter and for social work practice in general. Explore your observations and reactions in a one-page essay. Save your document as EX 17-6.

7. Turn to **Reading 26: Leonard Timms** and **Reading 27: The Omar Family.** Review the case studies and reflect on the evaluation processes and procedures used by the social worker in providing services to Leonard Timms and his family and the Omar family, respectively. Explore your observations and reactions in a one-page essay. Save your document as EX 17-7.

8. Arrange to interview an executive of a local social service agency—perhaps where you are undertaking or have completed a field placement—to learn about the ways that programs, services, and practices are evaluated to determine their safety and effectiveness. Prepare a one-page essay in which you summarize the agency's philosophy, purpose, and approach to program and practice evaluation. In your summary, discuss how evidence about what does or does not work has affected agency policies, programs, or practices. Save your document as EX 17-8.

9. Goal attainment scaling procedures can be used in any situation where objectives are set; thus, goal attainment scaling can be learned without actually working with clients. Prepare a one-page outline in which you (1) set personal learning objectives for yourself and (2) develop a set of goal attainment scales to measure the extent to which you accomplish your objectives. Save your document as EX 17-9.

Chapter 18

Endings in Social Work

Many social workers find that concluding a working relationship with a client is one of the most difficult aspects of the problem-solving process. In this chapter, we consider the following:

- Types of endings
- Client reactions
- Preparing clients for endings
- Endings as learning experiences
- Worker reactions to endings

◆ Types of Endings

Endings may occur in various ways and circumstances. They may occur when the service agreement has been satisfactorily completed and the client no longer requires continuing services. Sometimes a social worker and client may conclude that nothing more can be done, even though the goals have not been fully realized. Clients sometimes end the relationship because they are relocating to another area or for various personal reasons. Occasionally, clients decline to continue because of dissatisfaction with the service or because they decide the costs exceed the potential benefits. Sometimes, the relationship ends because a social worker leaves the agency or assumes different duties. Under such circumstances, clients are typically transferred to another worker within the agency.

Section 1.16 of the NASW Code of Ethics (National Association of Social Workers, 1999) contains several passages that relate to termination of services. One principle requires social workers to conclude profes-sional services to clients "when such services and relationships are no longer required or no longer serve the clients' needs or interests" (Section 1.16.a). "Social workers should take reasonable steps to avoid abandoning clients who are still in need of services. Social workers should withdraw services precipitously only under unusual circumstances, giving careful consideration to all factors in the situation and taking care to minimize possible adverse effects. Social workers should assist in making appropriate arrangements for continuation of services when necessary" (Section 1.16.b). "Social workers who anticipate the termination or interruption of services to clients should notify clients promptly and seek the transfer, referral, or continuation of services in relation to the clients' needs and preferences" (Section 1.16.e), and those "leaving an employment setting should inform clients of appropriate options for the continuation of services and of the benefits and risks of the options" (Section 1.16.f). In general, the code suggests that social workers are responsible for informing clients about and preparing them for the ending process, and assisting them with any reactions they might experience.

◆ Client Reactions

Clients may react to the conclusion of a helping relationship in various ways. Many conclude the work with a great deal of satisfaction, a sense of achievement, and feelings of gratitude toward the worker. Some experience few feelings, having approached the service in a business-like fashion. Others, however, may do any of the following:

- Deny or minimize the reality and behave as if the ending will not actually occur
- Reintroduce previously resolved problems
- Experience a "relapse" into earlier problematic behavior patterns
- Angrily assert that they cannot possibly manage without the worker's continued help
- Feel guilty that they did not work as hard as they could have or progress as far as they hoped
- Precipitously discontinue service or miss appointments—perhaps in an indirect expression of anger or an attempt to avoid feelings associated with the ending process.

Occasionally, clients may feel deserted, abandoned, or perhaps betrayed. Some may conclude that you do not really care about them. Clients who have experienced major losses or rejections in personal or familial relationship may become quite emotional. This ending may evoke some of the accumulated pain of prior separations. Of course, the intensity of the reactions depends partly on the nature of the working relationship. For example, suppose a social worker is reassigned to other duties and must transfer leadership responsibilities for a task-centered group working toward community change. The group members may be concerned about the competence and expertise of the new worker. In such circumstances, feelings of loss and separation may be secondary to the motivation to achieve the agreed-upon goals.

Endings sometimes provoke unexpectedly strong reactions. Notice the reactions of several adolescent girls to the conclusion of a five-session group experience as described in Exhibit 18-1.

Consider this example. A worker informed his client, Sal, that he was leaving the agency in six weeks. He promised to introduce Sal to the new probation officer and help them to get started together. Sal, an adolescent with a long history of theft and assault, had never experienced a trusting relationship with anyone until he met the worker. Over the year they worked together, Sal made remarkable progress. He had not re-offended at all during that time. Therefore, the worker was surprised to hear that Sal had stolen a car and resisted arrest when apprehended. When the two met, Sal greeted the worker by saying, "Now you can't leave. I'm in a new mess and you can't leave until you go to court with me and get me straightened out again."

◆ Preparing Clients for Endings

Social workers should discuss anticipated service endings well in advance of the termination date (Northen, 1969; Philip, 1994). Sometimes referred to as "pointing-out endings" (Shulman, 1992), social workers identify or remind clients about the forthcoming conclusion of their work together. Some service agreements are open-ended in nature. Although they do not include a precise termination date, they usually reflect an understanding that the relationship will end following achievement of agreed-upon goals. Other service agreements are time-limited. A specific number of sessions or an ending date is part of the agreement. For example, a family may agree to participate in meetings with a social worker for eight sessions or a communications skills group might be scheduled to meet on six consecutive Tuesday evenings. Endings are less hurtful and destructive when there is time for client and worker to deal with their reactions. In the case of transfers, the time provides an opportunity for new workers to become involved in an orderly manner—perhaps through a few joint meetings where both the outgoing and the incoming worker meet with the client.

Encourage clients to participate with you in planning the steps to the ending process—whatever form that ending might take. Invite clients to discuss their feelings about termination and help them prepare for the transition. Clients may sometimes be ready to terminate before the social worker is ready to let them end. Exhibit 18-2 contains a discussion of common issues associated with group termination.

When services are successful in helping clients accomplish agreed-upon goals, termination usually follows. In such cases, both clients and workers tend to experience a sense of pride and accomplishment (Fortune, Pearlingi, & Rochelle, 1991, 1992). A brief ending or "graduation" ceremony may facilitate the process of marking the conclusion of important work.

When clients choose to discontinue because of dissatisfaction with agency services or lack of progress, openly discuss the situation. When possible, encourage exploration of other means to pursue outstanding goals. Leave the door open for clients to return when they require assistance in the future. Clients who leave the agency when their work is finished should also be made aware that they can initiate future contact. Many individuals and families need social services on an intermittent basis.

EXHIBIT 18-1
Should the Group End?

The Let's-Talk-About-It group was composed of five adolescent girls, all on probation. The girls were selected for the group because they appeared to be shy, somewhat withdrawn, and lacking in social skills. The group leader was an outgoing, knowledgeable, yet sensitive volunteer with the probation agency. Each girl had discussed the group with her probation officer, and with the volunteer group worker, before the first group meeting. The group volunteer worker had also had a joint meeting with all the girls and their parents to arrive at a contract for the group.

The purpose of the group was to improve the girls' social skills, including their ability to communicate. The group agreed to meet for five sessions. At the first meeting, after a period of initial nervousness and giggling, the girls showed excellent ability to become part of a group, to enter into discussions, and to plan. One girl, the 17-year-old, quickly established herself as a spokesperson for the group and at one point in the first meeting expressed her feelings, as well as the temperature of the group, by saying, "We all feel a little tongue-tied and have to have time to think that over." Later, when she heard a tape-recording of a portion of the previous week's meeting, she remarked with a smile that she hadn't realized she talked so much.

They chose to have a hair stylist talk to them in the second meeting, and a modeling instructor in the fourth meeting, leaving the third and fifth meetings open for general discussion and to plan a group social event. Initially, the girls seemed uninterested in the social event. However, we soon learned that their relative silence did not mean disinterest. In fact, several of the girls asked their probation officers to suggest ideas about possible activities so they could help plan the social event. They were interested but afraid to come across as ignorant or naïve.

During the course of the five weekly meetings, they engaged in active discussions of issues such as whether to drop out of school, what to do when a boy asks them out and they want to go but are too shy to say yes, and whether adults can ever really help kids who are in trouble. A question such as, "Has anything happened since last week that anyone would like to talk about?" was enough to get the discussion started. The girls made good use of the discussions as evident by comments such as, "Maybe now we won't be so scared," as well as in their improved ability to communicate in the group meetings and in individual interviews.

The termination of the group provided both professional staff and volunteers with some insight and learning. None of the girls appeared for the fifth and final meeting. All but one did, however, contact the group worker by phone or in person. One girl arrived 20 minutes after the scheduled meeting time and explained that she had missed her bus. Another girl phoned to explain that she was ill and that her sister, also a member of the group, would miss the meeting because she had to stay after school. A fourth girl arrived 45 minutes later with her boyfriend, and explained that she was delayed and therefore could not attend the meeting. The fifth girl, reached later by phone, explained her absence by saying she had to stay after school and explained her failure to call in by saying she had been unable to use the phone at school.

The next day, one of the sisters phoned the group worker at home to say that she and her sister wondered if they really had to end the group meetings. She was told that this could be discussed at the rescheduled final session.

During a meeting with probation agency staff, the group worker hypothesized that the difficulties with the fifth session might well suggest that the girls were reluctant to conclude the experience. She offered to lead several more group sessions with the girls, if the probation staff decided it would be a good idea.

EXHIBIT 18-2
Ending a Group

The purposeful nature of social work implies that from time to time it is necessary to assess the desirability of continuing the group. One criterion for termination is that progress toward the achievement of goals has been sufficient and further help is not necessary, so the group should be terminated. In addition to the achievement of specific goals, there should be an expectation that the members will be able to function without the group but will use appropriate resources in the community for meeting their needs. Workers have anticipated termination from the beginning of their work with a group and have clarified with the members its possible duration, so that the goals and the means of achieving them have been related to plans for both individuals and the group.

When the members have made little progress and there seems to be little potential for changing the situation, the service may need to be terminated. But every effort should be made then to find a more suitable form of service for the members. There are times, too, when entropy takes over; the group disintegrates owing to the loss of members or unresolvable problems in the relationships between the members or in the group's structure and processes. In such instances, the social work goals have not been achieved. If it is too late for the worker to help the members to work through the problems, then there is no choice but to terminate the group. (pp. 408–409)

As the group moves toward readiness for termination, the . . . members exhibit anxiety about separation and ambivalence about the loss of relationships with the social worker and other members. They mobilize their defenses against facing termination. Although they accept each other, there is a movement toward the breaking of interpersonal ties as members find satisfaction in relationships outside the group. . . . Some members may feel ready to terminate before the time set for the group; others may want to drop out owing to insecurity, feeling they have been left behind by members who have made more rapid progress. The structure tends to become more flexible, for example, by the giving up of official roles within the membership or by changes in time, place, and frequency of meetings. . . . Group controls are lessened, and an increase in inner controls occurs on the part of the members. Cohesiveness weakens as the members begin to find satisfactions and new relationships outside the group. (p. 399)

The need for termination should be discussed in advance of the termination date to allow sufficient time to make of it a positive experience for the members. . . . The time span between the initial information about termination and the final meeting of the group will vary with many factors, including the group's purpose, the length of time the group has been together, the problems and progress of the members, their anticipated reactions to termination, and the press of the environment on them. (p. 412)

Source: Northen, H., & Kurland, R. (2001). *Social work with groups* (3rd ed.). New York: Columbia University Press.

In helping to prepare clients for endings, consider these guidelines:

- Incorporate within the service agreement an ending point or a description of the process by which the decision about ending will occur.
- Point-out and discuss endings well in advance of the termination point—even when an ending date is included within the service agreement.
- When ending occurs by transfer, introduce the client to the new worker before the ending. Invite the incoming worker to at least one joint meeting with you and the client.
- Help clients cope with their reactions to the end of the helping relationship.

◆ Endings as Learning Experiences

Planning for endings often provides an opportunity for personal growth and development (Siebold, 1991, 1992). Clients may experience the anticipated ending with some degree of distress. They may react with previously established coping strategies—some of which may relate to the agreed-upon problems for work. The ending process offers an opportunity to review the reactions and consider alternative ways to deal with stressors of various kinds.

Remember Sal, the youngster who stole another car in a misguided effort to avoid losing his worker? In talking with Sal, a social worker might explore the possibility that previous offenses may have partly involved attempts to retaliate against others or to control unwanted situations. The worker might engage Sal in assessing the effectiveness of the reactive strategy in helping him to accomplish his goals. They might be able to identify alternate ways to handle disappointment and distress that would have fewer unpleasant consequences for him or others. Reviewing the reactions and considering other options might serve as a learning experience for Sal and contribute to his growth and development.

The teenagers described in Exhibit 18-1 may be engaged in a similar fashion. The social worker might help them consider how often they use avoidance behavior as a means to handle distress or frustration. They might examine the use and effectiveness of that reaction and consider alternate strategies. The worker might help them to practice talking about and sharing their sense of loss. In this instance, the girls had a very positive experience with the group. The worker would also encourage expression about their sense of progress and satisfaction. In addition, the worker might meet with the clients and their probation officers and help them identify other groups in the community that could offer a similar experience.

◆ Worker Reactions to Endings

Endings are often difficult for social workers. After all, you are also concluding a meaningful relationship. You may well experience a sense of loss and sadness. Other feelings may emerge as well. For example, you may feel that you could have done a better job or might have provided better service if you had more time. You may worry about the client. When a client discontinues service because of dissatisfaction, you may feel guilty, concerned about your competence, or perhaps frustrated with the client. In the case of transfers, you may wonder if the incoming worker will care as much or provide as high quality services. If you are leaving the agency, you may experience painful feelings of separation. You may be so anxious about the demands of a new job that you do not give the process of transfer your full attention.

Termination may stir complex and conflicting feelings, emotions about yourself, your professional competence, and your clients. You may feel pleased about clients' progress while experiencing a sense of loss and perhaps grief. Endings with valued clients may lead you to consider establishing a different kind of relationship—perhaps a social relationship or a friendship. Several ethical principles pertain to this issue. For example, the NASW code indicates, "Social workers should not terminate services to pursue a social, financial, or sexual relationship with a client" (NASW, 1999, Section 1.16.d) and "should not engage in dual or multiple relationships with clients or former clients in which there is a risk of exploitation or potential harm to the client" (Section 1.06.c).

Worker-initiated contacts with former clients are seldom helpful. Professional relationships should not be converted to personal or social relationships. However, you should feel free to greet and speak briefly with former clients that you might see on the street or in a social setting. Say hello and exchange a few words, especially if the client acknowledges you. You may occasionally receive an invitation to a former client's college graduation or wedding. You are not obligated to attend such functions but you may do so as long as the former client initiates the invitation and you do not use the occasion to establish a longer-term social relationship.

Transfers may also pose problems for clients' new workers, who may wonder whether they can adequately replace their predecessors. As a result, they may become hesitant to meet with transferred clients or perhaps feel a special determination to prove themselves. Some workers may move too rapidly with advice and suggestions. During the transition period, clients may still have mixed feelings about the transfer and retain some loyalty to their former workers. Some clients may need to settle into the relationship before they are willing to move forward again. When clients anticipate that a newly assigned worker may be temporary, their trust for the agency and its workers may decrease. Clients may be reluctant to establish a relationship with another professional who could also leave. New workers must recognize clients' understandable feelings and take time to address and resolve them.

◆ Chapter Summary

Endings occur when services are complete, when you leave the agency or assume different responsibilities, or when you refer a client to another agency that can provide needed assistance. Most people find it difficult to conclude significant relationships. Clients are no different. Anticipate that many clients will experience various psychosocial reactions associated with the sense of loss. Clients may develop new problems, express anger or sadness, or avoid you by missing appointments.

You have a responsibility to prepare clients for endings. When providing a time-limited service, identify the anticipated ending date during the beginning phase of work. If the time frame for service is unclear at the onset of service, briefly outline the process by which an ending point may be determined. If you are transferring a case, inform the client as soon as you become aware of the pending change. Remind clients several sessions in advance of the expected ending, and plan to use one or two of your final sessions for review and evaluation. Prepare clients for transfer or referral by introducing them to the new worker and, when possible, arranging for a joint meeting so that both social workers and the client may review progress and identify areas for further work.

Explore and discuss clients' reactions to the ending process and, if appropriate, help them to cope. Clients often react to termination by resorting to their usual mechanisms for coping with stress. You may be able to help clients identify and consider other ways of handling their feelings or to reinforce other work you have undertaken. Through such explorations, endings may represent a learning and growth enhancing experience for clients. A modest closing ceremony may facilitate the ending process, especially when the objectives of the service plan have been accomplished.

Endings may also be difficult for social workers. Attend to and take responsibility for your own feelings. You may feel sadness, regret, or numerous other complex feelings—similar in nature to those that many clients experience. At times, you may be tempted to establish a personal or social relationship, perhaps motivated partly by your own unresolved feelings. Worker-initiated contacts with former clients are usually unwise, although you may accept invitations to special events such as graduations or weddings and engage in brief conversations when you have chance

meetings on the street or in the grocery store. However, resist temptations to initiate a continuing social relationship.

Finally, recognize that clients and social workers may begin and end with each other several times over time. Clients frequently address and resolve one problem only to have another issue emerge some months or years later. Former clients routinely make contact with agencies and social workers who have helped them in the past. Ensure that clients feel free to return to the agency if they require future assistance. Like health services, social work services may be an ongoing resource in many clients' lives.

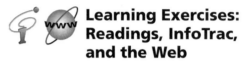

Learning Exercises: Readings, InfoTrac, and the Web

1. Use your word-processing computer program to enter the important terms and concepts presented in this chapter in alphabetical order. Place a question mark by any terms that you do not clearly understand. Save your document as EX 18-1.

2. Log on to the InfoTrac College Edition Web site. Conduct a keyword search (using either Keyword Search or Advanced Search) to locate the articles entitled "Ending Clinical Relationships with People with Schizophrenia" (Walsh & Meyersohn, 2001) and "Correlates of Recommended Aftercare Service Use After Intensive Family Preservation Services" (Staudt, 2000). Read the articles and prepare a two-page essay in which you reflect on their implications for ending processes in social work practice. Save your document as EX 18-2.

3. Turn to **Reading 24: Termination in Context.** Review this article, in which Howard Hess and Peg McCartt Hess provide a context for understanding termination. They note that even though endings often prompt denial and avoidance by both clients and social workers, endings also offer an opportunity to build a bridge between the service provided and the client's subsequent problem-solving activities. Prepare a one-page essay to explore your observations and reactions. Be sure to summarize the authors' suggestions for effective endings. Save your document as EX 18-3.

4. Turn again to **Reading 7: The Stover Family.** Prepare a brief, one-page reaction paper in which you address the following questions: How much time elapsed between the worker's suggestion that Mrs. Stover's case be closed and the actual closing of the case? What do you think was accomplished by engaging the client in an evaluation of what had been accomplished? What did the worker do to preserve the gains that Mrs. Stover had made? Save your document as EX 18-4.

5. Turn again to **Reading 9: Betty Smith.** Prepare a brief, one-page reaction paper in which you address the following questions: How was the process of ending in the Betty Smith case different from that for Mrs. Stover? Which ending do you think is less helpful for the client? Why do you think so? What would you do differently? Save your document as EX 18-5.

6. Turn to **Reading 26: Leonard Timms.** Prepare a brief, one-page reaction paper in which you address the following questions: How was the ending in the Timms case handled? What would you do differently? Save your document as EX 18-6.

7. Turn to **Reading 27: The Omar Family.** Prepare a brief, one-page reaction paper in which you address the following questions: How was the ending in the Omar case handled? What would you do differently? Save your document as EX 18-7.

8. Refer to Exhibit 18-1: Suppose you were the social worker responsible for supervising the volunteer group leader. Prepare a brief, one-page reaction paper in which you address the following questions: How might you respond to the problems associated with the ending process? Would you extend the group or let it end as scheduled? Why would you do so? Save your document as EX 18-8.

9. Suppose that you have served as a social worker for Sara, age 35, who recently moved to the area to be near her aging mother. For three months, you have supported her decision to place her mother in a nursing home and worked with her to minimize her feelings of grief, loss, and guilt. You are now preparing to terminate the professional relationship. Prepare a brief, one-page reaction paper in which you address the following questions: What would you say to Sara if she asks if you can be friends, especially because she has no friends or family in the area, now that you're completing your professional work together? What is the rationale for your response? What ethical principles from the NASW or CASW code of ethics guide your decision making? Save your document as EX 18-9.

Chapter 19

Self-Care

Social work is an extraordinarily rewarding profession. Assisting others in their efforts to overcome obstacles, resolve problems, and achieve goals tends to satisfy our fundamental human needs for purpose and meaning. Although social workers are unlikely to become rich in monetary terms, many of us become wealthy in other ways. We become richer each time we participate with clients in their often-heroic journeys. Social work involves work of substance. In a sense, it is holy work—worthy of respect and reverence.

Social workers face enormous challenges in our efforts to serve others. We need a sophisticated knowledge base and advanced expertise. We also require an insatiable appetite for personal and professional growth. Given the complexity and interdependence of human beings and the demands associated with problem solving, the learning requirements for effective practice are large and ever changing.

Most social workers seem to find practice both stimulating and satisfying. We hope you care deeply about your clients, stand with them as they address problems and pursue goals, and respect their wisdom and courage as they do so. We urge you to appreciate the often-powerful influences of the social and physical environment on human experience—both for your clients and for yourself.

At times, you will almost certainly experience stress and tension, ambiguity and confusion, frustration, disappointment, and conflicts of various kinds. They accompany professional service. Accordingly, you must find ways to recognize and address them. As Jones (1993) points out, the way professionals respond to stress and conflict partially determines whether the impact is positive or negative. Some social workers

are stimulated by the challenges; others become distressed and, over time, experience personal and professional burnout.

In this chapter, we explore the following dimensions of self-care:

- Stress and distress
- Self-awareness
- Control issues
- Social support

◆ Stress and Distress

Research about stress and its effects has occurred from several different perspectives. In his early animal experiments, Selye focused on the physiological reactions to demands on the organism (1946, 1950). Holmes and Rahe investigated the relative stress of various life events that significantly affect people (1967). Some researchers emphasize the psychological aspects of human stress (Endler, 1980), whereas others address its interactional nature and consider situational, psychosocial, and physiological factors (Selye, 1980; Spielberger, 1979; Weiman, 1977).

Social workers often use the term *stress* to refer to something unpleasant and undesirable. Despite that connotation, stress is not necessarily negative. Indeed, some stress is probably essential for optimal biopsychosocial functioning. Moderate stress seems to enhance motivation, promote concentration and quality of thought, enhance stamina, and improve performance. The extremes of either low-stress or high-stress are probably associated with negative effects

(Weiman, 1977). Selye recognized four categories of stress: (1) overstress (hyperstress), (2) understress (hypostress), (3) good stress (eustress), and (4) bad stress (distress) (Selye, 1980). As social workers, our task is often to strike a balance between overstress and understress while reducing distress and maximizing eustress—both for our clients and ourselves.

Social workers who suffer from burnout often proceed from mild stress to extreme distress through a series of stages. The first stage involves a more or less natural stress response in which the worker experiences increased energy and activity, and a sense of excitement. The professional work seems interesting, stimulating, and significant. Many social workers become most aware of this natural stress reaction when they intervene in a crisis situation or serve others in emotionally charged circumstances. When this moderate form of stress occurs periodically, workers tend to experience it as positive. However, if the stress is continuous, extreme, or both, it may have negative effects.

The second stage involves a transition from stress to distress. Social workers at this level may begin to experience uneasiness, worry, loss of energy, diminished motivation and energy, impairment in memory and concentration, and often physical symptoms such as frequent headaches or stomach upsets. Job performance and relationships with colleagues may also be affected partly because of greater irritability and fatigue. Service to clients may also suffer as lapses in professional responsibility and mistakes of judgment increase. Many workers begin to isolate themselves from colleagues and sometimes friends. Signs of distress at this stage are recognizable to the self-aware social worker. Others, however, may minimize or deny the indicators, perhaps hoping that they will diminish over time.

The third stage reflects major distress that becomes increasingly obvious to friends, family members, and professional colleagues. Clients often notice signs as well. Seriously impaired memory and concentration, sleep disturbances, apathy, extreme anxiety or significant depression along with stress-related physical illnesses tend to accompany this stage. Maladaptive efforts to cope through alcohol or drug usage may become more apparent. The quality of work often drops substantially. Required meetings may be ignored, paperwork may be neglected, and other fundamental responsibilities completed in a haphazard, incomplete, or otherwise unprofessional manner. Increased egocentrism and decreased empathy sometimes lead to conflicted family and collegial relationships. Encoun-

ters with clients may also become strained. In this stage of distress, many social workers become confused about their personal and professional goals and plans. Some adopt a detached, disinterested, and fundamentally cynical approach to their work whereas others voluntarily or involuntarily change jobs or leave the profession altogether.

The fourth and final stage of distress often involves a serious breakdown in personal and professional functioning. Some social workers suffer severe physical or psychiatric illness—often requiring hospitalization. Others exhibit bizarre behavior, reach odd and illogical conclusions, or adopt strange beliefs. Serious impairment prevents completion of basic professional tasks, commonly resulting in an enforced leave of absence or perhaps discharge from employment.

In efforts to establish an optimal balance of stress within the context of the challenging world of social service, social workers must recognize relevant factors within our person-and-environmental contexts. You should consider (1) stressors within your external world, (2) the way you interpret and appraise those stressors, (3) your coping and adaptation strategies, and (4) relevant external assets and resources. Cournoyer proposed a formula for personal and professional distress (PPD) among social workers: PPD = fPS (I × WC × WS × OS) × (CS + ER). Within the context of this formula, PPD is a "function (f) of the dynamic interaction of perceived stressors (PS) within the individual (I), in the context of work with client systems (WC), in the work setting (WS), and in other social systems (OS). The severity of the distress may be moderated by those coping skills (CS) and external resources (ER) available to the worker" (1988, p. 261).

Perceived individual stressors (I) include those that exist within the person of the social worker. They may be biological, psychological, emotional, practical, or moral in nature. Certain traits, characteristics, and personal styles may be involved. For example, social workers who reflect a "Type A" personality may be at greater risk of perceived stress than are those who are less driven (Freidman & Rosenman, 1974), those who over-identify with clients (Maslach, 1976, 1978, 1982; Maslach, Schaufeli, & Leiter, 2001), and those who have yet to come to terms with traumatic personal experiences (Freudenberger, 1974; Freudenberger & North, 1985).

Perceived stressors involved in direct service to clients (WC) include threatening words and actions directed toward the social worker, exposure to potentially or actually violent situations, legal actions and court hearings, emergencies of various kinds, sudden terminations with clients, removal of children from unsafe situations, conflicting roles and competing demands, and responsibility for decisions that directly affect people's lives (Barrett & McKelvey, 1980). Perceived stressors in the work setting (WS) include loud or crowded office conditions, arbitrary or discriminatory administrative policies, incompetent management or supervision, inadequate salary and low status, poor collegial relationships, and excessive caseloads (Barrett & McKelvey, 1980). Perceived stressors in other social systems (OS) include major life changes, family and household difficulties, legal or financial problems, conflicts with friends or neighbors, and inadequate social support network (Holmes & Rahe, 1967; McCubbin & Figley, 1983).

Coping skills (CS) help moderate the negative effects of perceived stressors. Among a vast array of coping strategies that social workers might adopt include positive self-talk and imagery (Burns, 1980; Lazarus, 1984), breathing exercises, meditation, deep muscular relaxation (Jacobson, 1970), vigorous exercise, creative hobbies and recreation, and adequate nutrition (Berger, 1985). Like coping skills, external resources (ER) can also mediate perceived stressors. Such resources include a safe and comfortable living environment, adequate financial reserves, practice relevant knowledge, social recognition, and social support from diverse sources.

◆ Self-Awareness

Earlier, we discussed how social workers require self-awareness to serve others effectively. Self-awareness also represents a critical aspect of professional self-care. You must cultivate both self-knowledge and self-acceptance to recognize what you can accomplish and accept what you cannot. You need to recognize your particular vulnerabilities and identify ways to address them. Feeling empathy for clients is essential, but you may lose your sense of objectivity if you over-identify (Koeske & Kelly, 1995). Over-identification and other forms of counter-transference are more likely when you serve clients who remind you of yourself or another significant person in your life, or who describe problems that you have personally experienced.

Some social workers hold extremely low expectations for themselves whereas others adopt excessively high standards. Expecting too little or demanding too much of ourselves or others often contributes to distress. Minimal expectations tend to be associated with low quality performance and limited productivity that eventually causes problems for clients and the agency. Disproportionately high expectations may initially yield high quality results but, over time, generate distress and perhaps burnout.

A philosophical sense of perspective and the ability to forgive yourself and others are needed to deal with the inevitable frustrations, mistakes, and disappointments. Adopt a person-in-environment perspective in your own life—just as you do with clients. When you become stressed, identify it as a problem to be addressed through the problem-solving process. Enlist a trusted colleague or perhaps consult with another professional to address the issue. Treat personal and professional distress as a problem to understand and resolve. We must notice, identify, and examine our cognitive, emotional, and behavioral reactions that involve our professional responsibilities—especially those that affect clients. If you blame yourself for mistakes, or feel shame and guilt for inappropriate thoughts and feelings, try to shift to a problem-solving perspective. Analyze the interaction, assess the problem, and attempt to resolve it. If you become irritated at a client's behavior, consider whether it results from your particular attitudes and expectations, or whether it might be the kind of response most people would have. If your reaction derives from your own issues, address them—perhaps through conversations with a colleague or supervisor. If it seems to be the kind of response that people in general would have, your reaction may represent information that could help the client become more aware of the effect of the behavior on others.

Self-awareness requires a thorough examination of your expectations for yourself, your clients, and the outcomes of your work. Problems that clients confront are usually the result of complex biopsychosocial interactions, some of which may have occurred in the distant past. Even the most expert social workers cannot undo the past, remake lives, or perform magic. Sometimes we must help clients accept reality, seek and give forgiveness, and find satisfying ways to live the lives they now have.

Consider the amount of time that the worker invested in efforts to serve Mrs. Stover (Reading 7). Although Mrs. Stover did not directly express her appreciation to the worker, she was very aware of change, and the school noted significant changes in the children's behavior. This evidence suggests that the service benefited Mrs. Stover and her children and helped them address the problems of concern. If, however, you expect clients to like and value you or to express gratitude and appreciation for your efforts, you may set yourself up for disappointment. Distinguish your personal from your professional needs. Try to find satisfaction in the process and outcomes of your work with clients rather than from their affection and approval. Do not build your whole life around your profession. Meet your personal needs and wants in your personal life. If you do not have a personal life—get one immediately! You must have relationships and interests outside of work. Some social workers become so invested in work that their entire sense of meaning in life derives from interaction with their clients and colleagues. Develop relationships, supports, and pleasurable activities unrelated to your professional work as well. Creative hobbies, arts, civic activities, various forms of recreation, or neighborhood groups contribute to the development of a support system with persons outside your agency and help divert your attention from the immediate stresses of work.

If you invest everything into your professional life, you may eventually lose a sense of balance and perspective. At some point, you may begin to resent your clients and your work when the primary source of distress is the absence of a satisfying personal life.

◆ Control Issues

The urge to control is a common motivation among social workers. Many of us seek to "fix problems," "remedy wrongs," or perhaps even "guide people toward the right path." Although most social workers do not usually have a great deal of social status or monetary wealth, we often have enormous power within the context of our professional service. Clients turn to social workers for help. The special trust they often feel for us, along with our access to agency and community resources and our professional knowledge and expertise, leave us in a potentially controlling position. If you believe you know "the right" solution to a problem, you may be strongly tempted to use your power to control clients' decisions and

behavior. If you were to do so, however, you would assume moral responsibility for them and their lives—much as a parent who decides for and directs the actions of a child. Indeed, there are certain occasions when helping professionals must assume parent-like responsibility for others. For example, when someone is intoxicated, suicidal, psychotic, violent, or at risk of serious, imminent harm, we cannot ignore our duty to care and protect. However, these are usually relatively rare occurrences—often involving life-threatening emergencies of some kind.

In general, assuming responsibility for and control of others violates the principles of collaboration and partnership, diminishes clients' power, and leaves social workers at risk of personal and professional distress. Attempts to control other people are likely to leave you emotionally exhausted, burdened, and perhaps even cynical about human beings who "don't do what they should." As a knowledgeable, ethical professional you may—and indeed should—share information, offer guidance and suggestions, and propose various intervention approaches that are consistent with the agreed-upon service agreement. However, do so in a manner that encourages clients to consider alternate perspectives and weigh the likely implications and consequences of various courses of action for themselves, for significant others, and for the achievement of their goals.

Control can take subtle forms. Unnecessarily "doing for" clients, for example, may be an indirect form of control that can deprive them of opportunities to experience themselves as competent and effective. Excessively intense services, especially if unwanted by the client, may also represent a form of control. Knowledge can be used to control clients rather than used as a resource to help them reach agreed-upon goals. Furthermore, efforts to regulate and control clients often leads to frustration and failure. Other strategies tend to be much more effective (Miller & Rollnick, 1991, 2002; Rollnick, 2002; Rollnick & Miller, 1995).

A written statement of the agreed-upon problems, goals, and plans helps social workers maintain focus and perspective. As a social work professional, your purpose is to help people address and solve problems in living. Do not try to "fix" or "transform" them into an image that you might prefer. Rather, attend to the identified problems and goals, and be alert to clients' strength, potential, growth, and achievement. Help them examine and celebrate gains. Indeed, clients may be aware of positive changes about which you are unaware. Unless you explore, you may never know. Ask clients about their pleasurable activities, their successes and satisfactions, and their progress toward goals.

◆ Social Support

A sense of personal well-being (Koeske & Kirk, 1995) and a sustaining social support system (Himle, Jayaratne, & Thyness, 1991; Koeske & Koeske, 1989, 1993) help social workers withstand the stresses of this challenging work. Regular, informal group meetings with colleagues provide an opportunity for workers to talk about the complex thoughts and feelings associated with social work practice. They may share their successes and failures, give and receive advice and support, and participate in a sense of common purpose and connection. An increasing number of social workers establish "journal clubs" where they read and discuss recent findings from practice relevant research studies, and consider their implications for their current programs and practices. Others participate in "practice effectiveness networks" through which nomothetic and ideographic evidence of best practices are disseminated, analyzed, and applied. Groups of this kind help social workers manage the challenges of this extraordinarily difficult work and simultaneously improve the quality of their service. Social support of various kinds represents a natural and obvious means for us to buffer the stresses of our professional work.

Historical accounts of social work and biographies of famous social workers may help you develop a broader and longer view of the profession. Familiarity with the circumstances, lives, and struggles of those who have gone before us may add perspective to help you cope with current issues. For example, you may understandably feel angry and frustrated when you encounter instances of sexism, racism, and classism in the 21st century. By reading about female social workers' attempts to secure federal legislation to support maternal and child health efforts early in the 20th century, you may come to appreciate the magnitude of their accomplishments in the face of great hostility from many United States senators and representatives. During its more than 100-year history in North America, social workers have contributed a great deal toward improving the lives of vulnerable people. Some of that work took decades of effort and unrelenting determination. Recognize that sometimes progress toward goals—including those identified by individual, family, group, organization, and community clients—requires patience, stamina, and an unyielding persistence.

◆ Chapter Summary

Although social workers in general may experience lower rates of burnout than do some comparable occupational groups (Söderfeldt, Söderfeldt, & Warg, 1995), we remain very much at risk (Meyerson, 1994). Personal and professional distress remains a major problem for thousands of practitioners (Cherniss, 1980a, 1980b). Burnout represents an occupational hazard with which you must contend. None of us is immune (Poulin & Walter, 1993). We suggest these guidelines for making your working life more satisfying and enjoyable (Koeske & Koeske, 1989; Pines, 1983):

- Adopt self-awareness of your own thoughts, feelings, attitudes, and behavior as a personal goal.
- Be especially alert to the way your ideas and beliefs influence your feelings and reactions, and affect your perception of others.
- Recognize that the beliefs you hold about yourself, others, and events in the world powerfully influence the nature and extent of stress or distress.
- Take full responsibility for your own thoughts and behavior, and develop strategies for changing them when needed.
- Acknowledge that although you are indeed responsible for your own thoughts, feelings, and behavior, you are not responsible for those of other competent persons or for the consequences of their decisions and actions.
- Recognize that attempting to control others tends to be time-consuming, emotionally draining, and usually ineffective.
- In your efforts to serve others, maintain your focus on the identified problems and agreed-upon goals.
- Develop support systems within your agency, profession, and community.
- Maintain an active personal life and pursue interests outside of social work so that your sense

of self-worth does not depend entirely on your professional identity and your job.

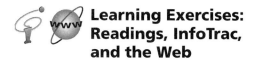

Learning Exercises: Readings, InfoTrac, and the Web

1. Use your word-processing computer program to enter the important terms and concepts presented in this chapter in alphabetical order. Place a question mark by any terms that you do not clearly understand. Save your document as EX 19-1.

2. Log on to the InfoTrac College Edition Web site. Conduct a keyword search (using either Keyword Search or Advanced Search) to locate the articles entitled "Skills Training in the Long-Term Management of Stress and Occupational Burnout" (Rowe, 2000) and "Job Burnout" (Maslach et al., 2001). Read the articles and prepare a two-page essay in which you reflect on their implications for managing your own distress within the context of social work and social work practice. Save your document as EX 19-2.

3. Turn to **Reading 25: Burnout: An Occupational Hazard for Social Workers.** Review this article, and reflect on Jan Hagen's observations in relation to the topics addressed in this chapter. Prepare a one-page essay to explore your observations and reactions. Save your document as EX 19-3.

4. Develop your own self-care plan. First, consider the categories of stressors identified in Jan Hagen's Reading 25: the individual, the helping relationship, the work environment, and societal factors. Second, make a list of at least one stressor from each category that does or might personally affect you. Third, determine the degree to which you might control each stressor. We suggest two categories: those stressors that you can reasonably expect to control and those over which you have limited control. Fourth, develop a plan to manage each of the stressors over which you have some control and then prepare another plan to "let go" of those stressors over which you have limited control. Prepare a two-page essay to discuss your observations and reflections, and to outline your plans to reduce distress and minimize the risk of burnout. Save your document as EX 19-4.

Readings

READING 1
Mrs. Warren's Profession[1]

George Bernard Shaw[2]

Mrs. Warren: You! you've no heart. [She suddenly breaks out vehemently in her natural tongue—the dialect of a woman of the people—with all her affectations of maternal authority and conventional manners gone, and an overwhelming inspiration of true conviction and scorn in her] Oh, I won't bear it: I won't put up with the injustice of it. What right have you to set yourself up above me like this? You boast of what you are to me—to me, who gave you the chance of being what you are. What chance had I? Shame on you for a bad daughter and a stuck-up prude!

Vivie: [sitting down with a shrug, no longer confident; for her replies, which have sounded sensible and strong to her so far, now begin to ring rather woodenly and even priggishly against the new tone of her mother] Don't think for a moment I set myself above you in any way. You attacked me with the conventional authority of a mother. I defended myself with the conventional superiority of a respectable woman. Frankly, I am not going to stand any of your nonsense; and when you drop it I shall not expect you to stand any of mine. I shall always respect your right to your own opinions and your own way of life.

Mrs. Warren: My own opinion and my own way of life! Listen to her talking! Do you think I was brought up like you? able to pick and choose my own way of life? Do you think I did what I did because I liked it, or

thought it right, or wouldn't rather have gone to college and been a lady if I'd had the chance?

Vivie: Everybody has some choice, mother. The poorest girl alive may not be able to choose between being Queen of England or Principal of Newnham; but she can choose between ragpicking and flowerselling, according to her taste. People are always blaming their circumstances for what they are. I don't believe in circumstances. The people who get on in this world are the people who get up and look for the circumstances they want, and, if they can't find them, make them.

Mrs. Warren: Oh, it's easy to talk, very easy isn't it? Here! Would you like to know what my circumstances were?

Vivie: Yes: you had better tell me. Won't you sit down?

Mrs. Warren: Oh, I'll sit down: don't you be afraid. [She plants her chair farther forward with brazen energy, and sits down. Vivie is impressed in spite of herself] D'you know what your gran'mother was?

Vivie: No.

Mrs. Warren: No, you don't. I do. She called herself a widow and had a fried-fish shop down by the Mint, and kept herself and four daughters out of it. Two of us were sisters; that was me and Liz; and we were both good-looking and well made. I suppose our father was a well-fed man: mother pretended he was a gentleman; but I don't know. The other two were only half sisters: undersized, ugly, starved-looking, hard-working, honest, poor creatures: Liz and I would have half-murdered them if mother hadn't half-murdered us to keep our hands off them. They were the respectable ones. Well, what did they get by their respectability? I'll tell you. One of them worked in a whitelead factory twelve hours a day for nine shillings a week until she died of lead poisoning. She only expected to get her hands a little paralyzed; but she died. The other was always held up to us as a model because she married a Government laborer in the Deptford victualling yard, and kept his room and the three children neat and tidy on eighteen shillings a week—until he took to drink. That was worth being respectable for, wasn't it?

Vivie: [now thoughtfully attentive] Did you and your sister think so?

Mrs. Warren: Liz didn't, I can tell you: she had more spirit. We both went to a church school—that was part

---

[1] Source: Shaw, Bernard. (1965, First published in 1898). *The Complete Plays of Bernard Shaw.* London: Paul Hamlyn, pp. 75–76.

[2] George Bernard Shaw wrote *Mrs. Warren's Profession* in 1894. The play, published in 1898, was so controversial that it was banned in London and was not produced until 1905 in New York. (The American producer was arrested for producing the play but was acquitted.) Mrs. Warren was an entrepreneur and successful businesswoman who had amassed considerable wealth. She had put her daughter, Vivie, through the University of Cambridge, where Vivie was one of the first female students and excelled in mathematics. Mrs. Warren worked as a prostitute and owned a chain of brothels across Europe. The play centers around the mother-daughter relationship as Vivie becomes aware of the nature of her mother's business; Mrs. Warren has hopes that Vivie will take over management of the business. This dialogue occurs in Act 2.

of the ladylike airs we gave ourselves to be superior to the children that knew nothing and went nowhere—and we stayed there until Liz went out one night and never came back. I know the schoolmistress thought I'd soon follow her example; for the clergyman was always warning me that Lizzie'd end up jumping off Waterloo Bridge. Poor fool: that was all he knew about it! But I was more afraid of the whitelead factory than I was of the river; and so would you have been in my place. That clergyman got me a situation as scullery maid in a temperance restaurant where they sent out for anything you liked. Then I was waitress; then I went to the bar at Waterloo station: fourteen hours a day serving drinks and washing glasses for four shillings a week and my board. That was considered a great promotion for me. Well, one cold, wretched night, when I was so tired I could hardly keep myself awake, who should come up for a half of Scotch but Lizzie, in a long fur cloak, elegant and comfortable, with a lot of sovereigns in her purse.

Vivie: [grimly] My aunt Lizzie!

Mrs. Warren: Yes; and a very good aunt to have, too. She's living down at Winchester now, close to the cathedral, one of the most respectable ladies there. Chaperones girls at the county ball, if you please. No river for Liz, thank you! You remind me of Liz a little: she was a first-rate business woman—saved money from the beginning—never let herself look too like what she was—never lost her head or threw away a chance. When she saw I'd grown up good-looking she said to me across the bar, "What are you doing there, you little fool? Wearing out your health and your appearance for other people's profit!" Liz was saving money then to take a house for herself in Brussels; and she thought we two could save faster than one. So she lent me some money and gave me a start; and I saved steadily and first paid her back, and then went into business with her as her partner. Why shouldn't I have done it? The house in Brussels was real high class; a much better place for a woman to be in than the factory where Anne Jane got poisoned. None of our girls were ever treated as I was treated in the scullery of that temperance place, or at the Waterloo bar, or at home. Would you have had me stay in them and become a worn out old drudge before I was forty?

Vivie: [intensely interested by this time] No; but why did you choose that business? Saving money and good management will succeed in any business.

Mrs. Warren: Yes, saving money. But where can a woman get the money to save in any other business? Could you save out of four shillings a week and keep yourself dressed as well? Not you. Of course, if you're a plain woman and can't earn anything more; or if you have a turn for music, or the stage, or newspaperwriting: that's different. But neither Liz nor I had any turn for such things at all: all we had was our appearance and our turn for pleasing men. Do you think we were such fools as to let other people trade in our good looks by employing us as shopgirls, or barmaids, or waitresses, when we could trade them in ourselves and get all the profits instead of starvation wages? Not likely.

READING 2
The Strengths Perspective: Principles and Practices[1]

Dennis Saleebey[2]

Over the past decade or so, strengths-based approaches to case management and direct practice have been developed in a number of fields of practice—mental health (Kisthardt, 1997; R. Rapp, 1997; Sullivan, 1997), juvenile justice (Clark, 1997), gerontological social work (Fast & Chapin, 1997; Parsons & Cox, 1994), families (Kaplan & Girard, 1994), substance abuse (Miller & Berg, 1995; C. A. Rapp, 1997), communities (Kretzmann & McKnight, 1993), schools (Benard, 1997a, 1997b; Bricker-Jenkins, 1991), and public welfare (Bricker-Jenkins, 1997). In addition, there are parallel developments in other areas of research, program, and practice; developmental resilience and youth development (Henderson, 1997; Werner & Smith, 1992); health and wellness (Gazzaniga, 1992; Mills, 1995; Weil, 1995); social constructionism (Franklin, 1995; Freedman & Combs, 1996); and solution-focused therapy (de Jong & Miller, 1995).

Significantly, some of the impetus for the development of a strengths/resilience-based practice comes from our society's unabashed fascination with pathology, problems, moral and interpersonal aberrations, violence, and victimization. Add to that the unstinting effort to medicalize

---

[1] An original reading for *Social Work Processes*.
[2] Professor, School of Social Welfare, University of Kansas, Lawrence.

and pathologize almost every human behavior pattern, habit, and trait, and you have a heady mix of diagnoses, labels, and identities at the ready—all advertising our abnormalities, disorders, weaknesses, fallibilities, and victimization. An influential cartel of professions, institutions, businesses, and individuals—from medicine to the pharmaceutical industry, from the insurance business to the media—stands to assure us that we all have a storehouse of vulnerabilities and failings born of toxic and traumatic experiences (usually in childhood) that put us at risk for an astonishing array of pathologies: from caffeine addiction to posttraumatic stress syndrome to dissociative identity disorder (Kaminer, 1993; Peele, 1989; Peele & Brodsky, 1991; Reiff, 1991). Victimhood has become big business, as many adults—prodded by a variety of therapies, gurus, and ministers—search out their wounded inner children and memories of the poisonous ecology of their family background. This phenomenon blurs the distinction between people who have been seriously traumatized and victimized and those who experience the expectable trials and tribulations of real life (Dineen, 1996).

To practice from a strengths perspective does not require us to blithely ignore or mute the real pains and troubles that afflict children, groups, families, and classes of people. Child sexual abuse is real; violence is real; cancer is real; schizophrenia is real; racism is real. But from the vantage point of a strengths perspective, it is as wrong to deny the possible as it is to deny the problem.

The strengths perspective decries the fact that the recovery movement, now so far beyond its original boundaries and intent, has

> Pumped out a host of illnesses and addictions that were by earlier standards, mere habits, some good, some bad. Everywhere in public we find people talking freely, if not excitedly, even proudly about their compulsions—whether it be gambling, sex, exercise, or the horrible desire to please other people. We are awash in a sea of codependency, wounded inner children, and intimacy crises. (Wolin & Wolin, 1993, p. 7)

The strengths perspective calls us back to a more balanced view of the human condition: a view in which we respect the power of human beings to overcome and surmount adversity.

PRINCIPLES OF THE STRENGTHS PERSPECTIVE

Like any theory, the strengths orientation is a construction of symbols, language, rhetoric, and diction. In this case, the language is ordinary. As Goldstein points out:

> Strength and resilience are social constructions with some vintage built into, over time, the ordinary, plebeian, or folk vocabulary. Terms—or really value judgments—such as virtue, willpower, integrity, fortitude are common, culturally defined ways of referring to the character and worth displayed in the face of the travails of living. (1997, p. 28)

I would add words such as empowerment, membership, competence, potential, responsibility, growth, assets, and vision. These stand in stark contrast to the esoteric and sometimes remote vocabulary of the medical, mental health, and human service professions. Words have power: They can elevate and ennoble; or they can subvert and destroy. They can encourage and motivate; or they can dishearten and enervate.

In a sense, we are asking those who have been hurt and discouraged—those who have been clients, often unwilling, of the human service industry—to engage in both insurrection and resurrection. Many people who are thought to have disorders are the objects of a totalizing discourse (Gergen, 1991). This discourse, based on a wildly expanding deficit language and taxonomy, eventually suffuses into the identities of individuals, so that they become their designation—a schizophrenic, a borderline, a victim, an alcoholic, and so on. Insurrection involves getting the stories of oppressed and suffering people out to those who need to hear them—schools, agencies (maybe your agency), hospitals, legislators, other professionals, even family members. Unfortunately, the media and various therapeutic enterprises are now busily creating cultural stories from which many of us draw our sense of who we are—the adult child of an alcoholic, the codependent, the hapless victim. Resurrection refers to an individual's or family's or even a community's rediscovery of their capacities and resiliencies once they begin to shed the mantle of totalizing discourse and to get their own stories and narratives heard. We need to heed the words of Edward Roberts (1992), the late president and founder of the World Institute on Disability and an individual with severe disabilities since childhood: "Never underestimate the power within any individual. Their limbs may be withered and useless but their spirit and souls are intact." Once people begin to remember and weave their own stories, their own realities, and get the word out, they often experience a resurrection of will and hope.

Major Principles of the Strengths Perspective

We know that strengths-based approaches differ from pathology-based approaches in their language. They also differ in the basic principles that guide and direct practice.

Every Individual, Every Family, Every Community Has Strengths, Assets, and Resources   While sometimes hard to invoke, this principle asks you to discern the resources and competencies that people have and to respect those strengths and the potential they have for reversing misfortune, countering illness, easing pain, and reaching goals. To detect strengths, you must be genuinely interested in, and respectful of, clients' stories, narratives, and accounts—the interpretive slants they take on their own experience; these are the most important theories that guide practice. You need to assume a respectful and open mindset.

Trauma and Abuse, Illness and Struggle May Be Devastating, But They Also May Be Opportunities for Growth and Sources of Challenge and Opportunity   Clearly, there are traumas that can overwhelm the coping capacities of any child or adult. Sometimes extraordinary measures are required to help such individuals get back on track. But the literature on the resilience of children and adults shows that most individuals—even children—when confronted with persistent or episodic crisis, disorganization, stress, trauma, or abuse somehow are able to surmount the adversity. They do not fall into a welter of psychopathology and the replication of their own family's chaos and disorganization. Children are active and developing individuals who, through these trials, learn skills and develop attributes that stand them in good stead in adulthood (Masten, 1994; Werner & Smith, 1992; Wolin & Wolin, 1993). In almost every study, the majority—sometimes a significant majority—of children who have experienced a very painful childhood develop into competent adults who have avoided many pitfalls and created a relatively satisfying and productive life for themselves (Benard, 1997b; Swadener & Lubeck, 1995). Not that these children and adults don't suffer or bear the scars of past hurts and cruelties; they certainly do. But along the way, thanks to resources within themselves and factors in their environments, they acquire knowledge, traits, and capacities that are preservative and life affirming.

Assume That You Do Not Know—Nor Can You Know—the Upper Limits of Any Individual's Capacity to Grow and Change   A diagnosis or assessment seems to set limits on what professionals think is possible for an individual or family. Being diagnosed as schizophrenic closes doors, abridges possibilities and opportunities, subverts hopes and dreams. But we cannot know, except in the crudest of ways, what the limits are. We cannot know that; we cannot even know that about ourselves.

And, if we cannot know it, then why assume it? Why not assume at the outset that there are many unknown possibilities (Deegan, 1996)? Why not assume that all of us have innate wisdom and health even though it may lie uncultivated? In his health/realization/community empowerment projects, Roger Mills noticed that

> if we treated people as healthy and showed confidence in their healthy side, they gained hope and managed things better . . . When we treat people as if they are one and the same as their problems . . . they tend to become more and more diseased. (1995, pp. 52–53)

> We concluded that we could help people much more by teaching them to elicit their own intrinsic health, rather than encouraging them to explore their dysfunctions. (1995, pp. 53–54)

The limitations we assume are often a product of the diagnosis and the process of being diagnosed.

Take Individual, Family, and Community Visions and Hopes Seriously   The basic equation of the strengths perspective is disarmingly simple. You account for and summon up the strengths, resources, and capacities of individuals and families and put them in the service of meeting needs, minimizing risks, and realizing hopes and dreams. To do this, of course, you have to know the assets of individuals and families and their environments and to take their dreams seriously. As George Vaillant notes,

> Our capacities for creativity, for mature self-deception, and for religious wonder are all facilitated in *dreaming*—both day and night dreams—as we review the past and rehearse the future. (1993, p. 338)

Dreams fuel hopes; hopes fuel intention; intention fuels action. It does not even matter if the dream is never fully achieved in the drama of daily life. What does matter is that it is taken seriously, it is made palpable through belief and elaboration, and steps are taken to move, however haltingly, in that direction. It is, in other words, a project.

Every Environment Is Full of Resources   No matter how harsh an environment, no matter how it may test the mettle of its inhabitants, it is also a potentially lush topography of assets and resources (Kretzmann & McKnight, 1993; McKnight, 1995; Shaffer & Anundsen, 1993; Sullivan, 1997) containing informal consolidations of individuals, families, and groups, associational networks of peers, systems of intergenerational mentoring, and individuals willing to give time and succor. In the strengths model of case management (C. A. Rapp, 1997), natural resources are preferred and sought before seeking resources in the service system. In the words of McKnight, the community vision of society

> understands the community as the basic context for enabling people to contribute their gifts. It sees community associations as contexts in which to create and locate jobs, provide opportunities for recreation and multiple friendships, and become the political defender of the right of labelled people to be free from exile. (1995, p. 169)

Subsidiary Principles of the Strengths Perspective

There are other principles of the strengths perspective, many of which flow from those just discussed.

Don't Take No for an Answer   People who are in trouble or in crisis don't tend to think in terms of their strengths. It takes some diligence and artful demonstrations on your part to move them in the direction of seeing some of their virtues.

Help Correct the Effects of Being Labeled   Many people who have been a part of the welfare, social service, mental health, or health systems have been taught deficit- and problem-based self-definitions very well. For some, these designations have become a central part of their identity. You must be active in pointing out (in terms of their daily life, in their real time, in their actual place) how, in fact, they are much more than a label, a reputation, or a case.

Take Advantage of the Considerable Resources of Culture and Ethnicity   Every culture is rich in resources—people, rituals, symbols, healing practices, support systems, spiritual bounty—that may be used in helping people right and redirect the course of their life. Curanderismo, the medicine wheel, sweatlodge, and other rituals and healing practices will serve to provide support, tranquility, instruction, and healing. Cultural narratives of origins, of migration and settlement, of triumph over adversity and oppression may solidify identity, provide comfort, stimulate pride, and suggest future paths.

Normalize and Externalize   To normalize requires that we work with individuals and families to turn problems into wants and possibilities. People often get stuck in a rut of conflict, disorganization, and confusion when they are trying to solve a problem, to figure out what the problem is, or to meet needs. Helping people to look toward what they want, how they would like to be, or how they might otherwise meet needs often helps to break the logjam of difficulties and stresses. Externalizing means getting people's

stories out to those individuals, associations, agencies, and institutions that need to hear them.

The problem-based approach and the strengths approach are compared in Exhibit R2-1; the contrast is drawn a little dramatically to make the point.

ASSESSMENT

The strengths perspective requires that we broaden the scope of our work and our assessment. It reminds us that individuals and families have not always had problems, and that they do not have these difficulties every waking moment; they also have successes. The emphasis is on knowing them in a more holistic way: acknowledging their hopes and dreams, their needs, their resources and the resources around them, their accomplishments, their capacities, and their gifts. The strengths perspective invites a more affirming interaction with individuals and families; as a professional, you engage them conversationally as collaborators and peers, recognizing that they and you are both experts and have a mutual interest in improving their quality of life.

Part of the work during assessment is toward normalization—understanding problems as expressions, in part, of attempts to meet needs and realize possibilities. Many problems have evolved as distorted, anguished ways to meet common human needs—for love, respect, control, tranquility, choice, stability, security, and so on. Assessment is based on an exploration of the needs that are crying to be met, the hopes and dreams of individuals and family members, and the strengths and resources that they have at their disposal or can develop.

The strengths approach to assessment does not come naturally for many of us. It has to be learned, and many conceptual, professional, institutional, and interpersonal barriers need to be overcome. If the strengths and assets of colleagues are not acknowledged and employed, it will be hard for you to affirm and summon up the capacities of your clients. Mills (1995) argues strongly that the first order of business is to create the organizational and interpersonal conditions for the health of staff. In our assessments, we should always strive to be possibility-focused, goal-focused, solution-focused, and strengths-focused. The rankest amateur can find pathology in some individuals and families; it takes skill, determination, and a different standpoint to find strengths.

What Are Strengths, and How Do You Find Out about Them?

Almost anything might turn out to be a strength, depending on the context, the contingencies, and the demands in

EXHIBIT R2-1
Comparison of Strengths- and Problem-Based Approaches

Problem/dysfunction	Strengths
Safety and security of children and vulnerable family or group members is first concern	Safety and security of children and vulnerable family or group members is first concern
Individuals/groups are seen as vulnerable and at risk and characterized in terms of pathologies/disorders/trauma	Individuals/groups are seen as having innate resilience, strengths, and assets in spite of problems
Individuals/groups are defined as cases and/or problems to be dealt with	Individuals/groups are defined as unique: the sum total of their talents, resources, capacities, and assets, as well as their problems
Problem- and pathology-focused vocabulary of victimization and recovery	Possibility- and development-focused vocabulary of resilience and mastery
Individual/familial/group accounts sought in service of naming the problem, deficit, abuse, pathology	Individual/familial/group accounts sought in the service of discovering who this individual or family is
Knowing the individual/family/group from the outside in	Knowing the individual/family/group from the inside out
Skeptical of individual/family accounts, which are seen as excuses, rationalizations	Disposed to believe individual/family accounts, which are seen as stories/narratives
Centerpiece of work is the treatment/work plan: goals set by professionals and protocols	Centerpiece of work is the goals and aspirations, the needs and strengths of the individual, family, or group
Professional is the ultimate expert on and arbiter of the individual's/family's/group's life	Individual/family/group are the experts on their lives—past, present, and future
Professional designs and carries out the plan of helping or treatment	Work is a collaborative effort driven by the aspirations of the individual/family/group
Possibilities for choice, control, and development are seriously limited by age and the effects of abuse, addiction, pathology	Possibilities for choice, control, and development are always open
Resources for work are primarily the knowledge and skills of the professional/service delivery system	Resources for work are primarily the strengths, capacities, and assets of the individual or family/group members and the community
Help is centered on solving the problems, controlling the symptoms, eliminating the addiction, etc.	Help is centered on getting on with life, affirming and developing values and commitments, making and finding membership in the community

people's daily lives. Following are some of the experiences, traits, and environmental and interpersonal transactions that have been found to be strengths at one time or another.

What People Learn as They Struggle   People discover inner resources as they confront demands and challenges—whether abuse, illness, death, oppression, or chronic stress. Or they may develop personal traits and qualities that help

them master the trauma. As Wolin and Wolin (1993) point out, children in chaotic, disorganized, or violent families often learn interpersonal skills and develop intrapsychic habits of mind that help them survive—a sense of humor, insight into others' motives and behavior, a strong moral imagination, and creativity, for example. Some people not only learn from the successes but from their trials as well, even those they may inflict upon themselves. For example, most people quit or moderate drinking on their own because they do not like what they see in the mirror, and because they have come to cherish other values and principles of living (Peele & Brodsky, 1991).

What Individuals/Families Know People learn intellectually or educationally about their world as well as discerning and distilling things through their own life experience. Perhaps an individual who, as a child, cared for an ailing parent has developed the frame of mind and interpersonal skills to tend to the needs of vulnerable or sick individuals. Another individual may be able to use an artistic medium to entertain and educate others. We cannot know what it might be unless we take the time to find out.

Personal Qualities and Virtues Forged in the fires of trauma and hardship, these qualities might include loyalty, perseverance, independence, insight, steadfastness, self-discipline, and a sense of humor and fun; the list could be extended indefinitely. To balance the considerable invalidating weight of *DSM,* we need a Diagnosis of Strengths Manual, in which we account for, develop criteria of, and describe in detail the substantial virtues that people may possess.

Talents That People Have These talents may surprise not only the professional but also the talented individual, in whom they may have lain dormant for years. Playing a musical instrument, carpentry, telling stories, cooking, landscaping, painting, home repair—it could be anything. Like all strengths, these may provide tools and resources to assist individuals, families, groups, and communities in reaching their goals. In addition, they may be assets that can be shared and given to others, thereby fostering solidarity, strengthening mentorship, or cementing friendship.

Cultural and Family Rituals, Beliefs, Stories, and Lore Often profound sources of strength, guidance, stability, comfort, or transformation, these resources tend to be overlooked, minimized, or distorted by official or professional orientations and definitions.

Survivor's Pride People who have confronted and surmounted challenges to their integrity, health, and even existence often have, deep inside, survivor's pride. As Wolin and Wolin (1992, p. 6; 1993) note, "survivor's pride drives the engine of change, shame jams the gears!"

Dreams and Hopes Individual and family dreams and hopes are as much a motivating dynamism as pride. Strengths-based practitioners aim to give palpable shape to aspirations and then help people employ their strengths and resources in a project designed to take steps toward their dreams.

The Community Any community, even the most impoverished, has people, institutions, associations, organizations, and natural resources that may contribute to the well-being of individuals and families. Asked to help out another child or adult, many individuals in a public housing community, for example, will be able and willing to provide succor, respite, guidance, or material resources.

Spirituality/Faith For many individuals and families, the wellspring of strength and resilience is the belief in some transcendent power and in the possibility of transformation, surcease of pain, or the summoning of strength to face life's challenges.

Discovering and Uncovering Strengths

Look Around You When you are with a client, do you see evidence of interests, talents, competencies? A young social work student who was visiting Mrs. G. a 35-year resident of public housing who had successfully raised 11 children, noticed the family pictures and cross-stitching with Biblical quotations on the walls. Prompted by this observation, she and Mrs. G. developed a plan in which Mrs. G. would lead a Bible study course for young mothers. It was the student's hope that Mrs. G. would also teach the young women about parenting. Mrs. G. adamantly declared that she would stick strictly to Bible instruction. But in the course of the study, Mrs. G. did pass along a lot of information about parenting. Interestingly enough, in all her years as a resident, Mrs. G. had never been asked to share her wisdom.

Here's another example. Michael, with moderate mental retardation, lived in a group home. Now an adult, he was assigned a new case manager. The social worker noticed at their first meeting that the walls of Michael's room were decorated with elegantly wrought maps of the local area, the state, and the nation. Michael told the worker that he had hand drawn them from memory; there was no record of this in Michael's extensive file. Impressed with Michael's uncanny ability, the social worker, with Michael's collaboration, brought the maps to public attention through a feature story in the Sunday supplement. As a result, Michael's maps were displayed at a local art museum. However, Michael's pride in his accomplishments was perhaps the most important outcome—an outcome that was evident when the worker looked around.

EXHIBIT R2-2
Questions to Discover Strengths

Survival questions. How have you managed to survive (or thrive) thus far, given all the challenges you have had to contend with? How have you been able to rise to the challenges put before you? What have you learned about yourself and your world during your struggles? Which of these difficulties have given you special strength, insight, or skill?

Support questions. What people have given you special understanding, support, and guidance? Where are they now? What did they respond to in you? What associations, organizations, or groups have been especially helpful to you up to now?

*Exception questions.** When things are going well in life what is different? In the past, when you felt that your life was better, more interesting, or more stable, what about your world, your relationships, and your thinking was special or different? In those times in your life when your problems did not seem to be troubling you, what was different?

Possibility questions. What do you want out of life now? What are your hopes, visions, and aspirations? How far along are you toward achieving these? Which of your special talents and abilities will help you realize your dreams? How will you know when things are going well in your life— what will you be doing, who will you be with, how will you be feeling, thinking, and acting? How can I help you achieve your goals? What do you think is the first step we can take in reaching your goals?

Esteem questions. When people say good things about you, what are they likely to say? What is it about your life, yourself, and your accomplishments that gives you real pride? What gives you genuine pleasure in life? When did you begin to believe that you might achieve some of the things you wanted in life?

---

*Thanks to the practitioners of solution-focused therapy for the "exceptions" terminology (de Jong, P., & Miller, S. D. (1995). How to interview for client strengths. *Social Work, 40*(6), 729–736.).

Listen to Client Stories   Stories—especially stories of survival—are often the richest source of clues about interests, hopes, strengths, and resources. When Jonelle told the story of her struggle with alcoholism, she mentioned that drawing was an important, though tenuous, source of respite for her. However, no one knew she had this talent. The social worker wondered if Jonelle would be willing to use her talent in planning a mural that children were going to paint in the community recreation room. She agreed. This project brought Jonelle great satisfaction and a little notoriety. Her struggle with alcohol continued, but she clearly had more reserves to draw upon and more determination to become sober.

Let People Know You Are Interested in Their Capacities, Hopes, and Dreams   We have to let people know that we want to hear about their talents, their accomplishments, their virtues, and the resources within and around them.

We should never dismiss their dreams as impracticable. Jim, diagnosed with chronic undifferentiated schizophrenia, wanted to work; to him, this was the sign of being a fully endowed citizen. His previous case managers, because of Jim's demeanor and appearance and his occasional hallucinations, thought that this was not practicable. A new case manager took Jim's dream seriously. They worked together to get Jim ready for the job market, rehearsing, giving shape to his dream of real work. Soon after, Jim interviewed for a job and was hired; he has now worked for two years. Jim, in fact, had much to offer any employer, but it was buried underneath official designations and opinions of who he was and what his limitations were.

Exhibit R2-2 provides several kinds of questions you might ask to discover strengths. These obviously do not exhaust likely questions; and they are not meant to be a protocol or format. Rather, they are designed to stimulate possible lines of thinking during engagement and conversation. Exhibit R2-3 is an example of a form that can be used to record strengths.

EXHIBIT R2-3
Strengths Assessment Form

Life Domains:
> *Survival/daily living:* Shelter, safety, security, food, health
> *Economic well-being:* Income, employment, education, training
> *Personal and social well-being:* Personal/spiritual growth, values, mutual support, hopes and visions, physical
>   and mental health, citizenship, connection

Life domain to be worked on: _____

Aspirations, interests, and needs (what do we want?)_____

_____

_____

Individual and family strengths and exceptions: _____

_____

_____

_____

Community and social resources available for meeting needs, achieving aspirations, and fostering a healing mind and environment:

_____

_____

_____

Immediate goal: _____

Steps to be taken toward goal	Persons and resources involved	Target date
1.		
2.		

ELEMENTS OF STRENGTHS-BASED PRACTICE

Acknowledging the Pain

For many individuals and families, there is real use and purpose in addressing, acknowledging, reexperiencing, and putting into perspective the pains and trauma of life, especially those that now seem insistent. Catharsis, grieving, expression of rage and anxiety, and the metabolization of these feelings are important in developing an understanding of where individuals have been, what their current struggles are, and what emotional and cognitive baggage they carry with them. This is also an important step in letting go of the past and conceiving a different, and better, present and future. For some, it may even be beneficial to explore the roots of trauma in family, community, and culture. It is also important to assess current risks—for example, in a family in which there has been abuse. But the purpose is always to look for the seeds of resilience and rebound, the lessons taken away from the adversity; the cultural, ethnic, and familial sources of adaptability; and resources to be used in lessening risk factors. This is the resiliency attitude (Henderson, 1997) in action!

EXHIBIT R2-4
Language of the Seven Resiliencies

The Wolins have created a model of resiliency that includes not only the damage done to individuals but seven resiliencies that individuals may develop over time—from childhood to adolescence to adulthood. These personal qualities, traits, and capacities, forged in the fire of trauma, include:

Insight: What begins in childhood as a sense that there is something wrong ends in adulthood as a deep understanding of oneself and other people.

Independence: What begins in childhood as a moving away from painful family scenes ends in adulthood as a rational and reasoned separation from (or redefined relationship with) their family.

Relationship: What begins in childhood as a search for connection to available, positive adults ends in adulthood as the ability to consciously form gratifying attachments to others.

Initiative: What begins in childhood as a way of exploring the world away from parents ends in adulthood as the ability to become focused on goals and aims and to accomplish them with energy and purpose.

Creativity and humor: What begins in childhood as playing, supposing, and pretending that one is something valued or powerful ends in adulthood as the ability to compose and make things out of nothing or to mix the terrible with the ironic and absurd and to laugh at what one has created.

Morality: What begins in childhood as questions about why one is hurt and judgments regarding the rights and wrongs of one's life ends in adulthood as dedicated service to others or to an ideal.

Source: Wolin, S. J., & Wolin, S. (1993). *The resilient self: How survivors of troubled families rise above adversity.* New York: Villard.

Stimulating the Discourse and Eliciting Narratives of Resilience and Strength

Individuals often exhibit great resistance to acknowledging their competence, reserves, and resourcefulness. In addition, many traits and capacities that are signs of strength are hidden by years of self-doubt, the blame of others, and a diagnostic label.

The revelation of individual strengths may be hindered by lack of words, by disbelief, or by lack of trust. The social worker may have to begin to provide the language—to look for and give name to those resiliencies that people have demonstrated in the past and in the present. Some names for resiliencies are listed in Exhibit R2-4. To develop such a language in the context of clients' lives, the social worker elicits stories and narratives of their daily struggles and triumphs—what they have done, how they survived, what they want, and what they want to avoid. People need to acknowledge their strengths, play them out, see them in the past and the present, feel them, and have them affirmed by the worker and others. In this way, they write a better text for themselves. The social worker can assist by reframing—not in the manner of so many family therapies, but by adding brush strokes that depict the clients' capacity and ingenuity.

Stimulating a strengths discourse involves at least two acts on your part: providing a vocabulary of strengths (in the language of the client); and mirroring—providing a positive reflection of the client's abilities and accomplishments and helping the client to find other positive mirrors in the environment (Wolin & Wolin, 1994).

Acting in Context: Education, Action, Advocacy, and Linkage

Education is the process by which individuals learn about their capacities and resiliencies, as well as their hopes, goals, and visions. Having found such competencies, the individual is encouraged to take the risk of action. Through continuous, collaborative action with the worker, individuals begin to employ their strengths as they move toward well-formed, achievable goals. The goals should be positive and verifiable and should reflect changes in behavior, knowledge, status, and/or feelings. This process is not easy for many clients. But as they decide and act, as they identify multiple strategies for achieving outcomes, they are encouraged to put their assets, resources, strengths, and re-siliencies to work. Inevitably, they will also discover the limits of their resilience and the effect of still-active sore spots and scars. But, in the end, their decision making and activity, along with the mobilization of internal and external resources, will lead to changes in thinking, feeling, and relationship that are more congruent with their goals and their strengths.

It is important that the individual or family begin to use available community resources to move toward their goals. For you, this means advocacy: You must discover what natural or formal resources are available and accessible, and to what extent they are adequate and acceptable to the client (Kisthardt, 1993). The environment is full of resources: people, institutions, associations, and families who are willing and able to provide instruction, succor, relief, services, time, and mirroring. When people begin to plan ways of achieving their goals and to exercise their strengths, the effect is synergistic. They can do more personally, and they find themselves closer to connection to a community. Here's an example. The director of a respite program identified a creative strategy for providing respite to parents of children with special needs. In collaboration, a worker from the agency and the family developed a plan for the scheduling of respite, including the parents' particular needs. The worker and the parents identified potential respite givers among friends, relatives, or neighbors. The worker then assisted the family in making requests for respite. When someone agreed, all the parties worked together to formulate a contract for care. The worker also helped the respite providers identify what they expected to receive in return for their services. In some cases, parents swapped respite services. In others, the agency gave $10 to the parents, who, in turn, paid the provider (Rupe, 1997).

Normalizing and Capitalizing on Strengths

Over a period of time—often a short period of time—you and the individual or family will begin to consolidate the strengths that have emerged, reinforce the new vocabulary of strengths and resilience, and bolster the capacity to discover resources. Furthermore, you and the family periodically make an accounting of and celebrate the goals and successes that have been realized. The purpose is to cement the strengths and to assure the synergy of their continuing development and articulation. One important avenue to normalization for many who have been helped through a strengths-based approach is to teach others what they have learned in the process, a kind of mentorship. This also facilitates disengagement between worker and client, with the assurance that the personal strengths and the communal resources are in place.

CONCLUSION

The strengths perspective requires that you and your clients develop a different way of looking at what you do together. Practitioners who apply the strengths perspective report that, once clients are engaged in building up strengths and employing assets in daily living, they develop a desire to do more, to become more absorbed in daily life, and to be drawn by future possibilities.

By way of summary, Kaplan and Girard suggest that we can empower families (and individuals) in six ways:

- By believing in their ability to change and helping them to believe in that ability
- By providing families with a perspective that is hopeful and full of possibilities
- By educating families and helping them increase their own skills
- By recognizing and building upon their assets and strengths and the resources around them
- By helping families realize that they do have options and alternatives
- By designing strategies that support and strengthen cultural and ethnic backgrounds (1994, p. 41).

READING 3
The House on Sixth Street[1]

Francis P. Purcell[2] and Harry Specht[3]

The extent to which social work can affect the course of social problems has not received the full consideration it deserves.[4] For some time the social work profession has taken account of social problems only as they have become manifest in behavioral pathology. Yet it is becoming increasingly apparent that, even allowing for this limitation, it is often necessary for the same agency or worker to intervene by various methods at various points.

In this paper, the case history of a tenement house in New York City is used to illustrate some of the factors that should be considered in selecting intervention methods. Like all first attempts, the approach described can be found wanting in conceptual clarity and systematization. Yet the vital quality of the effort and its implications for social work practice seem clear.

The case of "The House on Sixth Street" is taken from the files of Mobilization For Youth (MFY), an action-research project that has been in operation since 1962 on New York's Lower East Side. MFY's programs are financed by grants from several public and private sources. The central theoretical contention of MFY is that a major proportion of juvenile delinquency occurs when adolescents from low-income families do not have access to legitimate opportunities by which they can fulfill the aspirations for success they share with all American youth. The action programs of MFY are designed to offer these youths concrete opportunities to offset the debilitating effects of poverty. For example, the employment program helps youngsters obtain jobs; other programs attempt to increase opportunities in public schools. In addition, there are group work and recreation programs, a program for released offenders, and a narcotics information center. Legal services, a housing services unit, a special referral unit, and a community development program among other services that have been developed or made available. Thus, MFY has an unusually wide range of resources for dealing with social problems.

THE PROBLEM

"The House on Sixth Street" became a case when Mrs. Smith came to an MFY [Mobilization for Youth] Neighborhood Service Center to complain that there had been no gas, electricity, heat, or hot water in her apartment house for more than four weeks. She asked the agency for help. Mrs. Smith was 23 years old, black, and the mother of four children, three of whom had been born out of wedlock. At the time she was unmarried and receiving Aid to Families with Dependent Children. She came to the center in desperation because she was unable to run her household without utilities. Her financial resources were exhausted—but not her courage. The Neighborhood Service Center worker decided that, in this case the building—the tenants, the landlord, and circumstances affecting their relationships—was of central concern.

A social worker then visited the Sixth Street building with Mrs. Smith and a community worker. Community workers are members of the community organization staff in a program that attempts to encourage residents to take independent social action. Like many members in other MFY programs, community workers are residents of the particular neighborhood. Most of them have little formal education; their special contribution being their ability to relate to and communicate with other residents. Because some of the tenants were Puerto Rican, a Spanish-speaking

---

[1] Purcell, F. P., & Specht, H. (1965). The house on sixth street. *Social Work, 10*(4), 69–76. Copyright © 1965. National Association of Social Workers, Inc. Reprinted with permission. This classic case has been used by social work educators for some 40 years to help students appreciate the interactional nature of social problems and the value of a generalist, problem-solving approach to social work practice.

[2] Chief (deceased), Training and Personnel, Mobilization for Youth, New York; Professor and Director, School of Social Work, San Francisco State University, San Francisco.

[3] Professor (deceased), School of Social Welfare, University of California, Berkeley.

[4] Social work practitioners sometimes use the term *social problem* to mean "environmental problem." The sense in which it is used here corresponds to the definition developed by the social sciences: That is, a social problem is a disturbance, deviation, or breakdown in social behavior that (1) involves a considerable number of people and (2) is of serious concern to many in the society. It is social in origin and effect, and is a social responsibility. It represents a discrepancy between social standards and social reality. Also, such socially perceived variations must be viewed as corrigible. *See* Robert K. Merton and Robert A. Nisbet, eds., *Contemporary Social Problems* (New York: Harcourt, Brace, and World, 1961), pp. 6, 701.

community worker was chosen to accompany the social worker. His easy manner and knowledge of the neighborhood enabled him and the worker to become involved quickly with the tenants.

Their first visits confirmed Mrs. Smith's charge that the house had been without utilities for more than four weeks. Several months before, the city Rent and Rehabilitation Administration had reduced the rent for each apartment to one dollar a month because the landlord was not providing services. However, this agency was slow to take further action. Eleven families were still living in the building, which had 28 apartments. The landlord owed the electric company several thousand dollars. Therefore, the meters had been removed from the house. Because most of the tenants were welfare clients, the Department of Welfare had "reimbursed" the landlord directly for much of the unpaid electric bill and refused to pay any more money to the electric company. The Department of Welfare was slow in meeting the emergency needs of the tenants. Most of the children (48 from the 11 families in the building) had not been to school for a month because they were ill or lacked proper clothing.

The mothers were tired and demoralized. Dirt and disorganization were increasing daily. The tenants were afraid to sleep at night because the building was infested with rats. There was danger of fire because the tenants had to use candles for light. The 17 abandoned apartments had been invaded by homeless men and drug addicts. Petty thievery is common in such situations. However, the mothers did not want to seek protection from the police for fear that they would chase away all men who were not part of the families in the building (some of the unmarried mothers had men living with them—one of the few means of protection from physical danger available to these women—even though mothers on public assistance are threatened with loss of income if they are not legally married). The anxiety created by these conditions was intense and disabling.

The workers noted that the mothers were not only anxious but "fighting mad"; not only did they seek immediate relief from their physical dangers and discomforts but they were eager to express their fury at the landlord and the public agencies, which they felt had let them down.

The circumstances described are by no means uncommon, at least not in New York City. Twenty percent of all housing in the city is still unfit, despite all the public and private residential building completed since World War II. At least 277,500 dwellings in New York City need major repairs if they are to become safe and adequate shelters. This means that approximately 500,000 people in the city live in inferior dwelling units and as a many as 825,000

people in buildings that are considered unsafe (Emergency Committee for More Low Income Housing, 1963). In 1962, the New York City Bureau of Sanitary Inspections reported that 530 children were bitten by rats in their homes and 198 children were poisoned (nine of them fatally) by nibbling at peeling lead paint, even though the use of lead paint has been illegal in the city for more than 10 years. Given the difficulties involved in lodging formal complaints with city agencies, it is safe to assume that unreported incidents of rate bites and lead poisoning far exceed these figures.

The effect of such hardships on children is obvious. Of even greater significance is the sense of powerlessness generated when families go into these struggles barehanded. It is this sense of helplessness in the face of adversity that induces pathological anxiety, intergenerational alienation and social retreatism. Actual physical impoverishment alone is not nearly so debilitating as poverty attended by a sense of unrelieved impotence that becomes generalized and internalized. The poor then regard much social learning as irrelevant, since they do not believe it can effect any environmental change (Purcell, 1964).

INTERVENTION AND THE SOCIAL SYSTEMS

Selecting a point of intervention in dealing with this problem would have been simpler if the target of change were Mrs. Smith alone, or Mrs. Smith and her co-tenants, the clients in whose behalf intervention was planned. Too often, the client system presenting the problem becomes the major target for intervention, and the intervention method is limited to the one most suitable for that client system. However, Mrs. Smith and the other tenants had a multitude of problems emanating from many sources, any one of which would have warranted the attention of a social agency. The circumstantial fact that an individual contacts an agency that offers services to individuals and families should not be a major factor in determining the method of intervention. Identification of the client merely helps the agency to define goals; other variables are involved in the selection of method. As Burns and Glasser have suggested:

> It may be helpful to consider the primary target of change as distinct from the persons who may be the primary clients. . . . The primary target of change then becomes the human or physical environment toward which professional efforts via direct intervention are aimed in order to facilitate change. (1963, p. 423)

The three major factors that determined MFY's approach to the problem were (1) knowledge of the various social systems within which the social problem was located (i.e., social systems assessment), (2) knowledge of the various methods (including non–social work methods) appropriate for intervention in these different social systems, and (3) the resources available to the agency. (Specht & Reissman, 1963)

The difficulties of the families in the building were intricately connected with other elements of the social system related to the housing problem. For example, seven different public agencies were involved in maintenance of building services. Later, other agencies were involved in relocating the tenants. There is no one agency in New York City that handles all housing problems. Therefore, tenants have little hope of getting help on their own. In order to redress a grievance relating to water supply (which was only one of the building's many problems) it is necessary to know precisely which city department to contact. The following is only a partial listing:

No water—Health Department

Not enough water—Department of Water Supply

No hot water—Buildings Department

Water leaks—Buildings Department

Large water leaks—Department of Water Supply

Water overflowing from apartment above—Police Department

Water sewage in the cellar—Sanitation Department

The task of determining which agencies are responsible for code enforcement in various areas is not simple, and in addition, one must know that the benefits and services available for tenants and for the community vary with the course of action chosen. For example, if the building were taken over by the Rent and Rehabilitation Administration under the receivership law, it would be several weeks before services would be reestablished, and the tenants would have to remain in the building during its rehabilitation. There would be, however, some compensations: tenants could remain in the neighborhood—indeed, in the same building—and their children would not have to change schools. If, on the other hand, the house were condemned by the Buildings Department, the tenants would have to move, but they would be moved quickly and would receive top relocation priorities and maximum relocation benefits. But once the tenants had been relocated—at city expense—the building could be renovated by the landlord as middle-income housing. In the Sixth Street house, it was suspected that this was the motivation behind the landlord's actions. If the building were condemned and renovated, there would be 28 fewer low-income housing units in the neighborhood.

This is the fate of scores of tenements on the Lower East Side because much new middle-income housing is being built there. Basic services are withheld and tenants are forced to move so that buildings may be renovated for middle-income tenants. Still other buildings are allowed to deteriorate with the expectation that they will be bought by urban renewal agencies.

It is obvious, even limiting analysis to the social systems of one tenement, that the problem is enormous. Although the tenants were the clients in this case, Mrs. Smith, the tenant group, and other community groups were all served at one point or another. It is even conceivable that the landlord might have been selected as the most appropriate recipient of service. Rehabilitation of many slum tenements is at present nearly impossible. Many landlords regard such property purely as an investment. With profit the prime motive, needs of low-income tenants are often overlooked. Under present conditions it is financially impossible for many landlords to correct all the violations in their buildings even if they wanted to. If the social worker chose to intervene at this level of the problem, he might apply to the Municipal Loan Fund, make arrangements with unions for the use of non-union labor in limited rehabilitation projects, or provide expert consultants on reconstruction. These tasks would require social workers to have knowledge similar to that of city planners. If the problems of landlords were not selected as a major point of intervention, they would still have to be considered at some time since they are an integral part of the social context within which this problem exists.

A correct definition of interacting social systems or of the social worker's choice of methods and points of intervention is not the prime concern here. What is to be emphasized is what this case so clearly demonstrates: that, although the needs of the client system enable the agency to define its goals, the points and methods of intervention cannot be selected properly without an awareness and substantial knowledge of the social systems within which the problem is rooted.

DEALING WITH THE PROBLEM

The social worker remained with the building throughout a four-month period. In order to deal effectively with the problem, he had to make use of all the social work methods as well as the special talents of a community worker, lawyer, city planner, and various civil rights organizations. The social worker and the community worker functioned as generalists; with both individuals and families calling on caseworkers as needed for specialized services or at especially trying times, such as during the first week and when the families were relocated. Because of the division of labor in the agency, much of the social work with individuals was done with the help of a caseworker. Group work, administration, and community organization were handled by the social worker, who had been trained in community organization. In many instances he also dealt with the mothers as individuals, as they encountered one stressful situation after another. Agency caseworkers also provided immediate and concrete assistance to individual families, such as small financial grants, medical care, homemaking services, baby-sitting services, and transportation. This reduced the intensity of pressures on these families. Caseworkers were especially helpful in dealing with some of the knotty and highly technical problems connected with public agencies.

With a caseworker and a lawyer experienced in handling tenement cases, the social worker began to help the families organize their demands for the services and utilities to which they were legally entitled but which the public agencies had consistently failed to provide for them.

The ability of the mothers to take concerted group action was evident from the beginning, and Mrs. Smith proved to be a natural and competent leader. With support, encouragement, and assistance from the staff, the mothers became articulate and effective in negotiating with the various agencies involved. In turn, the interest and concern of the agencies increased markedly when the mothers began to visit them, make frequent telephone calls, and send letters and telegrams to them and to politicians demanding action.

With the lawyer and a city planner (an agency consultant), the mothers and staff members explored various possible solutions to the housing problem. For example, the Department of Welfare had offered to move the families to shelters or hotels. Neither alternative was acceptable to the mothers. Shelters were ruled out because they would not consider splitting up their families, and they rejected hotels because they had discovered from previous experience that many of the "hotels" selected were flophouses or were inhabited by prostitutes.

The following is taken from the social worker's record during the first week:

> Met with the remaining tenants, several black men from the block, and [the city planner]. . . . Three of the mothers said that they would sooner sleep out on the street than go the Welfare shelter. If nothing else, they felt that this would be a way of protesting their plight . . . One of the mothers said that they couldn't very well do this with most of the children having

colds. Mrs. Brown thought that they might do better to ask Reverend Jones if they could move into the cellar of his church temporarily. . . . The other mothers got quite excited about this idea because they thought that the church basement would make excellent living quarters.

After a discussion as to whether the mothers would benefit from embarrassing the public agencies by dramatically exposing their inadequacies, the mothers decided to move into the nearby church. They asked the worker to attempt to have their building condemned. At another meeting, attended by tenants from neighboring buildings and representatives of other local groups, it was concluded that what had happened to the Sixth Street building was a result of discrimination against the tenants as Puerto Ricans and Negroes. The group—which had now become an organization—sent the following telegram to city, state, and federal officials:

> We are voters and Puerto Rican and Negro mothers asking for equal rights, for decent housing and enough room. Building has broken windows, no gas or electricity for four weeks, no heat or hot water, holes in floors, loose wiring. Twelve of forty-eight children in building sick. Welfare doctors refuse to walk up dark stairs. Are we human or what? Should innocent children suffer for landlords' brutality and city and state neglect? We are tired of being told to wait with children ill and unable to attend school. Negro and Puerto Rican tenants are forced out while buildings next door are renovated at high rents. We are not being treated as human beings.

For the most part, the lawyer and city planner stayed in the background, acting only as consultants. But as the tenants and worker became more involved with the courts, and as other organizations entered the fight, the lawyer and city planner played a more active and direct role.

RESULTANT SIDE EFFECTS

During this process, tenants in other buildings on the block became more alert to similar problems in their buildings. With the help of the community development staff and the housing consultant, local groups and organizations such as tenants' councils and the local chapter of the Congress of Racial Equality were enlisted to support and work with the mothers.

Some of the city agencies behaved as though MFY had engineered the entire scheme to embarrass them—steadfastly disregarding the fact that the building had been unlivable for many months. Needless to say, the public agencies are overloaded and have inadequate resources. As has been documented, many such bureaucracies develop an amazing insensitivity to the needs of their clients (Bendix, 1952). In this case, the MFY social worker believed that the tenants—and other people in their plight—should make their needs known to the agencies and to the public at large. He knew that when these expressions of need are backed by power—either in numbers or in political knowledge—they are far more likely to have some effect.

Other movements in the city at this time gave encouragement and direction to the people in the community. The March on Washington and the Harlem rent strike are two such actions.

By the time the families had been relocated, several things had been accomplished. Some of the public agencies had been sufficiently moved by the actions of the families and the local organizations to provide better services for them. When the families refused to relocate in a shelter and moved into a neighborhood church instead, one of the television networks picked up their story. Officials in the housing agencies came to investigate and several local politicians lent the tenants their support. Most important, several weeks after the tenants moved into the church, a bill was passed by the city council designed to prevent some of the abuses that the landlord had practiced with impunity. The councilman who sponsored the new law referred to the house on Sixth Street to support his argument.

Nevertheless, the problems that remain far outweigh the accomplishments. A disappointing epilogue to the story is that in court, two months later, the tenants' case against the landlord was dismissed by the judge on a legal technicality. The judged ruled that because the electric company had removed the meters from the building it was impossible for the landlord to provide services.

Some of the tenants were relocated out of the neighborhood and some in housing almost as poor as that they had left. The organization that began to develop in the neighborhood has continued to grow, but it is a painstaking job. The fact that the poor have the strength to continue to struggle for better living conditions is something to wonder at and admire.

IMPLICATIONS FOR PRACTICE

Social work helping methods as currently classified are so inextricably interwoven in practice that it no longer seems valid to think of a generic practice as consisting of the application of casework, group work, or community organization skills as the nature of the problem demands. Nor does it seem feasible to adapt group methods for traditional casework problems or to use group work skills in community organization or community organization method in casework. Such suggestions—when they appear in the literature—either reflect confusion or, what is worse, suggest that no clear-cut method exists apart from the auspices that support it.

In this case it is a manifestation of a social problem—housing—that was the major point around which social services were organized. The social worker's major intellectual task was to select the points at which the agency could intervene in the problem and the appropriate methods to use. It seems abundantly clear that in order to select appropriate points of intervention the social worker needs not only to understand individual patterns of response, but the nature of the social conditions that are the context in which behavior occurs. As this case makes evident, the social system that might be called the "poverty system" is enduring and persistent. Its parts intermesh with precision and disturbing complementarity. Intentionally or not, a function is thereby maintained that produces severe social and economic deprivation. Certain groups profit enormously from the maintenance of this system, but larger groups suffer. Social welfare—and, in particular, its central profession, social work—must examine the part it plays in either maintaining or undermining this socially pernicious poverty system. It is important that the social work profession no longer regard social conditions as immutable and a social reality to be accommodated as service is provided to deprived persons with an ever increasing refinement of technique. Means should be developed whereby agencies can affect social problems more directly, especially through institutional (organizational) change.

The idea advanced by MFY is that the social worker should fulfill his professional function and agency responsibility by seeking a solution to social problems through institutional change rather than by focusing on individual problems in social functioning. This is not to say that individual expressions of a given social problem should be left unattended. On the contrary, this approach is predicated on the belief that individual problems in social functioning are to varying degrees both cause and effect. It rejects the notion that individuals are afflicted with social pathologies, holding, rather, that the same social environment that generates conformity makes payment by the deviance that emerges. As Nisbet points out, "socially prized arrangements and values in society can produce socially condemned results" (Merton & Nisbet, 1961, p. 7). This should direct social work's attention to institutional arrangements and their consequences. This approach does not lose sight of the individual or group, since the social system is composed of various statuses, roles, and classes.

It takes cognizance of the systemic relationship of the various parts of the social system, including the client. It recognizes that efforts to deal with one social problem frequently generate others with debilitating results.

Thus it is that such institutional arrangements as public assistance, state prisons, and state mental hospitals, or slum schools are regarded by many as social problems in their own right. The social problems of poverty, criminality, mental illness, and failure to learn that were to be solved or relieved remain, and the proposed solutions pose almost equally egregious problems.

This paper has presented a new approach to social work practice. The knowledge, values, attitudes, and skills were derived from a generalist approach to social work. Agencies that direct their energies to social problems by effecting institutional change will need professional workers whose skills cut across the broad spectrum of social work knowledge.

READING 4
An Ecosystemic Approach to Assessment[1]

Jane F. Gilgun[2]

A defining characteristic of social work practice is its focus on the person-environment interaction. Such a focus requires an assessment and an intervention plan that encompasses the person, the environment, and the interactions between them. An ecosystemic approach to assessment involves understanding the "interrelated, complex reality in people's lives" (Meyer, 1983b, p. 30). The starting point for an ecosystemic assessment is the client's perception of the environment. Its major emphasis is on observation of the client's interaction with members of the interpersonal environment, usually the family.

The environment can be sliced into several categories. The client's most immediate environment is interpersonal, composed of individuals with whom the client interacts. This slice of the environment frequently is called the micro level (Bronfenbrenner, 1979; Garbarino, 1982). The family, friendship networks, and relationships in schools, the workplace, and governmental agencies are examples of settings where interpersonal connections are made. The interpersonal environment also can be historical, such as the family of origin or the death or birth of persons who affect present interactions. Interpersonal patterns from the past often influence present interactions.

Another dimension of the interpersonal environment is the stage of the individual and family life cycle. Interactions change depending on developmental stage. For example, parents are doomed to frustration when they attempt to force a 2-year-old to share toys happily; sharing is not characteristic of a child at this age. The family with three young children under 5 will have far different issues and interactions with each other than they will when the children are between the ages of 10 and 15, although there also will be continuities.

A person's environment is also physical—for example, the presence or absence of businesses or other facilities that can offer employment. Access to schools, job training programs, grocery stores, playgrounds, and recreation can have an enormous impact on the person's quality of life and opportunity. The relationship that exists between two micro-level settings is called the meso level by Bronfenbrenner (1979) and Garbarino (1982). The school-home, church-home, and work-home relationships are examples. An isolated family has few meso-level relationships, while a socially integrated family is characterized by numerous, rich, and supportive meso-level relationships.

Often, environments with which individuals do not come into direct contact may have a profound impact on their interpersonal interactions. The workplace environment can affect family life; actions of the federal government can affect taxation and thus the individual and the family; changes in policy made by the county welfare office can deeply affect many individuals who have no direct contact with the office itself. This is the exo level of the environment (Bronfenbrenner, 1979; Garbarino, 1982).

Even more nebulous than the effects of the exo level of the person's environment is the macro level. Here, aspects of the environment are shaped by customs, norms, and practices that can be—and often are—fair to most people but can also be racist, sexist, and ageist. These aspects of the environment can be thought of as part of a stratification system where opportunity, power, privilege, and prestige

---
[1] An original reading for *Social Work Processes*.
[2] Professor, School of Social Work, University of Minnesota, Minneapolis.

are allocated along the dimensions of age, sex, social class, race, and sexual orientation, to name just a few. The consequences of stratification systems are experienced through social, economic, and political policy and practice, which often are exo-level influences, as well as by the daily micro-level interactions. These interpersonal interactions give individuals feedback on their social standing and either open or close opportunity for education, income, and social and political power.

Individuals usually are not aware of how profoundly macro-level forces affect the course of their lives. Thus, a 27-year-old divorced mother of three children under age 10 may believe that her personal inadequacies are causing the family's financial troubles. She may become depressed and isolated. When she does seek opportunities for education and job advancement, there may be nothing available for her, resulting in more depression, feelings of inadequacy, and isolation. In fact, more than her individual choice has led to her poverty and discouragement. Through public policy, as well as more individualized micro-level actions, many women live in poverty because of lack of encouragement and opportunity—and sometimes outright negation of their potential to develop a well-paying and meaningful career. The status that most persons have achieved results largely from socialization practices, opportunity structures, and beliefs, all macro-level forces, over which individuals have little control and of which they usually are unaware.

This reading provides an example of how to conduct an ecosystemic assessment. Guidelines for doing this assessment will be developed out of case material. Thus, the approach is presented as it would be experienced by the practitioner: from the assignment of the case, to gathering and organizing assessment data, to thinking about the data, and, finally, to developing an initial intervention plan. You, in effect, will be looking over the shoulder of an experienced practitioner who does an ecosystemic assessment; the reader will be privy to the practitioner's self-talk.

AN INITIAL ASSESSMENT

You are a social work practitioner in a family service agency. Your supervisor gives you a face sheet and a file folder that is empty except for a few lines recording a phone intake. Your supervisor says, "I'd like you to take this case." The face sheet tells you the initial contact was made by Mary Smith, 23, married to John Smith, 23, for five years. They have a 2½-year-old son, Billy, and a 1½-year-old daughter, Kelly. Mary is at home with the chil-

dren, although prior to the birth of Kelly, she worked as a computer operator. John is a diesel mechanic, earning $32,000 a year. He also has a tow truck business that provides a net income of $25,000 a year. Both are white and high school graduates. They went to the same high school. Their last names are Anglo-Saxon, and their religion is Catholic. Mary's parents are alive, and she has two older sisters and one younger sister. John's mother died when he was 14, and he left his father's home at 16 to live with an aunt and uncle. He has one younger brother. John's father has not remarried.

The intake note states that Mary has requested help in dealing with John's physical violence. She left the family home three times in the last six months. Twice she left without the children, and she feels guilty about that; one time, she left home with slippers on, and it was December and cold outside. She told the intake worker that John would not come in for consultation.

Knowledge of Content Area

Trained in ecosystemic thinking, you also have some knowledge of violence against women in families. Your first thought is whether Mary has a protection plan, which is a preplanned set of actions she will take in the event of an abusive episode. When you phone to make an appointment, you will check on the protection plan. You also intend to make an early appointment because, in domestic abuse situations, a person's life may be in danger. If the case had involved an area with which you weren't familiar, you would have discussed the case in depth with your supervisor before making the appointment, and you would also have gone to the agency library to educate yourself about the subject area. Accurate knowledge of the content area of a case is essential for effective practice.

You are, in fact, knowledgeable about violence against women in families, and through experience you have gained confidence in your ability to deal effectively with such cases. Knowledge in a content area goes hand in hand with doing the assessment. You would not have known about the centrality of a protection plan had you not had knowledge of domestic abuse as a content area.

You phone Mary, and she answers with a soft "Hello." You hear children crying in the background. You identify yourself and tell her you've called to schedule a time when she can come into the office for an appointment. Mary says, "I'm so glad it's you. I've been walking on eggs around here. John's tow business has been slow, and he's been so touchy. The kids are driving me crazy. I can't get Billy to play with Kelly, and they fight all day long. Just a few minutes ago, Billy hit Kelly with a toy truck. I'm afraid he's going to be just like his father." The softness is gone from her voice; she sounds hoarse and distraught.

You negotiate a mutually agreeable time to meet with Mary. You check to see if she is willing to ask John to come in, too, and she says that she doesn't want him there this time. "I need to see someone all by myself," she said. For most forms of work with married persons, the agency has a strict policy that the couples are seen together, but an exception can be made for domestic abuse situations. If, after a few sessions, it appears that the husband and wife both want to remain together, the policy is to involve the other spouse in treatment. The rationale for involving both spouses is that each spouse is a significant part of the other's interpersonal environment. Each spouse mutually influences the behavior of the other, although a host of mediating variables may influence the couple's interaction. When a spouse in a domestic abuse situation is seen alone, the purposes are: (1) to develop a protection plan; (2) to establish that responsibility for stopping the abuse lies with the batterer; and (3) to clarify whether the spouse wants to remain with the batterer. Thus, there are very good reasons to see a married person alone in such cases. The agency has a similar policy when the presenting problem is alcohol or drug abuse, compulsive gambling, and compulsive sexual acting-out.

You ask Mary if she would like to take a few minutes to talk about ways of protecting herself from battering. She says she would. You give her an example of a typical protection plan: having the names and phone numbers of shelters and of friends and family who will provide refuge if she finds herself in physical danger; keeping a spare car key and some money where she can get to them in an emergency; and not hesitating to call the police if she finds herself in danger. She listens intently and tells you she hadn't thought of calling the police, and she doesn't know the names and phone numbers of any shelters. You encourage her to call the police, and you provide her with information on the shelters. You tell her that she can phone the shelter at any time to get advice and support. You also tell her that the shelters have ongoing groups for women in battering relationships. She expresses a great deal of gratitude for the information and for your interest in her well-being. She cries just a little. When she has left the home during episodes of violence in the past, she has gone to stay at her parents. "They let me stay, but they don't understand. It gets tense there after a while, and I go home," she says.

Initial Assessment of Environmental Supports

Because you think in terms of systems, you are able within a few minutes to assess Mary's environmental supports. She does have her parents' home as a safe environment during the violent periods, but she had no knowledge of shelters and the police as resources. When you discover this, you provide her with the necessary information. Thus, when doing ecosystemic assessments, the interventions can follow immediately, as they did in this case. Mary did not know about some key resources, and the practitioner immediately provided her with the information.

Before you ask about the children's safety during the battering episodes, Mary tells you that John does not hit the children. A few times, he has thrown objects at Mary and just missed the tops of the children's heads, but that is the extent of his physical violence toward them. Mary said that, when she has left the home only to return within an hour or two, John has fed the children, bathed them, and read them bedtime stories. "He loves the kids," she said, "and he says he loves me. I don't know if he really loves me, but he works on being a good father."

You are concerned that the children are witnesses to their father's violence. There is ample evidence that simply witnessing violence can affect children negatively. Children tend to identify with victims and have affects similar to persons who are the direct target of violence. In addition, children who witness violence are at risk of perpetrating violence themselves, while they are still children and later, in adolescence and adulthood.

As you hang up the phone, you realize that this case has serious issues, but there is reason to hope for a good outcome. Mary is bright and articulate. Despite being in a battering situation, she has her wits about her. Although she is speaking for John, he appears to have some strengths: He states his love for Mary and the children, and apparently he enjoys parenting his children. You are not clear about the strengths of the marital relationship. That Mary is not saying she wants to leave John suggests that the marriage may provide a degree of satisfaction.

The face sheet, the intake data, and your initial phone call have provided you with the beginnings of an ecosystemic assessment. This type of assessment involves the generation of a great deal of data. The genogram and the eco-map are two ways of organizing data.

The Genogram

A genogram is a diagram of the family's generational configuration (Guerin & Pendagast, 1976; Hartman, 1979). It helps organize both historical and contemporary data on the major figures in the client's interpersonal environment. Thus, it helps the social worker understand how family patterns are affecting the current situation. Births, deaths, mental illness, alcoholism, divorce, separation, adoption, incest, and family occupation are some of the types of

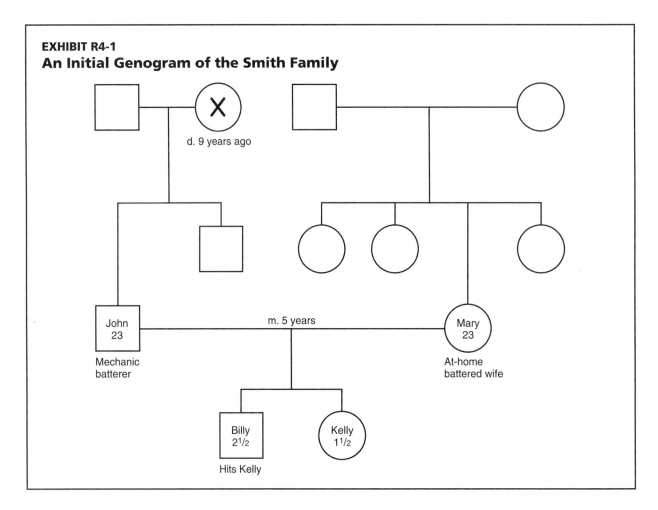

EXHIBIT R4-1
An Initial Genogram of the Smith Family

d. 9 years ago

John
23

m. 5 years

Mary
23

Mechanic
batterer

At-home
battered wife

Billy
2½

Kelly
1½

Hits Kelly

family data present on genograms, which provide a concise means for organizing complex and significant information helpful to intervention planning. The following symbols signify family events and relationships.

○ = Female   □ = Male
▽ = Pregnancy   – – – = Marital separation
× = Death   . . . . = Divorce

Names and ages customarily are placed on the genogram. Exhibit R4-1 is a genogram of the Smith family, based on the information the practitioner has gathered so far. As work with the family proceeds, information will be added to the genogram. The genogram provides a representation of the family generational structure. The initial information suggests John might have issues related to his mother's death, and his reasons for leaving his father's home at age 16 might be important. Neither set of grandparents was divorced, and John's father did not remarry.

This, along with the couple's Catholicism, suggests the possibility that divorce is discouraged by family tradition. On the basis of the genogram information, the worker hypothesizes that John and Mary may be committed to staying together and that John may need to do some family-of-origin work—that is, to work out his thoughts and feelings regarding his mother's death and possible cutoff from his father. Mary is likely to have family-of-origin issues related to her parents, but there are no data yet to support or disconfirm this.

The Eco-Map

An eco-map is a diagram of the family within its social context, and it includes the genogram (Hartman, 1978; Seabury, 1985). The purpose of the eco-map is to organize and clarify data on the supports and stresses in the family's environment. The major meso-level and exo-level social systems that affect the family are placed within cir-

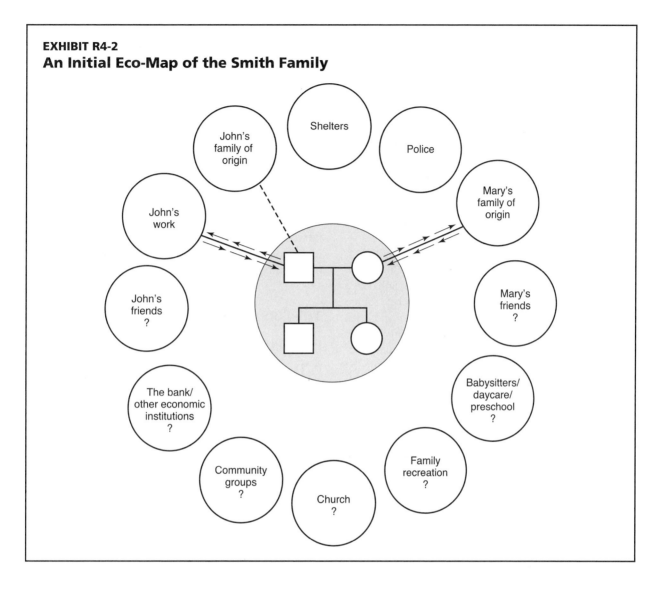

EXHIBIT R4-2
An Initial Eco-Map of the Smith Family

cles; and the family genogram is placed within the center circle. The symbols for the eco-map are

strong relationship ⇄

stressful relationship ┼┼┼┼┼┼┼┼┼┼┼

tenuous relationship – – – – – –

No line at all means no relationship. Exhibit R4-2 is an initial eco-map of the Smith family.

Many of the possible community groups, support groups, and friendship networks are not known at this time. During your first interview with Mary, you intend to explore some of the other environmental supports she might have. The only two types of outside relationships

that are known to you are John's with his work and Mary's with her parents. Chances are good that there are a few more relationships outside the family. Typically in families who come in for treatment, however, a major task is helping them to hook into the already-existing support networks within their communities. As the practitioner, you expect to explore ways that Mary and her family can make more connections outside of the nuclear family.

The Stratification Assessment

The face sheet information also provides a set of facts that will help you do a stratification assessment. A stratification assessment involves looking at the family's and the individual family members' place in the social structure. Race, age, social class, and gender-role issues all are involved in a stratification assessment. These attributes greatly influence a person's access to opportunities, power, and prestige. Mary and John are both white European Americans and, thus, are not likely to have suffered from racism. Because they are Catholic, and the area in which they live is predominantly Catholic, religious prejudice might also not be an issue for them. They are a working-class couple, and they have a good income. Thus, they are not suffering from economic deprivation, but they are not likely to be leaders and policy makers in their communities or on a wider level; their social power, therefore, is likely to be limited.

Gender-role issues in this family may be significant. John has two jobs, while Mary appears to have almost sole responsibility for the children. This suggests an imbalance in parenting and breadwinner roles, which may be a source of stress in the family. Possible support for this hypothesis comes from Mary's report that the kids are driving her crazy and the sound of children screaming at each other during your phone conversation with Mary. John may be overworking, and you wonder what motivates him to work two jobs when his income from one job appears adequate. You wonder if Mary would like to go back to work. You know that, in families where battering occurs, the battering spouse often has traditional gender-role expectations. You plan to explore whether this is contributing to the battering.

You also wonder if child care is available in the neighborhood or if there is a play group. This would provide Mary with some respite from child care and offer her the possibility of adult company. John is likely to have control over the family assets, which would contribute to his power in the family. Mary, on the other hand, is not earning money and is home with children a great deal of the time. She may feel quite powerless within the family.

Developmental Assessment

It is important to analyze the stages of individual and family development in assessing families. John and Mary are the same age, and they married at age 18, right after high school graduation. Thus, they are in a high-risk group for divorce, and they are likely to have had to struggle with late-adolescent issues at the same time they were adapting to marriage and then to parenthood. Because they were married for about two years before Mary became pregnant with Billy, they had some opportunity to establish themselves as a couple before becoming parents. Identity issues, which are salient in adolescence, might still be a source of contention. These might be related, in part, to

gender-role practices, as already noted. They have two very young children, which might be stressful to both parents: John might be worried about financial support, and Mary might be overburdened with parenting.

The children are not at an age where they would play quietly with each other. If they are cooped up in a house all day with each other, and with Mary, the stress level of the mother-children interaction might be quite high. John's battering of Mary not only increases her stress level but may be undermining the children's sense of security, which would make them even more difficult to manage. John's working two jobs would contribute further stress: He would provide Mary with minimal companionship, and he would not be available to share child-care responsibilities. In sum, they are likely to be in a tough spot developmentally, as individuals and as members of a family.

THE FIRST INTERVIEW

Planning for the First Interview

After completing the genogram, the eco-map, and the stratification and developmental assessments, and after thinking about the data you've gathered so far, you make a plan for your initial interview with Mary. Your first priority is to assess whether she has developed an adequate protection plan. Then you plan to gather more data on her perception of the presenting problem—the battering and its effects on her and the children. You intend to allow Mary to tell her story in her own words, but you also intend to guide her gently, so that you can continue to assess the extent to which she has a supportive or potentially supportive environment.

As you do the initial assessment, you are hoping that the process itself will help Mary to see her own situation more clearly. If this happens, she may, on her own, discover some action plans that could protect her from further violence. You intend to keep yourself open to many possibilities. You are taking no stand on whether she should stay with John. You simply don't have enough information on which to make a judgment. You also don't know how strongly Mary feels about working on her relationship with John. Out of respect for the client and because you truly want to start where Mary is, you plan not to make premature judgments about what you think she should do. If she or the children are in danger of serious physical or psychological injury, you will recommend physical separation from John until she and the children are safe.

As you listen to Mary and draw her out, you will be on the alert for data on environmental supports and stresses.

How much time does John spend working? How might this affect the couple and family interactions? What kinds of friendship networks do John and Mary have? What kinds of recreation does the family enjoy? Is the interpersonal environment outside the nuclear family supportive or is it a source of additional stress? As Mary tells you about the presenting problem and family interaction, you are confident that much of these data will be part of her narrative. If there are some blanks, such as information on friendship networks or recreation, you intend to ask about these.

You also will be interested in understanding how stratification and gender-role issues play out in the family. Who makes decisions for the family? Is there conflict over family roles? Does Mary wish she were back at work? Does she want John to work less and spend more time with her and the children? You expect to gather a lot of information about these issues as Mary tells you her story.

As Mary describes the presenting problem, you plan to observe her account of her interactions with John, examining such issues as hearing the other out versus interrupting; asking for clarification and drawing the other out versus assuming knowledge of what the other is thinking and feeling; the ability to express a range of thoughts and feelings versus being able to express a limited range; self-centeredness versus other-centeredness; taking responsibility for one's self versus blaming; patterns of pushing the other around versus cooperation; and the extent of problem-solving behavior versus premature closure of discussion, unilateral actions, and high-handedness. These interactions are part of the interpersonal environment and form a significant part of an ecosystemic assessment.

You also realize that much of what you will learn from Mary's description will be self-report data. If Mary decides that she would like to work on the marital relationship and John comes in for marital therapy, then you will have an opportunity to observe their interactions at first hand. However, Mary will be reporting her perceptions of the interactions, and it is on the basis of her perceptions that she thinks, feels, and acts.

The Presenting Problem

Your intercom buzzes. "Mary Smith is here," the receptionist announces. You walk to the waiting room. Sitting on the edge of the red vinyl chair and biting her lower lip is a fair-skinned, freckled young woman with full, dark hair. "Mrs. Smith?" you say. You introduce yourself and exchange the usual pleasantries as you walk to your office. "No," she says, "I had no trouble finding the office. The kids' pediatrician is right across the street." You note that she takes the children to a pediatrician, and the environment of the agency is familiar to her.

Mary quickly unburdens herself. She loves her husband, but he flares up and hits her. He gets mad at the drop of a hat. You ask her to describe a recent incident when he became angry and hit her. She said, "John always has two of his buddies over. They sit around and drink beer, eat chips, and watch football on TV. I'm the maid. John orders me around. I fetch the beer and fill up the chip bowls." You wonder if John wants to show his friends that he has a wife who is willing to wait on him. Is having such a wife some kind of proof that he is a competent male? Why does Mary wait on the men? Does she think that is her role? These kinds of thoughts relate to the stratification section of the assessment. You are trying to understand the gender-role structure of the couple. Often, traditional gender roles work very well for couples, but when the partners each have different ideas of appropriate gender-role behavior, or if partners are being exploited, the scene is set for conflict.

Mary reports that all three of the men make fun of her: They say she's got a fat can, tell her she ought to smile more, and ask why she doesn't keep the kids quiet. Last Saturday, she got angry and told them to leave her alone. She refused to wait on them. "I slammed the door of the bedroom shut, and Kelly started to cry and banged on the door. Then Billy cried. John yelled at the kids to be quiet. I took the kids to the playground." Mary says that when she got home, John was alone. "He started yelling at me for humiliating him in front of his friends. I yelled back, demanding that he apologize for treating me like a maid and for letting his friends make fun of me. He yelled that they were only kidding. I started swearing, and then he did. He hit me on the side of the head, and I swore some more. He started punching. I ran out of the house. I remember hearing the kids cry. I walked around for about an hour. When I came home, John was calmly feeding the kids. We didn't talk about the fight. In bed that night, he wanted to make love. I didn't feel like it. He got mad again, but we didn't fight. After a while, we went to sleep." The next day was Sunday. They hardly spoke, and John was out all day and night towing cars with his two buddies. Mary was alone with the children.

Assessing the Content of the Presenting Problem

When doing an ecosystemic assessment, asking for a description of a recent incident related to the presenting problem is an efficient way of obtaining data on which to base your continuing assessment.

The material for the eco-map, the stratification assessment, and the interactional assessment is plentiful. John has two close friends with whom he spends a lot of time. Certainly these men provide John with companionship, but they also might be a wedge between John and Mary if, indeed, they are always at the house. Mary feels rejected by them. Whether or not their teasing is intended to be good-natured, she feels put down by their remarks. These men also seem to think that it is appropriate for Mary to serve them beer and chips and to keep the children quiet. If Mary wanted to protest these assigned roles, John would be able to cite the rightness of the roles because he and his two friends all think they are appropriate. Thus, on the eco-map, Mary's relationship to these two men would be characterized as stressful, while John's relationship to them would be strong. That Mary did not call on anyone else when she left the home suggests that she has a tenuous support system. No new lines showing social support for Mary can be drawn. The presence of a playground is a positive aspect of the environment, and it should be indicated on the eco-map.

The material for the stratification assessment is quite rich. Mary and John are not in agreement about roles when John has friends over. Mary does not want to wait on them, while John expects her to. John also expects her to go along with teasing, which Mary doesn't like and wants stopped. The disagreement over appropriate roles was the reason Mary went to her room and then left the home to take the children on an outing. That she took the children instead of leaving them in John's care suggests that she considers child care her responsibility. John did not object when she took the children. Thus, he is likely to agree that the children are largely her responsibility. Drinking beer, eating chips, and watching football on television also are activities strongly associated with the male gender role. It is possible that John is a traditional male, behaving in ways the culture suggests males ought to behave. John's two jobs suggest that he values work highly. Some men believe that their value lies in their wallets: If they earn more money, they feel more valued and more confident that they are competent men. You wonder what Mary's and John's beliefs are about this.

The interactional assessment leads to the hypotheses that John and Mary apparently have few problem-solving skills; that they are not able to draw each other out and hear each other's point of view; that they have a restricted range of expressiveness of thoughts and feelings; and that much of their behavior is unilateral and each becomes frustrated. After a cooling-down period, they are not able to discuss or resolve conflict. They deal with frustration by swearing, yelling, and leaving the field. John has one additional and dangerous behavior: He beats his wife.

Assessing Strengths

As you are listening to Mary and making your assessment, you decide that you need a clearer picture of what the couple's strengths might be. You ask Mary to describe a recent incident in which things went smoothly between her and John. She says, "Three weeks ago on a Saturday morning, before John went off on his towing business, I suggested we go on a picnic next to a lake where we could swim. I know he likes picnics and swimming. His mother used to take him and his brother swimming a lot. I like picnics, and so do the kids. John wanted to go. He agreed to be home by noon. He got home by 12:30, and we were off by 12:45. We had a great day. John cooked. I set the table and cleaned up. He played with the kids in the water. I did, too. The kids fell asleep on the way home. We both unloaded the car and put the kids to bed. We made love that night." This story shows that the couple does share some recreation. Again, the tasks performed generally fall along gender-typed lines, but there was a great deal of cooperative effort also. The couple apparently can take great pleasure in shared activities. The story also provides further data on the amount of time John spends at work and Mary spends with the children. Further data gathering will clarify the reasons for the amount of time the couple spends apart. You hypothesize that staying away is a means of avoiding conflict, a way for John to earn extra money, and an opportunity for John to be with his friends.

Without much pause, Mary's story about the happy family outing spills into her telling you how much John had wanted a family when they were going out. His father used to beat his mother. One time, John drew a knife on his father to stop the beating. His father didn't beat John, but he used to make fun of him and had little time for him. John sees his father once a year at Christmas. She says her own father was not a batterer, but he was an alcoholic and was verbally abusive.

Developmental and Historical Assessment

Mary's narrative provides a great deal of developmental and historical information. As a young family, they are able to participate in appropriate family activities. A picnic outing at a lake is something both the children and the adults enjoy, and they were able to interact with each other in mutually pleasurable ways. Some of the information, however, was Mary's interpretation of John's history, and you would prefer hearing John's story from John. Since, however, you have the data, it does help you to formulate additional hypotheses about the wife battering and the future of the marital relationship. John may well have had a

EXHIBIT R4-3
Genogram of the Smith Family After the First Interview

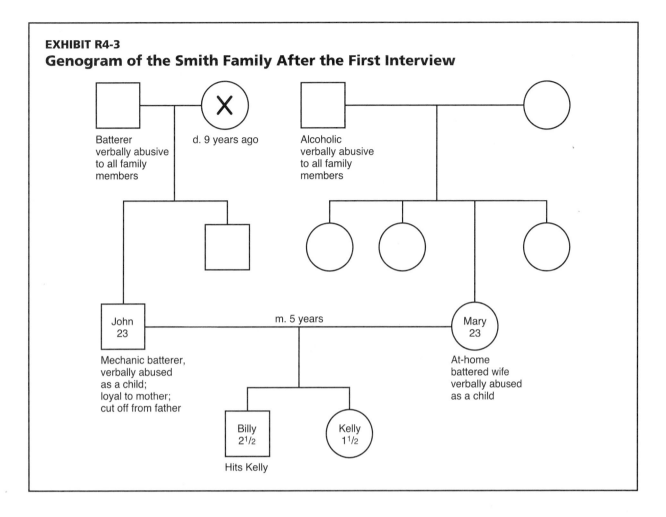

Batterer verbally abusive to all family members

d. 9 years ago

Alcoholic verbally abusive to all family members

John 23

m. 5 years

Mary 23

Mechanic batterer, verbally abused as a child; loyal to mother; cut off from father

At-home battered wife verbally abused as a child

Billy 2½

Hits Kelly

Kelly 1½

close relationship with his mother. Her death may have been a serious and difficult loss. That his father used to beat his mother suggests that John had very poor modeling for problem-solving and for conflict management and resolution. He may well be bringing what he knows into his marriage. John, like all of us, would carry his earlier environment with him. If he had a close relationship with his mother, that might provide a basis for building a nonviolent relationship with Mary. Mary's report of her father's verbal abuse and drinking behavior suggests that she, too, came from a family with poor interpersonal skills of problem-solving and conflict management and resolution. Finally, John's history of witnessing his father's beating of his mother adds to your thinking that John's children—especially Billy—are at risk for becoming physically violent themselves. You've learned that Mary's father is an alcoholic and is verbally abusive, that John's

father also was verbally abusive and beat his wife but not the children, and that John defended his mother against his father. You will place that information on the genogram when the interview is over.

These developmental and historical data provide you with a context in which to understand Mary and John. That there is a dovetailing of the family histories of each spouse does not surprise you. Commonalities in background, particularly emotional constellations, are the rule rather than the exception in couples work. The dovetailing makes the job of intervention much simpler. Each spouse has a part to play in clearing up communication difficulties. John, of course, has the additional task of coming to terms with his physical violence and learning and using alternatives to violence. The interview has given you rich data, and you add information to the genogram and the eco-map (Exhibits 4-3 and 4-4).

EXHIBIT R4-4
Eco-Map of the Smith Family After the First Interview

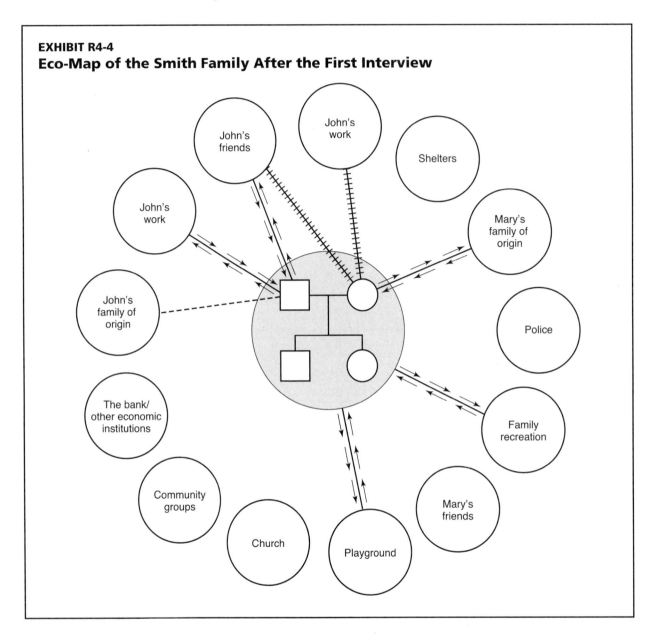

PLANNING INTERVENTIONS

Your initial assessment with Mary has provided you with multiple intervention points. If she were a computer, you could easily reprogram her: You could hook her up to day care, play groups, a battered women's group, a job, a host of supportive friends, and the entire gamut of interpersonal skills. If John were a computer, you could program him to stop the violence immediately and come in for marital therapy. You could hook him up to a group for battering men and some friends who would help him to foster his relationship with Mary. He could instantly acquire a gamut of interpersonal skills and motivation to work less and spend more time with Mary and the children. Neither, of course, is a computer, nor are they programmable. These lists of changes you would like to make, however, are based on your ecosystemic assessment; they are, in fact, the recommendations you intend to make to the couple over the course of your work with them. Exhibit R4-5 shows how you would like the family eco-map to look. The eco-map, then, helps you visualize treatment goals.

EXHIBIT R4-5
Eco-Map of the Smith Family as You Would Like It to Be

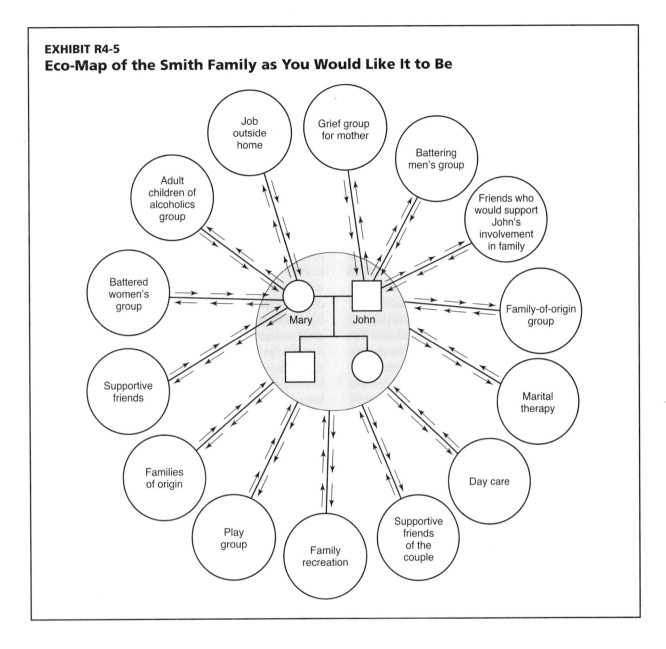

Your assessment, of course, is not complete. As you continue your work with Mary, and possibly John, you will gather further data, which will suggest further possible points of intervention. The data you have thus far, however, touches on all the levels of ecosystemic assessment. From this point on, your assessment will continue, but the balance of your work will tip toward ecosystemic interventions and evaluation of the effectiveness of the interventions.

You start the intervention planning at the place where the client is. Mary is the client you have in your office, and it is with her that you plan the interventions. What she wants and experiences as most pressing will be the focus of the intervention planning. The most pressing issues for her are likely to be: (1) stopping the battering; (2) improving communication; and (3) redistribution of breadwinner and parenting roles. As you continue to work with her, she is likely to be ready to look at and change other aspects of her interpersonal environment. John may also come in for service. This is likely to facilitate more change in the couple's ecosystem.

The work you do with the family will proceed in microsteps, building on the foundation the clients provide. Your ecosystemic assessment will prove a blueprint for how you would like the family to be. The assessment will help you keep your focus as you work on small pieces of the couple's ecosystem. The couple, however, is ultimately in charge of the directions taken. Client self-determination is a fundamental right, superseded only by the right to protection of life. It is also a therapeutic necessity. Your assessment and intervention planning may be first-rate, but careful, respectful, and empathic work with clients to help them define their goals is the means by which you will achieve some of the goals suggested by the ecosystemic assessment.

In doing ecosystemic interventions, practitioners have many choices. You will be working on more than one level. Often major issues are on the micro level—that is, the interpersonal, interactional level—but the micro-level issues often are supported by, affected by, and affect meso-level, exo-level, and macro-level issues. In short, interactional, stratification, developmental, historical, exo-level, and meso-level issues are in dynamic and reciprocal interaction. Concurrent interventions at two or more systems levels appear to be more effective than interventions on one level alone. Advocacy, lobbying for legislative change, working toward policy changes in your own agency, and setting up special community service programs may develop from your micro-level work with individual client systems.

SUMMARY AND DISCUSSION

In doing an ecosystemic assessment, practitioners are gathering data on mutually interacting environmental systems. The genogram helps to organize some of the historical and developmental data that influence present interactions. The eco-map helps organize meso-level and exo-level environmental contingencies that are part of the client's ecosystem. The interactional assessment provides information on the micro level. The stratification assessment helps organize data on gender roles, distribution of power (in decision making, for example), and the family's and the individual's place in the social structure, as determined by age, gender, race, ethnicity, social class, sexual orientation, and occupation, to name a few. The influence of the macro level is seen in all four types of assessments.

The starting point for the ecosystemic assessment is the clients' perceptions of their multiple environments. Observation is often an important source of assessment data, but an ecosystemic assessment can be done with an individual client. An ecosystemic assessment provides many possible points of intervention. Where to start the intervention is determined by where the client is—that is, what the client wants and experiences as most pressing.

In involuntary situations, where a client is court-ordered into treatment, an ecosystemic assessment is especially desirable, because the client might experience many aspects of the environment as painful. If the practitioner begins where the client is and contracts to facilitate changes that the client requests, the client may be more likely to work to change behavior that is harmful and illegal. For example, abusive parents are often court-ordered into treatment. By definition, they are not choosing to work with a practitioner, and they may be quite reluctant to set treatment goals. An ecosystemic assessment might help client and practitioner discover environmental contingencies that support the abusive behavior. Some of these contingencies might be experienced by the client as noxious. Feelings of isolation are common among abusive parents and often are both a source of pain and a contributing factor to the abuse. An eco-map would quickly reveal social isolation. If the client would like to decrease social isolation, then this goal would be responsive to the client's request. Increased social integration might also decrease the likelihood of the parent abusing again. Many other mutually agreed-upon ecosystemic goals would need to be developed and pursued in order to deal with the complex problem of child abuse. The ecosystemic assessment is a solid foundation on which to plan intervention into such complex situations.

Ecosystemic assessments and interventions respond to the heart of the definition of social work direct practice. As social workers, we are enjoined to treat the person-environment interface, and we are enjoined to start where the client is. The ecosystemic approach helps us do this. In involuntary situations, this approach has a great deal of promise in bringing about change in the client's interactions with the myriad aspects of an environment that the client undoubtedly experiences as painful. Finally, the ecosystems approach can also help us accept that there are some situations that we, together with our clients, may not be able to change. Sometimes, the effects of racism, sexism, ageism, and classism on an individual client or family have been so devastating that we are practically helpless. Widespread change in the social structure is the intervention that would facilitate solution of the client's presenting problem. Social workers have a part to play in changing the social structure through research, client advocacy, lobbying legislators, and writing model laws and policy, and by becoming planners, policymakers, or managers in human service agencies. The ecosystems approach, then, opens up many possibilities for intervention on the micro, meso, and macro levels both for direct practitioners and for social work planners, managers, policy makers, researchers, and educators.

READING 5
Social Work and the Medicine Wheel Framework[1]

Lyle Longclaws[2]

The ecological or person-in-situation approach is used by social workers to better understand the person and environment. This approach cannot be appreciated in isolation of cultural factors. This paper describes cultural factors associated with the Anishinaabe (Ojibway/Saulteaux Indians) medicine wheel and compares principles central to the ecological and medicine wheel models.

THE ECOLOGICAL MODEL AND SOCIAL WORK

Social work has always been interested in the person and the environment, despite an emphasis on one or the other throughout the development of the profession. Several decades ago, social workers may have been viewed more as psychologists than as sociologists, with only a secondary and indirect interest in peoples' relationships with their environments. However, since the late 1960s, a definite reciprocal interest in environment has emerged. Brower (1988) recognizes that the ecological model, often defined as the social environmental approach, developed from the profession's dual commitment to the person and environment; it grew directly from the profession's roots. Germain and Gitterman (1980) adopt the ecological perspective and view social work as being at the interface between people and the environment. They see a reciprocal relationship between the person and environment, in which each shapes the other, and advocate treatment of the person within the context of the environment. Bryant (1980) applies an ecological formula to treatment of inner-city families, while Compher (1982) limits his analysis to the educational environment. Both suggest that it is possible for social workers to effectively intervene in order to ensure appropriate relationships and productivity within such settings.

The ecological framework assists us in organizing information about people and environments in order to understand the interconnectedness. In this approach, human beings are regarded as engaging in constant adaptive and evolutionary interchange with all elements of their environments. Human needs and problems are generated by the transactions between people and their environments.

Additionally, like all living systems, people need to maintain a notion of fit in order to match human needs to environmental resources.

Stress results from lack of fit and the cognitive appraisal of imbalance between perceived demand and perceived capability. Produced by either external or internal demands, stress occurs in a cyclical form: One stressful event leads to another. In this way of thinking, stress is part of any transaction; social workers may intervene in the cycle to help mobilize the client's ability to deal with the perceived demand. Social workers may also reframe the situation or provide supportive interventions.

The client's ability to cope depends on personality attributes and also situational elements such as the incentive system and societal preparation and support for coping. The social work profession forms part of the social environment and acts a mediator with the external environment. Social workers offer emotional support by providing problem-solving skills and may be responsible for advocating at the case level while working with the person. Further, social workers may advocate on behalf of a class, such as single mothers, and in areas of policy.

Individuals move through a series of life transitions, all of which require environmental supports and coping skills and may result in stress if there is not a good fit between internal and external demands and resources (Germain & Gitterman, 1980). Common life transitions include stages of human development, changes in occupation, and relocation from rural to urban areas. In general, the environment may either assist or hinder life transitions. It is helpful to think of different layers in the environment. The first two layers include the natural world and the built world and their effects on people's behavior. The third layer, which consists of three sublayers, is the social world and deals with people in terms of organizations. Examples of the first sublayer include neighbors and self-help groups. The second sublayer includes service organizations, such as school systems. The last sublayer consists of culture, which is broadly shared across families and organizations and includes values and political systems. Most of the attention of social work has been on the third layer. Meanwhile, the built and social worlds are in continual interaction among these layers and the individual.

The profession of social work is interested in the person, the environment, and transactions between the two. In contrast to labeling that fosters a deficit view of the

---

[1] An original reading for *Social Work Processes*.
[2] Social worker and consultant, and member of the Waywayseecappo First Nation, Winnipeg, Manitoba.

person, transactional concepts can help focus assessment and intervention on the relations between person and environment. Transactional ideas view adaptation as a process of shaping physical and social environments; people in turn are also shaped by the environment. The goal of intervention in transactions is to release adaptive capacities and to improve the environment. Social workers are interested in transactions that either promote or inhibit growth and development.

Thus, social workers assess the nature of transactions and intervene in them. Such interventions are often oriented toward stress reduction and enhancement of coping. Network intervention tries to increase mutual aid among those within the social network and supports the development of self-esteem, personal autonomy, sovereignty, and other experiences that will increase individuals' well-being. An adaptation evaluation takes account of emotional and situational stress in order to help people discover their inner resources and enhance their self-esteem and confidence.

The ecological approach is appealing to social workers of Anishinaabe ancestry because it suggests the possibility of culturally appropriate treatment for the Anishinaabe Indian people within their environments. Redhorse and his colleagues (Redhorse, Lewis, Fest, & Decker, 1978) challenge the profession to apply ecological standards to Indian families, who may be vanishing as rapidly as the buffalo. However, caution is necessary; the Anishinaabe social worker cannot afford to be drawn to yet another mirage in hopes of quenching a very real thirst in the midst of a vast desert.

THE ANISHINAABE MEDICINE WHEEL TEACHINGS

Medicine wheel teachings are passed down orally by Anishinaabe elders from Waywayseecappo First Nation (located in West Central Manitoba, near the town of Rossburn). Waywayseecappo elders teach that four laws or ceremonies were given to the Anishinaabe in order for them to obtain balance and harmony. These are the midewewin, aniba-qwayshimoong, anishanabe-nee-midewing, and ape-tong. (Exhibit R5-1 provides a glossary of selected Anishinaabe concepts.) Of the four, the midewewin is most frequently practiced by Anishinaabe.

Over the years, several traditions have evolved. The council dance, for example, is now held for peaceful purposes, and not for war as in traditional tribal times. Elders continue to practice age-old ceremonies in which the four laws are handed down. In order to fully appreciate and participate in

the four major ceremonies, or laws, Anishinaabe must travel the medicine wheel journey. Exhibit R5-2 presents a diagram of the medicine wheel, which serves as a framework for learning the significance of ceremonies and rituals.

The medicine wheel approach views the universe and a person's position in it as critical to understanding the meaning of a good life. It acknowledges the interconnection of all beings and forces existing on physical and spiritual worlds. The medicine wheel framework has teachings essential for the physical world, while recognizing the direct link to oda aki (centeredness). Centeredness, the ultimate goal to be achieved within the medicine wheel circle, is the achievement of balance—peace and harmony with oneself and all other living things. Individuals travel within their own medicine wheel but are guided by the teachings given to all Anishinaabe. Each life affects all others in the circle of life, in both the present and the future. All living things are born with a spirit, but only human beings must find harmony within the circle, because all other living things, such as the plants, animals, and elements, are already in balance with the universe. A philosophy of interdependence is paramount to achieving harmony and balance in the medicine wheel. The medicine wheel demonstrates the absence of a hierarchy. It has no top or bottom; all living things have their place and responsibility in the natural order of life within the wheel. People and nature are viewed as interdependent and connected. Whatever happens to one happens to all. Thus, utmost respect and reciprocity is practiced within the medicine wheel circle.

Given this worldview, the purpose of the medicine wheel is to provide a framework for ensuring the balance and harmony of Anishinaabe within the circle of life. Those who disregard the medicine wheel teachings experience imbalance and disharmony with all around them. To ensure balance and harmony, the medicine wheel proposes a way of living that emphasizes responsibilities, values, and ethics. Ceremonies assist individuals in centering themselves and give them strength to participate in a lifelong learning process. People are born good. Throughout life, the teachings of the medicine wheel provide guidance and protection from evil forces that can lead people astray—off the good or red road. These evil forces are found all across Turtle Island, mother earth, and Indian country. Evil forces of the spiritual world are manifested in the physical world through the use of bad medicine. Evil forces are also found in physical substances such as alcohol and drugs. The values of materialism, greed, jealousy, and dishonesty are also seen as evil forces, as they prevent the individual from reaching personal centeredness. People who are involved with these evil forces are lost, not only to themselves but

EXHIBIT R5-1
Glossary of Anishinaabe Concepts

Aniba-qwayshimoong: one of the four lodges or laws of the Anishinaabe.

Anishinaabe: literally, the original people (in the Ojibway/Saulteaux language).

Anishinaabe-nee-midewing: one of the four lodges or laws of the Anishinaabe.

Ape-tong: one of the four lodges or laws of the Anishinaabe.

Bad medicine: the destructive use of medicine and knowledge to harm an individual.

Council dance: ceremony traditionally performed in time of war but now modified to promote peace and goodwill.

Eshkabes: individuals who assist a teacher elder during ceremonies. These individuals may also be apprentices who are learning the teachings.

Giveaway: traditional ceremony in which personal possessions are distributed to those in attendance.

Indian Country: common term for land traditionally held by First Nations.

Kitche Manitou or *Manitou:* literally, the great mystery.

Medicine wheel: an organizing and clarifying framework, dynamic in nature, for thinking about existence in the universe.

Midewewin: lodge or law of the Anishinaabe; currently, the most frequently practiced of the laws.

Mother earth: the earth as giver and sustainer of life.

Naming ceremony: a ceremony in which an individual is given his or her spiritual or Indian name.

Oda aki: literally, heart of the earth or center.

Ojibway: common English term for the Anishinaabe.

Powwow: a social gathering usually with dancing and feasts.

Saulteaux: common French term for the Anishinaabe—specifically, those who historically lived at present-day Sault Ste. Marie and later migrated to present-day Manitoba and Saskatchewan.

Shake tent: sacred ceremony practiced for specific purposes and only on rare occasions.

Sundance: ceremony held for four days every June, commencing on the longest day of the year; the general purpose is to strengthen the commitment of participants in the ways of the medicine wheel teachings.

Sweatlodge: purification and healing ceremony.

Sweetgrass: one of four sacred cleansing medicines used by the Anishinaabe.

Turtle Island: North America.

to the nation. Therefore, feeling a direct connection to the spirit world, Anishinaabe are careful not to offend any of their relations, living or dead, through their actions or thoughts, lest they be the recipient of that spirit's wrath. This worldview reinforces the ethics and values of the Anishinaabe. Most aspects of life are defined and given significance within the context of the spiritual world.

Central life principles of the Anishinaabe include respect, kindness, caring, sharing, honor, and the attainment of wisdom, strength, and truth. These values are operationalized within extended family groups and clans, which take on specific roles and responsibilities; the bear clan, for example, is responsible for protection within the nation or tribe, while the responsibility of extended family groups is to ensure the survival of the family.

Particular ethical principles are defined for use within the extended family groupings, within the tribe, and in

dealings with other nations. All Anishinaabe are either part of an extended family or members of a clan. They participate in the circle of life, with different responsibilities in different phases. The circle is a powerful symbol of the interconnection and interdependence of all the phases.

A child enters the circle at birth. The parents make a gift of tobacco and cotton cloth to an elder who will conduct a naming ceremony, so that Manitou will recognize the child's spirit. Later in life, if the child states his or her Indian name before praying, Manitou will hear the prayers. The naming ceremony reinforces group identification, as family members accept their responsibilities to raise the child in a prescribed way. The ceremony includes the burial of the child's umbilical cord, signifying that the child is forever a member of the nation. The child is not the property of the parents; the name reinforces a deep connection to all of mother earth and enables the child to grow

EXHIBIT R5-2
The Anishinaabe Medicine Wheel

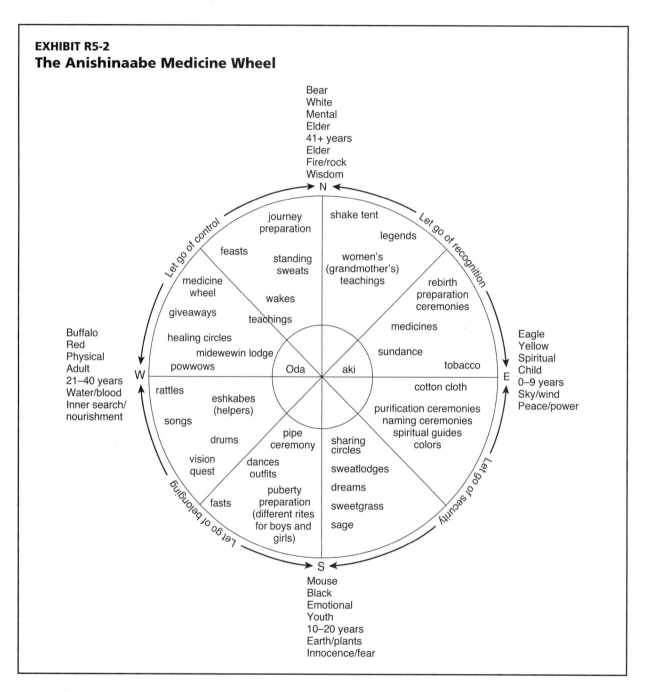

Bear
White
Mental
Elder
41+ years
Elder
Fire/rock
Wisdom

Buffalo
Red
Physical
Adult
21–40 years
Water/blood
Inner search/
nourishment

Eagle
Yellow
Spiritual
Child
0–9 years
Sky/wind
Peace/power

Mouse
Black
Emotional
Youth
10–20 years
Earth/plants
Innocence/fear

Let go of control
Let go of recognition
Let go of security
Let go of belonging

journey preparation
shake tent
legends
feasts
standing sweats
women's (grandmother's) teachings
medicine wheel
wakes
rebirth preparation ceremonies
giveaways
teachings
healing circles
medicines
midewewin lodge
sundance
powwows
Oda
aki
tobacco
rattles
cotton cloth
eshkabes (helpers)
purification ceremonies
naming ceremonies
spiritual guides
colors
songs
pipe ceremony
sharing circles
drums
sweatlodges
vision quest
dances outfits
dreams
fasts
puberty preparation (different rites for boys and girls)
sweetgrass
sage

N
W   E
S

in spirit. The name also provides guidance; with deepening understanding of the name, the child begins to distinguish his or her individual gifts. Frequently, the child receives personal colors, related to the name; the meaning of the colors is elaborated in traveling through the circle. When worn by the child, colors are believed to give strength.

After receiving traditional gifts, the elder prepares for the ceremony. When the time is right to share the naming celebration, a pipe ceremony is conducted at sunrise with family members. Prayers of gratitude are expressed. Through the dreams of the elder, the spirits give the name to the child. The name signifies the belief that a spirit guide will protect and direct the child over the life journey. As part of the ceremony, the extended family holds a feast to celebrate its commitment to the child.

As clan members travel through the circle of life, they grow in ways of knowledge, spirit, and wisdom. The four directions of the medicine wheel possess teachings to assist in the search for knowledge and wisdom. Anishinaabe believe that the east is associated with illumination, peace, and spiritual influence. These gifts are represented by the eagle, who flies closest to Manitou and is believed to have great vision or farsightedness. Because the sun rises in the east, this is the direction of the child and of the color yellow, signifying the sun's rays. In recent interpretations, the east is associated with Asian peoples. The eastern direction is also represented by the elements such as wind and is the domain of the sky.

Moving in the direction of the sun as it crosses the sky, the next direction is south. The south is represented by the mouse; the gifts received there include innocence and fear. This direction corresponds to the emotional realm; within the circle of life, it is associated with the ages of 10–20 years. The south represents the worlds of plants; mother earth is represented by the color black, signifying a time of letting go of security and belonging, which can be a dark or unknown time. Ceremonies such as sweatlodges, pipe ceremonies, vision quests, and male and female puberty rites are introduced to assist youth. These ceremonies are enriched with sharing circles, songs, chants, and dancing. The young Anishinaabe person may be given the right to hold sharing circles in which sweetgrass, sage, and other medicines are used, depending on his ability to respect these gifts. The south begins making contact with the center of the circle, known as oda aki. The individual is conscious of experiences of harmony and balance. As the frequency of these experiences increases, the individual begins to develop the ability to visit the spiritual world, and the likelihood of having a meaningful journey increases.

The next direction in the medicine wheel is the west, represented by the buffalo. Buffalo are leaders of the hoof clan and represent the gifts of nourishment and introspection. This direction is associated with people aged 21–40 and is the physical domain of the circle. The corresponding color is red, representing the setting sun and the blood or water of the physical world. Like buffalo, people in this phase of life protect and provide nourishment for their young and also protect the weak and old. In this phase, there is opportunity for searching inwardly, which provides the strength for letting go of control; this is necessary in order to remain in balance and harmony with all living things. During this phase, the vision received in youth is given meaning and is strengthened by participating as an

eshkabe (helper) to an elder or medicine person. Gifts of songs, drums, and rattles reinforce the teachings and provide greater insight. With greater understanding of the medicine wheel teachings at this phase, the individual has greater influence in healing circles and a place of credibility in the midewewin lodge. Giveaways are a necessary part of benefiting from such spiritual nourishment. This phase is associated with a different style of songs and dances at social gatherings such as powwows.

The fourth direction is the north, represented by the bear. The gifts of this direction are knowledge, guidance, and wisdom. This phase is the mental sphere in the circle of life; having lived more than 40 years, Anishinaabe are teachers of young and old alike. This direction is represented by the color white, to denote the blanket of wisdom in the winter of an Anishinaabe's life cycle. The elements of fire and rock are powerful symbols of completing the foundation within the medicine wheel. The rocks, as the oldest substance on mother earth, are referred to as grandfathers and used in the sacred sweatlodge ceremony. They are heated in a fire and then placed with great reverence in the center of the sweatlodge. Water is sprinkled on the rocks with medicines, so that the spirits of grandfather rocks are released and heal the participants in the sweatlodge ceremony. In this phase in life, having practiced the ways of the people as outlined in the medicine wheel teachings, the elder will now be prepared to assume leadership in ceremonies. Elder Anishinaabe conduct the sweatlodge, pipe ceremonies, standing sweats, sundance, shake tents, council dance, naming ceremonies, burial rites, and feasts, and pass on teachings through stories. They are healers, with knowledge of the medicines available from the plant world. Anishinaabe are very respectful of elders and their wisdom and look forward to taking this role in the clan. Elders have let go of control and recognition, so that they live life for their Manitou and all creation. In addition, elders are seen as returning to the beginning of the circle, which is the spiritual world; they are becoming a child once again, particularly toward the end of their life in the physical world.

The last three directions within the Anishinaabe medicine wheel are the vertical, which represents Kitche Manitou; the horizontal, which represents mother earth; and the inward, which represents the heart or center. There are many ways of traveling on the medicine wheel circle. For example, contrary people will do everything backward; others may travel vertically or horizontally within the circle; still others will start at a certain direction and work their way around the circle. The process is not linear but cyclical. Anishinaabe may be born in one direction, learn those teachings, but never progress throughout their lifetime; these people are referred to as warriors. A chief or clan mother will travel through two phases and receive the teachings and gifts. An elder will travel and obtain the gifts and teachings of three phases, while the medicine person will have completed or traveled through all four phases and will be knowledgeable of the teachings and gifts. Medicine people supervise others in their journey through the medicine wheel.

ECOLOGICAL PRACTICE AND ANISHINAABE HEALING PRINCIPLES

The ecological and medicine wheel frameworks have been presented as independent models. However, they overlap. For example, the respect of person and environment embraced within the ecological approach has parallels in Anishinaabe belief. Another similarity is that both approaches recognize the value of intervention by an expert within the culture; when people require assistance, they involve another party. As part of the process, all experts identify problems in relationship to the environment as they understand it. In social work, experts exercise authority that they have obtained through academic preparation and certification that emphasizes intellectual ways of helping clients. These experts often operate within a spiritual anomie and consider spiritual values taboo; help is secular in nature. Professional principles hold that experts must be objective in order to be effective. Emotional and personal involvement with clients is discouraged, in the belief that this will cloud the expert's judgment.

The Anishinaabe tradition offers useful insights to ecological practitioners. One is the importance of expertise based on life experience, wisdom, and recognition within one's culture. Further, for the Anishinaabe, spirituality is an essential element of centeredness, although spiritual needs are often ignored by social workers. The individual is seen as part of an extended family and clan network, with reciprocal responsibilities to other members of the extended family and clan.

The Anishinaabe healing principles recognize the inherent rights and dignity of the individual but assert the interconnectedness of all, so that the healing of the individual is necessary not only for the person, but for family and clan. Holistic values, with ceremonial supports, contribute balance to the spiritual dimensions of life. Anishinaabe experts base their qualifications on life experience and giftedness. The key is to respect the family and clan in order to establish a relationship, so that reciprocity can occur. Reciprocity is necessary for the person to be-

come centered, so that balance and harmony can be restored both to the person and to those affected, such as family and clan; in this way relationships within the environment are strengthened.

Because elders have gained the wisdom to understand the family's reality, they can use the dynamics of that reality to guide people to healthier lives. Therefore, elders serve as mentors in guiding unhealthy families beyond their trapped reality. This guidance, provided within the medicine wheel framework, suggests that behavior is determined by environment. To change behavior means that the environment must be changed. Yet, the principle of a centered self (including harmony with spiritual needs) will effectively balance the realities of the physical world or environment.

Becoming centered is an empowering process. Less emphasis is placed on expertise; self is the principal resource. The utilization of extended family is encouraged to support this self-empowering process and contributes to the overall healing of the person within the environment. The process includes isolating parts of the person that do not permit self to provide leadership. Ceremonial activities support the person in reaching an agreement with all parts of the self. These healing practices are driven by spiritual principles. Holistic principles are rooted in ancient wisdom, are humanistic in nature, and do not permit the isolation of person or problem from environment.

The interconnectedness of all cannot be overemphasized, but assistance is personalized in order to provide meaning and mutual healing. The person is not viewed as a client but referred to as family. This is in direct contrast to labeling people as clients or patients, where the emphasis is on the problem. A person-oriented focus exists throughout an indefinite treatment time span. Unlike short-term intervention, where independence is viewed as progress, the Anishinaabe healing principles emphasize the restoration of balance and harmony, which can only occur if there is interdependence.

CONCLUSION

This comparison of the ecological approach to social work and Anishinaabe healing principles suggests that there are similarities—in particular, the idea of interconnectedness and a focus on both person and environment. But there are different emphases. Elders identify problems in terms of the spiritual relationship to environment. Healing occurs primarily from the inside out (in the spiritual realm) and not from the outside in (in the environment). Can social workers, with their secular traditions, accommodate spiritual aspects within their practice?

The involvement of extended family is central to Anishinaabe healing. The extended family is also a part of the ecological system of all people. How can extended-family involvement be made a more central part of social work practice?

The encouragement of professional resources that provide arms-length treatment will discourage voluntary requests for assistance from most Anishinaabe people. The authoritarian attitude that the expert knows what is best for the client will not result in client independence. Can a personal relationship evolve if the person seeking assistance is viewed simply as a client in the worker's overflowing caseload? Is it reasonable to expect a professional to ig-nore an academic training that encouraged objectivity and authority in order to practice Anishinaabe beliefs when helping people in need?

The Anishinaabe medicine wheel is not a model of social work, but the teachings can provide social workers with useful tools. Social workers need to recognize the important roles played by elders, ceremonies, spirituality, and family in the ecological systems of clients from Native cultures. Supporting the client's participation in traditional culture, and not getting in the way of these practices, may be the most useful way of restoring balance and harmony between the person and environment.

READING 6
The Birky Family[1]

INITIAL CONTACT

John Birky is a 4-year-old white boy enrolled in a full day-care program. The day care center is located in a predominantly African American public housing project in a southern city of 90,000. This center provides services to low-income families where both parents work or the only parent works or is disabled. John was referred to the staff social worker a few weeks after his enrollment because he demonstrated possible neglect. He usually arrived at the center at 8:00 A.M. unfed and inadequately dressed, and his frequent illnesses (cold, strep throat) were very often untreated. His language development was limited, and he was poorly toilet trained. Staff members were required to change his clothes frequently and expressed resentment of and dislike for the child. The center teaching staff had made routine attempts to contact the mother—sent notes home, phoned—but thus far with no success.

On the social worker's first phone call, she reached the mother, who was obviously upset; only the day before, her 2-year-old son had drowned in the uncovered drainage ditch behind the apartment. This incident had been on the late news broadcast the night before, but none of the staff had realized it was John's brother. The ditch ran the length of the housing project, which was located in an under-served, low-income part of the city and had been the scene of a previous drowning. Although the city had promised to cover the ditch, there were no indications of any efforts to do so.

The social worker made an immediate visit and found the mother in tears but pathetically eager to talk to someone. She said her mother and most of her large extended family were coming for the funeral the next day; they lived about 75 miles away in a rural Appalachian section of the state. From what the mother said, the social worker gathered that Mr. and Mrs. Birky had grown up there together and married very early. Their first child had been stillborn. Tears rolled down Mrs. Birky's cheeks when she told this. "It looks like God don't want us to raise no children," she said. She had resented the day-care staff changing John's clothes; he never soiled himself at home. She also said, "They told John to eat breakfast before he came. John eats when we eat—don't none of us eat much. But we have enough and we never, none of us, been on welfare." The remains of a lunch of hominy and red beans could be seen on a card table in the almost-bare living room.

Wiping her eyes, Mrs. Birky explained that the 2-year-old, Robert, was too young for the day care center, which takes only ages 3–5. A neighbor had been keeping Robert and several children who were under 3 or otherwise ineligible, but Robert was at home with his father the day he drowned because Mr. Birky had been laid off from his service station job. The phone had rung and Mr. Birky had run into the next room to answer it, hoping it was about his job. Somehow Robert got out the back door and was gone. Mr. Birky hadn't missed him at first. Here Mrs. Birky broke off. Then she said, "Children are bound to get into things. I don't know—it's the Lord's will, I guess. My whole family has had a lot of sadness." She said her husband had gone to see about the funeral. She hoped they

---

[1] An original case study for *Social Work Processes*.

EXHIBIT R6-1
Service Plan for the Birky Family

Problem:

An uncovered ditch creates a safety risk for children in the housing project in which Mr. and Mrs. Birky live. Two children, including their 2-year-old son, have drowned in the ditch.

Objectives:

1. To get the city to fulfill its commitment to cover the ditch.
2. To secure damages from the city for failure to follow through on a previous commitment to cover the ditch.

Service Plan:

Tasks	To be done by	Completion date
1. Contact legal aid and the family's minister to identify attorneys who specialize in this type of case	Mr. & Mrs. Birky	October 15
2. Make inquiries of legal experts to identify attorneys who have successfully sued the city for damages and accept cases on a contingency fee basis	Social worker	October 15
3. Meet to review the list of possible attorneys and develop a short list of three attorneys	Social worker and Mr. & Mrs. Birky	October 20
4. Arrange visits with the attorneys to discuss the case and fee arrangements	Mr. & Mrs. Birky	October 25
5. Meet with the three attorneys	Mr. & Mrs. Birky and social worker	November 10
6. Meet to discuss whether to retain an attorney to file suit against the city	Mr. & Mrs. Birky and social worker	November 15
7. If decision is to retain an attorney, secure and review retainer agreement	Mr. & Mrs. Birky and social worker	November 20
8. Sign retainer agreements	Mr. & Mrs. Birky	November 24
9. If, after consultation with their attorney, the decision is against suing the city, meet to consider other possible alternatives	Mr. & Mrs. Birky and social worker	November 25

could borrow some money to pay for it when the families arrived.

Mrs. Birky said she felt strange in the city. Most of her neighbors were "colored—I mean black." She explained, as if for the benefit of the African American social worker, that there were no blacks where she grew up and their ways were strange to her, "but there's good and bad in all people." But she didn't like living around people who were on welfare, "colored or white." Her family would "do without" first.

Although the day-care center's records show Mrs. Birky's age as 20, she looked 35 or more, was thin, and needed dental work. She picked up a book from the battered coffee table and said she had enrolled in a GED course; that's where she was "the day it happened." Her husband, aged 21, could barely read and write, and she wanted to "learn more so I can help him." She had never done "public work" and had no plans to get a job, though some of her sisters did waitress work or factory work "back home." Mr. Birky had worked in a factory that closed; that was why they had moved to the city.

SERVICE PLAN FOR THE BIRKY FAMILY

Suppose that the service plan in Exhibit R6-1 has been developed with Mr. and Mrs. Birky to get the ditch covered and to secure damages from the city for the loss of their son. The principle of equifinality discussed in Chapter 2 indicates that there are many ways to move from a problem to accomplish an objective; you may think of other alternative plans to accomplish the goal of getting the ditch covered.

READING 7
The Stover Family[1]

This family was referred to Family Service Agency by the Child Protection Unit of the State Department of Health and Human Services. At the time of referral, the family household included Earl (husband), age 43; June (wife and mother), age 39; and three children. George, age 12, and Larie, age 5, are from her second marriage. Eileen, age 4, was born four months after the Stovers married.

Mr. and Mrs. Stover had been involved with numerous social agencies during the past 15 years. Most contacts addressed issues related to the children's welfare although approximately 8 years ago, Mrs. Stover received psychosocial services following a suicide attempt. Mrs. Stover has had three marriages, the first after she became pregnant in high school. She never lived with her first husband and the baby was adopted immediately after birth. Her second husband had a serious developmental disability for which he received state-sponsored financial support. Three of her children with him were placed for adoption. She became involved with Mr. Stover approximately 5 years ago while still married to her second husband. Eileen arrived four months after their marriage.

Mr. Stover has received services on and off from the Veterans Administration since his psychiatric discharge from the U.S. Army 20 years ago. He evidently suffers from a serious anxiety disorder and alcoholism. During contacts with Family Service 3 years ago, Mrs. Stover reported that Mr. Stover had physically abused her and the children on several occasions.

During the past four years, there have been six complaints of neglect of the children. These have originated

from Mrs. Stover's relatives, her former husband and his relatives, the school nurse, and their minister. The Child Protection Unit has found insufficient evidence to proceed on these charges. Workers have found it difficult to work with Mrs. Stover. When initially interviewed, she appears superficially cooperative but subsequently avoids workers whenever possible. She typically is not home for scheduled appointments. Family Service Agency was reluctant to reopen the case. Past experience with Mrs. Stover indicated that she would not participate in the process. However, on plea from the Child Protection Unit, we decided to make another attempt to provide service. Child protection workers were especially concerned about Eileen Stover, the 4-year-old, who has a condition believed to be muscular dystrophy. They thought that Mrs. Stover underestimated the seriousness of Eileen's condition and did not always ensure that the girl received adequate medical care.

March 20 to April 15   Since we accepted the case, I have tried on numerous occasions to contact the Stover family without success. The Child Protection worker reports that Mrs. Stover stays away from home if she knows who is coming. The worker also expressed the opinion that Mrs. Stover simply cannot be trusted at all; she agrees to everything and does nothing: On April 13, I sent a note saying I would call on April 15. This time Mrs. Stover was home.

The Stovers have two rooms on the second floor of a large house, the ground floor of which is in the process of being remodeled. Mrs. Stover indicated that she couldn't talk to me since her husband was sleeping and she did not want to wake him. She is of medium height and seems to be pregnant. Mrs. Stover appears quite dirty and somewhat

---

[1] An original case study for *Social Work Processes*.

disheveled. Barefooted, she is dressed in old slacks and a stain-covered man's white shirt. I introduced myself and said I would speak very quietly to avoid disturbing Mr. Stover. I referred to the previous contacts she had had with our agency, Child Protection, and other agencies and explained we recognized that she faced a number of difficult problems. I said we wanted to help. I referred to Eileen's health condition and to the fact that Mrs. Stover had temporarily left her husband last March. I said I knew such separations often result in difficulties for the family as a whole. Mrs. Stover's reaction was to say that the situation has cleared up and she feels that the marital relationship is now okay. She did, however, appear responsive to my interest in her problems and accepted an office interview for April 23.

April 23 Mrs. Stover did not keep the scheduled office appointment. I then attempted several home visits, but she was never home when I arrived. I made two other appointments by telephone, neither of which she kept.

June 24 I finally located the Stover family when Child Protection called to say they had moved to Jonesville. On this date, I visited the new residence and found both Mr. and Mrs. Stover at home. Their present housing is a four-room shack raised about five feet from the ground on stilts beside the river. The home was flooded out two years ago. There is no foundation; the beams and supporting joists in the house were seriously weakened by the flood. The sides and interior partitions are still caked with river dirt.

There is no sign of paint on the interior or exterior of the house, which is barely habitable. The front door has a drop of about four feet to the ground, with only a crude ladder. The home has two bedrooms, a living room, and kitchen; these are adequate in size. Toilet facilities are outdoors. The shack was previously owned by an elderly bachelor who died. The house was in estate when the Stovers moved in, and they are paying a low rent, which may be applied toward a purchase price if the Stovers decide to stay.

Mr. Stover is a small-built man, neatly dressed, unshaven, and quiet. Mrs. Stover had told him that I had seen her earlier. He said that they were getting on well now. However, he said he lost his job and is now unemployed. He stated that the previous marital difficulties had been due largely to his alcohol problem. He said he got angry when he drank and that led to fights with his wife. He reported that they haven't fought with each other for the last 10 months. I asked him to what he attributed the change. He feels that difficulties arose because of his nervousness

and unemployment. When he is nervous, he starts drinking, and they go round and round again. He said that he had been employed pretty steadily during the last summer and fall, mostly on temporary jobs. He says he cannot get full-time employment as a carpenter because he would be unable to pass the medical examination required for insurance. He indicates that's the reason he must take odd jobs and casual labor. He also reports that he becomes especially nervous when he works too close to too many people and that he dislikes working for other people. He says that small things bother him and he is easily irritated. He states that he would prefer to work for himself. His ambition would be to get a small farm of his own where he could grow vegetables for market. The problem is lack of capital, and he doubts if he will get a chance to do this. During this visit, the Stovers present a united front. However, Mrs. Stover neither nodded nor spoke in support of much of what her husband said. She did say in his presence that she felt his drinking had improved.

July 17 Again, I failed to find the Stovers at home on visits I made by appointment. When I visited the home on July 15, it appeared that they had moved again. Child protection had no new address. However, on July 17, to my surprise Mrs. Stover came into the office. She was neatly dressed in a clean dress and had carefully brushed her hair. She seemed anxious and uncomfortable. Mrs. Stover said she had decided to leave her husband because he has been drinking heavily, mostly wine, and had beaten her and the kids. She is afraid of what will happen. She said he had been on the wagon until July 4 when he started drinking again. Mrs. Stover felt this had something to do with the troubles with housing. She also said that Mr. Stover has picked up with a neighbor who drinks, and they have been going out together. Mr. Stover, she said, "gets nervous and edgy. He orders the kids and me around. Nothing I do pleases him. He calls me all sorts of names when he gets drunk. He even pushed me down in the yard when I got in his way."

Mrs. Stover said she is out of money and food, and the baby is due shortly. I helped her secure groceries from the local food pantry and asked if she wanted to go into a shelter to ensure her own safety as well as that of the children. She declined, saying that they were safe enough for the time being. I then asked about making application for Temporary Assistance for Needy Families (TANF). She was hesitant. She reported that she had briefly received assistance before but that she had lost her benefit because she failed to look for work. I asked if she wanted my help making another application. She said yes and agreed to return to the office tomorrow to do so.

July 18 to September 1 Mrs. Stover arrived at the office as scheduled. Together, Mrs. Stover and I made application for TANF and arranged for child care during the week before and after her hospitalization for the birth of the baby. She went into the hospital two days later. I visited with her twice during her stay in the hospital. After the baby's birth, Mrs. Stover moved in with her sister. However, she failed to notify her TANF caseworker of her new address and circumstances. I suggested that if she kept her caseworkers informed, they might respect her more. Mrs. Stover said her caseworkers didn't trust her. I challenged her to prove them wrong. She then said she was planning to move again soon. She said, "I'll notify my caseworker before and after the move." This time she did exactly what she said she would.

September 15. Visit to the Stover Home When I visited on this date, Mrs. Stover, Eileen, and Peter, the baby, were at home. Eileen played happily in the apartment while the baby slept. Eileen has come to know me. The apartment consists of three good-sized rooms in an old apartment building. The apartment is neat and clean. Mrs. Stover was dressed in slacks and a clean blouse. Her hair was neatly brushed. She was noticeably cleaner and was obviously paying more attention to her appearance. Mrs. Stover mentioned she has bought some winter clothes for the children, but she needs to buy a few more things. She showed me her TANF budget, which includes funds to be signed over by Mr. Stover from his disability pension. Mr. Stover held up signing the documents, but instead gave Mrs. Stover some money himself in September, and is offering to do this every month. Mrs. Stover refused this offer and reported the whole matter to the VA office. By law, she feels, he will be required to sign the document because part of his disability pension is for his wife and children. She feels Mr. Stover is still trying to punish her and spoil her plans. She also suspects he wants to move back in with her and the kids. I asked Mrs. Stover about her plans regarding the marriage. Mrs. Stover seems quite sure at this point that she wants a permanent separation. She would want a rule that Mr. Stover would visit the children, but only when sober, and could only visit his two children—that is, Peter and Eileen. Mrs. Stover acknowledged she had ambivalent feelings about Mr. Stover. She regards him as an intelligent man who was fairly easy to get along with when he wasn't drinking. She said she had always felt that she needed him and couldn't get along without him. She said she was afraid to be alone in the world. She indicated that she had been willing to put up with his drinking to some extent. However, she now feels his drinking has got-

ten to the point where he can't control it, and he won't admit it. She says that reconciling with him would represent a risk to her own safety and that of the children, and might lead Child Protection to take the kids from her. She seems quite determined to remain separated from Mr. Stover. She says she's a bit worried though because she doesn't know where Mr. Stover is living now.

September 22 During this visit, Mrs. Stover reported that her kitchen stove had broken and she doesn't have enough money to repair it or to buy another. I asked if she owned the stove. She said it had come with the apartment. We then explored ways she could request that the landlord make the necessary repairs. We practiced what she would say and how she would say it. She smiled after we finished that exercise.

I then asked how things were going with the TANF program. She said it seemed to be going okay but she wondered why the checks were sometimes held up and why they hadn't yet forced Mr. Stover to pay child support yet deducted the amount from the stipend. She said there were all these rules and regulations and she was afraid she'd slip up and lose the little money she received to care for her children. She then said she constantly worried that Child Protection Services would come and take the children from her. I asked what she thought might lead them to take her kids into protective custody. She said she was pretty sure that the Child Protection caseworkers believed she was an unfit mother—especially because of the men she'd married and the places she'd lived before. I asked her to identify the changes that she'd made since she'd separated from Mr. Stover and gotten her own place. She smiled and said she'd made more changes than she'd even imagined. She said she now lives quite a peaceful life. She reads books to the children and they play board games almost every evening.

I added that it seemed to me that she began to take better care of herself, the children, and her home almost immediately after Peter's birth when she separated from Earl. I said she looked happier, seemed to have more energy—even with a new baby—and a better sense of humor since we first met. I also indicated that the children were certainly at risk when she was with Mr. Stover. After all, he had beaten her and the kids. But, I added, she seemed to be doing a much better job caring for the kids since the separation. I commented that the dangers to the children seemed to lie more in Mrs. Stover's disturbed marriages than in her. I told her that, in my opinion, she seems to love her children, wants to keep them, and appears quite capable of caring for them. On the other hand, I said, we do have to be aware of the needs of the children for safety and security. We have to try to protect them from the kinds of violence they had experienced in her previous marriages. Mrs. Stover again said she knows that my primary concern is with the children. She indicated that she doesn't resent my concern, because she knows I support her efforts to get out of the tangled marital situation. She said, however, that she does resent the Child Protection workers because they never took the time to understand what was really going on.

Mrs. Stover said that she thinks perhaps they regard her as unintelligent. I challenged this by saying I personally experienced her as exceptionally bright and pointed out that previous testing indicates that she has a superior intelligence. Mrs. Stover said that she knows her IQ is 142, though she couldn't recall who told her this. I explained this placed her within the upper 1% of the population in intelligence, whereupon Mrs. Stover demanded, "Where has it got me?" She went on to say, "My life is a complete mess," pointing out her three unhappy marriages at 39. She mentioned that she didn't do as well in school as she should have, always had her nose in a book, has always had a liking for books, but cannot use this information in her own life. She said she always wanted to be a librarian and dreams about getting some kind of training or education for library work. She said she would love to work in a library and have enough money to support her children without anyone else's help. She then said that she wants *no more men!*

Mrs. Stover asked how she could have made such a mess of her life. I pointed out that feelings are often as important as brains in determining what we do and suggested that she work on the problem of how her experiences and her feelings have landed her where she is. She can still use books to acquire knowledge and training, but this is not enough by itself. Mrs. Stover seemed very taken by this.

October 13   During today's visit, Mrs. Stover volunteered that she is not feeling well and has been cranky lately. She attributed her mood to her current concerns about her husband. She said that most of the time she is content to stay apart from him but that she sometimes feels lonely. I asked her what she did when she felt lonely. She said, when she feels that way, she gets up and starts to clean and rearrange the apartment. I commented that the children seem happier, cleaner, and better clothed than ever. I also said that I noticed how she had given reasonable instructions to the children and that they seemed to obey her willingly. Mrs. Stover said, yes, she had made progress since she left Earl. She now lives in a better place and is less stressed and less confused. She said she actu-ally finds housework somehow relaxing. She also expressed satisfaction about being able to make decisions without having to turn to either her husband or her mother.

October 20   On this date, I talked by telephone with Mrs. Stover. I informed her that the Child Protection caseworker wanted a conference meeting to discuss our work together over the past few months. Mrs. Stover became upset, angry, and anxious. She suspected that Child Protection was planning to remove the children from her custody. I said that was not my impression. I asked her to remember that I first became involved with her because of a referral by the Child Protection Unit. I added that it seemed quite reasonable that the referring agency would be interested in the children's safety and status. I asked her to remember the large number of positive changes and the amount of progress she has made over these past several months. That seemed to ease her mind somewhat. I then asked her for permission to participate in the conference meeting and share information about our work together. She readily agreed and said, "I'm glad you're going to be there."

October 26. Conference with the Child Protection Unit Caseworker   On today's date, Mrs. Stover, the Child Protection caseworker, and I gathered for a conference meeting at Mrs. Stover's apartment. Mrs. Stover was noticeably nervous. The caseworker introduced herself and thanked us for meeting. She said she wanted to explore Mrs. Stover's and the children's current situation and learn about the changes that have occurred since March. Mrs. Stover glanced at me—as if to ask me what to do. I nodded and smiled—encouraging her to tell her story. She did just that, talking for about 15 minutes straight about Peter's birth, the separation from Mr. Stover, the improvement in housing, and the status of each child. As she talked, she invited us to tour the apartment so we could see the children's sleeping areas, their clothes, books, and toys.

The caseworker seemed impressed with Mrs. Stover's comments and with the apartment. She then asked Mrs. Stover about her relationship with Mr. Stover, saying that she remained concerned about the children's safety in light of the men she had been involved with in the past. Mrs. Stover said that she had fully separated from Mr. Stover and neither she nor the children had had any contact with him since August. The caseworker asked if she thought she would be able to keep Mr. Stover and other men who might be dangerous to her or her children at arm's length. Mrs. Stover said, "I have sworn off men altogether!"

I then added that this was one of the issues that Mrs. Stover and I were addressing in our work together. I mentioned that Mrs. Stover was gaining greater awareness about this relationship pattern and said that as she continued to develop a sense of her own ability to make independent decisions and to take care of herself and her children, we hoped her ability to make judgments about men would also improve.

The caseworker asked about a few other matters and then thanked us for the meeting. She made a point to recognize Mrs. Stover's progress and wished her the best for the future.

November 3. Visit to Mrs. Stover by Appointment On this date, I visited Mrs. Stover at her apartment. Eileen and Peter were taking their regular afternoon naps, and the other children were in school. Mrs. Stover had the household well organized. The apartment was neat and clean. All floors were swept, the furniture dusted, and the kitchen was nearly spotless. Mrs. Stover was dressed in blue denims for housework, but her clothes were clean and ironed. She reflected a positive mood and seemed pleased to see me. The interview began with a discussion of the meeting with the Child Protection caseworker. Mrs. Stover acknowledged that she had been quite afraid before the meeting. She had been especially concerned that she might lose custody of her children. She said, however, that the meeting had helped a great deal. She now felt more secure that the Child Protection Unit was sincerely interested in her children's welfare and would not unfairly take them away from her. She said that she thought as long as she stayed away potentially abusive men, Child Protection would leave her and her kids alone.

We talked about past relationship patterns and the temptations she would probably face at some point in the future. We explored how she responded in the past when a man expressed interest in her at times she felt lonely or insecure, and how she might respond in the future under similar circumstances. She grinned when she thought about things she could say to herself, and to men, to maintain her sense of self-respect and dignity and ensure the safety of her children.

Mrs. Stover brought up a further problem in connection with running the household. As she gets more interested in cooking, she is realizing how little she knows. She attempted to cook a goose for the family but spoiled it through lack of proper cleaning. She claims the food that she knows how to prepare is plain and unattractive. The children do some complaining about the food; George recently pointed out that other children he knows get more variety. I arranged to bring Mrs. Stover a recipe file containing a large variety of recipes and some instructions on food preparation and menus. Mrs. Stover is also interested in tackling her budget problems in a more organized fashion; using budget envelopes from the agency, she will be able to keep track of her expenses for two months, to gain a more accurate idea of where her money is going.

November 10. Visit to Mrs. Stover by Appointment During today's visit, Mrs. Stover indicated that she had initiated divorce proceedings against Mr. Stover. She said she was pleased with the decision and proud of herself for taking action. However, she said that since starting divorce action, she has also felt edgy and reported that she had trouble sleeping last night. Mrs. Stover said she has begun to think about marriage again and feels she has a need to get married. She indicated that once she was divorced, she could make another mistake with another man. She worried that she might fall back into old patterns despite her determination to be "through with men." Mrs. Stover seems quite insightful about this issue. She said that she must first learn to become comfortable as an independent, unmarried woman without a man in the household. She shared her opinion that she may have picked damaged men that she pities. She observed that her father was just such a man, and she may have chosen men who were like him. At this point, I mentioned that her case record contained information about her father, to the effect that he was a smooth-talking, dapper man who had an alcoholic problem and was openly unfaithful to his wife. Mrs. Stover said this described him to a T. She thought that her mother had tried to reform her father, and she wondered if she might behave in the same way toward the men she had married. Mrs. Stover expressed considerable hostility toward her father, pointing out that all he did was "take" from others; he never "gave" to either his wife or his children. She said her mother had played right into his hand because she always did whatever he wanted and never drew the line. Mrs. Stover added that she learned from her mother that men boss women around and it's women's lot to learn to live with abuse and neglect. She said she had always deferred to her husbands—even when she knew their demands were wrong. She described how she had catered to her husbands, did everything possible to pacify them, didn't complain about their drinking or abusive behavior, and didn't draw a clear line about what was acceptable and unacceptable. Instead, she had let the abuse go on without really confronting them until, in the case of Mr. Stover, she finally ran out on the situation. She pointed again to her mother, saying that her mother was partly to blame because she tolerated her father's behavior. Mrs. Stover said that during her adolescence, she became aware that her mother was far too forgiving of her father's behavior. Mrs. Stover added that she now realizes that she has followed her mother's pattern with men.

These realizations about herself contribute to Mrs. Stover's feelings of guilt, shame, and anxiety. At the same time, she is now more clear and determined about what she wants to do. I pointed out that anxiety is a natural part of finding out about herself and a necessary aspect of the process of change. Mrs. Stover admitted that she still has ambivalent feelings about her husband—a feeling of loneliness and the realization that she could have him back just by asking. She says that even now she is sometimes tempted to do so. However, she has stuck with her decision and, as she accomplishes more, the temptation diminishes. At the moment, she realizes the need for larger housing, since there is no privacy for George. She handles periods of anxiety by getting busy in the apartment—cleaning, preparing meals, or sewing. Time doesn't hang heavily on her hands, especially with the young children. She feels that she is now giving them more attention than ever, and maybe giving Peter too much attention. She says she frequently interrupts her housework to play with him. Mrs. Stover admits that she has a tendency to do too much for the children. She said that Larie hasn't yet fully learned how to dress herself because Mrs. Stover has done it for her.

I asked Mrs. Stover if, at some point in the future, she ever decided to remarry what she would look for in a husband. Mrs. Stover said she wanted someone who didn't drink or smoke, who could look after her, and could be a good father for her children. She laughed at how little her actual choice of husbands reflected these qualities.

November 25. Home Visit to Mrs. Stover by Appointment When I arrived for today's visit, Mrs. Stover was up on a ladder installing new curtains. I helped her finish and then we began to talk. Mrs. Stover said that she realized that these last few months represent the first time that she has really ever lived in a home without either her mother or a man. She said that when she first moved to this apartment, her mother told her that she would be lonely living by herself, that she would never make a go of it, that she ought to stay in the mother's home. Mrs. Stover realized that her mother wanted her to remain dependent. She also recognized that she had previously been a willing participant in this pattern. Her mother wanted Mrs. Stover to depend on her and Mrs. Stover wanted to depend on her mother. Mrs. Stover said that she had never before felt she was capable of managing her own life or making decisions on her own. She had always turned to her mother, or to her husbands, for even small decisions. She said she felt proud

that she had selected the fabric and designed, cut, and sewed the curtains without any help from her mother. She then described how she had been the good little girl at home all her life. She said her mother had expected her to take responsibility for the care of her younger brother and later her sister. She changed, dressed, and bathed them when they were toddlers, though at the time she was only 9 or 10 herself. She said that her mother's poor health contributed to this pattern. When Mrs. Stover was 15, her mother was hospitalized for several months. That left Mrs. Stover with total responsibility for the household. She became worried, depressed, and distressed. It was probably not coincidental that she became involved with her first husband at this time. He was an older man who offered her companionship and comfort. He was affectionate, supportive, and did not criticize her, as her father so often did. The man took it for granted that she would sleep with him, and she did. At the time, she acted largely on impulse, meeting her needs—or the man's needs—without much thought. She became pregnant and they married. However, that marriage only lasted a few days. Her first husband abandoned her almost immediately after the ceremony.

December 8. Visit with Mrs. Stover by Appointment
On today's date, I visited Mrs. Stover at her apartment. I suggested that we might use part of today's meeting to review how the children were doing. Mrs. Stover agreed and chuckled as she did so. She said the children seemed to be doing well. She laughingly commented, "I'm all tangled up with the school around planning parties." The school had asked some parents to act as party room mothers, to help look after the children. Mrs. Stover and a neighbor, Mrs. Kirby, had done so and have been asked by the school to recruit 11 more mothers. Mrs. Stover has been on the phone a lot about this. Although it is a chore and a nuisance, she enjoys it, and she has a lot of respect for the school principal. It makes her feel good to know the school trusts her with such a job.

Mrs. Stover mentioned she has other nice neighbors in addition to Mrs. Kirby. She said her neighbors are friendly, considerate, and cooperative. She feels genuinely supported by them. For example, family members from across the hall drive her to the supermarket because there aren't any grocery stores in the immediate area.

Mrs. Stover then shared her concerns about Eileen, who will be old enough to start school next fall. Mrs. Stover doubts if this will be possible, however, because Eileen clings to her mother. Mrs. Stover said that because of the muscular dystrophy, Eileen simply can't keep up with the other children, nor can she follow their games. She said she is less worried about Eileen's present behavior than she is about Eileen's ability to begin kindergarten next fall. She hopes to use the time between now and next fall to foster Eileen's independence. I supported this idea, pointing out several ways in which Mrs. Stover could achieve this: through encouraging Eileen's outdoor play with other children and deliberately encouraging her to stay with the neighbor—for short periods at first and longer periods later. I also suggested rewarding Eileen for small steps toward independent functioning through the use of praise and reinforcers.

I also mentioned that Eileen could have an aptitude test at the school's Guidance Office and mentioned the possibility of Eileen's enrolling in a preschool. Mrs. Stover was skeptical about this plan. She wasn't sure she wanted to ask the school about this. I pointed out that she was sometimes hesitant to share problems with the very people who could offer the greatest help. I said that things seemed to have worked out better during the last few months when she shared her concerns with others. She said, "Yes. I was so afraid of that meeting we had with the Child Protection caseworker but it turned out just fine when I simply answered her questions truthfully."

I then shared my observation that she had grown more independent since her separation from Mr. Stover. I said, "You also want to help Eileen become more independent as well." I asked her to reflect upon what she has done to enable her to make changes in her own life in such a relatively short time. Mrs. Stover mentioned her increased self-confidence. She related this to her contact with the Family Service Agency and the caseworker from the Child Protection Unit because we have demonstrated confidence in her ability. She said, "You must have this confidence in me or you wouldn't have spent as much time helping me as you did." She said she also used to lie awake at night worrying about whether the Child Protection Unit would take her children. Now, she doesn't worry about that anymore. She mentioned that she feels that I and others at Family Service would be available to her if things go wrong or get difficult.

Mrs. Stover also brought up some negatives. She said that her increasing self-knowledge leads her to worry more about other people. She mentioned that she feels uncomfortable when she sees other mothers making the same mistakes with men she has. She would like to help them avoid the problems she's had but doesn't know how to offer that assistance.

January 16 On this date, Mrs. Stover called to inquire whether I thought she should move. She has been offered an apartment in the same building a floor above her exist-ing apartment. It has more closet space and has been freshly painted. Mrs. Stover wound up by wondering if I ought to look at and approve the new apartment. I indicated willingness to do this but said that I trusted her decision on the matter.

January 19 During a telephone call on this date, Mrs. Stover announced that she had decided against moving. As soon as she talked it over with the children, they became very anxious and uncomfortable. This made her realize the extent to which the children had been upset by previous moves. She said, "I figured I'd be losing more than I gained by moving now." Mrs. Stover had also been concerned about the fire hazard on the third floor, because she had recently heard that the old building is a big firetrap and would burn rapidly. This is a particular problem for Mrs. Stover because both Peter and Eileen would need special help in any emergency.

February 8. Home Visit by Appointment During our visit on this date, Mrs. Stover reported that Mr. Stover had sent toys for the children. His mother had delivered them. Mrs. Stover had accepted them without question, because she thought the mother-in-law possibly didn't know that she was averse to taking anything from him. Mrs. Stover was very angry that Mr. Stover had used this deception. I wondered if Mrs. Stover could explain her attitude in this matter-of-fact manner as soon as possible to the mother-in-law, to prevent any repetitions of this ploy. Mrs. Stover accepted this idea. She said she was on good terms with her mother-in-law and felt that she could explain the situation to her quite readily.

February 15 Mrs. Stover called to say that Mr. Stover has telephoned her several times during the past week. She said he wanted to get back with her. She said she talked with him a few times but soon realized that it was not wise to do so. She observed that he had not once asked about the children. She now uses her answering machine to screen his calls. She says she knows the best policy is to avoid personal contact with him.

March 15 In a telephone call, Mrs. Stover reported that Mr. Stover has stopped calling her but has begun to telephone the lady upstairs. Her neighbor then passes on the messages. I made a suggestion to Mrs. Stover for handling these calls as follows: Ask the person calling to leave his name and number. If he calls again, encourage the neighbor to tell him that she is not taking any more calls for Mrs. Stover. Mrs. Stover seemed pleased with this plan.

March 22   Mrs. Stover said that Eileen is starting to go outside on her own without being urged to do so. Since our recent clarification, Mrs. Stover has felt more relaxed about this and is also letting Eileen go out on the back porch. She formerly had done this, but kept running out every few minutes. I brought out again that I thought there was an intermediate stage between school and home—that is, a stage in which Eileen would have a place to go to develop a range of activity and to play with other children.

Mrs. Stover said that she feels more confident about Eileen now and that much of the problem was probably her own attitude. She brought up the possibility of the East School summer program for prekindergarten children, which she had heard about last year. The idea of this program, as Mrs. Stover understands it, is to give the children some experience of being away from their parents and getting used to the school building. This was discussed at the last PTA meeting that Mrs. Stover had attended.

George continues to receive favorable reports from school but does not like some aspects of schoolwork. He doesn't like to write things down. Mrs. Stover says she handles this by encouraging George to recognize that school can't be all pleasurable activities, nor will he necessarily like all of his teachers. The thing for him to do is to try to put up with these unpleasant aspects because there are so many things about school he likes. I supported Mrs. Stover in this, pointing out the desirability of consistently encouraging George in responsible attitudes.

April 12   During today's meeting, Mrs. Stover said she had taken Eileen with her to a holiday party at school. She reported that Eileen initially held on to her leg. However, after a short time, Eileen cheerfully went to play with the other children and allowed Mrs. Stover to talk with the kindergarten teacher by herself. After learning about the muscular dystrophy and observing Eileen, the teacher said that she thought Eileen would be able to start with the others in kindergarten. The teacher apparently liked Eileen and said she would be glad to have her in the class. She had indicated to Mrs. Stover that, at the end of the kindergarten year, a decision could be made regarding special education services for Eileen.

April 15   On this date, we received the psychologist's report regarding Eileen. The intelligence test results suggested that Eileen reflected a borderline level of intellectual functioning, with an IQ score of 74.

April 18. Visit to Mrs. Stover by Appointment   During this visit, Mrs. Stover and I discussed the report from the psychologist. Mrs. Stover struggled with the news. She found it difficult to believe that Eileen suffers from developmental disability as well as muscular dystrophy. She was visibly upset. I tried to convey empathy and support. She began to sob almost immediately. She said, "Maybe she's not Mr. Stover's child after all." After a few minutes, however, she sat up and said she'd do whatever she needed to help her daughter. She said she thought she might enroll Eileen in the regular kindergarten group the first year and see how she did. She thought she could use the kindergarten year as a time to undertake a more complete evaluation of Eileen's potential and decide about a special education class or program after that. Mrs. Stover said she preferred to try it this way first rather than enrolling Eileen in a special preschool before she had a chance to try.

May 3. Home Visit by Appointment   Mrs. Stover and I met at her apartment on this date. She began the meeting by saying she thought she was coming to terms with the news about Eileen. She felt more confident about her ability to manage and mentioned that Eileen continued to play outside and seemed to grow somewhat more independent with each passing day.

I asked Mrs. Stover about Mr. Stover. She said he had not bothered her at all in recent weeks. She said she was in no rush to proceed with the divorce and would take action only if Mr. Stover becomes a problem. In the meantime, she is keeping her mind open on the whole subject. I wondered if that meant she was reconsidering reconciliation with Mr. Stover but she said no. It was really a matter of money and convenience. At that time, she didn't have enough money to pay for the divorce.

Mrs. Stover then asked to talk about her kids. She said she was concerned about George, who is having problems in school. He sometimes comes home in tears. Mrs. Stover felt that one of George's teachers is extremely punitive toward him. George had been ill on Monday, and Mrs. Stover notified the school by telephone. She was told to phone back when George was ready to return. She did so on Tuesday morning as George returned to school. Later in the morning, Mrs. Stover received a call from the teacher claiming that George had skipped school, although it was subsequently verified that George actually was in school. George didn't even have a class with the teacher that morning. Mrs. Stover believed the teacher had something against George and perhaps against her as well.

Mrs. Stover went on to describe a recent incident in which George made a mistake on his arithmetic calculations. The teacher made him stay after school and redo them 200 times. Shortly after this, the teacher sent home a paper that she refused to grade because the writing was too faint. Mrs. Stover showed the paper to me, and the writing was quite legible and clear. George says that when he gets out of school he feels like killing somebody. As a result of the punitive treatment by the teacher, George is now taking the attitude "to heck with school." Mrs. Stover says that George really knows he must attend school and he is unlikely to be truant even with the problems with this one teacher.

I offered to visit the school and to review the problem with the principal and the school social worker, with Mrs. Stover present or not as she desired. In advance of this, we could discuss how to present the problem to the school— not strictly as a complaint against the teacher, but because of concern about George and his discouragement about the school situation. Mrs. Stover said she liked this approach, but she wanted to try it out on her own first.

This led to a discussion of how she should handle this with George. Mrs. Stover has been very careful not to side completely with George and paint the teacher as the villain. When he comes home crying, she puts her arm around him and comforts him. On the other hand, she has tried to help him see that he is likely to meet other teachers like this one, that this is part of going to school. George wants to transfer to another school but Mrs. Stover recognizes that it's probably too late in the year to do so. I supported Mrs. Stover in her stand with George and her plan to go to the school to discuss it.

May 10   In today's meeting, Mrs. Stover talked about her interest in getting a job and getting off welfare. I asked her to examine this carefully in terms of what it would mean to try to manage the children and work at the same time. I concurred in the idea of her working as a long-term goal but suggested very careful consideration of this as something she could do soon. After this, Mrs. Stover calmed down and said she realized this was not a constructive thing to do. I brought up the possibility of using a home economist as a consultant to help Mrs. Stover get the most out of her present budget. Mrs. Stover said, "I'm all for that," but added that she felt she is managing pretty economically at present.

I later saw the agency home economist and arranged for her to visit Mrs. Stover on May 24.

May 25   On a brief home visit, I took clothing supplied by the home economist, including a dress for Mrs. Stover, three small comforters for the younger children, and a jacket for Eileen.

June 6. Visit to Mrs. Stover by Appointment   During this visit, we discussed Mrs. Stover's arrangements with the home economist regarding the budget. Mrs. Stover said, "She showed me how I could cover all my expenses and a little extra." She remained somewhat skeptical, but she planned to give it a try and to confer further with the home economist on any difficulties that come up.

She has recently heard indirectly that Mr. Stover is planning to get married. I asked Mrs. Stover how she felt about this. She said she feels greatly relieved. She feels more free of him than ever before. She also said it also made her realize how protective she still feels toward him. She had always felt that it was her duty to stay with Mr. Stover no matter what he did because he needed her. She wondered if this fact, perhaps even more than the cost, had delayed her from taking divorce action. The latest news took the decision out of her hands. He will have to initiate the divorce, not her. It gets her off the hook and he will have to pay for the divorce expenses.

I asked about Mrs. Stover's current thoughts about men and relationships. She described her former pattern of running from one situation into a worse one; she wouldn't allow anybody to help her or to get close enough to help her. She said she now understands how and why she got involved with these damaged men and believes she won't make the same mistake again.

Mrs. Stover said that she now feels she has something of her own and she is no longer afraid. She indicated that she feels comfortable about her current attitude about men. She said, "My way of looking at a man now is in terms of what can he give me as a husband that is better than what I've got now. So far I haven't met anybody that I thought could measure up to this." She said she has enough to do to care for herself and her children; she "refuses to assume responsibility for yet another injured man."

She added that she and men just don't mix. She said that she no longer believes that men can be trusted and wants nothing more to do with them She indicated, however, that she does worry about the effects of her attitudes on the children. She doesn't want her daughters to be prejudiced against all men, and she doesn't want her attitudes to affect her son.

I suggested that we use our next meeting to discuss how she might help her children develop nonprejudicial attitudes toward both men and women. She said she'd like that.

June 14   In this meeting, Mrs. Stover and I returned to the question of helping the kids develop constructive attitudes about men and women. I provided Mrs. Stover with a recently published book for parents about dealing with adolescents' attitudes toward the opposite sex. Mrs. Stover said that she felt the book would be useful to her. She said the children do not volunteer much in this area, nor do they ask many questions. She said she tries to deal with issues as they come up.

Mrs. Stover indicated that she thinks her own attitudes are more of a problem than her children's and she hopes to avoid transferring to the children a biased attitude toward men. I suggested that when she talks with the children about Mr. Stover and his problems, she do so in as favorable a light as possible to avoid putting him down in their presence. Mrs. Stover thought she could do that. She mentioned that the children rarely speak of Mr. Stover but seem to accept that he doesn't want to be with the family. George occasionally expresses some resentment, commenting that they are better off now that Mr. Stover is not around. Mrs. Stover accepted my suggestion that, when George makes such remarks, she could point out that Mr. Stover has his problems but also has his good points, and had wanted to be a father to the family but hadn't been equal to the task.

June 28. Visit to Mrs. Stover by Appointment   On this visit, Mrs. Stover was visibly upset and agitated. She said she couldn't talk with me very long. A new Child Protection caseworker had visited three days earlier and informed her that a larger, subsidized apartment was currently available through the housing authority. To get it she would have to apply right away and be prepared to move within three days. Mrs. Stover talked at first as though she hadn't any choice in the matter. When I inquired further about this, however, she agreed that it really was her decision. She said that she knew they needed a larger place but she was also afraid of offending the Child Protection Unit. She felt that circumstances forced her to move quickly while there is a vacancy.

July 6. Home Visit to Mrs. Stover's New Apartment in the Housing Project   I visited Mrs. Stover at her new apartment. The family has a two-bedroom unit. Mrs. Stover and the girls share one bedroom and the boys have the other.

Mrs. Stover said she was still angry with the Child Protection Unit about the move—even though she was now satisfied with the apartment. She said when she first arrived, the electricity was not connected. It took two days for the electric company to come out to connect it. Mrs. Stover said, "I feel so rushed about the move. It's true that the other apartment was too small for me and the children, but it was neat and clean, and I had such great neighbors. We liked it there and felt comfortable. This place is so different."

I asked her to take a moment and think through what she would have done if she had had more time to think

about it. She thought for a moment and then said, "I would have moved anyway. I knew that place was too small. The children needed more privacy." I then asked how she goes about making big decisions such as this one about the move to a larger apartment. She described how in this instance, she really didn't think much about the decision. When Child Protection called about the larger apartment, she felt terribly afraid and pressured to do whatever they wanted. She said how she would have done just about anything to keep Child Protection off her back. Mrs. Stover went on to describe how she would prefer to remain more calm and think about the pros and cons before rushing to take action.

In the remainder of the interview, we discussed future plans and goals. Mrs. Stover was aware of my upcoming vacation and the possibility that she may have made so much progress that we might consider concluding our work together. Mrs. Stover talked about what the relationship with me and the Family Service Agency means to her at this point. She said our relationship serves as a control on her impulsive behavior. She says that most of the time, she now telephones me before making decisions or taking action and that helps her to think things through, so that she doesn't act on the spur of the moment. Despite this rushed decision about relocating to a larger apartment, she feels stronger and more mature. She also said things with her children are better as well. They have greater trust in her and she some greater trust in them. Then, too, she has had less difficulty with Mr. Stover for quite some time and has made some progress in getting Eileen ready for school. In the light of all this, she feels that her situation is better and she can probably handle it more easily than in the past. The vacation could be a kind of planned period to see how she manages. A tentative appointment was set for a follow-up visit in August.

August 30   During this visit, Mrs. Stover and I discussed plans for termination. She obviously had mixed feelings about concluding our relationship. On the one hand, she reiterated her view that she has fewer problems and is better able to manage them. On the other, she said she values our relationship and the security that implies. She said that, if things do take a negative turn, she can always turn to the agency. I explained that she could do this in any case, but she wants to defer termination. I agreed, at least for the present.

September 18   On this date, the school social worker telephoned regarding Eileen. Mrs. Stover started Eileen in kindergarten at the beginning of this month. Unfortunately, the teacher she had met in the spring has left the school. The school is aware of Eileen's physical and intellectual status. The teacher had spoken to the social worker about this, wanting further clarification. The teacher had also observed that Eileen was essentially unable to relate to other children in her group.

The school social worker felt that continuing Eileen in kindergarten might be good in view of the mother's overprotection of Eileen and the mother's continuing work on her own behavior. If Eileen's limitations are accepted in the group and not too much is expected of her in the way of either skills or sociability, it is quite likely that she will be able to make an adjustment to the kindergarten situation. Failing this, special education services should be considered. Matters were left that the school social worker will call us in about six weeks, and that period will be used to see how Eileen gets along.

Later in the day, I dropped in on Mrs. Stover to discuss the school's report. Mrs. Stover said that she recognized Eileen is behind the group in sociability, and we briefly reviewed the report obtained in April regarding her intellectual capacity.

At the same time, Mrs. Stover was pleased Eileen had been able to separate herself from her mother and sister without apparent difficulty. Mrs. Stover wants to visit the school soon, to see the teacher and get more information for herself.

A further appointment will be scheduled in a month, after Mrs. Stover visits the school. Despite the previous plan to terminate, both Mrs. Stover and the school want the agency to remain involved, at least until Eileen's problems have been resolved.

Summary. October 18 Through December 1   Mrs. Stover visited the school in October and received a favorable report about Eileen. The teacher told Mrs. Stover that Eileen cannot comprehend things with the rest of the children, but her behavior is not abnormal, nor does it in any way hamper the class or harm the other children. Eileen plays very little with the other children, but the teacher pointed out that lots of children play by themselves in the classroom. On November 16, a further brief report from the school social worker confirmed the information from Mrs. Stover.

Summary. December 1 Through January 8   The two interviews with Mrs. Stover during this period were concerned largely with working through her feelings about the agency closing its case.

February 15. Last Visit   In this termination interview, Mrs. Stover summed up her feelings as follows: "We've changed a lot during our time together. We are more settled, more of a family instead of five separate people. Each is different, that is to be expected, but we are more united, kind of. That's the biggest change, more secure in ourselves as a family. Larie and George and I each worried about ourselves instead of all of us. Now it isn't so much a personal worry as how is this family going to get along. We think of the good of the family rather than for each one. It's not so much what you've said and done as what you've listened to. I could talk things over and sort them out, kind of. I could bring up things that I wouldn't ordinarily be able to tell people. If I told these things to others, they would get all mixed up in my problem, but you don't."

I shared my view of the progress she had made during our work together and thanked her for letting me become involved with her and her family. We hugged and both cried a bit as we said our goodbyes.

Entry for Record: April 23   On this date, I received a call from Mrs. Stover who wanted information about special education programs for Eileen. She wanted to begin planning for the next academic year. I referred her to Miss Bithy, the social worker at the department of education who specialized in special education services.

Entry for Record: June 5   Mrs. Stover called to describe the end of year reports she received from her children's schools. She said, the teachers have told her that Larie is the "top girl in her class," Eileen has made a great deal of progress in relating to other children, and George is doing wonderfully. She said she was so proud she wanted to tell me about it.

Entry for Record: September 11   On this date, Mrs. Stover called to say that Eileen is enrolled in a special education program and is enjoying the experience. Eileen is very tired when she gets home. However, she leaves the home readily in the morning, much to Mrs. Stover's surprise.

READING 8
Variations on the Problem-Solving Theme[1]

Ralph Woehle[2]

Perlman (1957) wrote that any attempt to describe case-work should be regarded as an exercise in problem solving, because the subject matter is complex and in motion. It was necessary, she said, to carve out some essential qualities of the whole and to view them as parts on a continuum. In this paper, weaving variations on Perlman's theme, we will examine problem solving as part of a continuum in a systems context. The problem-solving model will be combined with the strengths perspective of Saleebey (1996) and incorporated within the general model of mixed scanning provided by Etzioni (1986).

PROBLEM SOLVING

Originally, Perlman (1957) saw three components in the problem-solving process: (1) study or fact finding; (2) organizing the facts into a goal-oriented explanation; and (3) implementing the conclusions in some action on the problem. She recognized that these three steps did not differ radically from the three steps of the previous diagnostic schools; the major difference was that problem solving was conceived as a cooperative process with the client. Therefore, problem solving had to abandon the Freudian preoccupation with the unconscious, and adopt an emphasis on conscious rationality.

Many other writers have outlined problem-solving processes. Sheafor, Horejsi, and Horejsi (1997) drawing from Epstein (1988) and the problem-solving approach of Pincus and Minahan (1973), as well as other authors, describe a change process having five stages: (1) intake and engagement; (2) data collection and assessment; (3) planning and contracting; (4) intervention and monitoring; and (5) evaluation and termination.

Epstein (1988), along with Reid (1978), has integrated client tasks and time limits into the problem-solving framework. The task-centered model focuses on the achievement of tasks and problem reduction (Epstein, 1988), by restating the particular problem, undertaking continuous assessment, generating alternatives, negotiating support from other agencies, and implementing agreed-upon task strategies. Implementation of the strat-

egy includes further development of the tasks; support of task performance; and verification and monitoring of tasks, effects, and problem reduction. Finally, termination may lead to extension of the work if the client wants and is committed to further services, to monitoring (if required by some authority), or simply to ending the services. The task-centered work is to be completed within a limited time period, which is clearly stated at the beginning of the process.

More recently, Saleebey (1996) has cautioned that the language of problem solving tends to become the language of pathology, in which professionals name clients according to their problems. Such naming can entrap clients in the pathologizing system, a contention supported by this writer's research (Woehle, 1994). Saleebey (1996) would have us honor the ability of the self, with environmental help, to heal.

By the mid-1980s, Macht and Quam (1986) claimed that problem solving and planned change had become accepted as the key commonality of social work. This has placed rational thought at the core of social work. However, few social work writers have made this rational base explicit. Exceptions include policy analysts, who have drawn on a rich literature in political science and sociology (DiNitto, 1995).

As DiNitto (1995) has indicated, social science has fallen far short of the requirements for purely rational change. All of the alternative actions and outcomes cannot be specified in advance; neither are actions easily related to effects. As Fox (1987) has further pointed out, facilitative, or incremental, goals may be easier to see than goals describing outcomes. Such short-term goals are also easier to relate to specific actions than are outcomes. The functional or normative goals Fox (1987) identified may be more consistent with systems theory. However, such goals are not specific solutions to problems. Finally, decision-making parties often disagree. As Barker (1987a) has indicated, incremental social change is an effort to take into account a variety of political and pluralistic influences. In brief, incrementalist theories have questioned whether it is possible to consciously bring about solutions to problems.

Lindblom's (1977, 1980) work spanned the range of thought on rationality and incrementalism. He referred to the first as the root approach and to the latter as the branch approach. Originally, he preferred the branch approach,

---

[1] An original reading for *Social Work Processes*.
[2] Professor and Chair, Department of Social Work, University of North Dakota, Grand Forks.

which he called muddling through. In his magnum opus, however, Lindblom (1977) came to praise the possibilities of both approaches and their traditions. On a practical level, Etzioni (1986) integrated the two approaches in his mixing-scanning model.

SYSTEMS THEORY IN SOCIAL WORK

Social work theory has considered the limitations of rational thought via systems theory. Systems theory takes account of the environment and usually adds a feedback loop to the problem-solving model. Feedback loops provide the client and social worker with information about reactions to the problem-solving activities, including reactions from the environment (Fordor, 1976). However, some social work writers using the systems approach have not altered the problem-solving model significantly. Pincus and Minahan (1973) did not move beyond traditional problem solving. Others adopt a more complex cybernetic model (Fordor, 1976), in which the traditional problem-solving model is expanded to include feedback loops. Such views are consistent with systems theory but avoid major issues raised by systems theory. They leave rational and scientific reductionist assumptions in place, even if they are multicausal (Auerswald, 1987). The causes have remained additive in such models, whereas in ecological systems the whole is greater than the sum of its parts.

The ecological issues raised by systems theory are its greatest contribution. In fact, Auerswald (1987) says this is a new epistemology. Unlike the old epistemology, which saw things as true or false on the basis of the scientific method, this epistemology sees truth as heuristic. Science and rationality are also heuristic devices in this new epistemology and are therefore acceptable ways of understanding. However, Auerswald no longer represents science and rationality as an underlying truth. Thus, systems theory is important because it takes us from a static view of rationality as a reflection of the underlying truth to rationality as an abstraction of the far more complex and socially structured reality, which cannot be fully expressed by the abstraction.

Systems theory is also important because it points to the environmental factors in the functioning of systems. In this respect, it has had great impact on social work.

Pincus and Minahan (1973) moved social work boldly into the social environment with their practice model. Similarly, Etzioni (1986) pointed to the importance of structural factors in decision making in his mixed-scanning model. But he later indicated that considerations of the mixed-scanning approach had largely ignored such factors. By combining the contributions of systems theory, the strengths perspective, problem-solving, and mixed scanning, it is possible to generate variations of the problem-solving model that are compatible with practice as social workers have always found it.

SYSTEMS, SCANNING, STRENGTHS, AND PROBLEM SOLVING

Lantz (1986) added to the problem-solving model in family therapy by adding reflexive feedback loops. He saw 10 stages. The first six were conventional problem solving. Then Lantz added a problem-escalation stage, which followed task preparation; this stage limited the ability to resolve the original problem. In one possible feedback loop, escalation leads back to assessment; in another, task preparation is followed by resistance, reflection, and insight. The therapist must respect the resistance, Lantz (1986) said, and explore the family's catastrophic expectations about the dangers of change. Insight might then reveal the nature of the family's resistance, and the therapist and family would be able to move back to the task preparation stage. Thus, Lantz added feedback loops within the client system.

Auerswald (1987) drew on systems theory to describe an approach to family therapy that was very similar to problem solving, especially to the task-centered approach. However, he added problem-solving sequences that went outside the client system. While he recognized that work might have been directed at the client's larger environment, and he claimed to draw on a revolutionary development, he did not go as far as he might have. His model still appeared to consist primarily of reductionist, sequential problem solving.

Etzioni's (1986) mixed-scanning approach, while originally intended for policy-making processes, might also be used in personal decisions about careers, marriage, health, and financial security. Mixed scanning is a hierarchical mode of decision making. Fundamental decisions are seen as of a high order; within them are nested lower-order, more incremental decisions. Scanning, according to Etzioni (1986), consists of the gathering, evaluation, and use of information in order to come to conclusions. In social work terms, scanning is assessment. But the hierarchical nature of the decision making offers something more: It recognizes that most decisions are made in the larger context, a context partly consisting of larger policy decisions and organizational structures. The limitations imposed by the context make the rational consideration of all alternatives less productive, because many alternatives are not possible in that context. Scanning is therefore less demanding than the full rational search for solutions, but it is more strategic than pure incrementalism. Rational approaches demand an evaluation of all possible solutions, and incrementalism deals with just the trouble spots; scanning strikes some middle ground.

Etzioni (1986) listed four major steps that made the mixed-scanning approach operational. First, all relevant known alternatives should be listed on strategic occasions. (In social work terms, alternatives are explored). Second, the implementation should be fragmented (or in social work, partialized) into several sequential steps. Third, steps should be reviewed as they are implemented. (This resembles continued assessment.) And, fourth, a rule for the allocation of time and assets (strengths) among the various levels of scanning should be formulated. (Policies should be reviewed.)

Scanning or assessment of the alternatives might lead to elimination of those that will not be pursued. Etzioni (1986) suggested three criteria for elimination: (1) utilitarian—the lack of means or strengths to pursue the alternatives; (2) normative—the violation of basic values of the decision makers; and (3) political—the violation of values or interests of the actors whose support seems necessary for making a decision and implementing it. For alternatives not so rejected, examination in greater detail is in order. Basically, this involves repetition of the scanning process in ever greater detail, until only one or some other small number of alternatives remain.

Before implementing a remaining alternative, it should be broken down into parts in three ways (Etzioni, 1986). First, for administrative clarity, it is broken down into sequential parts. Second, for political purposes, commitment to implement is made in serial steps. Resources or strengths are committed a piece at a time, while maintaining a strategic reserve. Furthermore, arranging commitments so that the most costly ones can be made later will make the process more reversible and less costly. Finally, scanning or assessment should continue on scheduled occasions and as the need arises. At important turning points, assessment at higher system levels would be desirable.

As each subset of increments is completed, scanning or assessment at the level of that subset should be undertaken (Etzioni, 1986). Even if things seem to be working, assessment should continue, though less intensively. Trouble requires more intensive assessment. Alternative strategies may appear more desirable in light of experience with the present alternative. If the goal has been achieved or become undesirable or too costly, the effort may be discontinued. Use of resources or strengths is required for assessment itself (Etzioni, 1986). Assessment takes time and energy,

some of which should be reserved for occasions when its use is triggered by set intervals or by emergencies.

Assessment proceeds on the assumption of limited foresight. Each step is a hypothesis that needs evaluation; or, in more practical terms, each step is a trial that may be more or less successful. Likewise, each set of steps, which constitutes a larger step, is a trial. When a course of action is failing, assessment is a way of learning about the reasons for failure and considering alternative courses of action.

This literature review suggests several generalizations and task processes that modify problem solving. Let's consider each of these in turn.

GENERALIZATIONS

On the basis of the literature, some conclusions may be drawn regarding the continual use of assessment; the recognition of higher-order decisions in which task decisions are nested; the generation, elimination, and prioritization of alternative tasks; and the commitment of system strengths. Each of these topics will now be discussed in greater detail.

Assessment

Assessment is present in every part of the social work process. Everything that happens provides information to the worker and client. Participants in the process do not adhere strictly to a particular task process, even when they have agreed to do so; assessment continues naturally as practitioners and clients look at their situations and adjust their work. However, the assessment process must be orderly if the work is to maintain some direction. Clients and workers can strategically guide the assessment process by emphasizing it at certain times and deemphasizing it at others. There are at least three occasions when assessment should be the primary work of the process. The first is the assessment associated with problem, strength, and task identification in each task process; this is assessment as described traditionally in problem-solving and task-centered approaches to social work.

The second strategic use of assessment occurs on specified occasions. Often these occasions are specified by institutional or individual policies—for example, by governmental policy for review of cases or by a supervisor's practice of directing a periodic case review. Alternatively, the need for further assessment may emerge from the process itself. For instance, if a task process develops a problem that requires the ongoing task process to be modified, the worker and client may need to shift the work to assessment of the emerging problem and the strengths needed to address it.

Finally, assessment occurs at the end of each task process. This is usually referred to as evaluation but, given that one task flows from another, evaluation will often be the assessment for the next task.

Assessment should review strengths as well as problems. In fact, a problem is not a problem unless some available system has the means to resolve it. Thus, by definition, problems can only be assessed in relation to the strengths of systems that can address those problems.

Nested Decisions

A second important modification of the traditional problem-solving process is the recognition that decisions in the work process are nested in higher-order decisions. Generally, this means that social work occurs within the context of decisions made in larger social structures. Such structures might include the agency and the larger public bureaucracy in which the agency is typically located; professional associations; client interest groups; and communities with their particular cultural values. For example, Rothman, Smith, Nakashima, Peterson, and Mustin (1996) report that practice is sometimes directed by client protection policies and procedures, which may give rise to ethical quandaries. Thus, both agency and professional/licensing organizations nest the practice decisions, and their directives may conflict.

In some circumstances, higher-order decisions may themselves emerge as social work issues. If so, the work will move out of the client system to some external system. For example, changing agency policy may be a proper work task if a particular policy limits desirable tasks at the client level.

As we have already noted, all client-worker efforts are nested within a professional association and licensing agency and also within governmental agencies and policy-making bodies, all of which have procedures to guide social work decisions and practice (Rothman et al., 1996). This nesting implies the political nature of work decisions; decisions will often be political compromises between competing prescriptions rather than rational conclusions. If rationality is to limit pure muddling, however, it must also guide decision making. The compromise between these two approaches is to make relatively limited commitments to tasks that we are quite certain we will be able to complete.

Finally, since the problems and strengths may be located in a variety of systems and at various system levels, assessment may at times be directed at systems other than the one where work is presently located. It is therefore necessary to assess such issues not just when they emerge in relation to an individual case, but in some systematic fashion. Such assessments must take account of strengths as well as problems.

Generating Feasible Alternatives

Although Epstein (1988) also recommended the generation of alternatives, this account will focus on Etzioni's (1986) approach. First, Etzioni suggested the generation of known alternatives on strategic occasions, following assessment. Basically, this is a matter of working with the client to identify as many options as strengths and knowledge allow. Thus, even in the initial assessment, social workers recognize that their job is limited by present knowledge and strengths.

Second, Etzioni (1986) recommended the elimination of alternatives by tests of feasibility—by looking at resources or strengths and at the values of participating parties. In social work, the relevant values are those of clients, workers, and sanctioning bodies such as agencies and professional associations. This is closely related to Epstein's (1988) suggestion that tasks be prioritized in terms of clients', workers', and referral-source priorities, since a low-priority task will probably be eliminated.

Note that, as the assessment of strengths and problems continues, priorities may change, or new tasks of high priority, consistent with available strengths, may emerge.

Use of Strengths

Commitment to tasks may change if the availability of system strengths to complete tasks changes. Available strengths of social service agencies are subject to fluctuation, because society's commitment is politically unstable and demands for services fluctuate. Economic conditions and fluctuations, as well as a variety of individual, family, and macrosystem conditions, may otherwise affect available strengths. Consequently, long-term tasks always face uncertainties with regard to systems strengths. Furthermore, the ability to judge strengths in advance is limited. Thus, it is generally not rational to commit to a long-term task at any cost.

Etzioni (1986) suggests a fragmented commitment of resources to task completion. Basically, this means limiting the early commitment of strengths to small amounts, pending the accomplishment of small tasks. He also suggests leaving the biggest commitments to last, where possible. The short-term tasks of Reid (1978) and Epstein (1988) obviously help to meet this requirement.

Just as it should not be assumed that strengths will be adequate, it should not be assumed that they are nonexistent. Workers should be prepared to work with clients to seek support for task completion from the larger social environment, inside or outside of the agency's network, as Epstein (1988) suggests. This is the essence of Cowger's (1994) assessment for strengths.

TASK PROCESS

Given the generalizations identified here, various modifications of the task process can be suggested. Modifications suggested here are: extended sequential task processes, three task processes with feedback loops, the terminated task process, and simultaneous-task processes.

Sequential Task Processes

As Epstein (1988) recognizes, the work with the client does not necessarily end when a specific set of tasks is completed. If the worker, client, and other involved parties agree, additional tasks may be undertaken. If this work begins after the completion of a task cycle, then the next set of tasks is a repetition of the original process, with different goals, tasks, and so on. In brief, this variation is merely the sequential continuation of repetitions of the problem-solving process.

Processes with Feedback

As already noted, variations of the task-centered approach with internal feedback loops have been identified by Lantz (1986). Lantz indicated that two types of feedback loops involving work with the family may emerge. One such loop may occur when tasks are being identified. If family members resist at this stage, exploration of that resistance can lead to reflection, insight, and return to the prescribed tasks. Alternatively, if problem escalation occurs as tasks are being undertaken, it may be necessary to return to the assessment stage to redefine tasks. Lantz sees these loops as reflexive, and both involve work within the family system.

Auerswald (1987) did not describe the diagram suggested by his approach. He might, in fact, have disagreed with an attempt to reduce it to a diagram. While his model was described earlier as sequential, it can also be represented as feedback loops that spiral into the social environment or into subsystems. Auerswald recognized that the family's problem may not exist in the family system. Thus, problem solving undertaken in the family might not work. Returning to assessment may indicate that the problem may lie in an individual or in the larger environment—the school, for example. If such problems are identified, the worker then takes up the problem-solving process in the appropriate system.

Whether the problem lies within or outside of the system, the strength to resolve the problem must be located in a system that can be brought to bear on the problem. It follows that strength assessment must also move between systems and may be successful in a system other than that in which the problem is located.

The Terminated Process

Because feasibility is continually being evaluated, the process may be discontinued at any stage. Indeed, the process may end almost as soon as it begins. The inability to bring strengths to bear on a problem may end the process. For example, if an agency refers a client with goals for certain services but the services are not authorized by some overriding authority, then the start-up suggested by Epstein (1988) may lead to discontinuation of services. In fact, tasks may be discontinued at any time that the ongoing assessment reveals a lessening of the priority of the problem or unavailability of requisite strengths.

Simultaneous Task Processes

Simultaneous task processes are appropriate when an initial task process can proceed only if another is undertaken. For example, if a family has a child with behavior problems, the parents may undertake consistent discipline as a task. But the child also has to develop behavior control. A task for the child may include working on positive behavior. Thus, simultaneous work on discipline and the behavior of the child may be undertaken.

CONCLUSION

The new ecosystem paradigm has suggested that rational problem solving is an analogy for the social work process. However, it does not represent the underlying truth of the process. Thus, it would also be possible to propose another model for the work process and to reject scientific rationality. Rather than rejecting traditional social work, however, this paper suggests that there is much to be said for the traditional approaches to social work.

Nevertheless, once we begin to challenge the assumption of rationality underlying the idea that social work is a linear process, we are free to consider nonlinear approaches. Information about such processes suggests several modifications of traditional problem-solving: (1) the liberal use of assessment, both on a continuous basis and on special occasions; (2) the nesting of decisions in higher-order decisions, which directs work to other levels on occasion and situates decisions within political processes; (3) limitation of the number of alternatives generated, on the basis of the feasibility of problem solving with the available strengths; and (4) the need to commit strengths appropriately among prioritized alternatives. Task processes may be modified from the traditional problem-solving model by (1) making them sequential; (2) adding feedback loops at various system levels; (3) terminating them at any point; and (4) running them simultaneously.

This paper represents a small step. Two larger steps seem obvious at this point. First, any or all of the above task processes may be used in a given case; case diagrams may be permutations and combinations of those here described. Second, the release from scientific rationality as an underlying truth frees us to consider a wide variety of nonrational approaches.

READING 9
Betty Smith[1]

Betty Smith was a disgusting hunk of humanity. That was clear. At least it was clear to all of the previous caseworkers, who didn't hesitate to moralize at length about her in the case record.

A 22-year-old woman who had dropped out of school in the 10th grade, Ms. Smith had gotten pregnant twice by men old enough to be her father. She received Temporary Assistance for Needy Families (TANF) support for her two children, Angelia, 5, and Tommy, 3. She was described as a poor housekeeper, a negligent mother, and a person without any motivation. She had been active with protective services for some time because of concern about neglect of her children.

On the first visit, I went to her apartment and knocked several times without receiving an answer. As I was leaving, a neighbor came out and said in a disgusted voice: "She's in there. You just have to pound and pound." She directed me back to the apartment, a partially converted garage, and loudly knocked and shouted. After a while, an obese woman in a dirty robe came to the door. She looked much older than 22 years old, and her skin was crusted over with eczema sores. She acted sleepy but warmly invited me in. The other woman left after making a snide remark.

The front room of the apartment served as a living room and a bedroom to Ms. S; it was small, dreary, and dirty. The shades were drawn and the temperature was in the high 80s with a heater going full blast, although it was a beautiful, bright afternoon outside. In the first interview, I introduced myself and attempted to establish rapport. I didn't mention the condition of the house nor the fact that she could not adequately supervise the children when she

was asleep. Fortunately, the second point was not of immediate importance since the neighbor I'd met was Ms. S's aunt and was keeping an eye on them. Betty Smith went to get the children, at her own initiative, to introduce them to me. She talked with pride of their accomplishments. Angelia seemed to be an alert, bright child but somewhat shy. Tommy seemed quite affectionate and outgoing but mentally slow.

My initial impression was not of disgust, but more of pity. I felt Ms. S was bright and articulate and had a great deal of affection for her children. I was impressed by the fact that she wanted me to meet them and by the obvious interest she had in them. She seemed to have so little meaning in her life other than the children.

THE PRELIMINARY ASSESSMENT

I made five more weekly visits. In these visits, I tried to understand Ms. Smith's view of her problems, to collect data, and to establish a relationship of trust.

My assessment was based on the three members of the S family. Biogenetically, there were several problems. Ms. S had medical problems, most noticeably obesity and eczema. I suspected that she had metabolism problems, which possibly contributed to obesity, to her desire for high temperatures, and to her lethargy. There were indications that the children were not receiving balanced, nutritious meals, partly as a result of their mother's inattention.

Cognitively, Ms. S showed her greatest strength. She was not only bright and articulate but was easily motivated in this area. Angelia appeared to share her talents, but Tommy appeared slow for his age.

Psychosocially, this was a poorly adjusted family. Ms. S had spent a short time as a child with her mother, who had grown up in a middle-class family. All the other family

---

[1] An original case study for *Social Work Processes* prepared by a student at Indiana University School of Social Work.

members had gone to college and had been successful, but Ms. S's mother had shocked the family by becoming pregnant repeatedly, by men whom the family classed as undesirable. An aunt who had no children of her own had offered to take Ms. S and raise her. Already under financial strain, the mother agreed. As a result, Ms. S was raised in a city quite distant from her mother; her aunt and uncle provided material support but gave her little emotional support. The aunt was cold and punitive, and her attitude toward sex was extremely prudish.

My contacts with the aunt confirmed what Ms. S told me of her. The aunt informed me at length that Betty was worthless and would end up in the gutter. Ms. S was subjected to these lectures daily. Ms. S disliked her aunt but felt that she was dependent upon her and that she had a moral obligation to be thankful for what the aunt has done for her. She blamed her mother for having rejected her and for having given her to an aunt who was so devoid of human emotion.

Ms. S wanted to provide more warmth and love for her children than she had experienced but she was hampered by an inadequate model of family functioning. In addition, her own problems interfered with her ability to nurture the children. She gave them sincere, showy affection at times but was inconsistent in her behavior.

Because of the long hours of sleeping each day, she mainly avoided them. Sometimes she would express her frustration by shouting at them; then she would feel guilty and hug and kiss them. She did not show preference toward either of them, in spite of Angelia's obviously superior intelligence. She recognized that they had different areas of strength and encouraged them in these areas.

The environment in which Ms. S lived was overwhelmingly hostile. Her aunt was constantly nagging her about what she should do (get out of bed and clean the house), what she was (a no-good tramp), and what she should not do (get into trouble again). This advice had been reinforced by a long series of social workers. She had no positive social experience and indeed had become a total recluse. She spent large portions of her time in bed, seemingly as an escape. Her children had few experiences; their great-aunt occasionally took them someplace.

The situation is a good example of a mismatch of coping patterns and impinging environment, which results in feedback that creates further mismatching. This vicious circle involves an increasing number of people (basically offspring) and contributes to an ever greater dysfunction. Ms. S's strengths were her hopes and aspirations for her children and her desire to do more for them. The fact that she was bright and articulate and enjoyed discussing her situation was also positive.

I hoped to break the circle of mismatchings, but I had to decide the most effective point of intervention. Alleviation of medical problems seemed a logical starting point. My efforts in providing access to medical resources would be a concrete example of nurturing and supporting. If medical problems could be overcome, then the family members might be able to function at maximum physical strength and to cope more effectively with their other problems. It would also provide an opportunity to assess Ms. S's motivation and willingness to follow through on a plan mutually developed.

I decided to explore with Ms. S the necessity of seeking treatment and to suggest possible treatment resources. With her permission, I would make a referral to the visiting public health nurse, who could explain health problems and give advice on how to minimize them. She would also be able to help Ms. S plan balanced diets. For Tommy, it might be advisable to make use of a special fund available for a work-up to explore the possibility of developmental disability. In the event of disability, appropriate plans could be made before he began school.

The community had two nursery schools, which could offer the children a wider range of experiences. I hoped to interest Ms. S in the cooperative school because this would involve her in an activity and would help her to develop techniques of child care.

THE WORKING ASSESSMENT

At the next interview, I had hoped to explore these suggestions with Ms. S, but I was so appalled by the condition of the house that I changed my plans. The living room bedroom had debris piled four or five inches thick over the entire floor. In order to sit down, I had to remove a pile of records and clothing from a chair and then clear off a section of the floor on which to set the chair. Ms. S was lying between sheets so incredibly filthy that it was hard to believe they had ever been gray, much less white; they must not have been washed in weeks. The condition of the apartment represented a health and safety hazard to the children and Ms. S. A confrontation was necessary. I decided to focus on the children's welfare, a matter with which she was concerned.

I pointed out, firmly and directly, that it was unfair to subject the children to these kinds of conditions and that rats and cockroaches were inevitable if things did not improve. She listened attentively and then admitted that she had not considered the possible effect on the children nor the likely health and safety hazards. It seemed to make an impression on her that I was rational and unemotional and did not couch the discussion in terms of how evil she was. I tried to show her that I respected her even though I did not like her behavior in this instance. She promised to clean up the house if I would return in a week to see it. Far more importantly, however, the incident presented an opportunity for her to unleash her feelings about herself.

She informed me that her apartment was like herself—dirty. Having her aunt nag at her constantly only served to reinforce this opinion. When I explored why she felt she was dirty, she was surprised that it was not obvious to me. This appeared to be her first feedback that others might not agree with her self-perception. (Generally, they probably did.) She explained that having had three illegitimate pregnancies, having dropped out of school, and having to depend on welfare support were indications that she was dirty. In fact, everything she did was an indication that she was a worthless, dirty person.

This was the first that I had heard of a third child. Her aunt had arranged for her first child to be given to a friend. Betty had no choice in the matter, just as she had no choice when her aunt declared that she was to keep the second child as punishment for having gotten into trouble again. This left her with unresolved feelings about her first child; she had a desire to see the child and feared that the child would feel rejected by her. Unavoidably, she also had feelings that Angelia was a source of punishment, even though she loved her very much.

The incident and the new knowledge I had of Ms. S changed my assessment and my strategy of intervention. I decided that I could expect little movement until her self-image was improved and that this would have to take priority over the other goals. I knew she would have to feel that a change in self-esteem was necessary and possible and that this would have to be incorporated into her value system. Since the topic had arisen and she seemed receptive to discussing her feelings, I felt that we should begin immediately. We discussed on a very intellectual plane how one develops a self-image and the philosophical idea of the basic worth of each person.

She was then able to apply the abstract ideas to her own life experiences and to examine how she came to have a negative self-image. She recalled how miserable she had been as a teenager. Her aunt lectured her continually on the evils of sex. These ideas were in contradiction to those of her peers. Sex was an area in which she could most threaten her aunt, and in retrospect she sees her actions as a way of punishing her aunt. In addition, she felt that she was searching for a relationship that provided warmth and love, which she had never received from her mother or her aunt and uncle. She did not find this type of relationship,

however. All three children were the result of casual affairs with older men whom she saw as socially undesirable. She felt unworthy of any other man, however. The parallel between her actions and those of her mother hardly seems accidental. In a sense, it was a self-fulfilling prophecy. Many times her aunt had accused her of being like her mother, and it was small wonder that she chose this way in which to rebel.

As a result of the second pregnancy, she was moved into her present apartment, which was fashioned out of one half of a garage. The other half housed the latest-model Cadillac. Ms. S felt that moving from the house was both punishment and rejection. She offered to show the worker the apartment, and it became apparent that Angelia did not live with her. Ms. S said that Angelia had a room in the house (and by implication, room in the aunt's heart) but ate with Tommy and her. The aunt had special affection for Angelia and had strongly hinted that Angelia should stay with her if Ms. S were ever to break the ties and move from her present situation. Ms. S thought that this might be the best situation for her daughter, since she had so little to offer Angelia.

At this point, I felt that we had begun to define and prioritize problems and had a more adequate assessment of Ms. S's situation. She had expressed awareness of problems and the desire for change. With the relationship that had already been established, it appeared that a plan of action could be mutually worked out and first steps at redirection taken.

Our plan was to begin by helping Ms. S to become independent from her aunt. Separation from the hostile environment was valuable in itself but, in addition, it would prove to Ms. S that she was capable of managing on her own and could be self-sufficient. It would also mean leaving the dreary surroundings, hopefully for more pleasant ones. Separation presented a financial problem, however, because the public welfare grant provided a small housing allowance that was inadequate to pay the rent anywhere else. Finally, separation would force her to address her feelings about Angelia. If she gave her daughter up, she would be behaving in the same way as her own mother. She needed to realize that she had a real contribution to make to her daughter.

The original goal of getting medical treatment could be incorporated into the self-image building attempts. Improving her body image could help boost her self-esteem.

On the next few visits, rapid movement was evident. We began to explore alternative ways to the goals we had set. Ms. S made strides toward cleaning her house, and I praised her. But I looked forward to a day when she would do it for herself, not for me. We discussed her situation and I shared what I saw as her strengths. She was flattered by my feeling that she was bright and enthusiastically agreed to be tested by City College. Our interview served to strengthen her self-esteem.

Ms. S began to make actual change efforts in the next three months. Her testing at City College showed that she had a high IQ, and her aptitude scores for college subjects were so good that the school was willing to accept her as a freshman without a high school diploma. She went for counseling and decided to take a review course and get her General Educational Development (GED) diploma before going to college; she felt that it would give her more security. She was showing a great deal of maturity in her decisions. She got psychology and philosophy books from library to enlighten herself (and to impress me). She was able to understand Freud's concepts of id, ego, and superego with little difficulty. Health problems had been explored. Extracting teeth improved her general state of health; the gum disease had been depressing her immune system.

Tommy was found to have an average IQ but was behind his age group developmentally because of very severe hearing loss. He was referred to a charity for children with disabilities, which sponsored corrective surgery.

The public health nurse came weekly to help plan a balanced diet for the children and a weight reduction diet for Ms. S. I coordinated my efforts with the nurse, and she reinforced my efforts to build Betty's self-esteem.

During this upward climb, there were periods of regression. I had to get Ms. S out of bed on many occasions. More often, however, the house was cleaner, the shades were up, and the heat was reasonable. I could see improvement in her skin, and she seemed happier.

The children were visited, and they finally enrolled in the nursery school. When I visited, they would run up to tell me what they had been doing, and I got the same kind of excited reaction from Ms. S.

Each success Ms. S achieved helped convince her that she could build a satisfying life.

THE CONTINUING REASSESSMENT

A point came at which we were ready to begin the generalization and stabilization of change. Two major considerations marked this period. One was that Ms. S's aunt decided to tear down the garage and build several apartment units instead. This meant that Ms. S would be forced by circumstances to make the desired separation. The second was the need to counteract Ms. S's attempts at structuring our relationship into a friendship rather than a professional relationship. The present relationship had been used purposefully to motivate Ms. S to follow through on proposed projects. However, I had had to resist her attempts to let visits become book review sessions or social calls. In a sense, she was resisting attempts to go further and to use the knowledge she had gained to help herself; it was a tactic to resist change. I decided to clarify the nature of the relationship and to set a new goal—that of widening social contacts so that others in the community could provide the friendship she so much desired.

Thus, successful separation from her aunt and successful establishment of social contacts became goals during this period. She used agency policy to give her support in moving Angelia with her: She explained to her aunt that the public welfare agency could not give her money for a child who was not living with her. Ms. S had come to believe that she had more to offer Angelia but was still finding it difficult to confront her aunt directly.

The new apartment was larger and more cheerful, and the neighbors were friendly. She thrived in the new environment and this helped her to broaden her social contacts. She began going to church fellowship meetings and did volunteer work for a civil rights group while the children were in nursery school. She was so efficient that she soon became an officer in the group. She made a good child care arrangement with a neighbor for her evenings at the GED review course. At Christmas, she got a job as a gift wrapper at a large department store.

Ms. Smith developed enough friends so that she was happy to use our relationship in a professional way. She discussed her feelings toward people visiting in the home. She became anxious and did not want people in her apartment for too long. She had used her apartment as a protective womb for such a long time that she was threatened by friends coming there. We worked through many such fears, or at least relieved her anxiety about holding such beliefs.

Her apartment was consistently clean, partly because she knew guests might drop in at any time. Her eczema was rapidly disappearing, and she bragged of having lost 50 pounds. Her change of attitude was reflected in the behavior of the children and in her care of them. She was more consistent in her discipline, and they were more responsive.

She took the children on a bus trip to visit her mother. It was a very good experience. Her mother was glad to see her and the children, and Ms. S was able to satisfy herself that her mother loved her. She felt she had made peace with her mother after all these years.

Soon afterward, she began dating a man who was a college graduate, an accountant. After several months, she became engaged to him and was extremely happy. Problems arose, however. His parents were unhappy that he had chosen a high school dropout who had illegitimate children. Their pressure was sufficient to break up the relationship. As soon as I learned of the broken engagement, I made a home visit. I was sure that this would result in regression, and I wanted to head it off. I could visualize a dirty apartment, drawn shades, and extreme temperature. When I arrived, the apartment was spotless, and she was smiling. I told her what I had expected and she laughed. "The relationship was a good one for me. I know now that someone who is handsome, intelligent, and well-educated can love me. But I wouldn't touch Robert with a ten-foot pole; he's a momma's boy. Any man who can't make decisions for himself isn't worth having. I'm going to college next year and will have the opportunity to meet all kinds of men. I'm not going to settle for a weak man; I want one that will think of me first." It appeared we were ready to terminate our relationship. Betty Smith no longer needed me. She had the inner strength to make her own decisions and to motivate herself.

READING 10
The Record of Change: Client-Focused Recording[1]

Susan Steiger Tebb[2]

Social work recording has changed over time in response to concerns about cost-effectiveness and worker accountability and to changes in practice, in the role of the social worker, in agency services, and in technology—from the advent of the typewriter to the use of the computer and Internet (Kagle, 1995). The effort to develop a record that reflects accountability and changing services and technologies has sacrificed a basic value of social work—client self-determination (Tebb, 1991).

Recording often lacks relevance to social work practice, because popular recording methods do not recognize documentation as a tool that can reflect the thinking and responsibility of both the social worker and client (Monnickendam, Yaniv, & Geve, 1994; Tebb, 1991). A record is a data vessel of client history. The file, however, can provide very little on plans for client change; it does not usually present a clear picture of the relationship between the social worker and client, nor does it assist practitioners in their reflection, planning, and thinking. Records are often written after the important work between client and worker is done (Gelman, 1992).

"It is not the recording, as a wise case worker once said, which is difficult; it is the thinking which precedes it. If we can think clearly about a client's needs, his circumstances, and the treatment proposed, the record will shape itself easily and simply" (Hamilton, 1946, p. 207). Recording is used traditionally as an administrative aid (an agency-based file). A client-focused record, however, furthers client change and improves practice. The thesis of this article is that client involvement in record writing can strengthen the role of self-determination in social work practice.

GROUNDWORK FOR RECORD CHANGE

Background

Weed's (1969) problem-oriented record was introduced in the late 1960s and offered the medical field a way of reforming unwieldy and ineffective medical records. This model provided a very organized and simple framework for recording. The problem-oriented record (POR) consists of four segments: (1) a database that gives both demographic and medical patient information; (2) a problem list gleaned from the database; (3) strategies to solve each problem; and (4) ongoing plans for each problem. The acronym SOAP (*subjective* data, *objective* data, *assessment* of the subjective and objective data, and *plan*) is the outline for this recording model. This model was soon adapted to social work recording (Beinecke, 1984; Hartman & Wickey, 1978; Johnson, 1978; Kagle, 1984, 1991; Kane, 1974; Wilczynski, 1981). The social worker uses subjective information to decide which problem(s) to address; the problem-oriented medical record is often criticized for its subjectivity (Tebb, 1991).

Another criticism of the problem-oriented record is that it does not address the interrelationship of client problems. Because problems are disconnected from clients, practitioners are able to view clients as objects, instead of knowledgeable resources and partners in the change process. The client's problems or weaknesses are observed, rather than the client's strengths, and these problems are regarded as

---

[1] An original reading for *Social Work Processes*.
[2] Dean, School of Social Service, Saint Louis University, St. Louis, Missouri.

outside the client's control (Tebb, 1991). The social worker selects the problem, gathers the objective and subjective information, makes an assessment, and develops a plan. The client is not expected to play an active part in this process. If what clients say about themselves is described as subjective and what social workers say is objective, the implication is that client information is only in the client's mind, whereas the practitioner's information is factual and verifiable. This method of recording places the social worker outside the client's situation; the social worker's role is then to observe and manipulate the client's situation.

Using the POR method, the professional accepts total responsibility for determining a plan for change and resolution of the problem. This method of recording violates the value of client self-determination. The emphasis of the POR is on biomedical rather than psychosocial factors and does not show the ongoing process or the complexity of services provided through the client-worker relationship. Although described as objective, the social worker's findings are actually observations. Addressing this concern, Donnelly and Brauner (1990) suggest that client data be described as the story and practitioner data as observations, but they maintain that, no matter what words are substituted, the mantra of subjective, objective, assessment, and plan will continue to be used, and a more radical solution needs to be developed. They note that social workers are only observers and can only understand clients through interaction and collaboration.

Client Involvement

The U.S. Privacy Act of 1974 provided clients with access to their files. In our litigious society, one of the best protections from possible liability is to collaborate with the client in writing the file (Gelman, 1992; Kagle, 1995).

Several social workers (Badding, 1989; Doel & Lawson, 1986; Gelman, 1992; Houghkirk, 1977; Kagle, 1991, 1993, 1995; McDevitt, 1994; Monnickendam et al., 1994; Schrier, 1980; Wilczynski, 1981) have involved the client in the recording process as part of the social work intervention and report that the experience is positive for all. Further, a record written together is less likely to be denied as evidence when subpoenaed by a court. Client involvement adds to the quality of the record.

Badding (1989) reports on a study to determine whether client involvement in the recording process had potential for improving practice and the client's ability to change. Practitioners used their judgments and included the client's input in the file, along with their own assessment; the record was then shared with the client. The findings indicated that this procedure increased client autonomy and encouraged the client to take responsibility for his or her actions and changes. This process helped the client express feelings more openly and enhanced communication between the social worker and client. It enabled both to correct any inaccuracies in their perceptions of the work. According to Goldstein (H. Goldstein, 1988) using a recording process that highlights capability and potential "encourages clients to discover the richness of choice and the cornucopia of opportunity" (pp. 16–17). In collaboration with the client, the worker can use recording to construct an understanding of the situation and begin to look at ways to change it. Clients who share in recording tend to remember their plans better than those who do not (Badding, 1989).

Gelman's (1992) work with adolescents reinforced Badding's (1989) findings. Client changes were observed as a result of active client involvement in the recording process. While access to their file was important, actual involvement in the creation and writing of the file provided adolescents with a sense of investment in their change process (Gelman, 1992). Client participation also resulted in records that were better written and organized, shorter, more factual, and easier to read and use.

Child welfare agencies now require practitioners to involve families in developing service plans (McDevitt, 1994); what better way than to record together? In this approach, files are open for review by clients, and planning is conducted with client participation. Client access to records can lead to improvement in the quality of recording, and recording together tends to empower clients. The Family Service Association of America found that client reading of the file should be seen as part of the counseling process (Kagle, 1991). At the very least, clients should be given access to information requested by others, with the opportunity to amend or correct it and comment. Informed consent implies that the client should know what records say before authorizing their release to others. Writing the record together is a natural way to reassure clients regarding the content of their file, and also eliminates the need to amend or correct. In addition, access to files can promote client-worker communication and trust.

Client Satisfaction

Higher levels of client satisfaction with the social work relationship and with outcomes were reported when the client was actively involved in the creation of the record (Kagle, 1991). Wilczynski (1981) found that the client's active involvement in the change process is as therapeutic as the achievement of a successful outcome. Recording enables the social worker to communicate the process of change and growth. By recording together, the worker and client can look critically at the meanings of this process.

CLIENT-FOCUSED RECORDING MODEL

The client-focused recording method has evolved out of dissatisfaction with SOAP, the problem-oriented medical record, which is incompatible with social work values (H. Goldstein, 1988; Weick, 1983, 1987). At the core of social work process is change, which is the norm in any intervention. Questions about change were used in generating a client-focused recording model that recognizes clients as knowledgeable participants in the social work process (Tebb, 1991). The questions were (Weick, 1987):

1. How might such change occur?
2. What factors seem to contribute to change?
3. What forces constitute resistance to change?
4. How can change be fostered?

By answering these questions, the client and the social worker address the initial change process.

A replacement for the problem-oriented medical record should retain the strengths of the POR model: organization, simplicity, and ability to be remembered. One client-focused alternative to SOAP is known as CREW. The acronym is apt: A crew (the word is derived from the French verb *creistre,* to grow, according to *Webster's Ninth New Collegiate Dictionary,* 1991) is a group of people banded together to work toward a goal.

In using this acronym as a guide in recording, the following questions are asked (Tebb, 1991):

Contributors: What factors contribute to the need for change?

Restraints: What factors constitute restraints or barriers to change?

Enablers: What factors seem to be enabling or contributing to change?

Ways: How can change be fostered?

Client-focused recording examines worker and client perceptions of the immediate situation; this method is not solely oriented toward the problems. Collaboration between worker and client provides the client with the opportunity to make choices, take responsibility, and practice self-determination (Badding, 1989). If the client is involved in the recording process, meanings can be examined, and ongoing review of the actual process and the overall plans for change is possible, with informed determination of the next steps. In client-focused recording, re-

sponsibility for change no longer rests exclusively with the professional, but is shared by the social worker and the client; the client is acknowledged as a knowledge source. Asking the CREW questions facilitates the active involvement of the client in the recording process. Exhibit R10-1 summarizes the differences between the CREW and SOAP approaches.

Exhibit R10-2 is an example of a CREW record. It concerns Jane, who has recently reunited with her husband. Her husband has a history of alcoholism but has regained sobriety; Jane's intention is to make the marriage work. By addressing the CREW together, Jane and I were able to identify, evaluate, and assess Jane's concerns and establish ways to use the available resources to help her move on with her current marriage.

As we wrote the record together, Jane had the opportunity to recall childhood memories of abuse and was convinced of the importance of continuing work on her parenting skills. The process of collaborative writing reassured Jane that I had heard her point of view.

The answers to the four CREW questions can be incorporated into any agency recording format. McDevitt (1994) suggests a flexible format consisting of three parts:

1. A structured set of summary sheets with demographic information on health, family, schooling, and goals.
2. Ongoing service plans and assessments with shared client-worker recording.
3. Comprehensive closing and/or transfer summary.

The CREW record in Exhibit R10-3 was prepared with Mabel, who is the full-time caretaker for her husband, a person with Alzheimer's disease. The ability to establish control and time for herself added sparkle to Mabel's eyes. She began attending the hospital's caregiver support group and actively encouraged other caregivers to use respite services and reconnect with friends. Reading the file validated for Mabel that she needed to begin to consider herself and her needs and not to internalize them. Our sharing in the writing also provided me with examples of what George was like before he became ill. By working with the four CREW questions, we were able to make plans that could bring Mabel some enjoyment and hope again.

CONCLUSION

Client-focused recording (CREW) provides a method for social worker and client to critically address and examine the meanings that are made and those that need to be made. This recording process reflects the continuous

EXHIBIT R10-1
Comparison of Client-Focused and Problem-Oriented Recording

	CREW (client-focused record)	SOAP (problem-oriented medical record)
View of problem, need for change	1. Client defines the need for change and shares it with the professional.	1. Professional defines the problem through careful observation.
	2. Client sees self as an active player in the problem and need for change.	2. Problem externally caused and separate from client.
Client-professional relationship	1. Professional relies on client's personal knowledge.	1. Client reliant on professional's expert knowledge.
	2. Professional supports client with expert knowledge as a consultant and enabler for change.	2. Client is passive; professional is the leader and expert.
	3. Professional's knowledge and relationship strengthen client's ability for change.	3. Specialized expert knowledge separates professional from client.
Nature/process of change	1. Client with the support of the professional is the change agent.	1. Professional is the change agent.
	2. Client, in partnership with the professional, defines personal meaning of problem and change.	2. Professional is given power to create client's meaning of problem and change.
	3. Client designs plans for change with professional input.	3. Change is initiated by the professional and client follows professional's plans.
	4. Change is a naturally occurring process directed by client with support of professional.	

Source: Adapted from: S. Tebb, Client-focused recording: Linking theory and practice. *Families in Society, 72*(7), 429 (1991).

growth of meaning constructed by the client and worker in their collaborative relationship. If social workers understand the process of continuous change, they will be able to facilitate the change procedure in the best interests of their clients.

It would behoove our profession to begin, once again, to learn about, discuss, and examine social work recording. Besides serving the needs of the agency, recording can also serve the needs of clients. Collaborative recording, as an integral part of the social work process, emphasizes the importance of values and self-determination.

In doing so, client-focused recording becomes an important bridge connecting social work values with social work practice. Records that reflect the mutuality of the client-worker relationship provide meaningful knowledge, and agency personnel can use the recording process to extend every possible choice to the client. As a result, social work values are expressed in action.

EXHIBIT R10-2
A CREW Recording Written with Jane

Remarried followed by two years of struggling. Her present husband, an alcoholic, maintained sobriety for the first year of marriage. He relapsed and Jane left him for six months. Able to renew his sobriety during the six-month separation, the couple is now back together and Jane has sought out help, wanting the marriage to have a chance.

Restraints

Jane is 28 years old, third youngest of seven children from a self-described very violent and turbulent childhood.

Her father, an alcoholic, was victim along with the children to a wife and mother who physically, mentally and sexually abused the family. Father often retreated to the basement to avoid his wife's abuse. Jane felt safe with her two older brothers and looked to her older sisters as "mom." She was not particularly attached to her younger two siblings; they were "just there." There were many rules in her home. One rule was you could not be sick. She remembers at four years of age getting sick to her stomach, vomiting, and being beaten by her mother for throwing up. She also had to clean up after herself.

Her parents divorced when she was 11 years old and the children resided with their mother. After the divorce her mother began to speak of suicide. Social Service was involved and there were social workers coming into the home often, sometimes placing the children for short periods of time in foster care.

One day when Jane was in junior high she came home to blood all over the house. Her mother had slit her wrists. At this point the children were either placed with her father and his new wife or with an aunt. Jane stayed with her father for nine months and then was returned to her mother's. It was at this time that the sexual abuse began. The mother would fondle her and bathe with her. If Jane locked the bathroom and refused to allow her mother in, the mother would beat her when she came out. Jane was also sexually abused by boarders whom her mother took in to help pay the rent. Her siblings were aware of what was happening but for their own self-preservation they withdrew. She tried to tell people what was happening to her but they did not believe her. She began to overeat and became involved with drugs and alcohol at 15 years of age. Following high school at 19 she became pregnant and married the father of her child. He had a history of prison. She divorced him when she was 24 and the child custody battle over the terms is still waging.

Enablers

There were two significant people in Jane's life who showed her kindness, a teacher and a neighbor.

Through all the turmoil at home she was able to finish high school. She quit drinking and abusing drugs at the time of the divorce and has been able to stay sober for over five years, through the current marriage's six-month separation and her husband's misuse of alcohol. She is not an abusive mother and continues to fight for the custody of her child. She believes her health, sobriety and ability to parent are due in part to help she received from support groups and an occasional social worker.

Ways

Jane acknowledges that couple counseling would probably be best but she knows she cannot make her husband participate. She is the one wanting the help and she is the one who will participate in counseling.

She asked the social worker to invite her husband and also to offer to meet individually with him. Jane will continue to attend a sobriety support group and also to participate in a parenting support group. She finds both groups a source of emotional and social help to her. She credits the parenting group with helping her to learn to parent.

EXHIBIT R10-3
A CREW Recording Written with Mabel

Mabel participated in the recording process by reading the record at the beginning of each of our sessions.

Contributors

Using an assessment tool together Mabel shared with me things that she only dreamed about doing since she had become a full-time caregiver to her husband, George. I learned that she missed a quilting group; she was a founding member and they had been meeting over twenty years. She also had not attended church nor exercised on a regular basis for over three years.

Restraints

Concerned about Mabel's appearance the nurse in George's outpatient clinic asked that I see Mabel. George's diagnosis of Alzheimer's disease had confined her to her home and she had no means of socializing or having regular contact with others. Mabel was tired, listless and her doctor was concerned about her health and whether she would be able to continue providing round the clock care to George who needed constant watching because he was now wandering.

Enablers

Mabel willingly sat with me and completed the assessment tool. It offered Mabel an opportunity to share her loneliness and her doctor's concerns. It offered me a better understanding of the restraints Mabel was experiencing in her caregiving role.

Ways

Keeping in mind Mabel's dreams we set about to make some changes in her caregiving situation. Mabel was supported to approach her minister and ask him to announce in church her need for volunteers to sit with her husband while she attended church. She would bring George to church with her if he was feeling well and a church volunteer would sit with him in an empty classroom while she attended early church. If it was not a good day the volunteer would come to her home. At my suggestion Mabel hired a neighbor high school boy to come over to her home each afternoon and sit with George while she went out walking. After much persuasion on my part and feeling renewed due to regular exercise and social contract, Mabel agreed to try the local Red Cross respite service. The respite worker came to her home once a week to be with George while Mabel attended her quilting group.

READING 11
Four Pennies to My Name: What It's Like on Welfare[1]

Addie Morris[2]

I had to get up at 3:30 A.M. and start getting the kids dressed. Sally was five and the oldest, so I started with her. Then I dressed Sam; he was three. I did the baby last. All I had to do was change her diaper and wash her face because I had dressed her before putting her to bed.

It was cool that morning and I didn't have a coat for Sam. He never had a chance to go any place in the winter anyway, so there had been no reason to buy him one. I decided to use Sally's coat that Aunt Jean had given her two years ago. He wouldn't know the difference, and I could care less about what people would say.

I wrapped the baby snugly and the four of us started off for the bus stop. At 4:45 a bus finally came and the four of us boarded. I put forty-five cents in the box and we took a seat in the rear. But I hadn't settled down before the driver called, "Lady, you owe me another fare." I had only forty-

[1] Reprinted with permission of the American Public Human Services Association from *Public Welfare* (Spring 1979), pp. 13–22. Copyright © 1979.
[2] Former Assistant Director, Education and Outreach, Arkansas Division of Mental Services, Little Rock, Arkansas.

five cents left and if I gave that to him, I wouldn't have any money to return home. I approached the front of the bus with the baby in my arms. By this time, I had tears in my eyes. Couldn't this black man understand what was happening to me? Didn't he realize that if I had the money I would have gladly put it in the box?

I stood holding on to the rail beside the driver, unable to say anything. Every time I tried to speak the words choked in my throat. Finally, I got the words out tearfully, "Mister, I am on my way to the social service office. I don't have but forty-five cents to my name. I will need that to return home on." A lady that was sitting a couple of seats behind the driver said, "Aw, let the woman go. Can't you see what she's going through?" The driver looked straight ahead and mumbled, "Go on and sit down, lady." That is exactly what I did. I returned to my seat too ashamed to look at anyone.

I sat in my seat silently with tears streaming down my cheeks. Sally put her arms around my neck and asked, "What's wrong, Mama? Do you need my shoulder?" I reached over Sam and gave Sally a big hug.

"No, darling, I don't need your shoulder," I replied.

I heard someone in back of me whisper, "Wasn't that sweet?"

It was a thirty-minute drive to the social service department. My kids and I went out the side door of the bus. I couldn't bear to face all of the people by walking out the front door. I felt relieved that only one other lady got off at the bus stop. She walked so fast ahead of us I thought she must be going to some place important. I had to take my time walking because I was carrying the baby and Sam couldn't walk too fast.

When we arrived at the social service office, it was 5:05. The door of the office was still locked, and people were standing around waiting for it to open. After standing for a few minutes, I decided it would be better if I sat on the steps for awhile. It was then that I noticed the lady who got off the bus with us. She quickly turned her head when she saw me looking at her. The door finally opened at 5:30. Everyone rushed in and took a number or crowded half in line around the desk. I didn't know what to do so I took a number, too. Then I went to the front desk. I waited in line for at least ten minutes before my turn came to talk to the receptionist.

I came straight to the point, saying, "I'd like to see someone about getting food, clothes, and shelter for me and my children." The receptionist told me I would have to wait and talk to an intake worker but they didn't just hand out money like that. Then she took my name and said someone would call me later. I felt a little sick to my stomach that she thought I was looking for a handout.

Around 9:00 the kids became restless. I kept getting up to give them a drink of water, but the water wasn't relieving their hunger. There was a snack bar next to the information desk and some people were buying things to eat. Naturally this made the kids want food even more. But the only money I had I needed for carfare to get home.

Finally, Sam stood up and said, "Mom, can I have one piece of candy?" I was embarrassed and I couldn't think normal. I slapped Sam hard. He began to cry loudly—maybe because he was hurt but also because he was hungry. I told him he better stop crying right away. And of course, not wanting another slap, he did.

By 11:00 the waiting room was crowded. Some people had to stand. However, when noon came everyone that worked there went out to lunch. By this time, my insides felt like they were melting together. I knew how Sally and Sam must feel. But I wasn't thinking much about them because I was too busy feeling sorry for myself.

All of the employees came back to work at 1 o'clock. I approached the receptionist again to find out why I hadn't been called. She told me flatly, "Everyone has to wait their turn; they will call you when they get to your name." I tried to explain that my two older children hadn't had breakfast or lunch and I couldn't afford to purchase them anything from the snack bar. She looked up from her scratch pad and said, "What do you expect me to do? I hear this kind of thing all day long." I quickly took my seat hoping too many people hadn't heard our conversation.

Finally, at 1:15 a lady came out and called, "Mrs. Morgan." My name never sounded so beautiful. I hurried to the front desk. A woman instructed me to follow her to a small room I assumed was her office. She began by saying, "I am Mrs. Jenkins and you are Mrs. Morgan."

"Yes," I replied.

She said, "What can I do for you?" I began, "My husband left me because he was constantly being laid off. He said we could make it better without him."

"Do you know where your husband is?"

"No, ma'am," I replied.

Giving me an application blank, she said, "Fill this out and bring it in tomorrow by 5:30."

It seemed Mrs. Jenkins had finished, but I continued to sit there. After a few seconds, she said, "You may go now."

"But . . . but Mrs. Jenkins, I don't have any food for my two older children. I do have some milk for my baby. Plus I don't have bus fare to return tomorrow." She went into another room and returned with two bus tickets. I said, "I brought two walking children with me that are sitting in the waiting room." She went out again and returned with two more tickets. Then she told me that she would be unable to provide me with a food order; my application would have to be approved first.

As I left the room I thought to myself, "Anyone who thinks being on welfare is fun has to be mentally unstable." The wait alone is enough to make you go out of your mind. Then after the long wait, what did I get? Four bus tickets. Well, at least the bus driver wouldn't be able to embarrass me.

I walked slowly to where Sally and Sam sat. I was thinking hard. I could tell they were glad to see me—it showed in their eyes. But they were afraid to show me because I had been acting so strange and they thought I might lash out at them again.

Someone was sitting in the chair that I was in earlier, so I asked Sam to stand so I could sit down and compose myself. I decided that since I didn't have to use forty-five cents for bus fare, I could buy a snack. I gave the baby to Sally and went to the snack bar. I bought one pack of potato chips and two candy bars. Now, all I had was four pennies to my name.

When I returned with the candy and potato chips, I could see the joy in Sally and Sam's eyes. I gave them each a candy bar and the three of us shared the potato chips. Afterwards, we filled up with water at the fountain.

As we left the building, I was thinking we might go to Aunt Jean's instead of going home. After all, she didn't live too far away. Maybe she would ask us to spend the night and then it would be easier to return to the social service office the next morning. Besides, we didn't have any food at home and she might offer us a little something to eat.

We took a bus going west toward Aunt Jean's house. I was pleased to have two tickets to put in the box when we boarded the bus. It wasn't long before we had arrived at our stop. We got off and started walking to Aunt Jean's home. Sally and Sam realized where we were going and started skipping instead of walking. I was sure they realized that they would get a meal there. Aunt Jean always gave us food.

Aunt Jean was happy to see us. She was even happier that John had finally decided to leave. I didn't bother to explain how desperate I was. It would have only encouraged her to remind me how bad John was. Right then, I could do without hearing that. I tried to make it appear that I was paying her one of those long awaited visits. She was really pleased and indicated that she knew that John was the reason I could never visit before.

Aunt Jean was full of southern hospitality and offered us food immediately. It wasn't long before Sally, Sam, and I were sitting down to a hot meal. It wasn't the greatest, but it was food: salmon, biscuits, syrup, and grapefruit to drink. I washed the dishes for Aunt Jean.

Then we sat down to talk and watch television. It wasn't long before Aunt Jean started to encourage me to spend the night. Of course, this was what I had been waiting for, but I didn't want to let on. "I am going to fool you this time," I said. "We are going to spend the night." She was happy with this. The children were pleased, too. And I was glad at the way Sally and Sam had been conducting themselves.

The next morning we were able to get up a little later because we were closer to social services. I didn't have to start dressing the children until 4:30. Either Aunt Jean didn't hear our noise or she didn't want to be bothered. I was hoping she would get up and offer us breakfast. At the last minute, she got up and fixed us coffee with a lot of cream. We enjoyed this because we love coffee with lots of cream.

As I boarded the bus, I thanked the Lord again that I was able to put two tickets in the box. I was also thankful that my insides were not clinging together from hunger.

We arrived just as the door of the social services office was opening. People rushed in to take a number. Others formed lines at the receptionist's desk. I rushed to take a number, too. Then I remembered that I had taken one the day before and hadn't returned it. The next number was fifteen. My number from the day before was six. Naturally, I kept the number six. Then I wondered if that was a wise decision. The worker I get with the number fifteen might help me more than the one I would get with the number six.

We waited in the waiting room the same as we did the previous day. People walked back and forth to buy snacks. I know that Sam and Sally were hungry, but neither of them asked for anything. They were probably afraid. In my heart I wanted to be able to buy goodies for my children just like everyone else. I knew this was why I lashed out at them for every little thing. I realized that I wasn't making things any better by doing this, so I promised myself that I would do better.

I was daydreaming about being able to afford things for my children when I heard my name over the paging system, "Mrs. Morgan, front desk." I rushed up to the front desk and identified myself.

A lady said, "This way, please."

She offered me a chair and identified herself as Mrs. Jones. I handed her my application and she began to look it over. She didn't say a word with her mouth, but she said a lot with her facial expressions. I would have felt better if she had spoken. I began perspiring until my hands felt slippery. My knees began to tremble so that it appeared I was shaking my baby. I wondered whether Mrs. Jones was enjoying my extreme anxiety. She certainly wasn't trying to alleviate it by breaking the silence.

I suppose it took Mrs. Jones ten minutes to read my application. To me it seemed like ten years. She finally looked up at me and said, "Mrs. Morgan, do you know where your husband is now?" I told her that I didn't have any idea of where he could be. Then she proceeded to tear apart each of my answers on the application. She asked, "Do all three of your children have the same father?" I suppose I was partly to blame on this one. I didn't indicate their last names on the form because I assumed anyone would know their last name was Morgan. Mrs. Jones wanted to know about the length of time I had lived at our address. She threw one question after another at me: "Why don't you have . . . ?" "What have you been doing up to now for . . . ?" "How come you haven't . . . ?" Either Mrs. Jones was asking the questions in a downgrading manner, or I had a complex and was taking all of her questions the wrong way. But I was meek as a lamb answering all of her questions.

My father always said, "Take it easy when you have your head in a lion's mouth." This was certainly true now, and I needed this woman for my survival.

As she continued to question me, I became choked up. When I began to answer her question on what I had been doing for food, I broke down. Here I was a grown woman crying. Mrs. Jones did or said nothing to comfort me. She just sat there. When I managed to control myself, she said, "Maybe I should tell you a little about what we can do for you. We are not intended to be an agency for people to live off. We are designed to help you out with aid until you are able to manage alone. We only take care of things that are essentials or necessities . . ." She rambled on and on but still wasn't saying anything that I wanted to hear. I wanted to know what they were going to give me.

Finally she told me she would work out a budget for me and tell me how much it was when she got back. She left and was gone for thirty minutes. I was relieved because I knew that at least I would be getting some help. I wasn't even angry when I saw her joking and laughing with her friends instead of working on my budget.

She came back with the budget that the department allowed for me. It included the following:

Rent	$100
Lights	15
Gas	20
Food, clothes	120
Total	$255

I was currently paying $130 for rent, but she said the department only allowed $100. She further explained that my checks would arrive on the first and sixteenth of each month. Each check would be for $127.50. She told me about the food stamp program that I was eligible for. The way I understood it I could pay $10 and get enough stamps to buy $15 worth of food.

I was very thankful. In fact, I was so happy I walked right out of her office without asking for bus tickets to get home or a food order to keep us until the following week. I turned around and went back into the office, stumbling over the chair I had been sitting in. "I don't have any food for my two older children," I told her. "I also don't have any money or bus tickets to get home."

"I see your kind every day," she said. "Want everything you can get. Have a seat outside and they will call your name to pick up the tickets and food order."

I was so thrilled. I went back outside, sat down next to my kids, and hummed "Thank You, Jesus." Suddenly, things had begun to look up for me. I could really pray to God now. Before, I was too depressed to pray as I should.

They didn't call my name until 3:00. When I went up to the front desk, Mrs. Jones gave me a $20 food order and $2 worth of bus tickets. I was so hungry and weak, I just thanked her, got the children, and left.

On the way to the bus stop I decided what I was going to do. I would take a bus to the supermarket that was six blocks from my house. We got off the bus and walked proudly to the supermarket. We were going to be able to buy some groceries.

I was careful to add up every item I put into the basket. I knew I couldn't go over $20. I bought potatoes, eggs, milk, bread, sugar, corn flakes, beans, spinach, beef neck bones, chicken livers, and other items that were reasonable and would stretch a long way. After I had finished, I only had a little over $18 worth of groceries. I told Sally and Sam they could go and pick one thing they wanted.

I've never seen two happier kids. Sam got a box of six Baby Ruth candy bars; Sally picked a box of vanilla wafer cookies. I was so full of pleasure with their joy that tears rose in my eyes.

When the cashier finished, I had two bags full of groceries. I realized I couldn't carry the groceries and my baby, too. There were drivers by the door calling, "Transportation. Transportation." I sure needed transportation, but I couldn't afford it.

I pushed my groceries outside and decided to give one of the bags to Sally to carry. I carried the other bag and the baby. But I hadn't gone very far when my load became unbearable. I absolutely couldn't go any farther. I managed to get my bag to the ground before it burst.

For about five minutes, I was out of breath. Sally and Sam seemed to sense what was happening to me because they stood there silently with me. I was trying to stuff some of the groceries into Sally's bag when a car pulled to the curb and stopped.

It was one of the men who was at the supermarket calling, "Transportation." He said, "Lady, do you need a ride?" I told him yes but I didn't have any money. "Get in," he said. Sally, Sam, and I crowded in as he held the seat forward. I told him where we lived. To make conversation, I talked about the weather. I offered him some of my groceries for pay but he refused.

The dinner I prepared that evening was a tasty one. I fried the chicken livers with onions and we had rice, spinach, and corn bread. We felt like saying grace before eating for a change. During our meal, I explained my success of the day. "Now we will be able to eat a meal three times a day. And I won't be so worried and upset."

Sam asked, "Is three times a day a lot of times?" I laughed and assured him that it was enough times that he wouldn't be hungry.

We had never been able to afford story books or television in our home. So I decided I must think of something to entertain the kids. As the three of us sat on the floor, I told them stories. I started with "The Three Little Pigs," continued with "Snow White," and ended up with "The Four Little Rabbits." When I finished, Sally said, "Mom, I didn't know you could tell stories."

The following week was beautiful: three meals each day, peace of mind, and most of all giving love and receiving my children's love.

Saturday was the sixteenth of the month and my check was due. My groceries were getting thin. However, I knew I could make it a few more days. I waited for the postman. He finally came around 1 P.M. He left something in my mailbox. I was so excited. I rushed downstairs and found a sample of Ultra Sheen.

I refused to let my disappointment get the best of me and told myself the check was delayed because of the weekend and would definitely be there on Monday. Meanwhile, things would be all right. I must admit that the weekend wasn't a pleasant one. In fact, it was the longest weekend I've known. I wasn't harsh with kids, though. I just wasn't motivated to talk, clean house, or do anything but the necessities.

Finally, Monday came. The postman always came earlier during the week. But today he didn't stop. My heart was beating so hard, I thought it was going to come through my skin. Without thinking, I ran outside after the postman with only my robe and slippers on. He stopped and went through his bag of mail again but didn't find anything for me.

I ran back inside and fumbled through my purse until I found Mrs. Jones' telephone number. I hurried out to the corner telephone booth with my last dime. I dialed the number but every time the line was busy. At twelve noon, I finally got through but no one answered. Then I realized everyone was out to lunch. But I was determined not to hang up until someone answered.

Around 1:00 someone finally answered the phone. I asked to speak to Mrs. Jones. When she came to the phone she asked, "Was that you letting the phone ring for a whole hour?" She hadn't identified herself.

"Yes," I said, "I'd been calling all morning, and the line was busy. I was determined to reach you." I identified myself and told her about my check not coming in the mail. She said that sometimes it takes two to three weeks for checks to get started. She told me to be down at the office at 8 A.M., and she would have a check for me.

Our food was more than thin at this point. We had been eating generously because we thought we'd be getting more food in two weeks. Anyway, I felt at ease because I would be getting a check the next day.

Tuesday morning I was up bright and early. But it suddenly dawned on me that I didn't have any money to take the bus. I decided I would have to walk. I awakened Sally and told her about feeding the baby and where she could find bread to toast for Sam and herself. I told her to give the baby one bottle in the morning and the other when she wakes from her nap. She agreed to do this faithfully and off I went.

It was a long walk. Although I wasn't wearing a watch, I could tell it was already much later than 8:00. I was so tired I thought my legs would fall from under me. But I couldn't stop. I had to get my check so I could buy food for my children.

Finally, I arrived. I was so exhausted that I had to lean on the receptionist's desk to ask to see Mrs. Jones. She told me to have a seat and Mrs. Jones would call me. There were no vacant seats in the waiting room so I went over to a large ash tray in the corner and sat on it. I was absolutely too tired to stand any longer. As I sat there catching my breath, I looked at the clock on the wall and it said 10:10. Gee whiz, it had taken me more than four hours to walk from home.

Mrs. Jones came out and called different people but not me. Some of the people she called I thought had come in after I had. But I didn't have any proof. And even if I had proof, there was nothing I could do about it. Just before noon Mrs. Jones came out and called me. As soon as I approached the desk, she handed me a check and two bus tickets. I reached out and tried to shake her hand but she refused. I said, "Thank you so very, very much!" I left humming an old spiritual, "Yes, God Is Real."

What a thrill it was to have a check of my own for $127.50. I had never had a check this large in my whole life. All I could do was sing and pray a thankful prayer all the way to the bus stop.

I got off the bus near the supermarket. Going inside, I asked them to cash my check. Of course, they asked, "Do you have any identification?" All I had was my marriage certificate that I had forgotten to take out of my purse after I'd taken it to the social service office two weeks before. I gave my marriage license to the clerk and told her that was the only identification I had. She smiled and initialed my check and told me that the cashier would cash it after I had made a purchase. Then she asked me whether I would like an identification card so I could cash all of my checks there. Of course, I was pleased and thanked the clerk. She gave me a wallet-size card.

I was so happy walking around the store picking up my groceries. I began to feel as though I was a princess.

After I finished getting my groceries, I still had $90 left. I felt great. The same men were across from the checkout counter saying, "Transportation. Transportation." I walked across and asked the one that had given the children and me a ride two weeks before.

After he had helped me take my groceries in, I asked him would $1 be enough. He said, "Whatever you want to give." So I gave him a dollar and he thanked me.

Then I noticed something different about my house.

My children had attempted to clean the house while I was gone. They jumped up and down with joy when they realized that I was bringing food home. I jumped right along with them for the good job they had done. Then Sam and Sally happily assisted me in putting the groceries away.

After I cooked dinner, we sat down to eat. Everyone was quiet. I thought I would break the silence by asking whether anyone had anything they would like to talk about. Sam spoke up, "Mama, aren't you glad Daddy is gone?"

I quickly replied, "No! Why?"

He began to stammer a bit and continued, "We can eat good food all the time since he's away. I hope he stay gone."

"Oh, don't talk like that," I said. I was sorry I had broken the silence. And I had spoken in such a defensive manner. I knew I wasn't letting my children open up and tell me what was on their minds. Yet, I couldn't seem to help myself.

The rest of the week went fine. I told the children stories and even played games with them—games like guessing who has the penny, or who is knocking at my door. All our games had to be things that didn't require a game set. I decided to do exercises and play running games, too. The house had very little furniture—only the necessities: stove, refrigerator, one bed, a mattress on the floor for Sally and Sam to sleep on, and a cradle. So, there was plenty of space available for running.

On Friday, Mr. Perry came over for the rent. I didn't want to give him all of the money that I had. And, even if I did give him all of the money I had, I would still have a balance due to him. The rent was $130 and I had a little more than $88. I decided to give Mr. Perry $65 of the rent and promised to mail him the balance in two weeks. He wasn't pleased because he'd had trouble with my husband in the past. But he agreed. And I felt more secure with the $23 I kept in case of an emergency.

I kept pretty much to myself the following two weeks and enjoyed my children and having decent food to eat. Before I expected it, my check arrived. It was the first of the month, but somehow I expected it to be late. I now had $150. Happy, I mean I was happy. I only owed a $15 gas bill and a $10 light bill.

I left my children alone, instructing them to keep the door closed and not open it for anyone. First I walked to the grocery store. This way I could get my check cashed. I decided not to get groceries until I was on my way home. After getting my check cashed, I took a bus to the post office and bought three stamped envelopes and three money orders to pay my light, gas, and rent balance.

Then I returned to the supermarket. I spent $30 for groceries. I also paid the driver $1 to take my groceries home. So I had $29 left—not a lot of money, but some in case of an emergency.

The money I received from social services could pay the rent, utilities, and buy some food. However, the food would have to be mostly second rate such as neck bones, chicken livers, or bacon ends. But I couldn't complain because I could at least live.

The time came for Sally to start school and I began to wonder what we would do for clothes. I started looking for a night job, but I couldn't find work doing anything. I would even have taken a job sweeping the street. I knew there had to be more to life than this. I was barely surviving.

The day before school, I made starch out of flour and ironed Sally's best dress which wasn't much. It was old plus it was up to her butt because she had gotten it two years before. I bought her a pair of gym shoes and socks at the supermarket.

The first day of school I dressed Sally along with Sam, the baby, and myself. Of course, today was Sally's day and the rest of us didn't matter that much. But as we waited in line to register, I noticed the way the other children were dressed.

After being in school for several weeks, Sally began to act strangely. One afternoon she came home and asked, "Mama, why do all of the children laugh at me?" I didn't want to tell her it was because I couldn't afford to buy her nice clothes like the others had. She seemed to sense that I didn't want to talk about it, so she never mentioned it again. But she began to withdraw and talk less and less. That winter she had a mental breakdown and was hospitalized for two weeks. When the doctor told me he thought this had happened because of the way she had been treated by her peers at school, I became even more determined to get a job so I could buy us some clothes.

I soon found the Lord was looking out for me. The day Sally was discharged from the hospital, her doctor told me about a job at a nursing home working nights as a nurse's aide. He said the man that was the administrator was a friend of his. He told him about me and the administrator had agreed to give me a try. I felt all I needed was a chance like this. I was so elated I had tears in my eyes when I thanked the doctor. He told me to take good care of my children.

I was due to start to work on Sunday night. I knew I couldn't afford to hire anyone to look after the children when I was at work. So I took time and explained to Sally what I was going to do. I told her in order to get money to buy a few toys and clothes like other people, I had to work. I would need her help with Sam and the baby. I assured her they would be asleep most of the time anyway.

I bought a white uniform with my light bill money and used the rest of my emergency savings to catch the bus to and from work.

It was three weeks before my first paycheck, but it was well worth the wait. I cleared $120 and had some money to buy clothes. I went to K-Mart and bought Sam a suit, Sally a dress, shoes and socks, and the baby a new dress, socks, and shoes because she had never had any shoes before.

That Sunday when I got home from work, I dressed everyone; and we all went to church. I was sleepy that night at work, but I was pleased we went. The kids enjoyed it and my heart felt all good inside.

From that time forward Sally kept the kids for me while I worked at night. We had better food and clothes—and I even started saving a little. We went to church every Sunday and sometimes during the week. Sally and Sam began to love Sunday school and looked forward to going.

Sometimes I felt a little guilty for accepting money from social services and working, too. But I rationalized to myself that I couldn't survive on either one alone. So I took the better of two evils and risked going to jail if I got caught.

One night at work an inservice instructor gave a class on "Treating the Patient As a Human Being Through Reality Orientation." I dearly enjoyed the class. Afterwards, I went to the instructor and asked her about continuing my education. She was happy about my interest, especially since I wanted to be a nurse. (I had been thinking about this for some time.) She agreed to bring me literature and an application to a junior college. Of course, I was happy about her promise, but I never expected her to fulfill it. So often people had made promises and never kept them.

The next evening when I arrived at work, I was surprised to find a catalog about a nearby community college and an application. During my lunch break that night I read as much as I could of the catalog and filled out the application.

I wrote a letter to my high school for my transcript. I felt like I was really doing something worthwhile. But in the back of my mind I kept reminding myself that I might not be accepted. Maybe my southern education hadn't been adequate. But I was optimistic. I talked about going back to school with my co-workers and they made fun of me. Even the licensed practical nurse in charge made sarcastic remarks. But this made me keep my head up and try harder.

In less than a month I received a letter from the school to come down for an interview. I became apprehensive, but I decided to go. Surely it couldn't be any worse than my first few visits to social services. Besides, all they can tell me is "yes" or "no." The interview wasn't as difficult as I expected. The director of nursing was black—although she talked and tried to act like she was white. She was blunt and direct. She informed me that with my academic background I would need one year of liberal arts before entering the nursing program.

I registered early in the summer for the fall semester. I planned to take four courses: English 1, Chemistry 1, Humanities 200, and Speech 200. My classes began at 8:00 A.M. and were over at 11:00. Two were on Monday and Wednesday, and the other two were on Tuesday and Thursday. This meant I would be home by 12:30 every day so Sally could go to school in the afternoon.

Soon summer was over and it was time for Sally and me to start to school. I sat down and explained my plans to Sally. I told her she would be caring for Sam and the baby (now a year and a half old) in the morning while I attended classes. She already knew how to prepare cereal for them. That would be all they would need until I returned home at 11:30. Then I would prepare lunch and dress Sally for school. (Sally was better now and able to return to school.)

This plan worked out well. During that first year, I made two A's in chemistry, four B's in my other courses, and two C's in English. I managed to pay my own way through school in addition to buying our clothing. (I enjoyed dressing Sally each morning after I arrived home from work. I continued to thank the Lord for decent clothes to dress her in.)

In April, I received a letter from the Nursing Evaluation Committee to come for an interview for the nursing program. I was put through the third degree at that interview. I managed to answer their questions and remain calm on the outside. But sometimes two of them would ask a question at the same time. I would answer one. Then, when the opportunity presented itself, I answered the other. At the end of the interview, the director of the program told me that I was accepted to the nursing program and was to begin classes in September. I couldn't have been happier.

The next week I made an appointment to see Mrs. Jones at social services. I told her of my acceptance in the nursing program. She questioned me about my getting into the program without prior preparation. I told her about attending classes for the past eight months. Then she asked me, "What do you want me to do?" I told her the first thing I would need was money for a babysitter. To this she replied, "You didn't seem to have any trouble getting a babysitter for the past eight months." At this point my hands became sweaty. Couldn't this lady see the sacrifices I had made? I composed myself and told her of the arrangement I had made with Sally.

But Mrs. Jones continued the questioning. She asked how I got the money to attend college. Silently I said, "Lord, forgive me for this lie," before I told her that my boyfriend had paid for my schooling. I added that we had broken up now and I wouldn't be receiving any more help from him. At last, she told me that social services could allow me $30 a week for child care but nothing for tuition. She told me to try the financial aid office at the school.

I did exactly as Mrs. Jones said and went to the financial aid office at the college. I was able to get a loan and a grant to cover my entire tuition. But I decided to continue to work. I planned to save the loan money in case I had to stop working. However, if I didn't use the loan money I could pay the loan back upon completion of the program.

So I continued to work at the nursing home. The jokes and remarks about my going to school became less frequent as I progressed in the nursing program. At the request of the nursing director, I even took charge when the supervisor was unable to come in.

At times, working along with going to school and taking care of my children would get the best of me. Sometimes I would catch myself nodding in class, and once I fell asleep. Everyone was leaving the classroom when I awakened. I was so embarrassed. I immediately went up and explained to my instructor that I was working nights.

Finally I graduated. It was a small graduation, but an extremely happy occasion for me and my children. As I walked across the stage for my associate degree in nursing, my baby Nell stood up in her seat in the rear of the auditorium and said, "That's my mama!" The audience turned to her and cheered and clapped.

I am now off AFDC and I am very thankful to God that he helped me through those years. I am very proud to be a nurse, and it feels great to be able to go to the supermarket and pay for my groceries with cash rather than food stamps. I always felt people were watching me when I paid with food stamps. It doesn't mean that I have that much more money now, but I do have more dignity which seems to make the money go further. Bank tellers and checkout clerks seemed to sneer at me when I cashed my welfare check. With a check I've earned, these people respect me and I feel that I am not a burden to society. I feel good about having earned that money.

I can see now that children act in the same way their parent acts. When I was on welfare and barely able to make ends meet from one month to the next, my kids were sad and struck out at each other. Now that I am more content, they are nice to each other. Another factor that has changed their attitude is that they can do things other children do and have things other children have. Now I am able to buy Sam a truck for his birthday. I can afford to take the kids to the zoo or on a picnic in the park. Sally has pajamas so she can spend the night with a friend. Our life is very different from before.

It's a great feeling to be off welfare.

READING 12
Approach and Companionship in the Engagement Process[1]

Craig Rennebohm[2]

The primary concern of the Mental Health Chaplaincy is for individuals on the streets of downtown Seattle who are homeless and mentally ill. The chaplain and volunteers seek out those who are most vulnerable, isolated, and lacking in care. Walking a daily route, the chaplain observes, gently approaches, builds trust, and assists with appropriate resources. The aim of the Chaplaincy is to share with each individual the journey from the street to stability and to do all we can to foster the healing process. Basic to our work is the notion of story. Each of us has a story—the narrative of our unique history and journey.[3]

Our story is neither right nor wrong. It may be deeply confused or disturbed, but it still our story. That is where the work begins. There may be profound difficulties or struggles affecting this individual's life; a person may be fearful or wary, hopeless or hostile; yet the story is there, waiting to be told, if we will be patient and listen.

I cannot stress enough the importance of beginning with deep respect for each person we meet. We regard each individual not as a client or patient or case, but as a brother or sister in the human family. Much of what we do in the Chaplaincy is guided by simple courtesy and kindness. Part of that is to understand that peoples about the world have their own ways and traditions; we don't just barge in.

Many individuals are hardly able to speak of their situation. One man stood in the doorway of a department store. He may have been waiting for a bus, or just waiting. Later in the day, he was still there, and again the next morning. His clothes looked a little slept in. I said hello; he nodded. A day or two later, he was again at his post. I stopped and asked him how things were going. He said ok. For a week or so, we exchanged greetings, perhaps a couple of sentences. One morning, I asked if he wanted to join me for coffee. He agreed. As we sat together he responded to a few questions. He was sleeping out. That was hard, I commented. The conversation quickly died; a spare narrative at best, almost nothing. A few days later, still with no job, the man went with me to a shelter, where he was able to get a regular mat each night, and I began seeing him there each morning. I found he had a pattern. At 7:00 A.M., when the shelter emptied, he looked for a newspaper on the ground or in the trash. He took it back to the shelter again at 9:00, when it opened for the day, and looked in the want ads. He circled one or two, and then sat.

This he explained in five or six sentences and with great effort at concentration. I told him that I had noticed how, after we talked a little, he would stop. I asked if he could tell me what happened; we were sitting on the floor, our backs to the wall. "It's embarrassing," he said. "I start something, then I just stop. I can't go on." A long pause. "Like right now. My thoughts are just floating away. Everything is just floating away." Silence.

I told him that I thought there was something we could do to help. "I'd like to talk to a friend here about this. See what she thinks. Just get some ideas." I looked at the man to see how this might seem to him. Slowly, he nodded. I consulted with one of the shelter counselors. Our sense was that this individual might be struggling with some form of thought disorder, a subtle type of schizophrenia. With the man's permission, I introduced him to the counselor. After a couple of visits in which he tried laboriously and valiantly to respond, we made a plan together to see the shelter psychiatrist. The four of us met. The man again shared his pain and embarrassment at being "so slow," and was unable to answer most of the questions or follow the mental status exam exercises. At the doctor's suggestion, he did begin with a small dose of medication. The physician explained that the medicine was intended to help the brain function better, to help the man keep his thoughts together, to take a few more steps each day.

The process was slow. The man continued to meet with the team. Gradually, he was able to stretch out his thinking and conversation over longer and longer periods of time. He began to talk a little of his family and past. We were able to pinpoint when the illness had begun to burden his life, several years earlier, and to trace how things had deteriorated for him into homelessness. We went together to apply for benefits, and shared a walk to a nearby clubhouse program specializing in helping folks prepare for and find work. Today, this man is employed; he has his own apartment; he is in touch with his family. It appears

---

[1] An original reading for *Social Work Processes*.
[2] Director, Mental Health Chaplaincy, Seattle, Washington.
[3] I acknowledge my colleagues in the Seattle Mental Health Chaplaincy and in the community who share this work of outreach and engagement. These thoughts have taken shape through continuing conversations and consultations with many good, wise, and caring souls.

that the medicine may be a lifetime necessity. The man tells his story with clarity and feeling. It includes the episode of illness and his ongoing vulnerability; it includes the experience of his isolation and also the account of his reconnection with others.

The process of reconnection involves four phases of relationship: approach, companionship, partnership, and mutuality. Each phase ends with a change in the relational field. The approach phase ends with the establishment of a one-to-one relationship. The companionship phase concludes as others begin to be part of the circle of healing and partnerships develop with other caregivers. As stability is reached in the community, healing and supportive partnerships may continue to be important, but our life is increasingly characterized by a growing number of mutual relationships with friends, peers, co-workers, family, and neighbors.

In the approach phase of outreach and engagement, the chaplain or volunteer first observes and then, on the basis of the observation, chooses a mode of introduction. These are quite natural behaviors. In observing, we simply evaluate how comfortable a person is with others, how formal or informal we might want to be, how close we may come, how much conversation a person may be able to tolerate, and what their actions may tell us of their condition and sensitivities.

Careful observation reveals moments appropriate for small introductory steps. The work is incredibly slow; at first a second or two, then four or five seconds of contact. After a month, our encounters may last less than a minute.

Often, when students or interns or guests are walking with me to learn a little about outreach and engagement, I suggest we stop for a while at the corner or in the park and just watch. We see who comes by, what occupies a person, how much space they claim or need. After a while, I ask my colleague simply to go and say hello to someone, nothing more. If the person responds and wants to talk, fine. Sometimes, my colleagues have difficulty with this. They want a reason; they want to have a role, a professional frame. You have what you need, I say. You are a neighbor; you share this world; it is enough.

One day, a man sat slumped on a park bench, the rain pouring off him. His hands were grimy from days without washing. On his feet were broken shoes with no laces; all he wore was a light jacket on the cold November day. I went toward him a few steps. He took no notice. Quietly, I asked if it would be all right if I shared the bench. He said nothing. Tentatively I sat down with him in the rain. Perhaps after ten minutes, I spoke again. "My name is Craig. I'm a Chaplain." A pause, then I asked, "Can I help?"

Again no response. From his demeanor, I guessed that the man might be experiencing a serious depression. I did not expect that it would be easy for him to speak. Minutes more went by. "It can be hard, very hard," I said. Once more, nothing. We sat together for almost half an hour. Slowly he lifted his head a little. "Nothing can be done," he said.

A bare thread, the merest, thinnest line between us. It took an hour or more to weave a few more such threads of conversation into enough of a connection that he was willing to go with me to a nearby drop-in center. There, over a cup of coffee, he was able to share a little of his story. He was homeless; he didn't know the shelters; he hardly ate any more; he didn't think anyone could help. I invited him to go with me to the shelter. His hopelessness was overwhelming, almost totally paralyzing. He just shook his head. We waited. I was prepared to let things rest and try again the next day. What we did or did not do, how far we got that day was not nearly so important as how we treated each moment together.

As it happened, we did go to the shelter. He was registered for the night, and I alerted the staff that he was new, and struggling. He had not wanted to talk with anyone else. We visited again together over several days. He had been in the army and afterward managed a law office. While in that job, he became "very tired," listless. He started drinking and lost his position. He went into an alcohol treatment program and had been sober ever since. But again, the great tiredness came. He stopped going to his aftercare appointments and simply stayed in bed. His benefits were stopped, and he was evicted. He had been to treatment, but it hadn't helped; he didn't know what to do. I suggested that one of the staff at the shelter had some knowledge of this sort of thing, and we could possibly talk with him. I let the idea sit for a while. The next week, with the man's agreement, a colleague from the mental health team joined us, just to get acquainted.

The three of us met several times informally, in the shelter or on the street. It was awhile before the man was ready to go to the counselor's office. The visits continued, and slowly the possibility of depression was raised as something to look at. A diagnosis can be hard to hear. Stigma, myth, fear of being crazy make it difficult to accept that this is something affecting our lives. A visit with a doctor was arranged, a time to ask questions and talk over what might be involved in care. Medications were explained and started. He applied for benefits again. A small apartment was arranged. Still, the man was doubtful. It was a month to six weeks before the medication took effect. Today, the man is an assistant manager of the building; he helps welcome and settle in others. He is a quiet and modest man, but very much part of our community, the man at the door.

All of our introductions rest on a basic truth: we are neighbors. Wherever I am, on the street, in the shelter or drop in center, on the bus, out for a walk, I try to practice the simple hospitality of greeting, a nod, a smile, a hello. I may introduce myself a number of times and begin a conversation again and again with a particular individual. When a person tells me his or her name and entrusts me with a little of its meaning and history, I feel that the approach has achieved some success.

In meeting another, few of us reveal all of ourselves at once. Who we are emerges a little at a time, as we begin to feel safe. Whether on the street or in the office, after I have met someone and talked a little, I thank the person, and ask if it would be ok to say hello or to meet again. I don't assume that privilege.

Partly, I think the response depends on how I have acted. Has there been some sharing back and forth? As in any conversation, the other person is interested in me. What do I do? Where I am from? What do I think and feel and believe? Always, I find that we have some common ground in our stories; we are never complete strangers to one another. I do take care with self-disclosure, just as the other is careful about how much to say to me. I try to be open, honest, thoughtful—not a blank screen, but a real person.

As we deepen our introductions, as we begin to share more of ourselves, we are entering into companionship. A companion is one who walks alongside, listens, helps with the road ahead, works with us to overcome obstacles and barriers, carries some of the load. A good companion helps us learn the way, interprets if necessary, reflects with us about our efforts and needs. A companion has sympathy, empathy, compassion for us. A companion knows what it is like and is able to feel with us as we move through our experiences.

First, a good companion needs to listen well. I have found it important to listen intently, to give the other my undivided attention, even through pauses and silences. People need time to find a word, to name a feeling, to remember, especially if their brain is disturbed or their life situation is fraught with struggle. Though colleagues have suggested I carry a pager or cell phone, I don't. I don't want to be interrupted when listening to another. When I am with someone in need, I want to listen as deeply and as long as is necessary, with as much attention and care as I can muster.

Second, I listen not so much for details as for feelings and for the themes of the conversation. How can I acknowledge the wealth of sensations, the emptiness or tur-

moil that another is going through? There are a range of common human themes: the need for shelter, food, survival, the yearning for safety and security, issues of relationship, struggles with decision, right and wrong, the desire for understanding and acceptance, questions of meaning and purpose, a desire for useful and productive work, health. What are the life themes that are important to this person?

Third, when I am listening, I keep in mind that no one thing ever defines or determines another person. Only over time and in the context of community can I begin to fully know and understand who an individual may be.

Fourth, I take great care with responses. I often ask for clarification. "Help me understand." "I'm not sure what that means. Could you say more?" "How so?" "What are you experiencing?" "Is this something that has happened with you before?"

Fifth, as I listen to another, I listen also to myself. What feelings are being stirred in me? What thoughts and memories are emerging? Not that I will share all this, but it helps me to begin to empathize. Listening to myself is a reminder that, in sharing this journey with another, I am opening myself to a new experience. In engaging, I will be affected.

Sixth, as I listen to another, I listen especially for the possibilities—the future that is available in this journey. What strengths, what resources, what capacities does this person carry and have available? I listen for the hope, the dreams, the meanings that are important to this person. What draws the person on? What gives the person a sense of purpose and power?

Seventh, as I listen, I ask how I can best promote the journey toward health and wholeness. I always test my intuitions and ideas with the other person and with the helping team. "What do you think?" "Is this agreeable?" "How do you feel about doing this?" "Does this seem helpful?" These ways of listening honor the other. More than anything I can give, these are the ways that make for companionship.

In approaching another person, we start with an understanding that, no matter how delicate or tenuous, a relationship is there. The question is what we will make of our encounter. Our task as we observe and introduce ourselves is to strengthen the fragile ties, to come to some gentle agreement that we can walk and perhaps work together.

It may be that this will not happen. Even then, my hope is that we will have approached in such a way that keeps open possibilities for someone else down the line to join the journey.

As companionship develops, our aim is also clear. The relationship we build seeks always to strengthen and encourage the other, to increase that person's capacity for choice, decision, life chance. Being a companion is an art; it requires a capacity to listen, a willingness to serve, and skill in helping find a way toward a worthy destination. As companions, we develop a common language. We discern the territory around us, scout out the best paths forward, and make connections with others who may be important for the journey.

As a circle of care and community forms, the process of engagement comes to fruition. Sustained in a period of companionship, a person is increasingly able to partner with other caregivers and enter into friendships, explore a vocation, exercise citizenship and civil rights, and take an active part in family home and neighborhood. In our view, companionship does not abruptly end. It is groundwork out of which a range of other helping relationships can grow.

Companionship honors our human needs and sows the seeds of mutuality. On the journey together, we talk about tomorrow, about our hopes, about the kind of life this person is working toward. Our aim is not to keep another dependent upon us or our services. In companionship, we recognize that we all require to be part of a circle of support and also that we are created for interdependence, for a life of sharing, for a life in community. None of us can make the journey alone.

As the journey continues, the experience of companionship takes its place in our relational memory; we can refer back to this fundamental experience of being accompanied and cared for.

A woman I once knew summed it up clearly. Involuntarily committed to a mental hospital, she was discharged after three months with a referral to a new mental health program, which declined to serve her. Homeless and without care, she rapidly deteriorated and ended up in jail. Her defense attorney arranged for me to visit before her trial; I agreed to assist when she was released on parole the next morning at 10:00 A.M. At midnight, the jail cut her loose, and she was long gone when I arrived. I began looking in the places where she mentioned she had found refuge in the past. Early that afternoon, we connected and began the journey together—to a nurse for medication, to a shelter, to the clothes bank, to a mental health center to start the process of enrollment once again. Sometime later, a note came to the Chaplaincy office. "Thank you for coming to find me," it read. "Thank you especially for not leaving me."

We are privileged to approach another and to share his or her journey in its most troubling moments. Of course, our efforts will not always be successful. Our approach may be declined, our companionship brief. Even then, I trust we have made an important attempt. Perhaps with the next person, the connection will hold.

READING 13
Basic Communications Skills for Work with Groups[1]

Barry R. Cournoyer[2] and Katharine V. Byers[3]

A well-developed competence in communications skills is important for all forms of social work practice. However, when you work directly with client systems of more than one person, proficiency in communications skills becomes indispensable. Communication with a dyad, a family, or a small group for the purpose of problem solving is a much more complex interactional process than is communication with an individual client alone. In the group setting, you must attend closely not only to the communications between you and each group member but also to the communications between each member

and every other member and to communications between you and the group as a whole.

As Schwartz (cited in Shulman, 1992) and others so significantly suggest, the group worker has two clients: the individual and the group. Shulman (1992) extends this idea to all social work practice, terming it the *two-client construct*. Social workers, because of our dual emphasis on person and environment, always consider elements beyond the individual person. In group work, the two-client construct is especially applicable. As a group leader, you continuously shift focus and redirect communications from the individual to the group and from the group to the individual. These connecting processes occur over and over again throughout the life of the group. In such complex contexts, accurate reception and understanding of messages require close observation and careful listening. Similarly, accurate transmission of messages to the several

---
[1] An original reading for *Social Work Processes*.
[2] Professor, School of Social Work, Indiana University, Indianapolis.
[3] Associate Professor and BSW Program Director, School of Social Work, Indiana University, Bloomington.

potential recipients requires well-developed skills in direct and clear communication.

Two general forms of communication have relevance for social work with dyads, families, and small groups: communication based on empathic skills, and communication based on expressive skills. The major distinction between them, which is of remarkable significance for both the sender and receiver of messages, is that empathic communications from the worker to a client—whether individual or group—derive from the client's frame of reference, whereas expressive communications derive from the worker's frame of reference and only indirectly—if at all—from the client's. In empathic communications, you attempt to reflect or mirror the client's expressions. You paraphrase, as accurately as possible, the client's own message. Expressive skills enable you to share knowledge, ideas, experience, feelings, and expectations for the purpose of helping clients go beyond where they are likely to progress on their own.

EMPATHIC COMMUNICATION SKILLS

From its inception, social work has recognized the importance of empathy. The frequent references to starting where the client is and the concept of client self-determination reflect an emphasis on understanding, appreciating, and respecting clients' feelings, thoughts, and experiences: "Empathy is an understanding *with* the client, rather than a diagnostic or evaluative understanding *of* the client" (Hammond, Hepworth, & Smith, 1977, p. 3). Cournoyer states that it "is not an expression of 'feeling for' or 'feeling toward,' as in pity or romantic love. Rather it is a conscious and intentional joining with others in their subjective experience" (1996, p. 7). In most contexts, empathic understanding is probably the single most important quality that you must regularly demonstrate in your work with clients.

Empathic communication skills are responsive or reflective in nature. The content of empathic reflections originates in the subjective experience of the client; such reflections may be responsive to the nonverbal as well as to the verbal expressions of the client. When you communicate empathically, you help clients feel understood, respected, and accepted. Empathic reflections encourage clients to continue their exploration of thoughts, feelings, and experiences that are meaningful to them. Their use also supports the development of the rapport with the social worker, which helps clients feel valued and facilitates the "use of existing strengths to develop a more positive self-image" (Brown, 1991, p. 59).

Consistent with the groupwork notion of two clients, the individual and the group, empathic communications may reflect the expressions of an individual member, one or more subgroups, or the group as a whole. For example, when you observe a group member smiling and laughing and you say, "Bill, you seem pleased today," you are using an empathic skill. Of course, even when your empathic communications are directed toward one individual, they often affect other members in the group and the group as a whole. Your responses promote the development of an empathic culture. As the group members follow your empathic lead, the group becomes a context to communicate understanding, acknowledge strengths, and celebrate positive outcomes.

You can also empathically communicate understanding of the expressions of subgroups or the whole group. For example, suppose you observe that, when one group member, Joan, begins to talk, most other members cross their arms or legs, change facial expressions, or tilt their heads and eyes downward. In response, you may use an empathic communication by saying, "The group seems to be impatient with Joan just now."

As a social worker, you may communicate empathy through the use of several distinct skills. All of the empathic skills, however, require that you (1) nonverbally attend, observe, listen, and remember; and (2) accurately reflect what the client has communicated. In doing so, you acknowledge the individual and cultural meanings of the client's nonverbal and verbal expressions.

Attending (Kadushin, 1995) involves communicating nonverbally that you are open and available to others. Keep your hands, arms, shoulders, and legs in appropriate but relaxed positions. In group settings, you should periodically make eye contact with each and every member. For many social workers, this occurs naturally as a part of listening. However, be sure to also establish occasional eye contact when a group member is not talking. By attending in this way, you demonstrate recognition that members contribute to the group through their interest and involvement as well as through their words and actions. Keep in mind, however, that patterns of eye contact are usually culturally determined. "In many cultures, regular eye contact is experienced as positive, but in several others it is not" (Cournoyer, 1996, p. 83). As Ivey notes, "Some cultural groups (for instance, certain Native American, Eskimo, or aboriginal Australian groups) generally avoid eye contact, especially when talking about serious subjects" (1988, p. 27). Sensitivity to these differences will help you avoid misinterpretations of eye contact and other culturally relevant nonverbal behaviors. Your knowledge in these areas may also aid you in facilitating communication among group members with different ethnic and cultural backgrounds. Head nods and facial expressions that are congruent with the other's communications represent further aspects of nonverbal attending. In meetings with families and groups, be aware that, if you attend more intently to one person, others may experience you as taking sides or having favorites. In addition to listening closely and remembering the verbal expressions of the clients, attending also involves observing carefully the nonverbal communications of group members. Observing, listening, and remembering are essential if you are to engage in accurate reflections of what group members have expressed. You may convey your understanding of clients' expressions through specific empathic communication skills: reflection of content; reflection of feelings; reflection of thinking or meaning; combined reflection; and summarization.

Reflection of Content

Reflection of content involves communicating your understanding of the clients' expressions about problems, circumstances, or other aspects of their lives (Carkhuff & Anthony, 1979). Frequently, you begin by inviting group members to talk about their problems and situations. After someone makes a few statements, you may reflect your understanding of the content, by accurately paraphrasing the message. For example, a group member might share a problem by saying, "I didn't see it coming. She just packed her bags and left without a word. Two weeks ago I received a notice that she is filing for divorce." You might empathically reflect the content of the message by saying, "She left suddenly without telling you and now she wants to end the marriage."

You may also reflect content expressed by subgroups or the group as a whole. Such a response might begin, "So the group is saying . . . ," followed by a statement that demonstrates your understanding of a group-identified concern or situation. For example, several members of a group might express their difficulties in meeting at the time and on the days scheduled. You might reflect the content by saying, "Meeting at this time represents a real problem for many of you."

Reflection of Feeling

Reflection of feeling (Carkhuff & Anthony, 1979) involves communicating understanding of the client's verbal and nonverbal expressions of feelings about the problem or situation, other group members, or the worker. A typical reflection of feeling might begin, "You feel . . ." or "You're feeling . . . ," followed by a restatement of the feeling or feelings expressed. Be sure to use an equivalent feeling word, rather than repeating the words used by the other person. You are a human being, not a tape recorder; exact repetitions can seem mechanical and phony.

When you wish to reflect expression of a subgroup or the group as a whole, you might begin by saying, "Johnny and Sue feel . . ." or "The group seems to feel . . ." For example, following another group member's comments concerning marital conflict, Jack says, "I'm very ashamed about the way I berated my wife in our arguments. I don't know how I can make it up to her." You could reflect the feelings by saying, "You're feeling guilty and despondent about how you treated your wife."

Should you observe downcast eyes, slouched body positions, and yawns by a large number of the group members, you might reflect their probable feelings by stating, "The group seems to be tired and perhaps a little bored just now." Sometimes, feelings expressed by an individual or the group relate specifically to you, the group worker. For example, a member might express frustration and resentment when questioning the effectiveness of your style of group leadership. When you accurately reflect such feelings, you accomplish a great deal indeed. First, you demonstrate that you are personally and professionally competent enough to respond to all kinds of messages, including those about yourself. Second, you immediately increase the safety within the group. If you can communicate understanding of feelings, even those that relate personally to you, others may feel safe to express their feelings as well. Third, by reflecting these feelings as you would others, you encourage a greater level of cohesion and intimacy.

For example, suppose that a social worker asked a member of a teenage group to leave a meeting because the youth had been drinking beer; the smell of alcohol was obvious. After the boy left, the remaining members became silent. They furtively looked at one another and at the worker. In such a context, the worker might reflect the group's feelings by suggesting, "The group seems to be feeling kind of stunned right now. Are you surprised that I would ask Johnny to leave because he had been drinking?" By demonstrating to Johnny that professional service sometimes extends to the maintenance of agreed-upon rules, the worker may help to enhance his individual functioning. By reflecting the other members' feelings about Johnny's departure, the worker contributes significantly to the group's growth and development.

Reflection of Thinking or Meaning

Reflection of thinking or meaning (Carkhuff & Anthony, 1979) involves communicating your understanding of the thoughts or the meaning that an experience has for a client.

A group member might share a beginning description of the problem or situation and perhaps express some associated feelings. You may encourage the individual to explore the thoughts about these experiences by saying, "You think . . ." and then reflecting the message the client has implicitly or explicitly sent. When reflecting messages from the group you may begin with, "Do you mean . . . ?" Alternatively, you could lead into the reflection by saying, "The group seems to think . . ."

For example, suppose a group member describes concerns in this manner: "I am really mad at my folks. They want me to get all A's in school, to help out at home, and to work part-time too." The meaning can be reflected by suggesting, "You think that your parents expect too much of you; you believe that their demands are unreasonable."

In one meeting, following several group sessions in which one person had taken up a large and disproportionate share of the group's time, several other members began to express their disapproval. A social worker might reflect the meaning of their message by asking: "Are you thinking it might be time to explore the issue of timesharing? By timesharing, I mean the process by which we as a group assure that each member has a fair opportunity to speak. Is that what you're thinking about just now?"

Combined Reflection

Combined reflection involves responding to a client's direct or indirect expression of a mixture of content, feelings, thought, and meaning. Such expressions may reflect the client's view that two or more experiences seem to relate to one another but are not necessarily linked in a causal way. At other times, the client may see one experience as the result of, or caused by, another. When the relationship is associational rather than causal, you may connect the two or more empathic reflections with the words *and, but,* or *yet.* When the relationship is seen by the client as causal, the connecting word changes to *because.* Consider the following examples of combined reflections:

- "You have just lost your job *and* you feel devastated, as if the world just caved in."
- "You feel devastated *because* you lost your job."
- "You feel devastated *because* right now you think you will never get another decent job."
- "You just lost your job *and* you think you'll never get another one."

Combined reflections may also be used to respond empathically to expressions from the group as a whole. Here are three examples:

- "The group feels annoyed with me just now because I carried out my obligation to report to the judge those of you who failed the drug-screening tests."
- "Jean, you're angry with Judy because she told you to grow up."
- "You feel proud that Susan has progressed so far but, since it means that she will be leaving the group, you also feel sad."

Summarization

In summarization (Kadushin, 1995), the worker reflects a number of expressions communicated by one or more of the group members over a period of time. It may involve a single empathic skill, such as reflection of content or feeling; often, however, it takes the form of a combined reflection. A summarization might begin with a statement such as, "You've shared a number of important things here today. Let me try to summarize what the group members have said." You would then go on to outline the major elements of the session. For example, you might summarize a group meeting in the following way:

> We've explored a number of personal experiences and concerns today. Let's see if I have understood the major ones accurately, and maybe I can pull some of them together. Joseph and William are going through divorces and are experiencing feelings of guilt, anger, and loss. Maria's husband has recently died, and this has left her feeling uncertain about the future; she wonders whether she'll be able to make it on her own. Wanda has lost her job and thinks she may never find another one. It seems that, in one way or another, all of you in this group are trying to cope with some major changes in your lives, and it's really a struggle to see any bright spots, any hope.

Summarization can contribute to the identification of concerns, issues, and themes that the group members may choose to explore. Especially when used to highlight commonalities among clients' experiences, summarization can aid in the development of cohesiveness—an important ingredient in successful groups (Schopler & Galinsky, 1995). This process of finding common ground is especially important in heterogenous groups, where members differ from one another in age, race, socioeconomic class, or sexual orientation. For example, suppose that, during one session of a grief therapy group for parents whose children have died, the members discuss the ways in which death is handled in their respective cultures. In summarizing that discussion, the worker could make special note of the common feelings of loss experienced by all the parents in the group. By mentioning the commonalities while respecting the differences, the worker contributes to a sense of group membership and belonging.

Although groups composed of diverse members can be quite challenging to social workers, they can also be extremely energizing (Chau, 1990). Heterogenous groups can be especially successful when "group members get to know each other, appreciate and value the vitality of diversity, learn how to use their diversity for creative problem solving and enhanced productivity, and internalize a common superordinate identity that binds them all together" (Johnson & Johnson, 1994, p. 449).

EXPRESSIVE COMMUNICATION SKILLS

In expressive communication, the worker communicates from his or her own frame of reference, rather than the client's. You will introduce new material or extend client-initiated material. When you share knowledge, feelings, perceptions, expectations, judgments, or hypotheses, you are using expressive skills. Your selection and use of expressive skills should be guided by professional values, knowledge, and experience. In groups, a worker most often uses group theory, communication theory, role theory, and the values and ethics of the social work profession. Group workers today also rely on strengths (Weick, Rapp, Sullivan, & Kisthardt, 1989) and ethnic-sensitive (Devore & Schlesinger, 1996) and ethnic competence (Green, 1982) perspectives to guide their use of expressive skills, especially in work with at-risk, vulnerable, and diverse population groups. Because the expressive skills are generated by the worker rather than the client, they must be used with sensitivity, care, and respect.

Expressive communication skills also help group members understand your role, the purpose of the group experience, and your expectations of the participants. The expressive skills help clients to become aware of additional resources and to consider new ways of thinking, feeling, and behaving. They may also be used to promote and enhance the interaction among group members. Among the expressive communication skills commonly used in work with groups are clarification of purpose, roles, and expectations; questioning; partializing; focusing; sharing information; self-disclosure; reframing; and confrontation.

Clarification of Purpose, Roles, and Expectations

Perhaps the most fundamentally important of all the expressive skills used by social workers is the clarification of purpose, roles, and expectations (Shulman, 1992). This is usually among the very first communication skills used by social workers as they meet with a new individual client or a group. Through such clarification, a preliminary direction for work is established. In addition, this process constitutes an important aspect of informed consent.

As they begin a group experience for the first time, many members commonly experience a good deal of ambivalence and anxiety. They may ask themselves, "What will this be like? What will the social worker think of me? Who are these other people? Will they understand my concerns? Will they like me? Will they reject me?" Because of their cultural backgrounds and previous experiences, certain people (for instance, some Asian Americans) may be uncomfortable with the prospect of sharing private feelings and family issues within a group context.

You can help to alleviate many of these concerns by clearly stating your view of the general purpose for the group, by clarifying your role in regard to the group's work, and by outlining the expectations you have for the group members. You may also outline some of the norms to be observed within the group. Meeting with each group member individually before the first group session provides a context for initial explanation of purpose and roles. Later, during the first group meeting, further exploration and clarification can follow from the foundation established during the individual meetings.

You should, of course, vary the way in which you clarify purpose and roles according to the nature of each group experience. For example, suppose you were beginning a group for women who had been battered by their spouses. You might initiate the exploration and clarification of roles, purpose, and expectations in the following way:

> Now that we are seated, I'd like to introduce myself and share my views about how we might use these times together. My name is Sue Walker and I'm a social worker here at the counseling center. As we have discussed individually, the general purpose for this group is to provide an opportunity to share your problems, concerns, and hopes with others who are also experiencing violence and aggression in their homes. I don't see myself as an expert who listens to your problems and then tells you what you should do. Rather, I see my role as helping you help each other. Together, you have an enormous amount of wisdom that, I hope, you will share with one another. I'll get things started each time we meet and try to make sure that everybody gets a chance to be heard. I'll also identify some topics and share information about family violence that may be helpful to you. What I'd like each of you to do in the group is to share your own concerns, experiences, and ideas with one another; to listen to others express themselves; and to join in as together we work to resolve the problems that are presented. How does this approach sound to you?

Of course, your use of the clarification skills will also vary according to the particular purpose for each group, the role that the social worker assumes in regard to the group, and the characteristics of group members. Typically, clarification of purpose, role, and expectations needs to be more elaborate with groups than with individuals. Groups are inherently more complex and, during the beginning stages, there tend to be relatively high levels of anxiety and ambivalence among the members. With clients who are more or less forced to participate, the clarification process should be quite extensive and detailed. Also, because differences among group members (in gender, ethnicity, age, and so on) may initially inhibit free and full expression, you can contribute to the development of a climate of trust and safety by clarifying group guidelines for interaction. By verbalizing norms (Middleman & Wood, 1990) early in the process, you can encourage respect for differences within the group.

Questioning

The communication skill of questioning (Kadushin, 1995) or probing (Cournoyer, 1996) typically occurs when the worker asks questions or makes comments that function as questions. Questioning is a powerful, multipurpose tool that social workers may use in helping clients learn and grow. Too many questions, however, especially when asked one after another, may lead clients to feel interrogated rather than interviewed. Fortunately, after a group has been together for a while, members tend to ask questions of one another. Also, if you regularly use empathic reflecting skills, you will probably find that fewer questions are needed.

Questions may be open-ended or closed-ended. Open-ended questions encourage clients to express themselves freely and openly: "How did that occur?" "What were your thoughts?" "How do you feel?" "What did that mean to you?" "How do you explain that?" Closed-ended questions, on the other hand, tend to yield short responses, sometimes even yes or no, but they can provide a great deal of information in a short period: "How many children do you have?" "Are you married?" "When did you move there?" "Have you ever been in a group before?"

When asking questions, be aware that some questions may contain an implied suggestion or judgment. For example, you might say to a group member, "John, have you told your mother yet?" You may intend this as a simple request for information. However, John may conclude that you think he would not follow through on his commitment to discuss the topic with his mother; or he might believe that you would be disappointed in him if he had not yet talked with his mother; or he might interpret this as a suggestion that, if he has not yet done so, he *should* tell his mother as soon as possible.

Questioning skills are often especially appropriate in conjunction with certain other expressive skills, such as clarifying purpose and roles or sharing information. In such contexts, you may use questions to check clients' reactions to what you have said. For example, you could ask, "How does that sound?" or "Does that make sense?" or perhaps, "I'm wondering what you think about this?"

In problem-solving groups, questions are not only used to encourage members to share personal experiences but also as a means of facilitating group interaction. For example, one group member, Miki, might have talked about the fear and embarrassment she felt when her son had a seizure in the grocery store. You might then seek input from another group member whose daughter has epilepsy: "Kenji, I wonder if you'd share with Miki some of the experiences you've had with your daughter." Other examples of a social worker using the questioning skill include, "Consuella, I'd be interested in your reaction to that" or "Manuel, would you like feedback from the group as to how we see you?"

As the group proceeds and develops a sense of cohesion, you can become more active in promoting interaction. For example, you could say, "Sanji, would you move over next to Tamara and speak directly to her about this?" You can also facilitate interaction by seeking expression from the group as a whole. For example, you might say, "I'd like to hear how the group feels about what Stephen just said." As the group continues to develop and becomes more cohesive, the members themselves often facilitate group interaction by asking questions of one another and directly expressing their thoughts and feelings.

Partializing

Partializing (Cournoyer, 1996) is a skill that helps clients to break down problems, concerns, and other complex phenomena into more manageable parts to greater facility in problem solving. When problems are viewed individually or in small pieces, they tend to seem less overwhelming and can be more readily addressed in a logical or prioritized order. For example, following a lengthy list of concerns by a group member, the worker might say, "You have a lot going on right now. I wonder if it might be easier for you and the other group members if you identified one concern that we could focus upon first. Could you select one that we could explore today?"

Focusing

Focusing (Bertcher, 1979) is an expressive communication skill through which social workers highlight or call attention to something that is, or could be, of importance to the group's work. In their discussions, group members may sometimes wander away from their agreed-upon purpose and goals; you may need to redirect them back toward the work to be done. Also, there could be interpersonal dynamics or processes that should be highlighted for the group. For example, a social worker leading a group for persons experiencing depression might focus by saying, "I noticed that, when Sheila said she sometimes thinks of doing away with herself, the rest of us suddenly got quiet and then went on to some other topic. I'd like to back up a little and really respond to what Sheila tried to say." If a group member has expressed a desire to improve interpersonal relationships, a worker using the focusing skill might say, "Rita, you've said that you have experienced the men in your life as irresponsible and undependable. Since I'm a man and there are other men in the group, I wonder if you'd share what reactions you have had to us?"

In heterogenous groups, prejudices and biases may need your specific attention and intervention. If unaddressed, such attitudes may interfere with group functioning and inhibit group cohesiveness. For example, suppose you are leading a group composed of two noticeable subgroups: a younger set of people in their early 20s, and an older set of individuals in their late 40s. You observe that the younger members consistently fail to respond to pertinent comments made by the older members. In using the focusing skill to address this issue, you might say, "I noticed that when Esther and Nellie made suggestions based on their life experience, Julie and Heather, who are quite a bit younger, did not respond. What do you think? Might the age differences in this group affect the way we interact with one another?"

Sharing Information

Sharing information (Kadushin, 1995; Shulman, 1992) or educating (Cournoyer, 1996) is a vital skill in social work practice. Sometimes, clients do not readily identify available resources within their own natural environment. When appropriate, social workers will share information about community programs and services, which can be very tangible resources for some clients. There are less tangible resources, as well. By helping group members identify unrecognized assets and underutilized strengths, a worker may contribute to a sense of individual and group empowerment (Delgado & Humm-Delgado, 1982). In the real world, social workers frequently function as educators or trainers. When conducting training sessions or leading educationally oriented groups, social workers regularly share large amounts of information in their teaching function.

Social workers leading problem-solving groups may sometimes encourage group members to discover certain information on their own. Indeed, seeking out information can be empowering to individual members and to the group as a whole. For example, members of a support group for parents of disabled children may seek information about ways to involve their boys and girls in community recreation programs from which they have previously been excluded. When successful, such independent knowledge seeking can be enormously satisfying for all group members. On occasion, however, group members individually or collectively may not be able to access relevant, accurate, or complete data. As a group leader, you may appropriately offer information that is relevant to the purpose and current work of the group. Indeed, in many cases, you would have a professional responsibility to do so. In sharing information, however, you should clearly distinguish between fact and opinion, and you should convey the data in such a way that clients are free to accept or reject it. When sharing opinions, you should qualify your expressions by saying, "In my view . . ." or "It's my opinion that . . ." Here are two examples of a social worker sharing information:

- "I know something about the topic you're discussing. The fees for that particular program are based on a family's ability to pay. The more income a family has, the more services cost. The lowest fee is $5 and the highest fee is $80 per visit. Most of the members of this group would pay between $15 and $25 each week."
- "In my opinion, as their children grow older, parents would usually be wise to gradually loosen the rules and modify their methods of discipline. I think that most adolescents of 13 should be treated in a manner quite different from most young adults of 17. What do you think?"

Self-Disclosure

When, as a social worker, you appropriately disclose your own feelings and experiences (Hammond et al., 1977), the group members are likely to perceive you as a sincere and genuine human being. You may also contribute to group cohesion and mutual understanding when you share some of your personal feelings and experiences. Through your own self-disclosure, you also help to model open communication for the group members. However, you should be careful not to share so many feelings and experiences that group meetings become contexts for you to focus on yourself. Group members may find it difficult to deal with their own concerns when the social worker takes up most of the time with self-disclosure. It is helpful to ask yourself, "Will my self-disclosure support the group's work in relation to its purpose and goals?" If your answer is yes, you may appropriately disclose relevant personal feelings and experiences. However, even in that case, you should express yourself in such a way that you maintain ultimate responsibility for your own feelings and actions. Other persons—and especially clients—should not be identified as the cause of your feelings and behavior. For example, suppose a social worker says to a group member, "You make me feel very sad today." This sentence suggests that the client is causing the social worker's feelings; in effect, the worker holds the client responsible for the worker's own emotional reaction. Such a communication is neither personally nor professionally appropriate. It would be better to say, "When I listen to your feelings of loss and sadness, I feel like crying right along with you." In this form of self-disclosure, the social worker maintains personal responsibility for his or her own feelings and actions.

Here are some examples of a social worker using the skill of self-disclosure:

- "Jim, your feelings about your Vietnam experience really hit home with me. I, too, was in Nam and, when I came back, I felt more like a foreigner than an American."
- "I'm feeling uneasy about what just happened here. Judy was talking about her disappointment in us as a support group and we just seemed to skip over her feelings. I'd like to go back to that point now and tell you, Judy, what I felt when you expressed your feelings of disappointment. Honestly, I felt defensive when you complained about the group. I felt that if the group isn't meeting your needs then it must be my fault. I began to feel guilty and wondered what I could do to fix it for you."
- "Jack, when you raise your voice and point your finger at me, I begin to think that you're angry at me. At that point, I start to feel angry, too."
- "Yes, I do feel annoyed when you arrive late for our group meetings. Sure, I'd like it better if you were here on time. However, I'd be much more disappointed if you didn't come at all."

Reframing

Reframing (Brown, 1991; Cournoyer, 1996; Toseland & Rivas, 1995) can help group members view a problem or situation in a new or different way. Often this involves identifying positive aspects of a negative situation. For example, a parent who experiences her teenager's rebellious attitude as a complete negative may benefit from the idea

that her daughter's capacity for independent thinking will help her manage the complexities of life as she enters young adulthood. Reconceptualizing negatives as positives may help group members feel hopeful about the potential for change and may contribute to the problem-solving process. Such reframing processes can lead to individual and group empowerment, as members realize that many problems and situations can be viewed from several perspectives. They may experience a genuine sense of personal competence and freedom when they recognize that alternate explanations exist and that they can select the perspective that best fits their own particular circumstances. For example, when a group member complains about the inquisitiveness and interference of her mother-in-law, the group worker might say, "It sounds like your husband's mother cares very deeply about her son and continues to be concerned about his welfare. How would you like her to show her interest and concern in him?"

Confrontation

The use of confrontation (Cournoyer, 1996) involves directly pointing out to a client a discrepancy or an inconsistency between statements and actions. In effect, the social worker asks an individual or group to examine an apparent contradiction or inconsistency in thoughts, feelings, and behavior. This skill should be used with considerable caution, since some clients will experience strong emotional reactions when confronted. Typically, when confrontation is used in groups, it is communicated with warmth, understanding, and concern for the members. It is good practice to use empathic communications before and after confrontations. Also, be sure to deliver confrontations in such a way that you assume responsibility for the content of the messages and acknowledge that others may see things differently. Here are a few examples of confrontations used by social workers in their work with groups:

- "Jason, you say that you want to get good grades but you also tell us that you don't do much studying. Help us understand how your desire to get good grades fits with your reluctance to put in time with the books."
- "Jorge, you've identified a number of goals that you want to work on in the group. Some of them seem terribly ambitious—more than what most of us could achieve and more than anything you've been able to accomplish in the past. What do you think? Are you setting up goals that are impossible to reach?"
- "Each one of you is in this group because you accepted the judge's offer to participate in counseling sessions rather than go to jail. All of you have come

to the meetings, but several of you arrive late and do not participate in the group discussions. Could it be that some of you are just going through the motions?"

SUMMARY

Successful work with groups requires that you maintain a dual focus at all times. As a group worker, you have two clients: each individual member and the group as a whole. You must continuously attend to them both, through the use of two major categories of social work skills. Through empathic skills, you communicate understanding of the experiences of the group members. By accurately reflecting their verbal and nonverbal messages, you help to build cohesion and facilitate group development. When you regularly convey empathic understanding, you contribute to the growth of an active, interactive group culture, where thoughts, feelings, and experiences are freely shared. Through expressive communication skills, you contribute your own thoughts, feelings, and information from your social work frame of reference. The expressive skills enable you to assist the group members as they proceed into uncharted territory, exploring and experimenting with new information, new experiences, and new perspectives.

READING 14
A Framework for Establishing Social Work Relationships Across Racial/Ethnic Lines[1]

Joan Velasquez,[2] Marilyn E. Vigil,[3] and Eustolio Benavides[4]

It is well documented that disproportionately large numbers of social work clients, particularly in public agencies, are racial or ethnic group members. When we examine the use of social work services by these clients, we find a substantially higher rate of discontinuance than among white clients (Miranda, 1976). It is our assumption that many of these clients drop out of service because they do not perceive what they are offered as helpful and that the partnership which ideally evolves from engaging a client in a positive, purposeful relationship does not develop.

Our purpose here is to explore the development of the social work relationship across racial ethnic lines within a framework of biculturalism. Although this framework has evolved primarily from social work with Latinos, we believe it applies to work with any ethnic or racial group.

If we define culture as a relatively unified set of shared values, ideas, beliefs, and standards of action held by an identified people, numerous cultural groups can be identified within this country. The dominant culture integrated the values and norms of European immigrant groups, as each was encouraged to drop its language and become assimilated by the majority. Groups with recognizable physical characteristics—notably, skin color—have also been pushed to accept the dominant culture as their own, yet have been responded to as separate and inferior groups and thus not allowed to participate fully in it. As a result of this exclusion and a desire on the part of some to retain their original culture, distinct groups continue to exist. We view the retention of one's culture of origin as desirable and see multiculturalism as a perspective that encourages acceptance of difference and the capacity to work with it.

Let us diagram a bicultural continuum to reflect this perspective.

Relationship

Dominant Anglo/ white culture	Other group culture
Values, norms, role expectations	Values, norms, role expectations

Each group's cultural system is based on a set of values manifested in norms and role expectations that are distinct from those of the dominant cultural system. Though a wide range of individual differences exists within each group and parts of one group's system may be similar to that of others, recognizable boundaries exist and must be bridged if relationships are to be developed across them.

[1] An original reading for *Social Work Processes.*
[2] Research Director (retired) Ramsey County Community Human Services Department, St. Paul, Minnesota.
[3] Associate Professor, Department of Social Work, Metropolitan State University, St. Paul, Minnesota.
[4] Organizational Development Consultant, St. Paul, Minnesota, and professor, Metro State University, St. Paul.

At either end of the continuum are located those who function within the boundaries of that cultural system. They identify and interact primarily with other members of the same group, govern their behavior according to its values and norms, and often speak a common language. Movement across the continuum in either direction indicates exposure to another cultural system and generally occurs as one interacts with members of the other group. At least one participant in a relationship which crosses racial or ethnic lines must move toward the other in order to develop common ground for communication. If movement does not occur, interaction remains on a superficial level. As noted earlier, such movement in society has generally been from right to left on this continuum. Members of the dominant group have traditionally expected others to move toward them—to understand their cultural system and adapt to it. We maintain that the preferred alternative is for the social worker to develop the capacity to move across the continuum to wherever the client is located on it.

Let us consider the implications of this perspective for social work practice. Movement across the continuum essentially requires that one understand the values and norms of another cultural system and of one's own system, be aware of where differences lie, and accept both as legitimate. The Anglo/white worker, then, must acquire a substantial knowledge base, including the values, expected role behaviors, historical experiences, and language of the group to which the client belongs. It is essential that the worker accept both self and other before this knowledge can be integrated and applied effectively. Workers, as they offer service to the client, then draw from this understanding and acceptance to assess where the particular individuals involved are located on the continuum.

Social workers who are members of a nondominant racial or ethnic group have, when working with other members of the same group, the advantage of understanding from life experience what is expected and appropriate within the group. They also have the advantage of being identified by physical characteristics as people with common experiences, more likely to be trusted than Anglo/white workers, who must overcome this immediate barrier if service is to be used. In addition to understanding their own system, however, workers from nondominant cultures must develop the capacity to interact effectively within the Anglo/white system as well, since its members predominantly control needed services and resources. When working with members of other groups, such workers move across two continua, developing their capacity to interact within both the dominant culture and the clients' culture.

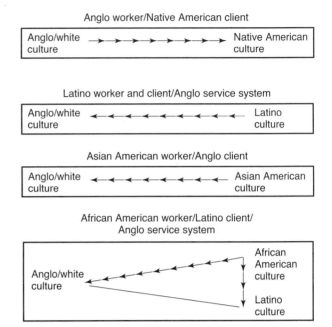

Worker movement across the bicultural continuum is diagrammed in the accompanying examples. The arrows indicate that workers move from wherever they are located both to where the client is and toward competence in interacting with the Anglo/white system.

In order to establish helpful, purposeful relationships across racial/ethnic lines, workers of all groups must be able to move along each continuum to interact within the cultural context that has meaning for the client.

The purpose of the social work relationship is to help clients to become the kind of people they want to become, or to do something they have chosen to do, by overcoming barriers and dealing more effectively with the stresses of life. The magnitude of this task for the client will not be understood by a worker who lacks empathy—the capacity to enter into the feelings and experiences of another without losing oneself in the process.

Unless workers have some knowledge of the values, norms, and expectations of the culture of the client and of this particular client, they will not be able to understand either the client's goals or the barriers impeding progress toward these goals. It is easier for each of us to work with clients who share the same cultural values, norms, expectations, and worldview, since it is easier to be appropriately empathic with such clients. A more conscious effort is required to work effectively with clients of another culture, who have a different frame of reference, particularly in regard to perceptions of the importance of activity, the dynamics of relationships, and human nature.

Empathy, which requires openness to the reality of another person's feelings, experiences, and perceptions, facilitates the conscious efforts of workers in establishing relationships with clients of a different culture. Work with clients of a different culture requires, in addition, an openness on the part of workers to values, norms, and worldviews that their own culture may not share. This requires workers to understand and respect their own culture and the role it has played in their development and to feel free to respect the culture of the other. It demands from workers a belief that no culture is inherently superior to another, but that each is merely different.

We have chosen three dimensions of Latino culture—the culture with which we are most familiar—in order to illustrate factors relevant to the development of the social work relationship across racial or ethnic lines. The three dimensions considered—language, locus of control, and worldview—are not the only, or perhaps even the most important, dimensions of Latino culture. However, they provide examples of how the bicultural framework can be applied in client-worker situations and illustrate points of possible incongruities between the perceptions of the worker and those of a Latino client.

Although these incongruities may not exist if either the Latino client or the worker has ease of movement on a bicultural continuum, nevertheless the onus of movement on the bicultural continuum is on the worker if he is to meet the client wherever the client is and if there is going to be any possibility of establishing a working relationship.

Verbal and nonverbal communications express a person's feelings, ideas, and worldview developed in a particular cultural context. The meanings assigned to verbal and nonverbal communication can result in incongruities between worker and client.

A nonverbal gesture, such as lowering of the eyes or not looking at someone directly, is interpreted by some persons as a sign of respect and deference to authorities and elders, but by others as a sign of lack of veracity. Nonverbal communication is much more open to misinterpretation than is verbal communication. However, verbal communication can also be misinterpreted when one language does not allow for full expression of the nuances and concepts behind another language. This is especially true in regard to Spanish and English.

In Spanish, there are two means of addressing another person, depending on their status in terms of both age and social role. *Tu* is the personal pronoun used to address peers or persons who are younger, whereas *Usted* is used to address elders and persons in positions of authority. To address an authority or an elder by using *tu,* the familiar form, is not seen as a misuse of language but rather as a lack of respect to that individual. This is not a cause for embarrassment, for there is no such term in Spanish. Rather, it is a cause for shame, since disrespect is never seen as a matter to be taken lightly.

The use of *you,* the familiar pronoun in English, is appropriate at all times, since English usage does not distinguish its salutation according to either function or age. The general trend in the usage of English in this country is to do away with distinctions and to become acquainted with one another on a first-name basis. To do the opposite, in English, is sometimes viewed as an attempt to create an artificial distance between the two parties.

In dealing with persons who are of Spanish heritage, the emphasis is not on creating an artificial distance but rather on acknowledging what is already so—namely, that some people have more power by virtue of position and some have more experience by virtue of age. To address another who is older or in authority on a first-name basis is not viewed as an attempt to get closer to the other but rather as an attempt to challenge authority or to discount experience. A person who did this would be viewed as ill-bred or, at a minimum, ill-mannered and disrespectful.

Respect, then, becomes the key for dealing with authority. Respect, however, is not the same as *respeto.* In English, one can respect another while *strongly* opposing the opinions that that person holds; the word *respect* does not contain the element of acceptance of another's view as one's own. *Respeto,* on the other hand, means that one must not challenge the opinions of others. It means that, if one chooses not to adopt the opinions of another, one must at least pay deference to the other person's views by not saying anything. Thus, for Latinos, the locus of control tends to be much more external than internal, whether the locus is God, fate, nature, authority, or age, and this condition is constantly reinforced by means of language.

Because the respect for authority is essential to the highly structured and hierarchical worldview of Latinos, relationships do not occur as often between equals as they do in the dominant culture. Relationships are perceived as occurring between one who is in authority and one who is not. A social worker is seen as a person with authority. The purpose of the social work relationship—the conscious and deliberate use of self for the benefit of the client—remains the same. However, the way that the purpose is viewed by Latino clients may be different from the way it is viewed by Anglo clients.

A Latino client entering a social work relationship views the relationship as unequal. The worker is assigned a sense of authority and *respeto*. The client may disagree with the worker but remain silent rather than appear disrespectful. A worker unaware of this culturally determined approach may view the silence as resistance. Errors in assessment resulting from culture-based misinterpretations lead to antagonistic relationships and the selection of inappropriate methods of intervention. Consider the discordant perceptions that may result from differences on the dimensions of locus of control and worldview. Latinos tend to see many aspects of their lives in which the control is external. Anglos consider more aspects of their lives to be under internal control. Efforts to foster independence and self-reliance, if taken at face value, can be viewed by Latinos as a lack of concern for others and as representing a pompous and unrealistic attitude. This logically follows from a Latino worldview in which there is a balance of pain and pleasure and the natural order is controlled by God. In the white/Anglo worldview, the individual is the powerful force; individuals are in charge of themselves and can change what they want to change about themselves or their world. Latinos view themselves as much more interdependent and not solely in charge of themselves. What they, as individuals, can do is more dependent on others and the external environment.

If not recognized and addressed, such contrasting views impede work toward common goals. For example, the worker may decide to deal with an adolescent client on a one-to-one basis. However, the Latino mother may view this as inappropriate, since she sees herself as in control of her child. Failure to recognize and acknowledge the mother's position is likely to result in discontinuance from service. The reason might never be shared with the worker, because of the authority element in the relationship.

In empathizing with a Latino client, a worker may want to move too quickly from recognizing the difficulty the client is experiencing to identifying what could be done to help. For the client, it may be more helpful to dwell on the difficulty longer—even to the point where the worker might interpret this as resistance or as evidence that the client does not have the capacity to use the service. From the Latino client's point of view, dwelling on the difficulty could be viewed as helpful, since the client knows that pain is balanced by pleasure. The worker could acknowledge that cultural element and use it with the client, to prepare for the more pleasant phase of life; this would result in a more useful service for the client.

We have presented a framework for viewing cross-cultural social work relationships as developing across a bicultural continuum. The dimensions of language, locus of control, and worldview illustrate points of possible incongruities between the perceptions of an Anglo worker and a Latino client, which, in turn, create difficulties in establishing effective social work relationships. Empathy is required if workers of one culture are to move on a bicultural continuum toward clients of a different culture. We believe that recognizing the necessity of, and developing the capacity for, such movement will increase the likelihood of engaging clients of a different culture in positive, purposeful, and effective relationships.

READING 15
Family Group Decision Making[1]

Gale Burford,[2] Joan Pennell,[3] and Susan MacLeod[4]

Social workers have a historic commitment to enabling people to take charge of their individual and collective lives—what we today refer to as empowerment. At the same time, social workers are keenly aware of the dangers of leaving families to their own devices, especially in situations of violence against children and women (Pennell, 1995; Schecter, 1982; Sinclair, 1985). While social workers must be watchful that empowerment does not become

[1] An original reading for *Social Work Processes*. Based on a demonstration project that received funding from the Canadian federal departments of Health, Human Resources Development, Justice, Solicitor General, and Heritage, as well as the Newfoundland & Labrador Department of Social Services. In Nain, the project was cosponsored by the Labrador Inuit Health Commission. Support for the project also came from the Newfoundland & Labrador Department of Justice, Public Service Commission, Women's Policy Office; Correctional Services of Canada; Royal Newfoundland Constabulary; Royal Canadian Mounted Police; and the Provincial Association Against Family Violence.

[2] Professor and Director of Child Welfare Partnership, Department of Social Work, University of Vermont, Burlington.
[3] Professor and Head, Department of Social Work, North Carolina State University, Raleigh.
[4] Social Worker, Health and Community Service, St. John's, Newfoundland.

a rationale for government cutbacks and off-loading of responsibilities onto families and communities, they still need to move ahead with strategies for advancing people's self-determination in safe and effective ways. This chapter provides an example of one means—family group decision making—by which social workers can fulfill their mandate, through encouraging partnerships in which family, community, and government representatives work together to resolve family violence.

In the Canadian province of Newfoundland and Labrador, the Family Group Decision Making Project tested the New Zealand approach of family group conferencing in situations of family violence—that is, abuse against child and adult family members. In this reading, the model is overviewed, and then a case example is used to highlight relevant practice elements, particularly for ensuring the safety of the participants.

BACKGROUND TO THE PROJECT

New Zealand's Children, Young Persons and Their Families Act (1989) outlines how the extended family is to be brought together and resourced as a decision-making body in cases of child protection and youth justice. The model of family group conferencing has been described in detail, and some research has been carried out, especially on youth justice conferences (Atkin, 1991; Connolly, 1994; Maxwell & Morris, 1993; Paterson & Harvey, 1991; Walker, 1996).

To adapt an imported model to the Newfoundland and Labrador context, the university researchers teamed up with representatives from a broad cross section of groups, including women's groups, cultural organizations, police, child welfare, and correctional services. They formed into a provincial committee and local advisory committees in each site where the model was to be tested. This effort in itself took nearly two years and involved first working out a clear statement of philosophy and then policies for the project.

In discussion with local leaders, three sites in the province were selected for demonstration: Nain, an Inuit community in northern Labrador; the Port au Port Peninsula, a rural Newfoundland area with people of British Isles, French, and Micmac heritage; and St. John's, the province's capital and largest urban center, with residents of largely British and Irish descent.

During the course of the project, 37 conferences were held (32 families; four had reconvened conferences), with a total of 472 participants, of which the large majority were family, relatives, or other close supports (384) rather than professionals (88). In order to enhance the validity and reliability of the findings, research and evaluation information on the family group conferencing was collected through diverse methods and from a range of perspectives (Ristock & Pennell, 1996). Descriptions of the model and the results of an implementation study are available (Burford & Pennell, 1995a, 1995b, 1996; Burford, Pennell, & MacLeod, 1995; Burford, Pennell, MacLeod, Campbell, & Lyall, 1996; Pennell, 1995; Pennell & Burford, 1994, 1995, 1996). Reports will be available on the findings from a follow-up study and economic analysis of the project.

PHILOSOPHY AND MODEL

Family group decision making was predicated on the assumption that, in order for anyone in a family to be safe, everyone has to be safe. Focusing only on the abuse of a child when older teens or adults are also being abused does not solve the problem and may even put further at risk those other people who are being abused. In particular, a rationale was developed for avoiding the kind of blaming of mothers that can go on in child protection when the only leverage the authorities have is to intervene on behalf of the child, rather than strengthening families by empowering women (Callahon, 1993). The model challenges mandated authorities to work together with the extended family to bring a halt to the abuse, as an alternative to the marginalization of the family, that can occur in fragmented service systems (Stark & Flitcraft, 1988; Swift, 1991) and in judicial proceedings (Braithwaite, 1989).

Inherent in this philosophy is the notion that families can only come together safely and make appropriate decisions if emotional support and protection is provided throughout the process and if needed resources are made available to assist them in carrying out their decisions. In our adaptation of the model, safety was provided in a variety of ways. The university hired site coordinators who were known for their community work, especially in efforts to end violence. Training in the approach was provided not only to the coordinators but to a broad range of community and government participants, so that they could work together effectively.

In addition to a local advisory committee already mentioned, each site had either a community panel to advise the coordinator on working with the families or a professional consultant in the case of Nain, where the advisory committee recommended that the Labrador Inuit Health Commission both cosponsor and provide the consultancy. Each coordinator worked from the general guidelines provided by the project to flesh out specific procedures for safety at the local level (MacLeod & Campbell, 1996).

THE FAMILY GROUP CONFERENCE (FGC)

The coordinator then began to accept referrals from any protective services agency, or combination of agencies, who could pay for the costs of bringing the extended family together and could resource the family's decisions if they agreed with the plans the family developed. At first, some practitioners were reluctant to refer families, because they were concerned about safety issues, worried that the families could not come up with quality decisions or would not follow through on plans, and wondered if the government would actually resource the plans and if involvement in the project would create extra work for them. The coordinators' tasks at this stage involved working to overcome systemic resistance to the use of an empowerment approach; some of the people who spoke the language of empowerment balked in the moment of letting go, as is often the case during times of restructuring and transition when powerful groups are seeking to reinvent themselves (Burford, 1994).

The coordinator contacted family members, assisted them in identifying who their family members were, prepared all persons for the meeting, facilitated the meeting, and ensured that the plan was specific before submitting it to the referring authorities. The meetings themselves consisted of an opening phase, during which the coordinator worked to set a climate of respect, safety, and clarity of purpose; an information-giving phase, in which the coordinator promoted a sense of authenticity and understanding by having the investigating authorities and other professionals express their concerns and provide information about the identified problems; a phase of family private deliberations, at which time the professionals left the room to foster ownership by family members over the plan that they developed; and a phase of firming up the plan, in which the coordinator returned to the room with the family and worked to anchor their ideas and clarify roles in writing.

REFERRAL AND PREPARATION

Wendy's story illustrates the model. Wendy, age 15, was referred to the Family Group Decision Making Project by a child protection worker, with the endorsement of the police, after she showed up at school with a black eye. She alleged that her father had hit her because she had taken some of his drugs to sell at school. Wendy's friend convinced her to talk to the guidance counselor outside of school. The guidance counselor subsequently contacted the child welfare department, as is mandatory, and an investigation was started. The investigation involved the po-

lice, because of the implication of drugs and the alleged assault. It was brought out during the investigation that the father had a lengthy criminal record and a history of violence; he admitted that he was currently an alcoholic. It also came out during the investigation that Wendy's younger sister, Natalie, and her father had had many physical altercations previously, including an occasion on which he assaulted her. Wendy's older sister, Melanie, maintained that "none of this involves me." No charges were laid against Wendy for her alleged drug dealing, and no charges were laid against the father for assaulting Wendy, as he agreed to move out of the house. Everyone in the family admitted that the incidents as described by Wendy were true. This was the family's first involvement with the police and with child welfare in the province since their return a few months earlier.

Preparation is very important to the success of the meeting. Laying the groundwork for the conferences was the most time-consuming of all the coordinator's activities and usually took place over a period of three to four weeks. Tasks included:

1. Compiling the invitation list—ensuring that all sides of the family (including those of the biological fathers) were invited to the conference.
2. Identifying support persons—requiring that all young survivors be accompanied at the conference by an adult who would stay by them to provide support; and encouraging the same for all adult survivors, as well as for abusers and others who might feel at risk during the conferences.
3. Securing personal statements—having the participants (especially young people, mothers, and abusers) prepare in advance a written statement of their views, to be presented at the conference.
4. Training professionals—preparing the child protection workers, police, and other professionals on how to present their reports at the conference.

The coordinator's notes reveal her anxiety during the preparation phase of Wendy's case: "This is the one I was most concerned with in terms of safety of family members during the FGC process. The dad . . . has . . . history of violence, alcohol and drug abuse, and criminal behavior yet at present there are no social controls (parole or probation) monitoring his behavior." But she felt that she had paid careful attention throughout the planning to the safety of the family members:

> This family was a perfect example of how the safety measures this project utilizes are effective in keeping people safe . . . The offender as well as the mom and kids in the family chose

a support person. He identified this as a way he could feel more in control of his emotions and a way that would ensure he would not blow up or leave during the FGC.

THE CONFERENCE

The hours leading up to the conference were typically an anxious time. The coordinators' skill in turning a last-minute obstacle into an opportunity was tested time and time again. InWendy's case, the family decided three days prior to the conference to change its location. As the co-ordinator observed, "While this was a nightmare for me it was obviously the right thing for the family and added to their ownership of the process and the FGC." The arrival of the family members, their seeing one another's faces, and joining together in the circle demonstrated their willingness to overcome what were often considerable odds. For the children and young people, seeing their relatives come into the room "for them" proved therapeutic.

Opening the Conference

The task of the coordinator was to set a climate of respect for the family, including any rituals that might be important to them, while at the same time making the purpose of the meeting very clear. The coordinator would have had the opportunity to find out from the family members what would be a good way to open the meeting, in what order to introduce people in attendance, and who should be called upon to give an opening comment or prayer, if this was the family's preference. The coordinator would typically name the abused person or persons at this stage and repeat, for example, "We are here for Wendy, to make sure she is safe," thereby reinforcing the purpose of the conference.

The mother's eldest brother opened Wendy's conference with words of welcome. This was fitting, as all family members demonstrated a great deal of respect for this man; years before, he had taken on the role of parent with his younger siblings when both their parents died. He was now clearly viewed as the head of the family. In addition, he had organized the use of the meeting space at his community hall and was therefore also in the role of the host for the conference.

Information Giving

First, the authorities were asked to present the facts from the investigation or assessment, then other professionals or community leaders were invited to provide information on the general area of concern, and finally personal statements by family members were read to the group. When the authorities gave their reports, the conferences tended to be quite emotional, not only because the family—along with their relatives and other close supports—heard the facts, but because they witnessed each other's reactions. The co-ordinator's successful efforts in rehearsing the authorities for the presentations paid high dividends at this stage.

Reflecting back on Wendy's conference, where both the child protection worker and a police officer were present, the coordinator wrote:

> The impact of having the officer speak was significant in that it emphasized the seriousness of the situation for the family and criminalized for them what had become part of their daily life. Both the officer and the Child Protection Worker were respectful, clear and detailed in their presentations.

Later, when discussing the conference, the coordinator noted that the police officer

> made it clear what charges could have resulted . . . I think the family saw the police in a more positive role than in the past. The kids in the family have grown up with a "Don't tell the cops" ethic . . . They saw [the child welfare social worker] in a very positive light. She was clear and specific, didn't gloss over anything. She had good rapport with them. She hadn't antagonized any of them. No one [in the family] disputed the facts that the police officer and social worker presented.

Invited guests gave information to the family on a specific topic, such as the impact of sexual abuse, handling attention deficit disorder, or, in Nain, traditional practices of family support. Normally, the coordinators and investigative authorities were discouraged from acting in the role of information giver in order to keep their roles distinct. In Wendy's family, the guest speaker on alcohol and violence was unexpectedly unable to attend, as the coordinator noted in her journal, "The child protection worker and I shared this role of information provider and in this instance it worked fine because the family had a great deal of respect for this worker and saw her as a helper."

One of the most poignant moments in the conference was when the family members' prepared statements were shared:

> Most family members had their support person read their statement (except Mom). The children's statements had a major impact on the family. Dad used his statement as a way of taking responsibility for his behavior and expressing his sorrow to his family. The uncle (mom's brother) who was his support person, cried when reading the Dad's statement as did most family members, however they did not let him off the hook at all and the statement was sincere rather than an attempt to glean sympathy and minimize the behaviors . . . The two uncles who attended the meeting were people the dad had respect for and he wanted their approval. It was imperative

that they be present at the FGC as this ensured the Dad's attendance and his good behavior. It was they who made him feel shame about what he had done, not the officials present.

It was important at the end of this stage for the coordinator to again check with the family to find out if they still agreed that there was a problem. If they did not, we were always prepared to call the conference to a halt, thank everyone for coming, and refer the case back to the referring worker.

THE FAMILY'S PRIVATE TIME

Once the information stage was complete, including an opportunity to ask questions, and reassurances had been given that people could be brought back if the family had further questions, the moment came when the coordinator facilitated the transition to the family's private deliberation time. Of course, the coordinator was instructed not to leave if violence was imminent but that didn't happen at any of the 37 conferences. The professionals—especially the therapist—felt nervous at the idea of leaving the family on their own, with just themselves and their chosen support people; doubts were expressed that these dysfunctional families could talk purposefully without a professional in the room. Initially, even our own coordinators, and some family members, were skeptical, but any time a professional person was allowed to stay in the room the professional took over overtly or subtly, for lack of the patience to wait the family out, let them express their pain, and coalesce.

Perhaps the professionals had a blueprint in mind for how a family ought to reach a decision. In practice, our research confirms, it is not always by everyone having an equal say. In Wendy's conference, the observer's notes report that Natalie was

> very vocal . . . Wendy was the opposite. She hardly spoke at all, but quietly sanctioned any decisions by interpreting and writing all family decisions, thereby giving them her seal of approval. Melanie, unfortunately, said virtually nothing throughout the conference.

The families each had their own way of expressing themselves and of approaching their purpose. Like other groups who come together to work out solutions to problems, their strategies were not always orderly or elegant, but they got the job done. Only one of the 32 families failed to come up with a plan.

FIRMING UP THE PLAN

When the family groups felt that they had addressed all the issues in the plan, the coordinator and the referring worker were invited back into the room to review what the family was recommending. The emphasis was on making sure that roles and tasks were clear. At Wendy's conference, the plan was well in hand by the time the coordinator returned to the room:

> Wendy ensured she had control of the plan and the decisions agreed upon at the FGC by being the note taker during private deliberation time. She did a fabulous job and had all decisions recorded in great detail. When I asked her at the end of the FGC if she was satisfied with the plan, she grinned and said, "I wrote it, didn't I?"

Key points from the plan included:

- Counseling for the two younger daughters
- Counseling for the parents to deal with their addictions, their relationship, and their parenting, and the father's violent behaviors
- Regular family outings (without involving intoxicants)
- Curfews for the daughters
- Separate housing for the father until he had completed his treatment
- A safety plan (for example, calling the police and relatives) in case the father arrived at the home inebriated or became violent
- A review meeting of the family and child protection to determine if and when it would be safe for the father to return home
- Consistent monitoring by the child protection worker

The costs for the counseling and transportation were to be paid by Child Protection.

But what about the oldest daughter Melanie, who never spoke up? Does this plan represent her interests? It appears so. At the end of the conference, all the family members and the professionals said that they were quite satisfied with all aspects of the conference; the same was true two weeks later, when the researcher interviewed family members about the conference. The researcher wrote, "The three [daughters] seem to be very happy with their lives now that there is peace in the house and some routine in their lives." During the follow-up interview a year later with the aunt, the researcher reported:

> Overall, [the aunt] felt that the FGC left the family better off. It essentially eliminated the abuse evident in the family and made [the mother] a "better person." [The mother] quit drinking, smoking and did all of the extra counseling that was suggested in the plan. According to [the aunt], up until their departure to [another province], [the mother] was doing quite well. The girls also held up their end of the deal by keeping

their curfews [and attending counseling]. [The father] on the other hand, did not put as much effort into it, in [aunt's] opinion. She's pretty sure that he did not attend any of the counseling sessions that he said he would.

The aunt's progress report corresponds with the national police records and provincial child welfare records, which indicated that there had been no further reports, allegations, or investigations of abuse with this family during the 12 months following the conference.

Reflecting on her experience with the family and the conference, the social worker from children's protection services said: "As a worker, we are so used to going out and confronting people on the issues . . . it's so much more effective with everyone there." Before transferring the family to another worker, she visited the family home two months after the conference and again at six months. The father was even present for the second visit but was not living in the home. The mother and daughters said on both occasions that the plan was working and, in particular, the father was not drinking.

STRENGTHS AND LIMITATIONS OF THE MODEL FOR SOCIAL WORK

The strengths of the model for social work are numerous:

1. The abuse is brought out in the open where it can be discussed.
2. The abuser is shamed in a way that does not endanger, but rather serves to safeguard, survivors.
3. The family group is empowered to make important decisions.
4. Nonadversarial relationships between the family and the professionals are fostered.
5. Family and community resources are mobilized on behalf of survivors.

On the other hand, the model calls for a substantial commitment to community development and requires coordinators with considerable communication skills.

The model will seem counterintuitive to administrators in many service delivery systems, which are operated in a top-down, expert-driven manner, and some professionals are not used to a more collaborative environment that empowers families nor to the pressure for accountability. It is best used in systems that are committed to developing thorough and ongoing case review and planning models. Moreover, the use of the model illuminates problems of interdisciplinary collaboration, especially around cooperative resource allocation. The idea that different departments will flexibly allocate their resources in the service of an individual family's plan challenges the status quo. Typically, a block of services is purchased in the hope that the professionals' assessments and recommendations will mesh up with those purchases.

The model also challenges the ways in which many professionals like to work, because it operates around the family's needs; hence, the conferences typically took place outside of normal working hours and lasted on average around six hours. We did not experience resistance from professionals to meetings in the evenings or on weekends, but this was a demonstration project. Would the same cooperation exist on an ongoing basis?

The entire process lends itself to the empowerment philosophy of the social work profession. After a number of conferences had been held, and general anxiety about the use of the model had dissipated, the assistant director of child welfare commented, "Once you understand it, family group decision making seems . . . well, really, it's just good social work practice."

READING 16
The Clinical Utility of Models and Methods of Assessment in Managed Care[1]

Cynthia Franklin and Catheleen Jordan

Social work practice is changing with the advent of managed care and managed behavioral health care. Managed care is a way of financing health, mental health, and social services in which the focus is on cost containment and increasing the quality of clinical services delivered (Strom-Gottfried, 1997). Managed care systems are changing the way that social workers and other professionals conduct their practices in both public and private agencies. Indeed, the managed care context is blurring the boundaries so that the distinction between public and private practice no longer applies (Franklin & Johnson, 1996).

The current trend in managed behavioral health care is to finance brief and effective service delivery models (Corcoran & Vandiver, 1996; Franklin & Johnson, 1996; Strom-Gottfried, 1997; Winegar, 1993). These systems mandate the development of best practices, accurate assessment, and diagnosis to see that clients are referred to the most effective, cost-efficient interventions, with an emphasis on the measurement of case outcomes. To compete in market-driven social services and mental health care delivery systems, practitioners will need a variety of skills in empirically based assessment and an ability to monitor systematically the effectiveness of their practices (Blackwell & Schmidt, 1992; Corcoran & Gingerich, 1994; Giles, 1991; Lazarus, 1995; Sabin, 1991).

Therefore, greater sophistication in assessment and measurement techniques is necessary for competent practitioners. In social work practice, assessment denotes different but related processes: (1) the determination of what interventions and resources are needed to help a client solve problems; (2) an evaluation that leads to a clinical diagnosis—for instance, assignment of an accurate diagnostic label from *DSM-IV;* (3) a set of interventions that reveal relevant information about the client but also introduce information that produces change; and (4) an ongoing evaluation of a client's progress toward treatment goals.

Over the past 20 years, social work has moved toward the use of standardized measures as part of clinical assessment; a broad literature advocates that single-case designs be used to monitor the progress of outcome goals (Blythe & Trippodi, 1989; Fischer & Corcoran, 1994; Hudson, 1989; Jordan & Franklin, 1995; Levitt & Reid, 1981).

Many academic social workers saw the need to produce clinical researchers and wanted students to practice in ways that would contribute to the empirical knowledge base concerning practice effectiveness. The impulse to train practitioners as researchers arose, in part, out of social work's failure to produce outcome studies that contribute to its own knowledge base (Franklin & Brekke, 1994).

This approach did not prove very successful. The responsibility for producing clinical research should be the role of the academic social workers whose job description entails research; it should not be a primary role of practitioners, who have little time to produce clinical research—and are likely to have even less time in the managed care environment. Practitioners are required to familiarize themselves with research incorporating the best-known empirically based practices for different problems. Further, they must demonstrate that what they are doing with their clients is cost-effective. Diverse skills in assessment and outcome measurement are needed in order to practice in an effective and accountable manner.

In this reading, we build on previous work (Franklin & Jordan, 1992; Jordan & Franklin, 1995) to provide a knowledge of various assessment models that may be useful in managed care. We review four practice models—the psychosocial, cognitive-behavioral, life, and family systems models—and identify the assessment strategies of each. We further discuss the utility of these models in managed care environments. An integrative framework for combining the best practices from the models is presented, along with an integrative skills checklist to guide decisions concerning what is needed in a brief assessment.

PSYCHOSOCIAL ASSESSMENT MODEL

In the psychosocial and related ego approaches, associated with Florence Hollis, Gordon Hamilton, and others (Blanck & Blanck, 1974; Goldstein, 1986; E. G. Goldstein, 1988; Hollis & Woods, 1981; Maluccio, 1981; Parad & Miller, 1963; Perlman, 1957, 1986; Woods & Robinson, 1996), the goal is to determine a diagnosis of the client. Factors such as past history and developmental processes are taken into account in making this diagnosis and in implementation of the change efforts. Ego psychology provides the psychosocial assessment framework, and an appreciation for the interplay of biopsychosocial processes is built into the

---

[1] An original reading for *Social Work Processes.*

model. Goldstein (1986) explains that, compared to the classical psychoanalytical ideas dominant in early social work practice, ego psychology presented a more optimistic and sociocultural view of human behavior:

> Ego psychology concepts were used to refocus the study and assessment process on (1) the client's person-environment trans-actions in the here and now, and particularly the degree to which he is coping effectively with major life roles and tasks; (2) the client's adaptive, autonomous, and conflict free areas of ego functioning, as well as her ego deficits and maladaptive defenses and patterns; (3) the key developmental issues affecting the client's current reactions; and (4) the degree to which the ex-ternal environment is creating obstacles to successful coping.

Psychosocial theory has integrated ego psychology with other ideas, including role theory, systems theory, and factors such as ethnicity, values, and power (Turner, 1988). Over the years, psychosocial assessment and treatment have incorporated new ideas from the social sciences. The current model emphasizes more of a systems perspective; the focus of the social worker is on modifying the aspects of persons and environments that are easiest to change. Psychosocial theory has incorporated many ideas from systems theory—for instance, that a change in one part of a system may influence other parts of a system, and that small changes may create a big difference in client func-tioning. Practitioners focus on clients' strengths and cop-ing abilities and work to help people make the best adaptations possible. The model has taken on a more col-laborative approach, with a focus on problem solving, al-though it retains the major assumptions of ego psychology concerning personality functioning.

Psychosocial Assessment in Current Practice Environments

One of the strengths of the psychosocial model in today's practice environments is that it is consistent with the med-ical model, which involves study, diagnosis, and treatment. Its biopsychosocial perspective meshes with that of med-ically based behavioral health care settings. The focus of the psychosocial model on support, strengths, coping, problem solving, and a quick return to adaptive function-ing also meets the current demands of managed care. The model's basis in ego psychology, however, may prove to be a challenge. In managed care settings, there is little time for detailed history taking and study of the developmental processes associated with problem patterns; and there is no time for the long-term fostering and use of the thera-peutic relationship in the psychosocial approach (Budman & Armstrong, 1992; Sabin, 1991).

Current practice environments offer short-term treat-ment sessions; evidence suggests that clients rarely see practitioners for more than six to eight sessions, regard-less of therapeutic orientation (Koss & Shiang, 1994). Some practitioners have advocated a course of intermit-tent work, similar to a primary care model; in this ap-proach, practitioners would offer fewer sessions spaced over a long period of time (Cummings & Sayama, 1995). Another model being used is intensive outpatient treat-ment, where clients are seen two to three times a week for a short period. Even single-session therapies are being used (Talmon, 1990). In general, psychoanalytic ego psy-chologies and associated treatment models that rely on long-term therapy have fallen out of favor. Some social work authors have linked the advent of managed care to the demise of psychodynamic theories (Alperin & Phillips, 1997). There have also been efforts to develop shorter-term psychodynamic models that can be used in brief ther-apy (Davanloo, 1980; Levenson & Butler, 1994; Sifneos, 1992; Worchel, 1990). The psychosocial model has aligned itself with brief psychodynamic perspectives.

Over the years, the psychosocial model has adapted by taking on variations of other models—for example, aspects of the functional casework model, which de-emphasizes history and focuses on solving problems in the here and now through the use of agency resources. Some of these adaptations include abbreviating history taking in the di-agnostic interview and working more collaboratively with the client to solve problems (Woods & Robinson, 1996). To offer a viable assessment model for today's practice en-vironment, the psychosocial model will need to continue to move toward a shorter-term perspective that relies less on history and ongoing therapeutic relationship and more on rapid assessment and helping clients to quickly resolve their presenting problems.

The psychosocial model's usefulness for managed care settings is also limited by the paucity of empirical outcome research demonstrating that this model is successful at re-solving a client's presenting problems. Most research on the psychosocial model has been based on qualitative case studies (Woods & Robinson, 1996), which do not provide the efficacy and effectiveness data required if the method is to become an acceptable treatment alternative. Qualita-tive methods are useful in practice but may have limited utility for managed care (Franklin & Jordan, 1995).

Methods Used in Psychosocial Assessment

Turner (1988) suggested that psychosocial diagnosis is an ongoing process involved with the identification and la-beling of problems and with the recognition of client

---

EXHIBIT R16-1
Evaluation Form for Standardized Assessment Measures

Name of measure:	Scoring procedures:
Author:	Level of training needed:
Date of publication:	Purpose of the measure:
Purchase availability:	Theoretical orientation:
Availability of manual:	Standardization and appropriateness of norms:
Cost:	Evidence for validity:
Time for administration:	Evidence for reliability:
Ease of use:	Evidence for clinical utility:
Clarity of directions:	

Source: Jordan, C., & Franklin, C. (1995). *Clinical assessment for social workers: Quantitative and qualitative methods*. Chicago: Lyceum Books/Nelson Hall, p. 89.

---

strengths. Detailed psychosocial interviewing has become a key component of assessment in the model. Specific assessment techniques include: (1) classical psychiatric interviewing for the purposes of making a diagnosis; (2) the use of standardized and projective testing to aid accurate diagnosis; (3) psychosocial and developmental study to identify problem patterns; and (4) observations and interpretations of the client-social worker relationship for the purpose of helping clients understand their problem patterns and providing a corrective emotional experience. Social workers in managed care environments will particularly appreciate two aspects of the psychosocial model: the use of standardized interviews to obtain an accurate mental health diagnosis; and the monitoring of symptoms to make sure that they change during the treatment plan.

To practice in managed care, social workers need to be skillful in various types of diagnostic assessments and the use of the *DSM-IV* (Jarman-Rohde, McFall, Kolar, & Strom, 1997). Increasing the validity of these assessment activities is consistent with the historic focus of the psychosocial model on detailed study leading to a diagnosis. Many diagnostic tools are currently available to help practitioners make an accurate diagnosis on the basis of established criteria; several involve semistructured interviews using standardized formats. Interviewing for diagnostic purposes is an important part of the psychosocial model.

To use the best practices in clinical assessment, practitioners must learn to identify and evaluate various standardized assessment tools on the basis of their psychometric properties and clinical utility. Exhibit R16-1 provides a useful evaluation form for assessment instruments.

Standardized interviews guide the practitioner in making a quick and accurate diagnosis and allow the practi-

tioner to closely scrutinize diagnostic decisions. In other words, practitioners are no longer relying only on their own clinical judgments in an informal interview process but have a valid measure to aid their judgments. This will decrease the likelihood of inaccurate diagnosis, which leads to time wasted on treatments that do not match the problems, and increase the likelihood that clients will receive treatments in a timely manner.

Managed care companies are very concerned that clients receive the correct level of care necessary to solve problems. In particular, most managed behavioral health care companies require a *DSM-IV* diagnosis as a basis of payment for mental health treatment. The practitioner has to communicate to the payor (the managed care company) that the client actually has the diagnosis and needs a certain level of treatment. Companies usually prefer that problems be solved at the outpatient level, instead of automatically opting for more expensive residential treatments. Managed care companies have review panels and experts who evaluate the practitioner's treatment plan and determine if his or her clinical judgments concerning diagnosis and treatment are warranted. Being able to establish diagnosis through the use of standardized interviewing adds credibility, so that it is easier to justify a regimen of treatment. It may also provide methods to monitor changes in symptoms during the course of treatment, in which the payor is also interested. Sauter and Franklin (1998), for example, review five instruments for assessing posttraumatic stress disorder in children.

COGNITIVE BEHAVIORAL ASSESSMENT MODELS

Cognitive behavioral therapy focuses on clients' present functioning and attributes clients' problem behavior to learning processes, the formation of maladaptive cognitive schemas, information processing, and proactive cognitive structures or meaning systems. It has moved to the forefront in psychotherapy within professional psychology and is also one of the most popular forms of brief psychotherapy (Turner, 1992). In social work, it has been integrated into competency-based, problem-solving, and task-centered models, as well as the empirical practice model (Berlin, 1996; Brower & Nurius, 1993; Franklin & Jordan, 1998; Franklin & Nurius, 1996; Gambrill, 1983; Gambrill, Thomas, & Carter, 1971; Granvold, 1996; Mattaini, 1990; Rose, 1977, 1988; Shorkey & Sutton-Simon, 1983; Stuart, 1980; Thyer, 1983, 1985, 1987, 1988). Brower and Nurius (1993) have integrated the knowledge from cognitive science into a new practice model, the cognitive-ecological model. The cognitive behavioral model is more a school of thought than a unitary set of practices or theory; it has been influenced by theoretical positions ranging from psychoanalytic to behavioral therapies.

The underlying theoretical base of the cognitive behavioral model is taken from experimental psychology—particularly, learning theories and work in cognition and memory, information processing, and social cognition. Recently, cognitive theory has also borrowed from developmental theories such as attachment theories, and integrated newer systems theories, such as complexity systems theory (Guidano, 1991; Mahoney, 1991, 1995). Meichenbaum (1993) describes how cognitive behavior therapy has changed over time by identifying three metaphors that have guided the model.

1. Conditioning as a metaphor: Cognitions are viewed as covert behaviors subject to the same laws of learning as overt behavior.
2. Information processing as a metaphor: The mind is a computer. The language of information processing and social learning theory (for example, decoding, encoding, retrieval, attributional bias, cognitive structure, schemata, belief systems, cognitive distortion, and cognitive errors) is employed.
3. Constructive narrative as a metaphor: Humans construct their personal realities and create their own representational models of the world. Personal meanings, multiple realities, and consequences of cognitive constructions are emphasized. The therapist helps clients to alter their narratives and life stories and to reframe stressful life experiences and emotions as normal. The focus is on strengths, resources, coping abilities, and narrative reconstruction.

Cognitive behavioral models are beginning to emphasize that behavioral and cognitive sequences are complex, interactional, circular, and self-perpetuating (Arrington, Sullaway, & Christensen, 1988; Mattaini, 1990). Constructivism is a central theoretical construct for contemporary cognitive therapies (Ellis, 1989b; Mahoney, 1991; Meichenbaum & Fitzpatrick, 1993).

According to Mahoney (1991), constructivism

(1) emphasizes the active and proactive nature of all perception, learning and knowing, (2) acknowledges the structural and functional primacy of abstract (tacit) over concrete (explicit) processes in all sentient and sapient experience; (3) views learning, knowing and memory as phenomena that reflect the ongoing attempts of body and mind to organize (and endlessly reorganize) their own patterns of action and experience—patterns that are, of course, related to changing and highly mediated engagements with their momentary worlds. (p. 95)

Many of the principles of the newer cognitive therapies are supported by research relating to memory (Brower & Nurius, 1993), social cognition (Fiske & Taylor, 1991), ecological psychology (Greenberg & Pascual-Leone, 1995), narrative psychology (Van den Broek & Thurlow, 1991), new social cognitive, applied developmental, and learning theories (Aldridge, 1993; Bandura, 1989; Prawat, 1985), complexity systems theory (Mahoney, 1995; Warren, Franklin, & Streeter, 1998), and evolutionary epistemology, which is the study of how humans construct knowledge (Mahoney, 1991). Brower and Nurius (1993), for example, review empirical research from cognitive, personality and social psychology, as well as ecological psychology, and describe the importance of the constructivist perspectives (Franklin, Waukechon, & Larney, 1996).

Cognitive Behavioral Assessment in Current Practice Environments

Cognitive behavioral assessment has considerable promise for work in managed care settings. In fact, given the compatibility of cognitive behavior therapy with brief practice settings, some social workers have advocated that student training focus on cognitive behavioral methods (Jarman-Rohde et al., 1997). Cognitive behavioral therapies have rejected Freudian psychology, with its emphasis on long-term treatment and pathology. Instead, these therapies developed an understanding of human behavior based on learning and cognitive theories, the importance of environmental modification, self-efficacy, and adaptive change. The principle of parsimony was incorporated in the models, and practitioners were taught to be pragmatic, efficient, and effective in their approach to human problems. For these reasons, cognitive therapy has always been a brief form of therapy (Wilson, 1981).

In cognitive therapy, practitioners are active, and sessions are structured and goal-directed. The relationship between the client and worker is collaborative; there is an emphasis on gathering evidence and exploring personal hypotheses, with the notion of testing out faulty ideas and personal coping strategies. Efforts are made to develop a clear conceptualization of the case on the basis of theory, and cognitive behavioral techniques are chosen according to the client's goals. In general, the practitioner's tasks are psychoeducation, increasing client cognitive and behavioral skills for better functioning, and helping the client plan for relapse prevention. This active and systematic approach is very consistent with brief treatment models and managed care.

Four attributes of the cognitive behavioral model make it especially useful for managed care:

1. It is a short-term model that focuses on the rapid assessment and treatment of mental disorders. Cognitive behaviorists primarily emphasize the resolution of the presenting problem; they work with history only as it relates to the client's current functioning. The main focus is to identify faulty learning and cognitive mechanisms that maintain the presenting problem and then to guide, educate, and facilitate the client in getting past the current difficulties.

2. Cognitive behavior therapies are the best researched of all psychotherapies. The methods that they use rest on a strong empirical base. Researchers in academic psychology and psychiatry have supported the efficacy studies on cognitive behavioral therapies and produced impressive outcome studies on their effectiveness.

3. Cognitive behavior therapists have provided detailed treatment manuals that guide practitioners in helping clients resolve problems such as depression, substance abuse, personality disorders, and post-traumatic stress disorders (Barkley, 1997; Beck & Freeman, 1990; Beck, Rush, Shaw, & Emery, 1987; Beck, Wright, Newman, & Liese, 1993; Linehan, 1993; Meichenbaum, 1994). Such manuals make practice more systematic and outline procedures that are known to work. By following the manuals, practitioners can be sure that they are using the best practices, which is an important consideration in managed behavioral health care.

4. Cognitive behavior therapies advocate that practitioners systematically monitor the effectiveness of their practices; many of the early behavior therapists advocated the use of single-case designs (Barlow &

Hersen, 1984). This emphasis is very consistent with managed care principles.

Methods Used in Cognitive Behavioral Assessment

The goal of cognitive behavioral assessment is to specify the behavior (thoughts, feelings, or overt behavior) that is to be changed, along with its antecedents and consequences and underlying cognitive mechanisms. From a nine-step procedure (Gambrill et al., 1971), behavioral assessment today has evolved into a multidimensional contextual model (Barth, 1986; Gambrill, 1983; Mattaini, 1990; Whittaker & Tracy, 1989). Gambrill (1983) identified sources of influence over clients' behavior, including the actions of others, thoughts, emotions, physiological factors, setting, events, physical characteristics of the environment, ethnic and cultural factors, material and community resources, past history, societal factors, and developmental factors. Specific assessment techniques used in the cognitive behavioral model include behavioral analysis theory, interviewing, identifying underlying cognitive schemas, logs, self-anchored scales, and standardized measures (Bellack & Herson, 1988; Hudson, 1982; Kanfer & Schefft, 1988; Shorkey & Sutton-Simon, 1983).

In assessment systems, cognitive behaviorists focus on theoretically and experimentally based approaches for identifying and tracking specific behaviors and cognitions that need to be changed. Popular earlier models, such as the ABC model, focused on tracking antecedents, behaviors, and consequences of a particular problem. Collecting data on the frequency and duration of cognitions and behaviors is important for observing the difficulties that clients are experiencing and monitoring their changes. Self-observation, self-monitoring, and self-recording are hallmarks of assessment approaches; in newer constructivist models, these activities are also central to change efforts (Brower & Nurius, 1993).

With a focus on developing standardized measures to assess maladaptive cognition and behavior (Clark, 1988), cognitive behavior therapists have been forerunners in advocating valid and reliable methods for client assessment. Computerized assessment systems (Hudson, 1990; Jordan & Franklin, 1995; Nurius & Hudson, 1988) systematically track behaviors using standardized measures. For instance, the Hudson (Hudson, 1982, 1989) Clinical Assessment System (CAS) provides approximately 20 scales to measure intrapersonal and interpersonal client problems, such as generalized contentment and marital satisfaction. The system is designed so that clients (or the practitioner) may enter and graph the data on computer for single-system analysis. Standardized rapid assessment instruments

EXHIBIT R16-2
Essential Questions for a Brief Therapy Assessment Interview

1. Why is the client entering therapy now?
2. Are there any signs of psychosis, delusions, or thought disorders that would indicate that the client needed immediate medical or psychiatric treatment?
3. Are there signs of organicity indicating the need for neurological or other medical treatment?
4. Is there evidence of depression or of suicidal or homicidal ideations?
5. What are the presenting complaints?
6. What important factors are antecedent to the client's problem and to seeking help?
7. Who or what is maintaining the problem?
8. What does the client wish to derive from therapy?
9. What are the client's preferences for therapy style? How can you match that style?
10. Are there clear indications for a specific modality for treatment based on the BASIC ID?
11. Can a therapeutic alliance be maintained or should the client be referred?
12. What are the client's positive attributes and strengths?

(RAIs) are becoming popular in social work practice (Fischer & Corcoran, 1994; Jordan & Franklin, 1995). Behavioral practitioners also endorse computer-based expert systems, which aim to help practitioners make clinical decisions—for example, in child welfare and in mental health (Mullen & Schuermann, 1990; Stein, 1990; Wakefield, 1990).

It is impossible to describe a full spectrum of cognitive behavioral approaches to assessment, because of the increasing numbers (currently more than 20, according to Franklin [1995]) of specific models and their unique features. One comprehensive assessment framework developed from the cognitive behavioral approach is multimodal assessment, which helps practitioners evaluate client problems in great depth and detail across different modalities, including behavior, affect, sensory, imagery, cognitions, interpersonal relationships, and physiological factors of client functioning, as well as their interactive effects (Lazarus, 1989). Lazarus (1991) developed a Multimodal Life History Inventory to help practitioners gain information about the different modalities. The comprehensive components that go into a behavioral assessment are summarized by the acronym BASIC ID: Behavior, Affect, Sensation, Imagery, Cognition, Interpersonal, and Drugs; the latter represents the broader biological realm.

In the multimodal model, practitioners formulate a brief but comprehensive assessment by developing a modality profile, which organizes information according to the BASIC ID assessment. Using the BASIC ID, practitioners can make differential decisions about effective treatments. It is also possible to scale the modality preferences, so as to determine whether a client shows a more favorable response to treatment in particular areas (Lazarus, 1981). For example, some clients may experience their difficulties more through their behavior, while others have more difficulties with affects. Even a client with a presenting problem such as anxiety (an affect) may respond to treatments that focus on another modality. For example, one of the authors had a client who experienced anxiety attacks mainly as physiological sensations (rapid heart, tight muscles). The modality profile suggested a treatment focused on the sensation modality. As it turned out, the client difficulties were effectively helped by teaching him progressive muscle relaxation exercises. Using the BASIC ID, it is possible for a practitioner to plan interventions systematically on the basis of the client's assessment profile.

Exhibit R16-2 lists the 12 essential questions that a practitioner should ask in a brief therapy interview, according to the multimodal model.

LIFE MODEL ASSESSMENT

The life model for social work practice was developed by Germain and Gitterman (Gitterman, 1988). The underlying theory is ecological, concerned with interactions between people and their environments (Johnson, 1981). Important concepts include stress, coping, and adaptation, as well as competence, autonomy, social networks, and organizations. The goal of the life model assessment is for client and worker to collaborate together in order to understand the problem, and then to set objectives and plan the intervention (Johnson, 1981). Gitterman (1996) explains assessment as concerned with "the interplay of dynamic forces within the life space, including the influence of the agency as a presence in the client's ecological context" (p. 391). The primary tool of assessment is the problems-in-living formulation, which distinguishes between three areas of the life space: life transitions, environmental pressures, and maladaptive interpersonal processes (Gitterman, 1996).

Gitterman (1988) identified five major aims of the life model: (1) to develop a perspective that gives equal attention to people and to the environment; (2) to develop a model of practice that bridges the traditional specializations of casework, administration and planning, and family therapy; (3) to mirror life processes closely, so that social workers fit in with clients, instead of requiring clients to fit in with their theoretical orientation; (4) to build on people's strengths, rather than on their pathologies and to avoid labeling, which is seen as blaming clients for their problems; and (5) to build bridges between treatment and social reform.

Life Model Assessment in Current Practice Environments

While considerable information can be conveyed through the ecological assessment, this information does not provide a direct set of interventions to address the various difficulties in functioning. This limits the life model's utility as a set of practice activities for managed care. The assessment phase of the life model relies on a detailed social study, which is inconsistent with the time and resource constraints of brief therapy environments. In the managed care setting, assessment information must permit immediate selection of a solution to a problem. The life model has yet to provide this degree of specificity. Mattaini's (1990, 1992a) efforts to combine the ecological assessment model with specific targeted interventions from behavioral practice may be a step in the right direction.

Wakefield (1996a, 1996b, 1996c) has pointed out several weaknesses of ecological systems theory that limit its clinical utility in managed care. First, this approach is not an intervention model but, rather, relies on other social science theories—such as cognitive therapy and ego psychology—for its interventions. Wakefield suggests that, because the life model does not add anything new to existing models, it is unnecessary. We might add that ecological models such as the life model impose a cumbersome overlay of metatheory on other theoretical approaches, with no benefit for managed care. Second, Wakefield suggests that to integrate different areas of social work practice, as the ecological systems theory hopes

to do, is not possible, because each field has to develop its own unique perspectives and interventions on the basis of extant theories. We might add that direct practice in managed behavioral health care requires very specialized skills in clinical assessment and intervention. While some knowledge of community systems, management, and policies (for example, information technology, advocacy, and health care reforms) is needed, generalist training and skills will not serve clinical practitioners very well. Finally, Wakefield argues that ecological systems theory is nonempirical and does not offer a research base for its effectiveness. The nonempirical status of the life model also limits its clinical utility for managed care.

According to Warren, Franklin, and Streeter (1998), some of the difficulties of the ecological systems theory mentioned by Wakefield can be transcended through the use of newer systems theories, which concentrate on how ordered systems—such as human social systems—develop and change. These theories, based on chaos and complexity systems theory, come from empirical research in other fields, such as mathematics and biology, and provide mathematical and empirical tools to study systems. Such tools have been lacking in the life model and other ecological approaches. In addition, with their focus on change, these approaches may be useful for modeling change processes in brief therapies and may provide decision tools for facilitating naturally occurring change processes in current practice environments.

Methods Used in Life Model Assessment

Assessment techniques include the interview, eco-maps or social network mapping, and standardized social support assessment instruments (Cheers, 1987; Hartman & Laird, 1983; Streeter & Franklin, 1992). Social support can be linked empirically to improvements in social and mental health functioning and is an important area for assessment (Streeter & Franklin, 1992). Tracy and Whittaker (1990) have improved upon the information that can be obtained through eco-mapping by combining it with card sort techniques and an interview grid approach to perform clinical assessment of social network characteristics. In its current form, however, this assessment instrument is too cumbersome for use in brief therapy. Mattaini (1992b) has provided computer software for developing eco-maps and a variety of graphic-based assessments within the ecosystems approach. In their brevity and clarity, the computerized versions of these assessments are promising for integration into managed care settings, especially when computerization of graphic methods is combined with a specific set of treatment recommendations.

Reviewing the literature on social support, Streeter and Franklin (1992) identify eight measures that may be used in clinical practice. The use of standardized measures for social support may greatly improve social work assessments.

FAMILY SYSTEMS ASSESSMENT MODELS

The family therapy field has developed multiple methodologies for assessing families as a system. These new methods focus on whole-systems functioning and assess the interactional, interpersonal, and systemic functioning of family groups. Assessment of whole-systems family functioning is based on systems theory and assumes that the interactions of a family group take on measurable and/or observable behavior patterns and characteristics that extend beyond the individual behaviors of each of its family members (Franklin & Jordan, 1998).

Family systems assessment focuses on the systemic or relational network characteristics of family functioning and the associated presenting problems. Systemic functioning specifically refers to the circular, patterned ways in which family groups are believed to behave. Behavior patterns in family systems are nonlinear, recursive, repetitive, and reflexive (Becvar & Becvar, 1988; de Shazer, 1982; Hoffman, 1981; O'Hanlon & Wilk, 1987; Selvini, Boscolo, Cecchin, & Prata, 1980; Tomm, 1987). Some family clinicians believe that systemic family patterns have meaning or serve a function for the family system—by helping the family to stay intact or to avoid marital conflict, for example (Haley, 1987; Madanes, 1984; Palazoli, Cirillo, Selvini, & Sorrentino, 1989). Other clinicians focus more on the behavioral aspects of the systemic functioning or the self-reinforcing nature of the pattern and make few interpretations about its meaning or function (Cade & O'Hanlon, 1993; Fisch, Weakland, & Segal, 1982; Watzlawick, Weakland, & Fisch, 1974).

To effectively assess family systems, clinicians need methods that can focus on the interactive sequences and relational network patterns of the entire family. Assessment is both a way to discover how a family system is functioning and a method for intervening in the patterns of a family system. Correspondingly, assessment and change interventions are not distinct but, rather, are interactive and circular; assessment methods may function both as information-gathering strategies and as interventive methods (Tomm, 1987). Viewing assessment as intervention blurs the boundaries between which methods are for assessment and which are for change (Franklin & Jordan, 1998; O'Hanlon & Weiner-Davis, 1989).

Family Assessment in Current Practice Environments

Family assessment methods focus on introducing rapid change and are especially suited for brief therapy settings. The brevity of this approach adds to its utility for managed behavioral care. However, all the interventions are based on systems theory, which holds that the presenting problem will be resolved if we alter the functioning of the whole system. Although some family approaches, such as the Mental Research Institute (MRI) and solution-focused therapy—have the resolution of the presenting problem as a goal, not all approaches are so goal-directed. Managed care companies may accept the idea that family relationships are an important target of intervention when the client's difficulties are primarily interpersonal (for instance, marital conflict or battering); greater reluctance is likely, however, in the case of individual mental health issues (for instance, depression or psychosis).

Fortunately, a body of empirical literature points to the importance of relationship issues in mental health problems such as depression (Jacobson & Christensen, 1996; O'Leary & Beach, 1990), although some of the theoretical notions concerning the possibility of eliminating client problems by changing family patterns remain open to question. Nevertheless, there is support for the effectiveness of family therapy with a variety of mental health disorders (Pinsof & Wynne, 1995). The process-driven nature of the family assessments and interventions may make it difficult to tell where the assessment ends and the intervention begins. In family therapy, assessment is treated as just another intervention or change effort. This is positive in that there are no delays in treatment, but negative in that it is difficult to specify what assessment means. For example, how does assessment help us determine which interventions to choose or monitor the progress in treatment? The development of standardized family assessment measures may clarify this question.

Methods Used in Family Assessment

Assessment methods designed for family systems may also be used to facilitate change within those systems. Change happens as the system is assessed; assessment and change are part of the same process, as patterns are successively identified and modified. Family assessment relies on questioning techniques that are used to simultaneously gather information and introduce information into a family system. Franklin and Jordan (1998) review such techniques, including circular questions; conversational/therapeutic questions; hypothesizing, circularity, and neutrality; tracking problems, solutions, and/or exceptions to problems; and pretherapy change assessment.

Family assessment models and standardized measures derived from research on the classification and assessment of family systems functioning include the Olson circumplex family model (Olson, 1986; Olson et al., 1985; Olson, Sprenkle, & Russel, 1979), Beavers' levels of family functioning and competence model (Beavers, 1981; Beavers & Hampson, 1990; Beavers & Voeller, 1983); and the McMaster family model (Epstein, Baldwin, & Bishop, 1982, 1983).

INTEGRATIVE SKILLS ASSESSMENT

To master a range of effective skills in assessment, it is important to learn assessment techniques from the various practice models. We call this approach an integrative skills assessment approach (Franklin & Jordan, 1992). The following assumptions underlie the integrative skills assessment approach:

1. Practice is empirically based.
2. Assessment is brief but comprehensive enough to be effective.
3. A larger-lens or systems approach is useful in grasping the complexities of problems.
4. Measurement is essential.
5. Ethical practitioners evaluate their clinical work.
6. Well-qualified practitioners are knowledgeable about numerous assessment methods and can apply multiple methods in developing assessments.

Such an approach to assessment is compatible with the demands of managed care and will prepare practitioners to be effective in their work. The integrative skills approach to assessment assumes that practice methods from different theoretical models may be used together, without consideration for inconsistencies in the underlying assumptions among the models. This approach is based on the theory of technical eclecticism (Hepworth & Larsen, 1990).

Technical eclecticism assumes that the complexities of practice require effective practitioners to be eclectic but acknowledges that the inconsistencies inherent in the underlying assumptions and principles of the different models preclude integration at the theoretical level (Lazarus, 1981). Instead, without necessarily embracing any underlying theory, technical eclecticism allows practitioners to borrow techniques (outcome-producing methods) from various treatment models, to seek empirical validation for the choices made, and to exercise some flexibility in trying out techniques on an exploratory basis (Rosen, 1988).

Integration of skills, therefore, relies on the empirical connections between methods and client outcomes. Technical eclecticism is a prescriptive, problem-solving, and outcome-driven approach. Any treatment techniques may be used together if empirical evidence suggests they can solve client problems. A technique with no empirical support—in particular, a technique from the practice wisdom—may be used on an exploratory basis, as long as the practitioner seeks to monitor its effectiveness. This type of tinkering with practice methods is similar to the approach recommended by Blythe and Briar (1985) in developing empirically based models of practice.

Within technical eclecticism, the practitioner selects a battery of assessment techniques from different treatment models in order to produce a valid and reliable assessment of client attributes. Techniques and empirical outcomes are organically connected. Assessment and treatment techniques are chosen because of their effective outcomes, and positive outcomes happen on account of effective techniques. There is a continuous interaction between knowledge derived from clinical techniques and knowledge derived from empirical outcomes. This approach is consistent with the managed care context and will serve practitioners well.

The integrative skills checklist in Exhibit R16-3 formulates a brief assessment model on the basis of the four assessment models considered here and allows practitioners to make decisions about which techniques to use in any assessment. The focus of the checklist is assessing the client in the environmental context. Not every question or technique may be relevant for every client, but the checklist gives a sense of areas that could be important in obtaining an accurate picture of the client and outlines several methods by which this information may be collected. In brief assessment, the practitioner must be able to determine which areas to focus on and must develop a method for including some data and excluding others. The following guidelines are suggested:

1. Always begin by reviewing information on the presenting problems (for instance, the client's depression and anxiety).
2. Focus the assessment initially on the resolution of the presenting problems, by forming concrete and specific goals for change. How does the client experience the presenting problem? How is it a problem for him or her? What is needed to make immediate progress on the depression and anxiety?
3. Next, focus on the resolution of associated or secondary problems that may prevent the resolution of the

EXHIBIT R16-3
Checklist for Brief Integrative Skills Assessment Protocol

I. Identifying information
____ 1.–12.

II. Nature of presenting problem
____ 13.a.   List all problems
____ 14.a.–k. Specification of particular, discrete problem behavior(s)
____ 15.a.   Prioritize problem(s)

III. Client
____ 16.a.–i. Intrapersonal issue
____ 17.a.–d. Interpersonal—family
____ 18.a.–b. Interpersonal—work or school
____ 19.a.   Interpersonal—peers

IV. Context and Social Support Networks
____ 20.a.–b. Agency consideration
____ 21.a.–c. Client's environmental context

V. Assessment Measures
____ 22.   Family functioning
____ 23.   Marital (or significant other) functioning
____ 24.   Individual functioning
____ 25.   Social supports

VI. Strengths and Resources
____ 26.   Client strengths
____ 27.   Environmental strengths

VII. Assessment Summary and Treatment Recommendation
____ 28.a.   Baseline
____ 29.a.   Practitioner impressions
____ 30.   DSM

____ 31.a.   Problem(s) targeted for intervention
____ 32.a.–b. Recommended treatment alternatives

VIII. Methods Used in Assessment
____ 33.   Standardized interview
____ 34.   Ethnographic interview
____ 35.   Nonstandardized interview
____ 36.   Background information sheets and questionnaires
____ 37.   Standardized assessment measures
____ 38.   Behavioral observations
____ 39.   Projective measures
____ 40.   Self-anchored or self-rating scales
____ 41.   Client logs or diaries
____ 42.   Graphs or maps
____ 43.   Experiential and task assignments
____ 44.   Information from collateral sources
____ 45.   Previous treatment or other social service records
____ 46.   Other (PLEASE SPECIFY):

_____

_____

_____

Source: Jordan, C., & Franklin, C. (1995). *Clinical assessment for social workers: Quantitative and qualitative methods.* Chicago: Lyceum Books/Nelson Hall.

presenting problem or that need attention once the presenting problem is resolved (such as marital conflicts).

4. Think about the other sections (developmental history, family situation, and so on) and decide what information is affecting the presenting problems and how it needs to be considered in the treatment process (for instance, the client's report of childhood abuse). Just skim these sections to see if anything might be relevant for maintenance and relapse prevention (for example, a cognitive schema of lack of self-worth that perpetuates the depressive pattern).

5. Look at all the assessment information and treatment goals you have obtained and construct a set of recommendations for the client that can begin to be implemented in the first session.

SUMMARY

Managed care demands that social workers develop sophisticated skills in clinical assessment; they need to know the most effective empirically based techniques. Redressing the lack of information on assessment methods for managed care, we have evaluated four assessment models—the psychosocial, cognitive behavioral, life, and family systems models—in terms of their clinical utility for managed behavioral health care settings. We have examined the potential for integrating diverse methods across practice models within the framework of technical eclecticism and presented an integrative skills checklist that aids practitioners in making decisions about which areas to cover and which techniques to use in a brief assessment.

READING 17
A Brief Solution-Focused Practice Model[1]

Michelle MacKenzie[2]

Families often provide social workers with vague or conflicting descriptions of what they want to change. The worker typically attempts to help families articulate clear and specific goals and to develop a service plan against which the effectiveness of the treatment can be judged (de Shazer, 1975, 1982; Fisch, Weakland, & Segal, 1982; Haley, 1963; Jacobson, 1985; Weakland, Fisch, Watzlawick, & Bodin, 1974). Solution-focused brief therapy (de Shazer, 1984, 1985) is designed to assist in developing a clear idea of the goals of service and in creating a positive context for change. De Shazer (1985) maintains that families often cannot recognize the solutions to their own problems that they already have at their disposal. Solution-focused therapy is designed to promote expectations of change and to shift the focus from the past to the present and especially the future; and from problems to strengths, assets, and resources. The service focus emphasizes family resources and creates a context in which "change is not only possible but inevitable" (de Shazer, 1985, p. 137).

The solution-focused brief therapy model is optimistic and proactive (de Shazer et al., 1986) and offers both the family and social worker an efficient and practical means for solving problems. Because the focus is on solutions and what is working, the model promotes cooperation and hope.

The model focuses on solution construction with clients. What clients find helpful often has no direct relationship to the problems presented (de Shazer, 1985). Rather than trying to understand the problem, the worker asks clients questions and identifies tasks that help them focus on their own perception of needs and goals and their own existing and potential resources for solutions (Lipchik & de Shazer, 1986; Molnar & de Shazer, 1987). Discovering

exceptions—times when the problem wasn't a problem (or was less severe)—is more helpful than asking about the times it was a problem (Molnar & de Shazer, 1987).

The approach is based on Milton Erickson's ideas about people's resources (de Shazer, 1982; Durrant, 1992). Erickson was not particularly interested in helping people consciously understand their predicaments; he thought that insight and interpretation were largely useless. Three primary principles of Erickson's work have been assimilated into the solution-focused brief therapy model (de Shazer, 1982):

- Meet the patient where he is at, and gain rapport.
- Modify the patient's productions and gain control.
- Use the control that has been established to structure the situation so that change, when it does occur, will occur in a desirable manner and a manner compatible with the patient's inner wishes and drives.

Brief therapy is time-limited; Weakland prefers to call his work efficient therapy (Weakland et al., 1974), as does Steve de Shazer (1988a): "Therapy should be as efficient and effective as possible, and brief therapy is built around ways of knowing when therapy is finished" (p. 29). Brevity is a metaphor for clarity about what needs to be changed, an attitude of being task-oriented (Budman & Gurman, 1988). Brief therapy has also been termed problem-solving therapy (Miller, 1992; Molnar & de Shazer, 1987). The premise is that problems are maintained by repetitive interactional patterns. Once the pattern has been identified, a solution can be developed to interrupt it and reduce or extinguish the problem (Haley, 1987).

Solution-focused practitioners do not accept that the problem and its underlying causes must be known in order to find a solution. Rather, they relate the continuation of the problem to the context in which it occurs and the expectation that it will continue (de Shazer, 1988a). Consequently, the focus is on the situation, rather than on the person. Solutions can be developed by amplifying nonproblematic

---

[1] An original reading for *Social Work Processes*.
[2] Social Worker, Halton Regional Police Service, Oakville, Ontario.

patterns, without attempting to determine what caused the problem (de Shazer & Berg, 1988). The solution-focused brief therapist shifts from changing problems to constructing and initiating solutions (Lipchik & de Shazer, 1986).

Solutions, like problems, vary a great deal from individual to individual, but they are similar enough to allow researchers to formulate a description that fits for most (Miller, 1992). Solutions may be described "as the behavior and/or perceptual changes that the therapist and client construct to alter the identified difficulty, the ineffective way of overcoming the difficulty, and/or the construction of an acceptable, alternative perspective that enables the client to experience the complaint situation differently" (de Shazer et al., 1986, p. 210).

Problems or complaints requiring service are typically defined as involving a limited set of behaviors, perceptions, thoughts, expectations, and feelings (de Shazer, 1988a). The role of the therapist is to assist clients in discovering the solutions outside the complaint. "The solution focus emphasizes exceptions to the rules of the problem rather than the rules of the problem itself" (Molnar & de Shazer, 1987, p. 350). The therapist engages clients in developing solutions by asking when the complaint does not occur. By "generating discussion about such exceptions to the complaint, the clinician and client system create the opportunity for solutions to completely emerge" (Miller, 1992, p. 3). Any exception to the complaint is a potential solution, since it lies outside the constraint of the problem and the accompanying worldview. Often, clients can describe exceptions to the problem, but do not regard them as significant. "For the clients, these are not differences that make a difference; making these differences make a difference is the heart of the therapist's job" (de Shazer & Berg, 1988, p. 42).

To do so, the therapist needs to explore the constraints of the complaint (de Shazer et al., 1986). The solution needs to fit within those constraints (de Shazer, 1985, 1988a). The quality of fit will depend on the relationship between the social worker and the client(s) (in particular, the feelings of closeness and responsiveness within that relationship), the pathway the interview takes, and the goals (de Shazer, 1988b; Lipchik & de Shazer, 1986).

The solution-focused brief therapy model promotes collaboration between social worker and client system (de Shazer, 1984). Resistance is reframed as the client's way of informing the worker that the present intervention does not fit (de Shazer, 1988a). To promote and encourage collaboration,

> First we connect the present to the future (ignoring the past), then we compliment clients on what they are already doing that is useful and/or good for them, and then—once they

know we are on their side—we can make a suggestion for something new that they might do which is, or at least might be, good for them. (de Shazer, 1988a, p. 15)

People come to therapy because they want to change their situation but their attempts to change have not worked (de Shazer, 1985; de Shazer et al., 1986). A small change in one person's behavior can produce far-reaching differences; specifically, a change in one part of the system leads to changes in the system as a whole. Accordingly, smaller changes are promoted because "the bigger the goal or the desired change, the harder it will be to establish a cooperative relationship and the more likely the therapist and client will fail" (de Shazer et al., 1986).

A primary task of intervention is to help clients change their method of constructing experience. If clients construct—and talk about—their experiences in a different way, they may begin to have different experiences, which, in turn, will prompt different depictions or reports in subsequent sessions (de Shazer, 1988a).

In the initial interview, the therapist works to build rapport and create a workable, task-centered, and cooperative therapeutic alliance with the client (Lipchik & de Shazer, 1986). The establishment of rapport leads to fit between the client and the social worker. Understanding and accepting the client's worldview is essential for the development of useful solutions and, correspondingly, the quality of the therapeutic alliance established in the first session predicts the outcome of contracted, short-term therapy (Marziali, 1984; Marziali & Alexander, 1991; Moras & Strupp, 1982). Furthermore, rapport promotes hopefulness about the therapeutic process, which is also significantly associated with a favorable outcome.

It is optimal to contract the goals of therapy early in the therapeutic process—preferably during the first interview—as success in therapy depends upon establishing criteria for change (Thomlison, 1986). Lipchik (1986, cited in Fox, 1987) states that goals must be set "by the end of the first session so that there is a focus for the therapy and some way to evaluate progress" (p. 494). Also, "the family, in forming goals and in establishing the conditions to be changed, leads the therapy" (p. 495) and "the setting of goals fosters a truly collaborative effort that offers a paradigm for continuing problem-solving activity outside the therapeutic situation" (p. 495). The focus on goals is associated with positive change, as it is based on the principle of starting where the client is (Reid, 1990).

The solution-focused model differentiates clients as visitors, complainants, and customers (de Shazer, 1988a; Kral, 1990). The client is the person most irritated with the situation and, therefore, the person most willing to do something about it (Kral, 1990). Visitors are there because they have to be, the problem at hand is not a major concern for the visitor; some visitors do not even recognize that there may be a problem. Complainants are willing to discuss the problem but lack the desire to take any action. Finally, a customer relationship exists when clients explicitly identify the problem and their goals and are willing to do something (Kral, 1990). An essential task for the therapist is to identify these differing roles within families and to assist and encourage visitors and complainants to become customers.

The initial interview includes the search for exceptions to the problem. The search for exceptions is central to a solution-focused interview; exceptions are the beginnings of solution construction. If exceptions cannot be articulated, the therapist should continue exploration of the identified problem or complaint until exceptions emerge (Lipchik & de Shazer, 1986). The worker complements the search for exceptions by maintaining the attitude that change will occur. This positive, proactive attitude promotes the amplification of nonproblematic patterns of behavior within the system (de Shazer, 1984).

The solution-focused brief therapy model utilizes the miracle question. "Suppose one night there is a miracle and while you are sleeping the problem is solved: What will you notice different the next morning that will tell you there has been a miracle? What else?" (Berg & Gallagher, 1991, p. 96). When clients pretend that their complaint has miraculously been resolved, they see solutions more clearly. Further, the steps toward the solution become clearer; "clients queried in such a manner have been observed to become more concrete and behaviorally specific as well as become more self-confident, smile and even burst out laughing" (Miller, 1992, p. 5).

As an illustration of solution-focused work, consider the Davis family. Bobby and his family were referred to the Community Intervention Program (CIP) by the school guidance counselor on account of his low self-esteem, his emotional difficulties following the death of his grandmother, and his parents' concerns about his defiance and acting-out behaviors. Ten months earlier, at the recommendation of the guidance counselor, the family had attended one family therapy session but then declined further service. This second referral was prompted by the parents' increasing concerns about Bobby's behavior. The disposition summary written by the previous worker advised that the family was resistant to counseling and unwilling to engage. The family consists of Ben (37) and Mary (34), who have been married for 10 years, and their children Eve (9)

and Bobby (7). This family is interracial; Ben is Jamaican Canadian and Mary is Anglo-Canadian. Mary works full time for Bell Canada, and Ben has been unemployed for almost a year on account of a back injury. He conducts some sporadic car repair work from his garage.

All sessions occurred within the family's home. In the first visit, the worker briefly explored perceptions of the problem; used the miracle question to search for exceptions, as a way of moving toward solutions; assessed the perceived seriousness of the problem and the motivation for change by means of scaling questions; and identified tasks to assist Ben and Mary in moving toward the solution they wanted.

Both Ben and Mary cited Bobby as a major source of anger and frustration because of his verbal defiance and increasing aggression. They had similar—but less intense—concerns about Eve. Eve advised that her parents yelled a lot, which she found upsetting. Bobby remained very quiet and appeared withdrawn and uncomfortable, despite attempts at demystifying any possible misconceptions regarding therapy and/or therapists. Ben and Mary had told Bobby that they were in therapy because of him and his behaviors. The worker let Bobby know that lots of families have difficulties and/or problems and that he was not the problem; rather, it was the family as a whole that was experiencing some difficulties. However, Bobby remained relatively quiet throughout therapy and only engaged in discussions unrelated to any stated family issues.

During the first session, individual perceptions regarding the initial problem/complaint were explored. Ben and Mary concurred that Bobby had been a difficult child since the age of about 4 and that both children's behaviors had significantly deteriorated over the last two years, since the maternal grandmother's death. Both children were frequently defiant and did not follow simple parental instructions or directives. Ben clearly identified Bobby as their biggest problem, as he was increasingly aggressive and easily became frustrated and aggravated. In addition, Ben was concerned that Bobby seemed uninterested in school and his grades were not as good as his sister's. However, school personnel reported that, while Bobby did exhibit some difficulties with his reading, he was improving. Bobby remained relatively quiet throughout this session and became aloof when discussing personal issues that were problematic to his parents. He would not state his perceptions of why the family was seeking service and did not display any reaction to his parents' stated concerns. Eve advised that she and Bobby had a bad attitude and were at times bad, which made her parents very mad and upset.

Both children were quiet and presented as being shy and uncomfortable. They remained close to their mother and frequently hugged and kissed her or hid behind her as a means of declining to answer a question. In addition, before choosing to answer a question, they would look toward their father for approval and/or permission to continue. Mary spoke openly about her feelings and emotions, in a quiet voice, while Ben presented as a very logical and pragmatic person who spoke about facts and realities. Mary thought that Bobby's problem behaviors could possibly be attributed to the loss of his grandmother. On the other hand, Ben thought that these behaviors were based on Bobby's inability and/or unwillingness to follow simple rules and also his laziness. Whereas Mary said that Bobby and Eve required love, support, and guidance, Ben was punitive and said that reprimanding the children was the only way to rectify the situation. Ben frequently interrupted Mary and the children when they were speaking and often finished their statements or comments, with little consideration for their thoughts or what they were going to say. This obviously irritated Mary, who would comment, "Ben, you're not listening now, just like you never listen" or else would remove herself from the table, wave her arm, and laugh, as though saying, "Here he goes again."

Each family member was asked the miracle question: "If a miracle happened tonight while each of you was sleeping, what would you notice the next morning that was different and that would let you know that a miracle had occurred?" This was a little confusing for both Bobby and Eve, but they appeared interested and intrigued. Therefore, the question was restated. "If you had a magic wand and could wave it to make a wish so that something about your family would be different, what would your wish be?" Mary said that she would like to get along better. Asked what it would take to get along better, she said that she would like the family's communication to improve, so that they felt better about each other, and she would like her husband to listen to her and understand her feelings more. Ben agreed with Mary and also said that he would like his wife to yell less at the children and his children to listen more and do as they were told. Eve said that she too would like less conflict within the home. In addition, she would like her parents not to yell as often and wished that everyone would be happier. Bobby remained quiet and said that he did not know. In exploring the exceptions, Mary, Ben, and Eve said that there is less upset when the family does things together.

There appeared to be a lot of conflict between Mary and Ben and a sense of hopelessness, which was expressed both verbally and nonverbally, via their eye contact (or lack of it) and sighs indicating discomfort and/or difference of opinion. Given the children's increasing irritability, the worker asked if they could be excused for the rest of the session; Ben and Mary agreed.

The worker then shared some observations regarding the level of marital conflict. In response to this feedback, Ben and Mary engaged in a heated discussion regarding their unmet emotional needs. Mary reacted strongly to Ben interrupting her and to his oppositional demeanor; Ben appeared confused and upset by the exchange. Both appeared embarrassed by the worker's presence. The worker focused their attention on exceptions—times they had been able to share their differences of opinions, feelings, and thoughts without such heated conflict.

The next step in the interview was to ask scaling questions, which are used to measure clients' progress before and during therapy, to determine clients' investment in change, and to assess perceptions of solutions. An example of a scaling question is: "On a scale of 1 to 10, where 10 is when these problems are solved and 1 is the worst they have ever been, where are you today?" The score itself is not as important as the change that was accomplished to get to that point or the change expected to get to the next level. Thus, follow-up questions might be: "How did you manage to get to a 3? What would be different if you were at 4?"

The worker used: three scaling questions with Ben and Mary. The first was: "On a scale of 1–10, where 10 is the highest, where would you rate your sense of family satisfaction?" Ben answered, a little hesitantly, with a 6; Mary chose 4. To search for exceptions, the worker asked both Mary and Ben what it would take to move one number up the scale. Both advised that they would like to argue less; to understand each other better; to enjoy each other more, without feeling as though they were always stepping on eggshells; and to spend more positive time with the children, instead of yelling and disciplining them.

The second and third scaling questions, also based on a 10-point scale, concerned their personal motivation regarding therapy and their optimism that therapy would be worthwhile and beneficial. Mary rated her personal motivation at 9 and her sense of optimism at 7. Ben assigned a 5 in both cases. Mary appeared to be the customer of service, as she presented as the person most irritated with the situation and therefore, probably the person most willing to do something about it. Ben could be termed a complainant of service as he was willing to discuss the problem, but he was not as motivated to do anything about it.

Mary, Ben, and the worker contracted the following goal of therapy: to process and attempt to improve marital communication in order to decrease marital conflict, thereby decreasing family conflict.

In the remainder of the session, the worker delivered compliments and acknowledged Ben and Mary's strengths. Two tasks were discussed and assigned. The first was the formula first task: "Between now and next session, I want you to observe, so that you can tell me what happens in your family life and/or relationship that you want to continue." Formula first tasks are used to shift the focus from past to present and future and from problems to strengths and to promote expectations of change (Molnar & de Shazer, 1987). They are often provided at the end of a session.

Secondly, Mary and Ben were asked to do something different every time they felt the urge to argue and as soon as they sensed the stirrings of conflict or tension. Mary and Ben were both very receptive to these tasks. In addition, they decided to try to prioritize family outings and togetherness time, which were enjoyable for the whole family and appeared to reduce their conflict. Mary and Ben both said that they felt comfortable working on the contracted goal and agreed that Eve and Bobby did not need to be involved in subsequent sessions. All subsequent sessions were spent with Mary and Ben.

The worker visited this family's home for four additional sessions over the next three months. By the third session, Mary and Ben agreed that they had a better appreciation of each other and were able to come up with some interesting and unique ways of implementing the do-something-different task. Both agreed that they enjoyed spending time together without the children, as it decreased their feelings of animosity and conflictual exchanges and increased their ability to understand one another. Furthermore, Mary said that, since she and her husband had been spending more time together, she felt more supported and better equipped to deal with her children's behaviors and to meet their needs without yelling.

The conflict between Mary and Ben decreased as they directed increased energy and time to their marital relationship. They continued to have disputes and differences of opinions, but both felt better understood and were able on occasion to agree to disagree, without any unspoken or repressed feelings of anger or remorse. As their communication became more direct and open, Mary and Ben acknowledged that communication had also improved with their children. There was less yelling and conflict. Both Mary and Ben noted that they were enjoying their children more and did not feel as antagonistic toward them for insignificant negative behaviors and occasional disrespect and/or defiance.

From one session to the next, there was an observable increase in positive communication and affect between Ben and the children. Ben was not as ill-tempered when talking to the children or asking them to do something, and he was more affectionate with them; he gave hugs and allowed Bobby to sit on his lap. The worker shared this observation with the parents, because it was such a sharp contrast to the first session.

At the fifth and termination session, both parents said that they had achieved their goal of improved marital communication and decreased marital conflict. They understood how the high level of marital conflict had affected not only their relationship but also their ability to deal with their children's needs. Their improved communication had a positive impact on their relationship with the children; it had served to decrease their children's negativity and increase their family's sense of cohesion.

During the initial session, the parents were able to identify the exceptions to their complaint/problem as times when they did things together. By the termination session, they had implemented activities to make these exceptions occur more frequently; they had become more the rules of family functioning, rather than the sporadic exceptions. Throughout the course of service, the family allocated more time and energy in discussing and planning family activities, which created increased family communication and positive time spent together.

Preliminary data indicated that clients reported clearer treatment goals following this intervention (de Shazer, 1985). Moreover, clients were judged to be optimistic about the possibility of change and more cooperative in therapy and often reported improvement in the presenting problem. According to de Shazer (1985), therapists also appeared more optimistic about the possibility of change.

Between 1978 and 1983, therapists from the Brief Family Therapy Center in Milwaukee saw 1600 cases for an average of six sessions per case (de Shazer et al., 1986). Follow-up phone calls by a person who had no connection with the case were made to a representative sample of 25%. Of this sample, 72% either met their goals for therapy or felt that significant improvement had been made, so that further therapy was not necessary (de Shazer et al., 1986). An earlier study (Weakland et al., 1974) reported similar success rates, with an average of seven sessions per client.

In 1988, David Kiser conducted a follow-up study (Sykes Wylie, 1990) by tracking the progress of 164 clients for 6, 12, and 18 months after therapy. Of 69 clients receiving 4–10 sessions, 93% (64) reported they had met, or made progress on, their treatment goal. At the 18-month follow-up, 51% reported that the presenting problem was still resolved, while about 34% said that it was not as bad as when they had initiated therapy. In other words, 85% of the clients reported full or partial success; further, 94% of the group had received 10 or fewer sessions. These findings suggest continued improvement, rather than deterioration after solution-focused brief therapy (de Shazer et al., 1986).

READING 18
Goal Setting with Biological Families[1]

Edith Fein[2] and Ilene Staff[3]

"Goal-setting is one of the critical tasks of the social work problem-solving process" (Anderson, 1989). Goal-setting encourages procedures that give a clear picture of problems, support treatment planning and assessment of progress, and facilitate review and evaluation of outcomes.

This chapter presents policy and practice in setting goals with biological families whose children have been removed because of abuse or neglect. Using the experience of a demonstration program in operation since 1989 as illustration, the authors examine guidelines for the goal-setting process; set forth tools for helping workers in assessment, decision-making, and treatment planning; discuss policy and practice aspects; and consider the application of results and conclusions from this example to family reunification practice in general.

THE FAMILY REUNIFICATION PROJECT

Casey Family Services is a voluntary long-term foster care and permanency planning agency founded in 1976 in Connecticut, currently serving over 200 children in six New England states. This chapter draws from the agency's experience with its Family Reunification Project, which assists families whose children are in foster care primarily because of abuse or neglect and who need a broad range of intensive or special services if the family is ever to be reunited. The program offers families case management and clinical intervention services in their own homes. Unlike most time-limited, crisis-oriented family preservation programs, family reunification services may be provided for periods as long as two years. Professionals assigned to the families have low caseloads and are able to give sustained attention to the families.

Each family is assigned to a reunification team consisting of a social worker and a family support worker. The team provides such services as training in parenting skills; mental health counseling; respite care; group support; and assistance with housing, job training, transportation, and legal problems. Services begin before the child returns home, when the reunification team and the biological family create a service agreement setting forth treatment goals and plans, and continue after reunification for as long as needed, up to a two-year total.

Referrals to the program come from state agency workers who determine that reunification should be the permanent plan for an abused or neglected youngster, but who are not optimistic that it can be achieved unless intensive services are provided. The biological family must be willing and able to participate in formulating a service agreement and to work with the reunification team. In addition, the foster parents or residential care facility staff must be willing to work with the team, and the child must have been removed from the home within the previous 18 months. To protect children and ensure the safety of workers, cases are not accepted if a sibling has died because of abuse or neglect or if life threatening abuse has taken place in the past; if the child's safety would be jeopardized by reunification; if sexual abuse has taken place and the perpetrator lives in the home or is an active member of the family; if violence has taken place (or a potential for violence exists) toward people outside the family; or if caregivers are substance abusers with no willingness to participate in treatment.

GOAL-SETTING IN CHILD WELFARE

Since the 1970s, goal-setting has found expression in several areas of practice, including the development of task-oriented

---

[1] From Fein, E., & Staff, I. (1993). *Together Again: Family Reunification in Foster Care,* Washington, DC: Child Welfare League of America, pp. 67–97. Reprinted by special permission.
[2] Research Director, Dunne, Kimmel, & Fein, LLC, Hartford, Connecticut.
[3] Senior Scientist, The Institute for Outcomes Research and Evaluation, Hartford Hospital, Hartford, Connecticut.

casework (Reid & Epstein, 1972), time-limited therapy (Mann, 1973), and goal-attainment scaling (Garwick & Lampman, 1972). The child welfare field has benefited from this emphasis on goals. Permanency planning—the mainstream movement in delivering child welfare services—stresses explicit formulation of problems, treatment planning, identification of permanent placement options, case management, review of plans, and timely decision-making based on the implementation of service agreements (Maluccio, Fein, & Olmstead, 1986). Permanency planning thus epitomizes goal-setting.

Functions

Service planning for family reunification using a goal and plan orientation, as Maluccio et al. (1986) suggest, fulfills the following functions:

- Encourages systematic thinking about many areas of family needs
- Structures service delivery activity so workers, supervisors, and clients are fully aware of what is occurring
- Aids in case planning and management, allowing for timely decision making and corrective action when necessary
- Helps clients participate in what is happening to their families in achieving reunification
- Ensures program accountability
- Documents case progress for possible court testimony

In the child welfare field, intensive family preservation programs have given further impetus to the goal-setting orientation. Intensive family preservation programs typically are in-home, time-limited, crisis-oriented services, and are designed to prevent foster care placement of children at risk of removal from their homes (Whittaker, Kinney, Tracey, & Booth, 1990). Various family preservation training courses and handbooks underscore the usefulness of focus and goal-setting in delivering these services (Lloyd & Bryce, 1985; Tracy, Haapala, Kinney, & Pecora, 1991; Whittaker et al., 1990).

Some family preservation program advocates believe the family preservation model might make family reunification efforts more timely and more successful than they are at present (Maluccio, Kreiger, & Pine, 1991; Nelson, 1990). Many family reunification programs are superficially similar to family preservation services, having developed from the same roots. However, there are important differences. Most important, in intensive family preservation programs a family's motivation to develop and achieve goals and to work with service providers is tied to

the fear that children will be removed from the home—a strong authoritative mandate. Families of children already in foster care, however, have different concerns.

First, family reunification readily occurs two-thirds to three-fourths of the time in the course of normal service delivery by state agencies (Fein, Maluccio, Hamilton, & Ward, 1983; Tatura, 1989); parental motivation is not necessarily an issue. Second, those children not reunified with their families are typically victims of one or more unfortunate circumstances: the state agency may not be able to deliver the kind or depth of services the family needs; the children present almost insurmountable problems in adjusting to family life; or the families are too troubled to make use of the services available. Third, even children who are quickly reunited with their families face difficulties (Turner, 1984). When children stay out of the home for long periods, families achieve a new equilibrium without them, and parents may feel ambivalent about having the children return. As a result, reunification programs, which by their nature work with many families in situations such as those described above, are forced to deliver services without the motivation and authoritative mandate that family preservation programs command.

For all these reasons, goal-planning is an essential feature of family reunification practice and was made an integral part of the Casey program model. Family members and social workers alike can use the focus and structure that goal-planning provides, particularly when reunification aims at a level of reconnection short of living in the same household. In those cases, the goal-planning process enables the family and the social worker to identify the appropriate level of reconnection and achieve some success in attaining the selected level despite the family's inability to live together.

THE SERVICE PLANNING PROCESS

The process of service planning requires that workers and clients together (1) identify appropriate goals, (2) build on existing strengths and resources, and (3) create action plans to help the clients' progress toward the goals. Of the three, identifying and explicitly stating the goals is probably the most difficult, but all are crucial for a successful case plan.

Identifying and Stating Goals

To create a goal statement, the worker must consider what problems the family is facing (see Exhibit R18-1), what must change about the family's functioning to allow reunification to take place, and what the family will be like if the goals are achieved.

EXHIBIT R18-1
Problem Areas

In creating goals and plans, each of the following problem areas should be considered for families whose children are in care because of abuse or neglect:

1. Parents' feelings toward selves
2. Parents' relationship, including sexual relations
3. Parents' recognition of problems
4. Parents' capacity for child care
5. Parents' approval of children
6. Discipline of children
7. Supervision of children
8. Incidence of sexual abuse
9. Child's behavior
10. Relationship between parents and child
11. Child's relationship to family
12. Child's feelings toward self
13. Child's disabling condition
14. Child's developmental lags
15. Child's relationship to peers
16. Child's relationship to foster family
17. Child's educational needs
18. Health care
19. Home management (nutrition, clothing, sanitation, hygiene, physical safety)
20. Money management
21. Housing and transportation needs
22. Employment needs
23. Social networks

Building on Strengths and Resources

Goals are positive statements about changes the family can achieve; strengths and resources are abilities, ways of functioning, personal characteristics, environmental conditioning, social connections, or any positive aspects of the family's life that are present or that can be found or mobilized in behalf of the family (see Exhibit R18-2).

Creating Action Plans

Particular actions must be taken by the reunification team and the family, separately and together, to achieve progress toward the family's goals. The plans should be specific, indicate a date by when they will be accomplished, and identify who will be working on each plan. For example, consider goal #1 in Exhibit R18-2. Ms. Parker and Mr. Vega will not abuse drugs or alcohol. Plans for them might include the following actions:

- Ms. Parker will no longer associate with the drug dealers she knew in the past, beginning immediately. *Responsibility:* Ms. Parker.

- Weekly until May 1, Ms. Parker and the social worker will discuss Ms. Parker's drug cravings, how she feels about herself, and how she is managing her new life. *Responsibility:* Social worker and Ms. Parker.

- Mr. Vega will continue attending AA meetings. *Responsibility:* Mr. Vega.

GUIDELINES FOR SETTING GOALS AND CREATING CASE PLANS

The following guidelines should be applied in developing an effective service plan.

Goals

A. A goal should state how the family situation will be different, not what the reunification team or family will do to make it happen.

Confusing goals and plans is the problem most frequently encountered in writing goal statements. The goal is the end-state that is sought; details of the work that needs to be done will be written in the plans. They are related as strategy and tactics are related.

Not a goal: Mother will visit with her two sons.
Goal: Mother will give her children the affection and attention they need.

B. Each goal should be explicit and germane to the family's functioning and ability to cope. The language should be direct and informal.

To participate productively in their plans, client families have to understand the concepts and language of their goal statements. Technical jargon is not helpful. The goals should define what the clients' life situation must be to have their children live with them.

Unclear goal: Mother will have a responsive support network.

EXHIBIT R18-2
Goals and Strengths

Goals	Strengths and Resources
Ms. Parker and Mr. Vega will not abuse drugs or alcohol.	Mr. Vega has enrolled in a drug rehabilitation program. Ms. Parker has already completed Phase 1 of day treatment and has been regularly attending AA meetings.
Ms. Parker and Mr. Vega will have enough money to pay for the basic needs of life, including housing, clothing, food, and utilities, and will manage their money carefully.	Ms. Parker currently has a stable job. Mr. Vega is actively looking for a job.
Ms. Parker and Mr. Vega will set limits and teach Jacob right from wrong. Ms. Parker and Mr. Vega will have a good understanding of Jacob's needs. Ms. Parker and Mr. Vega will develop a good relationship, free from abuse.	Ms. Parker and Mr. Vega want very much to learn better ways to be good parents. Ms. Parker and Mr. Vega intend to visit Jacob regularly and will provide their own transportation. Mr. Vega and Ms. Parker are involved in counseling to improve their communication with each other.

Clear goal: Mother will be close to other people she can talk to and get help from them when she needs it.

C. Goals should be formulated to balance explicit and assessable expectations with the family's social and emotional needs.

The goals must specify the changes necessary for the family to attain reunification. Goals that define a better state but are irrelevant to the original reason for placement should not be identified.

Irrelevant goal: Mother should volunteer her time to help others.

Relevant goal: Mother will locate and use community resources.

D. Family members should be able to make progress on some goals in a fairly short time period so that a feeling of success can emerge from their interactions with the worker.

Long-term goals should include more easily attainable short-term goals, to encourage the confidence that family members must have to work toward their larger achievements.

Long-term goal: Mother will earn sufficient money from employment to support her children on her own.

Short-term goal: Mother will obtain services to have enough to pay for such basic needs as housing, clothing, food, and utilities.

E. Goals should be stated in such a way that progress toward their achievement can be assessed.

Progress toward a goal is an important concept. Some of the goals will never be fully reached—improvement is always possible in such areas as understanding a child's needs or providing needed affection. Goal achievement, moreover, is not always easily measured. Sufficient progress toward the goal, however, can be evaluated through the social worker's observation of parent-child interactions.

Limited goal: Mother will interact with her children.

Assessable goal: Mother will give her children more of the affection and attention they need.

Strengths and Resources

F. Family strengths and resources should be articulated so workers and family members begin to think positively about the family's potential.

Strengths may be dispositional attributes such as motivation, biological predispositions such as intellectual capacity, or positive events. They should always be the focus when formulating goals. Strengths should be germane to the particular case and explicitly stated.

Strength: Mother has had her own apartment in the past. Mother has begun to look at classified ads for affordable housing.

Goal #1: Mother will provide a home with space, furnishings, appliances, utilities, and so forth, adequate for essential household functions and for meeting the personal needs of family members.

Strength: Mother already receives food stamps and has dealt with state and local welfare offices.

Goal #2: Mother will have enough money to pay for basic needs, such as housing, clothing, food, and utilities, and will manage her money carefully.

Action Plans

G. Each action plan should be explicit, doable in a specified time period, and assessable.

The plans proposed to achieve each goal, that is, the work to be done, should be reasonable and specific enough so that the worker's and the family's actions can be monitored and measured.

Goal: Mother will give her children more of the affection and attention they need.

Plans: (A) Mother will visit children once a week at the agency office; (B) Social worker will bring children to mother's home once a week starting June 1st; (C) Mother will attend parent support group.

SUPPORTIVE RECORDKEEPING

Effective goal-planning requires a systematic recordkeeping procedure that is consonant with a program's philosophy and practice. The procedures suggested here are based on earlier work in goal-planning (Jones & Biesecker, 1980; Maluccio et al., 1986; Miller, Fein, Howe, Claudio, & Bishop, 1984), and incorporate concepts and techniques developed in permanency planning work in child welfare. The recordkeeping system is a logical extension of the service-planning process and guidelines discussed above, and was developed by the staff of the project on which this chapter is based.

The recordkeeping system uses a variety of forms to establish goals with the family, outline the plan of action, define responsibilities, document case activity, and monitor and evaluate case progress. The forms are described briefly below, and in the following section their use is illustrated with a case example.

The Case Plan Form

The case plan form (Exhibit R18-3) is the central document upon which most of the others depend. It defines what the case is about and what planning will lead to progress toward specified goals. The case plan requires that workers consider a multitude of potential problems, define applicable goals with the client, delineate resources and strengths that may be brought to bear, create plans that will help the client progress toward the goals, and identify responsibility for completion of the plans.

The Monthly Goal and Plan Rating Form

The monthly goal and plan rating form (Exhibit R18-4) allows for monthly review of goal and plan progress. It tracks changes in the amount of effort expended, monitors continuance or completion of the plan, and evaluates the past month's efforts. The form is completed by the reunification team and reviewed with the family. The monthly evaluation enables both team and family to be supported in the successes they have had and to be aware of the work that remains.

Other Forms

Additional forms include a referral sheet (see Exhibit R18-5), containing information provided by the state agency; a face sheet, with full demographic information; an assessment, using the Family Risk Scales (Magura, Moses, & Jones, 1987), at several key points in case progress; a status change form, documenting milestones in case progress; narrative recordings, comprising an intake summary, periodic case updates, and case notes; an expense form; and the service agreement described above. The following case example illustrates the use of some of these forms for service planning and goal setting and for case documentation.

> Five-year-old Josh has been in family foster care for the past three months. Months before, he was admitted to a hospital clinic along with his two-year-old brother, Philip. Both had bruises, head lice, and scabbed sores around the hairline severe enough for the clinic to refer them to state care. Josh was not yet toilet trained, Philip seemed to be developmentally delayed, and both boys were poorly socialized.
>
> This was not the first time the two boys had been removed from their family. Earlier in the year they had been placed in family foster care and later returned home. But now their mother was not keeping medical appointments and was known to be associating with drug dealers. In light of this information, social workers from the public child welfare agency were pessimistic about the outcome of a second effort to reunite the family, but they referred the family to a private agency for intensive reunification services.

EXHIBIT R18-3

Sample Case Plan

Family Name:	Smith	*Case #:*	01
Workers:	J. Jones		

Use as many pages as needed to identify all goals and plans to be worked on. Add new goals and plans as they emerge. In the right columns, please indicate the date each goal and plan was identified and who will be working on each.

	Date	Who
GOAL #: 1		
Mother will give her children the affection and attention they need.	2/10/90	
Strengths and Resources		
Mother loves to play with the boys when they visit.	2/10/90	1
Mother likes to read magazine articles about child care.	2/10/90	1
Plan A.		
Mother will visit children once a week at the agency office.	2/10/90	1
Plan B.		
Worker will discuss discipline and other child-rearing problems	2/10/90	2
at each home visit.		
Plan C.		
School worker will bring children to mother's home	3/10/90	3
at each home visit.		
Plan D.		
Mother will attend parent support group.	3/10/90	1

Codes: 1–Family, 2–Family Support Worker, 3–Social Worker, 4–Other (specify)

EXHIBIT R18-3
Sample Case Plan *(continued)*

Family Name: Smith   Case #:   01

Workers: J. Jones

Use as many pages as needed to identify all goals and plans to be worked on. Add new goals and plans as they emerge. In the right columns, please indicate the date each goal and plan was identified and who will be working on each.

GOAL #: 2	Date	Who
Mother will have enough money to pay for the basic needs of life,	2/10/90	
including housing, clothing, food, and utilities, and will manage her		
money carefully.		
Strengths and Resources		
Mother already receives food stamps and has dealt with state and local		
welfare offices.		
Plan A.		
Worker will help mother draw up a budget.	2/10/90	2
Plan B.		
Worker will go with mother to open a bank account.	2/10/90	1, 2
Plan C.		
Mother will not buy anything on layaway or credit.	2/10/90	1
Plan D.		
Worker will help mother with shoppping to take advantage of	2/10/90	1, 2
coupons, sales and bargains.		

Codes: 1–Family, 2–Family Support Worker, 3–Social Worker, 4–Other (specify)

(continued)

EXHIBIT R18-3
Sample Case Plan (continued)

Family Name:	Smith	*Case #:*	01
Workers:	J. Jones		

Use as many pages as needed to identify all goals and plans to be worked on. Add new goals and plans as they emerge. In the right columns, please indicate the date each goal and plan was identified and who will be working on each.

	Date	Who
GOAL #: 3		
Mother will not abuse drugs or alcohol.	2/10/90	

Strengths and Resources

Mother has been free of drugs for extended periods in the past.

Mother is determined to stay clean in the future.

Plan A.

	Date	Who
Mother will no longer associate with the drug dealers she knew in the past.	2/10/90	1

Plan B.

	Date	Who
Mother will attend AA meetings each Wednesday evening.	2/10/90	1

Plan C.

	Date	Who
Mother and social worker will discuss mother's cravings, how she feels about herself, and how she is managing her new life.	2/10/90	1, 3

Plan D.

	Date	Who
Mother will attend parent support group at the agency.	3/10/90	1

Codes: 1–Family, 2–Family Support Worker, 3–Social Worker, 4–Other (specify)

EXHIBIT R18-4
Sample Monthly Goal and Plan Rating Form

Family Name:	Smith	*Case #:*	01
Workers:	J. Jones, O. Doe	*Rating Date*	2/28/90

INSTRUCTIONS: At month's end, list all goals and plans by describing them briefly in the space provided. Rate goals and plans on focus and status; indicate this month's progress for goals, and an evaluation for plans, in the third column. The codes and scales are listed on the bottom of the form.

GOAL #: 1	*Focus*	*Status*	*Goal Progress*
Mother will give her children the attention and affection they need.	1	C	2

Plan	*Focus*	*Status*	*Eval.*
A. Mother will visit.	1	C	3
B. Worker will discuss discipline, etc.	1	C	2
C.			
D.			
E.			
F.			
G.			
H.			
I.			
J.			
K.			
L.			

Codes:

Focus:
Over the past month, how much time has been spent by the family or the team on this plan? Toward achieving this goal?
1. A major amount of time.
2. A minor amount of time.
3. Goal or plan not worked on this month.

Status:
At this time this goal or plan is:
C. Continued
D. Discontinued

Plan Evaluation:
Over the past month, how well was this plan working?
1. Not at all.
2. Working a little.
3. Working very well.

Goal Progress:
How much progress, if any, has there been this month in approaching this goal?

0	1	2	3	4	5
Regress from goal	None	A little progress	Moderate progress	A lot of progress	Goal achieved

EXHIBIT R18-5
Sample Referral Form

Case # _____ Referral Date _____ Taken by _____ Team Assigned _____

State Worker _____ Phone # _____

Child Information

Name _____ DOB _____

Current Placement: Type _____ Name _____ Removal Date _____

Address _____

_____ Phone # _____

Sex _____ Race _____ Grade _____ School _____

Previous Placements: ☐ No   ☐ Yes   How many? _____

To be reunified with

Name _____ Relationship to child _____

Address _____

_____ Phone # _____

Biological Parents	Mother	Father
Name	_____	_____
Address	_____	_____
	_____	_____
Phone #	_____	_____

Comments (mention siblings to be reunified)

_____
_____
_____
_____
_____
_____
_____
_____
_____
_____
_____
_____
_____
_____
_____
_____

Josh and Philip's case plan contained seven goals, three of which are illustrated in Exhibit R18-3. The mother was involved in the creation of the goals and for each goal, family strengths were defined and plans made. The case plan identifies the date each goal and plan was established, as well as who is responsible for the plan. Note that for goals 1 and 3, additional plans were made a month after the original plans.

The Monthly Goal and Plan Rating Form (Exhibit R18-4) illustrates the first month's rating of progress on goal 1. (A rating form is normally completed for each goal.) The social worker and family support worker team complete the form together. This form is shared with the mother or can be completed with her participation. The rating form charts progress, shows where more work needs to be done, and keeps the goals and plans in everyone's consciousness.

PROGRAM AND PRACTICE ISSUES

As discussed above, the goal-setting process is a familiar, if not completely comfortable, procedure for social workers. When it is used systematically, benefits for clients and staff members are well documented (Klier, Fein, & Genero, 1984; Miller et al., 1984). Agency reunification programs, however, have not generally directed themselves to the particular fit between their reunification objectives and a goal-setting orientation. For goal-setting (or goal-oriented service planning) to be an integral feature of family reunification programs, a number of factors must be considered.

WORKERS' SKILLS AND ATTITUDES

Social workers are often uncomfortable at first with formulating goals and plans. "We were struck by the meager reporting we found in most of the case records about the social worker's definition of clinical tasks and description of ongoing therapeutic work. A well-articulated service plan was often not present in the records" (Fanshel, Finch, & Grundy, 1989, p. 477). Indeed, many programs are not clear about their continuum of goals (Videka-Sherman, 1989). Even training courses designed to teach the procedure can add to the confusion—some define goals as the most general of the plans, others equate goals with mission statements, and still others confuse the workers' efforts with the clients' needs (Anderson, 1989).

Despite training and the availability of written guidelines, staff members may vary widely in their ability to articulate goals. Some workers may write goals that are action-oriented, rather than ones that describe new situations for the client. Consensus may not exist on the degree of specificity that differentiates a goal from a plan. Moreover, in some cases goals may correctly describe an improved family situation but their relationship to reunification may not be clear. A client's goal, for example, might be to become self-supporting, but having a job might not result in managing money well enough to achieve reunification.

To assist workers in the goal-setting process—in effect, to come to agreement on the proper scope for goals in relation to plans—the authors examined all the early goals and plans in the family reunification project being presented in this chapter. These goals and plans fell into fairly clear categories, addressing financial stability, child care, substance abuse treatment, and educational and vocational attainment. These categories were congruent with factors in the Family Risk Scales (Magura et al., 1987), already used in the project to assess families at intake, reunification, and case closing.

From this examination, a list of representative goals was created, amalgamating the workers' experience and the Family Risk Scale factors (see Exhibit R18-6). Workers and family members can select a pertinent goal from the list or use one as a guide or model. This procedure, used in other goal-oriented programs (McCroskey & Nelson, 1989), can smooth out variations in specificity of goals and plans, and help to create goals that are germane to the reunification effort.

Role of Supervisor

The supervisor's importance in formulating, documenting, and monitoring goals and service delivery plans cannot be overestimated. Although an evaluation component within a program can help with monitoring and assuring consistency, it does not replace the supervisor. Service quality and oversight are managed by monitoring responsibility. For example, the case plan sets forth a clear overview of expected action for each case, indicates who is responsible for the action, and often provides a timeline. The supervisor can use the case plan to determine whether appropriate planning is taking place.

Supervisors also can use the Monthly Goal and Plan Rating form (Exhibit R18-4) as a summary of progress and a basis for case conferences with workers and families. The goal concentration minimizes the sometimes rambling nature of presentations based on narrative recordings.

Number of Goals

As discussed elsewhere by Fein and Staff (1991), various issues arise in goal-oriented reunification services that are not readily dealt with by extra effort or training. In particular,

---

EXHIBIT R18-6
Representative Goals

The (parents) (family):

1. Will have and keep a clean, safe home, without physical dangers.
2. Will provide a home with space, furnishings, appliances, utilities, and so forth, adequate for essential household functions and meeting the personal needs of family members.
3. Will have enough money to pay for the basic needs of life, including housing, clothing, food, and utilities, and will manage their money carefully.
4. Will keep themselves and their children healthy by eating healthy, balanced meals and by getting medical and dental care when needed.
5. Will be close to other people they can talk to and get some help from when they need it.
6. Will get and use community services.
7. Will have a good relationship, free of abuse, with other adults in the home.
8. Will each feel that he or she is a good person and deserves to be treated well.
9. Will not abuse drugs or alcohol.
10. Will give their children the affection and attention that they need.
11. Will make sure that their children are safe from harm at all times, and that they are not left alone or left with someone who is not able to take care of them.
12. Will set limits and teach their children right from wrong without hurting them physically or with words.
13. Will have a good understanding of their children's needs.
14. Will make sure their children attend school regularly.

---

how many goals should be set at the beginning of service? Some workers believe that it is most respectful of families if family members know from the beginning of service all they will need to do to have their families reunited. These workers advocate starting with as complete a list of goals as is necessary to effect reunification, with the understanding that other goals can be added if the situation changes during the course of the case. They reason that beginning with only a few goals and then adding others as early successes occur makes families feel they will never achieve the ultimate reunification.

Other workers fear that a complete list of goals will dishearten a family, that a few goals will lead to early successes, and that the original goals can easily be amended because the family will have had that understanding from the beginning. Some writers suggest that developing a complete list of goals is important; clients then rank goals and the most pressing receive attention first (Pomerantz, Pomerantz, & Colca, 1990).

No evidence documents that one method is superior to the others. Examination of various questions about goal-setting as a client motivator is sorely needed, particularly for neglectful families (Videka-Sherman, 1989).

CONCLUSION

The project described in this chapter is part of a small, financially healthy, voluntary agency that can afford the small caseloads, specialized programs, and individualization of clients good case management and effective casework for reunification require. How well would the method apply to large, publicly funded reunification services in public agencies? If a public agency has the resources, it can implement a goal-oriented intensive service. Alternatively, it can contract for such services from voluntary agencies. The principles of goal orientation and careful and systematic documentation, however, can be used to support any agency's reunification efforts.

READING 19
Action as a Vehicle for Promoting Competence[1]

Anthony N. Maluccio[2]

Human beings are involved, to one degree or another, in a perpetual struggle toward control of their lives. In this struggle, some of them directly or indirectly ask for help and come to the attention of social workers in diverse settings. Building on an ecological perspective and a problem-solving framework, we address, in this reading, how social workers can respond to this struggle by using action as a vehicle for promoting client competence.

COMPETENCE AND ACTION

Competence

Human or social competence is generally defined as the repertoire of skills that enable the person to function effectively. However, a distinction should be made between discrete skills or competencies and the broader ecological or transactional concept of competence, which, as suggested by Exhibit R19-1 may be defined as the outcome of the interplay among (Maluccio, 1981):

- A person's capacities, skills, potentialities, and other characteristics
- A person's motivation—that is, her interests, hopes, beliefs, and aspirations
- The qualities of the person's impinging environment—such as social networks, environmental demands, and opportunities.

From this perspective flows a set of attitudes, principles, skills, and strategies designed to promote effective functioning in human beings by:

- Promoting their empowerment
- Focusing on their unique coping and adaptive patterns
- Mobilizing their actual or potential strengths
- Using their life experiences in a planful way

---

[1] An original reading for *Social Work Processes*. This reading draws from earlier papers by the author, including Maluccio (1974, 1981, 1983), Maluccio & Libassi (1984), and Libassi & Maluccio (1986). The author appreciates Robin Warsh's contribution of several case examples.

[2] Professor, Graduate School of Social Work, Boston College, Chestnut Hill, Massachusetts.

- Emphasizing the role of natural helping networks
- Using environmental resources as major instruments of help

Action

Action is an integral component of this competence oriented perspective; it consists of coping, striving, and goal-directed activities by which individuals endeavor to meet life challenges, attain appropriate control over their lives, achieve their goals, and grow. In this perspective, clients are regarded as active, striving human beings who are capable of organizing their lives and realizing their potentialities, as long as they have appropriate family, community, societal, and environmental resources and supports.

Action includes both natural activities—everyday experiences such as work, play, or social interaction—and artificial activities, including role-playing, play therapy, and participation in activity groups. Artificial activities are used as vehicles for learning, as media of communication, or as opportunities to practice desired behaviors. The client's participation in such activities can serve as preparation for engagement in life itself. Furthermore, the action should be specifically related to people's goals and consonant with their natural growth processes, lifestyles, and significant life events.

Artificial and natural activities may prove complementary. For example, a school social worker found that, following participation in a discussion group on parenting, a mother in an urban school was able to successfully confer with school personnel on behalf of her underachieving child. When she shared her experience with other mothers in the group, she felt a real sense of satisfaction. The example in Exhibit R19-2 suggests that natural activities may be more meaningful and more effective than artificial ones, since they are more closely related to the individual's life processes of growth and adaptation.

An extensive knowledge base supports the use of action as a vehicle for promoting competence (Maluccio, 1983). Especially pertinent are integrative themes from ecology, general systems theory, ego psychology, crisis theory, and learning theory:

1. The concept of human beings as open systems involved in dynamic transactions with their environment. Each person is constantly influenced by—and

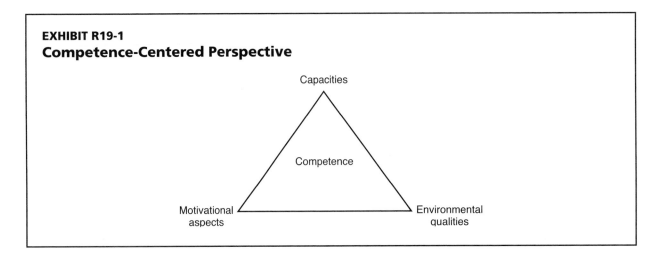

EXHIBIT R19-1
Competence-Centered Perspective

Capacities

Competence

Motivational aspects — Environmental qualities

EXHIBIT R19-2
Assistance by Means of Natural Activities

A family service agency worker had tried to involve Mr. A, an isolated elderly man, in social activities at a neighborhood center. These efforts were unsuccessful, as Mr. A seemed disinterested in contact with his peers or in leaving his home. Eventually, he was faced with the need to relocate owing to demolition of his building.

As the social worker accompanied him on various apartment-hunting trips in different parts of the city, Mr. A began to reminisce about his life experiences, showed much interest in the ways the city had changed, and expressed his desire to move into a setting with opportunities for companionship.

---

in turn exerts influence upon—other systems such as family, school, community, and work.

2. The related idea of the goodness of fit, or complementarity. In the complex transaction between human beings and their environment, the goodness of fit between people's needs and qualities, on the one hand, and the environment's characteristics and demands, on the other, influences human competence and adaptation.

3. Knowledge about competence development. Knowledge from systems theory, ego psychology, and other disciplines is valuable in understanding how human beings achieve competence and effective functioning through action and through life experiences. Relevant concepts include coping, adaptation, autonomy, and resilience, along with the premise that human beings have an innate motivation to achieve competence.

4. The role of learning. The crucial role of learning in human behavior is central to a competence-centered and action-oriented perspective, and essential to the problem-solving process. Despite their different philosophical assumptions, such perspectives as behaviorism, learning theory, ego psychology, and socialization theory agree that learning through life experiences is a major influence on competence development and human behavior.

PRACTICE PRINCIPLES AND STRATEGIES

These perspectives suggest a range of principles and strategies for the effective use of action in problem solving within diverse agency settings. In problem solving, client and worker employ action—natural or otherwise—to help meet client needs, support client strengths and adaptive strivings, and promote client competence.

Mobilizing Motivation for Change

Early in the helping process, the practitioner needs to consider the readiness of the client to undertake certain activities. As well as the capacity to perform a given action, readiness implies some tension needing release and some motivation toward an objective. The tension and motivation can be expressed in different forms, such as anxiety, dissatisfaction, guilt, or even a hopeless dream or a fanciful ambition. The quantity and quality of the client's tension influence the timing of the activity, which should be geared to the person's readiness and spontaneity. In some situations, however, an impulse-ridden person may need help to delay action.

The traditional view of motivation as a client trait is less valuable than "a transactional model dealing with motivation as a process that takes into account the interactions among client, worker, and the environment" (Moore-Kirkland, 1981, p. 33). Such a model builds on the original formulation of the dynamic interaction among motivation, capacity, and opportunity by Ripple, Alexander, and Polemis (1964), especially their emphasis on the pivotal role of motivation in social work intervention. Following such an orientation, the worker redefines resistive behavior as motivation and considers questions such as the following in formulating the assessment and service goals (Moore-Kirkland, 1981).

1. What is the level of anxiety regarding the problem(s), the services, or the relationship with the worker, and what are the specific sources of anxiety or lack of anxiety?
2. How does the client perceive the consequences of achieving the goals of the change effort?
3. What are the effective motivators in the client's life at this time?
4. What practical factors might impede change?

Exhibit R19-3 illustrates ways of mobilizing motivation so as to facilitate effective action and promote competence in a situation involving child abuse, family breakdown, and mother-child separation and eventual reunion.

Redefining Assessment as Competence Clarification

In social work practice, interventive plans are based on careful understanding of the client—that is, the special needs, qualities, problems, goals, and behaviors of the person, family, or group. A major purpose of the assessment phase is to understand the client's readiness and competence for change. To do so effectively, the worker needs to complement clinically based assessment procedures with other methods, such as participant observation. As much as feasible and appropriate, the worker should become involved in the client's life situation and seek to understand, through direct experience, what is going on with the client in relevant contexts, such as the family, neighborhood, or school.

Workers should understand, as clearly as possible, each client's competence and the multiple factors affecting it, in order to make professional use of life experiences and strengths as resources for change. Accordingly, the following guidelines will be helpful in assessment (Maluccio, 1981):

1. Clarify the competence of the client. What are the unique capacities, skills, attitudes, motivations, strengths, and potentialities of the client? What are the particular areas of coping strengths? What are indicators of resilience in the person? Which areas of competence need to be reinforced or supported? Which life experiences may be mobilized to stimulate or support the process of change?
2. Clarify the environmental characteristics that influence the coping and adaptive patterns of the client. What are the critical environmental challenges confronting the client? What actual or potential supports are available in the environment? What are the risks and vulnerabilities in the client system? What blocks, obstacles, and deficits interfere with each person's life processes and adaptive strivings?
3. Clarify the goodness of fit between the client system and its environment. Does the environment contain the elements necessary to support, nourish, and challenge the person? What needs to be changed to make the transaction more mutually rewarding, to achieve a better adaptive fit, and to help the person to build on his life experiences? What new experiences or activities should be planned?

The focus on competence clarification also requires that human difficulties be viewed as problems in living or as manifestations of the poor fit between people and their environments. These problems include developmental crises, such as adolescence; life transitions, such as marriage or divorce; and discrepancies between a person's needs and environmental resources, such as a lack of day-care services near to a single mother's home.

Problems, needs, or conflicts are not seen as specific weaknesses or properties of the person. They are redefined in transactional terms, so as to suggest ways of intervening in the person-environment transaction. In particular,

EXHIBIT R19-3
Mobilizing Motivation

Marie W, now divorced, had been married to Tom W for ten years. They have a 9-year-old son, Kevin. Mr. W was physically abusive to both his wife and child. When Kevin was five, his day care provider reported to the state child welfare agency her concerns that Kevin might have been sexually abused. The evaluation, though inconclusive, suggested that the child might have been victimized by a woman. At the same time, Mrs. W, distraught over the breakup of her marriage and ensuing financial difficulties, asked her sister and brother-in-law to provide temporary care for Kevin in their home. The agency then required that Mrs. W participate in a sexual abuse evaluation prior to Kevin's return to her care. Following a long series of delays in initiating the evaluation, which the agency viewed as evidence of Mrs. W's noncompliance, the court awarded Kevin's aunt and uncle temporary guardianship and required that visits with the parents be supervised.

Mrs. W participated in supervised visits at an agency-based visitation center for six months. Each of the visits between Kevin and his mother went very well. However, when a new job took her to a distant part of the state, Mrs. W did not contact her son for seven months. Mrs. W then relocated nearer to Kevin and petitioned the court for his return. The judge appointed a social worker to improve the relationship between Kevin and his mother. Several months into the therapy, Mrs. W disclosed her alcohol abuse. She explained that the trauma of losing her husband and son was overwhelming; she could not tolerate the pain of just visiting with her son, and for that reason she could not participate in parent-teacher conferences, watch Kevin's softball games, or involve herself in other parenting tasks. She indicated that alcohol helped ease the pain, but that more than anything she wanted her son back.

The social worker recognized Mrs. W's disclosure as evidence of the client's trust in her, willingness to confront her problems, and motivation to become a better parent. She used the disclosure to point to Mrs. W's courage and newly found hope that the future might be brighter than she had once thought. With the social worker's support and encouragement, Mrs. W began to attend Alcoholics Anonymous meetings. After a period of proven sobriety, Mrs. W began weekly unsupervised visits with Kevin that were gradually lengthened to a full day and then overnight. She began to feel motivated and confident enough to become more integrated in her son's life.

Mrs. W's sister objected to the social worker's recommendations to increase Mrs. W's time with Kevin. Her sister's attitude initially prompted despair but, helped by the social worker's encouragement, Mrs. W developed a new set of strategies to control her anger and maintain her focus on the goal of reunifying with her son. After two years of continued growth and change by Mrs. W, Kevin returned to his mother's home.

---

problems are translated into adaptive tasks or meaningful life experiences, which provide the client with opportunities for action and for competence development. Change efforts can then be directed toward supporting the client's resilience and coping strategies, learning necessary skills, and, in many situations, rising above adversity (Wolin & Wolin, 1993). For example, a parent referred for child neglect is viewed as needing to learn skills in child care and is provided with a homemaker and a parent aide, who offer concrete help and also serve as role models. A couple experiencing marital discord is encouraged to clarify factors that lead to their persistent arguments. A young unmarried mother is seen as having a problem in role transition rather than an underlying personality conflict and is provided with activities that help her to gain competence as a new parent. The use of these principles as a part of the assessment process is illustrated in Exhibit R19-4. Problem definition can lead to the conscious use of life experiences as instruments of change and as opportunities for competence development. Above all, the worker regards clients as human beings who are striving toward growth, can be resources on their own behalf, and have the potential to learn through more positive life experiences.

EXHIBIT R19-4
Assessment as Competence Clarification

A worker in a halfway house located on the grounds of a large psychiatric hospital began to work with a resocialization group of five middle-aged women who had been diagnosed with schizophrenia. Every one of them had been in the hospital at least four years. They had recently been transferred to the halfway house to test their readiness to return to the community.

In examining the functioning of group members from a competence perspective, the worker was impressed by the variety of existing skills and strengths. For instance, three of the women had been successfully holding part-time jobs in the hospital; one was an excellent cook; another one wrote poetry that delighted the other patients. All of them had been regularly attending group activities. The worker thus identified each client's skills and potentialities for competent functioning. At the same time, she recognized various environmental blocks.

As a result of having been labeled as sick, the women were not receiving positive feedback from their family or from staff members.

The worker set out to improve the goodness of fit between these persons and their environment by changing other people's perceptions of them and their qualities, by offering encouragement and support, and by providing further opportunities for development of their skills and talents. She planned a structured life skills workshop for group members and then helped them to practice their new skills through a variety of specific and repeated activities, such as shopping in local supermarkets, going to the movies in town, and taking the bus to a nearby city. These activities were developed on the basis of the worker's assessment of each person's needs and qualities and were purposively related to specific goals formulated with each client.

Choosing Alternative Courses of Action

Another practice strategy is to provide opportunities for clients to consider alternative courses of action—to evaluate various possibilities, test their readiness, and choose the most appropriate alternative. Furthermore, the deliberative process can stimulate clients' cognitive growth and mastery, mobilize their decision-making function, and reinforce the sense of autonomy that comes from involvement in purposive activities consonant with their needs as well as societal requirements. The worker plays an important role through the provision of information concerning the potential effects of the action, feedback to heighten clients' awareness of their reality, and support in taking a risk. Client-worker interaction becomes more meaningful and productive as both parties go through the process of reaching agreement on specific goals, tasks, and procedures.

It is useful to keep in mind the systems theory principle of equifinality—the notion that the same result can be achieved in different ways. If diverse opportunities for action are identified, the individual is able to look at the world in novel ways and to select the activity most suited to her personal style of coping and drive for competence. People cope differently with similar life crises. Exhibit

R19-5 illustrates how a worker who understands the person's unique ways of coping and adapting is able to perceive appropriate opportunities for action.

Choosing the most appropriate course of action also involves negotiating short-term goals and formulating specific action plans with clearly defined tasks for members of the client system. Exhibit R19-6 illustrates this in work with a 15-year-old with a learning disability.

Implementing Differential Client and Practitioner Roles

As another feature of a competence-oriented perspective, social work practitioners need to view their clients more explicitly as resources—as human beings with assets and potentialities that can be mobilized on their own behalf—and to help clients to see themselves as resources. Such a perspective suggests that clients should play active roles in such areas as assessment, goal formulation, and the selection of interventive strategies. By exercising their own decision-making powers in these areas, clients increase their autonomy and competence.

As clients take action on their behalf, the role of the social worker is defined in complementary terms. In particular, as suggested by Studt (1968), workers are viewed

---

EXHIBIT R19-5
Helping a Family Cope with a Father's Sudden Death

Mrs. F was a middle-aged woman who seemed incapable of functioning following her husband's recent death. She became extremely dependent on her adolescent children, who were frightened and frustrated by her behavior. The children avoided her, thus contributing to her loneliness and depression. The family physician referred them to a family service agency.

After helping Mrs. F to work through some of her grief reaction, the social worker involved her and the children in the formulation of multiple tasks designed to promote her independent functioning and to change the family's interactional patterns. For example, instead of constantly avoiding their mother, the children agreed to go with her to visit relatives at least once weekly. Mrs F agreed to let them go out on their own during the week, rather than feeling that all of them should always stay home to keep her company. The worker instructed the children to sit down individually with their mother and share with her their hopes for the future—something that they had routinely done

with their father. The worker encouraged Mrs. F to make decisions in such areas as planning for necessary housing repairs and also helped her to pursue a variety of activities, such as shopping for some badly needed clothes for herself and beginning to look for a job.

As they performed these varied tasks, Mrs. F and her children developed a new equilibrium in their family system, which had been severely threatened by the loss of the husband and father. New role behaviors and communication patterns emerged, enabling them to offer each other some gratification as a changed family unit.

In addition, as she gradually performed her individual tasks with the worker's and children's support, Mrs. F increased her sense of autonomy, gained some desperately needed feelings of competence, and improved her skills in dealing with the environment. All family members thus benefited from engagement in a variety of individual and joint activities and experiences.

---

primarily as catalysts—as enabling agents who help the client to identify and use appropriate experiences or to create new experiences and resources. The worker uses a variety of approaches to help provide the conditions necessary for clients to achieve their purposes. In addition to the role of therapist, a worker may need to serve as guide, strategist, teacher, broker, or advocate.

These changes also affect the relationship between client and practitioner: "The relationship is redefined as one in which two people are working on a shared project. Each brings a special expertise to the task" (Hartman, 1979, p. 264). Moreover, the relationship should be characterized by encouragement of client autonomy, reduction of the authority and power invested in the worker, and the elimination of any hidden agenda (Hartman, 1979).

As much as possible, workers should reduce social distance and promote a relationship in which openness, authenticity, and human caring are nurtured (Germain & Gitteman, 1996). Studies find that clients seem to value the worker's human qualities more than their technical skills.

One such study indicated that, from the perspective of clients, the "composite picture of the good or ideal worker is that of someone who is warm, accepting, understanding, involved, natural, genuine, competent, objective, and able to share of himself with the client" (Maluccio, 1979, p. 125). The focus on a redefined client-worker relationship can lead to benefits that at times go beyond the client's immediate need. Exhibit R19-7 provides examples.

As our examples show, mobilizing the potentialities and motivation of clients requires practitioners to select actions that provide opportunities for clients to build on their strengths (Saleebey, 1997). This involves identifying issues of primary concern around which motivation can be awakened and taking into consideration the person's strengths and potentialities and ethnic and racial characteristics, as well as environmental resources and deficits (Iglehart & Becerra, 1995). Above all, it means emphasizing interventions that empower human beings to take action in their own behalf (Parsons & Cox, 1994; Pinderhughes, 1989).

EXHIBIT R19-6
Negotiating Short-Term Goals and Action Plans

Ryan, a shy 15-year-old, had been diagnosed with attention deficit disorder and a learning disability that resulted in poor language comprehension and production. He was doing very poorly in school, which compounded his already low self-esteem. To make matters worse, his older brother, Charley, was an outstanding college freshman, excelling both academically and on the football field. With the school year coming to a close, Ryan told his social worker that he was preparing to quit his part-time job so that he could take the summer off and "just sleep."

The social worker noted that the only time Ryan seemed to talk with any passion and sense of hopefulness was when he described his guitar playing. He played frequently with a group of his friends with whom he had formed a band and wished that someday he might earn his living as a musician. She explored with Ryan the possibility of his using the summer to work toward this goal. Together they created a list of action steps that he would need to take, such as establishing a regular practice schedule for the band; creating a two-hour show; identifying venues; purchasing a new amplifier; and developing a publicity campaign.

By the end of the summer, Ryan and his friends had accomplished all of their goals and were scheduled to play at a host of school dances through the end of the year. Even Ryan's parents, who had begun to see Ryan as a failure and "just plain lazy," had to admire the energy and drive that their son displayed once he was helped to focus on an aspect of his life that was a strength and that really mattered to him.

EXHIBIT R19-7
Redefining the Worker-Client Relationship

A social worker in a day-care center became acquainted with a young mother, Mrs. J, when she dropped off and picked up her child each day. Mrs. J began to linger for short conversations with the worker. Eventually, she asked the worker to visit her at home so that they could talk further about some of her concerns.

Mrs. J expressed much dissatisfaction with her life; she felt lonely, unfulfilled, and unhappy over the lack of contact with other adults. People in her neighborhood tended to keep to themselves. Although she was yearning for opportunities to develop her interests and form close relationships with others, her environment provided little challenge or inspiration.

As the worker became aware of Mrs. J's needs and qualities, she encouraged Mrs. J to try to create an informal support system in the neighborhood, thus making the environment more nurturing. Mrs. J brought considerable knowledge and skills to this task. She had a good understanding of the needs and characteristics of the community and also had skills in arts and crafts. The worker, on the other hand, had information about—and access to—formal agencies and was able to involve appropriate ones in the project.

Mrs. J and the worker began to hold informal arts and crafts events at the day-care center for parents and children in the neighborhood. This not only provided an opportunity for families to have fun together but also began to produce the kind of informal support that Mrs. J had wanted.

While serving as facilitator and community organizer, the worker respected and supported Mrs. J and helped her to create opportunities that were responsive to her needs and talents. In turn, Mrs. J, as an effective leader, attained satisfaction through her participation in meaningful activities and enhanced her sense of competence. At the same time, with the worker's encouragement, she created an environment that was more supportive and challenging for herself, as well as for other mothers in the area.

EXHIBIT R19-8
Targeting Environmental Transactions

Mrs. T, a woman in her mid-70s, went to a primary health care facility with health problems, and also complained to the physician that she was lonely and often very blue. The doctor diagnosed her as depressed and referred her to a social worker, who, in turn, made a home visit. Mrs. T's apartment was rather barren and neighbors were cut off from each other, leaving Mrs. T with no one to talk to or confide in. Time hung heavy on her hands. The environment provided neither social supports nor opportunities for activity and involvement.

Building on the competence-centered orientation, the worker found that Mrs. T was an energetic woman who enjoyed people, was motivated toward an active life, was well organized, and had good cognitive skills. She and the worker discussed her interests and potential volunteer jobs that would facilitate socialization, productive activity, and, in essence, a meaningful new role. Eventually, a job was selected in a local library as part of the Retired Seniors Volunteer Program, and opportunities for successful action to promote competence emerged.

The first days on the job were difficult for Mrs. T; she was apprehensive and sensitive to what she perceived as criticisms on the part of the library staff, and she considered resigning. Rather than perceiving these difficulties as a failure on Mrs. T's part, the worker located the problem in the transaction between Mrs. T and the librarian, a busy younger person who was not sufficiently aware of the needs and skills of her new volunteer. The worker's subsequent talk with the librarian was successful in changing the person-environment transaction so that it became mutually satisfying. In other words the worker, as enabler, supported Mrs. T's coping and intervened in restructuring the environment with and for her, until a good match was created.

At termination, after only a few highly focused sessions, Mrs. T had increased her autonomy, enjoyed her new role as a volunteer, and found friends in her apartment and in her work environment. Mrs. T. had learned and practiced new coping skills. In addition, her environment had changed and now provided support and nourishment. The competence-centered approach resulted in increased self-confidence and self-esteem—in sum, positive mental health.

Restructuring the Environment

Competence also flourishes through a nutritive environment that is suited to people's needs and qualities and supports their life processes. Consequently, the worker needs to understand the environment with all of its complexities and to find ways of enriching or restructuring it in a systematic fashion. In many situations, the client environment needs to be modified so as to facilitate coping efforts and adaptive strivings; social networks are especially important in this regard. Indeed, a key characteristic of competent persons is that they are able to identify and use natural helping networks. Some people, however, need help to make effective use of resources within their own actual or potential networks.

Emphasis on the environment of the client system is not new in social work. Typically, however, we have focused on modifying the environment as a means of influencing the helping process. We need to regard environmental resources and supports as instruments of help, rather than simply as influences on help; we need to appreciate the environment's potential to release or inhibit human potentialities for growth, adaptation, and competence. Doing so can lead to more accurate environmental assessment and more effective environmental intervention (Kemp, Whittaker, & Tracy, 1997).

Much can be accomplished by identifying and using environmental instruments—that is, people, resources, social networks or supports, and facilities that exist in the environment or can be added to it. These instruments are integral to intervention (Germain & Gitteman, 1996). In the area of child welfare, for instance, homemakers or parent aides are found to be effective instruments of help in working with parents who abuse or neglect their children. In short, as Exhibit R19-8 suggests, emphasis on changing the environment is as important as—if not more important than—attention to changing people themselves.

Using Client Feedback

It is important to obtain, on a regular basis, clients' views concerning our helping efforts. Although this may change with the emphasis on consumer satisfaction and outcome evaluation in a managed care environment, workers in general do not systematically elicit client feedback, as worker comments in research interviews illustrate (Maluccio, 1979, p. 175):

- "I often wish I knew what clients think of me—and what we're doing together . . . Maybe I should ask them."
- "How did the client view the objectives of our work together? I don't really know . . . You keep asking me this question and it makes me think about my approach."
- "I think that she [the client] in general felt positive toward me. But I couldn't say specifically how she saw me . . . As you ask about this, I realize that these are things we rarely discuss with our clients."

Client feedback can serve various purposes. It can be a means for the agency to monitor services, carry out program evaluation, and improve service delivery; and it can also be an effective device for workers to monitor practice and improve their skills:

> By being tuned into the clients' perspectives, workers might be better able to determine for themselves which methods or techniques are effective, what they need to modify in their approach in order to make it more relevant to client needs and qualities, and what questions they need to ask about their underlying assumptions regarding human behavior and interpersonal helping. (Maluccio, 1979, p. 202)

Obtaining feedback in each situation can help ensure that the practitioner is attuned as much as possible to the client's feelings, needs, views, and qualities. Moreover, eliciting the client's view can have positive consequences for the client—by, for instance, providing the individual with opportunities for decision making, reducing the social distance between client and worker, enhancing the sense of mutuality between them, and increasing the client's sense of power and control. In sum, it can promote competence by enhancing the client's self-esteem and autonomy.

More emphasis on client feedback can serve to engage clients even more actively in the helping process. At the same time, it can help workers to examine and revise their approach.

CONCLUSION

Systematic attention to the use of action in social work practice can help to enhance the problem-solving process and ultimately promote client competence. We have delineated a range of practice principles and strategies that can help practitioners achieve such purposes:

- Mobilizing motivation for change by building on each person's anxiety and struggles
- Viewing human difficulties as manifestations of the poor fit or lack of mutuality between people and their environments
- Redefining assessment as the process of clarifying the competence of the client system, the characteristics of the environment, and the goodness of fit between clients and their environment
- Helping clients to choose alternative courses of action
- Implementing differential client and practitioner roles, by regarding clients as resources and workers as enabling agents
- Restructuring or enriching the client's environment in a purposive and systematic fashion
- Obtaining client feedback so as to engage clients more actively in the helping process, enhance their self-esteem, monitor and improve services, and improve practitioner skills

Through deliberate emphasis on action and competence, social workers can promote their own personal and professional growth and redirect the trajectory of coping and adaptation in clients from frustration and despair toward satisfaction, self-fulfillment, and effective functioning.

READING 20
The Social Work Process of Social Care Planning[1]

Miriam M. Johnson[2] and W. David Harrison[3]

At various points in the human life cycle, we all must be cared for by others, and we must in turn care for others (Aldous, 1994). Mutual caring is one of the essential foundations of human community (Bulmer, 1987; Dokecki, 1992). Social workers are professionally involved in helping people to take care of one another. Using problem-solving processes, they help individuals to meet their social care wants and needs from the community resources available. Often, practitioners strive to make the social care processes of the community more functional (Hadley, Cooper, Dale, & Stacy, 1987).

SOCIAL CARE PLANNING

In this reading, we look at the basic ideas of social care planning and counseling as an application of the problem-solving model. You will encounter an enormous diversity of problems and circumstances in social care planning and counseling. You may need, for instance, to develop a cooperate plan of care for an adolescent in a group home; to coordinate services for an individual moving from a mental hospital to a board and care home; to negotiate the legal system in order to secure permanent homes for the children of an abusive mother; to provide support for long-term caregivers of adults with developmental disabilities; or to persuade a day-care provider to take a child with a minor disability.

Services such as foster family and group care or the community care of people with mental disabilities involve what Morris (1977) called caring for as well as caring about people. Social care is central to the personal social services (Harrison & Hoshino, 1984; Kahn & Kamerman, 1982). It involves helping to provide the socialization, developmental, and counseling services and resources that people need in today's complex societies. Demographic trends in Western societies suggest that the need for social care will grow very rapidly (Briar & Kaplan, 1990); already, in many parts of the world, social care and social work are virtually synonymous.

Social care work usually involves integrated planning and counseling. When done well, social care planning is truly social; it involves cooperation between individuals and their communities (for example, Harrison, 1989, 1991; Harrison, Smale, & Hearn, 1992; Johnson, 1992; Martinez-Brawley, 1990; Smale, Tuson, Cooper, Wardle, & Crosbie, 1988; Specht, 1990). This kind of social work is sometimes called case management. However, while case managers often integrate services constructively and provide a supportive relationship (Johnson, 1985), this term is problematic, because it implies that clients are inanimate cases to be managed by someone else, rather than active, self-determining human beings. Where case managers lack professional values and skills, clients may be treated disrespectfully (Netting, 1992). In the United Kingdom, the equivalent term is social care planning (Barclay, 1982), which, in practice, encompasses not only planning but also the emotional, informational, and decision-making aspects of counseling. Regardless of the terminology, it is crucial to recognize the importance of partnership in social care planning. Keith-Lucas' (1973) concept of coplanning is particularly valuable, because cooperative planning is ethically right for social work and is far more productive than planning done to or for people.

The most important human relationships involve caring for others. As infants, we are almost totally dependent on others for our care. As adults, we take care of those we love—our children, our aging parents, our partner, or our friends—when they are sick or in need. When our patterns of care change or break down or when especially difficult needs for care emerge, we often call on specialists, institutions, neighbors, and relatives for assistance, or we seek special training. Social care planning involves helping people to make use of these resources and to come to grips with the difficulties their lives present, so as to improve the quality of care. It encompasses very practical, concrete arrangements, as well as basic issues of human emotion and meaning.

Not limited to work with individuals and families, social care planning also includes collective projects such as adult day care, meals on wheels, and mobility programs. As societal patterns and attitudes change, new needs for social care arise. In particular, new opportunities for women in the workplace demand new arrangements for fulfilling their traditional family care roles. Social workers can help

---

[1] An original reading for *Social Work Processes*.
[2] Associate Professor, College of Social Work, University of South Carolina, Columbia, South Carolina.
[3] Professor and Dean, School of Social Work and Criminal Justice, East Carolina University, Greenville, North Carolina.

individuals, families, communities, and even larger systems adapt to, and shape, these social forces.

Social workers also deal with more severe care problems, such as the difficulty of providing sound socialization and humane care to individuals with serious physical or mental disabilities. In these situations, social care work will often involve a therapeutic dimension.

PROBLEM-SOLVING CONCEPTS IN SOCIAL CARE

Good social care work uses the problem-solving model of practice. The model offers direction as workers focus on providing quality care and helping people cope.

Cognitive psychologists have found that successful problem solving usually involves two processes. First, people must achieve some understanding of the problem. This implies a personally meaningful idea of the current situation and also of a preferred way for things to be—that is, an objective. The current situation may be that things are getting worse, and the objective may be simply to halt the trend. It is often difficult for individuals to see their predicament clearly and to envision something different without skilled and patient help.

Second, humans solving problems invoke some kind of plan—deliberate or haphazard—to reduce the discrepancy between the way things are and the preferred situation (Anderson, 1980; Hayes, 1978; Newell & Simon, 1972; Rubinstein, 1974). Often what appears to be irrational or self-defeating behavior reflects individuals' attempts to deal with problems without some plan or to reduce anxiety without addressing problems directly. A plan is an organized way of working toward solutions; it involves a set of actions and responsibilities, usually with some sequential order. In social care planning, workers and clients must develop this plan together. The problems that they face will be complex and open to a variety of definitions and possible plans of action. Emotions may cloud planning, just as they complicate problem definition. "As problems become less well-defined, greater importance is attached to activities such as interpreting the problem, generating solution possibilities that are minimally suggested by the information given, and evaluating solution attempts" (Bourne, Dominowski, Loftus, & Healy, 1986, p. 237).

Creativity and expertise are important in problem solving. Social workers exercise their creativity by helping people develop plans that fit the situation and lead to desirable results. Hayes (1978) suggests that creativity is promoted by a large knowledge base, an atmosphere that encourages new and more effective ways to deal with problems, and a deliberate search for analogies between the current situation and others.

THE MILTON-CLAY FAMILY

Work with the Milton-Clay family illustrates many aspects of the problem-solving model of social work. James Milton had expected his late 50s to be the golden years. He anticipated that his daughter, Sharon, would be married, and his grandchildren would be a source of pleasure and pride. With his earning power at its peak, his wife Mildred could stay at home and pursue hobbies or take long vacations with him. Unfortunately, a back injury had forced him to quit his construction job. Although he was receiving disability pay, Mildred needed to keep her full-time secretary position in order to cover the monthly bills and to maintain the family's health insurance. His mother-in-law, whom everyone called Nana, lived in their spare bedroom; it meant a loss of privacy, but he'd appreciated her company since his injury. Now the doctor said she needed hip replacement surgery. Mildred would have to be out of work to help out during the long weeks of recovery at home. At the same time, their 31-year-old daughter was again asking for help with her two teenage children. She still seemed more of an adolescent than an adult much of the time, and the Miltons found it hard not to step in when their grandchildren were unsupervised and the home was a wreck. Living within a few blocks of her small apartment was both a convenience and a nuisance.

The Miltons had no close friends. Occasional attendance at church was their only real community contact. It was difficult for them to socialize with people, because their daughter and grandchildren inevitably came up in conversation.

Concerned about his grandchildren, Mr. Milton went to Northwood Family Services, a voluntary agency that he knew had a group foster home program. He spoke to the Family Care Unit worker, Tameeka Arthur, in very precise words and diction, his chin held high. Ms. Arthur could not help but feel for him in his turmoil. Mr. Milton had tried to be supportive to his daughter, but he was afraid that he had actually made matters worse. He explained to Ms. Arthur that his daughter had been a single parent for ten years, since she and her husband divorced. Sharon had a 14-year-old son, Henry, and a 12-year-old daughter, Tina. The Miltons had mixed feelings about Sharon's marriage. She got pregnant during her senior year in high school. Hank Clay seemed like a nice enough fellow, but he had to drop out of his classes at the community college to support her and the baby. After the divorce, Hank moved to another state, remarried, and started a second family. Now his contacts with his first two children were limited to birthday and holiday phone calls. His small child-support checks were often late or didn't come at all, and Sharon had to apply for public assistance when she was between jobs.

After Henry's birth, Sharon spent about six weeks in the state psychiatric hospital with postpartum depression. The Miltons started taking on parental duties for their grandchildren, and there had been little relief in the last 14 years. They were glad to do their part, Mr. Milton stressed, but things had gotten out of hand. Mildred had used up her paid sick leave taking her mother to the doctor, and they couldn't keep running back and forth whenever Sharon's neighbors called to complain that the children had been left without supervision.

Ms. Arthur acknowledged that it seemed now a great strain on the Miltons to feel responsible for three generations at the same time, and indicated that she might be able eventually to help the family make a plan. She asked Mr. Milton what finally had made him decide to ask for help.

Mr. Milton said that he was afraid Sharon was again experiencing a serious bout of depression, although she had been doing well for several months. She had finally put her mind to practical matters and had gotten a job. She had been working 8 to 10 hours a day as a clerk at an auto parts shop, with great enthusiasm. Every night, she was at one nightspot or another, almost going without sleep, the children said. Mr. Milton abruptly changed the subject, as if he felt uncomfortable. He said that Mrs. Milton was very stressed with trying to balance her work and care for her mother. He didn't see how she could take on any more, even with his help. In the most measured tones, Mr. Milton said that he and his wife wondered whether their daughter had become a drug addict.

Ms. Arthur said that it was, of course, a possibility, but that it was important not to jump to conclusions. Mr. Milton said that he had never seen any evidence of drug use but he was concerned about the variations in Sharon's mood. He had talked to the children about drugs in the neighborhood and had the impression that they were truly appalled at the idea of drug abuse. He had not been able to confront the issue directly with Sharon.

"Is this not the sort of situation your homes are designed for?" asked Mr. Milton. Ms. Arthur said that sometimes a plan involving group care could be helpful but in these situations, unlike in medicine, it was hard to find the remedy solely on the basis of the symptoms and a diagnosis. She said that usually it was very important to dis-

cuss these matters with everyone involved so as to explore the various ways of looking at the situation. She noted that fairly common psychiatric problems other than drug abuse might lead to Sharon's symptoms and that these might be amenable to treatment. Mr. Milton did not think that his daughter had had a mental health consultation recently. He said that he was willing to listen to Ms. Arthur's advice.

Ms. Arthur wondered whether it might be useful for Ms. Clay and maybe her ex-husband to talk with the Miltons and with her about the situation. Mr. Milton thought it would be hard for his wife to take any more time off work. He felt that Hank Clay wouldn't want to be involved and that Sharon, although willing to meet, would probably not want to drive so far without some idea that it would be helpful. In her depressed state, she would see the situation as hopeless. Ms. Arthur wondered what Henry and Tina thought of the situation. She asked whether anyone knew that Mr. Milton was making contact with the agency. He said that Mildred knew. Henry and Tina did not, but they talked very openly about their mother's condition. It might be good to talk with them as soon as possible, Mr. Milton said, because they often felt like they had to tell their mother what to do, anyway. They usually got angry when action was taken without their knowledge and responded by disappearing for a day or two. Even the Department of Social Services had been looking for them once, after the neighbors called to say that something was wrong.

Ms. Arthur said that there was a legal responsibility to inform the Department of Social Services if there was reason to believe that children might have been neglected. She suggested that it might be worthwhile for Mr. Milton to talk to Mr. Bowen from that department, to let him know that she and her agency might be getting involved and to make sure that he knew about the children's situation. Mr. Milton was a bit surprised at this, but he agreed to make the call, saying that he was afraid that everyone was going to know about the situation before they were through.

When Mr. Milton called DSS, he learned that a social worker had been assigned to the family, but that the case had been inactive since Henry and Tina had last come home. Mr. Bowen suggested that Ms. Arthur try to meet with Ms. Clay and get back in touch with him afterward.

Ms. Arthur suggested that Mr. Milton discuss today's conference with his wife and daughter. She asked whether there were any other people in the community who helped Ms. Clay or could look after the children. Mr. Milton said that he had often discussed this with his daughter, but that Sharon seemed completely isolated. Ms. Arthur said that she would be available to meet with them all or with Ms. Clay alone, but that it was not possible to jump in and intervene in Ms. Clay's affairs; that would probably lead to more confusion and friction. If Ms. Clay preferred not to come to the agency at this point, Ms. Arthur could go to her home or to the Miltons'. Ms. Arthur said that she could contact Ms. Clay if necessary. However, since Mr. Milton had made the first move, it might be best to let him work things out, assuming he still thought that it would be helpful to work with the agency after more thought and discussion.

They talked at some length about how it felt to be a potential client and how Northwood Family Services worked with its clients. The agency tried to work with the whole family; sometimes group home care was part of a plan, but often they were able to work out child-care problems without anyone having to move. If placement was part of the plan, they worked very hard on both long-term solutions and the immediate needs and interests of the youngsters. They worked carefully with the Department of Social Services which now had a Permanency Planning Program to make sure that no youngsters got lost in the system without the prospect of a permanent, stable home. Ms. Arthur reassured Mr. Milton that she was not putting down his idea that his grandchildren might benefit from a group home but said that in the light of experience and research, it was most useful to get everyone together working on the same problems, if possible. He said he would consider what he had learned and agreed to call back no matter what they decided.

Three days later, Mildred Milton telephoned Ms. Arthur. Mrs. Milton said she was glad that Jim had taken it upon himself to do something because, much as she cared for her daughter and her grandchildren, she was too exhausted to even think about the problems anymore. All of her energy was used up worrying about how she was going to care for her mother after surgery. She was glad that someone could help the family think through its options.

Ms. Arthur said she appreciated Mrs. Milton taking her coffee break to call and offered to schedule an evening appointment for the family if needed. She asked if Mrs. Milton had talked to anyone at the Northwood Council on Aging about her mother's needs or if she had requested temporary homemaker chore services. When Mrs. Milton said she had no idea such services existed, Ms. Arthur gave her the name of a colleague at the Council office.

Mrs. Milton thanked Ms. Arthur for her support and told her that she and Jim had talked with their daughter. Since Ms. Arthur had taken some of the fear out of mentioning drug abuse, they had found it possible even to discuss that subject. "Sharon said that she had had nothing to do with drugs." Mrs. Milton asked whether Ms. Arthur could come to the Miltons' home for a conference, not worrying Henry and Tina about a move unless it seemed a real possibility. Ms. Arthur agreed, saying that she would need to involve them as soon as possible if she began to work with their mother.

The meeting occurred at the Milton home as planned. Ms. Arthur came in the evening, so that neither Mrs. Milton nor Sharon Clay had to miss any time from work. Mrs. Milton's mother joined them at the kitchen table. Almost immediately Ms. Arthur noted that Ms. Clay was seriously depressed; she sat with her eyes fixed on the pattern in the linoleum floor. She talked very little and with an air of complete hopelessness. She confirmed that she had severe ups and downs and had even been tempted to drive off the side of the road at times. She had not consulted any mental health professionals since her hospitalization years before. She said that she had often wondered if the children would be better off somewhere else, but she really had not thought beyond the possibility of her ex and his wife taking them for a while. In her last contact with Hank, two months ago, he said there was no way they could take the kids, but he promised to try to be more prompt with the child-support payments.

Ms. Arthur thought that Sharon might be suffering from a serious cyclic mood disorder. At the same time, the Miltons' need to deal with Nana's upcoming surgery was straining the resources of the family. Ms. Arthur had long ago learned that it was important to share her observations in a deliberate, honest way so that they could really be used by the family; she had not yet even met Henry and Tina. Ms. Arthur suggested that she could probably help develop a plan to support the family now that they were under such stress. She discussed all of the ways that the family had adapted over the years to cope with whatever happened. She said that she hoped that she and the agency might be seen as a new source of support. She wondered whether the adults felt that it would be helpful for Henry and Tina to talk with her and, after some initial uncertainty, they agreed. Ms. Clay said that she would tell her children what was being discussed, and she agreed to telephone Ms. Arthur the next morning. Given the level of concern Ms. Arthur felt over Ms. Clay's depression, she was glad to gain this commitment.

The next day Mr. Milton telephoned Ms. Arthur to thank her for her time. He said that Mildred had called the Council on Aging and was pleased with the alternatives they suggested; she was feeling much less overwhelmed. Mr. Milton said that they would do whatever they could to help Sharon and the children, but they knew that their time might become much more limited soon. Ms. Arthur thought that that would probably be a good way to proceed, letting Ms. Clay take as much responsibility for herself as she could. Mr. Milton did wonder whether Ms. Arthur thought Sharon should see a psychiatrist, and Ms. Arthur said that she was going to suggest a consultation, since she was not really an expert on mental disorders and psychotherapy.

Sharon Clay called as she agreed; and Ms. Arthur made an appointment to meet her at home about an hour before Tina and Henry were to return from school.

The contrast between the Milton home and Sharon Clay's apartment was dramatic. Images of rock stars were on most of the walls, and Henry's collection of baseball caps was prominently displayed on the shelves in the living room. Tina's CDs and tapes were piled high on the floor near the stereo. The house appeared clean, but definitely cluttered. Ms. Clay mumbled an apology for the mess. Pointing to a large pile of papers on the kitchen table, Ms. Clay said that she would have to do something about all these bills and receipts, but she had spent the day just getting them together. She said that she didn't have the energy even to decide what to wear, much less to determine which of her creditors could be paid this month. She went on to say that she had been looking for her will when she found the bills, and she wasn't sure whether to ask her father to sort them out. She hated to do that, but she probably would have to eventually anyway. After asking direct, tactful questions about Ms. Clay's previous reference to driving off the road and her comment about the will, Ms. Arthur learned that the first thing Ms. Clay wanted to do was to go to the hospital for some rest. She said she was worn out, and did not see how she could continue. Ms. Arthur was concerned that Ms. Clay was working on a suicide plan. She shared some of her concern by reflecting how grim the situation seemed to look to Ms. Clay and offered, rather insistently, to take Ms. Clay to the Mental Health Center that afternoon. Ms. Clay seemed relieved that someone was hearing how desperate she felt. Ms. Arthur suggested that Ms. Clay phone the Mental Health Center to see if someone could be prepared for their coming, but Ms. Clay asked Ms. Arthur to call for her. An emergency appointment was scheduled for 5:30 P.M. that day.

Ms. Clay said that she had mentioned going to live with the Miltons to Tina and Henry, but they all knew that plan would not work for long. Henry had been the first to mention a group home, not very seriously. He knew someone who lived in a group home where the boys went on regular camping trips, and that was of real interest to him. Ms. Clay wondered if the children could be cared for in a group home, at least for the time she was in the hospital. She had told her children that Ms. Arthur was coming, but they seemed not to pay much attention.

Ms. Clay went on to say that she did not really think she could handle the job of parent anymore, that the children were beyond her, and that she was not able to supervise them. They had stopped listening to her and acted as if she were not there much of the time. Now their test grades were dropping, and they were starting to get into trouble at school—nothing serious, just constant hassles. The teacher wanted her to come in for a meeting. The guidance counselor had sent home a note asking permission to test Tina for a learning disability; Ms. Clay thought she still had the permission form somewhere. She had hesitated to sign it for fear that the school would "put Tina in one of those special classes."

The school bus stopped out front and Henry burst in. Far from being disinterested, he was extremely curious about Ms. Arthur's visit. He asked a number of questions about where she came from and what she knew about him. He wondered if she knew that his sister had threatened to run away before they put her away somewhere. Before he could finish, Tina arrived. Ms. Arthur introduced herself. Tina mumbled her name but, when Ms. Arthur asked if she had any questions about what they were discussing, all she would say was, "I don't know."

For the benefit of the children, as well as to make sure that Ms. Clay understood, Ms. Arthur decided to summarize the discussion to that point. She said that several people, including their grandparents and great-grandmother, were concerned about how the family was managing. Ms. Clay had been trying very hard, but she was feeling overwhelmed, and something had to be done.

Tina pointed to her mother and said, "She's what's wrong. She's weird!" Ms. Clay started to cry; she said Tina was right.

"Is my momma crazy?" Tina asked. Ms. Arthur explained that Ms. Clay wasn't crazy; she was just very tired and very unhappy. The situation wasn't anybody's fault—not Ms. Clay's, not the kids', not the grandparents', and not Nana's. But they would all have to work together to figure out what to do next, because Ms. Clay might need to go into the hospital for some tests, to get a rest, and to see if some medicine would help her.

Ms. Clay told the children that they would have to go to the Miltons for the night. The children actually seemed quite happy about this idea. Henry asked if they could rent a video on the way; Ms. Arthur told them that would be up to their grandparents and suggested that they gather a few changes of clothing.

Ms. Clay called her parents, who agreed to pick up the children and even take them out for supper at the local burger place. That done, Henry asked about what life in a group home might be like. Ms. Arthur reminded him that no solution had been selected from the several alternatives available; they hadn't even decided how long the children would need a place to stay. She hoped that their school attendance wouldn't be interrupted. Ms. Arthur asked about the possibility of talking with others who might care for them in their own neighborhood, but the children could think of no one who had extra space. Ms. Arthur suggested that a foster family home might be an alternative and is usually a first choice—after relatives—for younger children, but that a final placement choice depended on current vacancies. Usually group home facilities were better able to respond to emergencies and to sibling groups. Many teenagers were happier in a group with others their own age, rather than trying to adjust to another family's home. Ms. Arthur was at least happy that they were not actively opposing the idea of placement, as many parents and children did. They would have to work toward some idea of what problems they were up against, and whether a plan for living in a group home would be helpful. Ms. Arthur assured the children that, if they did need to live somewhere other than with their grandparents, they would be encouraged to visit the place first and to meet the adults and some of the children who lived there.

Ms. Arthur agreed to contact the children the following morning at the Miltons. Her overwhelming impression was that they were eager to have someone to help them bring order to their unhappy and sometimes frightening situation. The ambivalence of the children toward their mother was clear. They wished she would act more like other mothers. Sometimes she embarrassed them, and other times they felt they should be taking care of her. Henry, in particular, was worried about how she would manage if he weren't there to be the man of the house.

After Mr. Milton picked up the children, Ms. Arthur and Ms. Clay went to the Mental Health Center. The social worker and psychiatrist there thought that Ms. Clay was seriously depressed and suicidal, probably suffering from a bipolar affective disorder that would respond well to medication. As Ms. Arthur had anticipated, they recommended immediate hospitalization to stabilize Ms. Clay's condition for now and to begin medical treatment. The next morning, Ms. Arthur called to update Mr. Bowen and said that she would be in touch if the children were in need of more attention or if a plan of care were arrived at.

Over the next week, Ms. Arthur had almost daily contact with the hospital staff, Henry and Tina, the Miltons,

and Sharon Clay. Nana found the children to be a distraction from worries about her health. Jim and Mildred Milton were happy that Sharon was getting started on a medicine that held promise for her and that Ms. Arthur seemed to be a steadying influence. Nevertheless, the Miltons worried that Sharon would not be able to care for her children right away and that they could not continue to do it after Nana had her surgery.

After a second week, it appeared that Ms. Clay would soon be ready to leave the hospital. A conference was held in which she discussed her situation with the hospital staff, Ms. Arthur, and, at Ms. Clay's request, Mr. Milton. Mr. Milton said that a date had been set for his mother-in-law's surgery and his wife had made arrangements to take off work for three weeks to be with her at the hospital and when she returned home. Ms. Clay asked if the group home placement could be worked out while she got a fresh start. She wanted to stabilize her medicine, attend a day treatment program, take care of the paperwork she had left behind, and maybe apply for a new job.

It was agreed that Ms. Arthur would work with Ms. Clay, Tina, and Henry to pursue this alternative. They decided to arrange for the Clays to meet the counselors and see the facilities that had space available. Ms. Arthur would also need permission to talk over the school situation with the principal and teachers and to have them share the planning with the school in the group home's district. Ms. Clay agreed to go along, but she wanted Ms. Arthur to do the talking. Henry and Tina seemed reassured to learn that, even though the boys and girls were in different homes, they were almost next door to one another.

On the way to the group home, Ms. Arthur told the Clays to think about questions they wanted to ask. She suggested that all three Clays be prepared to discuss why they thought the placement might be useful. She had already talked about how many staff and other children lived there, and had given Henry and Tina a copy of the house rules. She reminded all of them that most families feel anxious and awkward during these visits and that the group home staff understood that.

The visit went smoothly. The children were asked what they were interested in, how they might adapt to some rules and routines, and what specific goals they might want to achieve. Neither Henry nor Tina had thought about things in quite this way before, and it seemed like something of a challenge, especially when they considered some of the privileges and recreational opportunities that went with living in the home. Henry was taken on a tour of the boys' home with his mother, and Tina saw the girls' home with Ms. Arthur. Each child had an opportunity to

EXHIBIT R20-1
A Family Care Plan

This is a family plan of care developed by Northwood Family Services and Sharon, Henry, and Tina Clay, with the support of the Social Services Department Permanency Planning Program.

The problem leading to this plan is that Ms. Clay is for now unable to provide the care she wants for her children. In the past she has depended on her parents for financial and task support. They have other demands on their time and resources and the Clays would like to be more independent. Ms. Clay has sought psychiatric care for her mental illness and continues to be responsible in following up on medications. Henry and Tina agree that they were reacting to their mother's condition in a way that was unsatisfactory to them and to her. They would like to do better in school.

The objectives developed by the Clay family are as follows:

1. Pleasant, productive living arrangements for Henry and Tina for the next six months (when the plan may be extended) at the Northwood group homes.
2. A return to the Clays living independently as a family.
3. Ms. Clay stabilizing her condition and obtaining steady employment.
4. Less friction and conflict between Henry, Tina, and Ms. Clay than in the recent past.
5. Better academic attendance and grades for both Henry and Tina Clay.

Responsibilities include the following:

Northwood Family Services agrees to provide ongoing group care services, planning, and counseling. The agency agrees to develop individualized plans with Henry and Tina to find interests they want to pursue and needs they may have and to find ways to achieve their goals while living in the homes. Northwood agrees to work with community resources (for example, schools, employers, neighbors) as much as possible to support reunion of the Clay family.

Sharon Clay agrees to continue her medical treatment, to enroll in an education or job-training program, and to work with Ms. Arthur on planning for the return of Henry and Tina to her care. Ms. Clay agrees to contact her children by telephone at least twice per week, and to visit at least once a week, working out the details with the Northwood staff. Ms. Clay agrees to turn over her child support checks to pay toward the cost of care for her children. Ms. Clay agrees to work with the Department of Social Services as required by law in order to allow for their financial support of the children's care and in documenting her plans and progress.

Henry Clay agrees to work with his counselors on his objectives and needs while living in the home, to continue to work with Ms. Arthur and Ms. Clay on the goal of returning home, and to attend school. Henry has identified his hot temper and outbursts aimed at his mother as the main things he would like to learn to change.

Tina Clay agrees to work with her counselors on her objectives and needs while living in the home, to continue to work with Ms. Arthur and Ms. Clay on the objective of returning home, to attend school, and to take new tests to help the school staff figure out the best ways to teach her arithmetic and reading.

The Department of Social Services agrees to provide an outside review of this planning process at the end of six months and to provide financial and medical support for the children while they are living in the group homes.

A *review* of this plan can be asked for by anyone involved at any time. At the end of six months a conference will be held to review the plan jointly and to evaluate it and to plan ahead. Everyone involved will have a copy, and the plan will guide everyone's efforts to achieve their goals.

Signed:
Tameeka Arthur
Richard Bowen
Bob Bloom (Group Care Counselor)
Robin Maple (Group Care Counselor)
Sharon Clay
Tina Clay
Henry Clay

Date:

ask questions of the other teens, who reported that they got tired of some of the rules but that generally things were OK and sometimes even fun. The counselors told Tina she could bring her tapes and told Henry he could put up a poster in his room. Ms. Clay and the children were surprised and reassured to learn that ordinarily there were no restrictions on family visits and telephone calls; in fact, a specific section on family contact was included in the written care plan.

Later, Ms. Arthur commented that Ms. Clay and Henry and Tina seemed to have decided group care would help them take charge of their lives. They agreed, and Ms. Arthur said that it would be important to come to an agreement about their situation and put together a formal plan—a sort of contract to help everyone know what was happening and what they were trying to do. Ms. Arthur said that the staff and the families had found written plans to be particularly helpful. After a good deal of discussion and deciding which points to focus on and which to leave out, a formal plan was drawn up (Exhibit R20-1). Most of it was in the Clays' own words, the product of their own discussions and various perspectives. It was hard to imagine just how much work had gone into such a simple document, but Henry and Tina learned that most of the other residents had been through the same process.

This plan was not a complete solution to the Clays' problems, but it did become an important part of their work on many fronts with Ms. Arthur and others.

A great deal of work had to be done with Henry over the separation from his mother, because he feared she would not be safe without him nearby. One night, he even ran away from the group home with some of the other residents, but he showed up at his mother's front door several hours later. Ms. Clay had already been notified that he was missing, and she was able to reach Ms. Arthur through the agency's after-hours emergency number. Ms. Arthur thanked Ms. Clay for calling to let them know Henry was safe. They agreed that Ms. Arthur would pick him up the next day. On the way back to the group home, Ms. Arthur and Henry talked about how getting pressured into misbehaving with peers can be a special problem in group care. Ms. Arthur also said she knew that Henry was worried about his mother. Eventually, with a great deal of support and reassurance, he overcame both the realistic aspects of this fear and also the fantasies involved.

Tina was tested for learning disabilities by the agency's counseling psychologist. He met with her teachers to recommend some special classroom techniques and adaptive study assignments; the recommendations were put in her school file, so that they could be implemented when she returned to her home school.

Ms. Clay benefited greatly from her lithium medication. She saw a psychiatrist at the Mental Health Center once a month to monitor her medication, and participated in a bi-weekly therapy group. She met every two weeks with Ms. Arthur, usually around specific plans for Henry and Tina and practical things she could do to take control of her life and to become more independent. She became acquainted with relatives of children in the agency's care during parent support group meetings. She remained skeptical of close attachments to new people, but she did seem to feel the other parents understood her situation better than some professionals with whom she had worked. Together with some other mothers, she worked out plans to make treats for the children for special occasions. When Mr. Bowen helped her sign up at DSS for a special program designed to help single mothers get off welfare, Sharon was pleased to learn that one of the other Northwood parents was also involved.

After nine months in care, Henry and Tina returned to live with their mother on a full-time basis. Each maintained contact with some of the adults and teenagers at Northwood. Henry went back for a short-term aftercare counseling group and Tina continued to see the Big Sister who had been assigned to her. One of the clearest changes was that now the entire family seemed able to make use of some of the community supports that were available.

Six months after Tina and Henry returned to her home, Ms. Clay and Ms. Arthur had their last interview. They reviewed the entire agency file, especially the progress detailed in the plans. The last contact of any sort they had was about three months later, when Ms. Clay called to tell Ms. Arthur that she had received her G.E.D. and that both kids had made the Honor Roll. She also reported that Nana was fully recovered and feeling better than ever and that her parents were taking a well-deserved vacation.

READING 21
Social Work, Social Care, Care Management, and User Involvement[1]
Reima Ana Maglajlic[2]

This reading considers social workers' relationships with politicians, policymakers, other professionals, superiors, and service users within the arena of social and community care. Parton (1994) argues that these relationships reflect a "hole at the centre of the enterprise" (p. 30).

Social care is an established form of practice in the United Kingdom. In the U.K., as in most of Western Europe, social care refers to a range of activities and care resources provided by the local public social service agencies, informal support (families, friends, and neighbors), and independent (not-for-profit and for-profit) agencies (Munday, 1993). Social care is only a tiny part of government activity but draws individuals and families to the governmental agenda (Parton, 1994). It could be viewed as a method of indirect social regulation, important for the liberal ideal of maintaining autonomous free individuals who are at the same time governed.

SOCIAL WORK AND THE NEW RIGHT

Social work in the U.K. has had to contend with the disintegration of political consensus about the welfare state (Harris, 1996). Expenditures on social welfare have been declining since the mid-1960s, under the impact of worldwide economic and social trends. The rationale combines fiscal responsibility—the need to halt the steady increase in the social security budget and in residential care costs (Holman, 1993; Lewis, Bernstock, Bovell, & Wookey, 1997)—with the New Right dogma of a permanent underclass that is beyond help (Holman, 1993). During the 1970s, social work malpractices were widely publicized, and the profession came to personify the problems of welfarism (Parton, 1994).

For their part, professional, community, and other interest groups (including feminists, radical social workers, and user groups) also wanted changes, but for very different reasons. Concerned about the needs of service users within the welfare state, they were a growing voice for independence from patronizing professional domination. These groups advocated a shift from a medical to a social model of care, as explained by Bewley and Glendinning (1994).

> A medical model of disability focuses on specific, individual impairments, and does not recognize links among the experiences of disabled people in each of the systems of health and social service provision. A social model of disability defines people's experience of disability in terms of institutionalised discrimination against disabled people. The distinction is experienced by disabled people with physical, sensory or mental "impairments." The medical model says that people are disabled by their medical impairments, a social model says that people are disabled by the discriminatory social and political response to their impairment. (p. 5)

The social model does not deny the problems of disability, but locates it "squarely within the society" (Hampshire Coalition of Disabled People, 1995, p. 2).

Community care reforms in the 1980s and the 1990s began to transform the welfare state into welfare pluralism (Department of Health and Social Services Inspectorate and Scottish Office Social Work Group, 1991a, 1991b; Her Majesty's Stationary Office, 1989). For the New Right, the new paradigm included subordination to market forces, a strong managerial class, and the idea of the welfare recipient as a consumer of services, within a new contract culture (Harris, 1996; Holman, 1993). The interest groups saw community-based care and user empowerment. The most visible changes are copious legislation, reduced bureaucracy, budgetary constraints, and an emphasis on private enterprise management (Holman, 1993).

There is a difference of opinion regarding how much resistance social workers mounted to these New Right inroads into the profession. Clapton (cited in Holman, 1993) found no criticisms of the proposals in a two-year search of the social work press, and the same silence is reported from practice (La Valle & Lyons, 1996b).

Brandon and Atherton (1997), however, report long experience of protesting injustices and malpractices within the work setting, as well as the personal and professional consequences of that. According to Cooper (1991), we forgot to ask the most important question. Who needs change?

Today, 15 years after the emergence of community care, the serious consequences of these changes are more apparent: "New welfare can be delivered . . . without anyone having to form a relationship or even see a poor . . .

---

[1] An original reading for *Social Work Processes*.
[2] Social worker and consultant, HealthNet International, Bosnia and Herzegovina, Sarajevo.

sorry, financially challenged . . . person at all" (Harris, 1996; Middleton, 1996, p. 4). Within agencies, decision making is increasingly the domain of elite managers removed from the grassroots work (Holman, 1993).

MANAGERIALISM IN THE MIXED ECONOMY OF CARE

The managers of the mid-1990s present a professional equivalent of the Mafia—"the macho controllers," as Holman (1993, p. 28) calls them. The historical tensions between social workers and managers, dating back to the Seebohm reforms of 1968 (La Valle & Lyons, 1996a), have become more acute. The older managers are former social workers, although some of those in the Social Service Department are from business backgrounds (Holman, 1993; Lewis et al., 1997; Thompson, 1995). However, even managers with social work background lack recent experience, because they carry no caseloads (Holman, 1993; Thompson, 1995). Managers, in the practitioners' view, have lost social work skills. "They do not feel that principles and ethics of services are their direct concern— that is a problem of the Quality Assurance division" (Anonymous for legal reasons, 1997). There is a lack of shared professional themes between managers and practitioners (La Valle & Lyons, 1996a). Rather than client problems, managers are focused on the wishes of the chief executive and other superiors.

At best, managers and practitioners are uneasy bedfellows (Bamford, cited in La Valle & Lyons, 1996a). Social workers feel like cogs in the managerial chain (Holman, 1993). The major problem is that managers do not consult practitioners regarding the many changes that affect practice (Balloch, 1996), which impairs practitioners' role as change agents (La Valle & Lyons, 1996b).

The emergence of underground newsletters underlines the extent of this communication problem and the feeling of powerlessness among social workers. *News from Sammy's Dad* emerged in one local authority because the climate in social services was perceived as discouraging professional comment on matters that concerned practice; the title is a bitter joke derived from the Russian term *samizdat,* used by dissidents in the former Soviet Union for their underground publications (*Sammy's Dad*, 1997). Balloch (1996) found that 58% of approximately 1,200 social workers interviewed were dissatisfied with department management; almost as many did not perceive managers as a source of support.

These tensions lead to high staff turnover, reduce the numbers of social work staff who see their future as including a managerial post (La Valle & Lyons, 1996a), and open the door for more business professionals.

More importantly, who is most affected by this troubled relationship within the mixed economy of care? A letter to *Sammy's Dad* (1997) gives the answer: "I cannot remember being asked in any recent supervision session what impact a recommendation of mine might have on a client" (Anonymous for legal reasons, 1997, p. 8).

SOCIAL WORKERS AS CARE MANAGERS

The Concept of Care Management

Social workers at the grassroots level assess need and plan care; these functions are performed under the title of care manager. Care management has no widely accepted definition, embraces a variety of meanings, and thus contains both open and hidden agendas (Brandon & Brandon, 1988). One view is that care management is an appropriate tool that offers users a choice of services, and hence a measure of control over their lives (Richardson, 1995), while "containing minimal assumptions about the kind of services people should want" (Hudson, 1993). Care management is the point at which welfare objectives and resource constraints meet—where social and economic criteria must be integrated to balance needs and resources, scarcity and choice (Challis, 1994).

Care management refers to any method of linking, managing, or coordinating services to meet individuals' needs. It evolved in North America during the 1970s and 1980s, as a result of concerns about service fragmentation and cost containment in long-term care (Challis, 1995). Services were to be more flexible and related to needs.

Care management has been defined as an "administrative service that directs client movement through a series of phased involvements with the long-term care system" (Capitman, Haskins, & Bernstein, 1986, p. 399). These phased involvements are the seven core tasks of care management:

- Publishing information
- Determining the level of assessment
- Assessing needs
- Planning care
- Implementing the care plan
- Monitoring
- Reviewing

Some contrast care management with social casework and service management, because its emphasis is on tailoring services to the individual needs of particular clients, rather than fitting clients into existing service provision

(Beardshaw & Towell, 1991). Care managers are generally expected to make a holistic assessment of client needs, encompassing physical and social environments and informal care networks, and then to construct and manage a range of service or living options for clients. These goals are yet to be achieved.

O'Connor (cited in Moore, 1990) made an often neglected distinction between care management practice and care management systems. Care management practice is direct practice that contributes to the implementation of a care plan. Care management systems are the administrative structures, integration networks, and formal and informal community resources within which care management practice takes place. Dimensions of care management systems include personnel, status, functions, roles, and focus on target and technology. This distinction is helpful in thinking about changes in care management. Such changes must address not only user experiences but the dynamics—or stasis—of the overall system.

In my own research (Maglajlic, 1996), informants (nine care managers, three other professionals, a residential care worker, nine day-care workers, and three parents) were asked for their definitions of care management. Some struggled: "I haven't really thought about it." "I guess it's about different types of services on offer." Some stressed the primacy of the practitioner: "You take in all their needs and you monitor it." "It's about how they should be cared for." Others placed the service user at the center of the process: "It's a system where you find what is important to someone and translate it into practical support." "It's about getting the best deal that I can for an individual in terms of meeting his needs-led assessment." No one mentioned a partnership with service users.

All informants were pessimistic about how much these processes are needs-led as opposed to service-led. Most pointed to financial restraints and bureaucracy as major barriers: "In the economics-led climate, people tend to go for what is around." "It's not user led; it's led by finances, bureaucracy, everything but the user."

The Practice of Care Management

In practice, care management is characterized by a preoccupation with agency procedures (Lewis et al., 1997); rigid institutional structures inhibit flexible responses (La Valle & Lyons, 1996b). In the new system, social workers perceive themselves as deskilled and pinned down under large caseloads that allow little client contact. "Community care assessments (form based) are a deskfull; an exercise in administration co-ordination and deforestation" (Anonymous for legal reasons, 1997, p. 8).

Care management practice lacks the expected holistic approach. Professionals in different settings (residential, day services, specialist services) are seldom involved in a coordinated manner (Challis, 1994). Existing communication channels are not used, but there is no incentive to create new ones around the care management process. In a rapidly changing environment, the different professions fear a loss of status or relevance; attacks on professionalism of all kinds in the 1980s and 1990s contributed to this fear. As a result, debates on boundaries among different professions overshadow the ostensible purpose, which is to get the best deal for the service users (Carrier & Kendall, 1995). Interprofessionalism, which requires a willingness to surrender work roles, share knowledge, and integrate procedures on behalf of the service users, may be less useful than a multidisciplinary approach, in which practitioners retain their specific knowledge but are willing to collaborate across professional boundaries.

The community care reforms introduced a split between the purchaser (usually a public agency) and the provider. The rationale for this was that providers are driven primarily by their own interests, and not those of clients. The split was supposed to remedy this and increase the quality of services on offer. At the same time, market forces were introduced by public encouragement of private and voluntary providers; in 1993/1994, the first year of the community care reforms, local governments were to spend 85% of their allocated budget on the private and voluntary sector (Holman, 1993). Evidence is now accumulating that the purchaser-provider split has encouraged an overly administrative and mechanistic (Lewis et al., 1997) approach.

Within the purchaser-provider split, commitment to a process led by user needs was to be achieved through budget devolution to the lowest possible level; devolution to the care manager level was proven to be most effective (Sainsbury Centre for Mental Health, 1996). In reality, however, devolution usually stopped at the management level. Care managers thus work toward requirements set by management and administration, and not by service users (Social Services Inspectorate, 1995a). Such a system is disempowering to practitioners and users.

A crisis is slowly developing. Social workers are burdened by lack of resources, vision, and support and by an increase in demand and statutory control requirements (Thompson, 1995). Practitioners who once saw themselves as enthusiastic identifiers of need are now turning into strict rationers (Lewis et al., 1997). One mechanism to resolve conflicts between responsiveness to users' needs and cost containment is advocacy (Challis, 1994). In advocacy, individuals and groups with disabilities press their cases with influential others about situations that affect them directly or try to prevent proposed changes that will leave them worse off (Brandon, Brandon, & Brandon, 1995). Advocacy attracted many social workers into the profession; yet involvement in advocacy on behalf of service users might injure social workers' chances of promotion (Brandon & Atherton, 1997).

The service is no longer universal. Most social service departments now impose eligibility criteria for services. Assessment is offered solely to clients with more complex needs. The judgment regarding whose needs is complex— a new version of the distinction between the deserving and undeserving poor—is not made by social workers but by managers higher up in the hierarchy. While care management is most effective for the clients with the most complex needs (Lightfoot, cited in Cnaan, 1994), there is no justification for the accompanying lack of preventive work (Sainsbury Centre for Mental Health, 1996). This neglect of prevention further de-skills social workers, since it is inconsistent with their values and training.

Workers have little time to maintain relationships with service users. "No-one mentions the complexity of relationship building, the invasion of personal space by the carer. Surely these two issues alone make all purchased care complex? We should be encouraging agencies to employ people able to grasp these issues and not just anyone prepared to accept the lowest rate of pay" (Annoyed social worker, 1997, p. 8).

Although most social workers are employed in the public sector, they are a minority of the total staff in social service departments; administrative staff predominates (Cooper, 1991; Lewis et al., 1997). While agency guidelines leave some latitude for creative interpretation by workers (Elizabeth, 1997; Lewis et al., 1997), half of the social workers in one study reported lack of clarity over what is expected (Balloch, 1996); thus, they were highly dependent on the personality and preferences of managers (Holman, 1993). Services operate in an ideological vacuum, resorting to whatever works (Thompson, 1995). Whatever it is, "it isn't what we were trained to do" (practitioner cited in Lewis et al., 1997, p. 22). The consequence is disillusionment and cynicism among front-line staff.

In a care management context, social work practice must contend with these circumstances (Harris, 1996):

- The social market exacerbates the inequalities between different service users.
- Users are generally uncomfortable with the definition of themselves as consumers.

- Markets are efficient when individuals have the information and knowledge to be the best judge of their own needs.
- Little attention is paid to users' opinions.
- Divisions of class, race, gender, age, disability, and sexual orientation that produce disadvantages within and among social groups are ignored.

The idea of the mixed economy of care lacks the fundamental condition of access to resources (La Valle & Lyons, 1996b). For example, the Community Care (Direct Payments) Act (1997) for which many user groups and professionals campaigned, is still in line with the legacy of the New Right. Many service users—for instance, older individuals—will have no access to the direct payments that the law mandates. Local governments decide who is willing and able to manage their payments, just as they decide, with other community care providers, what need is to be addressed. Rather than service users, the local governments exercise choice and power under the Act.

Service users are also deprived of choice and power under the direct-payment system because of the lack of appropriate information systems. The problems begin when individuals enter the care management system. People who are referred and denied assessment are not provided with any information about care management (Sainsbury Centre for Mental Health, 1996), while people preparing for assessment are commonly unaware of the elements and possible consequences of the process (Audit Commission, 1995) or are swamped by tides of inappropriate information— written, jargonized, and/or only in English.

IMPROVING CARE MANAGEMENT

Documenting Unmet Need

The challenge to social work posed by care management can be partly remedied by making unmet need a political issue (Lewis et al., 1997). This will entail collecting information about the extent and the nature of needs of service users. Doing so may provide a common ground for partnership between social workers and users, but will require the use of advocacy skills (Brandon & Atherton, 1997).

Notable shortcomings of care provision are a chronic shortage of valued services in the community (Beeforth, Conlon, & Graley, 1994) and the difficulty of ensuring continuity of service for the neediest of users, even with good monitoring (Sainsbury Centre for Mental Health, 1996). These issues should be set in a wider context; the question is not how to prioritize resources but how we can change a delivery structure in which priorities are not openly negotiated. The criteria governing resource management should be made explicit, with decisions open to challenge and change (Ellis, 1993).

User Involvement

User involvement became a statutory requirement under the National Health Service and Community Care Act (1990). However, it was legally recognized four years before, in the unimplemented sections of the Disabled Persons Act (1986), which gave individual users and carers the rights to consultation, representation, and information. The Act sought to ensure that service providers were accountable to people with disabilities by conferring these procedural rights at both an individual and collective level of decision making.

Social workers have developed a whole new jargon—quality assurance, consultation, satisfaction surveys, charters, empowerment, partnership, self-advocacy—to make sure that power remains in a firm professional grasp, rather than having more than 50% of users actively involved in all the decision-making bodies (Croft & Beresford, 1993). Few agencies involve users (Arblaster, Conway, Foreman, & Hawtin, 1996). Organizations often suffer from the DATA syndrome: "We're doing all that already" (Fisher & Marsh, cited in Parsloe, 1997).

Users should be involved:

- Across all aspects of system organization—within care planning, consultation, strategic planning, and provision of services (Arblaster et al., 1996)
- In trying to influence existing services and developing their own user organizations (Croft & Beresford, 1993)
- In tackling oppression and discrimination and changing organizational culture (User-Centred Services Group, 1993)
- In addressing common needs of all members of the user group and specific, individual requirements (Poole, 1993)

To promote user involvement, changes will be required in the social care system (Statham, 1996):

- Efficiency should be evaluated on the basis of the use of time, relationships among service users, professionals, and management, or number of episodes rather than criteria that relate to the nature of the task.
- Organizational and management systems must promote user involvement, not the culture of blame.
- The environment in which service users and staff operate is crucial to what can be achieved and should focus on the social nature of needs and social networks.
- Support networks are needed for workers, who are disempowered and not involved.
- The influence of the infrastructure of social care (hierarchies and the interdisciplinary approach) must be acknowledged.
- The goal of independent living must be adopted.
- Social workers need to learn how to utilize policy conflicts and contradiction in order to secure constructive change for users.

The time has come to move beyond an obligatory, tokenistic consultation that doesn't involve setting the agendas but only comments on decisions already made (Orme, 1996). "Users feel like optional extras, brought in to fine-tune details, but not valued enough to have a central role, so that services they need are flawed" (User-Centred Services Group, 1993, p. 20). Even in such limited form, user consultation was implemented in only 4 out of 19 authorities studied by the Social Services Inspectorate (Social Services Inspectorate, 1995b). No attempts were made to specify the machinery for user consultation in legislation, despite its normative recognition (Means & Randall, 1994).

We should remove the hindrances of inappropriate language, incomprehensible and complex systems, and inappropriate meeting style and develop a shared language with service users (Department of Health, 1994). This will require detailed and resourced strategies (Bowl, 1996) to train, inform, and support users (with attention to cultural and disability issues). We need to allow time and flexibility for their involvement, at venues agreeable to all, to pay them for their involvement, to outline the kind of change that is possible, and to secure it as part of the decision-making structures (Arblaster et al., 1996; Croft & Beresford, 1993). Involvement should not focus solely on users' experiences within the system, but should also consider other aspects of their lives and their expectations for the future. This will maintain a framework in which people's lives are more important than service outcomes.

Effective involvement also means providing information: "Victims may not be aware they are victims and do not always know all their real interests" (Means & Randall, 1994, p. 72). Users may be content with receiving services which currently exist, though disillusioned about the nature of services (Brandon & Atherton, 1997). They should not be content with second best (Gibbs & Priestley, 1996). Information should be available through a one-stop-shop approach (People First, 1990), because contacts with many different people intensify the powerlessness of service users. In addition, information systems are presently constrained by decisions made in crisis (Means & Randall, 1994).

Currently, progress toward user involvement is uneven (Statham, 1996). On the one hand, user groups and radical professional groups are developing new ways of working together. On the other hand, users still do not get a picture of what assessments are about and what options exist, are not actively involved in the process, and do not receive a copy of the assessment (Carpenter & Sberiani, 1996). Also, little attention is given to the users who do not meet eligibility criteria and thus do not receive an assessment (Means & Randall, 1994).

All the stakeholders have fears about user involvement. Users fear that their services will be withdrawn if they complain. Professionals and managers fear that they will be swamped by demands that they cannot meet. There is a history of deep mistrust and unequal power between users and professionals. Professionals are driven by their values and personal commitment, which can be both a force for change and an obstacle (Morris, 1994). Users seek allies within the system (User-Centred Services Group, 1993), but those efforts are complicated by their need to rely on professionals for advice (Dowson, 1991).

Management may attempt to subvert user involvement by arguing that the service users who do get involved are not representative. As service users have commented, "When we agree with them, we are representative, when we don't, we aren't" (Croft & Beresford, 1993, p. 28). The growing practice of paying users for their involvement and the stronger voice of user organizations may lead to the emergence of professional users. In this context, it is important to support the involvement of users with severe and complex needs—that is, people who have never been heard (Brandon et al., 1995)—and to pressure organizations to provide the training and resources necessary for user involvement (Arblaster et al., 1996). Effective user involvement will depend on strong political commitment at the government level (Arblaster et al., 1996).

Effective involvement requires an acceptance of people, not just as service users, but as equal citizens with equal rights (Croft & Beresford, 1993). Social rights are conceived in terms of needs, not resources (Orme, 1996). They should be legally based, not procedural; most fundamental is the right to income and nondisabling environments (Means & Randall, 1994).

Such an approach is essential for the protection of users against arbitrary professional power (Means & Randall, 1994). We might contrast user involvement with em-

powerment, which highlights the importance of power (Croft & Beresford, 1993). Empowerment implies citizen control, delegated power, and partnership, all of which are still significantly lacking from the practice of user involvement. We have to keep in mind that the rights that exist are limited. They concern issues that the rest of us take for granted—deciding where to live and what to do during the day, having access to education and employment opportunities. What we call self-advocacy should be part of everyday lives and require no special label; it means, for instance, having the opportunity to say what you want and think and knowing your voice will be heard (Dowson, 1991).

Some social workers (Arblaster et al., 1996; Brandon & Atherton, 1997; Holman, 1993) are advocating a primary relationship with community groups, which thrive on user involvement. Their leaders are elected by local residents and often have first-hand experience of what it means to be a service user. They are also knowledgeable about local needs. Such an approach would alter or remove social works' link to the local government, which is corrosive to professional independence and vitality (Brandon & Atherton, 1997).

Social workers themselves are not consulted within the system, although their input would help to change services (Social Services Inspectorate, 1995b). Mutual partnership between social workers and service users would benefit both groups; in that context, social workers would need to demonstrate their skills in supporting those they are dedicated to serve. An alliance of social workers and service users can provide a sense of vision by communicating outwards and upwards into policymaking (Cooper, 1991; Thompson, 1995). Currently, peer support and development work is not financed by the state because it is not seen as care; the terminology of care should be replaced with one of support (Gibbs & Priestley, 1996).

Concern About Poverty

Concern with poverty has declined among social workers, and yet it should be a major issue because most people who approach social service departments have serious financial problems (Holman, 1993). "The existing government is keen to give the status of consumer to parents whose children are at school, patients in hospitals—but extremely reluctant to give it to those who are poor and disabled" (Brandon & Atherton, 1997, p. 18). We may not have skills to abolish poverty, but we should maintain our role as campaigners to keep it on the national agenda, since it adversely affects most of our user groups, particularly young people and the retired (Brandon & Atherton,

1997). Most social work practice ignores the economic and social deficits of poverty, unemployment, bad housing, urban decay, racism, class discrimination, and inadequate public services (Cooper, 1991).

LOOKING TO THE FUTURE

The deficiencies of social work may be traced to its intensely individualistic values (Holman, 1993), which

- Never explain just why all clients are to be valued and have the right to be regarded as citizens
- Tend to stress individual practice rather than collective action
- Fail to acknowledge that social work may in practice disempower people
- Are not a part of the social framework
- Are limited to what happens at work and do not extend to the way social workers live their lives

In order to combat managerialism, services, training, and research need to be more closely coordinated (Thompson, 1995).

The profession is beset with internal tensions. Academics are perceived as stuck in their ivy tower, and practitioners have yet to be retrieved from stacks of paper and stress-related sick leaves. We have poor skills in taking care of ourselves, which is a paradox in light of the profession we practice. As Walsh (1996) notes, "The cobbler's children are the poorest shod."

A recent study of job satisfaction (Balloch, 1996) shows that 21% of social workers employed by social service departments want to leave the profession; a further 48% want to become independent consultants. British social work has little tradition of private practice (Cooper, 1991). In the United States, by contrast, 15% of all NASW members work privately as primary employment and a further 43% are involved in private practice as secondary, part-time employment (Suppes & Cressy Wells, 1996). An emphasis on private practice would involve rethinking the nature of both social work provision and education in the U.K. In the United States, consumers are making increasing demands for the licensing and certification of social workers. Any move to private social work practice can also be viewed as a move away from the social control of the state over social workers and their practice and, consequently, over service users. My biggest fears are about the generation of social workers born and raised into the profession in the era of marketization. Both privately and professionally, we remember no other practice. Unless we embrace social rights and partnership with service users, we stand an even greater chance of losing the best of our profession (advocacy and community work) and assimilating the worst (market-based, cost-unit thinking and form filling).

READING 22
Self-Help in African American Communities: A Historical Review[1]

Elijah Mickel[2]

The traditional approaches to studying poverty and social policy (Federico, 1984; Friedlander, 1968; Harrington, 1962; Huberman, 1963; Jansson, 1990; Merton & Nisbet, 1961; Myrdal, 1962; Prigmore & Atherton, 1986; Rainwater & Yancey, 1967), as well as related issues such as structural adjustment (Meldrum, 1991; Stein & Nafziger, 1991), have not fully appreciated African Americans' contribution to the development of American social welfare (Pollard, 1978; Ross, 1978). The primary form of social welfare in the African American community has been self-help.

The practice of racism has structured the parameters of social welfare in the United States. Discriminatory practices in large part determined who was served and who served. These practices ignored the many strengths of the oppressed and embellished the contributions of the oppressor.

The Africans dragged in chains to these shores came with a range of skills and abilities—as artisans, artists, priests, farmers, and leaders. Colonial slavery was a continuation of the European serf system, with the modification that individuals could be sold apart from the land (Huberman, 1963; Rodney, 1982). Among African Americans, resistance has largely been linked to the religious community, since the early revolts led by Mackandal, Boukman, Gabriel Prosser, Denmark Vessey, Nat Turner,

---

[1] An original reading for *Social Work Processes*.
[2] Professor, Department of Social Work, Delaware State University, Dover.

Gullah Jack, and others. Resistance to slavery was the first expression of self-help among Africans in America. The examples in Exhibit R22-1 indicate that resistance began with the first contact with the slavers.

THE BLACK CHURCH IN AMERICA

The Black Church in America can be traced from the mystery system in ancient Egypt. According to Herodotus (1909), "Almost all the names of the gods came into Greece from Egypt" (p. 252). The secret societies grew out of this system and developed in parallel in other parts of the African continent. When Africans were transported to the American continents, they brought with them memories of these church forms.

During slavery, the principal occasions of worship were ancestral ceremonies, the most important of which in North America was the ring shout (Stuckey, 1987). The Africans brought memories of home, family, and history, as well as a desire to be free. This desire was rooted in their culture and expressed through their religion:

> The slaves, tempered and toughened by the annealing heat of adversity, turned American Christianity inside out, like a glove, infusing it with African-oriented melodies and rhythms and adding new patterns, such as the ring shout, ecstatic seizure and communal call-and-response patterns. The grand outcome was a new creation, which differed strikingly from the white original. The emblem of this creation was the invisible black church of slavery, which centered in the portable "hush-harbors." (Bennett, 1961, p. 99)

One of the first Black Churches in the Americas was at Silver Bluff, South Carolina; Jesse Peters took control of this church in 1783 (Quarles, 1987; Simms, 1888). The first Black Baptist church was founded in Savannah, Georgia, in 1788 (Simms, 1888). According to the Georgia historic marker commemorating the church,

> On January 20, 1788, the Reverend Abraham Marshall (white) and the Reverend Jessie Peters (Colored) ordained Andrew Bryan and certified the congregation at a Brampton Barn as the Ethiopian Church of Jesus Christ. The Reverend Bryan moved from place to place with his congregation and was even imprisoned and whipped for preaching . . . He persevered and finally bought his and his family's freedom and purchased this lot for his church.

The First African Baptist church in Philadelphia, the African Baptist Church of Boston, and the Abyssinian Baptist Church in New York City were all established in 1809. By 1840, there were more than 300 separate northern black churches (Berry & Blassingame, 1982).

Today, there are thousands of Black churches, with millions of members. These churches are the most powerful, independent social change organizations in the Black community; any intervention in that community must include those institutions if it is to be effective.

SELF-HELP BEYOND THE CHURCH

Self-help organizations also formed independently of churches. In Newport, Rhode Island, for example, a mutual aid society formed in 1780 to record births, marriages, and deaths, to provide for decent burials, to assist members in times of distress, and to apprentice youths to skilled artisans. Under its auspices, the first Black church in Newport was formed in 1824 (Meier & Rudwick, 1966).

From the 1720s on, laws forbidding the formation of fraternal and mutual aid societies were enacted by several states, including Maryland, Virginia, and North Carolina (Berry & Blassingame, 1982). Undaunted, African Americans continued to develop self-help organizations. The African Institute (1835) was the forerunner of Cheney University in Pennsylvania; it began as a program for talented, orphaned African American males.

Self-help organizations embody a basic value system of cooperation, self-determination, and unity. "Regardless of the region, tribe, or community, the helping tradition was deeply rooted in the African way of life. It was to be found almost everywhere that African people existed" (Martin & Martin, 1985, p. 16). African culture mandated an interdependence between free Africans and those who were slaves; it gave Africans a sense of self.

The self-help movement provided a formal structure within which the social service needs of the African American community could be met. Self-help organizations enabled African Americans to develop collective responsibility, economic interdependence, creative purpose, and a belief in themselves.

The early colonizers, too, accepted an obligation to help the needy, but that obligation did not extend to people of color (Trattner, 1979), who had no alternative but to rely on self-help. Mutual support was directed to the alleviation of problems such as hunger, illness, separation, physical disability, physical and spiritual discomfort, and bereavement (Rhone, 1973). Commitment to mutual support is illustrated in the objectives of the Phoenix Society (Exhibit R22-2).

African Grand Lodge 459, founded in 1792 was the first Black freemasons' society in the United States (Crawford, 1914). "The lodge provided its members not just with social recreation, but, more important, with protection

EXHIBIT R22-1
Significant Instances of Resistance

Year	Event
1640	Maryland. John Punch and two white servants found guilty of trying to run away from their master. The whites were given four additional years. John Punch was sentenced to a lifetime of servitude.
1663	Gloster County. African Americans and whites discovered in a conspiracy to overpower their masters and make a break for freedom.
1676	Bacon's Rebellion. Scores of African Americans joined white indentured servants, unemployed workers, and other whites.
1681	Maria and two male companions tried for attempting to burn down the home of their master. One man hanged, one banished. Maria burned at the stake
1708	Newton, Long Island. A band of slaves killed seven whites. Three of the male slaves were hanged. (One was a Native American.) The women were burned at the stake.
1712	New York City. Twenty-three slaves armed themselves and gathered to set fire to a slaveholder's house. Nine whites killed, six injured. Twenty-one slaves were executed.
1732	Slave plot in Louisiana. One African American woman hanged, four males broken on the wheel. Their heads were stuck on poles at each end of New Orleans.
1739	Stone, South Carolina. Slave revolt led by Jemmy. Twenty-five whites were killed before the insurrection was put down.
1741	Kate and African American boatswain convicted of trying to burn down the entire community of Charlestown, Massachusetts.
1766	Slave woman in Maryland executed for setting fire to her master's home, tobacco house, and outhouse, burning them all to the ground.
1791–1804	Haiti. The second republic in the Western Hemisphere. First successful slave revolt against European domination in history.

Year	Event
1800	Gabriel Prosser and Nancy Prosser. Probably the largest slave revolt in the United States took place near New Orleans in 1811. Four to five hundred slaves gathered after a rising at the plantation of a Major Andry. Armed with cane knives, axes, and clubs, they wounded Andry, killed his son, and began marching from plantation to plantation, their numbers growing. They were attacked by U.S. army and militia forces; 66 were killed on the spot, and 16 were tried and shot by a firing squad.
1822	Charleston, South Carolina. Denmark Vessey led a revolt involving thousands of African Americans, 37 of whom were hanged.
1829	Cincinnati, Ohio. Race riot that resulted in more than 1000 African Americans leaving for Canada.
1831	Southampton County, Virginia. Nat Turner's Rebellion. Some 60 whites were killed.
1811–1839	Florida became a haven for escaped slaves and Native Americans. A point of resistance until 1839.
1839	Joseph Cinquez with fellow slaves killed the captain and took the slave ship *Amistad*. (Thirty-five *Amistad* survivors returned to Africa in 1841.)
1841	Slave revolt on the *Creole*. The ship was sailed to the Bahamas, where the slaves received asylum and freedom.
1848	Seventy-five enslaved individuals armed themselves and attempted to leave Fayette County, Kentucky. All were killed or recaptured.
1850s	During the 1850s about a thousand slaves a year escaped into the North.
1859	John Brown's Rebellion, Harpers Ferry, Virginia. Ended with the capture of John Brown.

Sources: Bennett, L. (1961). *Before the Mayflower.* Chicago: Johnson; Giddings, P. (1984). *Where and when I enter: Impact of Black women on race and sex in America.* New York: Murrow; and Zinn, H. (1980). *A people's history of the United States.* New York: Harper & Row.

EXHIBIT R22-2
Objectives of the Phoenix Society (1833)

To visit every family in the ward, and make a register of every colored person in it—their name, sex, age, occupation, if they read, write and cypher—to induce them, old and young, and of both sexes, to become members of this society, and make quarterly payments according to their ability—to get the children out to infant, Sabbath, and week schools, and induce the adults also to attend school and church on the Sabbath—to ascertain those persons who are able to subscribe for a newspaper that advocates the cause of immediate abolition of slavery and the elevation of the colored population to equal rights with the whites—to encourage the females to form Dorcas Societies; to help to clothe poor children of color, if they will attend school—the clothes to be loaned, and to be taken away from them if they neglect their schools, and to impress on the parents the importance of having the children punctual and regular in their attendance at school—to establish circulating libraries, formed in each ward, for the use of people of color, on very moderate pay—to establish mental feasts, and also lyceums for speaking and for lectures on the sciences—and to form moral societies—to seek out young men of talents and good moral character, that they may be assisted to obtain a liberal education—to report to the Board all mechanics who are skillful and capable of conducting their trades to procure places at trades, and with respectable farmers, for lads of good moral character—giving a preference to those who have learned to read, write and cypher—and in every other way to endeavor to promote the happiness of the people of color, by encouraging them to improve their minds and to abstain from every vicious and demoralizing practice.

against the possibility of enslavement for delinquent debts. It participated in the abolitionist movement and sponsored regular programs to aid the poor" (Carson, 1993, p. 12). Other secret orders—the International Order of Good Samaritans, the Ancient Sons of Israel, the Grand United Order of True Reformers, and the Independent Order of St. Luke—offered insurance against sickness and death, aided widows and orphans of deceased members, and gave opportunities for social interaction (Franklin, 1980).

The Grand United Order of Odd Fellows was founded in 1787, and the Independent Order of Good Samaritans in 1847. "The Odd Fellows burgeoned after the Civil War. It is reported to have had 89 lodges and 4,000 members in 1868 . . . and more than 4,000 lodges and almost 300,000 members by 1904" (Carson, 1993, p. 17).

Some mutual aid organizations assumed an oppressive role within the African American community. In Charleston, South Carolina, for example, the Brown Fellowship Society, founded in 1790, excluded dark-skinned African Americans and prohibited discussions of controversial issues such as slavery (Meier & Rudwick, 1966).

Black benevolent associations met the basic needs of the poor and offered free or subsidized education. They also provided financial and human resources for African Americans to promote their own improvement and confront social injustices (Carson, 1993). In line with the patriarchal attitudes of the time, many of these associations excluded women, who responded by forming their own clubs. One of the first women's organizations was Boston's African American Female Intelligence Society, established in 1832. The society sponsored forums and lectures for the general public and provided its members with health insurance and other services. Other early Bostonian women's organizations were the Daughters of Zion, founded in 1845, and the Female Benevolent Firm, founded in 1850 (Carson, 1993). African American women organized for many purposes:

> The Daughters of Tabor, founded in 1855, was an antislavery society. The Women's Loyal Union was founded in 1892 to help combat lynching. The White Rose Industrial Association, established in New York in 1898, helped young black women migrating from the South find jobs and provided them with a place to live so they would not be lured into prostitution. (Carson, 1993, p. 18)

A TALE OF TWO CITIES

Philadelphia

After 1780, when the Act for the Gradual Abolition of Slavery decreed that no child born in Pennsylvania should be a slave, the city of Philadelphia was regarded as a haven for free African Americans. The city's African American population increased by 176% between 1790 and 1800 (DuBois, 1899). An 1847 study found that African Americans in Philadelphia were employed as mechanics, laborers, seafarers, coachmen, carters, shopkeepers, traders, waiters, cooks, hairdressers, musicians, preachers, physicians, and schoolteachers; the majority of African American women were employed in laundry work or domestic service, while a smaller number were employed in needlework or in other trades (Frazier, 1966).

These Philadelphians donated a portion of their income to mutual aid societies; the Free African Society was founded as early as 1787. "In 1853, there were 108 incorporated Mutual Beneficial Societies in Philadelphia having 8,762 members with an annual income of $29,600 . . . A total of 1385 families was assisted to the amount of $10,292.38" (Jackson, 1973, p. 37). Many of the societies were connected with churches, and others were organized by occupation—for example, the Coachman's Benevolent Society and the Humane Mechanics Society. "The Philadelphia Library Company of Colored Persons maintained a well-furnished room with several hundred volumes and scheduled public debates on moral as well as literary topics" (Meier & Rudwick, 1966, p. 106).

As a result of the self-help organizations, the general conditions of the Black population improved. Although oppressed and excluded, this population used its resources to advance the conditions of the general population in the city.

The condition of the Negroes of the city in the last decade of the eighteenth and the first two decades of the nineteenth century, although without doubt bad, slowly improved; an insurance society, in 1796, took the beneficial features of the old Free African Society. Some small essays were made in business, mostly in small street stands, near the wharves; and many were in the trades of all kinds. Between 1800 and 1810 the city Negro population continued to increase, so that at the latter date there were 100,688 whites and 10,522 blacks in the city, the Negroes thus forming the largest percent of the population of the city that they have ever attained. The free Negroes also began to increase from the effect of the abolition law. The school established in 1770 continued, and was endowed by bequests from whites and Negroes. It had 414 pupils by 1813. In this same year there were 6 Negro churches and 11 benevolent societies (DuBois, 1899, p. 23).

The number of societies in Philadelphia reflected the sense of community. It showed the commitment of the African American community to freedom. Self-help was perceived as the vehicle that would move the community

toward freedom. This was exhibited by their involvement in the number of organizations as well as their faith in the interrelationship of one to the other.

New York

The move toward freedom, equality, and justice is exemplified through Africans in America coming together and using every measure at their disposal to overcome oppression. This included the court system. African Americans were from the beginning convinced that the legal system could be used in their own best interest.

> In 1644, some eighteen years after their arrival, the "Dutch Negroes," as they were called, filed a petition for freedom, the first black legal protest in America. The petition was granted by the Council of New Netherlands, which freed the blacks because they had "served the Company seventeen or eighteen years" and had been long since promised their freedom on the same footing as other free people in New Netherlands. (Bennett, 1961, p. 41)

In New York, as elsewhere in the North, free African Americans formed and funded vigilance committees to protect themselves from those who wished to enslave them. These committees also raised money for the support of the sick and infirm and for widows and orphans of deceased members (Hirsch, 1931).

Testimony to the effectiveness of self-help may be seen in the gradual amelioration in the economic conditions of African Americans in New York:

> A decided improvement in this respect was noted by 1851. So evident was this progress that the colonizationists who had repeatedly referred to the poverty of the Negroes and the prejudice against them in the laboring world as a reason why they should migrate to Africa, thereafter ceased to say very much about their poverty. (Lindsay, 1921, p. 196)

Frederick Law Olmsted wrote that in New York, during the severe winter of 1854, he did not see a single African American "among the thousands of applicants for soup, bread, and fuel, as charity . . . The poor blacks always manage to keep themselves more decent and comfortable than poor whites" (cited in Hirsch, 1931, p. 435).

African Americans demonstrated their continuing efforts to overcome the oppression inherent to the society. Although at times it was reported that free Africans were only servants, they obtained and maintained skilled jobs. According to Frazier (1966, p. 149), "In spite of the prejudice in New York City against Negro labor, Negroes were engaged in skilled as well as unskilled occupations. Although in the census for 1850 they were listed chiefly as servants and laborers, some had found a place in the skilled occupations as carpenters, musicians, and tailors."

Mutual aid may also be given much of the credit for a decrease in African American mortality rates in New York and Philadelphia. It appears that a joint population of 37,000 free colored have diminished their ratio of mortality from 1 in 17 in Philadelphia, and 1 in 21 in New York in 1820; to 1 in 40, in both places in 1843, being a distinct improvement in condition of at least 100 percent in 23 years!" (Aptheker, 1951, p. 241).

IMPLICATIONS FOR PRACTICE

The major themes within the history of African American self-help are freedom, justice, mutuality, and social change. These values are fundamental to social work. Practitioners can draw upon an understanding of secret orders and societies, mutual aid organizations, and self-help groups in developing community practice. The history of self-help demonstrates the efficacy of participation by the oppressed in their own liberation struggle and reminds us of the need to mobilize client strengths. Community organizations must be involved in decisions that affect their lives.

The financial basis of self-help organizations is of particular interest. The church-based organization was a successful model. Church organizations existed on the financial contribution of members, as well as their volunteer labor. The leader was charged with building the budget and the goal was usually defined before the collection was taken. This model still exists within many communities.

In times of crisis, practitioners must evaluate many models for self help. Practitioners should not be afraid to look at successful self-help models regardless of the political implications. Simply because we do not agree with the theoretical underpinnings, dare we ignore the possible contribution? Social workers must take a serious look at the women's clubs, secret societies, fraternal and benevolent groups, many of which began with only the desire to change social conditions and the concomitant practices emanating from the community's attitude and oppressive structure. There are answers which can be gleaned from the past. African Americans have provided a successful methodology. Practitioners must do a thorough analysis of the contribution of the past and relate it to the present using it to prepare for the future. Utilizing a nonpathological approach, practitioners can assess the self-help movement and use its strengths.

The historic vision underpinning African American self-help provides a foundation for current social work practice. This vision allowed the self-help groups to effectively challenge poverty and to resist mental, physical, and spiritual oppression.

READING 23
Does My Intervention Make a Difference? Single System Research[1]

Robert W. Weinbach[2]

Relatively few social workers have the opportunity to design and implement program evaluations; a larger percentage participate in them. But *all* social workers should be involved in evaluating whether their methods of intervention are achieving their objectives. The most common method for doing so is single system research (also known as single subject research, $N = 1$ research, single case designs, or ideographic research).

ACCOUNTABILITY AND PRACTICE

The impetus for social work practitioners to evaluate the effectiveness and efficiency of their practice cannot be traced to any one event. Over the past 30 years, many interrelated phenomena have contributed to this impetus, including

- Conservative politicians who spotlight the supposed failures of human service programs (especially public assistance) and demand proof that tax dollars are being used productively
- A reduction in resources for human services, with an accompanying withdrawal of government and charitable funding from programs and services that cannot demonstrate that they work
- Attempts by human service professionals, faced with financial constraints, to identify those services that, if cut, would represent the least loss to client groups
- The argument by vocal consumer advocates that clients have a right to be involved in planning for

[1] An original reading for *Social Work Processes*.
[2] Distinguished Professor Emeritus, College of Social Work, University of South Carolina, Columbia.

services and a right to expect that programs and services will accomplish their objectives

- Mushrooming litigation in which consumers of services seek compensation not only for professional malpractice, but also for promised results that have not been achieved
- Meta-analysis of research reports on the effectiveness of intervention methods
- Professional organizations' emphasis, for over a decade, on the utilization of research by practitioners (Grasso & Epstein, 1992)
- The advent of managed care in the 1990s, with its emphasis on cost containment
- Recent action by the Council on Social Work Education (Council on Social Work Education, 1992a, 1992b, 2001), which accredits social work education programs, ensuring that future social workers will have some understanding of methods for evaluating the effectiveness of their practice

RESEARCH FOR AND BY THE PRACTITIONER

Methods for evaluating the effectiveness of programs and services employ many of the established procedures of scientific inquiry. But they also differ markedly from more traditional research in a number of ways, most dramatically in their objectives. For example, most traditional group research studies attempt to study a sample or portion of the research population. Their goal is to identify relationships between variables within the sample. Statistical methods are used to determine whether the relationships within the sample are likely to be true of the population. In this way, general knowledge is developed for use by others. In program evaluation and single system research, by contrast, we are less concerned with developing general knowledge than with determining whether a given program is working within a given organization (program evaluation) or whether a given treatment appears to be effective with a given case (single system research). The external validity, or generalizability (Rubin & Babbie, 1997), of findings from a program evaluation—that is, the likelihood that those findings would be true of similar or identical programs—is assumed to be low. No two programs are exactly alike; what we learn about one may not be true of another. The results of a single system study are also assumed to have little or no external validity (Marlow, 1998), because, as we know, no two clients or client systems are alike.

With single system research, the social worker wants to know, "Does my intervention method appear to be effective in my work with *this* client or client system?" Single

system research is conducted by responsible practitioners to provide feedback for their own use.

There is little reason why a client or client group should object to being a part of single system research. It involves doing what clients expect a good social worker to do anyway—to conscientiously and objectively monitor their progress toward some objective. For this reason, single system research generally does not require prior approval from an institutional review board or other similar groups that protect the rights of research participants within more traditional group research studies.

When conducting single system research with families, individuals, or groups, there is rarely any need for deception. Clients often participate in identifying and setting treatment objectives. Thus, there is no reason why they cannot be aware that research is occurring; they often participate in collecting and recording data.

In many ways, single system research is more like good practice than like research. Its similarities to traditional group research designs are quite superficial (Yegidis & Weinbach, 1996). Single system research studies a single case, but that is about the only similarity to the exploratory, qualitative research design that researchers usually call a case study. It makes repeated, ongoing measurements of the same variable (such as a behavior or attitude that the social worker is seeking to influence); that is a characteristic of all forms of longitudinal research, but longitudinal studies usually have a slightly different purpose—to learn when and under what conditions certain changes occur. As we have noted, single system research does not seek to make generalizations, as most longitudinal research does.

Single system research has been compared to experimental research. Some authors even refer to certain single system designs as experimental (Bloom, Fischer, & Orme, 1995). Single system research uses a kind of quasi-control group (observations of those times when the intervention is not being offered). It also introduces or manipulates what can be regarded as the independent or predictor variable (the intervention). But it does not meet all of the requirements of a classical experimental research design. Most importantly, the sample (the client system studied) is not selected randomly; it is selected for study because it seems especially appropriate for single system research.

While it is probably employed most with individual clients, single system research is equally suitable for work with couples, families, groups, organizations, or communities (Thyer, 1993). It can be used as long as the social worker can: (1) conceptualize and specify the intervention method being used; and (2) operationalize and accurately measure the behavior, attitude, or other problem that the intervention is designed to influence. Of course, these conditions are not always present.

Sometimes, single system research is not appropriate for another reason. It requires the presence of a clear pattern in the target problem (the dependent or criterion variable, in research terminology). That pattern can be rising, falling, steady, or even fluctuating in some consistent way over time. But it cannot appear to be simply random in its incidence.

The target problem in single system research is most often a behavior, but it may be some other attribute like an attitude or a perception that can be measured repeatedly and accurately. It may be the principal problem experienced by a client or client system, or it may be just one symptom or manifestation of the problem. The target problem may be something undesirable or dysfunctional that the intervention is designed to decrease or extinguish. But it can also be something desirable (for example, assertiveness) that the intervention is designed to increase.

The target problem is measured at regular time intervals, and these measurements are systematically recorded. Any one of several aspects of a problem might be used; the measurements thus generated would reflect different levels of measurement precision (Tripodi, 1994). For example, we could record the frequency (ratio level), duration (interval level), or magnitude (ordinal level) of temper tantrums by a client's 3-year-old child or the length of the interval between them (ratio level). Or we could simply note whether a tantrum occurred during the previous week (nominal level). Which of these measurements would a social worker choose? It depends on the objective of intervention, which should have been agreed upon in partnership with the client. Relevant questions might include:

1. What type of change is sought and what realistic objectives have been set?
2. What is the best way to demonstrate whether or not progress is being made toward achieving the objective of intervention?
3. What would success or lack of success for the intervention look like?

There is an almost infinite number of target problems that a social worker might select as the dependent variable in single system research, for example:

- The number of hours that a mother helps a child with homework
- The number of self-esteem enhancing comments to a child by a parent
- The intervals between family activities

- The number of times that spouses disagree without blaming
- The duration of meals with all family members present
- The number of discussions about child-rearing issues between parents
- The percentage of members who verbally participate in a treatment group
- The number of participants in a group who have sought employment
- The number of workdays lost because of calling in sick
- The number of times that legislators request a social worker's opinion on pending social legislation
- The percentage of registered voters within a community
- The incidence of hate crimes within a community

Note that most of these target problems are expressed in positive terms. While this is not always feasible, it is desirable, because it is consistent with social work values and processes: We seek to increase what is positive, rather than focusing on the negative aspects of problems. Note also that most of these examples involve a behavior that is easily measured. With single system research, simple is almost always better.

Often, single system research involves an innovative intervention that we think may prove effective, or an intervention that is generally believed to be effective with one problem or client but has yet to be tried with another one. Single system research is exploratory; the social worker thinks, "I wonder if I can demonstrate that this is associated with a difference?" It is often the precursor to replication with other similar clients who have the same target problem or, ultimately, to various forms of group research designed to have more external validity.

SINGLE SYSTEM RESEARCH AS GOOD SOCIAL WORK PRACTICE

Do good social workers evaluate their practice using single system research, or is single system research really just a form of good social work practice? That's an academic question. The truth is that single system research methods are very consistent with good practice. Much of what is done in conducting single system research is what a good practitioner would do anyway—except that, perhaps, single system research helps us to do it in a more systematic way. For example, it has been suggested elsewhere in this book that, in social work practice, the independent variable (the

---

EXHIBIT R23-1
Planning for Single System Research

1. Briefly describe the client's problem or at least its manifestation.
2. Specify the target behavior, attitude, or other factor (the dependent variable) and how you propose to measure it. Remember, it may be just a symptom of an underlying problem if that symptom is to be the focus of some intervention.
3. Identify what pattern of the dependent variable exists (stable, rising, falling, and so on).
4. In 50 words or (preferably) less, specify the treatment or intervention to be used (the independent variable), and how it will relate to other, ongoing services to the client.
5. Conduct a literature review. Identify research studies or professional literature suggesting that your treatment may produce the desired results.
6. Select the single system design most suitable for examining the relationship between the independent and dependent variables. Specify why it is the best, given such factors as time and ethical constraints.
7. Determine which pattern of the dependent variable would indicate that your intervention may be related to a desired effect with your client—that is, the goal of treatment that you and the client have agreed upon.
8. Determine what pattern(s) would suggest the possibility that your intervention may have promoted unhealthy dependency or some other unintended consequence.
9. Conduct the research, carefully graphing the fluctuations in the dependent variable.
10. Carefully analyze the research results relative to steps 7 and 8. If the pattern in step 7 is observed, speculate on what other clients might find the intervention helpful.
11. Replicate the research with similar clients or with other clients who might benefit from the intervention.

---

intervention) is often poorly conceptualized. One of the most important steps in planning for single system research is to develop a clear conceptualization and specification of the intervention. It is not enough to merely conduct research that asks, "Did my intervention make a difference?" We want to know exactly *what* made a difference; that is the only way that we can learn from our efforts.

Similarly, measuring the dependent (or criterion) variable forces the social worker to clearly define and specify the treatment goal and to develop or find objective ways of measuring it. This is also very consistent with sound social work practice. For example, if alcohol abuse is the general problem, what is the treatment objective—total abstinence, not drinking on the job, drinking that does not involve abuse of family members, or some other type of alcohol-related behavior? In the participatory planning process, what did the social worker and the client adopt as a realistic objective? Would the substitution of another substance be indicative of treatment success or failure? Should the dependent variable be the amount of alcohol consumed over a time period, the frequency of bouts of drinking, their duration, their magnitude, or the length of time between them? The specification and measurement

of the dependent variable will inevitably depend on what objective was agreed upon, as will any good treatment planning. Note the other similarities between the steps in planning single research in Exhibit R23-1 and the usual questions asked in good social work assessment and treatment planning.

Step 6 in Exhibit R23-1 alludes to ethical concerns. On the surface, it might seem that single system research can produce numerous ethical dilemmas for the social worker. However, most of these concerns stem from a misunderstanding. Whenever single system research is conducted, strict adherence to professional ethical standards is emphasized. Clients are not denied access to needed treatment. Rather, the intervention method that the social worker is evaluating is offered as an adjunct to the usual treatment or intervention—not usually as a replacement for it. For example, while a patient in an inpatient psychiatric facility participates in occupational therapy, group treatment, physical therapy, and medication therapy, a social worker might employ intervals during which some other intervention is alternately offered and not offered. Then, the data could be examined to see if the presence or absence of the intervention is associated with some behavior—for example, a reduction in acting-out. In this way, the withdrawal of the intervention (a requirement of the research design) is not an ethical problem.

In accordance with social work values, single system research must always be subordinate to clients' welfare. It can be terminated prior to its completion for ethical reasons. If, for example, a social worker concludes that an intervention is associated with an undesirable fluctuation in the target problem, it should not be reintroduced, even if the research design calls for its reintroduction. Conversely, another social worker may decide that, in the client's best interest, an intervention that appears to be highly effective should be continued indefinitely, even though the research design calls for its withdrawal.

The various single system research designs are all, in a sense, variations on a theme. In all such designs, the target problem is subjected, alternately, to periods when the specific intervention is offered (B phases) and periods when it is not (baseline or A phases); a chart is kept of its fluctuations. The simplest design, known as AB, consists of an observation period in which the dependent variable is measured and recorded but the intervention (independent variable) is not offered (A) and then a period in which the dependent variable is measured and recorded with the inclusion of the intervention (B). This design is generally used when the social worker believes that the effects of the intervention are likely to be permanent. For example, an intervention to increase assertiveness might be tested using an AB design because it is believed that assertiveness, once learned, is self-reinforcing.

Other designs add one or more A or B phases. For example, an ABA design adds a second A phase after intervention to see if the dependent variable changes when treatment is withdrawn. An ABAB (reversal) design adds both second baseline (A) and second intervention (B) phases to see what happens to the dependent variable when the intervention is withdrawn and then re-introduced. Another specialized design is ABCABC, which monitors the effects of twice introducing two different successive interventions on a single dependent variable, while multiple baseline designs measure outcomes across clients, across settings, and across clients' multiple target problems (Thyer, 1993). More complicated designs attempt to ensure that any difference in the dependent variable is indeed a function of an intervention; that is, they try to increase the internal validity (Rubin & Babbie, 1997). Such designs probably produce more definitive answers about a social worker's practice effectiveness, but they involve a loss of simplicity. They may require that a social worker receive advanced research training and devote more time to single system research than can be justified.

Ideally, research begins in an A phase of observation, with no intervention, so that a baseline can be established; longer A phases are desirable because they "contain enough points to establish the unlikelihood that extraneous events affecting the target problem will coincide only with the onset of intervention" (Rubin & Babbie, 1997, p. 322). However, requiring an initial A phase may pose ethical concerns. What if the dependent variable is a behavior that represents a serious problem or is even life threatening, such as unsafe sex practices? Sometimes a valid retrospective baseline can be based on a recollection of what has occurred in the recent past. If this is impossible, can we ethically withhold a potentially effective intervention during the baseline phase? Of course not! We could select a research design that begins with an intervention phase (such as BAB), even though it may not be the design of choice from a purely research perspective.

Note that the research can start after treatment has been in progress for months or even years. Alternatively, if a design calls for the research to end in an A phase (for example, an ABA design), an intervention that seems to correlate with desirable changes in the target problem can always be reinstituted after the final A phase.

INTERPRETING FINDINGS

Once a design is selected and implemented, the social worker records and plots the frequency, duration, and other aspects of the target problem at regular intervals and observes the patterns that develop. Computer software packages for personal computers store and graphically display data and provide appropriate statistical analysis (Bloom et al., 1995); hand-generated graphs can also be used. The time dimension (hours, days, weeks, months, number of interviews, and so on) is displayed along the horizontal axis, while the measurements of the dependent variable are displayed along the vertical axis. The social worker can use the chart for ongoing feedback and is constantly seeking to interpret it. The research graph or chart might provide the focus for a discussion of treatment progress with the client. For example, the social worker might suggest that, according to the graph, a recovering stroke patient seems to be spending more time in performing activities of daily living. Client and worker might also examine together the degree of consistency of any pattern observed. When the research has been completed, the social worker and client can look at the entire pattern of the dependent variable. Practice knowledge, values, and skills will suggest many questions, for example:

1. What else was going on in the client's life during the research?
2. What components of the treatment package besides the independent variable may have contributed to changes in the dependent variable?
3. How may the passage of time or normal physical processes have influenced the dependent variable?
4. How much dependency on the social worker is reflected in the fluctuations in the dependent variable, and is this desirable?
5. How efficient (costly) is the intervention, given the results documented?
6. How likely is the pattern to continue after permanent discontinuation of the intervention?
7. Overall, how consistent are the results with treatment goals and objectives?

AN EXAMPLE:
INTERVENTION IN A SUPPORT GROUP

The social work research literature includes many examples of single system research with individual clients. The following case illustrates its use in a group context.

Rhoda, a social worker in a large general hospital, was leading a support group for 10 children with Type I (insulin dependent) diabetes who were having trouble controlling their blood sugar. In reading about juvenile diabetes and talking to colleagues, she learned that many children continue to eat sugar-flavored foods, despite the hazards to their health, because they think they won't like the taste of foods prepared with sugar substitutes. She wanted to see if regular exposure to a pleasant-tasting snack made with sugar substitutes and other low-calorie ingredients might contribute to better control of blood glucose level among her group members. She defined her intervention as "bringing in a home-cooked sugar-free snack and spending five minutes of each group session with all group members tasting it and discussing it." Her dependent variable was a measurement already in use and available—the results of the children's blood test taken three days after each group session. At the testing, clinic staff recorded whether each child was within the optimum blood glucose range.

Rhoda selected an ABAB design for her research. Since the target problem was not immediately life threatening for the children, she felt that, ethically, she could begin her research in a nonintervention (A) phase. She also believed that ABAB, with its four phases, would allow a pattern of relationship between the dependent and independent variables to develop, if the intervention made a difference. She recognized the major limitations of the research. She knew

that the glucose reading taken in the hospital may not have been typical for any or all of the children. She also could not control the other two major influences on blood glucose level (besides diet): insulin intake and exercise. But, she knew that single system research seeks association between variables and does not attempt to uncover relationships of cause and effect. Rhoda implemented her research and kept a chart of the results (Exhibit R23-2). Was her intervention effective? As with most single system research efforts, there were few conclusive findings. But she made three important observations that influenced her future practice as a group leader:

1. Overall, the children showed a desirable change in the dependent variable over the course of the research.
2. There were no dramatic changes when the intervention was introduced or withdrawn.
3. Verbal participation by group members, while not a target for change, increased dramatically over the course of the research. By week 16, all children were active participants.

These findings suggested many questions, for instance:

1. Given that the percentage of children with their blood glucose level in control consistently and dramatically improved over the 16 weeks, should the intervention be regarded as successful?
2. If so, does the research suggest that the periodic reinforcement method used is the best way to employ the intervention?
3. Does the lack of a decline in the dependent variable when the treatment was withdrawn indicate that the treatment was not closely associated with changes in the dependent variable or that it had a healthy carryover effect?
4. Would a decline at these points have been consistent with treatment goals of independent blood sugar management?
5. Would the changes in the dependent variable have occurred even without the intervention, because of experience, learning, maturation, time, or some other factor?
6. Did the increased verbal interaction within the group contribute to change in the dependent variable or was it, perhaps, the other way around?
7. Did the intervention contribute more to increased verbal participation in the group than to changes in the dependent variable? If so, what are the treatment implications?

EXHIBIT R23-2
ABAB Design for the Tuesday Afternoon Group

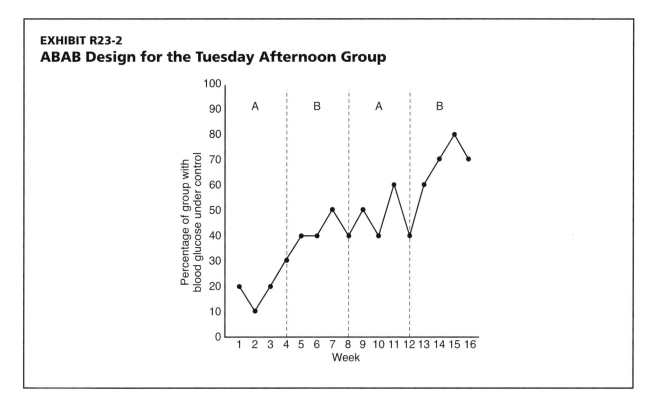

Rhoda could not isolate any cause-effect relationships between her intervention and the dependent variables using the ABAB design. However, the intervention had been associated with two desirable changes—the group's improved blood glucose level and the increase in their verbal participation—both of which, in her experience, did not usually occur until later in a group's existence. Did it matter exactly how and why these desirable changes occurred? Probably not, at least not at this early stage of her inquiry. She decided to replicate her research with a diabetic support group that was about to begin.

STRENGTHS AND WEAKNESSES

Single system research will never replace group research as a means of generalized knowledge building for the social work profession. Findings derived from single system research have limited external validity; only through replication with similar clients can more generalized knowledge regarding practice effectiveness be generated. Single system research is also vulnerable to charges that it lacks internal validity (Marlow, 1993), in that we can only speculate on the degree to which changes in the dependent variable might have resulted from something other than the intervention. Further, single system research is difficult to use with some problems, especially those that are not easily measured. It is most suitable when the client has one major problem, rather than in situations where the client system has a multitude of equally severe and interrelated problems. However, if the problems are mutually reinforcing, single system research can be used to see if an interaction is associated with changes in one of them that may help to break up the cycle.

Single system research requires administrative support and encouragement. The results should be used only for candid feedback to the individual social worker; they should never be used for administrative evaluation by a supervisor.

The limitations of single system research are common to social work practice, which must often depend on the self-report of clients or their significant others for data on the dependent variable. The social worker must assume that the information received is truthful, which is questionable when working with problems characterized by denial or distortion. It is also difficult to know about—much less to control—other factors that may be influencing the target behavior. Moreover, when clients substitute one problem for another—for example, cocaine dependency for alcohol dependency—how can the success of an intervention be judged? Defining the dependent variable broadly—for example, as substance abuse—will help in this case.

The advantages of single system research clearly outweigh its limitations and demands. It is inexpensive, both in dollars and in time required. The basics are easily taught and understood in a one-day workshop. Single system research raises few ethical issues because it is consistent with good professional practice. In contrast to many group research studies, utilization of findings is virtually guar-anteed. Findings, while always tentative, can provide good early feedback on the effectiveness of a new intervention, which can be discarded if it appears to make no difference or reevaluated through replication.

Single system research is well-suited to task-centered, problem-solving methods of practice. It is consistent with a wide variety of methods and social work processes that stress the importance of sound, accountable social work practice. It is also well suited to the participatory methods of social work practice described elsewhere in this book.

READING 24
Termination in Context[1]

Howard Hess[2] and Peg McCartt Hess[3]

A distinctive characteristic of the worker-client interaction—whether a single interview for the purpose of assessment and referral or a therapeutic relationship, extending over a series of interviews—is that it must end. Termination raises issues of separation and self-sufficiency and will also require both client and social worker to evaluate their work together. Because of these issues of separation and evaluation, ending can be difficult for both client and practitioner (Fox, Nelson, & Bolman, 1969; Shulman, 1992; Siebold, 1991; Siporin, 1975; Webb, 1985). In many instances, ambivalence about the ending causes both to vacillate in their judgments about an appropriate conclusion to their work. Their ability to resolve this ambivalence determines the quality of the termination experience.

In mastering termination, clients must accomplish two general tasks: First, they must confront and begin to accept the impending separation from their helpers; and, second, they must come to terms with the outcome of the helping process. Client awareness of both loss and outcome is stimulated by the encroaching time limit. At no other phase in the process is time such a powerful influence.

Because clients and practitioners often form close attachments, termination typically involves working through the grief associated with a break in these ties; as well as a clear evaluation or review of accomplishments. If the goals of working together have been accomplished, clients can be helped to acknowledge the appropriateness of ending. Conversely, if the goals have not been accomplished, the client can be helped to determine whether the goals were realistic and how problem solving can continue after the end point with the practitioner. When the helping process is disrupted, the termination work should clarify the nature of the necessary referral or transfer. As the work is reviewed, clients often experience a blend of pride in accomplished change, hope for the future, and sorrow about the loss of a valued resource.

The interrelationship between loss and evaluation during termination is clear in the following extract from a final interview:

Student: We haven't talked very much about the fact that this is my last visit to you. I just wanted to hear how you're feeling about that.

Client: I'd rather you'd stay on . . . and still come . . . In a way I hated for you even to come today because I said I won't see her from now on . . . I said, well maybe I'll just leave the house and that way she might have to come back . . . I said no, I'll just wait.

Student: Endings are hard, C, and it's hard for me, too, because you've been a very important person to me these last months.

Client: You've helped me a lot. When nobody else could. Just sitting down and talking. Other people say you're wrong, you're wrong. You're crazy. You think you are crazy. What's wrong with you? That's all I ever hear from B. I can't talk to B about nothing.

Student: It feels good to be able to talk and to say what's on your mind and not be judged. I'm glad that it has been helpful to you to have someone to talk to. I think

---

[1] An original reading for *Social Work Processes.*

[2] Rector, St. Christopher's Episcopal Church, Kingsport, Tennessee and formerly Associate Dean, Fordham University Graduate School of Social Service

[3] Professor and Director of Doctoral Studies, College of Social Work, University of South Carolina, Columbia.

you've done some things for yourself, too, C. That's kind of what I'd like to pay attention to just now.

Client: What?

Student: I'd like to talk about what you've been doing for yourself that has been helping.

Client: Yeah, but you know I just started almost not wanting to go back to the doctor's and the only thing that made me really want to go back was that I started bleeding yesterday.

Student: Uh-huh.

Client: 'Cause I really started feeling again like I just didn't care no more.

Student: I wonder . . .

Client: Easy let down . . . It's easy for me to feel let down like that. Very easy.

Student: I wondered . . . I was thinking about what you had said last time. That you didn't want to be dependent on anybody and so forth. If that might have something to do with the fact that you had grown dependent on me over these past few months and that I was going to let you down just like everybody else has.

Client: I was thinking about how I'll feel about that other social worker. I don't know if I'll be able to talk to her like I've been able to talk to you. I might feel angry toward her. I've been thinking about that and feeling if maybe I'd feel angry because she's trying to take S's place. And it won't be the same.

THE CONTEXT OF TERMINATION

Although the termination phase is unique, it cannot be accurately understood except in the context of an entire course of treatment. Decisions made early about focus and goals directly determine the potential for review during termination. A theme that continues throughout the entire treatment process is the attachment between client and helper that develops during early and middle phases. Consequently, the practitioner's awareness of differential relationship patterns is crucial in planning and managing termination. In addition, termination always occurs within a specified social context, including the organization that sponsors and shapes the helping process.

Problem Definition

Clarity about the focus of the helping process is necessary to successful termination. The determination of how long the treatment will continue and how activities will be structured follows from the specification of client problems and agreement about objectives. The objectives are then reworked throughout the helping process and re-

flected in the specific termination plan. In this respect, the quality of review at termination depends directly on the clarity of the treatment objectives. Lack of precision in the early and middle phase of the work creates difficulty in measuring the extent to which the objectives have been achieved. Correspondingly, the point of termination is more difficult to establish, and relationship may become the focus of the work, rather than the vehicle.

If client problems are developmental, the termination might be designed to allow periodic checking in with the practitioner as the developmental progression continues (Golan, 1981). If the client problems are related to specific material or physical difficulties, on the other hand, a fixed end point might be appropriate. When the expectations of the outcome of the helping process are shared and based upon a skillful assessment, the format of termination will have already been suggested.

Clients' expectations concerning what will be derived from the helping process are maintained by hopes for specific change, as well as the subjective meaning or value of the helping relationship. As the work progresses, the practitioner must monitor and maintain the appropriate balance between objective achievement and relationship gratification. Termination decisions should reflect that balance.

The Helping Relationship

The attachment between client and social worker is one source of the feelings experienced in termination. The impending separation runs counter to many clients' hope that this attachment would continue indefinitely. Accordingly, termination may engender ambivalence in both client and practitioner; in a sense, this ambivalence mirrors the ambivalence about the beginning of the work together. Our knowledge about the separation or individuation process verifies the presence of strong and often contradictory feelings about leaving valued others (Kauff, 1977). Mastery of termination requires both client and practitioner to experience and share a variety of reactions to the ending.

One way that social workers can prepare for termination is to teach clients about the predictable reactions to loss and to assist them in identifying those reactions when either directly or indirectly expressed. Various authors have written about the predictable stages of the grief process: denial, anger, sadness, acceptance, and disengagement (Germain & Gitterman, 1996; Kubler-Ross, 1969; Lindemann, 1956; Webb, 1985). For example, clients who have previously experienced multiple or traumatic losses may react with sadness and feelings of abandonment. On the other hand, clients who have succeeded in achieving desired gains in treatment may be particularly proud and self-confident during termination (Fortune, 1987). Do not assume that all clients uniformly transverse these stages in lockstep fashion or that all clients react to termination with the same intensity. However, both clients and practitioners tend to deal with termination initially with denial and/or distancing. This may take many forms, varying from general detachment to premature discontinuation of sessions. Initially, these reactions may provide the client with space for adaptation; appropriate focus by the practitioner often aids in surmounting the denial and allows open exchange about the discomfort and confusion associated with loss. If they experience uncertainty about their own capacity to deal with the ending, however, practitioners may encourage clients to remain in a state of denial as a form of self-protection. As noted earlier, separation and ending inevitably evoke self-examination regarding competence and accomplishment; social workers and clients alike are forced to confront their own limitations.

It is the responsibility of the practitioner to guide the ending process, through appropriately timed interventions and self-disclosure. Honest expression of the practitioner's own reactions during the termination phase facilitates the client's expression of responses stimulated by termination. Through this mutual exchange or sharing of reactions, the reality of the ending is verified.

A major task of termination is to construct a bridge between the services provided and the clients' subsequent problem-solving efforts. In part, this may be accomplished through a synthesis of termination evaluation and future planning. Clients should be empowered, through termination, to embark on a self-directed course of action based upon a realistic assessment of their problem-solving strengths. Successful termination supports client self-esteem, reinforces the client's hope that progress will continue, and also frees the client to reinvest energy in appropriate life tasks and ongoing relationships that support problem solving.

DIFFERENTIAL PATTERNS OF ATTACHMENT

So far, feelings related to loss in termination have been discussed in the context of the open-ended helping relationship between an individual client and practitioner. However, individual counseling is only one type of social work process. Many clients present problems related to inadequate resources or information and have limited need for counseling. In addition, many clients are best helped within their families or in small groups.

Variations in client problems and goals and in the modality used are associated with important qualitative differences in the nature of termination. In different types of work, the nature of the client-practitioner attachment varies, as does the focus and length of time required for the termination phase. Variations in termination as a function of the primary intervention activities and system size are summarized in Exhibit R24-1. Let's consider these variations in more detail, for each of the primary activities.

Counseling

Individual counseling often allows for the development of a high degree of mutual attachment, which tends to increase as the process continues. Termination of individual counseling is quite likely to prompt elements of the grieving process for client and practitioner. Termination of a predominantly counseling relationship may be time-consuming. For example, in treatment of a year's duration, the last eight weeks would be utilized for ending, as would two of the last 8–12 interviews in short-term treatment (Reid & Epstein, 1972; Shulman, 1992; Webb, 1985). Inattention to termination or prolonged denial may provoke regression and circumvent solidification of gains. The practitioner's role is to monitor and persistently call attention to the dynamics of the ending phase.

Counseling with families and small groups can also entail an intense relationship between clients and practitioner. The major distinction between family or group and individual treatment is that any single client's attachment is to multiple others. In fact, one of the practitioner's major goals in work with families and small groups is to facilitate individuals' communication with others, as well as to solidify members' attachments with one another; the attachment between the individual client and practitioner is diffused throughout the client system. Although a family's termination with the practitioner may be difficult for individual family members, the experience of loss is often modified by the reality that the family is likely to remain intact and members can turn to one another for support. The practitioner's role during termination is to underscore the family's interpersonal resources. Loss of the practitioner is moderated by the attachments shared by family members and by review of the system's shared treatment accomplishments.

In the group, several phenomena may be present (Shulman, 1992). If the group is ongoing or naturally formed—for instance, a neighborhood group, classroom, or cottage unit—individual group members may turn to one another for assistance during and following termination. In a group that disbands at termination (a formed group, in the terminology of Exhibit R24-1), termination can be quite emotionally charged, because members lose the group as

EXHIBIT 24-1
Variations in Termination

Primary activities	System size		
	Individual	*Group*	*Family*
Counseling	Attachment may be intense	Attachment may be intense but shared among group worker, group as a whole, and other members.	Attachment may be intense, but is shared with other family members.
	Loss in termination may include considerable avoidance and/or grief, which must be openly managed and processed in mutual interaction.	Grief may be considerable; when formed groups terminate, focus must be on ending and multiple separations. In natural groups, loss is moderated by ongoing ties between members. Termination should include support of group's ongoing motivation to support members.	Loss moderated by family's continuation. Termination focus is on improved attachments and communication within family system.
Education	Attachment may be of moderate intensity.	Attachment usually more moderate in intensity.	Attachment often more moderate in intensity.
	Ending often preset in original plan and focuses on success in learning and generalization beyond treatment setting.	Differences persist between formed and natural groups, but have less impact upon the nature of termination. Emphasis in both groups is on evaluation of learning. Some formed groups may continue after treatment ends.	As family is usually ongoing, termination includes focus on members' mutual support and application of learning that has occurred.
Resource mobilization (referral, brokerage, mediation, advocacy)	Attachment may be intense, but transitional and/or intermittent.	Attachment may be intense but is present among multiple group members.	Attachment may be intense and may have strengthened family relationships.
	Loss moderated by attachment to new resource and/or need satisfaction. Focus is on evaluation of mobilization, with door open for return. Loss not usually a theme in termination discussion.	Termination should enhance group's capacity to locate and utilize resources independently. During this phase, some formed groups will develop into natural groups and maintain their ties.	Termination should enhance the family's capacity to locate and utilize resources independently. Specific skills regarding resource use may be consolidated during termination.

a whole, other group members, and the group worker. The group practitioner must facilitate the members' ability to detach from the group. In this instance, the practitioner places major emphasis on the group members' efforts to deal with the loss of one another and acts as a catalyst, encouraging member interactions.

Educational Interventions

Educational interventions tend to maintain a focus upon cognitive processes; the major goal is learning, rather than emotional change or stabilization. Although intimate relationships certainly can develop when the helping goals and supporting interventions are educational, the attachment between client and practitioner may be less intense than in counseling situations. The point of termination is often preset by the nature and amount of material to be learned. There is typically less client concern that termination will endanger the maintenance of what has been learned and more emphasis on utilization of the new skills beyond treatment. The practitioner's educational interventions encourage generalization of learning through rehearsal, practice, and positive reinforcement in the client's natural environment. A clear focus on evidence of the client's learning and self-sufficiency is the most effective method of solidifying gains during the ending period. Educational interventions with families (family life education) or groups (parent education groups) are not likely to result in intense attachments between clients and practitioners or, correspondingly, in feelings of loss at termination.

Resource Mobilization

Interventions focused on resource mobilization may include referral, mediation, brokerage, and/or advocacy. In these instances, the relationship is often intense, and attachment develops rapidly between client and practitioner, either because of the urgency of the identified problem or because client and worker participate closely in a mobilization effort directed toward an outside source. However, in spite of the intensity of the effort, the worker is acting as a way station to an additional helping resource somewhere else. Consequently, termination is focused heavily on the success of resource mobilization and less on the attendant interaction between client and practitioner. Resource mobilization with families and groups is also highly task-focused. Termination is expected when the resource is activated but might include a provision for additional contact should resource problems reappear. Although attachments may be strong throughout a specific period, the relationship expectations are clearly limited. Therefore, termination may be less emotionally charged and may re-

quire an emphasis on evaluation of outcomes rather than issues of loss or grief.

Certain general statements can be made about differences in the helping relationship associated with the primary activities and the system size:

1. More exclusive relationships between client and practitioner will usually result in more intense attachment. Greater intensity of attachments typically necessitates greater attention to the grieving process. Generally, family and group systems provide multiple resources for resolution of grief; feelings of loss are diffused and shared with other clients.

2. Termination is likely to be more emotionally charged as the attachment between client and practitioner increases. The ending phase of such relationships will require sensitive support and encouragement toward self-sufficiency. As already noted, certain interventions more typically result in greater client reliance on the practitioner.

3. Reactions to the loss of the practitioner will be more limited if clients can continue in relationships that were a part of the helping process. Clients in families and ongoing groups are more likely to substitute one another for the lost practitioner and thereby more readily resolve the grieving process.

4. Themes of loss and evaluation can be expected in the termination of each helping relationship, and therefore clients' ideas and feelings with regard to each theme should be recognized and explored.

ORGANIZATIONAL INFLUENCES UPON TERMINATION

Termination will also be shaped by the organizational context within which social work intervention occurs. The organizational mission sets limits on the nature of the client problems that can be addressed and the typical or preferred treatment modalities utilized. Intra- and interorganizational factors may also affect the timing and character of termination.

The impact of the organizational mission is most evident in settings where social workers provide a secondary service, such as hospitals, schools, emergency shelters, and the workplace. In such settings, clients are typically eligible for the practitioner's assistance only for the duration of their involvement with the primary service. Thus, the relationship with a social worker is usually terminated when patients are discharged from the hospital, children reach the end of the school year, clients leave an emergency shelter, or employees quit or are fired. While such setting-specific endings are planned and anticipated openly by the client and practitioner together, the ending itself may be experienced as an unnatural or premature closure. A social worker in a children's hospital comments, "Each morning when I come in to work, the first thing I do is check the census to see who's missing." Such abrupt endings may be accompanied by a brief follow-up period for attention to termination issues or by referral of the client for continuing services. However, provision of time to accomplish the tasks of termination is crucial both for clients, whether or not they seek services elsewhere, and for practitioners.

Settings in which social services are the primary organizational mission also structure beginnings and endings of client-practitioner relationships through available program options and preferred treatment modalities. For example, a public agency mandated to serve all persons requesting services in a geographic area, such as a community mental health center, may develop guidelines limiting the duration of client services or designating the modalities to be utilized, such as crisis intervention, solution-focused treatment, or group treatment. In negotiating the service agreement, you should inform clients of such agency guidelines, to ensure the realistic definition of treatment goals.

Other organizational factors also affect the helping process. For example, requirements for practitioners' productivity or for third-party reimbursement for agency services may place subtle or explicit pressures upon practitioners. There may be an expectation that social workers will continue with clients beyond contracted services in order to inflate the direct service time or will terminate prematurely because the client's reimbursement benefits have been exhausted. Practitioners may also be expected to extend services up to a client's benefit limit regardless of need (Strom-Gottfried, 1997) or to terminate prematurely in order to shrink the agency's waiting list. Managed care companies may also preempt decisions about the timing of termination: "For clients who have been approved for some managed care payments, the social worker's report of positive treatment outcomes frequently inclines the case reviewer to stop payment for further services because the client's needs are then determined to be not great enough" (Davidson & Davidson, 1996, p. 209). The possibility that a client's personal information is maintained in the managed care company's file after termination is also troubling (Davidson & Davidson, 1996). Pressures regarding the timing and management of termination increasingly present ethical dilemmas for the individual social worker, as well

as for the organization. These dilemmas require skillful balancing of client need and organizational demands (Reamer, 1995b) and inevitably impact on the practitioner's feelings about the employing agency and about beginnings and endings with clients.

If clients have been referred involuntarily by the courts or other systems, such as the workplace or a school, potential difficulties in termination arise when the problem definition and/or length of treatment are determined externally and as a condition for a child's return home from foster care, an employee's return to work, or a continuation of probation.

Organizational commitments to professional training also shape the termination process. An exploratory study of students' termination of individual clinical work at the end of an academic year found that students in the sample appeared to learn about termination primarily from their agency supervisors (Gould, 1978). Students' first-year field agency supervisors, as well as several of the second-year supervisors, had encouraged students not to discuss the predictable training-related ending of treatment with their clients until the latter part of treatment (Gould, 1978). This policy could potentially have a destructive impact on the helping process, particularly in the termination phase. "By contrast, where agencies are open and direct about their training function and present their students as supervised learners, clients expect the student's departure at the end of the academic year, and termination and transfer are likely to be viewed as legitimate (though some people do 'forget' they were told at the start)" (Germain & Gitterman, 1996, pp. 312–313).

Because the organizational context influences the nature of the help offered and received, it is crucial that inter- and intraorganizational factors be fully and openly weighed early in the process, as the client and practitioner explore goals, options, and tasks together, and in the ending phase, as feelings and ideas regarding loss and evaluation emerge.

SELF-AWARENESS IN TERMINATION

In the ending phase, the worker must be open to a range of intense feelings and reactions from the client, including sadness, anger, and negative evaluation of their work together. Clients may also express relief, increased self-esteem, and diminished need for the worker's assistance. These predictable themes suggest important areas for the social worker's introspection and action.

Continuing self-examination and self-awareness is fundamental to professional competence. Social workers necessarily explore their own attitudes, values, experiences, and feelings in order to ensure that their interactions with clients are guided by the clients' needs and concerns, rather than their own. In termination, these include the worker's lifelong experiences with and feelings about separations generally; feelings and concerns about the worker's competence as a helping person; and feelings about a specific client system and the ending of work together.

The predictable stirring of memories and feelings associated with separation is the major theme in descriptions of termination: "The ending process in a helping relationship can trigger feelings of the deepest kind in both worker and client. This is the reason why there is potential for powerful work during this phase as well as ineffective work if the feelings are not dealt with" (Shulman, 1992, p. 174). The social worker's ability to deal with these feelings in the helping interaction builds on awareness of the personal meaning of separation. Therefore, the practitioner's own experiences with separation and assumptions about clients' feelings emerge as areas for reflection. Thus, practitioners' experiences with death, divorce, geographic moves, or other losses or transitions may affect their ability to individualize the meaning of the ending to specific clients. Painful or recent separation experiences may prompt a practitioner to deny the importance of the ending to the client, in order to avoid remembering or reexperiencing painful feelings.

When the termination is based upon the practitioner's own timetable and needs, rather than those of the client, self-awareness is particularly important. For example, practitioners leaving an agency or students completing a semester of agency-based practicum training may experience conflict because they are acting out of self-interest rather than concern for the client (Gould, 1978; Moss & Moss, 1967; Siebold, 1991). As a second-year social work student commented, "I haven't yet had any real terminations with clients—all my cases have ended when the placement is over. I feel so guilty to quit working with my clients because my time is over, not because we're through. I have offered to volunteer here at the agency when the placement is over." At the end of professional training, student practitioners are also typically in the process of separating from the university, from the student role, from practicum agency and field instructor, and from classmates. Therefore, client terminations become part of a broader separation experience. It is important for the student practitioner to explore and understand the multifaceted nature of this transition period (Husband & Scheunemann, 1972).

Inevitably, the evaluative component of ending raises the questions: "Have I done well by this client? Could I have done more?" It is not possible to evaluate and review client goal accomplishment without scrutiny of the practitioner's sensitive and skilled use of self in the process. Practitioners must be aware of their reactions to the evaluation of their own performance. While the major reason for professional inattention to termination as a phase of treatment "seems to be the general sensitivity to loss and separation" (Fox et al., 1969, p. 62), another contributing factor may be the profession's general sensitivity to accountability and evaluation. However, as Germain and Gitterman (1996) emphasize, "Endings are especially valuable in building professional knowledge and refining skills. Joint assessment of outcomes with clients, identifying what was helpful and what was not helpful, and why, can be gradually generalized to practice principles" (p. 335). Objective evaluation and conceptualization of one's own practice is preceded by self-examination and acknowledgement of one's level of training and experience, as well as the professional expectation of continued growth. Each termination provides further information regarding the practitioner's strengths and professional learning needs.

Feelings of inadequacy or guilt about difficulties in helping a particular client, however, should be shared and examined with one's supervisor, consultant, or colleagues to determine the reality of this assessment and to prevent transmission of the message that the client should either reassure the practitioner of his or her worth or confirm the lack of worth.

The specific meaning for the practitioner of a particular client and of that client's termination also merits self-examination. For example, has this client been particularly gratifying? Or ungratifying? Is this client terminating with little accomplished? Has the client's success or lack of success taken on a special meaning for the practitioner personally or within the organization? Does the practitioner wish to have a continuing relationship with the client? Is there relief at the idea of terminating with this client? Have organizational pressures become an issue in the treatment and termination? As Levinson (1977) notes, "During treatment the therapist has an opportunity to participate in a creative process in which a new or modified self emerges . . . Saying good-bye to the patient by the therapist can be akin to saying good-bye to a part of himself" (p. 483). The meanings of termination are uniquely personal to the practitioner. Anticipating these meanings is an important aspect of preparation for the disciplined and conscious use of self in termination with the client.

SUMMARY

The intent of the helping process, whether brief or long-term, is to make a positive difference in the life of the client. This difference can be understood, evaluated, and maintained by means of skillful termination. The major task of the practitioner during this phase is to help the client move from denial or avoidance of the inevitable ending to exploration of ideas and feelings related to the outcome of the helping process and to termination of the helping relationship. The ability to accomplish this task will depend upon the practitioner's self-awareness and skills, as well as the practitioner's understanding of the context within which termination occurs: the client's problems and goals, the particular helping relationship, and the sponsoring organization. Thus, each termination can be uniquely anticipated and sensitively completed.

READING 25
Burnout: An Occupational Hazard for Social Workers[1]

Jan L. Hagen[2]

In general, social workers are regarded as being at high risk for burnout. As Meyerson (1994) notes, "Social workers face ambiguity in their technologies (e.g., talking to clients), their goals (e.g., to provide empathy and caring), their evaluation criteria (e.g., sensitivity) and occupational boundaries (e.g., who is and is not a social worker)" (p. 629). Social workers often enter the profession with an idealized sense of mission to help others and yet they must work within sometimes-severe bureaucratic constraints. Accordingly, burnout may be particularly high during the initial years of practice, as social workers confront the realities of their jobs, their clients, and their own competence (Cherniss, 1980a, 1980b; Edelwich & Brodsky, 1980). Practitioners may describe their dissatisfaction in various ways:

- "I am only 31 years old and feel that my job has stifled my ability and drive. I hope to get a job which will bring my old self out; where I can think for myself, plan, use my brain again. It is hard to recover from burnout but I plan to."
- "Workers here are unappreciated. Administrators do not care about their people and it filters down from there. Only failures are noted, so morale is very low. The goal of 100% excellence is impossible to reach. Therefore, some stop trying while others get ulcers trying to stay afloat."

Burnout is costly to practitioners, organizations, and clients. For the individual practitioner, burnout may mean physical and emotional exhaustion; depression and general malaise; feelings of helplessness and hopelessness; physical problems such as headaches, ulcers, hypertension, fatigue, and backaches; and the development of personal problems such as marital conflict and drug and alcohol abuse (Maslach, 1976, 1982; Pines, Aronson, & Kafry, 1981). For the organization, burnout results in inefficient workers, low morale, absenteeism, and high turnover. For clients, burnout among service providers means impersonal, dehumanized, and uncaring services.

Burnout, however, is not yet a clearly defined concept, nor has a clearly articulated theoretical model been developed. This reading reviews definitions of burnout, specifies variables contributing to it, and examines strategies for prevention and intervention by both individuals and agencies. Practitioners will be better prepared to prevent and alleviate burnout by knowing the personal, organizational, and societal variables that contribute to it.

DEFINING BURNOUT

Freudenberger (1974), a psychoanalyst, first used the term *burnout* to describe emotional and physical exhaustion brought about by conditions at work and identified types of personalities prone to burnout: the dedicated worker who takes on too much work with an excess of intensity; the overcommitted worker whose outside life is unsatisfactory; and the authoritarian worker who needs extensive control in his or her job (Karger, 1981). Freudenberger's conceptualization of burnout highlights the role of individual psychological characteristics and excludes the interactions between people and their environments.

Maslach and Pines propose a broader social/psychological view of burnout that examines the relationship

---

[1] An original reading for *Social Work Processes*.
[2] Distinguished Teaching Professor, School of Social Welfare, University of Albany, New York.

between individuals and their work environments (Maslach, 1976, 1978, 1982; Pines, 1983; Pines et al., 1981; Pines & Kafry, 1978; Pines & Maslach, 1978). Based on her numerous investigations, Maslach (1978) has concluded that

> burn-out is best understood (and modified) in terms of the social and situation sources of job related stresses. Although personality variables are certainly relevant in the overall analysis, the prevalence of the phenomenon and the range of seemingly disparate staff people who are affected by it suggest that the search for causes is better directed away from identifying the bad people and toward uncovering the characteristics of the bad situations where many good people function. (p. 114)

For Maslach (1982), burnout is a

> syndrome of emotional exhaustion, depersonalization, and reduced personal accomplishment that can occur among individuals who do "people work" of some kind. It is a response to the chronic emotional strain of dealing extensively with other human beings, particularly when they are troubled or having problems. (p. 3)

The variables to consider in this formulation of burnout include: (1) the personal characteristics of the practitioner; (2) the job setting, in terms of supervisory and peer support as well as agency rules and regulations; and (3) the actual work with individual clients.

On a societal level, Karger (1981) argues that professional burnout is very similar to industrial alienation as defined by Marx. In Marxian theory, burnout and dissatisfaction are logical outgrowths of a capitalist system in which workers become alienated from work; they are "reactions to the fragmentation of work, to competition within the workplace, and to the loss of worker autonomy" (Farber, 1983, p. 8). By including larger societal issues—how work is structured and valued in society—a Marxist analysis is helpful in conceptualizing burnout among human service providers. However, as Farber (1983) has noted, the helping professions are unique in numerous ways, and a class analysis of their role within society is inadequate.

As we see, these approaches disagree about the nature of burnout and its causes; they do agree, however, that the symptoms of burnout include attitudinal, physical, and emotional components.

It is most useful to think of burnout as a work-related strain, the "outcomes of experienced stress emotions and behaviors that deviate from the individual's normal response" (Jayaratne, Tripodi, & Chess, 1983). It is distinct from, although not unrelated to, job dissatisfaction, which is another work-related strain. As a strain, burnout pro-

duces at least three outcomes: (1) emotional exhaustion—a lack of emotional energy to use and invest in others; (2) depersonalization—a tendency to respond to others in callous, detached, emotionally hardened, uncaring, and dehumanizing ways; and (3) a reduced sense of personal accomplishment and a sense of inadequacy in relating to clients (Maslach, 1982).

STRESSORS THAT CONTRIBUTE TO BURNOUT

Stressors that contribute to burnout may be identified in the individual, the helping relationship, the work environment, and society. There is still little agreement as to which of these are most important.

The Individual

The initial work on burnout focused on individual psychology and personality structures. These certainly play a role in burnout, though not the only role. While excessive emotional demands in a work situation place anyone at risk for burnout, personality characteristics make some individuals more vulnerable. Low self-esteem and lack of confidence increase vulnerability to burnout, as does a lack of understanding about self-limitations, strengths, and weaknesses. As Maslach (1982) notes, "All too often providers feel completely responsible for whether a client succeeds or fails, lives or dies—and are emotionally overwhelmed by this heavy burden" (p. 65). When asked why they entered social work, practitioners often note the desire to help others, to make a contribution to the betterment of others, or to create a just world. The loftiness of these ideals contributes to burnout (Cherniss, 1980a, 1980b; Edelwich & Brodsky, 1980). Practitioners will quickly become disillusioned with both themselves and their clients if these ideals generate unrealistic goals and expectations—for example that clients' problems require only simple solutions, that problems will be solved quickly, that practitioners can work effectively with anyone, that practitioners' work will drastically alter clients' lives, and that clients will show the utmost appreciation for the practitioners' efforts (Edelwich & Brodsky, 1980).

Other reasons for entering social work include personal needs such as recognition, approval, affection, power and control, and intimacy. In and of themselves, these needs neither help nor hinder work with clients. The risk of burnout increases, however, if practitioners expect clients to fulfill these personal needs.

In general, men and women experience burnout similarly, although some gender differences have been noted.

Women are more likely to experience emotional exhaustion and to experience it more intensely, whereas men are more prone to depersonalization, characterized by callousness toward clients (Jayaratne et al., 1983; Maslach, 1982). Vulnerability to burnout appears to be related to age: Younger workers are more likely to experience burnout than older workers, who not only have more time on the job but also tend to have a more balanced perspective (Maslach, 1982; Poulin & Walter, 1993).

Investigating the role of education, Maslach (1982) found that those who had some college but did not graduate were at lower risk for burnout than those with postgraduate education; those with four years of college were at highest risk for burnout. This, too, may be related to age and practitioners' unrealistic expectations.

Relationships with family members and friends also influence burnout. As part of the practitioner's social support system, family and friends can have a buffering effect on the stresses of work (Koeske & Koeske, 1989). Research indicates that, as these personal relationships become more positive, the likelihood of burnout falls (Pines et al., 1981). A longitudinal study of intensive case managers suggests that it is the level of current, rather than previous, social supports that affects worker outcomes (Koeske & Kirk, 1995). However, if relationships with family members and friends are stressful, they may contribute to burnout by creating additional demands and obligations that conflict with work roles (Cherniss, 1980b).

The Helping Relationship

The helping relationship is a major contributor to burnout. In fact, burnout has been defined as the "result of constant or repeated emotional pressure associated with an intense involvement with people over long periods of time" (Pines et al., 1981, p. 15). The helping relationship exists for the primary benefit of the client, and the emotional giving in the relationship is exclusively from the practitioner to the client. Constant emotional giving and sharing the intense feelings of others may result in emotional depletion. Some client problems are more emotionally draining than others: Incest, child abuse, wife battering, and rape, for example, place tremendous emotional demands on the practitioner. Moreover, what is emotionally stressful and depleting will be different for different individuals, depending on previous life experiences. Nevertheless, unless practitioners have an adequate knowledge base, a commitment to individualization, and sufficient awareness of personal responses, they may develop callous and hostile attitudes toward clients as a result of prolonged exposure to emotionally charged situations. Additionally, burnout is likely if practitioners overidentify with clients and get caught up in their emotions (Koeske & Kelly, 1995).

When clients come for services, they are not functioning at their optimal level. Often, by the time they reach a social worker, they have exhausted their own resources—including informal social supports—in trying to solve their problems. They may feel hopeless and at their wit's end. Many times, work focuses exclusively on clients' problems and deficiencies; their strengths, abilities, and resources are ignored. This not only limits practitioners' effectiveness but also fosters cynical attitudes to clients and depersonalization.

Social work practitioners tend to focus on unsuccessful interventions with clients. Certainly, evaluation of failed interventions can be helpful, as a means of building knowledge and skills, but successes need to be evaluated as well. In general, client feedback reduces the likelihood of burnout (Pines & Kafry, 1978). Practitioners need to build ongoing and systematic evaluation into their practice.

The Work Environment

Within the past few years, research has begun to address the larger social, organizational, and societal factors that contribute to burnout. Arches (1991) identified two factors: the worker's perceived lack of autonomy and the influence of funding sources on agencies. In this section, we'll look at the impact of workload, role ambiguity, and role conflict; relationships with co-workers and supervisors; and agency goals and procedures.

An early study (Pines & Kafry, 1978) identified caseload size as related to burnout, particularly the development of negative attitudes toward clients. Maslach (1982) also links excessive caseload to emotional withdrawal and impersonal service. More recent studies suggest that the critical factor is not the actual size of the workload but the worker's perception that the workload is too large. Additionally, the role of workload dissatisfaction in burnout seems to be different in different settings—for example, child welfare services or family services (Jayaratne & Chess, 1984).

Important stressors in the work environment are role ambiguity, defined as lack of clarity regarding a worker's rights, responsibilities, methods, goals, status, or accountability, and role in which the practitioner experiences conflict, inconsistent, incompatible, or inappropriate demands (Farber, 1983). Role ambiguity and role conflict reduce the clarity of goals and expectations in work with clients and impair relationships with co-workers and supervisors, on account of confusion regarding work responsibilities.

Using job satisfaction as an indirect indicator of burnout, Harrison (1980) found that high levels of role ambiguity and role conflict related to low levels of job satisfaction among child protective workers. However, in studies of social workers generally, Jayaratne and Chess (1983) found that role conflict and role ambiguity "do not play a significant role in either the assessment of job satisfaction or in the reporting of burnout" (p. 137). Again, however, the importance of role ambiguity and role conflict in burnout may vary by job position and setting (Jayaratne & Chess, 1984). For example, a qualitative study of public child welfare administrators suggests that role conflict may be energizing for individual administrators and that the process of resolving conflicts contributes to team work, coalition building, and networking among diverse groups (Jones, 1993).

Relationships with co-workers and supervisor also have a bearing on burnout. These relationships may be an additional source of stress if they are competitive or conflicted. However, co-workers and supervisors are an important source of social support; they play vital roles in helping practitioners learn new skills, evaluate the effectiveness of their work, develop competence in their positions, and understand the purpose and function of the agency. A study of social service workers found that workers who had positive relationships with co-workers, had someone to discuss work problems with, and received feedback from both co-workers and supervisors were less likely to experience burnout (Pines & Kafry, 1978). Poulin and Walter (1993) note that an increase in supervisor support helped to decrease burnout among social workers. Informational and instrumental support from supervisors and co-workers have also been found to buffer the impact of various work stresses on burnout (Himle, Jayaratne, & Thyness, 1991).

Agency goals and procedures may foster burnout. If the agency's goals are unclear or ambiguous, role ambiguity or role conflict result. Ambiguous goals contribute to difficulties in measuring the effectiveness of interventions and hinder the provision of helpful feedback from co-workers and supervisors. Agency procedures—such as the mandatory collection of certain data on all clients, regardless of its relevance to the clients' problems—also interfere with the client-worker relationship and with worker effectiveness.

Research suggests that many sources of job-related stress—such as financial rewards, mastery, predictability, and workload—may be reduced if an agency setting is culturally sophisticated—that is, promotes policies and practices facilitating appropriate services for culturally diverse clients (Gant, 1996). However, culturally sophisticated workplaces

did little to reduce worker burnout, and Gant (1996) suggests that "psychological stresses may simply be an enduring consequence of working in the human services" (p. 168).

Adequacy of organizational resources has been related to burnout (Poulin & Walter, 1993). If funding is inadequate, agency staff has insufficient resources and support to meet demands for service. While staff may be reduced, the workload of the agency seldom is, and practitioners must contend with increased and often inappropriately large caseloads.

Societal Factors

Three societal factors are particularly relevant to social work: social welfare policy, changing expectations of work, and sexism.

The development of social welfare policy in the United States is primarily a political process. Although this is one of the strengths of a democratic society, the policy directions and program goals that result are often vaguely stated, which may lead to conflicting, ambiguous, and excessive role demands on social workers. If legislation is intended as a symbolic statement and its objectives exceed its funding, service providers must negotiate high consumer expectations with inadequate resources. Further, ambiguous legislation results in a lack of job specificity, lack of program structure, and excessive paperwork in pursuit of accountability (Dressel, 1982).

Cherniss (1980b) has identified unfulfilled expectations as a major source of burnout among human service providers, especially with "the growing belief during the last 40 years that . . . a job had to be a vehicle for self-actualization as well as economic security" (p. 150). Seeking self-actualization through work—and only through work—fosters burnout by creating unrealistic expectations for the work setting.

Discrimination based on gender has been well documented in society and in social work. Sexism contributes to burnout among women through its influence on salary levels, promotions, organizational influence and power, job assignments, and role expectations (Edelwich & Brodsky, 1980). Sexism in the workplace may foster a sense of helplessness and powerlessness, decrease the availability of feedback on performance, and interfere with social support from co-workers and supervisors (Finn, 1990).

PREVENTING AND ALLEVIATING BURNOUT

Techniques recommended for stress management and stress reduction include relaxation techniques, physical exercise, proper nutrition and rest, and the reduction of coffee, cigarette, drug, and alcohol consumption. Important as they are for health promotion and well-being, these methods address the symptoms of burnout, rather than the causes. Strategies for addressing burnout must focus on stressors at the individual level, including the client-worker relationship, and the organizational and societal level.

Individual Strategies

While the importance of organizational factors cannot be denied, individual practitioners bear some responsibility for burnout. New practitioners, driven by idealized notions of professional performance, may experience a crisis of competence (Cherniss, 1980a). Building on White's theory (1959, 1963) that a sense of competence may be developed by acting in the environment and meeting its challenges, Harrison (1980) suggests that "workers are able to develop positive affective responses to their jobs only if there is some certainty that what they do is valuable and makes a difference in the lives of clients" (p. 42). One aspect of competence is "the worker's skill, including techniques, judgment, and the ability to use him or herself effectively" (Harrison, 1983, p. 32). Thus, by developing skill, the individual contributes toward a positive work experience.

Practitioners have an ongoing responsibility to expand their knowledge base by keeping up with the professional literature, participating in continuing education programs and in-service trainings, and learning from clients, peers, and supervisors. A strong knowledge base is vital for understanding the client's current situation and goals and designing appropriate practice interventions. It is particularly important to develop an awareness of, and sensitivity to, cultural factors in the client's situation.

Practitioners must learn to set realistic goals. By establishing realistic goals for the work environment, the practitioner will be able to measure progress, to have a sense of accomplishment, and to feel mastery. While noble ideals of fighting injustice or providing well-being to all motivate many social workers, progress toward those goals is difficult to measure without more specific and realistic indicators along the way. The same principles apply to direct work with clients. In partnership, client and practitioner must formulate realistic goals, accompanied by specific subgoals to mark progress. By attending to the client's wishes, the practitioner is less likely to set inappropriate goals, and the chance of a successful outcome is increased. Worker-practitioner partnership also tends to reduce beginning practitioners' sense of total responsibility for clients' well-being.

Focusing on clients' strengths, abilities, and resources reduces the risk of burnout. With an understanding of these assets, the practitioner develops a more complete and realistic perspective of clients and of appropriate interventions. A practitioner who focuses solely on problems and deficiencies will be less able to design effective interventions and more likely to adopt a negative attitude to clients.

Self-awareness also reduces the likelihood of burnout. First, if we understand our personal limitations, we will not accept inappropriate responsibility, we will set achievable goals, and our work expectations will be realistic. Second, if we are aware of our personal needs, we might realize that they are being inappropriately met in work with clients; in that case, we can develop other resources to address these needs. Third, if we are self-aware, we can recognize and deal with our subjective reactions to clients that hinder effective work. Because the use of self is critical in work with clients, awareness of our emotional responses is vital for the well-being of both client and practitioner.

To develop competence and to avoid burnout, practitioners must actively seek feedback about their work with clients. This includes direct feedback from clients, through systematic and continual evaluation of progress toward goals. Developments in clinical research have provided resources for gathering information about effectiveness. Additionally, feedback may be gathered indirectly by evaluation of the clients' progress in treatment. Colleagues and supervisors are also essential sources of feedback.

Building a social support system at work is critical in reducing the likelihood of burnout. Co-workers and supervisors fulfill a number of social support functions, including listening without judgment, technical support, technical challenge, emotional support, emotional challenge, and sharing social reality (Pines, 1983). Energy invested in developing relationships with colleagues is repaid many times over through access to their expertise and support.

Research indicates that a fulfilling and enriching personal life contributes to more positive attitudes toward work. As Maslach (1982) notes:

> When your whole world is your work and little else, then your whole world is more likely to fall apart when problems arise on the job. Your sense of competence, your self-esteem, and your personal identity are all based on what you do in life, and they will be far more shaky and insecure if that base is a narrow one. (p. 104)

Setting boundaries on your work is often the first step toward a satisfying personal life (Maslach, 1982). Taking leisure time is not enough, however; it must be used for personally rewarding activities, such as fostering personal relationships and exploring personal interests.

Organizational and Societal Strategies

Agencies must assume responsibility for creating work environments that decrease vulnerability to burnout. A strategy frequently suggested is the development of training programs. Programs in stress or time management are less important than programs designed to increase practitioners' skills and knowledge—in particular, interpersonal skills and information about the clients served, realistic goals for that population, and practice models appropriate for intervention, as well as information about evaluation techniques. This type of training enhances practitioners' sense of competency.

To reduce burnout, agencies should review their policies. First, agency policies and procedures must be responsive to client needs. If the requirements regarding data collection and documentation or the mandated procedures for intervention interfere with the helping relationship, they will contribute to burnout. Second, agency policies and procedures, both formal and informal, must provide clarity of job function and tasks, to minimize role ambiguity and conflict for both supervisors and practitioners. Third, agency policy that fosters the development of supportive relationships with co-workers and supervisors will reduce burnout. Fourth, agency policies and procedures, both formal and informal, should be nonsexist. All workers, regardless of gender, expect to be treated equally and equitably in the work environment.

Specific strategies have been proposed to deal with the emotional energy that work with clients demands (Daley, 1979; Pines & Kafry, 1978; Zastrow, 1984). One alternative is to rotate assignments. This allows practitioners to experience variety—and perhaps challenge—in their work but, unless employed with caution, it may undermine the development of competency. A more useful alternative is to balance work assignments so that particularly demanding cases are distributed among the staff. Work assignments should also be flexible, so as to meet individual practitioner needs in terms of caseload composition; providing a variety of case assignments reduces the risk of burnout. Another alternative is time-outs, which allow practitioners to assume less stressful work assignments for a time. As a general rule, agencies should make efforts to reduce caseload size if they want to minimize burnout, with its costly consequences of absenteeism, worker inefficiency, and turnover. Other options include job sharing, job splitting, quality circles for participatory management, and flexible benefit plans (McNeely, 1988).

Finally, it is appropriate for both agency representatives and individual practitioners to become involved in the political process—for instance, by designing social welfare legislation responsive to clients' needs, with realistic program goals and adequate funding. In political action, it is usually more effective to join an organized group. The National Association of Social Workers actively lobbies on both state and federal levels in support of legislation consistent with the principles and goals of the profession.

CONCLUSION

Social workers are at risk for burnout by virtue of who they are, the work they do, and the environments in which they work. Once burnout has developed, it is extremely difficult to reverse, and the costs of burnout are a burden for the client, the practitioner, and the agency. Prevention is a more successful strategy. Agencies have a responsibility to create a work environment that does not foster burnout. However, the individual practitioner is able to reduce the risk of burnout by becoming aware of the various stressors and implementing strategies for their minimization.

READING 26
Leonard Timms[1]

Robert B. Bennett[2]

Intake Information

Date: February 22   **Case #:** 032-LT1
Name: Leonard Timms   **Age:** 14

---

[1] An original case study for *Social Work Processes*.
[2] Assistant Professor, School of Social Work, Indiana University, Indianapolis.

Address: 2250 Scrub Oak Circle
City/State/Zip: Indianapolis, IN 46240
Parents: William (stepfather) and Carla Durst (biological mother). Biological father deceased.
Home Phone: 317-076-3333
Family Members in the Home: William, Carla, Susan Durst (16-year-old stepsister)

Father's Employer: Central Cleaning Company
Job Description: Janitor
Number of Years at Current Place of Employment: 6 Months
Mother's Employer: NA   **Job Description:** NA
Number of Years at Current Place of Employment: NA
Referral Source: Leslie McDermott, Probation Officer
Previous Counseling: Youth Ministry Services, 3 or 4 visits, 9 years ago
Current Physical Illnesses and/or Disabilities: None
Medications: None
Insurance Information: Medifirst Preferred
Reasons for Seeking Service At This Time: Leonard was arrested for a sexual offense against his 8-year-old cousin. He acknowledged exposing his penis and asking her to touch it. He was court ordered to obtain an assessment and treatment recommendation. His probation officer helped Mrs. Durst (Leonard's mother) arrange the initial meeting at this agency.

ENGAGEMENT: FIRST FACE-TO-FACE CONTACT

Leonard Timms was referred by his probation officer, Leslie McDermott, as required by court order. For this first face-to-face meeting, Leonard was accompanied by his mother, Carla Durst, and his stepfather, William Durst. Leonard's biological father is deceased. The purpose of this initial meeting was to discuss the nature of the assessment process, determine if Leonard and his parents wanted to have the assessment completed at this agency, and—if they agreed—to conduct the assessment. Mrs. Durst had previously made contact with the agency to set up the appointment, provide intake information, and discuss the financial arrangements.

I introduced myself to all members of the family and invited them into my office. Leonard and his parents appeared somewhat nervous. Each family member was attentive and cooperative. There was no evidence of hostility directed toward me or toward the legal system despite the court order to obtain the evaluation. Leonard smiled shyly and the Dursts were somewhat quiet and reserved. I offered them a cup of coffee or glass of water. They each asked if they could have a glass of water. I told them I had reviewed the information Mrs. Durst had provided earlier and proceeded to describe the agency, its programs, and the usual process by which we formulated assessments and recommendations to the court in such circumstances. I also explained that if the assessment process indicated that psychosocial services were warranted, they could decide later whether to obtain them through our agency or through other programs in the community. I indicated that about one week following the initial assessment, we would meet again to review and discuss the assessment and recommendations.

I asked if they had any questions. Leonard asked how long it would take. He sighed when I told him that it was about three hours. I then reviewed the informed consent policy and discussed confidentiality—noting that the probation officer and judge would receive copies of the assessment and recommendations report. I then asked if they had any other questions. No one did. I explained that if they wanted to proceed with the evaluation, they would need to sign the consent form so indicating. They each signed their consent for the assessment to proceed.

At that point, I provide Leonard with several self-report forms to complete in a separate room while I interviewed his parents. Later, I asked the Dursts to fill out self-report forms while I spent time with Leonard. On the basis of the written information and the data obtained through the interview process, I prepared the following *Assessment and Recommendations Report.*

ASSESSMENT AND RECOMMENDATIONS REPORT

Presenting Problem

Leonard Timms, age 14, was referred by Leslie McDermott for the purpose of obtaining an assessment and treatment recommendation, as ordered by the county judge. Ms. McDermott is a probation officer for the county. His mother, Carla Durst and stepfather William Durst accompanied Leonard to the agency on February 22. All three consented to and actively participated in the assessment process.

Leonard molested an 8-year-old cousin (Shania) in September of last year. The events appear to have transpired as follows: During a family gathering when he and Shania were alone in a bedroom, Leonard took his penis from his pants and asked his cousin to touch it. She said that she did not want to do that and he then put his penis back in his pants. His cousin subsequently told her mother (Leonard's maternal aunt). His aunt then told Leonard's mother and called the police. Leonard initially denied the allegation. When his mother told him to tell the truth, he then said that he had only asked his cousin to touch him on top of his pants. He later acknowledged that he had taken his penis out of his pants to show her and had then asked her to touch him. He also reported that he first asked his cousin if she wanted to see his penis. Leonard said that she told him she wanted to see his penis.

Initial Interactions

Leonard is an engaging young man who cooperated throughout the interview. He was dressed in casual attire. He is of average height for his age. He is approximately twenty pounds overweight. Leonard was uncomfortable during the discussion of the sexual acting out behaviors. He stated that he felt terrible about what happened and acknowledged that he was at fault because he was older than his young cousin. He said he should not have tried to take advantage of her for his own satisfaction. When asked why he committed the offenses, he stated that he was not thinking about anything other than being "horny" and desiring to get his own needs met.

Both his mother and stepfather also seemed cooperative and concerned. They said they were totally shocked when they initially learned about the offense. They indicated that their initial anger and disappointment with Leonard has changed to concern. They remain confused about why he would do "such a thing" but support him in his attempt to get counseling for his offense so "it won't happen again."

History of Prior Offenses

Leonard reported he had not done anything like this before. Leonard's parents reported they are unaware of other such incidents. There is no record of prior sexual offenses or other contacts with the Juvenile Court.

Family Situation

Leonard lives with his biological mother, Carla Durst (35 years old), his stepfather, William Durst (43 years old), and his stepsister, Susan Durst (16 years old). Leonard's biological father, John Timms, died in an automobile accident about 9 years ago.

Mrs. Durst reported that she married Leonard's father, John Timms, when she was 16 years old and divorced him approximately 2 years later. However, the relationship continued, off and on, for approximately 8 years. Mrs. Durst shared that she was abused by Mr. Timms and sought counseling to help her deal with the problems in the relationship. Her ex-husband reportedly did not physically abuse Leonard. Mrs. Durst also said that she had been sexually molested by her brother when she was 9 years old and her brother was 16 years old. Mrs. Durst also has been in treatment for depression and anxiety. She currently takes prescription medication for these problems and is being monitored by her physician.

Mrs. Durst has been married to William Durst for 6 years. Mr. Durst has recently gotten custody of his 16-year-old daughter Susan. Susan has been living with the family for the past two years.

Leonard gets along "OK" with his stepsister. He states that he does not always trust her. He shared that he has gotten in trouble before when Susan told him she would do his chores if he would take care of her chores so she could go shopping with friends. She did not follow through on her promise and he got in trouble with his mother for not doing his chores. Mrs. Durst also reported that Leonard and Susan have an "on again, off again type of friendship." She feels that Susan is able to manipulate Leonard to get what she wants and this is often at Leonard's expense.

Areas of concern that Carla Durst identified regarding Leonard are

- Fighting with family members
- Disobedience
- School grades
- Low self-esteem
- Being picked on
- Sexual issues
- Boy/girl relationships

In the family, members generally keep their feelings to themselves and don't readily share emotions with each other. Major life events that have occurred in the past 12 months have been

- Changes in work schedules and jobs for both parents
- Legal problems
- Financial problems and debt
- Marital stresses

During their marriage, the Dursts have moved approximately 15 times. Thus, the children have never had the opportunity to stay long in one school or neighborhood. Ability to form relationships and attachments has undoubtedly been affected in an adverse manner due to these frequent moves.

School Performance and Adjustment

Leonard is in the 7th grade at Melton Junior High School in Indianapolis, Indiana. This is his first year at the school. Last year he attended Prairie Elementary School in Layton County. He is reportedly doing well in school this year. His grades are A's, B's, and C's this year. Last year he got D's and F's in school. He shared that he enjoys using the computer and his favorite subject is spelling. He has not had any behavior problems in school.

Social Development

Leonard's social relationships appear to be sparse at best. He speaks of some friends at school. He states that he does not have any friends in the neighborhood. Due to the number of moves that the family has made during his lifetime, it would be difficult for Leonard to have developed long-lasting social relationships. The primary social relations and play relationships have been with other extended family members. Leonard's mother indicates that he has often been picked on by peers. In addition, one has the sense that the family is a rather closed system. This is yet another reason why making and maintaining close peer relationships are difficult for Leonard.

Sexual Knowledge and Development

As stated above, Leonard was initially self-conscious and uncomfortable when questioned about sexual knowledge and development. He stated that no adult had ever talked with him about sexual development and he did not know much about it until he was given a book about sexual development, by a social worker from his school. He stated that the book had been helpful. He felt he could talk with his mother about questions he might have regarding sexual development and feelings. It appears that what Leonard knows about sexual development has been learned from discussions with his school-age peers. He was able to say that he did know about masturbation and felt that it was all right, because it did not hurt anyone else and "makes you feel better when you are horny." He has seen nudity in some movies. These have not been pornographic movies. He has seen *Playboy* magazines that belonged to an older male cousin. Mrs. Durst shared that she had discovered a photograph of the torso of a woman with exposure of naked breasts. The face was not in the photo, thus, identity could not be established. The photo was found in the door jam of Leonard's bedroom. When asked about the photo, Leonard claimed he had never seen it before.

Leonard's information about sexuality is sparse. A great deal of his information is inaccurate and he appears to be misinformed. He has not had a trusted adult to confide in about sexuality. He was able to share that he knew it was wrong to look in windows, expose oneself to another, and to force any kind of sexual behavior onto another. He did state that "everyone knows that blonde women are the most highly sexually active." When asked where he got that information, he stated that a classmate at school told him. Of the 50 items on the Sexual Attitudes Questionnaire, Leonard only answered 15 items. He is obviously unsure of many of the areas addressed on the questionnaire. This is again illustrated on the Sexual Knowledge Inventory where he only answered two of the 20 questions.

Leonard states that he has not been sexually active with anyone and has not committed any other sexual offenses

with anyone other than his cousin. He has not kissed any girls. He would like to have a girlfriend, but does not see any prospects at this time. He also is very fearful of being removed from the home and going to Boys School (juvenile correction facility) if he does anything else of a sexual nature with anyone. He states that he will not offend again because he knows it is wrong, and he does not want to be put in a residential program, or go to Boys School.

Past History of Abuse

No sexual or physical abuse was reported by Leonard or his parents. Mrs. Durst stated that there was an incident about 5 years ago when she and Mr. Durst were investigated by Child Protective Services due to an allegation of child neglect. Leonard was temporarily removed from the home but returned within a week. The problem, as recalled by Mrs. Durst, was that both adults were unemployed at the time and they could not afford to heat their rented home during the winter. Leonard had also asked his teacher for lunch money. Mr. and Mrs. Durst stated that they soon were able to receive temporary assistance and Mr. Durst began working again within two weeks.

Drug and Alcohol Use

Leonard said he has not used drugs or alcohol. Mrs. Durst felt this was accurate to the best of her knowledge.

Prior Treatment for Emotional/Mental Health Problems

According to Mrs. Durst, Leonard briefly received counseling from a youth minister following the accidental death of his biological father about 9 years ago.

Risk Status

On the Estimate of Risk of Adolescent Sexual Offense Recidivism (ERASOR) (Worling & Curwen, 2001), Leonard scores at the level of low risk. Prominent factors contributing to his risk for reoffending include the following:

- Nature of offense with younger child
- Lack of intimate peer relationships/social isolation
- High stress family environment
- No development or practice of realistic prevention plan/strategy
- Incomplete sexual-offense-specific treatment

Individual and Family Strengths and Resources

Leonard is a likeable and verbal 14-year-old. He can be engaging and positive. He appears to be genuinely remorseful for his sexual behavior with his cousin. Leonard

500 PART IV Additional Readings

has demonstrated that he responds well to feedback and input, as evidenced by his current progress in school.

This family has struggled to maintain on a day-to-day basis. They have faced financial and emotional crises for extended periods. They do seem to be desirous of obtaining help for Leonard and assuring the safety of younger children in their extended family. Mr. Durst is currently working and trying to provide as best as he can for the family. Both appear to be very positive about the past counseling that the children and Mrs. Durst have obtained.

Recommendations

As previously mentioned, Leonard's current risk status places him in the low-risk category. Consistent with his score at the lower end of that category, it is recommended that he attend an outpatient sex offender treatment program. The program should include an active parent component. Leonard would benefit most from a program which involves peer group counseling and addresses areas of human sexuality, responsibility for one's behavior, victim empathy, problem-solving, thinking errors, and triggers for reoffending as well as a strong reoffense prevention plan. He should be considered for treatment in the sexual adjustment group for adolescents offered through this agency.

Continued monitoring of the family situation is considered crucial to the success of Leonard not reoffending. The Dursts will need continued support and input with regard to limit setting and establishment of appropriate boundaries and roles within the family. Any reoffending behaviors on Leonard's part would prompt strong consideration for him to be placed out of the home in a residential sex offender program.

Robert Bennett, DSW, LSCW, ACSW
Licensed Clinical Social Worker
Date: February 26

ASSESSMENT:
SECOND MEETING WITH THE FAMILY

The purpose for this session was to discuss the results of the assessment and my recommendations with Leonard and his parents. I gave a copy of the report to each of them and reviewed the assessment results. I then talked with the family about my recommendation that Leonard participate in a time-limited, psycho-educational treatment group for adolescents at low risk of reoffense. I indicated that different agencies might offer somewhat different programs but that the typical format consists of 12 consecutive weekly 90-minute sessions. I also noted my recommen-

dation that family sessions occur at least once each month and more often if the worker, the family, or Leonard needed or wanted them. Initially, Leonard was unhappy about the group recommendation. He was afraid that he might not "fit in" and might be disrespected by the other kids. I briefly explored some of his fears, outlined the topics typically addressed, and gave examples of how members generally interacted with each other. That seemed to lessen his fears somewhat.

I explained that the family had the right to seek other professional opinions if they disagreed with the assessment or the recommendations. I also restated that if they chose to follow the recommendations, they could obtain services from our agency or from others within the community. The Dursts indicated that they supported the assessment and recommendations and would like Leonard to participate in our program because they had heard positive things about it from their probation officer and the local mental health center. I then asked them for formal consent to provide group and family services. Leonard and his parents readily signed the applicable treatment consent forms. Leonard signed the group contract form that outlined his responsibilities as a group member and his commitment to attend all 12 group meetings. We concluded the meeting with the understanding that Leonard would attend the first group session in two weeks and that we would meet again as a family in about three weeks.

SOCIAL WORKER'S COMMENTARY

Engagement

Most adolescents who have been court ordered to receive a psychosocial or mental health assessment following commission of a sex offense are unwilling "respondents." Their parents or guardians are in a similar position—responding to the court's expectations—even when they are simultaneously concerned about the youth. I always wonder how the offense has affected family relationships. Some parents view the offensive behavior as a form of youthful "experimentation" and resent the involvement of the courts. Many abhor the term "sex offender." Although Leonard and his parents were fully and actively involved in the process of assessment, the court and the probation department were the primary initial clients. In theory, the judge, probation officer, and I—in my role of assessor—attempt to serve on behalf of the best interests of the general community. Therefore, my assessment of adolescents charged with or convicted of sex offenses must include an evaluation concerning the likelihood of an additional offense. The issue of community safety is a primary consideration at the time of assessment (National Adolescent Perpetrator Network, 1993).

I often find it difficult to assume this role of "community protector." However, my initial clients—the court and probation department—refer youthful offenders and their families to our agency for precisely that purpose. Understandably, most adolescents and their families initially view me as an extension of the criminal justice system rather than their advocates. They usually recognize that the assessment may lead to a recommendation for residential placement or perhaps even incarceration. As a result, most adolescents and their parents are highly anxious about the evaluation and usually attempt to present themselves in the best possible light.

Leonard's mother and his stepfather joined him for the assessment process. I took that as a good sign. A significant number of court-ordered youth and their families fail to attend the originally scheduled first meeting or are accompanied by one adult—perhaps a biological or foster parent, a guardian, older sibling, or grandparent. Sometimes, the attending adult is angry, uncooperative, and unsupportive of the process. In Leonard's case, both parents were concerned about Leonard and supportive of him. They also actively participated in the process.

I first met with Len, Carla, and William to educate them about the process. I wanted them to understand the nature and implications of the assessment before they provided informed consent for the assessment. I indicated that they would receive a copy of the assessment and recommendations report that I would send to the court and the probation department. I also described our policies about confidentiality and the exceptions to that policy. When they had signed the required informed consent forms, I escorted Leonard to a computer workstation where he could complete several self-report inventories. While he did that, I met with Carla and William to obtain background and developmental information. I generally prefer to meet with the parents or guardians first and the adolescent later. The computerized self-report forms contain many items about sexuality and sex offenses. Many adolescents seem to find it easier to write or type than talk about such sensitive material—at least at first. Most seem less anxious following their completion of the computerized self-reports. The time also provides me an opportunity to talk with the parents or guardians about the family situation, the effects of the offense on the household, and obtain a social and family history. During the interview, I try to elicit their views about the adolescent and the offense. One of the risk factors associated with reoffenses involves the lack of cooperation

and support of treatment by parents or guardians (Worling & Curwen, 2001). Therefore, I try to assess the degree of investment in and support for the process. In this instance, both Carla and William Durst actively engaged in the interview process. They were open, involved, and cooperative. At one point, William said, "He just asked her to touch his penis." When adults minimize the nature or potential impact of the act, offending adolescents may find it difficult to develop empathy for victims. They may conclude—like their parents or guardians—that their actions were essentially insignificant. In this instance, however, Carla quickly disagreed with William who then reconsidered his position. I took this as a positive as well. Following a brief discussion, William recognized that it might be a problem if he described the act as a "minor offense" when talking with Len.

I was not surprised to learn that Carla's previous husband had abused her. This is often true of mothers of adolescent sex offenders (Kaplan, Becker, & Martinez, 1990). I did wonder if she and William had a combative relationship. It turned out that they did not. However, the family has struggled at times to make ends meet. Financial issues were often at the heart of their arguments with each other.

When I met with Len alone as part of the assessment, he was fairly open and expressive. As with most adolescents, he had difficulty discussing the offense in detail. I usually begin with other aspects of the adolescent's life first, rather than to jump in with a discussion of the offense. This gives me an opportunity to establish some positive rapport before asking for details about the offense itself. I want to learn about the youngsters as people, appreciate their dreams and aspirations, and understand their social lives to gain a sense of the context of the sexual offense. I try to resist the term "sex offender" in my thoughts as well as my spoken or written words. If I adopt the label, I may only experience the adolescent through the "sex offender" lens. I especially like to inquire about pleasurable activities and pastimes and learn about their friends. Following this, discussion about the sex offense itself seems easier for most adolescents. Indeed, Len readily shared information about himself, his friends, and his family and then provided details about the offense. I was encouraged when he accepted responsibility for and felt remorse about his action, and did not hold the victim responsible for any part of it.

Sharing the Assessment

When I met with Len and Mr. and Mrs. Durst to discuss the assessment and recommendations, I was pleased that both parents supported Len's participation in the group treatment. The also agreed to participate in the family meetings as well. Even though this was only our second meeting, they seemed more than willing to approach the process as a team effort. They wanted to be involved.

Len's initial reluctance about participating in a group experience was expected. Most adolescents are hesitant about group services. Len also has had problems with peers in the past. He remained somewhat anxious about the prospect even after I explained the rationale for and the contents of the group. I find this aspect of my work troublesome. I knew that Len felt uneasy about the group and might well prefer individual or family services instead. In fact, he had little choice in the matter. He could not easily refuse the recommendation. The cost of refusal might include incarceration or placement in a residential facility, the disappointment of his parents, or another courtroom appearance. If he refused treatment, he would be in violation of his probation. I was afraid he might conclude that his feelings were being discounted.

Although families have a right to a second opinion and another assessment from another agency, few take advantage of that option. Most accept the recommendations I propose—despite the fact that we do not currently have "clear scientific evidence to favor any particular treatment approach, or even to demonstrate that adolescent sexual offender treatment is effective at all" (Chaffin, 2001, p. 91). Perhaps the most commonly accepted and widely employed clinical practice includes peer group therapy and the use of cognitive behavioral approaches (Chaffin, 2001; Murphy, Page, & Hoffmann, 2003; National Adolescent Perpetrator Network, 1993). Time-limited, closed-ended groups are advantageous in that all participants begin and end the experience together. They also quickly develop "common ground" and "common purpose" because all are court ordered due to a sex offense. The group helps to normalize their feelings about the experience and contributes to a sense of universality: "We're all in the same boat." Generally, the group members begin to provide each other with support and understanding within the first two meetings. Mutual aid and social support (Yalom, 1995) are readily apparent in the group and operate as powerful therapeutic factors in conjunction with intervention components such as:

- Psychoeducation about the consequences of abusive behavior
- Increasing victim empathy
- Identifying personal risk factors
- Promoting healthy sexual attitudes and beliefs
- Social skills training
- Sex education

- Anger management
- Relapse prevention (Chaffin, 2001, p. 91)

We also use the ERASOR instrument (Worling & Curwen, 2001) for assessment and evaluation purposes. ERASOR helps to identify dynamic and static factors associated with the risk for sexual reoffense. In addition, we use various questionnaires and response forms at various points during the process to assess the impact of each module. For example, Len completed the Sexual Attitudes Questionnaire and Sexual Knowledge Inventory during the initial meeting and again at the conclusion of the group experience. These instruments serve as pre- and post-test indicators to reveal the nature, direction, and extent of change before and after treatment. They serve, of course, as indirect measures. The most direct measure of outcome involves actual behavior. We consider our program successful to the degree that service recipients actually abstain from subsequent sexual offenses.

INTERVENTION AND EVALUATION

Group Session 1: March 11

Data   This was the first group session for all of the boys. Introductions included name, age, grade, school, and type of sex offense. Leonard indicated that he would like to be called Len in the group. I reviewed the overall purpose of the group, discussed the importance of confidentiality, and outlined the group rules and expectations. I discussed the topics we would cover during the group experience. I also asked for input from the members regarding additional topics or rules that they would like to see. No one had suggestions or questions. Len was cooperative and participated when called upon but did not volunteer information. He and two other group members downplayed the nature of their sexual offenses. Len said, "I just showed her my penis." These comments led to discussion about "taking ownership for one's actions" and the process of minimization. Later, we discussed rationalization as well.

Assessment   Len was somewhat anxious in this first meeting. He seemed to minimize his offense—but since he talked after two other group members who did so as well, he may have followed their lead. He appeared interested in the discussion and attentive although he occasionally looked at his watch and tapped his toe. I wonder if Len's modest discomfort may be due in part to past difficulties in social situations.

Plan   Discussion for next group session will focus upon further discussion of member's offenses as well as discussion of legal issues with regard to sex offenses.

Worker's Commentary   In the first group session, I described the purpose of the group and outlined the topics we would address. I offered a rationale for selecting these particular topics and identified some of the methods we would use, such as discussion, handouts, videotapes, simulations, and role plays. I encouraged members to ask questions about the content or process, and offer suggestions about additional material they would like to explore. Although few members propose changes, the invitation itself may encourage a sense of ownership in the process—even though they are involuntary clients (Behroozi, 1992). In the first group, Len was generally quiet although participated when called upon. I asked many open-ended questions in an effort to avoid yes or no answers. I also tried to link the members by commenting on their commonalities. At first, Len and two other boys seemed to minimize the nature and impact of their sexual offenses. There may be a contagion effect in adolescent groups. If one starts out by minimizing, others often do so as well. The influence of peers may be for better or worse. Indeed, some parents express the fear that their sons might develop even more problematic behaviors if they are exposed to other offenders. This is a legitimate concern. I try to address this possibility by forming groups on the basis of similar levels of offense severity and risk factors. I seek to include low-severity, low-risk youth in one group; moderate in another; and extreme-severity, high-risk in a third. Accordingly, the risk of developing more problematic behaviors from others is somewhat mitigated.

Group Session 2: March 18

Data   Len was more active today than he had been during the first meeting. He seemed very interested in the presentation about and discussion of sex offenses and legal issues. At first, he again minimized his offense saying, "I did not force her to do anything. I even asked her if she wanted to see it. And, when I wanted her to touch it, I did not make her do that." He also stated that he did not know that it was illegal (based upon age of consent) even if force was not used. I inquired more about this and asked if he knew what he was doing was wrong. He acknowledged that he knew it was wrong but maintained that he thought it was wrong from a religious (moral) point of view and did not know it was illegal. He said that had he known that he would get in trouble with the law, he would not have

done it. At the end of the group, each member filled out a response form indicating what they had learned in that session. Len indicated that he now had an understanding of his sex offense from a legal standpoint.

Assessment   Len feels that he broke a moral commandment but states that he did not know that his action was illegal. He seems to have the belief that it was ok to break a moral commandment but claimed that he did not intend to break the law. This would indicate that he is still reliant upon external controls more than internal controls. He did not see that the consequence of his actions could cause harm to the victim; but rather, was more concerned with the consequences for him. His response form, at the end of group, indicates that he felt he had gained knowledge regarding the legal issues and his offense.

Plan   Continue with group. The issue of victim empathy will be an important one for Len to understand. Also, schedule a family session.

Worker's Commentary   I was encouraged by Len's level of participation during the second group session. He continued to minimize the offense in the group context, however, that is something that I've come to expect with this population. The youngsters often experience a great deal of shame and attempt to manage it through minimization or rationalization. For example, some adopt the ignorance excuse as justification by saying they did not understand about the legal age of consent. In effect, they assert that they did not know their actions were wrong. I try to adopt a gentle, supportive approach to confrontation around these issues. When I first began to work with this population, I felt obligated to be forceful in challenging minimization, denial, and rationalization. However, I found that a "get in your face" form of confrontation led to reduced expressiveness and diminished trust. The therapeutic relationship suffered as a result. My observations in this regard seem consistent with the motivational interviewing approach discussed by Miller and Rollnick (1991, 2002). Now I try to use the group process for confrontation and encourage the members to point out thinking errors to each other in a respectful manner. I also use "Socratic questioning" to promote self-analysis of their own thinking.

Family Intervention Session 1: March 23

Data   The purpose for this family session was to provide Len and his parents an opportunity to discuss the group experience and address any relevant questions and issues.

Len indicated that the group sessions "have not been as bad as I thought." He said that he wanted to finish the program. He voluntarily discussed the general topics of the first two group sessions and said he had already learned some things he hadn't known before. He also said he felt pretty comfortable with the other group members. I asked Len if he would care to share a topic that especially affected him. He said that he felt bad when the group talked about the pain and suffering experienced by the victims. Mrs. Durst began to tear up at this. She shared that she had been sexually abused for several years between the ages of 6 and 12 by a maternal uncle. She was tearful as she explained this to Len. He was very attentive to her and said that he was sorry that happened to her. She expressed to him how the abuse affected her and how it still affects her in some ways. She said, "I have never completely gotten over it." At this point, William stated that what Len did wasn't as bad as what happened to Carla. Carla got angry with William telling him any sexual abuse is bad and is not excusable.

Assessment This information from his mother was very sobering to Len. He appeared to be genuinely distressed about her pain. It seems that he was able to be in touch with victim empathy due to the feelings he expressed toward his mother.

Plan The group session this week will focus upon victim empathy.

Worker's Commentary This was an emotional session. Mrs. Durst disclosed that she had been sexually molested repeatedly during childhood. This was new information to me and to Len—despite my awareness that many parents of adolescent sex offenders have themselves been victimized (Kaplan et al., 1990). When Mr. Durst tried to dismiss Len's offense as not being as bad, I had mixed emotions. On one hand, I felt he was trying to be supportive of Len but I also thought he was minimizing Len's offense. I wasn't sure exactly what to say. I was relieved when Carla reacted to his comment and felt that what she said was much more meaningful than anything I could have interjected. I also felt positive about Len's response to his mother's pain. I thought that his empathy and compassion for his mother was a positive sign that attested to the strength of their relationship. A strong mother-son relationship may be a protective factor against further offending (Kobayashi, Sales, Becker, Figueredo, & Kaplan, 1995).

Group Session 3: March 25

Data The purpose of this group session was to aid members in developing empathy for their victims. Group members first wrote down on a piece of paper how they thought their victims felt at the time of the offense. Each member read what he or she wrote. Len first wrote that his victim was "OK." I asked him what that meant. He said she seemed "OK" because she didn't act afraid. Another member asked if she seemed nervous. Len said "probably." Next, the group was shown a videotape in which victims of sexual abuse told their stories how the abuse affected them. The group members then again wrote down what they thought their victims felt. We then discussed their answers in light of the new information. Len's answers after the video were more in-depth than those of some of the other group members. He said his victim was probably nervous because she was afraid of what he was going to do. He also was able to be more active in today's discussion without as much prompting from the leaders.

Assessment Len seems to have retained the information from the family session and the impact of his actions on his victim has registered with him. He was much more focused today.

Plan Continue with group. Next group session will deal with appropriate and inappropriate sexual behaviors.

Worker's Commentary During this session, the group members interacted more easily with each other. We began to explore the impact of sexual offenses upon victims. I thought Len might add to the discussion—in light of his mother's disclosure during the most recent family session. I was disappointed that he did not share what he had learned from his mother about the pain of victimization.

I could not discuss his mother's experience with the group. I had not explored that possibility with her and did not have her permission to do so. Although I sometimes discuss with families what information might be shared in the group experience, I had not done so in the family session. I reminded myself to consider that aspect with all of the group members' families. Some information discussed in the family sessions would be helpful to the group experience. When I met with the families, we needed to decide if some information might be shared within the group as well. I missed an opportunity to do so during the last session with Len's family.

Group Session 4: April 2

Data The purpose of today's session was to discuss sexual behaviors that group members felt were appropriate or inappropriate. They each made a list of sexual behaviors they felt were "OK" (appropriate) and "Not OK" (inappropriate) for their age. Len said that it was important to have consent from a partner and to respect when the partner did not want to participate. He agreed with another member when it was brought up that it was important to have a positive relationship with the partner and to be within the legal age limits of consent. Len also said that he thought some girls were "teases" and that they let boys think that there would be sex but changed their mind at the last minute. I also brought up the concept of "flirting" and that often it did not lead to sexual activity but it was a way that guys and girls expressed interest in each other. He said that girls could get away with more of that than could boys. He thought that boys were often blamed for making sexual advances when flirting and that girls were not blamed. We talked about the notion that one still must respect the boundaries of others. The discussion focused upon the concept that when someone said "no" it meant that the sexual activity should stop, or should not start in the first place. The members completed a checklist at the end of group indicating what they now thought about appropriate and inappropriate sexual behaviors. One of Len's responses indicated that kissing was an appropriate behavior as long as it was with people you cared about and they were your age.

Assessment Len showed a good grasp of inappropriate and appropriate sexual behaviors. He seems to understand the concepts of consent and boundaries. He participates in the group process and seems interested in learning. He shares his opinions but seems open to input from others. He appears engaged with the other group members and seems to be processing information well at this point.

Plan Next group session will deal with incidents where group members have felt victimized. The intent is to promote further victim empathy on the part of the offenders.

Worker's Commentary In this session, we began to explore the distinction between acceptable and unacceptable sexual behavior. Len became more spontaneously expressive during the exchange. He suggested that many girls were "teases" and led boys on. The boys in the sex offense groups often find it difficult to differentiate between words

and behavior that reflect flirtation and those that indicate consent for sex. Adolescents who commit sexual offenses often operate on the basis of misinformation, strange beliefs, and atypical attitudes. Many routinely make decisions based upon erroneous perceptions (Lakey, 1994). Although I've led these groups for many years, I am still frequently surprised at the sexual ignorance, naiveté, and distorted beliefs of youngsters in the sexual offense groups. In this evening's session, for example, someone suggested that certain girls "get what they ask for and deserve what they get." Indeed, blaming victims is a common pastime in early sessions. When I asked that group member how he came to believe that a male person became entitled to rape or beat a female person because of the words she used, the clothes she wore, or the way she walked, he became flustered. Other group members then contributed their thoughts. This led to an interesting and somewhat philosophical discussion about personal responsibility. Len pointed out the need to respect personal boundaries saying that people's bodies are theirs and theirs alone. No one has a right to touch others in any way without their permission. I was pleased with his comments and wondered if he might be thinking about his mother's experience during childhood and later during her first marriage. I also wondered if he worried that he might turn out to be like his own biological father.

Group Session 5: April 9

Data The agenda for group discussion was to focus upon identifying times that each member felt victimized in some way. This topic is intended to aid members in further development of victim empathy as well as to obtain information about their past experiences. Len talked about how he has often felt picked on and teased by peers in school. They make fun of his weight and his clothing. Len said he hoped to lose about 50 pounds and wished his family could afford to buy him nicer clothes. He said when he gets teased he has several different feelings but mostly he feels angry and would like to strike back at those who hurt him. He rarely says anything, however, because when he has, they usually tease him even more. He was able to make the connection that his victim may also have had some of the same feelings he has about being used in some way by others. During this discussion, I noticed that Len was on the verge of tears and commented to him that recalling these incidents appeared to be painful for him. He said he didn't like to talk with others about them because "They don't understand."

Assessment Len was able to take risks in group today and allow himself to be vulnerable. His pain was obvious as he struggles with means to respond to teasing by peers. In that he doesn't seem to feel he has adequate resources, it will be important to help him to identify some.

Plan Schedule a family session to further discuss these issues and explore how family can be a resource for Len.

Worker's Commentary In this session, we continued our exploration about victimization. I hoped the discussion would encourage further development of victim empathy. At about this stage in the group, some youngsters begin to share their own experiences as victims. I am no longer surprised when group members reveal histories of sexual abuse at the hands of relatives, neighbors, and older children. Many offending adolescents have been sexually victimized—perhaps as many as 52 percent—and tend to become more willing to discuss their experiences as the group progresses (Worling, 1995). Although Len has not been sexually abused, he has often felt victimized and bullied in school. Youngsters who commit sexual offenses often lack basic social and interpersonal skills (Fagan & Wexler, 1988). Like Len, many find it difficult to develop and maintain close peer relationships. I also discovered that Len believed that others would be unable or unwilling to understand his problems and concerns. I wondered if he felt that I or the group might be able to understand.

Family Intervention Session 2: April 13

Data This was the first family session that included Len's stepsister Susan. I felt it was important to include her in the session to determine if she can be a positive resource for Len regarding the issues with teasing. I had not previously met Susan. She is an attractive young woman. She was somewhat put out that she was required to come to the session. I asked her how she felt about attending the family session. She said, "I don't know why I have to be here. I didn't do anything wrong and there isn't anything I can do to help him with this sex problem thing Lenny has going on." I thanked her for coming to the session and explained that I thought family members could be an important resource for Len with regard to supporting him in his treatment and being available for him regarding difficulties he was having with self-esteem issues. I asked Len if he would tell his family members about some of the struggles he had with regard to being teased. He was able to explain the situations that caused him stress at school and with peers. Both parents were supportive and con-

cerned about those feelings. Carla stated "You always tell us that things are fine at school when we ask you. I wish you would open up more so we can help you." Susan said that she would also try to help out by being available for him to talk to her after school. However, she also said that she wanted him to stop "sneaking around trying to peak at me when I'm undressing." I asked her to describe what she's noticed. She said that Lenny frequently tried to see her naked or in various stages of undress. Len became embarrassed and blurted out that he had not done that for a long while. She agreed that he seemed to have stopped it after his offense with his cousin was discovered. I suggested to Len that it would be important for him to talk about that issue in group. I also reminded him that he could be found in violation of his probation agreement if he was still doing that because it was considered to be re-offending behavior. He said he would bring it up in group and said that he knew that he had invaded Susan's privacy previously. He also told her that he had not attempted to "peep" after he had been charged with an offense. He apologized to her and assured her it would not happen again.

We then shifted topics and discussed a plan for Len to talk about how his school day went after school with either his mother or sister. William is usually working when Len gets home but said he would also like to be involved and would "check in" with Len when he got home in the evenings.

Assessment The family was supportive to Len and identified a plan to help Len process his day at school and to aid him in problem solving about issues with peers. A surprise in the session was the discussion regarding his stepsister's feelings that he had been trying to "see her naked." This issue was addressed and it appears that the behavior has not occurred since the discovery of his offense. However, it is an issue that still needs attention in group. The voyeuristic behavior was clearly offensive to his sister and may represent a contributory factor to the offense with his cousin.

Plan Address this issue in the next group session.

Worker's Commentary Len's sister Susan attended this family session at my request. The parents thought she would be reluctant, so I was not surprised by her initial reaction. However, I felt that there must be some reason that she chose to come to the session. She could have refused. I think her reason for coming was to bring up Len's "peeping" behavior. I was somewhat surprised by this disclosure despite the fact that many adolescents under-report their sexual offensive behavior. I was glad she felt comfortable enough to express it during the session and was relieved to learn that it had not occurred since Len's offense. I would have had to make a report to his probation officer and Len may have been placed in a residential or juvenile justice setting for probation violation. I do not see Len as a chronic offender but probation violations often lead to a more restrictive level of care. I was also pleased by the response of Len's family to his dilemma at school. Again, this is an indicator of a supportive environment that will be a protective factor against recidivism.

Group Session 6: April 16

Data During the check-in, Len brought up his family session and told the group what had occurred. When he shared that he had "tried to peak at Susan when she was undressing" the other group members had various reactions. One member asked if Susan was "hot." Len said that she was "really pretty." We then talked about the issue of boundaries and sex offenses such as voyeurism, which represent violations of personal privacy. Len was adamant that he had not done that since the offense. He was asked why he hadn't revealed this before. He said that he didn't want to get in more trouble than he was already in and was afraid he would get sent to Boys School (a juvenile correction facility). He also said that Susan had told him that she would "beat the shit out of me if she ever caught me doing it again." Some of the group members got into "victim bashing" stating that some girls bring these things on themselves by the way they dress and act around guys. I reiterated that they would be guilty of reoffending if they were found to be "peeping" at others. The group also discussed that "peeping" at others could be sexually stimulating and might increase the risk of committing an even more serious sex offense.

Assessment Len seems to have an understanding of how his past behavior was wrong with regard to his stepsister. Of concern is the fact that he had not previously reported this behavior and also that he is so reliant upon external control to monitor the behaviors. This will have to be monitored closely and if it reoccurs the decision as to whether Len can stay in the home will be re-visited.

Plan Deal with sexual attitudes during the next group session.

Worker's Commentary We instituted a "check-in" process in group today. I felt that the group members have become attached and interested in each other; thus, it seems like a check-in process would continue to aid in establishing mutual aid. However, today's group consisted totally of "checking in"! I allowed that to occur because I felt that the members were using the time appropriately. The problem is that I did not introduce any new content. Since this is a time-limited program, it is always difficult to balance content and process. I will need to pay closer attention to this in the ensuing weeks. I tend to enjoy the process groups more and feel that in this shorter-term group we too often neglect the open discussions. Yet, there is a certain amount of content that needs to be covered.

Group Session 7: April 23

Data At check-in Len reported that he had a good week at school. He felt supported by his mom and stepdad with regard to some of the teasing issues. His mom also offered to help him with a diet to control weight. And, his sister had offered some tips on grooming and choices in what to wear so he didn't feel so "out of style." He said that he had also apologized to her for past behavior and promised he would not do anything to make her uncomfortable again.

Today's topic was about sexual attitudes. During the group discussion, several of the group members talked about their attitudes about women and how they formed those attitudes. Len said that his biological father had often made comments about women and their bodies when they were driving around town. He also said that when other guys are making sexual comments about women he often tries to join in so they won't "think I'm gay or something." We then watched a videotape on the topic of sexual harassment in high school. Further discussion focused upon how group members felt the video pertained to them and their behaviors with girls. Len shared that he has different feelings about the inappropriateness of his behaviors as a result of what his mother shared about being molested and his stepsister feeling violated by his attempts to see her naked. One of the other members laughed when Len said this and told Len that he didn't believe that he would stop looking for opportunities to see his sister naked. Len got very angry and called him an "ass-hole" that should concentrate on his own problems. When I asked Len what would stop him from trying to look, he said "I just won't do it anymore." The group members pointed out to him that he needed to have a better reason and a more complete plan to resist the temptations to "peep."

At the end of the group session, members completed an open-ended response form that required them to list three things that they had learned from today's group. Len indicated that he had learned more specifics about sexual harassment; the source of some of his beliefs; and that he needs to give more thought to prevention efforts.

Assessment   It would appear that Len is developing a good understanding of how his sexually offending behaviors have affected others. He seems to be integrating information and content from the family sessions with that from the group. He still needs to develop more specific prevention plans with alternatives to "just won't do it."

Plan   Next group session will focus on healthy expression of sexuality.

Worker's Commentary   I was pleased to hear how Len's family has come to his aid at home. One group of researchers (Blaske, Borduin, Henggeler, & Mann, 1989) found that supportive communication was limited in families of adolescent sex offenders and that interruptions as well as aggressive statements were common. Adolescent sex offenders seem to be more disengaged from and receive less emotional support from their families than other adolescents. These factors may leave them more vulnerable to stress and temptation, and less able to form positive attachments with peers and adults (Bischof, Stith, & Wilson, 1992; Bischof & Stith, 1995). Len's family situation may counter this pattern. They seem to care about Len and appear willing to help him deal with everyday issues at school. Len may have a stronger support system than he realized. His parents and his sister seem committed to helping him feel better about himself and learn to control temptations and sexual impulses.

Group Session 8: April 30

Data   During check-in, Len said that he received a week's suspension from school for fighting with another boy. The boy teased Len about being overweight and also referred to him as a "sex pervert with little girls." The other boys asked how the other kid knew Len had committed a sexual offense. Len said he didn't know. The boys gave Len credit for standing up for himself and thought he did the right thing by fighting back. We talked about the fighting as a new form of behavior and explored whether he felt it had worked out for him or not. He said he was glad he hit the other boy but thought it would not really change anything. He predicted that other kids would probably tease him more. The group members gave Len some ideas about how to handle it the next time. In general, they suggested that he should ignore the teasing and talk to the principal or school counselor for support.

The topic for discussion in today's group was building friendships and participating in social activities with peers. This is difficult for Len. He said he did not feel confident around his peers and especially in conversations with girls. He said he is afraid others will tease him about other things or laugh at him. Group members made some suggestions as to how Len might be able to meet more people. One of the suggestions was to list the activities/hobbies he enjoys and try to find an after school activity to participate in that focuses on those things.

Assessment   Len adopted a new form of behavior in an interaction with a boy at school. When teased, he hit the other boy and engaged in a fight. His suspension from school for fighting might represent a violation of his probation agreement. He will need to develop further coping skills and problem-solving techniques for these situations. Len also is socially isolated. He lacks confidence in talking with other young people—especially girls—and is skeptical that others will like him.

Plan   Schedule a family session to explore how things are at home. Len also agreed to explore possible extracurricular activities, which may be of interest to him.

Worker's Commentary   My initial gut reaction to Len's striking out at the boy who teased him was to think "good for you." I did not share this reaction with Len and the group. Obviously, fighting does not represent a functional response and, in Len's case, it could also constitute a violation of the terms of his probation. However, Len was at least trying a new behavior. I think this was the first fight of his life. I also hoped the other group members would provide support and offer alternate suggestions. Students and teachers often scapegoat adolescent sex offenders and lump them into the same category as chronic adult offenders. These kids are frequently stigmatized by family members and neighbors. Certain family relatives may refuse any and all contact with a sexual offending adolescent. Peers can be unmerciful in their treatment of the adolescent offender in school. If the word spreads in their neighborhood about the offense, families sometimes must relocate to another neighborhood or community due to the harassment they receive.

We must support youth and their families in their efforts to cope with harassment and, further, to help them develop social skills needed to build positive relationships with peers. Lack of intimate peer relationships and social isolation may leave adolescent sex offenders at higher risk for sexual reoffense (Worling & Curwen, 2001).

Family Intervention Session 3: May 3

Data   This session focused upon how things are going at home with regard to Len's use of family supports. Carla and William have been pleased by Len's willingness to express himself more freely during the past few weeks. Susan expressed how that she was proud of Len for standing up for himself in school and thought he did the right thing. We talked about this at length because it also turned out that the kid who teased Len and called him a "pervert" was a brother of one of Susan's friends who learned about the offense through Susan. Susan said she was sorry that her friend had told her brother. The family brainstormed ideas as to how Len might deal with teasing situations. Len agreed to try to ignore any teasing at school and to walk away from the situation. If it continues, he said he would report it to the principal. Len felt he could try it although he wasn't sure how well it would work.

Assessment   The family seems to be positive and active in supporting Len. Interventions discussed at the last family session have been helpful and family members have rallied around Len. He is in a difficult situation at school now that other students have learned about the sex offense. At this point, he feels angry. Previously teased about his weight and appearance, he is now being harassed because of the offense. Given his low self-esteem and the possibility that the teasing might increase, it will be important to watch for signs of depression.

Plan   Continue with group. Next session topic is human sexuality.

Worker's Commentary   This family session revealed the importance of caution in family members' sharing information about sexual offenses with others. In this particular situation, Susan shared information with a friend, who then shared it with her brother. Often, families ask me who should have information; or, who really needs to know about the offense. Due to the stigma associated with adolescent sex offenses, families often find it difficult to determine with whom they may safely share information with and to whom they can turn for support. Of course, we must protect those vulnerable to victimization by the sexual offending adolescents. The degree of supervision must increase in proportion to the risk of reoffense. Sometimes this means that friends, relatives, and neighbors must be informed so that they don't leave vulnerable children alone in the presence of an adolescent at risk of reoffensive. Indeed, some supportive friends and relatives may provide proper supervision for the adolescent offender at times when the parents are unavailable. In this particular situation, Susan shared information about Len's offense with a trusted friend—expecting it to remain confidential. Her friend violated that trust by telling her brother who then harassed Len at school, in front of others.

Group Session 9: May 6

Data   Len returned to school today without any incidents. He stated he just wants to make it through the next month until summer break. He received a great deal of support from the group with regard to his plan. Several of the other group members said they thought he should ignore the teasing and harassment. They expressed concern that he might violate the probation agreement if he got into any more trouble. One group member also suggested that peers who tease in a mean spirited way are not worth wasting energy on.

The remainder of the group session was educational in nature. Following completion of a sexual information inventory that focused upon reproduction and contraception, members received accurate knowledge about reproduction, contraception, and sexually transmitted diseases. We also viewed two videotapes. Afterward, I asked several questions and offered the boys the opportunity to ask questions as well. Len was an active participant. He said that he had learned several new facts about reproduction and contraception. Specifically, he had always believed that condoms were foolproof but he didn't realize that there were certain ways to put them on and that there were many different kinds of condoms. He also said that he had always thought that birth control was the girl's responsibility. He said he now realized it is a joint responsibility that should be addressed by both partners in a sexual relationship. At the end of the session, group members completed the same inventory as they had before the discussion. This serves as a post-session indicator of the nature and degree of learning during this session.

Assessment   Len's comments about making it through the next month seem to be a realistic appraisal of the situation at school. His mood appeared to be boosted by the feedback from other group members and their concern for him. He also took some risks in sharing his thoughts about the sex education materials and contributed to the discussion.

Plan   We will explore the relationship between thinking errors and sex offenses during the next group session.

Worker's Commentary   Group members supported Len and offered suggestions for dealing with teasing, harassment, and bullying behaviors. Many adolescents—especially those who have engaged in sexual offenses—lack problem-solving and conflict resolution skills. These and other social skills must be introduced to this population and opportunities for them to use them must be provided. The group format provides an ideal context for such learning and allows group members to gain information from other members who may experience similar difficulties.

The primary content of the group had to do with sex education. Many adolescent sex offenders operate on the basis of inaccurate and distorted information about sexuality (Lakey, 1994). Sex education represents one of the most important program components (Chaffin, 2001; Knopp, Freeman-Longo, & Lane, 1997). Most of the group members in today's session lacked basic knowledge about birth control.

Group Session 10: May 13

Data   Len reported one teasing incident at school this week. He was again called a "pervert" by the same kid as before. He said that a teacher overheard the kid call him that name and immediately took both of them into a classroom. Len was smiling as he related that the teacher really "lit that kid up and read him the riot act." The teacher then insisted that the kid apologize to Len and he also told the kid he better not hear of any other harassment of Len. The other group members were surprised to hear that a teacher would stand up for Len especially in regard to the sex offense. Len said he was also surprised but he felt great about the whole situation.

We then introduced the concept of thinking errors. Each group member wrote down some of the thinking errors they believed were present at the time they committed the offense. Then, they discussed the thinking errors. Len told his offense story after two other members told theirs. Other group members helped him to identify certain thinking errors. For example, Len thought that "It is OK as long as the girl does not specifically say 'no' or fight him off." He also identified two others: "As long as I don't physically hurt her she won't be harmed" and "It's OK if I only do it once and never do it again." Next, the members identified and wrote down thoughts they could substitute for the thinking errors. Len struggled somewhat with this but was able to do it with input from me and the other members. At one point he stated, "I think I get it. Instead of thinking that it won't harm her physically, I should also have thought about how she might feel and

could be affected that way. I could also think about her rights as a human being."

Assessment   Len seems to have a beginning understanding of some thinking errors associated with the sex offense. He voices genuine understanding of some of the emotional harm that his cousin probably experienced. I think Len demonstrated genuine insight today when he said that he hadn't really thought about his cousin—he had only thought about himself.

Plan   During the next group session, we will explore other factors that may contribute to sexually offensive behavior. We will also discuss the issue of termination and ending the group in two weeks.

Worker's Commentary   In this group session, Len expressed his pleasure and satisfaction when a teacher stood up for him in spite of the fact that he was a sex offender. This support from a significant adult can aid in the adolescent feeling that they are more than a "sex offender" and offer hope that things can be different.

We explored various thinking errors in the group today. Len identified several that are common among adolescent sex offenders. He and the other boys seemed to understand the concept of thinking errors and to recognize their significance to the offensive behavior. This cognitive dimension is a common component of most programs for adolescent sex offenders (Chaffin, 2001; Murphy et al., 2003). As indicated by his participation in group and his pre- and post-response questionnaires, Len has a good grasp of this concept. Importantly, he exhibited an ability to move beyond a self-centered viewpoint by taking into account how his victim might have been feeling rather than to focus on a thinking pattern that rendered the behavior acceptable. I feel that Len has continued to engage well in the group and is grasping the concepts as indicated by his ability to discuss and apply them to his own experience.

Group Session 11: May 20

Data   During check-in Len said he had a good week except for an argument with his mother about going to the swimming pool by himself. His mother refused to let him go telling him that he should not be in an area with a lot of young kids and without supervision. He said this made him angry even though he understood that it was part of the safety plan that was in place for him as a sex offender. This led to a general discussion about prevention plans and the importance of managing situations that could cause temptation. Many of the boys had strong feelings about how unfair it is to be constantly punished for past mistakes—especially now that they have gotten help for the problem. We talked a lot about the often-lengthy process necessary for rebuilding trust once that basic sense of trust had been lost.

We then discussed how sexually offensive behavior can occur for various reasons. Each of the boys talked about what feelings they were having prior to the offense. Len said that he had been looking at pornography on the Internet the night before he committed his offense. He became sexually aroused and also began to wish that he were more popular and that he had a girlfriend. As he thought about that he also began to feel angry about how he was often teased and wondered if he would ever have a girlfriend. The next day, these thoughts were still present when he visited with his cousin. He wanted to have a sexual experience and thought that she would be "safe" and would not turn him down. I asked Len to talk more about the feelings of anger and hurt regarding girlfriends. He became tearful and said he was afraid he would never meet a girl that found him attractive. He stated, "Look at me. I'm fat and ugly. How will I ever get a girlfriend?" I asked him to consider what qualities he thought he had that would be attractive to girls. He shrugged his shoulders and said he couldn't think of any. Another group member (Sam) told Len that he thought he had a good sense of humor. John then told Len that he thought he was a good listener and came up with good suggestions. Len began to relax and had a slight smile. He then cracked a joke, which caused others to confirm what Sam had said about Len's sense of humor.

We also discussed termination and the ending process. The group's final meeting is scheduled for next week. We talked about ending feelings. Each member shared how he felt they had done and gave feedback to each other. Len was positive regarding his progress and talked about the various things he had learned in the group. I commended them for the work they had done and said that I would be sad to see them go, even though I was happy they completed the program. There was an awkward moment after this and I said, "Goodbyes can be difficult. We'll talk more about it next week."

Assessment   Len's triggers for reoffending seem to involve a sense of low self-esteem, fears that girls will not find him attractive, and sexual stimulation through pornography. He has difficulty getting in touch with his strengths and becomes depressed and hopeless.

Plan   Next group is the last session in this sequence. The focus will be on prevention plans. Len and the other boys will also complete the Sexual Attitudes Questionnaire and the Sexual Knowledge Inventory as post-test measures at the conclusion of the last group.

Worker's Commentary   Supervision is often a difficult issue for adolescent offenders and their parents. This generally has to do with the hope that the offense was an anomaly and will not recur. Supervision means that there may be continuing restrictions in which the teen and parent are inconvenienced. In Len's situation, it also means that there are some activities that he may need to avoid or carefully manage if they put him at risk for reoffending. This might inhibit the establishment of social relationships and contribute to continued feelings of shame and stigma.

The content of the session focused upon factors contributing to sex offenses. Certainly, there are multiple reasons and not all offenders are the same. This is a very heterogeneous population. Understanding the idiosyncratic life events, circumstances, and internal struggles the adolescent experienced at the time of the offense is crucial to progress. Len identified a relationship among the factors of pornography, sexual stimulation, and poor self-esteem and the sexual offense. Exposure to pornographic material led to myriad feelings on his part. It was obvious that Len suffered from low self-esteem and had many negative self-attributions. The group members were able to aid Len in coming up with positive attributes and provided considerable social and emotional support. I am always excited to experience this aspect of the group process. It is touching to see how much group members connect with and show concern for each other. There is a genuine sense of interest in caring for each other.

Group Session 12: May 27

Data   Len thanked the guys in the group for helping him feel better about himself last week. He said he had also talked with Susan (stepsister) and she had confirmed that he had those positive qualities that the group members identified. He also shared that he had lost seven pounds in the past 6 weeks and was continuing his work on reducing his weight with exercise and a program that involved fewer snacks.

In group, we focused on the prevention plans that each of the boys worked on during the week. Len's prevention plan was well formulated. He identified being alone with younger children as one of the high-risk factors for reoffense. His prevention plan called for him to avoid those situations. We did a role-play with regard to how he could respond if asked to baby-sit for a younger child. He also identified looking at pornography as risky for him in that he became stimulated and wanted to have sex. He indicated that he could use masturbation as a healthy outlet at times when he was over-stimulated but also planned to avoid pornography. In addition, he identified the feeling triggers of anger and sadness. These are the feelings that might cause him to be more vulnerable and to inappropriately seek out sexual contact. He was able to come up with a plan to deal with these feelings. His plan was to seek out a friend or family member to talk with him about his feelings. Group members asked him what he would do if a friend or family member were not immediately available to talk to him. He said he guessed he would "just have to wait." I observed that waiting could be difficult when we have strong feelings we need to talk about. By waiting, he might put himself in a higher risk category to act out sexually again. Len became frustrated and said he didn't know what else to do. I asked if any of the other group members had suggestions. There were two suggestions that Len thought would be good to use. The first was to find something active to do such as, go outside and shoot baskets, walk around the block, clean up his room. The second was to use a journal to express his feelings. Then he could also use techniques he has learned in group to identify thinking errors and substitute more positive self-talk. He seemed intrigued by this idea.

The second part of group was devoted to termination and saying goodbye to each other. Each boy reviewed what he learned from the experience and what had been most helpful. Len stated that what had been the most helpful to him was the support and concern of the other members. He felt that the most significant learning experience was that he should always remember how victims are hurt by abuse and that he needed to deal with his issues and sexuality in more appropriate ways. We did a "go around" in which everyone said something positive that they had gotten from each of the other members. Len and the other boys completed the post-test questionnaires at the conclusion of the group. Then we invited the parents to join us for cake and ice cream.

Assessment   Len appears to have used the group experience in a positive manner. He was able to discuss what he learned and accept modifications to his prevention plan. Of continuing concern is Len's vulnerability regarding low self-esteem, periods of depression, and his ability to cope

with stressful situations. He has received needed input about sexually inappropriate behaviors and he has a well-formulated prevention plan. He probably could benefit from further work on social skill building, enhancement of self-esteem, and management of depressed feelings.

Plan   Our last family session is scheduled for next week. Len and his family members will review progress and I will make recommendations. I feel that further therapy is warranted for the purpose of social skill enhancement and building self-esteem. Since Len has made good use of group, I will refer him to a social skills group for adolescents at this agency. I also will recommend that the family continue family sessions in that this has been useful to Len. I do not feel that further specific sex offender treatment is necessary. This is based upon the progress and contributions made in group, the pre-, post-questionnaires, and the most recent scoring on the ERASOR with regard to risk of reoffending.

Worker's Commentary   This is the last group session. The original client contract has been fulfilled with regard to participation in this time-limited group. This session dealt with review and termination issues. As a part of the final session, the group members are required to present their prevention plans. They present to the group and their families plans for identifying and managing triggers associated with reoffending. Len presented a clear prevention plan. He addressed the essential dimensions of a well-formulated plan. When he became frustrated, he was able to accept input from others and continue to problem solve. I thought it was a good sign that he could accommodate to the feedback and put it to good use. The members also discussed and evaluated the group experience. They talked about what had been most helpful. I am sometimes disappointed when group or family members continue to reflect denial and minimization. Len was able to come up with something that the entire group had given him (support and concern for him); and, something that he thought had been helpful regarding victimization of another child. The celebration at the end of the session is always a highlight for me. I have enjoyed working with this group, and particularly with Len. He has many positive qualities and it has been rewarding to see him benefit from the group experience. When the parents joined the boys to celebrate the ending, they reflected a sense of accomplishment as well as hope and optimism. These feelings are quite different from those they experienced at the beginning of the process!

Family Session 4: June 2

Data   I asked Len to describe his prevention plan, thinking errors, and feeling triggers to the family. He did so and asked them if they had any questions. All members said they were proud of him. He talked about how he was still working on his diet and exercise. Len and Susan have become "buddies" and Len said it really helps to have someone close to his age to talk to. Susan is giving him tips on how to talk to girls at school. I asked Len how he would feel about attending another group for the purpose of continuing to build social skills. His first comment was "Do I have a choice?" I told him that he did. He has fulfilled the requirements of his probation and is not mandated for further treatment. He then said he would like to try the new group and stated that he thought the prior group had been surprisingly helpful to him. I also asked the rest of the family how they felt about Len continuing in a social skills group. All members were supportive of that. In addition, we reviewed and discussed each member's thoughts about the family sessions. Again, the feedback was positive. Len thought the sessions had really benefited him especially with regard to his relationship with Susan. William and Carla said that there was significantly less fighting and disobedience at home and they each felt that communication among all family members was more positive. I asked them what they would like to do regarding the family sessions. Each of the members felt that they would like to continue to meet with me as a family until Len had completed the social skills group. I stated that I would be able to do that and we agreed to meet on a monthly basis for the next three months.

Assessment   This family has come together well and utilized the sessions in an effective way to address needed changes. They obviously care about each other and are willing to consider alternate means for solving problems.

Plan   Refer to Social Skills Group. I will continue to work with the family since the relationship is established. I will invite the group therapist to join us for family sessions.

Worker's Commentary   This session served as a review of the therapeutic process. Len talked with his family about what he had learned from the group process and gave specific details about his prevention plan, thinking errors, and feeling triggers. I am encouraged by the degree in which Len's responses on the sexual information and sexual attitude questionnaires demonstrates learning in those areas. I am still concerned about Len's social relationships and isolation. This is a primary risk factor. However, he seems motivated to develop more sophisticated social skills and he wants to develop relationships with other young people. This is the basis of my recommendation that he continue in a social skills group. Len was interested in knowing whether this is "required." Once he learned that there were no further probation requirements, he and the family readily agreed to continued service.

I think this case serves as a useful example of how clients who are required to receive treatment often move from involuntary to voluntary status. My work with Len and his family has been enjoyable. I appreciate the difficulties of their struggles and have been impressed at how well they have come together during this crisis in their lives.

READING 27
The Omar Family[1]

Khadija Khaja[2]

Intake Information

Date: July 10
Name: Mr. Majid Omar (age 36)
Residence: 17 Perdue Court, Indianapolis, Indiana 46202
Contact Information: (H) 234–6213 (W) 361–9000

---

[1] An original case study for *Social Work Processes*.
[2] Visiting Assistant Professor, School of Social Work, Indiana University, Indianapolis.

Family Context: Mr. Majid Omar (age 36); Mrs. Amina Omar (age 35). One child, Sara (age 6).
Ethnicity: Somalian   **Religion:** Muslim
Current Employment: Engineer
Initial Concern: Mr. Omar telephoned the agency from his place of work. He sounded very upset. He reported that he had overheard his wife, Mrs. Omar, talking to some friends over the telephone telling them that she wanted to perform female circumcision on their six-year-old

daughter, Sara. Mr. Omar reported that he informed his wife that female circumcision was banned in the United States. He stated that female circumcision was a traditional Somalian practice which involved cutting the vaginal area of girls. Mr. Omar said that previously his wife agreed to forgo the procedure for their daughter. He was frustrated because his wife continued to raise the topic and they constantly argued about female circumcision. Mr. Omar said he was concerned because his wife did not appear to understand why female circumcision was banned in North America or accept that his daughter would be unable to participate in this traditional practice. He reported that his wife believed he had turned against Somalian cultural beliefs because he did not support female circumcision. Mr. Omar stated that he and his wife wanted counseling because their conflicting views were driving them apart.

Other Pertinent Information: Mr. Omar and his family are Muslim. He requested an appointment time that would not interfere with their daily prayer schedule. Mr. Omar said that he and his wife had never previously sought or received counseling.

Disposition: An appointment was set with the social worker, Ms. Khaja for July 11 at 2:00 P.M.

ENGAGEMENT

First Meeting: Contact

During the first interview session I introduced myself and asked how the couple wished to be addressed. They requested that I refer to them as Amina and Majid. I then reviewed the information contained in the telephone intake report to ensure that everything was accurate. I told them that information they shared with me would remain confidential within the agency unless there were indications of child abuse or neglect, or someone's life were in danger. Under those circumstances, I might need to share confidential information to safeguard children or protect human life.

I briefly outlined the costs associated with service. Mr. Omar indicated they could afford to pay for five counseling sessions. In repeating my name, Mrs. Omar asked if I was Muslim. I confirmed her hunch, which seemed to comfort both of them.

Majid indicated that he was looking forward to counseling sessions. He wanted to resolve this issue that caused such unhappiness between him and his wife. Amina suggested that she was hopeful but also hesitant about the counseling. She expressed concern that I might have already

judged her negatively because of her views on female circumcision. I thanked her for sharing this with me and suggested that I would try to be fair to each of them. She said that even though I was also a Muslim woman, I seemed quite Westernized. She was afraid that I had fully accepted popular Western views regarding the practice of female circumcision. She mentioned that the mass media always depicted female circumcision as a barbaric cultural practice. She thought I might be unable to see both sides of the issue because I was raised in a Western culture. I thanked her again for sharing her thoughts and concerns. I then acknowledged that I sincerely hoped to learn about her views concerning the traditional practice of female circumcision. I also said that I'd like to learn about Majid's perspective as well. My comments appeared to ease both partners.

I then asked the couple how they were referred to the agency. Majid said he had been referred by someone at their mosque. Amina said she was surprised that I did not wear a head covering (hijab) over my hair, a common practice among many Muslim women. I said that most women in my family wore hijabs and I did so as well when I prayed.

I then asked Amina and Majid what they hoped to achieve from the counseling experience. Majid said he hoped counseling would teach them how to communicate better as a couple. He said he wanted to learn how to discuss the issue of female circumcision in a more compassionate manner. He said he was tired of the arguments that occurred whenever they talked about female circumcision. Amina was less clear about what she wanted from counseling. During this first meeting, there were a few rather lengthy silences when Amina and Majid just looked at me.

About halfway through the scheduled meeting time, I received an emergency call. I learned my father had been admitted to the hospital. Although I did not share the news with Amina or Majid, I quickly moved to conclude the session. As the session ended, I said that in our next meeting, I hoped we would explore the conflict in greater detail, perhaps reach a better understanding of the nature of the problem, and establish goals for our work together. Then, we could develop plans to pursue those goals. I asked how that seemed to them. They both nodded and confirmed that would be helpful.

I then asked if we could meet again early the following week. I suggested times that I knew would not interfere with prayer times and mentioned that I was doing so. I could tell they appreciated my concern for their religious practices. However, I was also aware that they sensed I was rushing to conclude the session. I thanked the couple for coming in to see me and told them I looked forward to working with them.

Worker's Commentary

In a sense, the first session began even before I first met Majid and Amina. An intake worker had already noted some general information and decided when I would meet the family. When I read the intake sheet, I immediately became interested in the case. I had spent the last ten years studying female circumcision and had completed my doctoral dissertation on the topic. Given my knowledge of female circumcision, I had assumed that engaging Amina and Majid would be quite straightforward. However, when Amina seemed disappointed that I had not worn a hijab, my confidence ebbed. I found myself trying to align with her by sharing family information. I even told them I wore a hijab when I prayed. It was my attempt to show I was like them in at least some significant ways—but I wondered if I had shared too much.

Many people who seek social services expect the social worker to solve the problem for them by telling them exactly what to do. I wondered if Amina and Majid might expect that of me as well. They may have expected me to be more active and directive—even in this first meeting. Perhaps that's what those silences meant. They were probably waiting for me to provide direction. After all, they were not experienced in the process.

I was also extremely aware that to them—and especially to Amina—I was a stranger of a different ethnicity from a different culture. Although I was also Muslim, Amina viewed me as someone who had been assimilated into Western culture. Despite my statements about fairness to each of them, I am certain that she expected me to hold a negative view of female circumcision and probably to take her husband's side in the conflict.

I chose not to reveal that my doctorate dissertation addressed the topic of female circumcision. I wanted them to share their thoughts and feelings freely and openly. I was afraid they might become more cautious if they thought I was an expert in the field. In some ways, I felt deceptive. On the other hand, we had not yet specifically identified a problem and agreed upon goals for work. Therefore, it was premature to conclude that my knowledge about female circumcision would be especially helpful. Other areas of expertise, such as psychosocial issues associated with migration and acculturation, communication skills, or perhaps the processes of grieving might be more applicable.

I know myself well enough to recognize that I tend to be quite anxious during first meetings with clients. I try to cope by maintaining a clear focus on the purpose for the first session, following clients' leads, and being myself (Moursund & Kenny, 2002). The fact that Amina suspected that I had already seen her as the "problem" contributed to my anxiety. Her questions added even more. I started to worry that we were focusing too much on me as a person. However, Amina was probably asking these personal questions as a test to determine whether I had the capacity for fairness. Amina's comment about Westerners' belief that female circumcision was a barbaric practice might have been a way to ask if I thought she was barbaric too. She had every right to question if I could be fair and open-minded, and to test me as a way of addressing that concern.

There were quite a few silences during the first session. My heart started beating faster and I became aware that I wanted to end the session early—even before the emergency phone call about my father. I was probably more anxious than they were during that first meeting.

Interruptions in any session can be embarrassing and may interfere with the flow of the interview. I was surprised to receive a phone call during the meeting because they are taken by a secretary. When I learned that my father had been taken to the hospital, I became even more anxious. I then rushed to conclude the session. I should have explained that I had a family emergency. The Omars would have found that easier to understand than they did the abrupt ending without explanation. We can and should provide some information about emergency circumstances when they affect the professional work. Most clients readily understand that we are also human and face real-life problems too. In the absence of an explanation, Majid and Amina might think I was anxious to get rid of them (Dillon, 2003). Indeed, I wondered if Amina and Majid would return for our next scheduled meeting.

ASSESSMENT

Second Meeting: Engagement to Assessment

I greeted Amina and Majid warmly and asked how things were going. They said they were doing okay. I then outlined what I hoped we'd accomplish during today's meeting: to gain a better understanding of the nature of the conflict and establish goals for work. They agreed. I also mentioned that we would have more time for today's meeting than we did last time. I said that I wanted to apologize for concluding our first meeting in such an abrupt fashion. I told them about my father's hospitalization and said I wished I had shared that information at the time I received the phone call. They said they understood perfectly and asked how my father was doing. I told them. They seemed relieved. I'm certain that they had wondered why that first meeting had ended in such a strange fashion.

My apology and explanation seemed to set the stage for a much more comfortable session. We then proceeded to explore the issues that concerned them (Cormier & Nurius, 2003). One concern involved the issue of trust. Majid was not certain he could trust that Amina would not arrange to circumcise their daughter without his permission. Amina felt insulted and betrayed that Majid did not trust her. She said she had given her word and she would keep her word—just as she always had. Amina said she was tired of reassuring Majid that Sara would not be circumcised.

Amina also believed that Majid's disapproval of the practice of circumcision indicated that he had begun to reject his Somalian culture. She was concerned that Majid wanted their daughter raised in a Western manner. She said she wanted to raise Sara in a traditional Somalian way. They agreed that the debates about female circumcision involved differences of opinion about assimilation as well. They said they would argue about female circumcision instead of really listening to each other about their feelings.

Majid reported that following arguments he would often leave the house to visit his friends. Amina reported that his departures infuriated her such that she would not speak to Majid for a few days. He said he visited friends to get away from the anger, conflict, and hurt at home.

I inquired how they had tried to address these conflicts on their own. The partners indicated that their faith was extremely important to them and provided them with great comfort during stressful times. However, Amina reported that during their arguments Majid sometimes presents her with the Quran and asks her to identify any passages that mandate female circumcision. She said that he says there is absolutely no religious justification for the practice. Amina felt this puts her on the spot. She said she resented Majid's patronizing sermons about religion. She complained that Majid uses the Quran to justify his beliefs instead of respecting hers. He nodded at that point to indicate that she was accurate. He said he felt ashamed about that and he would not use the Quran in that way again.

Amina and Majid reported that arguments about female circumcision occur almost daily. They said they realized the situation was out of control when Sara started crying, begging them to stop fighting about her. Sara's reaction led the couple to seek professional assistance.

We continued to explore the issues of concern. Following the meeting, I prepared the following written assessment:

Description

Client System   Mr. Omar prefers to be addressed by his first name, Majid. He is of Somalian descent and considers himself a devout Muslim. He is about six feet tall and of normal build. He describes himself as a positive thinker and goal oriented. Mrs. Omar prefers to be addressed as Amina. She is also of Somalian descent and also follows the Muslim faith. She is five feet tall and of slim build. On the date of the interview Amina wore a long traditional Somalian dress and a hijab (Islamic head scarf which covers the hair). They did not bring their daughter, Sara, to the session as they did not want her involved in counseling.

Family and Household System   During the interview Amina and Majid reported they both have always had a good relationship. They stated that their life was devoted to their daughter, Sara. They appeared very proud of their Somalian heritage. They spoke fondly about Islamic principles guiding their home life. In 1990, Amina and Majid moved to Indiana as refugees from their country's civil war. Both of their parents had been killed in the Somalian conflict. Majid had been a professor of engineering in Somalia, but his doctorate was not recognized in the United States. Therefore, he had enrolled in a university and earned another engineering degree that enabled him to find employment.

Amina had been a schoolteacher in Somalia. However, when Sara was born, she decided to stay at home to look after Sara. She did not have extended family to support her as she would have had in Somalia. The couple said they were happy in Indiana but they were extremely upset at the death of so many Somalis back home due to malnutrition, famine, disease, unemployment, and other adverse consequences of the civil war in Somalia. They currently lived modestly in a two-bedroom apartment and regularly sent money to their relatives in Somalia. Before the war, they had lived quite well on their two salaries. They had been able to employ servants to help with household chores. Their lifestyle had changed dramatically. Nonetheless, they felt fortunate they had survived the civil war and seemed happy to live in the United States.

Community System   Amina and Majid said they regularly attend the mosque for Islamic prayers and to hear lectures by various invited speakers. They reported having many Somalian friends who live in their apartment complex. Amina said her Somalian friends provide her with great support and understanding, and help her maintain a sense of cultural identity. She also spoke passionately about her love for cooking. She sometimes caters Somalian community events and appears to take great pride in her cooking. She mentioned that it sometimes disturbed her when her white North American neighbors stared at her when she wore her traditional Somalian clothes. She thought that many North Americans looked down on Somalian cultural clothes.

Presenting Concerns   Majid said he became really concerned when he overheard Amina telling a friend that she wished that she could circumcise their daughter, Sara. This "frightened" him because female circumcision is banned in North America. Majid stated that female circumcision was a cultural tradition that involved cutting the genital area of young girls. He stated that generally this procedure was performed on girls in Somalia when they were around six or seven years old. He said that in Somalia 98% of girls were circumcised. He stated that most Somalis believed that circumcised girls were viewed as pure and would remain virginal until marriage. He also said, however, that he had always been disturbed by the practice of female circumcision because his sisters had suffered health complications and much discomfort as a result of the procedure. He added that he could not find any mention of female circumcision in the Quran. Therefore, he believed that God had not sanctioned the practice.

Amina said she had been circumcised by an elder at the age of six. She said she felt proud that she had been. She said that all her female ancestors had been circumcised and that she felt it was a sacred part of her heritage. She also believed that female circumcision was a sign of status, honor, and respect. She said that uncircumcised women were poorly regarded—almost as if they were prostitutes.

Majid was frustrated with Amina because she would not acknowledge that some girls suffered adverse physical consequences due to circumcision. He believed that Amina minimized the risks of the procedure. He wished Amina could understand why female circumcision was banned in North America. He said he was afraid that one day he might return home from work to find that Amina had taken their daughter back to Somalia to get her circumcised.

Amina felt angry and betrayed that Majid did not trust her. She said she would never have Sara circumcised because Majid was against it and she had given her word. However, she did not understand why she had to accept his views about female circumcision. She felt that Majid had become "too Americanized" and was rejecting his Somalian culture by not supporting female circumcision.

Strengths, Competencies, and Resources   Majid described himself as very task centered and well organized.

He said he adjusted to Indiana quite easily because he is fluent in English. He said he sometimes serves as an interpreter for social service agencies when they have Somalian clients who do not speak English. Majid says that he enjoys giving back to and being part of the community. He believes that his voluntary service as a Somali translator and interpreter provides him a means to do so.

Amina stated that she values the opportunity to maintain a Somalian home environment while living in a North American culture. She stated that this dual lifestyle is difficult to maintain. She complained about American television shows that showed kissing and explicit sexual scenes. However, she appeared particularly proud that she managed to adjust in North America even though her English was not as fluent as Majid's. She attributed this to her ability to read others' body language.

Social History   Amina and Majid did not want to bring their daughter, Sara, to the counseling session. They believed that the topic of female circumcision was a private family matter that should not be discussed in front of children. They described Sara as a bright six-year-old who was happy and energetic but a little shy. They said she is very sensitive to other children's teasing. Majid said that some of his friends had their daughters circumcised in Somalia prior to their migration to North America. He reported that sometimes these girls ask Sara why she remains uncircumcised. Majid says Sara feels different. As a result, she asks her mother to get her circumcised because she wants to be like the other Somalian children. Majid expressed his concern that Sara could pressure her mother to take her back home to have her circumcised. Although Amina assured Majid that she would not take Sara back to Somalia to get her circumcised without his consent, he remains unsettled.

Majid and Amina reported that they were very close to their own parents in Somalia. Each came from a financially well-to-do family. They said they miss the maids and servants they had back home. Amina said she tires of the household chores without anyone to help and often feels exhausted at the end of the day. Majid said that life in North America is especially difficult without the support of extended family members. Majid stated that he would like to take Amina out for pleasurable activities, but he can't afford a babysitter. He also stated that in his culture children are never left with strangers.

Referral Source and Process   Majid was referred to me by the mosque. He wanted a Muslim professional who could understand his culture. He said that most Muslims seek guidance from family members or the mosque when they need help or advice. He said that his positive experience with social workers when he served as an interpreter led him to seek help from a Muslim social worker.

Amina said that initially she did not want to talk with an outsider. She agreed only because Majid insisted on it. She would have preferred to consult with family members or community elders. She indicated that my Muslim faith helped some but she did not like the fact that I was younger than she and dressed like an American. She said that she would rather receive help from an elder.

Personal and Familial   Both Amina and Majid came from large families. Amina is the youngest of eight children. Her mother was the decision maker at home. Her father was a hardworking man who owned a transportation company. Amina lost her parents and four siblings during the civil war. All had been killed in the fighting. She said she terribly missed her three surviving siblings who remained in Somalia. She felt "guilty" that they had been left behind.

Majid had eight siblings. He was the middle child. Both his parents had been physicians in Somalia. He said he had been very close to his parents. They and three of his siblings died from the malnutrition that resulted after the civil war. Both Amina and Majid were devastated by deaths of their loved ones.

They spoke passionately about missing their conversations with elders about important matters. In Somalia, elders were honored and respected for their wisdom and life experience. However, few elders survived the civil war and there were hardly any in Indiana. Although Amina and Majid were glad to be alive and living safely in North America, they said they continued to feel depressed and isolated because of their move here. They shed tears as they described their escape to Kenya where they sought refugee status before coming to North America. They said they felt enormous guilt about leaving other family members in Somalia who later died in the civil war. They described the civil war as the most critical event of their lives. They said it altered the course of their lives forever. They said that they were still trying to recover from the loss of loved ones and the challenges of rebuilding a life in North America. They said that their faith in God and their desire to start another family helped them to manage during the most stressful times.

Sexual   Amina reported that she was a virgin before marriage. In her culture, virginity was seen as deeply sacred. A woman's honor largely rested on this fact alone. She re-ported that although she was proud she was circumcised, it took several months before she could engage fully in sexual intercourse with Majid. She said that Majid had been patient and supportive during this period. She mentioned that she sometimes wondered what sex would be like had she not been circumcised. However, she did not want North Americans to assume that circumcision made her less sexually active than other women. Majid said that their sex life was good but he remembers the pain that Amina experienced when they were first married. He said the female circumcision sealed the vaginal opening so tightly that sexual penetration was almost impossible. It had been very painful for Amina. He said that his memory of her pain was a major reason he could no longer support the practice of female circumcision.

Alcohol or Drug Use   Both Amina and Majid reported that they did not consume any form of alcohol or drugs. Their religious beliefs did not permit them to consume alcohol or drugs. Majid reported that sometimes at company parties he felt "different" because he did not drink alcohol as did most of his colleagues. However, he said he was quite comfortable telling people that his religion did not permit the consumption of alcohol.

However, both parents expressed concern about raising Sara in a North American environment. They worried that Western acceptance of alcohol use could lead Sara to experiment with alcohol as she gets older. Amina said that this is one reason she prefers that Sara have Muslim friends.

Medical or Physical   Amina and Majid said they were in good health. Amina mention that she felt awkward about doctors' visits because she expects them to stare at her circumcised vagina. Amina reported that when Sara was born, her doctor called several nurses and other doctors to observe the gynecological examination. The doctor said it would help them learn about female circumcision. Amina was extremely offended by this experience. She felt like a health specimen or object of study due to her circumcision. She was especially angry that the doctor had failed to ask her permission before inviting others to examine her. She has been reluctant to seek medical help ever since.

Recreational   Amina reports that she loves to spend time with her family and friends. Her recreational activities include walking and attending Somalian social events. She loves spending her evenings with other Somalian ladies, they gather together to talk, sing and dance. Majid plays tennis with some friends from work and likes to be in good physical shape. He enjoys reading, particularly spending time at the mosque to develop his knowledge on Islam.

Their daughter, Sara, is enrolled in a girls' soccer club. Sara is an active child who loves sports. Sara has many friends who are primarily Somalian. Amina prefers this so that Sara keeps her Somalian heritage, but Majid is concerned this will keep Sara from adjusting to North American culture.

Religious and Spiritual   Amina and Majid consider themselves strong Muslims. They are very involved with their Mosque and are excited that Sara is taking Islamic classes to learn how to read the Quran. Both have come from fairly religious families and report that faith is what keeps them going. Majid reports that he is struggling to try and understand why Amina is so convinced that female circumcision is part of Islam. He reports that even in the Muslim community there is heavy disagreement about whether the practice is part of Islam. However, he does believe that male circumcision is a mandatory code of conduct and that all Muslim boys must be circumcised.

Amina wears Somali traditional dresses according to how Muslim culture prefers women to dress. She always wears long sleeve shirts and loose clothing that covers her whole body. Her face is the only part of her body that is showing. She wears a head scarf to cover her hair. Majid is happy about the way that Amina dresses, but thinks that expecting Sara to dress in the same manner is not reasonable. Amina thinks Sara should be in Islamic dress, but Majid feels strongly that Sara should look like other Western children. He is worried that Sara will be ostracized in school if she dresses different from other Western girls.

Prior Psychological or Social Service   When Amina and Majid first arrived in North America they went on public assistance and were grateful to have received some help. Majid took on many odd jobs to pay for his engineering schooling. Majid does volunteer work for some social service agencies serving as a Somali translator and interpreter because he wants to help others. Both report no psychological problems. However, they were very sad, lonely, and depressed when they first came as refugees to Indiana. They did not take any antidepressant medication, feeling that prayers gave them the strength to cope with adjustment and migration issues.

Amina does experience some nightmares on occasions where she relives the civil war of Somalia. She is relieved that her nightmares are less. Sara does not appear to have any emotional problems. She was born and raised in Indiana and never saw the civil war of Somalia.

Summary Assessment

Amina and Majid appear to have a close relationship. They are committed to each other and to their daughter, Sara. They are devoted to their Islamic beliefs and Muslim religion. Amina is proud of her Somalian heritage and hopes to raise Sara according to those cultural traditions. Majid is supportive but also worries that Amina may prevent Sara from full integration into North American society. Their biggest disagreement involves the topic of female circumcision and the related issues of trust, respect, and understanding. Each is concerned that their conflicting views about female circumcision could cause problems in their marriage and perhaps trouble Sara. Both hope that the counseling will help them to resolve the conflict so that they will discontinue their heated arguments about the practice.

The couple seems well aware of both the substance of their conflict and the problematic patterns of communication that contribute to the arguments. I am fairly confident of their ability to address this issue and learn to communicate with each other in a more respectful, empathic, and loving manner. I'm not as certain that some of the conflict might be indicative of unresolved grief and the stresses associated with numerous transitions.

Have Majid and Amina fully expressed their grief about the loss of so many family members, the loss of their expected life as highly respected members of Somalian society, and the anticipated loss of their cultural identity? Sara is now about the age when most girls would already have been circumcised. Might this stimulate memories and regrets about family, community, and culture? Might they experience "survivors' guilt" and perhaps guilt that their siblings remain behind in Somalia? It's not clear that these are relevant factors but I'll keep them in mind as possible areas for exploration.

Goals and Plans

Approximately 98% of all Somalian girls are circumcised (Rahman & Toubia, 2000; Toubia & Izett, 1998). Obviously, the practice has held and continues to hold great meaning for most Somalian families. I thought we had to address the role and function of female circumcision and explore its cultural meaning. I also kept in mind that Majid and Amina were goal oriented and we would probably only meet a few times. I therefore suggested that we use the next few meetings to pursue several goals. In particular, I proposed that our work together might be considered successful if the couple becomes able to

1. Communicate with understanding, respect, and compassion
2. Discuss the topic of female circumcision in a non-argumentative manner
3. Appreciate each other's point of view on the topics of female circumcision and culture
4. Experience a sense of trust in each other

Majid and Amina readily approved these. They appeared pleased that I had somehow organized our far-ranging discussion into a manageable list of four goals. Amina seemed especially appreciative and perhaps somewhat surprised that I had been able to do so. Once we agreed upon these goals, I then suggested that we work together toward their achievement both within and between our meetings together. I said I'd offer ideas and suggestions but I hoped they would do so as well. They seemed pleased at this and looked at each other with genuine affection.

I asked them if they might be willing to do some "homework" during the interval before our next meeting. They smiled and agreed. I then asked them to take the next few days to think about the characteristics and actions of their partners that led them to trust each other for almost all of the years they've been together. After reflecting for several days, they were to prepare a written list of the trustworthy characteristics of their partners and bring it to share during our next session. I asked if they understood what I meant. They said they did.

I then asked if they could manage one more assignment during the next several days. They seemed pleased that I asked. I said that this task one would require both intelligence and creativity. I explained that during times of stress partners often attempt to protect themselves from additional pain by increasing the emotional distance between each other. I mentioned that the attempt to reduce distress through the greater distance frequently has exactly the opposite effect. I said that it was absolutely obvious to me—after only two meetings—that they loved and respected each other. I observed that their affection for each other was an incredibly valuable resource that we could use in our work together. I then requested that each of them think about some new and creative way to express affection and love for their partner one time per day. I referred to these as "loving gestures" and asked that they find ways to express their affection in ways that came from the heart rather than the wallet. In other words, the gestures should not cost any money. They seemed intrigued by this idea and agreed

to this activity as well. After ensuring that they understood and consented to both assignments, we arranged for a next meeting and said our goodbyes.

Worker's Commentary

As I reflected on this session, I again became aware of my tendency to collect a broader range of information than necessary. In my attempt to cover all areas, I sounded like a question-machine. As a result, clients may feel interrogated rather than interviewed. Although I probably covered too wide a range of areas, I was pleased that I had not focused exclusively on the topic of female circumcision (Dillon, 2003).

Had I done so, I might have missed important information about the impact of the Somalian civil war on Amina and Majid and the deaths of so many family members. I also could have underappreciated the barriers they faced when they migrated to North America.

I felt great satisfaction when both Majid and Amina seemed somewhat surprised but also very appreciative that I had listened carefully and understood the meaning of their words well enough to summarize in the form of four goals. I was pleased that we were able to identify and agree upon goals for our work together. I was delighted that they were intrigued by and interested in the "homework" activities that related to the goals we had established. The session ended well, but as I reflect upon the meeting as a whole, I wish I had encouraged them to explore a few issues in greater depth rather than attempting to cover an excessively wide range of topics.

INTERVENTION

Third Meeting: Cultural Meaning

I greeted Majid and Amina with a warm smile. They seemed pleased to see me. I asked how things were going. They said they were doing well. I then said that during our last meeting, we had identified a few goals for our work together and agreed upon a couple of homework activities. I asked if they recalled it as I had. They agreed and said that they had worked on both activities. I asked them to share their lists of trustworthy characteristics. Majid went first. He had brought a copy for Amina and one for me. It was a long list. He smiled broadly as he read them aloud. He was clearly proud of his wife and considered her to be extraordinarily trustworthy. Amina then shared her list. It was even longer. She cried as she described the actions Majid had taken to ensure her safety and secure their escape from Somalia. She also remembered the sacrifices he had made to complete another engineering degree in the United States while working full-time to provide food and shelter for them both. Majid reached for and held her hand as she expressed her gratitude.

After a pause, I asked Amina if she thought Majid respected her and could be trusted to keep his word. She agreed. When I asked Majid the same question about Amina, he said, "absolutely." I followed that by asking if he believed she would keep her promise not to arrange for a circumcision for Sara without his knowledge and consent. He said, "yes." Finally, I asked, do you believe that she would keep that promise even if she preferred that Sara were circumcised according to Somalian cultural traditions? He again agreed. I then asked both of them if they could imagine keeping a promise even if they personally held a different point of view about a topic. They each said yes, they could.

I paused at that point. The silence seemed appropriate and somehow meaningful. I hoped this experience might represent a first step toward recovering their trust for and faith in one another.

I then inquired about the other activity—the one that involved the expression of at least one loving gesture each day. They smiled. Amina said it was a wonderful week. She excitedly described some of the surprising ways that Majid had expressed his affection. Majid did so as well, providing details about Amina's creative ways to share her love for him. He added that he learned a great deal from this experience and would never again let a day pass without showing Amina how much he loved her.

I then asked what drew them together in the first place. Amina said she always respected Majid's openness and his fine intellect. Majid reported that he valued Amina's integrity and honesty, and her respect for traditional cultural values. Amina said that she appreciated that Majid was proud of her loyalty to Somali culture. She said she had wondered about that because he disagreed with her about female circumcision. She said she now realized he was not turning his back on their culture, he disagreed with one aspect.

I asked Amina and Majid if there were times when their disagreements about female circumcision were not so volatile. Amina reported that when Majid helped her with chores around the home, she was less likely to get upset. Majid stated that if he had a good day at work and got a lot done, then he was less prone to get into an argument about female circumcision. They agreed that external stresses often contributed to the arguments. Majid said he would help out more with the housework and would tell Amina if he had a bad day at work so that she could give

him some space and time to recover. They felt this would help their communication patterns.

I also asked them to imagine a scenario where they could actually talk about circumcision in a compassionate manner together. Majid said in that scenario he would want Amina to listen to him when he was expressing his feelings instead of yelling and interrupting him. Amina stated that she would want Majid to stop giving her sermons about female circumcision not being mentioned in the Quran because it felt like he was lecturing at her.

Amina also said she wanted to spend more leisure time with Majid because she felt stuck in the house. Majid reported that he would like to be able to do things with Amina and his daughter, Sara, after work so they could start having fun again because he was also frustrated at not having enough leisure time with his family. Both acknowledged that they would try and find a friend that could help look after Sara so they could do more fun things as a couple. Majid said he would also take more days off work so that he could spend more quality time with Amina and Sara.

I thanked them both for the work they had done and asked them if we might spend some time exploring various aspects of Somali culture. I said that although I was also Muslim, I was not from that part of the world and hoped to gain a better understanding of their traditions and the role that female circumcision played in their culture.

They seemed to appreciate my interest in their culture and began to tell me about Somali books as well as the dates and places of social events and religious ceremonies that I could attend. They offered to take me to a religious service, but I wanted to respect the boundaries of the professional relationship. I thanked them for the offer but indicated that I might learn more if I went on my own. They seemed to understand. I then asked them to identify a few of the most important Somali cultural experiences. Understanding how clients perceive the world is crucial to cultural sensitivity (Milne, 1999).

Understanding the meaning of nonverbal behavior is also critical for cross-cultural understanding. When I first met Majid, I had offered my hand as a way to greet him. He had stepped back somewhat abruptly and politely explained that he meant no offense but that in his culture men were not supposed to touch women—even in a handshake. I was grateful for his kind explanation and referred to it as I talked about the significance of cultural beliefs and practices. I thanked him for helping me to understand and asked them as gently as I could if we could explore the cultural meaning of female genital mutilation. Suddenly, the atmosphere in the room changed. They both sat upright in a stiff and tense manner. Amina said quite curtly that she was offended by the term female genital mutilation and preferred to refer to the procedure as female circumcision. I apologized profusely and thanked her for pointing this out to me. I said I understood completely and would use the term female circumcision from that point forward.

Amina remained cautiously tense and quiet. I asked directly if she had other thoughts or feelings that she would be willing to share. She reported that female circumcision was a long-standing aspect of Somalian heritage. She said that she felt insulted when I used the term "female genital mutilation." She said it was as if I suggested that she was a mutilator, a torturer, or perhaps a child abuser because she valued the practice of female circumcision. She said sarcastically that her country must be filled with mutilators. My insensitive language nearly ruined our relationship that, until that point, seemed to be developing quite well.

Amina and Majid then informed me that nearly every woman in Somalia had experienced some type of circumcision. This tradition had occurred for generations in Somalia and was a normal part of life back home. They also told me that many other countries in Africa engaged in the practice. In fact, female circumcision was an accepted norm in many parts of Africa. Majid mentioned, however, that some people in Africa have discontinued the practice, but it remained ingrained in many countries.

I then asked why female circumcision was so important in their culture. Amina said that circumcised women were highly valued and honored whereas those who remained uncircumcised were devalued and dishonored. I then asked Amina what it would mean to her if Sara were not circumcised. She responded by telling me stories of young girls who ran away from home to avoid circumcision. She said that those girls were ostracized by their families and communities. Amina said that uncircumcised women were usually cut off from their families and community, and were viewed with dishonor as impure. Majid added that he was not worried about being cut off from his community if he failed to support female circumcision. However, he acknowledged that women often were ostracized. Amina said she found it difficult to distinguish her own beliefs from those of her community. She was concerned that Sara might be rejected by the Somali community, especially if they ever returned home to Somalia.

I asked about the procedure itself. Majid said that there were several forms of female circumcision—some of which were less invasive and had fewer adverse health effects. Amina said she understood why milder forms of circumcision were becoming more accepted. She had undergone an extreme form and, as a result, suffered a great deal of pain during the first few months of marriage. I asked how medical information and news reports about the health risks of female circumcision had influenced community beliefs and practices. Majid said that already many Somali are adopting milder forms of female circumcision and some have discontinued it altogether. Amina quickly added that circumcision was never intended as punishment. Rather, it was meant to signify purity. She said that it was difficult for uncircumcised girls to get married in Somalia and she worried that Somali men might refuse to marry Sara if she remained uncircumcised. Even if she did marry a Somali man, his family might reject and ridicule her. She was very concerned about Sara's future as a wife, mother, and member of the Somali community. Majid said that fewer Somalian men raised in North America expected circumcised brides and many men back home were changing their attitudes as well.

I then asked Majid to take a moment to put into words his understanding of Amina's concerns for their daughter Sara. After a short pause, he said to Amina, "You're afraid that she might be considered impure, might never marry a respectable Somali man, and might be rejected by the Somali community." Following another short pause, he added, "You're afraid that Sara might have to give up her Somali culture to have a decent life." Amina responded by saying quietly, "Yes, exactly."

Following this exchange, I asked them if they remembered the goals for our work together. When they looked somewhat quizzical, I refreshed their memories by handing each of them copy of the list of goals: (1) communicate with understanding, respect, and compassion; (2) discuss the topic of female circumcision in a nonargumentative manner; (3) appreciate each other's point of view on the topics of female circumcision and culture; and (4) experience a sense of trust in one another.

I asked them to reflect upon the discussion we had just completed in light of these goals. They seemed genuinely surprised and quite pleased to realize that the conversation about the meaning of female circumcision in Somali culture represented progress toward the first three goals and probably the fourth as well. I then asked if I could make an observation. They invited me to do so. I said, "As we explored this complex topic of Somali culture and the important tradition of female circumcision, I was struck by the fact that each of you is concerned about the well-being of your daughter Sara. Each of you loves her and wants the best for her. You are absolutely alike in this regard. You have exactly the same hopes for her—that she will have a safe and happy life with someone who loves her and a community that respects her." Each of them nodded in agreement. I then said that Sara was a fortunate girl indeed to have two parents who cared so much about her.

Before concluding the meeting, I asked them to continue the daily practice of finding some special way to express love and affection for each other—since it had worked so well during this past week. I also asked them to do the same with Sara as well. I said I was absolutely certain that Sara already felt their love for her and knew they already regularly expressed their affection. I said, however, that sharing a loving gesture with Sarah each day might help Majid and Amina remember that they both have her best interest in mind. We then moved to conclude the meeting by agreeing to meet again at the same time next week.

Worker's Commentary

I had extremely mixed feelings about this meeting. I was delighted they had completed the "homework" assignments and pleased that they represent a step toward our established goals. However, I was horrified that I had used the term "mutilation." They had always referred to the practice as circumcision and done so with a great deal of respect. The word mutilation came from my own frame of reference and from the research literature I had studied. I felt terrible about this lapse in sensitivity. It had just slipped out. Although I had expressed my sincere apology, I was worried that my insensitive use of the term mutilation might seriously damage our relationship and diminish the probability of a positive outcome (Luborsky, Barber, & Crits-Christoph, 1990; Moursund & Kenny, 2002). I was pleased, however, that both Amina and Majid seemed to recover enough from my error to explore the cultural meaning of female circumcision. I also felt some professional satisfaction that the discussion represented a step toward goal achievement and that they saw that as well.

As I reflected about this session, I again recognized the importance of cultural sensitivity. I reminded myself to acknowledge my own cultural traditions and remember how they influenced my thoughts and feelings about Amina and Majid (D'Ardennes & Mahtani, 1989). Like them, I am an African-born Muslim. I felt a kindred spirit with Amina and Majid. I understood the importance and role faith played in their lives. My family also left Africa abruptly due to civil war. I remember the stress of coming to North America and my parents starting all over again. I felt enormous compassion for Amina and Majid's experience because my family went through it as well. However, I needed to recognize that I could easily over-identify with them and lose my professional perspective. I also had to be aware that any self-disclosure about my family's experience must be related to our goals for work. If I shared personal information, it should be for their sake and not my own. In reflecting about this session, I wondered if self-disclosure might have helped Majid and Amina in some way. I know I was tempted to talk about my family's experience but remained unsure if my motives were personal or professional.

As I considered the issue of self-disclosure, my thoughts turned again to my insensitive use of the term mutilation. I wondered if my slip might reflect a cultural bias or prejudice of my own (D'Ardennes & Mahtani, 1989). I fully agreed that Western media depictions of female circumcision were almost universally negative. Almost all my colleagues were highly critical of the practice. I tried to consider the topic in a more objective fashion. I asked myself why most Westerners did not consider breast implantation a form of genital mutilation and why male circumcision was widely practiced while female circumcision represented a criminal offense. I also wondered if I had underappreciated the significance of community for Majid and especially for Amina. I have been raised in a Western culture that celebrates the individual. Amina and Majid came from a culture that valued the group, the community, and the collective whole. In Somalia, individuals were recognized in terms of their contribution to the community rather than their personal achievements. Western views of the world also tend to reflect a future orientation while other cultures may place more emphasis on the past and the continuity between the past and the present (Milne, 1999). Female circumcision represented a valued cultural tradition, widely respected and honored, saved via oral tradition, passed from one generation to another, and practiced out of respect for ancestors (Milne, 1999). I knew that giving up a prized cultural practice that had meant so much to so many people for so long could not occur easily. It represented a major loss—especially for Amina but also for Sara and probably Majid as well. I wondered how they might recognize and appropriately grieve this loss.

Fourth Meeting: Addressing the Loss

Following my greeting, I asked how things were going. Each said things were better. I inquired about the experience of expressing daily gestures of love to Sara as well as to one another. They said it had been great. Majid said that the first couple of days were somewhat awkward—almost as if Sara was unsettled by these demonstrations of affection. Then, he said, they became more natural. He said that he has noticed a difference in Sara already—that she seems to enjoy his company more than before. Amina added that she valued the experience as well. She mentioned that until this week, she had focused more upon guidance and discipline with Sara. She said that the increased affection seems to have helped both Sara and herself feel more relaxed and at ease with each other.

I thanked them for the information and asked about their interest in continuing the practice of daily loving gestures. They said they wanted to continue it. I then observed that maintaining behavior over the long term usually requires some planning and some system of reminders. I said that the demands of everyday life often lead us to forget about the most important things as we take care of less important but pressing matters. They nodded in agreement. I then asked how they might remind themselves to express their love to each other and to Sara each day for the next year or longer. Majid immediately said he would put it into his daily calendar so that he would see the reminder each and every day. Amina took some time to respond. She looked at her hands and said she would assign new meaning to the ring on her finger. She said from this time forward it would signify love not only for her husband but also for Sara. It would become a family ring as well as a wedding ring and would represent a daily reminder to express her love for both members of her immediate family.

I thanked them both and then suggested that we resume our conversation about Somali culture and the significance of female circumcision. Almost immediately, Amina said that she felt ashamed that Sara would not be circumcised, that it represented a profound insult. She said she dishonored her elders and her ancestors through her failure to circumcise Sara. She reported that almost all elders in Somalia supported female circumcision and that all of her ancestors had as well. Amina seemed extremely concerned that she might offend her elders and her ancestors if she did not continue the traditional practice of circumcision with Sara. Majid said he was less concerned about what the elders thought but understood Amina's concern. He said he wanted to maintain the respect of his ancestors as well.

A somewhat awkward silence followed this exchange. Initially, I could not identify the problem. However, after a few moments Amina said she was afraid that her extended family in Somalia would be disappointed in her and reject her and her daughter if Sara remained uncircumcised. Majid listened carefully and offered support and understanding to Amina as she shared these feelings.

I asked Amina to think about specific family members back home and imagine how they would respond to information that Sara would not be circumcised. She said she expected them to judge her severely, to conclude that she had accepted Western cultural beliefs, and to think that she had rejected Somali traditions. She said that the family

might not completely reject her and Sara but they would almost certainly become more emotionally distant. I then asked Majid to anticipate Somali family members' reactions as well. He said he expected some disapproval but did not anticipate they would be ostracized.

I asked if they intended to share the information with their Somali relatives back home. They said they did. I then inquired how they planned to present this information. At that point, Majid and Amina began to exchange ideas about how to best communicate this news to their relatives. They talked about how they might show respect for traditions and deference to their elders while also respecting the laws of the United States. I asked them to elaborate about that aspect of the process. Majid said that Somalis are expected to follow the laws of the nation where they reside while remaining faithful to their own culture. For example, he said it would be wrong to arrange for an illegal circumcision in this country but it would be perfectly acceptable to travel to Somalia, have the procedure, and then return here. He said he expected that some of their relatives and some elders might question why they did not arrange for Sara to have the procedure in Somalia.

I asked them to imagine three scenarios in relation to sharing the news with their relatives in Somalia. The first scenario reflects the worst possible outcome, perhaps complete rejection or banishment along with other negative effects upon the two of you and Sara. The second scenario involves the best possible outcome, perhaps complete acceptance and understanding. The third scenario is somewhere in between—not the best but not the worst. As they considered these scenarios, I asked them to recognize that while they could influence some people they might be unable to influence everyone—that different people might well have different responses to the news that Sara would not be circumcised in the traditional manner.

I then asked if they could take some time within the next couple of days to develop a plan for sharing the information with family members back home. They could decide whether to communicate by telephone or by letter, outline what they wanted to share, and identify the particular person or persons they hoped to inform. I asked them to bring their plans with them for our meeting next week when we could review them together and make whatever changes might be useful. They agreed. We said our goodbyes and concluded the meeting.

Worker's Commentary

As clients make progress toward resolution of the identified problems, they sometimes conclude that the social worker's help is no longer needed. While I try to respect clients' experience, I sometimes feel frustrated when they conclude that everything is okay when it is not. Changing long-established behavioral patterns is usually quite difficult. Clients may require some information about these processes—including the tendency to resume old patterns—during the middle phase of interventive work (Moursund & Kenny, 2002).

I am sometimes tempted to "dazzle" clients with various interventions that might help them address a particular problem. However, the intervention process is often nonlinear. Clients may move forward, backward, or perhaps plateau during this time. One challenge I faced in my work with Amina and Majid was accepting the reality and legitimacy of their uncertainty and confusion. The fact that they now openly acknowledge their confusion about what to do probably represents genuine progress. They are beginning to express their real thoughts and feelings—even when it is difficult to do so. They seem to have avoided a common pattern—which is to please the social worker and create an appearance of progress or resolution when the issue remains far from resolved.

Silences appeared awkward at different moments during the session. I continue to feel a strong temptation to fill in the silent periods with words of my own. I worried that if we were silent at times, Majid and Amina would think they were wasting my time or perhaps their own. I am gradually learning that when I don't know what to say, I am better off saying nothing at all (Moursund & Kenny, 2002). During the intervention stage, I often feel pressured to produce some type of change. Perhaps especially because we have agreed to only a few sessions together, I wanted to help the couple resolve the problems. Silences seemed a waste of precious time. However, silence can sometimes help clients reflect upon important issues. Majid and Amina struggled with means to cope with their different viewpoints regarding female circumcision. By respecting clients' need for some silent reflection, clients may feel that their inner experience is both recognized and honored (Moursund & Kenny, 2002). I found it extremely difficult to conclude the session on time when I sensed that Amina and Majid were still struggling with their different perspectives. I wanted to end the session in a positive way that reflected continued progress and encouraged optimism. When it ended poorly, I felt disappointed and questioned my own competence.

Moursund and Kenny (2002) observe that counselors who expect absolute predictability during the middle phase of work are likely to be both ineffective and disappointed. In an interesting way, giving ourselves and our clients permission to experience some confusion may contribute to rather than inhibit progress (Moursund & Kenny, 2002).

EVALUATION

Fifth Meeting: Ending

As we began, I mentioned that this was our last session. When we first met, we had agreed to five meetings. Amina and Majid seemed surprised. I had assumed they had remembered our initial contract. They suddenly started to bring up why they came to see me all over again, as though they were afraid of leaving counseling. I informed them that endings were never easy. I said they were also difficult for me. That seemed to comfort them.

We explored how things were going. Amina and Majid said they were learning to communicate better and had fewer arguments about female circumcision. Majid reported that he had come to trust Amina much more. He was certain that she would not circumcise their daughter without his consent. Amina indicated that she felt more relaxed around Majid since he had become less suspicious of her. She felt much less defensive when they discussed the topic of female circumcision. Both reported that they now listened more carefully to each other and interrupted each other less frequently. They also said they spent more leisure time together especially since Majid had begun to take more days off to spend time with Amina and Sara.

They said they had decided that they could not determine whether female circumcision was absolutely right or wrong. Instead they came to an agreement that many Somali cultural traditions were important to them and they hoped to find a way to incorporate another ritual to replace female circumcision. Amina reported that she was happy with her cultural tradition of respecting elders, ancestors, family, and community. She also said she enjoyed attending Somali events. She said she now realized that Sara's uncircumcised status did not mean she disrespected Somali culture because she remained very much involved in the community. Majid added that he was more involved in the Somali community now because he wanted to show Amina that he also respected their culture. Amina said this helped her to realize that he was not turning his back against his culture just because he was against female circumcision.

I thanked the couple for coming to see me. I shared my pleasure at meeting them and my sadness that we would not be meeting again. I also observed that they had made a great deal of progress in a short time and hoped they would continue to express loving gestures toward each other and Sara each and every day. They said they would. We then said our goodbyes.

Worker's Commentary

After I mentioned this was our last meeting, I realized I had made another mistake. I should never have assumed that Amina and Majid would keep track of how many sessions were left. I should have reminded them in either the third or fourth session. Preparation for ending starts with the first interview. Workers should talk about endings at different points to help prepare clients for termination and to gradually assume greater personal responsibility for their own growth and change (Moursund & Kenny, 2002).

The best endings occur when both social workers and clients sense they are ready to end at the same time. Understanding our own motives for wanting to hang onto clients is imperative (Moursund & Kenny, 2002). When Amina and Majid brought up old issues we had already addressed, it was clear they were fearful of ending. Talking openly about that helped them to address that fear. Clients often express a desire for continuing support. While I am hesitant to promise unlimited availability, I do inform clients they may call again at some point in the future should issues arise that they would like to address.

As I reflected upon the ending process, I realized I tried to pack too much in at the end because I want to make sure that I have covered everything. It felt rushed and somewhat abrupt especially since Majid and Amina had not realized this was our last meeting. I wondered if I had neglected to remind them about ending in earlier sessions in an effort to protect myself from their possible reaction and avoid their possible experience of loss or abandonment. It was clear from this experience that I should have discussed the ending issue earlier—probably in the third and certainly in the fourth of our five meetings. Although Majid and Amina seemed to have benefited from our work together, the abrupt nature of the ending left me feeling somewhat unfinished. I was certainly pleased they had progressed toward accomplishment of their goals but wished the process had been smoother and more complete. Of course, I feel that way when I end with most clients!

References

Abraham, F. D. (1995). *Chaos theory in psychology.* Westport, CT: Greenwood Press.

Abramson, J. S. (1988). Participation of elderly patients in discharge planning: Is self-determination a reality? *Social Work, 33*(5), 443–448.

Abramson, J. S., Donnelly, J., King, M. A., & Mailick, M. D. (1993). Disagreements in discharge planning: A normative phenomenon. *Health and Social Work, 18*(1), 57–64.

Abramson, M. (1984). Collective responsibility in interdisciplinary collaboration: An ethical perspective for social workers. *Social Work in Health Care, 10*(1), 35–43.

Abramson, M. (1990). Keeping secrets: Social workers and AIDS. *Social Work, 35*(2), 169–173.

Ad Hoc Committee on Advocacy. (1969). The social worker as advocate: Champion of social victims. *Social Work, 14*(2), 16–22.

Adams, P., & Nelson, K. (1995). *Reinventing human services: Community and family practice.* Hawthorne, NY: Aldine de Gruyter.

Adams, R. G., & Blieszner, R. (1993). Resources for friendship intervention. *Journal of Sociology and Social Welfare, 28*(4), 159–175.

Alberti, R. E., & Emmons, M. L. (1995). *Your perfect right: A guide to assertive living* (7th ed.). San Luis Obispo, CA: Impact.

Alcoholics Anonymous. (2003). *Welcome to Alcoholics Anonymous.* Retrieved October 6, 2003, from www .alcoholics-anonymous.org/

Aldous, J. (1994). Someone to watch over me: Family responsibilities and their realization across family lives. In E. Kahana, E. E. Biegel & M. L. Wykle (Eds.), *Family caregiving across the lifespan* (pp. 42–68). Thousand Oaks, CA: Sage.

Aldridge, J. (1993). Constructivism, contextualism, and applied developmental psychology. *Perceptual and Motor Skills, 76*(3), 1242.

Allen, J. A. (1995). African Americans: Caribbean. In R. L. Edwards (Ed.), *Encyclopedia of social work* (19th ed., Vol. 1, pp. 121–130). Washington, DC: NASW Press.

Allen-Meares, P., Deroos, Y. S., & Siegel, D. (1994). Are practitioner intuition and empirical evidence equally valid sources of professional knowledge? In W. W. Hudson & P. S. Nurius (Eds.), *Controversial issues in social work research* (pp. 37–49). Boston: Allyn & Bacon.

Allen-Meares, P., & Lane, B. A. (1987). Grounding social work practice in theory: Ecosystems. *Social Casework: The Journal of Contemporary Social Work, 68*(9), 515–521.

Allen-Meares, P., & Lane, B. A. (1990). Social work practice: Integrating qualitative and quantitative data collection techniques. *Social Work, 35*(5), 452–458.

Alperin, R. M., & Phillips, D. G. (1997). *The impact of managed care on the practice of psychotherapy: Innovation, implementation, and controversy.* New York: Brunner/Mazel.

American Academy of Pediatrics. (2000). Clinical practice guideline: Diagnosis and evaluation of the child with attention-deficit/hyperactivity disorder. *Pediatrics, 105*(5), 1158–1170.

American Academy of Pediatrics Committee on Bioethics. (1995). Informed consent, parental permission, and assent on pediatric practice. *Pediatrics, 95*(2), 14–17.

American Hospital Association. (1987). *Case management: An aid to quality and continuity of care (AHA Council Report: Council on Patient Services).* Chicago: Author.

American Psychiatric Association. (2000). *Diagnostic and statistical manual* (4th ed., text rev.). Washington, DC: Author.

Anderson, C. M., & Stewart, S. (1983). *Mastering resistance: A practical guide to family therapy.* New York: Guilford.

Anderson, J. R. (1980). *Cognitive psychology and its implications.* San Francisco: Freeman.

Anderson, S. C. (1989, October.). *Goal setting in social work practice.* Paper presented at the Annual Meeting of the National Association of Social Workers, San Francisco.

Anderson, S. G., & Gryzlak, B. M. (2002). Social work advocacy in the post-TANF environment: Lessons from early TANF research studies. *Social Work, 47*(3), 301–314.

Annie E. Casey Foundation. (1994). Community empowerment: Making human services a community enterprise. *AEC Focus, 4*(1), 3.

Annoyed social worker. (1997). The personal and social costs of the market philosophy. *News from Sammy's Dad* (Underground Newsletter) (3), 7–8.

Anonymous for legal reasons. (1997). Why my authority suspended me on suspicion. *News from Sammy's Dad* (Underground Newsletter) (3), 8–10.

Anthony, E. J. (1987). Risk, vulnerability and resilience. In E. J. Anthony & B. J. Cohler (Eds.), *The vulnerable child* (pp. 3–49). New York: Guilford.

Antonovsky, A. (1980). *Health, stress and coping.* San Francisco: Jossey-Bass.

Aptheker, H. (1951). *A documentary history of the Negro people in the United States.* New York: Carol.

Arblaster, L., Conway, J., Foreman, A., & Hawtin, M. (1996). *Asking the impossible? Inter-agency working to address the housing, health and social care needs of people in ordinary housing.* Bristol: Policy Press.

Arches, J. (1991). Social structure, burnout, and job satisfaction. *Social Work, 36*(3), 202–207.

Arrington, A., Sullaway, M., & Christensen, A. (1988). Behavioral family assessment. In I. R. H. Falloon (Ed.), *Handbook on behavioral family therapy* (pp. 78–106). New York: Guilford.

Asamoah, Y. W. (1997). *Innovations in delivering culturally sensitive social work services.* Binghampton, NY: Haworth Press.

Asay, T. P., & Lambert, M. J. (1999). The empirical case for the common factors in therapy: Quantitative factors. In B. L. Duncan & M. A. Hubble (Eds.), *The heart and soul of change: What works in therapy* (pp. 23–55). Washington, DC: American Psychological Association.

Association of Social Work Boards. (2004). *Content outlines.* Retrieved May 10, 2004, from http://www.aswb.org/

Atkin, B. (1991). New Zealand: Let the family decide: The new approach to family problems. *Journal of Family Law, 29*(2), 387–397.

Audit Commission. (1995). *Joint review of social service authorities (Consultation document).* London: Her Majesty's Stationary Office.

Auerswald, E. H. (1987). Epistemological confusion in family therapy and research. *Family Process, 26*(3), 317–330.

Austin, C. D. (1993). Case management: A systems perspective. *Families in Society: The Journal of Contemporary Human Services, 74*(8), 451–459.

Austin, D. M. (2001). Guest editor's foreword. *Research on Social Work Practice, 11*(2), 147–151.

Axinn, J., & Levin, H. (1982). *Social welfare: A history of the American response to need.* New York: Longman.

Bachelor, A. (1995). Client's perception of the therapeutic alliance: A qualitative analysis. *Journal of Counseling Psychology, 42*(3), 323–337.

Bachelor, A., & Horvath, A. (1999). The therapeutic relationship. In B. L. Duncan & M. A. Hubble (Eds.), *The heart and soul of change: What works in therapy* (pp. 133–178). Washington, DC: American Psychological Association.

Badding, N. C. (1989). Client involvement in case recording. *Social Casework, 70*(9), 539–548.

Baer, B. L., & Federico, R. C. (Eds.). (1978). *Educating the baccalaureate social worker: Report of the undergraduate social worker curriculum development project.* Cambridge, MA: Ballinger.

Baer, J. (2001). Evaluating practice: Assessment of the therapeutic process. *Journal of Social Work Education, 37*(1), 127–136.

Baer, J. S., Kivlahan, D. R., & Donovan, D. M. (2000). Combining skills training, motivational enhancement proves effective. *Brown University Digest of Addiction Theory and Application, 19*(1), 1.

Baily, T., & Baily, W. (1983). *Child welfare practice.* San Francisco: Jossey-Bass.

Baker, R. A. (Ed.). (1988). *Child sexual abuse and false memory syndrome.* Amherst, NY: Prometheus Books.

Balloch, S. (1996). Working in the social services: Job satisfaction, violence and stress. In *Participating in change: Social work profession in social development (Proceedings of the Joint World Congress of IFSW and IASSW)* (pp. 329–332). Hong Kong.

Bandura, A. (1977). Self-efficacy: Toward a unifying theory of behavior change. *Psychological Review, 84,* 191–215.

Bandura, A. (1989). Human agency in social cognitive theory. *American Psychologist, 44,* 1175–1184.

Bandura, A. (1992). Exercise of personal agency through the self-efficacy mechanism. In R. Schwarzer (Ed.), *Self-efficacy: Thought control of action* (pp. 355–394). Washington, DC: Hemisphere.

Bandura, A. (1995a). Exercise of personal and collective efficacy in changing societies. In A. Bandura (Ed.), *Self-efficacy in changing societies* (pp. 1–45). New York: Cambridge University Press.

Bandura, A. (Ed.). (1995b). *Self-efficacy in changing societies.* New York: Cambridge University Press.

Bandura, A. (1997). *Self-efficacy: The exercise of control.* New York: Freeman.

Bandura, A., & Walters, R. (1963). *Social learning and personality development.* New York: Holt, Rinehart, & Winston.

Banks, C. K., & Mangan, M. (1997). *The company of neighbours: Community development action research.* Toronto: University of Toronto Press.

Barber, J. G. (1995). Politically progressive casework. *Families in Society: The Journal of Contemporary Human Services, 76*(1), 30–37.

Barclay, P. M. (1982). *Social workers: Their roles and tasks.* London: National Institute for Social Work, Bedford Square Press.

Barker, R. L. (1987a). *The social work dictionary.* Silver Spring, MD: NASW Press.

Barker, R. L. (1987b). Spelling out the rules and goals: The written worker-client contract. *Journal of Independent Social Work, 1*(2), 67–77.

Barker, R. L. (1988). Just whose code of ethics should the independent practitioner follow? *Journal of Independent Social Work, 2*(4), 1–5.

Barker, R. L. (1995). *The social work dictionary* (3rd ed.). [CD-ROM] Washington, DC: National Association of Social Workers.

Barker, R. L. (2003). *The social work dictionary* (5th ed.). Washington, DC: NASW Press.

Barkley, R. A. (1997). *A clinician's manual for parent training.* New York: Guilford.

Barlow, D. H., & Hersen, M. (1984). *Single case experimental designs: Strategies for studying behavior change*. New York: Pergamon.

Barnard, C. P., & Kuehl, B. P. (1995). Ongoing evaluation: In session procedures for enhancing the working alliance and therapy effectiveness. *American Journal of Family Therapy, 23*(2), 161–172.

Barnes, D. (1994). Survival tips when the diagnosis is poor communication. *Family-Centered Care Networks, 11*(1), 4–5.

Barrett, L. (1997). *Independent living: Adult children's perceptions of their parents' needs*. Washington, DC: American Association of Retired Persons.

Barrett, M., & McKelvey, J. (1980). Stresses and strains on the child care worker. *Child Welfare, 59,* 270–280.

Barsky, A. E. (1995). Mediation in child protection. In H. Irving & M. Benjamin (Eds.), *Family mediation: Contemporary issues* (pp. 377–406). Thousand Oaks, CA: Sage.

Barsky, A. E. (1997a). Child protection mediation. In E. Kruk (Ed.), *Mediation and conflict resolution in social work and human services* (pp. 117–139). Chicago: Nelson-Hall.

Barsky, A. E. (1997b). Mediation and empowerment in child protection cases. *Mediation Quarterly, 14*(2), 111–134.

Barth, R. P. (1986). *Social and cognitive treatment of children and adolescents*. San Francisco: Jossey-Bass.

Bartholomew, R. E. (2000). *Exotic deviance: Medicalizing cultural idioms*. Boulder, CO: University Press of Colorado.

Bartlett, H. M. (1958). Working definition of social work practice. *Social Work, 3*(2), 5–8.

Bartlett, H. M. (1964). The place and use of knowledge in social work practice. *Social Work, 9*(3), 36–46.

Bartlett, H. M. (1970). *The common base of social work practice*. New York: NASW Press.

Bartlett, H. M. (2003). Working definition of social work practice. *Research on Social Work Practice, 3*(2), 267–270.

Basadur, M. (1995). *The power of innovation*. Langham, MD: Pitman.

Bassin, A. (1993). The reality therapy paradigm. *Journal of Reality Therapy, 12*(2), 3–13.

Bateson, G., Jackson, D., Haley, J., & Weekland, J. (1963). A note on the double bind. *Family Processes, 2*(1), 154–161.

Beard, J., Propst, R., & Malamud, T. (1982). The Fountain House model of psychiatric rehabilitation. *Psychosocial Rehabilitation Journal, 5*(1), 47–53.

Beardshaw, V., & Towell, D. (1991). *Assessment and care management: Implications for the implementation of caring for people (Briefing Paper No. 10)*. London: Department of Health.

Beardslee, W. R. (1989). The role of self-understanding in resilient individuals: The development of a perspective. *American Journal of Orthopsychiatry, 59*(2), 266–278.

Beavers, C. (1986). A cross-cultural look at child abuse. *Public Welfare, 44,* 18–22.

Beavers, W. R. (1981). A systems model of family for family therapists. *Journal of Marital and Family Therapy, 7,* 229–307.

Beavers, W. R., & Hampson, R. B. (1990). *Successful families: Assessment and intervention*. New York: Norton.

Beavers, W. R., & Voeller, M. N. (1983). Family models: Comparing the Olson circumplex model with the Beavers systems model. *Family Process, 22*(1), 85–98.

Beck, A., & Freeman, A. (1990). *Cognitive therapy of personality disorders*. New York: Guilford.

Beck, A., Rush, J., Shaw, B. F., & Emery, G. (1987). *Cognitive therapy of depression*. New York: Guilford.

Beck, A., Wright, F. D., Newman, C. F., & Liese, B. S. (1993). *Cognitive therapy of substance abuse*. New York: Guilford.

Becker, G. (1964). *Human capital*. New York: National Bureau of Economic Research.

Becker, H. (1963). *The outsiders: Studies in the sociology of deviance*. New York: Free Press.

Becvar, D. S., & Becvar, R. J. (1988). *Family therapy: A systemic integration*. Needleham, MA: Allyn & Bacon.

Beeforth, M., Conlon, E., & Graley, R. (1994). *Have we got views for you: User evaluation of care management*. London: Sainsbury Centre for Mental Health.

Beeman, S. K. (1997). Reconceptualizing social support and its relationship to child neglect. *Social Service Review, 71*(3), 421–440.

Behroozi, C. S. (1992). A model for social work with involuntary applicants in groups. *Social Work with Groups, 15*(2/3), 233–238.

Beinecke, R. H. (1984). PORK, SOAP, STRAP, and SAP. *Social Casework: Journal of Contemporary Social Work, 65*(9), 554–558.

Belcher, J. R. (1993). The trade-offs of developing a case management model for chronically mentally ill people. *Health and Social Work, 18*(1), 20–31.

Belenky, M., Clinchy, B., Goldberger, N., & Tarule, J. (1986). *Women's ways of knowing: The development of self, voice and mind*. New York: Basic Books.

Bellack, A. S., & Herson, M. (1988). *Behavioral assessment: A practical handbook* (3rd ed.). Elmsford, NY: Pergamon.

Bellair, P. E. (1997). Social interaction and community crime: Examining the importance of neighbor networks. *Criminology, 35*(4), 677.

Benard, B. (1997a). Fostering resiliency in children and youth: Promoting protective factors in the school. In D. Saleebey (Ed.), *The strengths perspective in social work practice* (2nd ed., pp. 167–182). New York: Longman.

Benard, B. (1997b). Resiliency research: A foundation for youth development. *Resiliency in Action, 2,* 13–18.

Benard, B. (2002). Turnaround people and places: Moving from risk to resilience. In D. Saleebey (Ed.), *The strengths perspective in social work practice* (3rd ed., pp. 213–227). New York: Longman.

Bendix, R. (1952). Bureaucracy and the problem of power. In R. K. Merton, A. Gray, B. Hockey & H. C. Sebrin

(Eds.), *Reader in bureaucracy* (pp. 114–134). New York: Free Press.

Benedict, R. (1959). *Patterns of culture* (2nd ed.). Boston: Houghton Mifflin.

Benjamin, A. (1987). *The helping interview: With case illustrations*. Boston: Houghton Mifflin.

Benn, C. (1991). Social justice, social policy and social work. *Australian Social Work, 26*(3), 239–244.

Bennett, L. (1961). *Before the Mayflower*. Chicago: Johnson.

Bennis, W. G., Benne, K. D., & Chin, R. (Eds.). (1969). *The planning of change* (2nd ed.). New York: Harcourt College.

Berenson, D. (1987). Alcoholics Anonymous: From surrender to transformation. *Family Therapy Networker, 11,* 24–31.

Berg, I. K., & de Jong, P. (1996). Solution-building conversations: Co-constructing a sense of competence with clients. *Families in Society: The Journal of Contemporary Human Services, 77*(6), 376–391.

Berg, I. K., & Gallagher, D. (1991). Solution focused brief treatment with adolescent substance abusers. In T. C. Todd & M. Selekman (Eds.), *Family treatment of adolescent substance abusers* (pp. 93–111). Boston: Allyn & Bacon.

Berg, I. K., & Miller, S. D. (1992a). Working with Asian American clients: One person at a time. *Families in Society: The Journal of Contemporary Human Services, 73*(6), 356–363.

Berg, I. K., & Miller, S. D. (1992b). *Working with the problem drinker: A solution focused approach*. New York: Norton.

Bergel, V. R. (1994). The many (unexpected) advantages of volunteering. *New Social Worker, 1*(1), 22–23.

Berger, S. M. (1985). *Dr. Berger's immune power diet*. New York: New American Library.

Bergmark, A., & Oscarsson, L. (1992). The limits of phenomenology and objectivity: On the encounter between scientism and practice. *British Journal of Social Work, 22*(2), 121–132.

Berg-Weger, M., Rubio, D. M., & Tebb, S. S. (2001). Strengths-based practice with family caregivers of the chronically ill: Qualitative insights. *Families in Society: The Journal of Contemporary Human Services, 82*(3), 263–272.

Berlin, S. B. (1983). Single-case evaluation: Another version. *Social Work Research and Abstracts, 19*(1), 3–11.

Berlin, S. B. (1996). Constructivism and the environment: A cognitive-integrative perspective for social work practice. *Families in Society: The Journal of Contemporary Human Services, 77*(6), 326–335.

Berman-Rossi, T., & Rossi, P. (1990). Confidentiality and informed consent in school social work. *Social Work in Education, 12*(3), 195–207.

Bernier, J. C., & Siegel, D. H. (1994). Attention deficit hyperactivity disorder: A family and ecological systems perspective. *Families in Society: The Journal of Contemporary Human Services, 75*(3), 142–151.

Berry, M. F., & Blassingame, J. W. (1982). *Long memory: The Black experience in America*. New York: Oxford University Press.

Bertcher, H. J. (1979). *Group participation: Techniques for leaders and members*. Newbury Park, CA: Sage.

Bertsch, E. F. (1992). A voucher system that enables persons with severe mental illness to purchase community support services. *Hospital and Community Psychiatry, 43*(11), 1109–1113.

Betancourt, J. R., Green, A. R., Carrillo, J. E., & Ananeh-Firempong-II, O. (2003). Defining cultural competence: A practical framework for addressing racial/ethnic disparities in health and health care. *Public Health Reports, 118*(4), 293–302.

Bewley, C., & Glendinning, C. (1994). *Involving disabled people in community care planning*. London: Community Care & Joseph Rowntree Foundation.

Biddle, B. J., & Thomas, E. J. (Eds.). (1966). *Role theory: Concepts and research*. New York: Wiley.

Biddle, W. W., & Biddle, L. J. (1965). *The community development process: The rediscovery of local initiative*. New York: Holt, Rinehart & Winston.

Bidgood, B., Holosko, M. J., & Taylor, L. E. (2003). A new working definition of social work practice: A turtle's view. *Research on Social Work Practice, 13*(3), 400–408.

Biehal, N. (1993). Changing practice: Participation, rights and community care. *British Journal of Social Work, 23*(5), 443–458.

Biestek, F. P. (1957). *The casework relationship*. Chicago: Loyola University Press.

Biestek, F. P. (1994). Revisiting our heritage: An analysis of the casework relationship. *Families in Society: The Journal of Contemporary Human Services, 75*(10), 245–257.

Billingsley, A. (1992). *Climbing Jacob's Ladder*. New York: Simon & Schuster.

Bilsker, D., & Goldner, E. M. (2000). Teaching evidence-based practice in mental health. *Research on Social Work Practice, 10*(5), 664–670.

Birdsall, B. A., & Miller, L. D. (2002). Brief counseling in the schools: A solution-focused approach for school counselors. *Counseling and Human Development, 35*(2), 1–10.

Bischof, G. P., Stith, S. M., & Wilson, S. M. (1992). A comparison of the family systems of adolescent sexual offenders and non-sexually delinquents. *Family Relations, 41,* 318–322.

Bishof, G. P., & Stith, S. M. (1995). Family environments of adolescent sex offenders and other juvenile delinquents. *Adolescence, 30*(117), 157–171.

Bisno, H. (1969). A theoretical framework for teaching social work methods and skills with particular reference to undergraduate social welfare education. *Journal of Education for Social Work, 5*(2), 5–17.

Bitensky, R. (1978). Social work: A non-existent profession in search of itself. *New University Quarterly, 33,* 65–73.

Blackwell, B., & Schmidt, G. L. (1992). The educational implications of managed mental health care. *Hospital and Community Psychiatry, 43*(10), 962–964.

Blanck, G., & Blanck, R. (1974). *Ego psychology in theory and practice*. New York: Columbia University Press.

Blanck, R., & Blanck, G. (1986). *Beyond ego psychology: Developmental object relations theory*. New York: Columbia University Press.

Blaske, D. M., Borduin, C. M., Henggeler, S. W., & Mann, B. J. (1989). Individual, family, and peer characteristics of adolescent sex offenders and assaultive offenders. *Developmental Psychology, 24*, 846–855.

Bloom, A. (1980). Social work and the English language. *Social Casework, 60*(6), 332–338.

Bloom, M., & Fischer, J. (1982). *Evaluating practice: Guidelines for the accountable professional*. Englewood Cliffs, NJ: Prentice-Hall.

Bloom, M., Fischer, J., & Orme, J. (1995). *Evaluating practice: Guidelines for the accountable professional* (2nd ed.). Boston: Allyn & Bacon.

Blüml, J., Gudat, U., Langreuter, J., Martin, B., Schettner, H., & Schumann, M. (1989). Changing concepts of social work in foster family care. *Community Alternatives: International Journal of Family Care, 1*(1), 11–22.

Blundo, R. (2001). Learning strengths-based practice: Challenging our personal and professional frames. *Families in Society: The Journal of Contemporary Human Services, 82*(3), 296–304.

Blythe, B. J. (1992). Should undergraduate and graduate social work students be taught to conduct empirically-based practice? Yes! *Journal of Social Work Education, 28*(3), 260–263.

Blythe, B. J. (1995). Single-system design. In R. L. Edwards (Ed.), *Encyclopedia of social work* (19th ed., Vol. 3, pp. 2164–2168). Washington, DC: NASW Press.

Blythe, B. J., & Briar, S. (1985). Developing empirically based models of practice. *Social Work, 30*, 483–488.

Blythe, B. J., & Tripodi, T. (1989). *Measurement in direct practice*. Newbury Park, CA: Sage.

Bodde, R., & Giddings, M. (1997). The propriety of affiliation with clients beyond the professional role: Non-sexual dual relationships. *Areté, 22*(1), 58–70.

Boehm, W. (1958). The nature of social work. *Social Work, 3*(2), 10–19.

Boehm, W. (1959). *Objectives of the social work curriculum of the future* (Vol. 1). New York: Council on Social Work Education.

Bogie, M. A., & Coleman, M. (2002). Facing a malpractice claim. *Understanding risk management: Practice pointers, 3*(2). Retrieved May 16, 2003, from http://www.naswinsurancetrust.org/understanding_risk_management/pointers/v03n03.asp

Boisjoly, J., Duncan, G. J., & Hofferth, S. (1995). Access to social capital. *Journal of Family Issues, 16*(5), 609–631.

Bolen, R. M. (2003). Child sexual abuse: Prevention or promotion? *Social Work, 48*(2), 174–185.

Borenzweig, H. (1981). Agency vs. private practice: Similarities and differences. *Social Work, 26*(3), 239–244.

Boughner, S. R., Hayes, S. F., Bubenzer, D. L., & West, J. D. (1994). Use of standardized assessment instruments by marital and family therapists: A survey. *Journal of Marital and Family Therapy, 20*(1), 69–75.

Bourne, E. J. (1998). *Overcoming specific phobia: Therapist protocol*. Oakland, CA: New Harbinger.

Bourne, L. E., Dominowski, R. L., Loftus, E. F., & Healy, A. F. (1986). *Cognitive processes* (2nd ed.). Englewood Cliffs, NJ: Prentice-Hall.

Bowen, G. L., Martin, B. R., & Nelson, J. P. (2002). A community capacity response to family violence in the military. In A. R. Roberts & G. J. Greene (Eds.), *Social workers' desk reference* (pp. 551–557). New York: Oxford University Press.

Bowl, R. (1996). Involving service users in mental health services: Social services departments and the NHS and community care act. *Journal of Mental Health, 5*(3), 287–303.

Bowlby, J. (1947). *Forty-four juvenile thieves: Their characters and home-life*. London: Baillière, Tindall & Cox.

Bowlby, J. (1951). *Maternal care and mental health*. Geneva: World Health Organization.

Bowlby, J. (1979). *The making and breaking of affectional bonds*. London: Tavistock.

Bowlby, J. (1982). *Attachment*. New York: Basic Books.

Bowlby, J. (1988). *A secure base: Parent-child attachment and healthy human development*. New York: Basic Books.

Bowler, T. D. (1981). *General systems thinking: Its scope and applicability*. New York: North Holland.

Boyd-Franklin, N. (1989). *Black families in therapy: A multisystem approach*. New York: Guilford.

Brager, G. A., & Jorcin, V. (1969). Bargaining: A method in community change. *Social Work, 14*(4), 73–83.

Braithwaite, J. (1989). *Crime, shame and reintegration*. New York: Cambridge University Press.

Brams, S. J., & Taylor, A. D. (1999). *The win-win solution: Guaranteeing fair shares to everybody*. New York: Norton.

Brandon, D., & Atherton, K. (1997). *A brief history of social work in Britain*. Cambridge: School of Community, Health & Social Studies, Anglia Polytechnic University.

Brandon, D., & Brandon, A. (1988). *Putting people first: A handbook on the practical application of ordinary living principles*. London: Good Impressions.

Brandon, D., Brandon, A., & Brandon, T. (1995). *Advocacy: Power to people with disabilities*. Birmingham: Venture Press.

Breen, J. (1985). Children of alcoholics: A subterranean grieving process. *Psychotherapy Patient, 2*, 85–94.

Brennan, J. P., & Kaplan, C. (1993). Setting new standards for social work case management. *Hospital and Community Psychiatry, 44*(3), 219–222.

Brenner, C. (1955). *An elementary textbook in psychoanalysis*. New York: Doubleday.

Breton, M. (1994a). On the meaning of empowerment and empowerment-oriented social work practice. *Social Work with Groups, 17*(3), 23–37.

Breton, M. (1994b). Relating competence-promotion and empowerment. *Journal of Progressive Human Services, 5*(1), 27–44.

Breton, M. (1995). The potential for social action in groups. *Social Work with Groups, 18*(2/3), 5–13.

Briar, K. H., & Kaplan, C. (1990). *The family caregiving crisis.* Silver Springs, MD: NASW Press.

Briar, S. (1967). The current crisis in social casework. In National Conference on Social Welfare (Ed.), *Social Work Practice* (pp. 19–33). New York: Columbia University Press.

Briar, S., & Miller, H. (1971). *Problems and issues in social casework.* New York: Columbia University Press.

Brice-Baker, J. (1996). Jamaican families. In M. McGoldrick, J. K. Pearce, & J. Giordano (Eds.), *Ethnicity and family therapy* (2nd ed., pp. 85–96). New York: Guilford.

Bricker-Jenkins, M. (1991). The propositions and assumptions of feminist social work practice. In M. Bricker-Jenkins, N. R. Hooyman, & N. Gottlieb (Eds.), *Feminist social work practice in clinical settings* (pp. 271–303). Thousand Oaks, CA: Sage.

Bricker-Jenkins, M. (1997). Hidden treasures: Unlocking strengths in the public social services. In D. Saleebey (Ed.), *The strengths perspective in social work practice* (2nd ed., pp. 133–150). New York: Longman.

Brill, C. K. (2001). Looking at the social work profession through the eye of the NASW Code of Ethics. *Research on Social Work Practice, 11*(2), 223–234.

Brocato, J., & Wagner, E. F. (2003). Harm reduction: A social work practice model and social justice agenda. *Health and Social Work, 28*(2), 117–125.

Bronfenbrenner, U. (1977). Toward an experimental ecology of human development. *American Psychologist, 32,* 513–530.

Bronfenbrenner, U. (1979). *The ecology of human development: Experiments by nature and design.* Cambridge, MA: Harvard University Press.

Bronfenbrenner, U. (1989). Ecological systems theory. In R. Vasta (Ed.), *Annals of child development, 6* (pp. 187–251). Greenwich, CT: JAI.

Bronfenbrenner, U. (1992). Ecological systems theory. In R. Vasta (Ed.), *Six theories of child development: Revised formulations and current issues* (pp. 187–249). London & Philadelphia: Jessica Kingsley.

Bronfenbrenner, U. (1997). Systems vs. associations: It's not either/or. *Families in Society: The Journal of Contemporary Human Services, 78*(2), 124.

Bronfenbrenner, U. (2000). Ecological systems theory. In A. E. Kazdin (Ed.), *Encyclopedia of psychology* (Vol. 3, pp. 129–133). New York: American Psychological Association and Oxford University Press.

Brooks, J., & Shaw, G. (1973). *Origin and development of living systems.* New York: Academic Press.

Bross, D., Krugman, R., Lenherr, M., Rosenburg, D., & Schmitt, B. (1988). *The new child protection team handbook.* New York & London: Garland.

Brower, A. M. (1988). Can the ecological model guide social work practice? *Social Service Review, 62*(3), 411–429.

Brower, A. M., & Nurius, P. S. (1993). *Social cognition and individual change: Current theory and counseling guidelines.* Newbury Park, CA: Sage.

Brown, J., Dreis, S., & Nace, D. K. (1999). What really makes a difference in psychotherapy outcome? Why does managed care want to know? In B. L. Duncan & M. A. Hubble (Eds.), *The heart and soul of change: What works in therapy* (pp. 389–406). Washington, DC: American Psychological Association.

Brown, J. A. (1980). Child abuse: An existential process. *Clinical Social Work Journal, 8*(2), 108–115.

Brown, L. N. (1991). *Groups for growth and change.* New York: Longman.

Brown, P. (1990). Social workers in private practice: What are they doing? *Journal of Clinical Social Work, 18*(4), 407–421.

Brown, P., & Barker, R. (1995). Confronting the "threat" of private practice: Challenges for social work educators. *Journal of Education for Social Work, 31*(1), 106–115.

Brown, R. A. (1973). Feedback in family interviewing. *Social Work, 18*(5), 52–59.

Browne, C., & Mills, C. (2001). Theoretical frameworks: Ecological model, strengths perspective, and empowerment theory. In R. Fong & S. Furuto (Eds.), *Culturally competent practice* (pp. 10–32). Boston: Allyn & Bacon.

Brownlee, K., & Taylor, S. (1995). CASW Code of Ethics and non-sexual dual relationships. The need for clarification. *The Social Worker/Le Travailleur Social, 63*(3), 133–136.

Bruce, T. J., & Sanderson, W. C. (1998). *Specific phobias: Clinical applications of evidence-based psychotherapy.* Northvale, NJ: Aronson.

Brun, C., & Rapp, R. C. (2001). Strengths-based case management: Individuals' perspectives on strengths and the case manager relationship. *Social Work, 46*(3), 278–288.

Bryant, C. (1980). Introducing students to the treatment of inner-city families. *Social Casework, 61*(10), 629–636.

Buckley, W. (1967). *Sociology and modern systems theory.* Englewood Cliffs, NJ: Prentice-Hall.

Budd, R. J., & Rollnick, S. (1996). The structure of the Readiness to Change Questionnaire: A test of Prochaska & DiClemente's transtheoretical model. *British Journal of Health Psychology, 1,* 365–376.

Budman, S. H., & Armstrong, E. (1992). Training for managed care setting: How to make it happen. *Psychotherapy, 29,* 416–421.

Budman, S. H., & Gurman, A. S. (1988). *Theory and practice of brief therapy.* New York: Guilford.

Buffum, W. E., & MacNair, R. H. (1994). Commitment to social action: Introduction. *Journal of Community Practice (special issue), 1*(2), 1–4.

Bullis, R. K. (1990). Cold comfort from the Supreme Court: Limited liability protection for social workers. *Social Work, 35*(4), 364–366.

Bulmer, M. (1987). *The social basis of community care.* London: Allen & Unwin.

Burford, G. (1994). Editorial: Getting serious about humanism in administration: The real unsolved mystery. *Journal of Child and Youth Care, 9*(3), v–viii.

Burford, G., & Pennell, J. (1995a). *Family group decision making project: Implementation report summary.* St. John's, Newfoundland: Family Group Decision Making Project, School of Social Work, Memorial University of Newfoundland.

Burford, G., & Pennell, J. (1995b). Family group decision making: An innovation in child and family welfare. In J. Hudson & B. Galaway (Eds.), *Child welfare in Canada: Research and policy implications* (pp. 140–153). Toronto: Thompson Educational.

Burford, G., & Pennell, J. (1996). Family group decision making: Generating indigenous structures for resolving family violence. *Protecting Children, 12*(3), 17–21.

Burford, G., Pennell, J., & MacLeod, S. (1995). *Family group decision making: Manual for coordinators and communities.* St. John's, Newfoundland: Family Group Decision Making Project, School of Social Work, Memorial University of Newfoundland.

Burford, G., Pennell, J., MacLeod, S., Campbell, S., & Lyall, G. (1996). Reunification as an extended family matter. *Community Alternatives, 8,* 2.

Burgess, L. (1994). Myths are the greatest barriers. *Modern Maturity, 37*(1), 6–7.

Burns, D. D. (1980). *Feeling good: The new mood therapy.* New York: Morrow.

Burns, M. E., & Glasser, P. H. (1963). Similarities and differences in casework and groupwork practice. *Social Service Review, 37*(4), 416–428.

Burr, W. R., & Christensen, C. (1992). Undesirable side effects of enhancing self-esteem. *Family Relations, 41*(4), 460–464.

Butz, R. (1992). Reporting child abuse and confidentiality in counseling. *Social Casework, 66*(2), 83–90.

Byrne, C., & Sebastian, L. (1994). The defining characteristics of support. *Journal of Psychosocial Nursing, 32*(6), 33–38.

Cade, B., & O'Hanlon, W. H. (1993). *A brief guide to brief therapy.* New York: Norton.

Callahan, J. (1996). Documentation of client dangerousness in a managed care environment. *Health and Social Work, 21*(3), 202–207.

Callahon, M. (1993). Feminist approaches: Women recreate child welfare. In B. Wharf (Ed.), *Rethinking child welfare in Canada* (pp. 172–209). Toronto: McClelland & Stewart.

Cameron, G. (1990). The potential of informal support strategies in child welfare. In M. Rothery & G. Cameron (Eds.), *Child maltreatment: Expanding our concept of helping* (pp. 145–168). Hillsdale, NJ: Erlbaum.

Cameron, G., & Rothery, M. (1985). *An exploratory study of the nature and effectiveness of family support measures in child welfare.* Paper presented at the Ontario Ministry of Community and Social Services, Toronto.

Campaign for Forgiveness Research. (2001). *Forgiving can heal individuals, marriages, families, communities, and even entire nations.* Retrieved October 2, 2003, from www.forgiving.org.

Campbell, D. T. (1969). Reforms as experiments. *American Psychologist, 24*(4), 409–429.

Campbell, J. (1995). *Understanding John Dewey: Nature and cooperative intelligence.* Chicago: Open Court.

Canadian Association of Social Workers. (1994). *Social work code of ethics.* Ottawa, ON: Canadian Association of Social Workers.

Canda, E. R. (1988a). Conceptualizing spirituality for social work: Insights from diverse perspectives. *Social Thought, 14,* 30–46.

Canda, E. R. (1988b). Spirituality, religious diversity, and social work practice. *Social Casework, 69*(4), 238–247.

Canda, E. R. (1991). East/west philosophical synthesis in transpersonal theory. *Journal of Sociology and Social Welfare, 18*(4), 137–152.

Canda, E. R. (1995). Spirituality. In R. L. Edwards (Ed.), *Encyclopedia of social work* (19th ed., Vol. 1997 Supplement, pp. 299–309). Washington, DC: NASW Press.

Capelle, R. G. (1979). *Changing human systems.* Toronto: International Human Systems Institute.

Capitman, J. A., Haskins, B., & Bernstein, J. (1986). Case management approaches in community-oriented long-term care demonstrations. *Gerontologist, 26,* 398–488.

Caplan, E. (2001). *Mind games: American culture and the birth of psychotherapy.* Berkeley: University of California Press.

Caplan, P. J. (1995). *They say you're crazy: How the world's most powerful psychiatrists decide who's normal.* Reading, MA: Addison-Wesley.

Capra, F. (1996). *The web of life: A new scientific understanding of living systems.* New York: Anchor Books.

Carkhuff, R. R. (1984). *Helping and human relations: Vols. 1 & 2.* Amherst, MA: Human Resource Development.

Carkhuff, R. R., & Anthony, W. A. (1979). *The skills of helping.* Amherst, MA: Human Resource Development.

Carpenter, J., & Sberiani, S. (1996). Involving service users and carers in the care programme approach (CPA). *Journal of Mental Health, 5*(5), 483–488.

Carrier, J., & Kendall, I. (1995). Professionalism and interprofessionalism in health and community care: Some theoretical issues. In P. Owens, J. Carrier, & J. Horder (Eds.), *Interprofessional issues in community and primary health care* (pp. 9–36). Basingstoke, England: Macmillan.

Carson, E. D. (1993). *Early roots of Black philanthropy.* Washington, DC: Joint Center for Political and Economic Studies.

Cascio, T. (1998). Incorporating spirituality into social work practice: A review of what to do. *Families in Society: The Journal of Contemporary Human Services, 79*(5), 523–532.

Cassel, J. (1974). Psychosocial processes and stress: Theoretical formulations. *International Journal of Health Services, 4*(3), 471–482.

Ceballo, R., & McLoyd, V. C. (2002). Social support and parenting in poor, dangerous neighborhoods. *Child Development, 73*(4), 1310–1321.

Chaffin, M. (2001). Adolescent sex offender treatment. In B. E. Saunders, L. Berliner, & R. F. Hanson (Eds.), *Guidelines for the psychosocial treatment of intrafamilial child physical and sexual abuse (Final Draft Report: July 30, 2001)* (pp. 87–89). Charleston, SC: Author.

Challis, D. (1994). *Implementing caring for people: Care management—Factors influencing its development in the implementation of community care.* London: Her Majesty's Stationary Office.

Challis, D. (1995). Case management: A review of UK developments and issues. In M. Titterton (Ed.), *Caring for people in the community: The new welfare* (pp. 91–112). London: Jessica Kinglsey.

Chambless, D. L., Baker, M. J., Baucom, D. H., Beutler, L. E., Calhoun, K. S., Crits-Christoph, P., et al. (1998). An update on empirically validated therapies, II. *Clinical Psychologist, 51*(1), 3–16.

Chambless, D. L., Sanderson, W. C., Shoham, V., Johnson, S. B., Pope, K. S., Crits-Christoph, P., et al. (1996). An update on empirically validated therapies. *Clinical Psychologist, 49*(2), 5–18.

Chamlin, M. B., & Cochran, J. K. (1997). Social altruism and crime. *Criminology, 35*(2), 203–227.

Chapin, R. K. (1995). Social policy development: The strengths perspective. *Social Work, 40*(4), 506–514.

Chapman, A. B. (1995). *Entitled to good loving: Black men and women and the battle for power and love.* New York: Holt.

Chau, K. L. (1990). Social work with groups in multicultural contexts. *Groupwork, 3*(1), 8–21.

Checkoway, B. (1995). Six strategies of community change. *Community Development Journal, 30*(1), 2–20.

Cheers, B. (1987). The social support network map as an educational tool. *Australian Social Work, 40*(3), 18–24.

Chen, H.-T. (1996). Epilogue: Synthesizing formative/summative evaluation. *Evaluation Practice, 17*(2), 163–167.

Chernesky, R. H., & Grube, B. (2000). Examining the HIV/AIDS case management process. *Health and Social Work, 25*(4), 243–253.

Cherniss, C. (1980a). *Professional burnout in human service organizations.* New York: Praeger.

Cherniss, C. (1980b). *Staff burnout.* Beverly Hills, CA: Sage.

Choi, N. G., & Wodarski, J. S. (1996). The relationship between social support and health status of elderly people: Does social support slow down physical and functional deterioration? *Social Work Research, 20*(1), 52–63.

Christiansen, J. M., Thornley-Brown, A., & Robinson, J. A. (1982). *West Indians in Toronto: Implications for helping professionals.* Toronto: Family Service Association of Metropolitan Toronto.

Chung, W. S., & Pardeck, J. T. (1997). Treating powerless minorities through an ecosystem approach. *Adolescence, 32*(127), 625–634.

Clancy, J. (1995). Ecological school social work: The reality and the vision. *Social Work in Education, 17*(1), 40–47.

Clark, D. A. (1988). The validity of measures of cognition: A review of the literature. *Cognitive Therapy and Research, 12*(1), 20.

Clark, M. (1997). Strengths-based practice: The new paradigm. *Corrections Today, 59*(2), 110–111.

Cleary, P. D., & Demone, J. H. (1988). Health and social service needs in a Northeastern metropolitan area: Ethnic group differences. *Journal of Sociology and Social Welfare, 15*(4), 63–76.

Cnaan, R. A. (1994). The new American social work gospel: Case management of the chronically mentally ill. *British Journal of Social Work, 24*(5), 553–557.

Coady, N. F. (1993). The worker-client relationship revisited. *Families in Society: The Journal of Contemporary Human Services, 74*(5), 291–297.

Cohen, B. Z. (1986). Written communication in social work: The report. *Child Welfare, 65*(4), 399–407.

Cohen, B. Z. (1999). Intervention and supervision in strengths-based social work practice. *Families in Society: The Journal of Contemporary Human Services, 80*(5), 460–466.

Cohen, M. B. (1989). Social work practice with homeless mentally ill people: Engaging the client. *Social Work, 34*(6), 505–509.

Cohen, M. B., & Wagner, D. C. (1992). Acting on their own behalf: Affiliation and political mobilization among homeless people. *Journal of Sociology and Social Welfare, 19*(4), 21–40.

Cohen, S., Doyle, W. J., Skoner, D. P., Robin, B. S., & Gwaltney, J. M. (1997). Social ties and susceptibility to the common cold. *Journal of the American Medical Association, 227*(24), 1940–1944.

Cohen, S., & Wills, T. A. (1985). Stress, social support and the buffering hypothesis. *Psychological Bulletin, 98*(2), 310–357.

Coleman, J. S. (1988). Social capital in the creation of human capital. *American Journal of Sociology, 94*(Supplement), S95–S120.

Collins, B. G. (1986). Defining feminist social work. *Social Work, 31*(3), 214–219.

Collins, M. E., Mowbray, C. T., & Bybee, D. (1999). Establishing individualized goals in a supported education intervention: Program influences on goal-setting and attainment. *Research on Social Work Practice, 9*(4), 483–507.

Compher, J. V. (1982). Parent-school-child systems: Triadic assessment and intervention. *Social Casework, 63*(7), 415–423.

Compher, J. V. (1987). The dance beyond the family system. *Social Work, 32*(2), 105–108.

Compton, B. R. (1979). *Family-centered project revisited.* Paper presented at the Family Centered Project, School of Social Work, University of Minneapolis.

Compton, B. R., & Galaway, B. (1984). *Social work processes* (3rd ed.). Homewood, IL: Dorsey.

Compton, B. R., & Galaway, B. (1989). *Social work processes* (4th ed.). Belmont, CA: Wadsworth.

Compton, B. R., & Galaway, B. (1994). *Social work processes* (5th ed.). Pacific Grove, CA: Brooks/Cole.

Compton, B. R., & Galaway, B. (1999). *Social work processes* (6th ed.). Pacific Grove, CA: Brooks/Cole.

Congress, E. P. (2000). What social workers should know about ethics: Understanding and resolving ethical dilemmas. *Advances in Social Work, 1*(1), 1–25.

Connidis, I. A., & McMullin, J. A. (1994). Social support in older age: Assessing the impact of marital and parent status. *Canadian Journal of Aging, 123*(4), 510–527.

Connolly, M. (1994). An act of empowerment: The Children, Young Persons, and Their Families Act (1989). *British Journal of Social Work, 24*(1), 87–100.

Conrad, P., & Schneider, J. W. (1992). *Deviance and medicalization: From badness to sickness.* Philadelphia: Temple University Press.

Cook, J. A., & Jonikas, J. A. (2002). Self-determination among mental health consumers/survivors: Using lessons from the past to guide the future. *Journal of Disability Policy Studies, 13*(2), 87–95.

Cooper, J. (1991). The future of social work: A pragmatic view. In M. Loney, B. Babcock, J. Clarke, A. Cochrane, P. Graham & M. Wilson (Eds.), *The state or the market: Politics and welfare in contemporary Britain* (pp. 58–69). London: Sage/The Open University.

Cooper, S. (1978). A look at the effect of racism on clinical work. *Social Casework, 54*(2), 78.

Coplon, J., & Strull, J. (1983). Roles of the professional in mutual aid groups. *Social Casework: The Journal of Contemporary Social Work, 64*(5), 259–266.

Corcoran, J. (2000). *Evidence-based social work practice with families: A lifespan approach.* New York: Springer.

Corcoran, J. (2002). Evidence-based treatments for adolescents with externalizing disorders. In A. R. Roberts & G. J. Greene (Eds.), *Social workers' desk reference* (pp. 793–797). New York: Oxford University Press.

Corcoran, K., & Fischer, J. (2000a). *Measures for clinical practice: A sourcebook, Vol. 1: Couples, families, and children* (3rd ed.). New York: Free Press.

Corcoran, K., & Fischer, J. (2000b). *Measures for clinical practice: A sourcebook, Vol. 2: Adults* (3rd ed.). New York: Free Press.

Corcoran, K., & Vandiver, V. (1996). *Maneuvering the maze of managed care.* New York: Free Press.

Corcoran, K. J., & Gingerich, W. J. (1994). Practice evaluation in the context of managed care: Case recording methods for quality assurance reviews. *Research on Social Work Practice, 4*(3), 326–337.

Cormican, J. D. (1978). Linguistic issues in interviewing. *Social Casework, 59*(3), 145–151.

Cormier, S., & Nurius, P. S. (2003). *Interviewing and change strategies for helpers: Fundamental skills and cognitive behavioral interventions* (5th ed.). Pacific Grove, CA: Brooks/Cole.

Cormier, W. H., & Cormier, L. S. (1985). *Interviewing strategies for helpers: Fundamental skills and cognitive behavioral interventions* (2nd ed.). Monterey, CA: Brooks/Cole.

Council on Social Work Education. (1992a). *Curriculum policy statement for BSW programs in social work education.* Alexandria, VA: Author.

Council on Social Work Education. (1992b). *Curriculum policy statement for master's degree programs in social work education.* Alexandria, VA: Author.

Council on Social Work Education. (2001). *Educational Policy and Accreditation Standards.* Alexandria, VA: Author.

Cournoyer, B. R. (1988). Personal and professional distress among social caseworkers: A developmental-interactional perspective. *Social Casework, 69*(5), 259–264.

Cournoyer, B. R. (1996). *The social work skills workbook* (2nd ed.). Belmont, CA: Brooks/Cole.

Cournoyer, B. R. (2000). *The social work skills workbook* (3rd ed.). Pacific Grove, CA: Brooks/Cole.

Cournoyer, B. R. (2004). *The evidence based social work (EBSW) skills book.* Boston: Allyn & Bacon.

Cournoyer, B. R. (2005). *The social work skills workbook* (4th ed.). Belmont, CA: Brooks/Cole.

Cournoyer, B. R., & Powers, G. T. (2002). Evidence-based social work: The quiet revolution continues. In A. R. Roberts & G. J. Greene (Eds.), *Social workers' desk reference* (pp. 798–807). New York: Oxford University Press.

Cournoyer, B. R., & Stanley, M. J. (2002). *The social work portfolio: Planning, assessing, and documenting lifelong learning in a dynamic profession.* Pacific Grove, CA: Brooks/Cole.

Coursey, R. D., Farrell, F. W., & Zahniser, J. H. (1991). Consumers' attitudes toward psychotherapy, hospitalization, and after care. *Health and Social Work, 16*(3), 155–161.

Cowger, C. D. (1994). Assessing client strengths: Clinical assessment for client empowerment. *Social Work, 39*(3), 262–268.

Cowger, C. D. (1996). Assessment of client strengths. In D. Saleebey (Ed.), *The strengths perspective in social work practice* (2nd ed., pp. 59–73). New York: Longman.

Cowley, A. D. (1993). Transpersonal social work: A theory for the 1990's. *Social Work, 38*(5), 527–534.

Cowley, A. D., & Derezotes, D. (1994). Transpersonal psychology and social work education. *Journal of Social Work Education, 30*(1), 32–41.

Cox, C. B. (2002). Empowering African American custodial grandparents. *Social Work, 47*(1), 45–54.

Cox, E. O. (1991). The critical role of social action in empowerment oriented groups. *Social Work with Groups, 14*(3/4), 77–90.

Coyle, G. L. (1948). *Group work with American youth.* New York: Harper & Row.

Crampton, C. (2002). I'm listening . . . Bedlam, mesmerism and psychoanalysis. *Psychology Review, 8*(4), 2–6.

Crawford, G. W. (1914). *Prince Hall and his followers.* New York: The Crisis.

Croft, S., & Beresford, P. (1993). *Getting involved: A practical manual.* London: Open Services Project/Joseph Rowntree Foundation.

Cross, T. (1988). Cultural competence continuum. *Focal Point: A National Bulletin on Family Support and Children's Mental Health, 3*(1).

Croxton, T. (1988). Caveats on contract. *Social Work, 33*(2), 169–171.

Cullen, F. T. (1994). Social support as an organizing concept for criminology. *Justice Quarterly, 11,* 527–559.

Cummings, N. A., & Sayama, M. (1995). *Focused psychotherapy: A casebook of brief, intermittent psychotherapy throughout the life cycle.* New York: Brunner/Mazel.

Cunningham, M., & Zayas, L. H. (2002). Reducing depression in pregnancy: Designing multimodal interventions. *Social Work, 47*(2), 114–123.

Curtis, P., & Lutkus, A. (1985). Client confidentiality in police social work settings. *Social Work, 30*(4), 355–360.

Daley, M. R. (1979). Burnout: Smoldering problem in the protective services. *Social Work, 24*(5), 375–379.

Dana, R. H. (1993). *Multicultural assessment perspectives for professional psychology.* Boston: Allyn & Bacon.

Dana, R. H. (Ed.). (2000). *Handbook of cross-cultural and multicultural personality assessment.* Mahwah, NJ: Erlbaum.

Dane, B. O., & Simon, B. L. (1991). Resident guests: Social workers in host settings. *Social Work, 36*(3), 208–213.

Daniel, J. H. (1985). Cultural and ethnic issues: The Black family. In E. H. Newberger & R. Bourne (Eds.), *Unhappy families: Clinical and research perspectives on family violence* (pp. 145–153). Littleton, MA: PSG.

D'Ardennes, P., & Mahtani, A. (Eds.). (1989). *Transcultural counseling in action.* London: Sage.

Davanloo, H. (1980). *Short-term dynamic psychotherapy.* New York: Aronson.

Davenport, J. (1992). Continuing social work education: The empirical base and practice guidelines. *Journal of Continuing Social Work Education, 5*(3), 27–30.

Davenport, J., & Reims, N. (1978). Theoretical orientation and attitudes toward women. *Social Work, 23*(4), 306–311.

David, M. (1970). *Game theory.* New York: Basic Books.

Davidson, J., & Davidson, T. (1996). Confidentiality and managed care: Ethical and legal concerns. *Health and Social Work, 21*(3), 208–215.

Davidson, J. P. (1997). *The complete idiot's guide to assertiveness.* New York: Alpha Books.

Davidson, J. R. (1992). White clinician-black client: Relationship problems and recommendations for change from a social influence theory perspective. *Journal of Multicultural Social Work, 1*(4), 63–76.

Davidson, M. (1983). *Uncommon sense: The life & thought of Ludwig von Bertalanffy (1901–1972), Father of general systems theory.* Boston: Houghton Mifflin.

Davies, B. (1992). *Care management, equity and efficiency: The international experience.* Canterbury, England: University of Kent, Personal Social Services Research Unit.

Davies, B. (1999). *Exploring chaos: Theory and experiment.* Reading, MA: Perseus Books.

Davis, L. E., & Gelsomino, J. (1994). An assessment of practitioner cross-racial treatment experiences. *Social Work, 39*(1), 122.

Davis, L. V. (1985). Female and male voices in social work. *Social Work, 30,* 106–113.

Davis, L. V. (1989). Empirical clinical practice from a feminist perspective: A response to Ivanoff, Robinson, and Blythe. *Social Work, 34*(6), 557–558.

De Hoyos, G., & Jensen, C. (1985). The systems approach in American social work. *Social Casework, 66*(8), 490–497.

de Jong, P., & Berg, I. K. (1998). *Interviewing for solutions.* Pacific Grove, CA: Brooks/Cole.

de Jong, P., & Berg, I. K. (2001). Co-constructing cooperation with mandated clients. *Social Work, 46*(4), 361–374.

de Jong, P., & Berg, I. K. (2002). *Interviewing for solutions* (2nd ed.). Pacific Grove, CA: Brooks/Cole.

de Jong, P., & Miller, S. D. (1995). How to interview for client strengths. *Social Work, 40*(6), 729–736.

de Shazer, S. (1975). Brief therapy: Two's company. *Family Process, 14,* 78–93.

de Shazer, S. (1982). *Patterns of brief family therapy: An ecosystemic approach.* New York: Guilford.

de Shazer, S. (1984). The death of resistance. *Family Process, 23,* 11–17.

de Shazer, S. (1985). *Keys to solution in brief therapy.* New York: Norton.

de Shazer, S. (1988a). *Clues: Investigating solutions in brief therapy.* New York: Norton.

de Shazer, S. (1988b). An indirect approach to brief therapy. *Family Therapy Collection, 19,* 48–55.

de Shazer, S., & Berg, I. K. (1988). Constructing solutions. *Family Therapy Networker, 12*(5), 42–43.

de Shazer, S., Berg, I. K., Lipchik, E., Nunnally, E., Molnar, A., Gingerich, W., et al. (1986). Brief therapy: Focused solution development. *Family Process, 25*(2), 207–221.

Dean, R. G. (1993). Constructivism: An approach to clinical practice. *Smith College Studies in Social Work, 63*(2), 127–146.

Dean, R. G. (2001). The myth of cross-cultural competence. *Families in Society: The Journal of Contemporary Human Services, 82*(6), 623–630.

Deci, E. L., & Ryan, R. M. (1980). The empirical exploration of intrinsic motivational processes. In L. Berkowitz (Ed.),

Advances in experimental social psychology (Vol. 13, pp. 40–80). New York: Academic.

Deci, E. L., Spiegel, N. H., Ryan, R. M., Kowstner, R., & Kauffman, M. (1982). Effects of performance standards on teaching styles: Behavior of controlling teachers. *Journal of Educational Psychology, 74*(6), 852–859.

Deegan, P. (1996). Recovery as a journey of the heart. *Psychiatric Rehabilitation Journal, 19,* 91–97.

Degen, K., Cole, H., Tamayo, L., & Dzerovych, G. (1990). Intensive case management for the seriously mentally ill. *Administration and Policy in Mental Health, 17*(4), 265–269.

Delaney, R., Brownlee, K., Sellick, M., & Tranter, D. (1997). Ethical problems facing northern social workers. *The Social Worker/Le Travailleur Social, 65*(3), 55–65.

Delaney, R. T., & Kunstal, F. R. (1997). *Troubled transplants: Unconventional strategies for helping disturbed foster and adopted children* (2nd ed.). Oklahoma City, OK: Wood 'N Barnes.

Delgado, J. R., & Rose, M. K. (1994). Caregiver constellations: Caring for persons with AIDS. *Journal of Gay and Lesbian Social Services, 1*(1), 1–14.

Delgado, M. (1995). Puerto Rican elders and natural support systems: Implications for human services. *Journal of Gerontological Social Work, 24*(1), 115–130.

Delgado, M. (1996). Community asset assessments by Latino youths. *Social Work in Education, 18*(3), 169–176.

Delgado, M., & Humm-Delgado, D. (1982). Natural support systems: Source of strength in Hispanic communities. *Social Work, 27*(1), 83–89.

Department of Health. (1994). *Implementing caring for people: "It's our lives." Community care for people with learning disabilities.* London: Her Majesty's Stationary Office.

Department of Health and Social Services Inspectorate and Scottish Office Social Work Group. (1991a). *Care management and assessment: Managers' Guide.* London: Her Majesty's Stationary Office.

Department of Health and Social Services Inspectorate and Scottish Office Social Work Group. (1991b). *Care management and assessment: Practitioners' Guide.* London: Her Majesty's Stationary Office.

Derezotes, D. S. (1995). Spirituality and religiosity: Neglected factors in social work practice. *Areté 20*(1), 1–15.

Derezotes, D. S., & Evans, K. E. (1995). Spirituality and religiousity in practice: In depth interviews of social work practitioners. *Social Thought, 18*(1), 19–56.

Desgranges, K., Desgranges, L., & Karsky, K. (1995). Attention deficit disorder: Problems with preconceived diagnosis. *Child and Adolescent Social Work Journal, 12*(1), 3–17.

Deutsch, K. (1968). Toward a cybernetic model of man and society. In W. Buckley (Ed.), *Modern system and research for the behavioral scientist* (pp. 387–400). Hawthorne, NY: Aldine de Gruyter.

Devore, W., & Schlesinger, E. G. (1996). *Ethnic-sensitive social work practice* (4th ed.). Boston: Allyn & Bacon.

Dewey, J. (Ed.). (1910). *How we think.* Lexington, MA: D. C. Heath.

Di Blasio, F. A. (1993). The role of social workers' religious beliefs in helping family members forgive. *Families in Society: The Journal of Contemporary Human Services, 74*(3), 163–170.

Di Blasio, F. A., & Proctor, J. H. (1993). Therapists and the clinical use of forgiveness. *American Journal of Family Therapy, 21*(2), 175–184.

Dickson, D. T. (1997). *Confidentiality and privacy in social work.* New York: Free Press.

Dillon, C. (2003). *Learning from mistakes in clinical practice.* Pacific Grove, CA: Brooks/Cole.

Dillon, P. A., & Emery, R. E. (1996). Divorce mediation and resolution in child custody disputes: Long term effects. *American Journal of Orthopsychiatry, 66*(1), 131–140.

Dilworth-Anderson, P. (1992). Extended kin networks in black families. *Generations, 17*(3), 29–32.

Dineen, T. (1996). *Manufacturing victims: What the psychology industry is doing to people.* Montreal: R. Davies Multimedia.

Dinerman, M. (1992). Managing the maze: Case management and service delivery. *Administrators in Social Work, 16*(1), 1–9.

DiNitto, D. M. (1995). *Social welfare: Politics and public policy.* Boston: Allyn & Bacon.

Diorio, W. D. (1992). Parental perceptions of authority of public child welfare caseworkers. *Families in Society: The Journal of Contemporary Human Services, 73*(4), 222–235.

Doel, M., & Lawson, B. (1986). Open records: The client's right to partnership. *British Journal of Social Work, 16*(4), 407–430.

Dokecki, P. R. (1992). On knowing the community of caring persons: A methodological basis for the reflective-generative practice of community psychology. *Journal of Community Psychology, 20,* 26–35.

Donnelly, W. J., & Brauner, D. J. (1990). *Why SOAP is bad for the medical record.* Unpublished manuscript.

Doublet, S. (2000). *The stress myth.* Chesterfield, MO: Science & Humanities Press.

Dougherty, S. J. (1994). The generalist role in club house organizations. *Psychosocial Rehabilitation Journal, 18*(1), 95–108.

Douville, M. L. (1993). Case management: Predicting activity patterns. *Journal of Gerontological Social Work, 20*(3/4), 43–55.

Downes, B. R. (1992). Guardianship for people with severe mental retardation: Consent for urgently needed treatment. *Health in Social Work, 17*(1), 13–15.

Dowson, S. (1991). *Keeping it safe.* London: Values into Action.

Drake, B. (1994). Relationship competencies in child welfare services. *Social Work, 39*(5), 595–602.

Dressel, P. L. (1982). Policy sources of work dissatisfaction: The case of human services in aging. *Social Service Review, 56*(3), 406–423.

Drolen, C. S., & Harrison, D. W. (1990). State hospital social work staff: Role conflict and ambiguity. *Administration and Policy in Mental Health, 18*(2), 127–129.

Dubin, M. (1996, July 23). Adults fear helping kids of others. *Omaha World-Herald,* 42.

DuBois, B., & Miley, K. K. (1996). *Social Work: An empowering profession.* Boston: Allyn & Bacon.

Du Bois, W. E. B. (1899). *The Philadelphia Negro.* New York: Benjamin Blom.

Dugan, T. F. (1989). *The child in our times: Studies in the development of resiliency.* New York: Brunner/Mazel.

Dumont, M. (1968). *The absurd healer.* New York: Viking Press.

Dungee-Anderson, D., & Beckett, J. O. (1995). A process model for multicultural social work practice. *Families in Society: The Journal of Contemporary Human Services, 76*(8), 459–468.

Durkheim, E. (1951). *Suicide, a study in sociology.* New York: Free Press.

Durrant, M. (1992). Solution focused brief therapy: Work shop package. Bradford, ON: Knowledge Unlimited.

Durst, D. (1992). The road to poverty is paved with good intentions: Social interventions and indigenous peoples. *International Social Work, 35*(2), 191–202.

Duryea, M. L., & Gundison, J. B. (1993). *Conflict and culture: Research in five communities in Vancouver, British Columbia.* Victoria, BC: University of Victoria Institute for Dispute Resolution.

Dyer, C. (2003). Unjustified seclusion of psychiatric patients is breach of human rights. *British Medical Journal, 327*(7408), 183.

D'Zurilla, T. J. (1986). *Problem solving therapy: A social competence approach to clinical intervention.* New York: Springer.

Earley, P. C., & Kanfer, R. (1985). The influence of component participation and role models on goal acceptance, goal satisfaction and performance. *Organizational Behavior and Human Decision Processes, 36,* 378–390.

Earley, P. C., & Perry, B. C. (1987). Work plan availability and performance: An assessment of task strategy priming on subsequent task completion. *Organizational Behavior and Human Decision Processes, 39,* 279–302.

Early, T. J., & Poertner, J. (1993). Case management for families and children. *Focal Point, 7*(1), 1–4.

Edelwich, J., & Brodsky, A. (1980). *Burn-out.* New York: Human Services Press.

Ekman, P., & O'Sullivan, M. (1991). Who can catch a liar. *American Psychologist, 46*(9), 913–920.

Elgin, S. H. (1993). *Genderspeak.* New York: Wiley.

Elizabeth. (1997). Management by whim. *News from Sammy's Dad* (Underground Newsletter) (3), 1–2.

Elks, M. A., & Kirkhart, K. E. (1993). Evaluating effectiveness from the practitioners perspective. *Social Work, 38*(5), 554–563.

Elliott, O. (1993). Social work and social development: Towards an integrative model for social work practice. *International Social Work, 36*(1), 21–36.

Ellis, A. (1975). *A new guide to rational living.* Englewood Cliffs, NJ: Prentice-Hall.

Ellis, A. (1986). Fanaticism that may lead to a nuclear holocaust: The contributions of scientific counseling and psychotherapy. *Journal of Counseling & Development, 65,* 146–150.

Ellis, A. (1989a). Dangers of transpersonal psychology: a reply to Ken Wilber. *Journal of Counseling & Development, 67*(6), 336–337.

Ellis, A. (1989b). Is rational emotive therapy (RET) "rationalist" or "constructivist"? In A. E. Ellis & W. Dryden (Eds.), *The essential Albert Ellis* (pp. 114–141). New York: Springer.

Ellis, A. (1990). Reply to Walsh on transpersonal psychology. *Journal of Counseling & Development, 68*(3), 344–345.

Ellis, A., & Yeager, R. J. (1989). *Why some therapies don't work: The dangers of transpersonal psychology.* Buffalo, NY: Prometheus Books.

Ellis, K. (1993). *Squaring the circle: User and carer participation in needs assessment.* London: Joseph Rowntree Foundation.

Else, J. F., & Raheim, S. (1992). AFDC clients as entrepreneurs. *Public Welfare, 50*(4), 36–41.

Emergency Committee for More Low Income Housing. (1963). *Facts about low income housing.* New York: Author.

Endler, N. S. (1980). Person situation interaction and anxiety. In I. L. Kutash & L. B. Schlesinger (Eds.), *Handbook on stress and anxiety* (pp. 249–266). San Francisco: Jossey Bass.

Epstein, L. (1980). *Helping people: The task-centered approach.* St. Louis: C. V. Mosby.

Epstein, L. (1985). *Talking and listening: A guide to the helping interview.* St. Louis: Times Mirror/Mosby.

Epstein, L. (1988). *Helping people: The task-centered approach.* Columbus, OH: Merrill.

Epstein, N. B., Baldwin, L. M., & Bishop, D. S. (1982). *McMaster family assessment device (FAD) version 3, manual.* Providence, RI: Brown University/Butler Hospital Family Research Program.

Epstein, N. B., Baldwin, L. M., & Bishop, D. S. (1983). The McMaster family assessment device. *Journal of Marital and Family Therapy, 9*(2), 171–180.

Erickson, G. D. (1984). A framework and themes for social network interventions. *Family Process, 23*(2), 187–198.

Erikson, E. H. (1968). *Identity, youth and crisis* (2nd ed.). New York: Norton.

Esten, G., & Wilmott, L. (1993). Double bind messages: The effects of attitude toward disability on therapy. *Women and Therapy, 14*(3/4), 29–41.

Etzioni, A. (1986). Mixed scanning revisited. *Public Administration Review, 46,* 8–14.

Evans, D. R., Hearn, M. T., Uhlemann, M. R., & Ivey, A. E. (1998). *Essential interviewing: A programmed approach to effective communication* (5th ed.). Pacific Grove, CA: Brooks/Cole.

Evans, E. H. (1992). Liberation theology, empowerment theory and social work practice with the oppressed. *International Social Work, 35*(2), 135–147.

Ewalt, P. L., Freeman, E. M., Kirk, S. A., & Poole, D. L. (Eds.). (1996). *Multicultural issues in social work.* Washington, DC: NASW Press.

Ewalt, P. L., & Mokuau, N. (1996). Self-determination from a Pacific perspective. In P. L. Ewalt, E. M. Freeman, S. A. Kirk, & D. L. Poole (Eds.), *Multicultural issues in social work* (pp. 255–268). Washington, DC: NASW Press.

Ezell, M. (1991). Administrators as advocates. *Administration in Social Work, 15*(4), 1–17.

Ezell, M. (1993). The political activity of social workers: A post Reagan update. *Journal of Sociology and Social Welfare, 20*(4), 81–97.

Ezell, M. (1994). Advocacy practice of social workers. *Families in Society: The Journal of Contemporary Human Services, 75*(1), 36–46.

Ezell, M. (1995). Juvenile and family courts. In R. L. Edwards (Ed.), *Encyclopedia of social work* (19th ed., Vol. 2, pp. 1553–1562). Washington, DC: NASW Press.

Fabricant, M., & Burghardt, S. (1992). *The welfare state crisis and the transformation of social service work.* New York: Sharpe.

Fabricant, M., & Fisher, R. (2002). Agency based community building in low income neighborhoods: A praxis framework. *Journal of Community Practice, 10*(2), 1–22.

Fagan, J., & Wexler, S. (1988). Explanations of sexual assault among violent delinquents. *Journal of Adolescent Research, 3,* 363–385.

Fairbairn, B., Bold, J., Fulton, M., Ketilson, L. H., & Ish, D. (1991). *Cooperatives and community development: Economics in social perspective.* Saskatoon: University of Saskatchewan.

Falck, H. S. (1988). *Social work: The membership perspective.* New York: Springer.

Fanshel, D., Finch, S. J., & Grundy, J. F. (1989). Foster children in life-course perspective: The Casey family program experience. *Child Welfare, 68*(5), 467–478.

Fanshel, D., Finch, S. J., & Grundy, J. F. (1990). *Foster children in a life course perspective.* New York: Columbia University Press.

Farber, B. A. (1983). Introduction: A critical perspective on burnout. In B. A. Farber (Ed.), *Stress and burnout in the human service professions* (pp. 1–20). New York: Pergamon.

Fargason, C. A., Barnes, D., Schneider, D., & Galloway, B. W. (1994). Enhancing multi-agency collaboration in the management of child sexual abuse. *Child Abuse and Neglect, 18*(10), 859–869.

Fast, B., & Chapin, R. (1997). The strengths model with older adults: Critical practice components. In D. Saleebey (Ed.), *The strengths perspective in social work practice* (2nd ed., pp. 115–132). New York: Longman.

Fatout, M. F. (1995). Using limits and structures for empowerment of children in groups. *Social Work with Groups, 17*(4), 55–69.

Federico, R. C. (1984). *The social welfare institution.* Lexington, MA: D.C. Heath.

Fein, E., Maluccio, A. H., Hamilton, V. J., & Ward, D. (1983). After foster care: Outcomes of permanency planning. *Child Welfare, 62*(6), 485–558.

Fein, E., & Staff, I. (1991). Implementing reunification services. *Families in Society: The Journal of Contemporary Human Services, 72*(6), 335–343.

Feit, M. D. (2003). Toward a definition of social work practice: Reframing the dichotomy. *Research on Social Work Practice, 13*(3), 357–365.

Festinger, T. B. (1983). *No one ever asked us: A postscript to foster care.* New York: Columbia University Press.

Festinger, T. B. (1996). Going home and returning to foster care. *Children and Youth Services Review, 18*(4/5), 383–402.

Figueira-McDonough, J. (1995). Community organizing and the underclass: Exploring new practice directives. *Social Service Review, 69*(1), 57–85.

Finn, J. (1995). Computer-based self-help groups: A new resource to supplement support groups. *Social Work with Groups, 18*(1), 109–117.

Finn, J., & Lavitt, M. (1994). Computer-based self-help groups for sexual abuse survivors. *Social Work with Groups, 17*(1/2), 21–46.

Finn, J. L. (1990). Burnout in the human services: A feminist perspective. *Affilia, 5*(4), 55–71.

Fisch, R., Weakland, J. H., & Segal, L. (1982). *Tactics of change: Doing therapy briefly.* San Francisco: Jossey-Bass.

Fischer, A. R., Jome, L. M., & Atkinson, D. R. (1998). Reconceptualizing multicultural counseling: Universal healing conditions in a culturally specific context. *Counseling Psychologist, 26*(4), 525–561.

Fischer, J. (1971). A framework for the analysis of clinical theories of induced change. *Social Service Review, 45,* 440–454.

Fischer, J. (1993). Empirically-based practice: The end of an ideology? *Journal of Social Service Research, 18*(1), 19–64.

Fischer, J., & Corcoran, K. (1994). *Measures for clinical practice: A Sourcebook, Vol. 2: Adults* (2nd ed.). New York: Free Press.

Fisher, R. (1994). *Let the people decide: Neighbourhood organizing in America.* New York: Twayne.

Fiske, S. T., & Taylor, S. T. (1991). *Social Cognition* (2nd ed.). New York: McGraw-Hill.

Fleuridas, C., Leigh, G. K., Rosenthal, D. M., & Leigh, T. E. (1990). Family goal recording: An adaptation of goal attainment scaling for enhancing family therapy and assessment. *Journal of Marital and Family Therapy, 16*(4), 389–406.

Flexner, A. (1915). Is social work a profession? In National Conference of Charities and Corrections (Ed.), *Proceedings of the National Conference of Charities and Corrections at the Forty-second annual session held in Baltimore, Maryland, May 12–19, 1915* (Vol. 42). Chicago: Hildmann.

Flexner, A. (2001). Is social work a profession? *Research on Social Work Practice, 11*(2), 152–165.

Folger, J., Poole, M., & Stautman, R. (1993). *Working through conflict: Strategies for relationships, groups, and organizations.* New York: Harper Collins.

Fong, R., & Furuto, S. (Eds.). (2001). *Culturally competent practice.* Boston: Allyn & Bacon.

Fook, J. (1993). *Radical casework: A theory of practice.* St. Leonards, Australia: Allen & Unwin.

Ford, M. E., & Ford, D. H. (Eds.). (1987). *Humans as self-constructing living systems: Putting the framework to work.* Hillsdale, NJ: Erlbaum.

Fordor, A. (1976). Social work and systems theory. *British Journal of Social Work, 6*(1), 8–14.

Fort, R., & Associates. (1990). *Spices of life: A well being handbook for older Americans.* Washington, DC: Center for Responsive Law.

Fortune, A. E. (1979). Problem-solving processes in task-centered treatment with adults and children. *Journal of Social Service Research, 2*(4), 357–371.

Fortune, A. E. (1987). Grief only? Client and social worker reactions to termination. *Clinical Social Work Journal, 15*(2), 159–171.

Fortune, A. E., Pearlingi, B., & Rochelle, C. (1991). Criteria for terminating treatment. *Families in Society: The Journal of Contemporary Human Services, 72*(6), 366–370.

Fortune, A. E., Pearlingi, B., & Rochelle, C. (1992). Reactions to termination of individual treatment. *Social Work, 37*(2), 171–178.

Fox, E., Nelson, M., & Bolman, W. (1969). The termination process: A neglected dimension in social work. *Social Work, 14*(4), 53–63.

Fox, R. (1987). Short-term, goal-oriented family therapy. *Social Casework, The Journal of Contemporary Social Work, 68*(8), 494–499.

Fraley, Y. L. (1969). A role model for practice. *Social Service Review, 43*(2), 145–154.

Frank, J. D. (1978). Expectation and therapeutic outcome: The placebo effect and the role induction interview. In J. D. Frank, R. Hoehn-Saric, S. Imber, B. Liberman, & A. Stone (Eds.), *Effective ingredients of successful psychotherapy* (pp. 1–34). New York: Brunner/Mazel.

Frankel, A. J., & Gelman, S. R. (1998). *Case management: An introduction to concepts and skills.* Chicago: Lyceum.

Frankenstein, R. (1982). Agency and client resistance. *Social Casework, 52*(1), 24–28.

Frankl, V. E. (1963). *Man's search for meaning: An introduction to logotherapy.* New York: Washington Square Press.

Franklin, C. (1995). Expanding the vision of the social constructionist debates: Creating relevance for practitioners. *Families in Society: The Journal of Contemporary Human Services, 76*(7), 395–407.

Franklin, C. (2001). Coming to terms with the business of direct practice social work. *Research on Social Work Practice, 11*(2), 235–244.

Franklin, C., & Brekke, J. S. (1994). Must social workers continually yield current practice methods to the evolving empirically supported knowledge base? In W. W. Hudson & P. S. Nurius (Eds.), *Controversial issues in social work research* (pp. 271–282). Boston: Allyn & Bacon.

Franklin, C., & Johnson, C. (1996). Family social work practice: Onward to therapy and policy. *Journal of Family Social Work, 1*(3), 33–47.

Franklin, C., & Jordan, C. (1992). Teaching students to perform assessment. *Journal of Social Work Education, 28*(2), 222–241.

Franklin, C., & Jordan, C. (1995). Qualitative assessment: A methodological review. *Families in Society: The Journal of Contemporary Human Services, 76*(5), 281–295.

Franklin, C., & Jordan, C. (1998). *Family practice: Brief systems methods for social work.* Pacific Grove, CA: Brooks/Cole.

Franklin, C., & Jordan, C. (2002). Treatment planning with families: An evidence-based approach. In A. R. Roberts & G. J. Greene (Eds.), *Social workers' desk reference* (pp. 252–255). New York: Oxford University Press.

Franklin, C., & Nurius, P. S. (1996). Constructivist therapy: New directions in social work practice. *Families in Society: The Journal of Contemporary Human Services, 77*(6).

Franklin, C., Waukechon, J., & Larney, P. S. (1996). Culturally relevant school programs for American Indian children and families. In P. L. Ewalt, E. M. Freeman, S. A. Kirk, & D. L. Poole (Eds.), *Multicultural issues in social work* (pp. 351–365). Washington, DC: NASW Press.

Franklin, D. L. (1990). The cycles of social work practice: Social action vs. individual interest. *Journal of Progressive Human Services, 1*(2), 59–80.

Franklin, J. C. (1997). Industry output and employment projections to 2006. *Monthly Labor Review* (November), 39–57.

Franklin, J. H. (1980). *From slavery to freedom: A history of Negro Americans.* New York: Knopf.

Fraser, M. W. (1995). Violence overview. In R. L. Edwards (Ed.), *Encyclopedia of social work* (19th ed., Vol. 3, pp. 2453–2460). Washington, DC: NASW Press.

Fraser, M. W. (1996). Aggressive behavior in childhood and early adolescence: An ecological developmental perspective on youth violence. *Social Work, 41*(4), 347–361.

Fraser, M. W. (Ed.). (1997). *Risk and resilience in childhood: An ecological perspective.* Washington, DC: NASW Press.

Fraser, M. W., Taylor, M. J., Jackson, R., & O'Jack, J. (1991). Social work and science: Many ways of knowing? *Social Work Research and Abstracts, 27*(4), 5–15.

Frazier, E. F. (1966). *The Negro family in the United States.* Chicago: University of Chicago Press.

Fredman, N., & Sherman, N. (1987). *Handbook of measurements for marriage and family therapy.* New York: Brunner/Mazel.

Freedberg, S. (1989). Self-determination: Historical perspectives and effects on current practice. *Social Work, 34*(1), 33–38.

Freedman, J., & Combs, G. (1996). *Narrative therapy: The social construction of preferred realities.* New York: Norton.

Freedman, M. (1993). *The kindness of strangers: Adult mentors, urban youth, and the new voluntarism.* San Francisco: Jossey-Bass.

Freedman, M. (1997). Towards civic renewal: How senior citizens could save civil society. *Journal of Gerontological Social Work, 28*(3), 243–263.

Freidman, M., & Rosenman, R. H. (1974). *Type A behavior and your heart.* New York: Knopf.

French, T. M. (1952). *The integrating behavior: Basic postulates.* Chicago: University of Chicago Press.

Freng, S. A., Carr, D. I., & Cox, C. B. (1995). Intensive case management for chronic public inebriates: A pilot study. *Alcoholism Treatment Quarterly, 13*(1), 8–90.

Freud, S. (1992). Dropping out: A feminist approach. In C. W. LeCroy (Ed.), *Case studies in social work practice* (pp. 228–234). Pacific Grove, CA: Brooks/Cole.

Freudenberger, H. J. (1974). Staff burn-out. *Journal of Social Issues, 30*(1), 159–165.

Freudenberger, H. J., & North, G. (1985). *Women's burnout: How to spot it, how to reverse it, and how to prevent it.* Garden City, NY: Doubleday.

Friedlander, W. A. (1968). *Introduction to social welfare.* Englewood Cliffs, NJ: Prentice-Hall.

Friedson, E. (1970). Dominant professions, bureaucracy, and client services. In W. R. Rosengren & M. Leften (Eds.), *Organization and clients* (pp. 71–93). Columbus, OH: Merrill.

From sandals to suits. (1997, February 1). Microlending and the microcredit summit. *Economist, 342,* 75.

Fuchs, D. (1993). Building on the strengths of family and neighborhood social network ties for the prevention of child maltreatment: An ecological approach. In M. R. Rodway & B. Trute (Eds.), *The ecological perspective in family-centered therapy* (pp. 69–98). Queenston, ON: Edwin Mellen.

Fulero, S. M. (1988). Tarasoff: 10 years later. *Professional Psychology: Research and Practice, 19,* 184–190.

Fuller, R. W. (2002). *Somebodies and nobodies: Overcoming the abuse of rank.* Gabriola Island, BC: New Society.

Fulton, M. (Ed.). (1989). *Capital formation in cooperatives: Social and economic considerations.* Saskatoon: University of Saskatchewan.

Furstenberg, A. L., & Rounds, K. A. (1995). Self-efficacy as a target for social work intervention. *Families in Society: The Journal of Contemporary Human Services, 76*(10), 587–595.

Galambos, C. M. (1998). Preserving end-of-life autonomy: The Patient Self-Determination Act and the Uniform Health Care Decisions Act. *Health and Social Work, 23*(4), 275–281.

Galaway, B. (1981). Social services and criminal justice. In N. Gilbert & H. Sprecht (Eds.), *Handbook of the social services* (pp. 250–280). Englewood Cliffs, NJ: Prentice-Hall.

Galaway, B., & Hudson, J. (1996). *Restorative justice: International perspectives.* Monsey, NY: Criminal Justice Press.

Galinsky, M. J., & Schopler, J. H. (1994). Negative experiences in support groups. *Social Work in Health Care, 20*(1), 77–95.

Gambrill, E. (1983). *Casework: A competency-based approach.* Englewood Cliffs, NJ: Prentice-Hall.

Gambrill, E. (1999). Evidence-based practice: An alternative to authority-based practice. *Families in Society: The Journal of Contemporary Human Services, 80*(4), 341–350.

Gambrill, E. (2001). Social work: An authority-based profession. *Research on Social Work Practice, 11*(2), 166–175.

Gambrill, E. (2003). A client-focused definition of social work practice. *Research on Social Work Practice, 13*(3), 310–323.

Gambrill, E., Thomas, E., & Carter, R. (1971). Procedure for sociobehavioral practice in open settings. *Social Work, 16,* 51–62.

Gant, L. M. (1996). Are culturally sophisticated agencies better workplaces for social work staff and administrators? *Social Work, 41*(2), 163–171.

Garbarino, J. (1982). *Children and families in the social environment.* New York: Aldine de Gruyter.

Garbarino, J. (1986). Where does social support fit into optimizing human development and preventing dysfunction? *British Journal of Social Work, 16* (supplement), 23–37.

Garcia, J. A., & Floyd, C. E. (1999). Using single system design for student self-assessment: A method for enhancing practice and integrating curriculum. *Journal of Social Work Education, 35*(3), 451–461.

Garland, D. R. (1995). Church social work. In R. L. Edwards (Ed.), *Encyclopedia of social work* (19th ed., Vol. 1, pp. 475–483). Washington, DC: NASW Press.

Garmezy, N. (1971). Vulnerability research and the issue of primary prevention. *American Journal of Orthopsychiatry, 41*(1), 101–115.

Garmezy, N. (1987). Stress, competence, and development: Continuities in the study of schizophrenic adults, children vulnerable to psychopathology, and the search for stress-resistant children. *Journal of Orthopsychiatry, 57*(2), 159–174.

Garmezy, N. (1993). Children in poverty: Resilience despite risk. *Psychiatry, 56*(1), 127–136.

Garrett, A. (1995). *Interviewing: Its principles and methods.* Milwaukee, WI: Families International.

Garrett, K. J. (1994). Caught in a bind: Ethical decision making in schools. *Social Work in Education, 16*(2), 97–105.

Gartner, A., & Reissman, F. (Eds.). (1984). *The self-help revolution.* New York: Human Sciences Press.

Garwick, G., & Lampman, S. (1972). Typical problems bringing patients to a community mental health center. *Community Mental Health Journal, 8*(4), 271–280.

Gaudin, J. M., Polansky, N. A., Kilpatrick, A. C., & Shilton, P. (1993). Loneliness, depression, stress and social supports in neglectful families. *American Journal of Orthopsychiatry, 63*(4), 597–605.

Gaudin, J. M., Wodarski, J. S., Arkinson, M. K., & Avery, L. S. (1990). Remedying child neglect: Effectiveness of social network interventions. *Journal of Applied Social Sciences, 15,* 97–123.

Gaylin, W., Glasser, I., Marcus, S., & Rothman, D. J. (1978). *Doing good: The limits of benevolence.* New York: Pantheon Books.

Gazzaniga, M. S. (1992). *Nature's mind: The biological roots of thinking, emotions, sexuality, language, and intelligence.* New York: Basic Books.

Gelman, S. R. (1992). Risk management through client access to case records. *Social Work, 37*(1), 73–79.

Gelman, S. R., & Reamer, F. G. (1992). Is Tarasoff relevant to AIDS-related cases? In E. Gambrill & R. Pruger (Eds.), *Controversial issues in social work* (pp. 342–355). Boston: Allyn & Bacon.

Gelman, S. R., & Schnall, D. J. (1995). Jewish communal services. In R. L. Edwards (Ed.), *Encyclopedia of social work* (19th ed., 1997 Supplement, pp. 169–178). Washington, DC: NASW Press.

General Assembly of the United Nations. (1948). *Universal declaration of human rights.* New York: Author.

General Assembly of the United Nations. (1989). *Convention on the rights of the child.* New York: Author.

Gerdes, K. E., Edmonds, R. M., Hoslam, D. R., & McCartney, T. L. (1996). A statewide survey of licensed clinical social workers' use of practice evaluation procedures. *Research on Social Work Practice, 6*(1), 27–39.

Gergen, K. J. (1991). *The saturated self: Dilemmas of identity in contemporary society.* New York: Basic Books/Harper.

Germain, C. B. (1973). An ecological perspective in casework practice. *Social Casework, 54,* 323–330.

Germain, C. B. (1976). Time: An ecological variable in social work practice. *Social Casework, 57,* 419–426.

Germain, C. B. (1978). Space: An ecological variable in social work practice. *Social Casework, 59,* 515–522.

Germain, C. B. (1979a). Ecology in social work. In C. B. Germain (Ed.), *Social work practice: People and environments—An ecological perspective* (pp. 1–22). New York: Columbia University Press.

Germain, C. B. (Ed.). (1979b). *Social work practice: People and environments—An ecological perspective.* New York: Columbia University Press.

Germain, C. B. (1981). The ecological approach to people-environment transactions. *Social Casework, 62*(6), 323–331.

Germain, C. B., & Gitterman, A. (1980). *The life model of social work practice.* New York: Columbia University Press.

Germain, C. B., & Gitterman, A. (1995). Ecological perspective. In R. L. Edwards (Ed.), *Encyclopedia of social work* (19th ed., Vol. 1, pp. 816–824). Washington, DC: NASW Press.

Germain, C. B., & Gitterman, A. (1996). *The life model of social work practice* (2nd ed.). New York: Columbia University Press.

Gibbs, D., & Priestley, M. (1996). The social model and user involvement. In *Conference Report: Disability rights symposium of the European regions* (pp. 139–150). Southhampton, England: Hampshire Coalition of Disabled People.

Gibbs, J. T. (1980). The interpersonal orientation in mental health consultation: Toward a model of ethnic variations in counseling. *Journal of Community Psychology, 8,* 195–207.

Gibbs, J. T. (1993). *After the L.A. riots: Social work's role in healing cities.* San Francisco: Many Cultures.

Gibbs, J. T., & Moskowitz-Sweet, G. (1991). Clinical and cultural issues in the treatment of biracial and bicultural adolescents. *Families in Society: The Journal of Contemporary Human Services, 72*(10), 579–592.

Gibbs, L. E. (2002a). *Evidence-based practice for the helping professions.* Belmont, CA: Wadsworth.

Gibbs, L. E. (2002b). How social workers can do more good than harm: Critical thinking, evidence-based clinical reasoning, and avoiding fallacies. In A. R. Roberts & G. J. Greene (Eds.), *Social workers' desk reference* (pp. 752–756). New York: Oxford University Press.

Gibson, A., & Lewis, C. (1985). *A light in the dark tunnel: Ten years of West Indian concern and Caribbean House.* London: Centre for Caribbean Studies.

Giddings, P. (1984). *Where and when I enter: Impact of Black women on race and sex in America.* New York: Murrow.

Gilbert, N., & Sprecht, H. (1976). Advocacy and professional ethics. *Social Work, 21,* 288–293.

Giles, T. R. (1991). Managed mental health care and effective psychotherapy: A step in the right direction? *Journal of Behavior Therapy and Experimental Psychiatry, 22,* 83–86.

Gilligan, C. (1984). *In a different voice.* Cambridge, MA: Harvard University Press.

Gitterman, A. (1988, March). *Alternative practice explanatory frameworks: A debate.* Paper presented at the Annual Program Meeting of the Council on Social Work Education, Atlanta, GA.

Gitterman, A. (1996). Life model theory and social work treatment. In F. J. Turner (Ed.), *Social work treatment: Interlocking theoretical approaches* (4th ed., pp. 389–408). New York: Free Press.

Gitterman, A., & Schaeffer, A. (1972). The white professional and the black client. *Social Casework, 53*(5), 280–291.

Gitterman, A., & Shulman, L. (1994). *Mutual aid groups: Vulnerable populations and the life cycle.* New York: Columbia University Press.

Glaser, G. (2001). Reflections of a social work practitioner: Bridging the 19th and 21st centuries. *Research on Social Work Practice, 11*(2), 190–200.

Globerman, J., & Bego, M. (1995). Social work and the new integrative hospital. *Social Work in Health Care, 21*(3), 1–21.

Golan, N. (1981). *Passing through transitions.* New York: Free Press.

Gold, D. (1987). Sibling in older age: Something special. *Canadian Journal of Aging, 6*(3), 199–227.

Goldberg, E. M., & Stanley, S. J. (1985). Task-centered casework in a probation setting. In E. M. Goldberg, J. Gibbons, & I. Sinclair (Eds.), *Problems, tasks and outcomes* (pp. 89–159). London: Allen & Unwin.

Goldberger, N. R., Tarule, J. M., Clinchy, B. M., & Belenky, M. F. (Eds.). (1996). *Knowledge, difference, and power: Essays inspired by "Women's Ways of Knowing."* New York: Basic Books.

Goldstein, E. G. (1986). Ego psychology. In F. J. Turner (Ed.), *Social work treatment: Interlocking theoretical approaches* (3rd ed., pp. 375–404). New York: Free Press.

Goldstein, E. G. (1988, March). *Alternative practice explanatory frameworks: A debate.* Paper presented at the Annual Meeting, Council on Social Work Education, Atlanta, GA.

Goldstein, E. G. (2001). *Object relations theory and self psychology in social work practice.* New York: Free Press.

Goldstein, H. (1973). *Social work practice: A unitary approach.* Columbia: University of South Carolina.

Goldstein, H. (1988, May). *Strength of pathology: Ethical and rhetorical contrasts in approaches to social work practice.* Paper presented at the School of Social Welfare, University of Kansas.

Goldstein, H. (1997). Victors or victims? In D. Saleebey (Ed.), *The strengths perspective in social work practice* (2nd ed., pp. 21–36). New York: Longman.

Gomez, L. (1997). *An introduction to object relations.* Washington Square: New York University Press.

Goodman, C. (1990). Evaluation of a model self-help telephone program: Impact on natural networks. *Social Work, 35*(6), 556–562.

Goodman, J. A. (1973). Preface. In J. A. Goodman (Ed.), *Dynamics of racism in social work practice* (pp. ix–xiii). Washington, DC: NASW Press.

Googins, B., & Davidson, B. N. (1993). The organization as client: Broadening the concept of employee assistance programs. *Social Work, 38*(4), 477–488.

Gordon, R. C. (1992). *Basic interviewing skills.* Itasca, IL: Peacock.

Gordon, W. E. (1962). A critique of the working definition. *Social Work, 7*(4), 3–13.

Gordon, W. E. (1965). Knowledge and value: Their distinction and relationship in clarifying social work practice. *Social Work, 10*(4), 32–39.

Gordon, W. E. (1969). Basic concepts for an integrative and generative conception of social work. In G. Hearn (Ed.), *The general systems approach: Contributions toward an holistic conception of social work* (pp. 5–11). New York: Council on Social Work Education.

Gorey, K. M., Thyer, B. A., & Pawluck, D. E. (1998). Differential effectiveness of prevalent social work practice models: A meta-analysis. *Social Work, 43*(3), 269–278.

Gorlick, C., & Pomfret, D. (1993). Hope and circumstance: Single mothers exiting social assistance. In J. Hudson & B. Galaway (Eds.), *Single parent families: Perspectives on research and policy* (pp. 253–270). Toronto: Thompson Educational.

Gottlieb, B. H. (1978). The development and application of a classification scheme of informal helping behaviors. *Canadian Journal of Behavioral Science, 10*(2), 105–115.

Gottlieb, B. H., & Todd, D. M. (1979). Characterizing and promoting social support in natural settings. In R. F. Muñoz, L. R. Snowden & J. G. Kelly (Eds.), *Social and psychological research in community settings* (pp. 183–242). San Francisco: Jossey-Bass.

Gottschalk, L. (1973). A study of prediction and outcome in a mental health crisis clinic. *American Journal of Psychiatry, 130,* 1107–1111.

Gould, R. (1978). Students' experience with the termination phase of treatment. *Smith College Studies in Social Work, 48*(3), 235–269.

Goulding, M. M. (1990). Getting the important work done fast: Contract plus redecision. In J. Zeig & S. Gilligan (Eds.), *Brief therapy: Myths, methods, and metaphors* (pp. 303–317). New York: Brunner/Mazel.

Granvold, D. K. (1996). Constructivist psychotherapy. *Families in Society: The Journal of Contemporary Human Services, 77*(6), 345–357.

Grasso, A. J., & Epstein, I. (Eds.). (1992). *Research utilization in the social services: Innovations for practice and administration.* New York: Haworth Press.

Gray, L. A., & Harding, A. K. (1988). Confidentiality limits with clients who have the AIDS virus. *Journal of Counseling and Development, 66,* 219–223.

Graybeal, C. (2001). Strengths-based social work assessment: Transforming the dominant paradigm. *Families in Society: The Journal of Contemporary Human Services, 82*(3), 233–242.

Graybeal, C. T., & Rulf, E. (1995). Process recording: It's more than you think. *Journal of Social Work Education, 31*(2), 169–181.

Green, J. W. (1982). *Cultural awareness in the human services.* Englewood Cliffs, NJ: Prentice-Hall.

Greenberg, L., & Pascual-Leone, J. (1999). A dialectical constructivist approach to experiential change. In R. A. Neimeyer & M. J. Mahoney (Eds.), *Constructivism in psychotherapy* (pp. 169–191). Washington, DC: American Psychological Association.

Greene, G. J. (1989). Using the written contract for evaluating and enhancing practice effectiveness. *Journal of Independent Social Work, 4*(2), 134–155.

Greene, R. R., & Ephross, P. H. (Eds.). (1991). *Human behavior theory and social work practice.* New York: Aldine de Gruyter.

Greene, R. R., & Frankel, K. (1994). A systems approach: Addressing diverse family forms. In R. R. Greene (Ed.), *Human behavior theory: A diversity framework* (pp. 147–172). New York: Aldine de Gruyter.

Greer, J. H., Davidson, G. C., & Gatchel, R. I. (1970). Reeducation of stress in humans through non-veridical perceived control of aversive stimulation. *Journal of Personality and Social Psychology, 16*(4), 731–738.

Griffith, J. E., & Villavicencio, S. (1985). Relationship among acculturation, sociodemographic characteristics, and social support in Mexican American adults. *Hispanic Journal of Behavioral Sciences, 7,* 75–92.

Grinnell, R. M. (1997). *Social work research and evaluation* (5th ed.). Itasca, IL:. Peacock.

Gross, M. L. (1978). *The psychological society: A critical analysis of psychiatry, psychotherapy, psychoanalysis and the psychological revolution.* New York: Random House.

Grosser, C. (1965). Community development programs serving the urban poor. *Social Work, 10*(3), 15–21.

Guerin, P. J., & Pendagast, C. G. (1976). Evaluation of family system and genogram. In P. J. Guerin (Ed.), *Family therapy theory and practice* (pp. 450–464). New York: Gardner.

Guidano, V. F. (1991). *The self in process.* New York: Guilford.

Gurowka, K. J., & Lightman, E. S. (1995). Supportive and unsupportive interactions as perceived by cancer patients. *Social Work in Health Care, 21*(4), 71–83.

Gutierrez, L. M. (1995). Understanding the empowerment process: Does consciousness make a difference? *Social Work Research, 19*(4), 229–237.

Gutierrez, L. M. (1996). Understanding the empowerment process: Does consciousness make a difference? In P. L. Ewalt, E. M. Freeman, S. A. Kirk, & D. L. Poole (Eds.), *Multicultural issues in social work* (pp. 43–59). Washington, DC: NASW Press.

Gutierrez, L. M., GlenMaye, L., & DeLois, K. (1996). The organizational context of empowerment practice: Implications for social work administration. In P. L. Ewalt, E. M. Freeman, S. A. Kirk, & D. L. Poole (Eds.), *Multicultural issues in social work* (pp. 60–76). Washington, DC: NASW Press.

Guttman, D. (1996). *Logotherapy for the helping professional: Meaningful social work.* New York: Springer.

Hadley, R., Cooper, M., Dale, A., & , & Stacy, G. (1987). *A community social worker's handbook.* London: Tavistock.

Haley, J. (1963). *Strategies of psychotherapy.* New York: Grune & Stratton.

Haley, J. (1987). *Problem solving therapy* (2nd ed.). San Francisco: Jossey-Bass.

Halfton, N., Berkowitz, G., & Klee, L. (1993). Development of an integrated case management program for vulnerable children. *Child Welfare, 72*(4), 379–396.

Hall, J. A., Carswell, C., Walsh, E., Huber, D. L., & Jampoler, J. S. (2002). Iowa case management: Innovative social casework. *Social Work, 47*(2), 132–141.

Halle, J. (1998). Fidelity: A crucial question in translating research to practice. *Journal of Early Intervention, 21*(4), 294–296.

Halmos, P. (1966). *The faith of the counsellors: A study in the theory and practice of social case work and psychotherapy.* New York: Schocken Books.

Hamilton, G. (1940). *Theory and practice of social case work.* New York: Columbia University Press.

Hamilton, G. (1946). *Principles of social case recording.* New York: Columbia University Press.

Hamilton, G. (1951). *Theory and practice of social casework* (2nd ed.). New York: Columbia University Press.

Hammond, D., Hepworth, D., & Smith, V. (1977). *Improving therapeutic communication.* San Francisco: Jossey-Bass.

Hampshire Coalition of Disabled People. (1995). *The language of disability.* Southampton, England: Author.

Hanson, B. G. (1995). *General systems theory: Beginning with wholes.* London: Taylor & Francis.

Hardina, D. (1995). Do Canadian social workers practice advocacy? *Journal of Community Practice, 2*(3), 97–121.

Hardman, D. (1960). The constructive use of authority. *Crime and Delinquency, 6*(3), 245–254.

Hardman, D. (1975). Not with my daughter you don't. *Social Work, 21,* 278–285.

Harlow, H. F. (1974). *Learning to love.* New York: Aronson.

Harlow, H. F. (1986). *From learning to love: The selected papers of H. F. Harlow.* New York: Praeger.

Harlow, H. F., & Mears, C. (1979). *The human model: Primate perspectives.* New York: Wiley.

Harper, K. V., & Lantz, J. (1996). *Cross-cultural practice: Social work with diverse populations.* Chicago: Lyceum.

Harrington, M. (1962). *The other America: Poverty in the United States*. Baltimore: Penguin.

Harris, J. (1996). Enforced participation in change: British social work in a changing policy context. In *Participating in change: Social work profession in social development (Proceedings of the Joint World Congress of IFSW and IASSW)* (pp. 274–276). Hong Kong.

Harris, J. R. (1998). *The nurture assumption: Why children turn out the way they do*. New York: Free Press.

Harris, M. B., & Franklin, C. G. (2003). Effects of a cognitive-behavioral, school-based, group intervention with Mexican American pregnant and parenting adolescents. *Social Work Research, 27*(7), 71–83.

Harrison, W. D. (1980). Role strain and burnout in child protection service workers. *Social Service Review, 54*(1), 31–44.

Harrison, W. D. (1983). A social competence model of burnout. In B. A. Farber (Ed.), *Stress and burnout in the human service professions* (pp. 29–39). New York: Pergamon.

Harrison, W. D. (1989). Social work and the search for postindustrial community. *Social Work, 34*, 73–75.

Harrison, W. D. (1991). *Seeking common ground: A theory of social work in social care*. Brookfield, VT: Gower.

Harrison, W. D., Drolen, C. S., & Atherton, C. R. (1989). Role discrepancies in state hospital social work. *Social Casework: The Journal of Contemporary Social Work, 70*(10), 622–626.

Harrison, W. D., & Hoshino, G. (1984). Britain's Barclay report: Lessons for the United States. *Social Work, 29*(3), 213–218.

Harrison, W. D., Smale, G. G., & Hearn, B. (1992, March). *Toward a practice theory for community social work: Britain's practice and development exchange*. Paper presented at the Council on Social Work Education Annual Program Meeting, Kansas City, MO.

Hart, C. G. (1993). "Power in the service of love": John Dewey's logic and the dream of a common language. *Hypatia, 8*(2), 190–212.

Hartman, A. (1970). To think about the unthinkable. *Social Casework, 51*(8), 467–474.

Hartman, A. (1978). Diagrammatic assessment of family relationships. *Social Casework, 59*, 465–476.

Hartman, A. (1979). The extended family as a resource for change: Ecological approach to family-centered practice. In C. B. Germain (Ed.), *Social work practice: People and environments* (pp. 239–266). New York: Columbia University Press.

Hartman, A. (1990). Many ways of knowing. *Social Work, 35*, 3–4.

Hartman, A. (1993). The professional is political. *Social Work, 38*(4), 365–366.

Hartman, A., & Laird, J. (1983). *Family-centered social work practice*. New York: Free Press.

Hartman, B. L., & Wickey, J. M. (1978). The person-oriented record in treatment. *Social Work, 23*(4), 296–299.

Hatcher, H. A. (1978). *Correctional casework and counseling*. Englewood Cliffs, NJ: Prentice-Hall.

Hayes, J. R. (1978). *Cognitive psychology: Thinking and creating*. Homewood, IL: Dorsey Press.

Hazel, N. (1989). Adolescent fostering as a community resource. *Community Alternatives: International Journal of Family Care, 1*(1), 1–10.

Hazel, N., & Fenyo, A. (1993). *Free to be myself: The development of teenage fostering*. St. Paul, MN: Human Service Associates.

Healy, J. (1991). Linking local services: Coordination in community centers. *Australian Social Work, 44*(4), 5–13.

Heidrich, S. M., & Denny, N. W. (1994). Does social problem solving differ from other types of problem solving during the adult years? *Experimental Aging Research, 20*(2), 105–126.

Henderson, N. (1997). Resiliency and asset development: A continuum for youth success. *Resiliency in Action* (2), 23–27.

Hennessy, C. H. (1993). Modeling case management decision making in a consolidated long-term care program. *Gerontologist, 33*(3), 333–341.

Henry, C. S., Stephenson, A. L., Hanson, M. F., & Hargett, W. (1993). Adolescent suicide families: An ecological approach. *Adolescence, 28*(110), 292–308.

Hepworth, D. H. (1993). Managing manipulative behavior in the helping relationship. *Social Work, 38*(6), 674–682.

Hepworth, D. H., & Larsen, J. (1990). *Direct social work practice: Theory and skills* (3rd ed.). Belmont, CA: Wadsworth.

Herberg, C. D. (1995). *Frameworking for cultural and social diversity: Teaching and learning for practitioners*. Toronto: Canadian Scholars' Press.

Herbert, M., & Levin, R. (1996). The advocacy role in hospital social work. *Social Work in Health Care, 22*(3), 71–83.

Her Majesty's Stationary Office. (1989). *Caring for people: Community care in the next decade and beyond*. London: Her Majesty's Stationary Office.

Herman, T. (1943). Pragmatism: A study in middle-class ideology. *Social Forces, 22*, 405–410.

Hernandez, M. (2000). Using logic-models and program theory to build outcome accountability. *Education & Treatment of Children, 23*(1), 24–40.

Herodotus. (1909). *The history of Herodotus*. (Translated from the ancient Greek by G. Rawlinson). New York: Tandy-Thomas.

Herrenkohl, E. C., Herrenkohl, R. C., & Egolf, B. (1994.). Resilient early school-age children from maltreatment homes: Outcomes in late adolescence. *American Journal of Orthopsychiatry, 64*(2), 301–309.

Hersen, M., & Hasselt, V. B. (Eds.). (1998). *Basic interviewing: A practical guide for counselors and clinicians*. Mahwah, NJ: Erlbaum.

Hess, P. M., & Mullen, E. J. (Eds.). (1995). *Practitioner-researcher partnerships: Building knowledge from, in, and for practice*. Washington, DC: NASW Press.

Hetherington, E. M. (1996). *Stress, coping, and resiliency in children and families.* Mahwah, NJ: Erlbaum.

Hickman, L. (1997). Inquiry: A core concept of John Dewey's philosophy. *Free Inquiry, 17*(2), 21–22.

Hickman, S. (1994). Social work licensing—What's it all about? *New Social Worker, 1*(1), 4–7.

Himle, D. P., Jayaratne, S., & Thyness, P. (1991). Buffering effects of four social support types on burnout among social workers. *Social Work Research and Abstracts, 27*(1), 22–27.

Hirsch, L. H. (1931). The Negro and New York, 1783–1865. *Journal of Negro History, 16,* 415–473.

Ho, C. G. T. (1993). The internationalization of kinship and the feminization of Caribbean migration: The case of Afro-Trinidadian immigrants in Los Angeles. *Human Organization, 52*(1), 32–40.

Hodge, D. R. (2001). Spiritual assessment: A review of major qualitative methods and a new framework for assessing spirituality. *Social Work, 46*(3), 203–214.

Hoff, M. D. (1995). The welfare state and social justice: An interdisciplinary study. In G. Magill & M. D. Hoff (Eds.), *Values and public life* (pp. 169–198). Landham, MD: University Press of America.

Hoff, M. D., Huff, D. D., & Ord, L. M. (1996). The social worker's ethical obligation to society: An assessment of charity and justice contributions of social workers. *Areté, 21*(1), 47–60.

Hoffman, L. (1981). *Foundations of family therapy.* New York: Basic Books.

Hollis, F., & Woods, M. E. (1981). *Casework: A psychosocial therapy* (3rd ed.). New York: Random House.

Holman, B. (1993). *A new deal for social welfare.* Oxford: Lion.

Holmes, T. H., & Rahe, R. H. (1967). The Social Readjustment Rating Scale. *Journal of Psychosomatic Research, 11,* 213–218.

Holosko, M. J. (2003a). Guest editor's foreword. *Research on Social Work Practice, 13*(3), 265–266.

Holosko, M. J. (2003b). The history of the working definition of practice. *Research on Social Work Practice, 13*(3), 271–283.

Holosko, M. J. (2003c). Special issue. *Research on Social Work Practice, 13*(3), 265–408.

Holosko, M. J., & Leslie, D. (1998). Obstacles to conducting empirically based practice. In J. S. Wodarski & B. A. Thyer (Eds.), *Handbook of empirical social work practice: Social problems and practice issues* (Vol. 2, pp. 433–451). New York: Wiley.

Holosko, M. J., & Leslie, D. R. (2001). Is social work a profession? The Canadian response. *Research on Social Work Practice, 11*(2), 201–209.

Homan, M. S. (1994). *Promoting community change: Making it happen in the real world.* Pacific Grove, CA: Brooks/Cole.

Hooker, C. E. (1976). Learned helplessness. *Social Work, 21*(3), 194–198.

Hornstra, R. K., Bruce-Wolfe, V., Sagduyu, K., & Riffle, D. W. (1993). The effect of intensive case management on hospitalization of patients with schizophrenia. *Hospital and Community Psychiatry, 44*(9), 844–847.

Horowitz, R. (1991). Reflections on the casework relationship. Beyond empiricism. *Health and Social Work, 16*(3), 170–175.

Hoshino, G. (1994). Contracting in social work: Another fad? In B. R. Compton & B. Galaway, *Social work processes* (5th ed., pp. 406–407). Pacific Grove, CA: Brooks/Cole.

Houghkirk, E. (1977). Everything you've always wanted your clients to know but have been afraid to tell them. *Journal of Marriage and Family Counseling, 3*(2), 27–33.

Houston-Vega, M. K., & Nuehring, E. M. (1996). *Prudent practice: A guide for managing malpractice risk.* Washington, DC: NASW Press.

Howitt, D. (1993). *Child abuse errors: When good intentions go wrong.* New Brunswick, NJ: Rutgers University Press.

Hubble, M. A., Duncan, B. L., & Miller, S. D. (1999). Directing attention to what works. In B. L. Duncan & M. A. Hubble (Eds.), *The heart and soul of change: What works in therapy* (pp. 407–447). Washington, DC: American Psychological Association.

Huberman, L. (1963). *Man's worldly goods.* New York: Monthly Review Press.

Hudson, B. (1993). *Busy person's guide to care management.* Sheffield: Joint Unit for Social Services Research, Sheffield University.

Hudson, J., & Galaway, B. (Eds.). (1994). *Community economic development: Perspectives on policy and research.* Toronto: Thompson Educational.

Hudson, J., & Grinnell, R. (1989). Program evaluation. In B. R. Compton & B. Galaway, *Social work processes* (4th ed., pp. 691–710). Belmont, CA: Brooks/Cole.

Hudson, J., Maxwell, G., Morris, A., & Galaway, B. (Eds.). (1995). *Family group conferences: Perspectives on policy and practice.* Monsey, NY: Criminal Justice Press.

Hudson, W. (1982). *The clinical measurement package: A field manual.* Homewood, IL: Dorsey.

Hudson, W. W. (1989). *Computer assisted social services manual.* Tempe, AZ: Walmyr.

Hudson, W. W. (1990). Computer-based clinical practice: Present status and future possibilities. In L. Videka-Sherman & W. J. Reid (Eds.), *Advances in clinical social work research* (pp. 105–117). Silver Spring, MD: NASW Press.

Hughes, R., Good, E. S., & Candell, K. (1993). A longitudinal study of the effects of social support on the psychological adjustment of divorced mothers. *Journal of Divorce and Remarriage, 19*(1/2), 37–56.

Hurdle, D. E. (2002). Native Hawaiian traditional healing: Culturally based interventions for social work practice. *Social Work, 47*(2), 183–192.

Husband, D., & Scheunemann, H. (1972). The use of group process in teaching termination. *Child Welfare, 51*(5), 505–513.

Huslage, S., & Stein, F. (1985). A systems approach for the child study team. *Social Work in Education, 7*(2), 114–123.

Huxley, P. (1993). Case management and care management in community care. *British Journal of Social Work, 23*(4), 365–381.

Iglehart, A. P., & Becerra, R. M. (1995). *Social Services and the ethnic community.* Boston: Allyn & Bacon.

Indyk, D., Belville, R., Lachapolle, S., Gordon, G., & Dewart, T. (1993). A community-based approach to HIV case management: Systematizing the unmanageable. *Social Work, 38*(4), 380–387.

Ingersoll-Dayton, B., Schroepfer, T., Pryce, J., & Waarala, C. (2003). Enhancing relationships in nursing homes through empowerment. *Social Work, 48*(3), 420–424.

International Federation of Social Workers. (2000). *Definition of social work.* Retrieved June 20, 2003, from www .ifsw.org/Publications/4.6e.pub.html

International Federation of Social Workers. (2003). *Ethics in Social Work Statement of Principles (Second Draft).* Retrieved August 31, 2003, from www.ifsw.org/GM-2004/GM-Ethics-2draft.html

International Forgiveness Institute. (2003). *Welcome to the International Forgiveness Institute.* Retrieved October 2, 2003, from www.forgiveness-institute.org

Itzhaky, H. (1991). Client participation and the effectiveness of community social work intervention. *Research in Social Work Practice, 1*(4), 387–398.

Itzhaky, H., & York, A. S. (1994). Different types of client participation and the effects in community social work intervention. *Journal of Social Service Research, 19*(1/2), 85–98.

Ivanoff, A., Blythe, B., & Tripodi, T. (1994). *Involuntary clients in social work practice: A research based approach.* Hawthorne, NY: Aldine de Gruyter.

Ivanoff, A., Blythe, B. J., & Briar, S. (1987). The empirical clinical practice debate. *Social Casework: The Journal of Contemporary Social Work, 68*(5), 290–298.

Ivanoff, A., Robinson, E., & Blythe, B. (1987). Empirical clinical practice from a feminist perspective. *Social Work, 32*(5), 417–423.

Ivey, A. E. (1988). *Intentional interviewing and counseling: Facilitating client development* (2nd ed.). Pacific Grove, CA: Brooks/Cole.

Ivey, A. E., & Ivey, M. B. (2003). *Intentional interviewing and counseling: Facilitating client development in a multicultural society* (5th ed.). Pacific Grove, CA: Brooks/Cole.

Ivry, J. (1992). Teaching geriatric assessment. In M. J. Mellors & R. Solomon (Eds.), *Geriatric social work education* (pp. 3–22). New York: Haworth Press.

Jackson, R. L., Purnell, D., Anderson, S. B., & Sheafor, B. W. (1996). The clubhouse model of community support for adults with mental illness: An emerging opportunity for social work education. *Journal of Social Work Education, 32*(2), 173–180.

Jackson, T., Weiss, K. E., Lundquist, J. J., & Soderlind, A. (2002). Perceptions of goal-directed activities of optimists and pessimists: A personal projects analysis. *Journal of Psychology, 136*(5), 521–532.

Jackson, W. S. (1973). *Social service delivery system in the Black community during the ante-bellum period (1619–1860).* Atlanta: Atlanta University School of Social Work.

Jacobson, E. (1970). *You must relax.* New York: McGraw-Hill.

Jacobson, N. S. (1985). Family therapy outcome research: Potential pitfalls and prospects. *Journal of Marital and Family Therapy, 11*(2), 149–158.

Jacobson, N. S., & Christensen, A. (1996). *Integrative couple therapy: Promoting acceptance and change.* New York: Norton.

Jahn, K. (1986). The usefulness of DSM-III and systematic interviews in treatment planning. *Women and Therapy, 5*(1), 91–99.

Jandt, F. E. (1985). *Win-win negotiating: Turning conflict into agreement.* New York: Wiley.

Janis, I. L. (1982). *Groupthink: Psychological studies of policy decisions and fiascoes.* Boston: Houghton Mifflin.

Jansson, B. (1990). *Theory and practice of social welfare policy.* Belmont, CA: Wadsworth.

Jarman-Rohde, L., McFall, J., Kolar, P., & Strom, G. (1997). The changing context of social work practice: Implications and recommendations for social work education. *Journal of Social Work Education, 33*(1), 29–46.

Jayaratne, S., & Chess, W. A. (1983). Job satisfaction, burnout, and turnover: A national study. In B. A. Farber (Ed.), *Stress and burnout in the human service professions* (pp. 129–141). New York: Pergamon.

Jayaratne, S., & Chess, W. A. (1984). Job satisfaction, burnout, and turnover: A national study. *Social Work, 29*(5), 448–453.

Jayaratne, S., & Levy, R. L. (1979). *Empirical clinical practice.* New York: Columbia University Press.

Jayaratne, S., Tripodi, T., & Chess, W. A. (1983). Perceptions of emotional support, stress, and strain by male and female social workers. *Social Work Research and Abstracts, 19*(2), 19–27.

Johnson, A. G. (2000). *The Blackwell dictionary of sociology: A user's guide to sociological language* (2nd ed.). Malden, MA: Blackwell.

Johnson, D. W., & Johnson, F. P. (1994). *Joining together: Group theory and group skills.* Boston: Allyn & Bacon.

Johnson, H. C. (1978). Integration the problem-oriented record with a systems approach to case assessment. *Journal of Education for Social Work, 14*(3), 71–77.

Johnson, L. (1981). *Social work practice: A generalist approach.* Boston: Allyn & Bacon.

Johnson, M. (1992). Describing the population we serve: Viewing children in a family context. *R & D: Research and Evaluation in Group Care, 21*(1), 18–21.

Johnson, P. J. (1985). Case management. In A. E. Fink, J. H. Pfouts, & A. Dobelstein (Eds.), *The field of social work* (8th ed., pp. 269–296). Hollywood, CA: Sage.

Johnson, W. (1951). Being understanding and understood: Or how to find a wandered horse. *ETC.: A Review of General Semantics, 8*(1), 161–179.

Jones, L. P. (1991). Unemployment: The effect on social networks, depression, and reemployment organizations. *Journal of Social Service Research, 15*(1/2), 1–22.

Jones, M., & Biesecker, J. (1980). *Goal planning in children and youth*. Washington, DC: U.S. Government Printing Office.

Jones, M. L. (1993). Role conflict: Causes of burnout or energizer? *Social Work, 38*(2), 137–141.

Jordan, C., & Franklin, C. (1995). *Clinical assessment for social workers: Quantitative and qualitative methods*. Chicago: Lyceum Books/Nelson Hall.

Joyce, B., Stanley, D., & Hughes, L. (1990). Staying well: Factors contributing to successful community adaptation. *Journal of Psychosocial Nursing and Mental Health Services, 28*(6), 18–24.

Jung, C. G. (1933). *Modern man in search of a soul*. New York: Harcourt Brace & World.

Kabadaki, K. (1995). Rural African women and development. *Social Development Issues, 16*(2), 23–35.

Kadushin, A. (1972). *The social work interview*. New York: Columbia University Press.

Kadushin, A. (1995). Interviewing. In R. L. Edwards (Ed.), *Encyclopedia of social work* (19th ed., Vol. 2, pp. 1527–1537). Washington, DC: NASW Press.

Kadushin, A., & Kadushin, G. (1997). *The social work interview: A guide for human service professionals* (4th ed.). New York: Columbia University Press.

Kadushin, A., & Martin, J. (1988). *Child welfare services* (4th ed.). Pacific Grove, CA: Brooks/Cole.

Kagle, J. D. (1984). *Social work records*. Homewood, IL: Dorsey Press.

Kagle, J. D. (1991). *Social work records* (2nd ed.). Belmont, CA: Wadsworth.

Kagle, J. D. (1993). Record keeping: Directions for the 1990s. *Social Work, 38*(2), 190–196.

Kagle, J. D. (1995). Recording. In R. L. Edwards (Ed.), *Encyclopedia of social work* (19th ed., Vol. 3, pp. 2027–2033). Washington, DC: NASW Press.

Kagle, J. D., & Giebelhausen, N. (1994). Dual relationships and professional boundaries. *Social Work, 39,* 213–220.

Kagle, J. D., & Kopels, S. (1994). Confidentiality after Tarasoff. *Health and Social Work, 19*(3), 217–222.

Kahn, A. H., & Kamerman, S. B. (1982). *Helping America's families*. Philadelphia: Temple University Press.

Kallies, L. (1997). *Task-centered social work with young offenders. MSW practicum report*. Winnipeg: Faculty of Social Work, University of Manitoba.

Kamerman, S. B., Dolgoff, R., Getzel, G., & Nelson, J. (1973). Knowledge for practice: Social science in social work. In J. Kahn (Ed.), *Shaping the new social work* (pp. 97–148). New York: Columbia University Press.

Kaminer, W. (1993). *I'm dysfunctional, you're dysfunctional*. New York: Vintage Books.

Kamya, H. A. (2000). Hardiness and spiritual well-being among social work students: Implications for social work education. *Journal of Social Work Education, 36*(2), 231–240.

Kane, R. A. (1974). Look to the record. *Social Work, 19*(4), 412–419.

Kane, R. A. (1982). Teams: Thoughts from the bleachers. *Health and Social Work, 7*(1), 2–4.

Kanfer, F. H., & Schefft, B. K. (1988). *Guiding the process of therapeutic change*. Champaign, IL: Research Press.

Kaplan, A. (1964). *The conduct of inquiry: Methodology for behavior science*. San Francisco: Chandler.

Kaplan, L. (1986). *Working with multiproblem families*. Lexington, MA: Lexington Books.

Kaplan, L., & Girard, J. L. (1994). *Strengthening high-risk families: A handbook for practitioners*. New York: Lexington Books.

Kaplan, M. S., Becker, J. V., & Martinez, D. (1990). A comparison of mothers of adolescent incest versus non-incest perpetrators. *Journal of Family Violence, 5*(3), 209–214.

Karenga, R. (1995). Making the past meaningful: Kwanzaa and the concept of Sankofa. *Reflections, 1*(4), 36–46.

Karger, H., & Stoesz, D. (1994). *American social welfare policy*. New York: Longman.

Karger, H. J. (1981). Burnout as alienation. *Social Service Review, 55*(2), 270–283.

Karls, J. M., & Lowery, C. T. (1997). The use of the PIE (person-in-environment) system in social work education. *Journal of Social Work Education, 33*(1), 49–59.

Karls, J. M., & Wandrei, K. E. (1992a). The person-in-environment system for classifying client problems. A new tool for more effective case management. *Journal of Case Management, 1*(3), 90–95.

Karls, J. M., & Wandrei, K. E. (1992b). PIE: A new language for social work. *Social Work, 37*(1), 80–85.

Karls, J. M., & Wandrei, K. E. (1994a). *PIE manual: Person-in-environment system: The PIE classification system for social functioning problems*. Washington, DC: NASW Press.

Karls, J. M., & Wandrei, K. E. (Eds.). (1994b). *Person-in-environment system: The PIE classification system for social functioning problems*. Washington, DC: NASW Press.

Karls, J. M., & Wandrei, K. E. (1995). Person-in-environment. In R. L. Edwards (Ed.), *Encyclopedia of social work* (19th ed., Vol. 3, pp. 1818–1827). Washington, DC: NASW Press.

Karr, J. (1990). Goal attainment scaling in the treatment of children with behavior disorders. *School Social Work Journal, 15*(1), 14–20.

Kauff, P. (1977). The termination process: Its relationship to the separation individuation phase of development. *International Journal of Group Psychiatry, 27*(1), 3–18.

Keenan, L. D., Dyer, E., Morita, L., & Shaskey-Setright, C. (1990). Toward an understanding of mentoring in rural communities. *Human Services in the Rural Environment, 14*(2), 11–18.

Keith-Lucas, A. (1972). *Giving and taking help.* Chapel Hill: University of North Carolina Press.

Keith-Lucas, A. (1973). Philosophies of public social service. *Public Welfare, 31*(1), 21–24.

Kelley, M. L., McKay, S., & Nelson, C. H. (1985). Indian agency development: An ecological practice approach. *Social Casework: Journal of Contemporary Social Work, 66*(10), 594–602.

Kelly, T. B. (1994). Paternalism and the marginally competent: An ethical dilemma, no easy answers. *Journal of Gerontological Social Work, 23*(1/2), 67–84.

Kemp, S. P., Whittaker, J. K., & Tracy, E. M. (1997). *Person-environment practice: The social ecology of interpersonal helping.* New York: Aldine de Gruyter.

Kenemore, T. (1987). Negotiating with clients: A study of clinical practice experience. *Social Science Review, 61*(1), 132–144.

Kerpelman, J. L., Shoffner, M. F., & Ross-Griffin, S. (2002). African American mothers' and daughters' beliefs about possible selves and their strategies for reaching the adolescents' future academic and career goals. *Journal of Youth and Adolescence, 31*(4), 289–303.

Kettner, P. M. (1975). A framework for comparing practice models. *Social Service Review, 49*(4), 629–642.

Ketzenbach, J. R., & Smith, D. K. (1993). *The wisdom of teams: Creating a high performance organization.* Cambridge, MA: Harvard Business School Press.

Kiam, R., Green, C., & Pomeroy, E. (1997). *Families empowering families through community partnerships.* Orlando: School of Social Work, University of Central Florida.

Kidneigh, H. C. (1969). A note on organizing knowledge. In H. Cassidy (Ed.), *Modes of professional education: Functions of field instruction in the curriculum* (Tulane Studies in Social Welfare, Vol. XI, pp. 153–160). New Orleans: School of Social Work, Tulane University.

Kiel, L. D. (1996). *Chaos theory in the social sciences: Foundations and applications.* Ann Arbor: University of Michigan Press.

King, H. (1991). A telephone reassurance service: A natural support system for the elderly. *Journal of Gerontological Social Work, 16*(1/2), 159–177.

Kiresuk, T., & Sherman, R. E. (1968). Goal attainment scaling: A general method for evaluating comprehensive community health programs. *Community Mental Health Journal, 4,* 443–453.

Kiresuk, T. J., & Garwick, G. (1974). *Basic goal attainment scaling procedures. Program Evaluation Report (Chapter 1).* Minneapolis, MN: Program Evaluation Project.: Hennipen County Health Center.

Kiresuk, T. J., & Lund, S. H. (1977). Goal attainment scaling. In C. C. Attkisson, W. A. Hargreaves, M. J. Horowitz, & S. E. Sorenson (Eds.), *Evaluation of human service programs.* New York: Academic.

Kiresuk, T. J., Smith, A., & Cardillo, J. E. (Eds.). (1994). *Goal attainment scaling: Applications, theory & measurement.* Mahwah, NJ: Erlbaum.

Kirk, S., & Kutchins, H. (1994). The myth of the reliability of the DSM. *Journal of the Mind and Behavior, 15*(1/2), 71–86.

Kirk, S., Osmalov, M., & Fischer, J. (1976). Social workers involvement in research. *Social Work, 21*(2), 121–132.

Kirk, S. A., & Kutchins, H. (1988). Deliberate misdiagnosis in mental health practice. *Social Service Review, 62*(2), 225–237.

Kirk, S. A., & Kutchins, H. (1992). *The selling of DSM: The rhetoric of science in psychiatry.* Hawthorne, NY: Aldine de Gruyter.

Kirk, S. A., & Reid, W. J. (2001). *Science and social work: A critical appraisal.* New York: Columbia University Press.

Kirk, S. A., Wakefield, J. C., Hsieh, D. K., & Pottick, K. J. (1999). Social context and social workers' judgment of mental disorder. *Social Service Review, 73*(82), 82–98.

Kisthardt, W. E. (1993). A strengths model of case management: Principles and functions of a helping partnership with persons with persistent mental illness. In M. Harris & H. Bergman (Eds.), *Case management for mentally ill patients: Theory and practice* (pp. 165–182). Langhorne, PA: Harwood Academic.

Kisthardt, W. E. (1997). The strengths model of case management: Principles and helping functions. In D. Saleebey (Ed.), *The strengths perspective in social work practice* (2nd ed., pp. 97–114). New York: Longman.

Klein, B. (1986). A piece of the world: Some thought about Ruth. *Women in Therapy, 5,* 33–40.

Klein, W. C., Bloom, M., & Chandler, S. M. (1994). Is there an ethical responsibility to use practice methods with the best empirical evidence of effectiveness? In W. W. Hudson & P. S. Nurius (Eds.), *Controversial issues in social work research* (pp. 100–112). Boston: Allyn & Bacon.

Klenk, R. W., & Ryan, R. M. (1974). *The practice of social work* (2nd ed.). Belmont, CA: Wadsworth.

Klier, J., Fein, E., & Genero, C. (1984). Are written or verbal contracts more effective in family therapy? *Social Work, 29*(3), 298–299.

Kline, M., Sydnor-Greenberg, N., Davis, W. W., Pincus, H. A., & Frances, A. J. (1993). Using field trials to evaluate proposed changes in DSM diagnostic criteria. *Hospital and Community Psychiatry, 44*(7), 621–623.

Klockars, C. B. (1972). A theory of probation supervision. *Journal of Criminal Law, Criminology and Police Science, 63*(4), 550–557.

Knopp, F. H., Freeman-Longo, R., & Lane, S. (1997). Program development. In G. R. S. Lane (Ed.), *Juvenile sexual offending* (pp. 183–200). San Francisco: Jossey-Bass.

Kobayashi, J., Sales, B. D., Becker, J. V., Figueredo, A. J., & Kaplan, M. S. (1995). Perceived parental deviance, parent-child bonding, child abuse, and child sexual aggression. *Sexual Abuse: A Journal of Research and Treatment, 7*(1), 25–43.

Koeske, G. F., & Kelly, T. (1995). The impact of over-involvement on burnout and job satisfaction. *American Journal of Orthopsychiatry, 65*(2), 282–292.

Koeske, G. F., & Kirk, S. A. (1995). The effects of characteristics of human service workers on subsequent morale and turnover. *Administration of Social Work, 19*(1), 15–31.

Koeske, G. F., & Koeske, R. D. (1989). Workload and burnout: Can social support and perceived accomplishment help? *Social Work, 34*(3), 243–248.

Koeske, G. F., & Koeske, R. D. (1990). The buffering effect of social support on parental stress. *American Journal of Orthopsychiatry, 60*(3), 440–451.

Koeske, G. F., & Koeske, R. D. (1993). A preliminary test of a stress-strain-outcome model of reconceptualizing the burnout phenomenon. *Journal of Social Service Research, 17*(3/4), 107–135.

Kokotovic, A. M., & Tracey, T. J. (1990). Working alliance in the early phase of counseling. *Journal of Counseling Psychology, 37*(1), 16–21.

Kondrat, M. E. (1995). Concept, act, and interest in professional practice: Implications of an empowerment perspective. *Social Service Review, 69*(3), 405–422.

Konopka, G. (1963). *Social group work: A helping process.* Englewood Cliffs, NJ: Prentice-Hall.

Kopels, S., & Kagle, J. D. (1993). Do social workers have a duty to warn? *Social Service Review, 67*(1), 101–126.

Koren, P. E., DeChillo, N., & Friesen, B. J. (1992). Measurement empowerment in families whose children have emotional disabilities: A brief questionnaire. *Rehabilitation Psychology, 37*(4), 305–321.

Korr, W. S., & Cloninger, L. (1991). Assessing models of case management: An empirical approach. *Journal of Social Service Research, 14*(1/2), 129–146.

Koslyk, D., Fuchs, D., Tabisz, E., & Jacyk, W. R. (1993). Combining professional and self-help group intervention: Collaboration in co-leadership. *Social Work With Groups, 16*(2), 111–123.

Koss, M. P., & Shiang, J. (1994). Research on brief psychotherapy. In E. Bergin & S. L. Garffield (Eds.), *Handbook of psychotherapy and behavior change* (4th ed., pp. 664–700). New York: Wiley.

Kowert, P. (2002). *Groupthink or deadlock: When do leaders learn from their advisors?* Albany: State University of New York Press.

Kral, R. (1990). *Strategies that work: Techniques for solutions in the school.* Milwaukee, WI: Brief Family Therapy Centre.

Kramer, K. D., & Nash, K. B. (1995). The unique social ecology of groups: Findings from groups of African Americans affected by sickle cell disease. *Social Work with Groups, 18*(1), 55–65.

Kretzmann, J. P., & McKnight, J. L. (1993). *Building communities from the inside out.* Evanston, IL: Northwestern University, Center for Urban Affairs and Policy Research.

Kropf, N. P., Lindsey, F. W., & Carse-McLocklin, S. (1993). The eligibility worker role in public welfare: Worker and client perceptions. *Areté, 18*(1), 34–42.

Kruk, E. (1997). *Mediation and conflict resolution in social work and human services.* Chicago: Nelson-Hall.

Krystal, S., & Zweben, J. (1989). The use of visualization as a means of integrating the spiritual dimension into treatment: Part 2. Working with emotions. *Journal of Substance Abuse Treatment, 6*(4), 223–229.

Kubler-Ross, E. (1969). *On death and dying.* New York: Macmillan.

Kunz, J., & Kunz, P. R. (1995). Social support during the process of divorce: It does make a difference. *Journal of Divorce and Remarriage, 24*(3/4), 111–119.

Kurtz, L. F. (1990). The self-help movement: Review of the post decade of research. *Social Work with Groups, 13*(3), 101–115.

Kutchins, H., & Kirk, S. (1987). DSM-III and social work malpractice. *Social Work, 32*(3), 205–211.

Kutchins, H., & Kirk, S. (1989a). DSM-III-R: The conflict over new psychiatric diagnoses. *Health and Social Work, 14*(2), 92–102.

Kutchins, H., & Kirk, S. (1989b). Human errors, attractive nuisances, and toxic wastes: A reply to Anello. *Social Work, 34*(2), 187–189.

Kutchins, H., & Kirk, S. A. (1986). The reliability of DSM-III: A critical review. *Social Work Research and Abstracts, 22*(4), 3–12.

Kutchins, H., & Kirk, S. A. (1993). DSM-IV and the hunt for gold: A review of the treasure map. *Research on Social Work Practice, 3*(2), 219.

Kutchins, H., & Kirk, S. A. (1995). Should DSM be the basis for teaching social work practice in mental health? No! *Journal of Social Work Education, 31*(2), 159–165.

Kutchins, H., & Kirk, S. A. (1997). *Making us crazy: DSM, the psychiatric Bible and the creation of mental disorders.* New York: Free Press.

La Valle, I., & Lyons, K. (1996a). The social worker speaks: Management of change in the personal social services. *Practice, 8*(3), 63–71.

La Valle, I., & Lyons, K. (1996b). The social worker speaks: Perceptions of recent changes in British social work. *Practice, 8*(2), 5–14.

Ladewig, B. H., McGee, G. W., & Newell, W. (1990). Life strains and depressive affect among women: Moderating effects of social support. *Journal of Family Issues, 11*(1), 36–47.

Lajoie, D. H., & Shapiro, S. I. (1992). Definition of transpersonal psychology: The first twenty-five years. *Journal of Transpersonal Psychology, 24,* 79–98.

Lakey, J. F. (1994). The profile and treatment of male adolescent sex offenders. *Adolescence, 29*(116), 755–761.

Lamb, D. H., Clark, C., Drumheller, P., Frizzell, K., & Surrey, L. (1989). Applying Tarasoff to AIDS-related psychotherapy issues. *Professional Psychology: Research and Practice, 20*(1), 37–43.

Lamb, H. R. (1994). A century and a half of psychiatric rehabilitation in the United States. *Hospital and Community Psychiatry, 45*(10), 1015–1020.

Lambert, M. J. (1982). Relation of helping skills to treatment outcome. In E. K. Marshall & P. D. Kurtz (Eds.), *Interpersonal helping skills: A guide to training methods, programs, and resources* (pp. 26–53). San Francisco: Jossey-Bass.

Lambert, M. J. (Ed.). (1983.). *A guide to psychotherapy and patient relationships.* Homewood, IL: Dow Jones-Irwin.

Lambert, M. J. (1992). Implications of outcome research for psychotherapy integration. In J. C. Norcross & M. R. Goldfried (Eds.), *Handbook of psychotherapy integration* (pp. 94–129). New York: Basic Books.

Lambert, M. J. (Ed.). (2003). *Bergin and Garfield's handbook of psychotherapy and behavior change* (5th ed.). Hoboken, NJ: Wiley.

Lambert, M. J., & Bergin, A. E. (1994). The effectiveness of psychotherapy. In A. E. Bergin & S. L. Garfield (Eds.), *Handbook of psychotherapy and behavior change* (4th ed., pp. 143–189). New York: Wiley.

Lambert, M. J., & Cattani-Thompson, K. (1996). Current findings regarding the effectiveness of counseling: Implications for practice. *Journal of Counseling and Development, 74,* 601–608.

Lambert, M. J., Christensen, E. R., & DeJulio, S. S. (Eds.). (1983). *The assessment of psychotherapy outcome.* New York: Wiley.

Lantz, J. (1986). Integration of reflective and task-oriented techniques in family treatment. *Child Welfare, 65*(3), 261–270.

Lantz, J., & Greenlee, R. (1990). Existential social work with Vietnam veterans. *Journal of Independent Social Work, 5*(1), 39–52.

Larsen, J. A., & Mitchell, C. T. (1980). Task-centered, strength-oriented group work with delinquents. *Social Casework, 61*(3), 154–163.

Lasch, C. (1979). *The culture of narcissism: American life in an age of diminishing expectations.* New York: Norton.

Lasch, C. (1981). *The minimal self: Psychic survival in troubled times.* New York: Norton.

Laszlo, E. (1996). *The systems view of the world: A holistic vision for our time.* Cresskill, NJ: Hampton Press.

Lauber, M. B. (1992). A taxonomy of case management tasks in community health facilities. *Social Work Research and Abstracts, 28*(3), 3–10.

Laursen, E. K. (2002). Seven habits of reclaiming relationships. *Reclaiming Children and Youth, 11*(1), 10–14.

Laursen, E. K., & Oliver, V. (2003). Recasting problems as potentials in group work. *Reclaiming Children and Youth, 12*(1), 46–49.

Lazarus, A. (1981). *Multi-modal therapy.* New York: McGraw-Hill.

Lazarus, A. (1984). *In the mind's eye: The power of imagery for personal enrichment.* New York: Guilford.

Lazarus, A. (1989). Multi-modal therapy. In R. Corsini & D. Wedding (Eds.), *Current psychotherapies* (4th ed., pp. 503–544). Itasca, IL: Peacock.

Lazarus, A. (1991). *The multi-modal life history inventory.* Champaign, IL: Research Press.

Lazarus, A. (1995). Preparing for practice in an era of managed competition. *Psychiatric Services, 46,* 184–185.

Lee, E. (2003). *Abortion, motherhood, and mental health: Medicalizing reproduction in the US and Britain.* Hawthorne, NY: Aldine de Gruyter.

Lee, J. (1994). *The empowerment approach to social work practice.* New York: Columbia University Press.

Lee, L. J., & Sampson, J. F. (1990). A practical approach to program evaluation. *Evaluation and Program Planning, 13*(2), 157–164.

Lee, P. R. (1937). *Social work as cause or function and other papers.* New York: Columbia University Press.

Lefcourt, H. M. (1966). Belief in personal control: Research and implications. *Journal of Individual Psychology, 22*(2), 185–195.

Leffers, M. R. (1993). Pragmatists Jane Addams and John Dewey inform the ethic of care. *Hypatia, 8*(2), 64–77.

Leiby, J. (1978). *A history of social welfare and social work in the United States.* New York: Columbia University Press.

Leigh, J. W. (1998). *Communicating for cultural competence.* Needham Heights, MA: Allyn & Bacon.

Lemert, E. (1967). *The juvenile court quest and realities.* Washington, DC: President's Commission on Law Enforcement and Administration of Justice, Task force report: Juvenile delinquency and youth crime.

Lenqua, L. J., Wolchik, S. A., & Brauer, S. L. (1995). Understanding children's divorce adjustment from an ecological perspective. *Journal of Divorce and Remarriage, 22*(3/4), 25–63.

Lens, V. (2000). Protecting the confidentiality of the therapeutic relationship: *Jaffee v. Redmond. Social Work, 45*(3), 273–276.

LePage-Lees, P. (1997). *From disadvantaged girls to successful women: Education and women's resiliency.* Westport, CT: Praeger.

LeResche, D. (1992). Comparison of the American mediation process with a Korean-American harmony restoration process. *Mediation Quarterly, 9*(4), 323–339.

Lerner, B. (1972). *Therapy in the ghetto.* Baltimore: Johns Hopkins University Press.

Leslie, D. R., & Cassano, R. (2003). The working definition of social work practice: Does it work? *Research on Social Work Practice, 13*(3), 366–375.

Leutz, W., Abrahams, R., & Capitman, J. (1993). The administration of eligibility for community long term care. *Gerontologist, 33*(1), 92–104.

Levenson, H., & Butler, S. F. (1994). Brief dynamic individual psychotherapy. In R. Hales & S. Yudofsky (Eds.), *Textbook of psychiatry* (2nd ed., pp. 947–967). Washington, DC: American Psychiatric Press.

Levinson, D. J. (1978). *The seasons of a man's life.* New York: Knopf.

Levinson, H. (1977). Termination of psychotherapy: Some salient issues. *Social Casework, 58*(8), 480–498.

Leviton, S. C., & Greenstone, J. C. (1997). *Elements of mediation.* Pacific Grove, CA: Brooks/Cole.

Levitt, J. L., & Reid, W. J. (1981). Rapid assessment instruments for practice. *Social Work Research and Abstracts, 17*(1), 13–19.

Levy, C. S. (1972). Values and planned change. *Social Casework, 53*(8), 488–493.

Levy, C. S. (1973). The value base of social work. *Journal of Education for Social Work, 9*(1), 34–42.

Levy, C. S. (1993). *Social work ethics on the line.* New York: Haworth Press.

Lewis, E. A., & Kissman, K. (1989). Factors linking ethnic-sensitive and feminist social work practice with African-American women. *Areté, 14*(2), 23–31.

Lewis, J., Bernstock, P., Bovell, V., & Wookey, F. (1997). Implementing care management: Issues in relation to the new community care. *British Journal of Social Work, 27,* 5–24.

Lewis, R. G., & Ho, M. K. (1975). Social work with Native Americans. *Social Work, 20*(5), 379–382.

Libassi, M. R., & Maluccio, A. N. (1986). Competence-centered social work: Prevention in action. *Journal of Primary Prevention, 6,* 168–180.

Liberman, B. (1978). The role of mastery in psychotherapy: Maintenance of improvement and prescriptive change. In J. Frank, R. Hoehn-Saric, S. Imber, B. Liberman, & A. Stone (Eds.), *Effective ingredients in successful psychotherapy* (pp. 35–72). New York: Brunner/Mazel.

Lifton, D. E., Seay, S., & Bushko, A. (2000). Can student "hardiness" serve as an indicator of likely persistence to graduation? Baseline results from a longitudinal study. *Academic Exchange Quarterly, 4*(2), 73–81.

Lindblom, C. E. (1977). *Politics and markets.* New York: Basic Books.

Lindblom, C. E. (1980). *The policy making process.* Englewood Cliffs, NJ: Prentice-Hall.

Lindemann, E. (1956). Symptomatology and management of acute grief. In H. Parad (Ed.), *Crisis intervention: Selected readings* (pp. 7–21). New York: Family Service Association.

Lindenthal, J., Jordan, T., Lentz, J., & Thomas, C. (1988). Social workers' management of confidentiality. *Social Work, 33*(2), 157–159.

Lindsay, A. G. (1921). The economic condition of the Negroes of New York prior to 1861. *Journal of Negro History, 6*(2), 190–199.

Lindsey, D., & Kirk, S. A. (1992). The continuing crisis in social work research: Conundrum or solvable problems? An essay review. *Journal of Social Work Education, 28*(3), 370–382.

Linehan, M. (1993). *Skills training manual for treating borderline personality disorders.* New York: Guilford.

Linhorst, D. M., Hamilton, G., Young, E., & Eckert, A. (2002). Opportunities and barriers to empowering people with severe mental illness through participation in treatment planning. *Social Work, 47*(4), 425–434.

Lipchik, E., & de Shazer, S. (1986). The purposeful interview. *Journal of Strategic and Systemic Therapies, 5*(1/2), 88–90.

Livermore, M., & Neustrom, A. (2003). Linking welfare clients to jobs: Discretionary use of worker social capital. *Journal of Sociology and Social Welfare, 30*(2), 87–103.

Lloyd, J. C., & Bryce, M. E. (1985). *Placement prevention and family reunification: A handbook for the family-centered service practitioner.* Iowa City: National Resource Center on Family Based Services, University of Iowa.

Locke, E. A. (1996). Motivation through conscious goal setting. *Applied and Preventive Psychology, 5,* 117–124.

Locke, E. A., & Latham, G. P. (1990). *A theory of goal setting and task performance.* Englewood Cliffs, NJ: Prentice Hall.

Locke, E. A., & Latham, G. P. (2002). Building a practically useful theory of goal setting and task motivation: A 35-year odyssey. *American Psychologist, 57*(9), 705–717.

Locke, E. A., Shaw, K. N., Saari, L. M., & Latham, G. P. (1981). Goal-setting and task performance, 1969–1980. *Psychological Bulletin, 90,* 125–135.

Locke, J. (1689, 1995). *An essay concerning human understanding.* Retrieved July 2, 2003, from www.ilt.columbia.edu/publications/locke_understanding.html

Lockhart, A. (1982). The insider-outsider dialectic in native socioeconomic development: A case study in process understanding. *Canadian Journal of Native Studies, 2*(1), 159–168.

Loewenberg, F., & Dolgoff, R. (1988). *Ethical issues for social work practice* (3rd ed.). Itasca, IL: Peacock.

Loewenberg, F. M., & Dolgoff, R. (Eds.). (1992). *Ethical decisions for social work practice* (4th ed.). Itasca, IL: Peacock.

Loewenberg, F. M., & Dolgoff, R. (1996). *Ethical decisions for social work practice* (5th ed.). Itasca, IL: Peacock.

Loewenberg, F. M., Dolgoff, R., & Harrington, D. (2000). *Ethical decisions for social work practice* (6th ed.). Itasca, IL: Peacock.

Logan, S. M. L., Freeman, E. M., & McDay, R. G. (Eds.). (1990). *Social work practice with Black families*. New York: Longman.

Loneck, B., Garrett, J., & Banks, S. M. (1997). Engaging and retaining women in outpatient alcohol and other drug treatment: The effect of referral intensity. *Health and Social Work, 22*(1), 38–46.

Long, D. D. (1995). Attention deficit disorder and case management: Infusing macro social work practice. *Journal of Sociology and Social Welfare, 22*(2), 45–55.

Longclaws, L. (1996). New perspectives in healing. In J. Oaks & R. Rieve (Eds.), *Issues in the North* (Vol. 1, Occasional Publication Series No. 4). Winnipeg: Department of Native Studies, University of Manitoba.

Luborsky, L., Barber, J. P., & Crits-Christoph, P. (1990). Theory based research for understanding the dynamic process of psychotherapy. *Journal of Consulting and Clinical Psychology, 58*(3), 281–287.

Lubove, R. (1977). *The professional altruist: The emergence of social work as a career 1880–1930*. New York: Antheneum (originally published Cambridge: Harvard University Press, 1965).

Luckey, I. (1994). African American elders: The support network of generational kin. *Families in Society: The Journal of Contemporary Human Services, 75*(2), 82–89.

Lum, D. (Ed.). (2003). *Culturally competent practice: A framework for understanding diverse groups and justice issues* (2nd ed.). Pacific Grove, CA: Brooks/Cole.

Lundy, M. (1993). Explicitness: The unspoken mandate of feminist social work. *Affilia, 8*(2), 184–199.

Lynch, E. W., & Hanson, M. J. (1992). *Developing cross-cultural competence: A guide for working with young children and their families*. Baltimore: Brookes.

MacDonald, S. (1988). Social work interviewing and feminism. *Australian Journal of Social Work, 41*(2), 13–16.

Macht, J., & Quam, J. (1986). *Social work: An introduction*. Columbus, OH: Merrill.

MacLeod, S., & Campbell, S. (1996). Family group decision making: A strategy to help families and communities keep women and children safe. In M. Russell, J. Hightower & G. Gutman (Eds.), *Stopping the violence: Changing families, changing futures* (pp. 170–174). Vancouver, BC: Benwell Atkins.

MacNeil, T. (1994). Governments as partners in community economic development. In J. Hudson & B. Galaway (Eds.), *Community economic development: Perspectives on policy and research* (pp. 178–181). Toronto: Thompson Educational.

Madanes, C. (1984). *Behind the one-way mirror: Advances in the practice of strategic therapy*. San Francisco: Jossey-Bass.

Maddi, S. R., Wadhwa, P., & Haier, R. J. (1996). Relationship of hardiness to alcohol and drug use in adolescents. *American Journal of Drug and Alcohol Abuse, 22*(2), 247–258.

Maddock, J. W. (1993). Ecology, ethics, and responsibility in family therapy. *Family Relations, 42*(2), 116–123.

Maglajlic, R. A. (1996). *Four case studies of care planning for adults with learning difficulties who have no speech*. Unpublished master's thesis. School of Community, Health and Social Studies, Anglia Polytechnic University, Cambridge, England.

Magnusson, D., & Allen, V. L. (1983a). *Human development: An interactional perspective*. New York: Academic Press.

Magnusson, D., & Allen, V. L. (1983b). An interactional perspective for human development. In D. Magnusson & V. L. Allen (Eds.), *Human development: An interactional perspective* (pp. 3–34). New York: Academic Press.

Magura, S., Moses, B. S., & Jones, M. A. (1987). *Assessing risk and measuring change in families*. Washington, DC: Child Welfare League of America.

Mahaffey, M. (1972). Lobbying and social work. *Social Work, 17*(1), 3–11.

Maher, C. A. (1987). Involving behaviorally disordered adolescents in instructional planning: Effectiveness of the goal procedure. *Child and Adolescent Psychotherapy, 4*(3), 185–189.

Maher, T. F. (1992). The withering of community life and the growth of emotional disorders. *Journal of Sociology and Social Welfare, 19*(2), 125–146.

Mahoney, M. J. (1991). *Human change processes*. New York: Basic Books.

Mahoney, M. J. (1995). Continuing evolution of cognitive sciences and psychotherapy. In R. A. Neimeyer & M. J. Mahoney (Eds.), *Constructivism in psychotherapy* (pp. 39–67). Washington, DC: American Psychological Association.

Mailick, M., & Ashely, A. (1981). Politics of interprofessional collaboration: Challenge to advocacy. *Social Casework: The Journal of Contemporary Social Work, 62*(3), 131–137.

Malpractice: How to sidestep the pitfalls. (1997, February). *NASW News*, 5.

Maluccio, A. N. (1974). Action as a tool in casework practice. *Social Casework, 55*, 30–35.

Maluccio, A. N. (1979). *Learning from clients: Interpersonal helping as viewed by clients and social workers*. New York: Free Press.

Maluccio, A. N. (Ed.). (1981). *Promoting competence in clients: A new/old approach to social work practice*. New York: Free Press.

Maluccio, A. N. (1983). Planned use of life experiences. In A. Rosenblatt & D. Waldfogel (Eds.), *Handbook of clinical social work* (pp. 134–154). San Francisco: Jossey-Bass.

Maluccio, A. N., Fein, E., & Olmstead, K. (1986). *Permanency planning for children: Concepts and methods.* London & New York: Tavistock.

Maluccio, A. N., Kreiger, R., & Pine, B. A. (1991). Preserving families through reunification. In E. M. Tracey, D. A. Haapala, J. Kinney, & P. J. Pecora (Eds.), *Intensive family preservation services: An instructional source book* (pp. 215–235). Cleveland, OH: Mandel School of Applied Social Sciences, Case Western Reserve University.

Maluccio, A. N., & Libassi, M. R. (1984). Competence clarification in social work practice. *Social Thought, 10*(2), 51–58.

Maluccio, A. N., & Marlow, W. (1974). The case for the contract. *Social Work, 19*(1), 28–36.

Maluccio, A. N., Washitz, S., & Libassi, M. F. (1992). Ecologically oriented, competence-centered social work practice. In C. W. LeCroy (Ed.), *Case studies in social work practice* (pp. 5–13). Pacific Grove, CA: Brooks/Cole.

Mandros, J., & Wilson, S. (1994). *Organizing for power and empowerment.* New York: Columbia University Press.

Mann, J. (1973). *Time-limited psychotherapy.* Cambridge, MA: Harvard University Press.

Manz, C., & Sims Jr., H. P. (1995). *Business without bosses: How self-managing teams are building high performance companies.* New York: Wiley.

Marin, M. V., & Vacha, E. F. (1994). Self-help strategies and resources among people at risk of homelessness: Empirical findings and social services policy. *Social Work, 39*(6), 649–657.

Marlow, C. (1990). Management of family and employment responsibilities by Mexican American and Anglo American women. *Social Work, 35*(3), 259–265.

Marlow, C. (1993). *Research methods for generalist social work.* Pacific Grove, CA: Brooks/Cole.

Marlow, C. (1998). *Research methods for generalist social work* (2nd ed.). Pacific Grove, CA: Brooks/Cole.

Martin, E., & Martin, J. (1985). *Helping tradition in the black family and community.* Silver Spring, MD: NASW Press.

Martinek, T., & Hellison, D. (1998). Values and goal-setting with underserved youth. *JOPERD—The Journal of Physical Education, Recreation & Dance, 69*(7), 47–52.

Martinez-Brawley, E. E. (1990). *Perspectives on the small community: Humanistic views for practitioners.* Silver Spring, MD: NASW Press.

Marziali, E. (1984). Three viewpoints of the therapeutic alliance. *Journal of Nervous and Mental Disease, 7,* 417–423.

Marziali, E., & Alexander, L. (1991). The power of the therapeutic relationship. *American Journal of Orthopsychiatry, 61*(3), 383–391.

Maslach, C. (1976). Burned-out. *Human Behavior, 5*(9), 16–22.

Maslach, C. (1978). The client role in staff burn-out. *Journal of Social Issues, 34*(4), 111–124.

Maslach, C. (1982). *Burnout: The cost of caring.* Englewood Cliffs, NJ: Prentice-Hall.

Maslach, C., Schaufeli, W. B., & Leiter, M. P. (2001). Job burnout. *Annual Review of Psychology, 52,* 397–422.

Maslow, A. (1943). A theory of human motivation. *Psychological Review, 50,* 370–396.

Maslow, A. (1979). *The journals of A. H. Maslow.* Monterey, CA: Brooks/Cole.

Maslow, A. (1982). *Toward a psychology of being* (4th ed.). New York: Van Nostrand Reinhold.

Mastboom, J. (1992). Forty clubhouses: Model and practices. *Psychosocial Rehabilitation Journal, 16*(2), 9–23.

Masten, A. S. (1994). Resilience in individual development: Successful adaptation despite risk and adversity. In M. C. Wang & E. W. Gordon (Eds.), *Educational resilience in inner-city America: Challenges and prospects* (pp. 3–25). Hillsdale, NJ: Erlbaum.

Mathie, A., & Cunningham, G. (2002). *From clients to citizens: Asset-based community development as a strategy for community-driven development.* Antigonish, NS: Coady International Institute, St. Francis Xavier University.

Mattaini, M. A. (1990). Contextual behavior analysis in the assessment process. *Families in Society: The Journal of Contemporary Human Services, 71*(4), 236–245.

Mattaini, M. A. (1992a). *More than a thousand words: Graphics for clinical practice.* Washington, DC: NASW Press.

Mattaini, M. A. (1992b). Visual Ecoscan for clinical practice (software for Macintosh and MS DOS). Washington, DC: NASW Press.

Mattaini, M. A., & Kirk, S. A. (1991). Assessing assessment in social work. *Social Work, 36*(3), 260–266.

Mattison, M. (2000). Ethical decision making: The person in the process. *Social Work, 45*(3), 201–212.

Maxwell, G., & Morris, A. (1993). *Family, victims and culture: Youth justice in New Zealand.* Wellington, New Zealand: Social Policy Agency and Institute of Criminology, Victoria University of Wellington.

Mayer, J. E., & Timms, N. (1969). Clash in perspective between worker and client. *Social Casework, 50*(1), 32–40.

Mayer, J. E., & Timms, N. (1970). *The client speaks: Working class impressions of casework.* New York: Atherton Press.

McClendon, R., & Kadis, L. (1990). A model of integrating individual and family therapy: The contract is the key. In J. Zeig & S. Gilligan (Eds.), *Brief therapy: Myths, methods, and metaphors* (pp. 135–150). New York: Brunner/Mazel.

McCroskey, J., & Nelson, J. (1989). Practice-based research in the family support program: The family connection project example. *Child Welfare, 63*(6), 573–587.

McCubbin, H. I., & Figley, C. R. (Eds.). (1983). *Stress and the family.* New York: Brunner/Mazel.

McCullagh, J. G. (1987). Social workers as advocates: A case example. *Social Work in Education, 9*(4), 253–263.

McDermott, J. F., Jr., Tseng, W. S., Char, W. F., & Fukunaga, C. S. (1978). Child custody decision making. The search for improvement. *Journal of the American Academy of Child Psychiatry, 17*(1), 104–116.

McDevitt, S. (1994). Case records in public child welfare: Uses and a flexible format. *Child Welfare, 73*(1), 41–55.

McFadden, E. J. (1992). The inner world of children and youth in care. *Community Alternatives: International Journal of Family Care, 4*(1), 1–17.

McGoldrick, M. (1988). Ethnicity and the family life cycle. In B. Carter & M. McGoldrick (Eds.), *The changing family life cycle: A framework for family therapy* (2nd ed., pp. 69–90). New York: Gardner.

McGoldrick, M., Garcia-Preto, N., Hines, P. M., & Lee, E. (1989). Ethnicity and women. In M. McGoldrick, C. M. Anderson, & F. Walsh (Eds.), *Women in families: A framework for family therapy* (pp. 169–199). New York: Norton.

McIvor, G. (1991). Social work intervention in community service. *British Journal of Social Work, 21*(6), 591–609.

McKnight, J. (1989). Do no harm: Policy options that meet human needs. *Social Policy, 20*(1), 5–15.

McKnight, J. (1996). *A twenty-first century map for healthy communities and families.* Evanston, IL: Institute for Policy Research, Northwestern University.

McKnight, J. L. (1995). *The careless society: Community and its counterfeits.* New York: Free Press.

McKnight, J. L., & Kretzmann, J. P. (1990). *Mapping community capacity* (rev. ed.). Evanston, IL: Institute for Policy Research, Northwestern University.

McNeely, R. L. (1988). Five morale enhancing innovations for human services. *Social Casework, 69*(4), 204–213.

McNulty, C., & Wardle, J. (1994). Adult disclosure of sexual abuse: A primary cause of psychological distress? *Child Abuse and Neglect, 18*(7), 549–555.

Mead, G. H. (1934). *Mind, self and society.* Chicago: University of Chicago Press.

Means, R., & Randall, S. (1994). *Community care: Policy and practice.* Basingstoke, England: Macmillan.

Mecca, W. F., Rivera, A., & Esposito, A. J. (2000). Instituting an outcomes assessment effort: Lessons from the field. *Families in Society: The Journal of Contemporary Human Services, 81*(1), 85–89.

Mech, E. V., Pryde, J. A., & Rycraft, J. R. (1995). Mentors for adolescents in foster care. *Child and Adolescent Social Work Journal, 12*(4), 317–328.

Meenaghan, T. M., & Gibbons, W. E. (1998). *Generalist practice and skills in larger systems.* Chicago: Lyceum.

Meichenbaum, D. (1993). Changing conceptions of cognitive behavior modification: Retrospect and the prospect. *Journal of Consulting and Clinical Psychology, 61,* 202–204.

Meichenbaum, D. (1994). *A clinical handbook/practical therapist manual for assessing and treating adults with post-traumatic stress disorder (PTSD).* Waterloo, ON: University of Waterloo, Institute Press.

Meichenbaum, D., & Fitzpatrick, D. (1993). A constructionist, narrative perspective on stress and coping: Stress inoculation applications. In L. Goldberg & S. Breznitz (Eds.), *Handbook of stress: Theoretical and clinical aspects* (2nd ed., pp. 706–723). New York: Free Press.

Meier, A., Galinsky, M. J., & Rounds, K. A. (1995). Telephone support groups for caretakers of persons with AIDS. *Social Work with Groups, 18*(1), 99–108.

Meier, A., & Rudwick, E. M. (1966). *From plantation to ghetto: An interpretive history of American Negroes.* New York: Hill & Wang.

Meldrum, A. (1991). ESAP'S fables. *Africa Report* (November–December), 56–60.

Memmott, J. L. (1993). Models of helping and coping: A field experiment with natural and professional helpers. *Social Work Research and Abstracts, 29*(3), 11–21.

Menninger, K. (1968). *The crime of punishment.* New York: Viking Press.

Mercier, C., & Racine, G. (1995). Case management with homeless women: A descriptive study. *Community Mental Health Journal, 31*(1), 25–27.

Merriam-Webster. (1989). *The Merriam-Webster dictionary of English usage.* Springfield, MA: Author.

Merriam-Webster. (2003). *The Merriam-Webster online dictionary.* Retrieved June 20, 2003, from www.m-w.com/dictionary.htm

Merton, R. K. (1968). *Social theory and social structure* (4th ed.). New York: Free Press.

Merton, R. K., & Nisbet, R. A. (1961). *Contemporary social problems.* New York: Harcourt Brace Jovanovich.

Messner, S. F., & Rosenfeld, R. (1994). *Crime and the American dream.* Belmont, CA: Wadsworth.

Meyer, C. H. (1970). *Social work practice: A response to the urban crisis.* New York: Free Press.

Meyer, C. H. (1983a). Selecting appropriate practice models. In D. Waldfogel & A. Rosenblatt (Eds.), *Handbook of clinical social work* (pp. 731–749). San Francisco: Jossey-Bass.

Meyer, C. H. (Ed.). (1983b). *Clinical social work in the eco-systems perspective.* New York: Columbia University Press.

Meyer, C. H. (1988). The eco-systems perspective. In R. Dorfman (Ed.), *Paradigms of clinical social work* (pp. 275–279). New York: Brunner/Mazel.

Meyer, C. H. (1992). Social work assessment: Is there an empirical base? *Research on Social Work Practice, 2*(3), 297–305.

Meyer, C. H. (1993). *Assessment in social work practice.* New York: Columbia University Press.

Meyer, C. H. (1995). Assessment. In R. L. Edwards (Ed.), *Encyclopedia of social work* (19th ed., Vol. 1, pp. 260–270). Washington, DC: NASW Press.

Meyerson, D. E. (1994). Interpretation of stress in institutions: The cultural production of ambiguity and burnout. *Administrative Science Quarterly, 39*(4), 628–653.

Middleman, R. R. (1973). Just one question. *Social Work, 18*(4), 4.

Middleman, R. R., & Wood, G. G. (1990). *Skills for direct practice in social work*. New York: Columbia University Press.

Middleman, R. R., & Wood, G. G. (1991). Communicating by doing. *Families in Society: The Journal of Contemporary Human Services, 72*(3), 153–156.

Middleton, L. (1996). Editorial. *Practice, 8*(2), 1–4.

Midgley, J. (1993). Promoting a development focus in the community organization curriculum: Relevance of the African experience. *Journal of Work Education, 29*(3), 269–278.

Midgley, J. (1995). *Social development: The development perspective in social welfare*. London: Sage.

Midgley, J. (1996). Social work and economic development. *International Social Work, 39*(1), 5–12.

Miley, K. K., O'Melia, M., & Dubois, B. L. (1995). *Generalist social work practice: An empowering approach*. Toronto: Allyn & Bacon.

Miller, D. D., & Berg, I. K. (1995). *The miracle method: A radically new approach to problem drinking*. New York: Norton.

Miller, H. (1968). Value dilemmas in social casework. *Social Work, 13*(1), 27–33.

Miller, J. G. (1978). *Living systems*. New York: McGraw-Hill.

Miller, K., Fein, E., Howe, G., Claudio, C., & Bishop, G. (1984). Time-limited goal focused parent aide services. *Social Casework, 68*(8), 472–477.

Miller, P. (1990). Covenant model for professional relationships: An alternative to the contract model. *Social Work, 35*(2), 121–125.

Miller, S. D. (1992). The symptoms of solution. *Journal of Strategic and Systemic Therapies, 11,* 1–11.

Miller, S. D., Hubble, M. A., & Duncan, B. L. (Eds.). (1996). *Handbook of solution-focused brief therapy*. San Francisco: Jossey-Bass.

Miller, W. B., Baum, R. C., & McNeil, R. (1968). Delinquency prevention and organizational relations. In S. Wheeler (Ed.), *Controlling delinquents* (pp. 61–100). New York: Wiley.

Miller, W. R., Benefield, R. G., & Tonigan, J. S. (2001). Enhancing motivation for change in problem drinking: A controlled comparison of two therapist styles. In C. E. Hill (Ed.), *Helping skills: The empirical foundation* (pp. 243–255). Washington, DC: American Psychological Association.

Miller, W. R., & Rollnick, S. (Eds.). (1991). *Motivational interviewing: Preparing people to change addictive behavior*. New York: Guilford.

Miller, W. R., & Rollnick, S. (2002). *Motivational interviewing: Preparing people for change* (2nd ed.). New York: Guilford.

Mills, R. (1995). *Realizing mental health*. New York: Sulzberger & Graham.

Millstein, K. H. (1993). Limit setting, coping, and adaptation: A theoretical context for clinicians and caregivers. *Child and Adolescent Social Work Journal, 10*(4), 289–300.

Milne, A. (1999). *Teach yourself counseling*. London: Hodder & Stoughton, Ltd.

Minahan, D. J. (1993). Assessment of dementia patients and their families: An ecological family centered approach. *Health and Social Work, 18*(2), 123–131.

Miranda, M. R. (1976). *Psychotherapy with the Spanish-speaking: Issues in research and service*. Los Angeles: Spanish-Speaking Mental Health Center.

Mizrahi, T. (2001). The status of community organizing in 2001: Community practice context, complexities, contradictions, and contributions. *Research on Social Work Practice, 11*(2), 176–189.

Modai, I., & Rabinowitz, J. (1993). Why and how to establish a computerized system for psychiatric case records. *Hospital and Community Psychiatry, 44*(11), 1091–1097.

Molnar, A., & de Shazer, S. (1987). Solution-focused therapy: Towards the identification of therapeutic tasks. *Journal of Marital and Family Therapy, 13*(4), 349–358.

Moncher, R. J. (1995). Social isolation and child abuse risk. *Families in Society: The Journal of Contemporary Human Services, 76*(7), 421–433.

Mondros, J. B., & Wilson, S. M. (1994). *Organizing for power and empowerment*. New York: Columbia University Press.

Monkman, M. M. (1991). Outcome objectives in social work practice: Person and environment. *Social Work, 36,* 253–258.

Monnickendam, M., Yaniv, H., & Geve, N. (1994). Practitioners and the case record: Patterns of use. *Administration in Social Work, 18*(4), 73–87.

Moon, A., & Williams, O. (1993). Perceptions of elder abuse and the help-seeking patterns among African-American, Caucasian-American, and Korean-American elderly women. *Gerontologist, 33*(3), 386–394.

Moore, C. W. (1986). *The mediation process*. San Francisco: Jossey-Bass.

Moore, S. (1992). Case management and the integration of services: How service delivery systems shape case management. *Social Work, 37*(5), 418–423.

Moore, S. T. (1990). A social work practice model of case management: The case management grid. *Social Work, 35*(5), 444–448.

Moore, S. T. (1995). Efficiency in social work practice and administration. *Social Work, 40*(5), 602–608.

Moore, S. T., & Kelly, M. J. (1996). Quality now: Moving human service organizations toward a consumer orientation to service quality. *Social Work, 41*(1), 33–40.

Moore-Kirkland, J. (1981). Mobilizing motivation: From theories to practice. In A. N. Maluccio (Ed.), *Promoting competence in clients: A new/old approach to social work practice* (pp. 27–54). New York: Free Press.

Mor Barak, M. E. (2000). The inclusive workplace: An ecosystems approach to diversity management. *Social Work, 45*(4), 339–352.

Morales, A. T., & Sheafor, B. W. (1998). *Social work: A profession of many faces* (8th ed.). Boston: Allyn & Bacon.

Moras, K., & Strupp, H. (1982). Pretherapy interpersonal relations, patients, alliance and outcome in brief therapy. *Archives of General Psychiatry, 39,* 405–509.

Moreau, M. J. (1990). Empowerment through advocacy and consciousness-raising: Implications of structural approach to social work. *Journal of Sociology and Social Welfare, 17*(2), 53–67.

Morgan, R. (1962). Role performance in a bureaucracy. In National Conference on Social Welfare (Ed.), *Social work practice* (pp. 111–126). New York: Columbia University Press.

Morin, R., & Balz, D. (1996). Americans losing trust in each other and institutions. *The Washington Post,* January 28, A1, A6.

Morris, J. (1994). *The shape of things to come? User-led social services (Social Service Policy Forum Paper No. 3).* London: National Institute of Social Workers.

Morris, P. M. (2002). The capabilities perspective: A framework for social justice. *Families in Society: The Journal of Contemporary Human Services, 83*(4), 365–373.

Morris, R. (1977). Caring for versus caring about people. *Social Work, 22*(5), 353–359.

Morrison, J. D. (1991). The Black church as a support system for Black elderly. *Journal of Gerontological Social Work, 17*(1/2), 105–120.

Morrow-Howell, N., Chadiha, L. A., Proctor, E. K., Hourd-Bryant, M., & Dore, P. (1996). Racial differences in discharge planning. *Health and Social Work, 21*(2), 131–139.

Morrow-Howell, N., Lott, L., & Ozawa, M. (1990). The impact of race on volunteer helping relationships among the elderly. *Social Work, 35*(5), 395–404.

Moss, S., & Moss, M. (1967). When a caseworker leaves an agency: The impact on worker and client. *Social Casework, 48*(7), 433–437.

Motivation. Encyclopædia Britannica. Retrieved July 13, 2003, from www.search.eb.com/eb/article?eu=115598

Moursund, J., & Kenny, M. C. (2002). *The process of counseling and therapy* (4th ed.). Upper Saddle River, NJ: Prentice-Hall.

Mouzakitis, C., & Goldstein, S. (1985). A multidisciplinary approach to treating child neglect. *Social Casework: The Journal of Contemporary Social Work, 66*(4), 218–224.

Moxley, D. P. (1989). *The practice of case management.* Newbury Park, CA: Sage.

Moxley, D. P., & Washington, O. G. M. (2001). Strengths-based recovery practice in chemical dependency: A transpersonal perspective. *Families in Society: The Journal of Contemporary Human Services, 82*(3), 251–262.

Moyers, B., & Woodruff, P. (2003). *Now with Bill Moyers: Interview with Paul Woodruff (transcript of January 3, 2003 broadcast).* Retrieved August 15, 2003, from www.pbs.org/now/transcript/transcript_woodruff.html

Mullen, E. J., & Goldstein, H. (1992). *Should social workers base practice decisions on empirical research?* Boston: Allyn & Bacon.

Mullen, E. J., & Schuermann, J. R. (1990). Expert systems and the development of knowledge in social welfare. In L. Videka-Sherman & W. J. Reid (Eds.), *Advances in clinical social work research* (pp. 119–142). Silver Spring, MD: NASW Press.

Munday, B. (1993). Introduction: Definitions and comparisons in European social care. In B. Munday & P. Ely (Eds.), *Social care in Europe* (pp. 1–20). London: Prentice-Hall/Harvester Wheatsheaf.

Murdach, A. D. (1980). Bargaining and persuasion with nonvoluntary clients. *Social Work, 25*(6), 458–461.

Murdach, A. D. (1982). A political perspective in problem solving. *Social Work, 27*(5), 417–421.

Murdach, A. D. (1996). Beneficence re-examined: Protective intervention in mental health. *Social Work, 41*(1), 26–32.

Murphy, K., & Schneider, B. (1994). Coaching socially rejected early adolescents regarding behaviors used by peers to infer liking: A dyad-specific intervention. *Journal of Early Adolescence, 14*(1), 83–95.

Murphy, L. B., & Moriarity, A. (1976). *Vulnerability, coping, and growth: From infancy to adolescence.* New Haven, CT: Yale University Press.

Murphy, W. D., Page, I. J., & Hoffmann, M. L. (2003). Adolescent sex offenders. In P. Allen-Meares & M. W. Fraser (Eds.), *Intervention with children and adolescents: An interdisciplinary perspective* (pp. 477–492). Boston: Allyn & Bacon.

Musolf, G. R. (2001). John Dewey's social psychology and neopragmatism: Theoretical foundations of human agency and social reconstruction. *Social Science Journal, 38*(2), 277–295.

Myrdal, G. (1962). *An American dilemma: The Negro problem and modern democracy.* New York: Pantheon.

Nakhaima, J. M. (1994). Network family counseling: The overlooked resource. *Areté, 19*(1), 46–56.

Nason, F. (1983). Diagnosing the hospital team. *Social Work in Health Care, 9*(2), 25–45.

NASW National Committee on Racial and Ethnic Diversity. (2001). *NASW standards for cultural competence in social work practice.* Retrieved May 15, 2003, from www.socialworkers.org/sections/credentials/cultural_comp.asp

National Adolescent Perpetrator Network. (1993). The revised report from the National Task Force on Juvenile Sexual Offending. *Juvenile and Family Court Journal, 44*(4), 1–120.

National Association of Social Workers (NASW). (1977). Special issue on conceptual frameworks. *Social Work, 22*(5), 338–444.

National Association of Social Workers. (1981a). *NASW working statement on the purpose of social work.* Silver Spring, MD: Author.

National Association of Social Workers. (1981b). Special issue on conceptual frameworks II. *Social Work, 26*(1), 6–75.

National Association of Social Workers. (1999). *Code of ethics of the National Association of Social Workers.* Retrieved April 10, 2003, from www.socialworkers.org/pubs/code/code.asp

National Association of Social Workers. (2003). Client self-determination in end-of-life decisions. In National Association of Social Workers (Ed.), *Social work speaks: NASW policy statements, 2003–2006* (6th ed., pp. 46–49). Washington, DC: NASW Press.

Nelson, D. (1990). Recognizing and realizing the potential of family preservation. In J. K. Whittaker, J. Kinney, E. M. Tracy, & C. Booth (Eds.), *Reaching high-risk families: Intensive family preservation in human services* (pp. 13–30). Hawthorne, NY: Aldine de Gruyter.

Nes, J. A., & Iadicola, P. (1989). Toward definition of feminist social work: A comparison of liberal, radical and socialist models. *Social Work, 25*(1), 12–21.

Netting, F. E. (1992). Case management: Service or symptom? *Social Work, 37,* 160–164.

Newell, A., & Simon, H. A. (1972). *Human problem-solving.* Englewood Cliffs, NJ: Prentice-Hall.

Nezu, A., & D'Zurilla, T. J. (1981). Effects of problem definition and formulation on the generation of alternatives in the social problem solving process. *Cognitive Therapy and Research, 5,* 265–271.

Nicholson, B., & Matross, G. (1989). Facing reduced decision-making capacity in health care: Methods for maintaining client self-determination. *Social Work, 25*(3), 234–238.

Norell, D., & Walz, T. (1994). Reflections from the field toward a theory and practice of reconciliation in ethnic conflict resolution. *Social Development Issues, 16*(2), 99–111.

Northen, H. (1969). *Social work with groups.* New York: Columbia University Press.

Northen, H. (1982). *Clinical social work.* New York: Columbia University Press.

Northen, H., & Kurland, R. (2001). *Social work with groups* (3rd ed.). New York: Columbia University Press.

Novak, J. M. (2002). Recalling John Dewey: Has he left the building? *Free Inquiry, 23*(1), 49–50.

Novak, M. W. (Ed.). (1997). *Aging and society: A Canadian perspective* (3rd ed.). Toronto: ITP Nelson.

Nugent, W. R., Umbreit, M. S., Winamaki, L., & Paddock, J. (2001). Participation in victim-offender mediation and re-offense: Successful replications? *Research on Social Work Practice, 11*(1), 5–23.

Nurius, P. S., & Hudson, W. W. (1988). Computers and social diagnosis: The client's perspective. *Computers in Human Services, 5*(1/2), 21–36.

O'Connor, G. (1972). Toward a new policy in adult corrections. *Social Service Review, 46*(4), 581–596.

Ogles, B. M., Lambert, M., & Masters, K. S. (1996). *Assessing outcomes in clinical practice.* Needham Heights, MA: Allyn & Bacon.

O'Hanlon, W. H., & Weiner-Davis, M. (1989). *In search of solutions: A new definition of psychotherapy.* New York: Norton.

O'Hanlon, W. H., & Wilk, J. (1987). *Shifting contexts: A generation of effective psychotherapies.* New York: Guilford.

O'Leary, K. D., & Beach, S. R. H. (1990). Marital therapy: A viable treatment for depression and marital discord. *American Journal of Psychiatry, 147*(2), 183–186.

Olsen, R. F. (1986). Integrating formal and informal social care: The utilization of social support networks. *British Journal of Social Work, 16* (supplement), 15–22.

Olson, D. H. (1986). Circumplex model VII: Validation studies and FACES III. *Family Process, 25*(3), 337–351.

Olson, D. H., McCubbin, H. I., Barnes, H., Larsen, A., Muxen, M., & Wilson, M. (1985). *Family inventories: Inventories in a national survey of families across the family life cycle* (rev. ed.). St. Paul: Family Social Science, McNeal Hall, University of Minnesota.

Olson, D. H., Sprenkle, D. H., & Russel, C. S. (1979). Circumplex model of marital and family systems: Cohesion and adaptability dimensions, family types, and clinical applications. *Family Process, 18,* 3–28.

Oppenheim, A. N. (1992). *Questionnaire design, interviewing, and attitude measurement.* New York: Pinter.

Oppenhein, L. (1992). The first interview in child protection: Social work method and process. *Children & Society, 6*(2), 132–150.

Orme, J. (1996). Paretic or patronage: Changes in social work practice brought about by community care policies in Britain. In *Participating in change: Social work profession in social development (Proceedings of Joint World Congress of IFSW and IASSW)* (pp. 250–252). Hong Kong.

Osterman, D., & Benbenishty, R. (1992). Keeping in touch: Ecological factors related to foster care visitation. *Child and Adolescent Social Work Journal, 9*(6), 541–554.

Overton, A. (1965). Establishing the relationship. *Crime and Delinquency, 11*(3), 120–124.

Owens, D. K., & Nease, R. F. (1993). Development of outcome-based practice guidelines: A method for structuring problems and synthesizing evidence. *Journal on Quality Improvement, 19*(7), 249–264.

Oxley, G. B. (1966). The caseworker's expectations in client motivation. *Social Casework, 47*(7), 432–437.

Painter, E. (1966). Ego building procedures that foster social functioning. *Social Casework, 47*(3), 139–145.

Palazoli, M. S., Cirillo, S., Selvini, M., & Sorrentino, A. M. (1989). *Family games: General model of psychotic processes in the family.* New York: Norton.

Palmer, N. (1997). Resilience in adult children of alcoholics: A nonpathological approach to social work practice. *Health and Social Work, 22*(3), 201–209.

Pappas, G. F. (1993). Dewey and feminism: The affective and relationships in Dewey's ethics. *Hypatia, 8*(2), 78–95.

Parad, H. J., & Miller, R. (Eds.). (1963). *Ego oriented casework*. New York: Family Service Association of America.

Parker, T. (1987). Dilemmas resulting from the application of extemporaneous ethics in interdisciplinary team decision-making. *Family Therapy, 14*(3), 201–211.

Parsloe, P. (1997). Everyday choices may be as important as the grand notion. *Care Plan, 3*(3), 9–12.

Parsons, R. J. (1991a). Empowerment: Purpose and practice principles in social work. *Social Work with Groups, 14*(2), 7–21.

Parsons, R. J. (1991b). The mediator role in social work practice. *Social Work, 36*(6), 483–487.

Parsons, R. J., & Cox, E. O. (1994). *Empowerment-oriented social work practice with the elderly*. Pacific Grove, CA: Brooks/Cole.

Parton, N. (1994). Problematics of government, (post) modernity and social work. *British Journal of Social Work, 24,* 9–32.

Paterson, K., & Harvey, M. (1991). *An evaluation of the organisation and operation of the care and protection family group conferences*. Wellington, New Zealand: Department of Social Welfare.

Patterson, S. L., & Brennan, E. M. (1983). Matching helping roles with the characteristics of older natural helpers. *Journal of Gerontological Social Work, 5,* 55–66.

Patterson, S. L., Germain, C. B., Brennan, E. M., & Memmott, J. L. (1988). Effectiveness of rural natural helpers. *Social Casework, 69*(5), 272–279.

Patterson, S. L., Memmott, J. L., Brennan, E. M., & Germain, C. B. (1992). Patterns of natural helping in rural areas: Implications for social work research. *Social Work Research and Abstracts, 28*(3), 11–21.

Pawlak, E. J. (1976). Organizational tinkering. *Social Work, 21*(5), 376–380.

Payne, J. E. (1972). Ombundsman roles for social workers. *Social Work, 17*(1), 94–100.

Pedersen, P. B., & Ivey, A. (1993). *Culture-centered counseling and interviewing skills: A practical guide*. Westport, CT: Praeger.

Peele, S. (1989). *The diseasing of America*. Lexington, MA: Lexington Books.

Peele, S., & Brodsky, A. (1991). *The truth about addiction and recovery*. New York: Simon & Schuster.

Penka, C., & Kirk, S. (1991). Practitioner involvement in clinical evaluation. *Social Work, 36,* 1513–1518.

Pennell, J. (1995). Encountering or countering women abuse. In P. Taylor & C. Daly (Eds.), *Gender dilemmas in social work: Issues affecting women in the profession* (pp. 89–105). Toronto: Canadian Scholars' Press.

Pennell, J., & Burford, G. (1994). Widening the circle: Family group decision making. *Journal of Child and Youth Care, 9*(1), 1–11.

Pennell, J., & Burford, G. (1995). *Family group decision making: New roles for "old" partners in resolving family violence: Implementation report*. St. John's, Newfoundland: Family Group Decision Making Project, School of Social Work, Memorial University of Newfoundland.

Pennell, J., & Burford, G. (1996). Attending to context: Family Group decision making in Canada. In J. Hudson, A. Morris, & B. Galaway (Eds.), *Family group conferences: Perspectives on policy and practice* (pp. 206–220). New York: Criminal Justice Press.

People First. (1990). *Oi! It's my assessment: Why not listen to me!* London: Author.

Perlman, H. H. (1957). *Social casework: A problem-solving process*. Chicago: University of Chicago Press.

Perlman, H. H. (1961). The role concept and social casework: Some explorations. *Social Service Review, 35*(4), 370–381.

Perlman, H. H. (1962). The role concept and social casework: Some explorations, II. *Social Science Review, 36*(1), 17–31.

Perlman, H. H. (1968). *Persona: Social role and personality*. Chicago: University of Chicago Press.

Perlman, H. H. (1970). *The problem-solving model in social casework*. Chicago: University of Chicago Press.

Perlman, H. H. (1971). *Perspectives on social casework*. Philadelphia: Temple University Press.

Perlman, H. H. (1975). In quest of coping. *Social Casework, 56*(4), 213–225.

Perlman, H. H. (1979). *Relationship: The heart of helping people*. Chicago: University of Chicago Press.

Perlman, H. H. (1986). The problem solving model. In F. Turner (Ed.), *Social work treatment: Interlocking theoretical approaches* (3rd ed., pp. 245–266). New York: Free Press.

Peters, T. (1992). *Liberation management*. New York: Knopf.

Peterson, K. J. (1979). Assessment in the life model: A historical perspective. *Social Casework, 60*(10), 586–596.

Peterson, S. M. P., Derby, K. M., Berg, W. K., & Horner, R. H. (2002). Collaboration with families in the functional behavior assessment of and intervention for severe behavior problems. *Education & Treatment of Children, 25*(1), 5–25.

Petri, H. L. (1996). *Motivation: Theory, research, and applications* (4th ed.). Pacific Grove, CA: Brooks/Cole.

Petrosino, A., Turpin-Petrosino, C., & Buehler, J. (2003). "Scared Straight" and other juvenile awareness programs for preventing juvenile delinquency (Cochrane Review). *Cochrane Database of Systematic Reviews*. Chichester, UK: Wiley.

Philip, C. E. (1994). Letting go: Problems with termination when a therapist is seriously ill or dying. *Smith College Studies in Social Work, 64*(2), 169–179.

Pierce, R. D. (2001, October). *Self-determination through the prism of community*. Paper presented at the University of Illinois National Research and Training Center on Psychiatric Disability's Annual Self-Determination Workshop Series, Chicago.

Pilsecker, C. (1994). Starting where the client is. *Families in Society: The Journal of Contemporary Human Services, 72*(3), 153–156.

Pincus, A., & Minahan, A. (1973). *Social work practice: Model and method.* Itasca, IL: Peacock.

Pinderhughes, E. (1983). Empowerment for our clients and for ourselves. *Social Casework: The Journal of Contemporary Social Work, 64*(6), 331–338.

Pinderhughes, E. (1989). *Understanding race, ethnicity, and power.* New York: Free Press.

Pines, A. (1983). On burnout and the buffering effects of social supports. In B. A. Farber (Ed.), *Stress and burnout in the human service professions* (pp. 158–160). New York: Pergamon.

Pines, A., Aronson, E., & Kafry, D. (1981). *Burnout: From tedium to personal growth.* New York: Free Press.

Pines, A., & Kafry, D. (1978). Occupational tedium in the social services. *Social Work, 23*(6), 499–507.

Pines, A., & Maslach, C. (1978). Characteristics of staff burnout in mental health settings. *Hospital and Community Psychiatry, 29*(4), 233–237.

Pinker, S. (2002). *The blank slate: The modern denial of human nature.* New York: Viking.

Pinsof, W. M., & Wynne, L. C. (1995). The efficacy of marital and family therapy: An empirical overview, conclusions and recommendations. *Journal of Marital and Family Therapy, 21*(4), 585–613.

Platt, A. M. (1977). *The child savers: The invention of delinquency* (2nd ed.). Chicago: University of Chicago Press.

Polansky, N. A., Bergman, R. D., & de Saix, C. (1973). *Child neglect: Understanding and reading the parent.* New York: Child Welfare League.

Pollard, W. L. (1978). *A study of Black self-help.* San Francisco: R & E Research Associates.

Polya, G. (1957). *How to solve it.* Princeton, NJ: Princeton University Press.

Pomerantz, P., Pomerantz, D. J., & Colca, I. A. (1990). A case study: Service delivery and parents with disabilities. *Child Welfare, 69*(1), 67–73.

Poole, B. (1993). Involving Careers. In User-Centred Services Group (Ed.), *Building bridges between people who use and people who provide services* (pp. 39–40). London: National Institute of Social Workers.

Poppendieck, J. E. (1992). Values, commitments, and ethics of social work in the United States. *Journal of Progressive Human Services, 3*(2), 31–45.

Poulin, J. E., & Walter, C. A. (1993). Social workers' burnout: A longitudinal study. *Social Work Research and Abstracts, 29*(4), 5–11.

Poulin, J. E., Walter, C. A., & Walker, J. L. (1994). Interdisciplinary team membership: A survey of gerontological social workers. *Journal of Gerontological Social Work, 22*(1/2), 93–107.

Powell, T. J. (1990). *Working with self-help.* Washington, DC: NASW Press.

Prawat, R. S. (1985). Affective versus cognitive goal orientations in elementary teachers. *American Educational Research Journal, 22*(4), 587–604.

Preston-Shoot, M. (1989). Using contracts in groupwork. *Groupwork, 2*(1), 36–47.

Prigmore, C. S., & Atherton, C. R. (1986). *Social welfare policy.* Lexington, MA: D.C. Health.

Prochaska, J. M. (2000). Transtheoretical model for assessing organizational change: A study of family service agencies' movement to time-limited therapy. *Families in Society: The Journal of Contemporary Human Services, 81*(1), 76–84.

Prochaska, J. O. (1999). How do people change, and how can we change to help many more people? In B. L. Duncan & M. A. Hubble (Eds.), *The heart and soul of change: What works in therapy* (pp. 227–255). Washington, DC: American Psychological Association.

Prochaska, J. O., & DiClemente, C. C. (1982). Transtheoretical therapy: Toward a more integrative model of change. *Psychotherapy: Theory, Research & Practice, 19,* 276–288.

Prochaska, J. O., Norcross, J. C., & DiClemente, C. C. (1994). *Changing for good: A revolutionary six-stage program for overcoming bad habits and moving your life positively forward.* New York: Avon.

Proctor, E., Vosler, N., & Sirles, E. (1993). The social-environmental context of child clients: An empirical exploration. *Social Work, 38*(3), 256–261.

Proctor, E. K., Morrow-Howell, N., & Lott, C. L. (1993). Classification and correlates of ethical dilemmas in hospital social work. *Social Work, 38*(2), 166–177.

Propst, R. (1992). Standards for Clubhouse programs: Why and how they were developed. *Psychosocial Rehabilitation Journal, 16*(2), 25–30.

Pruger, R. (1973). The good bureaucrat. *Social Work, 18*(4), 27–32.

Pruger, R. (1978). Bureaucratic functioning as a social skill. In B. L. Baer & R. C. Federico (Eds.), *Educating the baccalaureate social worker: Report of the undergraduate social worker curriculum development project* (pp. 149–168). Cambridge, MA: Ballinger.

Pumphrey, M. (1959). *The teaching of values and ethics in social work education.* Paper presented at the Council on Social Work Education, New York.

Pumphrey, M. (1991). Mary Richmond—the practitioner. *Social Casework, 42*(10), 375–385.

Pumphrey, R., & Pumphrey, M. (1961). *The heritage of American social work.* New York: Columbia University Press.

Purcell, F. P. (1964). The helping professions and problems of the brief contact. In F. Reissman, J. Cohen, & A. Pearl

(Eds.), *Mental health of the poor* (pp. 431–434). New York: Free Press.

Putnam, R. D. (1993, March 21). The prosperous community: Social capital and public life. *American Prospect, 4*(13), 35–42.

Putnam, R. D. (1995a). Bowling alone: America's declining social capital. *Journal of Democracy, 6*(1), 65–78.

Putnam, R. D. (1995b). Tuning in, tuning out: The strange disappearance of social capital in America. *PS: Political Science & Politics, 28*(4), 664–683.

Putnam, R. D. (2000). *Bowling alone: The collapse and revival of American community*. New York: Simon & Schuster.

Putnam, R. D. (2002). *Democracies in flux: The evolution of social capital in contemporary society*. New York: Oxford University Press.

Putnam, R. D., Feldstein, L. M., & Cohen, D. (2003). *Better together: Restoring the American community*. New York: Simon & Schuster.

Putnam, R. D., Leonardi, R., & Nanetti, R. Y. (1993). *Making democracy work: Civic traditions in modern Italy*. Princeton, NJ: Princeton University Press.

Quarles, B. (1987). *The Negro in the making of America*. New York: Collier Books.

Quarter, J. (1992). *Canada's social economy: Cooperatives, non-profits, and other community enterprises*. Toronto: James Lorimer.

Raheim, S. (1996). Micro-enterprise as an approach for promoting economic development in social work: Lessons from the self-employment investment demonstration. *International Social Work, 39*(1), 69–82.

Raheim, S., & Bolden, J. (1995). Economic empowerment of low income women through self-employment programs. *Affilia, 10*(2), 138–154.

Rahman, A., & Toubia, N. (Eds.). (2000). *Female genital mutilation: A guide to laws and policies worldwide*. London: Zed Books.

Rainwater, L., & Yancey, W. L. (1967). *The Moynihan report and the politics of controversy*. Cambridge, MA: MIT Press.

Ramsay, R. F. (2003). Transforming the working definition of social work into the 21st century. *Research on Social Work Practice, 13*(3), 324–338.

Randour, M. L. (Ed.). (1993). *Exploring sacred landscapes: Religious and spiritual dimensions in psychotherapy*. New York: Columbia University Press.

Rapp, C. A. (1997). *The strengths model: Case management with people suffering from severe and persistent mental illness*. New York: Oxford University Press.

Rapp, R. (1997). The strengths perspective and persons with substance abuse problems. In D. Saleebey (Ed.), *The strengths perspective in social work practice* (2nd ed., pp. 77–96). New York: Longman.

Rapp, R. C., Li, L., Siegal, H. A., & DeLiberty, R. N. (2003). Demographic and clinical correlates of client motivation among substance abusers. *Health and Social Work, 28*(2), 107–115.

Rappaport, J. (1985). The power of empowerment language. *Social Policy, 16*(2), 15–21.

Raymond, G. T., Teare, R. J., & Atherton, C. R. (1996). Is "field of practice" a relevant organizing principle for the MSW curriculum? *Journal of Social Work Education, 32*(1), 19–30.

Raynor, P. (1986). *Social work, justice and control*. Oxford, England: Basic Blackwell.

Reamer, F. G. (1988). AIDS and ethics: The agenda for social workers. *Social Work, 33*(5), 460–464.

Reamer, F. G. (1991). AIDS, social work, and the duty to protect. *Social Work, 36*(1), 56–59.

Reamer, F. G. (1993a). AIDS and social work: The ethical and civil liberties agenda. *Social Work, 38*(4), 412–419.

Reamer, F. G. (1993b). *Ethical dilemmas in social service* (2nd ed.). New York: Columbia University Press.

Reamer, F. G. (1994). *Social work malpractice and liability: Strategies for prevention*. New York: Columbia University Press.

Reamer, F. G. (1995a). Ethics and values. In R. L. Edwards (Ed.), *Encyclopedia of social work* (19th ed., Vol. 1, pp. 893–902). Washington, DC: NASW Press.

Reamer, F. G. (1995b). Malpractice claims against social workers: First facts. *Social Work, 40*(5), 596–601.

Reamer, F. G. (1995c). *Social work: Values and ethics*. New York: Columbia University Press.

Reamer, F. G. (1998). *Ethical standards in social work: A critical review of the NASW Code of Ethics*. Washington, DC: NASW Press.

Reamer, F. G. (1999). *Social work values and ethics* (2nd ed.). New York: Columbia University Press.

Reamer, F. G. (2000). The social work ethics audit: A risk-management strategy. *Social Work, 45*(4), 355–366.

Reamer, F. G. (2002). Ethical issues in social work. In A. R. Roberts & G. J. Greene (Eds.), *Social workers' desk reference* (pp. 65–69). New York: Oxford University Press.

Reamer, F. G. (2003). Boundary issues in social work: Managing dual relationships. *Social Work, 48*(1), 121–134.

Reamer, F. G., & Conrad, S. A. P. (1995). Professional choices: Ethics at work [Video]. Washington, DC: NASW Press.

Recent cases. (2001). Recent cases: Evidence—Sixth Circuit holds that Tarasoff disclosures do not vitiate psychotherapist-patient privilege—*United States v. Hayes,* 227 F.3d 578 (6th Cir. 2000). *Harvard Law Review, 114*(7), 2194–2200.

Redhorse, J. G., Lewis, R., Fest, M., & Decker, J. (1978). Family behavior of urban American Indians. *Social Casework, 59*(2), 67–72.

Reeser, L. C. (1991). Professionalization, striving, and social work activism. *Journal of Social Science Research, 14*(3/4), 1–22.

Reeser, L. C. (1992). Professional role orientation and social activism. *Journal of Sociology and Social Welfare, 19*(2), 79–94.

Regan, J. J., Alderson, A., & Regan, W. M. (2002). Health care providers' duty to warn. *Southern Medical Journal, 95*(12), 1396–1399.

Reichertz, D., & Frankel, H. (1993). Integrating family assessment into social work practice. *Research on Social Work Practice, 3*(3), 243–257.

Reid, W. (1996). Task-centered social work. In F. J. Turner (Ed.), *Social work treatment: Interlocking theoretical approaches* (4th ed., pp. 69–93). New York: Free Press.

Reid, W. J. (1978). *The task-centered system.* New York: Columbia University Press.

Reid, W. J. (1990). An integrative model for short-term treatment. In R. A. Wells & V. J. Gianetti (Eds.), *Handbook of brief psychotherapies* (pp. 55–77). New York: Plenum.

Reid, W. J. (1992). *Task strategies: An empirical approach to clinical social work.* New York: Columbia University Press.

Reid, W. J. (1994). The empirical practice movement. *Social Service Review, 68*(2), 165–184.

Reid, W. J. (2002). Knowledge for direct social work practice: An analysis of trends. *Social Service Review, 76*(1), 6–33.

Reid, W. J., & Epstein, L. (1972). *Task-centered casework.* New York: Columbia University Press.

Reid, W. J., & Epstein, L. (1977). *Task-centered practice.* New York: Columbia University Press.

Reiff, D. (1991, October). Victims all? *Harper's Magazine, 283*(1697), 49–56.

Rein, M. (1970). Social work in search of a radical profession. *Social Work, 15*(2), 13–33.

Renger, R., & Titcomb, A. (2002). A three-step approach to teaching logic models. *American Journal of Evaluation, 23*(4), 493–503.

Reynolds, B. C. (1963). *Uncharted journey.* New York: Citadel Press.

Rhodes, M. (1986). *Ethical dilemmas in social work practice.* Boston: Routledge & Kegan Paul.

Rhone, J. (1973). Social services delivery system among slaves 1619–1790. In W. S. Jackson, J. V. Rhone, & C. L. Sanders (Eds.), *Social service delivery system in the Black community during the ante-bellum period (1619–1860)* (pp. 3–10). Atlanta: Atlanta University School of Social Work.

Ribner, D. S., & Knei-Paz, C. (2002). Client's view of a successful helping relationship. *Social Work, 47*(4), 379–387.

Richardson, A. (1995). Care management. In N. Malin (Ed.), *Services for people with learning disabilities* (pp. 240–249). London: Routledge.

Richey, C., Blythe, B., & Berlin, S. (1987). Do social workers evaluate their practice? *Social Work Research and Abstracts, 23*(23), 14–20.

Richmond, M. E. (1899). *Friendly visiting among the poor: A handbook for charity workers.* New York: Macmillan.

Richmond, M. E. (1917). *Social diagnosis.* New York: Russell Sage Foundation.

Ridley, M. (2003). *Nature via nurture: Genes, experience, and what makes us human.* New York: HarperCollins.

Ripple, L. (1955). Motivation, capacity, and opportunity as related to the use of casework service: Plan of study. *Social Service Review, 29,* 172–193.

Ripple, L. (1957). Factors associated with continuance in casework services. *Social Work, 2,* 87–94.

Ripple, L., & Alexander, E. (1956). Motivation, capacity, and opportunity as related to casework services: Nature of client's problem. *Social Service Review, 30*(1), 38–54.

Ripple, L., Alexander, E., & Polemis, B. W. (1964). *Motivation, capacity, and opportunity: Studies in casework theory and practice.* Chicago: University of Chicago School of Social Service Administration.

Risler, E., Lowe, L. A., & Nackerud, L. (2003). Defining social work: Does the working definition work today? *Research on Social Work Practice, 13*(3), 299–309.

Ristock, J., & Pennell, J. (1996). *Community research as empowerment: Feminist links, postmodern interruptions.* Toronto: Oxford University Press.

Roberts, C. S., Severinsen, C., Kuehn, C., Straker, D., & Fritz, C. J. (1992). Obstacles to effective case management with AIDS patients: The clinician's perspective. *Social Work in Health Care, 17*(2), 27–40.

Roberts, E. (1992, October). *Keynote Address.* Paper presented at the Annual conference of social workers and psychologists working with closed head and spinal cord injuries, Las Vegas, NV.

Robertson, R. (1995). *Chaos theory in psychology and the life sciences.* Mahwah, NJ: Erlbaum.

Rodney, W. (1982). *How Europe underdeveloped Africa.* Washington, DC: Howard University Press.

Rogers, C. R. (1957). The necessary and sufficient conditions of psychotherapeutic personality change. *Journal of Consulting Psychology, 21,* 95–103.

Rogers, C. R. (1966). Client-centered therapy. In C. H. Patterson (Ed.), *Theories of counseling and psychotherapy* (pp. 403–439). New York: Harper & Row.

Rogers, C. R. (1975). Empathic: An unappreciated way of being. *Counseling Psychologist, 5,* 2–10.

Rojek, C., & Collins, S. A. (1987). Contract or con trick? *British Journal of Social Work, 17*(2), 199–211.

Rojek, C., & Collins, S. A. (1988). Contract or con trick revisited: Comments on the reply by Gordon and Preston-Shoot. *British Journal of Social Work, 18*(6), 611–622.

Rollnick, S. (2002). A motivational interviewing perspective on resistance in psychotherapy. *Journal of Clinical Psychology, 58*(2), 185–193.

Rollnick, S., & Miller, W. R. (1995). What is motivational interviewing? *Behavioural and Cognitive Psychotherapy, 23,* 325–334.

Rooney, R. (1988). Socialization strategies for involuntary clients. *Social Casework: Journal of Contemporary Social Work, 69*(3), 131–140.

Rooney, R. (1992). *Strategies for work with involuntary clients*. New York: Columbia University Press.

Rooney, R. H. (1993). When the client is unwilling. *CURA Reporter, 23*(2), 11–14.

Rose, A. M. (Ed.). (1962). *Human behavior and social processes: An interactionist approach*. Oxford, England: Houghton Mifflin.

Rose, S. (1988, March). *Alternative practice explanatory frameworks: A debate. Presentation*. Paper presented at the Annual Program Meeting, Council on Social Work Education, Atlanta, GA.

Rose, S., Bisson, J., & Wessely, S. (2003). Psychological debriefing for preventing post traumatic stress disorder (PTSD) (Cochrane Review). *Cochrane Database of Systematic Reviews*. Chichester, UK: Wiley.

Rose, S. D. (1977). *Group therapy: A behavioral approach*. Englewood Cliffs, NJ: Prentice-Hall.

Rose, S. M. (1990). Advocacy/empowerment: An approach to clinical practice for social work. *Journal of Sociology and Social Welfare, 17*(2), 41–51.

Rose, S. M. (Ed.). (1992). *Case management and social work practice*. New York: Longman.

Rose, S. M. (2000). Reflections on empowerment-based practice. *Social Work, 45*(5), 403–412.

Rose, S. M., & Moore, V. L. (1995). Case management. In R. L. Edwards (Ed.), *Encyclopedia of social work* (19th ed., Vol. 1, pp. 335–340). New York: NASW Press.

Rosemond, J. K. (1996, March). Volunteering for kids: Help your children learn that service—not self-interest—holds our world together. *Rotarian*, 16–17.

Rosen, A. (1993). Systematic planned practice. *Social Service Review, 67*, 84–100.

Rosen, A. (1994). Knowledge use in direct practice. *Social Service Review, 68*(4), 561–571.

Rosen, A. (1996). The scientific practitioner revisited: Some obstacles and prerequisites for fuller implementation in practice. *Social Work Research, 20*(2), 104–111.

Rosen, A., & Lieberman, D. (1972). The experimental evaluation of interview performance of social workers. *Social Science Review, 46*(3), 395–412.

Rosen, A., & Proctor, E. K. (2002). Standards for evidence-based social work practice: The role of replicable and appropriate interventions, outcomes, and practice guidelines. In A. R. Roberts & G. J. Greene (Eds.), *Social workers' desk reference* (pp. 743–751). New York: Oxford University Press.

Rosen, A., Proctor, E. K., & Staudt, M. M. (1999). Social work research and the quest for effective practice. *Social Work Research, 23*(1), 4–15.

Rosen, H. (1988). Evolving a personal philosophy of practice: Towards eclecticism. In R. A. Dorfman (Ed.), *Paradigms of clinical social work* (pp. 388–412). New York: Brunner/Mazel.

Rosewater, L., & Walker, L. (1985). *Handbook of feminist therapy: Women's issues in psychotherapy*. New York: Springer.

Ross, E. L. (1978). *Black heritage in social welfare, 1860–1930*. Metuchen, NJ: Scarecrow Press.

Roth, A., & Fonagy, P. (Eds.). (1996). *What works for whom? A critical review of psychotherapy research*. New York: Guilford.

Rothery, M. (1980). Contracts and contracting. *Clinical Social Work Journal, 8*(3), 179–187.

Rothery, M. (1993). The ecological perspective and work with vulnerable families. In M. Rodway & B. Trute (Eds.), *The ecological perspective in family-centered therapy* (pp. 21–50). Queenston, ON: Edwin Mellen.

Rothman, G. (1985). *Philanthropists, therapists, and activists: A century of ideological conflict in social work*. Cambridge, MA: Schenleman.

Rothman, J. (1991). A model of case management: Toward empirically based practice. *Social Work, 36*(5), 520–528.

Rothman, J., Smith, W., Nakashima, J., Paterson, M. J., & Mustin, J. (1996). Client self determination and professional intervention: Striking a balance. *Social Work, 41*(4), 396–405.

Rothman, J., & Tropman, J. (1987). Models of community organization and macro practice perspectives: Their mixing and phasing. In F. Cox, J. Erlich, J. Rothman, & J. Tropman (Eds.), *Strategies of community organization* (4th ed., pp. 3–26). Itasca, IL: Peacock.

Rothman, J. C. (2002). Developing therapeutic contracts with contracts. In A. R. Roberts & G. J. Greene (Eds.), *Social workers' desk reference* (pp. 304–309). New York: Oxford University Press.

Rounds, K. A., Galinsky, M. J., & Despard, M. R. (1995). Evaluation of telephone support groups for persons with HIV disease. *Research on Social Work Practice, 5*(4), 442.

Rowe, M. M. (2000). Skills training in the long-term management of stress and occupational burnout. *Current Psychology, 19*(3), 215–228.

Rowe, W. (1996). Client-centered theory: A person-centered approach. In F. J. Turner (Ed.), *Social work treatment: Interlocking theoretical approaches* (4th ed., pp. 69–93). New York: Free Press.

Rowlands, A. (2001). Ability or disability? Strengths-based practice in the area of traumatic brain injury. *Families in Society: The Journal of Contemporary Human Services, 82*(3), 273–286.

Rubin, A. (1992). Is case management effective for people with serious mental illness? A research review. *Health and Social Work, 17*(2), 138–150.

Rubin, A., & Babbie, E. (1997). *Research methods for social work* (3rd ed.). Pacific Grove, CA: Brooks/Cole.

Rubington, E., & Weinberg, M. S. (1968). *Deviance: The interactionist perspective*. New York: Macmillan.

Rubinstein, M. F. (1974). *Patterns of problem-solving*. Englewood Cliffs, NJ: Prentice-Hall.

Ruckdeschel, R. A., & Farris, B. E. (1981). Assessing practice: A critical look at the single case design. *Social Casework, 62*(7), 413–419.

Rullo, D. (2001). The profession of clinical social work. *Research on Social Work Practice, 11*(2), 210–216.

Rupe, M. (1997). *Strengths model for family preservation and family reunification*. Lawrence: School of Social Welfare, University of Kansas.

Russell, M. (1989). Feminist social work skills. *Canadian Social Work Review, 6*(1), 69–81.

Russo, R. J. (1999). Applying a strengths-based practice approach in working with people with developmental disabilities and their families. *Families in Society: The Journal of Contemporary Human Services, 80*(1), 25–34.

Rutter, M. (1979). Protective factors in children's response to stress and disadvantage. In M. W. Kent & J. Rolf (Eds.), *Primary prevention of psychopathology, social competence in children* (Vol. III, pp. 49–79). Hanover, NH: University Press of New England.

Rutter, M. (1987). Psychosocial resilience and protective mechanisms. *American Journal of Orthopsychiatry, 57*(3), 316–331.

Rutter, M., Maughan, B., Mortimore, P., Ouston, J., & Smith, A. (1979). *Fifteen thousand hours: Secondary schools and their effects on children*. Cambridge, MA: Harvard University Press.

Ryan, C. C. (1988). The social and clinical challenges of AIDS. *Smith College Studies in Social Work, 59*(1), 3–20.

Rylance, G. (1996). Making decisions with children: A child's rights to share in health decisions can no longer be ignored (Editorial). *British Medical Journal, 312*(7034), 794.

Sabin, J. E. (1991). Clinical skills for the 1990's: Six lessons from HMO practice. *Hospital and Community Psychiatry, 42*, 605–608.

Sachs, J. (1991). Meaning and motivational complexities of practice interventions. *Journal of Sociology and Social Welfare, 18*(4), 83–99.

Safer, D. J. (1995). An outpatient/inpatient comparison of child psychiatric diagnosis. *American Journal of Orthopsychiatry, 31*(3), 298–303.

Sainsbury Centre for Mental Health. (1996). *Care management: Is it working? An executive summary*. London: Author.

Saleebey, D. (1992). *The strengths perspective in social work practice*. New York: Longman.

Saleebey, D. (1996). The strengths perspective in social work practice: Extensions and cautions. *Social Work, 41*(3), 296–305.

Saleebey, D. (Ed.). (1997). *The strengths perspective in social work practice* (2nd ed.). New York: Longman.

Saleebey, D. (1999). The strengths perspective: Principles and practices. In B. Compton & B. Galaway, *Social work processes* (6th ed., pp. 14–23). Pacific Grove, CA: Brooks/Cole.

Saleebey, D. (2001a). The Diagnostic Strengths Manual? *Social Work, 46*(2), 183–187.

Saleebey, D. (2001b). Practicing the strengths perspective: Everyday tools and resources (Guest Editorial). *Families in Society: The Journal of Contemporary Human Services, 82*(3), 221–222.

Saleebey, D. (Ed.). (2002). *The strengths perspective in social work practice* (3rd ed.). Boston: Allyn & Bacon.

Sallee, A. L. (2003). A generalist working definition of social work: A response to Bartlett. *Research on Social Work Practice, 13*(3), 349–356.

Salomon, E. L. (1967). Humanistic values and social casework. *Social Casework, 48*(1), 26–33.

Saltz, C. C., & Schaefer, T. (1996). Interdisciplinary teams in health care: Integration of family caregivers. *Social Work in Health Care, 22*(3), 59–70.

Salzer, M. S., McFadden, L., & Rappaport, J. (1994). Professional views of self-help groups. *Administration and Policy in Mental Health, 22*(2), 85–95.

Sammy's Dad. (1997). Editorial comment: The sterility of oppression. *News from Sammy's Dad* (Underground Newsletter), (3), 2–3.

Sands, R. G. (1994). A comparison of interprofessional and team parent talk of an interdisciplinary team. *Social Work in Education, 16*(4), 207–219.

Sands, R. G., & Nuccio, K. (1992). Postmodern feminist theory and social work. *Social Work, 37*(6), 489–494.

Sands, R. G., Stafford, J., & McClelland, M. (1990). I beg to differ: Conflict in the interdisciplinary team. *Social Work in Health Care, 14*(3), 55–72.

Santas, G. F. (1979). *Socrates: Philosophy in Plato's early dialogues*. London: Routledge.

Santiago, J. M. (1993). Hispanic, Latino, or Raza? Coming to terms with diversity. *Hospital and Community Psychiatry, 47*(7), 613.

Santiago-Irizarry, V. (2001). *Medicalizing ethnicity: The construction of Latino identity in a psychiatric setting*. Ithaca, NY: Cornell University Press.

Sanua, V. D. (1995). The family and sociocultural factors of psychopathology. In L. L'Abate (Ed.), *The handbook of family psychology and therapy* (Vol. 2, pp. 847–875). Homewood, IL: Dorsey.

Sarason, B. R., Sarason, I. G., & Pierce, G. R. (Eds.). (1990). *Social support: An interactional view*. New York: Wiley.

Sarason, I., Levine, H., Basham, R., & Sarason, B. (1983). Assessing social support: The social support questionnaire. *Journal of Personality and Social Psychology, 44*, 127–139.

Saulnier, M. R. (1996). Accessing support in times of need. *The Social Worker, 644*(3), 97–106.

Sauter, J., & Franklin, C. (1998). Assessing post-traumatic stress disorder in children: Diagnostic and measurement strategies. *Research on Social Work Practice, 8*(3), 251–270.

Savoury, G. R., Beals, H. L., & Parks, J. M. (1995). Mediation in child protection: Facilitating the resolution of disputes. *Child Welfare, 74*(3), 843–862.

Saxon, W. (1979). Behavioral contracting: Theory and design. *Child Welfare, 58*(8), 523–529.

Schecter, S. (1982). *Women and male violence: The visions and struggles of the battered women's movement.* Boston: South End Press.

Schilling, R. F. (1987). Limitations of social support. *Social Service Review, 61*(1), 19–31.

Schlossberger, E., & Hecker, L. (1996). HIV and family therapists' duty to warn: A legal and ethical analysis. *Journal of Marital and Family Therapy, 22*(1), 27–40.

Schmitt, M. H., Farrell, M. P., & Heinemann, G. D. (1988). Conceptual and methodological problems in studying the effects of interdisciplinary geriatric terms. *Gerontologist, 28*(6), 753–764.

Schneider, J. A. (2002). Social capital and community supports for low income families: Examples from Pennsylvania and Wisconsin. *Social Policy Journal, 1*(1), 35–55.

Schofield, R. F., & Amodeo, M. (1999). Interdisciplinary teams in health care and human services settings: Are they effective? *Health and Social Work, 24*(3), 210–219.

Schon, D. A. (1983). *The reflective practitioner: How professionals think in action.* New York: Basic Books.

Schopler, J. H., & Galinsky, M. J. (1995). Group practice overview. In R. L. Edwards (Ed.), *Encyclopedia of Social Work* (19th ed., Vol. 2, pp. 1129–1143). Washington, DC: NASW Press.

Schrier, C. J. (1980). Guidelines for record keeping under privacy and open-access laws. *Social Work, 25*(6), 452–457.

Schriver, J. M. (1990, March). *The gentrification of social work: Philosophical implications and value issues.* Paper presented at the Annual program meeting of the Council on Social Work Education, Reno, NV.

Schubert, M. (Ed.). (1991). *Interviewing in social work practice* (rev. ed.). Alexandria, VA: Council on Social Work Education.

Schubert, M. A., & Borkman, T. J. (1991). An organizational typology for self-help groups. *American Journal of Community Psychology. Special issue: Self-help groups, 19*(5), 769–787.

Schultz, T. (1961). Investment in human capital. *American Economic Review, 51,* 1–17.

Schur, E. (1973). *Radical non-intervention: Rethinking the delinquency problem.* Englewood Cliffs, NJ: Prentice-Hall.

Schwartz, B. (1993). Why altruism is impossible . . . and ubiquitous. *Social Service Review, 30*(1), 314–343.

Schwartz, G. (1989). Confidentiality revisited. *Social Work, 34*(3), 223–226.

Schwartz, R. C. (1995). *Internal family systems therapy.* New York: Guilford.

Schwartz, W. (1961). Social worker in the group. In National Conference on Social Welfare (Ed.), *Social welfare forum* (pp. 146–171). New York: Columbia University Press.

Seabury, B. A. (1976). The contract: Uses, abuses and limitations. *Social Work, 21*(1), 16–21.

Seabury, B. A. (1979). Negotiating sound contracts with clients. *Public Welfare, 37*(2), 33–38.

Seabury, B. A. (1985). The beginning phase: Engagement, initial assessment, and contracting. In J. Laird & A. Hartman (Eds.), *A handbook of child welfare* (pp. 335–359). New York: Free Press.

Selekman, M. (1993). *Pathways to change: Brief therapy solutions with difficult adolescents.* New York: Guilford.

Selekman, M. (1997). *Solution focused therapy with children.* New York: Guilford.

Seligman, M. E. (1995). The effectiveness of psychotherapy: The Consumer Reports study. *American Psychologist, 50,* 965–974.

Seligman, M. E. P. (1975). *Helplessness: On depression, development and death.* San Francisco: Freeman.

Seligman, M. E. P. (1991). *Learned optimism.* New York: Knopf.

Seligman, M. E. P. (1994). *What you can change and what you can't: The complete guide to successful self-improvement.* New York: Knopf.

Selvini, M. P., Boscolo, L., Cecchin, G., & Prata, G. (1980). Hypothesizing-circularity-neutrality: Three guidelines for the conduct of the session. *Family Process, 19*(1), 3–12.

Selye, H. (1946). The general adaptation syndrome and the disease of adaptation. *Journal of Clinical Endocrinology, 6,* 117–230.

Selye, H. (1950). *The physiology and pathology of exposure to stress.* Montreal: Acta.

Selye, H. (1976a). Forty years of stress research: Principal remaining problems and misconceptions. *Canadian Medical Association Journal, 15*(1), 53–56.

Selye, H. (1976b). *Stress in health and disease.* Boston: Butterworth.

Selye, H. (1980). The stress concept today. In I. L. Kutash & L. B. Schlesinger (Eds.), *Handbook on stress and anxiety* (pp. 127–143). San Francisco: Jossey Bass.

Sermabeikian, P. (1994). Our clients, ourselves: The spiritual perspective and social work practice. *Social Work, 39*(2), 178–183.

Sessa, V. I. (1996). Using perspective talking to manage conflict and affect in teams. *Journal of Applied Behavioral Science, 32*(1), 101–115.

Severson, M. M., & Bankston, T. V. (1995). Social work and the pursuit of justice through mediation. *Social Work, 40*(5), 683–690.

Shaffer, C. R., & Anundsen, K. (1993). *Creating community anywhere: Finding support and connection in a fragmented world.* New York: Tarcher/Putnam.

Shapiro, J. (1996). The downside of managed mental health care. *Clinical Social Work Journal, 23*(4), 441–451.

Sheafor, B. W., Horejsi, C. R., & Horejsi, G. A. (1997). *Techniques and guidelines for social work practice* (4th ed.). Boston: Allyn & Bacon.

Sheldon, B., & Chilvers, R. (2000). *Evidence-based social care: A study of prospects and problems.* Dorset, England: Russell House.

Shera, W., & Page, J. (1995). Creating more effective human service organizations through empowerment strategies. *Administration in Social Work, 19*(4), 1–15.

Sheridan, M. J. (2002). Spiritual and religious issues in practice. In A. R. Roberts & G. J. Greene (Eds.), *Social workers' desk reference* (pp. 567–571). New York: Oxford University Press.

Sheridan, M. J., Bullis, R. K., Adcock, C. R., Berlin, S. D., & Miller, P. C. (1992). Practitioners' personal and professional attitudes toward religion and spirituality: Issues for education and practice. *Journal of Social Work Education, 28*(2), 190–203.

Sheridan, M. J., Wilmer, C., & Atcheson, L. (1994). Inclusion of content on religion and spirituality in social work curriculum: A study of faculty views. *Journal of Social Work Education, 30*(3), 363–376.

Sherraden, M. S., Slosar, B., & Sherraden, M. (2002). Innovation in social policy: Collaborative policy advocacy. *Social Work, 47*(3), 209–221.

Shields, G., & Clark, R. D. (1995). Family correlates of delinquency: Cohesion and adaptability. *Journal of Sociology and Social Welfare, 22*(2), 93–106.

Shireman, C. H., & Reamer, F. (1986). *Rehabilitating juvenile justice.* New York: Columbia University Press.

Shirilla, J. J. (2002). *Case studies in infant mental health: Risk, resiliency, and relationships.* Washington, DC: Zero to Three.

Shorkey, C. T., & Sutton-Simon, K. (1983). Reliability and validity of the Rational Behavior Inventory with a clinical population. *Journal of Clinical Psychology, 39*(1), 34–38.

Shulman, L. (1992). *The skills of helping individuals, families and groups* (3rd ed.). Itasca, IL: Peacock.

Shulman, L. (1999). *The skills of helping individuals, families, groups, and communities* (4th ed.). Itasca, IL: Peacock.

Sieber, S. (1981). *Fatal remedies.* New York: Plenum.

Siebold, C. (1991). Termination: When the therapist leaves. *Clinical Social Work Journal, 19*(2), 191–204.

Siebold, C. (1992). Forced termination: Reconsidering theory and technique. *Smith College Studies in Social Work, 63*(1), 325–341.

Siegel, D. (1984). Defining empirically based practice. *Social Work, 29*(4), 325–337.

Sifneos, P. E. (1992). *Short-term anxiety provoking psychotherapy: A treatment manual.* New York: Plenum Press.

Silver, R. L., Boon, C., & Stones, M. H. (1983). Searching for meaning in misfortune: Making sense of incest. *Journal of Social Issues, 39*(2), 81–102.

Silverman, M. (1977). Children's rights and social work. *Social Service Review, 51*(1), 171–178.

Silverman, P. R. (1986). The perils of borrowing: Role of the professional in mutual help groups. *Journal for Specialists in Group Work, 11*(2), 68–73.

Silvestri, G. T. (1997). Occupation employment projections to 2006. *Monthly Labor Review* (November), 58–83.

Simmons, J. L. (1969). *Deviants.* Berkeley, CA: Glendessary Press.

Simms, J. M. (1888). *The first colored Baptist Church.* Philadelphia: Lippincott.

Simon, B. L. (1994). *The empowerment tradition in American social work: A history.* New York: Columbia University Press.

Simon, B. L., & Thyer, B. A. (1994). Point/Counterpoint: Are theories for practice necessary? *Journal of Social Work Education, 30*(2), 144–152.

Simon, H. A. (1952). Comments on the theory of organization. *American Political Science Review, 46*(4), 1130–1139.

Sinclair, D. (1985). *Understanding wife assault: A training manual for counselors and advocates.* Toronto: Publications Ontario, Publications Services Section.

Siporin, M. (1975). *Introduction to social work practice.* New York: Macmillan.

Siporin, M. (1985). Current social work perspectives on clinical practice. *Clinical Social Work Journal, 13,* 198–217.

Skyttner, L. (2001). *General systems theory: Ideas and applications.* River Edge, NJ: World Scientific.

Slaght, E. F. (1999). Focusing on the family in the treatment of substance abusing criminal offenders. *Journal of Drug Education, 29*(1), 53–62.

Smale, G., Tuson, G., Cooper, M., Wardle, M., & Crosbie, D. (1988). *Community social work: A paradigm for change.* London: National Institute of Social Workers.

Smalley, R. (1970). *The functional approach to casework practice.* Chicago: University of Chicago Press.

Smalley, R. E. (1967). *Theory for social work practice.* New York: Columbia University Press.

Smith, C., & Carlson, B. E. (1997). Stress, coping, and resilience in children and youth. *Social Service Review, 71*(2), 231–257.

Smith, E. D. (1995). Addressing the psychospiritual distress of death as reality: A transpersonal approach. *Social Work, 40*(3), 402–413.

Smith, K. G., Locke, E. A., & Barry, D. (1990). Goal setting, planning and organizational performance: An experimental simulation. *Organizational Behavior and Human Decision Processes, 46,* 118–134.

Smith, M. J. (1975). *When I say no, I feel guilty.* New York: Bantam Books.

Smokowski, P. R., & Wodarski, J. S. (1996). The effectiveness of child welfare services for poor, neglected children: A review of the empirical evidence. *Research on Social Work Practice, 6*(4), 504.

Snell, C. L. (1991). Help-seeking behavior among young street males. *Smith College Studies in Social Work, 61*(3), 293–305.

Soares, H. H., & Rose, M. K. (1994). Clinical aspects of case management with the elderly. *Journal of Gerontological Social Work, 22*(3/4), 143–156.

Social Services Inspectorate. (1995a). *Social services department information strategies and systems (with references to community care): Inspection overview.* London: Her Majesty's Stationary Office.

Social Services Inspectorate. (1995b). *Third overview: Report of care management inspection of the work of inspection units in 19 local authorities.* London: Her Majesty's Stationary Office.

Söderfeldt, M., Söderfeldt, B., & Warg, L.-E. (1995). Burnout in social work. *Social Work, 40*(5), 638–646.

Solomon, M., Pistrang, N., & Barker, C. (2001). The benefits of mutual support groups for parents of children with disabilities. *American Journal of Community Psychology, 29*(1), 113–132.

Solomon, P., & Draine, J. (1996). Service delivery differences between consumer and non-consumer case managers in mental health. *Research on Social Work Practice, 6*(2), 193–207.

Sosin, M., & Caulum, S. (1983). Advocacy: A conceptualization for social work practice. *Social Work, 28*(1), 12–17.

Sowers, K. M., & Ellis, R. A. (2001). Steering currents for the future of social work. *Research on Social Work Practice, 11*(2), 245–253.

Specht, H. (1986). Social support, social networks, social exchange, and social work practice. *Social Service Review, 60*(2), 218–240.

Specht, H. (1990). Social work and the popular psychotherapies. *Social Service Review, 64*(3), 345–356.

Specht, H., & Courtney, M. E. (1994). *Unfaithful angels: How social work has abandoned its mission.* New York: Free Press.

Specht, H., & Reissman, F. (1963, June). *Some notes on a model for an integrated social work approach to social problems (Mimeographed).* New York: Mobilization for Youth.

Spence, S. A. (1991). Social support for the black elderly: Is there a link between informal and formal assistance? *Journal of Sociology and Social Welfare, 18*(3), 149–158.

Spielberger, C. D. (1979). *Understanding stress and anxiety.* New York: Harper & Row.

Spitz, R. A. (1959). *A genetic field theory of ego formation: Its implications for pathology.* New York: International Universities Press.

Spitz, R. A. (1965). *The first year of life: A psychoanalytic study of normal and deviant development of object relations.* New York: International Universities Press.

Spitz, R. A. (1983). *René A. Spitz, dialogues from infancy: Selected papers.* New York: International Universities Press.

Srole, L., Langer, T. S., Michael, S. T., Opler, M. K., & Rennie, T. A. C. (1962). *Mental health in the metropolis: The midtown Manhattan study.* New York: McGraw-Hill.

Staples, L. H. (1990). Powerful ideas about empowerment. *Administration in Social Work, 14*(2), 29–42.

Stark, E., & Flitcraft, A. (1988). Women and children at risk: A feminist perspective on child abuse. *International Journal of Health Services, 18*(1), 97–118.

Statham, D. (1996). *The future of social and personal care: The role of social services organisations in the public, private and voluntary sectors.* London: National Institute of Social Workers.

Staudt, M. M. (2000). Correlates of recommended aftercare service use after intensive family preservation services. *Social Work Research, 24*(1), 40–50.

Stein, H., & Nafziger, E. W. (1991). Structural adjustment, human needs, and the World Bank agenda. *Journal of Modern African Studies, 29*(1), 173–189.

Stein, T. J. (1990). Commentary: Issues in the development of expert systems to enhance decision making in child welfare. In L. Videka-Sherman & W. J. Reid (Eds.), *Advances in clinical social work research* (pp. 503–546). Silver Spring, MD: NASW Press.

Stern, S. B., & Smith, C. A. (1995). Family processes and delinquency in an ecological context. *Social Service Review, 69*(4), 703–731.

Stoesz, D. (1986). Corporate welfare: The third stage of welfare in the United States. *Social Work, 31*(4), 245–249.

Stoesz, D. (1994). Is privatization a positive trend in social welfare? Yes. In H. J. Karger & J. Midgley (Eds.), *Controversial issues in social policy.* Boston: Allyn & Bacon.

Strauss, A., Corbin, J., Fagerhaugh, S., Glaser, B., Maines, D., Suczek, B., et al. (1984). *Chronic illness and the quality of life.* Toronto: Mosby.

Streeter, C. L., & Franklin, C. (1992). Defining and measuring social support: Guidelines for social work practitioners. *Research on Social Work Practice, 2*(1), 81–98.

Stretch, J. J. (1967). Existentialism: A proposed philosophical orientation for social work. *Social Work, 12*, 97–102.

Strom, K. J., & Gingerich, W. J. (1993). Educating students for new market realities. *Journal of Social Work Education, 29*(1), 78–87.

Strom-Gottfried, K. (1997). The implications of managed care for social work education. *Journal of Social Work Education, 33*, 7–18.

Strom-Gottfried, K. J. (2000). Ensuring ethical practice: An examination of NASW code violations, 1986–97. *Social Work, 45*(3), 251–261.

Strom-Gottfried, K. J. (2003). Understanding adjudication: Origins, targets, and outcomes of ethics complaints. *Social Work, 48*(1), 85–95.

Stuart, R. (1980). *Helping couples change: A social learning theory approach to marital therapy.* New York: Guilford.

Stuckey, S. (1987). *Slave culture.* New York: Oxford University Press.

Studt, E. (1968). Social work theory and implications for the practice methods. *Social Work Education Reporter, 16*(2), 22–24, 42–46.

Stuifbergen, A. K., Becker, H., Timmerman, G. M., & Kullberg, V. (2003). The use of individualized goal setting to facilitate behavior change in women with multiple sclerosis. *Journal of Neuroscience Nursing, 35*(2), 94–100.

Subby, R. (1990). *Healing the family within.* Deerfield Beach, FL: Health Communications.

Sullivan, W. P. (1997). On strengths, niches, and recovery from serious mental illness. In D. Saleebey (Ed.), *The strengths perspective in social work practice* (2nd ed., pp. 183–197). New York: Longman.

Sullivan, W. P., & Fisher, B. J. (1994). Intervening for success: Strengths-based management and successful aging. *Journal of Gerontological Social Work, 22*(1/2), 61–74.

Sullivan, W. P., Hartman, D. J., Dillon, D., & Wolk, J. L. (1994). Implementing case management in alcohol and drug treatment. *Families in Society: The Journal of Contemporary Human Services, 75*(2), 67–73.

Sullivan, W. P., Wolk, J. L., & Hartman, D. J. (1992). Case management in alcohol and drug treatment: Improving client outcomes. *Families in Society: The Journal of Contemporary Human Services, 73*(4), 195–204.

Suppes, M. A., & Cressy Wells, C. (Eds.). (1996). *The future and social work* (2nd ed.). New York: McGraw-Hill.

Sutherland, J. W. (1973). *A general systems philosophy for the social and behavioral sciences.* New York: George Braziller.

Swadener, B., & Lubeck, S. (Eds.). (1995). *Children and families "at promise": Deconstructing the discourse of risk.* Albany: State University of New York Press.

Swenson, C. R. (1994). Clinical practice and the decline of community. *Journal of Teaching in Social Work, 10*(1/2), 195–212.

Swift, K. (1991). Contradictions in child welfare: Neglect and responsibility. In C. T. Baines, P. M. Evans, & S. M. Neysmith (Eds.), *Women's caring: Feminist perspectives* (pp. 234–271). Toronto: McClelland & Stewart.

Sykes Wylie, M. (1990). Brief therapy on the couch. *Family Therapy Networker, 14*(3), 26–72.

Szasz, T. (1994). *Cruel compassion: Psychiatric control of society's unwanted.* New York: Wiley.

Taber, M. A., & Vattano, A. J. (1970). Clinical and social orientations in social work: An empirical study. *Social Service Review, 44*(1), 34–43.

Tafoya, T. (1989). Circles and cedar: Native Americans and family therapy. *Journal of Psychotherapy and the Family, 6,* 71–98.

Taft, J. (1935). *The dynamics of theory in a controlled relationship.* New York: Macmillan.

Talmon, M. (1990). *Single session therapy.* San Francisco: Jossey-Bass.

Tamura, T., & Lau, A. (1992). Connectedness versus separateness: Applicability of family therapy to Japanese families. *Family Process, 31*(4), 319–430.

Tannenbaum, F. (1951). *Crime and community* (2nd ed.). New York: Columbia University Press.

Tatura, T. (1989). Characteristics of children in foster care. *Division of Child, Youth, and Family Services Newsletter (American Psychological Association), 12*(3), 16–17.

Taussig, I. M. (1987). Comparative responses of Mexican-Americans and Anglo-Americans to early goal setting in a public mental health clinic. *Journal of Counseling Psychology, 34,* 214–217.

Taylor, R. J., Neighbors, H. W., & Broman, C. L. (1989). Evaluation by Black Americans of the social service encounter during a serious personal problem. *Social Work, 34*(3), 205–211.

Taylor, S., Brownlee, K., & Mauro-Hopkins, K. (1996). Confidentiality versus the duty to protect: An ethical dilemma with HIV/AIDS clients. *Social Worker/Le travailleur social, 64*(4), 9–17.

Taylor-Brown, S., Garcia, A., & Kingson, E. (2001). Cultural competence versus cultural chauvinism: Implications for social work. *Health and Social Work, 26*(3), 185–187.

Tebb, S. (1991). Client-focused recording: Linking theory and practice. *Families in Society: The Journal of Contemporary Human Services, 72*(7), 427–432.

Terrell, F., & Terrell, S. (1984). Race of counselor, client sex, cultural mistrust level, and premature termination from counseling among black clients. *Journal of Counseling Psychology, 31*(3), 371–375.

Terrified toddlers taken from home. (1992, October 1). *Winnipeg Free Press,* p. A16.

Thomlison, B., & Thomlison, R. J. (1996). Behavior theory and social work treatment. In F. J. Turner (Ed.), *Social work treatment: Interlocking theoretical approaches* (4th ed., pp. 39–68). New York: Free Press.

Thomlison, R. J. (1986). Behavior therapy in social work practice. In F. J. Turner (Ed.), *Social work treatment: Interlocking theoretical approaches* (3rd ed., pp. 131–154). New York: Free Press.

Thompson, D. L., & Thompson, J. A. (1993). Working the 12 Steps of Alcoholics Anonymous with a client: A counseling opportunity. *Alcoholism Treatment Quarterly, 10*(1/2), 49–61.

Thompson, M. S., & Peebles-Wilkins, W. (1992). The impact of formal, informal, and societal support networks on the psychological well-being of black adolescent mothers. *Social Work, 37*(4), 322–328.

Thompson, P. (1995). New directions for social services and education. *Practice, 7*(4), 53–61.

Thyer, B. A. (1983). Behavior modification in social work practice. In M. Hersen, P. Miller & R. Eisler (Eds.), *Progress in behavior modification* (Vol. 15, pp. 173–226). New York: Academic.

Thyer, B. A. (1985). Textbooks in behavioral social work: A bibliography. *Behavior Therapist, 8,* 161–162.

Thyer, B. A. (1987). Contingency analysis: Toward a unified theory for social work practice. *Social Work, 32,* 150–157.

Thyer, B. A. (1988). Radical behaviorism and clinical social work. In R. Dorfman (Ed.), *Paradigms of clinical social work* (pp. 123–148). New York: Brunner/Mazel.

Thyer, B. A. (1993). Single system research designs. In R. M. Grinnell (Ed.), *Social work research and evaluation* (4th ed., pp. 94–117). Itasca, IL: Peacock.

Thyer, B. A. (1996). Forth years of progress toward empirical clinical practice? *Social Work Research, 20*(2), 77–81.

Thyer, B. A. (2000). A decade of research on social work practice. *Research on Social Work Practice, 10*(1), 5.

Thyer, B. A. (2002). Principles of evidence-based practice and treatment development. In A. R. Roberts & G. J. Greene (Eds.), *Social workers' desk reference* (pp. 739–742). New York: Oxford University Press.

Thyer, B. A., Isaac, A., & Larkin, R. (1997). Integrating research and practice. In M. Reisch & E. Gambrill (Eds.), *Social work in the 21st century* (pp. 311–316). Thousand Oaks, CA: Pine Forge Press.

Thyer, B. A., & Myers, L. L. (1999). On science, antiscience, and the client's right to effective treatment. *Social Work, 44*(2), 501–505.

Thyer, B. A., & Seidl, F. W. (2000). Point/Counterpoint: Should licensure be required for faculty who teach direct practice? *Journal of Social Work Education, 36*(2), 187–200.

Thyer, B. A., & Wodarski, J. S. (1998a). First principles of empirical social work practice. In B. A. Thyer & J. S. Wodarski (Eds.), *Handbook of empirical social work practice* (Vol. 1, pp. 1–21). New York: Wiley.

Thyer, B. A., & Wodarski, J. S. (Eds.). (1998b). *Handbook of empirical social work practice* (Vol. 1). New York: Wiley.

Tillich, P. (1962). The philosophy of social work. *Social Service Review, 36*(1), 12–16.

Timimi, S. (2002). *Pathological child psychiatry and the medicalization of childhood*. London: Brunner-Routledge.

Tingley, J. C. (2001). *The power of indirect influence*. New York: AMACOM.

Tobias, M. (1990). Validator: A key role in empowering the chronically mentally ill. *Social Work, 35*(4), 357–359.

Toch, H. (1970). The care and feeding of typologies and levels. *Federal Probation, 34*(3), 15–19.

Toffler, A. (1983). *The third wave*. New York: Bantam.

Tolson, E. R. (1988). *The metamodel and clinical social work*. New York: Columbia University Press.

Tolson, E. R., McDonald, S., & Moriarty, A. R. (1992). Peer mediation among high school students: A test of effectiveness. *Social Work in Education, 14*(2), 86–93.

Tolson, E. R., Reid, W. J., & Garvin, C. D. (1994). *Generalist practice: A task-centered approach*. New York: Columbia University Press.

Tomm, K. (1987). Interventive interviewing. *Family Process, 26*(2), 167–183.

Torczyner, J. (1991). Discretion, judgment, and informed consent: Ethical and practice issues in social action. *Social Work, 36*(2), 122–128.

Toseland, R. W., & Hacker, L. (1985). Social workers' use of self-help groups as a resource for clients. *Social Work, 30*(3), 232–237.

Toseland, R. W., & Rivas, R. F. (1995). *Introduction to group work practice* (2nd ed.). Boston: Allyn & Bacon.

Toubia, N., & Izett, S. (1998). *Female genital mutilation: An overview*. New York: World Health Organization.

Tower, K. D. (1994). Consumer centered social work practice: Restoring client self-determination. *Social Work, 39*(2), 191–196.

Tracy, E. M. (1990). Identifying social support resources of at-risk families. *Social Work, 35*(3), 252–258.

Tracy, E. M., Haapala, D. A., Kinney, J., & Pecora, P. J. (1991). *Intensive family preservation services: An instructional source book*. Cleveland, OH: Mandel School of Applied Social Services, Case Western Reserve University.

Tracy, E. M., & Whittaker, J. K. (1990). The social network map: Assessing social support in clinical practice. *Families in Society: The Journal of Contemporary Human Services, 71*(8), 461–470.

Tracy, L. (1989). *The living organization: Systems of behavior*. New York: Praeger.

Trader, H. P. (1977). Survival strategies for oppressed minorities. *Social Work, 22*(1), 10–13.

Trattner, W. I. (1979). *From poor law to welfare state*. New York: Free Press.

Trattner, W. I. (1989). *From poor law to welfare state: A history of social welfare in America* (4th ed.). New York: Free Press.

Treacy, M., & Wiersema, F. (1995). *The discipline of market leaders*. Reading, MA: Addison-Wesley.

Tripodi, T. (1994). *A primer on single-subject design for clinical social workers*. Washington, DC: NASW Press.

Tripodi, T. (2002). Single-subject designs. In A. R. Roberts & G. J. Greene (Eds.), *Social workers' desk reference* (pp. 748–751). New York: Oxford University Press.

Tripodi, T., & Epstein, I. (1980). *Research techniques for clinical social workers*. New York: Columbia University Press.

Triseliotis, J. (1980). Growing up in foster care and after. In J. Triseliotis (Ed.), *New developments in foster care and adoption* (pp. 131–162). London: Routledge & Kegan Paul.

Tropman, J. E. (1997). *Successful community leadership: A working guide*. Washington, DC: NASW Press.

Truax, C., & Mitchell, K. (1971). Research on certain interpersonal skills in relation to process and outcome. In A. Bergin & S. Garfield (Eds.), *Handbook for psychotherapy and behavior. Change: An empirical analysis* (pp. 299–344). New York: Wiley.

Truax, D. B., & Carkhuff, R. R. (1967). *Toward effective counseling and pyschotherapy: Training and practice*. Chicago & New York: Aldine Atherton.

Truth and Reconciliation Commission. (2001). *Truth: The road to reconciliation*. Retrieved October 2, 2003, from www.doj.gov.za/trc/

Turner, F. J. (1988). Psychosocial therapy. In R. A. Dorfman (Ed.), *Paradigms of clinical social work* (pp. 106–122). New York: Brunner/Mazel.

Turner, F. J. (1994). Reconsidering diagnosis. *Families in Society: The Journal of Contemporary Human Services, 75*(3), 168–171.

Turner, F. J. (Ed.). (1995). *Differential diagnosis and treatment in social work* (4th ed.). New York: Free Press.

Turner, J. (1984). Reuniting children in foster care with their biological families. *Social Work, 29*(6), 501–505.

Turner, J., & Jaco, R. (1996). Problem-solving theory and social work treatment. In F. J. Turner (Ed.), *Social work treatment: Interlocking theoretical approaches* (4th ed., pp. 503–522). New York: Free Press.

Turner, J. C. (2003). Bartlett's definition of social work practice: A generalist educator's perspective. *Research on Social Work Practice, 13*(3), 339–348.

Turner, R. (1992). Launching cognitive behavioral therapy for adolescent depression and drug abuse. In H. Budman, M. F. Hoyt, & S. Friedman (Eds.), *The first session in brief therapy* (pp. 135–155). New York: Guilford.

Tutty, L. (1990). The response of community mental health professionals to clients' rights: A review and suggestions. *Canadian Journal of Community Mental Health, 9*(1), 1–24.

Ullman, M. (1969). A unifying concept linking therapeutic and community process. In F. Duhl & N. Rizao (Eds.), *General systems theory and psychiatry* (pp. 253–265). Boston: Little, Brown.

Umbreit, M. S. (1994). Crime victims confront their offenders: The impact of a Minneapolis mediation program. *Research on Social Work Practice, 4*(4), 436.

Umbreit, M. S. (1995). *Mediating interpersonal conflicts: A pathway to peace*. West Concord, MN: CPI.

United States Bureau of Labor Statistics. (2003). *Occupational outlook handbook, 2002–03 edition, social workers*. Retrieved June 23, 2003, from www.bls.gov/oco/ocos060.htm

U.S. Department of Energy Human Genome Program. *What is the human genome project?* Retrieved August 28, 2003, from www.ornl.gov/TechResources/Human_Genome/project/about.html

United Way of America. (1996). *Measuring program outcomes: A practical approach*. Retrieved October 10, 2003, from http://national.unitedway.org/outcomes/resources/What/intro.cfm

University of Kentucky School of Social Work. (2001). *Reworking the working definition*. Lexington: Author.

User-Centred Services Group. (1993). *Building bridges between people who use and people who provide services*. London: National Institute of Social Workers.

Vaillant, G. E. (1993). *The wisdom of the ego*. Cambridge, MA: Harvard University Press.

Valentich, M. (1986). *Feminism and social work practice*. New York: Free Press.

Valentine, D. P. (1993). Children with special needs: Sources of support and stress for families. *Journal of Social Work and Human Sexuality, 8*(2), 107–121.

Van den Broek, P., & Thurlow, R. (1991). The role and structure of personal narratives. *Journal of Cognitive Psychotherapy (Special Issue: Narrative), 5*(4), 247–259.

Van Hook, M. P. (1995). Christian social work. In R. L. Edwards (Ed.), *Encyclopedia of social work* (19th ed., Vol. 1997 Supplement, pp. 68–77). Washington, DC: NASW Press.

Van Hook, M. P., Berkman, B., & Dunkle, R. (1996). Assessment tools for general health care settings: PRIME-DM, OARS, and SF-36. *Health and Social Work, 21*(3), 230–234.

Van Ness, D., & Strong, K. (1997). *Restoring justice*. Columbus, OH: Anderson.

VandeCreek, L., & Knapp, S. (1993). *Tarasoff and beyond: Legal and clinical considerations in the treatment of life-endangering patients* (rev. ed.). Sarasota, FL: Professional Resource Press.

VandeCreek, L., & Knapp, S. (2001). *Tarasoff and beyond: Legal and clinical considerations in the treatment of life-endangering patients* (3rd ed.). Sarasota, FL: Professional Resource Press.

Vandiver, V. L. (2002). Step-by-step practice guidelines for using evidence-based practice and expert consensus in mental health settings. In A. R. Roberts & G. J. Greene (Eds.), *Social workers' desk reference* (pp. 731–738). New York: Oxford University Press.

Vazquez-Nuttall, E., Romero-Garcia, I., & DeLeon, R. (1987). Sex roles and perceptions of femininity and masculinity of Hispanic women: A review of the literature. *Psychology of Women Quarterly, 11*(4), 409–425.

Videka-Sherman, L. (1989). *Intervention for child neglect: The empirical knowledge base*. Paper presented at the National Centre on Child Abuse and Neglect Research Symposium on Child Neglect, Washington, DC.

Von Bertalanffy, L. (1969). *General system theory: Foundations, development, applications*. New York: Braziller.

Von Bertalanffy, L., & LaViolette, P. (1981). *A systems view of man: Collected essays*. Boulder, CO: Westview Press.

Vorrath, H. H., & Bendtro, L. K. (Eds.). (1985). *Positive peer culture* (2nd ed.). Chicago: Aldine de Gruyter.

Wagner, D. (1989). Fate of idealism in social work: Alternative experiences of professional careers. *Social Work, 34*(5), 389–395.

Wakefield, J. (1988a). Psychotherapy, distributive justice and social work, part 1. *Social Service Review, 62*(2), 187–210.

Wakefield, J. (1988b). Psychotherapy, distributive justice and social work, part 2. *Social Service Review, 62*(3), 353–382.

Wakefield, J. (1990). Commentary: Expert systems, Socrates, and the philosophy. In L. Videka-Sherman & W. J. Reid

(Eds.), *Advances in clinical social work research* (pp. 485–502). Silver Spring, MD: NASW Press.

Wakefield, J. (1993). Is altruism part of human nature? Toward a theoretical foundation for the helping professions. *Social Service Review, 67*(3), 406–458.

Wakefield, J. (1996a). Does social work need the ecological perspective: Reply to Alex Gitterman. *Social Service Review, 70*(3), 476–481.

Wakefield, J. (1996b). Does social work need the ecosystems perspective? Part 1. Is the perspective clinically useful? *Social Service Review, 70*(1), 1–32.

Wakefield, J. (1996c). Does social work need the ecosystems perspective? Part 2. Does the perspective save social work from incoherence? *Social Work Review, 70*(2), 183–213.

Wakefield, J. (2003). Gordon versus the working definition: Lessons from a classic critique. *Research on Social Work Practice, 13*(3), 284–298.

Walker, H. (1996). Whanau hui, family decision making and the family group conference. *Protecting Children, 12*(3), 8–10.

Waller, M. A., Carroll, M. M., & Roemer, M. (1996). Teaching writing in social work education: Critical training for agents of social change. *Journal of Teaching in Social Work, 13*(1/2), 43–56.

Walsh, E. (1996). Participating in change: The social work profession in social development—W(h)ither social work? In *Participating in change: Social work profession in social development (Proceedings of the Joint World Congress of IFSW and IASSW)* (pp. 31–33). Hong Kong.

Walsh, J., & Meyersohn, K. (2001). Ending clinical relationships with people with schizophrenia. *Health and Social Work, 26*(3), 188–195.

Walsh, M. E. (1981). Rural social work practice: Clinical quality. *Social Casework: The Journal of Contemporary Social Work, 623*(8), 458–464.

Wandrei, K. E., & Karls, J. M. (1994). Structure of the PIE system. In J. M. Karls & E. K. Wandrei (Eds.), *Person-in-environment system: The PIE classification system for social functioning problems* (pp. 23–40). New York: NASW Press.

Warren, K., Franklin, C., & Streeter, C. L. (1998). New directions in systems theory: Chaos and complexity. *Social Work, 43*(4), 357–371.

Warshaw, T. A., & Barlow, D. (1995). *Resiliency: How to bounce back faster, stronger, smarter.* New York: Master Media.

Wasel-Grimm, C. (1995). *Diagnoses for disaster: The devastating truth about false memory syndrome and its impact on accusers and families.* Woodstock, NY: Overlook Press.

Wasserman, H. (1970). Early careers of professional workers in a public child welfare agency. *Social Work, 15*(3), 98–101.

Watkins, S. (1989). Confidentiality and privileged communications: Legal dilemma for family therapists. *Social Work, 34*(2), 133–136.

Watzlawick, P., Weakland, J. H., & Fisch, R. (1974). *Change: Principles of problem formulation and problem resolution.* New York: Norton.

Weakland, J., Fisch, R., Watzlawick, R., & Bodin, A. (1974). Brief therapy: Focused problem resolution. *Family Process, 13,* 141–168.

Weaver, H. N. (1996). Social work with American Indian youth using the orthogonal model of cultural identification. *Families in Society: The Journal of Contemporary Human Services, 77*(2), 98–107.

Weaver, H. N. (2001). Organization and community assessment with First Nation people. In R. Fong & S. Furuto (Eds.), *Culturally competent practice* (pp. 178–195). Boston: Allyn & Bacon.

Weaver, H. N. (2003). Cultural competence with First Nations peoples. In D. Lum (Ed.), *Culturally competent practice: A framework for understanding diverse groups and justice issues* (2nd ed., pp. 197–216). Pacific Grove, CA: Brooks/Cole.

Webb, N. B. (1985). A crisis intervention perspective on the termination process. *Clinical Social Work Journal, 13*(4), 329–340.

Weber, M. (1947). *The theory of social and economic organization.* New York: Free Press.

Weed, L. L. (1969). *Medical records, medical education, and patient care.* Cleveland, OH: Press of Case Western Reserve University.

Weick, A. (1983). Issues in overturning a medical model of social work practice. *Social Work, 28*(6), 467–471.

Weick, A. (1986). The philosophical context of a health model of social work. *Social Casework, 67*(9), 551–559.

Weick, A. (1987). Reconceptualizing the philosophical perspective of social work. *Social Service Review, 61*(2), 218–230.

Weick, A. (1992). Building a strengths perspective for social work. In D. Saleebey (Ed.), *The strengths perspective in social work practice* (pp. 18–26). New York: Longman.

Weick, A., & Pope, L. (1988). Knowing what's best: A new look at self-determination. *Social Casework: Journal of Contemporary Social Work, 69*(1), 10–16.

Weick, A., Rapp, C., Sullivan, W. P., & Kisthardt, W. (1989). A strengths perspective for social work practice. *Social Work, 34*(4), 350–354.

Weick, A., & Saleebey, D. (1995). Supporting family strengths: Orienting policy and practice toward the 21st century. *Families in Society: The Journal of Contemporary Human Services, 76,* 141–149.

Weil, A. (1995). *Spontaneous healing.* New York: Knopf.

Weil, M. (1997). *Community practice.* Binghampton, NY: Haworth Press.

Weil, M., & Sanchez, E. (1983). The impact of the Tarasoff decision on clinical social work practice. *Social Service Review, 57,* 112–124.

Weil, M. O., & Gamble, D. N. (1995). Community practice models. In R. L. Edwards (Ed.), *Encyclopedia of social work* (19th ed., Vol. 1, pp. 577–594). Washington, DC: NASW Press.

Weiman, C. G. (1977). A study of occupational stressors and the incidence of disease/risk. *Journal of Occupational Medicine, 19,* 119–122.

Weinberg, G. M. (1975). *An introduction to general systems thinking.* New York: Wiley.

Weinberg, N., Schmale, J. D., Uken, J., & Wessel, K. (1995). Computer mediated support groups. *Social Work with Groups, 17*(4), 43–54.

Weinberg, N., Schmale, J. D., Uken, J., & Wessel, K. (1996). Online help: Cancer patients participate in a computer mediated support group. *Health and Social Work, 21*(1), 24–29.

Weinberger, J. (1993). Common factors in psychotherapy. In G. Stricker & J. R. Gold (Eds.), *Comprehensive handbook of psychotherapy integration* (pp. 43–58). New York: Plenum.

Weinberger, J. (1995). Common factors aren't so common: The common factors dilemma. *Clinical Psychology: Science and Practice, 2,* 45–69.

Weinberger, J. (2003). Common factors. In W. E. Craighead & C. B. Nemeroff (Eds.), *The Corsini encyclopedia of psychology and behavioral science.* New York: Wiley.

Weiss, J. O. (1993). Genetic disorders: Support groups and advocacy. *Families in Society: The Journal of Contemporary Human Services, 79*(4), 213–220.

Weissman, H. (1973). *Overcoming mismanagement in the human service professions.* San Francisco: Jossey-Bass.

Wells, T. L. (1994). Therapist self-disclosure: Its effects on clients and the treatment relationship. *Smith College Studies in Social Work, 65*(1), 23–41.

Werner, E., & Smith, R. (1992). *Overcoming the odds: High-risk children from birth to adulthood.* New York: Cornell University Press.

Werrbach, G. B. (1996). Family strengths-based intensive child care management. *Families in Society: The Journal of Contemporary Human Services, 77*(4), 216–226.

Westbrooks, K. L., & Starks, S. H. (2001). Strengths perspective inherent in cultural empowerment: A tool for assessment with African American individuals and families. In R. Fong & S. Furuto (Eds.), *Culturally competent practice* (pp. 101–118). Boston: Allyn & Bacon.

Wharf, B., & Clague, M. (Eds.). (1997). *Community organizing: Canadian experiences.* Toronto: Oxford University Press.

Whimspire, Inc. (1997). *Whimspire practice guide: A social integration model.* Grand Junction, CO: Author.

Whiseyjack, F. (2000). Medicine wheel. *Wind Speaker, 18*(2), 6–8.

White, F. A. (1996). Family processes as predictors of adolescents' preferences for ascribed sources of moral authority: A proposed model. *Adolescence, 31*(121), 133–144.

White, R. W. (1959). Motivation reconsidered: The concept of competence. *Psychological Review, 66*(5), 297–334.

White, R. W. (1963). *Ego and reality in psychoanalytic theory.* New York: International Universities Press.

Whitfield, C. L. (1987). *Healing the child within: Discovery and recovery for adult children of dysfunctional families.* Pompano Beach, FL: Health Communications.

Whitley, D. M., White, K. R., Kelley, S. J., & Yorke, B. (1999). Strengths-based case management: The application to grandparents raising grandchildren. *Families in Society: The Journal of Contemporary Human Services, 80*(2), 110–119.

Whittaker, J. K. (1986). Integrating formal and informal social care: A conceptual framework. *British Journal of Social Work, 16* (supplement), 39–62.

Whittaker, J. K., & Garbarino, J. (1983). *Social support networks: Informal helping in the human services.* New York: Aldine de Gruyter.

Whittaker, J. K., Kinney, J., Tracey, E. M., & Booth, C. (Eds.) (1990). *Reaching high-risk families: Intensive family preservation in human services.* Hawthorne, NY: Aldine de Gruyter.

Whittaker, J. K., & Tracy, E. (1989). *Social treatment: An introduction to interpersonal helping in social work practice* (2nd ed.). New York: Aldine de Gruyter.

Wholey, J. S. (1996). Formative and summative evaluation: Related issues in performance measurement. *Evaluation Practice, 17*(2), 145–149.

Wickman, E. (1993). *Group treatment in social work.* Toronto: Thompson.

Wiener, L. S., Spencer, E. D., Davidson, R., & Fair, C. (1993). National telephone support groups: A new avenue toward psychological support for HIV-infected children and their families. *Social Work with Groups, 16*(3), 55–71.

Wilcox, J. A., & Taber, M. A. (1991). Informal helpers of elderly home care clients. *Health and Social Work, 16*(4), 258–265.

Wilcoxon, S. A. (1991). Clarifying expectation in therapy relationships: Suggestions for written guidelines. *Journal of Independent Social Work, 5*(2), 65–71.

Wilczynski, B. L. (1981). New life for recording: Involving the client. *Social Work, 26*(4), 313–317.

Wilensky, H. L., & Lebeaux, C. N. (1958). *Industrial society and social welfare.* New York: Russell Sage Foundation.

Williams, B. C. (1988). Parents and patients: Members of an interdisciplinary team on an adolescent inpatient unit. *Clinical Social Work Journal, 16*(1), 78–91.

Williams, C. R. (2002). *Law, psychology, and justice: Chaos theory and the new (dis)order.* Albany: State University of New York Press.

Williams, G. P. (1997). *Chaos theory tamed.* Washington, DC: Joseph Henry Press.

Williams, J. B. W. (1981). DSM-III: A comprehensive approach to diagnosis. *Social Work, 26*(2), 101–107.

Williams, J. B. W. (1995). Diagnostic and statistical manual of mental disorders. In R. L. Edwards (Ed.), *Encyclope-*

dia of social work (19th ed., Vol. 1, pp. 729–739). Washington, DC: NASW Press.

Williams, J. B. W., Karls, J. M., & Wandrei, K. (1989). The Person-in-Environment (PIE) system for describing problems of social functioning. *Hospital and Community Psychiatry, 40*(11), 1125–1127.

Williams, J. B. W., & Spitzer, R. L. (1995). Should DSM be the basis for teaching social work practice in mental health? Yes! *Journal of Social Work Education, 31*(2), 148–153.

Williams, L. F., & Hopps, J. G. (1988). On the nature of professional communication: Publication for practitioners. *Social Work, 33*(5), 453–459.

Wilson, G. T. (1981). Behavior therapy as a short-term therapeutic approach. In S. H. Budman (Ed.), *Forms of brief therapy* (pp. 131–166). New York: Guilford.

Wilson, P. A. (1986). Informal care and social support: An agenda for the future. *British Journal of Social Work, 16,* 173–179.

Winegar, N. (1993). Managed mental health care: Implications for administrators and managers of community-based agencies. *Families in Society: The Journal of Contemporary Human Services, 74,* 171–177.

Wituk, S. A., Shepherd, M. D., Warren, M., & Meissen, G. (2002). Factors contributing to the survival of self-help groups. *American Journal of Community Psychology, 30,* 349–366.

Wodarski, J. S., & Bagarozzi, D. A. (1979). A review of the empirical status of traditional modes of interpersonal helping. *Clinical Social Work Journal, 7*(4), 231–255.

Wodarski, J. S., & Dziegielewski, S. F. (Eds.). (2002). *Human behavior and the social environment: Integrating theory and evidence-based practice.* New York: Springer.

Wodarski, J. S., & Thyer, B. A. (Eds.). (1998). *Handbook of empirical social work practice: Social problems and practice issues* (Vol. 2). New York: Wiley.

Woehle, R. (1994). Case management and labelling in rural family agency. In B. Locke & M. Egan (Eds.), *Fulfilling our mission: Rural social work in the 1990's.* Morgantown: West Virginia University.

Wolf, M. (1992). *A thrice-told tale: Feminism, postmodernism, and ethnographic responsibility.* Stanford, CA: Stanford University Press.

Wolin, S. (2003). What is a strength? *Reclaiming Children and Youth, 12*(1), 18–22.

Wolin, S. J., Muller, W., Taylor, F., & Wolin, S. (1999). Three spiritual perspectives on resilience: Buddhism, Christianity, and Judaism. In F. Walsh (Ed.), *Spiritual resources in family therapy* (pp. 121–135). New York: Guilford.

Wolin, S. J., & Wolin, S. (1992). The challenge model: How children can rise above adversity. *Family Dynamics of Addiction Quarterly, 2*(2), 1–9.

Wolin, S. J., & Wolin, S. (1993). *The resilient self: How survivors of troubled families rise above adversity.* New York: Villard.

Wolin, S. J., & Wolin, S. (1994, October). *The challenge model of helping.* Paper presented at a workshop sponsored by Kansas City Employee Assistance Programs, Kansas City, MO.

Woliver, L. R. (1993). *From outrage to action: The politics of grass-roots dissent.* Urbana: University of Illinois Press.

Wolk, J. (1981). Are social workers politically active? *Social Work, 26*(4), 283–288.

Wong, J. (2001). The state of the profession. *Research on Social Work Practice, 11*(2), 217–222.

Wood, G. G., & Middleman, R. R. (1991). Advocacy and social action: Key elements in the structural approach to direct practice in social work. *Social Work with Groups, 14*(3/4), 53–76.

Wood, K. M. (1978). Casework effectiveness: A new look at the research. *Social Work, 23*(6), 437–458.

Woodruff, P. (2001). *Reverence: Renewing a forgotten virtue.* New York: Oxford University Press.

Woods, M. E., & Robinson, H. (1996). Psychosocial theory and social work treatment. In F. J. Turner (Ed.), *Social work treatment: Interlocking theoretical approaches* (4th ed., pp. 555–580). New York: Free Press.

Worchel, J. (1990). Short-term dynamic psychotherapy. In R. A. Wells & V. J. Giannetti (Eds.), *Handbook of brief psychotherapies* (pp. 193–216). New York: Plenum.

Worell, J., & Remer, P. (1992). *Feminist perspectives in therapy: An empowerment model for women.* New York: Wiley.

Worling, J. R. (1995). Adolescent sibling-incest offenders: Differences in family and individual functioning when compared to adolescent non-sibling sex offenders. *Child Abuse and Neglect, 19,* 633–643.

Worling, J. R., & Curwen, T. (2001). *The "Erasor": Estimate of risk of adolescent sexual offense recidivism. Version 2.0. SAFE-T Program.* Ontario: Thistletown Regional Centre, Ontario Ministry of Community & Social Services.

Yalom, I. (1995). *The theory and practice of group psychotherapy* (4th ed.). New York: Basic.

Yegidis, B., & Weinbach, R. (1996). *Research methods for social work.* White Plains, NY: Longman.

Yegidis, B. W., Weinbach, R. W., & Morrison-Rodriguez, B. (1999). *Research methods for social workers* (3rd ed.). Boston: Allyn & Bacon.

Yellow Bird, M. J. (1995). Spirituality in First Nations story telling: A Spanish-Hidatsa approach to narrative. *Reflections, 1*(4), 65–72.

Zastrow, C. (1984). Understanding and preventing burn-out. *British Journal of Social Work, 14*(2), 141–155.

Zehr, H. (1990). *Changing lenses: A new focus for crime and justice.* Scottdale, PA: Herald Press.

Zinn, H. (1980). *A people's history of the United States.* New York: Harper & Row.

Zippay, A. (1995). Expanding employment skills and social networks among teen mothers: A case study of a mentor program. *Child and Adolescent Social Work Journal, 12*(1), 51–69.

Zuniga, M. E. (1992). Using metaphors in therapy: Dichos and Latino chants. *Social Work, 37*(11), 55–60.

Zuniga, M. E. (2001). Latinos: Cultural competence and ethics. In R. Fong & S. Furuto (Eds.), *Culturally competent practice* (pp. 47–60). Boston: Allyn & Bacon.

Zuniga, M. E. (2003). Cultural competence with Latino Americans. In D. Lum (Ed.), *Culturally competent practice: A framework for understanding diverse groups and justice issues* (2nd ed., pp. 238–260). Pacific Grove, CA: Brooks/Cole.

Index

A

absentee human service systems, 287
abstracts, 125, 126
abuse/neglect, 336
  child abuse, 45, 46, 167–168, 171
  Marie W. case example, 452
  reporting, 140
  spouse abuse, 237
  support networks for parents, 267–268
abuses of power, 100, 122, 123, 124, 154
acceptance, 150
accountability, 88–90, 110–111, 477–478
acquired status, 29
Act for the Gradual Abolition of Slavery, 475–476
action plans, 227–230. *See also* service plans/agreements
  creating, 439
  focusing on results, 228–229
  force field analysis for, 253
  legal/ethical principles affecting, 199
  negotiating, 455
  time limits on, 228
actions
  acting in context, 342–343
  choosing alternate course of, 453
  problem solving through, 450–457
  taking precipitous, 122
  as vehicle for promoting competencies, 449–457
action systems, 38
active listening, 212–213
activities, 304, 450
adaptability, of systems, 26
adaptedness/adaptation, 53
Addams, Jane, 1, 283
adopted children, 299
adversity, 44–45
advice, 248, 279–280
advocacy, 230, 342–343
  definition of, 233
  as focus of social work, 8
  misdirected, 186
  for policy changes, 115

primary relationships with community groups, 471
  for referrals, 262
  for social justice, 127–131
  teamwork and, 296–297
affective communication mode, 210
affective functions of ego, 41–42
affiliational supports, 31, 259
agencies
  authority to provide services through, 104–110
  boards of directors/administrators, 109–110
  as bureaucracies, 108–110
  as clients, 96, 100
  differences in cultures in, 296
  expectations of, versus professionals', 110–112
  functions of, 106–108
  interpreting agency functions, 230
  method-focused agency practices, 15
  mission statements, 306
  policy issues. *See* policies
  as practice contexts, 105
  preparing, for referrals, 262–264
  questioning culture of, 113–114
aggressive messages, 35
agreements, preliminary, 181
AIDS/HIV, 94, 133, 134
alcoholics, support networks for, 270–271
Alcoholics Anonymous, 283
alternative practice structures, 116–117
ambivalence, applicant, 164–165
Anishinaabe medicine wheel, 362–366
anomie, social/psychological, 252–253
antecedent conditions, 205–206
anticipating others, problem of, in listening, 161–162
applicants, 201. *See also* clients; respondents
  ambivalence of, 164–165
  applicant specific-global/specific-focused assessments, 197

clients versus, 76–78
  contributions to decision making of, 83
  data collection by, 214
  definition of, 77
  engaging, 72–73, 168–169
  preparing for contact with, 166–168
  starting with perspective of, 174–176
  understanding wants of, 177–181
approaches/models. *See also* interventions; methods
  for addressing mathematical problems, 67
  allegiance to particular, 20
  brief solution-focused, 432–437
  cognitive behavioral assessment models, 424–427
  CREW approach, 391–394
  ecological model, 361–367
  ecosystem approach to assessment, 349–360
  establishing relationships across racial/ethnic lines, 413–416
  ETHIC model, 134–135
  evaluation model, 304
  family group decision making, 416–421
  family systems assessment models, 429–430
  indirect approach, 185–186
  intervention, 10
  life model, 427–429
  logic, 305–306
  mixed-scanning approach, 381
  participatory model, 214–215
  problem-solving model, 1, 9–17, 201, 215, 310
  psychosocial assessment model, 422–424
  social, 466
  solution-seeking, 10–13
  strengths-based compared to problem-based, 338
  strengths-discovery, 10–13
ascribed status, 29
assertiveness skills, 35

TO THE OWNER OF THIS BOOK:

I hope that you have found *Social Work Processes, Seventh Edition* useful. So that this book can be improved in a future edition, would you take the time to complete this sheet and return it? Thank you.

School and address: _____

Department: _____

Instructor's name: _____

1. What I like most about this book is: _____

   _____

   _____

   _____

2. What I like least about this book is: _____

   _____

   _____

3. My general reaction to this book is: _____

   _____

   _____

4. The name of the course in which I used this book is: _____

   _____

5. Were all of the chapters of the book assigned for you to read? _____

   _____

   If not, which ones weren't? _____

   _____

6. In the space below, or on a separate sheet of paper, please write specific suggestions for improving this book and anything else you'd care to share about your experience in using this book.

   _____

   _____

   _____

   _____

FOLD HERE

THOMSON
★ ™

BROOKS/COLE

BUSINESS REPLY MAIL
FIRST-CLASS MAIL   PERMIT NO. 34   BELMONT CA

POSTAGE WILL BE PAID BY ADDRESSEE

Attn: Social Work/Lisa Gebo

BrooksCole/Thomson Learning
10 Davis Dr
Belmont CA 94002-9801

FOLD HERE

OPTIONAL:

Your name:_____ Date: _____

May we quote you, either in promotion for *Social Work Processes, Seventh Edition*, or in future publishing ventures?

Yes: _____   No: _____

Sincerely yours,

Burt Galaway
Barry Cournoyer